6 Producer Behavior

7 Costs

8 Supply in a Competitive Market

9 Market Power and Monopoly

10 Market Power and Pricing Strategies

11 Imperfect Competition

12 Game Theory

microeconomics

Austan Goolsbee
The University of Chicago Booth School of Business

Steven Levitt
The University of Chicago

Chad Syverson
The University of Chicago Booth School of Business

WORTH PUBLISHERS
A Macmillan Higher Education Company

Senior Vice President, Editorial and Production: Catherine Woods
Publisher: Charles Linsmeier
Senior Acquisitions Editor: Sarah Dorger
Developmental Editors: Jane Tufts, Bruce Kaplan
Consulting Faculty Editor: Linda Ghent
Media and Supplements Editors: Lukia Kliossis
Assistant Editor: Mary Melis
Associate Director of Digital Marketing: Scott Guile
Senior Director of Market Research and Development: Steven Rigolosi
Associate Market Development Manager: Kerri Russini
Marketing Assistant: Lindsay Neff
Art Directors: Babs Reingold, Kevin Kall
Interior Designer: Amanda Kavanagh
Photo Editor: Ted Szczepanski
Photo Researcher: Elyse Rieder
Director of Development for Print and Digital Products: Tracey Kuehn
Associate Managing Editor: Lisa Kinne
Project Editor: Robert Errera
Production Manager: Barbara Anne Seixas
Supplements Production Manager: Stacey Alexander
Supplements Project Editor: Edgar Bonilla
Composition and Illustrations: TSI Graphics
Printing and Binding: RR Donnelley

Library of Congress Control Number: 2012950731

ISBN-13: 978-0-7167-5975-1
ISBN-10: 0-7167-5975-6

Second printing

Worth Publishers
41 Madison Avenue
New York, NY 10010
www.worthpublishers.com

The Authors

Austan Goolsbee is the Robert P. Gwinn Professor of Economics at the University of Chicago Booth School of Business. He earned a bachelor's and a master's degree from Yale University and a PhD in economics from the Massachusetts Institute of Technology. Goolsbee's work focuses on the new economy, government policy, taxes, and technology. He was appointed chairman of the Council of Economic Advisers in 2010, returning to the University of Chicago in August 2011. Goolsbee serves as a member of the U.S. Census Advisory Committee, and as a research fellow for the American Bar Foundation.

Steven Levitt is the William B. Ogden Distinguished Service Professor of Economics at the University of Chicago, where he directs the Becker Center on Chicago Price Theory. He earned a bachelor's degree from Harvard University and his PhD from Massachusetts Institute of Technology. He has taught at the University of Chicago since 1997. In 2004, Levitt was awarded the John Bates Clark Medal, and in 2006, he was named one of *Time* magazine's "100 People Who Shape Our World." He co-authored *Freakonomics* and *SuperFreakonomics*, and is also the co-author of the popular *Freakonomics* blog.

Chad Syverson is a Professor of Economics at the University of Chicago Booth School of Business. His research spans several topics, with a particular focus on the interactions of firm structure, market structure, and productivity. His work has earned multiple National Science Foundation awards. He serves on the editorial boards of several economics and business journals and is a research associate of the National Bureau of Economic Research. He earned bachelor's degrees in economics and mechanical engineering from the University of North Dakota, and a PhD in economics from the University of Maryland. Syverson joined the Chicago faculty in 2001.

From Austan

To a young woman I met many years ago—the girl of my dreams. Thank you for marrying me.

From Steve

With love and appreciation to my dear wife, Jenny.

From Chad

To my wife, Genaya, and my children, Claire, Adam, and Victoria. Love you all.

From all

And to the University of Chicago, where people don't just study economics, they live it, breathe it, eat it, and sleep it. The world of economics would never be the same without you, and neither would we.

microeconomics annotated contents

The preferences of consumers (demand) combine with the decisions of firms (supply) to determine the quantity sold and price of goods. The benefits of market transactions at this price are split between consumers and producers. Many factors and policies can alter market outcomes.

How do consumers decide which goods, and how much of each, to consume, in the face of an enormous set of goods and services from which they can purchase?

How do companies decide which combination of inputs to use in production, and how does this decision affect their costs of production? Cost curves show how costs change with a firm's output level and are crucial in determining what a market's supply side looks like.

In perfect competition, all firms take the market price as given, and industry supply reflects the aggregation of the cost curves of individual firms. Industry supply combines with market demand to determine price and quantity movements in the short and long term.

In a monopoly, a firm has the ability to choose at what price it sells its product and this ability implies that the monopolist chooses to produce less than the competitive industry does. Pricing power can be exerted on the market in many ways, including schemes that charge higher prices to consumers with a greater willingness to pay.

Few firms are either pure monopolists or perfectly competitive price takers. Oligopolies operate with some market power, but must also consider their competitors' actions and strategize to maximize their profits. We use the tools of game theory to analyze the strategic interactions among firms and predict market outcomes.

In the real world, markets don't always function as smoothly as models lead us to believe. In the remaining chapters, we make our analysis more realistic. Understanding the role of investment, time, and uncertainty can help individuals and firms make better economic decisions.

Markets are interconnected and we can analyze the conditions that must hold for an economy to operate efficiently and maximize the social benefit of a good or service.

After seeing what must hold for markets to work well, we look at situations in which markets might not work well. Problems arise when information is not equally shared by all potential parties in a transaction, when transactions affect people who are neither the buying nor the selling party, and when a good's benefits are shared across many people at the same time.

The intersection of psychology and economics explores the notion that people can have deeply formed biases and social preferences that limit their ability to act in the completely rational and self-interested way often assumed in economic analysis. Such irrationality may mean that our basic analytical models might be inadequate for explaining economic decision making.

brief contents

contents

contents

contents

contents

contents

contents

contents

contents

contents

contents

contents

contents

contents

contents

contents

contents

preface

Microeconomics is the closest thing economics has to a canon. It comprises the essential base of knowledge for all the various forms and extensions of the discipline. Microeconomics is also extremely useful. It introduces tools that are fundamental to effective decision making in business, government, and everyday life. We believe that microeconomics should inspire and excite students with its elegance and usefulness, and that a textbook should support this goal.

Why this book?

We have had one main goal in writing this book. We want to help each student grow from someone who has learned some economic principles to someone who can apply the tools of economic analysis to real situations, as economists do.

We looked at the major intermediate microeconomics texts and wanted something different. We found that current micro texts do not effectively deal with two criticisms we hear regularly from students about the micro course: *Do people and firms really act as theory suggests*, and *How can someone use microeconomic theory in a practical way?* We sought to answer these questions with this book. Let's address each in turn.

Do people and firms really act as theory suggests?

All microeconomics texts present the standard tools and theory of economics and all have examples. In their presentations, however, they do little to address a student's natural skepticism and they expect students to take on faith that these theories work. They do not always show effectively that these theories can be used in specific and practical ways.

Furthermore, current texts have not fully kept up with the dramatic rise of empirical work in applied microeconomics research. Undergraduates and business school students will find a microeconomics text compelling if it explains the theory, demonstrates how to use it, and provides real-world data to back it up. We show students the reality behind the theory in our Theory and Data feature and Applications, with a clear eye toward *how* economists use real data to test ideas. By including this empirical dimension, *Microeconomics* shows, often in surprising ways, that the theories can explain real behavior; it also shows where theories need to be modified.

How can someone use microeconomics in a practical way?

Students often view the intermediate microeconomics course as abstract and theoretical. Because this course requires a high degree of effort from students, they should know why and how the material they learn will be useful. Without that knowledge, their motivation will lag.

We found that usefulness is not a primary focus in current microeconomics texts, and we wanted to write a book of useful economics. When done the right way, economics *is* extremely useful: useful for business, useful for policy, useful for life. By illustrating how theory and research can explain and illuminate everyday events, market characteristics, business strategies, and government policies, our book shows students how to take the tools they learn and *do* something with them.

One more thing. Our goals of connecting theory to reality and showing the usefulness of microeconomics to students cannot be met if explanations are incomplete, inexact, vague, dull, dry, or fuzzy. We have strived to combine an accessible and clear writing style with current, vivid, and occasionally quirky examples (some of them found in Steve's Freakonomics boxes) to help all readers see the beauty, power, utility, and practicality of economic thinking.

Why us?

The three of us have been friends for a long time. When we agreed to write this book together, we wanted to bring an important, practical, and diverse perspective to the presentation of intermediate microeconomics. We teach in economics departments and in business schools, and we are active empirical microeconomics researchers. Our grounding in different areas of empirical research allows us to present the evidence developed in the last 20 years that has tested and refined the fundamental theories. We are confident that our teaching and professional experiences are reflected in an outstanding presentation of theories and applications.

Teaching in both economics departments *and* business schools has a further benefit. As teachers, we are often challenged by students who want to make sure they are getting their money's worth. As we noted above, these students want to see how realistic theory can be used in practical settings. We wrote this book with such students in mind.

How does our book reveal the reality and practicality of microeconomic theory?

With carefully crafted features, the text moves students from understanding the basics of real economic principles to applying the powerful and revelatory tools of economic analysis. In particular, we have spent significant time choosing examples that offer unusual perspectives on the seemingly ordinary and that are more meaningful, timely, and universally interesting to students.

Three features connect microeconomic theory to the real world and illuminate how useful theory is in understanding much about what students observe.

1. **Theory and Data** sections summarize economic research and use an empirical dimension to reveal the reality behind the theory. The ease with which data can be collected and analyzed has led to a radical shift in microeconomics. With the canon of microeconomic theory in place, the major work in microeconomics now is focused on data, field and lab experiments, and empirics. Theory is being tested all of the time. Our book shows the results.

   Examples of Theory and Data sections include *Golfers' Backward-Bending Labor Supply Curves* (Chapter 5), *Determining a New Drug's Potential Market* (Chapter 9), *Incumbent Airlines' Responses to Threatened Entry by Southwest* (Chapter 12), and *The Positive Externality of LoJack* (Chapter 16). A complete list of Theory and Data sections appears on the inside front cover of this book.

2. **Application** sections in every chapter show how microeconomic theory informs consumer and producer decision making in real situations. These applications show the practical uses of theory and often draw on data from various sources.

   Examples of Applications sections include *Better eBaying through Microeconomics* (Chapter 1), *Technological Change in U.S. Manufacturing* (Chapter 6), *Why Do Film Studios Make Movies That They Know Will Lose Money?* (Chapter 7), *How Priceline Learned That You Can't Price-Discriminate without Market Power* (Chapter 10), and *Random Mixed Strategies in Soccer* (Chapter 12). A complete list of Application sections appears inside the front cover of this book.

3. **Freakonomics** essays encourage students to develop as economic thinkers by showing them how (in often surprising ways) economic analysis can illuminate not only common phenomena but also things not normally thought to be within the economist's purview. Just as the book *Freakonomics* helped the general public to better understand that economics is all around us, our Freakonomics essays help students understand the practicality of using microeconomic theory to understand things off the beaten track.

Examples of Freakonomics essays include *Thomas Thwaites's Toaster* (Chapter 1), *Even Animals Like Sales* (Chapter 5), *Why Do Indian Fishermen Love Their Cell Phones So Much?* (Chapter 6), *Victoria's Not-So-Secret Price Discrimination* (Chapter 10), and *Going to the Ends of the World (Literally) to Test Economic Theory* (Chapter 17). A complete list of Freakonomics essays appears on the inside front cover of this book.

How does our book make it easier to read and learn microeconomics?

Outstanding presentation in an economics text depends on two main factors. We have labored to be sure that our book delivers on each one.

■ First, we use **straightforward and accessible writing** without sacrificing rigor or depth of discussion. Powerful and complex ideas should not be conveyed in abstract, dry, or complicated language.

■ Almost as important as a clear verbal explanation is a **clear graphical presentation.** By using color, clear labels, and detailed explanatory captions, we have worked hard to ensure that each graph complements our words and provides students with a powerful tool for deeper understanding.

How do we make it easier for students to understand microeconomics?

Intermediate microeconomics is a challenging subject and many students struggle to learn its theory and apply it to a variety of situations. Our features will help students succeed in the course.

1. **Figure It Out worked-out problems.** Reviewers, focus group participants, and class testers continually told us that their students have difficulty translating what they have learned into the ability to solve problems *using* what they have learned. Each chapter has several Figure It Out exercises. These detailed, worked-out problems patiently and completely walk students through the process of how to use economic tools and analysis to think through a problem and develop its solution. The solutions to these exercises give students a thorough, step-by-step model for analyzing exactly what a problem asks them to do, identifying what tools they need to solve the problem, and using those tools to arrive at an answer. The Figure It Out exercises are carefully coordinated with the end-of-chapter Problems sets so that students are well prepared to successfully work out not only the end-of-chapter exercises, but also questions on quizzes and exams.

2. **Make the Grade essays** point out common pitfalls that students may encounter and help them navigate through the finer points of microeconomic theory. Make the Grade essays give practical advice on topics that frequently trip up students during homework and tests. Examples include *Simple Rules to Remember about Income and Substitution Effects* (Chapter 5), *Is It Really Price Discrimination?* (Chapter 10), and *The Check Method* (Chapter 12).

3. **End-of-chapter study aids** appear at the end of every chapter. Students will find a Summary, Review Questions, and an extensive set of multipart Problems to help them review and practice what they've learned in the chapter. The answers to all Review Questions and solutions to selected end-of-chapter problems may be found at the back of this book. Problems with solutions provided in the text are indicated by an asterisk.

We worked particularly hard to coordinate our Problems with the Figure It Out exercises in the main chapter. If students have worked through the Figure It Outs, they will be successful in tackling the solutions to each problem. In addition, each problem set was exhaustively reviewed by instructors to ensure its validity and usefulness in testing the chapter's coverage.

How do we deal with math?

Math is a powerful tool for economic analysis, and we want students of every skills set to be able to use it effectively. We have provided a text that will work for a diverse population of students and encourage them to use their math skills to unlock the potential of economic analysis. Our versatile text and its accompanying resources will allow you to use our book in a course with a standard algebraic and geometric focus or in one that relies more on calculus.

Our clear and accessible verbal and graphical presentations are supported by simple and thorough, step-by-step explanations. The whys and wherefores of each step in the mathematical development of concepts are always clearly explained, and allow even math-shy students to easily understand how the use of math can enhance and simplify economic analysis. The main text uses algebra and geometry, but our in-text and online calculus appendices and accompanying resources allow calculus to be integrated easily into the presentation of theory, practice, and application.

For those who use calculus

Calculus makes some microeconomic tools easier to use, so in planning our "useful" text, we agreed on the need to integrate some degree of calculus. The difficulty lay in how much to include and how to present it. In talking to instructors who use calculus in their courses, we found that few were satisfied with how calculus was presented in their current texts. The reasons varied widely: The calculus was too much or not enough; it was too intrusive and obscured the economics; it was too integrated or not integrated enough. Our handling of calculus was one of the more challenging puzzles we faced in defining our approach. We believe we have arrived at a solution that, for many, will be "just right."

Calculus is presented in appendices that employ the same conversational tone and intuitive approach as the text. These appendices include examples and Figure It Out problems, which are often the same as the algebra-based ones in the chapter. In this way, students can see how the calculus analysis buttresses the algebraic analysis. To give students an opportunity to practice what they have learned, each appendix includes problems that require the use of calculus. For courses using a moderate amount of calculus, we provide five calculus appendices in the book; to accommodate more extensive use of calculus, there are 10 additional appendices online.

To connect the material presented in the chapter with that in the appendices, we have placed marginal notes in the chapter. These notes direct students to the appropriate appendix, and explain specifically how calculus will be used to understand the concepts. We hope these notes will encourage students familiar with calculus to utilize it on their own.

The following is a complete listing of our in-text and online appendices. All online appendices can be found at **http://glsmicro.com/appendices.**

In-text calculus appendices

Chapter 4: *The Calculus of Utility Maximization and Expenditure Minimization*

Chapter 5: *The Calculus of Income and Substitution Effects*

Chapter 6: *The Calculus of Cost Minimization*

Chapter 7: *The Calculus of a Firm's Cost Structure*

Chapter 9: *The Calculus of Profit Maximization*

Online calculus appendices

Math Review Appendix

Most students entering this course will benefit from a math review, whether it is a review of basic algebra or calculus. Our text includes a Math Review Appendix at the back of the book that provides the review necessary to prepare students for the math they will use throughout the text.

How is our book organized?

Here is a brief snapshot of the chapters in the book with a bit of discussion on particular subjects that received some special attention or might be different from what you would find in other books. We consider Chapters 1–11 the "core" chapters that most instructors will teach. The remaining chapters, 12–17, can be taught independently of one another.

Chapter 1, Adventures in Microeconomics: We open the book with a brief introductory chapter and a story about the markets for making and for buying coffee to entice and excite students about the study of microeconomics. Through an Application, a Theory and Data section, and a Freakonomics box, we show students right away how the microeconomic tools developed in this course are useful, not just in the study of economics and business, but in the pursuit of everyday life.

Chapter 2, Supply and Demand: In Chapters 2 and 3, we lay a solid foundation by going deeply into supply and demand before we move on to consumer and producer behavior. Existing books usually separate the presentation and the application of this simple yet powerful model. Presenting all aspects of this model at the beginning makes logical sense, and we (and those who class-tested the book) have experienced success with this approach in classes.

Chapter 2 presents the basics of the supply-and-demand model. Of particular note is the section "Key Assumptions of the Supply and Demand Model," which exemplifies the care with which we develop and explain microeconomic theory.

Chapter 3, Using Supply and Demand to Analyze Markets: In Chapter 3, we use the supply-and-demand model to analyze extensively consumer and producer surplus, price and quantity regulations, and taxes and subsidies. We believe that the earlier these concepts are introduced and the more completely they are explained, the easier it is to use them throughout the course. Note that the presentation of the topics in Chapter 3 is designed to be flexible: You don't have to cover every topic in the chapter; you can pick and choose.

Chapter 4, Consumer Behavior: How do consumers decide what and how much to consume given the enormous variety of goods and services available to them? We begin this crucial chapter by clearly laying out, in one section, the assumptions we make about consumer behavior. Actual tests among professors consistently showed this approach as being especially helpful for their students. This chapter also introduces utility theory and consumers' budget constraints in a clear, yet rigorous, presentation.

Chapter 5, Individual and Market Demand: Here we show how consumer preferences are used to derive market demand. Section 5.3, "Decomposing Consumer Responses to Price Changes into Income and Substitution Effects," takes extra care in explaining this topic, which students often find challenging. Abundant applications and discussion of pitfalls to avoid make this material particularly accessible and interesting.

Chapter 6, Producer Behavior: How do companies decide which combination of inputs to use in production, and how does this decision affect production costs? In this chapter, we once again begin by clearly laying out the "Simplifying Assumptions about Firms' Production Behavior." Later in the chapter, we devote a complete section to the role technological change plays in firms' productivity over time. Several applications and examples (including a Freakonomics box on how cell phones have altered the behavior of producers in the Indian fish market) bring this material alive for students.

Chapter 7, Costs: Cost curves illustrate how costs change with a firm's output level and are crucial in deriving market supply. Because opportunity costs and sunk costs are often difficult concepts for students to master, we take extra care at the start of Chapter 7 to distinguish these concepts and illustrate the role they play in decision making. Our examples (including studies of gym membership usage and why movie studios release films they know will lose money) engage students so that they can better understand the often challenging concepts in this chapter.

Chapter 8, Supply in a Competitive Market: This chapter begins our coverage of market structure, and it uses real-life industries such as the Texas electricity industry and housing markets in Boston, Massachusetts, and Fargo, North Dakota, to explain how competitive markets work. We clearly, carefully, and patiently explain a firm's shutdown decision, a topic that students often find confusing.

Chapter 9, Market Power and Monopoly: This chapter begins with a thorough discussion of the origin of market power and how having such power affects a firm's production and pricing decisions. Our three-step process for determining profit maximization for a firm with market power clarifies this topic for students. We bring the concept of monopolistic market power to life using examples of real firms with near-monopoly power, such as Durkee-Mower, Inc., the firm that makes Marshmallow Fluff, and Dr. Brown's, a manufacturer of specialty sodas. Abundant applications, including a discussion of how Southwest Airlines enters the stronghold airports of incumbent carriers and drives down fares, further engage students' interest.

Chapter 10, Market Power and Pricing Strategy: This extremely practical and useful chapter will appeal especially to business students. We thoroughly discuss the many ways in which a firm can take advantage of pricing power, and we clearly describe pricing strategies that can be effective in a variety of situations. Particularly useful to students are Figure 10.1: *An Overview of Pricing Strategies* and a pedagogical device called When to Use It, which explains at the start of each strategy what a firm needs to know about its market and customers to use each pricing strategy most effectively.

Chapter 11, Imperfect Competition: This chapter looks at oligopolies and monopolistically competitive firms. Unlike perfectly competitive and monopolistic firms, these firms must consider their competitors' actions and strategize to maximize their profits. To help students understand the various models of imperfect competition, each section starts with a Model Assumptions box that lists the conditions an industry must meet for that model to apply.

Chapter 12, Game Theory: The tools of game theory can be used to explain strategic interactions among firms and to predict market outcomes. Students will find our game theory analysis (presented in one chapter for better comprehension) easy to follow and understand because of our use of the *check method* (page 489), which simplifies games and helps students easily identify Nash equilibria and dominant/dominated strategies. Varied topics from penalty kicks in soccer to celebrity winemaking to airlines' responses to threats of entry to the movie *Dr. Strangelove* show the usefulness of game theory in not just business, but also everyday decision making.

Chapter 13, Investment, Time, and Insurance: Understanding the role of risk and uncertainty over time helps individuals and firms make better economic decisions about investments and insurance. We clearly explain how current costs, future payoffs, time, and uncertainty play a fundamental role in the many decisions firms and consumers face every day. Reviewers especially appreciated our coverage of all these topics in one concise chapter.

Chapter, 14 General Equilibrium: We can analyze the conditions that must hold for an economy to operate efficiently. We explain intuitively the concepts of general equilibrium, using an extension of the supply-and-demand framework. Examples include the decline in teacher quality and the interaction between housing and labor markets. We also explain the connections among exchange, input, and output efficiencies and then tie them to the Welfare Theorems.

Chapter 15, Asymmetric Information: After learning in earlier chapters what conditions must hold for markets to work well, we look at situations in which markets might not work well. Chapter 15 shows how market outcomes are distorted when information is not equally shared by all potential parties in a transaction. As always, a variety of examples from auto insurance to real estate transactions to piracy shows students that concepts learned in microeconomics are useful in many areas of life.

Chapter 16, Externalities and Public Goods: This chapter continues our examination of market failure by looking at what happens to market outcomes when transactions affect people who are neither the buying nor the selling party, and what happens when a good's benefits are shared by many people at the same time. Our coverage makes clear to students why externalities occur and how they can be remedied (including a discussion of tradable emissions permits and the Coase theorem). In our coverage of public goods, we show why a fire department might have an incentive to allow a house to burn down.

Chapter 17, Behavioral and Experimental Economics: The recent growth of behavioral economics poses a challenge to traditional microeconomics because it questions whether people actually behave the way traditional theory predicts they will. This question puts any intermediate microeconomics book in a bit of a conundrum because embracing behavioral economics seems to undermine the methods learned in the book.

Our chapter on behavioral economics explains how to think rationally in an irrational world. If some people make irrational economic decisions (and we present the behavioral evidence of situations where they tend to make mistakes), other market participants can use this irrationality to their advantage.

Reviewer acknowledgments

We are indebted to the following reviewers, focus group participants, and other consultants for their suggestions and advice:

Senyo Adjibolosoo, *Point Loma Nazarene University*

David Anderson, *Centre College*

Anthony Andrews, *Governors State University*

Georgeanne Artz, *Iowa State University*

Kevin Beckwith, *Salem State University*

Scott Benson, Idaho State University

Tibor Besedes, *Georgia Institute of Technology*

Volodymyr Bilotkach, *Newcastle University*

David Black, *University of Delaware*

Victor Brajer, *California State University–Fullerton*

John Brock, *University of Colorado–Colorado Springs*

Keith Brouhle, *Grinnell College*

Bruce Brown, *California State Polytechnic University–Pomona*

Byron Brown, *Michigan State University*

Donald Bumpass, *Sam Houston State University*

Paul Byrne, *Washburn University*

Benjamin Campbell, *The Ohio State University*

Bolong Cao, *Ohio University*

Shawn Carter, *Jacksonville State University*

Fwu-Ranq Chang, *Indiana University–Bloomington*

Joni Charles, *Texas State University–San Marcos*

Ron Cheung, *Oberlin College*

Marcelo Clerici-Arias, *Stanford University*

John Crooker, *University of Central Missouri*

Carl Davidson, *Michigan State University*

Harold Elder, *University of Alabama*

Tisha Emerson, *Baylor University*

Michael Enz, *Framingham State University*

Brent Evans, *Mississippi State University*

Haldun Evrenk, *Boston University*

Li Feng, *Texas State University*

Chris Ferguson, *University of Wisconsin–Stout*

Gary Fournier, *Florida State University*

Craig Gallet, *California State University–Sacramento*

Linda Ghent, *Eastern Illinois University*

Alex Gialanella, *Manhattanville College*

Lisa Giddings, *University of Wisconsin–La Crosse*

Kirk Gifford, *Brigham Young University*

Darrell Glaser, *United States Naval Academy*

Tuncer Gocmen, *Shepherd University*

Jacob Goldston, *University of South Carolina*

Julie Gonzalez, *University of California–Santa Cruz*

Darren Grant, *Sam Houston State University*

Chiara Gratton-Lavoie, *California State University–Fullerton*

Thomas Grennes, *North Carolina State University*

Philip Grossman, *Monash University*

Steffen Habermalz, *Northwestern University*

Jennifer Hafer, *University of Arkansas*

James Halteman, *Wheaton College*

David Hammes, *University of Hawaii at Hilo*

Mehdi Haririan, *Bloomsburg University*

Daniel J. Henderson, *University of Alabama*

Paul Hettler, *California University of Pennsylvania*

Tia Hilmer, *San Diego State University*

Gary Hoover, *University of Alabama*

Jack Hou, *California State University–Long Beach*

Greg Hunter, *California State University–Pomona*

Christos A. Ioannou, *University of Southampton*

Miren Ivankovic, *Anderson University*

Olena Ivus, *Queen's University*

Michael Jerison, *State University of New York–Albany*

Bruce K. Johnson, *Centre College*

Daniel Johnson, *Colorado College*

Leo Kahane, *Providence College*

Raja Kali, *University of Arkansas*

Pari Kasliwal, *California State University–Long Beach*

John W. Keating, *University of Kansas*

Russell Kellogg, *University of Colorado–Denver*

Chris Kennedy, *George Mason University*

Rashid Khan, *McMaster University*

Vasilios D. Kosteas, *Cleveland State University*

Carsten Lange, *California State Polytechnic University, Pomona*

Jeffrey Larrimore, *Georgetown University*

Sang Lee, *Southeastern Louisiana University*

Daniel Lin, *American University*

Qihong Liu, *University of Oklahoma*

Jeffrey Livingston, *Bentley University*

Kristina Lybecker, *Colorado College*

Guangyu Ma, *State University of New York–Buffalo*

Teny Maghakian, *University of California–Merced*

Arindam Mandal, *Siena College*

Justin Marion, *University of California–Santa Cruz*

Timothy Mathews, *Kennesaw State University*

Ata Mazaheri, *University of Toronto–Scarborough*

John McArthur, *Wofford College*

Naranchimeg Mijid, *Central Connecticut State University*

Lijia Mo, *Kansas State University*

Myra Moore, *University of Georgia*

Tamah Morant, *North Carolina State University*

Thayer Morrill, *North Carolina State University*

Felix Munoz-Garcia, *Washington State University*

Kathryn Nantz, *Fairfield University*

Pascal Ngoboka, *University of Wisconsin–River Falls*

Hong V. Nguyen, *University of Scranton*

Michael Nieswiadomy, *University of North Texas*

Matthew J. Notowidigdo, *The University of Chicago*

Constantin Ogloblin, *Georgia Southern University*

Alex Olbrecht, *Ramapo College of New Jersey*

Heather O'Neill, *Ursinus College*

June O'Neill, *Baruch College, City University of New York*

Patrick O'Neill, *University of North Dakota*

Alexei Orlov, *Radford University*

Lydia Ortega, *San Jose State University*

Emily Oster, *The University of Chicago*

Orgul Ozturk, *University of South Carolina*

Alexandre Padilla, *Metropolitan State University of Denver*

James Payne, *University of South Florida*

Anita Alves Pena, *Colorado State University*

Marie Petkus, *Centre College*

Jeremy Petranka, *University of North Carolina–Chapel Hill*

Barry Pfitzner, *Randolph-Macon College*

Brennan Platt, *Brigham Young University*

James Prieger, *Pepperdine University*

Samuel Raisanen, *Central Michigan University*

Rati Ram, *Illinois State University*

Ryan Ratcliff, *University of San Diego*

Marie Rekkas, *Simon Fraser University*

Michael Reksulak, *Georgia Southern University*

Malcolm Robinson, *Thomas More College*

Juliette Roddy, *University of Michigan–Dearborn*

Brian Rosario, *American River College*

Nicholas Rupp, *East Carolina University*

Robert Rycroft, *University of Mary Washington*

Shane Sanders, *Western Illinois University*

Sudipta Sarangi, *Louisiana State University*

Tom Scheiding, *Cardinal Stritch University*

Helen Schneider, *University of Texas–Austin*

Barbara Schone, *Georgetown University*

Kathleen Segerson, *University of Connecticut*

Quazi Shahriar, *San Diego State University*

Carl Shapiro, *University of California–Berkeley*

Alexandre Skiba, *University of Wyoming*

Rachael Small, *University of Colorado at Boulder*

Christy Spivey, *University of Texas–Arlington*

Kevin Stange, *University of Michigan*

Lee Stone, *State University of New York–Geneseo*

David Switzer, *St. Cloud State University*

Ellen Szarleta, *Indiana University–Northwest*

Kerry Tan, *Loyola University Maryland*

Gwendolyn Tedeschi, *Manhattan College*

Jeremy Thornton, *Samford University*

Irene Trela, *Western University*

Regina Trevino, *Loyola University–Chicago*

Brian Trinque, *University of Texas–Austin*

Victoria Umanskaya, *University of California–Riverside*

Michael Vaney, *University of British Columbia*

Jennifer VanGilder, *Ursinus College*

Jose Vazquez, *University of Illinois at Urbana-Champaign*

Annie Voy, *Gonzaga University*

Bhavneet Walia, *Western Illinois University*

Joann M. Weiner, *The George Washington University*

Jeanne Wendel, *University of Nevada–Reno*

Benjamin Widner, *New Mexico State University*

Keith Willet, *Oklahoma State University*

Beth Wilson, *Humboldt State University*

Catherine Wolfram, *University of California–Berkeley*

Peter Wui, *University of Arkansas–Pine Bluff*

Erik Zemljic, *Kent State University*

Faculty advisers

We owe an enormous debt to Linda Ghent, Eastern Illinois University, our consulting faculty editor, a talented economist, and gifted teacher. So much of this book, from text to features to graphics, reflects her imprint. Her devotion to and belief in this book from its inception to its completion have been invaluable and it has been a real pleasure working with her.

Alan Grant, Baker College, produced end-of-chapter questions that don't just test the material in the book, but enhance it. Scott Houser, Colorado School of Mines, and Anita Pena, Colorado State University, shaped the calculus program for the book and with Skip Crooker and Kristina Lybecker, developed many of the resources needed to make this book useful for a broad range of instructors and students.

We were fortunate to have a core group of committed and supportive instructors on whom we could depend to provide feedback when the path wasn't readily apparent: Tibor Besedes, Georgia Institute of Technology; Lisa Giddings, University of

Wisconsin–La Crosse; Alan Grant, Baker College; Scott Houser, Colorado School of Mines; Kristina Lybecker, Colorado College; Naranchimeg Mijid, Central Connecticut State University; Kathryn Nantz, Fairfield University; Anita Alves Pena, Colorado State University; Jeremy Petranka, University of North Carolina–Chapel Hill; Sudipta Sarangi, Louisiana State University; Jennifer VanGilder, Ursinus College; and Annie Voy, Gonzaga University.

We are most appreciative of the classes of Lisa Giddings and Annie Voy, who were the first to use our material in their classes. The core chapters of the text benefitted especially from their experience.

We would especially like to thank the eagle-eyed Michael Reksulak, Georgia Southern University, for his vigilant accuracy checking of the entire book. The book is cleaner, easier to read, and more understandable because of his careful work. Michael could spot a typo half a mile away, and we're all better off for it.

Publisher acknowledgments

We owe a great deal of thanks to the many hardworking and creative people who have helped bring this book into existence.

Craig Bleyer, then publisher of the economics list at Worth, started us down this road with a knock on Austan's door many years ago. Craig, with the supportive management of Elizabeth Widdicombe and Catherine Woods, set up an expert book team. When Craig took a new job within the company, Charles Linsmeier succeeded Craig as publisher, and provided the thoughtful direction and steady hand needed to see through this project.

Each member of our book team brought unique talents and perspective to the work. Our able and accomplished economics editor at Worth, Sarah Dorger, managed this project with great expertise and devotion. Keeping the countless moving parts (authors, editors, reviewers, and consultants) coordinated and on track often required her heroic (and heroically patient) efforts.

Our developmental editor, Jane Tufts, has edited some of the discipline's finest texts, and her creative influence can be seen in every element and every page of the book. With her unparalleled ability to read manuscript with real empathy for the student's experience, she provided guidance and advice that transformed our initial drafts into a readable, student-focused, and engaging text.

Bruce Kaplan, our developmental editor at Worth, controlled and directed the editorial traffic generated by the extensive development and production process with unwavering intelligence, good judgment, practicality, calm, and skill. Under his guidance, Mary Melis, assistant editor, moved the manuscript expertly into the hands of our tireless production team. Melissa Pellerano provided her with essential support throughout the process.

Most especially, we would have been lost without the assistance of Erin Robertson, on the ground with us at the University of Chicago. With the experience she's gained assisting us with research, editing, proofreading, and publisher communications, she's ready to write her own book!

We are grateful to the many people at Worth who provided the knowledge and support needed to get this book into your hands. Tracey Kuehn, Barbara Seixas, and Lisa Kinne provided essential direction, from the earliest planning stages to the very end. Rob Errera saw our manuscript through the production process with superior attention to detail and resourcefulness in the wake of missed deadlines here and there (and there and there and there!) and Hurricane Sandy. And we are grateful for the careful eye of Patti Brecht, our copyeditor. Designer Kevin Kall deserves credit for the distinctive look of this text, a departure from most intermediate texts. Ted Szczepanski and Elyse Rieder worked to find interesting and entertaining photos for each chapter. A special thank you goes to Greg Ghent for providing the computer sketches that were transformed into our clear, useful graphs.

Intermediate microeconomics is a hands-on course for instructors and students, and there is a great need for quality instructional and learning tools to enhance their experiences in and out of the classroom. Our media and supplements editors at Worth, Lukia Kliossis and Jaclyn Ferry, with the guidance of Faculty Supplements Coordinator and Editor Linda Ghent, have worked to provide innovative and truly useful tools for both instructor and student. We are especially grateful to Lukia for turning the plans for a truly useful media and supplements program into reality. The resources she and her colleagues, Stacey Alexander, Edgar Bonilla, and Ashley Joseph, have delivered will enhance the course experience of instructors and students.

The marketing of a first edition has special challenges and opportunities that our marketing team at Worth met with creativity and zeal. Paul Shensa's wisdom and experience were invaluable as we navigated this market and learned about the diverse needs of instructors and students. The keen marketing direction and insight of Steve Rigolosi and Scott Guile throughout the book development process added to the book's usefulness. They managed the successful launch to an eager market, while Kerri Russini managed the details of class tests and reviews with good cheer and expert coordination.

Final thoughts

Heartfelt thanks to our families for their continued support of our work (especially when we are too busy to let them know how much we appreciate it).

Ultimately, any text is only a tool and a complement to what students learn in the classroom and from one another. We hope that this text will help you to start them on that journey to using economics.

Austan Goolsbee

September 30, 2012

Steven Levitt

Chad Syverson

TOOLS FOR TEACHING AND LEARNING WITH *MICROECONOMICS*

Worth Publishers has collaborated with a number of experienced and committed instructors of intermediate microeconomics to develop resources to complement the text and provide useful tools for teaching the course and learning the material.

HANDY AS A SWISS ARMY KNIFE

http://youreconportal.com

ECON**P⊕RTAL** Available for Fall 2013

We've taken most of the book's tools for teaching and learning microeconomics and stowed them neatly in EconPortal, Macmillan Higher Education's course management system. Much like the Swiss Army knife on the book's cover, EconPortal integrates and unifies a variety of online tools, including the interactive e-Book, to meet the needs of instructors and students in powerful yet simple ways—powerful enough to dramatically enhance teaching and learning, yet simple enough to use right away. And now it can be fully integrated into Blackboard, Canvas, and many other learning management systems.

Here are just some of the resources and functionality in the EconPortal for *Microeconomics*:

Launch Pad

Build a course in minutes Curated by experienced instructors and learning specialists, Launch Pad is a ready-made EconPortal course to use out of the box or as the basis for a customized course. The Launch Pad modules combine e-Book sections with activities such as interactive animations, adaptive quizzing, and a variety of additional multimedia assignments as well as pre-assembled quizzes and homework assignments. With these ready-to-use units, instructors can create a fully-functioning online course quickly and easily, either by using the modules as-is or by quickly dragging and dropping selections from the GLS resource library or by inserting their own materials.

*LEARNING*Curve

Personalized, research-based, formative assessments With powerful adaptive quizzing, a game-like format, and the promise of better grades, LearningCurve is a quickly implemented, effective way to get students engaged and learning. Learning-Curve creates activities individualized for each student in difficulty and topic, according to what the student does and does not understand. Questions come with hints, links to relevant e-Book sections, and feedback for incorrect answers. For more detailed information, visit **http://learningcurveworks.com**.

Interactive e-Book

Robust, interactive, and customizable The e-Book in EconPortal is a powerful study tool for students and an easy way for instructors to deliver additional materials to customize their course.

The student will benefit from a number of embedded resources including

- narrated eFigure animations that walk students through the development of key figures in the text.

- material from the book's study guide: helpful tips, worked out problems, and additional practice problems with detailed and instructive solutions.

- an easy to use note-taking tool.

Instructors can customize the text by rearranging e-Book sections and chapters and adding material, including notes, hyperlinks, slides, quizzes, and further examples. And everything is assignable!

Practice and Assessment

Powerful online quizzing, homework, and practice With EconPortal's state-of-the-art online assessment system, everything is assignable. Research shows that making online assignments a part of final grades consistently translates into higher overall student performance. Instructors can use pre-created assignments for each chapter or create their own assignments, drawing from a vast repository of resources for the GLS text including eFigures with assessment, study guide materials, additional problems, test bank problems, graphing questions, examples and readings, and adapted calculus materials.

COMPANION WEB SITE FOR STUDENTS AND INSTRUCTORS

http://glsmicro.com

The companion Web site for the Goolsbee, Levitt, and Syverson text delivers a number of useful tools for instructors and students.

Available to Students and Instructors

Online Mathematical Appendices

In addition to the five calculus appendices in the text, ten additional appendices, including Figure It Outs and problems, are available.

Calculus Complement

Organized by chapter, it includes

- an introduction to using calculus in the intermediate microeconomics course and the calculus appendices, both in-text and online.

- Figure It Out examples, adapted for calculus.

- end-of-chapter questions from the book, adapted for calculus.

Study Aids

- **Quizzing:** Students can test their knowledge of the material in the book by taking multiple-choice quizzes on any chapter.

- **Flashcards:** Students can quiz themselves on the definitions in the glossary with virtual flashcards.

Tools for Instructors

We queried hundreds of intermediate microeconomics instructors to determine what resources would be most valuable to them in teaching the course. We are pleased to provide a robust set of quality instructional resources.

Supplemental Content

Instructors made it clear that supplemental content for class presentation and practice was by far their greatest need. Instructors will find a wealth of material on the instructor's Web site, including the following:

- **Problems and Solutions:** These problems and solutions have been modeled after the end-of-chapter problems and include problems adapted for calculus.

- **Instructional Examples & Content:** Mirrored after the popular features of the text, additional applications, Freakonomics boxes, Theory and Data boxes, and Figure It Outs will keep the course fresh and provide new material for presentation or distribution to students.

Lecture PPTs

Organized by chapter, these PowerPoint slides feature an overview of key concepts, animated graphs, additional applications, and Figure It Outs.

Resources for Course Planning

- **Suggested Course Outlines and Transition Guide:** To help instructors develop syllabi using the GLS text and transition from their current text, we provide suggested course outlines and guides with helpful pointers to smooth the transition.

- **Chapter Notes:** Chapter notes include an outline of each chapter, teaching tips, suggestions for "flipping the classroom," and additional worked-out problems.

- **Solutions Manual:** The Solutions Manual includes solutions for all end-of-chapter problems, including the problems found in the in-text calculus appendices. This is also available as a print version.

- **Solutions Manual for Calculus Problems:** This Solutions Manual includes solutions for all problems found within the calculus complement, which includes all end-of-chapter problems that have been adapted for calculus and the in-text and online calculus appendix problems.

ADDITIONAL RESOURCES FOR STUDENTS AND INSTRUCTORS

Available to Students and Instructors

Study Guide

The study guide offers a review of key concepts, study tips, additional Figure It Outs, and practice problems for each chapter. Calculus material tied to the book's mathematical appendices has been integrated and is easily identified by the calculus icon used in the text. This resource is available as a print version that can be packaged with the text, and through EconPortal.

Calculus Complement

This free resource is available to students and instructors online at **http://glsmicro.com/calccomp** or in a print version that can be packaged with the text.

CourseSmart

The CourseSmart e-Book offers the complete book in PDF format. Students can save up to 60% off the price of print textbooks. With the CourseSmart e-Book, students have the ability to take notes, print pages, and more.

For Instructors

Test Bank

The test bank makes building tests easy with multiple-choice and short-answer problems for all of the text's chapters. The test bank is available in both print and on CD, as well as through EconPortal.

Learning Management System Integration

For fall of 2013, EconPortal, as well as many media resources for the text, will be fully integrated with Blackboard, Canvas, and many other learning management systems. This means we will offer not only single sign on, but e-books and assessment that will work within the LMS and report directly to the LMS gradebook. For more information, please visit **http://macmillanhighered.com/lms.**

We also offer certain resources that can be used as a free course pack on a number of course management systems, including Blackboard, WebCT, Canvas, Desire2Learn, Angel, Sakai, or Moodle. For more information, go to **http://worthpublishers.com/catalog/Other/Coursepack.**

EXPERT RESOURCES AUTHORED BY EXPERT INSTRUCTORS

The resources to accompany GLS were created by a team of dedicated and experienced intermediate micro instructors. This list of contributors and reviewers is comprehensive of those who have contributed at this time and will continue to grow as new resources are developed.

John Crooker, *University of Central Missouri*
Practice and Assessment Materials Author

Linda Ghent, *Eastern Illinois University*
Instructor Resources Author

Alan Grant, *Baker College*
Practice and Assessment Materials Author

Scott Houser, *Colorado School of Mines*
Calculus Materials Author and Editor

Christos Ioannou, *University of Southampton*
Solutions Manual Author

David Kalist, *Shippensburg University*
Test Bank Author

Chris Kennedy, *George Mason University*
Lecture PowerPoints Author

Anthony Lima, *California State University—East Bay*
LearningCurve Author

Constantin Ogloblin, *Georgia Southern University*
Study Guide Author

Anita Pena, *Colorado State University*
Calculus Supplements and Adaptations Editor and Author

Jeremy Petranka, *University of North Carolina—Chapel Hill*
eFigures Author and Narrator

Samuel Raisanen, *Central Michigan University*
Graphing Problems Author

Leonie Stone, *State University of New York—Geneseo*
Instructor Resources Author

using *microeconomics*

Intermediate microeconomics is the course that decides majors and introduces the tools that are fundamental to effective decision making in business, government, and everyday life. *Microeconomics* bridges the gap between the theory and practice of microeconomics. In a course that is too often overwhelmingly theoretical, we provide an empirical dimension that will make the course immediately relevant and useful to students. *Microeconomics* provides examples that offer unusual perspective on the seemingly ordinary. With carefully crafted features, the text moves students from understanding the basics of economic principles to applying the powerful and revelatory tools of economic analysis. See below and the pages following for examples of these features.

theory and data

Theory and Data discussions summarize research and provide an empirical dimension, revealing how economic theory relates to real-world data.

Golfers' Backward-Bending Labor Supply Curves

Tiger Woods is perhaps the most recognizable face in professional golf. He's won 71 PGA tour events and picked up 14 Majors. He's lent his name to campaigns for Nike and Titleist—and taken home a cool $40 million and $20 million, respectively, for the work. But it's not just his athletic skill that separates him from the average American laborer: He's probably one of the few people facing wages on the backward-bending portion of his labor supply curve. In other words, as his wages increase, he actually decreases the number of tournaments in which he plays.

PGA rules allow each golfer to elect which and how many events to play in, meaning the athlete considers the labor–leisure tradeoff separately for each tournament event. With tournament payoffs in the millions of dollars for just four rounds of golf, you probably think it a no-brainer to play. Indeed, for most golfers, it is. Generally, around 100 players sign up for any given event. This doesn't even include the over 1,000 hopefuls who play in brutal qualifying rounds, vying for just 25 spots on the PGA Tour.

Given the opportunity, these hopefuls would gladly play every tournament, but as economists Otis Gilley and Marc Chopin discovered, players like Tiger Woods don't.* In a 2000 paper, Gilley and Chopin looked at how low- and middle-income PGA players in the 1990s responded to increases in their wages and compared this result to the effects of wage increases on high-income players. Whereas low-level players entered more events as their event winnings increased, golfers at the top of their game decreased their tournament play as their wages increased. Top golfers were actually operating on the backward-bending portion of their labor supply curve! In particular, for every $1,000 increase in expected per-event winnings, the number of tournaments entered in a season by high-income players decreases by 0.05 to 0.1. For these select players, the income effect dominated the substitution effect, and faced with the leisure–labor tradeoff, they elected to consume more leisure.

Workers in other fields—including many economists—often spend their leisure time on the golf course. But for a professional golfer, a day on the green is work, not leisure. So just what does a PGA player do on his day off? Gilley and Chopin found that married golfers took more days off than did single golfers. Drawing on their own experiences as family men, the two hard-working economists concluded that golfers must be taking off work to spend more quality time with their wives and kids. The example of Tiger Woods, however, shows that the predictions of economic theory don't always hold up in the real world.

---

*Otis W. Gilley and Marc C. Chopin, "Professional Golf: Labor or Leisure." *Managerial Finance* 26, no. 7 (2000): 33–45.

(see page 189)

 application

The Cost of the Black-Liquor Loophole

A recent example of an (accidental) subsidy gone awry is the so-called black-liquor loophole in the law that gave companies tax credits for using alternative fuels. The tax credit is given to businesses that combine alternative fuels with traditional fossil fuels used in their operations, with the idea of encouraging companies to reduce their fossil fuel use in doing so.

It turns out that there is a chemical by-product of paper making called "black liquor" that paper companies have traditionally recycled to use as fuel in their plants. The government determined that this chemical qualified as an alternative fuel under the definition in the law. However, the paper companies couldn't qualify for the tax credit unless they *combined* the alternative fuel with a fossil fuel. So they started adding a bit of diesel fuel—a fossil fuel they weren't using at all before—to the black liquor before burning it. This led to two results. First, paper companies used more diesel than they did before, even though the point of the tax credit was to encourage movement away from use of fossil fuels. Second, paper companies got paid (in the form of tax credits) to burn the black liquor they were already using without payment. They got paid a lot too: This tax credit, originally projected to cost the government $61 million, ended up costing an estimated $6 to $8 *billion* in tax credits in 2009, almost all of it going to paper companies.

How does our analysis in this section explain what happened? The tax credit became, in practice, a diesel subsidy for the paper industry. By tying the credit to the use of blended fuels, it lowered the effective price of diesel that the paper companies faced. Before, when they had to pay the market price, their quantity demanded for diesel to fuel their plants was zero—they had a plentiful and cheap alternative in the black liquor. But now every gallon of diesel they bought came with a big tax credit attached—meaning they faced a downward-shifted supply curve for diesel. The quantity of diesel they demanded at these lower supply prices became positive.

As a result of this policy, the paper companies and the diesel sellers are better off because of the subsidy. (The former very much so in this case.) But the costs are large. First, there is deadweight loss: An industry that wasn't using diesel before because it had a superior alternative now demands it, even though the industry values it at less than the cost of supplying it. Second, the government has to pay the subsidy. And as noted above, that's a really big number. So big, in fact, that Congress closed the loophole in 2010 because they decided that we couldn't afford it. ∎

(see page 102–103)

freakonomics

Even Animals Like Sales

If you think the laws of economics only apply to humans, think again. Monkeys, and even rats, behave in ways that would make you think they've taken intermediate micro.

Some of the most intensive testing of the economic behavior of animals was carried out by Yale economist Keith Chen and his co-authors on a group of Capuchin monkeys. As a first step, Chen introduced the monkeys to the concept of money. He gave them "money" in the form of metal washers that they could exchange for various types of foods including Jell-O, grapes, and Marshmallow Fluff (Capuchin monkeys *love* sweet foods).

Just Like Us?

Courtesy M. Keith Chen

After about six exasperating months, these monkeys finally figured out that the washers had value. Chen observed that individual monkeys tended to have stable preferences: Some liked grapes the best, others were fans of Jell-O. How did he learn this? He would give a particular monkey a coin and then offer that monkey a choice between a bowl of three Jell-O cubes and a bowl of six grapes and see which one the monkey chose.

Next, Chen did what any good economist would do: He subjected the monkeys to price changes! Instead of getting three Jell-O cubes for one washer, he would offer the monkey, say, the choice between a single Jell-O cube per washer and a bowl of six grapes per washer. Thus, the relative price of Jell-O became three times as high. The monkeys responded exactly the way economic theory would predict, shifting their consumption away from the goods whose prices had risen.[*]

Perhaps it is not that surprising that monkeys, one of our closest relatives in the animal kingdom, would be sophisticated consumers. But there is no way rats understand supply and demand, is there? It seems they do. Economists Raymond Battalio and John Kagel equipped rats' cages with two levers, each of which dispensed a different beverage.[†] One of these levers gave the rat a refreshing burst of root beer. Rats, it turns out, love root beer. The other lever released quinine water. Quinine is a bitter-tasting substance initially used to treat malaria, and now used primarily to give vodka tonics their distinctive flavor. Rats are far less fond of quinine than they are of root beer, and they made that quite clear to the researchers by pressing the root beer lever far more often. Battalio and Kagel, like Chen, then explored changes in "prices" (how much liquid came out per press of the lever) and in the rats' budget constraint (how many times they could press the levers each day). Like monkeys (and humans), the rats consumed less of a drink when its relative price increased. Even more interesting is that when the rats were made very poor (i.e., they got very few lever presses each day), they shifted their consumption away from root beer toward quinine water. The researchers found that root beer is a luxury good for rats, and quinine water is an inferior good! Wonder what rats would make of a vodka tonic. . . .

[*] That wasn't the only human-like behavior these monkeys exhibited when exposed to money — for the whole amusingly sordid story, see the epilogue to *SuperFreakonomics*.

[†] A description of the work by Battalio and Kagel may be found in: Tim Harford, *The Logic of Life: The Rational Economics of an Irrational World.* (New York: Random House, 2008), pp. 18–21.

(see page 177)

2.1 figure it out

Suppose that the demand and supply curves for a monthly cell phone plan with unlimited texts can be represented by

$$Q^D = 50 - 0.5P$$
$$Q^S = -25 + P$$

The current price of these plans in the market is $40 per month. Is this market in equilibrium? Would you expect the price to rise or fall? If so, by how much? Explain.

Solution:

There are two ways to solve the first question about whether the price will rise or fall. The first is to calculate the quantity demanded and quantity supplied at the current market price of $40 to see how they compare:

$$Q^D = 50 - 0.5P = 50 - 0.5(40) = 50 - 20 = 30$$
$$Q^S = -25 + P = -25 + 40 = 15$$

Because quantity demanded is greater than quantity supplied, we can tell that there is excess demand (a shortage) in the market. Many people are trying to get texting plans, but are finding them sold out because few suppliers want to sell at that price. Prices will rise to equalize quantity supplied and quantity demanded, moving the market to equilibrium.

Alternatively, we could start by solving for the market equilibrium price:

$$Q^D = Q^S$$
$$50 - 0.5P = -25 + P$$
$$1.5P = 75$$
$$P = \$50$$

The current market price, $40, is below the market equilibrium price of $50. (This is why there is excess demand in the market.) Therefore, we would expect the price to rise by $10. When the market reaches equilibrium at a price of $50, all buyers can find sellers and all sellers can find buyers. The price will then remain at $50 unless the market changes and the demand curve or supply curve shifts.

(see page 28)

make the grade

Does quantity supplied equal quantity demanded in equilibrium?

Solving for the market equilibrium as we just did is one of the most common exam questions in intermediate microeconomics classes. The basic idea is always the same: Take the equations for the demand curve and the supply curve, solve for the equilibrium price, and then plug that equilibrium price back into either the supply curve or the demand curve (it does not matter which) to determine the equilibrium quantity. It is simple, but it is easy to make math errors under the time pressure of an exam, especially if the demand and supply curves take on more complicated forms than the basic examples we deal with here.

A simple trick will ensure that you have the right answer, and it takes only a few seconds. Take the equilibrium price that you obtain and plug it into *both* the demand and supply curves. If you don't get the same answer when you substitute the equilibrium price into the supply and demand equations, you know you made a math error along the way because the quantity demanded must equal the quantity supplied in equilibrium.

(see page 26)

Using Math: An Intuitive, Optional, and Versatile Presentation

Math is a powerful tool, and we want students of every skill set to be able to use it effectively. Our text works for a diverse population of students and encourages them to use their math skills to unlock the potential of economic analysis.

Integration

Calculus is integrated easily into the presentation of theory, practice, and application with in-text and online appendices. Marginal notes next to relevant passages in the chapters connect the material to the appendix presentations. These notes encourage students familiar with calculus to utilize the appendices on their own.

Notice that the left-hand side of this equation is equal to the negative of the slope of the indifference curve, or MRS_{XY}. We now can see a very significant connection: *The MRS_{XY} between two goods at any point on an indifference curve equals the inverse ratio of those two goods' marginal utilities*:

$$MRS_{XY} = -\frac{\Delta Q_{\text{t-shirts}}}{\Delta Q_{\text{socks}}} = \frac{MU_{\text{socks}}}{MU_{\text{t-shirts}}}$$

In more basic terms, MRS_{XY} shows the point we emphasized from the beginning: You can tell how much people value something by their choices of what they would be

∂ The end-of-chapter appendix uses calculus to derive the relationship between the marginal rate of substitution and marginal utilities.

Marginal note example from Chapter 4, page 123.

Coverage

We provide five calculus appendices in the book and ten additional appendices online for more extensive use of calculus. Online appendices are at **http://glsmicro.com/appendices.**

In-text calculus appendices:

Chapter 4	The Calculus of Utility Maximization and Expenditure Minimization
Chapter 5	The Calculus of Income and Substitution Effects
Chapter 6	The Calculus of Cost Minimization
Chapter 7	The Calculus of a Firm's Cost Structure
Chapter 9	The Calculus of Profit Maximization Online calculus appendices

Online calculus appendices:

Chapter 2	The Calculus of Equilibrium and Elasticities
Chapter 3	The Calculus of Consumer and Producer Surplus
Chapter 4	The Mathematics of Utility Functions
Chapter 5	The Calculus of Demand
Chapter 6	The Calculus of Production Functions and Input Demand
Chapter 7	The Calculus of a Firm's Cost Structure Expanded
Chapter 8	The Calculus of Long-Run Competitive Equilibria
Chapter 10	The Calculus of Price Strategies
Chapter 11	The Calculus of Cournot and Differentiated Bertrand Competition Equilibria
Chapter 12	The Mathematics of Mixed Strategies in Game Theory

Consistency

The appendices have the same conversational tone and intuitive approach as the text. They include examples and Figure It Out problems, often the same as the algebra-based ones in the chapter, so students can see how the calculus analysis buttresses the algebraic analysis. Each appendix includes problems that require the use of calculus.

This appendix begins on page 157.

Chapter 4 Appendix:
The Calculus of Utility Maximization and Expenditure Minimization

In the chapters you've read so far, you've probably noticed that we use several different approaches when explaining microeconomic theories and applications. One method is mainly intuitive: Tell a story to illustrate an economic concept or discuss the logic of a model and its implications. This method of economic analysis goes back to Adam Smith and the invisible hand. A second method is the graphical approach. You only have to say "supply and demand" to conjure up a simple but powerful representation of a market. Finally, you've seen some simple mathematical models such as the algebraic representations of supply and demand curves in Chapter 2 and the consumer's budget constraint in Chapter 4. Each of these approaches provides a different window into understanding economic concepts.

Those of you who are familiar with calculus have yet another way to approach microeconomics. The tools of calculus are a natural fit with economics, and most economic models are formally derived using calculus. For some people (especially economists), it's easy to become so caught up in the math that the real economic ideas get lost. We don't want you to fall into that trap. That's why we present the calculus as a supplement to the intuition that we develop in the chapter. The calculus appendices provide an additional set of tools to examine the economic decisions and interactions discussed in the chapter. The logic of the models and the intuition from the chapter are still here in the calculus, only in another form.

So, don't think of the calculus that we explore in the appendices as a substitute for the logic, graphs, and algebra we use to explain microeconomics in the chapters. Instead, think of these techniques and the calculus as complements. As you learn more about microeconomics, you will find that each of these different approaches to understanding microeconomics may be more or less useful depending on the circumstances.

$$\max_{B,F} U = B^{0.5}F^{0.5} \text{ s.t. } 20 = 5B + 2F$$

5A.1 figure it out

...und that Antonio consumes 2 burgers and ...rs of fries, and his utility for this bundle is ...$5 = 2^{0.5}5^{0.5} = 10^{0.5}$.

...When the price of hamburgers doubles to ...ch, Antonio faces a new budget constraint: ...$0B + 2F$. Antonio's new utility-maximization ...m is

$$\max_{B,F} U = B^{0.5}F^{0.5} \text{ s.t. } 20 = 10B + 2F$$

...ore, we should write his constrained optimiza-...oblem as a Lagrangian and solve for his new ...al bundle at the higher burger price:

$$\mathcal{L}(B,F,\lambda) = B^{0.5}F^{0.5} + \lambda(20 - 10B - 2F)$$

$$\frac{\partial \mathcal{L}}{\partial B} = 0.5B^{-0.5}F^{0.5} - 10\lambda = 0$$

$$\frac{\partial \mathcal{L}}{\partial F} = 0.5B^{0.5}F^{-0.5} - 2\lambda = 0$$

$$\frac{\partial \mathcal{L}}{\partial \lambda} = 20 - 10B - 2F = 0$$

...e the first two conditions to solve for λ and ...olve for F as a function of B:

$$\lambda = 0.05B^{-0.5}F^{0.5} = 0.25B^{0.5}F^{-0.5}$$

$$F^{0.5}F^{0.5} = 20(0.25)B^{0.5}B^{0.5}$$

$$F = 5B$$

To see the entire Figure It Out, go to page 211.

Resources

Calculus Complement This free resource is available to students and instructors online at **http://glsmicro.com/calccomp** or in a print version that can be packaged with the text. Organized by chapter, it includes

- an introduction to using calculus in the intermediate microeconomics course.
- the calculus appendices, both in-text and online.
- Figure It Out examples, adapted for calculus.
- end-of-chapter questions from the book, adapted for calculus.

Instructors can find the solutions to all calculus problems at **http://glsmicro.com.**

Study Guide Calculus material tied to the book's mathematical appendices has been integrated into the study guide for the book and is easily identified by the calculus icon used in the text. The study guide offers a review of key concepts, study tips, additional Figure It Outs, and practice problems for each chapter. This resource is available as a print version that can be packaged with the text, and through EconPortal.

microeconomics

Adventures in Microeconomics

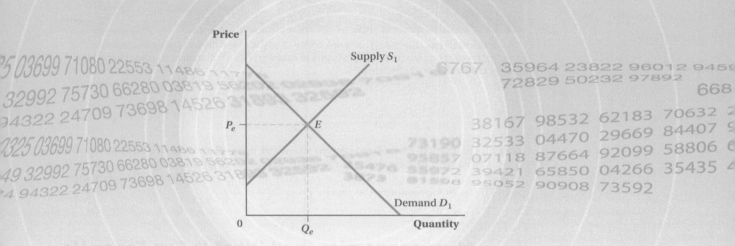

I t is morning in Peru's Selva Alta hills, and the sun has been up for a few hours. Rosa Valencia looks admiringly at the coffee plants she's grown. The coffee plants' fruits, called *cherries* because of the red hue they take on when ripe, are ready for harvest. Rosa's workers handpick the fruit and carry it to the outbuilding where it is processed. There, other workers sort the cherries, then remove the fruits' flesh to expose the two seeds—the coffee beans—inside. The beans are washed and prepared for drying and roasting.

That same morning, about 5,000 miles away in Seattle, Washington, home of Starbucks, Lauren Russell grapples with a physics problem. She's at her favorite coffee shop, a block off campus, for her mid-morning break. Sitting on the table next to her book is her usual, a skinny cappuccino. Every few moments, between calculations, Lauren takes a sip and savors the deep, rich flavor of the coffee.

Lauren and Rosa have never met each other, and likely never will. Yet, their morning routines are connected to one another because the two women are part of the same

Marshall Ikonography/Alamy; Fancy Collection/SuperStock

A woman peels back the red skin of a ripe coffee cherry to reveal the two coffee beans inside. The market for coffee connects coffee producers to consumers, like this student enjoying her coffee while she studies at a coffee shop.

market, the market for coffee. Lauren's taste in drinks connects her to Rosa, who provides a critical input for that drink. Both women benefit from this connection: Rosa profits from growing coffee and Lauren gets a cappuccino at a price she is willing to pay. This is microeconomics at work.

1.1 Microeconomics (and What It Can Teach Us about Rosa and Lauren)

Rosa and Lauren's connection is the consequence of a large number of decisions and transactions that combine to make Rosa believe that growing coffee is worth her time and effort, and make Lauren feel that her skinny cappuccino is worth the money. This book is about investigating those many decisions and transactions, and how they interact in markets.

Before we delve deeper into this book's topics, we need to be very clear about how we're going to approach the study of markets. We will be looking at these decisions through the framework of *micro*economics. **Microeconomics** is the branch of economics that studies the specific choices made by consumers (like Lauren) and producers (like Rosa). In contrast, *macro*economics looks at the world through a wider lens and is a description of the larger, complex system in which consumers and firms operate. Macroeconomics takes hundreds of millions of individual producers and consumers like Rosa and Lauren, and tries to describe and predict the behavior and outcome of the combined total of their individual decisions. In this book, we steer clear of the macroeconomic questions.

Although the basic outline and content of this course are similar to those of the principles of microeconomics course, there are some important differences. First, we incorporate mathematics into our models along with graphs. Remember that at its very root economics is concerned with resource allocation, so we want to be able to create precise models that can be solved for optimal quantities. For example, we often want to know exactly how much of a good a consumer will want to consume to maximize his happiness (utility) given that he has limited income. We also want to model how a firm maximizes its profit when choosing its output level and the amounts of inputs it uses to make that quantity of output. Although graphs and

microeconomics
The branch of economics that studies the specific choices made by consumers and producers.

verbal explanations are helpful, using math allows us to better quantify these economic agents' decisions.[1]

Second, the level of analysis in intermediate microeconomics is deeper. No longer do we take relationships such as the law of demand or the law of supply for granted—we examine the details of *why* the relationship exists.

Finally, intermediate microeconomics has a greater policy focus than the principles of microeconomics course. Understanding the economic behavior of consumers and producers is the key to developing appropriate policies. We can also use this deeper knowledge to attempt to predict how various policies (proposed or in place) alter individuals' and firms' incentives and change their behaviors.

Learning the Tools of Microeconomics

Microeconomics does not address every question about the economy, but it does provide tools to answer a dazzling number of questions about the choices individuals and firms make. The set of tools microeconomics gives you can be used to solve almost any economic problem an individual person or firm faces.

What sorts of tools will we learn to use as we explore the study of microeconomics? We always start with **theories** and **models,** explanations of how things work that help us understand and predict how and why economic entities (consumers, producers, industries, governments, etc.) behave as they do. To learn the intricacies of the theories and models, we use the tools of graphs and mathematics.

theories and **models**
Explanations of how things work that help us understand and predict how and why economic entities behave as they do.

We then use the theories and models to look at how people and firms actually behave in real life (including some seemingly noneconomic situations). The interaction between microeconomic theory and the events, decisions, and empirical data from the real world lies at the heart of microeconomics. Each chapter includes the following sections that illustrate this interaction:

■ *Application* sections help us understand theory at work by showing how microeconomics can be used to inform economic decision making in a variety of interesting, real-world situations. Want to know how members of OPEC decide how much oil to produce? Or, how the NBA sets contracts for rookie players? Or, how and why consumers and producers act as they do in the markets for housing, movies, electricity generation, corn, satellite radio, music, and concrete? Applications delve into the specifics of how consumers and producers act in real life.

■ *Theory and Data* sections look at current microeconomic research to see how the data gathered by microeconomists inform and test the predictions of theory across a wide range of topics, such as golf tournaments, phone service, cigarette smoking among college graduates, the use of gym memberships, the relationship between hospital input choices and Medicare, and determining the market for a new (legal) drug.

■ *Freakonomics* essays reveal the surprising ways in which economic analysis provides a unique perspective for exploring a huge variety of phenomena in the world around us. These essays look at topics as diverse as a homemade toaster, White House photography, football stadiums, Indian fishermen's cell phones, cheating, blackmail, the illegal drug industry, and Victoria's Secret pricing. Such stories give us a framework for thinking about the economic phenomena that surround us.

---

[1] For students who might need a review of basic mathematical tools, there is an appendix that provides such a review at the back of this text. While we use only algebra throughout the chapters, several chapters have appendices that show you how the use of simple calculus skills (such as taking a first derivative) can greatly simplify the analysis.

freakonomics

Thomas Thwaites's Toaster

Thomas Thwaites must really like toast. Not content simply to buy a toaster to make his toast, in 2009 Thomas Thwaites set out on a mission to make a toaster from scratch. He started with the raw materials, gathering copper, mica, nickel, and oil (to make plastic), some of which he extracted himself from abandoned mines in the English countryside. He even built his own version of a microwave smelter in order to smelt the iron ores needed for the toaster's grill and spring. In the end, his homemade contraption was indeed capable of making toast about as well as the cheapest toaster you can buy at Walmart for under $20. If you factor in time, effort, and money spent, Thwaites' toaster cost thousands of times more to make than the store-bought version.

A very expensive custom-built toaster.

Courtesy Thomas Thwaites

It should not have come as a surprise to Thwaites that making a toaster from scratch would be hard work, at least not if he knows anything about economics. Think about the goods and services you've consumed so far just *today,* and all the different materials, technology, workmanship, and coordination that went into making them. The modern economy is nothing short of miraculous. All of us—Thwaites included—have become completely dependent on the market's amazing ability to deliver a nearly infinite variety of products to us at a tiny fraction of the cost and effort it would cost us to produce them ourselves.

Compared to other things we use as consumers, a toaster is fairly simple. Imagine trying to build a computer or an automobile completely from scratch, starting from the rawest materials. Even making your own dinner, if you had to grow the food, would be life-consuming.

No doubt Thomas Thwaites' toaster experiment taught him—the hard way—about the modern economy. If his goal is to learn economics, we suggest a different approach the next time he gets a craving, say, for ice cream. Rather than raising cows, growing sugar cane, and hand-harvesting vanilla beans, we suggest he visit his local convenience store and enjoy some store-bought ice cream while he finishes reading Chapter 2 of this book.

Using the Tools of Microeconomics

An old joke tells of a tourist in New York City who asks a local, "How do you get to Carnegie Hall?" "Practice, practice, practice," the New Yorker replies. So it is with microeconomics. Practice with using the tools of microeconomics is how you get good at it, and there's plenty of help on this front as you progress through this book.

- In each chapter you will find several worked out problems titled *Figure It Out* (see p. 33 for an example). These problems are typical of the problems you will encounter in your homework sets, quizzes, and exams, and they appear throughout the chapters to illustrate how to translate your understanding of theory, graphs, and mathematics into successful problem-solving skills. Each Figure It Out shows you, step-by-step, how to understand what, exactly, a problem is asking you to do, and then how, exactly, to solve it using the tools you've just learned.

- At the end of each chapter, you will find a set of *Problems* to solve. The variety of problems will prepare you well for applying the tools you've learned to new

Holding the Rest of the World Constant

As you have probably seen in your previous economics courses, economists often use simplifying assumptions in their models to make the world an easier place to understand. One of the most important assumptions we use time and time again in this text is *ceteris paribus*—that is, "all else is equal." For example, suppose you are contemplating your friend Max's demand for an ice cream cone and considering how his demand is affected by an increase in the price of an ice cream cone. To see this impact, you need to hold constant everything else that may influence Max's decision: the amount of money he has, the outside temperature, the prices of other things Max buys, even his preferences for ice cream itself. This "all else equal" assumption then allows you to focus on the factor that you are interested in, the *price* of an ice cream cone.

It is easy to get tripped up on this assumption when you're asked to dissect an application or example, so be careful! Don't read more into a scenario than the facts you are given, and don't drive yourself crazy by dragging into the problem all kinds of hypothetical situations beyond those provided in the problem you are analyzing (e.g., what if Max is lactose intolerant? what if it's a cold, windy day? or what if Max just lost his job?).

It is also important to remember that the "all else equal" assumption applies, in addition, to the goods we are considering. When we talk about a particular good, we assume that all units of that good are the same; that is, we hold all the characteristics of the good constant. This means that when we talk about ice cream cones, we are talking about cones of a particular size and quality. Do not think that the price of an ice cream cone has risen if the ice cream inside it is now a premium brand, or if the same ice cream now comes in a chocolate-dipped waffle cone. By introducing either of those changes, you're changing the nature of the good itself, not just its price. By allowing something other than the cone's price to change, you would be violating the "all else equal" assumption.

Bruno Crescia Photography/Getty Images; Ildar Akhmerov/iStockphoto

Things are not held constant between these two cones.

situations, scenarios, and dilemmas. You should try to solve as many of these problems as you can, and for selected problems, you can check your answers with the solutions provided in the back of the text. If you get stuck on a problem, go back through the Figure It Out examples to review the steps you should take to solve for the correct answer.

- In many chapters, you will find a *Make the Grade* box with hints and explanations about how to successfully navigate the sometimes-confusing path through microeconomic theory and its application. Read these boxes carefully before exams and quizzes to help you avoid some common mistakes that students often make in the intermediate micro course.

1.2 This Book (and How Rosa and Lauren Would See It)

We begin our investigation of microeconomics with an overview of how the preferences of consumers like Lauren (the demand side of a market) combine with the decisions of firms like Rosa's coffee plantation (the supply side) to determine the quantity sold and price of goods such as coffee. We explore, for example, why consumers' and suppliers' responses to price changes differ, and how these differences affect what happens when consumer preferences or production technologies change. And we see how the benefits of a market transaction, such as buying a cappuccino, are split between consumers like Lauren and producers like the coffee shop and Rosa.

Consumers' and Producers' Decisions

After taking this overview, the next section of the book digs a lot deeper into each side of the market, starting with consumers' decisions. Lauren could have had some drink other than coffee that morning—tea, milk, juice, or a smoothie—or she could have done something completely different with her time and money, such as buy an Egg McMuffin or download songs from iTunes. What determines how often she has coffee instead of tea, or how often she goes to Starbucks instead of somewhere else? If Lauren becomes richer, will her choices change? We answer the question of how consumers decide which goods, and how much of each, to consume, in the face of the enormous number of goods and services they are offered. Then we see how adding up these decisions across all consumers gives us the total market demand curve.

After investigating consumer behavior in detail, we explore questions dealing with producers' decisions. For example, how do companies like Rosa's plantation decide which combination of inputs such as agricultural machinery (capital) and workers (labor) to use in production? As we see, it turns out that those types of decisions for firms are similar in many respects to the decisions consumers make when deciding what products to buy.

Once we've described firms' input mix choices, we look at how these affect their costs of production. We pay particular attention to how these costs change with a firm's output level, as embodied in firms' cost curves. If Rosa doubles her production, for example, will her total costs double, more than double, or less than double? We focus on cost movements as a firm's output changes because they are crucial in determining what a market's supply side looks like.

 application

Better eBaying through Microeconomics

Hemera/Thinkstock

Deciding when to put a product on the market is one of many production decisions. It wouldn't be a good decision to put these Halloween decorations up for auction in December.

In microeconomics, we focus in large part on two key economic players, consumers (buyers) and producers (firms). We all have ample experience as consumers. Every time we go to the supermarket or the college bookstore, we are consumers. This makes it easier to grasp the economic intuition of the consumer's problem. It's often more difficult to understand producers and the issues they face because the majority of us will make far fewer production decisions over our lifetimes.

When we think about production, big firms like Procter & Gamble or United Airlines might come to mind. But, there are also a surprisingly large number of small producers including, among thousands of others, mom and pop stores, plumbers, cabdrivers, and people selling anything and everything on eBay. In fact, nearly 1.3 million people worldwide make their living off of eBay.[2] These small sellers face the same sorts of choices as the world's largest corporations.

[2] AC Nielsen International Research, June 2006.

Let's look at the production decisions you would have to make as an eBay seller. Your first decision is *what* to sell. This may be dictated, in part, by what you have lying around your attic. You are also likely to be influenced by the market, however. After pop star Michael Jackson died, for example, interest in him went sky high. That would have been the right time to ditch your old Michael Jackson lunch box. If the economy is in a recession, though, you will probably hang onto your great-grandfather's diamond-encrusted cuff links until most people have more disposable income.

Pricing is one of the most important choices every eBay seller has to make. There are two facets of eBay pricing. The first is what to set as the opening bid. Ask for too much, and you might not receive any bids. Set the opening price too low, and you may end up selling at a price so low you regret it. You also have to decide whether to include shipping in the bid price or to add it on separately. (By the way, economists have found that offering a low starting bid but charging a high price for shipping yields greater returns.[3])

There are also many other, less obvious choices that you need to make, including:

■ **Taking a photo.** You'll want to post a picture of your product. Potential bidders may be drawn to a sharper picture of your item, but it's costly to purchase a high-quality camera rather than to continue to rely on, say, your cell phone. Buying a new camera is a capital investment in your eBay business.

■ **Writing the product description.** How long you spend writing a product description may affect your final sale price, but there is a tradeoff to consider: The labor and time you spend writing elaborate and entertaining descriptions are perhaps better spent going to yard sales and thrift stores in search of hidden treasures you can buy cheaply and then turn into a profit by selling for a higher price.

■ **Deciding on the auction characteristics.** How long will the auction last? And when will you put your product on the market? Over the weekend? Close to a holiday like Halloween or Christmas? Hitting the market at the right time can mean the difference between selling at a high price or a low one.

The microeconomics of production decisions may not come as easily to you as the microeconomics of consumer decisions, but understanding the production side of things will help you make more informed and perhaps wiser choices should you find yourself running your own or someone else's business. ■

Market Supply

The book's next section compares many possible configurations through which firms supply output to markets. We start with the canonical case of perfect competition. In a perfectly competitive market, all firms take the market price as given (they don't have any ability to choose the price at which they can sell their products) and decide how much they want to produce. This is close to Rosa's case. The international coffee market is large and supplied by coffee growers all over the world, so how much coffee Rosa decides to put on the market is not going to noticeably affect its market price. In a perfectly competitive industry, supply reflects the aggregation of the cost curves of Rosa and every other coffee grower, and industry supply combines with market demand to determine price and quantity movements over both the short and long runs.

After perfect competition, we move to the other extreme: monopoly. When only one firm supplies a good to a market, the situation differs in several ways from perfect competition. Key is that the firm now has the ability to choose the price at which it sells its products. We see that this ability implies that if Rosa were a monopolist selling

[3] For example, Tanjim Hossain and John Morgan, ". . . Plus Shipping and Handling: Revenue (Non) Equivalence in Field Experiments on eBay," *The B.E. Journal of Economic Analysis & Policy* 6, no. 2 (2006): Article 3.

to the world's coffee consumers, she would choose to produce less than a competitive industry would—even if she had the capacity needed to produce more. This is because limiting the amount she produces raises the price at which she could sell her coffee. We see why governments might want to (and sometimes do) step into such situations using antitrust laws. Next, we discuss other ways monopolists use their pricing power. This includes ways to charge higher prices to consumers with a greater willingness to pay, or combining products together and selling them as a single bundle to consumers.

In the book's final look at forms of a market's supply side, we investigate oligopolies. Oligopolies exist when multiple firms interact strategically in the same market. In such markets, firms have some ability to choose their prices, but their fortunes are determined, in part, by the actions of the other firms in the market. (They dish it out as well as they take it, though: Their own actions impact other firms as well.) These sorts of situations are common; few firms are either pure monopolists or perfectly competitive price takers. Strategic interactions among firms raise all sorts of interesting questions that we can analyze using the tools of game theory. For example, how might we expect a firm like Lauren's favorite coffee shop, say, to respond to a new coffeehouse opening across the street?

Beyond the Basics

After these detailed looks at the basics of markets' supply and demand sides, we study several specific subjects in the final section of the book. The economic concepts covered here are present in many markets. In some applications, these concepts deepen our understanding of markets by supplementing the basic analytical structure we introduce in the first parts of the book. In other cases, the basic structure may be inadequate to grasp all the necessary elements of economic interactions, so these concepts will be absolutely necessary to understanding the behavior of particular markets.

The first specific topic we explore is the combined role of risk, uncertainty, and time in economic decision making. These features are especially prominent in investment decisions—choices that typically involve paying an upfront cost with the hope of earning a future return—so these decisions are a focus of our exploration. Understanding risk, uncertainty, and time's interactions in investment choices helps us answer questions such as whether Rosa should invest in a new bean-drying facility, or whether Lauren should go to business school.

Next, we explore how markets are interconnected. Changes in the supply or demand of one good can lead indirectly to similar or opposite shifts in other markets. After studying this interconnectedness, we can see how a supply disruption in China's tea-growing areas can raise the price at which Rosa can sell her coffee and the price that Lauren must pay for her cappuccino. Once we're able to tie markets together, we can analyze the conditions that must hold for an economy to operate efficiently. For example, are producers supplying the "right" mix of coffee and tea, and doing so at the lowest possible cost? Being able to answer such questions allows us to determine whether markets are working to maximize the social benefit of a good or service.

After seeing what must hold for markets to work well, we look in detail at a series of situations in which markets might *not* work well. One set of situations involves markets in which information about tastes, costs, or product quality is not equally shared by all potential parties in a transaction. For example, if Rosa wants to buy a used tractor for the plantation, she wouldn't know with 100% accuracy how well the tractor works before buying it, and she might be especially concerned that the current owner was selling the tractor precisely *because* it didn't operate up to par. How does this lack of accurate information affect her decision? Or, if Lauren wants to convince a potential employer she would be a hard-working employee before she gets the job, how might she do it?

A second set of situations in which markets may not operate efficiently includes transactions that affect people who are neither the buying nor the selling party, or markets in which a good's benefits are shared across many people at the same time.

An example would be Rosa's decision whether or not to apply pesticides to her crop. Doing so would not only affect the economics of her own operation, but would also have spillover effects on others. A neighboring coffee plantation might benefit from facing a smaller population of local insects, for instance. On the other hand, other neighbors, workers, and maybe coffee consumers could be harmed by the chemical pollution that pesticide use involves. What makes these situations interesting—and what causes markets to have difficulty delivering the socially optimal outcome—is that Rosa is likely to take into account the pesticide's impact on her own production when deciding whether to use it or not, but is less likely to consider its effects on neighboring farms, the local population, and coffee drinkers in Seattle.

The book concludes with an exploration of behavioral economics. This study of the intersection of psychology and economics has become an increasingly prominent part of economic research. People often have deeply formed biases and social preferences that limit their ability to act in the completely rational, self-interested way that we often assume in economic analysis. If this is true, then our basic analytical structure—even when supplemented with knowledge of the deeper concepts discussed above—may be inadequate for explaining economic decision making.

Focus on Data

All of these topics provide you with microeconomic tools to study the world around you. Over the past fifty years, this set of tools has expanded and changed. Microeconomics has evolved into a more **empirical** discipline, that is, one that uses much more data analysis and experiments, and not just abstract theory, to explore economic phenomena. In the 1960s, if you wanted to analyze data, a slide rule (a two-piece sliding ruler used primarily for multiplication and division) was your weapon. The computing revolution changed this. As you'll learn in this book, when the price of a good (like computing) decreases, the quantity consumed of that good increases. Much more of modern-day economists' effort toward understanding the economy centers on data and measurement than before. In fact, go see your microeconomics professor during her office hours today, and you'll most likely find her typing away at her desktop computer, completing empirical research.

empirical
Using data analysis and experiments to explore phenomena.

theory and data

The Benefits of Studying Economics

There are many reasons to study economics. Maybe you are one of the lucky few with a burning passion to understand economics. Or, maybe you just need an economics course to graduate. Either way, you will learn a set of tools in this class that will better equip you to make all sorts of decisions, not just economic ones. There's even evidence that if you become an economics major, it will make you richer.

Economists Dan Black, Seth Sanders, and Lowell Taylor analyzed the question of how much people earn depending on their choice of major.[4] They approached the question in typical economic fashion: with a sizable dataset and quantitative statistics. Using the National Survey of College Graduates combined with information from the U.S. Census, they found that economics majors earn almost 20% more than graduates with degrees in any of the other social sciences. (Accounting, finance, and marketing students do about the same as economics majors.) Music majors don't fare so well in salary terms: Their incomes are approximately 40% lower than those of economics majors. The absolute

[4] Dan A. Black, Seth Sanders, and Lowell Taylor, "The Economic Reward for Studying Economics," *Economic Inquiry* 41, no. 3 (2003): 365–377.

worst major for your bank account? Philosophy majors earn only half as much as economics majors, on average.[5]

One thing you might worry about in this analysis is whether it is actually learning economics that leads to higher wages, or perhaps just that the kind of people who major in economics are different from, say, sociology majors, and would have earned more money, regardless of what they studied. To at least partially address that critique, Black, Sanders, and Taylor took a look at earnings within narrower career paths. For instance, looking only at students who go on to law school, they determined that those who studied economics as undergrads earn more than students with other majors—up to 35% more, in the case of former sociologists. An economics degree is similarly beneficial to those who eventually pursue an MBA.

We hope that you will be so enthralled by economics that you want to make it your focus. But if you are in it just for the money, you could do worse.

[5] While the data available for the study dated back a few years, these patterns have been quite consistent. For example, in the 2011–2012 PayScale survey of mid-career median salaries for 120 different majors, economics ranked 12th, behind only several engineering degrees, computer science, applied math, and physics (http://www.payscale.com/best-colleges/degrees.asp).

Let the Fun Begin!

By the end of your microeconomics course, you will have the resources necessary to examine the world as an economist does. We've already used microeconomic tools to broadly describe a very specific economic exchange between coffee producer Rosa and university student Lauren. But what's so powerful about microeconomics is that it can be applied to any market, not just to a market like the one inhabited by Rosa and Lauren. You can use microeconomics to think rationally about any of the dozens of choices (economic and noneconomic) you face each day. By the end of your study of intermediate microeconomics, you'll not only *be able to* think like an economist—you'll see *how useful* it is.

Summary

1. **Microeconomics** relies on **theories** and **models** to study the choices made by individuals and firms. Intermediate microeconomics builds on the principles of microeconomics course by adding mathematical models to the examination of consumer and producer behavior. Practicing the mathematics underlying microeconomic theory is the key to becoming a skilled economist. In addition, intermediate microeconomics has a strong focus on policy and its effects on behavior. [**Section 1.1**]

2. Microeconomics looks at a variety of decisions made by consumers and producers as they in-teract in the markets for goods and services, and at the different market structures in which consumers and producers operate. A wide range of topics deepens our understanding of the microeconomics of consumer and producer interaction, including risk and uncertainty, the role of information, and the study of behavioral economics. In recent years, microeconomics has evolved from a discipline that relied primarily on theory to one based in **empirical** studies (data analysis and experiments). [**Section 1.2**]

Review Questions

1. What differentiates microeconomics from macro-economics?
2. Name one instance in which you were a *consumer*.
3. How are consumption and production inter-connected?

4. What tools do we use to study microeconomics?
5. Why has microeconomics evolved into an empirical discipline?

Supply and Demand

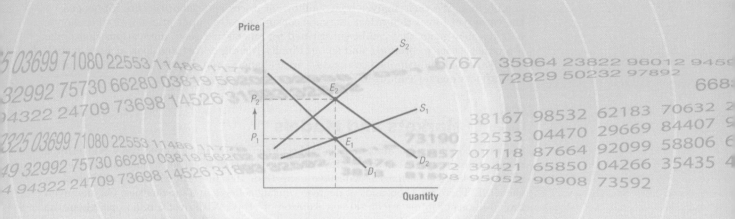

The pursuit of gold has driven people to extremes for centuries. Much of the initial exploration of the Americas was funded with the hope of acquiring gold. Centuries later, the discovery of gold at Sutter's Mill in Coloma, California, in 1848 triggered a gold rush that led 300,000 men, women, and children to migrate to California, turning San Francisco from a sleepy hamlet to a thriving city.

In recent years, the search for gold has taken on a decidedly modern flavor. It might surprise you to know that as many as 400,000 Chinese workers currently spend their days mining for gold. But they aren't panning for gold in a stream or working in a gold mine. Rather, they are seated in front of computer screens, logged onto online games like *World of Warcraft,* using virtual picks and axes to mine virtual gold that they sell on eBay to players willing to pay real money for the virtual gold that serves as the game's currency.

Whether the gold is real or virtual, the economic forces at work that determine its price and how much of it is "mined" are the same. In this chapter, we explore these forces, the two most powerful forces in economics: supply and demand.

Armed with an understanding of supply and demand, we can begin to tackle some of the fundamental questions in economics: How do consumers and producers interact in the market for a good or service to determine how much is sold and at what price? What happens to the market if tastes change, new technologies are invented, the government intervenes, or any one of a wide range of other forces changes?

This chapter outlines the basics of the supply and demand model. We first introduce the concept of the demand curve, which embodies consumers' desires for goods, and then move on to the supply curve, which embodies producers' willingness to make those goods available. We explain why these concepts are so useful in describing and analyzing markets, especially when we combine them to understand the concept of market equilibrium. We then analyze how equilibrium prices and quantities are influenced by the variety of forces that affect markets: consumer tastes, input prices, overall economic activity, new goods that can be substituted for an existing good, innovations that make a product easier to produce, and so on. Finally, we dig deeper and look at how quantities demanded and supplied respond to price changes, and discuss how this responsiveness affects market equilibrium.

2.1 Markets and Models

Modern economies are amazingly complex. Producers from all over the world offer a nearly unlimited number and variety of goods and services from which consumers can choose. A large supermarket will have more than 100 different kinds of cold cereal on the shelf. There are thousands of degree-granting colleges and universities. On any given day, millions of items are on sale on Amazon or eBay. With over 6 billion people in the world, each of them with different tastes and incomes, and 10s of millions of businesses that supply goods and services to these people, how do consumers decide what products, and how much of each, to buy? And how do producers know what products to produce? And who decides at what price the products sell?

Answering these questions might seem like a hopelessly complex task. Indeed, if we tried to tackle them all at once, it *would* be hopeless. Instead, we follow the economist's standard approach to complexity: Simplify the problem until it becomes manageable.

The supply and demand model represents the economist's best attempt to capture many of the key elements of real-world markets in a simple enough way to be easily analyzed. We start exploring that model by first defining what we mean by a market, and then discussing the model's most important assumptions. As you will see, the simplifying assumptions underlying the model are fairly strong. While actual markets don't often conform to all of these assumptions, the supply and demand model has proven to be remarkably useful for thinking about how an economy functions. We'll see the broad usefulness of the supply and demand model once we assemble it and put it to work.

What Is a Market?

The idea of a market is central to economics. What do we mean when we use the term "market"? In the strictest sense, a market is defined by the specific product being bought and sold (e.g., oranges or gold), a particular location (a mall, a city, or maybe the Internet), and a point in time (January 2012, maybe, or even 8:13 P.M. on January 4, 2012). In principle, the buyers in a market should be able to find the sellers in that market, and vice versa, although it might take some work (what economists call "search costs") to make that connection.

In practice, the kinds of markets we talk about tend to be much more broadly defined than these examples. They might be broader in terms of the product (e.g., fruit or groceries rather than oranges), the location (often we consider all of North America or even the world as the geographic market), or the time period (the year 2012 rather than a specific day). These broader markets often have more general interest and more data to analyze, but as we will see, defining markets this broadly makes the assumptions of the supply and demand model less likely to hold. Thus, we face a tradeoff between studying small, less consequential markets that closely match the underlying assumptions and broader, more important markets that do not match our assumptions well.

Now that we have defined a market, we are ready to tackle the key assumptions underlying the supply and demand model.

Key Assumptions of the Supply and Demand Model

There are four basic assumptions that underpin our development of the supply and demand model. Table 2.1 summarizes these assumptions. You will notice that the assumptions of the supply and demand model are in many cases very unrealistic, and few of the markets you participate in satisfy all these assumptions. It turns out, however, that a strength of this model is that when some (or even most) of the specific assumptions of the model fail, it still manages to provide a good description of how markets work in the real world. No model is perfect, but the supply and demand model has survived the test of time and is the workhorse of economics because of its flexibility and broad applicability. Developing a deep understanding of the basic supply and demand model is one of the most important tools you can have as an economist, even if the model does not perfectly fit every market. Plus, economics isn't completely wedded to the most stringent form of the model. Much of the rest of this book, and the field of economics more generally, are devoted to examining how changing the model's assumptions influences its predictions about market outcomes.

1. **We restrict our focus to supply and demand in a single market.** The first simplifying assumption we make is that rather than trying to tackle all markets at once, we look at how **supply** (the combined amount of a good that all producers in a market are willing to sell) and **demand** (the combined amount of a good that all consumers are willing to buy) interact in just one market to determine how much of a good or service is sold and at what price it is sold. In focusing on one market, we won't ignore other markets completely—indeed, the interaction between the markets for different kinds of products is fundamental to supply and demand. (We'll focus extensively on these interactions in Chapter 14.) For now, however, we only worry about other markets to the extent that they influence the market we're studying. In particular, we ignore the possibility that changes in the market we're studying might have spillover effects on other markets.

   supply
   The combined amount of a good that all producers in a market are willing to sell.

   demand
   The combined amount of a good that all consumers are willing to buy.

2. **All goods bought and sold in the market are identical.** We assume that all the goods bought and sold in the market are homogeneous, meaning that a consumer is just as happy with any one unit of the good (e.g., an ounce of gold or a tomato) as any other unit.[1] If we use the supply and demand model to analyze the market for "cars," it is only really a crude approximation to

Table 2.1	**The Four Key Assumptions Underlying the Supply and Demand Model**
1.	We focus on supply and demand in a single market.
2.	All goods sold in the market are identical.
3.	All goods sold in the market sell for the same price, and everyone has the same information.
4.	There are many producers and consumers in the market.

[1] Throughout this book, we often use the word "good" to mean both tangible goods, like trucks, computers, jewelry, and so on, and services, like haircuts, dog walking, financial planning, and so on. In this usage, anything a consumer values—tangible or not, concrete or abstract—is a good.

automobile markets in the real world. There are many different types of cars in reality, and consumers do not view them as identical. Most consumers would not be as happy with a Kia as they would be with a Ferrari sold at the same price. In the strictest sense, cars of the same make and model might not even be considered a single market. For instance, if a consumer wants only a silver Toyota Prius, then the market relevant to her is the market for silver Toyota Prii. To simplify our analyses, we often ignore such detail and treat groups of goods as though they were identical.

commodities
Products traded in markets in which consumers view different varieties of the good as essentially interchangeable.

The kinds of products that best reflect this assumption are **commodities,** which are traded in markets where consumers view different varieties of the good as essentially interchangeable. Goods such as wheat, soybeans, crude oil, nails, gold, or #2 pencils are commodities. Custom-made jewelry, the different offerings on a restaurant's menu, and wedding dresses are unlikely to be commodities; the consumer typically cares a lot about specific varieties of these goods.

3. **All goods sold in the market sell for the same price and everyone has the same information about prices, the quality of the goods being sold, and so on.** This assumption is a natural extension of the identical-goods assumption above, but it also implies that there are no special deals for particular buyers and no quantity discounts. In addition, everyone knows what everyone else is paying.

4. **There are many buyers and sellers in the market.** This assumption means that no particular consumer or producer has a noticeable impact on anything that occurs in the market and on the price level in particular. This assumption tends to be more easily justified for consumers than for producers. Think about your own consumption of bananas, for instance. If you were to stop eating bananas altogether, your decision would have almost no impact on the banana market as a whole. Likewise, if you thought you were potassium-deprived and increased your banana consumption fourfold, your effect on the market quantity and price of bananas would still be negligible. On the producer side, however, most bananas (and many other products) are produced by a few big companies. It is more likely that decisions by these firms about how much to produce or what markets to enter will substantially affect market prices and quantities. We're going to ignore that possibility for now and stick with the case of many sellers. Starting in Chapter 9, we analyze what happens in markets with one or a few sellers.

Having made these assumptions, let's see how they help us understand how markets work, looking first at demand and then at supply.

2.2 Demand

Pike Place Market, one of the best known public markets in the world, spans several blocks in the northwest corner of downtown Seattle. It has operated continually since 1907, and on any given day hosts hundreds of vendors selling everything from fish and meat to produce and flowers to crafts and antiques. The market sees approximately 10 million visitors per year.

Factors That Influence Demand

Tomatoes are a popular item for shoppers at farmers' markets like Pike Place Market. All sorts of factors influence how many tomatoes consumers purchase at the market. Let's discuss the most important.

Price The price of tomatoes is probably the most important consideration. Few consumers would pay $40 per pound for tomatoes. At $1 a pound, however, there would be many interested customers.

The Number of Consumers   All else equal, the more people there are in a market, the greater the quantity of the good desired. If there are a lot of people visiting the market on a given day, a relatively large amount of tomatoes will be sought for purchase.

Consumer Income or Wealth   As a consumer becomes richer, he will buy more of most goods. Tomatoes (and clothes and cars and jewelry and porterhouse steaks) probably fall in that category for most people. Sometimes, however, when a consumer becomes richer, he buys less of a good. For example, he might buy a car and stop taking public transportation and might stay in nice hotels instead of youth hostels. The consumption of these goods still responds to income or wealth, but in a different direction.

Consumer Tastes   A change in consumer preferences or tastes for tomatoes (given the consumer's income and tomato prices) will change the amount of tomatoes the consumer wants to purchase. Taste changes can be driven by all sorts of forces. For example, news about the health benefits of eating tomatoes would make many consumers want to eat more of them. On the other hand, news about salmonella being found in some tomato crops will make consumers reluctant to purchase them. For other products, taste changes might arise due to a really popular advertising campaign, fads, changes in demographics, and so on.

Prices of Other Goods   Produce vendors at Pike Place Market sell other goods such as onions and peppers that consumers can use to make their salads or top their burgers. Goods that can be used in place of another good are called **substitutes.** When the price of a substitute good falls, consumers will want to buy more of it and less of the initial good. The lower the prices of onions and peppers relative to the price of tomatoes, the fewer tomatoes consumers will want to buy. We can also think of tomatoes in some other market (say, at another location, like a consumer's neighborhood grocery store) as substitutes for tomatoes at Pike Place Market. If grocery store tomatoes become cheaper, shoppers at Pike Place are going to want to buy fewer tomatoes there.

Vendors at Pike Place Market also sell goods that consumers like to use with tomatoes. Goods that are often purchased and used in combination with a certain good are called **complements.** When the price of a complement falls, consumers will want to buy more of it and more of the initial good. There are some goods that people like to consume with tomatoes—basil, for instance, or mozzarella cheese or lettuce. If basil prices fall, consumers are likely to want to buy *more* tomatoes as a result.

The prices of substitutes and complements both affect how much of a good consumers want to buy, but they have opposite effects. A price decrease in a good's substitute will cause consumers to want less of the good; a price decrease in a good's complement will cause consumers to want more of the good.

substitute
A good that can be used in place of another good.

complement
A good that is purchased and used in combination with another good.

Demand Curves

In economics, "demand" is a catch-all word that captures the many different factors that influence the willingness of consumers to purchase a good. With so many factors influencing demand, it is difficult to wrap our minds around what would happen if all those various factors changed at the same time. We simplify the problem by considering what happens to the amount consumers demand when only a good's price changes, while everything else that determines consumer demand stays the same. (Later in the chapter, we look at how changes in all the other factors that influence demand affect the quantity of a good consumers demand.)

demand curve

The relationship between the quantity of a good that consumers demand and the good's price, holding all other factors constant.

Graphical Representation of the Demand Curve   The result of this simplifying assumption is a **demand curve.** Figure 2.1 depicts a demand curve for tomatoes at the Pike Place Market. The curve shows how the quantity of tomatoes that consumers want varies with the price of tomatoes. Price is on the vertical axis and quantity demanded is on the horizontal axis. This demand curve shows that when the price of tomatoes is $5 per pound, no tomatoes are desired. At a price of $4 per pound, consumers are willing to buy 200 pounds of tomatoes. At prices of $3, $2, and $1, the quantities of tomatoes demanded rise to 400, 600, and 800 pounds, respectively.

The point about demand curves holding all factors other than price constant is so important that it is worth saying it again: A demand curve is drawn with the assumption that there is no change in *any* of the other factors—such as consumers' incomes, tastes, or the prices of other goods—that might also affect how much of a good consumers buy. This means the demand curve in Figure 2.1 embodies the results of the following thought experiment (demand curves for other goods reflect similar thought experiments specific to their own contexts). We show up at Pike Place market some weekend and observe both the price of tomatoes and the total amount that consumers buy. Imagine that we have magical powers that allow us to go back in time. We use those powers to replace the price tags on tomatoes at the market, lowering their price by $1 per pound. Then we let the weekend happen all over again—the same weather, the same visitors to the market, the same set of items on display, and so on; the only difference is that tomatoes are $1 per pound cheaper. We then count up the total amount of tomatoes consumers buy at this new price. We continue using our magic powers to keep reversing time over and over, adjusting tomato prices up and down and by a different amount each time. When we connect all of the price and quantity combinations we have collected in this way, we have a demand curve.

The demand curve in Figure 2.1 exhibits a fundamental characteristic of demand curves: They slope downward.[2] This is another way of saying that, all else equal, the lower the price of a good, the more of it consumers will buy.

Figure 2.1 | **Demand for Tomatoes**

The demand curve D_1 for tomatoes at Pike Place Market shows how the quantity of tomatoes demanded varies with the price. As the price of tomatoes decreases, consumers demand greater quantities of tomatoes, creating a downward-sloping demand curve. At a price of $5 per pound, consumers demand no tomatoes; at $4, $3, $2, and $1, consumers are willing to purchase 200, 400, 600, and 800 pounds of tomatoes, respectively.

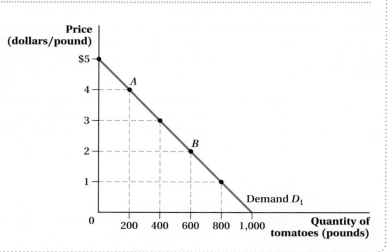

---

[2] An interesting but unusual exception to this is a Giffen good, which has an upward-sloping demand curve. We will discuss such goods in Chapter 5. Demand curves for regular (non-Giffen) goods can also sometimes be flat, as we discuss in the next section. We explore the deeper reasoning behind why demand curves usually slope down in Chapters 4 and 5.

Mathematical Representation of the Demand Curve   The demand curve in Figure 2.1 can also be represented mathematically by the equation

$$Q = 1{,}000 - 200P$$

where Q is the quantity demanded (in pounds) and P is the price (in dollars per pound). This equation implies that every \$1 per pound increase in price leads to a 200-pound decline in the quantity of tomatoes demanded.

Because of the odd condition in economics of plotting price on the vertical axis and quantity on the horizontal axis, and because it is easier to work with in certain contexts, economists often write demand curve equations in the form of the price as a function of quantity. This approach results in an **inverse demand curve.** The inverse demand curve simply rearranges the demand curve to put price in terms of quantity rather than the other way around.

We can find the inverse demand curve by solving for P:

$$Q = 1{,}000 - 200P$$

$$200P + Q = 1{,}000$$

$$200P = 1{,}000 - Q$$

$$P = 5 - 0.005Q$$

inverse demand curve
A demand curve written in the form of price as a function of quantity demanded.

One thing this inverse demand curve makes clear is that no consumer will be willing to buy tomatoes at a price greater than \$5 per pound, because the vertical intercept of the inverse demand curve (i.e., the price when the quantity demanded Q equals zero) is \$5 per pound. This level is also called the **demand choke price.**

demand choke price
The price at which no consumer is willing to buy a good and quantity demanded is zero; the vertical intercept of the inverse demand curve.

Shifts in Demand Curves

A given demand curve such as D_1 in Figure 2.1 illustrates how the quantity demanded of a good changes as its price, and only its price, changes. When one of the other (nonprice) factors that affect demand changes, the change can affect the quantity of tomatoes consumers want to buy at every price. For example, if there is an outbreak of salmonella poisoning, and public health officials believe that tomatoes may be the source of the outbreak, consumers' tastes will change. They will want fewer tomatoes at any given price than they did before and the demand curve will shift down and to the left to D_2, as shown in Figure 2.2. Mathematically, the demand curve D_2 corresponds to $Q = 500 - 200P$.

Figure 2.2   :   **Shifts in the Demand Curve**

The demand curve D_1 shifts with a change in any nonprice factor that affects demand. If tomatoes are suspected to be a source of salmonella, consumers will demand fewer tomatoes at any given price and the demand for tomatoes will shift inward, from D_1 to D_2. In contrast, if tomatoes are found to have cancer-fighting properties, the demand for tomatoes will shift outward, from D_1 to D_3.

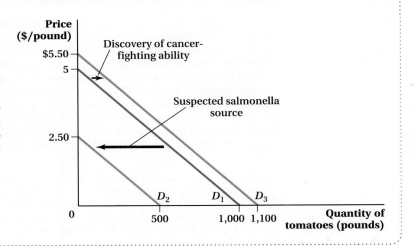

Similarly, if scientists discover that tomatoes help prevent cancer, consumers who wanted to buy 200 pounds of tomatoes at $4 per pound may now want to buy 300 pounds at $4. Those who wanted to buy 600 pounds at $2 per pound will now want to buy 700 pounds, and so on. Because consumers demand a higher quantity of tomatoes at any given price, the whole demand curve for tomatoes will shift out to the right from D_1 to D_3, illustrated in Figure 2.2. Mathematically, the new demand curve D_3 is described by the equation $Q = 1,100 - 200P$. Note that we are shifting the demand curves in the simplest way—sliding them over with the same slope. In real markets, this doesn't need to be true. The new curve can change steepness too, if demand becomes more or less sensitive to price.

The changes in the quantity demanded at every price that occur when any nonprice factor changes illustrate an essential distinction. When a good's price changes but nothing else does, this change creates a movement *along* a fixed demand curve. Changes in any of the other factors that influence demand create *shifts* in the demand curve. To clarify this distinction, economists distinguish **changes in quantity demanded,** which happen when a change in a good's price creates movement along a given demand curve (e.g., the move from point A to point B in Figure 2.1), from **changes in demand,** which happen when a good's entire demand curve shifts (e.g., the shifts from D_1 to D_2 and D_3 in Figure 2.2).

Quantity demanded is a single number, expressed in units of the good: 400 pounds of tomatoes, 30 cars, or 20 movie downloads, for example. Different prices imply different quantities demanded; the combination of all such price–quantity combinations is represented by the demand curve. Shifts in consumers' desired quantities caused by changes in any (or all) other factors move this entire combination of prices and quantities demanded—that is, they shift the demand curve.[3]

We motivated the shifts from D_1 to D_2 and D_3 in Figure 2.2 as changes in consumer tastes. But similar pictures occur for a change in any other nonprice factor that affects consumers' quantity demanded. The increase in demand reflected by the shift to D_3 would also occur if beautiful weather leads to higher attendance at the market. Of course, had the weather been cold and rainy, the number of customers at the market would fall, and the demand curve would have shifted inward to, perhaps, D_2.

change in quantity demanded
A movement *along* the demand curve that occurs as a result of a change in the good's price.

change in demand
A shift of the entire demand curve caused by a change in a determinant of demand other than the good's own price.

theory and data

Changes in Taste and the Demand for Cigarettes

If you were a cigarette company executive in 1960, you had to feel optimistic. Between 1940 and 1957, the share of Americans over the age of 25 who smoked had risen from 38% to 46%. Affluent people were more likely to smoke than the poor, so with people getting richer over time, the demand for cigarettes was likely to skyrocket.

But things didn't turn out as the executives planned. Today, only about 20% of the adult population smokes. Moreover, among those who currently do smoke, the number of cigarettes smoked per day is smaller than it was for the average smoker 50 years ago.

Why has the quantity demanded for cigarettes shrunk so much? One factor that no doubt has contributed to the decline is a rising price. In 1960 a pack of cigarettes cost around 30 cents. Adjusting for inflation, that's equivalent to $2.20 in 2010 dollars. But the

---

[3] Economists often draw demand curves as straight lines, and we do so as well throughout much of this book. This is really just for convenience. As their name suggests, demand curves in reality can be, and probably quite often are, *curves.* Also, when we use the word "shift," this includes not only parallel shifts of the demand curve as shown in Figure 2.2, but also rotations (which change the steepness or slope of a demand curve). We'll later discuss in further detail what economic forces affect the slopes of demand curves.

average price for a pack of cigarettes today is $4.80, more than twice as high. Much of that price increase is the result of heavy taxation — taxes that now account for more than half of the price of cigarettes. Price changes are unlikely to be the whole story, however. Based on economists' measurements of smokers' sensitivity to price changes, a price increase of this size explains only about half the drop in quantity demanded. Looking at changes in who smokes further reinforces the idea that price increases are not the whole story: Currently, fewer than 15% of Americans with college degrees smoke, compared to more than 25% of people with less education. That is the reverse of the pattern in the 1950s. In general, we expect high-income people to be *less* sensitive to price changes than the poor, so it is unlikely that rising prices would lead cigarette consumption to shift sharply toward those with low education. Clearly, something else happened.

One major "something" was the realization on the part of consumers that smoking is dangerous. The 1964 Surgeon General's Report, considered one of the top news stories that year, broadly disseminated information on the link between lung cancer and cigarette smoking that had been steadily growing in the academic community. In 1970 the addition of the ubiquitous Surgeon General's Warning to all cigarette packages sold in the United States furthered the spread of this information. Knowledge of the health risks associated with smoking led the demand curve for cigarettes to shift inward. What does it mean for a demand curve to shift inward? It means that *holding price constant,* the quantity demanded is lower.

Thus, the observed decline in demand for cigarettes reflects both movements along the demand curve (the rising price) and shifts in the demand curve (awareness that smoking is dangerous), as shown in Figure 2.3. Economist Damien de Walque studied whether these types of shifts in the demand curve are also related to the fact that the highly educated smoked more in the 1950s, but smoke much less today.[*] There is a growing body of evidence suggesting that more education pays off not just in the labor market, but in many other activities as well. (The benefits are especially great when you study economics — well, at least that's what economists will tell you.) People with more education have better access to information and are better prepared to properly interpret the information they receive, so it makes sense that the highly educated would react more to information about the risks of smoking than would the less educated. That is exactly what de Walque found in his study.

Figure 2.3　|　**Prevalence of Smoking by Education Category in the United States, Age 25 and Older, 1940–2000**

Prior to the mid-1960s, smoking prevalence was high across all educational groups, ranging from approximately 40 to 45% of the population. After the Surgeon General's Warning in 1964, the percentage of smokers declined more among the highly educated than among those with a high school education or below. In 2000 approximately 30% of people with a high school education or below smoked, while only around 15% of people with more than a college degree were smokers.

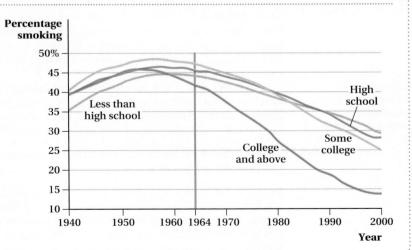

---

[*] Damien de Walque, "Education, Information, and Smoking Decisions: Evidence from Smoking Histories in the United States, 1940–2000," *Journal of Human Resources* 45, no. 3 (2010): 682–717.

Why Is Price Treated Differently from the Other Factors That Affect Demand?

Why do prices get special treatment relative to the other determinants of demand? After all, nothing prevents us from putting, say, income on the vertical axis in Figure 2.1 instead of price.

There are at least three reasons why economists focus on the effects of a change in a good's price. First, price is typically one of the most important factors that influence demand. Second, prices can usually be changed frequently and easily. Therefore, when we contemplate how markets respond to changes or "shocks," price fluctuations are likely to be a common response. Third, and most important, of all the factors that influence demand, price is the only one that also exerts a large, direct influence on the other side of the market—on the quantity of the good that producers are willing to supply. Price therefore serves as the critical element that ties together demand and supply. Let's turn to that other side of the market now.

2.3 Supply

We have one half of the demand and supply model assembled. In this section, we present the supply half. By supply we mean the combined amount of a good that all producers in a market are willing to sell.

Factors That Influence Supply

Just as there are many factors that determine demand, so too with supply. Let's discuss these again in the context of our Pike Place Market tomatoes example.

Price   Just as it does with demand, price plays an important role in supply decisions. If farmers expect to be able to sell tomatoes at $40 a pound at Pike Place Market, the market will be loaded with them. The farmers will grow more tomatoes and choose to sell them at Pike Place rather than other outlets. If they expect the price to be only $1 per pound, there will be a much smaller quantity available for sale.

Suppliers' Costs of Production   Suppliers' production costs will change when input prices and production technology change. There are many inputs a supplier must use to produce tomatoes and bring them to market, including land, tomato seeds, fertilizer, harvesting equipment, booth rental prices at markets like Pike Place, and the gasoline needed to ship tomatoes to markets, to name just a few. If the prices of these inputs change, the suppliers' costs will change and will influence the quantity of tomatoes supplied to the market.

production technology
The processes used to make, distribute, and sell a good.

Similarly, changes in **production technology,** the processes used to make, distribute, and sell a good such as tomatoes, will change the costs of production. The more efficient these processes are, the lower the costs to sellers of providing tomatoes for sale. Lower costs will raise sellers' willingness to supply tomatoes.

The Number of Sellers   More farmers bringing tomatoes to Pike Place will raise the available supply.

Sellers' Outside Options   Farmers who are busy selling tomatoes at Pike Place Market aren't selling some other product or selling tomatoes at some other place. A change in farmers' prospects for doing business in markets for other goods or in other markets for tomatoes can affect their willingness to supply tomatoes at Pike Place Market. These prospects depend on factors such as the prices of other goods the farmers might be growing and selling (radishes, peppers, or green beans) or tomato prices at markets other than Pike Place.

Supply Curves

Just as we introduced demand curves as a way to think in a more focused way about demand, we can do the same thing for supply. Supply curves, like demand curves, capture the idea that factors that influence supply can be divided into two sets: price and everything else. Supply curves isolate the relationship between price and quantity supplied.

Graphical Representation of the Supply Curve   Figure 2.4 depicts a supply curve for tomatoes at the Pike Place Market. The vertical axis reflects the price of the good, and the horizontal axis is the quantity supplied. The curve indicates that, for example, if the price of tomatoes is $2 per pound, 200 pounds of tomatoes will be offered for sale. If the price is $5 per pound, the quantity supplied will be 800 pounds.

The **supply curve** in the figure slopes upward: Holding everything else equal, producers are willing to supply more of a good as price rises.[4] The simple intuition behind the upward slope of most supply curves is that, given their costs of production and other nonprice factors, firms want to supply a greater quantity to the market when prices are high. For example, many firms experience increasing costs of production as their output rises. When this is the case, they need to earn a higher price in the market in order to induce them to produce more output.

supply curve
The relationship between the quantity supplied of a good and the good's price, holding all other factors constant.

Mathematical Representation of the Supply Curve   The supply curve in Figure 2.4 is expressed mathematically as

$$Q = 200P - 200$$

where Q is the quantity supplied (in pounds of tomatoes) and P is the price in dollars per pound. This indicates that holding everything else constant, for every dollar increase in price, the quantity supplied of tomatoes increases by 200 pounds.

Figure 2.4   Supply of Tomatoes

The supply curve S_1 for tomatoes at Pike Place Market shows how the quantity of tomatoes supplied varies with the price. As the price of tomatoes increases, producers supply greater quantities of tomatoes, creating an upward-sloping supply curve. At a price of $1 per pound, producers supply no tomatoes; at $2, $3, $4, and $5, respectively, producers supply 200, 400, 600, and 800 pounds of tomatoes.

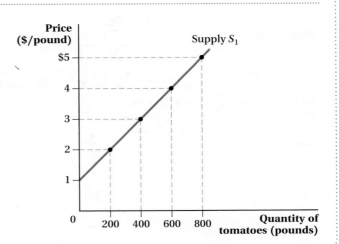

---

[4] We typically expect that supply curves slope upward, although in some cases (especially in the long run), they may be horizontal, and in others they might be perfectly vertical. We will discuss these special cases later.

inverse supply curve
A supply curve written in the form of price as a function of quantity supplied.

Just as it is common to write demand curves as inverse demand curves (price as a function of quantity demanded), economists often use **inverse supply curves** as well:

$$Q = 200P - 200$$

$$200P = Q + 200$$

$$P = 0.005Q + 1$$

The inverse supply curve makes clear that no firm will be willing to supply tomatoes at a price of $1 per pound (or less), because the vertical intercept of the supply is $1 per pound (i.e., the price at which the quantity supplied Q equals zero). This is often called the **supply choke price.**

supply choke price
The price at which no firm is willing to produce a good and quantity supplied is zero; the vertical intercept of the inverse supply curve.

Shifts in the Supply Curve

A given supply curve such as S_1 in Figure 2.4 illustrates how the quantity supplied of a good changes as its price, and only its price, changes.

When one of the other (nonprice) factors that affect supply changes, the change affects the quantity of tomatoes that suppliers want to sell at every price. For example, if someone invents a machine that can harvest tomatoes faster and at lower cost, producers who wanted to produce 600 pounds of tomatoes at $4 per pound will now be willing to supply 800 pounds of tomatoes at $4. Those who were willing to supply 200 pounds at $2 will now be willing to supply 400 at $2, and so on. Because producers supply more tomatoes at every price, the whole supply curve will shift out to the right from S_1 to S_2, as shown in Figure 2.5. The way we've drawn it, that additional quantity is the 200 pounds at any price, though there's nothing that says all supply shifts must exhibit this pattern.[5] Mathematically, the supply curve S_2 is described by the equation $Q = 200P$.

Similarly, if there is a drought, it will cost producers more to irrigate their fields. They will want to supply fewer tomatoes at any given price than they did before and the supply will shift up and to the left, to S_3. Mathematically, the supply curve S_3 corresponds to $Q = 200P - 600$.

Analogous to demand curves, the changes in a good's price when everything else stays constant lead to **changes in quantity supplied,** movements *along* a supply

change in quantity supplied
A movement *along* the supply curve that occurs as a result of a change in the good's price.

Figure 2.5   **Shifts in the Supply Curve**

The supply curve S_1 shifts when any nonprice factor that affects supply changes. If a faster harvesting method is developed, the supply of tomatoes will shift outward, from S_1 to S_2. In contrast, if there is a drought, the supply of tomatoes will shift inward, from S_1 to S_3.

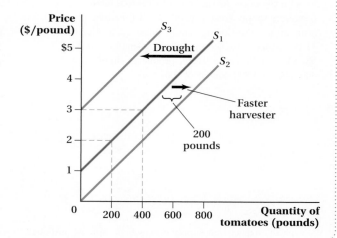

---

[5] Note that, just like demand curves, there's no requirement that supply curves be linear. We just draw them as such for simplicity.

curve. Changes in any other factors that influence supply change the quantity supplied at any given price and create *shifts* in the supply, which is called a **change in supply.**

Quantity supplied is a single number, such as 600 pounds of tomatoes, 100 iPads, or 40 haircuts, and different prices imply different quantities supplied. Supply curves show all possible price–quantity combinations producers would supply. Changes in any (or all) other factors move the entire combination of prices and quantities supplied—that is, they shift the supply curve.

> **change in supply**
> A shift of the entire supply curve caused by a change in a determinant of supply other than the good's own price.

Why Is Price Also Treated Differently for Supply?

Supply curves isolate the effect of prices on supply just as demand curves isolate price effects on demand. We mentioned one of the big reasons for this focus on price in the demand curve is that price is the only factor that has a direct influence on both demand and supply. Price is the critical element that ties together the two sides of a market. Price's roles in both the demand and supply sides of a market mean that prices can adjust freely to make the quantity demanded by consumers equal to the quantity supplied by producers. When this happens, we have a market in which everyone who wants to buy at the current price can do so, and everyone who wants to sell at the current market price can do so as well.

As we see in the next section, we can also use the supply and demand model to predict how changes in nonprice factors affect market outcomes. To get to the point where we *can* do that, however, we need to identify an initial market price and quantity sold. Treating price as special allows us to do that.

2.4 Market Equilibrium

The true power of the demand and supply model emerges when we combine demand and supply curves. Both relate quantities and prices, so we can draw them on the same graph, with price on the vertical axis and quantity on the horizontal axis. Figure 2.6 overlays the original demand and supply curves for tomatoes at Seattle's Pike Place Market. As a reminder, expressed as equations, the demand curve is $Q = 1,000 - 200P$ (with an equivalent inverse demand curve $P = 5 - 0.005Q$), and the supply curve is $Q = 200P - 200$ (with an inverse supply curve of $P = 1 + 0.005Q$).

The point where the supply and demand curves cross is the **market equilibrium.** The equilibrium is labeled as point E on Figure 2.6, and the price and quantity

> **market equilibrium**
> The point at which the quantity demanded by consumers exactly equals the quantity supplied by producers.

Figure 2.6   Market Equilibrium

The intersection of the supply curve S_1 and the demand curve D_1 at point E represents the market equilibrium. The equilibrium price and quantity of tomatoes are $3 per pound and 400 pounds, respectively.

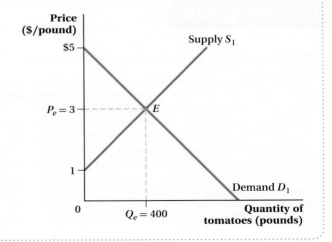

associated with this point are labeled P_e and Q_e. The **equilibrium price** P_e is the *only* price at which quantity supplied equals quantity demanded.

The Mathematics of Equilibrium

So what is the market equilibrium for our Pike Place tomatoes example? We can read off Figure 2.6 that the equilibrium price P_e is $3 per pound, and the equilibrium quantity Q_e is 400 pounds. But we can also determine these mathematically by using the equations for the demand and supply curves. Quantity demanded is given by $Q^D = 1,000 - 200P$ (we've added the superscript "D" to quantity just to remind us that equation is the demand curve), and quantity supplied is $Q^S = 200P - 200$ (again, we've added a superscript). We know that at market equilibrium, quantity demanded equals quantity supplied; that is, $Q_e = Q^D = Q^S$. Using the equations above, we have

$$Q^D = Q^S$$

$$1,000 - 200P = 200P - 200$$

$$1,200 = 400P$$

$$P_e = 3$$

At a price P of $3 per pound, quantity demanded Q^D equals quantity supplied Q^S, so the equilibrium price P_e is $3, as we see in Figure 2.6. To find the equilibrium quantity Q_e, we plug this value of P_e back into the equation for *either* the demand or supply curve, because both quantity demanded and quantity supplied will be the same at the equilibrium price:

$$Q_e = 1,000 - 200P_e = 1,000 - 200(3) = 1,000 - 600 = 400$$

We just solved for the equilibrium price and quantity by using the fact that the quantity demanded equals the quantity supplied in equilibrium, and substituting the demand and supply curve equations into this equality. We could have obtained the same answer by instead using the fact that the price given by the *inverse* demand and supply curves is the same at the market equilibrium quantity. That is,

$$5 - 0.005Q_e = 1 + 0.005Q_e$$

Solving this equation gives $Q_e = 400$ pounds, just as before. Plugging $Q_e = 400$ back into either the inverse demand or supply equation indicates that the market price P_e is $3 per pound, as expected.

make the grade

Does quantity supplied equal quantity demanded in equilibrium?

Solving for the market equilibrium as we just did is one of the most common exam questions in intermediate microeconomics classes. The basic idea is always the same: Take the equations for the demand curve and the supply curve, solve for the equilibrium price, and then plug that equilibrium price back into either the supply curve or the demand curve (it does not matter which) to determine the equilibrium quantity. It is simple, but it is easy to make math errors under the time pressure of an exam, especially if the demand and supply curves take on more complicated forms than the basic examples we deal with here.

A simple trick will ensure that you have the right answer, and it takes only a few seconds. Take the equilibrium price that you obtain and plug it into *both* the demand and supply curves. If you don't get the same answer when you substitute the equilibrium price into the supply and demand equations, you know you made a math error along the way because the quantity demanded must equal the quantity supplied in equilibrium.

Why Markets Move toward Equilibrium

When a market is in equilibrium, the quantity demanded by consumers and the quantity supplied by producers are equal at the current market price. To see why equilibrium is a stable situation, let's look at what happens when price is at a non-equilibrium level. If the current price is higher than the equilibrium price, there will be excess supply. If the price is lower, there will be excess demand.

Excess Supply   Suppose the price in a market were higher than the equilibrium price, say, at P_{high} instead of P_e, as shown in Figure 2.7a. At that price, the quantity supplied, Q^S_{high}, is greater than the quantity demanded, Q^D_{high}. Producers come out of the woodwork wanting to sell at this high price, but not all producers can find willing buyers at that price. The excess quantity for sale equals $Q^S_{high} - Q^D_{high}$, the horizontal distance between the supply and demand curves at P_{high}. This excess quantity supplied is known as a **surplus.** To eliminate this surplus, producers need to attract more buyers, and to do this, sellers must lower their prices. As price falls, quantity demanded rises and quantity supplied falls until the market reaches equilibrium at point E.

Excess Demand   The opposite situation exists in Figure 2.7b. At price P_{low}, consumers demand more of the good (Q^D_{low}) than producers are willing to supply (Q^S_{low}). Buyers want a lot of tomatoes if they are this cheap, but not many producers will deliver them at such a low price. At the low price, the quantity demanded Q^D_{low} is greater than the quantity supplied Q^S_{low}, and a **shortage** exists. To eliminate this shortage, buyers who cannot find the good available for sale will bid up the price and enterprising producers will be more than willing to raise their prices. As price rises,

surplus
The amount by which quantity supplied exceeds quantity demanded when market price is higher than the equilibrium price.

shortage
The amount by which quantity demanded exceeds quantity supplied when market price is lower than the equilibrium price.

Figure 2.7   **Why P_e Is the Equilibrium Price**

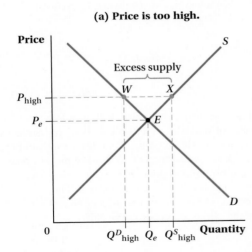

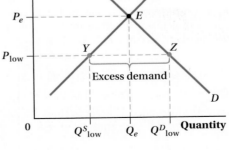

(a) Price is too high.

(b) Price is too low.

(a) At the price P_{high} above the equilibrium price P_e, producers supply the quantity Q^S_{high}, while consumers demand only Q^D_{high}. This results in a surplus of the good, as represented by the distance between points W and X. Over time, price will fall and the market will move toward equilibrium at point E.

(b) At the price P_{low} below the equilibrium price P_e, producers supply the quantity Q^S_{low}, while consumers demand Q^D_{low}. This results in a shortage for the good, as represented by the distance between points Y and Z. Over time, price will rise and the market will move toward equilibrium at point E.

quantity demanded falls and quantity supplied rises until the market equals equilibrium at point E.[6]

Adjusting to Equilibrium   It is important to note that in the real world an equilibrium can be mysterious. In our stylized model, we're acting as if all the producers and consumers gather in one spot and report to a sort of auctioneer how much they want to produce or consume at each price. The auctioneer combines all this information, computes and announces the market-clearing price, and only then do all the sellers and buyers make their deals at the announced market-clearing price. But few markets work this way in the real world. Real markets must rely on what the great eighteenth-century Scottish economist Adam Smith called the "invisible hand." Producers independently decide how much to produce of their products given what price they expect to be able to sell them at, and consumers show up at stores, gas stations, or Web sites to buy the good. Sometimes producers might supply too much or too little in the short run, but through the market, these mistakes tend to be corrected. Economists typically assume that the market reaches equilibrium one way or another, without being too specific about the process.

2.1 figure it out

Suppose that the demand and supply curves for a monthly cell phone plan with unlimited texts can be represented by

$$Q^D = 50 - 0.5P$$
$$Q^S = -25 + P$$

The current price of these plans in the market is $40 per month. Is this market in equilibrium? Would you expect the price to rise or fall? If so, by how much? Explain.

Solution:

There are two ways to solve the first question about whether the price will rise or fall. The first is to calculate the quantity demanded and quantity supplied at the current market price of $40 to see how they compare:

$$Q^D = 50 - 0.5P = 50 - 0.5(40) = 50 - 20 = 30$$
$$Q^S = -25 + P = -25 + 40 = 15$$

Because quantity demanded is greater than quantity supplied, we can tell that there is excess

demand (a shortage) in the market. Many people are trying to get texting plans, but are finding them sold out because few suppliers want to sell at that price. Prices will rise to equalize quantity supplied and quantity demanded, moving the market to equilibrium.

Alternatively, we could start by solving for the market equilibrium price:

$$Q^D = Q^S$$
$$50 - 0.5P = -25 + P$$
$$1.5P = 75$$
$$P = \$50$$

The current market price, $40, is below the market equilibrium price of $50. (This is why there is excess demand in the market.) Therefore, we would expect the price to rise by $10. When the market reaches equilibrium at a price of $50, all buyers can find sellers and all sellers can find buyers. The price will then remain at $50 unless the market changes and the demand curve or supply curve shifts.

---

[6] Prices can sometimes remain at levels other than their equilibrium value for extended periods of time, especially if there are policy-based interventions in the market, such as price ceilings (maximum prices allowed by law) or price floors (minimum prices prescribed by law). We discuss these sorts of situations in Chapter 3.

The Effects of Demand Shifts

As we have learned, demand and supply curves hold constant everything else besides price that might affect quantities demanded and supplied. Therefore, the market equilibrium depicted in Figure 2.6 will hold only as long as none of these other factors change. If any other factor changes, there will be a new market equilibrium because either the demand or supply curve will have shifted.

Suppose the demand for tomatoes falls when, as in our example on the previous pages, a news story reports that tomatoes are suspected of being the source of a salmonella outbreak. The resulting change in consumer tastes causes the demand curve to shift in (i.e., to the left), as Figure 2.8 shows, from D_1 to D_2.

How does the market equilibrium change after this demand shift? The equilibrium price and quantity both fall. The equilibrium quantity falls from Q_1 to Q_2, and the equilibrium price drops from P_1 to P_2. The reason for these movements is that if prices stayed at P_1 after the fall in demand, tomato farmers would be supplying a much greater quantity than consumers were demanding. The market price must fall to get farmers to rein in their quantity supplied until it matches the new, lower level of demand.

We can solve for the new equilibrium price and quantity using the same approach we used earlier, but using the equation for the new demand curve D_2, which is $Q = 500 - 200P$. (The supply curve stays the same.)

$$Q^D = Q^S$$

$$500 - 200P_2 = 200P_2 - 200$$

$$400P_2 = 700$$

$$P_2 = 1.75$$

So the new equilibrium price is $1.75 per pound, compared to $3 per pound from before the demand shift. Plugging this into the new demand curve (or the supply curve) gives the new equilibrium quantity:

$$Q_2 = 500 - 200(1.75) = 150$$

The new equilibrium quantity is 150 pounds, less than half of what it was before the negative demand shift.

Figure 2.8   **Effects of a Fall in the Demand for Tomatoes**

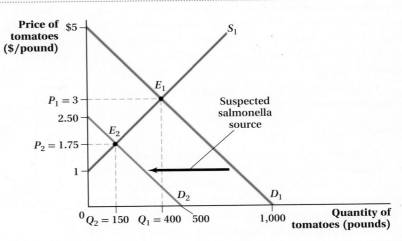

After a salmonella outbreak, the demand for tomatoes decreases, causing a leftward shift of the demand curve from D_1 to D_2. This fall in demand results in a new equilibrium point E_2 lower than the initial equilibrium point E_1. The equilibrium quantity falls from Q_1 (400 pounds) to Q_2 (150 pounds), and the equilibrium price falls from P_1 ($3) to P_2 ($1.75).

We could have just as easily worked through an example in which demand increases and the demand curve shifts out. Perhaps tastes change and people want to drink their vegetables by downing several cans of tomato juice a day or incomes rise or substitute produce items become more expensive. In the face of a stable supply curve, this increase in demand would shift the curve up to the right and cause both the equilibrium price and quantity to rise. At the initial (pre-shift) market price, the post-shift quantity demanded would outstrip sellers' willingness to supply. The price would have to rise, causing a movement along the supply curve until the quantities supplied and demanded are equal.

Shifts in Curves versus Movement along a Curve   This analysis highlights the importance of distinguishing between shifts in a demand or supply curve and movements along those curves. This distinction can sometimes seem confusing, but understanding it is critical to much of the analysis that follows in this book. We saw in Figure 2.8 what happens to a market when there is a change in consumers' tastes that make them view a product more negatively. That change in tastes made consumers want to buy less of the product at any given price—that is, caused an inward *shift* in the demand curve. Remember, anything that changes how much consumers want to buy of a good at any particular price must shift the demand curve. At the same time, this change in tastes had no effect on how much producers wish to sell at any given price. It doesn't affect their costs of producing or their outside options. So supply does not change, and the supply curve doesn't shift. However, the *quantity supplied* does change. It falls in response to the reduced demand. This change in quantity supplied is a movement *along* the supply curve. The only reason that the quantity supplied falls in this example is because the shift in the demand curve has made the equilibrium price lower, and at a lower price, suppliers produce less of the good. Therefore, a *shift* in the demand curve causes a movement *along* the supply curve to the new equilibrium.

2.2 figure it out

Draw a supply and demand diagram of the market for paperback books in a small coastal town.

a. Suppose that a hurricane knocks out electrical power for an extended period of time. Unable to watch television or use a computer, people must resort to reading books for entertainment. What will happen to the equilibrium price and quantity of paperback books?

b. Does this change reflect a change in demand or a change in quantity demanded?

Solution:

a. Books are a substitute good for television shows and computer entertainment. Because there is no power for televisions or computers (effectively raising the price of these substitutes), the demand for books will rise, and the demand curve will shift out to the right. As the figure shows, this shift will result in a

higher equilibrium price and quantity of books purchased.

b. Because the hurricane changes the availability (and therefore the effective price) of substitute goods, this shifts the amount of books demanded at any given price. This is a change in the demand for paperback books.

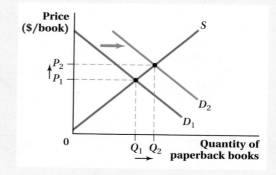

freakonomics

The Price of Fame: President Obama and the Paparazzi

Being president of the United States has its perks—you are the most powerful person in the world, people wait on you hand and foot, and you get to live in a pretty nice house rent-free. But being the president also has its downsides. For instance, every step you and your family take is in the public spotlight. Media coverage of the Obama family has been intense, even by White House standards. The president was particularly troubled by the toll on his daughters Sasha and Malia, so he asked his staff to come up with some solutions to the paparazzi problem.

The White House provided the media with this photo of Malia and Sasha Obama leaving for their first day of school in 2010.

The Obama-Biden Transition Project

Their solution shows that someone in the Obama administration knows some economics. White House staff recognized that the number of paparazzi photos represents a market equilibrium. Because of the public's strong demand for pictures of the Obama family, media outlets are willing to fork over large sums of money for high-quality photos. At those prices, many photographers are willing to devote a lot of time to stalking the First Family and supply the market with a huge number of photographs. A hypothetical initial equilibrium in the market for photographs of the Obama family is illustrated in Figure A.

Figure A

One way to reduce the number of paparazzi taking photos to supply the equilibrium quantity would be to decrease the demand for the photos and shift the demand curve inward. If that were to happen, both the price and quantity of paparazzi photos would decline. How could the White House reduce the demand for paparazzi photos? One thing we know from economics is that if two goods are substitutes, the demand for one good will fall if the price for the other good decreases because consumers will shift away from buying the first good and toward buying the second, cheaper good. So the administration needed a substitute for paparazzi pictures. The answer? Staged photos taken by White House photographers, given to media outlets for free.

Each White House–approved picture of Sasha and Malia hunting for Easter eggs or of the First Dog Bo running around the lawn lowered the demand for paparazzi photos, leading to a decrease in the price unauthorized paparazzi photos could command. As a result, fewer paparazzi spent their days milling around the White House lawn, and the number of unauthorized photos being published decreased, as shown in Figure B. Perhaps most important to President and Mrs. Obama, it meant that Sasha and Malia could go to their first day of school like normal kids—or, at least, like normal kids who happen to have several secret servicemen, the D.C. police, and the White House photographer with them.

After seeing the initial success of this photo project, the administration ventured into the world of social media and created Facebook and Flickr accounts with photo albums depicting everything from staff meetings in the Oval Office to the president instigating a snowball fight on the White House lawn. Up next for the White House presidential photo project? Given the current budget deficit, perhaps they should consider selling the pictures—just as long as they keep the price below the market equilibrium price!

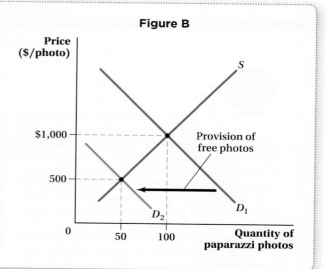

Figure B

The Effects of Supply Shifts

Now let's think about what happens when the supply curve shifts, but the demand curve does not. Figure 2.9 shows the case in which the supply of tomatoes rises, shifting the supply curve out from S_1 to S_2. This shift implies that, at any given price, farmers are willing to sell a larger quantity of tomatoes than before. Such a shift would result from a reduction in farmers' input costs—for example, if fertilizer prices fell. The logic of why a cost reduction increases quantity supplied at any given price is straightforward: If the farmers can make an average profit of (say) $1 per pound when the price is $3 per pound, then a $1 decrease in cost (which increases their profit) will lead farmers to offer more for sale. Note, however, that this cost change has no direct impact on the demand curve. Holding price fixed, consumers are no more or less willing to buy tomatoes than they were before.

Figure 2.9 shows how the equilibrium changes. The supply curve has shifted from its original position S_1 (given by the equation $Q = 200P - 200$) to S_2 (given by the equation

Figure 2.9   Effects of an Increase in the Supply of Tomatoes

With cheaper fertilizer, farmers supply more tomatoes at every given price and the supply curve shifts outward from S_1 to S_2. The equilibrium quantity increases from Q_1 (400 pounds) at E_1 to Q_2 (600 pounds) at E_2, while the equilibrium price falls from P_1 ($3/pound) to P_2 ($2/pound).

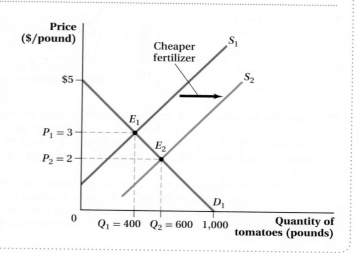

$Q = 200P + 200$). If the price stayed at the original equilibrium price P_1 after the supply shift, the amount of tomatoes that sellers would be willing to supply would exceed consumers' quantity demanded. Therefore, the equilibrium price must fall, as seen in the figure. This drop in price causes an increase in quantity demanded along the demand curve. The price drops until the quantity demanded once again equals the quantity supplied. The new equilibrium price is P_2, and the new equilibrium quantity is Q_2.

We can solve for the new equilibrium price and quantity using the equations for the original demand curve and the new supply curve:

$$Q^D = Q^S$$

$$1{,}000 - 200P_2 = 200P_2 + 200$$

$$400P_2 = 800$$

$$P_2 = 2$$

The cost drop and the resulting increase in supply lead to a fall in the equilibrium price from \$3 to \$2 per pound. This is intuitive: Lower farmers' costs end up being reflected in lower market prices. We can plug this price into either the demand or new supply equation to find the new equilibrium quantity:

$$Q_2 = 1{,}000 - 200(2) = 600$$

$$Q_2 = 200(2) + 200 = 600$$

The equilibrium quantity of tomatoes increases from 400 to 600 pounds in response to the increase in supply and the fall in the equilibrium price.

Again, we could go through the same steps for a decrease in supply. The supply curve would shift up to the left. This decline in supply would increase the equilibrium price and decrease the equilibrium quantity.

2.3 figure it out

Suppose that the supply of lemonade is represented by $Q^S = 40P$, where Q is measured in pints and P is measured in cents per pint.

a. If the demand for lemonade is $Q^D = 5{,}000 - 10P$, what are the current equilibrium price and quantity?

b. Suppose that a severe frost in Florida raises the price of lemons and thus the cost of making lemonade. In response to the increase in cost, producers reduce the quantity supplied of lemonade by 400 pints at every price. What is the new equation for the supply of lemonade?

c. After the frost, what will be the equilibrium price and quantity of lemonade?

Solution:

a. To solve for the equilibrium price, we need to equate the quantity demanded and quantity supplied:

$$Q^D = Q^S$$

$$5{,}000 - 10P = 40P$$

$$50P = 5{,}000$$

$$P = 100 \text{ cents}$$

To solve for the equilibrium quantity, we want to substitute the equilibrium price into either the demand curve or the supply curve (or both!):

$$Q^D = 5{,}000 - 10(100) = 5{,}000 - 1{,}000 = 4{,}000 \text{ pints}$$
$$Q^S = 40(100) = 4{,}000 \text{ pints}$$

b. If the quantity supplied of lemonade falls by 400 pints at every price, then the supply curve is shifting left (in a parallel fashion) by a quantity of 400 at each price:

$$Q^S{}_2 = Q^S - 400 = 40P - 400$$

The new supply curve can be represented by $Q^S{}_2 = 40P - 400$.

c. To solve for the new equilibrium, we would set $Q^D = Q^S{}_2$:

$$Q^D = Q^S{}_2$$
$$5{,}000 - 10P_2 = 40P_2 - 400$$
$$50P_2 = 5{,}400$$
$$P_2 = 108 \text{ cents}$$

Solving for equilibrium quantity can be done by substituting the equilibrium price into either the demand or supply equation:

$$Q^D = 5{,}000 - 10(108) = 5{,}000 - 1{,}080 = 3{,}920 \text{ pints}$$
$$Q^S = 40(108) - 400 = 4{,}320 - 400 = 3{,}920 \text{ pints}$$

As we would expect (see Table 2.2 below), the equilibrium price rises and the equilibrium quantity falls.

∂ This partial derivative symbol indicates that further insight into the topic using calculus is available in an end-of-chapter or online calculus appendix.

∂ The online appendix describes the effect of changes in variables other than the good's own price on a good's equilibrium price and quantity. (http://glsmicro.com/appendices)

Summary of Effects

Table 2.2 summarizes the changes in equilibrium price and quantity that result when either the demand or supply curve shifts while the other curve remains in the same position. When the demand curve shifts, price and quantity move in the same direction. An increase in demand leads consumers to want to purchase more of the good than producers are willing to supply at the old equilibrium price. This will tend to drive prices up, which in turn induces producers to supply more of the good. The producers' response is captured by movement along the supply curve.

When the supply curve shifts, price and quantity move in opposite directions. If supply increases, the supply curve shifts out, and producers want to sell more of the good at the old equilibrium price than consumers want to buy. This will force prices down, giving consumers an incentive to buy more of the good. Similarly, if supply shifts in, the equilibrium price has to rise to reduce the quantity demanded. These movements along the demand curve involve price and quantity changes in opposite directions because demand curves are downward-sloping.

Table 2.2 | **Effect of Shifts in Demand and Supply Curves in Isolation**

Curve that Shifts	Direction of Shift	Impact on Equilibrium Price	Quantity
Demand Curve	Out (increase in D)	↑	↑
	In (decrease in D)	↓	↓
Supply Curve	Out (increase in S)	↓	↑
	In (decrease in S)	↑	↓

application

Supply Shifts and the Video Game Crash of 1983

People love video games. About two-thirds of households in the United States have at least one game-playing member. Sales of video game consoles and software were around $15.5 billion in the United States in 2010. To put that number in perspective, it is almost 50% more than 2010's total domestic box office haul of $10.5 billion, and about the same size as the total combined U.S. sales of McDonald's and Burger King restaurants that year.

Seeing these numbers, you'd never know that in the industry's early days, there was a point when many people declared video games a passing fad and a business in which it was impossible to make a profit. Why did they say this? The problem wasn't demand. Early video games, from *Pong* to *Space Invaders* and consoles like the Atari 2600, were a huge hit and cultural touchstones. The problem was supply—way too much of it. In 1983 a set of factors combined to lead to a massive supply shift for the industry in North America that ended up crippling it for years.

Two primary factors led to the supply shift. Home video consoles, led by the Atari 2600 but also including popular machines from Mattel and Coleco, had taken off in the early 1980s. At this early point in the industry, console producers hadn't yet learned the best way to handle licensing arrangements with third-party games producers. As a result, just about anyone could write a game title for a console if they wanted to. And just about everyone did. Even Quaker Oats had a video games division! The pet food company Purina contracted with a software developer to create a game that would publicize its Chuck Wagon brand dog food. (The game, *Chase the Chuck Wagon*, involved a dog chasing a chuck wagon through a maze.) In essence, there was a gold rush: Too many producers, each hoping to capture just a part of the fast-growing market, all entered at the same time, leading to a much larger total supply than any producer expected individually beforehand. The same phenomenon occurred in console production as well. Several companies made clones of Atari's market-leading console, and others produced their own machines and lines of games.

The leading console makers didn't help themselves any with their own game-production decisions either. The most infamous failures were Atari's self-produced games *Pac-Man* and *E.T. the Extra-Terrestrial*. Atari management expected unprecedented sales for both, due to the extreme popularity of the arcade version of the former and the movie tied to the latter. In fact, Atari produced 12 million copies of *Pac-Man* even though there were only 10 million consoles in existence at the time, presuming that not only would just about every owner of a console buy the game, but also millions of others would buy a console just to play the game. Both were rushed through production to take advantage of the holiday shopping seasons. The games were a mess, and quantity supplied well exceeded quantity demanded even at the depressed prices in the market.

The sudden rush of producers to put product on the market created an outward shift in the supply curve—producers' behavior made clear that they were willing to produce more at any given price in early 1983 than they were just a couple years earlier, in early 1981. And while the demand for home video games had been trending upward as the technology diffused through households, the rush to produce new titles and consoles probably didn't have much of an effect on the demand curve. (In fact, because of the poor quality of the new games, it may have even shifted the demand curve inward.) It's reasonable to assume, then, that the demand curve was unmoved by the producer gold rush. The supply and demand model predicts the consequences of this supply shift on the market. A shift out in the supply curve in the face of constant demand will lead to an increase in quantity and a drop in prices, as shown in Figure 2.10. (These days, video game companies take more care in rolling out new games.)

That's exactly what happened in the video game industry. Price changes, in particular, were precipitous. Games that had been selling a year earlier at list prices of $35–$50 were being sold for $5 or even $1. Console prices fell by double-digit percentages as well. With games going at these rates, quantities increased somewhat, but nowhere near enough to

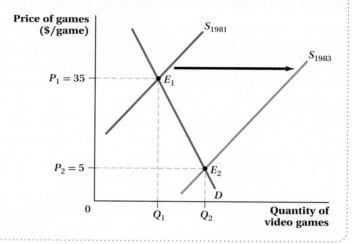

Figure 2.10 : **Effects of an Increase in the Supply of Video Games**

In 1983 a sudden increase in the number of video game producers shifted the supply curve from S_{1981} to S_{1983}. At the equilibrium, the price of video games dropped from P_1 ($35) to P_2 ($5), while the quantity increased from Q_1 to Q_2.

make them profitable for their producers. Dozens of firms—console and games makers alike—went out of business. Atari, which until then had been a cash cow, was sold by its parent Warner Communications and never recovered. The carnage was so total that some retailers, figuring the market was hopeless, refused to stock games anymore. It essentially wiped out producers from the market for three to four years, an eternity in this fast-moving industry where technological races are seemingly never-ending. Things finally turned around when a company known as Nintendo managed to convince retailers that its all-new 8-bit Nintendo Entertainment System would revitalize the moribund industry. ■

2.4 figure it out

Last month, you noticed the price of asparagus rising, and you also noted that there was less asparagus being sold than in the prior month. What inferences can you draw about the behavior of the supply and demand for asparagus?

Solution:

We need to work backwards to determine what could have happened to either supply or demand to lead to the change described in this question. Let's start with the change in price. The equilibrium price of asparagus is *rising*. This must mean one of two things: Either the demand for asparagus rose or the supply of asparagus fell. (If you have trouble seeing this, draw a couple of quick figures.)

We also know that the equilibrium quantity of asparagus fell. A drop in the equilibrium quantity can only have two causes: either a decrease in the

demand for asparagus or a fall in the supply of asparagus. (Again, you may want to draw these out to see such results.)

Which shift leads to both a rise in equilibrium price and a fall in equilibrium quantity? It must be a decrease in the supply of asparagus, as shown in the figure.

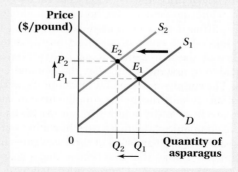

Did the curve shift, or was it just a movement along the curve?

A common type of exam question on demand and supply will involve one or more "shocks" to a market—changes in factors that influence demand or supply. Your job will be to sort out how those shocks affect demand and supply, and by extension, the equilibrium price and quantity in the market. Generally, the trickiest part of questions like these is figuring out whether changes in price and quantity are the result of moving along a given demand or supply curve, or whether the curves are shifting.

If you follow a few simple steps, this type of question need not be too difficult.

1. **Figure out what the shock is in any particular problem.** It is the change that causes a shift in either the supply curve, the demand curve, or both. There is a nearly infinite variety of shocks. A pandemic could wipe out a large number of consumers, a new invention might make it cheaper to make a good, a different good that consumers like better might be introduced, or inclement weather may damage or kill off a large portion of a certain crop.

   Importantly, though, a change in either the price or the quantity of the good *in the market being studied* cannot be the shock. The changes in price and quantity in this market are the *result* of the shock, not the shock itself. Be careful, however: Changes in prices or quantities in some *other* market can serve as a shock to this market. If the price of chunky peanut butter falls, for example, that could be a shock to the market for grape jelly or the market for creamy peanut butter.

2. **Determine whether the shock shifts the demand or supply curve.**

   a. *To figure out whether a shock shifts the demand curve and how it shifts it,* ask yourself the following question: If the price of this good didn't change, would consumers want to buy more, less, or the same amount of the good after the shock? If consumers want more of the good at the same price after the shock, then the shock increases the quantity demanded at every price and shifts the demand curve out (to the right). If consumers want less of the good at the same price after the shock, then the shock decreases demand and the demand curve shifts in. If consumers want the same amount of the good at the same price, then the demand curve doesn't move at all, and it's probably a supply shock.

   Let's go back to the grape jelly example. Our shock was a decline in the price of peanut butter. Do consumers want more or less grape jelly (holding the price constant) when peanut butter gets cheaper? The answer to this question is probably "more." Cheap peanut butter means consumers will buy more peanut butter, and since people tend to eat peanut butter and jelly together, consumers will probably want more jelly even if the price of jelly stays the same. Therefore, the decline in peanut butter's price shifts the demand for grape jelly out.

   b. *To figure out whether a shock shifts the supply curve and how it shifts it,* ask yourself the following question: If the price of this good didn't change, would suppliers want to produce more, less, or the same amount of the good after the shock? In the jelly example, a change in the price of peanut butter doesn't affect the costs of making jelly—it's not an input into jelly production. So it's not a supply shock. An increase in the price of grapes, however, would be a supply shock in the market for grape jelly.

3. **Draw the market's supply and demand curves before and after the shocks.** In the jelly example, we would draw the original demand and supply curves, and then add the new demand curve (to the right of the initial demand curve) that results from the increase in the demand for jelly because of lower peanut butter prices. From this, it's easy to execute the final step, interpreting what impact the shock has on equilibrium price and quantity. For grape jelly, the increase in demand will result in a higher equilibrium price and quantity for jelly because the demand shift creates movement up and to the right along the jelly supply curve.

Practice in following this recipe will make manipulating supply and demand curves second nature.

What Determines the Size of Price and Quantity Changes?

Thus far, the analysis in the chapter (summarized in Table 2.2) tells us about the *direction* in which equilibrium price and quantity move when demand and supply curves shift. But we don't know the size of these changes. In this section, we discuss the factors that determine how large the price and quantity changes are.

Size of the Shift One obvious and direct influence on the sizes of the equilibrium price and quantity changes is the size of the demand or supply curve shift itself. The larger the shift, the larger the change in equilibrium price or quantity.

Figure 2.11 │ **Size of Equilibrium Price and Quantity Changes, and the Slopes of the Supply and Demand Curves**

(a) Demand curve shift with flatter supply curve

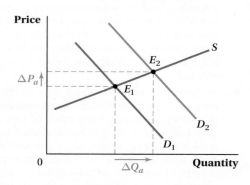

(b) Demand curve shift with steeper supply curve

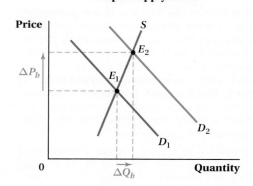

(c) Supply curve shift with flatter demand curve

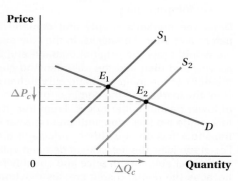

(d) Supply curve shift with steeper demand curve

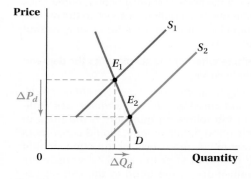

(a) With a relatively flat supply curve, a shift in demand from D_1 to D_2 will result in a relatively small increase in equilibrium price ΔP_a and a relatively large increase in equilibrium quantity ΔQ_a. (b) With a relatively steep supply curve, a shift in demand from D_1 to D_2 will result in a relatively large increase in equilibrium price ΔP_b and a relatively small increase in equilibrium quantity ΔQ_b.

(c) With a relatively flat demand curve, a shift in supply from S_1 to S_2 will result in a relatively small decrease in equilibrium price ΔP_c and a relatively large increase in equilibrium quantity ΔQ_c.
(d) With a relatively steep demand curve, a shift in supply from S_1 to S_2 will result in a relatively large decrease in equilibrium price ΔP_d and a relatively small increase in equilibrium quantity ΔQ_d.

Slopes of the Curves Even for a fixed-size demand or supply curve shift, the magnitudes of the resulting equilibrium price and quantity changes can vary. Specifically, the *relative* sizes of the price and quantity changes depend on the steepness of the demand and supply curves. If the demand curve shifts, then the slope of the supply curve determines whether the shift leads to a relatively large equilibrium price change and a relatively small equilibrium quantity change, or vice versa. If the supply curve shifts, it's the slope of the demand curve that matters.

Figure 2.11 demonstrates this. Panels a and b show the same shift in the demand curve, from D_1 to D_2. In panel a, the supply curve is relatively flat, while in panel b, it's relatively steep. When the demand curve shifts, if the supply curve is flat, the change in the equilibrium quantity (ΔQ_a) will be relatively large but the change in price (ΔP_a) will be small. When the supply curve is steep (panel b), the price change (ΔP_b) is large and the quantity change (ΔQ_b) small. Similarly, panels c and d show the same supply curve shift, but with differently sloped demand curves. The same results hold for shifts in the supply curve—flatter (steeper) demand curves result in larger (smaller) changes in quantity relative to price changes.

This analysis raises an obvious question: What affects the slope of demand and supply curves? We discuss the economic forces that determine the steepness or flatness of demand or supply curves next.

 application

The Supply Curve of Housing and Housing Prices: A Tale of Two Cities

From panels a and b of Figure 2.11, we can see that, when the demand curve shifts, the slope of the supply curve determines the relative size of the change in equilibrium price and quantity. Data for housing prices provide a good application of this idea. Specifically, we can look at how urban housing prices respond to an increase in the demand for housing caused by population growth.

Consider housing in the cities of New York City and Houston. New York is incredibly dense. Because the metropolitan area is so built up, it is expensive for developers to build additional housing. As a result, developers' costs rise so quickly with the amount of housing they build, the quantity of housing supplied doesn't respond much to price differences. There's only so much the developers can do. This means the supply curve of housing in New York is steep—the quantity supplied isn't very responsive to changes in price. Equivalently, it would take a very large increase in housing prices to induce housing suppliers to be willing to increase the quantity of housing they build. (We'll talk more in the next section about the factors that determine the price sensitivity of quantity supplied and quantity demanded.)

New York City.

Houston, on the other hand, is much less dense. It is surrounded by farm and ranch land, and there is still a lot of space to expand within the metro area. This means developers can build new housing without driving up their unit costs very much; they can just buy another farm and build housing on it if the price is right. For this reason, the quantity of housing supplied in Houston is quite responsive to changes in housing prices. That is, the housing supply curve in Houston is fairly flat.

Theory predicts that in response to an outward shift in the demand for housing in the two cities, New York (with its steep supply curve) should see a relatively large increase in the equilibrium price and very little change in the equilibrium quantity of housing. Houston, on the other hand, with its flatter supply curve, should see a relatively small increase in price and a large increase in quantity for an equal-size shift in demand.

Houston, Texas.

Figure 2.12 ⋮ Population Indices for New York and Houston, 1977–2009

Between 1977 and 2009, the population in New York grew by about 15%, while the population in Houston more than doubled.

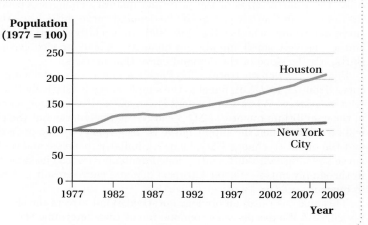

So let's look at some data. Look first at Figure 2.12, which shows how the populations of the New York and Houston metro areas changed from 1977 to 2009. (The figure shows the population index for each metro area, giving the city's population as a percentage of its 1977 value.) Population in both cities rose over these 32 years. New York metro area's population grew about 15%, while Houston's population saw a far greater rise, more than doubling.

We can think of these population influxes as being tied to outward shifts in the demand curve for housing in each city. Again, the prediction of the supply and demand model is that the equilibrium price response to a given-sized shift in demand should be larger in New York, where the supply curve of housing is steep (like that in Figure 2.11b), than in Houston, with its flatter supply curve (as in Figure 2.11a).

Looking at Figure 2.13, it's clear this prediction holds. The figure depicts a housing price index for both the New York and Houston metro areas, showing the price of housing in the cities (again, as an index based on their 1977 values). Despite having a considerably smaller increase in population, New York saw a tenfold rise in average housing

Figure 2.13 ⋮ Housing Price Indices for New York and Houston, 1977–2009

From 1977 to 2009, housing prices in New York rose at a much faster rate than those in Houston.

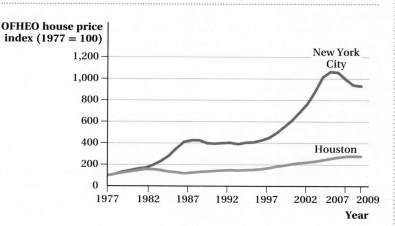

prices over the past 30 years. House prices went up in Houston too, as you would expect in a city that more than doubles in population, but by only a fraction of the increase seen in New York. In comparing these two cities, we see a clear pattern that the price effects of demand shifts in a market depend on the shape of the supply curve. ■

Changes in Market Equilibrium When Both Curves Shift

Sometimes, we are faced with situations in which supply and demand curves move simultaneously. For example, Figure 2.14 combines two shifts: decreases (inward shifts) in both supply and demand. Let's return to the tomato market at Pike Place Market and suppose that there is a big increase in oil prices. This increase drives up the cost of production because harvesting and distribution costs rise for sellers. Increased oil prices also decrease the demand for tomatoes. Because driving to the market gets more expensive for consumers, there are fewer people buying at any given price. The original equilibrium occurred at the intersection of D_1 and S_1, point E_1. The new equilibrium is at point E_2, the intersection of D_2 and S_2.

In this particular case, the simultaneous inward shifts in supply and demand have led to a substantial reduction in the equilibrium quantity and a slight increase in price. The reduction in quantity should be intuitive. The inward shift in the demand curve means that consumers want to buy less at any given price. The inward shift in the supply curve means that at any given price, producers want to supply less. Because both producers and consumers want less quantity, equilibrium quantity falls unambiguously, from Q_1 to Q_2.

The effect on equilibrium price is not as clear, however. An inward shift in demand with a fixed supply curve will tend to reduce prices, but an inward shift in supply with a fixed demand curve will tend to raise prices. Because both curves are moving simultaneously, it is unclear which effect will dominate, and therefore whether equilibrium price rises or falls. We have drawn the curves in Figure 2.14 so that equilibrium price rises slightly, from P_1 to P_2. But had the supply and demand curves shifted by different amounts (or had they been flatter or steeper), the dual inward shift might have led to a decrease in the equilibrium price, or no change in the price at all.

As a general rule, when both curves shift at the same time, we will know with certainty the direction of change of either the equilibrium price or quantity, but never both. This result can be seen by a closer inspection of Table 2.2. If the demand

---

Figure 2.14   Example of a Simultaneous Shift in Demand and Supply

An inward shift of both the supply and demand curves results in a new equilibrium point E_2 at the intersection between S_2 and D_2. At E_2, the price has increased slightly from P_1 to P_2, and the quantity has decreased from Q_1 to Q_2.

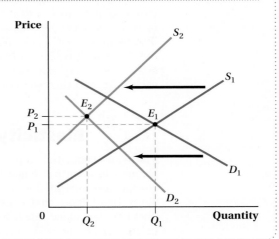

Figure 2.15 **When Both Curves Shift, the Direction of Either Price or Quantity Will Be Ambiguous**

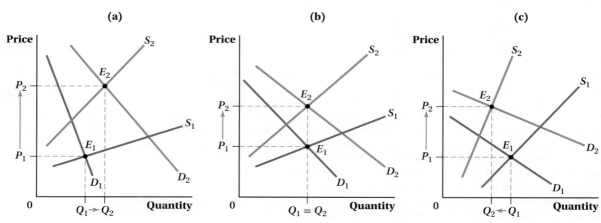

(a) **(b)** **(c)**

(a) In all three panels, there is an outward shift in demand (D_1 to D_2) and an inward shift in supply (S_1 to S_2). Here, both equilibrium price (P_1 to P_2) and quantity (Q_1 to Q_2) increase as a result.

(b) Equilibrium price increases from P_1 to P_2, while equilibrium quantity stays the same ($Q_1 = Q_2$).
(c) Equilibrium price increases from P_1 to P_2, while equilibrium quantity decreases from Q_1 to Q_2.

and supply curve shifts are both pushing price in the same direction, which would be the case if (1) the demand curve shifted out and the supply curve shifted in or (2) the demand curve shifted in and the supply curve shifted out, then the same shifts 1 or 2 will push quantities in opposite directions. Likewise, if the shifts in both curves serve to move quantity in the same direction—either (3) demand and supply both shift out or (4) demand and supply both shift in—the shifts 3 and 4 have opposing effects on equilibrium prices. The example we just looked at in Figure 2.14 involved a case of form 4.

This ambiguity is also apparent in the example in Figure 2.15. The directions of the shifts in the demand and supply curves are the same in each panel of the figure: Supply shifts inward from S_1 to S_2, and demand shifts outward from D_1 to D_2. Both of these shifts will lead to higher prices, and this is reflected in the change in the equilibrium (from point E_1 to E_2). But as can be seen, whether the equilibrium quantity rises, falls, or stays the same depends on the relative size of the shifts and the slopes of the curves. The figure's three panels show examples of each possible case. When examining a situation in which both supply and demand shift, you might find it helpful to draw each shift in isolation first, note the changes in equilibrium quantity and price implied by each shift, and then combine these pieces of information to obtain your answer.

2.5 Elasticity

Mathematically, the slopes of demand and supply curves relate changes in price to changes in quantity demanded or quantity supplied. Steeper curves mean that price changes are correlated with relatively small quantity changes. When demand curves are steep, this implies that consumers are not very price-sensitive and won't change their quantity demanded much in response to price changes. Similarly, steep supply curves mean that producers' quantities supplied are not particularly sensitive to price changes.

Flatter demand or supply curves, on the other hand, imply that price changes are associated with large quantity changes. Markets with flat demand curves have consumers whose quantities demanded change a lot as price varies. Markets with flat supply curves will see big movements in quantity supplied as prices change.

The concept of elasticity expresses the responsiveness of one value to changes in another (and here specifically, the responsiveness of quantities to prices). An **elasticity** relates the percentage change in one value to the percentage change in another. So, for example, when we talk about the sensitivity of consumers' quantity demanded to price, we refer to the **price elasticity of demand:** the percentage change in quantity demanded resulting from a given percentage change in price.

Slope and Elasticity Are Not the Same

You might be thinking that the price elasticity of demand sounds a lot like the slope of the demand curve: how much quantity demanded changes when price does. While elasticity and slope are certainly related, they're not the same.

The slope relates a change in one level (prices) to another level (quantity). The demand curve we introduced in the tomato example was $Q = 1,000 - 200P$. The slope of this demand curve is -200; that is, quantity demanded falls by 200 pounds for every dollar per pound increase in price.

There are two big problems with using just the slopes of demand and supply curves to measure price responsiveness. First, slopes depend completely on the units of measurement we choose. Suppose we measured tomato prices P in cents per pound rather than dollars. Now the demand curve would be $Q = 1,000 - 2P$, because the quantity of tomatoes demanded would fall by 2 pounds for every 1 cent increase in price. But the fact that the coefficient on P is now 2 instead of 200 doesn't mean that consumers are 1/100th as price-sensitive as before. Nothing has changed about consumers' price responsiveness in this market: The quantity demanded still falls by 200 pounds for each $1 increase in price. The change in the slope simply reflects a change in the units of P. The second problem with slopes is that you can't compare them across different products. Suppose we were studying consumers' grocery shopping patterns, and wanted to compare consumers' price sensitivity for tomatoes in the market at Pike Place Market to their price sensitivity for celery hearts, for instance. Does the fact that consumers demand 100 fewer celery hearts for every 10 cent per celery heart increase in price mean that consumers are more or less price elastic in the celery market than in the tomato market? The slope of the celery demand curve implied by these numbers is -100 (if we measure quantity demanded in hearts and price in cents per celery heart). How could we ever compare this slope to the -200 slope for tomatoes?

Using elasticities to express responsiveness avoids these tricky issues, because everything is expressed in relative percentage changes. That eliminates the units problem (a 10% change is a 10% change regardless of what units the thing changing is measured in) and makes magnitudes comparable across markets.

The Price Elasticities of Demand and Supply

The price elasticity of demand is the ratio of the percentage change in quantity demanded to an associated percentage change in price. Mathematically, its formula is

Price elasticity of demand = (% change in quantity demanded)/(% change in price)

The price elasticity of supply is exactly analogous:

Price elasticity of supply = (% change in quantity supplied)/(% change in price)

To keep the equations simpler from now on, we'll use some shorthand notation. E^D will denote the price elasticity of demand, E^S the price elasticity of supply, $\%\Delta Q^D$ and

elasticity
The ratio of the percentage change in one value to the percentage change in another.

price elasticity of demand
The percentage change in quantity demanded resulting from a 1% change in price.

$\%\Delta Q^S$ the percentage change in quantities demanded and supplied, respectively, and $\%\Delta P$ the percentage change in price. In this shorthand, the two equations above become

$$E^D = \frac{\%\Delta Q^D}{\%\Delta P} \text{ and}$$

$$E^S = \frac{\%\Delta Q^S}{\%\Delta P}$$

So, for example, if the quantity demanded of a good falls by 10% in response to a 4% price increase, the good's price elasticity of demand is $E^D = -10\%/4\% = -2.5$. There are a couple of things to note about this example. First, because demand curves slope downward, the price elasticity of demand is always negative (or more precisely, always nonpositive; in special cases that we will discuss below, it can be zero). Second, because it is a ratio, a price elasticity can also be thought of as the percentage change in quantity demanded for a 1% increase in price. That is, for this good, a 1% increase in price leads to a −2.5% change in quantity demanded.

The price elasticity of supply works exactly the same way. If producers' quantity supplied increases by 25% in response to a 50% increase in price, for example, the price elasticity of supply is $E^S = 25\%/50\% = 0.5$. The price elasticity of supply is always positive (or again more precisely, always nonnegative) because quantity supplied increases when a good's price rises. And just as with demand elasticities, supply elasticities can be thought of as the percentage change in quantity in response to a 1% increase in price.

Price Elasticities and Price Responsiveness

Now that we've defined elasticities, let's use them to think about how responsive quantities demanded and supplied are to price changes.

When demand (supply) is very price-sensitive, a small change in price will lead to large changes in quantities demanded (supplied). That means the numerator of the elasticity expression, the percentage change in quantity, will be very large in magnitude compared to the percentage change in price in the denominator. For price elasticity of demand, the change in quantity will have the opposite sign as the price change, and the elasticity will be negative. But its magnitude (its absolute value) will be large if consumers are very responsive to price changes.

Examples of markets with large-magnitude price elasticities of demand would be those where consumers have a lot of ability to substitute away from or toward the good in question. (We also saw above how substitute products can lead to shifts in the demand curve. Substitutes are therefore an example of a force that can rotate demand curves as they shift.) The demand for apples at the grocery store is probably fairly price-responsive because consumers have an array of other fruits they could buy instead if apple prices are high; if apple prices are low, they will buy apples instead of other fruits. The price elasticity of demand for apples might be something like −4: for every 1% increase in price, consumers' quantity demanded would fall 4%.

Markets with less price-responsive demand have elasticities that are small in magnitude. The demand for candy at the circus (certainly for the parents of small children) probably has a fairly small price elasticity of demand. In this case, the price elasticity of demand might be something like −0.3: for every 1% increase in price, quantity demanded would fall by 0.3%. (If you prefer, you could also express this as saying for every 10% price increase, quantity demanded would drop by 3%.)

Markets with large price elasticities of supply—where the quantity supplied is sensitive to price differences—would be those where it was easy for suppliers to vary their amount of production as price changes. Perhaps they have a cost structure that allows them to make as many units as they'd like without driving up their per-unit costs too much. In the market for software, for example, if a program is wildly popular and drawing a high price, it's fairly easy for the game's producer to print more DVDs or make additional copies available for download. So, the elasticity of supply might be quite large in this market, something like 12 (a 1% increase in price leads to a 12% increase in quantity supplied).

Markets with low price elasticities of supply have quantities supplied that are fairly unresponsive to price changes. This would occur in markets where it is costly for producers to vary their production levels, or it is difficult for producers to enter or exit the market. The supply curve for tickets to the Super Bowl might have a very low price elasticity of supply because there are only so many seats in the stadium. If the ticket price rises today, the stadium owners can't really put in additional seats. The supply elasticity in this market might be close to zero. It's probably slightly positive, however, because the owners could open some obstructed-view seats or make other temporary seating arrangements.

 **application**

Demand Elasticities and the Availability of Substitutes

We discussed how the availability of substitutes can affect the price elasticity of demand. When consumers can easily switch to other products or markets, they will be more responsive to changes in price of a particular good. This means that, for any small rise in price, there will be a large decline in quantity demanded and the price elasticity of demand will be relatively large (in absolute value).

Economists Glenn and Sara Ellison found an extreme example of the effect of substitution possibilities and extreme demand elasticities to match.[7] They look at the markets for different CPUs and memory chips on a price search engine Web site. The Web site collects price quotes for well-defined chips and chipsets from hardware suppliers and then groups the quotes together (ranked by price) with links to the corresponding suppliers. While Ellison and Ellison show that suppliers make heroic efforts to frustrate the search engine, it still makes it extremely easy to compare multiple suppliers' prices for certain products. Because the product in this case is so standardized, little distinguishes one chip from another. As a result, consumers are able and willing to respond strongly to any price differences across the suppliers of the chips.

This easy ability for consumers to substitute across suppliers means the demand curve for any given supplier's CPUs and memory chips is extremely elastic. If a supplier's price is even a slight bit higher than that of its competitors, consumers can easily buy from someone else. Ellison and Ellison, using data collected from the Web site, estimated the price elasticity of demand for any single chip to be on the order of −25. In other words, if the supplier raises its price just 1% higher than that of its competitors (which works out to a dollar or two for the chips listed on the Web site), it can expect sales to fall by 25%! This is a huge price response, and it's due to the many substitution possibilities the search engine makes available to consumers. Thus, the availability of substitutes is one of the key determinants of the price elasticity of demand. ∎

Elasticities and Time Horizons   Often, a key factor determining the flexibility consumers and producers have to respond to price differences, and therefore the price elasticity of their quantities demanded and supplied, is the time horizon.

In the short run, consumers are often limited in their ability to change their consumption patterns, but given more time, they can make adjustments that give them greater flexibility. The classic example of this is in the market for gasoline. If there is a sudden price spike, many consumers are essentially stuck having to consume roughly the same quantity of gas as they did before the price spike. After all, they have the same car, the same commute, and the same schedule as before. Maybe they can double up on a few trips, or carpool more often, but their ability to respond to prices is limited. For

---

[7] Glenn Ellison and Sara Ellison, "Search, Obfuscation, and Price Elasticities on the Internet," *Econometrica* 77, no. 2 (2009): 427–452.

this reason, the short-run price elasticity of gasoline demand is relatively low; empirical estimates by economists that specialize in the market suggest it is around −0.2. That is, for a 1% change in the price of gas, the quantity demanded changes by only −0.2% in the direction opposite the price changes. Over longer horizons, however, individuals have greater scope to adjust their consumption. If the gas spike is permanent, or at least persistent, they can set up a permanent ride-sharing arrangement, buy a more efficient car, or even shorten their commute by moving closer to where they work. The long-run price elasticity of demand for gasoline is therefore much larger in magnitude; empirical studies typically find it is something like −0.8. This means that in the long run, consumers can make four times the quantity adjustment to price changes they can make in the short run.

The same logic holds for producers and supply elasticities. The longer the horizon, the more scope they have to adjust output to price changes. Manufacturers already producing at capacity might not be able to increase their output much in the short run if prices increase, even though they would like to. If prices stay high, however, they can hire more workers, build larger factories, and new firms can set up their own production operations and enter the market.

For these reasons, the price elasticities of demand and supply for most products are larger in magnitude (i.e., more negative for demand and more positive for supply) in the long run than in the short run. As we see in the next section, larger-magnitude elasticities imply flatter demand and supply curves. As a result, long-run demand and supply curves tend to be flatter than their short-run versions.

Terms for Elasticities by Magnitude Economists have special terms for elasticities of particular magnitudes. Elasticities with magnitudes (absolute values) greater than 1 are referred to as **elastic.** In the above examples, apples have elastic demand and software has elastic supply. Elasticities with magnitudes less than 1 are referred to as **inelastic.** The demand for circus candy and the supply of previous wine vintages are inelastic. If the price elasticity of demand is exactly −1, or the price elasticity of supply is exactly 1, this is referred to as **unit elastic.** If price elasticities are zero—that is, there is no response in quantity to price changes, the associated goods are called **perfectly inelastic.** Finally, if price elasticities are infinite in magnitude (−∞ for demand, +∞ for supply)—the quantity demanded or supplied changes infinitely in response to any price change—this is referred to as **perfectly elastic.**

Elasticities and Linear Demand and Supply Curves

As we discussed above, economists often use linear (straight-line) demand and supply curves, mostly for the sake of convenience. Because they are so common, it's worth discussing how elasticities are related to linear curves. Even more important, drawing this connection shows exactly how curves' slopes and elasticities, the two measures of price responsiveness we've been using, are related but still different.

We can rewrite the elasticity formula in a way that makes it easier to see the relationship between elasticity and the slope of a demand or supply curve. A percentage change in quantity ($\%\Delta Q$) is the change in quantity (ΔQ) divided by the original quantity level Q. That is, $\%\Delta Q = \Delta Q/Q$. Similarly, the percentage change in price is $\%\Delta P = \Delta P/P$. Substituting these into the elasticity expression from above, we have

$$E = \frac{\%\Delta Q}{\%\Delta P} = \frac{\Delta Q/Q}{\Delta P/P}$$

where E is a demand or supply elasticity, depending on whether Q denotes quantity demanded or supplied.

elastic
A price elasticity with an absolute value greater than 1.

inelastic
A price elasticity with an absolute value less than 1.

unit elastic
A price elasticity with an absolute value equal to 1.

perfectly inelastic
A price elasticity that is equal to zero; there is no change in quantity demanded or supplied for any change in price.

perfectly elastic
A price elasticity that is infinite; any change in price leads to an infinite change in quantity demanded or supplied.

Rearranging terms yields

$$E = \frac{\Delta Q/Q}{\Delta P/P} = \frac{\Delta Q}{\Delta P} \cdot \frac{P}{Q}$$

or

$$E = \frac{1}{\text{slope}} \cdot \frac{P}{Q}$$

where "slope" refers to $\Delta P/\Delta Q$, the slope of the demand curve in the standard price-versus-quantity space.

Elasticity of a Linear Demand Curve   Suppose we're dealing with the demand curve in Figure 2.16. Its slope is −2, but its elasticity varies as we move along it because P/Q does. Think first about the point A, where it intercepts the vertical axis. At $Q = 0$, P/Q is infinite because P is positive ($20) and Q is zero. This, combined with the fact that the curve's (constant) slope is negative, means the price elasticity of demand is $-\infty$ at this point. The logic behind this is that consumers don't demand any units of the good at A when its price is $20, but if price falls at all, their quantity demanded will become positive, if still small. Even though this change in quantity demanded is small in numbers of units of the good, the *percentage* change in consumption is infinite, because it's rising from zero.

As we move down along the demand curve, the P/Q ratio falls, reducing the magnitude of the price elasticity of demand. (Remember, the slope isn't changing, so that part of the elasticity stays the same.) It will remain elastic—that is, have a magnitude larger than 1—for some distance. Eventually, the absolute value of the elasticity will fall to 1, and at that point the demand curve is unit elastic. For the curve in Figure 2.16, this happens to be when $P = 10$ and $Q = 5$, because $E^D = -(1/2) \times (10/5) = -1$. This is labeled point B in the figure.[8] As we continue down and to the right along the demand curve, the magnitude of the elasticity will fall further and demand will become inelastic.

Figure 2.16   **Elasticity of a Linear Demand Curve**

The ratio between price and quantity (P/Q) and the magnitude of the elasticity of a demand curve decrease as we move down the curve. At point A, $Q = 0$, $P/Q = \infty$, and the price elasticity of demand is $-\infty$. Between points A and B, the demand curve is elastic with a price elasticity of demand less than −1. At point B, the demand curve is unit elastic, or the price elasticity of demand equals −1. Between points B and C, the demand curve is inelastic with a price elasticity of demand greater than −1. At point C, $P = 0$, $P/Q = 0$, and the price elasticity of demand equals zero.

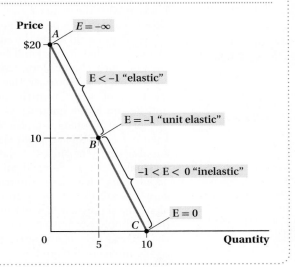

---

[8] For a linear demand curve that intersects both the price and quantity axes, the point where the demand curve is unit-elastic is always the midpoint. The curve's slope equals the price where it crosses the vertical axis (call this P_Y) divided by the quantity where it crosses the horizontal axis (call this Q_X), so 1 over the slope equals $-Q_X/P_Y$. The price-to-quantity ratio at the midpoint equals $(P_Y/2)/(Q_X/2)$, or simply P_Y/Q_X. The elasticity, which is the product of these two ratios, must therefore equal −1.

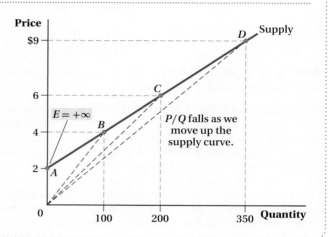

Figure 2.17   **Elasticity of a Linear Supply Curve**

The ratio between price and quantity (P/Q) and the magnitude of the elasticity of a supply curve decrease as we move up the curve. At point A, $Q = 0$, $P/Q = \infty$, and the price elasticity of supply is ∞. From B to C to D, the decrease in P/Q is reflected in the decrease of the slopes of the rays from these points to the origin. Unlike the demand curve, the price elasticity of supply will never reach zero because the supply curve never intercepts the quantity axis.

At the point where the demand curve hits the horizontal axis (point C in the figure), price is zero, so $P/Q = 0$, and the price elasticity of demand is zero.

To recap, the price elasticity of demand of changes from $-\infty$ to zero as we move down and to the right along a linear demand curve.

Elasticity of a Linear Supply Curve   A somewhat similar effect is seen as we move along a linear supply curve, like the one in Figure 2.17. Again, because the slope of the curve is constant, the changes in elasticity along the curve are driven by the price-to-quantity ratio. At point A, where the supply curve intercepts the vertical axis, $Q = 0$ and P/Q is infinite. The price elasticity of supply is $+\infty$ at this point. The same logic holds as with the demand curve: For the smallest increase in price, the quantity supplied rises from zero to a positive number, an infinite percentage change in quantity supplied.

As we move up along the supply curve, the P/Q ratio falls. While it's probably obvious to you that it must fall from infinity, you might wonder whether it keeps falling, because both P and Q are rising. It turns out that, yes, it must keep falling. The way to see this is to recognize that the P/Q ratio at any point on the supply curve equals the slope of a ray from the origin to that point. (The rise of the ray is the price P, and its run is the quantity Q. Because slope is rise over run, the ray's slope is P/Q.) We've drawn some examples of such rays for different locations on the supply curve in Figure 2.17. It's clear from the figure that as we move up and to the right along the supply curve, the slopes of these rays from the origin continue to fall.

Unlike with the demand curve, however, the P/Q ratio never falls to zero because the supply curve will never intercept the horizontal axis. Therefore, the price elasticity of supply won't drop to zero. In fact, while the P/Q ratio is always falling as we move up along the supply curve, you can see from the figure that it will never drop below the slope of the supply curve itself. Some linear supply curves like the one in Figure 2.17 intercept the vertical axis at a positive price, indicating that the price has to be at least as high as the intercept for producers to be willing to supply any positive quantity. Because the price elasticity of supply equals $(1/\text{slope}) \times (P/Q)$, such supply curves approach becoming unit elastic at high prices and quantities supplied, but never quite get there. Also, because P/Q never falls to zero, the only way a supply curve can have an elasticity of zero is if its inverse slope is zero—that is, if it is vertical. We discuss cases like this below.

The demand for gym memberships in a small rural community is $Q = 360 - 2P$, where Q is the number of monthly members and P is the monthly membership rate.

a. Calculate the price elasticity of demand for gym memberships when the price is $50 per month.

b. Calculate the price elasticity of demand for gym memberships when the price is $100 per month.

c. Based on your answers to (a) and (b), what can you tell about the relationship between price and the price elasticity of demand along a linear demand curve?

Solution:

a. The price elasticity of demand is calculated as

$$E = \frac{\Delta Q/Q}{\Delta P/P} = \frac{\Delta Q}{\Delta P} \cdot \frac{P}{Q}$$

Let's first calculate the slope of the demand curve. The easiest way to do this is to rearrange the equation in terms of P to find the inverse demand curve:

$$Q = 360 - 2P$$
$$2P = 360 - Q$$
$$P = 180 - 0.5Q$$

We can see that the slope of this demand curve is -0.5. We know this because every time Q rises by 1, P falls by 0.5.

So we know the slope and the price. To compute the elasticity, we need to know the quantity demanded at a price of $50. To find this, we plug $50 into the demand equation for P:

$$Q = 360 - 2P = 360 - 2(50) = 360 - 100 = 260$$

Now we are ready to compute the elasticity:

$$E = \frac{1}{-0.5} \cdot \frac{50}{260} = \frac{50}{-130} = -0.385$$

b. When the price is $100 per month, the quantity demanded is

$$Q = 360 - 2P = 360 - 2(100) = 360 - 200 = 160$$

Plugging into the elasticity formula, we get

$$E = \frac{1}{-0.5} \cdot \frac{100}{160} = \frac{100}{-80} = -1.25$$

c. From (a) and (b), we can see that as the price rises along a linear demand curve, demand moves from being inelastic ($0.385 < 1$) to elastic ($1.25 > 1$).

Perfectly Inelastic and Perfectly Elastic Demand and Supply

The formula relating elasticities to slopes also sheds some light on what demand and supply curves look like in two special but often discussed cases: perfectly inelastic and perfectly elastic demand and supply.

Perfect Inelasticity   We discussed above that when the price elasticity is zero, demand and supply are said to be perfectly inelastic. When would this be the case? We just saw that this will be true for any linear demand at the point where it intercepts the horizontal (quantity) axis. But what would a demand curve look like that is perfectly inelastic everywhere? A linear demand curve with a slope of $-\infty$ would drive the price elasticity of demand to zero due to the inverse relationship between elasticity and slope. Because a curve with an infinite slope is vertical, a perfectly inelastic demand curve is vertical. An example of such a curve is shown in Figure 2.18a. This makes intuitive sense: A vertical demand curve indicates that the quantity demanded by consumers is completely unchanged regardless of the price. Any percentage change in price will induce a 0% change in quantity demanded. In other words, the price elasticity of demand is zero.

While perfectly inelastic demand curves are uncommon (after all, there are almost always possibilities for consumers and producers to substitute toward or away from a good as prices hit either extreme of zero or infinity), we might see some approximations to this case. For example, diabetics might have very inelastic demand for insulin. Their demand curve will be almost vertical.

The same logic holds for supply: A vertical supply curve indicates perfectly inelastic supply and no response of quantity supplied to price differences. The supply of tickets for a particular concert or sporting event might also be close to perfectly inelastic, with a near-vertical supply curve, due to capacity constraints of the arena.

One implication of perfect inelasticity is that any shift in the market's demand or supply curve will result in a change only in the market equilibrium price, not the quantity. That's because there is absolutely no scope for quantity to change in the movement along a perfectly inelastic demand curve from the old to the new equilibrium. Likewise, for perfectly inelastic supply, if there is a demand curve shift, all equilibrium movement is in price, not quantity.

Perfect Elasticity   When demand or supply is perfectly elastic, on the other hand, the price elasticity is infinite. This will be the case for linear demand or supply curves that have slopes of zero—those that are horizontal. An example of such a curve is shown in Figure 2.18b. This shape makes intuitive sense, too. As flat demand or supply curves imply large quantity responses to price differences, *perfectly* flat curves imply infinitely large quantity changes to price differences. If price is just above a horizontal demand curve, the quantity demanded will be zero. But if price fell just a bit, to below the demand curve, the quantity demanded would be infinite. Similarly, a small price change from above to below a horizontal supply curve would shift producers' quantity supplied from infinite to zero.

Figure 2.18   Perfectly Inelastic and Perfectly Elastic Demand Curves

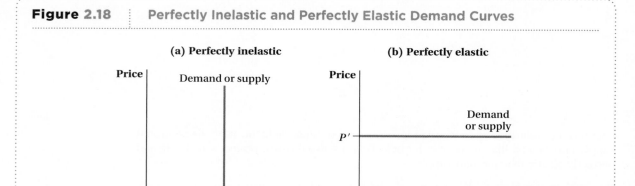

(a) When a demand or supply curve is vertical, its slope is infinite and it is perfectly inelastic. In other words, any change in price will result in a 0% change in quantity demanded or supplied.

(b) When a demand or supply curve is horizontal, its slope is zero and it is perfectly elastic. In other words, any change in price will result in an infinitely large change in quantity demanded or supplied.

When might we see perfectly elastic demand or supply curves? Small producers of commodity goods probably face demand curves for their products that are approximately horizontal. (We'll discuss this more in Chapter 8.) For instance, a small corn farmer can probably sell as many bushels of corn as she wants at the fixed price offered by the local grain elevator. While the elevator couldn't really handle an infinite amount of corn, it has the capacity to buy much more corn than the farmer could ever practically sell. So from the farmer's perspective, the quantity demanded at the offered price can grow as large as would ever matter for her. At the same time, if the farmer decided that the elevator's price was too low and insisted that she be paid more than the going rate, the elevator would likely refuse to buy any corn from the farmer. Effectively, then, it is as if the farmer faces an infinite quantity demanded for her corn at the going price (or below it, if for some reason she's willing to sell for less) but zero quantity demanded of her corn above that price. In other words, she faces a flat demand curve at the going market price.

Supply curves are close to perfectly elastic in competitive industries in which producers all have roughly the same costs, and entry and exit is very easy. (We'll also discuss this point more in Chapter 8.) These conditions mean that competition will drive prices toward the (common) level of costs, and differences in quantities supplied will be soaked up by the entry and exit of firms from the industry. Because of the strictures of competition in the market, no firm will be able to sell at a price above costs, and obviously no firm will be willing to supply at a price below costs. Therefore, the industry's supply curve is essentially flat at the producers' cost level.

As opposed to the perfectly inelastic case, shifts in supply in a market with perfectly elastic demand will only move equilibrium quantity, not price. There's no way for the equilibrium price to change when the demand curve is flat. Similarly, for markets with perfectly elastic supply, demand curve shifts move only equilibrium quantities and not prices.

The Price Elasticity of Demand, Expenditures, and Revenue

There's an interesting and useful relationship between consumers' expenditures on a good and the price elasticity of demand. Namely, expenditures rise with prices if demand is inelastic, but decrease with prices if demand is elastic. If demand is unit elastic, a change in price has no impact on expenditures. This same relationship holds between firm revenue and the price elasticity of demand.

To see why this is the case, recognize that expenditures and revenue are the products of price and quantity:

$$\text{Total expenditure} = \text{Total revenue} = P \cdot Q$$

Now think about how expenditure will change when price rises. (In the rest of this section, we examine what happens to expenditure when price changes, but we could instead focus on how prices change revenue and get the same result.) Obviously, the direct impact of the price increase will tend to raise expenditures. However, the higher price will also reduce quantity demanded, which tends to reduce expenditures. Which of these opposing effects is stronger depends on the price elasticity of demand.

We can be more specific. The percentage change in a product of two numbers is approximately equal to the sum of the percentage changes in the product's components. That means the percentage change in total expenditure due to a price change equals the percentage change in price plus the percentage change in quantity demanded that results. Of course, since price and quantity demanded move in opposite directions, when one of these changes is positive, the other change will be negative. For example, suppose that price rises. If the percentage increase in price is larger than the percentage drop in quantity demanded, expenditures will increase as a result of the price hike.

Expenditures will decrease if the opposite holds true and the percentage drop in quantity demanded is larger than the price change.

To see this more explicitly, remember the formula for the price elasticity of demand:

$$E^D = \frac{\%\Delta Q^D}{\%\Delta P}$$

If demand is inelastic (the elasticity is smaller than 1 in absolute value, or between –1 and zero if you prefer), then the percentage drop in quantity (the numerator) will be smaller than the percentage increase in price (the denominator). This means the direct effect of price outweighs the quantity effect, and expenditures rise. If demand is elastic (the elasticity is greater than 1 in absolute value) on the other hand, then the percentage drop in quantity (the numerator) will be larger than the percentage increase in price (the denominator). In this case, the indirect effect of the price increase is larger than the direct effect, and total expenditures fall. For unit elastic demand (an elasticity of –1), the percentage increase in price exactly equals the percentage decrease in quantity demanded, so expenditure doesn't change.

For a downward-sloping linear demand curve like the one shown in Figure 2.16 this property means that total expenditures will follow a particular pattern as we move along the demand curve. Let's start at the curve's intercept with the horizontal axis, point C. There, price is zero, so implied expenditure is also zero. Easy enough. Now let's start increasing the price, so we're moving up and to the left along the demand curve. As we know from our previous discussion, along the portion of the demand curve closest to the horizontal intercept, the demand is inelastic. Therefore, the percentage increase in price from moving up the demand curve is larger than the percentage decrease in quantity demanded, meaning expenditures must rise. As we keep increasing price and moving up the demand curve, demand will continue to be inelastic and expenditures will continue to rise until point B, where demand becomes unit elastic. At that point, we know that expenditures will not change when price increases. However, as we keep increasing price and moving further up the demand curve, demand becomes price elastic. This means that the percentage drop in quantity demanded is larger than the percentage increase in price, and expenditure starts to fall. This drop in expenditures continues as we keep raising price and moving up the demand curve. Eventually, we reach point A. There, quantity falls to zero and therefore so do implied expenditures.

If we plot these changes in expenditure along the demand curve versus the price, we get Figure 2.19. When price is zero at point C, so are expenditures (we've labeled the

---

Figure 2.19 | **Expenditures along a Linear Demand Curve**

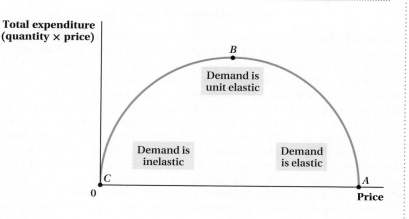

At point C, price and expenditures are zero along the demand curve. Between points C and B, the demand curve is inelastic, and expenditures increase with the increase in price along the demand curve. Point B is the maximum expenditures point; at B, the demand curve is unit elastic, and expenditures neither rise nor fall. Between points B and A, the demand curve is elastic, and expenditures decrease with the increase in price along the demand curve.

expenditure plot with points on the demand curve in Figure 2.16 to which they correspond). As price rises through the inelastic part of the demand curve, so do expenditures. When price hits the level at B, demand is unit elastic and expenditures are neither rising nor falling. At higher price levels, expenditure falls as price rises until finally hitting zero again at point A. Notice how expenditure is maximized at point B, where demand is unit elastic. This is because at lower prices demand is inelastic and expenditures rise with price, but at higher prices demand is elastic and expenditures fall in price.

Income Elasticity of Demand

We've been focusing on price elasticities to this point, and with good reason: They are a key determinant of demand and supply behavior and play an important role in helping us understand how markets work. However, they are not the only elasticities that matter in demand and supply analysis. Remember how we divided up all the factors that affected demand or supply into two categories: price and everything else? Well, each of those other factors that went into "everything else" has an influence on demand or supply that can be measured with an elasticity.

The online appendix calculates and applies different demand and supply elasticities. (http://glsmicro.com/appendices)

The most commonly used of these elasticities measure the impact of two other factors on quantity demanded. These are the income elasticity of demand and the cross-price elasticity of demand.

The **income elasticity of demand** is the ratio of the percentage change in quantity demanded to the corresponding percentage change in consumer income (I):

$$E^D{}_I = \frac{\%\Delta Q^D}{\%\Delta I} = \frac{\Delta Q^D}{\Delta I} \cdot \frac{I}{Q^D}$$

income elasticity of demand
The percentage change in quantity demanded associated with a 1% change in consumer income.

(Equivalently, it is the percentage change in quantity demanded associated with a 1% increase in consumer income.)

Income elasticities describe how responsive demand is to income changes. Goods are sometimes categorized by the sign and size of their income elasticity. Goods that have an income elasticity that is negative, meaning consumers demand a lower quantity of the good when their income rises, are called **inferior goods.** This name isn't a comment on their inherent quality; it just describes how their consumption changes with people's incomes. (Note, however, that low-quality versions of many product categories are inferior goods by the economic definition.) Examples of likely inferior goods are bus tickets, youth hostels, and hot dogs.

inferior good
A good for which quantity demanded decreases when income rises.

Goods with positive income elasticities (consumers' quantity demanded rises with their income) are called **normal goods.** As the name indicates, most goods fit into this category.

The subcategory of normal goods with income elasticities above 1 is sometimes called **luxury goods.** Having an income elasticity that is greater than 1 means the quantity demanded of these products rises at a faster rate than income. As a consequence, the share of a consumer's budget that is spent on a luxury good becomes larger as the consumer's income rises. (To keep a good's share of the budget constant, quantity consumed would have to rise at the same rate as income. Because luxury goods' quantities rise faster, their share increases with income.) Yachts, butlers, and fine art are all luxury goods.

normal good
A good for which quantity demanded rises when income rises.

luxury good
A good with an income elasticity greater than 1.

We will dig deeper into the relationship between incomes and consumer demand in Chapters 4 and 5.

Cross-Price Elasticity of Demand

The **cross-price elasticity of demand** is the ratio of the percentage change in one good's quantity demanded (say, good X) to the percentage change in price of *another* good Y:

cross-price elasticity of demand
The percentage change in the quantity demanded of one good associated with a 1% change in the price of another good.

$$E^D{}_{XY} = \frac{\%\Delta Q^D{}_X}{\%\Delta P_Y} = \frac{\Delta Q^D{}_X}{\Delta P_Y} \cdot \frac{P_Y}{Q^D{}_X}$$

own-price elasticities of demand

The percentage change in quantity demanded for a good resulting from a percentage change in the price of that good.

(To avoid confusion, sometimes the price elasticities we discussed above, which are concerned with the percentage change in quantity demanded to the percentage change in the price of the *same* good, are referred to as **own-price elasticities of demand.**)

When a good has a positive cross-price elasticity with another good, that means consumers demand a higher quantity of it when the other good's price rises. In other words, the good is a substitute for the other good: Consumers switch to the good when the other one becomes more expensive. Many pairs of goods are substitutes for one another—different brands of cereal, meals at restaurants versus dinners at home, colleges, and so on. Economist Aviv Nevo measured the substitutability of different cereals. He found that Froot Loops, for example, is a substitute for other kids' cereals, like Frosted Flakes and Cap'n Crunch ($E^D_{XY} = 0.131$ and 0.149, respectively). However, it is much less of a substitute for the more adult Shredded Wheat, which had a cross-price elasticity of only 0.020.[9]

When a good has a negative cross-price elasticity with another good, consumers demand less of it when the other good's price increases. This indicates that the goods are complements. Complements tend to be goods that are consumed together. If either of the goods within each pair were to become more expensive, consumers would buy not just less of that good itself, but of the other good in the pair as well. Milk and cookies are complements, as are tennis rackets and tennis balls, and computers and software.

2.6 figure it out

Suppose that the price elasticity of demand for cereal is -0.75 and the cross-price elasticity of demand between cereal and the price of milk is -0.9. If the price of milk rises by 10%, what would have to happen to the price of cereal to exactly offset the rise in the price of milk and leave the quantity of cereal demanded unchanged?

Solution:

The first step will be to see what happens to the quantity of cereal demanded when the price of milk rises by 10%. We can use the cross-price elasticity to help us with this. The cross-price elasticity for cereal with respect to the price of milk is equal to $\frac{\%\Delta Q_{cereal}}{\%\Delta P_{milk}} = -0.9$. Using the equation, we know that the denominator is 10 since the price of milk rose by 10%, so we get

$$\frac{\%\Delta Q_{cereal}}{\%\Delta P_{milk}} = \frac{\%\Delta Q_{cereal}}{10} = -0.9$$

$$\%\Delta Q_{cereal} = -9$$

Thus, when the price of milk rises by 10%, the quantity demanded of cereal falls by 9%.

Now we must consider how to offset this decline in the quantity of cereal demanded with a change in the price of cereal. In other words, what must happen to the price of cereal to cause the quantity of cereal demanded to *rise* by 9%? It is clear that the price of cereal must fall because the law of demand suggests that there is an inverse relationship between price and quantity demanded. However, because we know the price elasticity of demand, we can actually determine how far the price of cereal needs to fall.

The price elasticity of demand for cereal is $\frac{\%\Delta Q}{\%\Delta P} = -0.75$. To offset the decline in cereal consumption caused by the rise in the price of milk, we need the percentage change in quantity demanded to be +9%. Therefore, we can plug 9% into the numerator of the ratio and solve for the denominator:

$$\frac{\%\Delta Q}{\%\Delta P} = -0.75$$

$$\frac{9}{\%\Delta P} = -0.75$$

$$\%\Delta P = \frac{9}{-0.75} = -12$$

The price of cereal would have to fall by 12% to exactly offset the effect of a rise in the price of milk on the quantity of cereal consumed.

[9] Aviv Nevo, "Measuring Market Power in the Ready-to-Eat Cereal Industry," *Econometrica* 69, no. 2 (2001): 307–342.

2.6 Conclusion

This chapter introduced the concepts of supply and demand, two of the most important ideas in economics. Using the simplified supply and demand framework, we examined a variety of topics, including equilibrium price and quantity, the effects of shocks to supply and demand, and elasticities.

But, the various cases we looked at in this chapter are, for the most part, simplified and very abstract. In reality, measuring a market's demand and supply curves and determining the equilibrium price and quantity can be more challenging and complex. For example, firms hoping to make production decisions based on the types of analysis we've done here need to observe a wide range of data—prices, elasticities, demand curves, and so on—that are often not known exactly in the real world. As a result, producers might rely on more trial-and-error practices than allowed for in our simplified model. Indeed, our own experience with firms is that the people making the production decisions don't always approach and analyze them as economists would. If they did, firms might see more financial success. Beginning with Chapter 6 and continuing through Part 3, we talk more about situations that producers face in the real world, and the production decisions they have to make, such as how much of a product to produce, how to produce it, and whether they should enter a particular market at all. And we see how these decisions are reflected in a firm's supply curve. In the meantime, the simplified supply and demand framework we've developed here provides a valuable structure for delving into a deeper analysis of markets and equilibrium price and quantity in upcoming chapters.

Summary

1. Economists use models to analyze markets. Models employ simplifying assumptions to reduce the incredible complexity of the real world so that general insights can be learned. The **supply** and **demand** model is one of the most used analytical frameworks in economics. This model makes several assumptions about the market that is being analyzed, including that all goods bought and sold in the market are identical, they are all sold for the same price, and there are many producers and consumers in the market. [**Section 2.1**]

2. Demand describes the willingness of consumers to purchase a product. There are many factors that affect demand, including price, income, quality, tastes, and availability of **substitutes.** Economists commonly use the concept of a **demand curve,** which essentially divides these factors into two groups: price and everything else. A demand curve relates consumers' quantity demanded to the price of the good while holding every other factor affecting demand constant. A change in a good's price results in a movement along a given demand curve. If nonprice factors change, the quantity demanded at every price changes and the whole demand curve shifts. [**Section 2.2**]

3. Supply describes the willingness of producers to make and sell a product. Factors that affect supply include price, available **production technologies,** input prices, and producers' outside options. **Supply curves** isolate the relationship between quantity supplied and price, holding all other supply factors constant. A change in a good's price results in a movement along a given supply curve. If nonprice factors change, the quantity supplied at every price changes and the whole supply curve shifts. [**Section 2.3**]

4. Combining demand and supply curves lets us determine the **market equilibrium** price, which is where quantity demanded equals quantity supplied. This equilibrium can be determined because demand and supply curves isolate the relationships between quantities and the one factor that affects both demand and supply: price. At the equilibrium, every consumer who wants to buy at the going price can, and every producer who wants to sell at the current market price can as well. [**Section 2.4**]

5. Changes in the factors (other than price) that affect demand or supply will change the market equilibrium price and quantity. Changes that increase demand and shift out the demand curve

will raise **equilibrium price** and quantity in the absence of supply shifts; when the changes decrease demand and shift the demand curve in, price and quantity will fall. Changes that increase supply and shift out the supply curve, assuming no change in the demand curve, will increase equilibrium quantity and reduce price. Changes that decrease supply and shift in the supply curve decrease quantity and raise price. [**Section 2.4**]

6. If both supply and demand shift, either the effect on equilibrium price or the effect on equilibrium quantity will be ambiguous. If demand and supply move in the same direction, equilibrium quantity will follow, but the impact on price is unknown. On the other hand, if demand and supply move in opposite directions, equilibrium price will move in the same direction as demand (increase when demand rises, fall when demand decreases) but we cannot say with certainty what the effect on equilibrium quantity will be. [**Section 2.4**]

7. Economists typically express the sensitivity of demand and supply to various factors, but especially price, in terms of elasticities. An **elasticity** is the ratio of the percentage changes in two variables. The **price elasticity of demand** is the percentage change in quantity demanded for a 1% change in price, and the price elasticity of supply is the percentage change in quantity supplied for a 1% price change. [**Section 2.5**]

8. Total expenditure and total revenue are both equal to price times quantity demanded. When demand is **elastic** ($|E^D| > 1$), an increase in price will lead to a fall in expenditures (revenue), while a decrease in price will lead expenditures (revenue) to increase. When demand is **inelastic** ($|E^D| < 1$), expenditure (revenue) rises when price rises and falls when price falls. When demand is **unit elastic** ($|E^D| = 1$), a change in price has no effect on total expenditure (revenue). [**Section 2.5**]

9. Other common demand elasticities measure the responsiveness of quantity demanded to changes in income and the prices of other goods. The **income elasticity of demand** is positive for **normal goods** and negative for **inferior goods.** The **cross-price elasticity of demand** is positive for substitutes and negative for complements. [**Section 2.5**]

Review Questions

1. There are four key assumptions underlying the supply and demand model. Name these assumptions.

2. Complements and substitutes of a given good affect the demand for that good. Define complements and substitutes.

3. What simplifying assumption do we make to build a demand curve? Why is the demand curve downward-sloping?

4. What is the difference between a change in quantity demanded and a change in demand?

5. Why is the supply curve upward-sloping?

6. What is an inverse supply curve? Why do economists often represent supply using the inverse supply curve?

7. What is the difference between a change in quantity supplied and a change in supply?

8. Define market equilibrium. What is true of the quantity supplied and demanded at the market equilibrium?

9. What happens when price is below the equilibrium price? Why?

10. In what direction will price and quantity move as a result of a demand shift?

11. In what direction will price and quantity move as a result of a supply shift?

12. Why is the direction of change of *either* price *or* quantity unknown when both supply and demand shift?

13. What happens to equilibrium price when demand and supply shift in the same direction? What happens to equilibrium quantity in the same situation?

14. What is the difference between an elasticity and slope?

15. We learned that economists have special terms for elasticities of particular magnitudes. Name the magnitudes for the following: inelastic, elastic, unit elastic, perfectly elastic, and perfectly inelastic.

16. What is total expenditure? Total revenue?

17. Why must you know the price elasticity of demand to be able to predict the effect of a change in price on total expenditure?

18. Using the concept of income elasticity of demand, describe normal, luxury, and inferior goods.

19. Using the concept of cross-price elasticity of demand, describe substitutes and complements.

Problems (Solutions to problems marked * appear at the back of this book. Problems adapted to use calculus are available online at http://worthpublishers.com/GLS1e)

1. Is there a difference between movements along a demand curve and shifts in a demand curve? How would you explain this difference to a friend who is taking this course and is confused about the issue?

*2. The demand for organic carrots is given by the following equation:

$$Q^D{}_O = 75 - 5P_O + P_C + 2I$$

where P_O is the price of organic carrots, P_C is the price of conventional carrots, and I is the average consumer income. Notice how this isn't a standard demand curve that just relates the quantity of organic carrots demanded to the price of organic carrots. This demand function also describes how other factors affect demand—namely, the price of another good (conventional carrots) and income.

a. Draw the demand curve for organic carrots when $P_C = 5$ and $I = 10$.

b. Using the demand curve drawn in (a), what is the quantity demanded of organic carrots when $P_O = 10$?

c. Using the demand curve drawn in (a), what is the quantity demanded of organic carrots when $P_O = 5$?

d. Now, suppose $P_O = 10$ and $P_C = 15$ (I remains at 10). What is the quantity demanded of organic carrots? Compared with your answer in (b), has there been a change in demand or quantity demanded? Demonstrate using a graph.

e. What happens to the demand for organic carrots when the price of conventional carrots increases? Are organic and conventional carrots complements or substitutes?

f. What happens to the demand for organic carrots when the average consumer income increases? Are carrots a normal or an inferior good?

*3. Out of the following events, which are likely to cause the demand for coffee to increase? Explain your answers.

a. An increase in the price of tea

b. An increase in the price of doughnuts

c. A decrease in the price of coffee

d. The Surgeon General's announcement that drinking coffee lowers the risk of heart disease

e. Heavy rains causing a record-low coffee harvest in Colombia

4. How is each of the following events likely to shift the supply curve or the demand curve for fast-food hamburgers in the United States?

Make sure you indicate which curve (curves) is affected and if it shifts out or in.

a. The price of beef triples.

b. The price of chicken falls by half.

c. The number of teenagers in the economy falls due to population aging.

d. Mad cow disease, a rare but fatal medical condition caused by eating tainted beef, becomes common in the United States.

e. The Food and Drug Administration publishes a report stating that a certain weight-loss diet, which encourages the intake of large amounts of meat, is dangerous to one's health.

f. An inexpensive new grill for home use that makes delicious hamburgers is heavily advertised on television.

g. The dollar rises relative to foreign currencies, so that it becomes expensive for foreign tourists to travel to the United States on vacation.

h. The minimum wage rises.

5. Your roommate remarks that it is strange that a flight from New York to Chicago costs more than a flight from New York to Orlando, since New York and Chicago are closer than New York and Orlando. What is your roommate assuming about the relationship between distance and price? How do you explain these prices?

*6. Suppose that a hard freeze destroys a large portion of the Florida orange crop. At the same time, the *Journal of the American Medical Association* releases the results of a new study showing that drinking large quantities of orange juice substantially reduces one's risks of both heart disease and cancer. What is the likely effect of these two events on the price of orange juice? On the quantity of orange juice sold?

7. Suppose that you have been collecting vintage lightning rods for the past 30 years. When you began, finding lightning rods for sale meant drifting from town to town and antique store to antique store hoping that you would find a lightning rod for sale. The availability made possible by the Internet now means that you can easily find hundreds of lightning rods for sale at any given time.

a. Draw a diagram showing how the invention and popularization of the Internet have caused the demand curve for lightning rods to shift.

b. Suppose that the only change in the market for lightning rods is the change you described in (a). How would that change affect the equilibrium price of lightning rods and the equilibrium quantity of lightning rods sold?

8. In March 2002 the retail price of gasoline was $1.19 per gallon—exactly the same as it was in August 1990. Yet, total gasoline production and consumption rose from 6.6 million barrels per week in 1990 to 8.7 million barrels per week in 2002. Using the graph below, draw the appropriate shifts in the demand and supply curves to explain these two phenomena.

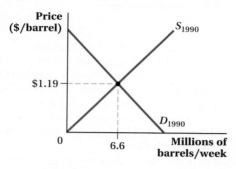

9. When the demand for toilet paper increases, the equilibrium quantity sold increases. Consumers are buying more, and producers are producing more.
   a. How do producers receive the signal that they need to increase production to meet the new demand?
   b. Does the increased production reflect an increase in supply, or an increase in the quantity supplied? Explain your answer, referring to (a).
*10. Suppose the demand for towels is given by $Q^D = 100 - 5P$, and the supply of towels is given by $Q^S = 10P$.
   a. Derive and graph the inverse supply and inverse demand curves.
   b. Solve for the equilibrium price and quantity.
   c. Suppose that supply changes so that at each price, 20 fewer towels are offered for sale. Derive and graph the new inverse supply curve.
   d. Solve for the new equilibrium price and quantity.
11. Your university has an honors program that accepts exactly 40 freshmen each year. Every year before soliciting applications, students are informed of the standards for program participation. The admissions staff observed that whenever the difficulty of the program requirements increased (decreased), they received fewer (more) applicants than in the previous year and have since begun to adjust requirements for each incoming group of students in an attempt to equate the number of applicants with the number of spots in the program. Though the system is not perfect, the administrators are able to estimate their applicant pool relatively accurately.
   a. In this situation, what is the "price" that determines how many students will apply to the honors program? Also, assume that the people who run the honors program do not plan to expand or contract it. Depict the demand and supply curves that represent this situation.
   b. How does the way "price" is determined in this situation differ from the way we normally think about the determination of equilibrium price?
   c. Assume that applicants to the honors program are usually the most qualified students at the university. If the university began offering merit scholarships to incoming students, how would we expect the difficulty of the program to change over the next few years? Demonstrate your answer with a graph.
   d. The president of the university became so impressed with the rigor of the first honors program that she decides to double its size. Assuming that the larger program accepts applicants in the same way, what will likely happen to the standards of the expanded honors program? Demonstrate your answer with a graph.
   e. Instead of expanding the first honors program, the faculty recommends introducing a whole new one. Suppose the first was an honors program in science. How would standards change for the science honors program if the new honors program were in math? How about art history? Explain your answers.
12. Consider the market for van Gogh paintings and assume no forgeries are possible.
   a. Is the supply of van Gogh paintings somewhat elastic, somewhat inelastic, perfectly elastic, or perfectly inelastic? Why?
   b. Draw the supply curve for van Gogh paintings.
   c. Suppose there are only 10 van Gogh paintings in the world, and the demand curve is $Q = 50 - 0.5P$. What is the equilibrium price?
   d. A tragic fire destroys five of the paintings. What is the new equilibrium price?
*13. Suppose the demand for down pillows is given by $Q^D = 100 - P$, and that the supply of down pillows is given by $Q^S = -20 + 2P$.
   a. Solve for the equilibrium price.
   b. Plug the equilibrium price back into the demand equation and solve for the equilibrium quantity.
   c. Double-check your work by plugging the equilibrium price back into the supply equation and solving for the equilibrium quantity. Does your answer agree with what you got in (b)?
   d. Solve for the elasticities of demand and supply at the equilibrium point. Which is more elastic, demand or supply?
   e. Invert the demand and supply functions (in other words, solve each for P) and graph them. Do the equilibrium point and relative elasticities shown in the graph appear to coincide with your answers?

14. Suppose that budding economist Buck measures the inverse demand curve for toffee as $P = \$100 - Q^D$, and the inverse supply curve as $P = Q^S$. Buck's economist friend Penny likes to measure everything in cents. She measures the inverse demand for toffee as $P = 10,000 - 100Q^D$, and the inverse supply curve as $P = 100Q^S$.
   a. Find the slope of the inverse demand curve, and compute the price elasticity of demand at the market equilibrium using Buck's measurements.
   b. Find the slope of the inverse demand curve, and compute the price elasticity of demand at the market equilibrium using Penny's measurements. Is the slope the same as Buck calculated? How about the price elasticity of demand?

15. Suppose that innovations in agriculture lower the cost of producing lettuce by 10%. This cost reduction effectively shifts the inverse supply curve downward by 10% at every quantity.
   a. Assume that the price of lettuce is determined by the forces of demand and supply. Graph the market for lettuce initially, and then illustrate the effects of the technological innovation.
   b. Will lettuce growers be able to capture the cost savings provided by the new technology, or will they end up passing the savings along to consumers? Explain, using your graph.
   c. How does your answer depend on the price elasticity of demand for lettuce? Explain, using two graphs to illustrate your point.

16. Some policy makers have claimed that the U.S. government should purchase illegal drugs, such as cocaine, to increase the price that drug users will face. Does this idea have any merit? Illustrate this logic in a simple supply and demand framework. How does the elasticity of demand for illegal drugs relate to the efficacy of this policy? Are you more or less willing to favor this policy if you are told demand is inelastic?

17. Consider the following problems on elasticity:
   a. When bottlers increased the price of canned soda from vending machines by 10%, sales dropped by 2.5%. Calculate the elasticity of demand for canned soda.
   b. Refer to part (a). The total revenue received by bottlers from their sales of canned soda is equal to the price of canned soda times the number of cans sold ($TR = P_{\text{soda}} \times Q_{\text{soda}}$). In approximate percentage terms, what was the impact of the bottlers' price change on total revenue?
   c. Sal the Sail Salesman's boss has just told him that if he fails to increase the volume of his sail sales by 8%, he'll be fired. In order to meet his goal, Sal is considering putting his sails on sale. If the price elasticity of demand for sales is −2.66, how much should Sal lower his price in order to meet his goal?
   d. Yogi eats a sizable quantity of pizza by the slice, and generally pays $5 per slice at a vending cart outside his office. When a new vendor on the block begins offering pizza at $3 per slice, Yogi finds that his monthly total expenditures on pizza rise. What can we say about Yogi's elasticity of demand for pizza?

*18. Suppose that a typical consumer has an inverse demand for frog's legs given by the following: $P = \dfrac{3}{Q^D}$. A graph of that inverse demand curve is given below:

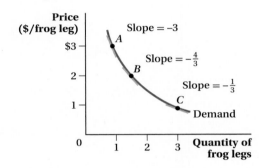

   a. Show that the demand curve is unit-elastic.
   b. If this customer came into your restaurant and asked for frog's legs, would you be better off charging a high price or a low price?

19. One type of elasticity that economists often use is the cross-price elasticity, which is measured as the percentage change in the quantity of a good when the price of a different good changes by 1%.
   a. What sign might you expect the cross-price elasticity to have if the two goods are shampoo and hair conditioner? Why?
   b. What sign might you expect the cross-price elasticity to have if the two goods are gasoline and ethanol? Why?
   c. What sign might you expect the cross-price elasticity to have if the two goods are coffee and shoes? Why?

20. One type of elasticity that economists often use is the income elasticity, which is measured as the percentage change in the quantity of a good when the income of consumers changes by 1%.
   a. What sign might you expect the income elasticity to have if the good in question is Swedish massages?
   b. What sign might you expect the income elasticity to have if the good in question is Ramen noodles?
   c. What sign might you expect the income elasticity to have if the good in question is table salt?

Using Supply and Demand to Analyze Markets

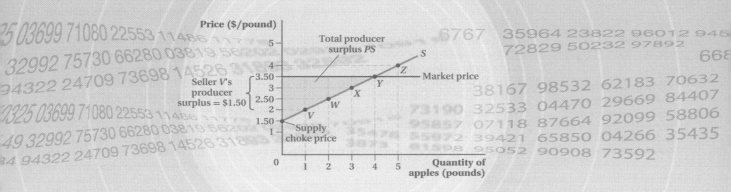

I n Chapter 2, we introduced the tools of supply and demand analysis. We learned about the economic decisions that supply and demand curves embody, and defined what it means for a market to be in equilibrium. In this chapter, we put those tools to work to take a deeper look at how markets operate. We study how to measure the total benefits that consumers and producers gain in any given market, and how these benefits change when demand or supply shifts. We also see how various government interventions into markets affect the well-being of consumers and producers.

Governments often enact policies that affect how markets work. The purpose of these policies can be to serve a particular constituency, to raise necessary tax revenue, or (as we'll see in Chapter 16) to correct a market failure. For example, every time gas prices rise above the public's tolerance, some politicians predictably call for a top limit on gas prices (called a *price ceiling*). Judging from the opinion polls that are usually taken at such times, this policy strikes many people as being a good idea. Are they right? Whether changes in market conditions are the result of government market interventions or changes in any of the many factors that affect supply, demand, or both, we can use supply and demand analysis to figure out not only what happens to price and quantity, but also who benefits, who loses, and by how much.

3.1 Consumer and Producer Surplus: Who Benefits in a Market?

To begin to understand the market impact of any policy, we need a way to measure the benefit consumers and producers obtain from buying and selling goods and services in a market. Economists measure these benefits using the concepts of consumer and producer surplus.

Consumer Surplus

consumer surplus
The difference between the amount consumers would be willing to pay for a good or service and the amount they actually have to pay.

Consumer surplus is the difference between the price consumers would be willing to pay for a good (as measured by the height of their demand curves) and the price they actually have to pay. Consumer surplus is usually measured as an amount of money.

To see why we define consumer surplus this way, let's think like an economist. Say a person is lost in the desert with no water, is getting extremely thirsty, and has $1,000 in his pocket. He stumbles upon a convenience store in this desert where he sees a bottle of Dr Pepper for sale. What is he willing to pay for the drink? Quite likely, his entire $1,000. Applying the concept of elasticity from Chapter 2, we can say this guy's demand for something to drink is almost perfectly inelastic: He will demand the one bottle of Dr Pepper almost regardless of its price. Let's say the store is asking $1 for the bottle of Dr Pepper. Mr. Thirsty was willing to pay $1,000 for the Dr Pepper but only had to pay the $1 market price. After the transaction, he has his drink *and* $999 left in his pocket. That $999—the difference between what he was willing to pay and what he actually paid—is his consumer surplus.

We can take this one-person example and extend the consumer surplus to the demand curve for an entire market. For example, let's return to Pike Place Market but now consider the market for apples. The market demand curve in Figure 3.1 tells us how many pounds of apples consumers are willing to buy at any given price. Let's assume that the market price of apples is $3.50 per pound.

If every point along the market demand curve represents a different person's willingness to pay for a pound of apples, we can measure each person's consumer surplus just as we did for Mr. Thirsty. The person at point *A* on the demand curve is willing to pay up to $5 for a pound of apples. If the price is $3.50 per pound, she will buy the apples and also keep $1.50 of consumer surplus. Person *B* is willing to pay $4.50 per pound and receives $1 of consumer surplus, while Person *C* receives $0.50 of consumer surplus. The person at point *D* is willing to pay $3.50 for a pound of apples and must pay the market price of $3.50 a pound. Thus, there is no consumer surplus for this individual.[1] Person *E* will not buy any apples; he is willing to pay only $3 per pound, which is below the market price. If you want to know the total consumer surplus for the entire market, add up all of the gains for each individual who buys apples—person *A*, person *B*, and so on.

After adding up all the gains, you will find that the total consumer surplus in the entire Pike Place apple market is the area under the demand curve and above the price, the area of the shaded triangle *CS* in Figure 3.1. The base of the consumer surplus triangle is the quantity sold. The height of the triangle is the difference between the

---

[1] Some years ago, there was an economist who was hired away by another university. As part of the deal to lure him, the new school gave him a big raise. When he arrived at the new university in the fall, his new dean said that the school was happy he had decided to come. The economist responded that if they really were happy, then he hadn't asked for enough money. He wanted to leave them with no consumer surplus.

market price ($3.50) and the **demand choke price** ($5.50 per pound), the price at which quantity demanded is reduced to zero.[2]

In this example, the demand curve represented a collection of consumers, each with a different willingness to pay for a unit of the good. Those with a high willingness to pay are located at the upper left portion of the curve; those with a lower willingness to pay are down and to the right along the curve. The same logic also applies to an individual's demand curve, which reflects his declining willingness to pay for each additional unit of the good. For instance, an apple buyer might be willing to pay $5 for the first pound of apples he buys, but only $4 for the second pound and $3.50 for the third pound (maybe he has limited ability to store them, or just plain gets a bit tired of eating apples after a while). If the market price is $3.50 per pound, he will buy 3 pounds of apples. His consumer surplus will be $1.50 for the first pound, $0.50 for the second, and zero for the third, a total of $2. Doing this calculation for all apple buyers and adding up their consumer surpluses will give a total consumer surplus of the same type shown in the triangular area in Figure 3.1.

Producer Surplus

Just as consumers gain surplus from engaging in market transactions, so do producers. **Producer surplus** is the difference between the price producers are willing to sell their goods for (measured by the height of the supply curve) and the price

demand choke price
The price at which quantity demanded is reduced to zero.

producer surplus
The difference between the price at which producers are willing to sell their good or service and the price they actually receive.

Figure 3.1   :   **Defining Consumer Surplus**

Consumer surplus is the difference between the amount consumers are willing to pay and the amount they actually have to pay. The market demand curve shows how many pounds of apples consumers are willing to buy at a given price. The consumer at point A is willing to pay $5 for 1 pound of apples; at a market price of $3.50, this person has a consumer surplus of $1.50. Similarly, at the market price of $3.50, consumers at points B, C, and D have consumer surpluses of $1, $0.50, and $0, respectively. The consumer at point E does not purchase any apples. The total consumer surplus is the area under the demand curve and above the price, represented by the area of the shaded triangle CS, with the base of the triangle the total quantity sold and the height the difference between the market price and the demand choke price.

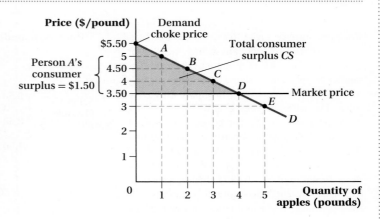

---

[2] There are two technicalities about this kind of calculation you should be aware of if you want to be completely precise. First, this area is a triangle only if the demand curve is a straight line. We use straight-line demand curves here because they are easy, but demand curves in real life are often curved. Second, calculating the total consumer surplus in dollars is only accurate if the marginal utility of income is constant. We discuss the idea of utility in Chapter 4. If a dollar of income is worth a lot more when income is low than when income is high, then we can't say for sure that all dollars of consumer surplus have the same impact on people's happiness.

they actually receive for the good. The supply curve in the Pike Place apple market (Figure 3.2) tells us how many pounds of apples producers are willing to sell at any given price. If we think of every point on the supply curve as representing a different apple seller, we see that Firm V would be willing to supply apples at a price of $2 per pound. Because it can sell apples at the market price of $3.50, however, it receives a producer surplus of $1.50.[3] Firm W is willing to sell apples for $2.50 per pound, and so receives $1 of producer surplus, while Firm X receives $0.50 of producer surplus. Firm Y, which is only willing to sell a pound of apples for $3.50, receives no surplus. Firm Z is shut out of the market; the market price of $3.50 per pound is less than its willingness to sell ($4). The total producer surplus for the entire market is the sum of producer surplus for every seller along the supply curve. This sum equals the triangle above the supply curve and below the price, the area of the shaded triangle PS in Figure 3.2. The base of the triangle is the quantity sold. The height of the triangle is the difference between the market price ($3.50) and the **supply choke price** ($1.50 per pound), the price at which quantity supplied equals zero. Here, that's $1.50 per pound; no seller is willing to sell apples below that price.

This particular supply curve represents a collection of producers that differ in their willingness to sell. The same logic applies to an individual producer's supply curve in cases where the firm's cost of producing additional output rises with its total output. In these cases, the firm must be paid more to sell additional units.[4] The firm's producer surplus is the sum of the differences between the market price and the minimum price the firm would need to receive to be willing to sell each unit.

supply choke price
The price at which quantity supplied equals zero.

The online appendix uses integration to find consumer and producer surplus.
(http://glsmicro.com/appendices)

Figure 3.2   Defining Producer Surplus

Producer surplus is the difference between the price at which producers are willing to sell their goods and the price they actually receive. The market supply curve shows how many pounds of apples sellers are willing to supply at a given price. The seller at point V is willing to sell his apples at a price of $2 per pound; at a market price of $3.50, this person receives a $1.50 producer surplus. Similarly, at the market price of $3.50, sellers at points W, X, and Y receive producer surpluses of $1, $0.50, and $0, respectively. The seller at point Z does not sell any apples. The total producer surplus is the area above the supply curve and below the price, represented by the area of the shaded triangle PS, with the base of the triangle the total quantity sold and the height the difference between the market price and the supply choke price.

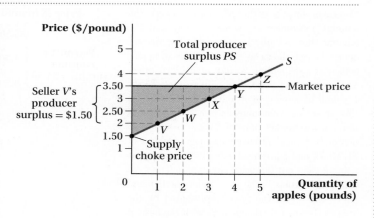

---

[3] Resist the temptation to call producer surplus "profit." While it seems natural to do this here, we will see in later chapters that the term "profit" has a precise meaning in economics, and it's not exactly this.

[4] We're also assuming here that the firm takes the market price as given. We'll discuss firms' supply behavior in this and the alternative case where a firm has price-setting power in Chapters 8 and 9.

The demand and supply curves for newspapers in a Midwestern city are given by

$$Q^D = 152 - 20P$$
$$Q^S = 188P - 4$$

where Q is measured in thousands of newspapers per day and P in dollars per newspaper.

a. Find the equilibrium price and quantity.

b. Calculate the consumer and producer surplus at the equilibrium price.

Solution:

a. Equilibrium occurs where $Q^D = Q^S$. Therefore, we can solve for equilibrium by equating the demand and supply curves:

$$Q^D = Q^S$$
$$152 - 20P = 188P - 4$$
$$156 = 208P$$
$$P = \$0.75$$

Therefore, the equilibrium price of a paper is $0.75. To find the equilibrium quantity, we need to plug the equilibrium price into either the demand or supply curve:

$$Q^D = 152 - 20P \qquad\qquad Q^S = 188P - 4$$
$$= 152 - 20(0.75) \qquad\qquad = 188(0.75) - 4$$
$$= 152 - 15 \qquad\qquad\quad = 141 - 4$$
$$= 137 \qquad\qquad\qquad\quad = 137$$

Remember that Q is measured in terms of thousands of papers each day, so the equilibrium quantity is 137,000 papers each day.

b. To calculate consumer and producer surplus, it is easiest to use a graph. First, we need to plot the demand and supply curves. For each curve, we can identify two points. The first point is the equilibrium, given by the combination of equilibrium price ($0.75) and equilibrium quantity (137). The second point we can identify is the choke price for demand and supply. These can be determined by setting Q^D and Q^S equal to zero and solving for P:

$$Q^D = 152 - 20P \qquad\qquad Q^S = 188P - 4$$
$$0 = 152 - 20P \qquad\qquad 0 = 188P - 4$$
$$20P = 152 \qquad\qquad\qquad 4 = 188P$$
$$P = 7.6 \qquad\qquad\qquad\quad P = 0.02$$

So the demand choke price is $7.60 and the supply choke price is $0.02.

The demand and supply curves are graphed in the figure on the next page. Consumer surplus is the area below demand and above the price (area A). Its area can be calculated as

$$CS = \text{area } A = \frac{1}{2} \times \text{base} \times \text{height} = (0.5) \times (137{,}000 - 0) \times (\$7.60 - \$0.75)$$
$$= (0.5) \times 137{,}000 \times \$6.85 = \$469{,}225$$

Producer surplus is the area below price and above supply (area B):

$$PS = \text{area } B = \frac{1}{2} \times \text{base} \times \text{height} = (0.5) \times (137{,}000 - 0) \times (\$0.75 - \$0.02)$$
$$= 0.5 \times 137{,}000 \times \$0.73 = \$50{,}005$$

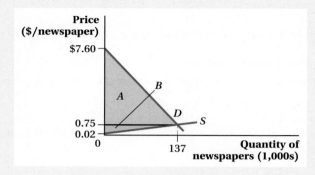

application

The Value of Innovation

Equipped with the concepts of consumer and producer surplus, we can do a quick analysis of one of the most important issues in economics—the introduction of new products. Economists emphasize the importance of innovation and new goods in raising a society's standard of living. In any discussion of the value of innovation, we need a way to compute how much benefit a new product gives to consumers.

A simple suggestion for valuing a new product would be to just add up what people paid for it. However, that approach would not be correct because, in reality, many consumers value the product at much more than the price they paid to get it. Consumer surplus, however, *does* measure the full benefit of the new product because it tells us how much consumers value the product *over and above* the price they pay.

A key factor in determining the amount of potential consumer surplus in a market for a new good is the steepness of the demand curve: All else equal, the steeper it is, the bigger the consumer surplus. That's because steep demand curves mean that at least some consumers (those accounting for the upper-left-hand side of the demand curve) have very high willingness to pay for the good. (You can see this on a price-quantity demand curve diagram. First, draw a horizontal line representing an equilibrium market price. Next, draw various demand curves with different slopes that intersect this price at the same point—i.e., so that the equilibrium quantity demanded is the same. You will see that the consumer surplus triangles will be larger for steeper demand curves.)

Let's look at eyeglasses as an example. Economist Joel Mokyr explained in his book *The Lever of Riches* that the invention of eyeglasses around the year 1280 allowed craftsmen to do detailed work for decades longer than they could before. If we think of glasses as a "new technology" circa 1280, we can visualize what the demand curve for glasses might have looked like. Because many people in 1280 would be quite blind without glasses, the demand curve was probably very steep—there was a set of individuals with a very high willingness to pay for glasses. This would also imply that demand wasn't particularly sensitive to prices. This steepness of the demand curve probably remained stable for the next 700 years, until the first commercially available contact lenses came on the market in the latter half of the twentieth century.

In Chapter 2, we learned that readily available substitute goods are likely to make demand more elastic. This is true of glasses, too: When contact lenses became available, the demand for glasses became more price elastic. How would this change in elasticity affect the consumer surplus people get from the existence of eyeglasses? Figure 3.3 illustrates the answer. Consumer surplus in 1950 is large because the demand for glasses D_1 is inelastic—if you want to see better, glasses are the only game in town. The consumer surplus is the area above the price and below D_1, or area $A + B$. Many people would be willing to buy glasses even if the price were much higher than P. (That's what having an inelastic demand means.)

When contact lenses become available, the demand for glasses becomes much more elastic, as shown by curve D_2. Even if just as many people buy glasses at the equilibrium price as before, a sharp rise in the price of glasses would cause many people to stop buying them because now they have an alternative. The figure shows that the consumer surplus from glasses declines after contacts come on the market. The area below the new, flatter demand curve and above the price is only area B.

After contacts are available, glasses are not worth as much to consumers because there are now other ways in which they can improve their eyesight. If glasses are the only way to fix your eyesight, you might be willing to pay thousands of dollars for them. Once you can buy contacts for $300, however, there is a limit to how much you would pay for glasses. You might still buy the glasses for $200, but you would certainly not be willing to pay $1,000 for them, and the change in consumer surplus reflects that change. Glasses are a miracle invention if they are the only way to correct one's vision (so they yield a higher consumer surplus). Remember that consumer surplus depends on the *most* that people would be willing to pay for the product. That maximum price goes down if alternatives are available. When alternative methods of vision correction are available, however, glasses are just another option rather than a virtual necessity, and the consumer surplus associated with them falls.

If you're concerned these examples imply that innovation destroys surplus, remember that the substitute goods create surpluses of their own. They have their own demand curves, and the areas under those curves and above the substitute goods' prices are also consumer surplus. For example, while the invention of contact lenses does reduce the consumer surplus provided by glasses, it creates a lot of surplus in the new contact lens market. ■

Figure 3.3   Consumer Surplus and the Elasticity of Demand

D_1 represents the demand for glasses in 1950 before a popular substitute good, contact lenses, were available. D_1 is relatively inelastic, and the total consumer surplus, $A + B$, is large. D_2 represents the demand for glasses after contact lenses were put on the market. D_2 is now relatively elastic, and the total consumer surplus B is relatively small.

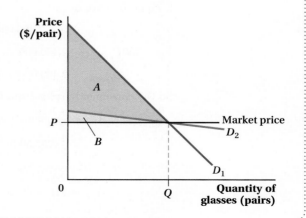

application

What is LASIK Eye Surgery Worth to Patients?

Laser-assisted in situ keratomileusis, commonly known as LASIK surgery, gives some people with vision problems an alternative to glasses and contact lenses. In the procedure, doctors use a laser to change the shape of the cornea to improve vision, usually to a point where patients can get rid of their corrective lenses.

Suppose we wanted to know how valuable LASIK surgery is to the patients who receive it. According to a market study commissioned by AllAboutVision.com, in 2010, the procedure cost about $2,150 per eye when performed by a reputable doctor. There were an estimated 800,000 LASIK procedures in 2010. A simple estimate for the value of this new procedure would be the number of surgeries times the cost (800,000 times $2,150, or about $1.7 billion). By now, however, you should realize that this measure of value is not a correct measure of the procedure's benefit to consumers because many people value the procedure at more than the price they paid. To determine the full benefit, we need to compute the consumer surplus—the benefit people receive from LASIK above and beyond what they have to pay for it.

To begin this computation, we need a demand curve for LASIK surgery. Because glasses and contacts are substitutes for LASIK, the demand curve will be flatter than if there were no substitutes. If LASIK were the only way to correct vision problems, then the nearly 70 million people now using corrective lenses in the United States would be willing to pay a lot for it. Because alternatives exist, however, if the price of LASIK goes up too much, many people will not opt for it, implying that LASIK's demand curve isn't very steep.

A hypothetical but realistic demand curve for LASIK procedures in 2010 is

$$Q_{\text{LASIK}} = 2,400,000 - 750 P_{\text{LASIK}}$$

where Q_{LASIK} is the quantity of LASIK procedures demanded and P_{LASIK} is the price per eye of the procedure. Plugging in a price of $2,150 per eye gives a quantity demanded of 787,500 procedures, right around the 2010 estimate. This demand curve is graphed in Figure 3.4. We can use this demand curve to determine the consumer surplus from LASIK.

We know the consumer surplus is the area of the triangle that is under the demand curve but above the price:

$$CS = \frac{1}{2} \times \text{base} \times \text{height}$$

$$= \frac{1}{2} \times (\text{quantity sold}) \times (\text{demand choke price} - \text{actual price})$$

Note that, for this demand curve, the demand choke price $(P_{D\text{Choke}})$ occurs where Q_{LASIK} is equal to zero, or

$$Q_{\text{LASIK}} = 0 = 2,400,000 - 750 P_{D\text{Choke}}$$

$$750 P_{D\text{Choke}} = 2,400,000$$

$$P_{D\text{Choke}} = 2,400,000/750 = 3,200$$

So the consumer surplus from LASIK is

$$CS = \frac{1}{2}(\text{quantity sold})(P_{D\text{Choke}} - \text{actual price})$$

$$= \frac{1}{2}(787,500)(\$3,200 - \$2,150)$$

$$= \frac{1}{2}(787,500)(\$1,050)$$

$$= \$413 \text{ million}$$

Figure 3.4 : Valuing LASIK Eye Surgery

The demand curve for LASIK is shown by the equation $Q = 2,400,000 - 750P$. The shaded triangle represents the consumer surplus in the LASIK market. We can use the actual price ($2,150), the choke price ($3,200), and the equilibrium quantity sold (787,500) to calculate the triangle's height (demand choke price – actual price) and base (quantity sold). The equation for the total consumer surplus thus becomes $CS = \frac{1}{2} \times$ (quantity sold) $\times$ (demand choke price – actual price), yielding a consumer surplus of approximately $413 million.

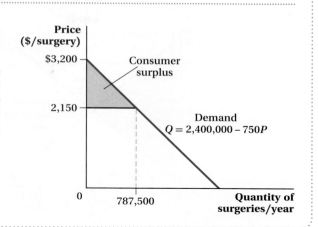

This calculation suggests that the people who got LASIK surgery in 2010 valued the surgery by about $413 million above and beyond what they paid for it. They paid about $1.7 billion for the surgery, but would have been willing to pay as much as 25% more. Because LASIK didn't exist as a product a couple of decades ago, that value was only created once the procedure was invented and a market established for it. This example suggests how important new goods can be for making consumers better off and raising the standard of living.

We can do the same sorts of calculations to compute the amount of producer surplus in a market. You'll see such an example in the next section. ■

The Distribution of Gains and Losses from Changes in Market Conditions

One nice thing about our definitions of producer and consumer surpluses is that we can analyze the impact of any changes on either side of a market in a way that builds on the analysis we started in Chapter 2. There, we learned how shocks to supply and demand affect prices, quantity demanded, and quantity supplied. Now we can show how these shocks affect the benefits producers and consumers receive from participating in a market.

Figure 3.5 shows the initial supply and demand in the market for donuts. We see that at the market price P_1, the donut buyers' benefit from buying donuts is greater than the price they pay for the donuts (reflected in the consumer surplus area $A + B + C + D$). Similarly, the donut makers' benefit from making the donuts is greater than the price at which they sell the donuts (reflected in the producer surplus area $E + F + G$).

Now let's suppose that a shock hits the donut market. Because of a poor berry harvest, the price of jelly filling goes up. (We're assuming that the filling the bakers use actually has some real fruit in it!) When this shock hits, the cost of making donuts rises, and suppliers are no longer willing to supply as many donuts at any given price. The supply of donuts falls, as reflected in the inward shift of the donut supply curve from S_1 to S_2. In response to the jelly shock, the equilibrium price of donuts rises to P_2, and the quantity of donuts bought and sold in the donut market falls to Q_2.

These changes affect both consumer and producer surplus. The higher equilibrium price and lower equilibrium quantity both act to reduce consumer surplus. Compared

Figure 3.5   Changes in Surplus from a Supply Shift

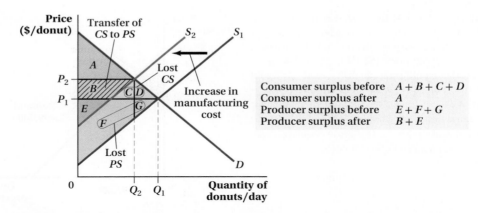

S_1 and D are the initial supply and demand for donuts. At market price P_1, consumer surplus is the area $A + B + C + D$, and producer surplus is the area $E + F + G$.

An increase in the manufacturing costs of donuts causes the supply curve to shift leftward from S_1 to S_2. At the new equilibrium price (P_2) and quantity (Q_2), consumer surplus has been reduced to the area A. The new producer surplus is shown by $B + E$. The effect of a supply shift on producer surplus is ambiguous. This ambiguity results because the lower equilibrium quantity acts to reduce producer surplus (by area $F + G$), while the higher equilibrium price increases producer surplus (by area B).

to triangle $A + B + C + D$ in Figure 3.5, triangle A is much smaller. While these price and quantity effects imply that inward supply shifts must reduce consumer surplus, there is no general rule for their impact on producer surplus. The lower equilibrium quantity that results from the supply shift reduces producer surplus, but the higher price increases it. These opposing effects can be seen in Figure 3.5. Some of the producer surplus before the shift—specifically, the space $G + F$ between the old and new supply curve and below the demand curve—is lost. But the price increase shifts some of what was consumer surplus before to producer surplus. This shifted surplus is area B. These effects on consumer and producer surplus are reversed for outward supply shifts.

We can also do a similar analysis for the effects of demand shifts. An inward shift in demand leads to a lower equilibrium price and quantity, both of which reduce *producer* surplus. The impact on consumer surplus, however, is ambiguous. Having a smaller equilibrium quantity reduces consumer surplus, but this reduction is counteracted by the drop in price. Similar to the supply shift case above (but in the opposite direction), the inward demand shift transfers to consumers part of what was producer surplus before. We see these effects in the application that follows.

 application

How Much Did 9/11 Hurt the Airline Industry?

After terrorists attacked the United States on September 11, 2001, the demand for air travel fell substantially, bringing the airline industry to its knees. Many congressional leaders wanted to compensate the airlines for the losses they suffered as a result, but there was a great debate over how much money was at stake. Using supply and demand industry analysis and our consumer and producer surplus tools, we can estimate the reduction in producer surplus that the airlines suffered after 9/11.

Statistics from the U.S. Department of Transportation (DOT) show that in the fourth quarter (October through December) of 2000, there were about 148.9 million enplanements (an enplanement is defined as one passenger getting on a plane).[5] In the fourth quarter of 2001, the first full quarter after the attack, there were only 123.6 million enplanements, a drop of 17% from the previous year. According to the DOT data, the average ticket price that airlines received per enplanement in the fourth quarter of 2000 was $122.22. In the fourth quarter of 2001, this average revenue had fallen to $104.82. This change in average revenue measures the price change over the period.

To figure out the damage to the industry, we need to compute the change to producer surplus.[6] Let's think of September 11th as creating a negative shift of the demand curve and assume no changes to the supply curve to make it easy: At every price, consumers demanded a lower quantity of plane travel. This shift is illustrated in Figure 3.6. Prices and quantities decreased in response to this event—just as the model suggests.

Figure 3.6 shows that the producer surplus fell when the demand curve shifted. Before the attack, producer surplus was the area above the supply curve and below the price, or $A + B + C$. After the attack, price and quantity fell and producer surplus fell to just area C. The loss to the airlines, then, was the area $A + B$.

Figure 3.6   **Airlines and September 11**

After September 11, the demand curve for air travel shifted inward, from D_{2000} to D_{2001}. In 2000 the equilibrium price and quantity were $122.22 and 148.9 million enplanements, respectively, and the producer surplus was the total shaded area, $A + B + C$. After September 11, the equilibrium price and quantity fell to $104.82 and 123.6 million enplanements, respectively, and the producer surplus was reduced to the area C. The area $A + B$ represents the loss in producer surplus to the airlines and was over $2.3 billion.

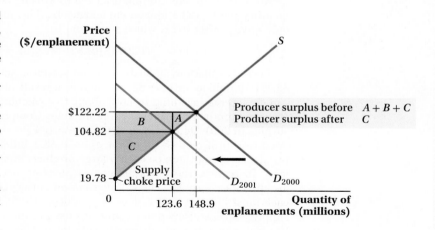

---

[5] Enplanements is one of many standard airline measures of quantity. If you fly a non-stop round-trip flight from Los Angeles to Chicago, for example, that would count as two enplanements because you got onto the airplane two times in your trip. We could have used a different measure of quantity such as revenue passenger miles (the number of miles that paying customers flew), and the answer would be very similar.

[6] We simplify our analysis by ignoring the modest supply effects of increases in costs from increased security requirements that the government did not pay for directly.

To calculate the producer surplus in this market, we need to know the equation for the supply curve. If we assume the supply curve is linear, we can use the data from our two equilibrium points to derive the equation for our inverse supply curve. The slope of the supply curve is the ratio of the change in equilibrium prices over the change in equilibrium quantities:

$$\text{slope} = \frac{P_2 - P_1}{Q_2 - Q_1} = \frac{\$122.22 - \$104.82}{148.9 - 123.6} = 0.688$$

Now that we have the slope, we can use either (or even better both!) equilibrium points to determine the supply choke price (the vertical intercept of the supply curve):

$$122.22 = P_{S\text{Choke}} + 0.688(148.9) \qquad \text{or} \qquad 104.82 = P_{S\text{Choke}} + 0.688(123.6)$$

$$P_{S\text{Choke}} = 122.22 - 102.44 \qquad\qquad P_{S\text{Choke}} = 104.82 - 85.04$$

$$= \$19.78 \qquad\qquad\qquad\qquad = \$19.78$$

So now we know that the industry's inverse supply curve is $P = 19.78 + 0.688Q$. Using the inverse supply equation allows us to match up the equation with the diagram in Figure 3.6.

With this inverse supply curve equation in hand, we can now calculate producer surplus before and after 9/11. Before 9/11, producer surplus is the area below the equilibrium price of $122.22 per enplanement and above the supply curve, for the entire quantity of 148.9 million enplanements. This would be areas $A + B + C$ in the graph. Since these three areas combine to form a triangle, we can calculate producer surplus before 9/11 as

$$\text{producer surplus} = \frac{1}{2} \times \text{base} \times \text{height} = \frac{1}{2}(148.9)(\$122.22 - \$19.78) = \$7,626.66$$

(The units of this producer surplus value are millions of dollars, because the quantity number is in millions of enplanements and the price is in dollars per enplanement.)

After 9/11, the equilibrium price fell to $104.82 per enplanement and the equilibrium quantity fell to 123.6 million enplanements. This means that producer surplus became only area C after 9/11, which was equal to

$$\frac{1}{2} \times \text{base} \times \text{height} = \frac{1}{2}(123.6)(\$104.82 - \$19.78) = \$5,255.47$$

These calculations indicate that the producer surplus in the airline industry fell by $2,371.19 million, or over $2.3 billion, as a result of the terrorist attack on 9/11.

One interesting thing to note about this calculation is that even after the 9/11 attack, the producer surplus is a big number. Comparing the $5.255 billion of producer surplus in 2001 Q4 to that quarter's reported (in the Air Carrier Financial Statistics) operating profit of −$3.4 billion (i.e., a $3.4 billion *loss*) for the industry leaves a puzzle. How can there be such a large producer surplus if the airlines had such a large loss? In reality, the puzzle is not so puzzling because producer surplus and profit are distinct concepts. The key distinction is the fixed costs firms pay—the expenses each must incur even if it doesn't produce a thing. Those costs aren't reflected in the supply curve, so they don't count against producer surplus. But they do come out of the firm's profits (and airlines have a lot of fixed costs). We learn more about fixed costs, the nature of the supply curve, and the connection between producer surplus and profit in Chapters 7 and 8.

By the way, if all we cared about was the drop in producer surplus after 9/11, there was another way to do the calculation we just did. We could have computed the size of areas A and B directly without actually solving for the supply curve. Rather than computing $A + B + C$ and subtracting C, we could have computed the size of rectangle B and triangle A using just the quantity and price data. This calculation would have given us the same answer for the *change* in producer surplus, but it would not have let us compute the *overall size* of the producer surplus before and after 9/11. ■

3.2 figure it out

A local tire market is represented by the following equations and in the diagram on the next page:

$$Q^D = 3{,}200 - 25P$$
$$Q^S = 15P - 800$$

where Q is the number of tires sold weekly and P is the price per tire. The equilibrium price is \$100 per tire, and 700 tires are sold each week.

Suppose an improvement in the technology of tire production makes them cheaper to produce so that sellers are willing to sell more tires at every price. Specifically, suppose that quantity supplied rises by 200 at each price.

a. What is the new supply curve?

b. What are the new equilibrium price and quantity?

c. What happens to consumer and producer surplus as a result of this change?

Solution:

a. Quantity supplied rises by 200 units at every price, so we simply add 200 to the equation for Q^S:

$$Q_2^S = 15P - 800 + 200 = 15P - 600$$

b. The new equilibrium occurs where $Q^D = Q_2^S$:

$$3{,}200 - 25P = 15P - 600$$
$$3{,}800 = 40P$$
$$P = \$95$$

We can find the equilibrium quantity by substituting the equilibrium price into either the supply or demand equation (or both):

$$Q^D = 3{,}200 - 25(95) \qquad\qquad Q_2^S = 15(95) - 600$$
$$= 3{,}200 - 2{,}375 \qquad\qquad\qquad = 1{,}425 - 600$$
$$= 825 \qquad\qquad\qquad\qquad\quad = 825$$

The new equilibrium quantity is 825 tires per week. Notice that because supply increased, the equilibrium price fell and the equilibrium quantity rose just as we would predict.

c. The easiest way to determine the changes in consumer and producer surplus is to use a graph such as the one on the next page. To calculate all of the areas involved, we need to make sure we calculate the demand choke price and the supply choke prices before and after the increase in supply.

The demand choke price is the price at which quantity demanded is zero:

$$Q^D = 0 = 3{,}200 - 25P$$
$$25P = 3{,}200$$
$$P = \$128$$

The demand choke price is \$128.

The supply choke price is the price at which quantity supplied is zero. Because supply is shifting, we need to calculate the supply choke price for each supply curve:

$$Q_1^S = 0 = 15P - 800$$
$$15P = 800$$
$$P = \$53.33$$
$$Q_2^S = 0 = 15P - 600$$
$$15P = 600$$
$$P = \$40$$

The initial supply choke price is $53.33 but falls to $40 when supply increases.

With the choke prices and the two equilibrium price and quantity combinations, we can draw the supply and demand diagram.

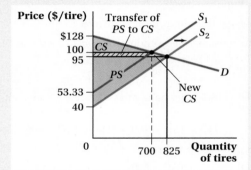

Consumer surplus: The initial consumer surplus is the area of the triangle below the demand curve but above the initial equilibrium price ($100):

$$CS_{\text{initial}} = \frac{1}{2} \times \text{base} \times \text{height}$$
$$= \frac{1}{2} \times (700 - 0) \times (\$128 - \$100) = (0.5)(700)(\$28) = \$9,800$$

The new consumer surplus is the area of the triangle below the demand curve and above the new equilibrium price ($95):

$$CS_{\text{new}} = \frac{1}{2} \times \text{base} \times \text{height}$$
$$= \frac{1}{2} \times (825 - 0) \times (\$128 - \$95) = (0.5)(825)(\$33) = \$13,612.50$$

So, after the outward shift in supply, consumer surplus rises by $3,812.50.

Producer surplus: The initial producer surplus is the area of the triangle below the initial equilibrium price and above the initial supply curve (S_1):

$$PS_{\text{initial}} = \frac{1}{2} \times \text{base} \times \text{height}$$
$$= \frac{1}{2} \times (700 - 0) \times (\$100 - \$53.33) = (0.5)(700)(\$46.67) = \$16,334.50$$

The new producer surplus is the area of the triangle below the new equilibrium price and above the new supply curve (S_2):

$$PS_{\text{new}} = \frac{1}{2} \times \text{base} \times \text{height}$$
$$= \frac{1}{2} \times (825 - 0) \times (\$95 - \$40) = (0.5)(825)(\$55) = \$22,687.50$$

The increase in supply also led to a rise in producer surplus by $6,353.

3.2 Price Regulations

Politicians call regularly for price ceilings on products whose prices have risen a lot. In this section, we explore the effects of direct government interventions in market pricing. We look both at regulations that set maximum prices (like a gas price ceiling) and minimum prices (price floors like a minimum wage).

Price Ceilings

A **price ceiling** establishes the highest price that can be paid legally for a good or service. Price ceilings get passed all the time. At various times, there have been price ceilings for cable television, auto insurance, flood insurance, electricity, telephone rates, gasoline, prescription drugs, apartments, food products, and many other goods.

> **price ceiling**
> A price regulation that sets the highest price that can be paid legally for a good or service.

To look at the impact of a price ceiling, let's suppose the city council of a college town passes a pizza price control regulation. With the intent of helping out the college's financially strapped students, the city council says no pizzeria can charge more than $8 for a pizza. Let's say the demand curve for pizzas in a month during the school year is described by the equation $Q^D = 20,000 - 1,000P$. The cheaper pizzas get, the more students will eat them, so the demand curve slopes downward as usual. If the price were zero, 20,000 pizzas would be sold per month (it's not that big a college, and there are only so many meals one can eat). The demand choke price is $20 per pizza—if the price were $20 per pizza, no pizzas would be sold.

Let's say the supply of pizzas is given by $Q^S = 2,000P - 10,000$. Supply slopes upward because when prices are higher, the pizzerias will make more pizzas. If the price is below $5, they make no pizzas. For each $1 increase in the price of a pizza after that, an additional 2,000 pizzas per month would be supplied.

Figure 3.7 graphs the supply and demand curves described by these two equations. It shows that the free-market equilibrium is at point w; that is, before price controls the equilibrium price for a pizza is $10, and at that price, 10,000 pizzas are supplied and demanded. Given these baseline market conditions, we can study the impact of the price ceiling using the graph or the equations. Let's start with the graph.

Figure 3.7   The Effects of a Price Ceiling

A price ceiling affects both producer and consumer surpluses. Before price controls in the pizza market, consumers pay $10 per pizza, and producers supply 10,000 pizzas per week at the equilibrium point w. Consumer surplus is the triangle $A + B + C$, and producer surplus is $D + E + F$. When a price ceiling of $8 is put in place, pizzerias supply only 6,000 pizzas (point x), but consumers demand 12,000 pizzas (point y), creating a shortage of 6,000 pizzas. Because pizzerias are now selling fewer pizzas at a lower price, producer surplus is reduced to area F. The new consumer surplus is the area $A + B + D$, and the net gain to consumers is $D - C$. The shaded area $C + E$ is the deadweight loss created by the price ceiling.

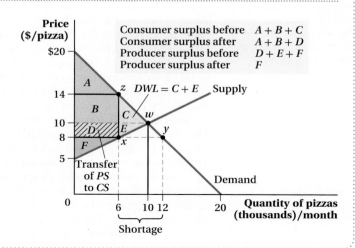

Consumer surplus before	$A + B + C$
Consumer surplus after	$A + B + D$
Producer surplus before	$D + E + F$
Producer surplus after	F

Graphical Analysis   Before any price controls, the consumer surplus for pizza-eating students is given by the area below the demand curve and above the $10 free-market price, $A + B + C$. The producer surplus is the area above the supply curve but below the price, $D + E + F$.

When the city council implements the price control regulation, the highest price the pizzerias can charge is $8 per pizza, which is less than the market-clearing price of $10. At $8, students demand a total of 12,000 pizzas (point y). This quantity demanded is larger than the 10,000 pizzas demanded at the free-market equilibrium because the price ceiling price is lower than the free-market price. At an $8 price, however, pizzerias are only willing to supply 6,000 pizzas. Because the quantity demanded exceeds the quantity supplied at that price, there is a shortage of 6,000 pizzas (sometimes this condition is also referred to as excess demand). Because the actual quantity of pizzas is limited to the number that suppliers are willing to sell, we end up with 6,000 pizzas sold at $8, and a large number of students frustrated that they cannot buy the additional 6,000 pizzas they would like to even though they are willing to pay the $8 per pie price.

Now let's consider the consumer and producer surplus to figure out how much better or worse off the two groups are as a result of the price controls. It's clear that the pizzerias are worse off. In the free market, they would have sold more pizzas (10,000 versus 6,000) at a higher price ($10 versus $8). The producer surplus after the price control law is everything below the capped price and above the supply curve; producer surplus shrinks from area $D + E + F$ to area F.

The law was passed to benefit students by lowering pizza prices. But we can't actually say for sure whether they are better off as a result. The new consumer surplus is the area below the demand curve and above the price, area $A + B + D$. The consumer surplus now includes area D because the price is lower. We call area D a **transfer** from producers to consumers, because imposing price controls shifted that area from being part of producer surplus to being part of consumer surplus. However, fewer pizzas are bought after the price cap law, resulting in consumers losing area C. Therefore, the net impact of the price cap on consumers depends on the relative sizes of the surplus transferred from the producers (area D) and loss reflected in area C. For those students who are able to buy the 6,000 pizzas in a month at a price that is $2 lower than they did before the law was enacted, life is good. They are the ones to whom area D is transferred. But for the students who would have enjoyed 4,000 more pizzas in the free market that they can no longer buy, life is a hungry proposition.

The producer surplus and consumer surplus represented by areas $C + E$ have disappeared because of the price ceiling. No one receives these surpluses anymore. Their combined areas are known as a **deadweight loss (DWL).** Deadweight loss is the difference between the maximum total surplus that consumers and producers could gain from a market and the combined gains they actually reap after a price regulation, and it reflects the inefficiency of the price ceiling. It's called a deadweight loss because it represents a set of surplus-generating transactions (pizza purchases, in this case) that would have occurred in an unregulated market with a customer who was willing to buy and a producer who was willing to sell at the market price. Area C is the deadweight loss suffered by consumers; area E is lost by producers.

Why is there a loss in consumer surplus if the students get to keep the money that they're not spending on pizza? Remember, the students missing out on the 4,000 pizzas after the price control law don't want to save the $10—they want the pizza! The reason there is a loss of consumer surplus is that the pizzas those students would have gotten in a market without a price control would be worth *more* than $10 to them. People who buy are on the part of the demand curve that is above the market price (except that individual right *at* the market price); their willingness to pay is greater than the price they have to pay. The price control results in their losing that difference.

Some producer surplus also becomes deadweight loss as a result of the price ceiling. There are pizzerias that would be willing to sell pizzas for more than $8 but less than

transfer
Surplus that moves from producer to consumer, or vice versa, as a result of a price regulation.

deadweight loss (DWL)
The reduction in total surplus that occurs as a result of a market inefficiency.

the $10 equilibrium price. Once the $8 price ceiling is in place, pizzerias will pull 4,000 pizzas off the market because $8 is not enough to cover their costs of making those extra pizzas. So both students and pizzerias were benefiting from transactions that took place before the price control; once the price ceiling is imposed, however, those transactions no longer take place and these benefits are lost.

Analysis Using Equations   Now let's compare the free and regulated markets for pizzas using the supply and demand equations we described earlier. To determine the free-market equilibrium using the equations, we set quantity supplied equal to quantity demanded and solve for the market clearing price P:

$$Q^S = Q^D$$

$$2,000P - 10,000 = 20,000 - 1,000P$$

$$3,000P = 30,000$$

$$P = \$10$$

Plugging that price back into either the supply or demand equation gives an equilibrium quantity of 10,000 pizzas:

$$Q^S = 2,000P - 10,000 \qquad \text{or} \qquad Q^D = 20,000 - 1,000P$$

$$= 2,000(10) - 10,000 \qquad\qquad\qquad = 20,000 - 1,000(10)$$

$$= 20,000 - 10,000 \qquad\qquad\qquad\quad = 20,000 - 10,000$$

$$= 10,000 \qquad\qquad\qquad\qquad\qquad = 10,000$$

The consumer surplus in the free market is the triangle $A + B + C$. The area of that triangle is

$$CS = \frac{1}{2} \times (\text{base}) \times (\text{height})$$

$$= \frac{1}{2} \times (\text{quantity sold}) \times (\text{demand choke price} - \text{market price})$$

The demand choke price is the price at which $Q^D = 0$. In this case,

$$0 = 20,000 - 1,000(P_{D\text{Choke}})$$

$$1,000(P_{D\text{Choke}}) = 20,000$$

$$(P_{D\text{Choke}}) = \$20$$

The consumer surplus triangle is

$$CS = \frac{1}{2} \times (\text{quantity sold}) \times (P_{D\text{Choke}} - \text{market price})$$

$$= \frac{1}{2}(10,000)(\$20 - \$10)$$

$$= (5,000)(\$10) = \$50,000 \text{ per month}$$

(Remember that quantities are measured in pizzas per month, so the consumer surplus is measured in dollars per month.)

The producer surplus is the triangle $D + E + F$ in the graph. The area of that triangle is $PS = \frac{1}{2} \times (\text{quantity sold}) \times (\text{market price} - \text{supply choke price})$.

The supply choke price is the price at which quantity supplied is zero:

$$Q^S = 2,000P - 10,000$$

$$0 = 2,000(P_{S\text{Choke}}) - 10,000$$

$$P_{S\text{Choke}} = 10,000/2,000 = \$5$$

Plugging this price into the equation for producer surplus, we find

$$PS = \frac{1}{2}(\text{quantity sold}) \times (\text{market price} - P_{S\text{Choke}})$$

$$= \frac{1}{2}(10{,}000)(\$10 - \$5)$$

$$= (5{,}000)(\$5)$$

$$= \$25{,}000 \text{ per month}$$

Now let's consider the impact of the price ceiling. The price of a pizza cannot rise to $10 as it did in the free market. The highest it can go is $8. We saw in the graphical analysis that this policy led to a shortage. The shortage is the difference between the quantity demanded and the quantity supplied at the price ceiling (P_c):

$$Q_{pc}^D = 20{,}000 - 1{,}000P_c$$

$$= 20{,}000 - 1{,}000(8)$$

$$= 12{,}000$$

$$Q_{pc}^S = 2{,}000P_c - 10{,}000$$

$$= 2{,}000(8) - 10{,}000$$

$$= 6{,}000$$

The shortage is 12,000 − 6,000 or 6,000 pizzas per month. This means that there are students ringing pizzerias' phones off the hook trying to order 6,000 more pizzas, but whose orders the pizzerias won't be willing to fill at the new market price.

Next, we compute the consumer and producer surpluses after the price control is imposed. Producer surplus is area F.

$$PS_c = \frac{1}{2}(Q_{pc}^S) \times (P_c - P_{S\text{Choke}})$$

$$= \frac{1}{2}(6{,}000)(\$8 - \$5)$$

$$= (3{,}000)(\$3) = \$9{,}000 \text{ per month}$$

which is just over one-third of the $25,000 of producer surplus pizzerias were making before the price ceiling. It is no wonder that producers fight against laws like this one.

The consumer surplus is now areas $A + B + D$. An easy way to figure the value for this surplus is to add the area of triangle A to the area of the rectangles B and D. Triangle A has an area of

$$\text{Area of } A = \frac{1}{2}(Q_{pc}^S) \times (P_{D\text{Choke}} - \text{price at point } z)$$

where the price at point z is the price at which quantity demanded equals the new quantity supplied of 6,000 pizzas. To figure out this price, set $Q^D = Q_{pc}^S$ and solve for the price:

$$Q^D = 20{,}000 - 1{,}000P_z = Q_{pc}^S$$

$$20{,}000 - 1{,}000P_z = 6{,}000$$

$$20{,}000 - 6{,}000 = 1{,}000P_z$$

$$P_z = 14{,}000/1{,}000 = \$14$$

This means that, if the price of a pizza were actually $14, exactly 6,000 pizzas would be demanded. With this value for the price at point z, we can now calculate:

$$\text{Area of } A = \frac{1}{2}(Q_{pc}^S) \times (P_{D\text{Choke}} - P_z)$$

$$= \frac{1}{2}(6{,}000)(\$20 - \$14)$$

$$= (3{,}000)(\$6)$$

$$= \$18{,}000 \text{ per month}$$

The area of rectangle B is

$$B = Q^S_{pc} \times (P_z - \text{free-market price})$$

$$= (6{,}000)(\$14 - \$10)$$

$$= \$24{,}000 \text{ per month}$$

and the rectangle D is

$$D = Q^S_{pc} \times (\text{free-market price} - P_c)$$

$$= (6{,}000)(\$10 - \$8)$$

$$= \$12{,}000 \text{ per month}$$

Adding these three areas, we find that total consumer surplus after the pizza price ceiling is $A + B + D = \$54{,}000$ per month.

Therefore, consumers *as a group* are better off than they were under the free market: They have $4,000 more of consumer surplus per month. However, this outcome hides a big discrepancy. Those students lucky enough to get in on the 6,000 pizzas for $8 rather than $10 are better off, but there are 4,000 pizzas that would have been available in the free market that are no longer being supplied. Students who would have consumed those missing pizzas are worse off than they were before.

What is the deadweight loss from the inefficiency of the price-controlled market outcome? The full DWL is the area of triangle $C + E$ in the figure, so

$$\text{DWL} = \frac{1}{2} \times (\text{free-market quantity} - Q^S_{pc}) \times (P_z - P_c)$$

$$= \frac{1}{2}(10{,}000 - 6{,}000)(\$14 - \$8)$$

$$= \frac{1}{2}(4{,}000)(\$6)$$

$$= \$12{,}000 \text{ per month}$$

The Problem of Deadweight Loss   As we have seen, a price ceiling creates a deadweight loss. This deadweight loss is just that: lost. It's surplus that was formerly earned by consumers (C) or producers (E) that neither gets when there is a price ceiling. This analysis has shown that price ceilings and other mandates and regulations can come with a cost, even if they don't involve any direct payments from consumers or producers (as taxes do).

A natural way to think about the size of the deadweight loss is as a share of the transfer D. Because the price control was designed to transfer surplus from pizzerias to students, the deadweight loss tells us how much money gets burned up in the process of transferring surplus through this regulation. In this case, the deadweight loss ($12,000) is just as large as the transfer. In other words, in the process of transferring income from pizzerias to students through the price ceiling, one dollar of surplus is destroyed for every dollar transferred.

This example illustrates the dilemma of using regulations to transfer income. If somehow the city council could get the producers to directly pay the consumers the amount $D - C$ without changing the price, the consumers would be just as happy as with the price control, because that's all they net in the deal after losing the deadweight loss. The producers would be better off as well. Rather than being left with just F, they would have their free-market producer surplus of $D + E + F$ minus their payment of $D - C$. The areas D in these two values cancel, leaving the pizzerias $E + F + C$, which is larger than the F in producer surplus they get under the price ceiling law. Deadweight loss occurs because the price-control regulation transfers income by changing prices, and price changes affect incentives and lead to inefficiency. Practically speaking, though, it's difficult to figure out how to organize the payment of $D - C$ without changing the price. A per pizza subsidy paid by pizzerias to students, for example, would have the same result as reducing the price and would thus have its own deadweight loss as we describe in Section 3.5.

Importance of Price Elasticities   The elasticities of supply and demand are the keys to the relative sizes of the deadweight loss and the transfer. Consider two different pizza markets in Figure 3.8. In panel a, the curves are relatively inelastic and show little price sensitivity. In panel b, the relatively elastic supply and demand curves reflect a greater amount of price sensitivity. It's clear from the figure that if the same price control rule is applied to both markets, the deadweight loss will be larger as a share of the transfer in the market with more elastic supply and demand.

The intuition behind this result is that the price ceiling's deadweight loss comes about because it keeps a set of sellers and buyers who would be willing to trade in the market at the free-market price from doing so. If the number of people in this set is small (in other words, the quantity after the regulation is close to the quantity before), then the deadweight distortion is small. How large that number of people is depends on how sensitive demand and supply are to prices. If demand and supply are relatively inelastic, the number of people and firms changing their quantity demanded or supplied will be small, and the DWL will be small. If demand and supply are relatively elastic, the number of people and firms who change their quantity demanded or supplied will be large.

Nonbinding Price Ceilings   In the pizza example, the price ceiling was below the free-market equilibrium price. What if a ceiling were set above the equilibrium price? Suppose the city council passed a law that limited the price of pizzas to $12 instead of $8, for example.

Figure 3.8   **Deagweight Loss and Elasticities**

(a)

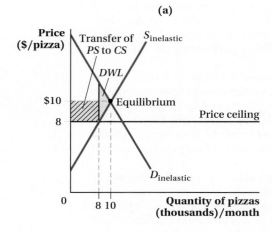

(b)

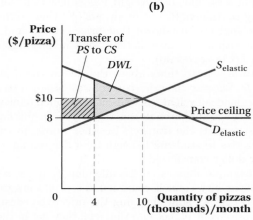

(a) $S_{\text{inelastic}}$ and $D_{\text{inelastic}}$ show little price sensitivity. With price controls, relatively few buyers and sellers who would have traded in the free market are kept out of the market, and the transfer is much larger than the deadweight loss created.

(b) In a market with a more elastic supply and demand curve, S_{elastic} and D_{elastic}, a relatively large group of buyers and sellers who would have traded in the free market are kept out of the market, and the deadweight loss created by the price control is much larger than the transfer.

In such cases, the price ceiling has no effect. Because it is set at a level above where the market would clear anyway ($10 in the pizza case), it won't distort market outcomes. There will be no impact on price, no excess demand, and no deadweight loss. Price ceilings at levels above the equilibrium price are said to be **nonbinding,** because they do not bind or keep the market from arriving at its free-market outcome.

If conditions in the market change, however, a price ceiling that was once nonbinding could become binding. Suppose, for example, that enrollment increases at the college, and as a result, the demand for pizzas shifts out to a point at which the equilibrium price would be $13. If this shift were to occur, a $12 price ceiling would start to bind, leading to excess demand and deadweight loss in the market. (A large inward shift in the supply curve from the original equilibrium could also make a formerly nonbinding ceiling start to bind.)

> **nonbinding price ceiling**
> A price ceiling set at a level above equilibrium price.

Price Floors

The other major type of price regulation is a **price floor** (sometimes called a **price support**), a limit on how low a product's price can go. Lawmakers around the world use price floors to prop up the prices of all sorts of goods and services. Agricultural products are a favorite, especially in wealthier countries. As early as the 1930s, the United States federal government began setting price supports for agricultural goods such as milk, corn, wheat, tobacco, and peanuts. The goal was to guarantee farmers a minimum price for their crops to protect them from fluctuating prices. Many of these price supports remain today. We will use the tools of consumer and producer surplus to analyze price floors just as we used them for price ceilings.

> **price floor (or price support)**
> A price regulation that sets the lowest price that can be paid legally for a good or service.

Let's look at the market for peanuts. The unregulated market for peanuts is shown in Figure 3.9. The equilibrium quantity of peanuts is 20 million tons, and the equilibrium price of peanuts is $500 per ton. The government decides that farmers should be getting more than $500 per ton for their peanuts, so it passes a regulation that peanuts must sell for no less than $1,000 per ton.

Immediately, we know there is going to be a problem. At the higher price, peanut farmers want to sell a whole lot of peanuts—30 million tons. But at that price, quantity demanded is much lower—only 10 million tons. (Peanut butter sandwiches are just too

---

Figure 3.9   The Effects of a Price Floor

A price floor affects both producer and consumer surpluses. Before price controls in the peanut market, consumers pay $500 per ton, and producers supply 20 million tons of peanuts. Consumer surplus is the triangle $A + B + C$, and producer surplus is $D + E + F$. When a price floor of $1,000 per ton is put in place, peanut farmers supply 30 million tons of peanuts (point y), but consumers demand only 10 million tons of peanuts (point x), creating an excess supply of 20 million tons of peanuts. Consumer surplus is reduced to A. Producer surplus is now $B + D + F$, and the net gain to producers is $B - E$. The deadweight loss is $C + E$.

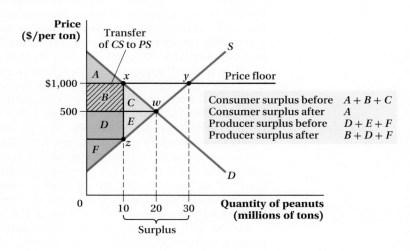

Consumer surplus before	$A + B + C$
Consumer surplus after	A
Producer surplus before	$D + E + F$
Producer surplus after	$B + D + F$

expensive when peanuts cost $1,000 per ton.) This imbalance leads to excess supply in the market: Sellers want to sell more of the product at that price than buyers want to buy. This is indicated in the figure by the 20-million-ton difference between the quantity of peanuts supplied and the quantity demanded at the price floor.

The goal of the price floor policy is to help farmers, so we need to look at the producer surplus to know how well the policy accomplishes its goal. Before the regulation, producer surplus was the area $D + E + F$. After the regulation, prices go up for all the peanut farmers who are still able to find buyers, so producers gain area B as a transfer from consumers. The farmers sell 10 million tons of peanuts and receive $500 per ton more than they were receiving in the free market. But peanut growers lose some of their market. The reduction in quantity demanded from 20 million to 10 million tons knocks out producers who used to sell peanuts at market prices and made a small amount of producer surplus from it. This area E then becomes the producers' part of the deadweight loss (DWL) from the regulation.

Overall, the producers gain surplus of $B - E$. If supply and demand are sufficiently elastic (i.e., if both curves are flat enough), producers could actually be made *worse off* from the price floor that was put in place to help them. This is because area E—the producers' share of the DWL—may be larger than the transfer from consumers, area B. This outcome is another application of our discussion above about how the deadweight loss grows as the supply and demand curves become more elastic.

How do consumers fare when the price floor is enacted? You can probably guess: Consumer surplus falls from $A + B + C$ to A. Area B is the surplus transferred from consumers to producers and area C is the consumer part of the DWL.

The price floor policy therefore transfers income from consumers to peanut farmers, but only by burning $C + E$ (the DWL) to do it. Again, if there were some way for the consumers to directly pay the peanut farmers a set amount equal to area B, the farmers would obtain more surplus than they get with the regulation (producer surplus of B versus $B - E$), and the consumers would be better off too (consumer surplus of $A + C$ instead of A). By changing the actual price of peanuts instead of making a transfer unrelated to quantity, the price support distorts people's incentives and leads to inefficiency as reflected by the DWL of $C + E$.

This analysis also illustrates the everlasting dilemma of price supports. The quantity supplied at the price floor is greater than the quantity demanded. So what happens to the extra peanuts? They accumulate in containers rather than being sold on the market. To avoid this outcome, a government will often pay the producers who can't sell their output in the regulated market to *stop* producing the extra output (20 million extra tons of peanuts in our example). The United States Department of Agriculture, for example, oversees various programs to reduce the surplus of price-supported crops on the market. One such program, the Conservation Reserve Program (CRP), paid farmers $1.85 billion in 2010 (an average of about $55 per acre) for holding land out of production. The program does have environmental benefits that mitigate some of the losses, but it also serves to reduce the quantity of subsidized crops that is grown, effectively by replacing those subsidies with CRP payments. There are also a number of programs that distribute millions of dollars annually ($871 million in 2010) of commodity foods—like peanut butter!—to school lunch programs and needy individuals on the condition that the foods will not be resold. Again, these programs serve to take surplus crops off the market.

Another example of a price support is a minimum wage. Here, the "product" is labor and the "price" is the wage, but the analysis is the same. If the government tries to help college students save tuition money by mandating that all summer internships pay at least $40 an hour, the quantity of labor supplied for internships will be much greater than the quantity demanded. As a result, there will be a lot of unemployed intern-hopefuls who would have been working at the equilibrium wage.

Just as with our earlier examples, how many people a minimum wage adds to the number of unemployed (the excess quantity supplied in the price floor figure), the amount of income transferred to workers (the change in producer surplus), and the size of the deadweight loss all depend on the elasticity of labor supply and labor demand. The price floor's deadweight loss arises because a set of sellers and buyers who would be willing to trade in the market at the free-market price will not do so at the regulated price. When suppliers and demanders are relatively insensitive to price, the number of transactions that the price floor prevents from happening is relatively small, and therefore so is the deadweight loss. Large price elasticities imply a large number of destroyed transactions and a large deadweight loss.

Nonbinding Price Floors   If a price floor is set below the free-market equilibrium price, it will have no effect on the market. **Nonbinding price floors** have no effect on price and do not create excess supply or deadweight loss. Just as with nonbinding price ceilings, however, conditions in a market may change to make a price floor that was once unbinding start to bind. Suppose the peanut price floor had been set at $400, below the equilibrium price of $500. If there is a sufficiently large outward shift in supply or inward shift in demand, the free-market equilibrium price may fall below $400, causing the price floor to start to affect the market.

nonbinding price floor
A price floor set at a level below equilibrium price.

3.3 Quantity Regulations

Sometimes, rather than regulating prices, governments impose quantity regulations. We discuss some of these regulations and analyze their effects on market outcomes in this section.

Quotas

A **quota** is a regulation mandating that a certain quantity of a good or service be provided. Quotas are occasionally used to force firms to produce a certain amount of a good (say, a vaccine in preparation for a flu epidemic or armaments during a war), but most often they are used to limit the amount of a good that is produced.

quota
A regulation that sets the quantity of a good or service provided.

For example, countries wanting to limit imports but not wanting to publicly announce tariffs (taxes on imports) can limit imports by establishing a quota. The U.S. government imposes quotas on the amount of sugar that can be imported from various countries, for example.[7] In other circumstances, a government may limit the amount of fish people can catch or the production of milk or oil.[8] The nation of Bhutan has a quota on the number of foreign tourists that can visit in a given year. France limits the amount of U.S. television shows that can be broadcast on TV. Singapore limits the number of cars that people can buy. London's Heathrow Airport limits the number of direct flights from U.S. airports. Taxis need medallions to operate, and doctors need licenses to practice.

Zoning laws impose another type of quota. Most towns and cities have zoning laws that limit the amount or type of construction that can go on in a certain area. A common zoning restriction limits the number of certain businesses considered by some to be unsavory, such as pawn shops or tattoo parlors. Such restrictions can be thought of as quotas on the amount of services these stores can provide in a local market. Let's consider as an example the impact of a quota on the amount of tattoo services that can be provided in the fictional town of River City.

---

[7] Legally, the current sugar quotas aren't completely binding. If a country goes over its quota allocation, it can still export sugar to the United States, but it must pay an additional tariff to do so. In practice, however, this tariff is so high that it all but eliminates shipments beyond the quota allocation.

[8] As we will see in Chapter 16 when we discuss externalities, there may be reasons for governments to limit the production of certain goods. For now, we just want to know what effects quotas have in a standard market situation.

Suppose the city's demand curve for tattoos is $Q_d = 2,500 - 20P$, and the supply curve is $Q_s = 100P - 3,500$, where the quantities demanded and supplied are both measured in the number of tattoos per year. We can analyze the effects of a quota on price and quantity by using graphs and equations.

Graphical Analysis In the free market, the equilibrium quantity of tattoos supplied and demanded for tattoos in River City is 1,500 tattoos per year and a price of $50 per tattoo (Figure 3.10). The consumer surplus in this market is $A + B + C$ and the producer surplus is $D + E + F$.

Suppose that River City's mayor becomes convinced that tattoo shops are a blight on society and rules that no more than 500 tattoos can be purchased per year in the city. He enforces this quota by requiring everyone who wants a tattoo to buy a tattoo permit before getting inked.

The quota creates a regulatory bend in the supply curve so that it becomes vertical at the quantity of 500. In other words, no matter what the price of tattoos is, parlors cannot supply more than 500. When this happens, the supply curve becomes perfectly inelastic at 500, making the new supply curve S_2 look like the red line in Figure 3.10. Now the demand curve intersects supply at point z rather than at point x, and the price rises from $50 to $100. Consumer surplus falls from area $A + B + C$ to area A, which is the only area that is below the demand curve and above the post-quota price P_{quota}. The post-quota producer surplus is above the supply curve and below the new price. This area $B + D + F$ includes a surplus transfer B from consumers to producers. The area $C + E$ is the deadweight loss.

Analysis Using Equations The equilibrium price is the price that exists when quantity supplied equals quantity demanded:

$$Q^D = Q^S$$

$$2,500 - 20P = 100P - 3,500$$

Solving for P and Q, we find

$$P = 50 \text{ and}$$

$$Q^D = 2,500 - 20(50) = 1,500 \quad \text{or} \quad Q^S = 100(50) - 3,500 = 1,500$$

Figure 3.10 **The Effects of a Quota**

In the free market for tattoos in River City, producers supply 1,500 tattoos per year at a price of $50 per tattoo at the equilibrium (point x). Consumer surplus is $A + B + C$, and producer surplus is $D + E + F$. After the mayor of River City enacts a law requiring a permit to get a tattoo, the supply for tattoos becomes vertical at the quantity of 500 tattoos. At the new equilibrium (point z), producers supply 500 tattoos at the increased price of $100 per tattoo. Consumer surplus is reduced to A. Producer surplus is $B + D + F$, and the net gain to producers is $B - E$. The deadweight loss is $C + E$.

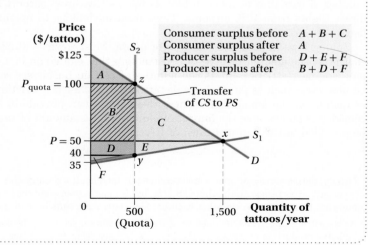

Consumer surplus before	$A + B + C$
Consumer surplus after	A
Producer surplus before	$D + E + F$
Producer surplus after	$B + D + F$

At the free-market equilibrium price and quantity, the consumer surplus is

$$CS = \frac{1}{2} \times (\text{base}) \times (\text{height})$$

$$= \frac{1}{2} \times Q \times (P_{D\text{Choke}} - P)$$

The demand choke price $P_{D\text{Choke}}$ is the price at which $Q^D = 0$, which in this case is

$$Q^D = 2{,}500 - 20(P_{D\text{Choke}}) = 0$$

$$20P_{D\text{Choke}} = 2{,}500$$

$$P_{D\text{Choke}} = \$125$$

Consumer surplus is therefore

$$CS = \frac{1}{2} \times Q \times (P_{D\text{Choke}} - P)$$

$$= (\tfrac{1}{2})(1{,}500)(\$125 - \$50)$$

$$= (750)(\$75) = \$56{,}250$$

The producer surplus is the triangle $D + E + F$ in the graph. That triangle's area is

$$PS = \frac{1}{2} \times Q \times (P - P_{S\text{Choke}})$$

The supply choke price $P_{S\text{Choke}}$ is the price at which quantity supplied is zero:

$$Q^S = 100 \times P_{S\text{Choke}} - 3{,}500 = 0$$

$$P_{S\text{Choke}} = 3{,}500/100 = \$35$$

Producer surplus in the unregulated tattoo market is then

$$PS = \frac{1}{2} \times Q \times (P - P_{S\text{Choke}})$$

$$= \frac{1}{2} \times 1{,}500 \times (\$50 - \$35)$$

$$= (750)(\$15) = \$11{,}250$$

After the 500-tattoo quota is implemented, the supply curve is the same up to $Q_S = 500$, at which point it becomes perfectly inelastic (point y). The equilibrium price will be

$$Q^S = Q^D$$

$$500 = 2{,}500 - 20P_{\text{quota}}$$

$$P_{\text{quota}} = \$100$$

At this price, the consumer surplus is the area A:

$$CS = \frac{1}{2} \times Q_{\text{quota}} \times (P_{D\text{Choke}} - P_{\text{quota}})$$

$$= (\tfrac{1}{2})(500)(\$125 - \$100)$$

$$= (250)(\$25) = \$6{,}250$$

This is dramatically reduced from the free-market surplus of $56,250. Sorry, River City tattoo fans.

The producer surplus is measured by the areas $B + D + F$. We can break out each of these areas separately:

$$\text{Area } F = \frac{1}{2} \times Q_{\text{quota}} \times (\text{price at point } y - P_{S\text{Choke}})$$

The price at point y is the price at which the quantity supplied is equal to the quota.

It can be determined by setting $Q^S = 500$ and solving for P:

$$Q^S = 100(\text{price at point } y) - 3{,}500 = 500$$

$$100(\text{price at point } y) = 4{,}000$$

$$\text{price at point } y = 4{,}000/100 = \$40$$

So this means

$$\text{Area } F = \frac{1}{2} \times 500 \times (\$40 - \$35) = \$1{,}250$$

The rectangle B is

$$\text{Area } B = Q_{\text{quota}} \times (P_{\text{quota}} - P)$$

$$= 500(\$100 - \$50) = \$25{,}000$$

and the rectangle D is

$$\text{Area } D = Q_{\text{quota}} \times (P - \text{price at } y)$$

$$= 500(\$50 - \$40) = \$5{,}000$$

Thus, the total producer surplus equals $F + B + D = \$31{,}250$.

Let's compare the quota outcomes to those of the free, unregulated River City tattoo market. Consumers are much worse off after the quota because their surplus has fallen from \$56,250 to only \$6,250. This decrease reflects, in part, the losses of the additional 1,000 people who would be willing to get a tattoo in River City in a free market but cannot with the quota in place. But the loss in consumer surplus also reflects the fact that the quota increases the price of tattoos even for those people who get one. This price increase shrinks the gap between what they are willing to pay for the tattoo and the price they actually have to pay.

On the supply side, the tattoo parlors do just fine. They lose the producer surplus in area E when the quota is imposed, but the quantity restriction leads to much higher prices for their output—they get a huge transfer from consumers (area B), which makes their total producer surplus \$31,250 under the quota instead of \$11,250 without it. This gain could explain why the tattoo parlors may not complain about an ordinance that would reduce the total number of tattoos they could sell, although a noneconomist might expect they would.

The quantity-restricting quota drives up the price of tattoos. In doing this, the quota transfers a bunch of surplus from tattoo buyers to tattoo parlors and creates a significant amount of deadweight loss (area $C + E$, which based on our calculations above totals \$25,000 + \$5,000 = \$30,000).

Government Provision of Goods and Services

The quota example we just discussed set a maximum quantity for the tattoo market. What if a government wanted to mandate a *minimum* amount of a good or service instead? For legal reasons, it can be difficult for a government to actually force companies to provide a certain quantity of a product that they do not want to produce. However, governments can and sometimes do produce goods themselves. In the market for higher education, for example, states run public colleges and universities that directly compete with private colleges and universities. In the insurance market, the government provides flood insurance. Research and development (R&D) conducted by private firms competes with R&D funded by the federal government through institutions like the National Institutes of Health or the National Science Foundation. Weather forecasting from the National Weather Service competes against Accuweather, The Weather Channel, and others. The U.S. Postal Service competes with UPS and Federal Express in package delivery.

To understand the effects of direct government provision of goods and services, let's use the supply and demand model to analyze the college education market. The price

| **Figure 3.11** | **The Effects of Government Provision of Education** |

In a market with only private colleges, supply would be S_{priv}, demand would be D, and the equilibrium price and quantity would be P_1, Q_1. When the government opens a new university, there is an outward shift in the supply curve equal to the number of credit hours provided by the government, the quantity Q_{gov}. At the equilibrium, the price decreases to P_{tot}, and the quantity increases to $Q_{tot} = Q_{gov} + Q_{priv}$. Because the increase in the equilibrium quantity is less than Q_{gov}, the quantity supplied by private universities must have been crowded out.

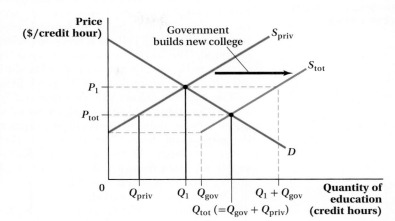

in this market is tuition per credit hour, and the quantity is the total number of credit hours taken.[9] In Figure 3.11, we start with the equilibrium that would exist in the market if higher education were provided only by private schools. The demand curve for education is D and the supply curve is S_{priv}. The equilibrium price and quantity are P_1 and Q_1.

If the government decides that getting more people to attend college is important, it can do so in many ways. It could help pay part of students' costs of attending a private school. (We analyze the impact of such payments, called subsidies, in Section 3.5.) Alternatively, the government could impose a price ceiling on college tuition so that more students could afford it. This price ceiling would have the disadvantage we learned about earlier in this chapter: There would be a shortage of education because more students would want a college education and fewer colleges would be willing to offer this education. Finally, the government could start a public university to directly enable more students to attend college. That's the case we'll look at here.

Let's say the government provides Q_{gov} credit hours at the new state-run university. This increase in credit hours shifts the supply curve from S_{priv} to S_{tot}. Notice that because the government's additional quantity supplied doesn't depend on price, this leads to a parallel outward shift in the supply curve by an amount Q_{gov}.

With this shift in supply, the market tuition falls from P_1 to P_{tot} per credit hour. However—and this is key—the number of credit hours taken will rise less than Q_{gov}, the amount provided by the government. We can see this in Figure 3.11. As we just noted, the horizontal distance between S_{priv} and S_{tot} is Q_{gov}. For the equilibrium quantity of credit hours to rise by an amount equal to Q_{gov}, the equilibrium price would have to remain at P_1, making the quantity of credit hours equal to $Q_1 + Q_{gov}$. The price doesn't stay at P_1, though, because the demand for credit hours is downward-sloping. The equilibrium price instead falls to P_{tot}, and the quantity rises by an amount less than Q_{gov}, to Q_{tot}. Because the total quantity of credit hours increases by less than the amount the government provides, private schools must now supply a number of credit hours (call this Q_{priv}) that is less than Q_1, the quantity they supplied before the government stepped in.

[9] In using the supply and demand model here, we are assuming that all colleges, private and public, offer identical educations.

crowding out
A reduction in private economic activity created by greater government presence in a market.

This decline in the quantity supplied by the private schools is known as **crowding out,** a reduction in private economic activity created by greater government presence in a market. Here, crowding out is the equivalent of the deadweight loss seen in our earlier examples. The government pays to provide Q_{gov} credit hours, but it increases the total number of credit hours in the market by less than this amount. Some credit hours formerly offered by private schools and willingly purchased by students are no longer produced. The larger the number of these lost credit hours—that is, the smaller the increase in the equilibrium quantity of credit hours relative to the government-provided quantity—the greater is the inefficiency from crowding out.

The intuition behind why crowding out occurs lies in the fact, seen in the example above, that the equilibrium quantity rises less than the quantity the government produces because demand is downward-sloping. By stepping in and increasing output, the government drives down the market price. This reduces the quantity supplied by private producers. At the original equilibrium price, private producers were willing to supply a certain quantity. At the lower, post-government market price, however, the private producers find it is no longer worth supplying their initial amount.

The same intuition explains how large crowding out will be in a market. When demand is relatively elastic, the increase in supply due to the government won't reduce the equilibrium price much. As a result, private producers won't cut back production a lot, and crowding out will be small. In the extreme case, when demand is perfectly elastic (i.e., if the demand curve were flat), government production won't change the equilibrium price at all. As we just discussed, in this case, the equilibrium quantity will rise by exactly the amount the government produces. On the other hand, if demand is relatively inelastic, government supply will reduce the equilibrium price a great deal. This will lead to large cutbacks in private production and a lot of crowding out. In the extreme case of perfectly inelastic (vertical) demand, crowding out is complete: Price falls and private firms cut back on production one-for-one for each unit the government produces. This makes sense: If quantity demanded is fixed at some specific amount regardless of price, any government provision will only serve to replace private production.

theory and data

Does Public Health Insurance Crowd Out Private Insurance?

The role of the government in providing health insurance is constantly debated in countries where coverage is provided by both private and public payers. The United States is a country with a heavy mix of the two. In 2010 about 150 million Americans were covered by private insurers, but another 50 or so million people were on Medicare, the government-provided health insurance for seniors, and just under 60 million were enrolled in Medicaid, government-provided insurance for low-income individuals and families. Another 50 million were uninsured.

In mixed-payer countries, government-provided coverage is often targeted at population segments like the elderly and poor that many believe would have a difficult time obtaining private coverage. Many policy makers and economists nevertheless believe that public coverage and private coverage might be close enough substitutes to cause expansion of public coverage to crowd out private coverage. In other words, if the government tries to expand coverage in order to reduce the number of uninsured, some of the increased enrollees will be individuals who would have still been covered by private insurance otherwise.

Figure 3.12 : **Government Provision of Health Insurance**

In a market with only private health insurance, supply would be S_{priv}, demand would be D, and the equilibrium price and quantity would be P_e, Q_e. When the government offers health insurance (in the form of Medicaid), the supply curve shifts out to S_{tot}. At the equilibrium, the price decreases to P_1, and the quantity increases to $Q_1 = Q_{priv} + Q_{gov}$. The quantity supplied by private insurers is crowded out since the total rise in the quantity of insurance coverage falls short of Q_{gov}.

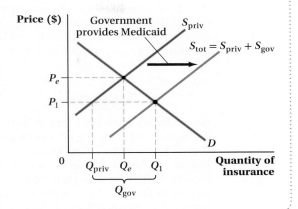

In a well-known study, health economists David Cutler and Jonathan Gruber measured the amount of crowding out that occurred during significant expansions of Medicaid.[*] Specifically, they used law changes that occurred in the late 1980s and early 1990s that greatly expanded the number of women and children eligible for Medicaid coverage. They measured crowding out by looking at the period of this large shift in the quantity of publicly provided insurance and determining if there were any corresponding drops in private insurance among the same population. In terms of Figure 3.12, they compared Q_{gov} (here, the amount of additional Medicaid coverage) to the difference between Q_e and Q_{priv} (respectively, the amount of private coverage before and after the Medicaid expansion).

Using this approach, Cutler and Gruber found evidence of substantial crowding out. For example, the expansion of coverage eligibility led to an additional 1.5 million children obtaining Medicaid coverage. Thus $Q_{gov} = 1.5$ million in Figure 3.12. However, they estimated about 600,000 of these new enrollees had been covered by private insurance beforehand; that is, $Q_e - Q_{priv} = 0.6$ million. Therefore the net change in children covered by medical insurance, $Q_1 - Q_{gov}$, was only about 900,000. This implies a crowd-out rate of 40 percent—for every 10 additional Medicare enrollees, 4 were simply exchanging their private insurance for public insurance. Another way to quantify this is in terms of the changes in uninsured children due to the policy. Before the expansion of coverage there were about 8.6 million uninsured children. Had all of the 1.5 million new enrollees come from this group, it would have cut the number of uninsured children by about 17 percent. But crowding out meant it reduced the number of uninsured by only 10 percent.

This result raises an interesting question about what the mechanism was through which the reduction in private insurance occurred. One possibility is that newly Medicaid-eligible individuals were less likely to pay for private coverage available to them through their employers or other channels. Another possible mechanism is that employers, knowing additional public coverage has been made available, reduced the quality or raised the price of the insurance plans they offered their employees. Cutler and Gruber found some evidence that employers did pare back their plans, but most of the crowding out appeared to have arisen because individuals who were newly eligible for Medicaid avoided using their employer-provided insurance options.

[*] David M. Cutler and Jonathan Gruber, "Does Public Insurance Crowd Out Private Insurance?" *Quarterly Journal of Economics* 111, no. 2 (1996): 391–430.

Just as with deadweight loss, the relative size of crowding out inefficiencies depends on elasticities. But there is a difference. While both supply and demand elasticities determine the amount of deadweight loss, only the demand elasticity matters for crowding out. This is because we've assumed the quantity supplied by the government doesn't depend on the price. As a result, for a given demand curve, the drop in equilibrium price after the government enters the market depends only on how much supply shifts (i.e., how much the government produces), not on the slope of the private supply curve.[10]

3.4 Taxes

Governments at all levels (local, state, federal) tax all kinds of things, and they do it in different ways. Sometimes, suppliers are legally required to remit the tax. Stores in the United States collect sales taxes and send them to state revenue agencies, for example, just as producers in Canada and Europe collect and remit value-added tax (VAT). Sometimes the legal burden falls on consumers, like "use taxes" that states levy on purchases their residents make in other states. In still other cases, the legal burden is shared. For instance, half of the U.S. federal payroll tax (which funds the Social Security and Medicare programs) is paid by employers before workers get their wages, and the other half is paid by workers through a deduction from their wages.

In this section, we use the supply and demand model to show one of the most striking findings in economics: In a competitive market, it doesn't matter whether the buyer or the seller is required by law to actually sign the check and remit the tax to the government; the impact on consumers and producers is always the same. That is, we could change the law so that consumers paid sales tax instead of sellers, or employers have to pay the entire payroll tax, and market outcomes would not change. The total impact of a tax on consumers and sellers depends only on the steepness of the supply and demand curves, not on the identity of the payer. Before we can understand why this is true, however, we first need to look at how taxes affect a market.

Tax Effects on Markets

We start with a no-tax market that is in equilibrium, the market for movie tickets in Boston, Massachusetts (Figure 3.13). The equilibrium is at point x, with a price of P_1, and the quantity of movie tickets sold is Q_1. In 2003 the mayor of Boston, Tom Menino, proposed adding a 50 cent tax to movie tickets to help balance a budget deficit. Many thought Menino proposed the tax because a large number of movie-goers in Boston are college students who live in the Greater Boston area but are not Boston voters. Regardless of his motivation, the tax was defeated by the state legislature.

If it had been enacted, the tax would have required theater owners to pay 50 cents per ticket to the government. Let's look at how such a change would affect the market for movie tickets. The tax is much like a 50 cent per ticket increase in the theaters' costs. We know from Chapter 2 that increases in production costs cause suppliers to supply a smaller quantity at any given price. Therefore, in response to the tax, the supply curve shifts up by the amount of the tax (50 cents) to S_2, and the equilibrium quantity of movie tickets sold falls to Q_2.[11]

But taxes do something different from a typical supply shift: They drive a wedge between the price buyers pay (the market price) and the price that producers actually

---

[10] If, for some reason, the government's quantity supplied *is* sensitive to price, then the elasticity of the supply curve (both the private and government components) will affect the amount of crowding out, just as the demand elasticity does.

[11] A tax expressed in percentage terms, such as a sales tax of 6%, is called an *ad valorem* tax (as opposed to a *specific tax* that is a set dollar amount, like the 50 cents per ticket here). An ad valorem tax version of this tax would shift the supply curve, but not by a fixed amount at every point. Instead, it would rotate the curve by a fixed percent around the point at which quantity supplied is zero.

Figure 3.13 ┊ Effect of a Tax on Boston Movie Tickets

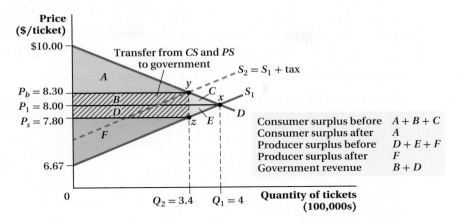

The figure shows the effect of a $0.50 movie tax on the market for Boston movie tickets. In the pre-tax market, supply S_1 and demand D intersect at the equilibrium price of $8 and the equilibrium quantity of 400,000 movie tickets. The consumer surplus is $A + B + C$, and the producer surplus is $D + E + F$. The addition of the $0.50 tax per movie ticket results in an inward shift of the supply curve from S_1 to S_2 by the amount of the tax and decreases the equilibrium quantity to 340,000 tickets. The resulting tax wedge creates two prices: $8.30, the price the buyer faces, and $7.80, the price the seller actually receives. The new consumer surplus is A, and the producer surplus is F. Area $B + D$ is government tax revenue, while area $C + E$ is the deadweight loss.

receive (the market price minus the tax). With a normal supply curve, the price at any point on the supply curve is the price a producer receives for selling its product. With a tax, the product sells for the price P_b (we denote the price the buyers pay with a "b"), but the sellers only receive P_s (we denote the price the seller receives with an "s"). This is the buyers' price minus the tax: $P_s = P_b - \text{tax}$. In other words, the buyers have to pay 50 cents more for any quantity, but the movie theaters don't get to keep the extra money—they receive only the higher price minus the tax.

Because of this wedge, the new equilibrium in the Boston movie market involves *two* prices. The first, point y, is the price ($8.30) that the buyers pay at the theater that includes the 50 cent tax. Thus, $8.30 is the market price. The second, point z, is the price ($7.80) that the suppliers receive after taking the 50 cents out of the higher market price and sending it to the government.

There are two key characteristics to note about the post-tax market equilibrium. First, the price of movie tickets increases, but not by the full 50 cents of the tax. This can be seen in Figure 3.13. The size of the tax is reflected in the vertical distance between P_b ($8.30) and P_s ($7.80). The rise in the price of movie tickets, however, is the distance between $8.30 and the equilibrium price with no tax, $8.00. The reason for this discrepancy is that the tax wedge drives some of the highest-cost theaters out of the market: Once the tax is added to the price, these theaters would have to sell their tickets at a price that is too high for buyers. The second characteristic to note is that the government generates revenue from the tax. The total revenue equals the 50 cent tax times Q_2, the new quantity of tickets sold.

We can apply all the familiar concepts from consumer and producer surplus analysis to this new equilibrium. We just need to remember that the tax creates a second supply curve that we have to keep track of, rather than moving a single supply curve as before. The supply curve that the theater owner cares about is S_1, the initial supply curve. The number of tickets that theaters are willing to supply at any particular price is still given by this curve, even after the tax is imposed, because the level of S_1 reflects the after-tax dollars theater owners take home from selling tickets. But the supply curve actually facing the buyers is S_2. It has been shifted up by the amount of the tax, because that is the price that moviegoers have to pay for a particular quantity supplied.

To make things clearer, let's work through this example in more detail. In Figure 3.13, the demand curve for movie tickets in Boston is $Q^D = 20 - 2P$ and the supply of movie tickets is $Q^S = 3P - 20$, where both quantities demanded and supplied in these curves are measured in hundreds of thousands of tickets. If the legislature passes the tax, all theater owners will be required to remit to the city 50 cents per ticket sold. We can analyze the tax's effect on the market using graphs or equations.

Graphical Analysis With no taxes, solving the model our usual way gives a free-market equilibrium price P_1 and quantity Q_1 and the resulting consumer and producer surpluses (Figure 3.13).

The tax means buyers now face a new supply curve S_2, equal to S_1 shifted up by $0.50, the amount of the tax. This reduces the number of movie tickets bought in the market from 400,000 to 340,000. At that quantity, the price the buyers are paying rises from $8.00 to $8.30. Because the law requires suppliers (the theater owners) to pay the government a 50 cent tax for every ticket they sell, the suppliers don't get to keep $8.30; they get to keep only $7.80 = $8.30 - 0.50.

What happens to consumer and producer surplus in the post-tax market? The new consumer surplus is smaller than before. In the no-tax market, consumer surplus was $A + B + C$. Now it is only A, the area below the demand curve but above the price that the buyers have to pay, $8.30.

The new producer surplus is also smaller than before. Before the tax, it was $D + E + F$. After the tax, it is only F, the area above the supply curve and below the price that the suppliers receive after they pay the tax, $7.80.

Imposing the tax reduces total producer and consumer surplus from area $(A + B + C) + (D + E + F)$ to just area $A + F$. Where has the surplus in areas B, C, D, and E gone? The area $B + D$ is no longer consumer *or* producer surplus; it is government tax revenue, the tax times the quantity sold after the tax is implemented. With a tax, there is no surplus transfer between producers and consumers, as we saw in earlier examples. Instead, both producers and consumers transfer some of their surpluses to the government. This tax revenue is then "returned" to consumers and producers in the form of government services, so it is not lost.

Areas C and E are the deadweight loss from the tax. They are surplus that moviegoers and theater owners formerly got from buying and selling tickets at the competitive price. This surplus is gone now because consumers buy fewer tickets at the higher post-tax price and sellers supply fewer tickets at their lower post-tax price.

Just as in the price regulation cases, a natural way to look at the size of the deadweight loss is as a fraction of the surplus transfer. Before, that transfer was from producers to consumers (for a price ceiling) or from consumers to producers (for a price floor). Now, it's from both to the government. The ratio in this case is the area $C + E$ to the area $B + D$, which is the DWL as a share of revenue.

Analysis Using Equations The no-tax market equilibrium equates quantity demanded and quantity supplied:

$$Q^D = Q^S$$
$$20 - 2P = 3P - 20$$
$$5P = 40$$
$$P_1 = 40/5 = \$8 \text{ per ticket}$$
$$Q^D = 20 - 2(\$8) = 4 \qquad \text{or} \qquad Q^S = 3(\$8) - 20 = 4$$

Therefore, before the tax, the equilibrium price is $8 and 400,000 tickets are sold.

The pre-tax consumer surplus is the triangle above the price and below the demand curve, as shown in Figure 3.13:

$$CS = \frac{1}{2} \times Q \times (P_{DChoke} - P_1)$$

Again, the choke price is found by determining the price that pushes the quantity demanded to zero:

$$Q^D = 20 - 2P_{DChoke} = 0$$

$$P_{DChoke} = \$10$$

In other words, this demand curve says that if tickets cost $10, no one will go to theaters in the city of Boston (perhaps because theaters in the suburbs are an attractive alternative).

Plugging the demand choke price into the CS formula gives a consumer surplus of

$$CS = \frac{1}{2}(400{,}000)(\$10 - \$8)$$

$$= \$400{,}000$$

The producer surplus is the triangle above the supply curve and below the price:

$$PS = \frac{1}{2} \times Q \times (P_1 - P_{SChoke})$$

The supply choke price is the price that moves quantity supplied to zero:

$$Q^S = 3P_{SChoke} - 20 = 0$$

$$P_{SChoke} = \$6.67$$

That is, at any price below $6.67 a ticket, no theaters would operate in Boston. Plugging this supply choke price into the PS formula gives a producer surplus of

$$PS = \frac{1}{2}(400{,}000)(\$8 - \$6.67)$$

$$= \$266{,}667$$

What happens to consumer and producer surplus when Mayor Menino applies his 50 cent tax? Theaters must pay the state for each ticket they sell. This creates a dual-supply-curve situation. The supply curve for the theater owners is the same as the initial supply curve. The theater is still willing to supply whatever number of tickets the supply curve says at the market price. But now, the supply curve facing buyers is shifted up by the amount of the tax: At each price, the tickets supplied to consumers now cost $0.50 more. The difference between the supply curve that the buyers face and the supply curve that the sellers face is the amount of the tax. In words, the theaters' supply curve says they would be willing to sell 400,000 tickets if they receive $8 per ticket (after the tax gets paid), but for theaters to get $8 per ticket, buyers would actually have to pay $8.50 per ticket because $0.50 of tax needs to be paid out of the price received by the theaters. The prices that result for both the buyer and the seller are summed up in the equation $P_b = P_s + \$0.50$.

To solve for the post-tax quantity and prices, we substitute this expression, which links the two supply prices into our supply and demand equations:

$$Q^D = Q^S$$

$$20 - 2P_b = 3P_s - 20$$

$$20 - 2(P_s + 0.50) = 3P_s - 20$$

$$20 - 2P_s - 1 = 3P_s - 20$$

$$5P_s = 39$$

$$P_s = 39/5 = \$7.80$$

Therefore, the buyers face the following price:

$$P_b = P_s + 0.50 = \$7.80 + 0.50 = \$8.30$$

Now if we plug the buyer price into the demand curve equation and the supplier price into the supply curve equation, they will both give the same after-tax market quantity:

$$Q_2 = 20 - 2(8.30) = 3.4 \qquad \text{or} \qquad Q_2 = 3(7.80) - 20 = 3.4$$

Only 340,000 tickets will be sold once the tax is put into place.

The consumer surplus after a tax is the area below the demand curve but above the price that the buyer pays:

$$CS = \frac{1}{2}(340,000)(\$10.00 - \$8.30)$$
$$= \$289,000$$

The producer surplus is the area above the supply curve and below the price that the suppliers receive:

$$PS = \frac{1}{2}(340,000)(\$7.80 - \$6.67)$$
$$= \$192,667$$

So the tax makes consumer surplus fall by \$111,000 and producer surplus fall by \$74,000 from their values in the no-tax market equilibrium. Some of that \$185,000 in lost surplus flows to the government in the form of revenue from the tax, however. That revenue is equal to \$0.50 per ticket times the number of tickets sold after the tax, or

$$\text{Revenue} = 0.50 Q_2$$
$$= \$0.50(340,000) = \$170,000$$

Notice that the total amount of the lost surplus, \$185,000, is more than the amount of revenue that the government generated, \$170,000. The difference of \$15,000 is the deadweight loss of the tax.

A different way to calculate DWL is to compute the area of the triangle whose base is the change in quantity and whose height is the amount of the tax:

$$\text{DWL} = \frac{1}{2} \times (Q_1 - Q_2) \times (P_b - P_s) = \frac{1}{2} \times (Q_1 - Q_2) \times \text{tax}$$

$$= \frac{1}{2}(400,000 - 340,000)(\$0.50) = \$15,000$$

That's about 9% of the revenue generated by the tax. In other words, this tax burns up about \$1 of surplus in DWL for every \$11 of revenue it generates.

Why Taxes Create a Deadweight Loss

Just as we showed in the case of price and quantity regulations, the main determinant of the DWL from a tax as a share of revenue is how much the quantity changes when the tax is added. The size of that change depends, in turn, on how sensitive supply and demand are to prices. The deadweight loss from pizza price controls, for example, came about because there were consumers and suppliers who would like to trade at market prices and would have earned surplus from doing so but were prevented from engaging in these transactions by the price ceiling. With taxes, there are no forbidden transactions. The source of the loss is the same, however. There are people who would have bought tickets at the market price without a tax and would have gained some surplus from doing so. Once the government adds a tax, the after-tax price rises enough so that these consumers no longer want to buy tickets. They get to keep their money, but they were previously able to buy something with it that gave them surplus. Likewise, movie houses lose surplus because some would have shown movies at the pre-tax market price but find the after-tax price too low to justify operating. These lost surpluses are the DWL of the tax.

Why a Big Tax Is Much Worse Than a Small Tax

An interesting result of our analysis is that it implies the inefficiency represented by the size of the deadweight loss gets much bigger as the size of a tax becomes larger. In the movie ticket tax example (Figure 3.13), we saw that the DWL from the tax was area $C + E$ and that the revenue generated was $B + D$. What would happen if Mayor Menino decided to *increase* the ticket tax? How much more revenue and how much more DWL would this large tax increase create?

Figure 3.14 illustrates the outcome for a general case. The larger tax reduces the quantity even further, from Q_2 to Q_3. The DWL under the larger tax is area $C + E + F + H$ (remember that it was only area F with the smaller tax). Government revenue, which was area $D + E$ with a smaller tax, is now area $B + D + G$. That is, the government gains areas B and G because the people who still buy tickets are paying more in taxes. However, the government loses area E, because some people stop buying movie tickets after the tax is raised. If we look at the DWL as a share of the revenue generated, it is clear that the *incremental* revenue generated by increasing this tax causes more inefficiency than the smaller tax did. Initially, the DWL was F, with a revenue gain of $D + E$. But the incremental DWL here is $C + E + H$, while the revenue gain is only $B + G - E$. In fact, if taxes are high enough, the increase in revenue per ticket from the tax will be more than offset by the reduction in the quantity of tickets sold, and there will be no revenue gain at all!

A general rule of thumb is that the DWL of a tax rises with the square of the tax rate.[12] That is, doubling the tax rate quadruples the DWL. That's why economists tend

---

Figure 3.14 ┆ **The Effect of a Larger Tax on Boston Movie Tickets**

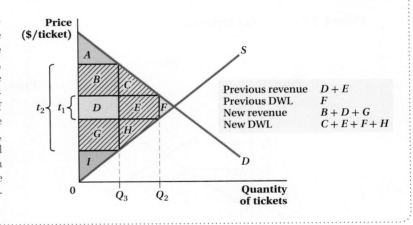

After an increase in the tax on movie tickets in Boston from t_1 to t_2, the tax wedge between the price consumers pay and the price movie theaters receive increases, while the quantity of movie tickets at the equilibrium (Q_3) decreases. The tax revenue is now $B + D + G$. Area E, a part of the government's tax revenues under the lower tax, is a part of the deadweight loss, $C + E + F + H$. Since the incremental DWL is $C + E + H$ and the revenue gain is only $B + G - E$, the incremental revenue created by the second larger tax is more inefficient than that of the first smaller tax.

Previous revenue	$D + E$
Previous DWL	F
New revenue	$B + D + G$
New DWL	$C + E + F + H$

---

[12] To see where this intuition comes from, notice that with linear supply and demand curves, the DWL from a tax is a triangle with a height equal to the quantity reduction caused by the tax and a base equal to the tax. Because the supply and demand curves are linear, the quantity reduction is proportional to the tax. Specifically, it will be $\Delta Q = A * t$, where A is some number that depends on the slope of the demand and supply curves. Therefore, the area of the DWL triangle is $\frac{1}{2} * A * t * t = \frac{1}{2} * A * t^2$. This area is proportional to the square of the tax. For nonlinear demand and supply curves, this formula is only an approximation, but if they aren't too nonlinear, the intuition remains the same.

to favor tax policies that exhibit what is called "low rates and broad bases." That is just a way of saying that, all else equal, taxing ten things at a low rate is better than taxing five things at zero and five things at a high rate. Because DWL rises with the square of the tax rate, the overall DWL will be larger with the five high rates than with the ten low rates.

The Incidence of Taxation: The Payer Doesn't Matter

An important thing to note about the movie ticket example is that although we supposed that it would be the theater owners who were legally obligated to remit the 50 cents per ticket tax to the City of Boston, they don't bear the complete burden of the tax. Before the tax came in, the theater owners received $8 per ticket and moviegoers paid $8 a ticket. After the $0.50 tax, moviegoers pay $8.30 a ticket. After they send in the tax, however, the theaters only end up with $7.80 per ticket. Therefore, of the 50 cents going to the government, 30 cents (60%) of it is coming out of consumers' pockets because their price went up by 30 cents. Movie theaters send the tax check to the government, but they are able to pass on much of the tax to consumers through higher prices. This means that the price realized by the suppliers goes down by only 20 cents. Who *really* bears the burden of a tax is called **tax incidence.** The incidence of this tax is 60% on the buyers and 40% on the suppliers.

tax incidence
Who actually pays a tax.

Now let's say Boston changed the rule for who pays the tax to the government. Instead of the theater sending the tax payment to the government, moviegoers would pay the tax by, after buying their ticket at whatever price the theater charges, dropping two quarters in a "Menino Box" as they enter the theater (silly, yes, but this is just to make a point).

Figure 3.15 : Tax Incidence

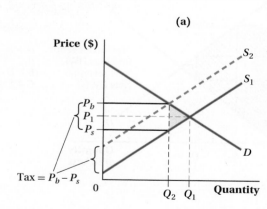
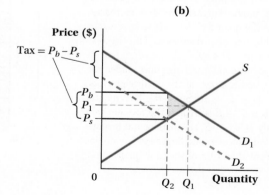

(a) The tax incidence is unaffected by whether the seller or buyer pays the tax. When the seller pays the tax, the supply curve shifts inward by the amount of the tax, $P_b - P_s$, from S_1 to S_2. The equilibrium quantity decreases from Q_1 to Q_2. The seller now faces price P_s at the equilibrium, while the buyer pays price P_b.

(b) When the buyer pays the tax, the demand curve shifts inward by the amount of the tax, $P_b - P_s$, from D_1 to D_2. The equilibrium quantity decreases from Q_1 to Q_2. As in panel a, the seller now faces price P_s at the equilibrium, while the buyer pays price P_b.

Does this change alter the tax incidence? It does not. The equations below show that the tax formula doesn't matter whether you subtract the tax from what the supplier receives or add the tax to what the buyer pays.

$$P_s = P_b - \text{tax}$$

is the same as

$$P_s + \text{tax} = P_b$$

This can also be seen graphically. The original case where the theater remits the tax is shown in Figure 3.15a. When the tax is instead paid by buyers, their quantity demanded depends on the price including the tax. But the price suppliers receive at this quantity demanded is only the price without the tax. To account for this difference, we shift down the demand curve by the amount of the tax, from D_1 to D_2 in Figure 3.15b. But the result hasn't changed: Quantity demanded is still Q_2 and the difference between the buyer's price and the seller's price still equals the amount of the tax. Thus, the incidence of a tax does not depend on who is legally bound to pay it.

That's why a helpful way to picture taxes on a graph is to just forget about whether the tax is moving the supply curve up or the demand curve down. Instead, start from the initial no-tax equilibrium point and move left until the vertical space between the supply and demand curves is the amount of the tax. This gives you the right answer regardless of whether the tax is being legally applied to suppliers or buyers.

This point about tax incidence is fundamental. If you have ever had a job, you probably know that the government takes many taxes out of your pay. Some of these are payroll taxes that appear on your pay stub as FICA (Federal Insurance Contributions Act). They are collected to pay for Social Security and Medicare. In the United States, payroll taxes are legally split evenly between workers and employers. In other words, if you earn wages of $1,000, you have to pay 7.65% of that in payroll taxes and the employer has to pay another 7.65% on its own.[13] Would U.S. workers be better or worse off if the law changed so that the company paid 15.3% and workers paid nothing, or if it instead made the employee pay 15.3% and his or her employers paid nothing? The analyses we've just completed suggest that such changes wouldn't make any difference. In a competitive market, the wage would adjust to the same level regardless of which side of the market actually pays the tax.

make the grade

Did I measure deadweight loss correctly?

A few simple tricks will help you nail problems involving deadweight loss. First, whenever the quantity consumed falls as a result of a government policy, a deadweight loss occurs. (This isn't *exactly* correct; if externalities are present, government policies can actually improve market outcomes. We learn more about externalities in Chapter 16.) If the quantity doesn't get distorted, no deadweight loss occurs. Second, the deadweight loss almost always takes the shape of a triangle, and moreover, that triangle points at the efficient market equilibrium with no market distortion. Why? Because deadweight loss measures the consumer and producer surplus destroyed. As we have seen, this loss in surplus grows as we move further and further away from the efficient equilibrium. The growing distance between the sides of the triangle reflects this fact.

---

[13] FICA taxes apply only to "earned" income like wages and salaries. In 2011 the Social Security tax applied to the first $106,800 of wages per person. After that, only the Medicare part of the tax applied (that rate is 2.9%). The limit is subject to increases from year-to-year, typically at a rate tied to inflation. Also in 2011, Congress temporarily reduced the Social Security rate workers were responsible for, making workers' legal share of the tax less than half.

It turns out that the only thing that matters about the economic effects of this tax is how elastic the supply and the demand for labor are. To see why, let's consider the two extremes.

Elastic Demand with Inelastic Supply   In a market characterized by an elastic demand and an inelastic supply, buyers are very sensitive to price and the suppliers are not. Most labor economists tend to think of the labor market in this way, so that the 15.3% FICA tax (the combined tax rate on the two sides) applies to a market in which labor supply is fairly inelastic (people work a similar amount even if their wage goes up or down) and firms' demand for labor is fairly elastic. This market is illustrated in Figure 3.16a.

Applying the methods we've used throughout this section, we see that the tax is borne almost entirely by the suppliers—here, workers supplying labor. With a tax, employers have to pay wages W_b that are a bit higher than wages without the tax, W_1. But after taxes, the workers receive a wage W_s that is much less than W_1. Therefore, workers are a lot worse off after the tax than employers. And we know from the discussion that we just had on tax incidence that even if the government switched the payroll tax rules so that employers paid the entire amount, workers would not do any better. Their wages would fall almost as much as the employers' tax went up.

Inelastic Demand with Elastic Supply   Figure 3.16b shows a market characterized by inelastic demand (buyers are not sensitive to price) and elastic supply (suppliers

---

Figure 3.16 | **Tax Incidence and Elasticities**

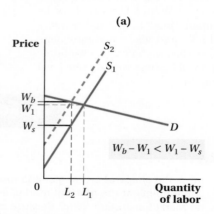

(a)

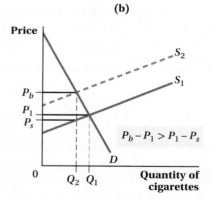

(b)

(a) In a labor market where demand is elastic and supply inelastic, we begin with supply curve S_1, demand D, and equilibrium price and quantity (W_1, L_1). The implementation of the tax $W_b - W_s$ shifts the supply curve inward from S_1 to S_2 and decreases the equilibrium quantity of labor from L_1 to L_2. Because laborers in this market are not very sensitive to price and employers are, the effect of the tax on the wages laborers receive is much larger than its effect on the wage employers pay, $W_b - W_1 < W_1 - W_s$.

(b) In the market for cigarettes where demand is inelastic and supply elastic, we begin with supply curve S_1, demand D, and equilibrium price and quantity (P_1, Q_1). The implementation of the tax $P_b - P_s$ shifts the supply curve inward from S_1 to S_2 and decreases the equilibrium quantity of cigarettes from Q_1 to Q_2. Because smokers in this market are not very sensitive to price and cigarette companies are, the effect of the tax on the price consumers pay is much larger than its effect on the price companies receive, $P_b - P_1 > P_1 - P_s$.

are very sensitive to price). In the market for cigarettes, for instance, many buyers are addicted and tend to buy a similar amount no matter how much the price goes up. Cigarette supply is more elastic. You can see in the figure that in this case, consumers bear the brunt of the tax. A tax on cigarettes causes the buyers' price to rise from P_1 to P_b, almost the entire amount of the tax. Suppliers are only a bit worse off than they were before, because they can pass on the higher costs to the inelastic consumers.

We could do this entire analysis using equations, as we did in the movie ticket example. It turns out that there is a general formula that will approximate the share of the tax that is borne by the consumer and the share borne by the producer. Not surprisingly given what we've just discussed, these shares depend on elasticities:

$$\text{Share borne by consumer} = \frac{E^S}{E^S + |E^D|}$$

$$\text{Share borne by producer} = \frac{|E^D|}{E^S + |E^D|}$$

If the price elasticity of supply (E^S) is infinite, the consumers' share is equal to 1; that is, consumers bear the whole burden when supply is perfectly elastic. If the absolute value of the price elasticity of demand ($|E^D|$) is infinite, the consumers' share of the tax burden is zero, and suppliers bear the whole burden of the tax.

3.3 figure it out

Consider the demand and supply for cola in a market represented by the following equations:

$$Q^D = 15 - 10P$$
$$Q^S = 40P - 50$$

where Q is millions of bottles per year and P measures dollars per bottle. The equilibrium price of cola is $1.30 per bottle, and 2 million bottles are sold each year.

a. Calculate the price elasticity of demand and the price elasticity of supply at the equilibrium price and quantity.

b. Calculate the share of a tax that would be borne by consumers and the share borne by producers.

c. If a tax of $0.15 per bottle is created, what would be the expected price buyers will have to pay? What price will sellers receive after the tax?

Solution:

a. The formula for price elasticity of demand is

$$E^D = \frac{\Delta Q^D}{\Delta P} \times \frac{P}{Q^D}$$

From the demand curve, we can calculate $\frac{\Delta Q^D}{\Delta P}$. Each time P changes by one unit, Q^D falls by 10. Therefore,

$$\frac{\Delta Q^D}{\Delta P} = -10$$

Substituting into the formula for elasticity, we get

$$E^D = \frac{\Delta Q}{\Delta P} \times \frac{P}{Q} = -10 \times \frac{1.3}{2} = \frac{-13}{2} = -6.5$$

The formula for price elasticity of supply is

$$E^S = \frac{\Delta Q^S}{\Delta P} \times \frac{P}{Q^S}$$

From the supply curve, we can see that $\frac{\Delta Q^S}{\Delta P} = 40$. Note that each time P increases by one unit, Q^S rises by 40.

Thus, the price elasticity of supply is

$$E^S = \frac{\Delta Q^S}{\Delta P} \times \frac{P}{Q^S} = 40 \times \frac{1.3}{2} = \frac{52}{2} = 26$$

b. The proportion of the tax borne by buyers will be

$$\frac{E^S}{E^S + |E^D|} = \frac{26}{26 + |-6.5|} = \frac{26}{32.5} = 0.8$$

The proportion of the tax borne by sellers will be

$$\frac{|E^D|}{E^S + |E^D|} = \frac{|-6.5|}{26 + |-6.5|} = \frac{6.5}{32.5} = 0.2$$

So buyers will bear 80% of the tax and sellers will bear only 20% of the tax.

c. If there is a tax of $0.15 per bottle, buyers will bear 80% of the tax:

$$\text{Increase in } P_b = (0.80)(\$0.15) = \$0.12$$

The price buyers pay will rise from $1.30 per bottle (the original equilibrium price) to $1.42.

Sellers will bear the other 20% of the tax:

$$\text{Decrease in } P_s = (0.2)(\$0.15) = \$0.03$$

The price sellers receive will fall from $1.30 per bottle to $1.27.

3.5 Subsidies

subsidy

A payment by the government to a buyer or seller of a good or service.

A **subsidy** is a payment by the government to a buyer or seller of a good or service. It is, in essence, the exact opposite of a tax. In fact, when we analyze the effects of subsidies on markets, we can treat the subsidy as a negative tax. Thus, the price the buyer pays is *lower* than the price the supplier receives after the subsidy. If the government subsidizes gasoline by $1 per gallon, for example, then buyers might pay $3.50 per gallon at the pump, but gas stations receive $4.50 per gallon because they get to add the government dollar to the $3.50. This relationship is

$$P_b + \text{subsidy} = P_s$$

where P_b is the price the buyer pays (the market price) and P_s is the price the seller receives after the subsidy is paid.

Governments tax a lot, but they also subsidize the production of many different goods and services. Let's look at the effects of the U.S. government subsidy for the domestic production of ethanol, a corn-based fuel additive that can be mixed with gasoline. (A common rationale given for the subsidy is to reduce the dependence of the United States on imported oil, though not coincidentally politicians from large corn-producing states have been vocal backers of the policy.) Let's say the government gives fuel producers \$1 for every gallon of gas-ethanol mix they sell. This means that if the original supply curve S_1 is what suppliers receive, the supply curve that buyers face will be *shifted down* by the amount of the subsidy, to S_2 (Figure 3.17). The supply curve that buyers face is lower because the amount people pay to fill their tank is less than the amount the gas station receives, since the government is footing part of the bill (the effects of a tax are just the opposite).

Before the subsidy was in place, consumer surplus was everything below the demand curve and above the price that consumers pay (P_1), area $A + B + C$ in Figure 3.17. After the subsidy, consumer surplus will change. But it will not get smaller, as in the case of a tax. It will get larger. The new consumer surplus is the area below the demand curve and above the price that the consumers have to pay (the new lower price, P_b). This is the old consumer surplus $A + B + C$ *plus* the new part $F + G + H$. This additional surplus comes from the lower price and the additional sales at that price.

Before the subsidy, the producer surplus was everything above the supply curve but below the price the suppliers received (P_1), area $F + G + J$. After the subsidy, producer surplus gets bigger, too. The area above the producers' own supply curve S_1 and below the price that the suppliers receive (P_s) is now $F + G + J$ plus $B + C + D$. (We calculate producer surplus using the *producers'* supply curve (S_1) to compute producer surplus because this is the supply curve that embodies the suppliers' costs of production.)

Note that parts of the consumer and producer surplus areas overlap in this case (areas $B + C + F + G$) because both sides are getting more surplus than before. The only way this is possible, however, is if someone else foots the bill. In this case, it's the government. The subsidy costs money. The cost of the subsidy is the subsidy

Figure 3.17   **The Impact of a Producer Subsidy**

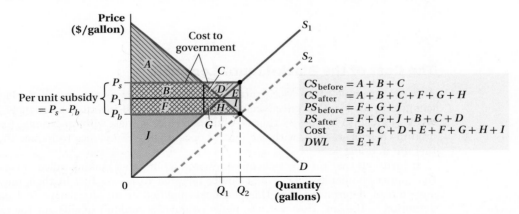

In the pre-subsidy market for gasoline, the supply curve S_1 intersects with the demand curve D at the equilibrium price P_1 and equilibrium quantity Q_1. The consumer surplus is $A + B + C$, and the producer surplus is $F + G + J$. After a government subsidy is put in place, the supply curve shifts down by the amount of the subsidy, $P_s - P_b$, to S_2. At the equilibrium, the quantity increases to Q_2, the price facing suppliers is P_s, and the price facing buyers is P_b. Consumer surplus is now $A + B + C + F + G + H$, and producer surplus is $F + G + J + B + C + D$. The cost of the subsidy is $B + C + D + E + F + G + H + I$, and the deadweight loss is $E + I$. Therefore, the costs associated with the subsidy are larger than the sum of the benefits to producers and consumers.

amount times the quantity produced, $Q_2 \times (P_s - P_b)$, which amounts to the rectangle $B + C + D + E + F + G + H + I$.

This isn't the only cost of the subsidy, however. Like any other price regulation, a subsidy also creates deadweight loss. It might seem odd at first that there would be DWL when both consumers *and* producers are better off after the subsidy. The key is to compare how much their surplus goes up to how much the subsidy costs the government. While consumer surplus went up by $F + G + H$ and producer surplus by $B + C + D$, total government outlays for the subsidy were $(F + G + H) + (B + C + D) + (E + I)$. Therefore, the subsidy's DWL is $E + I$. Society as a whole pays more for the subsidy than the added benefit it gave to consumers and producers. If somehow the government could just turn over the subsidy revenue to consumers without changing the price, society would be better off. By changing the price, it gets some extra people to buy gasoline (with ethanol added) who really were not interested in buying before.

When we looked at the market interventions earlier in this chapter, the DWL derived from the surplus lost by people who would have bought if there were no tax or regulation, but do not buy when the tax is in place and the price is too high. Here, it is the other way around. The DWL comes from people who would *not* have made a purchase in a competitive market. They only make a purchase because the subsidy lowers the price. The amount they value the extra quantity is less than it costs the government to move them to buy it.

A different way to see how this deadweight loss occurs is to think about people giving presents to each other. Economist Joel Waldfogel asked microeconomics students who received Christmas presents how much they thought the gifts they received cost the people who bought them.[14] Then he asked the students how much the gifts were worth to them, apart from the sentimental value. The students valued the presents they got by about 15% less than the cost of the presents. This 15% DWL from Christmas presents is just like the DWL from a subsidy. When the government subsidizes a product, it gives consumers a gift: The consumers value the gift (as measured by the consumer surplus) less than it costs the government to buy it (as measured by the revenue cost).

 ## application

The Cost of the Black-Liquor Loophole

A recent example of an (accidental) subsidy gone awry is the so-called black-liquor loophole in the law that gave companies tax credits for using alternative fuels. The tax credit is given to businesses that combine alternative fuels with traditional fossil fuels used in their operations, with the idea of encouraging companies to reduce their fossil fuel use in doing so.

It turns out that there is a chemical by-product of paper making called "black liquor" that paper companies have traditionally recycled to use as fuel in their plants. The government determined that this chemical qualified as an alternative fuel under the definition in the law. However, the paper companies couldn't qualify for the tax credit unless they *combined* the alternative fuel with a fossil fuel. So they started adding a bit of diesel fuel—a fossil fuel they weren't using at all before—to the black liquor before burning it. This led to two results. First, paper companies used more diesel than they

---

[14] Joel Waldfogel, "The Deadweight Loss of Christmas," *American Economic Review* 83, no. 5 (1993): 1328–1336. Leave it to an economist to point out the deadweight loss of Christmas!

did before, even though the point of the tax credit was to encourage movement away from use of fossil fuels. Second, paper companies got paid (in the form of tax credits) to burn the black liquor they were already using without payment. They got paid a lot too: This tax credit, originally projected to cost the government $61 million, ended up costing an estimated $6 to $8 *billion* in tax credits in 2009, almost all of it going to paper companies.

How does our analysis in this section explain what happened? The tax credit became, in practice, a diesel subsidy for the paper industry. By tying the credit to the use of blended fuels, it lowered the effective price of diesel that the paper companies faced. Before, when they had to pay the market price, their quantity demanded for diesel to fuel their plants was zero—they had a plentiful and cheap alternative in the black liquor. But now every gallon of diesel they bought came with a big tax credit attached—meaning they faced a downward-shifted supply curve for diesel. The quantity of diesel they demanded at these lower supply prices became positive.

As a result of this policy, the paper companies and the diesel sellers are better off because of the subsidy. (The former very much so in this case.) But the costs are large. First, there is deadweight loss: An industry that wasn't using diesel before because it had a superior alternative now demands it, even though the industry values it at less than the cost of supplying it. Second, the government has to pay the subsidy. And as noted above, that's a really big number. So big, in fact, that Congress closed the loophole in 2010 because they decided that we couldn't afford it. ■

3.4 figure it out

Suppose the demand for and supply of ethanol in a small town are as follows:

$$Q^D = 9{,}000 - 1{,}000P$$
$$Q^S = 2{,}000P - 3{,}000$$

where Q measures gallons per day and P represents price per gallon. The current equilibrium price is $4, and the current equilibrium quantity is 5,000 gallons per day.

Now suppose that the government wants to create a subsidy of $0.375 per gallon to encourage the use of ethanol.

a. What will happen to the price buyers pay per gallon, the price sellers receive per gallon, and the number of gallons consumed each day?

b. How much will this subsidy cost the government (and ultimately taxpayers)?

Solution:

a. Determining the prices that buyers and sellers face under a subsidy is done in a way similar to how we determined the prices for buyers and sellers in the presence of a tax. However, there is one big difference. Now, the price sellers receive is actually larger than the price paid by buyers (due to the subsidy):

$$P_s = P_b + \text{subsidy}$$

So now we know that in our problem

$$P_s = P_b + 0.375$$

Remember that we need to start with the supply and demand equations in the following form:

$$Q^D = 9{,}000 - 1{,}000P_b$$
$$Q^S = 2{,}000P_s - 3{,}000$$

Once we have these, we can substitute for P_s in the supply equation so that it becomes

$$Q^S = 2{,}000P_s - 3{,}000$$
$$Q^S = 2{,}000(P_b + 0.375) - 3{,}000 = 2{,}000P_b + 750 - 3{,}000 = 2{,}000P_b - 2{,}250$$

Now, we can equate Q^D and Q^S to solve for P_b

$$9{,}000 - 1{,}000P_b = 2{,}000P_b - 2{,}250$$
$$3{,}000P_b = 11{,}250$$
$$P_b = 3.75$$
$$P_s = P_b + 0.375$$
$$P_s = 4.125$$

To solve for the quantity of ethanol sold after the subsidy is put in place, we can substitute P_b into the demand equation or substitute P_s into the supply equation. (It is a good idea to do both to check your work.)

$$Q^D = 9{,}000 - 1{,}000P_b = 9{,}000 - 1{,}000(3.75) = 9{,}000 - 3{,}750 = 5{,}250$$
$$Q^S = 2{,}000P_s - 3{,}000 = 2{,}000(4.125) - 3{,}000 = 8{,}250 - 3{,}000 = 5{,}250$$

So, buyers will pay $3.75 per gallon, sellers will receive $4.125 per gallon, and 5,250 gallons will be sold each day. This can be seen in the figure below.

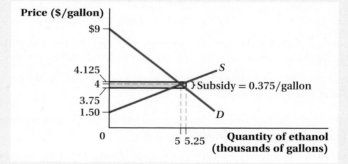

b. The cost of the subsidy will be the subsidy per gallon multiplied by the number of gallons sold:

Cost of subsidy = ($0.375)(5,250) = $1,968.75 per day

freakonomics

Can Economic Incentives Get You Pregnant?

In many countries around the world, the number of babies being born has declined dramatically. In places like China, which instituted a one child per family policy in 1978, the government wanted fewer babies to control the size of the population. In many other parts of the world, especially Europe and Japan, declining fertility poses a problem for governments. Fewer babies mean an aging population. In the next 20 years, the number of retired people worldwide who depend on government pensions will skyrocket, but there will be fewer people of working age to pay the taxes that fund these pensions.

What can governments do about this? One approach would be for governments to run budget surpluses now to cover potential shortfalls in the future. But that sort of austerity is not very popular among elected officials: They would pay the political price of high taxes today but wouldn't be in office 20 years from now to reap the benefits. Another approach would be to encourage additional immigration of working-age individuals. This is another tough sell politically in many countries. Instead, some countries such as France and Sweden are now considering adopting a different economic solution: paying cash to people who have babies.

Can government subsidies encourage the production of babies? You may think this is preposterous—that a couple's decision to become parents is completely unconnected to economics. If so, it just means you don't yet think like an economist. (It is only Chapter 3, though, so there is plenty of time to fix that.) The data suggest that the demand curve for babies slopes downward; that is, when the "price" of having a baby falls, people have more babies. In Israel, which has paid parents to have kids since 1959, economists Alma Cohen, Rajeev Dehejia, and Dmitri Romanov found sizable impacts of government subsidies on fertility.* In fact, they estimate that a 2003 reduction in the subsidy offered to new parents decreased the number of children born in 2004 by 12%. Given Israel's population, that amounts to approximately 5,400 babies who would have been born had the old, higher subsidy remained in effect. This pricing effect was seen across all ethnicities and religious groups too, with payouts affecting the family planning of Orthodox Jews as well as Arab Muslims in the country.

Countries of the former Soviet bloc didn't explicitly pay for children, but they encouraged baby-making in other ways. During the Communist reign, many of these countries such as Czechoslovakia and East Germany offered free child care, giving mothers the opportunity to quickly return to work. The allocation of housing was often tied to children; in Prague, for example, a couple had to be married with a child to be eligible for a government apartment.

The despotic ruler of Romania, Nicolae Ceausescu, used a different approach: In 1966, without warning, he banned abortion, which was the primary form of birth control in Romania at the time. The number of children born skyrocketed in the short run, with the fertility rate nearly doubling from 1.9 children per woman in 1966 to 3.7 children per woman, on average, in 1967. The large number of births accomplished Ceausescu's goal of having more boys who could eventually serve in his army. The problem with suddenly banning abortion, however, was that the babies who were born were not wanted or planned for by their parents. This outcome made the parents angry and led to unwanted children who faced much more difficult lives than the typical Romanian child born prior to 1966. Compared to Romanian children born just a year earlier, the cohorts of children born after the abortion ban would do worse in every measurable way: They would test lower in school, they would have less success in the labor market, and they would also prove much more likely to become criminals. Eventually, young protesters born after the abortion ban would overthrow Ceausescu in 1989, and he would be executed.

If Ceausescu had been a better economist, he would have realized that changing prices (in this case, by offering subsidies for babies) can be a more efficient way of incentivizing behavior than outright prohibition. In other words, economics might even have saved Ceausescu's life.

*Alma Cohen, Rajeev Dehejia, and Dmitri Romanov, "Do Financial Incentives Affect Fertility?" *NBER Working Paper,* 2007.

3.6 Conclusion

In this chapter, we took the supply and demand hammer and pounded every nail in sight. We saw how you can compute the consumer and producer surplus generated by transactions in a market, learned how to value new goods, and learned what deadweight loss is. We learned to use supply, demand, and total surplus to analyze industries and the ways in which they change in response to changes in the market, particularly to price and quantity regulations, taxes, and subsidies. Being able to do so much with such a simple model makes supply and demand the workhorse of microeconomics.

Summary

1. **Consumer surplus** is the value that consumers receive from participating in market transactions. It is the difference between the most they would pay for something and the price they actually have to pay for it. On a supply and demand graph, consumer surplus is measured by the area under the demand curve and above the price. **Producer surplus** is the benefit that producers receive from participating in market transactions. It is the difference between what they sell their product for and the least they would be willing to receive to sell their product. On a supply and demand graph, producer surplus is measured by the area above the supply curve and below the price. [**Section 3.1**]

2. Using consumer and producer surplus, we can compute how shifts in supply and demand affect the well-being of customers and of companies. An inward shift in supply will cause consumer surplus to fall because both the increase in the equilibrium price and the decrease in the equilibrium quantity this shift causes act to reduce consumer surplus. An outward shift in supply, on the other hand, raises consumer surplus. An inward shift in demand leads to a drop in producer surplus because it decreases both the equilibrium price and quantity. Outward demand shifts have the opposite effect. [**Section 3.1**]

3. If the government imposes a price regulation—either a maximum price or **price ceiling** like rent control or a minimum price or **price floor** like the minimum wage—the quantities supplied and demanded will differ at the market price, resulting in either excess demand or excess supply of the good. Such regulations also create a **deadweight loss** that arises because some of the surplus-creating transactions that took place before the regulation was enacted do not take place in the regulated environment. A direct transfer of income from one side to the other without changing the price would be a more efficient way to help consumers and suppliers. Deadweight losses are largest when supply and demand are most elastic. [**Section 3.2**]

4. If the government imposes a cap on output (a **quota**) or provides output itself, this action will change the market and create a deadweight loss, just as a price regulation does. These actions do not create excess demand or supply, though, because prices are able to adjust and clear the market. [**Section 3.3**]

5. Taxes reduce output and raise price. In doing so, they reduce consumer and producer surplus but generate tax revenue. The revenue they generate is less than the damage they do to surplus, and the difference is the deadweight loss of the tax. The concept of **tax incidence** tells us who really bears the burden of a tax: It does not matter who actually pays a tax by law. All that matters is the elasticities of demand and supply. The more elastic side of the market will bear less of the burden because it can more easily shift away from the taxed good. [**Section 3.4**]

6. **Subsidies** increase both consumer and producer surplus relative to the free-market equilibrium. They still create a deadweight loss, though, because the outlay cost of the subsidy exceeds the amount by which it increases the surplus of the two groups. [**Section 3.5**]

Review Questions

1. Define consumer and producer surplus.
2. What is the demand choke price? How does this price relate to consumer surplus?
3. What is the supply choke price? How does this price relate to producer surplus?
4. How does a supply shift affect consumer and producer surplus in a given market? Consider both inward and outward shifts of the supply curve.
5. How does a demand shift affect consumer and producer surplus in a given market? Consider both inward and outward shifts of the demand curve.
6. What is a price ceiling? Why does a price ceiling create excess demand for (shortage of) a good?
7. What is a price floor? Why does a price floor create an excess supply of (surplus of) a good?
8. What is a deadweight loss? If the price elasticity of a good is large, would you expect the deadweight loss to be large or small?
9. When is a price ceiling nonbinding? When is a price floor nonbinding?
10. What is a quota? How does it differ from a price ceiling or a price floor?
11. What is crowding out? Why does it occur?
12. Why is the relative size of crowding out inefficiencies dependent only on the elasticity of demand and not on the elasticity of supply?
13. What happens to the equilibrium price and quantity of a good when a tax is imposed on the good? Why does a tax create a wedge between the price the consumer pays and the price the producer receives?
14. How does a tax affect consumer and producer surplus? Why does a tax create a deadweight loss?
15. What is the tax incidence? What factors determine the tax incidence?
16. What is a subsidy?
17. How does a subsidy affect consumer and producer surplus?
18. Why does a subsidy create a deadweight loss?

Problems (Solutions to problems marked * appear at the back of this book. Problems adapted to use calculus are available online at http://worthpublishers.com/GLS1e)

1. If the supply curve for snowboards in the United States is described by the equation $Q^S = 400P - 8,000$ (where Q is the number of snowboards and P is in dollars per snowboard), compute the producer surplus at a price of $120. What happens to producer surplus if the price falls to $100?
2. The demand for air travel is summarized in the equation $Q^D = 800 - 2P$, where quantity is in millions of enplanements per quarter and price is in dollars per enplanement. How much would consumer surplus change if the rising cost of fuel led airlines to raise the price from $150 to $200?
3. Consider the demand for broadband Internet service, given as follows: $Q^D = 224 - 4P$, where Q is the number of subscribers in a given area (in hundreds) and P is the price in dollars per month. This demand relationship is illustrated in the diagram on the right. Assume that the price of broadband service is $25 per month. Determine the following, paying particular attention to the units in which quantity is denominated:
   a. The total number of subscribers at that price
   b. The total amount paid by subscribers for broadband service, area B
   c. The consumer surplus received by subscribers, area A
   d. The total value to consumers of the broadband service they received, areas A and B

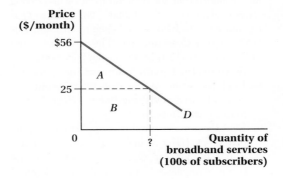

4. Consider the diagram on the next page, which depicts the supply of broadband Internet service. The supply of broadband service is given by $Q^S = 12.5P - 150$, where Q is the quantity of services (in hundreds) and P is the price per month. Assume that the price of broadband service is $25 per month. Determine the following, paying particular attention to the units in which quantity is denominated:
   a. The total number of services providers will supply at that price
   b. The total amount received by producers for that service, areas D and E
   c. The producer surplus received by suppliers, area D

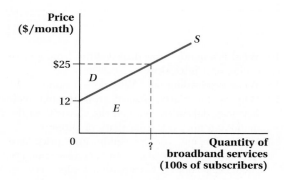

5. Combine the graphs and equations from questions 3 and 4 and determine the following:
   a. The equilibrium price of broadband Internet service
   b. The equilibrium quantity of broadband Internet service
   c. Consumer surplus
   d. Producer surplus
   e. The total surplus received by producers and consumers together

6. Holding price and quantity constant, why does the consumer surplus from a product decline if the demand curve becomes more elastic?

*7. The Ministry of Tourism in the Republic of Palau estimates that the demand for its scuba diving tours is given by $Q^D = 6,000 - 20P$, where Q is the number of divers served each month and P is the price of a two-tank dive. The supply of scuba diving tours is given by $Q^S = 30P - 2,000$.
   a. Solve for the equilibrium price and quantity.
   b. Find the value of the consumer surplus received by divers visiting Palau. (*Hint*: It may help to draw a graph.)
   c. Find the value of producer surplus received by dive shops. (*Hint*: It may help to draw a graph.)
   d. Suppose that the demand for scuba diving services increases, and that the new demand is given by $Q^D = 7,000 - 20P$. Calculate the impact of this change in demand on the values you calculated in parts (a) through (c).
   e. Are consumers better off or worse off as a result of the demand increase?

8. Is it possible that a regulation like the minimum wage, which is specifically designed to help low-income people, could actually reduce their income? If so, under what supply and demand conditions might this happen?

9. Low-skilled workers operate in a competitive market. The labor supply is $Q^S = 10W$ (where W is the price of labor measured by the hourly wage) and the demand for labor is $Q^D = 240 - 20W$. Q measures the quantity of labor hired (in thousands of hours).

   a. What is the equilibrium wage and quantity of low-skilled labor working in equilibrium?
   b. If the government passes a minimum wage of $10 per hour, what will be the new quantity of labor hired? Will there be a shortage or surplus of labor? How large?
   c. What is the deadweight loss of this price floor?
   d. How much better off are low-skilled workers in this case (in other words, how much does producer surplus change) and how much worse off are employers?

*10. The diagram below illustrates the market for beef. Suppose that the government has instituted a price support program for beef by placing a price floor at $4.00 per pound. Under the program, any unsold beef will be purchased by the government and placed in long-term storage.

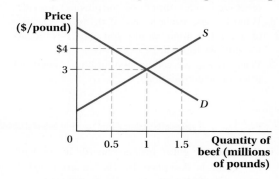

   a. What is the cost to consumers in lost surplus?
   b. What is the cost to taxpayers to purchase the unsold beef?
   c. How much producer surplus do sellers of beef gain?
   d. What is the loss to society of the beef program?
   e. The president of the National Cattleman's Association makes the following semi-extortionary offer to consumers: "Pay us $2.2 million per month forever and we'll lobby our congressmen to abandon the price support program." Should consumers pay the Cattleman's Association? Why or why not?

*11. Draw a graph illustrating the impact of imposing a quota on production in a market, where the quota is less than the current equilibrium quantity. What happens to the price of the good, producer surplus, and consumer surplus? Show the deadweight loss from the quota.

12. For decades, the mob ran a "numbers game" in which participants who matched three numbers chosen at random would win a prize. In the 1970s, state governments began authorizing state lottery commissions; those commissions typically offered games similar in structure to the numbers game. Using supply and demand analysis:

a. Predict the effect of the creation of state lotteries on the number of people playing numbers-type games.

b. Predict the effect of the creation of state lotteries on the number of people playing mob-run numbers games.

c. Predict the effect of the creation of state lotteries on the price of playing a numbers-type game.

d. Numbers games are unusual in that tickets don't typically vary in their nominal price—most tickets sell for exactly $1. Given that the nominal price is fixed, how might the price change you indicated in (c) be achieved?

13. Why do taxes create a deadweight loss the same way that regulations do? If a tax and a quota raise prices by the same amount, which causes more deadweight loss? Explain.

14. Consider the market for Cheese Puff Snacks (Q is in bags of Cheese Puffs). The demand for Cheese Puff Snacks is $Q^D = 30 - P$ and the supply is $Q^S = 3P - 10$. To pay for classes about healthy snacking, the government imposes a $4 per bag tax on Cheese Puffs.

a. What are the price paid by buyers, price received by sellers, and the number of bags of Cheese Puffs sold both before and after the tax?

b. What are the deadweight loss and revenue generated from this tax?

c. If the government decides to expand the healthy snacking program and raises the tax by $8 per bag (to the $12 total), what is the *additional* DWL and revenue from increasing taxes by this amount (that is in addition to the DWL and revenue that resulted from the $4 tax)?

*15. The demand for ice cream is given by $Q^D = 20 - 2P$, measured in gallons of ice cream. The supply of ice cream is given by $Q^S = 4P - 10$.

a. Graph the supply and demand curves, and find the equilibrium price and quantity of ice cream.

b. Suppose that the government legislates a $1 tax on a gallon of ice cream, to be collected from the buyer. Plot the new demand curve on your graph. Does demand increase or decrease as a result of the tax?

c. As a result of the tax, what happens to the price paid by buyers? What happens to the price received by sellers? How many gallons of ice cream are sold?

d. Who bears the greater burden of the tax? Can you explain why this is so?

e. Calculate consumer surplus both before and after the tax.

f. Calculate producer surplus both before and after the tax.

g. How much tax revenue did the government raise?

h. How much deadweight loss does the tax create?

16. Social Security taxes are taxes on the sale of labor services. Half of Social Security taxes are generally collected from the employer and half from the employee. Does this seem like a good way to structure the tax collection? Can the government dictate who bears what share of the burden of a tax? Explain.

*17. Draw a graph for a competitive market with a relatively elastic demand curve and inelastic supply curve. Illustrate on the graph the impact of imposing a per unit tax on the suppliers of the good in terms of consumer and producer surplus, prices and quantities, as well as how much deadweight loss the tax creates and the revenue it generates for the government. Who bears the larger burden of this tax?

18. The U.S. Senate is considering a bill that would tax the sale of laptop computers in order to fund a computer education program for presidential hopefuls. The Congressional Budget Office (CBO) estimates that if it implements a low tax of $12 per laptop, revenue should be sufficient to exactly fund the program. The CBO also estimates that a high tax of $230 per laptop will exactly fund the program.

a. How can a low tax and a high tax raise exactly enough money to fund the program? Illustrate your answer using a graph.

b. Suppose that you are an economic advisor to the Senate Finance Committee, tasked with analyzing the economic impact of the tax proposals. Which proposal do you recommend, and why?

*19. Consider the following fiscal scheme designed to directly transfer welfare from coffee drinkers to coffee vendors: The government will impose a $1.00 tax, collected from buyers, for each cup of coffee sold. The government will then subsidize coffee vendors $1.00 for each cup of coffee sold.

a. What will happen to the equilibrium price of coffee?

b. What will happen to the equilibrium quantity of coffee?

c. How will the outcome of this scheme differ from one in which the government collects a $1.00 tax for each cup of coffee sold, and divides the total tax collections equally among all coffee vendors? (It is safe to assume that all coffee vendors are identical.)

Consumer Behavior

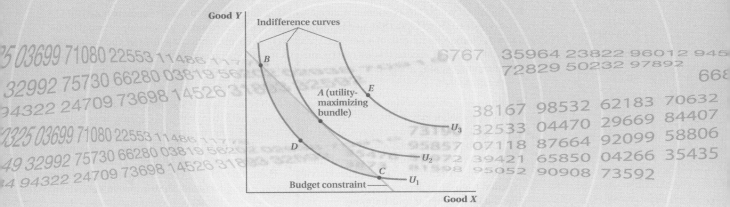

Suppose you're Jeff Bezos at Amazon in 2006, trying to develop the Kindle for introduction to the market the following year. What features do you want to include in this device to maximize profitability? Much of the answer to that question depends on consumers' preferences: what they like to read, where they read, their willingness to pay for screen size, and their distaste for carrying heavy objects, just to name a few examples. Your profitability will also depend on consumers' ability to pay—their income. If you can figure out how all those forces interact, Mr. Bezos, you can build an attractive, desirable digital text display device that could make you bazillions. (You must have figured well: Kindle books now outsell print books on

his chapter is about one key question: Given the seemingly unlimited array of products and services that consumers can buy, how do they decide which ones (and how much of each) to consume? In addition to serving as the building block for the demand curve in the basic supply and demand model, understanding the answer to this simple question is incredibly powerful and its potential applications are enormous.

Amazon, and while Amazon doesn't release figures on the number of devices it sells, some estimate that 8 million units sold in 2010, and Amazon's Kindle-generated revenue including both the devices and the books approached $5 billion a year.)

■ Suppose you manage a grocery store. Pepsi offers to cut your wholesale price if you run a promotion over the coming week. If you drop Pepsi prices by 20%, how much more shelf space should you give to Pepsi instead of Coke? How many customers will switch from buying Coke to Pepsi? How many customers who wouldn't have bought any soft drinks before the promotion will buy them now? Deciding how to handle this situation is another case in which understanding how consumers behave can help someone make the right decision and earn some profit by doing so.

■ Suppose you're an economic analyst working for a development nongovernmental organization (NGO) that needs projections of how a country's consumption patterns will change as its citizens become wealthier. Such projections will help the organization plan and create the infrastructure to move new goods to the country's growing markets. Again, a key part of the answer lies in understanding how consumers make their choices.

■ Suppose you are trying to decide whether to buy a ticket to see your favorite performer live or pay a share to rent a beach house with 10 friends for spring break. How do you make *all* your choices about what to spend your money on? Is your method of making such decisions "right," or could you do better? In this chapter, we examine some simple rules about how you (and other consumers) make choices. You might find that your decision-making methods violate these rules. If so, changing your behavior to take them into account will probably help you make decisions that improve your day-to-day well-being and happiness.

In addition to preparing you to analyze specific applications like these examples, this chapter illustrates a broader point about the study of economics. Like so many problems in economics (and life), the consumer's decision is a *constrained optimization* problem. Consumers try to do the best they can (they try to *optimize*) given that they are limited or *constrained* by the amount of money they have to spend. They have to make tradeoffs but do it in the smartest way they can. The set of techniques and ways of thinking we use to analyze consumers' constrained optimization problems will reappear over and over, in slightly modified ways and different settings, throughout this book and in any economics courses you may take in the future. If you become adept at solving the kind of constrained optimization problem we solve in this chapter, you will have gone a long way toward being able to answer *any* constrained optimization problem.

We begin the chapter by discussing the nature of consumers' preferences (what they like and don't like) and how economists use the concepts of utility—a measure of a consumer's well-being—and utility functions to summarize consumers' preferences. Consumers maximize their utility by trading off the purchase of one good against the purchase of others in a way that makes them the happiest. We'll see how such tradeoffs depend on a consumer's preferences, the amount of income the consumer has to spend, and the prices of the goods. Once we have these concepts in hand, we can combine them to analyze how real-world consumers behave, for example, why people buy less of something when its price rises (i.e., why demand curves slope down), and why they might consume not just more but different things as they become wealthier.

4.1 The Consumer's Preferences and the Concept of Utility

Consumers' preferences underlie every decision they make. Economists think of consumers as making rational choices about what they like best, given the constraints that they face when they make their choices.

Assumptions about Consumer Preferences

Consumers make many choices every day about what to buy and what not to buy. These choices involve many different goods: Buy a giant bag of Twizzlers and walk home, or buy a bus ticket and leave a sweet tooth unsatisfied? Buy a new video game or buy a new water pump for the car? Buy a ticket to the ball game or go to a bar for drinks with friends and watch the game on TV? To make it possible to understand how consumers form their preferences for thousands of goods and services, we need to make some simplifying assumptions. Specifically, we assume that all consumers' decisions about what to buy share four properties and that these properties help consumers determine their preferences over all the combinations of goods and services they might consume.

1. **Completeness and rankability.** This assumption implies consumers can make comparisons across all sets of goods that they consider. Economists use the term **consumption bundle** (or just *bundle*) to describe any collection of these goods. The assumption means that, given any two bundles, a consumer can determine whether she prefers the first bundle to the second bundle, the second to the first, or is indifferent between the two (i.e., views them equally). This assumption is important because it means that we can apply economic theory to any bundle of goods we want to discuss. Whether the bundle includes sapphires and SUVs; movies, motorcycles, modern art, and marshmallows; or iPods, Ikea furniture, and iceberg lettuce, the consumer can decide which bundle she likes better. This assumption does not, however, tell us what kinds of bundles the consumer will like more than others. It just implies she is able to determine if one is better than the other.

   > **consumption bundle**
   > A set of goods or services a consumer considers purchasing.

2. **For most goods, more is better than less (or at least more is no worse than less).** In general, we think that more of a good thing is good. If we like a car that is safe in a crash, we would like that car even better if it were even safer.[1] We also assume that consumers can discard unwanted goods at no cost, a concept economists call "free disposal." If you can get rid of things for free, then having more of something will never hurt you, even if it does not make you better off. The free disposal assumption may not always be strictly true in the real world, but it is a useful simplification in our basic economic model of consumer behavior.

3. **Transitivity.** For any three bundles of goods (call them A, B, and C), if a consumer prefers A to B and also prefers B to C, then the consumer must also prefer A to C. For example, if Claire prefers an apple to an orange, and prefers an orange to a banana, then transitivity implies that Claire must also prefer an apple to a banana. Note that, as always, we are holding everything else constant when making these comparisons. Transitivity does *not* mean that Claire has to prefer apples to bananas in all situations, but rather that at a given moment, she prefers apples to bananas. Transitivity imposes a logical consistency on the consumer.

4. **The more a consumer has of a particular good, the less she is willing to give up of something else to get even more of that good.** The idea behind this assumption is that consumers like variety. If you like birthday cake and haven't had cake lately, you might be willing to give up a lot for some cake. You might pay a high price for a cake, take the afternoon to bake a cake, or trade away your last carton of milk for some cake. On the other hand, if you've just polished off two-thirds of a cake, you are unlikely to be willing to pay much money for more, and you may very well want to trade the rest of the cake to get back some of that carton of milk. Like free disposal, it is possible to think of special cases in which the assumption of consumers liking variety will be violated

---

[1] There may come a point at which more of a good thing stops being better. Economists call this a *satiation point*. For instance, the first jelly bean may make us happy, but the 1,437th jelly bean might actually make us sick if we ate it, making us worse off than had we eaten only 1,436. However, because people can sometimes save extra jelly beans for later, trade them to someone else for something they want, or just give them away, satiation points tend not to be very important in practice.

(e.g., most people would prefer having either two water skis or two snow skis to having one of each). Nonetheless, we will almost always adopt this assumption because it holds true in a large number of situations and greatly simplifies our analysis.

The Concept of Utility

Given these assumptions about utility, we could create a list of a consumer's preferences between any bundles she might consume. The problem is that such a list would be a very long and unwieldy one. If we try to analyze a consumer's choices based on millions of pairwise comparisons over these bundles, we would get hopelessly lost.

Economists use the concept of utility and a mathematical relationship called a utility function to describe preferences more concisely. **Utility** describes how satisfied a consumer is. For practical purposes, you can think of utility as being a fancy word for happiness or well-being. It is important to realize that utility is *not* a measure of how rich a consumer is. Income may affect utility, but it is just one of many factors that do so.

A **utility function** summarizes the relationship between what consumers consume and their level of well-being. A function is a mathematical relationship that links a set of inputs to an output. For instance, if you combine the inputs eggs, flour, sugar, vanilla, butter, frosting, and candles in just the right way, you end up with the output of a birthday cake. In consumer behavior, the inputs to a utility function are the different things that can give a person utility. Examples of inputs to the utility function include traditional goods and services like cars, candy bars, health club memberships, and airplane rides. But there are many other types of inputs to utility as well, including scenic views, a good night's sleep, spending time with friends, and the pleasure that comes from giving to charity. The output of the utility function is the consumer's utility level. By providing a mapping between the bundles a consumer considers and a measure of the consumer's level of well-being—this bundle provides so much utility, that bundle provides so much utility, and so on—a utility function gives us a concise way to rank bundles.

Utility functions can take a variety of mathematical forms. Let's look at the utility someone enjoys from consuming Junior Mints and Milk Duds. Generically, we can write this utility level as $U = U(J, M)$, where $U(J, M)$ is the utility function and J and M are, respectively, the number of Junior Mints and Milk Duds the consumer eats. An example of a specific utility function for this consumer is $U = J \times M$. In this case, utility equals the product of the number of Junior Mints and Milk Duds she eats. But it could instead be that the consumer's (or maybe another consumer's) utility equals the total number of Junior Mints and Milk Duds eaten. In that case, the utility function is $U = J + M$. Yet another possibility is that the consumer's utility is given by $U = J^{0.7}M^{0.3}$. Because the exponent on Junior Mints (0.7) is larger than that on Milk Duds (0.3), this utility function implies that a given percentage increase in Junior Mints consumed will raise utility more than the same percentage increase in Milk Duds.

These are just a few examples from the large variety of possible utility functions we could imagine consumers having for these or any other combination of goods. At this point in our analysis of consumer behavior, we don't have to be too restrictive about the form any particular utility function takes. Because utility functions are used to represent preferences, however, they have to conform to our four assumptions about preferences (rankability and completeness, more is better, transitivity, and variety is important).

Marginal Utility

One of the most important concepts related to utility functions is **marginal utility,** the extra utility the consumer receives from a one-unit increase in consumption.[2] Each

utility
A measure of how satisfied a consumer is.

utility function
A mathematical function that describes the relationship between what consumers actually consume and their level of well-being.

marginal utility
The additional utility a consumer receives from an additional unit of a good or service.

[2] Marginal utility can be calculated for any given utility function.

good in a utility function has its own marginal utility. Using the Junior Mints and Milk Duds utility function, for example, the marginal utility of Junior Mints, MU_J, would be

$$MU_J = \frac{\Delta U(J, M)}{\Delta J}$$

where ΔJ is the small (one-unit) change in the number of Junior Mints the consumer eats and $\Delta U(J, M)$ is the change in utility she gets from doing so. Likewise, the marginal utility of consuming Milk Duds is given by

$$MU_M = \frac{\Delta U(J, M)}{\Delta M}$$

Later in this chapter, we see that marginal utility is the key to understanding the consumption choices a person makes.

Utility and Comparisons

One important but subtle point about the four preference assumptions is that they allow us to rank all bundles of goods for a particular consumer, but they do not allow us to determine how much more a consumer likes one bundle than another. In mathematical terms, we have an *ordinal* ranking of bundles (we can line them up from best to worst), but not a *cardinal* ranking (which would allow us to say exactly how much one bundle was preferred to another). The reason for this is that the units in which we measure utility are essentially arbitrary.

An example will make this clearer. Let's say we define a unit of measurement for utility that we call a "util." And let's say we have three bundles: A, B, and C, and a consumer who likes bundle A the most and bundle C the least. We might then assign these three bundles values of 8, 7, and 6 utils, respectively. The difficulty is that we just as easily could have assigned the bundles values of 8, 7, and 2 utils (or 19, 17, and 16 utils; or 67, 64, and 62 utils, etc.) and this would still perfectly describe the situation. Because there is no real-world unit of measure like dollars, grams, or inches with which to measure utility, we can shift, stretch, or squeeze a utility function without altering any of its observable implications, as long as we don't change the ordering of preferences over bundles.[3]

Does it matter that we have only an ordinal ranking of utility, rather than a cardinal ranking? For the most part, not really. We can still provide answers to the important questions about how individual consumers behave, and how this behavior results in a downward-sloping demand curve.

The one set of questions we will not be able to answer so easily is how to make *interpersonal comparisons*, that is, comparisons of one consumer's utility and another's. Based on utility functions alone, it's impossible to determine which consumer values, say, a set of concert tickets more, or whether society as a whole will be made better off if we take the tickets away from one consumer and give them to another. (We can determine, however, that if one person prefers, say, tickets to Concert A over tickets to Concert B, and the other person prefers Concert B to Concert A, then both consumers

---

[3] In mathematical parlance, these order-preserving shifts, squeezes, or stretches of a utility function are called *monotonic* transformations. Any monotonic transformation of a utility function will imply exactly the same preferences for the consumer as the original utility function. Consider our first example of a utility function from consuming Junior Mints and Milk Duds, $U = J \times M$. Suppose that it were $U = 8J \times M + 12$ instead. For any possible bundle of Junior Mints and Milk Duds, this new utility function will imply the same ordering of the consumer's utility levels as would the old function. (You can put in a few specific numbers to test this.) Because the consumer's relative preferences don't change, she will make the same decisions on how much of each good to consume with either utility function.

∂ The online appendix explores the mathematics of monotonic transformations of utility functions. (http://glsmicro.com/appendices)

will be better off if we give the tickets to Concert A to the first person and the tickets to Concert B to the second.) These important questions are addressed in the area known as **welfare economics,** which we discuss in several places in the book. For now, however, we focus on one consumer at a time.

Just as important as the assumptions we make regarding utility functions are the assumptions that we *do not* make. For one, we do not impose particular preferences on consumers. An individual is free to prefer dogs or ferrets as pets, just as long as the four preference assumptions are not violated. Moreover, we typically don't make value judgments about what consumers should or shouldn't prefer. It isn't "right" or "wrong" to like bluegrass music instead of R&B or classical; it is just a description of how a person feels. We also don't require that preferences remain constant over time. Someone may prefer sleeping to seeing a movie tonight, but tomorrow, the opposite may be true.

The concepts of utility and utility functions are general enough to let us account for a consumer's preferences over any number of goods and the various bundles into which they can be combined. As we proceed in building our model of consumer behavior, though, we focus on a simple model in which a consumer buys a bundle with only two goods. This approach is an easy way to see how things work, but the basic model works with more complicated situations, too. In the rare situations in which this is not the case, we will point out how and why things change once there are more than two goods.

welfare economics
The area of economics concerned with the economic well-being of society as a whole.

4.2 Indifference Curves

As we discussed in the previous section, the right way to think about utility is in relative terms; that is, in terms of whether one bundle of goods provides more or less utility to a consumer than another bundle. An especially good way of understanding utility is to take the special case in which a consumer is **indifferent** between bundles of goods. In other words, each bundle provides her with the same level of utility.

Consider the simple case in which there are only two goods to choose between, say, square feet in an apartment and the number of friends living in the same building. Michaela wants a large apartment, but also wants to be able to easily see her friends. First, Michaela looks at a 750-square-foot apartment in a building where 5 of her friends live. Next, she looks at an apartment that has only 500 square feet. For Michaela to be as happy in the smaller apartment as she would be in the larger apartment, there will have to be more friends (say, 10) in the building. Because she gets the same utility from both size/friend combinations, Michaela is indifferent between the two apartments. On the other hand, if her apartment were a more generous 1,000 square feet, Michaela would be willing to make do with (say) only 3 friends living in her building and feel no worse off.

Figure 4.1a graphs these three bundles. The square footage of the apartment is on the horizontal axis and number of friends is on the vertical axis. These are not the only three bundles that give Michaela the same level of utility; there are many different bundles that accomplish that goal—an infinite number of bundles, in fact, if we ignore that it might not make sense to have a fraction of a friend (or maybe it does!).

The combination of all the different bundles of goods that give a consumer the same utility is called an **indifference curve.** In Figure 4.1b, we draw Michaela's indifference curve, which includes the three points shown in Figure 4.1a. Notice that it contains not just the three bundles we discussed, but many other combinations of square footage and friends in the building. Also notice that it always slopes down: Every time we take away a friend from Michaela, we need to give her more square footage to leave her indifferent. (Equivalently, we could say every time we take away apartment space, we need to give her more friends in the building to keep her equally as well off.)

indifferent
The special case in which a consumer derives the same utility level from each of two or more consumption bundles.

indifference curve
A mathematical representation of the combination of all the different consumption bundles that provide a consumer with the same utility.

Figure 4.1 : **Building an Indifference Curve**

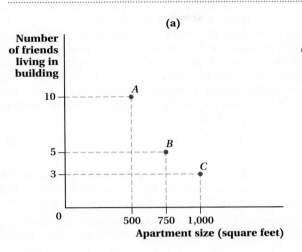

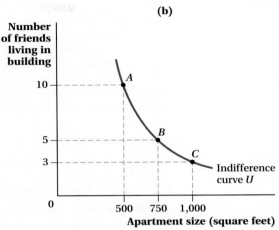

(a)

(b)

(a) Because Michaela receives utility from both the number of friends in her apartment building and the square footage of her apartment, she is equally happy with 10 friends in her building and a 500-square-foot apartment or 5 friends in her building and a 750-square-foot apartment. Likewise, she is willing to trade off 2 more friends in her building (leaving her with 3) to have a 1,000-square-foot apartment. These are three of many combinations of friends in her building and apartment size that make her equally happy.

(b) An indifference curve connects all bundles of goods that provide a consumer with the same level of utility. Bundles A, B, and C provide the same satisfaction for Michaela. Thus, the indifference curve represents Michaela's willingness to trade off between friends in her apartment building and the square footage of her apartment.

For each level of utility, there is a different indifference curve. Figure 4.2 shows two of Michaela's indifference curves. Which corresponds to the higher level of utility? The easiest way to figure this out is to think as a consumer would. One of the points on the indifference curve U_1 represents the utility Michaela would get if she had 5 friends

Figure 4.2 : **A Consumer's Indifference Curves**

Each level of utility has a separate indifference curve. Because we assume that more is preferred to less, an indifference curve lying to the right and above another indifference curve reflects a higher level of utility. In this graph, the combinations along curve U_2 provide Michaela with a higher level of utility than the combinations along curve U_1. Michaela will be happier with a 1,000-square-foot apartment than a 500-square-foot apartment, holding the number of friends living in her building equal at 5.

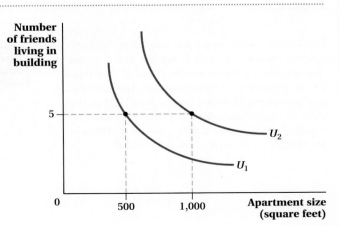

in her building and a 500-square-foot apartment. Curve U_2 includes a bundle with the same number of friends and a 1,000-square-foot apartment. By our "more is better" assumption, indifference curve U_2 must make Michaela better off. We could have instead held the apartment's square footage constant and asked which indifference curve had more friends in the building, and we would have found the same answer. Still another way of capturing the same idea is to draw a ray from the origin—zero units of both goods—through the two indifference curves. The first indifference curve the ray hits has bundles that give lower utility. Remember that by the definition of an indifference curve, utility is the same at every point on any given indifference curve, so we don't even need to check any other points on the two curves to know Michaela's utility is higher at every point on U_2 than at any point on U_1.

Characteristics of Indifference Curves

Generally speaking, the positions and shapes of indifference curves can tell us a lot about a consumer's behavior and decisions. However, our four assumptions about utility functions put some restrictions on the shapes that indifference curves can take.

1. **We can draw indifference curves.** The first assumption, completeness and rankability, means that we can always draw indifference curves: All bundles have a utility level, and we can rank them.

2. **We can figure out which indifference curves have higher utility levels and why they slope downward.** The "more is better" assumption implies that we can look at a set of indifference curves and figure out which ones represent higher utility levels. This can be done by holding the quantity of one good fixed and seeing which curves have larger quantities of the other good. This is exactly what we did when we looked at Figure 4.2. The assumption also implies that indifference curves never slope up. If they did slope up, this would mean that a consumer would be indifferent between a particular bundle and another bundle with more of *both* goods. There's no way this can be true if more is always better.

3. **Indifference curves never cross.** The transitivity property implies that indifference curves for a given consumer can never cross. To see why, suppose our apartment-hunter Michaela's hypothetical indifference curves intersect with one another, as shown in Figure 4.3. The "more is better" assumption implies she prefers bundle E to bundle D, because E offers both more square footage and more friends in her building than does D.

Figure 4.3   :   **Indifference Curves Cannot Cross**

Indifference curves cannot intersect. Here, Michaela would be indifferent between bundles D and F and also indifferent between bundles E and F. The transitivity property would therefore imply that she must also be indifferent between bundles D and E. But this can't be true, because more is preferred to less, and bundle E contains more of both goods (more friends in her building and a larger apartment) than D.

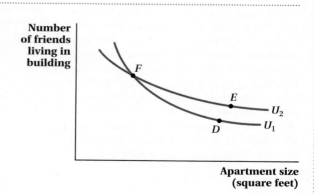

Now, because E and F are on the same indifference curve U_2, Michaela's utility from consuming either bundle must be the same by definition. And because bundles F and D are on the same indifference curve U_1, she must also be indifferent between *those* two bundles. But here's the problem: Putting this all together means she's indifferent between E and D, because each makes her just as well off as F. We know that can't be true. After all, she must like E more than D because it has more of both goods. Something has gone wrong. What went wrong is that we violated the transitivity property by allowing the indifference curves to cross. Intersecting indifference curves imply that the same bundle (the one located at the intersection) offers two different utility levels, which can't be the case.

4. **Indifference curves are convex to the origin.** The fourth assumption of utility—the more you have of a particular good, the less you are willing to give up of something else to get even more of that good—implies something about the way indifference curves are curved. Specifically, it implies they will be convex to the origin; that is, they will bend in toward the origin as if it is tugging on the indifference curve, trying to pull it in.

To see what this curvature means in terms of a consumer's behavior, let's think about what the slope of an indifference curve embodies. Again, we'll use Michaela as an example.

make the grade

Draw some indifference curves to really understand the concept

Indifference curves, like many abstract economic concepts, are often confusing to students when they are first introduced. But one nice thing about indifference curves is that preferences are the only thing necessary to draw your own indifference curves, and everybody has preferences! If you take just the few minutes of introspection necessary to draw your own indifference curves, the concept starts to make sense.

Start by selecting two goods that you like to consume—maybe your favorite candy bar, pizza, hours on Facebook, or trips to the movies (this is one of the nice things about economic models—they are designed to be very general). Next, draw a graph that has one good on the vertical axis and the other good on the horizontal axis (again, it doesn't matter which one goes where). The distance along the axis from the origin will measure the units of the good consumed (candy bars, slices of pizza, hours on Facebook, etc.).

The next step is to pick some bundle of these two goods that has a moderate amount of both goods, for instance, 12 pieces of candy and 3 slices of pizza. Put a dot at that point in your graph. Now carry out the following thought experiment. First, imagine taking a few pieces of candy out of the bundle and ask yourself how many additional slices of pizza you would need to leave you as well off as you are with 12 pieces of candy and 3 slices of pizza. Put a dot at that bundle. Then, suppose a couple more candy pieces are taken away, and figure out how much more pizza you would need to be "made whole." Put another dot there. Next, imagine taking away some pizza from the original 12-piece, 3-slice bundle, and determine how many extra candy pieces you would have to be given to be as well off as with the original bundle. That new bundle is another point. All those points are on the same indifference curve. Connect the dots, and you've drawn an indifference curve.

Now try starting with a different initial bundle, say, one with twice as many of both goods as the first bundle you chose. Redo the same thought experiment of figuring out the tradeoffs of some of one good for a certain number of units of the other good, and you will have traced out a second indifference curve. You can start with still other bundles, either with more or less of both goods, figure out the same types of tradeoffs, and draw additional indifference curves.

There is no "right" answer as to exactly what your indifference curves will look like. It depends on your preferences. However, their shapes should have the basic properties that we have discussed: downward-sloping, never crossing, and convex to the origin.

Figure 4.4 Tradeoffs Along an Indifference Curve

At point *A*, Michaela is willing to give up a lot of friends to get just a few more square feet, because she already has a lot of friends in the building but little space. At point *C*, Michaela has a large apartment but few friends around, so she now would require a large amount of space in return for a small reduction in friends to be left equally satisfied.

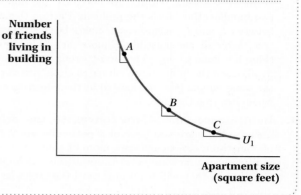

If the indifference curve is steep, as it is at point *A* in Figure 4.4, Michaela is willing to give up a lot of friends to get just a few more square feet of apartment space. It isn't just coincidence that she's willing to make this tradeoff at a point where she already has a lot of friends in the building but a very small apartment. Because she already has a lot of one good (friends in the building), she is less willing to give up the other good (apartment size) to have yet another friend. On the other hand, where the indifference curve is relatively flat, as it is at point *C* of Figure 4.4, the tradeoff between friends and apartment size is reversed. At *C*, the apartment is already big, but Michaela has few friends around, so she now needs to receive a great deal of extra space in return for a small reduction in friends to be left as well off.

Because tradeoffs between goods generally depend on how much of each good a consumer would have in a bundle, indifference curves are convex to the origin. Virtually every indifference curve we draw will have this shape. As we discuss later, however, there are some special cases in which either curvature disappears and indifference curves become straight lines, or where they become so curved that they have right angles.

The Marginal Rate of Substitution

Indifference curves are all about tradeoffs: how much of one good a consumer will give up to get a little bit more of another good. The slope of the indifference curve captures this tradeoff idea exactly. Figure 4.5 shows two points on an indifference curve that reflects Sarah's preferences for t-shirts and socks. At point *A*, the indifference curve is very steep, meaning Sarah will give up multiple t-shirts to get one more pair of socks. The reverse is true at point *B*. At that point, Sarah will trade multiple pairs of socks for just one more t-shirt. As a result of this change in Sarah's willingness to trade as we move along the indifference curve, the indifference curve is convex to the origin.

This shift in the willingness to substitute one good for another along an indifference curve might be a little confusing to you initially. You might be more familiar with thinking about the slope of a straight line (which is constant) than the slope of a curve (which varies at different points along the curve). Also, you might find it odd that preferences differ along an indifference curve. After all, a consumer isn't supposed to prefer one point on an indifference curve over another, but now we're saying the consumer's relative tradeoffs between the two goods change as one moves along the curve. Let's address each of these issues in turn.

Figure 4.5 | The Slope of an Indifference Curve Is the Marginal Rate of Substitution

The marginal rate of substitution measures the willingness of a consumer to trade one good for the other. It is measured as the negative of the slope of the indifference curve at any point. At point A, the slope of the curve is -2, meaning that the MRS is 2. This implies that, for that given bundle, Sarah is willing to trade 2 t-shirts to receive 1 more pair of socks. At point B, the slope is -0.5 and the MRS is 0.5. At this point, Sarah is only willing to give up 0.5 t-shirt to get another pair of socks.

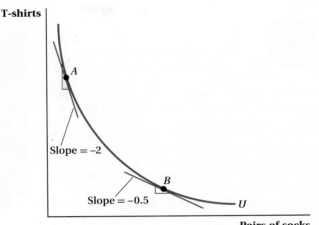

First, the slope of a curve, unlike a straight line, depends on where on the curve you are measuring the slope. To measure the slope of a curve at any point, draw a straight line that just touches the curve (but does not pass through it) at that point but nowhere else. This point where the line (called a tangent) touches the curve is called a tangency point. The slope of the line is the slope of the curve at the tangency point. The tangents that have points A and B as tangency points are shown in Figure 4.5. The slopes of those tangents are the slopes of the indifference curve at those points. At point A, the slope is -2, indicating that at this point Sarah would require 2 more t-shirts to give up 1 pair of socks. At point B, the slope is -0.5, indicating that at this point Sarah would require only half of a t-shirt to give up a pair of socks.

Second, although it's true that a consumer is indifferent between any two points on an indifference curve, that doesn't mean her relative preference for one good versus another is constant along the line. As we discussed above, Sarah's relative preference changes with the number of units of each good she already has.

Economists have a particular name for the slope of an indifference curve: the **marginal rate of substitution of X for Y (MRS_{XY})**. This is the rate at which a consumer is willing to trade off or substitute one good (the good on the horizontal axis) for another (the good on the vertical axis) and still be left equally well off:

$$MRS_{XY} = -\frac{\Delta Y}{\Delta X}$$

(A technical note: Because the slopes of indifference curves are negative, economists use the negative of the slope to make the MRS_{XY} a positive number.) The word "marginal" indicates that we are talking about the tradeoffs associated with small changes in the composition of the bundle of goods—that is, changes at the margin. It makes sense to focus on marginal changes because the willingness to substitute between two goods depends on where the consumer is located on her indifference curve.

Despite the intimidating name, the marginal rate of substitution is an intuitive concept. It tells us the relative value that a consumer places on obtaining a little more of the good on the horizontal axis, in terms of the good on the vertical axis. You make this kind of decision all the time. Whenever you order something off a menu at a restaurant, choose whether to ride a bicycle or drive, or decide on what brand of jeans to buy, you're evaluating relative values. As we see later in this chapter, when

marginal rate of substitution of X for Y (MRS_{XY})
The rate at which a consumer is willing to trade off one good (the good on the horizontal axis X) for another (the good on the vertical axis Y) and still be left equally well off.

freakonomics

Do Minnesotans Bleed Purple?

People from Minnesota *love* their football team, the Minnesota Vikings. You can't go anywhere in the state without seeing people dressed in purple and yellow, especially during football season. If there is ever a lull in a conversation with a Minnesotan, just bring up the Vikings and you can be certain the conversation will spring to life. What are the Vikings "worth" to their fans? The answer to that question is obvious: The Vikings are priceless. Or are they?

AP Photo/Paul Spinelli

There has often been discussion that the Vikings would leave the state because the owners were unhappy with the existing stadium. Two economists carried out a study to try to measure how much Minnesota residents cared about the Vikings.[*] The authors looked at the results of a survey that asked hundreds of Minnesotans how much their household would be willing to pay in extra taxes for a new stadium for the team. Every extra tax dollar for the stadium would be one less the household could spend on other goods, so the survey was in essence asking for the households' marginal rate of substitution of all other goods (as a composite unit) for a new Vikings stadium. Because it was widely perceived that there was a realistic chance the Vikings would leave Minnesota if they didn't get a taxpayer-funded stadium, these answers were also viewed as being informative about Minnesotans' marginal rate of substitution between all other goods and the Minnesota Vikings.[†]

It turns out that fan loyalty does know some limits. The average household in Minnesota was willing to pay $571.60 to keep the Vikings in Minnesota. Multiplying that value by the roughly 1.3 million households in Minnesota gives a total marginal value of about $750 million. In other words, Minnesotans were estimated to be willing to give up $750 million of consumption of other goods in order to keep the Vikings. That's a lot of money—imagine how much people might pay if the Vikings could actually win a Super Bowl.

Alas, stadiums aren't cheap. Officials estimate that a new stadium will cost about $1 billion. That might explain why a law passed by the state legislature in 2012 finally gave the Vikings the stadium they wanted but only agreed to provide $500 million of funding, with the team responsible for providing the remaining money.

The Los Angeles Vikings? Don't even bring up this possibility in conversation with a Minnesotan, unless, of course, you have a check for $571.60 that you're ready to hand over.

---

[*] John R. Crooker and Aju J. Fenn, "Estimating Local Welfare Generated by an NFL Team under Credible Threat of Relocation," *Southern Economic Journal* 76, no. 1 (2009): 198–223.

[†] An interesting feature of this study is that it measures consumers' utility functions using data on hypothetical rather than actual purchases. That is, no Minnesotan had had to actually give up consuming something else to keep the Vikings around. They were only answering a question about how much they would pay *if* it came time to actually make that choice. While economists prefer to measure consumers' preferences from their actual choices (believing actual choices to be a more reliable reflection of consumers' preferences), prospective choices are sometimes the only way to measure preferences for certain goods. An example of this is when economists try to measure the value of abstract environmental goods, such as species diversity.

prices are attached to goods, the consumer's decision about what to consume boils down to a comparison of the relative value she places on two goods and the goods' relative prices.

The Marginal Rate of Substitution and Marginal Utility

Consider point A in Figure 4.5. The marginal rate of substitution at point A is equal to 2 because the slope of the indifference curve at that point is -2:

$$MRS_{XY} = -\frac{\Delta Y}{\Delta X} = -\frac{\Delta Q_{\text{t-shirts}}}{\Delta Q_{\text{socks}}} = 2$$

Literally, this means that in return for 1 more pair of socks, Sarah is willing to give up 2 t-shirts. At point B, the marginal rate of substitution is 0.5, which implies that Sarah will sacrifice only half of a t-shirt for 1 more pair of socks (or equivalently, will sacrifice 1 t-shirt for 2 pairs of socks).

This change in the willingness to substitute between goods at the margin occurs because the benefit a consumer gets from another unit of a good tends to fall with the number of units she already has. If you already have all the bananas you can eat and hardly any kiwis, you might be willing to give up more bananas to get one additional kiwi.

Another way to see all this is to think about the change in utility (ΔU) created by starting at some point on an indifference curve and moving just a little bit along it. Suppose we start at point A and then move just a bit down and to the right along the curve. We can write the change in utility created by that move as the marginal utility of socks (the extra utility the consumer gets from a small increase in the number of socks consumed, MU_{socks}) times the increase in the number of socks due to the move (ΔQ_{socks}), plus the marginal utility of t-shirts ($MU_{\text{t-shirts}}$) times the decrease in the number of t-shirts ($\Delta Q_{\text{t-shirts}}$) due to the move. The change in utility is

$$\Delta U = MU_{\text{socks}} \times \Delta Q_{\text{socks}} + MU_{\text{t-shirts}} \times \Delta Q_{\text{t-shirts}}$$

where MU_{socks} and $MU_{\text{t-shirts}}$ are the marginal utilities of socks and t-shirts at point A, respectively. Here's the key: Because we're moving along an indifference curve (along which utility is constant), *the total change in utility from the move must be zero.* If we set the equation equal to zero, we get

$$0 = \Delta U = MU_{\text{socks}} \times \Delta Q_{\text{socks}} + MU_{\text{t-shirts}} \times \Delta Q_{\text{t-shirts}}$$

Rearranging the terms a bit will allow us to see an important relationship:

$$-MU_{\text{t-shirts}} \times \Delta Q_{\text{t-shirts}} = MU_{\text{socks}} \times \Delta Q_{\text{socks}}$$

$$-\frac{\Delta Q_{\text{t-shirts}}}{\Delta Q_{\text{socks}}} = \frac{MU_{\text{socks}}}{MU_{\text{t-shirts}}}$$

Notice that the left-hand side of this equation is equal to the negative of the slope of the indifference curve, or MRS_{XY}. We now can see a very significant connection: *The MRS_{XY} between two goods at any point on an indifference curve equals the inverse ratio of those two goods' marginal utilities*:

$$MRS_{XY} = -\frac{\Delta Q_{\text{t-shirts}}}{\Delta Q_{\text{socks}}} = \frac{MU_{\text{socks}}}{MU_{\text{t-shirts}}}$$

In more basic terms, MRS_{XY} shows the point we emphasized from the beginning: You can tell how much people value something by their choices of what they would be

∂ The end-of-chapter appendix uses calculus to derive the relationship between the marginal rate of substitution and marginal utilities.

willing to give up to get it. The rate at which they give things up tells you the marginal utility of the goods.

This equation gives us a key insight into understanding why indifference curves are convex to the origin. Let's go back to the example above. At point A in Figure 4.5, $MRS_{XY} = 2$. That means the marginal utility of socks is twice as high as the marginal utility of t-shirts. That's why Sarah is so willing to give up t-shirts for socks at that point—she will gain more utility from receiving a few more socks than she will lose from having fewer t-shirts. At point B, on the other hand, $MRS_{XY} = 0.5$, so the marginal utility of t-shirts is twice as high as that of socks. At this point, she's willing to give up many more socks for a small number of t-shirts.

As we see throughout the rest of this chapter, the marginal rate of substitution and its link to the marginal utilities of the goods play a key role in driving consumer behavior.

The Steepness of Indifference Curves

We've now established the connection between a consumer's preferences for two goods and the slope of her indifference curves (the MRS_{XY}). We have found that the slope of an indifference curve reveals a consumer's willingness to trade one good for another, or each good's relative marginal utility. We can flip this relationship on its head to see what the shapes of indifference curves tell us about consumers' utility functions. In this section, we discuss the two key characteristics of an indifference curve: how steep it is, and how curved it is.

Figure 4.6 presents two sets of indifference curves reflecting two different sets of preferences for concert tickets and MP3s. In panel a, the indifference curves are steep,

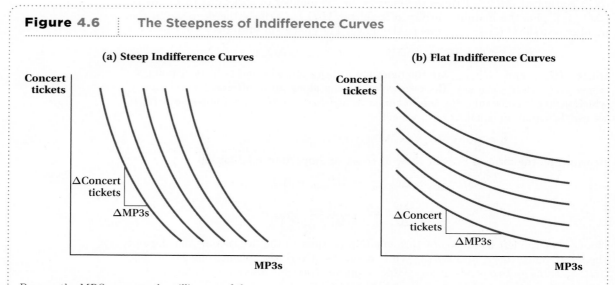

Figure 4.6 │ **The Steepness of Indifference Curves**

(a) Steep Indifference Curves

Concert tickets

ΔConcert tickets
ΔMP3s

MP3s

(b) Flat Indifference Curves

Concert tickets

ΔConcert tickets
ΔMP3s

MP3s

Because the MRS measures the willingness of the consumer to trade one good for another, we can tell a great deal about preferences by examining the shapes of indifference curves. (a) Indifference curves that are relatively steep indicate that the consumer is willing to give up a large quantity of the good on the vertical axis to get another unit of the good on the horizontal axis. Here, the consumer is willing to give up a lot of concert tickets for some additional MP3s. (b) Relatively flat indifference curves imply that the consumer would require a large increase in the good on the horizontal axis to give up a unit of the good on the vertical axis. The consumer with flat indifference curves will give up a lot of MP3s for one additional concert ticket.

while in panel b they are flat. (These two sets of indifference curves have the same degree of curvature so we don't confuse steepness with curvature.)

When indifference curves are steep, consumers are willing to give up a lot of the good on the vertical axis to get a small additional amount of the good on the horizontal axis. So a consumer with the preferences reflected in the steep indifference curve in panel a would part with many concert tickets for some more MP3s. The opposite is true in panel b, which shows flatter indifference curves. A consumer with such preferences would give up a lot of MP3s for one additional concert ticket. These relationships are just another way of restating the concept of the MRS_{XY} that we introduced earlier.

4.1 figure it out

Mariah consumes music downloads (M) and concert tickets (C). Her utility function is given by $U = 0.5M^2 + 2C^2$, where $MU_M = M$ and $MU_C = 4C$.

   a. Write an equation for MRS_{MC}

   b. Would bundles of ($M = 4$ and $C = 1$) and ($M = 2$ and $C = 2$) be on the same indifference curve? How do you know?

   c. Calculate MRS_{MC} when $M = 4$ and $C = 1$ and when $M = 2$ and $C = 2$.

   d. Based on your answers to question b, are Mariah's indifference curves convex? (*Hint*: Does MRS_{MC} fall as M rises?)

Solution:

   a. We know that the marginal rate of substitution MRS_{MC} equals MU_M/MU_C

We are told that $MU_M = M$ and that $MU_C = 4C$. Thus, $MRS_{MC} = \dfrac{MU_M}{MU_C} = \dfrac{M}{4C}$.

   b. For bundles to lie on the same indifference curve, they must provide the same level of utility to the consumer. Therefore we need to calculate Mariah's level of utility for the bundles of ($M = 4$ and $C = 1$) and ($M = 2$ and $C = 2$):

   When $M = 4$ and $C = 1$, $U = 0.5(4)^2 + 2(1)^2 = 0.5(16) + 2(1) = 8 + 2 = 10$

   When $M = 2$ and $C = 2$, $U = 0.5(2)^2 + 2(2)^2 = 0.5(4) + 2(4) = 2 + 8 = 10$

Each bundle provides Mariah with the same level of utility, so they must lie on the same indifference curve.

   c. and d. To determine if Mariah's indifference curve is convex, we need to calculate MRS_{MC} at both bundles. Then we can see if MRS_{MC} falls as we move down along the indifference curve (i.e., as M increases and C decreases).

   When $M = 2$ and $C = 2$, $MRS_{MC} = \dfrac{2}{(4)(2)} = \dfrac{2}{8} = \dfrac{1}{4} = 0.25$

   When $M = 4$ and $C = 1$, $MRS_{MC} = \dfrac{4}{(4)(1)} = \dfrac{4}{4} = 1$

These calculations reveal that, holding utility constant, when music downloads rise from 2 to 4, the MRS_{MC} rises from 0.25 to 1. This means that as Mariah consumes more music downloads and fewer concert tickets, she actually becomes *more* willing to trade concert tickets for additional music downloads! Most consumers would not behave in this way. This means that the indifference curve becomes steeper as M rises, not flatter. In other words, this indifference curve will be concave to the origin rather than convex, violating the fourth characteristic of indifference curves listed above.

theory and data

Indifference Curves of Phone Service Buyers

Harken back to ancient times—1999–2003—when broadband was still a novelty. Most households that wanted to connect to the Internet had to use something known as a dial-up connection. The way it worked was that you hooked your computer up to the phone line in your house, and when you wanted to connect to the Internet, your computer would dial the number of your local Internet service provider (ISP). Then you had to wait, often for a very long time, listening to your computer making a screeching, fingernails-on-a-blackboard sound as it attempted to make the connection. This call to your ISP tied up your phone line (you couldn't talk on the phone while you were connected to the Internet) and was charged just like any other call on your phone bill.

A study by economists Nicholas Economides, Katja Seim, and Brian Viard used data on New York consumers' choices of land-line phone services during 1999–2003 to measure consumer utility functions and indifference curves over two related goods: local and regional phone calls.[*] Their study gives us a clear example of how different types of consumers can have different marginal rates of substitution for the same set of goods. One of their key results is sketched out in the figure shown. The indifference curves of households with Internet access (Figure 4.7a), when drawn with local calls on the horizontal axis and regional calls on the vertical axis, are much steeper than the indifference curves of households without Internet access (Figure 4.7b). For example, they found that a typical household in their data (one of average size and income, owning at least one mobile phone, and making the average number of local and regional calls) had an *MRS* of local for regional calls of about 1.0 if the household had Internet access and 0.5 if it didn't. That means the Internet household would be willing to give up 1 regional call to get another local call and be no worse off. The non-Internet household, on the other hand,

---

Figure 4.7   New Yorkers' Preferences for Local and Regional Phone Calls, 1999–2003

(a) Households with Internet Service

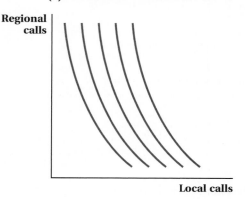

(b) Households without Internet Service

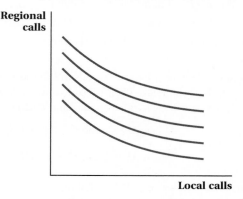

Households with dial-up Internet service (a) have a greater *MRS* (and steeper indifference curves) than households without Internet service (b). Accordingly, households with Internet service are more likely to use local minutes to purchase Internet usage, so they are less willing to trade local minutes for regional minutes.

[*] Nicholas Economides, Katja Seim, and V. Brian Viard, "Quantifying the Benefits of Entry into Local Phone Service," *RAND Journal of Economics* 39, no. 3 (2008): 699–730.

would have to get 2 extra local calls to be no worse off for giving up 1 regional call. (Note that there is nothing special about our choice to put local calls as the good on the horizontal axis and regional calls on the vertical axis. We could have swapped the goods and redrawn the graph.)

Can you guess why having Internet access raised households' *MRS* of local for regional calls? Remember that the *MRS* is the ratio of the household's marginal utility of local calls to the marginal utility of regional calls, or

$$MRS_{LR} = \frac{MU_{local}}{MU_{regional}}$$

If Internet households have higher *MRS* values, their marginal utility of local calls is larger relative to their marginal utility from regional calls. In other words, they obtain greater utility on the margin from consuming local calls than do non-Internet households. This difference in relative marginal utilities most likely reflected that most of these households connected to the Internet using dial-up connections. Every time they went online, they were making a billable local call to their ISP. Their desire to browse the Internet or send e-mails therefore raised the marginal utilities they received from making local calls, which explains the patterns Economides, Seim, and Viard found.

The Curvature of Indifference Curves: Substitutes and Complements

The steepness of an indifference curve tells us the rate at which a consumer is willing to trade one good for another. The curvature of an indifference curves also has a meaning. Suppose indifferences curves are almost straight, as in Figure 4.8a. In this case, a

---

Figure 4.8   The Curvature of Indifference Curves

(a) Almost Straight Indifference Curves

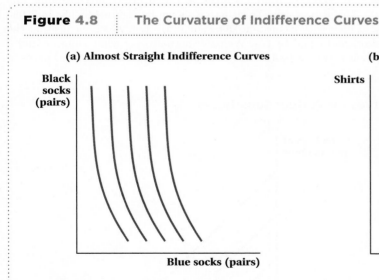

Black socks (pairs)

Blue socks (pairs)

(b) Very Curved Indifference Curves

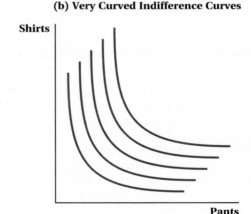

Shirts

Pants

The curvature of indifference curves reflects information about the consumer's preferences between two goods, just as its steepness does. (a) Goods that are highly substitutable (such as pairs of black socks and blue socks) are likely to produce indifference curves that are relatively straight. This means that the *MRS* does not change much as the consumer moves from one point to another along the indifference curve. (b) Goods that are complementary will generally have indifference curves with more curvature. For example, if Evan has many shirts and few pants, he will be willing to trade many shirts to get a pair of pants. If a consumer has many pants and few shirts, he will be less willing to trade a shirt for pants.

consumer (let's call him Evan) is willing to trade about the same amount of the first good (in this case, pairs of black socks) to get the same amount of the second good (pairs of blue socks), regardless of whether he has a lot of black socks relative to blue socks or vice versa. Stated in terms of the marginal rates of substitution, the *MRS* of black socks for blue ones doesn't change much as we move along the indifference curve. In practical terms, it means that the two goods are close substitutes for one another in Evan's utility function. That is, the relative value a consumer places on two substitute goods will typically not be very responsive to the amounts he has of one good versus the other. (It's no coincidence that we use in this example two goods, such as socks of two different colors, that many consumers would consider to be close substitutes for one another.)

On the other hand, for goods such as shirts and pants that are poor substitutes (Figure 4.8b) the relative value of one more pair of pants will be much greater when you have 10 shirts and no (or very few) pants than if you have 10 pairs of pants but no (or very few) shirts. In these types of cases, indifference curves are sharply curved, as shown. The *MRS* of shirts for pants is very high on the far left part of the indifference curve (where the consumer has few pants) and very low on the far right (when the consumer is awash in pants).

Perfect Substitutes   The intuition behind the meaning of the curvature of indifference curves may be easier to grasp if we focus on the most extreme cases, **perfect substitutes** and **perfect complements**. Figure 4.9 shows an example of two goods that might be perfect substitutes: 12-ounce bags of potato chips and 3-ounce bags of potato chips. If all the consumer cares about is the total amount of chips, then she is just as well off trading 4 small bags of chips for each large bag, regardless of how many of either she already has. These kinds of preferences produce linear indifference curves, and utility functions for perfect substitutes take on the general form $U = aX + bY$, where a and b are numbers that respectively indicate the marginal utility of consuming one more unit of X and Y. This is precisely the situation shown in Figure 4.9. The indifference curves are straight lines with a constant slope equal to $-1/4$, which means that the MRS_{XY} is also constant and equal to $1/4$. We can't actually say what values a and b take here, only that their ratio is 1 to 4—that is, $a/b = 1/4$. The indifference curves in

perfect substitute
A good that a consumer can trade for another good, in fixed units, and receive the same level of utility.

perfect complement
A good whose utility level depends on its being used in a fixed proportion with another good.

∂ The online appendix looks at the relationship between the utility function and the shape of indifference curves. (http://glsmicro.com/appendices)

Figure 4.9 : **Indifference Curves for Perfect Substitutes**

Two goods that are perfect substitutes have indifference curves that are straight lines. In this case, the consumer is willing to trade one 12-ounce bag of chips for four 3-ounce bags of chips no matter how many of each she currently has and the consumer's preference for chips does not change along the indifference curve. The *MRS* is constant in this case.

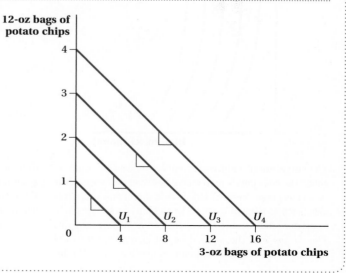

the figure would be the same if $a = 1$ and $b = 4$ or if $a = 40$ and $b = 160$, for instance. This is another demonstration of the point we made above: A transformation of a utility function that does not change the order of which goods the consumer prefers implies the same preference choices.

Different-sized packages of the same good are just one example of why two goods would be perfect substitutes.[4] Another way perfect substitutes might arise is if there are attributes of a product that a particular consumer does not care at all about. For instance, some people might not care about the color of their toothbrush, or whether a bottle of water is branded Aquafina or Dasani. Their indifference curves when comparing red and green toothbrushes or Aquafina and Dasani water would therefore be straight lines. On the other hand, other consumers who *do* care about such features would not view the goods as perfect substitutes, and their indifference curves would be curved.

It is crucial to understand that two goods being perfect substitutes does *not* necessarily imply that the consumer is indifferent between single items of the goods. In our potato chip example above, for instance, the consumer likes a big bag a lot more than a small bag. That's why the consumer would have to be given 4 small bags, not just 1, to be willing to trade away 1 large bag. The idea behind perfect substitutes is only that the tradeoff the consumer is willing to make between the two goods—that is, the marginal rate of substitution—doesn't depend on how much or little she already has of each but is instead constant at every point along an indifference curve.

Perfect Complements   When the utility a consumer receives from a good depends on its being used in fixed proportion with another good, the two goods are perfect complements. Figure 4.10 shows indifference curves for right and left shoes, which are an example of perfect complements (or at least something very close to it). Compare point A (2 right shoes and 2 left shoes) and point B (3 right shoes and 2 left shoes). Although the consumer has one extra shoe at point B, there is no matching shoe for

---

Figure 4.10   **Indifference Curves for Perfect Complements**

When goods are perfect complements, they have L-shaped indifference curves. For example, at point A, the consumer has 2 left shoes and 2 right shoes. Adding another right shoe while keeping left shoes constant does not increase the consumer's utility, so point B is on the same indifference curve as point A. In like manner, adding another left shoe will not increase the consumer's utility without an additional right shoe, so point C is on the same indifference curve as points A and B. Because shoes are always consumed together, 1 right shoe and 1 left shoe, the consumer's utility rises only when she has more of both goods (a move from point A to point D).

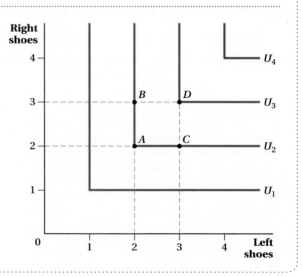

---

[4] You could think of reasons why the different-sized bags might not be perfect substitutes—maybe there's a convenience factor involved with the smaller ones because there's no need to worry about storing open, partially eaten bags. But even allowing for these small differences, they're fairly close to perfect substitutes.

the other foot, so the extra shoe is useless to her. She is therefore indifferent between these two bundles, and the bundles are on the same indifference curve. Similarly, comparing points A and C in the figure, we see that an extra left-footed shoe provides no additional utility if it isn't paired with a right-footed shoe, so A and C must also lie on the same indifference curve. However, if you add an extra left shoe *and* an extra right shoe (point D compared to point A), then the consumer is better off. That's why D is on a higher indifference curve.

Perfect complements lead to distinctive L-shaped indifference curves. Mathematically, this can be represented as $U = \min\{aX, bY\}$, where a and b are again numbers reflecting how consuming more units of X and Y affects utility. This mathematical structure means a consumer reaches a given utility level by consuming a minimum amount of each good X and Y. To be on the indifference curve U_2, for instance, the consumer must have *at least* 2 left shoes and 2 right shoes. The kink in the indifference curve is the point at which she is consuming the minimum amount of each good at that utility level.

This L-shape is the most extreme case of curvature of indifference curves. It is at the other extreme from the straight-line indifference curves that arise with perfect substitutes, and its shape produces interesting results for MRS_{XY}. The horizontal part of the indifference curve has MRS_{XY} equal to zero, while on the vertical portion, the marginal rate of substitution is infinite. As we've noted, indifference curves more generally will fall somewhere in between the shapes of the indifference curves for perfect substitutes and perfect complements, with some intermediate amount of curvature.

The proportion in which perfect complements are consumed need not be one-for-one, as in the case of our left- and right-shoe example. Chopsticks and Chinese buffet lunches might be perfect complements for some consumers, for example, but it's likely that they will be consumed in a proportion of 2 chopsticks to 1 buffet. It's hard to eat with just one chopstick.

Different Shapes for a Particular Consumer   One final point to make about the curvature of indifference curves is that even for a particular consumer, indifference curves may take on a variety of shapes depending on the utility level. They don't all have to look the same.

For instance, indifference curve U_A in Figure 4.11 is almost a straight line. This means that at low levels of utility, this consumer considers bananas and strawberries

---

Figure 4.11   **The Same Consumer Can Have Indifference Curves with Different Shapes**

Indifference curves for a consumer can take on a variety of shapes, depending on the utility level. For example, at low levels of utility, bananas and strawberries may be substitutes and the consumer may just want to buy fruit, not caring whether it is a banana or a strawberry. This means that the indifference curve will be fairly linear, as is the case of U_A. But, at higher levels of utility, the consumer may prefer to have a variety of fruit. This means that she will be willing to give up many bananas for another strawberry when she has a lot of bananas, but is not willing to do so when she only has only a few bananas. Here, the consumer's indifference curve will have more curvature, such as U_B.

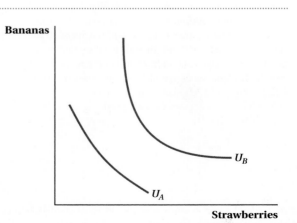

almost perfect substitutes. Her marginal rate of substitution barely changes whether she starts with a relatively high number of bananas to strawberries, or a relatively small number. If all she is worried about is surviving (which might be the case at really low utility levels like that represented by U_A), how something tastes won't matter much to her. She's not going to be picky about the mix of fruit she eats. This leads the indifference curve to be fairly straight, like U_A.

Indifference curve U_B, on the other hand, is very sharply curved. This means that at higher utility levels, the two goods are closer to perfect complements. When this consumer has plenty of fruit, she is more concerned with enjoying variety when she eats. This leads her to prefer some of each fruit rather than a lot of one or the other. If she already has a lot of one good, she will have to be given a very large additional amount of that good to make her willing to give up a unit of the good she has less of. This leads to the more curved indifference curve. Remember, though, that even as the shapes of a consumer's indifference curves vary with her utility levels, the indifference curves will never intersect.

4.2 figure it out

Jasmine can watch hours of baseball (B) or hours of reality shows (R) on TV. Watching more baseball makes Jasmine happier, but she really doesn't care about reality shows—good or bad. Draw a diagram showing a set of Jasmine's indifference curves for hours of baseball and hours of reality shows. (Put reality shows on the horizontal axis.) What is Jasmine's MRS_{RB} when she is consuming one unit of each good?

Solution:

The easiest way to diagram Jasmine's preferences is to consider various bundles of reality shows and baseball and determine whether they lie on the same or different indifference curves. For example, suppose she watches 1 hour of reality TV and 1 hour of baseball. Plot this in Figure A as point A. Now, suppose she watches 1 hour of reality TV and 2 hours of baseball. Plot this as point B. Because watching more hours of baseball makes Jasmine happier, point B must lie on a higher indifference curve than point A.

Now, try another point with 2 hours of reality TV and 1 hour of baseball. Call this point C. Now, compare point A with point C. Point C has the same number of hours of baseball as point A, but provides Jasmine with more reality TV. Jasmine neither likes nor dislikes reality TV, however, so her utility is unchanged by having more reality TV. Points A and C must therefore lie on the same indifference curve.

This would also be true of points D and E. Economists often refer to a good that has no impact on utility as a "neutral good."

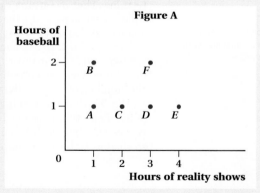

Figure A

Looking at Figure A, we see that there will be an indifference curve that is a horizontal line going through points A, C, D, and E. Will all of the indifference curves be horizontal lines? Let's consider another bundle to make sure. Suppose that Jasmine watches 3 hours of reality TV and 2 hours of baseball, as at point F. It is clear that Jasmine will prefer point F to point D because she gets more baseball. It should also be clear that Jasmine will be equally happy between points B and F; she has the same hours of baseball, and reality shows have no effect on her utility. As shown in Figure B, points B and F lie on the same indifference curve (U_2) and provide a greater level of utility than the bundles on the indifference curve below (U_1).

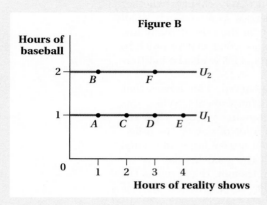

Figure B

To calculate the marginal rate of substitution when Jasmine is consuming one unit of each good, we need to calculate the slope of U_1 at point A. Because the indifference curve is a horizontal line, the slope is zero. Therefore, MRS_{RB} is zero. This makes sense; Jasmine is not willing to give up any baseball to watch more reality TV because reality TV has no impact on her utility. Remember that MRS_{RB} equals MU_R/MU_B. Because MU_R is zero, MRS_{RB} will also equal zero.

 application

Indifference Curves for "Bads"

All of the indifference curves we've drawn are for goods that a consumer likes and wants to consume. But sometimes we want to analyze consumer behavior with regard to things that a consumer doesn't want to consume—like air pollution, illness, commute time, or rutabagas. Instead of goods, these things are **bads,** things that would reduce a consumer's utility if she consumed more of them.

bad
A good or service that provides a consumer with negative utility.

Let's go back to Michaela and her apartment from Figure 4.2 and replace apartment size with distance to work. Greater distance to work is a bad because Michaela's commute time increases. Michaela's indifference curves between commute time (a bad) and the number of friends living in the building (a good) are shown in Figure 4.12.

We see that the result is that indifference curves now slope upward, not downward. Why? Let's first consider bundles A and B, which lie on the same indifference curve, U_1. Notice how bundle B has more commute time than A. Michaela doesn't like to commute, so she has to be given more friends at B to be as well off as she was at point A (in other

Figure 4.12   Indifference Curves for a "Bad"

An economic "bad" is a product that reduces a consumer's (Michaela's) utility falls as commute time increases. Therefore, to keep Michaela's utility constant, we must provide her with more friends in the building if we increase her commute time. This leads to upward-sloping indifference curves. Indifference curve U_2 provides more utility than U_1, because (holding friends constant) bundle B has more commute time than bundle C, making Michaela worse off. Alternatively, points A and C provide her with a constant amount of commute time, but she has more friends at point C. Thus, Michaela is better off at point C (on U_2) than at point A (on U_1).

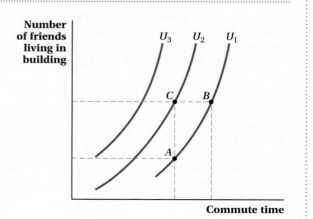

Figure 4.13   Indifference Curves for the Absence of a "Bad"

An economic "bad" can be converted into a "good." By changing the economic bad of "commute time" into the economic good of "saved commute time," we can have two goods that Michaela desires and produce typical downward-sloping, convex indifference curves. Michaela's utility increases with either an increase in the number of friends in the building or an increase in the amount of saved commute time.

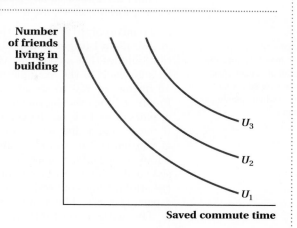

---

words, to keep her on the same indifference curve). Thus, Michaela receives the same level of utility from bundles A and B even though B has more of both products (we use the term "product" loosely). Bundle C has more friends than bundle A but the same commute time, so C must be preferred to A. Indifference curves that lie higher (more friends) and to the left (less commute time) indicate greater levels of utility. So do bads violate our assumption that more is better? Not really. We can keep all of our original assumptions by defining a particular good as an absence or reduction of a bad. In the case of commute time, "saved commute time" is a good. Graphing Michaela's indifference curves in terms of saved commute time—the opposite of a bad—produces the standard, downward-sloping indifference curves we've been working with, as in Figure 4.13. ■

4.3 The Consumer's Income and the Budget Constraint

In the preceding sections, we analyzed how a consumer's preferences can be described by a utility function, why indifference curves are a convenient way to think about utility, and how the slope of the indifference curve—known as the marginal rate of substitution—captures the relative utility that a consumer derives from different goods at the margin. Our ultimate goal in this chapter is to understand how consumers maximize their utility by choosing a bundle of goods to consume. Because consumers do not have an infinite amount of money and because goods are not free, consumers must make tradeoffs when deciding how much of each good to consume. That decision depends not only on the utility consumers get from each good, but also on how much money they have to spend and on the prices of the goods. We have to analyze the interaction among all of these factors.

We start looking at the interactions of utility, income, and prices by making some assumptions. To keep things simple, we continue to focus on a model with only two goods.

1. Each good has a fixed price, and any consumer can buy as much of a good as she wants at that price if she has the income to pay for it. We can make this assumption because each consumer is only a small part of the market for a good, so her consumption decision will not affect the equilibrium market price.

2. The consumer has some fixed amount of income to spend.

3. For now, the consumer cannot save or borrow. Without borrowing, she can't spend more than her income in any given period. With no saving, it means that unspent money is lost forever, so it's use it or lose it.

To incorporate prices and the consumer's income into our model of consumer behavior, we use a **budget constraint.** This constraint describes the entire set of consumption bundles that a consumer can purchase by spending all of her money. For instance, let's go back to the example of Sarah and her t-shirts and socks. Suppose Sarah has an income of $50 to spend on t-shirts (which cost $10 each) and socks ($5 a pair). Figure 4.14 shows the budget constraint corresponding to this example. The number of pairs of socks is on the horizontal axis; the number of t-shirts is on the vertical axis. If Sarah spends her whole income on socks, then she can consume 10 pairs (10 pairs at $5 each is $50) and no t-shirts. This combination is point A in the figure. If instead Sarah spends all her money on t-shirts, she can buy 5 shirts and no socks, a combination shown at point B. Sarah can purchase any combination of t-shirts and socks that lies on the straight line connecting these two points. For example, she could buy 3 t-shirts and 4 pairs of socks. This is point C.

The mathematical formula for a budget constraint is

$$\text{Income} = P_X Q_X + P_Y Q_Y$$

where P_X and P_Y are the prices for one unit of goods X and Y (pairs of socks and t-shirts in our example) and Q_X and Q_Y are the quantities of the two goods. The equation simply says that the total expenditure on the two goods (the per-unit price of each good multiplied by the number of units purchased) equals the consumer's total income.

Any combination of goods on or below the budget constraint (i.e., any point between the origin and the budget constraint, including those on the constraint itself) is **feasible,** meaning that the consumer can afford to buy the bundle with her income. Any points above and to the right of the budget line are **infeasible.** These bundles are beyond the reach of the consumer's current income. Figure 4.14 shows the feasible and infeasible bundles for the budget constraint $50 = 5Q_{\text{socks}} + 10Q_{\text{t-shirts}}$.

The budget constraint in Figure 4.14 is straight, not curved, because we assumed Sarah can buy as much as she wants of a good at a set price per unit. Whether buying the first pair of socks or the tenth, the price is assumed to be the same. As we'll see

budget constraint
A curve that describes the entire set of consumption bundles a consumer can purchase when spending all income.

feasible bundle
A bundle that the consumer has the ability to purchase; lies on or below the consumer's budget constraint.

infeasible bundle
A bundle that the consumer cannot afford to purchase; lies to the right and above a consumer's budget constraint.

Figure 4.14   The Budget Constraint

The budget constraint demonstrates the options available to a consumer given her income and the prices of the two goods. The horizontal intercept is the quantity of socks the consumer could afford if she spent all of her income (I) on socks, I/P_{socks}. The vertical intercept is the quantity of her t-shirts she could afford if she spent all of income on t-shirts, $I/P_{\text{t-shirts}}$. Given this, the slope of the budget constraint is the negative of the ratio of the two prices, $-P_{\text{socks}}/P_{\text{t-shirts}}$.

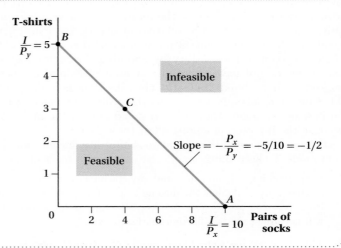

later, if the goods' prices change with the number of units purchased, the budget line will change shape depending on the amount of the goods purchased.

The Slope of the Budget Constraint

The relative prices of the two goods determine the slope of the budget constraint. Because the consumer spends all her money when she is on the budget constraint, if she wants to buy more of one good and stay on the constraint, she has to buy less of the other. Relative prices pin down the rate at which purchases of the two goods can be traded off between one another. If she wants to buy 1 more t-shirt (a cost of $10), for example, she'll have to buy 2 fewer pairs of socks at $5.

We can see the equivalence between relative prices and the slope of the budget constraint by rearranging the budget constraint:

$$\text{Income} = P_X Q_X + P_Y Q_Y$$

$$P_Y Q_Y = \text{Income} - P_X Q_X$$

$$Q_Y = \frac{\text{Income}}{P_Y} - \frac{P_X}{P_Y} Q_X$$

The equation shows if Q_X—the quantity purchased of good X—increases by one unit, the quantity of good Y or Q_Y that can be bought falls by P_X/P_Y. This ratio of the price of good X relative to the price of good Y is the negative of the slope of the budget constraint. It makes sense that this price ratio determines the slope of the constraint. If good X is expensive relative to good Y (i.e., P_X/P_Y is large), then buying additional units of X will mean you must give up a lot of good Y. In this case, the budget constraint will be steep. If on the other hand, good X is relatively inexpensive, you don't have to give up a lot of Y to buy more X, and the constraint will be flat.

We can use the equation for the budget constraint (Income $= P_X Q_X + P_Y Q_Y$) to find its slope and intercepts. Using the budget constraint ($50 = 5Q_{\text{socks}} + 10Q_{\text{t-shirts}}$) shown in Figure 4.14, we get

$$50 = 5Q_X + 10Q_Y$$

$$10Q_Y = 50 - 5Q_X$$

Dividing each side by 10—the price of Q_Y—yields a slope of $-1/2$:

$$Q_Y = 5 - \frac{1}{2} Q_X$$

As we noted earlier, if Sarah spends all her income on socks, she will buy 10 pairs of socks (the x-intercept), while she can purchase 5 t-shirts (the y-intercept) using all of her income. These relative prices and intercepts are shown in Figure 4.14.

As will become clear when we combine indifference curves and budget constraints in the next section, the slope of the budget constraint turns out to play an incredibly important role in determining what consumption bundles maximize consumers' utility levels.

Factors That Affect the Budget Constraint's Position

Because relative prices determine the slope of the budget constraint, changes in relative prices will change its slope. Figure 4.15a demonstrates what happens to our example budget constraint if the price of socks doubles to $10 per pair. The budget constraint rotates clockwise around the vertical axis, becoming twice as steep. That's because P_X/P_Y doubles (because P_X doubles). If Sarah spends all her money on socks, then the doubling of the price of socks means she can buy only half as many with the same income (the 5 pairs shown at A', rather than 10 pairs as before). If, on the other hand, she spends all her money on t-shirts (point B), then the change in socks' prices doesn't affect the bundle she can consume. That's because the price of t-shirts is still the same ($10). Notice that after the price increase, the set of feasible consumption bundles is smaller: There are now fewer combinations of goods that Sarah can afford with her income.

If instead the price of a t-shirt doubles to $20, but pairs of socks remain at their original $5 price (as in Figure 4.15b), then the budget constraint's movement is reversed: The budget constraint rotates counterclockwise around the horizontal axis, becoming half as steep. Someone who wants to buy only socks is unaffected, whereas someone who wants only t-shirts can obtain only half as many (if you could buy a half a t-shirt, that is; we'll assume you can for now), at bundle B'. Notice that this price increase also shrinks the feasible set of bundles just as the socks' price increase did. Always remember that when the price *rises*, the budget constraint rotates toward the origin, and when the price *falls*, it rotates away from the origin.

Now suppose Sarah's income falls by half (to $25) and prices stay at their original levels. With only half the income, Sarah can buy only half as many pairs of socks and t-shirts as she could before. If she spends everything on socks, she can now buy only 5 pairs. If she buys only t-shirts, she can afford 2.5. But because relative prices haven't changed, the tradeoffs between the goods haven't changed. To buy 1 more t-shirt, Sarah still has to give up 2 pairs of socks. Thus, the slope of the budget constraint remains the same. This new budget constraint is shown in Figure 4.15c.

Figure 4.15   The Effects of Price or Income Changes on the Budget Constraint

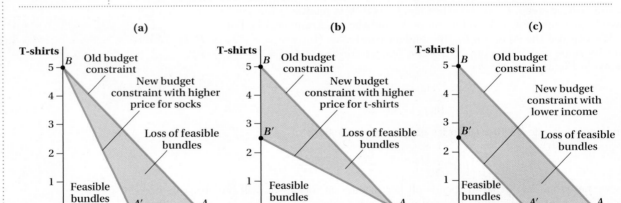

(a) When the price of socks increases, the horizontal intercept (I/P_{socks}) falls, the slope $(-P_{socks}/P_{t\text{-}shirts})$ gets steeper, the budget constraint rotates toward the origin, and the consumer (Sarah) has a smaller set of socks and t-shirt combinations from which to choose. The higher price for socks means that she can buy fewer socks, or if she purchases the same number of socks, she has less money remaining to buy t-shirts.
(b) When the price of t-shirts increases, the vertical intercept $(I/P_{t\text{-}shirts})$ falls, the slope $(-P_{socks}/P_{t\text{-}shirts})$ gets flatter, the budget constraint rotates toward the origin, and again, Sarah has a smaller choice set. The higher price for t-shirts means

that she can buy fewer t-shirts and, for a given purchase of t-shirts, she has less money available to buy socks.
(c) When Sarah's income is reduced, both the horizontal and vertical intercepts fall and the budget constraint shifts in. The horizontal intercept is lower because income I falls; thus, (I/P_{socks}) falls. The same holds for the vertical axis. Because the movement along both axes is caused by the change in income (the reduction in I is the same along both axes), the new budget constraint is parallel to the initial budget constraint. Given a reduction in income, Sarah's choice set is reduced.

Note that had both prices doubled while income stayed the same, the budget constraint would be identical to the new one shown in Figure 4.15c. We can see this more clearly if we plug in $2P_X$ and $2P_Y$ for the prices in the slope-intercept format of the budget constraint:

$$Q_Y = \frac{\text{Income}}{2P_Y} - \frac{2P_X}{2P_Y}Q_X$$

$$Q_Y = \frac{1}{2}\left(\frac{\text{Income}}{P_Y}\right) - \frac{P_X}{P_Y}Q_X$$

In both the figure and the equation, this type of change in prices decreases the purchasing power of the consumer's income, shifting the budget constraint inward. The same set of consumption bundles is feasible in either case. If Sarah's income had increased rather than decreased as in our example (or the prices of both goods had fallen in the same proportion), the budget constraint would have shifted out rather than in. Its slope would remain the same, though, because the relative prices of t-shirts and socks have not changed.

We've now considered what happens to the budget constraint in two situations: when income changes while prices stay constant and when prices change, holding income constant. What happens when prices and income both go up proportionally (e.g., all prices double and income doubles)? The budget constraint doesn't change at all. You have double the money, but because everything costs twice as much, you can only achieve the same bundles you could before the change in price and income. You can see this mathematically in the equation for the budget constraint above: If you multiply all prices and income by whatever positive constant you want (call this constant k), all the k's will cancel out, leaving you with the original equation.

4.3 figure it out

Braden has $20 per week that he can spend on video game rentals (R), priced at $5 per game, and candy bars (C), priced at $1 each.

   a. Write an equation for Braden's budget constraint and draw it on a graph that has video game rentals on the horizontal axis. Be sure to show both intercepts and the slope of the budget constraint.

   b. Assuming he spends the entire $20, how many candy bars does Braden purchase if he chooses to rent 3 video games?

   c. Suppose that the price of a video game rental falls from $5 to $4. Draw Braden's new budget line (indicating intercepts and the slope).

Solution:
   a. The budget constraint represents the feasible combinations of video game rentals (R) and candy bars (C) that Braden can purchase given the current prices and his income. The general form of the budget constraint would be Income $= P_R R + P_C C$. Substituting in the actual prices and income, we get $20 = 5R + 1C$.

To diagram the budget constraint (see the next page), first find the horizontal and vertical intercepts. The horizontal intercept is the point on Braden's budget constraint where he spends all of his $20 on video game rentals. The x-intercept is at 4 rentals ($20/$5), point A on his budget constraint. The vertical intercept represents the point where Braden has used his entire budget to purchase candy bars. He could purchase 20 candy bars ($20/$1) as shown at point B. Because the prices of candy bars and video game rentals are the same no matter how many Braden buys, the budget constraint is a straight line that connects these two points.

The slope of the budget constraint can be measured by the rise over the run. Therefore, it is equal to $\frac{\Delta C}{\Delta R} = -\frac{20}{4} = -5$. We can check our work by recalling that the slope of the budget constraint is equal to the negative of the ratio of the two prices or $-\frac{P_R}{P_C} = -\frac{5}{1} = -5$. Remember that the slope of the budget constraint shows the rate at which Braden is able to exchange candy bars for video game rentals.

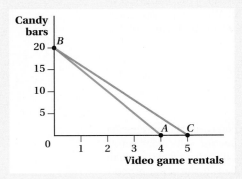

b. If Braden currently purchases 3 video game rentals, that means he spends \$15 (= \$5 × 3) on them. This leaves \$5 (= \$20 − \$15) for purchasing candy bars. At a price of \$1 each, Braden purchases 5 candy bars.

c. When the price of a video game rental falls to \$4, the vertical intercept is unaffected. If Braden chooses to spend his \$20 on candy bars, at a price of \$1, he can still afford to buy 20 of them. Thus, point B will also be on his new budget constraint. However, the horizontal intercept increases from 4 to 5. At a price of \$4 per rental, Braden can now afford 5 rentals if he chooses to allocate his entire budget to rentals (point C). His new budget constraint joins points B and C.

The slope of the budget constraint is $\dfrac{\Delta C}{\Delta R} = -\dfrac{20}{5} = -4$. Note that this equals the inverse price ratio of the two goods $\left(-\dfrac{P_R}{P_C} = -\dfrac{4}{1} = -4 \right)$.

Nonstandard Budget Constraints

In all the examples so far, the budget constraint has been a straight line. There are some cases in which the budget constraint would be kinked instead.

Quantity Discounts Suppose Alex spends his \$100 income on pizzas and phone calls. A pizza costs \$10; if he spends everything on pizzas, he can buy 10. If the price of phone minutes is constant at 10 cents per minute, he can buy as many as 1,000 minutes of phone time. Figure 4.16 portrays this example graphically. The budget constraint in the case where minutes are priced at a constant 10 cents is given by the solid section of the line running from zero minutes and 10 pizzas up to 1,000 minutes and zero pizzas.

Phone plans often offer quantity discounts on goods such as phone minutes. With a quantity discount, the price the consumer pays per unit of the good depends on the number of units purchased. If Alex's calling plan charges 10 cents per minute for the first 600 minutes per month and 5 cents per minute after that, his budget constraint will have a kink. In particular, because phone minutes become cheaper above 600 minutes, the actual budget constraint has a kink at 600 minutes and 4 pizzas. Because the price of the good on the y-axis (phone minutes) becomes relatively cheaper, the constraint rotates clockwise at that quantity, becoming steeper. To find where the budget constraint intercepts the vertical axis, we have to figure out how many minutes Alex can buy if he buys only cell phone time. This total is 1,400 minutes [(600 × \$0.10) + (800 × \$0.05) = \$100]. In Figure 4.16, the resulting budget constraint runs from 10 pizzas and zero minutes to 4 pizzas and 600 minutes (part of the solid line) and then continues up to zero pizzas and 1,400 minutes (the dashed line). It's clear from the figure that the lower price for phone time above the 600-minute threshold means that Alex can afford a set of phone minute and pizza combinations (the triangle above the initial budget constraint and below the dashed line) that he could not afford when phone minutes had a constant price of 10 cents.

Quantity Limits Another way a budget constraint can be kinked is if there is a limit on how much of one good can be consumed. For example, during World War II in the United States, certain goods like sugar and butter were rationed. Each family could buy only a limited quantity. During the oil price spikes of the 1970s, gas stations

Figure 4.16 : Quantity Discounts and the Budget Constraint

When the price of phone minutes is constant at 10 cents per minute, Alex's budget constraint for phone minutes and pizza has a constant slope, as represented by the solid line. If the phone company offers a quantity discount on phone minutes, however, Alex's budget constraint will be kinked. Here, Alex's calling plan charges 10 cents per minute for the first 600 minutes per month and 5 cents per minute after that, resulting in the kink at 600 phone minutes shown by the dashed line. The triangle above the initial budget constraint and below the dashed line represents the set of phone minute and pizza combinations Alex can afford under the new pricing scheme that he could not have purchased at a constant price of 10 cents per minute.

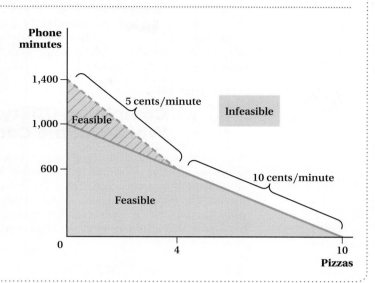

often limited the amount of gasoline people could buy. These limits have the effect of creating a kinked budget constraint.[5]

Suppose that the government (or maybe his parents, if he lives at home) dictates that Alex can talk on the phone for no more than 600 minutes per month. In that case, the part of the budget constraint beyond 600 minutes becomes infeasible, and the constraint becomes horizontal at 600 minutes, as shown by the solid line in Figure 4.17.

Figure 4.17 : Quantity Limits and the Budget Constraint

When there is a limit on how much of a good a person can consume, a budget constraint will be kinked. When Alex is limited to 600 minutes on the phone per month, his budget constraint is horizontal at that quantity. The triangle above the horizontal section of the budget constraint and below the dashed line represents the set of phone minutes and pizzas that are now infeasible for Alex to buy. Note that Alex can still afford these sets since his income and the prices have not changed, but the restrictions on how much he can purchase dictate that he cannot buy them.

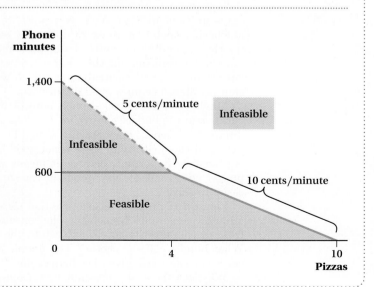

---

[5] Note that limits on how much a consumer can purchase are a lot like the quotas we learned about in Chapter 3, except now they apply to a single consumer, rather than to the market as a whole.

Note that neither Alex's income nor any prices have changed in this example. He still has enough money to reach any part in the area below the dashed section of the budget constraint that is labeled infeasible. He just isn't allowed to spend it. Consequently, for the flat part of the budget constraint, he will have unspent money left over. As we see in the next section, you will never actually want to consume a bundle on the flat part of the budget constraint. (You might want to see if you can figure out why yourself, before we tell you the answer.)

4.4 Combining Utility, Income, and Prices: What Will the Consumer Consume?

We now have in place all the pieces necessary to determine how much of each good a utility-maximizing consumer will consume. We know the consumer's preferences over all possible bundles of goods from the utility function and its associated indifference curves. The budget constraint shows us which bundles are feasible and which are beyond the consumer's reach given her income and the goods' prices. It's just a matter of combining this information in the right way.

Solving the Consumer's Optimization Problem

As we mentioned in the introduction to this chapter, the choice of how much to consume (like so many economic decisions) is a *constrained optimization* problem. There is something you want to maximize (utility, in this case), and there is something that limits how much of the good thing you can get (the budget constraint, in this case). And as we will see in the next chapter, the constrained optimization problem forms the basis of the demand curve.

Before we try to solve this constrained optimization problem, let's think for a minute about what makes it a tricky problem: It requires us to make comparisons between things (e.g., income and prices) measured in dollars and things (e.g., consumer utility) measured in imaginary units that we can't directly translate into dollars. How can you know whether or not you're willing to pay $3 to get some extra units of utility? Well, you can't, really. What you can figure out, however, is whether spending an extra dollar on, say, golf balls gives you more or less utility than spending an extra dollar on something else, like AAA batteries. It turns out that in figuring out this choice, you and other consumers use your indifference curves and budget constraints in such a way that solving the consumer's optimization problem becomes straightforward.

Maybe you didn't take much note of it earlier when we introduced indifference curves and the budget constraint, but look now at the axes we use to depict these two different concepts. They are the same: The quantity of some good is on the vertical axis, and the quantity of some other good is on the horizontal axis. This arrangement is extremely important, because it means we can display indifference curves and the budget constraint for two goods in the same graph, making the consumer's problem easier to solve.

Figure 4.18 presents an example that shows a combination of indifference curves and a budget constraint. Remember, the consumer wants to get as much utility as possible from consuming the goods, subject to the limits imposed by her budget constraint. What bundle will she choose? The bundle at point *A*. That's the highest indifference curve she can reach given her budget line.

Why is *A* the utility-maximizing consumption bundle? Compare point *A* to another feasible bundle, such as *B*. Point *B* is on the budget constraint, so the consumer can

Figure 4.18 : **The Consumer's Optimal Choice**

The consumer's optimal consumption bundle occurs at the point of tangency between her budget constraint and her indifference curve, shown here at point A. The consumer can afford the consumption bundles represented by points B, C, and D, but these are on a lower indifference curve (U_1) than is point A (U_2). Point E is on a higher indifference curve (U_3), but it lies outside the consumer's budget constraint and is thus infeasible.

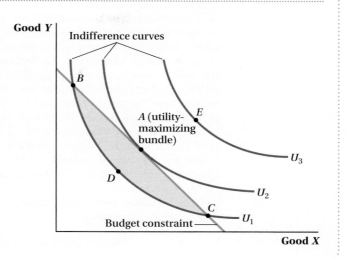

afford it with her income. However, because B is on a lower indifference curve (U_1) than A is (U_2), bundle B provides less utility than A. Bundles C and D are feasible too, but also leave the consumer worse off. The consumer would love to consume a bundle like E because it's on an indifference curve (U_3) that corresponds to a higher utility level than U_2. Unfortunately, the consumer can't afford E: It's outside her budget constraint.

A look at the consumer's optimal consumption bundle A in Figure 4.18 shows that it has a special feature: The indifference curve running through it, U_2, touches the budget constraint once and only once, exactly at A. Mathematically speaking, U_2 and the budget constraint are tangent at point A. As long as the assumptions about utility we established earlier hold, no other indifference curve we can draw will have this feature. Any other indifference curve will not be tangent, and therefore will cross the budget constraint twice or not at all. If you can draw another indifference curve that is tangent, it will cross the indifference curve shown in Figure 4.18, violating the transitivity assumption. (Give it a try—it is a useful exercise.)

This single tangency is not a coincidence. It is, in fact, a requirement of utility maximization. To see why, suppose an indifference curve and the budget constraint never touched. Then no point on the indifference curve is feasible, and by definition, no bundle on that indifference curve can be the way for a consumer to maximize his utility given his income. Now suppose the indifference curve instead crosses the budget constraint twice. This implies there must be a bundle that offers the consumer higher utility than any on this indifference curve and that the consumer can afford. For example, the shaded region between indifference curve U_1 and the budget constraint in Figure 4.18 reflects all of the bundles that are feasible and provide higher utility than bundles B, C, D, or any other point on U_1. That means no bundle on U_1 could be utility-maximizing; there are other bundles that are both affordable and offer higher utility. By similar reasoning, this outcome will be generally true not just for indifference curve U_1, but for any indifference curve that crosses the budget constraint twice.

This means that only at a point of tangency are there no other bundles that are both (1) feasible and (2) offer a higher utility level. This tangency is the utility-maximizing bundle for the consumer.

Mathematically, the tangency of the indifference curve and budget constraint means that they have the same slope at the optimal consumption bundle. This has a very important economic interpretation that is key to understanding why the optimal bundle is where it is. In Section 4.2, we defined the negative of the slope of the indifference curve as the marginal rate of substitution, and we discussed how the MRS_{XY} reflects the ratio of the *marginal utilities* of the two goods. In Section 4.3, we saw that the slope of the budget constraint equals the negative of the ratio of the *prices* of the two goods. Therefore, the fact that the consumer's utility-maximizing bundle is at a tangency between an indifference curve and the budget constraint (and that it's on the budget constraint rather than inside it) gives us this key insight: *When the consumer spends all her income, her optimal consumption bundle is the one at which the ratio of the goods' marginal utilities exactly equals the ratio of their prices.*

This economic idea behind utility maximization can be expressed mathematically. At the point of tangency,

$$\text{Slope of indifference curve} = \text{Slope of budget constraint}$$

$$-MRS_{XY} = -MU_X/MU_Y = -P_X/P_Y$$

$$MU_X/MU_Y = P_X/P_Y$$

Why are the marginal utility and price ratios equal when the consumer maximizes her utility level? If they were not equal, she could do better by shifting consumption from one good to the other. To see why, let's say Meredith is maximizing her utility over bottles of Gatorade and protein bars. Suppose bottles of Gatorade are twice as expensive as protein bars, but she is considering a bundle in which her marginal utilities from the two goods *are not* 2 to 1 as the price ratio is. Say she gets the same amount of utility at the margin from another bottle of Gatorade as from another protein bar, so that the ratio of the goods' marginal utilities is 1. Given the relative prices, she could give up 1 bottle of Gatorade and buy 2 more protein bars and doing so would let her reach a higher utility level. Why? Because those 2 extra protein bars are worth twice as much in utility terms as the lost bottle of Gatorade.

Now suppose that a bottle of Gatorade offers Meredith four times the utility at the margin as a protein bar. In this case, the ratio of Meredith's marginal utilities for Gatorade and protein bars (4 to 1) is higher than the price ratio (2 to 1), so Meredith could buy 2 fewer protein bars in exchange for 1 more bottle of Gatorade. Because the Gatorade delivers twice the utility lost from the 2 protein bars, she will be better off buying fewer protein bars and more Gatorade.

It is often helpful to rewrite this optimization condition in terms of the consumer's marginal utility per dollar spent:

$$\frac{MU_X}{MU_Y} = \frac{P_X}{P_Y} \Rightarrow \frac{MU_X}{P_X} = \frac{MU_Y}{P_Y}$$

∂ The end-of-chapter appendix uses calculus to solve the consumer's utility maximization problem.

Here, the utility-maximation problem can be restated as finding the consumption bundle that gives the consumer the most bang for her buck. This occurs when the marginal utility per dollar spent (MU/P) is equal across all goods. If this is not the case, the consumer is able to adjust her consumption of Good X and Good Y to improve her utility.

Suppose Antonio gets utility from consuming two goods, burgers and fries. His utility function is given by

$$U = \sqrt{BF} = B^{0.5}F^{0.5}$$

where B is the amount of burgers he eats and F the servings of fries. Antonio's marginal utility of a burger $MU_B = 0.5B^{-0.5}F^{0.5}$, and his marginal utility of an order of fries $MU_F = 0.5B^{0.5}F^{-0.5}$. Antonio's income is \$20, and the prices of burgers and fries are \$5 and \$2, respectively. What are Antonio's utility-maximizing quantities of burgers and fries?

Solution:

We know that the optimal solution to the consumer's maximization problem sets the marginal rate of substitution—the ratio of the goods' marginal utilities—equal to the goods' price ratio:

$$MRS_{BF} = \frac{MU_B}{MU_F} = \frac{P_B}{P_F}$$

where MU_B and MU_F are the marginal utilities of burgers and fries, respectively. P_B and P_F are the goods' prices. Therefore, to find the utility-maximizing quantities of burgers and fries, we set the ratio of marginal utilities equal to the goods' price ratio and simplify:

$$\frac{MU_B}{MU_F} = \frac{P_B}{P_F}$$

$$\frac{0.5B^{-0.5}F^{0.5}}{0.5B^{0.5}F^{-0.5}} = \frac{5}{2}$$

$$\frac{0.5F^{0.5}F^{0.5}}{0.5B^{0.5}B^{0.5}} = \frac{5}{2}$$

$$\frac{F}{B} = \frac{5}{2}$$

$$2F = 5B$$

$$F = 2.5B$$

This condition tells us that Antonio maximizes his utility when he consumes fries to burgers at a 5 to 2 ratio. We now know the ratio of the optimal quantities, but do not yet know exactly what quantities Antonio will choose to consume. To figure that out, we can use the budget constraint, which pins down the total amount Antonio can spend, and therefore the total quantities of each good he can consume.

Antonio's budget constraint can be written as

$$\text{Income} = P_F F + P_B B, \text{ or}$$

$$B = \frac{\text{Income}}{P_B} - \frac{P_F}{P_B}F$$

Substituting in the values from the problem gives

$$B = \frac{20}{5} - \frac{2}{5}F$$

$$B = 4 - 0.4F$$

Now, we can substitute the utility-maximization condition $F = 2.5B$ into the budget constraint to find the quantity of burgers Antonio will consume:

$$B = 4 - 0.4F$$

$$B = 4 - 0.4(2.5B)$$

$$B = 4 - B$$

$$B = 2$$

And because $F = 2.5B$, then $F = 5$.

Therefore, given his budget constraint, Antonio maximizes his utility by consuming 2 burgers and 5 servings of fries.

$$MRS_{xy} = \frac{MU_x}{MU_y} = \frac{P_x}{P_B}$$

Implications of Utility Maximization

The marginal-utility-ratio-equals-price-ratio result has another implication for the economy as a whole that can initially be quite surprising. Even if two consumers have very different preferences between two goods, they will have the *same* ratio of marginal utilities for the two goods, because utility maximization implies that MRS equals the ratio of the prices.[6]

This might seem odd. If Jack has consumed 9 packs of gum and 1 iTunes download, while Meg consumed 9 downloads and only 1 pack of gum, it seems that Jack likes gum a lot and would therefore be willing to pay more for another pack of gum (and a lot less for iTunes) than Meg. This assertion would be true *if both Jack and Meg had to consume the same bundle*, but they don't have to. They can choose how much of each good they want to consume. Because Jack likes gum a lot, he will consume so much of it that he drives down his marginal utility until, by the time he and Meg both reach their utility-maximizing consumption bundles, they both place the same relative marginal utilities on the two goods. Ultimately, the relative value they place on any two goods (on the margin) is dictated by the relative prices. Because Meg and Jack face the same prices, they have the same marginal values.

This situation is shown in Figure 4.19. To keep things simple, we assume Jack and Meg have the same incomes. Because they also face the same relative prices, their budget constraints are the same. Jack really likes gum relative to iTunes downloads, so his indifference curves tend to be flat: He has to be given a lot of iTunes to make up for any loss of gum. Meg has the opposite tastes. She has to be given a lot of gum to make her no worse off for giving up an iTunes download. Her indifference curves are therefore steep. Nevertheless, both Jack and Meg's utility-maximizing bundles are on the same budget line, and their marginal rates of substitution at those bundles are the same. We've drawn the indifference curves for Jack (U_J) and Meg (U_M) so that they are tangent to the budget line and therefore contain the utility-maximizing bundle.

While they have the same MRS_{XY}, what *is* different is the amount of each good they consume in their respective bundles. Jack, the gum lover, maximizes his utility by choosing a bundle (J) with a lot of gum and not many iTunes. Meg's optimal consumption bundle (M), on the other hand, has a lot of iTunes and little gum. Again, the idea is that the way both consumers end up with the same MRS in their utility-maximizing bundles

---

Figure 4.19 ⋮ **Two Consumers' Optimal Choices**

Although they have the same budget constraint, Jack and Meg have different relative preferences and, therefore, different optimal consumption bundles. Because Jack likes gum relative to iTunes downloads, his indifference curve (U_J) is flat and he consumes much more gum than iTunes at his optimal consumption bundle at point J. Meg's indifference curve (U_M) is much steeper and reflects her relative preference for iTunes downloads over gum; her utility-maximizing bundle is shown at point M. Although their consumption bundles are different, the MRS is the same at these points.

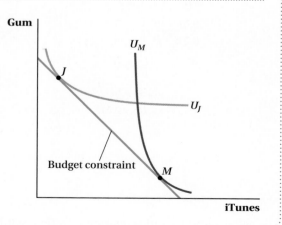

---

[6] Technically, this is true only of consumers who are consuming a positive amount of both goods, or who are at "interior" solutions in economists' lingo. We'll discuss this issue in the next section.

is that each consumes a large amount of the good for which he or she has the stronger preference. By behaving in this way, Jack and Meg drive down the relative marginal utility of the good they prefer until their marginal utility ratio equals the price ratio.

Note that these two indifference curves cross, although earlier we learned that indifference curves can never cross. If a consumer's indifference curves did cross, her preferences wouldn't have the transitivity property, and the bundle located where the indifference curves crossed would supposedly deliver two different utility levels. However, the "no crossing" rule applies only to the indifference curves of one individual. Figure 4.19 shows indifference curves for two different people with different preferences. Transitivity doesn't have to hold across people. If you like gum more than iTunes, and your friend likes iTunes more than, say, coffee, that doesn't imply you have to like gum more than coffee. So the same consumption bundle (say, 3 packs of gum and 5 iTunes downloads) can offer different utility levels to different people.

theory and data

Indifference Curves of Phone Service Buyers Revisited

From the Economides, Seim, and Viard study we discussed earlier, we learned that households with Internet access had higher relative marginal utilities for local phone calls than did non-Internet homes. Because the marginal utilities of regional calls were lower for Internet households, their *MRS* was higher than that for non-Internet households. Using the logic we just discussed, we can see that if the two types of households had the same budget constraint, the outcome would look something like Figure 4.20. Just like Jack and Meg above, consumers with different tastes end up consuming different bundles. Because households with the Internet had steeper indifference curves than those without Internet access, they ended up consuming a larger amount of local calls, shown at bundle *I*. (U_{Internet} is the indifference curve tangent to the budget constraint.) Non-Internet households' phone use was relatively heavy in regional calls instead, as seen in their optimal bundle *NI*. However, because we've assumed all households face the same budget constraint (and therefore the same relative prices), they will all have the same *MRS* at their optimal bundles.

Figure 4.20   **Optimal Choices of Internet and Non-Internet Households**

Non-Internet households and Internet households have the same budget constraint but different optimal bundles. Non-Internet households consume more regional calls than local calls at their utility-maximizing point (*NI*) because at any given level of local calls, they get higher marginal utility from regional calls. Internet households, on the other hand, consume more local calls than regional calls (point *I*) because they favor local calls on the margin more.

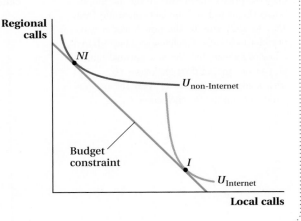

An interesting additional aspect of this market is that households actually have some choice in the relative prices they face. This is because they choose a specific calling plan from the many offered by the various competing phone companies. These menus typically let households trade off higher fixed monthly fees to face lower prices for additional calls on the margin. So, for example, a household could sign up for a billing plan that has a high fixed fee and a low marginal price for local phone service, but a low fixed fee with a high marginal price for regional service. Or vice versa.

How would these sorts of choices show up in our analysis? We know that the impact of different marginal prices would show up as a steeper or shallower budget constraint, depending on whether local or regional calls become relatively more expensive. How would a fixed fee affect the households' choices depicted in the figure drawn? You can think of paying a fixed fee as a reduction in the household's income. It doesn't affect relative prices on the margin, so in and of itself, it doesn't change the slope of the budget constraint. However, it does leave the household with less income to allocate between local and regional calls. Thus, if a household opts to pay a higher fixed fee, its budget constraint shifts in toward the origin.

A household might be willing to pay a higher fee and suffer the related income loss *if* the calling plan significantly lowers the price of the good it expects to consume a lot of. This is because the combination of these income and price changes would both shift (the result of the income change) and rotate (the result of the price change) the budget constraint, so that the household could still reach a higher utility level than before the shift.

An example of this is shown in Figure 4.21. An Internet household's original optimal bundle I from Figure 4.20 is shown (now labeled I_1), along with the original budget constraint (BC_1) and tangent indifference curve (now labeled $U_{\text{Internet},1}$). When the household pays a fee to reduce the price of local calls on the margin, the budget constraint shifts in and rotates counterclockwise, as shown. Notice that the household has suffered a loss in income—it can't even afford its old optimal bundle I_1 anymore; that point is now infeasible. Nevertheless, the new optimal bundle I_2 is on an indifference curve ($U_{\text{Internet},2}$) that corresponds to a higher utility level than the household received before.

By reducing the price of the good it has stronger relative preferences for, the household is actually able to make itself better off by paying a fee and, in effect, reducing its income. (In the next chapter, we spend a lot of time looking at how consumers respond to simultaneous changes in income and relative prices.)

Figure 4.21   Paying a Fixed Fee to Reduce the Price of Local Calls

By paying a fee, the Internet household can reduce the price of local calls on the margin, rotating the household's budget constraint from BC_1 to BC_2, due to the now lower relative price for local calls. The household has suffered a loss of income, but the new optimal bundle (I_2) is on an indifference curve ($U_{\text{Internet},2}$) with a higher utility level than the original bundle (I_1 on indifference curve $U_{\text{Internet},1}$).

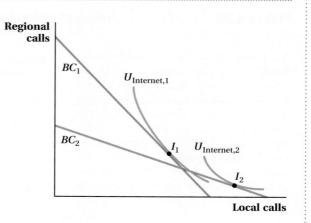

A Special Case: Corner Solutions

Up to this point, we have been analyzing situations in which the consumer optimally consumes some of both goods. This assumption usually makes sense if we think that utility functions have the property that the more you have of a good, the less you are willing to give up of something else to get more. Because the first little bit of a good provides the most marginal utility in this situation, a consumer will typically want at least *some* amount of a good.

Depending on the consumer's preferences and relative prices, however, in some cases a consumer will want to spend all her money on one good. Consuming all of one good and none of the other maximizes a consumer's utility given the budget constraint is called a **corner solution.** (Its name comes from the fact that the optimal consumption bundle is at the "corner" of the budget line, where it meets the axis.) If the utility-maximizing bundle has positive quantities of both goods, like all the cases we've looked at to this point, it is referred to as an **interior solution.**

Figure 4.22 depicts a corner solution. Greg, our consumer, has an income of $240 and is choosing his consumption levels of romance novels and economics textbooks. Let's say a hardcover romance novel costs $20, and an economics text costs $120. Because econ texts are more expensive than romance novels, Greg can afford up to 12 romance novels, but only 2 econ texts. Nonetheless, the highest utility that Greg can obtain given his income is bundle A, where he consumes all economics textbooks and no romance novels.

How do we know A is the optimal bundle? Consider another feasible bundle, such as B. Greg can afford it, but it is on an indifference curve U_1 that corresponds to a lower utility level than U_2. The same logic would apply to bundles on any indifference curve between U_1 and U_2. Furthermore, any bundle that offers higher utility than U_2 (i.e., above and to the right of U_2) isn't feasible given Greg's income. So U_2 must be the highest utility level Greg can achieve, and he can do so only by consuming bundle A, because that's the only bundle he can afford on that indifference curve.

In a corner solution, then, the highest indifference curve touches the budget constraint exactly once, just as with the interior solutions we discussed earlier. The only

---

Figure 4.22   :   A Corner Solution

A corner solution occurs when the consumer spends all his money on one good. Given Greg's income and the relative prices of romance novels and economics textbooks, Greg is going to consume 2 economics textbooks and zero romance novels at his optimal consumption bundle (A). All other feasible consumption bundles, such as point B, correspond to indifference curves with lower utility levels than the indifference curve U_2 at point A. Greg cannot afford consumption bundles at a higher utility level, such as U_3, with his current income.

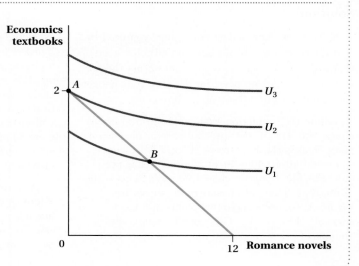

difference with a corner solution is that bundle A is not a point of tangency. The indifference curve is flatter than the budget constraint at that point (and everywhere else). That means Greg's *MRS*—the ratio of his marginal utility from romance novels relative to his marginal utility from textbooks—is *less* than the price ratio of the two goods rather than equal to it. In other words, even when he's consuming no romance novels, his marginal utility from them is so low, it's not worth paying the price of a novel to be able to consume one. The marginal utility he'd have to give up due to reduced textbook consumption would not be made up for by the fact that he could spend some of his textbook money on novels. In fact, if Greg were allowed to consume a negative quantity of romance novels (that would be kind of like Greg producing some romance novels to sell to other consumers), he would want to.

4.5 figure it out

A pizza chain recently offered the following special promotion: "Buy one pizza at full price and get your next three pizzas for just $5 each!" Assume that the full price of a pizza is $10, your daily income $40, and the price of all other goods $1 per unit.

a. Draw budget constraints for pizza and all other goods that reflect your situations both before and during the special promotion. (Put the quantity of pizzas on the horizontal axis.) Indicate the horizontal and vertical intercepts and the slope of the budget constraint.

b. How is this special offer likely to alter your buying behavior?

c. How might your answer to (b) depend on the shape of your indifference curves?

Solution:

a. To draw your budget constraint, you need to find the combinations of pizza and all other goods that are available to you before and during the promotion. The starting place for drawing your budget constraint is to find its x- and y-intercepts.

Before the promotion, you could afford 4 pizzas a day ($40/$10) if you spent all of your income on pizza. This is the x-intercept (Figure A). Likewise, you could afford 40 units of all other goods per day ($40/$1) if you purchased no pizza. This is the y-intercept. The budget constraint, shown in Figure A, connects these two points and has a slope of $-40/4 = -10$. This slope measures the amount of other goods you must give up to have an

additional pizza. Note that this is also equal to $-P_x/P_y = -\$10/\$1 = -10$.

Once the promotion begins, you can still afford 40 units of all other goods if you buy no pizza. The promotion has an effect only if you buy some pizza. This means the y-intercept of the budget constraint is unchanged by the promotion. Now suppose you buy 1 pizza. In that case, you must pay $10 for the pizza, leaving you $30 for purchasing all other goods. This bundle is point A on the diagram. If you were to buy a second pizza, its price would be only $5. Spending $15 on 2 pizzas would allow you to purchase $25 ($40 − $15) worth of other goods. This corresponds to bundle B. The third and fourth pizzas also cost $5 each. After 3 pizzas, you have $20 left to spend on other goods, and after 4 pizzas, you are left with $15 for other goods. These are points C and D on the diagram.

A fifth pizza will cost you $10 (the full price) because the promotion limits the $5 price to the next 3 pizzas you buy. That means if you choose to buy 5 pizzas, you will spend $35 on pizza and only $5 on other goods, as at bundle E. Now that you have again purchased a pizza at full price, you are eligible to receive the next 3 at the reduced price of $5. Unfortunately, you only have enough income for one more $5 pizza. Therefore, if you would like to spend all of your income on pizza, you can buy 6 pizzas instead of just 4.

As a result of the promotion, then, your x-intercept has moved out to 6, and your budget line has pivoted out (in a somewhat irregular way because of all the relative price changes corresponding to purchasing different numbers of pizzas) to reflect the increase in your purchasing power due to the promotion.

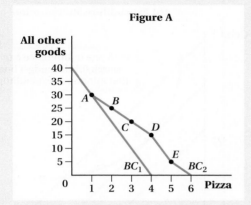

Figure A

b. It is likely that the promotion will increase how much pizza you consume. Most of the new budget constraint lies to the right of the initial budget constraint, increasing the number of feasible bundles available to you. Because more is preferred to less, it is likely that your optimal consumption bundle will include more pizza than before.

c. If your indifference curves are very flat, you have a strong preference for other goods relative to pizza. For example, look at U_A (Figure B). The slope of this indifference curve is relatively small (in absolute value). This means that the marginal rate of substitution of other goods for pizza is small. If your

indifference curves look like this, you are not very willing to trade other goods for more pizza, and your optimal consumption bundle will likely lie on the section of the new budget constraint that coincides with the initial budget constraint. The promotion would cause no change in your consumption behavior; pizza is not a high priority for you, as indicated by your flat indifference curve.

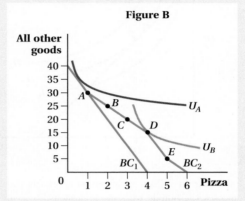

Figure B

On the other hand, if your indifference curves are steeper, like U_B, your marginal rate of substitution is relatively large, indicating that you are willing to forgo a large amount of other goods to consume an additional pizza. This promotion will more than likely cause you to purchase additional pizzas.

An Alternative Approach to Solving the Consumer's Problem: Expenditure Minimization

Up to this point, our strategy for determining what bundle of goods the consumer will consume has involved maximizing utility subject to the constraint that expenditure cannot exceed the consumer's income. As we discussed above, this is an example of a *constrained maximization* problem.

While this approach is natural and intuitive, any constrained maximization problem can also be solved by reversing the roles played by the constraint and the function being maximized. That is, we can also look at how a consumer decides what bundle to consume as a "constrained minimization" problem: The consumer minimizes expenditure (reflected in the budget constraint) subject to the constraint that she must achieve a given level of utility from this expenditure. Graphically speaking, utility maximization is about finding the highest indifference curve that is tangent to the budget constraint, while expenditure minimization is about finding the lowest budget constraint that is tangent to a given indifference curve.

Economists call this expenditure-minimization setup the "dual" to the utility-maximization problem. They're sort of mathematical mirror images.

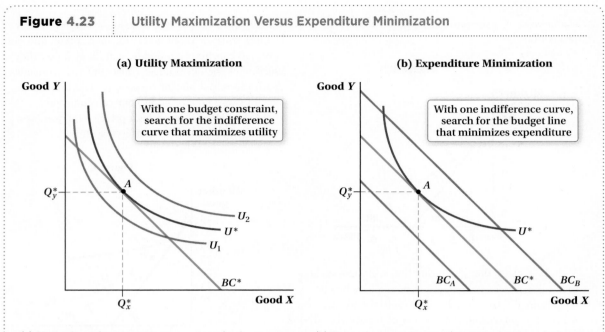

Figure 4.23 : **Utility Maximization Versus Expenditure Minimization**

(a) Utility Maximization

With one budget constraint, search for the indifference curve that maximizes utility

(b) Expenditure Minimization

With one indifference curve, search for the budget line that minimizes expenditure

(a) Using the utility-maximization approach, the consumer chooses the bundle with the highest utility level that she can afford given her budget constraint. This occurs at the point of tangency (bundle A) between the indifference curve U^* and the budget constraint BC^*.

(b) Using the expenditure-maximization approach, the consumer begins with an indifference curve of a given utility level, U^*. She then chooses the budget line, BC^*, tangent to U^*. As in panel a, the consumer chooses bundle A, where she consumes quantities Q_x^* and Q_y^*.

Figure 4.23 shows these two approaches graphically. Panel a on the left is an example of the standard utility-maximization approach. The consumer has a fixed income reflected in the budget constraint BC^* and various levels of utility as reflected by the three indifference curves shown. Bundle A, which is at the point of tangency between the budget constraint and the indifference curve labeled U^*, represents the utility-maximizing feasible bundle.

Panel b solves the same problem using the expenditure-minimization approach. In this case, we start with a level of utility that the consumer wants to achieve. Specifically, we start with a given level of utility U^*, which is the same utility level that the consumer has in panel a. Then, we search over different levels of income (or equivalently, expenditure) for the smallest amount of income or expenditure necessary to achieve U^*. Each expenditure level is associated with a different budget line. These budget *lines* are just like the budget *constraints* we have seen earlier—they are straight lines with the slope determined by the relative prices of the two goods. We call them budget *lines* not budget *constraints* because now it is the indifference curve U^* that is the constraint.

In panel b, we've drawn in a few budget lines. We know from before that budget lines further from the origin reflect higher levels of income. Because the consumer wants to achieve his chosen level of utility with the least amount of income/expenditure, he must find the budget line *closest* to the origin that touches U^*. The answer, as in our original approach, boils down to finding the point of tangency between the indifference curve and the budget line. And, as shown in panel b, that point is bundle A, the same bundle from the utility-maximization problem in panel a.

It is no coincidence that the optimal solution in the two panels is the same. The utility-maximization and expenditure-minimization approaches are just two different ways of solving the same problem. Either we fix a budget constraint and try to find the highest indifference curve that is tangent to it (utility maximization), or we fix

∂ The end-of-chapter appendix uses calculus to solve the consumer's expenditure minimization problem.

an indifference curve and try to find the lowest budget line that is tangent to it (expenditure minimization). The reason that the optimal solution in the two panels is the same consumption bundle is that when we set up the utility constraint in panel b's expenditure-minimization problem, we picked the same utility level reached in panel a's utility-maximization problem. If we had chosen any other utility level for our analysis, the minimum-expenditure budget line would be something other than BC^*, and the optimal consumption bundle would not be bundle A.

4.5 Conclusion

This chapter has looked at how consumers decide what to consume. This decision combines two characteristics of consumers, their preferences (embodied in their utility function) and their income, and one characteristic of the market, the goods' prices.

We saw that a consumer will maximize her utility from consumption when she chooses a bundle of goods such that the marginal rate of substitution between the goods equals their relative prices. That is, in this bundle the ratio of the goods' utilities equals their price ratio. Equivalently, the goods' marginal utilities per dollar spent are equal. If this property didn't hold, a consumer could make herself better off by consuming more of the goods with high marginal utilities per dollar and less of the goods with low marginal utilities per dollar.

There is another way to think about the consumer's problem of what and how much to consume. Rather than thinking of consumers as trying to maximize utility subject to a budget constraint, we could think of them as trying to minimize the expenditure necessary for them to reach a given level of utility. This is called the expenditure-minimization problem. We saw how it turns out that this delivers the same rule for optimal consumption behavior: The MRS of the goods should equal their price ratio.

Summary

1. **Utility** is the economic concept of consumers' happiness or well-being, and the **utility function** is the construct that relates the amount of goods consumed (the inputs) to the consumer's utility level (the output). There are properties that we expect almost all utility functions to share: the completeness, rankability, and transitivity of utility bundles, that having more of a good is better than having less, and that the more a consumer has of a particular good, the less willing she is to give up something else to get more of that good. [**Section 4.1**]

2. Consumers' preferences are reflected in their **indifference curves,** which show all the combinations of goods over which a consumer receives equal utility. The set of properties imposed on utility functions imply some restrictions on the shapes of indifference curves. Namely, indifference curves slope downward, never cross for a given individual, and are convex to the origin. [**Section 4.2**]

3. The negative of the slope of the indifference curve is the **marginal rate of substitution of good X for good Y (MRS_{XY}).** The MRS is the ratio of the marginal utilities of the goods in the utility function. [**Section 4.2**]

4. Consumer preferences lead to differences in the steepness and curvature of indifference curves. If a consumer views two goods as **perfect substitutes** or **perfect complements,** their indifference curves will be shaped like straight lines and right angles, respectively. [**Section 4.2**]

5. The consumer's decision about how much of each good to consume depends not only on utility, but also on how much money that person has to spend (her income) and on the prices of the goods. In analyzing the role of income in consumption decisions, we assume the following: Each good has a fixed price, and any consumer can buy as much of a good as she wants at that price if the consumer has sufficient income to pay for it; the consumer has some fixed amount of income to spend; and the consumer cannot save or borrow.

   The **budget constraint** captures both a consumer's income and the relative prices of goods. The constraint shows which **consumption bundles** are **feasible** (i.e., affordable given the consumer's income) and which are **infeasible**. The slope of the budget constraint is the negative of the ratio of the prices of the two goods $(-P_X/P_Y)$. [**Section 4.3**]

6. The consumer's decision is a constrained-optimization problem: to maximize utility while staying within her budget constraint. The utility-maximizing solution is generally to consume the bundle of goods located where an indifference curve is tangent to the budget constraint. At this optimal point, the consumer's marginal rate of substitution—the ratio of the consumer's marginal utilities from the goods—equals the goods' relative price ratio.

A **corner solution**, where the optimal quantity consumed of one good is zero, can occur when a consumer's marginal utility of a good is so low compared to that good's relative price that she is better off not consuming any of that good at all. In such cases, the MRS does not equal the price ratio even though the consumer is at the utility-maximizing consumption bundle. [**Section 4.4**]

7. The consumer's problem of what and how much to consume can be recast as an expenditure-minimization problem. That is, rather than thinking of consumers as trying to maximize utility subject to a budget constraint, we could think of them as trying to minimize the expenditure necessary for them to reach a given level of utility. The optimal choices for both problems result in the same criterion: The MRS of the goods should equal their price ratio. [**Section 4.4**]

Review Questions

1. We make four assumptions about preferences: completeness and rankability, "more is better," transitivity, and consumers want variety. Briefly describe each assumption.
2. What does the term "utility" mean? How does utility relate to a utility function?
3. Define "indifference curve." What does an indifference curve tell us about the consumer?
4. We learned that the slope of the indifference curve is called the marginal rate of substitution of X for Y. What does the MRS_{XY} tell us about a consumer's preferences between two goods?
5. Why does the slope of the indifference curve vary along the curve? What does this variability tell us about consumers' preferences?
6. What does a steep indifference curve indicate about a consumer's preferences? What does a flat indifference curve say?
7. When are two goods perfect substitutes? What does the indifference curve look like, or what is its *curvature*?

8. When are two goods perfect complements? What does the indifference curve look like?
9. In addition to utility, what other factors determine how much of a good to buy?
10. Describe the three assumptions we make when incorporating income into our model of consumer behavior.
11. What is a budget constraint?
12. What determines the slope of a budget constraint? What situation would change the slope of a budget constraint?
13. What do we call the bundle represented by the point of tangency between the consumer's indifference curve and her budget constraint?
14. At the point of tangency, what is true about the ratio of the goods' marginal utilities and the ratio of their prices?
15. What is the difference between these approaches: utility maximization and expenditure minimization?

Problems (Solutions to problems marked * appear at the back of this book. Problems adapted to use calculus are available online at http://worthpublishers.com/GLS1e)

1. Which assumption about consumer preferences does each of the following individuals violate?
   a. Randy likes basketball more than football; football more than baseball; and baseball more than basketball.
   b. Paula prefers prune juice to orange juice but cannot decide how she feels about grapefruit juice.
   c. Simon likes superhero comic books but prefers 5 comic books to 10 comic books.

2. By assumption, individual preferences must be transitive so that if A is preferred to B, and B is preferred to C, then A is preferred to C. Suppose that Marsha, Jan, and Cindy individually have transitive preferences over three goods: oranges, apples, and pears. If Marsha, Jan, and Cindy were to vote on whether to name oranges, apples, or pears the "fruit of the month," show that it is possible the preferences for the *group* might *not* be transitive.

3. In Arbitrageville, 1 orange can be exchanged for 4 apples, and 4 apples for 1 orange. The mayor of Arbitrageville likes oranges a lot. He buys 100 oranges and 1 apple at the grocery store. As the mayor piles oranges onto the checkout counter, he tells the clerk, "I just love these oranges. In fact, I think you'd need to offer me three apples to pry one orange from my hands."

   a. Explain why the clerk, a sharp entrepreneur, immediately reaches under the counter and offers the mayor 3 apples.

   b. What should the mayor have said about how many apples the clerk would need to offer him for 1 orange, assuming that the mayor was maximizing his utility? What equation tells us how the mayor's preferences relate to prices?

   c. If the mayor maintained his preferences, how could the clerk wind up with all of the mayor's oranges and the mayor (eventually) without a penny to his name?

*4. Draw two indifference curves for each of the following pairs of goods. Put the quantity of the first good on the horizontal axis and the quantity of the second good on the vertical axis.

   a. Paul likes pencils and pens.

   b. Rhonda likes carrots and dislikes broccoli.

   c. Emily likes hip-hop iTunes downloads and doesn't care about heavy metal downloads.

   d. Michael only likes dress shirts and cufflinks in 1 to 2 proportions.

*5. Suppose that John is indifferent between consuming bundle A, which consists of 4 apples and 1 peach, and bundle B, which consists of 4 peaches and 1 apple. If John were given the choice between bundle A and bundle C, which contained 3 peaches and 2 apples, which should he pick? (*Hint*: Draw an indifference curve or two.)

6. The table below displays the total utility $U(X)$ that corresponds to the number of units of X consumed by three different consumers (Abe, Barbara, and Chuck), holding everything else constant:

Abe		Barbara		Chuck	
U(X)	X	U(X)	X	U(X)	X
10	2	10	2	10	2
14	3	10	3	12	3
16	4	10	4	15	4
17	5	9	5	19	5
17.5	6	8	6	24	6

   a. Compute the marginal utility of X for each of the three consumers at each level of X.

   b. Based on the data in the table, can you tell whether any of these consumers are vio-

lating any of the standard assumptions about preferences?

   c. Is it possible that any of these three consumers have the exact same preferences, and that columns for the three consumers differ only because of the arbitrary units that are used to measure utility? Explain.

*7. A consumer's utility function is given by $U = XY$, where $MU_X = Y$ and $MU_Y = X$.

   a. What is the utility derived from 1 unit of X and 2 units of Y? What is the utility derived from 2 units of X and 1 unit of Y? What is the utility derived from 5 units of X and 2 units of Y?

   b. How does the consumer rank the following bundles?

Bundle	Quantity of X	Quantity of Y
A	2	2
B	10	0
C	1	5
D	3	2
E	2	3

   c. Graph an indifference curve that shows the bundles of X and Y for which $U = 6$ and $U = 8$. Is the "more is better" assumption satisfied for X and Y?

   d. What are MU_X and MU_Y for the following bundles?

Bundle	Quantity of X	Quantity of Y
F	1	2
G	2	2
H	1	3

   e. Does MU_X diminish, stay constant, or increase as X increases? (*Hint*: You must keep the values of all other variables fixed.)

8. Kelly's utility function is given by $U = 5X + 2Y$, where $MU_X = 5$ and $MU_Y = 2$.

   a. What is MRS_{XY}?

   b. What is MRS_{XY} when $X = 1$ and $Y = 5$? When $X = 2$ and $Y = 2.5$?

   c. Draw a sample indifference curve.

9. Andrea loves to eat burritos with hot sauce. In fact, she cannot enjoy a burrito (B) unless it has three servings of hot sauce (H). She gets no additional enjoyment from more than three servings per burrito. Thus, her utility function is $U = \min\{B, \frac{1}{3}H\}$. Graph Andrea's indifference curves for $U = 1$ and $U = 2$.

10. If Harry considers Cubs tickets a "good" and White Sox tickets a "bad," draw a set of indifference curves for Harry.

11. Josie gets satisfaction from both music and fireworks. Josie's income is $240 per week. Music costs $12 per CD, and fireworks cost $8 per bag.

    a. Graph the budget constraint Josie faces, with music on the vertical axis and fireworks on the horizontal axis.

    b. If Josie spends all her income on music, how much music can she afford? Plot a point that illustrates this scenario.

    c. If Josie spends all her income on fireworks, how many bags of fireworks can she afford? Plot a point that illustrates this scenario.

    d. If Josie spends half her income on fireworks and half her income on music, how much of each can she afford? Plot a point that illustrates this scenario.

    e. Connect the dots to create Josie's budget constraint. What is the slope of the budget constraint?

    f. Divide the price of fireworks by the price of music. Have you seen this number before, and if so, where?

    g. Suppose that a holiday bonus raises Josie's income temporarily to $360. Draw Josie's new budget constraint.

    h. Indicate the new bundles of music and fireworks that are feasible, given Josie's new income.

12. Suppose that only one person in the world sells ice cream. He employs a strange pricing policy: You can buy 1 ice cream cone for $1, but if you buy 2 cones, you have to pay $2 each. If you buy 3, you have to pay $3 each, etc., so that if you buy 10, you have to pay $10 each. You have $100 dollars to spend on ice cream cones and chocolate milk, and chocolate milk costs $1 per unit. Draw your budget constraint. This strange ice cream pricing, where buying more costs you more, is called a quantity surcharge.

13. Matthew is redecorating his apartment. The amount of utility he gets from chairs and couches is listed in the table below, where each number represents how much utility (in utils) he receives from the combination of chairs and couches:

	1 chair	2 chairs	3 chairs	4 chairs
1 couch	5	6	8	20
2 couches	6	7	10	21
3 couches	9	12	16	30

    a. What is the marginal utility from buying an additional chair if Matthew has 2 chairs and 2 couches?

    b. What is the marginal utility from buying an additional couch if Matthew has 2 chairs and 2 couches?

    c. If couches are the same price as chairs, and Matthew wants one more piece of furniture but already has 2 couches and 2 chairs, will he buy a couch or a chair? Explain.

14. Good X sells for $4, and good Y sells for $2. At your current level of consumption, the marginal rate of substitution between X and Y is 4.

    a. Are you maximizing your utility?

    b. If not, are you buying too much X or too much Y? Explain.

*15. For Mitzi, shampoo and conditioner are perfect complements. She likes to use 1 squirt of shampoo and 1 squirt of conditioner each time she washes her hair.

    a. Draw a set of indifference curves for Mitzi that illustrate the utility she derives from using shampoo and conditioner.

    b. Assume that shampoo costs $4 and conditioner costs $2. Construct a budget constraint for Mitzi and describe her purchasing habits. What is her optimal bundle likely to look like? (*Hint*: Assume some level of income for Mitzi.)

    c. Suppose that prices change so that shampoo costs $2 and conditioner costs $4. What is likely to happen to Mitzi's optimal bundle as a result? Explain.

    d. How would your answer to (c) change if Mitzi used 2 squirts of shampoo and 1 squirt of conditioner each time she washed her hair?

16. Suppose that there are only two goods, books and coffee. Wally gets utility from both books and coffee, but his indifference curves between them are concave rather than convex to the origin.

    a. Draw a set of indifference curves for Wally.

    b. What do these particular indifference curves tell you about Wally's marginal rate of substitution between books and coffee?

    c. What will Wally's utility-maximizing bundle look like? (*Hint*: Assume some level of income for Wally, and some prices for books and coffee; then draw a budget constraint.)

    d. Compare your answer to (b) to real-world behaviors. Does the comparison shed any light on why economists generally assume convex preferences?

*17. Anthony spends his income on fishing lures (L) and guitar picks (G). Lures are priced at $2, while a package of guitar picks cost \$1. Assume that Anthony has \$30 to spend and his utility function can be represented as $U(L,G) = L^{0.5}G^{0.5}$. For this utility function, $MU_L = 0.5L^{-0.5}G^{0.5}$ and $MU_G = 0.5L^{0.5}G^{-0.5}$.

a. What is the optimal number of lures and guitar picks for Anthony to purchase? How much utility does this combination bring him?

b. If the price of guitar picks doubles to \$2, how much income must Anthony have to maintain the same level of utility?

*18. A prominent online movie rental service mails rental DVDs to consumers. The service offers two pricing plans. Under the first plan, consumers face a flat \$10 fee each month and can rent as many DVDs as they wish for free. Under the second plan, consumers can rent DVDs for an à la carte price of \$2. Assume that a consumer has an income of \$20 and uses it to purchase DVD rentals and a "composite good" that costs \$1 per unit.

a. Draw a set of indifference curves for a representative consumer, putting DVD rentals on the horizontal axis.

b. Draw the budget constraint for the à la carte movie rental plan, making sure to indicate the horizontal and vertical intercepts. Find the consumer's optimum quantity of movie rentals. Label this point A.

c. Draw the budget constraint for the flat-fee plan, making sure to indicate the horizontal and vertical intercepts. Find the consumer's optimum quantity of movie rentals. Label this point B.

d. Under which plan does the consumer rent more movies?

e. Under which plan does the consumer end up with a lower marginal rate of substitution between movies and the composite good?

f. Under which plan is the consumer more likely to end up viewing *The Perils of Gwendoline in the Land of the Yik Yak*, widely acknowledged to be one of the worst movies of all time?

19. Suppose that doctors' visits cost \$20, and the typical consumer has an income of \$100. Consumers spend all of their incomes on doctors' visits and a "composite good" that costs \$1 per unit.

a. Draw a graph that illustrates the consumer's budget constraint, putting doctor's visits on the horizontal axis. Make sure you indicate the horizontal and vertical intercepts.

Now, suppose the local government is considering two health plans. Under plan A, the government will give out vouchers worth 2 free visits to the doctor. Under plan B, the government will give out four 50% coupons to be used at the doctor's office.

b. Draw the new budget constraint the consumer faces under plan A.

c. Draw the new budget constraint the consumer faces under plan B.

d. For whom is the choice of plan A or plan B not likely to matter—those who are quite well, or those who are quite sick? (*Hint*: Superimpose some indifference curves on your budget constraints.)

e. Which plan would someone who is generally well be likely to choose, if offered a choice?

20. Elaine loves receiving flowers and has a particular fondness for daisies and daffodils. Her relative preferences for the two flowers are illustrated by the set of utility curves in the diagram. The number at the bottom of each indifference curve indicates the amount of happiness she receives from the various combinations of daisies and daffodils on the curve. Elaine's boyfriend Jerry would like to give her enough flowers to provide her with 200 units of happiness, but would like to do so as inexpensively as possible.

a. If daisies sell for \$3 and daffodils sell for \$6, what is the minimum amount Jerry will have to spend?

b. Suppose that Jerry fails to make it to the flower store on time, so he quickly tucks the money he was planning to spend on flowers [as you determined in part (a)] in a card and gives it to Elaine. If Elaine spends the money on flowers, how much happiness will she receive from her purchase?

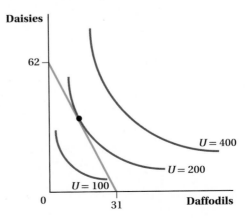

Chapter 4 Appendix:
The Calculus of Utility Maximization and Expenditure Minimization

In the chapters you've read so far, you've probably noticed that we use several different approaches when explaining microeconomic theories and applications. One method is mainly intuitive: Tell a story to illustrate an economic concept or discuss the logic of a model and its implications. This method of economic analysis goes back to Adam Smith and the invisible hand. A second method is the graphical approach. You only have to say "supply and demand" to conjure up a simple but powerful representation of a market. Finally, you've seen some simple mathematical models such as the algebraic representations of supply and demand curves in Chapter 2 and the consumer's budget constraint in Chapter 4. Each of these approaches provides a different window into understanding economic concepts.

Those of you who are familiar with calculus have yet another way to approach microeconomics. The tools of calculus are a natural fit with economics, and most economic models are formally derived using calculus. For some people (especially economists), it's easy to become so caught up in the math that the real economic ideas get lost. We don't want you to fall into that trap. That's why we present the calculus as a supplement to the intuition that we develop in the chapter. The calculus appendices provide an additional set of tools to examine the economic decisions and interactions discussed in the chapter. The logic of the models and the intuition from the chapter are still here in the calculus, only in another form.

So, don't think of the calculus that we explore in the appendices as a substitute for the logic, graphs, and algebra we use to explain microeconomics in the chapters. Instead, think of these techniques and the calculus as complements. As you learn more about microeconomics, you will find that each of these different approaches to understanding microeconomics may be more or less useful depending on the circumstances.

Consumer's Optimization Problem

One of the topics for which calculus provides additional insight is consumer behavior. Let's start by recalling the answer to the consumer's problem that we derived graphically in the chapter before seeing how we can get there using calculus. A consumer maximizes her utility $U(X,Y)$ when

$$MRS_{XY} = \frac{MU_X}{MU_Y} = \frac{P_X}{P_Y}$$

You may have noticed that to solve the optimization problem in the chapter, we just gave you the consumer's marginal utilities of goods X and Y—we didn't actually solve for them. This is because solving for the marginal utilities requires more than just the algebra and geometry we've relied on so far. Calculus allows us to derive the marginal utilities directly from the consumer's utility function. After determining the values of the marginal utilities, we can calculate the marginal rate of substitution. Calculus also provides us with another way to solve the consumer's problem—the Lagrangian—which yields some important insights into utility maximization.

The Marginal Rate of Substitution and Marginal Utility

In the chapter, we develop the connection between the marginal rate of substitution and marginal utility by thinking about how utility from each good changes as the consumer moves a little bit along one of her indifference curves. Here, we work in the opposite direction by starting with utility and seeing how we can use calculus to find the *MRS*. In this way, we examine what happens when we make small changes to the consumption bundle.

Take the consumer who has utility for goods X and Y, $U(X,Y)$. Any of the consumer's indifference curves show how the consumer trades off good X for good Y while keeping utility constant. We can choose any one of these indifference curves and call its level of utility $\overline{U}$:

$$U(X,Y) = \overline{U}$$

We are interested in how the utility from each good changes as we change the quantities of X and Y. So, we will totally differentiate the utility function, setting the total change in utility, dU, equal to zero because we are holding the level of utility constant:

$$dU = \frac{\partial U(X,Y)}{\partial X} \, dX + \frac{\partial U(X,Y)}{\partial Y} \, dY = 0$$

$$\frac{\partial U(X,Y)}{\partial X} \, dX = -\frac{\partial U(X,Y)}{\partial Y} \, dY$$

$$MU_X dX = -MU_Y dY$$

$$\frac{MU_X}{MU_Y} = -\frac{dY}{dX}$$

The right-hand side of this equation, $-dY/dX$, is the negative of the slope of the indifference curve or the marginal rate of substitution. Therefore,

$$MRS_{XY} = \frac{MU_X}{MU_Y}$$

Utility Maximization

The ratio of the marginal utilities is one piece of the puzzle—the preferences side. To finish the consumer's optimization, we need to relate consumer preferences to the prices of the goods and the consumer's income. Let's start by looking at a consumer whose utility function is the standard Cobb–Douglas functional form, $U(X,Y) = X^\alpha Y^{1-\alpha}$, where $0 < \alpha < 1$, and whose income is $I = P_X X + P_Y Y$. This consumer's utility-maximization problem is written formally as

$$\max_{X,Y} U(X,Y) = X^\alpha Y^{1-\alpha} \text{ subject to (s.t.) } I = P_X X + P_Y Y$$

This is known as a *constrained optimization problem*, in which $U(X,Y)$ is the objective function and $I = P_X X + P_Y Y$ is the constraint. In other words, how much utility the consumer can get is *constrained* by how much income she has to spend. In the chapter, we solved the same constrained optimization problem graphically with the objective of reaching the highest indifference curve while staying on the budget constraint.

If this were an unconstrained maximization problem, finding the optimal combination of variables would be fairly straightforward: Take the partial derivatives of the objective function with respect to each of the variables, set them equal to zero, and solve for the variables. But the presence of the budget constraint complicates the solution of the optimization problem (although without the constraint there wouldn't even be a finite solution to the utility-maximization problem because in an unconstrained world, the consumer consumes infinite amounts of each good).

There are two approaches to solving the consumer's utility-maximization problem using calculus. The first relies on what we already demonstrated in this chapter: At the optimum, the marginal rate of substitution equals the ratio of the two goods' prices. First, take the partial derivatives of the utility function with respect to each of the goods to derive the marginal utilities:

$$MU_X = \frac{\partial U(X,Y)}{\partial X} = \frac{\partial(X^{\alpha}Y^{1-\alpha})}{\partial X} = \alpha X^{\alpha-1}Y^{1-\alpha}$$

$$MU_Y = \frac{\partial U(X,Y)}{\partial Y} = \frac{\partial(X^{\alpha}Y^{1-\alpha})}{\partial Y} = (1-\alpha)X^{\alpha}Y^{-\alpha}$$

Next, use the relationship between the marginal utilities and the marginal rate of substitution to solve for MRS_{XY} and simplify the expression:

$$MRS_{XY} = \frac{MU_X}{MU_Y} = \frac{\alpha X^{\alpha-1}Y^{1-\alpha}}{(1-\alpha)X^{\alpha}Y^{-\alpha}} = \frac{\alpha}{(1-\alpha)}\frac{Y}{X}$$

Find Y as a function of X by setting MRS_{XY} equal to the ratio of the prices:

$$\frac{\alpha}{(1-\alpha)}\frac{Y}{X} = \frac{P_X}{P_Y}$$

$$Y = \frac{(1-\alpha)P_X}{\alpha P_Y}X, \text{ where } \frac{(1-\alpha)P_X}{\alpha P_Y} \text{ is a constant}$$

Now that we have the optimal relationship between Y and X, substitute the expression for Y into the budget constraint to solve for the optimal consumption bundle:

$$I = P_X X + P_Y\left[\frac{(1-\alpha)P_X}{\alpha P_Y}X\right]$$

$$I = P_X X\left[1 + \frac{(1-\alpha)}{\alpha}\right] = P_X X\left[\frac{\alpha}{\alpha} + \frac{(1-\alpha)}{\alpha}\right] = \frac{P_X}{\alpha}X$$

$$X^* = \frac{\alpha I}{P_X}$$

$$Y^* = \frac{(1-\alpha)P_X}{\alpha P_Y}\left(\frac{\alpha I}{P_X}\right) = \frac{(1-\alpha)I}{P_Y}$$

You can see that the resulting optimal bundle $\left(\frac{\alpha I}{P_X}, \frac{(1-\alpha)I}{P_Y}\right)$ is dependent on all three pieces of the consumer's problem: the consumer's relative preferences $(\alpha, 1-\alpha)$, the consumer's income I, and the goods' prices (P_X, P_Y).

Utility Maximization Using the Lagrangian

The first approach to finding the optimal consumption bundle is precisely the method we used in the chapter; the only difference is that we used calculus to derive the marginal utilities and then solved for the marginal rate of substitution. A second approach introduces something known as the Lagrange multiplier, or λ. The Lagrangian is a technique for transforming a constrained optimization problem into an unconstrained problem by combining the objective function and the constraint into one equation. λ is a variable that multiplies the constraint.

Suppose, for example, that the objective function is $f(x,y)$ and the constraint is $g(x,y) = 0$. The Lagrangian equation is

$$\mathcal{L}(x,y,\lambda) = f(x,y) + \lambda[g(x,y)]$$

Now maximize the equation by taking the partial derivatives of the equation with respect to x, y, and λ, and set them equal to zero. Partial derivatives in this form are known as first-order conditions, or FOC:

$$\frac{\partial \mathcal{L}}{\partial x} = \frac{\partial f(x,y)}{\partial x} - \lambda \frac{\partial g(x,y)}{\partial x} = 0$$

$$\frac{\partial \mathcal{L}}{\partial y} = \frac{\partial f(x,y)}{\partial y} - \lambda \frac{\partial g(x,y)}{\partial y} = 0$$

$$\frac{\partial \mathcal{L}}{\partial \lambda} = g(x,y) = 0$$

So, we have three equations and three unknowns and can solve the system of equations. Note that the third first-order condition is simply the constraint.

Let's see how the Lagrangian can be applied to our consumer facing the utility-maximization problem:

$$\max_{X,Y} U(X,Y) = X^\alpha Y^{1-\alpha} \text{ s.t. } I - (P_X X + P_Y Y) = 0$$

(Notice that we wrote the budget constraint so that it is equal to zero—this is important for how we set up the Lagrangian.) This equation can be rewritten in Lagrangian form as

$$\max_{X,Y,\lambda} \mathcal{L}(X,Y,\lambda) = X^\alpha Y^{1-\alpha} + \lambda(I - P_X X - P_Y Y)$$

Take the first-order conditions (FOCs):

$$\frac{\partial \mathcal{L}}{\partial X} = \alpha X^{\alpha-1} Y^{1-\alpha} - \lambda P_X = 0$$

$$\frac{\partial \mathcal{L}}{\partial Y} = (1-\alpha) X^\alpha Y^{-\alpha} - \lambda P_Y = 0$$

$$\frac{\partial \mathcal{L}}{\partial \lambda} = I - P_X X - P_Y Y = 0$$

Embedded in these three first-order conditions are the same three pieces of information we've seen before: the marginal utilities of X and Y, the goods' prices, and the consumer's income.

The Lagrange multiplier λ is in the first two first-order conditions. So, solve each of these equations for λ:

$$\lambda = \frac{\alpha X^{\alpha-1} Y^{1-\alpha}}{P_X} = \frac{(1-\alpha) X^\alpha Y^{-\alpha}}{P_Y}$$

How can we interpret this Lagrange multiplier? First, recognize that the numerators are the marginal utilities of X and Y. In other words, at the optimum, $\lambda = \frac{MU_X}{P_X} = \frac{MU_Y}{P_Y}$. Therefore, λ is the exchange rate between utility and income—an additional dollar of income allows the consumer to purchase additional goods that generate λ more units of utility. We can also see this in the Lagrangian: If income increases by \$1, maximum utility increases by λ units. In other words, λ measures the marginal utility of income. For example, let's say that λ is 0.5. Then, if you gain \$1 more in income, you'll gain 0.5 units of utility.

Note that this expression for λ is the optimization condition in terms of the consumer's marginal utility per dollar spent that we derived in the chapter. We can rearrange this to get exactly what we showed graphically in the text—that the marginal rate of substitution equals the ratio of the prices:

$$\frac{MU_X}{MU_Y} = MRS_{XY} = \frac{P_X}{P_Y}$$

We can then solve for (X^*, Y^*) exactly as we did in the first approach, starting by finding Y as a function of X using the equality from the first two conditions:

$$\frac{\alpha X^{\alpha-1}Y^{1-\alpha}}{P_X} = \frac{(1-\alpha)X^{\alpha}Y^{-\alpha}}{P_Y}$$

$$\frac{Y^{1-\alpha}}{Y^{-\alpha}} = \frac{(1-\alpha)P_X}{\alpha P_Y}\frac{X^{\alpha}}{X^{(\alpha-1)}}$$

$$Y = \frac{(1-\alpha)P_X}{\alpha P_Y}X$$

Using the last first-order condition, we can plug this value for Y into the budget constraint:

$$I - P_X X - P_Y Y = 0$$

$$I = P_X X + P_Y \frac{(1-\alpha)P_X}{\alpha P_Y}X$$

$$I = P_X X\left[1 + \frac{(1-\alpha)}{\alpha}\right]$$

$$I = P_X X\left[\frac{\alpha}{\alpha} + \frac{(1-\alpha)}{\alpha}\right]$$

$$I = \frac{P_X}{\alpha}X$$

$$X^* = \frac{\alpha I}{P_X}$$

$$Y^* = \frac{(1-\alpha)P_X}{\alpha P_Y}\left(\frac{\alpha I}{P_X}\right) = \frac{(1-\alpha)I}{P_Y}$$

4A.1 figure it out

Let's revisit Figure It Out 4.4. Antonio gets utility from burgers (B) and fries (F) in the form

$$U(B,F) = \sqrt{BF} = B^{0.5}F^{0.5}$$

His income is $20, the price of burgers is $5, and the price of fries is $2.

Find Antonio's optimal consumption bundle.

Solution:

To find the optimal consumption bundle, we need to solve the consumer's utility-maximization problem:

$$\max_{B,F} U = B^{0.5}F^{0.5} \text{ s.t. } 20 = 5B + 2F$$

The solution in the chapter uses the approach in which we solve for the MRS_{BF} from the marginal utilities. If instead we use the Lagrangian, we begin by writing Antonio's constrained optimization problem and then solve for the first-order conditions:

$$\max_{B,F,\lambda}\mathcal{L}(B,F,\lambda) = B^{0.5}F^{0.5} + \lambda(20 - 5B - 2F)$$

FOC:

$$\frac{\partial\mathcal{L}}{\partial B} = 0.5B^{-0.5}F^{0.5} - 5\lambda = 0$$

$$\frac{\partial\mathcal{L}}{\partial F} = 0.5B^{0.5}F^{-0.5} - 2\lambda = 0$$

$$\frac{\partial\mathcal{L}}{\partial\lambda} = 20 - 5B - 2F = 0$$

Use the first two conditions to solve for λ:

$$0.5B^{-0.5}F^{0.5} = 5\lambda$$

$$\lambda = 0.1B^{-0.5}F^{0.5}$$

$$0.5B^{0.5}F^{-0.5} = 2\lambda$$

$$\lambda = 0.25B^{0.5}F^{-0.5}$$

Set the two expressions for λ equal to each other and solve for F as a function of B:

$$\lambda = 0.1B^{-0.5}F^{0.5} = 0.25B^{0.5}F^{-0.5}$$

$$0.1F^{0.5}F^{0.5} = 0.25B^{0.5}B^{0.5}$$

$$F = (10)0.25B = 2.5B$$

So, for every burger Antonio consumes at the optimum, he will consume 2.5 orders of fries. Substitute $F = 2.5B$ into the third condition (the consumer's budget constraint) and solve for the optimal bundle (B^*, F^*):

$$20 = 5B + 2F$$
$$20 = 5B + 2(2.5B)$$
$$20 = 10B$$
$$B^* = 2 \text{ burgers}$$
$$F^* = 2.5B = 2.5(2) = 5 \text{ orders of fries}$$

This is where we stopped when we solved Antonio's constrained optimization problem using the first approach we presented in this appendix. But using the Lagrangian, we can also solve for one more variable: the marginal value of Antonio's income, λ, when Antonio is maximizing his utility.

$$\lambda = 0.1B^{-0.5}F^{0.5} = 0.1(2)^{-0.5}(5)^{0.5} \approx 0.16$$

Therefore, Antonio's utility increases by 0.16 units of utility for every extra dollar of income he has.

Expenditure Minimization

As we saw in the chapter, utility maximization—where you take income as given and find the combination of goods that will give you the greatest utility—is only one way to look at the consumer's optimization problem. Another is expenditure minimization, in which you start with a level of utility and find the cheapest bundle that achieves that utility level. In many ways, expenditure minimization is less intuitive—in real life, you probably do face a set income, but no contract you sign will ever specify your utility. But, ultimately, expenditure minimization leads to the same answer. What is more, the expenditure-minimization technique is extremely useful in the appendices for Chapters 5 and 7. In particular, this technique makes a lot more sense in the context of the producer's cost-minimization problem in Chapter 7.

Let's demonstrate the equivalence of utility maximization and expenditure minimization using Antonio's utility function from the Figure It Out and the Lagrangian method (the first approach is identical to that for utility maximization except that you plug into the utility constraint instead of the budget constraint in the last step). We write out Antonio's expenditure-minimization problem given a constant utility of $\sqrt{10}$ or $10^{0.5}$, the utility at his optimal consumption bundle from the utility-maximization problem above:

$$\min_{B,F} I = 5B + 2F \text{ s.t. } 10^{0.5} = B^{0.5}F^{0.5}$$

or

$$\min_{B,F,\lambda} \mathcal{L}(B,F,\lambda) = 5B + 2F + \lambda(10^{0.5} - B^{0.5}F^{0.5})$$

As before, solve for the first-order conditions:

$$\frac{\partial \mathcal{L}}{\partial B} = 5 - \lambda 0.5B^{-0.5}F^{0.5} = 0$$

$$\frac{\partial \mathcal{L}}{\partial F} = 2 - \lambda 0.5B^{0.5}F^{-0.5} = 0$$

$$\frac{\partial \mathcal{L}}{\partial \lambda} = 10^{0.5} - B^{0.5}F^{0.5} = 0$$

Then solve for λ in the first two conditions:

$$\lambda 0.5B^{-0.5}F^{0.5} = 5$$
$$\lambda = 10B^{0.5}F^{-0.5}$$
$$\lambda 0.5B^{0.5}F^{-0.5} = 2$$
$$\lambda = 4B^{-0.5}F^{0.5}$$

Set the two expressions for λ equal to each other and solve for F as a function of B:

$$\lambda = 4B^{-0.5}F^{0.5} = 10B^{0.5}F^{-0.5}$$

$$4F^{0.5}F^{0.5} = 10B^{0.5}B^{0.5}$$

$$F = 2.5B$$

Now substitute F as a function of B into the utility constraint:

$$10^{0.5} = B^{0.5}F^{0.5} = B^{0.5}(2.5B)^{0.5} = (2.5)^{0.5}B^{0.5}B^{0.5}$$

$$B^* = \left(\frac{10}{2.5}\right)^{0.5} = 4^{0.5} = 2$$

$$F^* = 2.5B^* = 2.5(2) = 5$$

This optimal bundle of goods costs Antonio

$$5B^* + 2F^* = 5(2) + 2(5) = \$20$$

the minimum expenditure needed to achieve $10^{0.5}$ units of utility.

Expenditure minimization is a good check of our cost-minimization problem because it should yield the same results. In this case, as with utility maximization, Antonio purchases 2 burgers and 5 orders of fries for a cost of \$20 and a total utility of $10^{0.5}$.

Problems

1. For the following utility functions,
   - Find the marginal utility of each good.
   - Determine whether the marginal utility decreases as consumption of each good increases (i.e., does the utility function exhibit diminishing marginal utility in each good?).
   - Find the marginal rate of substitution.
   - Discuss how MRS_{XY} changes as the consumer substitutes X for Y along an indifference curve.
   - Derive the equation for the indifference curve where utility is equal to a value of 100.
   - Graph the indifference curve where utility is equal to a value of 100.
   a. $U(X,Y) = 5X + 2Y$
   b. $U(X,Y) = X^{0.33}Y^{0.67}$
   c. $U(X,Y) = 10X^{0.5} + 5Y$
2. Suppose that Maggie cares only about chai and bagels. Her utility function is $U = CB$, where C is the number of cups of chai she drinks in a day, and B is the number of bagels she eats in a day. The price of chai is \$3, and the price of bagels is \$1.50. Maggie has \$6 to spend per day on chai and bagels.
   a. What is Maggie's objective function?
   b. What is Maggie's constraint?
   c. Write a statement of Maggie's constrained optimization problem.
   d. Solve Maggie's constrained optimization problem using a Lagrangian.

3. Suppose that there are two goods (X and Y). The price of X is \$2 per unit, and the price of Y is \$1 per unit. There are two consumers (A and B). The utility functions for the consumers are

$$U_A(X,Y) = X^{0.5}Y^{0.5}$$

$$U_B(X,Y) = X^{0.8}Y^{0.2}$$

   Consumer A has an income of \$100, and Consumer B has an income of \$300.
   a. Use Lagrangians to solve the constrained utility-maximization problems for Consumer A and Consumer B.
   b. Calculate the marginal rate of substitution for each consumer at his or her optimal consumption bundles.
   c. Suppose that there is another consumer (let's call her C). You don't know anything about her utility function or her income. All you know is that she consumes both goods. What do you know about C's marginal rate of substitution at her optimal consumption bundle? Why?
4. Katie likes to paint and sit in the sun. Her utility function is $U(P,S) = 3PS + 6P$, where P is the number of paint brushes and S is the number of straw hats. The price of a paint brush is \$1 and the price of a straw hat is \$5. Katie has \$50 to spend on paint brushes and straw hats.

a. Solve Katie's utility-maximization problem using a Lagrangian.

b. How much does Katie's utility increase if she receives an extra dollar to spend on paint brushes and straw hats?

5. Suppose that a consumer's utility function for two goods (X and Y) is

$$U(X,Y) = 10X^{0.5} + 2Y$$

The price of good X is $5 per unit and the price of good Y is $10 per unit. Suppose that the consumer must have 80 units of utility and wants to achieve this level of utility with the lowest possible expenditure.

a. Write a statement of the constrained optimization problem.

b. Use a Lagrangian to solve the expenditure-minimization problem.

Individual and Market Demand

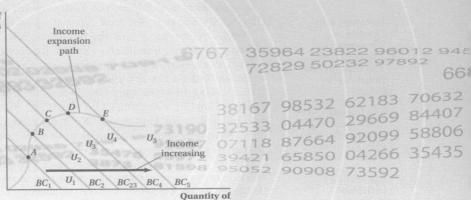

I n Chapter 4, we learned the basics of how consumers make choices: Preferences (embodied in the consumer's utility function and its associated indifference curves) and income and market prices (both embodied in the consumer's budget constraint) combine to pin down the consumer's utility-maximizing bundle of goods. Variations in preferences are reflected in the shapes of indifference curves, and variations in income and prices are reflected in the location and slope of the budget constraint.

Now that we've built our consumer choice framework, we can show how it forms the basis of the demand curves in Chapters 2 and 3. We'll see exactly where demand curves come from, when they shift, and how to add up individual consumers' demands to get market demand curves.

The importance of a deeper understanding of the determinants of demand is clear: Demand is half the story in any market. Knowing what drives consumer demand is crucial to understanding a number of issues, including:

- why shifts in tastes affect prices,

- the benefits that products offer consumers,

■ what happens to purchase patterns as consumers (or even entire countries) become wealthier,

■ how changes in the price of one good affect the demand for other goods, and

■ what factors determine consumers' responses to price changes.

We start this chapter by looking at what happens to a consumer's choices when prices stay fixed and his income goes up or down. This analysis involves finding the consumer's optimal bundle not just once for a particular income level (as we did in Chapter 4), but over and over for every possible amount of income.

Next, we determine how the bundle a given consumer chooses changes as the price of one good in the bundle changes, holding constant income and the price of the other good. Once again, this analysis involves finding the utility-maximizing optimal consumption bundle not just once, but for every possible price of the good in the bundle. By analyzing how the quantity desired of a good changes as the price of that good changes (holding everything else constant), we can map out an individual consumer's demand curve for that good. We'll see that consumers' responses to price changes have two components: the change in relative prices caused by the price change and the change in the purchasing power of the consumer's income caused by the price change.

We then see how changes in the price of *other* goods affect the consumer's decision about how much of a particular good to consume. This effect can increase or decrease the quantity of a good demanded, depending on whether one good is a substitute for the other or if the two goods are consumed together.

After we explore all these features of an *individual's* choices, we show how total *market* demand responds to the same changes. Once this is done, we'll have a full understanding of what determines the same market demand that we took as given in Chapters 2 and 3.

5.1 How Income Changes Affect an Individual's Consumption Choices

In Section 4.3, we learned how changes in income affect the position of a consumer's budget constraint. Lower incomes shift the constraint toward the origin; higher incomes shift it out. In this section, we look at how a change in income affects a consumer's utility-maximizing consumption decisions. This is known as the **income effect.** To isolate this effect, we hold everything else constant during our analysis. Specifically, we assume that the consumer's preferences (reflected in the utility function and its associated indifference curves) and the prices of the goods stay the same.

Figure 5.1 shows the effect of an increase in income on consumption for Evan, a consumer who allocates his income between vacations and fancy gourmet restaurant meals. Initially, Evan's budget constraint is BC_1 and the utility-maximizing consumption bundle is at point A, where indifference curve U_1 is tangent to BC_1. If the prices of vacations and gourmet meals remain unchanged, an increase in Evan's income means that he can afford more of both goods. As a result, the increase in income induces a parallel, outward shift in the budget constraint from BC_1 to BC_2. Note that, because we hold prices fixed, the slope of the budget constraint (the ratio of the goods' prices) remains fixed. The new optimal consumption bundle at this higher income level is B, the point where indifference curve U_2 is tangent to BC_2.

Because U_2 shows bundles of goods that offer a higher utility level than those on U_1, the increase in income allows Evan to achieve a higher utility level. Note that when we analyze the effect of changes in income on consumer behavior, we hold preferences (as well as prices) constant. Thus, indifference curve U_2 does not appear because of some income-driven shift in preferences. U_2 was always there even when Evan's income was lower. At the lower income, however, point B and all other bundles on U_2 (and any other higher indifference curves) were infeasible because Evan could not afford them.

income effect
The change in a consumer's consumption choices that results from a change in the purchasing power of the consumer's income.

Figure 5.1 | A Consumer's Response to an Increase in Income When Both Goods Are Normal

Evan allocates his income between two normal goods, vacations and gourmet restaurant meals. His initial budget constraint BC_1 is tangent to the utility curve U_1 at the optimal consumption bundle A. An increase in Evan's income is represented by the outward parallel shift of BC_1 to BC_2. Since the prices of the goods are unchanged, Evan can now afford to buy more vacations and meals, and his new utility-maximizing bundle is B, where utility curve U_2 is tangent to BC_2. At bundle B, Evan's consumption of vacations and restaurant meals rises from Q_v to Q_v' and Q_m to Q_m', respectively.

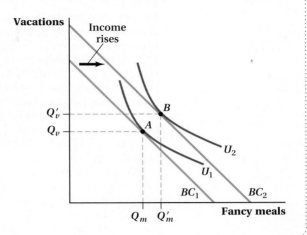

Normal and Inferior Goods

Notice how the new optimum in Figure 5.1 involves higher levels of consumption for both goods. The number of vacations Evan takes rises from Q_v to Q_v', and the number of gourmet meals increases from Q_m to Q_m'. This result isn't that surprising; Evan was spending money on both vacations and gourmet meals before his income went up, so we might expect that he'd spend some of his extra income on both goods. Economists call a good whose consumption rises when income rises—that is, a good for which the income effect is positive—a **normal good.** Vacations and gourmet meals are normal goods for Evan. As "normal" suggests, most goods have positive income effects.

It is possible that an increase in income can lead to a consumer optimally consuming a smaller quantity of a good. As we indicated in Chapter 2, economists refer to such goods as **inferior goods.** Figure 5.2 presents an example in which one of the goods is

normal good
A good for which consumption rises when income rises.

inferior good
A good for which consumption decreases when income rises.

Figure 5.2 | A Consumer's Response to an Increase in Income When One Good Is Inferior

When a good is inferior, an increase in a consumer's income decreases the consumer's consumption of that good. Here, mac and cheese is an inferior good, while steak is a normal good. When the consumer's income increases, shifting the budget constraint outward from BC_1 to BC_2, she consumes less mac and cheese and more steak at the optimal consumption bundle. From initial optimal consumption bundle A to her new optimal consumption bundle B, the quantity of mac and cheese consumed decreases from Q_{mac} to Q_{mac}' while her consumption of the normal good steak increases from Q_s to Q_s'.

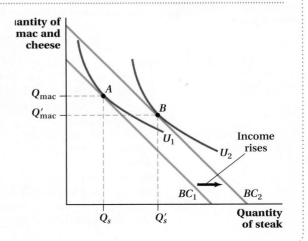

inferior. An increase in the consumer's income from BC_1 to BC_2 leads to more steak being consumed, but less macaroni and cheese. Note that it isn't just that the quantity of mac and cheese *relative to* the quantity of steak falls. This change can happen even when both goods are normal (i.e., they both rise, but steak rises more). Instead, it is the *absolute* quantity of macaroni and cheese consumed that drops in the move from A to B, because Q'_{mac} is less than Q_{mac}. Note also that this drop is optimal from the consumer's perspective—B is her utility-maximizing bundle given her budget constraint BC_2, and this bundle offers a higher utility level than A because indifference curve U_2 represents a higher utility level than U_1. The difference is the shape of the indifference curves for these goods (which comes from the utility function).

What kind of goods tend to be inferior? Usually, they are goods that are perceived to be low-quality or otherwise undesirable. Examples might include generic cereal brands, secondhand clothing, nights spent in youth hostels, and Spam. When we say Spam, we mean the kind you buy in the grocery store, not the kind you get via e-mail. Junk e-mail probably isn't a good at all, but rather a "bad."

We do know that *every* good can't be inferior, however. If a consumer were to consume a smaller quantity of everything when his income rises, he wouldn't be spending all his new, higher income. This outcome would be inconsistent with utility maximization, which states that a consumer always ends up buying a bundle on his budget constraint. (Remember there is no saving in this model.)

Whether the effect of an income change on a good's consumption is positive (consumption increases) or negative (consumption decreases) can often vary with the level of income. (We look at some of these special cases later in the chapter.) For instance, a good such as a used car is likely to be a normal good at low levels of income, and an inferior good at high levels of income. When someone's income is very low, owning a used car is prohibitively expensive and riding a bike or taking public transportation is necessary. As income increases from such low levels, a used car becomes increasingly likely to be purchased, making it a normal good. But once someone becomes rich enough, used cars are supplanted by new cars and his consumption of used cars falls. Over that higher income range, the used car is an inferior good.

Income Elasticities and Types of Goods

income elasticity
The percentage change in the quantity consumed of a good in response to a 1% change in income.

We've discussed how the income effect can be positive (as with normal goods) or negative (as with inferior goods). We can make further distinctions between types of goods by looking not just at the sign of the income effect, but at the **income elasticity** as well, which we discussed in Chapter 2. Remember that the income elasticity measures the *percentage* change in the quantity consumed of a good in response to a given *percentage* change in income. Formally, the income elasticity is

$$E_I^D = \frac{\%\Delta Q}{\%\Delta I} = \frac{\Delta Q/Q}{\Delta I/I} = \frac{\Delta Q}{\Delta I}\frac{I}{Q}$$

where Q is the quantity of the good consumed (ΔQ is the change in quantity), and I is income (ΔI is the change in income). As we noted in our earlier discussion, income elasticity is like the price elasticity of demand, except that we are now considering the responsiveness of consumption to income changes rather than to price changes.

The first ratio in the income elasticity definition is the income effect shown in the equations above: $\Delta Q/\Delta I$, the change in quantity consumed in response to a change in income. Therefore, the sign of the income elasticity is the same as the sign of the income effect. For normal goods, $\Delta Q/\Delta I > 0$, and the income elasticity is positive. For inferior goods, $\Delta Q/\Delta I < 0$, and the income elasticity is negative.

Within the class of normal goods, economists occasionally make a further distinction. The quantities of goods with an income elasticity between zero and 1 (sometimes called **necessity goods**) rise with income, but at a slower rate. Because prices are held constant when measuring income elasticities, the slower-than-income quantity growth implies the *share* of a consumer's budget devoted to the good *falls* as income grows. Many normal goods fit into this category, especially things that just about everyone uses or needs, like toothpaste, salt, socks, and electricity. Someone who earns $1 million a year may well consume more of these goods (or more expensive varieties) than an aspiring artist who earns $10,000 annually, but the millionaire, whose income is 100 times greater than the artist's, is unlikely to spend 100 times more on toothpaste (or salt, or socks . . .) than the artist spends.

necessity good
A normal good for which income elasticity is between zero and 1.

Luxury goods have an income elasticity greater than 1. Because their quantities consumed grow faster than income does, these goods account for an increasing fraction of the consumer's expenditure as income rises. Luxury goods tend to be those that one does not need to live, but that improve the quality of life: first-class airline tickets, jewelry, fancy coffee drinks, beach homes, and so on.

luxury good
A good with an income elasticity greater than 1.

The Income Expansion Path

Imagine repeating the analysis in the previous section for every possible income level. That is, for a given set of prices and a particular set of preferences, we can find the utility-maximizing bundle for every possible budget constraint, where each constraint corresponds to a different income level. Those optimal bundles will be located wherever an indifference curve is tangent to a budget line. In both of the examples above, they'll include bundles A and B.

Figure 5.3 demonstrates an example of such an exercise. In the figure, Meredith allocates her income between bus rides and bottled water. Points A, B, C, D, and E are the optimal consumption bundles at five different income levels that correspond to the budget constraints shown. Point A is Meredith's utility-maximizing bundle for the lowest of the five income levels, point B is the bundle for the second-lowest income, and so on. Note that the indifference curves themselves come from the individual's utility function. We have chosen various shapes here just to illustrate that these points can move around in different ways.

Figure 5.3   The Income Expansion Path

Meredith's income expansion path connects all of the optimal bundles of bottled water and bus rides for each income level. Points A, B, C, D, and E are optimal consumption bundles associated with budget constraints BC_1 through BC_5. Where both bottled water and bus rides are normal goods, the income expansion path is upward-sloping. At incomes higher than that shown at the budget constraint BC_4 and to the right of bundle D, bus rides become inferior goods, and the income expansion path slopes downward.

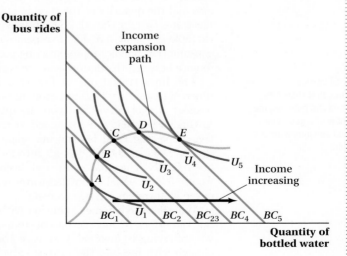

income expansion path
A curve that connects a consumer's optimal bundles at each income level.

If we draw a line connecting all the optimal bundles (the five here plus all the others for budget constraints we don't show in the figure), it would trace out a curve known as the **income expansion path**. This curve always starts at the origin because when income is zero, the consumption of both goods must also be zero. We've drawn in Meredith's income expansion path for bus rides and bottled water in Figure 5.3.

When both goods are normal goods, the income expansion path will be positively sloped because consumption of both goods rises when income does. If the slope of the income expansion path is negative, then the quantity consumed of one of the goods falls with income while the other rises. The good whose quantity falls is therefore inferior. Remember that whether a given good is normal or inferior can depend on the consumer's income level. In the example in Figure 5.3, for example, both bus rides and bottled water are normal goods at incomes up to the level corresponding to the budget constraint containing bundle D. As income rises above that and the budget constraint continues to shift out, the income expansion path begins to curve downward. This outcome means that bus rides become an inferior good as Meredith's income rises beyond that level. We can also see from the income expansion path that bottled water is never inferior, because the path never curves back to the left. When there are only two goods, it's impossible for both goods to be inferior at a given income level. If they were both inferior, an increase in income would actually lead to lower expenditure on both goods, meaning that the consumer wouldn't be spending all of her income.

The Engel Curve

The income expansion path is a useful tool for examining how consumer behavior changes in response to changes in income, but it has two important weaknesses. First, because we have only two axes, we can only look at two goods at a time. Second, although we can easily see the consumption quantities of each good, we can't see directly the income level that a particular point on the curve corresponds to. The income level equals the sum of the quantities consumed of each good (which are easily seen in the figure) multiplied by their respective prices (which aren't easily seen). The basic problem is that when we talk about consumption and income, we care about three numbers—the quantities of each of the two goods and income—but we have only two dimensions on the graph in which to see them.

A better way to see how the quantity consumed of one good varies with income (as opposed to how the relative quantities of the two goods vary) is to take the information conveyed by the income expansion path and plot it on a graph with income on the vertical axis and the quantity of the good in question on the horizontal axis. Panel a of Figure 5.4 illustrates this for the relationship between income and the quantity of bus rides from our example in Figure 5.3. The five points mapped in panel a of Figure 5.4 are the same five consumption bundles represented by points A, B, C, D, and E in Figure 5.3; the only difference between the figures is in the variables measured by the axes.

Engel curve
A curve that shows the relationship between the quantity of a good consumed and a consumer's income.

The lines traced out in Figure 5.4 are known as **Engel curves,** named for the nineteenth-century German economist Ernst Engel who first presented the data in this manner. Engel curves tell you the quantities of goods—bus rides and bottled water, in this case—that are consumed at each income level. If the Engel curve has a positive slope, the good is a normal good at that income level. If the Engel curve has a negative slope, the good is an inferior good at that income. In Figure 5.4a, bus rides are initially a normal good, but become inferior after bundle D, just as we saw in Figure 5.3. In panel b, bottled water is a normal good at all income levels and the Engel curve is always positively sloped.

Whether the income expansion path or Engel curves are more useful for understanding the effect of income on consumption choices depends on the particular question we are trying to answer. If we care about how the relative quantities of the two goods change with income, the income expansion path is more useful because it shows both quantities at the same time. On the other hand, if we want to investigate the impact

Figure 5.4   An Engel Curve Shows How Consumption Varies with Income

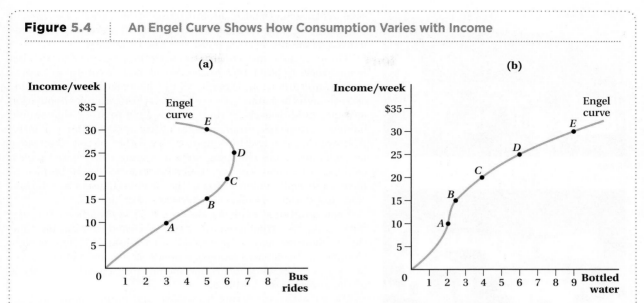

(a) In contrast to an income expansion path, an Engel curve compares the consumption of a single good to the consumer's income. As Meredith's income increases from $10/week to $25/week, her consumption of bus rides increases from 3 to a little over 6 bus rides. At income levels above $25/week, bus rides are inferior goods, and the number of bus rides she takes decreases.

(b) Bottled water is a normal good across all income levels shown here. At an income of $10/week at point A, Meredith consumes 2 bottles of water. At point E, Meredith's income is $30/week, and the number of bottles of water she buys increases to 9 per week.

of income changes on the consumption of one particular good, the Engel curve isolates this relationship more clearly. The most important thing to remember is that the two curves contain the same information displayed in different ways due to the limitations imposed by having only two axes.

 application

Engel Curves and House Sizes

Houses in the United States have been getting larger for several decades. In 1950 newly built houses had an average of about 1,000 square feet (93 square meters) of floor area, a little less than one-fourth the size of a basketball court. By 2008 the average new house was well over twice as large, at 2,519 square feet. Recent debates about "McMansions" and tear-downs, still present even after the housing crash, have highlighted this trend and how it has affected discussions of public policies like zoning laws.

Explanations for this trend vary. Some have suggested homeowners' utility functions have changed in a way that favors more space. But another (not mutually exclusive) possibility is that space is a normal good, so homeowners demand more space as they become wealthier. It isn't necessary for homeowners' utility functions to have changed to see such effects. It could just be that an increase in income has moved them to a different part of their utility function where they demand more space.

The historical patterns are consistent with those that would arise from an income effect at work. Figure 5.5 plots the average size of newly built homes (in square feet) and average inflation-adjusted household income (in thousands of dollars) from 1975 to 2009. Both house

Time & Life Pictures/Getty Images

Then

Brendel/Wikimedia Commons

Now

sizes and income trended upward through this period. The sizes of the changes in these variables were similar too; for every 10% increase in average income, average house size rose by about 11%.[1]

These trends are consistent with income growth driving homeowners to buy larger homes. We should be careful in leaping to this interpretation, though. Many things can trend over time even though they aren't closely related. (For example, population also increased over the period, but it's hard to argue that simply having more people around makes everyone want larger homes.) And even if income effects matter here, other factors that make larger homes more common, such as falling construction costs, could also be changing over time. It would therefore be nice to have additional evidence about the income–house size relationship that doesn't involve simple trends over time.

Such additional evidence does exist. The American Housing Survey (AHS) is conducted every two years and contains information on housing and demographics for thousands of households. Comparing home sizes to income levels across individual households at a given moment in time should complement our analysis of the average trends above.

We fit a curve relating home size and annual household income in the 2007 survey data (a survey containing about 35,000 households) in Figure 5.6. This is very similar to an Engel curve for home size: It shows how much a household's purchases of a good (square feet) varies with its income.[2]

Figure 5.5 | **Average New House Size and Household Income in the United States, 1975–2009**

House sizes and income trended upward between 1975 and 2009, increasing at almost the same rate.

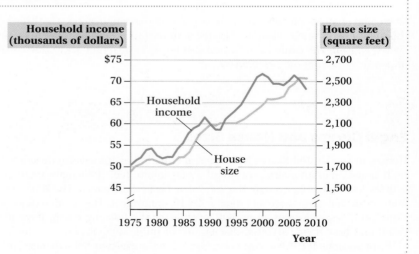

---

[1] These data are collected from various U.S. Census Bureau publications.

[2] It's not exactly an Engel curve for a few reasons. For one, we aren't able to hold constant everything else about households' choices. To read Figure 5.6 as an Engel curve, we're assuming that every household is the same except for its income level. In reality, households might differ in their preferences and size as well as incomes. Furthermore, different households might face various prices for square footage depending on where they live. If these prices are related to income levels (say, because people who live in urban areas both have higher average incomes and face higher house prices per square foot), this could mix up price and income effects. Nevertheless, the relationship in Figure 5.6 is probably close to the true Engel curve for square footage.

Figure 5.6   **An Engel Curve for House Size in the United States**

The Engel curve for housing slopes upward, indicating that housing is a normal good. However, for incomes between approximately $175,000 and $250,000 per year, house size does not change much as income grows.

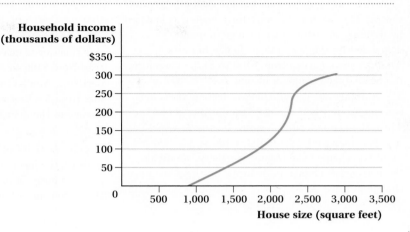

We can see that this Engel curve always slopes up. That is, based on these data, house size is always a normal good. However, there is a considerable income range—from about $175,000 to $250,000 a year—where the size of the income effect is fairly small and home size does not change much as income grows. It's also interesting to compare the average slope of this Engel curve to the size-income correlation we saw in the time trend data. In the time trends in Figure 5.5, 10% income growth was tied to an 11% increase in house size. This relationship is smaller when we look across households in Figure 5.6: People with 10% more income have houses that are around 2% larger. One reason why the relationship across people might be smaller than across time is that the cross section of people includes all houses, not just newly built ones. If home sizes are trending upward over time (which they did from 1950 to 2005), and not just the highest income households are buying new houses, this will reduce the correlation between size and income in the cross section because some higher-income households will be in older, smaller houses. It could also be that factors in addition to income growth (such as preferences) are driving the trends of the past several decades. Nevertheless, it's clear from both sets of data that income changes are strongly related to the demand for house size. ∎

5.1 figure it out

Annika spends all of her income on golf and pancakes. Greens fees at a local golf course are $10 per round. Pancake mix is $2 per box. When Annika's income is $100 per week, she buys 5 boxes of pancake mix and 9 rounds of golf. When Annika's income rises to $120 per week, she buys 10 boxes of pancake mix and 10 rounds of golf. Based on these figures, determine whether each of the following statements is true or false, and briefly explain your reasoning.

  a. Golf is a normal good, and pancake mix is an inferior good.

  b. Golf is a luxury good.

  c. Pancakes are a luxury good.

Solution:

  a. A normal good is one of which a consumer buys more when income rises. An inferior good is a good for which consumption falls when income rises. When Annika's income rises, she purchases more pancake mix and more rounds of golf. This means that both goods are normal goods for Annika. Therefore, the statement is *false*.

b. A luxury good has an income elasticity greater than 1. The income elasticity for a good is calculated by dividing the percentage change in quantity demanded by the percentage change in income. Annika's income rises from $100 to $120. Therefore, the percentage change in income is $\frac{\Delta I}{I} \times 100 = \frac{20}{100} \times 100 = 20$. When Annika's income rises, her consumption of golf changes from 9 rounds to 10. Thus, the percentage change in the quantity of rounds demanded is $\frac{\Delta Q}{Q} \times 100 = 100 = \frac{1}{9} \times 100 = 11.1$. To calculate the income elasticity, we divide the percentage change in quantity by the percentage change in price, $\frac{11.1}{20} = 0.555$. Golf cannot be a luxury good for Annika because the elasticity is not greater than 1. Therefore, the statement is *false*.

c. Again, we must calculate the income elasticity, this time for pancake mix. When Annika's income rises from $100 to $120 [a 20% rise as calculated in part (b)], Annika increases her purchases of pancake mix from 5 boxes to 10 boxes. Thus, the percentage change in the quantity of pancake mix demanded is $\frac{\Delta Q}{Q} \times 100 = \frac{5}{5} \times 100 = 100$. This means that the income elasticity of demand is $\frac{\%\Delta Q}{\%\Delta I} = \frac{100}{20} = 5$. Because the income elasticity is greater than 1, pancake mix is a luxury good for Annika. Therefore, the statement is *true*.

5.2 How Price Changes Affect Consumption Choices

In the previous section, we looked at how a consumer's choices change when we vary income, holding prices and preferences constant. In this section, we see what happens when the price of a good changes, holding income, preferences, and the prices of all other goods constant. *This analysis tells us exactly where a demand curve comes from.*

At this point, it is useful to recall exactly what a demand curve is because it has been a few chapters since we discussed the concept. We learned in Chapter 2 that many factors influence the quantity that a consumer demands of a good. The demand curve isolates how one particular factor, a good's own price, affects the quantity demanded while holding everything else constant. Changes in any other factor that influences the quantity demanded (such as income, preferences, or the prices of other goods) shift the location of the demand curve.

Up to this point, we know that demand curves slope downward because diminishing marginal utility implies that consumers' willingness to pay falls as quantities rise. That explanation is correct, but it skips a step. A consumer's demand curve actually comes straight from the consumer's utility maximization. A demand curve answers the following question: As the price of a good changes while holding all else constant, how does the quantity of that good in the utility-maximizing bundle change? This is exactly the question we're going to answer here.

Deriving a Demand Curve

To see how a consumer's utility-maximizing behavior leads to a demand curve, let's look at a specific example. Suppose Caroline is deciding how to spend her income on two goods, 2-liter bottles of Mountain Dew and 1-liter bottles of grape juice, and we want to know her demand curve for grape juice. Caroline's income is $20, and the price of Mountain Dew is $2 per 2-liter bottle. We'll hold these factors (income and price of Mountain Dew) and Caroline's preferences constant throughout our analysis. If we didn't, we would not be mapping out a single demand curve (which, remember, shows the relationship between price of a good and the quantity demanded of that good), but would instead be shifting the demand curve around.

To build the demand curve, we start by figuring out the consumer's utility-maximizing consumption bundle at some price for grape juice. It doesn't actually matter what price we use to start because we will eventually compute the quantity demanded at all prices. Let's start with a price of $1 per liter bottle of grape juice. (It makes the math easy.)

The top half of Figure 5.7a shows Caroline's utility-maximization problem. Her budget constraint reflects the combinations of bottles of Mountain Dew and bottles of grape juice that she can afford at the current prices. With an income of $20, she can buy up to 10 bottles of Mountain Dew at $2 per bottle if that's all she spends her money on, or up to 20 bottles of grape juice at $1 per bottle if she restricts her purchases to grape juice. The slope of the budget constraint equals the negative of the price ratio P_{MD}/P_G, which is −0.5 in this case. Caroline's indifference curve that is tangent to this budget constraint is also shown in the figure. We know that the point of tangency shown is the utility-maximizing bundle. Given her income, her preferences, and the prices of the two juices, Caroline's optimal quantities to consume are 3 bottles of Mountain Dew and 14 bottles of grape juice.

We now have one point on Caroline's demand curve for grape juice: At a price of $1 per liter, her quantity demanded is 14 bottles. The only problem is that the top panel of Figure 5.7a does not have the correct axes for a demand curve. Remember that a

Figure 5.7   Building an Individual's Demand Curve

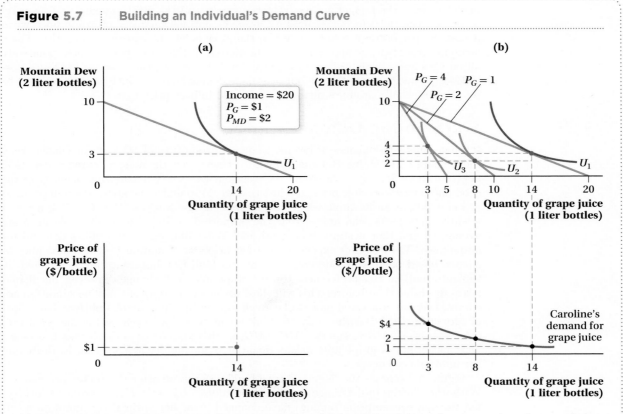

(a) At her optimal consumption bundle, Caroline purchases 14 bottles of grape juice when the price per bottle is $1 and her income is $20. The bottom panel plots this point on her demand curve, with the price of grape juice on the y-axis and the quantity of grape juice on the x-axis.

(b) A completed demand curve consists of many of these quantity-price points. Here, the optimal quantity of grape juice consumed is plotted for the prices $1, $2, and $4 per bottle. This creates Caroline's demand curve, as shown in the bottom panel.

demand curve for a good is drawn with the good's price on the vertical axis and its quantity demanded on the horizontal axis. When we graphically search for the tangency of indifference curves and budget constraints, however, we put the quantities of the two goods on the axes. So we'll make a new figure, shown in the bottom panel of Figure 5.7a, that plots the same quantity of grape juice as the figure's top panel, but with the price of grape juice on the vertical axis. Because the horizontal axis in the bottom panel is the same as that in the top—the quantity of grape juice—we can vertically transfer that dimension of the figure directly from the top to the bottom panel.

To finish building the demand curve, we need to repeat the process described above again and again for many different grape juice prices. When the price changes, the budget constraint's slope changes, which reflects the relative prices of the two goods. For each new budget constraint, we find the optimal consumption bundle by finding the indifference curve that is tangent to it. Because preferences are constant, the set of indifference curves corresponding to Caroline's utility function remains the same. It's just that the particular indifference curve that is tangent to the budget constraint will depend on where the constraint is. Each time we determine the optimal quantity consumed at a given price of grape juice, we have found another point on the demand curve.

Figure 5.7b shows this exercise for grape juice prices of $1, $2, and $4 per bottle. As the price of grape juice rises (holding fixed the price of Mountain Dew and Caroline's income), the budget constraint gets steeper, and the utility-maximizing quantity of grape juice falls. In our example, Caroline's optimal quantity of grape juice when it costs $2 per bottle is 8 bottles. When the price is $4, she consumes 3 bottles. These combinations of prices and quantities are plotted in the lower panel. These points are all on Caroline's demand curve for grape juice. Repeating this exercise for every possible grape juice price will trace out her whole demand curve, which we've drawn in the figure. Note that Caroline's quantity demanded falls as price rises.

Shifts in the Demand Curve

If a consumer's preferences or income change, or the prices of other goods change, then the demand curve shifts. But the process for tracing out the demand curve under these new conditions is exactly the same: We trace out the utility-maximizing quantity of the good under every possible price. It's just that we do so under the updated circumstances.

Let's look at an example where preferences change. Suppose that Caroline meets a scientist at a party who argues that the purported health benefits of grape juice are overstated and that it stains your teeth red. What happens to Caroline's demand for grape juice? We wouldn't expect the market prices of Mountain Dew or grape juice to change based on this private conversation, nor will Caroline's income be affected by this information. Her preferences toward grape juice will change, however. She'll find it less desirable than before. This will show up as a flattening of Caroline's indifference curves, because now she'll have to be given more grape juice to be indifferent to a loss of Mountain Dew. Another way to think about it is that, because the marginal rate of substitution (MRS) equals $-MU_G/MU_{MD}$, this preference shift shrinks Caroline's marginal utility of grape juice at any quantity, reducing her MRS—that is, flattening her indifference curves.

Figure 5.8 repeats the demand-curve building exercise after the preference change. With the flatter indifference curves (labeled U_1', U_2', and U_3'), Caroline's utility-maximizing consumption bundles have changed. Now her optimal consumption levels of grape juice at prices of $1, $2, and $4 per bottle are 9, 6, and 2 bottles, respectively. The bottom half of Figure 5.8 plots these points on Caroline's new demand curve D_2.

We can see that because Caroline's preferences have changed, she now demands a smaller quantity of grape juice than before at every price. As a result, her demand curve for grape juice has shifted in from D_1 to D_2. This result demonstrates why and how preference changes shift the demand curve. Changes in Caroline's income or in the price

freakonomics

Even Animals Like Sales

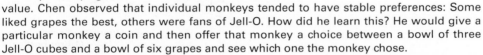

If you think the laws of economics only apply to humans, think again. Monkeys, and even rats, behave in ways that would make you think they've taken intermediate micro.

Some of the most intensive testing of the economic behavior of animals was carried out by Yale economist Keith Chen and his co-authors on a group of Capuchin monkeys. As a first step, Chen introduced the monkeys to the concept of money. He gave them "money" in the form of metal washers that they could exchange for various types of foods including Jell-O, grapes, and Marshmallow Fluff (Capuchin monkeys *love* sweet foods).

Just Like Us?

Courtesy M. Keith Chen

After about six exasperating months, these monkeys finally figured out that the washers had value. Chen observed that individual monkeys tended to have stable preferences: Some liked grapes the best, others were fans of Jell-O. How did he learn this? He would give a particular monkey a coin and then offer that monkey a choice between a bowl of three Jell-O cubes and a bowl of six grapes and see which one the monkey chose.

Next, Chen did what any good economist would do: He subjected the monkeys to price changes! Instead of getting three Jell-O cubes for one washer, he would offer the monkey, say, the choice between a single Jell-O cube per washer and a bowl of six grapes per washer. Thus, the relative price of Jell-O became three times as high. The monkeys responded exactly the way economic theory would predict, shifting their consumption away from the goods whose prices had risen.[*]

Perhaps it is not that surprising that monkeys, one of our closest relatives in the animal kingdom, would be sophisticated consumers. But there is no way rats understand supply and demand, is there? It seems they do. Economists Raymond Battalio and John Kagel equipped rats' cages with two levers, each of which dispensed a different beverage.[†] One of these levers gave the rat a refreshing burst of root beer. Rats, it turns out, love root beer. The other lever released quinine water. Quinine is a bitter-tasting substance initially used to treat malaria, and now used primarily to give vodka tonics their distinctive flavor. Rats are far less fond of quinine than they are of root beer, and they made that quite clear to the researchers by pressing the root beer lever far more often. Battalio and Kagel, like Chen, then explored changes in "prices" (how much liquid came out per press of the lever) and in the rats' budget constraint (how many times they could press the levers each day). Like monkeys (and humans), the rats consumed less of a drink when its relative price increased. Even more interesting is that when the rats were made very poor (i.e., they got very few lever presses each day), they shifted their consumption away from root beer toward quinine water. The researchers found that root beer is a luxury good for rats, and quinine water is an inferior good! Wonder what rats would make of a vodka tonic. . . .

---

[*] That wasn't the only human-like behavior these monkeys exhibited when exposed to money — for the whole amusingly sordid story, see the epilogue to *SuperFreakonomics.*

[†] A description of the work by Battalio and Kagel may be found in: Tim Harford, *The Logic of Life: The Rational Economics of an Irrational World.* (New York: Random House, 2008), pp. 18–21.

Figure 5.8 | **Preference Changes and Shifts in the Demand Curve**

(a) Caroline's indifference curves for grape juice flatten when her preference for grape juice decreases relative to her preference for Mountain Dew. At each price level, she now consumes fewer bottles of grape juice.

(b) Because she purchases fewer bottles of grape juice at each price point, Caroline's demand curve for grape juice shifts inward from D_1 to D_2.

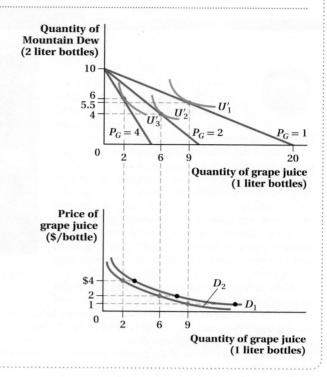

The online appendix derives the demand curve directly from the utility function. (http://glsmicro.com/appendices)

of Mountain Dew also shift her demand curve. (We saw earlier how income shifts affect quantity demanded, and we investigate the effects of price changes in other goods in Section 5.4.) Remember, however, that for any given value of these nonprice influences on demand, the change in the quantity demanded of a good in response to changes in its own price results in a movement along a demand curve, not a shift in the curve.

5.2 figure it out

Cooper allocates $200 of his weekly budget to entertainment. He spends all of this $200 on two goods: theater tickets (which cost $50 each) and movie tickets (which cost $10 each).

a. With theater tickets on the horizontal axis, draw Cooper's budget constraint, making sure to indicate the horizontal and vertical intercepts. What is the slope of the budget constraint?

b. Suppose that Cooper currently purchases 3 theater tickets per week. Indicate this choice on the budget constraint and mark it as point A. Draw an indifference curve tangent to the budget

constraint at point A. How many movie tickets does Cooper buy?

c. Suppose that the price of a theater ticket rises to $80, and Cooper lowers his purchases of theater tickets to 2. Draw Cooper's new budget constraint, indicate his choice with a point B, and draw an indifference curve tangent to the new budget constraint at point B.

d. Once again, the price of a theater ticket rises to $100, and Cooper lowers his purchases of theater tickets to 1 per week. Draw his new budget constraint, show his choice on the budget constraint with a point C, and draw an indifference curve tangent to this new budget constraint at C.

e. Draw a new diagram below your indifference curve diagram. Use your answers to parts (b)–(d) to draw Cooper's demand for theater tickets. Indicate his quantities demanded at $50, $80, and $100. Is there an inverse relationship between price and quantity demanded?

Solution:

a. To start, we need to calculate the horizontal and vertical intercepts for Cooper's budget constraint. The horizontal intercept is the point at which Cooper spends all of his income on theater tickets and purchases no movie tickets. This occurs when he buys $200/$50 = 4 theater tickets (Figure A). The vertical intercept is the point at which Cooper spends his entire income on movie tickets and buys no theater tickets. This means that he is buying $200/$10 = 20 movie tickets. The budget constraint connects these two intercepts. The slope of the budget constraint equals rise/run = −20/4 = −5.

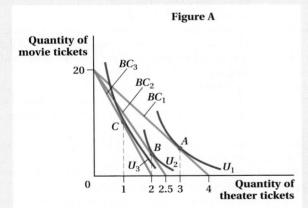

Figure A

Note that this slope is the negative of the ratio of the two prices $= -\dfrac{P_{\text{theater tickets}}}{P_{\text{movie tickets}}} = -\$50/\$10 = -5$.

b. Maximum utility occurs where the indifference curve is tangent to the budget constraint. Therefore, point A should be the point where this tangency takes place. If Cooper purchases 3 theater tickets a week, he will spend $50 × 3 = $150, leaving him $200 − $150 = $50 to spend on movie tickets. Since movie tickets cost $10 each, he purchases $50/$10 = 5 movie tickets.

c. Cooper's budget constraint will rotate in a clockwise direction. The vertical intercept is not

affected because neither Cooper's income nor the price of movie tickets changes. However, the price of theater tickets has risen to $80, and now if Cooper were to allocate his entire budget to theater tickets, he could afford only $200/$80 = 2.5 of them. This is the new horizontal intercept. If Cooper chooses to buy 2 theater tickets, he will have an indifference curve tangent to this budget constraint at that point (B).

d. The budget constraint will again rotate clockwise and the vertical intercept will remain unchanged. The new horizontal intercept will be $200/$100 = 2. Point C will occur where Cooper's indifference curve is tangent to his new budget constraint at a quantity of 1 theater ticket.

e. The demand curve shows the relationship between the price of theater tickets and Cooper's quantity demanded. We can take the information from our indifference curve diagram to develop three points on Cooper's demand curve:

Point	Price	Quantity of Theater Tickets Demanded
A	$50	3
B	$80	2
C	$100	1

We can then plot points A, B, and C on a diagram with the quantity of theater tickets on the horizontal axis and the price of theater tickets on the vertical axis (Figure B). Connecting these points gives us Cooper's demand curve for theater tickets.

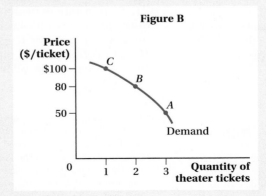

Figure B

5.3 Decomposing Consumer Responses to Price Changes into Income and Substitution Effects

When the price of a good changes, the demand curve for that good tells us how much consumption will change. This total change in quantity demanded, however, is a result of two distinct forces that affect consumers' decisions: the substitution effect and the income effect. Any change in quantity demanded can be decomposed into these two effects.

1. When the price of one good changes relative to the price of another good, consumers will want to buy more of the good that has become relatively cheaper and less of the good that is now relatively more expensive. Economists call this the **substitution effect.**

2. A price shift changes the purchasing power of consumers' incomes—the amount of goods they can buy with a given dollar-level expenditure. If a good gets cheaper, for example, consumers are effectively richer and can buy more of the cheaper good and other goods. If a good's price increases, the purchasing power of consumers' incomes is reduced, and they can buy fewer goods. Economists refer to consumption changes resulting from this shift in spending power as the **income effect.**

> **substitution effect**
> The change in a consumer's consumption choices that results from a change in the relative prices of two goods.

> **income effect**
> The change in a consumer's consumption choices that results from a change in the purchasing power of the consumer's income.

Any change in quantity demanded can be decomposed into these two effects. We introduce them in this book, but we are just scratching the surface. We're going to be upfront with you: The distinction between income and substitution effects is one of the most subtle concepts that you will come across in this entire book. If you go on to take more advanced economics courses, income and substitution effects will come up again and again.[3] There are two reasons why this topic is so difficult. First, we don't separately observe these two effects in the real world, only their combined effects. Their separation is an artificial analytical tool. Put another way, as a consumer you can (and do) figure out how much to consume without knowing or figuring out how much of the change is due to income effects and how much is due to substitution effects. Second, the income effect occurs even when the consumer's income as measured in dollars remains constant. How rich we feel is determined both by how much income we have and how much things cost. If your income stays at $1,000 but the prices of all goods fall by half, you are effectively a lot wealthier. The income effect refers to how rich you feel, not the number of dollar bills in your pocket.

In our overview, we demonstrate income and substitution effects using graphs. The appendix to this chapter describes these effects mathematically.

Figure 5.9 shows how a consumer, Carlos, who spends his income on rounds of golf and restaurant meals, reacts to a fall in the price of restaurant meals. This is just like the analysis we did in Section 5.2. Lower restaurant meal prices lead the budget constraint to rotate outward from BC_1 to BC_2 because Carlos can now purchase more restaurant meals with his income. As a result, the optimal consumption bundle shifts from A (the point of tangency between indifference curve U_1 and budget constraint BC_1) to B (the point of tangency between indifference curve U_2 and budget constraint BC_2). Because of the fall in the price of restaurant meals, the quantity of rounds of golf

---

[3] For instance, it is much easier to describe the properties of a demand curve when there is no income effect, only a substitution effect. Demand curves that reflect only substitution effects are known as "Hicksian demand curves" in honor of the economist Sir John Hicks. The demand curves that combine both effects—the kind you're accustomed to working with, and the kind we'll continue to use throughout the text—are called "Marshallian demand curves" after economist Alfred Marshall. Because we stick with this standard demand curve throughout the book, we'll skip the modifier and just keep calling them demand curves.

Figure 5.9 The Effects of a Fall in the Price of Restaurant Meals

When the price of restaurant meals decreases, Carlos's budget constraint rotates outward from BC_1 to BC_2. The total effect of the price change is shown by the increase in his optimal consumption bundle from point A to point B. In particular, the number of restaurant meals Carlos consumes increases from 3 to 5, and the number of rounds of golf he consumes increases from 5 to 6.

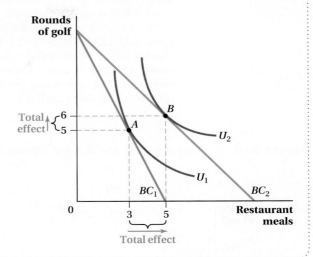

consumed increases from 5 to 6, and the number of restaurant meals Carlos purchases rises from 3 to 5. These overall changes in quantities consumed between bundles A and B are the **total effect** of the price change.

Note that just as in Section 5.2, we figured out the optimal bundle without any reference to income or substitution effects. In the next sections, we decompose the total effect into separate substitution and income effects. That is,

Total Effect = Substitution Effect + Income Effect

Breaking down the movement from A to B into income and substitution effects helps us understand how much of the total change in Carlos's quantity demanded occurs because Carlos switches what he purchases as a result of the reduction in the relative prices of the two goods (the substitution effect), and how much of the change is driven by the fact that the decrease in the price of restaurant meals gives Carlos more purchasing power (the income effect).

Note that all the examples we work through involve a drop in the price of a good. When the price of a good increases, the effects work in the opposite direction.

total effect
The total change (substitution effect + income effect) in a consumer's optimal consumption bundle as a result of a price change.

Isolating the Substitution Effect

Let's begin by isolating the substitution effect. This part of the change in quantities demanded is due to the change in relative prices, not to the change in Carlos's buying power. To isolate the substitution effect, we need to figure out how many rounds of golf and restaurant meals Carlos would want to consume if, after the price change, there was no income effect, that is, if he had the same purchasing power as before the price change and felt neither richer nor poorer.

For Carlos to feel neither richer nor poorer, *the bundle he consumes after the price change must provide him with the same utility he was receiving before the price change; that is, the new bundle must be on the initial indifference curve U_1.*

So where is this substitution-effect-only bundle on U_1? We know this bundle has to reflect the fact that the goods' relative prices have changed. Those new relative prices are embodied in the slope of the new budget line BC_2. The problem is that there isn't a point of tangency between U_1 and BC_2—as we can see in Figure 5.10. However, there *is* a point of tangency between U_1 and a budget line with the same slope (i.e., the same relative prices) as BC_2. The budget line we're talking about is BC', the dashed line in panel a of Figure 5.10, and the point of tangency is point A'.

Bundle A' is what Carlos would buy if the relative prices of rounds of golf and restaurant meals changed the way they did, but Carlos experienced no change in purchasing power. This is the definition of the substitution effect. Thus, the substitution effect in isolation moves Carlos's demanded bundle from A to A'. To find this effect, we have to shift the post-price-change budget line BC_2 back in parallel (to preserve the new relative prices) until it is tangent to the pre-price-change indifference curve U_1 (to

---

Figure 5.10   **Substitution and Income Effects for Two Normal Goods**

(a)

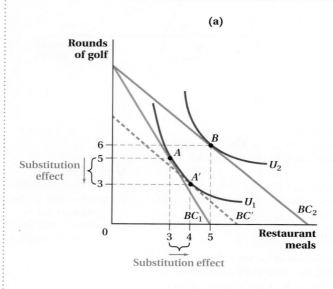

(b)

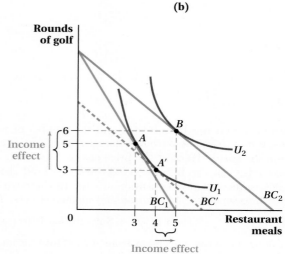

(c)

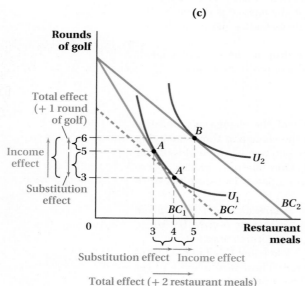

(a) The substitution effect is the change in quantities demanded due to the change in relative prices of restaurant meals and rounds of golf after the price of restaurant meals decreases. The budget constraint BC' is parallel to Carlos's new budget constraint BC_2 but tangent to his original utility level U_1. The point of tangency between BC' and U_1, consumption bundle A', is the bundle Carlos would purchase if relative prices changed but his purchasing power did not. The change from bundle A to bundle A' is the substitution effect.

(b) The income effect is the change in quantities demanded due to the change in the consumer's purchasing power after the change in prices. When the price of restaurant meals decreases, Carlos can afford to purchase a larger bundle than he could before the price change. The change in the quantity of goods consumed from bundle A' to B represents the income effect.

(c) The total effect is the sum of the substitution and income effects. In this case, Carlos consumes 1 more round of golf and 2 more restaurant meals.

keep the original utility level the same). *It's important to recognize that the budget line BC' is hypothetical—Carlos never actually faces it.* Instead, it is a conceptual device that lets us figure out what Carlos would do if he did face it; that is, if relative prices changed in the way they actually did while at the same time any income gains he enjoyed as a result were taken away from him.

There are a few things to notice about the change in quantities due to the substitution effect. First, the quantity of rounds of golf decreases (from 5 to 3), and the quantity of restaurant meals increases (from 3 to 4). The decrease in the quantity of rounds of golf demanded occurs because the price change has caused restaurant meals to become cheaper relative to rounds of golf, so Carlos wants to buy relatively more restaurant meals. Second, while points A and A' are on the same indifference curve (and Carlos therefore gets the same utility from either bundle), it costs Carlos less to buy bundle A' at the new prices than to buy A. We know this because point A is located above BC' and so is infeasible if the budget constraint is BC'. (A', however, being on BC', is feasible with this constraint.)

Carlos therefore responds to the decline in restaurant meal prices by substituting away from rounds of golf and toward restaurant meals. By moving down along U_1, Carlos has effectively made himself better off; he is getting the same utility (he's still on U_1) for less money (bundle A is no longer feasible even though A' is).

Isolating the Income Effect

The income effect is the part of the total change in quantities consumed that is due to the change in Carlos's buying power after the price change. Why is there an income effect even though only the price of a good changed, not the actual number of dollars that Carlos had to spend? The key to understanding this outcome is to recognize that when the price of a good falls, Carlos becomes richer overall. The reduction in a good's price means there's a whole new set of bundles Carlos can now buy that he couldn't afford before because he has more money left over. At the old prices, everything above and to the right of BC_1 was infeasible; at the new prices, only bundles outside BC_2 are infeasible (see panel b of Figure 5.10).

This increase in buying power allows Carlos to achieve a higher level of utility than he did before. The income effect is the change in Carlos's choices driven by this shift in buying power while holding relative prices fixed at their new level. Finding these income-effect consumption changes is fairly easy once we've isolated the substitution

∂ The end-of-chapter appendix uses calculus to decompose the total effect of a price change into substitution and income effects.

make the grade

Computing substitution and income effects from a price change

There are three basic steps to analyzing substitution and income effects. We start with the consumer at a point of maximum utility (Point A) where his indifference curve is tangent to his budget constraint.

1. When prices change, draw the new budget constraint (a price change rotates the budget constraint, altering its slope). Then find the optimal quantity at the point (Point B) where this new budget constraint is tangent to a new indifference curve.

2. Draw a new line that is parallel to the new budget constraint from Step 1 and tangent to the

original indifference curve at Point A'. The movement along the original indifference curve from Point A (the original, pre-price change bundle) to this new tangency (point A') is the substitution effect. This movement shows how quantities change when relative prices change, even when purchasing power of income is constant.

3. The income effect of the price change is seen in the movement from point A' to point B. Here, relative prices are held constant (the budget lines are parallel) but the purchasing power of income changes.

effect. Remember that to find bundle A', we shifted the new budget constraint back in parallel until it was tangent to the original indifference curve. Doing that shift in reverse reflects the income effect exactly: It is the shift in consumption quantities (from bundle A' to B in panel b of Figure 5.10) due to Carlos's ability to reach a higher indifference curve (U_2 instead of U_1) while holding relative prices fixed (BC_2 and BC' have the same slope).

Therefore, the income effect of the decline in the restaurant meal price is illustrated by the move from the substitution-effect bundle (point A') to the final bundle, point B. Because the decline in restaurant meal prices has, in effect, made Carlos wealthier, he can reach a higher indifference curve U_2 and consume more of both goods. Due to the income effect, his desired quantity of rounds of golf increases by 3 from 3 (at A') to 6 (at B) and his desired quantity of restaurant meals increases by 1 from 4 (at A') to 5 (at B).

In this particular example, the income effect led to increases in the quantities of both rounds of golf and restaurant meals. That means both goods are normal goods. In the next section, we show an example in which one of the goods is inferior.

The Total Effects

The total effects of the decline in restaurant meal prices are shown in panel c of Figure 5.10:

1. The quantity of rounds of golf Carlos desires rises by 1 round of golf from 5 in the initial bundle at point A to 6 in the final bundle at point B. (A decline of 2 caused by the substitution effect is counteracted by a rise of 3 caused by the income effect for a net gain of 1 round of golf.)

2. The quantity of restaurant meals Carlos desires rises by 2 restaurant meals, from 3 in the initial bundle A to 5 in the final bundle B. (A rise of 1 caused by the substitution effect plus a rise of 1 caused by the income effect.)

What Determines the Size of the Substitution and Income Effects?

The size (and as we'll see shortly, sometimes the direction) of the total effect of a price change depends on the relative sizes of its substitution and income effects. So it's important to understand what factors influence how large substitution and income effects are. We discuss some of the more important factors below.

The Size of the Substitution Effect   The size of the substitution effect depends on the degree of curvature of the indifference curves. This can be seen in Figure 5.11. The figure's two panels show the substitution effects of the same change in the relative prices of rounds of golf and restaurant meals for two different indifference curve shapes. (We know it's the same relative price change because the budget constraints experience the same change in slope in both panels.) When indifference curves are highly curved, as in panel a, the MRS changes quickly as one moves along them. This means any given price change won't change consumption choices much, because one doesn't need to move far along the indifference curve to change the MRS to match the new relative prices. Thus, the substitution effect is small. This is unsurprising, because we learned in Chapter 4 that indifference curves have more curvature in cases where the two goods are not highly substitutable. In panel a, the relative price change causes a substitution from A to A', and the consumer moves from purchasing a bundle with 2 restaurant meals and 2 rounds of golf to a bundle containing 3 restaurant meals and 1.25 rounds of golf.

When indifference curves are less curved, as in panel b, the MRS doesn't change much along the curve, so the same relative price change causes a much greater substitution effect. The substitution from A to A' in panel b involves much larger changes in golf and meals consumption than that caused by the same relative price change in

Figure 5.11   **The Shape of Indifference Curves Determines the Size of the Substitution Effect**

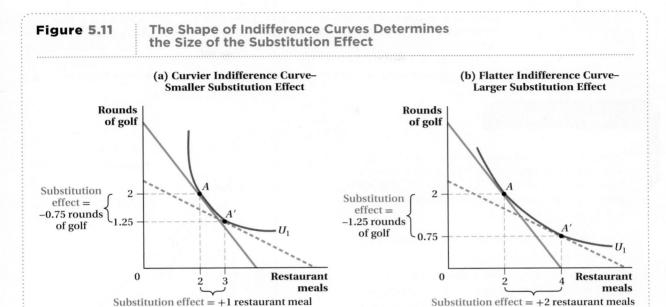

(a) Curvier Indifference Curve– Smaller Substitution Effect

(b) Flatter Indifference Curve– Larger Substitution Effect

(a) When the indifference curve is highly curved, the *MRS* changes quickly along the curve. Thus, any given price change will not change consumption choices by much. Here, the original consumption bundle *A* is 2 restaurant meals and 2 rounds of golf. After a change in prices, the new optimal consumption bundle is *A′*, and the consumer now demands 1.25 rounds of golf and 3 restaurant meals.

(b) When the indifference curve is less curved, the *MRS* does not change quickly along the curve. Thus, any given price change affects consumption choices more strongly. At the new optimal consumption bundle *A′*, the consumer now demands 0.75 rounds of golf and 4 restaurant meals.

panel a.[4] In panel b, the quantity of restaurant meals purchased grows to 4 (rather than 3) and the quantity of rounds of golf purchased falls to 0.75 (rather than 1.25). Again, we can relate this to what we learned about the curvature of indifference curves in Chapter 4. Indifference curves with little curvature indicate that the two goods are close substitutes. Thus, it makes sense that a price change will lead to a much greater adjustment in the quantities in the consumer's preferred bundle.

The Size of the Income Effect   The size of the income effect is related to the quantity of each good the consumer purchases before the price change. The more the consumer was spending on the good before the price change, the greater the fraction of the consumer's budget affected by the price change. A price drop of a good that the consumer is initially buying a lot of will leave him with more income left over than a price drop of a good with a small budget share (and a price increase will sap a greater share of the consumer's income). For example, consider the effects of a change in the

---

[4] This logic also explains why perfect substitutes, the special case we discussed in Chapter 4 with perfectly straight indifference curves, have the largest substitution effects. There, a small relative price change can lead the consumer to shift from one corner solution to another—that is, from consuming all of one good, *A*, and none of the other good, *B*, to consuming only *B* and no *A*. (To see this, suppose all a consumer cares about is the number of potato chips he consumes, and he views 3-ounce and 12-ounce bags of chips as perfect substitutes. If the price of 12-ounce bags is less than four times the price of 3-ounce bags, he will only buy 12-ounce bags. But if the price of 12-ounce bags is just a bit more than four times the price of 3-ounce bags, he will only buy 3-ounce bags.) It's also why perfect complements, with their right-angled indifference curves, have no substitution effect; they are always consumed in constant proportion regardless of relative prices.

prices of two goods homeowners deal with: electricity and pest control. A typical consumer spends much more of his budget on electricity. Therefore, a change in the price of electricity will affect his income and alter his purchases by more than a similar change in the price of pest control. (At the extreme, if the consumer currently purchases no pest control, a change in the price of pest control will have no income effect at all.)

5.3 figure it out

Pavlo eats cakes and pies. His income is $20, and when cakes and pies both cost $1, Pavlo consumes 4 cakes and 16 pies (point A in Figure A). But when the price of pies rises to $2, Pavlo consumes 12 cakes and 4 pies (point B).

a. Why does the budget constraint rotate as it does in response to the increase in the price of pies?

b. Trace the diagram on a piece of paper. On your diagram, separate the change in the consumption of pies into the substitution effect and the income effect. Which is larger?

c. Are pies a normal or inferior good? How do you know? Are cakes a normal or inferior good? How do you know?

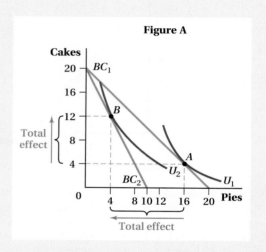
Figure A

Solution:

a. The price of cakes hasn't changed, so Pavlo can still buy 20 cakes if he spends his $20 all on cakes (the y-intercept). However, at $2 per pie, Pavlo can now afford to buy only 10 pies instead of 20.

b. The substitution effect is measured by changing the ratio of the prices of the goods but holding utility constant (Figure B). Therefore, it must be measured along one indifference curve. To determine the substitution effect of a price change in pies, you need to shift the post-price-change budget constraint BC_2 out until it is tangent to Pavlo's initial indifference curve U_1. The easiest way to do this is to draw a new budget line BC' that is parallel to the new budget constraint (thus changing the ratio of the cake and pie prices) but tangent to U_1 (thus holding utility constant). Label the point of tangency A'. Point A' is the bundle Pavlo would buy if the relative prices of cakes and pies changed as they did, but he experienced no change in purchasing power. When the price of pies rises, Pavlo would substitute away from buying pies and buy more cakes.

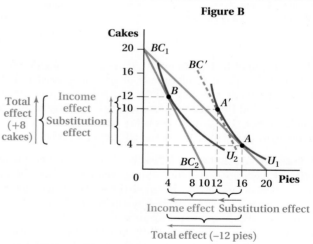
Figure B

The income effect is the part of the total change in quantities consumed that is due to the change in Pavlo's buying power after the price of pies changes. This is reflected in the shift from point A' on budget constraint BC' to point B on budget constraint BC_2. (These budget constraints are parallel because the income effect is measured holding relative prices constant.)

For pies, the income effect is larger than the substitution effect. The substitution effect leads Pavlo to purchase 4 fewer pies (from 16 to 12), while the income effect further reduces his consumption by 8 pies (from 12 to 4).

c. Pies are a normal good because Pavlo purchases fewer pies (4 instead of 12) when the purchasing power of his income falls due to the price increase. However, cakes are an inferior good because the fall in purchasing power actually leads to a rise in cake consumption.

 application

Backward-Bending Labor Supply and Income Effects in Leisure

The relative sizes of substitution and income effects can create an interesting phenomenon sometimes observed in individuals' willingness to work. Think for a minute about leisure time (no jokes about skipping class). For just about everyone, leisure is a good, just like rounds of golf, restaurant meals, cakes, pies, electricity, pest control, and all the other examples we have worked with. Consuming more of it raises people's utility.

But if leisure is a good, what is its price? Well, consuming leisure involves using up time. The price of leisure is the value of what one could be doing with that time if she wasn't being leisurely. The main alternative use of leisure time is work. (Economists often consider any time a person spends not working as leisure, whether or not that individual is doing something we might think of as leisurely.) What's the value of working? Aside from any inherent pleasure someone might get from her job, its value is the income she earns from it—or more precisely, the utility she would obtain by consuming goods and services bought with her work income. What this means is that by choosing to take an extra unit of leisure, a person is giving up the income she could have earned had she worked during that period. That lost income equals her wage rate. So that is the price of leisure: a person's wage, and the goods and services that she could have bought with that income.

Based on these ideas, then, we can think of a person's willingness to work as involving a choice between consuming leisure and consuming the goods and services that can be bought with her work income. If we treat those other goods and services as a single good (call it "consumption," with its quantity measured in dollars), the relative price between leisure and consumption is the wage. If a person's wage is $30 per hour, for example, and she chooses to take one more hour of leisure (i.e., work one hour less), she is giving up $30 in consumption.

Economists call the choice of how much to work an individual's labor supply choice, because it involves how much time the person offers to supply to the labor market as a function of the wage level. We can describe the work-leisure choice using the set of tools we've been working with in this chapter: A person has a utility function (with its associated indifference curves) that depends on both the amount of leisure time she spends and the consumption she enjoys from her work income. She maximizes her utility subject to a budget constraint for which the relative price of leisure and consumption equals her wage rate. The only thing that's a bit different in this case is that we aren't taking her income—how much she has to spend on the two goods—as a fixed number, as we usually do. Instead, her income will depend on her choice of how much leisure to take and, therefore, how much work. That would complicate things some, but it turns out we don't need to deal with this explicitly to understand the basic economics underlying how changes in the wage rate affect someone's willingness to work.

Suppose a person's wage goes up. (Maybe she gets a raise.) One consequence of this is that leisure now has a higher price relative to consumption. Choosing to work one less hour has become more expensive in terms of forgone consumption. This change is going to tend to make her choose less leisure (more work) and consume more goods and services. This is a substitution effect applied to these two goods, leisure and consumption.

The substitution effect therefore tends to make people want to work more when their wage rises. (If the wage were to fall instead, it would make leisure relatively cheap and tend to make workers want to work less.) This makes a person's labor supply curve, which shows how much she is willing to work at any given wage level, slope up. That shape is how we usually think of supply curves for anything: The higher the price of the good (the wage here), the higher the quantity of the product (work hours) the producer (worker) is willing to supply.

But there's another effect of an increase in the wage that we hinted at before. For any given level of work—or equivalently, any given level of leisure time—it raises the person's income. This means there is also an income effect of a wage increase, not just a substitution effect. What impact will the income effect have on someone's leisure choice? For most people, leisure is a normal good; they consume more of it as their income rises. If this doesn't seem obvious to you, imagine that you win a $100 million lottery prize, but your job doesn't change. This scenario is a pure income effect: an increase in income without a change in the relative price of leisure, the wage. Would you take more vacation time and work less after winning the lottery? Most people would.

The bottom line of the income effect from an increase in the wage, then, is to make a person want to work less. This is exactly the opposite of the substitution effect. The net effect of a wage change on how much a person is willing to work is the difference between the two. In principle, at least, if the income effect is large enough, a person's labor supply curve will no longer have a positive slope. Instead, there will be a negative relationship between wages and how much an individual is willing to work. An example of this is shown in Figure 5.12. At wages below w^*, the substitution effect dominates; increases in the wage will make the person willing to work more. Above w^*, however, the income effect begins to dominate, and the amount of work the person is willing to supply falls as wages rise. Economists call labor supply curves with this negative slope *backward-bending* labor supply curves.

Economists have found examples of backward-bending labor supply curves in certain markets. In one broad-ranging case, economic historian Dora Costa gathered surveys on the work habits of thousands of U.S. men working in the 1890s.[5] She found that low-wage workers spent more hours per day working than those earning high wages. Specifically, workers in the lowest wage decile (those being paid wages in the lowest 10% of all observed wage rates) averaged 11.1 hours of work per day, but those in the top wage decile (the top 10% of wage rates) only worked 8.9 hours per day. Workers in the highest wage group worked 5% fewer hours than those being paid the median wage, who in turn worked 14% less than those in the lowest wage group. In other words, the daily labor supply curve appeared to exhibit backward-bending patterns.

Figure 5.12 Backward-Bending Labor Supply

When the income effect dominates, laborers choose to consume more leisure and work fewer hours, creating a backward-bending labor supply curve. At wages below w^*, the substitution effect is dominant, and the supply curve is upward-sloping. For any given increase in wages, laborers will choose to work more hours. At wages above w^*, the income effect dominates, and the supply curve is backward-bending. For any given increase in wages, laborers will choose to work fewer hours.

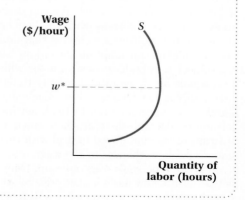

Interestingly, using other data, Costa also showed that the pattern had reversed itself by the 1990s. While workers in that period across the wage scale spent on average less time per day working than a century before, now those at the high end of the scale worked more than those at the low end. Those in the lowest wage decile averaged 7.6 hours per day, and those in the highest averaged 8.5 hours a day. Thus, over the course of the intervening century, the substitution effect became larger relative to the income effect, and eventually started to dominate in magnitude.

It's not clear what factors caused this shift. One possibility is that the overall decline in average daily hours for all workers (which may itself reflect an income effect that affected all workers as the country became wealthier over the twentieth century) meant workers had more free time during the day, reducing their willingness to pay on the margin for another hour of leisure when the wage rose. It might also be that higher-wage workers still want to take more leisure, but this shows up as an earlier retirement age in the later period rather than lower average daily hours. Thus, the income effect is still large in this case, but its effect on day-to-day work choice is smaller relative to its effect over a person's lifetime. ■

theory and data

Golfers' Backward-Bending Labor Supply Curves

Tiger Woods is perhaps the most recognizable face in professional golf. He's won 71 PGA tour events and picked up 14 Majors. He's lent his name to campaigns for Nike and Titleist—and taken home a cool $40 million and $20 million, respectively, for the work. But it's not just his athletic skill that separates him from the average American laborer: He's probably one of the few people facing wages on the backward-bending portion of his labor supply curve. In other words, as his wages increase, he actually decreases the number of tournaments in which he plays.

PGA rules allow each golfer to elect which and how many events to play in, meaning the athlete considers the labor–leisure tradeoff separately for each tournament event. With tournament payoffs in the millions of dollars for just four rounds of golf, you probably think it a no-brainer to play. Indeed, for most golfers, it is. Generally, around 100 players sign up for any given event. This doesn't even include the over 1,000 hopefuls who play in brutal qualifying rounds, vying for just 25 spots on the PGA Tour.

Given the opportunity, these hopefuls would gladly play every tournament, but as economists Otis Gilley and Marc Chopin discovered, players like Tiger Woods don't.[*] In a 2000 paper, Gilley and Chopin looked at how low- and middle-income PGA players in the 1990s responded to increases in their wages and compared this result to the effects of wage increases on high-income players. Whereas low-level players entered more events as their event winnings increased, golfers at the top of their game decreased their tournament play as their wages increased. Top golfers were actually operating on the backward-bending portion of their labor supply curve! In particular, for every $1,000 increase in expected per-event winnings, the number of tournaments entered in a season by high-income players decreases by 0.05 to 0.1. For these select players, the income effect dominated the substitution effect, and faced with the leisure–labor tradeoff, they elected to consume more leisure.

Workers in other fields—including many economists—often spend their leisure time on the golf course. But for a professional golfer, a day on the green is work, not leisure. So just what does a PGA player do on his day off? Gilley and Chopin found that married golfers took more days off than did single golfers. Drawing on their own experiences as family men, the two hard-working economists concluded that golfers must be taking off work to spend more quality time with their wives and kids. The example of Tiger Woods, however, shows that the predictions of economic theory don't always hold up in the real world.

[*] Otis W. Gilley and Marc C. Chopin, "Professional Golf: Labor or Leisure." *Managerial Finance* 26, no. 7 (2000): 33–45.

An Example of the Income Effect with an Inferior Good

Figure 5.13 provides another example of decomposing quantity changes into income and substitution effects. Here, however, one of the goods is inferior, at least over the price range explored in the example.

Figure 5.13 shows Judi's utility-maximizing bundles of steak and ramen noodles for two sets of prices. The optimal bundle at the original prices is shown at point A. The price of ramen noodles then drops, rotating the budget constraint outward. With the new budget constraint BC_2, Judi can reach a higher level of utility (U_2) and chooses bundle B to maximize her utility.

To decompose the shift from bundle A to bundle B into its substitution and income effects, we follow the steps we described in the previous section. To find the substitution effect, we shift in the budget constraint after the price change until it is tangent to the original indifference curve U_1. This is shown by the dashed line BC' in panel a of Figure 5.14. The point of tangency between BC' and U_1 is bundle A'. Because this is the bundle that provides the same utility as the original bundle A but with ramen noodles at their new, lower price, the shift from A to A' is the substitution effect. Just as before, the substitution effect leads Judi to consume more of the good that becomes relatively cheaper (ramen noodles) and less of the other good (steak).

The quantity shifts between bundle A' and bundle B, shown in panel b of Figure 5.14, are due to the income effect. As before, this is the change in quantities consumed due to the shift in the budget lines from BC' to BC_2: Judi's increase in buying power while holding relative prices constant. Notice that now the income effect actually *reduces* the quantity of ramen noodles consumed, even though the drop in their price makes Judi richer by expanding the set of bundles she can consume. This means ramen is an inferior good over this income range; an increase in income makes Judi want less of it.

Does the fact that a price drop leads to a reduction in the quantity consumed due to the income effect mean that the demand curve for ramen noodles slopes up? No, because the substitution effect increases the quantity demanded by more than the income effect decreases it. Thus, the quantity of ramen noodles demanded still rises when their price falls even though ramen noodles are an inferior good. We see this outcome in panel c of Figure 5.14 because the total effect on the quantity of ramen noodles is posi-

---

Figure 5.13 **A Fall in the Price of an Inferior Good**

When the price of ramen noodles decreases, Judi's budget constraint rotates outward from BC_1 to BC_2. The total effect of this price change is represented by the increase in quantities consumed from the original utility-maximizing bundle A to bundle B. Overall, Judi's consumption of both ramen noodles and steak increases.

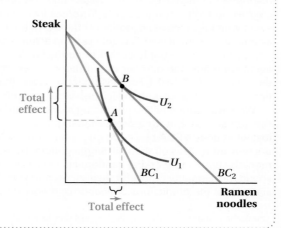

Figure 5.14 : **Substitution and Income Effects for an Inferior Good**

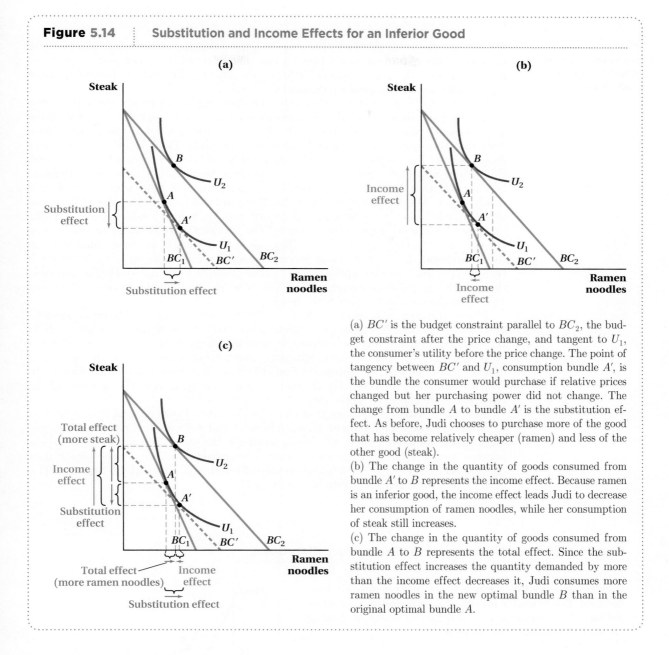

(a) BC' is the budget constraint parallel to BC_2, the budget constraint after the price change, and tangent to U_1, the consumer's utility before the price change. The point of tangency between BC' and U_1, consumption bundle A', is the bundle the consumer would purchase if relative prices changed but her purchasing power did not change. The change from bundle A to bundle A' is the substitution effect. As before, Judi chooses to purchase more of the good that has become relatively cheaper (ramen) and less of the other good (steak).

(b) The change in the quantity of goods consumed from bundle A' to B represents the income effect. Because ramen is an inferior good, the income effect leads Judi to decrease her consumption of ramen noodles, while her consumption of steak still increases.

(c) The change in the quantity of goods consumed from bundle A to B represents the total effect. Since the substitution effect increases the quantity demanded by more than the income effect decreases it, Judi consumes more ramen noodles in the new optimal bundle B than in the original optimal bundle A.

tive: The optimal bundle after ramen noodles become cheaper (bundle B) has a higher quantity of ramen than the optimal bundle before their price fell (bundle A). So the demand curve for ramen does indeed slope down. This is generally the case for inferior goods in the economy—while the income effect will make people want to consume less of them as their price falls, the substitution effect has a larger impact in the opposite direction, leading to a net increase in their consumption.

If the income effect is large enough, however, it is possible that a reduction in the price of an inferior good could actually lead to a net decrease in its consumption. A good that exhibits this trait is called a Giffen good.

Giffen Goods

Giffen goods are goods for which a fall in price leads the consumer to want *less* of the good. That is, an inverse relationship does not exist between price and quantity demanded and the demand curves of Giffen goods slope *up*! The more expensive a Giffen good is, the higher the quantity demanded.

This seemingly paradoxical effect arises because, for Giffen goods, the substitution effect of a price drop, which acts to increase the quantity a consumer demands of the good, is smaller than the reduction in the desired quantity caused by the income effect. Note that this means Giffen goods *must* be inferior goods. The income effect of a price drop can only reduce the desired quantity if the good is inferior; for all normal goods, the income effect of a price drop acts to increase the quantity demanded. Remember, though, that while all Giffen goods are inferior, not all inferior goods are Giffen goods—they are extremely rare. Typically, there will still be a net increase in the quantity demanded when price falls, just as we saw with the ramen noodles example before.

Figure 5.15 shows a graphical example. The two goods are potatoes and meat, and potatoes are the Giffen good. The utility-maximizing bundle at the original prices is shown at point A. When potatoes become cheaper, the budget constraint rotates out from BC_1 to BC_2 and the optimal bundle shifts from A to B. Notice that in this case, the quantity of potatoes consumed at point B is smaller than the quantity consumed at A even though potatoes are now cheaper.

The substitution and income effects underlying this change are shown in panels a and b of Figure 5.16. We isolate the substitution effect the same way as before: shifting the new budget constraint back in parallel until it is tangent to the original indifference curve. This creates changes in the quantity consumed corresponding to the shift from bundle A to bundle A'. As always, the substitution effect increases the quantity of the good that has become relatively cheaper, potatoes, and decreases the quantity of the relatively more expensive good, meat.

The income effect is the change in quantities associated with moving from bundle A' to B. Here, those changes are an increase in meat and a decrease in potatoes. Potatoes are therefore an inferior good, like ramen noodles in the previous example. But here, the negative income effect on potatoes has a larger magnitude than the positive substitution effect, so the net change in potatoes consumed from their drop in price is negative. This is what we saw in the shift from bundle A to B.

Figure 5.15   A Change in the Price of a Giffen Good

When the price of a Giffen good falls, the consumer consumes less of that good. Here, when the price of potatoes decreases, the consumer purchases fewer potatoes, as reflected in the change in quantities consumed from bundle A to bundle B.

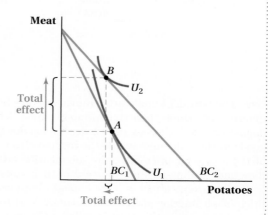

Figure 5.16 : **Substitution and Income Effects of a Giffen Good**

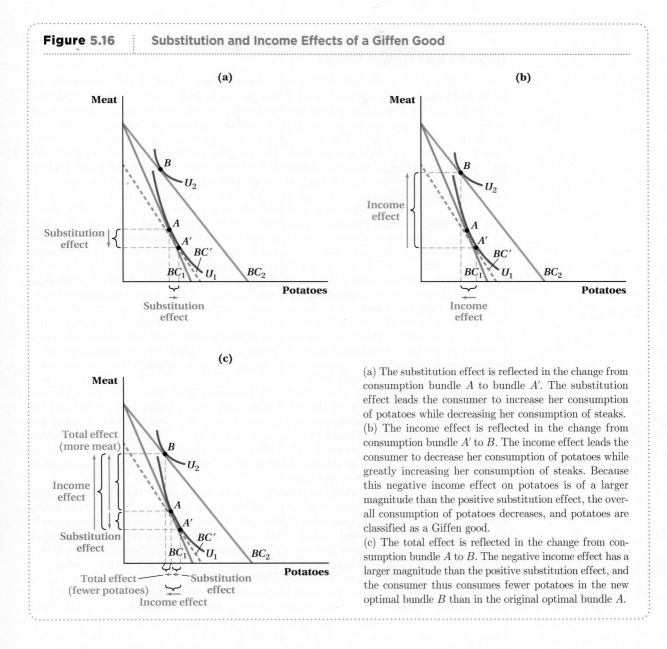

(a) The substitution effect is reflected in the change from consumption bundle A to bundle A'. The substitution effect leads the consumer to increase her consumption of potatoes while decreasing her consumption of steaks.
(b) The income effect is reflected in the change from consumption bundle A' to B. The income effect leads the consumer to decrease her consumption of potatoes while greatly increasing her consumption of steaks. Because this negative income effect on potatoes is of a larger magnitude than the positive substitution effect, the overall consumption of potatoes decreases, and potatoes are classified as a Giffen good.
(c) The total effect is reflected in the change from consumption bundle A to B. The negative income effect has a larger magnitude than the positive substitution effect, and the consumer thus consumes fewer potatoes in the new optimal bundle B than in the original optimal bundle A.

We discussed before that for a good to be a Giffen good, it must be an inferior good, and consumers' preferences for it must have an income effect that is larger in size than the substitution effect. When would we expect this? First, Giffen goods would have to have limited substitutability with other goods; that is, the substitution effect would need to be small, and therefore the indifference curves would have to be highly curved. Second, the income effect needs to be large; this is more likely if, before the price change, a large fraction of the consumer's budget is spent on the good. This way, if the price of the good falls because the consumer is already spending most of her income on it, she's likely to feel a larger bump in effective buying power than if the good were only a small share of her budget.

 **application**

In Search of Giffen Goods

While Giffen goods are a theoretical possibility, they are extremely rare in practice. An often cited example of a Giffen good is the potato in Ireland during the Irish famine of the mid-1800s. The story is that the famine-driven increase in potato prices drastically reduced the purchasing power of Irish families' incomes, shrinking the bundles of goods that they could afford because potatoes already consumed a very large fraction of a typical Irish family's meager cash income. The resulting income effect led to a decrease in the demand for other foods such as meat that were normal goods for Irish families and an increase in the demand for potatoes, an inferior good, that swamped any substitution effect. However, more recent reexaminations of the data by economists Gerald Dwyer and Cotton Lindsay, and later Sherwin Rosen in a separate study, found that even this canonical example proved not to be a Giffen good.[6]

These reexaminations differ in their explanations, but one common element between them is that the purported Giffen demand of Irish households just doesn't add up when confronted with what is known about the potato famine. Specifically, if potatoes were a Giffen good for individual households, then the total market demand curve for potatoes in Ireland should have also sloped up (quantity demanded would have increased as price increased). (We learn about how individuals' demand curves add up to total market demand later in this chapter.) But that would mean that the huge drop in supply due to the blight—about which there is no historical argument—should have led to lower potato prices. This is inconsistent with historical accounts reporting cases where no potatoes were available at any price, and when potatoes were available, they were sold at historically unprecedentedly high prices.

However, a recent policy experiment with extremely poor households in rural areas of China's Hunan province by Robert Jensen and Nolan Miller has produced what might be the most convincing documentation of a Giffen good to date.[7] Jensen and Miller subsidized the purchases of rice to a randomly selected set of such households, effectively lowering the price of rice that they faced. They then compared the change in rice consumption in the subsidized households to rice consumption in unsubsidized households of similar incomes and sizes.

Jensen and Miller found that the subsidy, even though it made rice cheaper, actually caused the households' rice consumption to fall. Rice was a Giffen good for these households. (Jensen and Miller conducted a similar experiment subsidizing wheat purchases in Gansu province and also found evidence that wheat was a Giffen good for some families, though the effect was weaker in this case.) The apparent mechanism behind this result is in accordance with our discussion above. Rice purchases took up so much of these households' incomes that the subsidy greatly increased the households' effective buying power. The resulting income effect made them want to consume less rice in place of other foods for the sake of dietary variety. This income effect was large enough to outweigh the substitution effect. To oversimplify things a little, the households were buying enough rice to meet their caloric needs and spending their leftover income on foods that added variety. When they could meet their caloric needs more cheaply, they used the now freed-up income to buy variety foods—enough to replace some of the calories formerly supplied by rice.

Interestingly, Jensen and Miller also found that while rice was a Giffen good for very poor households, it was not a Giffen good for the very poorest of the poor. Those extremely impoverished households basically ate only rice before the subsidy, and not really

---

[6] Gerald P. Dwyer, Jr. and Cotton M. Lindsay, "Robert Giffen and the Irish Potato," *American Economic Review* 74, no. 1 (1984): 188–192. Sherwin Rosen, "Potato Paradoxes." *Journal of Political Economy* 107, no. 6 (1999): S294–S313.

[7] Robert T. Jensen and Nolan H. Miller, "Giffen Behavior and Subsistence Consumption," *American Economic Review* 98, no. 4 (2008): 1553–1577.

enough to meet their basic caloric needs at that. When rice became cheaper, they bought more in order to meet some basic level of healthy subsistence. Essentially, even the subsidy didn't raise their income enough to allow them to buy any other foods besides rice. ∎

∂ The online appendix takes a deeper look into income and substitution effects using the Slutsky equation. (http://glsmicro.com/appendices)

make the grade

Simple rules to remember about income and substitution effects

It is easy to get tripped up when you're asked to identify income and substitution effects. First, remember to always start your analysis on the indifference curve associated with the consumption bundle *before* the price change. If you want to know why consumption changed going from one bundle to the other, you must start with the initial bundle. Next, keep in mind the key distinctions between the two effects listed in the table below.

SUBSTITUTION EFFECTS	INCOME EFFECTS
Involve comparisons of bundles that lie on the same indifference curve.	Involve comparisons of bundles that lie on two different indifference curves.
The direction of the effect on quantity consumed for a given change in the relative price of the good is unambiguous.	The direction of the effect on quantity consumed for a given change in the relative price of the good is ambiguous and depends on whether the good is normal or inferior.
If the good's relative price falls, the substitution effect causes the consumer to want more of it.	If the good is normal, then a fall in either its price or the price of the other good will cause the consumer to want more of it. (A drop in any price, even of another good, increases the effective income of the consumer.) If the good is inferior, then a price drop will cause the consumer to want less of it.
If the good's relative price rises, the substitution effect causes the consumer to want less of it.	If the good is normal, then a rise in either its price or the price of the other good will cause the consumer to want less of it. If the good is inferior, then a rise in either price will cause the consumer to want more of it.

Finally, remember that the total effect of a price change (for either good) on quantity consumed depends on the relative size of the substitution and income effects. If the price of one good falls, the quantities of both goods consumed may rise, or consumption of one good may rise and consumption of the other good may decline. But the quantities consumed of both goods cannot both decline, because this would mean the consumer would not be on her budget constraint.

5.4 The Impact of Changes in Another Good's Price: Substitutes and Complements

The two preceding sections showed how a change in the price of a good leads to a change in the quantity demanded of that same good. In this section, we look at the effects of a change in a good's price on the quantity demanded of *other* goods.

The approach to examining what happens when the price of another good changes is similar to that in the previous sections. We start with a fixed level of income, a set of indifference curves representing the consumer's preferences, and initial prices for the two goods. We compute the optimal consumption bundle under those conditions. Then, we vary one of the prices, holding everything else constant. The only difference is that as we vary that price, we focus on how the quantity demanded of the other good changes.

A Change in the Price of a Substitute Good

Figure 5.17 shows an example of the effects of a change in the price of a substitute good. Initially, the consumer's utility-maximizing bundle is 15 quarts of Pepsi and 5 quarts of Coke—the point labeled A. When the price of Pepsi doubles, the consumer can only afford a maximum of 10 quarts instead of 20. The maximum quantity of Coke the consumer can buy stays at 20 because the price of Coke has not changed. As a result, the budget constraint rotates inward to BC_2. In the new optimal consumption bundle B, the consumer demands more Coke (10 quarts) and less Pepsi (5 quarts).

> **substitute**
> A good that can be used in place of another good.

As we learned in Chapter 2, when the quantity demanded of one good (Coke) rises when the price of another good (Pepsi) rises, the goods are **substitutes.** More generally, the quantity a consumer demands of a good moves in the same direction as the prices of its substitutes. The more alike two goods are, the more one can be substituted for the other, and the more responsive the increase in quantity demanded of one will be to price increases in the other. Pepsi and Coke are closer substitutes than milk and Coke, for instance.

Changes in the prices of a good's substitutes lead to shifts in the good's demand curve. When a substitute for a good becomes more expensive, this raises the quantity demanded of that good at any given price level. As a result, the demand curve for the good shifts out (the demand for that good increases). When a good's substitutes become cheaper, the quantity demanded at any given price falls, and the good's demand curve shifts in.

> **complement**
> A good that is purchased and used in combination with another good.

When the quantity consumed of a good moves in the opposite direction of another good's price, they are **complements.** Complements are often goods that the consumer would use in tandem, like golf clubs and golf balls, pencils and paper, or home theater systems and installation services. Vanilla ice cream and hot fudge, for example, are complementary goods. Figure 5.18 shows how an increase in ice cream's price leads to a decrease in the quantity demanded of hot fudge. The higher ice cream price causes the budget constraint to rotate in, shifting the utility-maximizing bundle from A (30 quarts

---

Figure 5.17 | **When the Price of a Substitute Rises, Demand Rises**

At the original prices, the consumer consumes 15 quarts of Pepsi and 5 quarts of Coke at the utility-maximizing bundle A. When the price of Pepsi doubles, the consumer's budget constraint rotates inward from BC_1 to BC_2. At the new optimal consumption bundle B, the consumer decreases his consumption of Pepsi from 15 to 5 quarts and increases his consumption of Coke from 5 to 10 quarts. Since the quantity of Coke demanded rose while the price of Pepsi rose, Coke and Pepsi are considered substitutes.

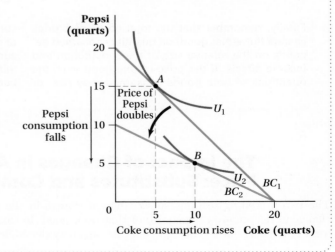

Figure 5.18 : **When the Price of a Complement Rises, Demand Falls**

At the original prices, the consumer consumes 20 gallons of ice cream and 30 quarts of hot fudge at the utility-maximizing bundle A. When the price of ice cream increases, the consumer's budget constraint rotates inward from BC_1 to BC_2. At the new optimal consumption bundle B, the consumer decreases his consumption of ice cream from 20 to 15 gallons and likewise decreases his consumption of hot fudge from 30 to 20 quarts. Since the quantities demanded of both ice cream and hot fudge decreased with an increase in price of only one of those goods, ice cream and hot fudge are considered complements.

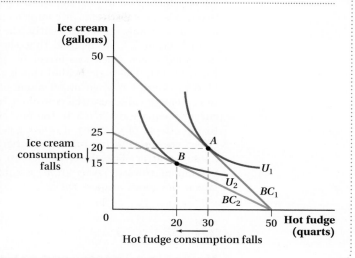

of hot fudge and 20 gallons of vanilla ice cream) to B (20 quarts of hot fudge and 15 gallons of vanilla ice cream). The quantity demanded of both goods falls; an increase in the price of ice cream not only causes the consumer to demand less ice cream (this is the own-price effect we've studied so far in this chapter), but less hot fudge, the complementary good, as well.

When the price of a complement of a good increases, the quantity demanded of that good at every price decreases and its demand curve shifts in. If the price of a complement of a good falls, the quantity demanded of that good rises at all prices and the demand curve shifts out. Changes in the price of a complementary good *shift* the demand curve for the other good. Changes in a good's own price cause a *move along* the same demand curve.

The effects of price changes in substitute and complementary goods on demand are summarized in Figure 5.19.

Figure 5.19 : **Changes in the Prices of Substitutes or Complements Shift the Demand Curve**

When the price of a substitute good rises or the price of a complement falls, the demand curve for good X shifts out. When the price of a substitute good falls or the price of a complement rises, the demand curve for good X shifts in.

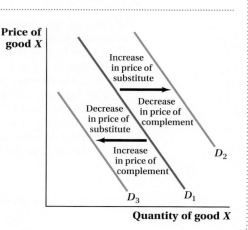

Indifference Curve Shapes, Revisited

As we touched on in Chapter 4, the shape of indifference curves is related to whether two goods are substitutes or complements. The more curved the indifference curve, the less substitutable (or, equivalently, the more complementary) are the goods.

In Section 5.3, we learned that the size of the substitution effect from a change in a good's *own* price was larger for goods with less-curved indifference curves (see Figure 5.11). The logic behind this is that, because the marginal rate of substitution (*MRS*) doesn't change much along straighter indifference curves, a given relative price change will cause the consumer to move a longer distance along his indifference curve to equate his *MRS* to the new price ratio. This logic holds true when it comes to the effects of changes in *other* goods' prices. All that matters to the substitution effect are the *relative* prices; whether it's Good *A*'s or Good *B*'s price that changes doesn't matter. Therefore, an increase (decrease) in a good's price will create a larger movement toward (away from) a substitute good when the indifference curves between the goods are less curved.

 **application**

Movies in a Theater and at Home—Substitutes or Complements?

If you own a movie theater company, one of the most important issues you face for the long-run viability of your firm is whether watching a movie on a home theater system and seeing a film in your movie-plex are substitutes or complements. Improvements in home electronics like large-screen, high-definition TVs, Blu-ray disc players, downloadable digital movies, and compact surround sound audio systems have greatly reduced the price of having a high-quality movie-watching experience at home. A middle-class family today can buy a home theater system that a multimillionaire could have only dreamed about a few decades ago. If movies at home are a substitute good for movies in a theater, this price reduction will reduce the number of people visiting their local movie-plex. This change will surely lead to some theaters going out of business sooner or later. If movies at home are instead a complement, theater-going will increase and bring newfound growth to the movie exhibition business.

Either case is plausible. On one hand, there is clear scope for substitution. If home electronics can better replicate the theater experience, people could find it less costly (in terms of either direct expenditures, convenience, or both) to watch a movie at home. On the other hand, if people become more interested in films in general because they now watch more at home—perhaps they develop a movie habit, or appreciate the art of film, or get caught up in following their favorite actors or watching their favorite movie again and again—then they might be more likely to see movies in theaters than they were before, particularly if theaters offer some component of the movie-watching experience that you can't get at home (audiences to laugh or be scared with, really big screens, super-greasy popcorn, etc.).

The data are not yet clear about the answer to this question. Figure 5.20 shows the trends in total U.S. box office sales receipts (inflation adjusted to 2010 dollars) and the number of tickets sold per capita since 1980.[8] The overall trend in total box office has been upward over the period, but it topped out in 2002 after a run-up in the 1990s. The decline between 2002 and 2010 was just under 5%, though this is

---

[8] The data in this application are from www.boxofficemojo.com.

Figure 5.20 | U.S. Total Box Office and Tickets Sold per Capita, 1980–2010

The overall trend in total box office was upward over the period, but leveled out after 2002.

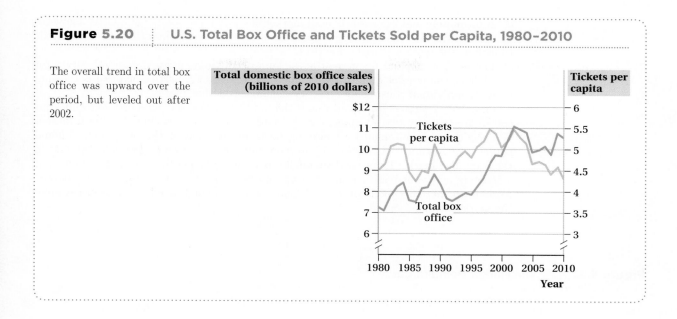

mitigated some by the fact that 2009 and 2010 were good years. The data on the number of tickets sold per capita—you can think of this as the average number of times a person goes to see a movie during the year—are more volatile, but show a similar pattern of a run-up in the 1990s and then a drop after 2002. The drop is larger relative to that for the total box office, though, falling about 20% from 5.5 to 4.3 movies a year by 2010.

The decrease in theater-going after 2002 suggests that watching movies at home is a substitute, because it coincides with the period of the increased availability of big-screen HDTV and disc players. However, the data are fairly noisy: That is, there is a large amount of variation across the years, so it's not completely clear if these are long-run trends or just temporary blips due to the quality of movies or changes in the prices of other entertainment goods such as video game systems. Furthermore, the widespread diffusion of VCRs, DVD players, and early surround-sound systems in the 1980s and 1990s didn't scar the movie exhibition industry because revenues and tickets per capita both rose, indicating that they may have been complements to watching films in a theater.

So perhaps movie-plex owners will be helped by cheap, high-quality home theater systems. Then again, in 1946, before TVs were in most people's homes, over 4 billion tickets were sold in the United States when the population was about 140 million (compared to over 310 million today). That's an average of over 28 movies a year per person! By 1956 attendance was half that. It seems quite likely that movie houses and TVs were substitutes then. Time will tell whether the same holds for movie houses and home theaters. ■

5.5 Combining Individual Demand Curves to Obtain the Market Demand Curve

When studying consumer demand, we're often more interested in the combined demand of all consumers, rather than any one consumer's demand. For instance, if you are a company trying to figure out how many scooters to make and what to charge for them, what ultimately matters is the overall market demand for scooters.[9] Similarly, a government that wants to figure out how much revenue a tax or tariff on tires will raise needs to look at the market demand for tires.

The market demand for a good is the sum of all the individual demand curves for it. That is, the market quantity demanded for a good at a particular price is the sum of every individual consumer's quantity demanded at that price.

Figure 5.21 shows graphically how this adding up works. Suppose you and your cousin are the only two consumers in the market for Razor scooters. The total market demand curve is obtained by summing horizontally each of the individual demand curves. For instance, at a price of $40, you and your cousin each want 3 scooters, so the combined market quantity demanded is 6 scooters. When the price is $20, you want 4 scooters and your cousin wants 8, for a market quantity demanded of 12 scooters. Adding up the individual consumers' quantities demanded at all possible prices gives the market demand curve.

Figure 5.21 The Market Demand Curve

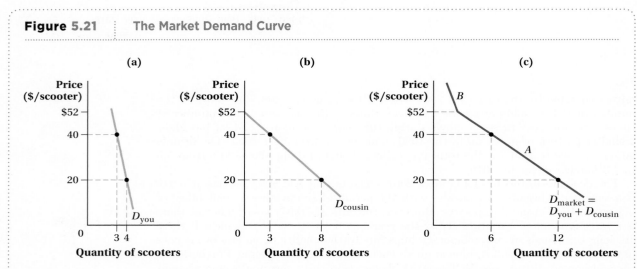

(a) Your market demand curve D_{you} shows the number of scooters you would demand at each price. At a price of $40 per scooter, you demand 3 scooters; at $20 per scooter, you demand 4 scooters.

(b) Your cousin's market demand curve D_{cousin} shows that he is more sensitive to price changes in scooters than you are. At a price of $40 per scooter, he similarly demands 3 scooters, but when the price of a scooter is $20, he demands 8 scooters.

(c) In a market consisting only of you and your cousin, the total market demand curve D_{market} is the sum of your demand curve D_{you} and your cousin's demand curve D_{cousin}. At a price of $40 per scooter, you and your cousin each demand 3 scooters, summing to 6 scooters on D_{market}. When scooters cost $20 each, you demand 4 scooters and your cousin demands 8 scooters, summing to 12 scooters on D_{market}. At prices above $52, your cousin's quantity demanded is zero, so D_{market} overlaps with D_{you}, and therefore D_{market} is kinked at a price of $52. Market demand will always be flatter and to the right of the individual demand curves.

[9] An exception to this rule would be when the firm can charge different prices to different consumers (what economists call *price discrimination*). In that case, which we explore in Chapter 10, the firm can take advantage of individual consumers' demand curves rather than just the overall market demand. By charging different prices to different consumers depending on their individual demand, the firm can make higher profits.

The Market Demand Curve

There are a few things to notice about market demand curves. First, a market demand curve will always be to the right of any individual demand curve, because all consumers combined must consume at least as much of a good at a given price as any single consumer does. For a similar reason, the slope of the market demand curve must also be as flat as or flatter than any of the individual demand curves. That is, for a given change in price, the change in quantity demanded for the market as a whole must be at least as great as the change in quantity demanded by any individual consumer.[10] Finally, if the price is so high that only one consumer wants any of the good, the individual demand curve for that consumer will lie directly on top of the market demand curve at that price. At that point, the consumer *is* the market.

Using Algebra to Move from Individual to Market Demand

We can move from individual to market demand algebraically as well as graphically. The formulas for the two demand curves in Figure 5.21 are

$$Q_{\text{you}} = 5 - 0.05P$$
$$Q_{\text{cousin}} = 13 - 0.25P$$

To find the market demand for the tickets, we start by adding up the two individual demand curves:

$$Q_{\text{market}} = Q_{\text{you}} + Q_{\text{cousin}} = (5 - 0.05P) + (13 - 0.25P)$$
$$Q_{\text{market}} = 18 - 0.3P$$

If we plug in the prices from Figure 5.21, they match the quantities in the figure as long as we are on the part of the curve labeled A in Figure 5.21 where both quantities demanded are above zero. According to the equation, market demand when $P = 40$ is $Q_{\text{market}} = 6$, which is what the figure shows, and when $P = 20$, $Q_{\text{market}} = 12$, just as on the figure.

We're not quite done yet, though. The prices at which you and your cousin will consume no scooters—the demand choke prices—are different. Yours is $100; your cousin's is $52. (You can check this by plugging these prices into the demand curves and verifying that the quantities demanded equal zero.) That means at prices above $52, the market demand is only *your* demand because your cousin's quantity demanded is zero. There is no negative demand allowed. This isn't accounted for when we add together the two demand curves above, however, because at prices above $52, the part of the market demand curve coming from the formula for Q_{cousin} is less than zero. Therefore, market demand is your demand, $Q = 5 - 0.05P$, for prices between $52 and $100 (quantity demanded is zero at prices higher than $100), and is $Q = 18 - 0.3P$ (yours plus your cousin's) for prices below $52. That is, the market demand has a kink at $P = 52$.

---

[10] Even though the *slope* of the market demand curve is always flatter than that of individual demand curves, it doesn't necessarily imply that the *elasticity* of the market demand curve is higher than that of individual demand curves (though this is often the case). This is because the elasticity doesn't just depend on the slope, but also on the level of demand. The percentage change in prices (the denominator in the elasticity equation) will be the same for both individuals and the market. While the change in quantity will be smaller for individuals, the level of demand will be lower too. If the level is small enough, the percentage change in quantities for the individual can be large enough to make individual demand as or more elastic than market demand.

make the grade

Adding demand curves horizontally, not vertically

Moving from individual demand curves to market demand is conceptually fairly simple. There's just one thing you have to be careful about. Market demand curves are derived by adding *quantities* of individual demand curves, not prices. That is, individual demands are graphically added horizontally, not vertically.

When you add horizontally, you are summing up all the individual quantities demanded, holding price fixed. This is exactly what you want to do because market demand is the total quantity demanded at any given price. If you add individual demand curves vertically, however, you are holding quantities demanded fixed while adding up the prices. That's a very different conceptual exercise and one that, in this case at least, doesn't really make any sense.

Likewise, if you are combining individual demand curves algebraically rather than graphically, make sure you've written out the individual demand curves as quantities demanded as a function of price. When you add those equations, you'll just be adding the quantities, which is again what you want to do. If you instead try to add equations where prices are a function of quantities (economists call these "inverse demand curves"), again you'll be doing the very different exercise of adding up prices across individuals while holding the quantities fixed.

5.4 figure it out

Suppose that at a rural gas station in Toby Acres, there are only two customers, Johnny (who drives a 4X4 pickup) and Olivia (who drives a Prius). Johnny's demand for gasoline is $Q_J = 32 - 8P$, while Olivia's demand is $Q_O = 20 - 4P$, where Q is measured in gallons and P is the price per gallon.

a. Solve for the market demand equation for gasoline at Toby Acres.

b. Draw a diagram showing the market demand curve for gasoline at Toby Acres.

Solution:

a. The market demand curve is the horizontal sum of the buyers' demand curves. Remember that summing horizontally means to add up quantities demanded at each price. This means that we can get the market demand by adding Q_J and Q_O:

$$Q_{\text{market}} = Q_J + Q_O$$
$$= (32 - 8P) + (20 - 4P)$$
$$= 52 - 12P$$

But there is more to the story than solving for the summation of the two demand curves. Johnny is not willing to buy any gas if the price is greater than or equal to $4 per gallon because that is his demand choke price:

$$Q_J = 32 - 8P$$
$$0 = 32 - 8P$$
$$8P = 32$$
$$P = 4$$

So, once the price hits $4, only Olivia will be in the market. Her demand choke price is $5:

$$Q_O = 20 - 4P$$
$$0 = 20 - 4P$$
$$4P = 20$$
$$P = 5$$

Thus, as long as the price is below $4 per gallon, the market demand for gasoline is the horizontal sum of the two buyers' demand curves. Between a price of $4 and $5, the market demand is simply the same as Olivia's demand. At a price greater than or equal to $5, quantity demanded is zero.

b. The figure here shows the market demand for gasoline in Toby Acres. Notice that the market demand curve is kinked as a result of the buyers' different choke prices. Segment A is the section of demand below the price of $4 and is the horizontal summation of Johnny's and Olivia's demand for gasoline. Segment B is the segment of market demand where Olivia is the only buyer (since the price is above Johnny's demand choke price). At a price of $5 or above, quantity demanded is zero.

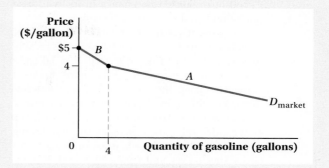

5.6 Conclusion

In this chapter, we used the consumer choice model of Chapter 4 to see where demand curves come from and what factors shift them. We studied how changes in various factors that drive consumer demand for a good—their income, the good's price, and the prices of other goods—affect the consumer's utility-maximizing bundle and, through this, the demand curve.

We decomposed the response of a consumer's choices to a price change in a good into two components: the substitution effect and the income effect. The substitution effect reflects changes in quantities consumed due to the new relative prices of goods after the price change. The income effect reflects the fact that a price change affects a consumer's buying power, and this in turn changes the consumer's optimal consumption bundle.

We also saw how individuals' demand curves for a good are added up to create the market demand curve for that good.

This chapter ends our examination of the factors that determine consumer demand. In the next chapter, we move on to producer behavior and the supply side of markets.

Summary

1. Shifts in income holding prices constant are reflected in parallel shifts in the budget constraint and affect a consumer's demand curve. An **Engel curve** shows the relationship between income and the quantity of a good demanded. Whether an increase in income raises or reduces the quantity demanded of a good depends on the type of good. **Normal goods** are those for which demand increases with income. **Inferior goods** are those for which demand decreases with income. Within normal goods, goods with an **income elasticity** between zero and 1 (those whose share of expenditure rises more slowly than income rises) are called **necessity goods.** Goods with an income elasticity greater than 1 (those whose share of expenditure grows faster than income) are called **luxury goods.** [Section 5.1]

2. The way in which changes in the price of a good affect the quantity demanded of that good is what creates the shape of the demand curve. We construct a consumer's demand curve by examining what happens to a consumer's utility-maximizing bundle as the price of one good changes, holding the price of the other good, income, and preferences fixed. Changes in income, holding preferences and prices constant, can shift the demand curve. Changes in preferences, holding income and prices constant, can shift the demand curve. [Section 5.2]

3. The **total effect** on the quantity demanded of a good in response to a change in its own price can be broken down into two components.

    The **substitution effect** causes the consumer to shift toward the good that becomes relatively cheaper and away from the good that becomes relatively more expensive. This shows up as a movement along the consumer's initial indifference curve, driven by the change in relative prices.

    The **income effect** occurs because a change in the price of a good changes the purchasing power of the consumer; a price drop increases purchasing power and expands the set of bundles a consumer may choose from, while a rise in price decreases purchasing power and reduces the consumer's options. The income effect shows up as a move to a new indifference curve, reflecting a change in utility for the consumer. The direction of the income effect on quantity demanded depends on whether the good is normal (where demand rises when income rises) or inferior (demand falls when income rises). If the income effect is large enough for inferior goods,

it is theoretically possible for the quantity demanded of a good to rise when its price rises. However, these types of goods, called **Giffen goods,** are exceedingly rare in the real world. [**Section 5.3**]

4. Changes in the prices of other goods shift the demand curve for a good. Which ways these cross-price effects shift demand depends on the nature of the relationship between the goods. Goods are **substitutes** if a price increase in one leads to an increase in demand of the other, due to consumers switching away from the now more expensive good and toward the substitute. Goods are **complements** if an increase in one's price causes demand of the other to fall. Complements are goods that are often consumed together. [**Section 5.4**]

5. Individuals' demand curves are aggregated to get total market demand. Market demand at a given price is the sum of all individual demands at that same price. Another way of saying this is that market demand is the horizontal (i.e., quantity) sum of individual demands. [**Section 5.5**]

Review Questions

1. Define the income effect. What variables do we hold constant in order to isolate the income effect?
2. What are the differences between normal goods, inferior goods, and luxury goods?
3. Both the income expansion path and the Engel curve show the effect of income on consumption choices. When might you choose to use the income expansion path? When might the Engel curve be more useful?
4. Describe how we can derive a consumer's demand curve from his indifference curves. Why would we expect the demand curve to slope downward?
5. Name at least three factors that can shift an individual's demand curve for pizza. Also describe the effect each factor has on demand (e.g., does it rise or fall?).
6. Define the substitution effect. How does it relate to the income effect?

7. Describe how to decompose the consumer's response to price changes into the substitution and income effects.
8. How do income and substitution effects differ between normal and inferior goods?
9. What is a Giffen good?
10. What are complements and substitutes?
11. When the cross-price elasticity of demand is positive, are the two goods complements or substitutes? What type of goods have a negative cross-price elasticity?
12. What can the shape of the indifference curve tell us about two goods?
13. How does the market demand relate to individual demand curves?
14. Why will a market demand curve always be at least as flat as a given individual demand curve?

Problems (Solutions to problems marked * appear at the back of this book. Problems adapted to use calculus are available online at http://worthpublishers.com/GLS1e)

1. A principles of microeconomics instructor regularly asks her class to give an example of an inferior good. "No matter how poor we might be," the students tell her, "ramen noodles are an inferior good." Explain why the students must be wrong in their reasoning.
2. Can you tell whether a good is normal or inferior by looking at the shape of a single indifference curve? Explain your answer.

*3. Andrew has an income of $30 he spends on cupcakes and cakes. The price of a cupcake is $5. Suppose that Andrew has the following preferences depicted below:

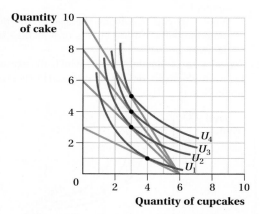

a. With this in mind, draw Andrew's demand curve for cake.
b. When the price of cake changes, which effect is stronger, the substitution effect or the income effect? Give your answer for every price change depicted in the figure.
c. If Andrew's preferences shifted toward not distinguishing between cake and cupcakes (i.e., if they became closer substitutes), all his indifference curves would become flatter. How would Andrew's demand curve for cake change?

4. Suppose that, holding prices constant, Alice has preferences over the number of books she purchases that look like:

Income (thousands of dollars)	Optimal number of books purchased
5	5
10	6
15	20
20	25
25	26
30	10
35	9
40	8
45	7
50	6

a. Draw a smooth approximation of Alice's Engel curve for books, indicating the ranges

over which books are inferior goods and over which they are normal goods.
b. A luxury good is a good that has an income elasticity greater than 1. Give the ranges in which books are luxury goods for Alice.

*5. Suppose that Sonya faces an increase in the price of pasta, as depicted below, moving her from an optimum bundle of rice and pasta at A to an optimal bundle at B.
a. Trace a copy of this diagram. Graphically depict the substitution and income effect.
b. Which effect is strongest? How can you tell?

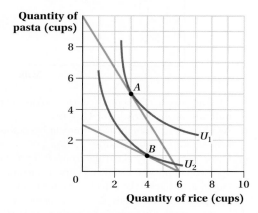

6. Kim's utility function is given by $U = 5X + 2Y$, where $MU_X = 5$ and $MU_Y = 2$.
a. Suppose that at the prices P_X and P_Y of good X and good Y, respectively, Kim is consuming (optimally) some positive amount of good X and some positive amount of good Y. What is the price of good X in terms of the price of good Y?
b. How will her consumption change if P_X doubles, while P_Y does not change?

7. You may have noticed that the market demand curve is always flatter than any individual demand curve. Is market price elasticity of demand also always lower than individual price elasticity of demand? Why or why not?

8. Indicate whether the following statements are true, false, or uncertain. If false or uncertain, explain why.
a. The price of a watch increases by 10%, and you spend a larger fraction of your income on it. The watch is a Giffen good.
b. Due to a flood, corn prices and soybean prices increase. If corn and soybeans are substitutes, the quantity of corn demanded falls.
c. Goods 1 and 2 are substitutes, and goods 2 and 3 are substitutes. This must mean that goods 1 and 3 are substitutes.

9. Suppose that Grover consumes two goods, cookies and milk. Grover's income expansion path is shown in the diagram below. Use the information in the diagram to explain whether each of the statements below is true or false. Provide an explanation for each answer.

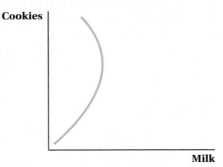

Cookies

Milk

a. At low levels of income, both cookies and milk are normal goods for Grover.
b. As Grover's income grows, eventually cookies become an inferior good.
c. Draw, intuitively, the Engel curve for Grover's consumption of milk at various incomes.
d. Draw, intuitively, the Engel curve for Grover's consumption of cookies at various incomes.

10. Josie gets great pleasure from eating flan. Her preferences for flan and tofu are given in the graph below:

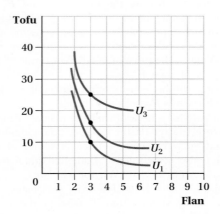

Tofu

Flan

Suppose that Josie's income is $40, and that tofu costs $1.

a. Draw budget constraints for Josie given three different prices for flan: $5, $8, and $10.

b. Find the optimal consumption of flan at each of those prices.
c. What will Josie's demand curve for flan look like? Describe it in terms of the elasticity of demand.
d. What can you say about the size of the income and substitution effects of a change in the price of flan?

*11. Consider the following graph, which illustrates Tyler's preferences for DVD rentals and in-theater movie tickets:

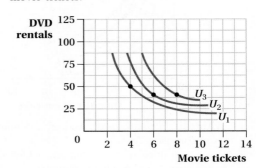

DVD rentals

Movie tickets

Suppose that DVD rentals always cost $1, and that Tyler's income is $100 per week.

a. If the price of a movie ticket is $10, draw Tyler's budget line. Be very careful to draw to scale. How many movies does he see in the theater?
b. In another graph, plot a point that reflects how many movies Tyler sees in the theater at a price of $10.
c. The movie theater changes the price of tickets to $12.50. Repeat your work in (a) and (b) using this new price.
d. Tyler's mother gives him a discount card that allows him to purchase movie tickets for $7.50. Repeat your work in (a) and (b) using this new price.
e. Connect the dots in your second graph to complete Tyler's demand curve for movie tickets.

12. Consider the following three graphs, which illustrate the preferences of three consumers (Bob, Carol, and Ted) regarding two goods, apples and peaches. Each consumer has an income of $30, and each consumer pays $2 for apples and $3 for peaches.

(a) Bob

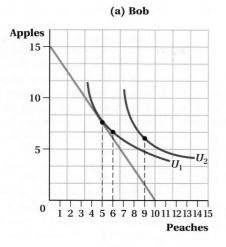

(b) Carol

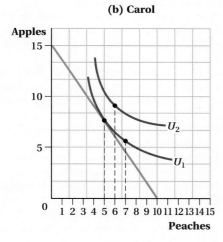

(c) Ted

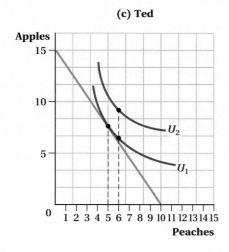

a. Suppose that the price of peaches falls to $2. Draw a new budget line for each consumer and find the new optimal bundle of apples and peaches each would buy. How does the new quantity of peaches compare to the original quantity? Indicate the change in the first column of the table below (an increase of one unit might be denoted as a +1).

b. For each consumer, determine the substitution effect of the price change by drawing a hypothetical budget line with the same slope as your new budget line, but just tangent to the consumer's original indifference curve. How much of a change in peach consumption does the substitution effect account for? Indicate that change in the first column of the table below.

c. Now add in the income effect. Compare each consumer's peach consumption in (b) to his or her final peach consumption in (a). Indicate the difference in column 3 of the table below. Double-check your work to ensure that the last two columns add up to the number in the first column.

d. Do Bob, Carol, and Ted consider peaches normal, inferior, or income-inelastic?

	Total Effect of Price Change	Substitution Effect of Price Change	Income Effect of Price Change
Bob			
Carol			
Ted			

*13. Carmen's preferences are such that she is always indifferent between watching two movies or seeing one basketball game.
   a. What must Carmen's indifference curves look like?
   b. Suppose that Carmen has an income of $90. If a movie costs $10 and a basketball game costs $18, what will Carmen's optimal consumption bundle be?

*14. Consider the following diagram, which illustrates Gaston's preferences for red beans and rice. Gaston has an income of $20. Rice costs $2 per serving.

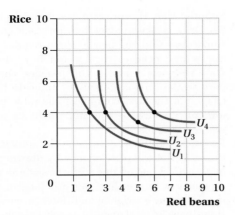

a. Derive Gaston's demand for red beans. Use prices of $2 and $4 in your analysis. Graph your results, and connect the points you plotted to yield Gaston's demand for red beans.

b. Suppose that the price of rice increases to $3. Again, derive Gaston's demand for red beans using the same prices you used in part (a).

c. Does Gaston's demand for red beans increase or decrease as a result of the increase in the price of rice?

d. Does your answer to (c) indicate that red beans and rice are substitutes or complements?

15. Consider Harry's indifference curve indicated in the graph below:

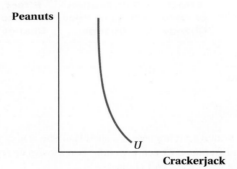

a. True or False (and explain): Peanuts and Crackerjack are clearly complements.

b. True or False (and explain): Peanuts and Crackerjack are clearly both normal goods.

16. True or False: If pizza and calzones are substitutes, then the substitution effect of a price change will be in a different direction than if pizza and calzones are complements. Explain, using a diagram.

17. Armen lives in Washington State, where grapes are grown. Armen's twin Allen lives in New York, where grapes must be trucked in from Washington at a fixed cost of $0.20 per pound of grapes. Armen and Allen have identical tastes, but Armen tends to purchase lower-quality grapes and Allen tends to purchase higher quality grapes. Use indifference curve analysis to explain this oddity.

18. Mitch cares only about how much he can write. Because a pen will write 7 miles of text and a pencil will write 35 miles of text, Mitch considers them perfect 5-to-1 substitutes. If the price of pens is given by P_{pen} and the price of pencils is given by P_{pencil}, and if Mitch's income is given by Y, use indifference curve analysis to *derive* the demand curve for pencils.

19. Brady, who has ordinary-shaped indifference curves, buys 16 ounces of salt each year. Even when the price of salt doubles, Brady continues to purchase exactly 16 ounces.

a. True or False (and explain): Salt is neither inferior nor normal to Brady.

b. What is Brady's price elasticity of demand for salt?

c. What can we say about Brady's income elasticity of demand for salt?

d. What can we say about the substitution and income effects of a change in the price of salt?

*20. At a price of $3 each, Yoshi (a typical New Yorker) drinks 200 44-ounce sodas each year. Concerned about burgeoning obesity, the Mayor of New York proposes a $0.50 tax on such drinks. He then proposes compensating consumers for the price increase by mailing each resident a check for $100.

a. What will happen to Yoshi's consumption of soda? Show, using an indifference curve diagram with soda on the horizontal axis and a composite good (price = $1) on the vertical axis.

b. Will Yoshi be better off, worse off, or indifferent to the change? Explain, using your diagram.

c. In terms of revenue, will the government be better off, worse off, or indifferent to the proposal? Explain.

Chapter 5 Appendix:
The Calculus of Income and Substitution Effects

We saw in this chapter that a price change in one good influences a consumer's consumption in two ways. The *substitution effect* is the change in a consumer's optimal consumption bundle due to a change in the relative prices of the goods, holding his utility constant. The *income effect* is the change in a consumer's optimal consumption bundle due to the change in his purchasing power. In the chapter, we solved for these two effects using a figure like the one below where good X is shown on the horizontal axis and good Y on the vertical axis. The consumer's original consumption bundle is A. Consumption bundle B is the optimal bundle after a decrease in the price of X, holding the price of Y constant. Finally, bundle A' shows what the consumer would buy if the price of X decreased but utility stayed the same as at bundle A (i.e., on indifference curve U_1). Graphically, the substitution effect is the change from bundle A to bundle A', the income effect is the change from A' to B, and the total effect is the sum of these two effects or the change from A to B.

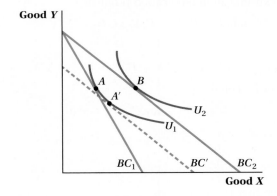

The graphical approach to decomposing the income and substitution effects can be a little messy. You have to keep track of multiple budget constraints, indifference curves, and their respective shifts. The calculus links the effects we observed in the graph to the techniques we learned for solving the consumer's problem in the Chapter 4 Appendix. Solving for these effects is a two-step process. We begin by finding the new consumption bundle B to solve for the total effect. Second, we solve for bundle A', which will allow us to identify both the substitution and income effects.

Let's start with a consumer with budget constraint $I = P_X X + P_Y Y$ (BC_1 in the graph) and a standard Cobb–Douglas utility function $U(X,Y) = X^\alpha Y^{1-\alpha}$, where $0 < \alpha < 1$. Point A in the figure is the solution to the constrained optimization problem:

$$\max_{X,Y} U = X^\alpha Y^{1-\alpha} \text{ s.t. } I = P_X X + P_Y Y$$

In the Chapter 4 Appendix, we derived the solution to this particular utility-maximization problem, and found that the optimal bundle A is $\left(X_A = \frac{\alpha I}{P_X}, Y_A = \frac{(1-\alpha)I}{P_Y} \right)$.

Now suppose that the price of good X, P_X, decreases to P_X'. The consumer has the same utility function as before, but because of the price change, his budget constraint rotates outward to $I = P_X'X + P_YY$ (BC_2 on the graph). Once again, we rely on utility maximization to solve for the optimal bundle:

$$\max_{X,Y} U = X^\alpha Y^{1-\alpha} \text{ s.t. } I = P_X'X + P_YY$$

Because we already know the generic solution to this problem, we can plug in the new price of X to find the new optimal bundle $B = \left(X_B = \frac{\alpha I}{P_X'}, Y_B = \frac{(1-\alpha)I}{P_Y}\right)$. This gives us the total effect of the price change on the consumer's consumption bundle—the difference between his new consumption bundle $\left(\frac{\alpha I}{P_X'}, \frac{(1-\alpha)I}{P_Y}\right)$ and his original consumption bundle $\left(\frac{\alpha I}{P_X}, \frac{(1-\alpha)I}{P_Y}\right)$. Note that in this instance the change in the price of X does not affect the quantity of Y the consumer purchases. That the demand for each good is independent of changes in the price of the other good is a quirk of the Cobb–Douglas utility function. This result is not necessarily true of other utility functions.

The solution to the utility-maximization problem gives us the final bundle B. But we want to know more than just the total effect of the price change on the consumption bundle. We want to decompose this total effect into its two components: the substitution and income effects. We can do this by solving for bundle A'.

What is the substitution effect? It is the effect of the change in relative price of two goods on the quantities demanded given the consumer's original level of utility. How can we solve for this effect? It's easy! When we know the consumer's original level of utility and the goods' prices, as we do here, expenditure minimization tells us the answer to the problem. Take the consumer's original level of utility U_1 as the constraint and set up the consumer's expenditure-minimization problem

$$\min_{X,Y} I = P_X'X + P_YY \text{ s.t. } U_1 = X^\alpha Y^{1-\alpha}$$

as a Lagrangian:

$$\min_{X,Y,\lambda} \mathcal{L}(X,Y,\lambda) = P_X'X + P_YY + \lambda(U_1 - X^\alpha Y^{1-\alpha})$$

Write out the first-order conditions:

$$\frac{\partial \mathcal{L}}{\partial X} = P_X' - \lambda\alpha X^{\alpha-1}Y^{1-\alpha} = 0$$

$$\frac{\partial \mathcal{L}}{\partial Y} = P_Y - \lambda(1-\alpha)X^\alpha Y^{-\alpha} = 0$$

$$\frac{\partial \mathcal{L}}{\partial \lambda} = U_1 - X^\alpha Y^{1-\alpha} = 0$$

Solve for Y using the first two conditions:

$$\lambda = \frac{P_X'}{\alpha X^{\alpha-1}Y^{1-\alpha}} = \frac{P_Y}{(1-\alpha)X^\alpha Y^{-\alpha}}$$

$$P_X'(1-\alpha)X^\alpha Y^{-\alpha} = P_Y\alpha X^{\alpha-1}Y^{1-\alpha}$$

$$Y^{1-\alpha}Y^\alpha = \frac{(1-\alpha)}{\alpha}\frac{P_X'}{P_Y}X^\alpha X^{1-\alpha}$$

$$Y = \frac{(1-\alpha)}{\alpha}\frac{P_X'}{P_Y}X$$

Plug this expression for Y as a function of X into the constraint to solve for bundle A':

$$U_1 = X^\alpha Y^{1-\alpha} = X^\alpha\left[\frac{(1-\alpha)}{\alpha}\frac{P_X'}{P_Y}X\right]^{1-\alpha}$$

$$U_1 = X^\alpha X^{1-\alpha}\left[\frac{(1-\alpha)}{\alpha}\frac{P_X'}{P_Y}\right]^{1-\alpha} = X\left[\frac{(1-\alpha)}{\alpha}\frac{P_X'}{P_Y}\right]^{1-\alpha}$$

$$X_{A'} = U_1\left[\frac{\alpha}{(1-\alpha)}\frac{P_Y}{P_X'}\right]^{1-\alpha}$$

Then plug this optimal value of X into the expression for Y as a function of X from above:

$$Y_{A'} = \frac{(1-\alpha)}{\alpha} \frac{P_X'}{P_Y} X_{A'} = \frac{(1-\alpha)}{\alpha} \frac{P_X'}{P_Y} U_1 \left[\frac{\alpha}{(1-\alpha)} \frac{P_Y}{P_X'} \right]^{1-\alpha}$$

To simplify, invert the third term and combine like terms:

$$= Y_{A'} \frac{(1-\alpha)}{\alpha} \frac{P_X'}{P_Y} U_1 \left[\frac{(1-\alpha)}{\alpha} \frac{P_X'}{P_Y} \right]^{\alpha-1}$$

$$= U_1 \left[\frac{(1-\alpha)}{\alpha} \frac{P_X'}{P_Y} \right]^{\alpha}$$

Solving the consumer's expenditure-minimization problem at the new prices and original utility level gives us the third piece of the substitution/income effect puzzle: bundle A'.[1] Having these three bundles (A, A', and B) allows us to solve for the substitution and income effects. The substitution effect is the difference between the consumer's original bundle and what he would buy at the new prices but at the old utility level, the difference between A and A'. The income effect is the difference between what he would buy at the new prices and original utility and what he buys with his original income at the new prices, the difference between A' and B. The total effect is the sum of the substitution and income effects or the difference between A and B.

5A.1 figure it out

A sample problem will make breaking down the total effect of a price change into the substitution and income effects even clearer. Let's return to Figure It Out 4.4, which featured Antonio, a consumer who purchases burgers and fries. Antonio has a utility function $U(B,F) = \sqrt{BF} = B^{0.5}F^{0.5}$ and income of $20. Initially, the prices of burgers and fries are $5 and $2, respectively.

a. What is Antonio's optimal consumption bundle and utility at the original prices?

b. The price of burgers increases to $10 per burger, and the price of fries stays constant at $2. What does Antonio consume at the optimum at these new prices? Decompose this change into the total, substitution, and income effects.

Solution:

a. We solved this question in the Chapter 4 Appendix, but the answer will be crucial to solving for the total, substitution, and income effects in part (b). When a burger costs $5 and fries cost $2, Antonio's original constrained optimization problem is

$$\max_{B,F} U = B^{0.5}F^{0.5} \text{ s.t. } 20 = 5B + 2F$$

We found that Antonio consumes 2 burgers and 5 orders of fries, and his utility for this bundle is $B^{0.5}F^{0.5} = 2^{0.5}5^{0.5} = 10^{0.5}$.

b. When the price of hamburgers doubles to $10 each, Antonio faces a new budget constraint: $20 = 10B + 2F$. Antonio's new utility-maximization problem is

$$\max_{B,F} U = B^{0.5}F^{0.5} \text{ s.t. } 20 = 10B + 2F$$

Therefore, we should write his constrained optimization problem as a Lagrangian and solve for his new optimal bundle at the higher burger price:

$$\max_{B,F,\lambda} \mathcal{L}(B,F,\lambda) = B^{0.5}F^{0.5} + \lambda(20 - 10B - 2F)$$

$$\frac{\partial \mathcal{L}}{\partial B} = 0.5B^{-0.5}F^{0.5} - 10\lambda = 0$$

$$\frac{\partial \mathcal{L}}{\partial F} = 0.5B^{0.5}F^{-0.5} - 2\lambda = 0$$

$$\frac{\partial \mathcal{L}}{\partial \lambda} = 20 - 10B - 2F = 0$$

We use the first two conditions to solve for λ and then solve for F as a function of B:

$$\lambda = 0.05B^{-0.5}F^{0.5} = 0.25B^{0.5}F^{-0.5}$$

$$F^{0.5}F^{0.5} = 20(0.25)B^{0.5}B^{0.5}$$

$$F = 5B$$

---

[1] One way to check our answer to bundle A' is to take the new prices, income, and utility function, and solve for the bundle using utility maximization. As we saw in the Chapter 4 Appendix, this approach will yield the same answer.

and substitute this value for F into the budget constraint:

$$20 = 10B + 2F$$
$$20 = 10B + 2(5B)$$
$$20 = 20B$$
$$B^* = 1 \text{ burger}$$
$$F^* = 5B = 5(1) = 5 \text{ orders of fries}$$

In response to the increase in the price of burgers from \$5 to \$10, then, Antonio decreases his consumption of burgers and leaves his consumption of fries unchanged. Therefore, the total effect of the price change is that Antonio's consumption of burgers declines by 1 and his consumption of fries remains the same at 5.

Next, we use expenditure minimization to find the substitution and income effects. Remember that we want to find out how many burgers and fries Antonio will consume if the price of burgers is \$10 but his utility is the same as his utility when burgers cost \$5. His third constrained optimization problem is

$$\min_{B,F} I = 10B + 2F \text{ s.t. } 10^{0.5} = B^{0.5}F^{0.5}$$

We could solve using the Lagrangian as we did above, but instead let's use what we know about the solution to the consumer's optimization problem and set the marginal rate of substitution of burgers for fries equal to the ratio of their prices and solve for F as a function of B:

$$\frac{MU_B}{MU_F} = \frac{P_B}{P_F}$$
$$\frac{0.5B^{-0.5}F^{0.5}}{0.5B^{0.5}F^{-0.5}} = \frac{10}{2}$$
$$\frac{F}{B} = \frac{10}{2}$$
$$F = 5B$$

Now plug this value for F into the consumer's utility constraint:

$$10^{0.5} = B^{0.5}F^{0.5} = B^{0.5}(5B)^{0.5}$$
$$10^{0.5} = B(5^{0.5})$$
$$B' = \frac{10^{0.5}}{5^{0.5}} = 2^{0.5} \approx 1.4 \text{ hamburgers}$$
$$F' = 5B' \approx 5(1.4) \approx 7 \text{ orders of fries}$$

Antonio's expenditure-minimizing bundle for the new prices and the original utility is approximately 1.4 hamburgers and 7 fries compared to his original bundle of 2 hamburgers and 5 fries. As intuition would tell you, the desired consumption of burgers decreases when burgers become relatively more expensive, while the desired consumption of fries increases as fries become relatively less expensive—that's the substitution effect in action. In particular, Antonio's substitution effect is to consume 0.6 fewer burgers (1.4 – 2 burgers = –0.6 burgers) and 2 more orders of fries (7 – 5 orders of fries = 2 orders of fries).

While this bundle gives Antonio the same level of utility as the original bundle, he would have to spend about \$8 more to buy it [his original expenditure was \$20; his new one is \$10(1.4) + \$2(7) = \$28]. Remember, however, that Antonio doesn't actually purchase this \$28 combination of burgers and fries. It's just a step on the way to his final consumption bundle (1 hamburger, 5 orders of fries) that we got from the utility-maximization problem above. We can use this final bundle to find the income effect. Here, the income effect is to consume 0.4 fewer burgers (1 – 1.4 burgers = –0.4 burgers) and 2 fewer orders of fries (5 – 7 orders of fries = –2 orders of fries) because the increase in the price of burgers reduces Antonio's purchasing power. Notice that the quantity of both goods declines as his purchasing power declines. This means that, for Antonio, they are both normal goods.

In the end, the price change only changes Antonio's consumption of hamburgers: The total effect on his consumption bundle is 1 fewer burger (1 – 2 burgers = –1 burger), which is the sum of the substitution effect (–0.6 burgers) and the income effect (–0.4 burgers). On the other hand, the total effect on his consumption of fries is zero because the substitution effect (2 more orders of fries) and the income effect (2 fewer orders of fries) exactly offset one another.

Let's review what we've learned about decomposing the total effect of a price change into the substitution and income effects. To find the original bundle, we solve the utility-maximization problem at the original prices and income. We identify the substitution effect after a price change by solving the expenditure-minimization problem using the new prices with the original level of utility as the constraint. This tells us how a consumer's bundle responds to a price change while leaving the consumer with the same level of utility—the substitution effect. Finally, to find the income effect, we solve the utility-maximization problem using the new prices and the consumer's actual income. Comparing this bundle with the bundle we found using expenditure minimization tells us how consumption responds to the change in purchasing power that is caused by the price change, or the income effect.

Problems

1. Malachi only consumes 2 goods: DVD rentals and coffee. His utility function is

$$U(R,C) = R^{0.75}C^{0.25}$$

where R is the number of rentals and C is cups of coffee. Malachi has $16 in his pocket right now, and he plans to spend all of the $16 on DVD rentals and coffee today.

   a. The price of one rental is $4 and the price of coffee is $2 per cup. Solve for Malachi's optimal bundle.

   b. Suppose that Malachi signs up for a membership that reduces the price of a rental to $2, while leaving his income unchanged. Find the substitution effect, the income effect, and the total effect of the decrease in the price of video rentals on Malachi's consumption of rentals and coffee.

   c. From your answer to part (b), are DVD rentals and coffee normal or inferior goods for Malachi? Explain.

2. Suppose that a consumer has utility given by $U(X,Y) = XY + 10Y$ and income of $100 to spend on goods X and Y.

   a. The prices of X and Y are both $1 per unit. Use a Lagrangian to solve for the optimal basket of goods.

   b. Suppose that the price of X increases to $5 per unit. Use a Lagrangian to solve for the new optimal basket of goods. Find the total effect of the price change on the consumption of each good.

   c. Use a Lagrangian to find the substitution effect of the increase in the price of good X on the consumption of each good. What income would the consumer need to attain the original level of utility when the price of X increases to $5 per unit?

   d. Find the income effect of the increase in the price of good X on the consumption of each good. Are the goods normal or inferior? Explain.

   e. Show that the total effect of the increase in the price of X is equal to the sum of the substitution effect and the income effect.

Producer Behavior

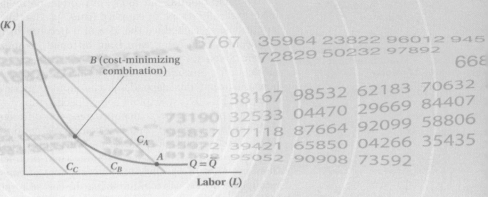

At the beginning of Chapter 4, we asked you to imagine you are Jeff Bezos trying to develop the Kindle for introduction to the market. Your task was to decide what features you wanted the Kindle to have so that consumers would find it desirable. Now suppose you've done your market analysis, developed your product concept, and selected the features. Your task at this point is to figure out how to produce the Kindle. How many do you want to make? What mix of inputs are you going to use to do so? What size factory? How many employees? How much plastic? What kind of microprocessor? What will all this cost? Suppose the Kindle is an even bigger hit than you predicted, and you want to ramp up production. If you can't easily adjust the size of your factory, will your factory's size limit your ability to make more units by hiring more employees? And how much will costs rise if you increase production levels?

Any producer of a good or service faces these types of questions and others like them. The economics driving those questions, and their answers, are the focus of our analysis over the next several chapters. Chapters 4 and 5 were about consumer behavior, which determines the demand side of markets. With this chapter, we turn our attention to producer behavior, which drives the supply side of markets.

6.1 The Basics of Production

For a good to be consumed, it must first be produced. **Production** is the process by which a person, company, government, or non-profit agency uses inputs to create a good or service for which others are willing to pay. Production can take many forms. For instance, some producers make **final goods** that are bought by consumers.[1] Others make **intermediate goods** that are inputs into another firm's production, such as electricity, sugar, or advertising services. The range of products is so extensive that formulating a general but still useful model of production presents a formidable challenge—not unlike that involved in building the model of consumer behavior in the previous two chapters.

We begin building our model of production by laying out the assumptions that economists typically adopt to simplify firms' production decisions.[2] Having clarified these assumptions, we introduce the idea of a **production function,** which relates the amount of output a firm can create from different combinations of inputs. We then show how a firm, given its production function, makes its choice about which inputs to use in production—how many workers to hire, how much equipment to buy, and so on. We see how this input mix depends on the inputs' prices and the properties of the production function. Finally, we explore some specific topics about production functions, including how they reflect technological progress and differences in the scale of operations.

Before we begin our detailed analysis, a word of advice: Students often find it more difficult to understand production and supply than consumption and demand because they have more experience consuming than producing. But as you'll see in this chapter, there are a lot of parallels in the economics of consumers' and producers' decisions. For example, a firm's task of minimizing the cost of producing its desired quantity of output is very much like a consumer's desire to minimize her cost of achieving a given utility level.

Simplifying Assumptions about Firms' Production Behavior

In the real world, production is a dizzyingly complicated task. Think about a local restaurant. It sells dozens, maybe hundreds, of items. It has multiple suppliers (of meat, fish, fruit, drinks, glasses, silverware), several employees, and requires decisions about table sizes and placement, décor, dinnerware, advertising, and more. Each of these elements requires hundreds of decisions to be made just to set up for business, and then many more on-the-spot decisions while the restaurant is operating. At large firms like Walmart, Apple, or BMW, with tens of thousands of employees and billions of dollars of annual revenues from sales all over the globe, the production process is incredibly complex.

If we want to draw general conclusions about optimal production behavior in the face of such a complex reality, we need to make some simplifying assumptions. These let us focus on the essentials of a situation, kind of like imagining away all the little ripples and eddies in a river so we can focus on which direction the river is flowing. As always in economics, the goal is to make assumptions that allow us to build a useful model; we do not want to assume away so much reality that the model becomes useless as a tool to understand real-world behavior. In our attempt to model producer behavior in this chapter, we make the following assumptions:

1. **The firm produces a single good.** If a firm sells many products, then the decisions a firm makes about each product can be intertwined in complicated ways. In our basic

production
The process by which a person, company, government, or non-profit agency creates a good or service that others are willing to pay for.

final good
A good that is bought by a consumer.

intermediate good
A good that is used to produce another good.

production function
A mathematical relationship that describes how much output can be made from different combinations of inputs.

---

[1] Throughout this book, we often use the word "good" to mean both tangible goods, such as trucks, computers, jewelry, and so on, as well as services, such as haircuts, dog walking, financial planning, and so on. In this usage, anything a consumer values—tangible or not, concrete or abstract—is a good.

[2] We use the word "firm" as a generic term for any producer. Many producers *are* firms, but the term can also mean persons, governments, or non-profit agencies that create products.

model of the firm, we avoid these complications by assuming that the firm makes just one good.

2. **The firm has already chosen which product to produce.** The firms we study already know what they want to produce; our task is to determine how they can make it most efficiently. Deciding what to produce is an extremely important aspect of a firm's success, but that analysis is a bit beyond the scope of what we analyze here. The branch of economics called *industrial organization* studies many aspects of firm behavior, including product choice.

3. **The firm's goal is to minimize the cost of producing whatever quantity it chooses to make.** There are a couple of reasons why economists assume cost minimization is a goal of the production process. First, *most* firms seem to act this way (do, however, see the Application on Minnesota iron ore producers on the next page). It would certainly seem bizarre for a firm to behave in a way that suggested it knew how to make the very same product it currently makes for a lower cost, but just didn't want to.

   Note that the cost we're talking about here is the firm's total cost of producing *any particular quantity it chooses to make*. The firm can always reduce its total production cost by making less output. In building our model, we want to analyze how a firm will produce a specific quantity of output. (A firm's choice about what specific quantity of output to make depends on the characteristics of the market for its product, including the demand for the product and the number and type of its competitors. We discuss firms' choices of output levels in Chapters 8–11.)

   Second, cost minimization is necessary if a firm is going to maximize its profits. Profit maximization is another standard assumption economists make about firm behavior. We can think of cost minimization as a first step in profit maximization. It's important to remember, however, that we don't need to assume a firm is maximizing profits for it to be minimizing costs. Producers such as non-profits or governments might have priorities other than profits, but they would still want to minimize their costs; they gain nothing from wasting resources to make their products.

4. **The firm uses only two inputs in making its product: capital and labor.** Capital encompasses the buildings, machinery, and raw materials needed to make the product. Labor refers to all of the human resources (such as factory workers, salespeople, and CEOs) that are used to produce the firm's output. In building our model, we lump together all different kinds of capital under one single label, and do the same for labor.[3]

5. **In the short run, a firm can choose to employ as much or as little labor as it wants, but it cannot rapidly change how much capital it uses. In the long run, the firm can freely choose the amounts of both labor and of capital it employs.** This assumption captures the fact that it takes time to put capital into use. For example, between acquiring permits and undertaking construction, it can take many years for an electric company to build a new power plant. In comparison to this, firms can easily adjust worker hours by allowing employees to leave early or asking them to work overtime. In addition, hiring new employees and putting them to work is relatively easy. Even though the company must take time to find and train these workers, such tasks do not usually take as long as building or integrating new capital.

6. **The more inputs the firm uses, the more output it makes.** This assumption is similar to the "more is better" assumption for consumers' utility functions that we discussed in Chapter 4. Here, the analogous implication for production is that if the firm uses more labor or capital, its total output rises.

---

[3] We can lump together different kinds of capital and labor in this way because we measure each input in common units that measure the productive ability of a given input. Economists call these units *efficiency units*, and they allow us to add up all the units across the various types of capital and of labor the firm employs. This simplifies our model by leaving the producer with only two inputs to purchase, labor and capital.

7. **A firm's production exhibits diminishing marginal returns to labor and capital.**
   If the amount of capital is held constant, each additional worker eventually generates less
   output than the one before. The same diminishing returns exist for capital when labor is
   held constant. This assumption captures a basic idea of production: A mix of labor and
   capital is more productive than labor alone or capital alone. Capital helps workers to be
   productive, and vice versa. Take, for instance, the case of digging a hole for a building's
   foundation. Even hundreds of workers will make little progress digging the hole if they have
   no capital—machinery, or even shovels for that matter—to dig with. Similarly, a large
   amount of the fanciest digging equipment is of no use without humans to operate it. Only
   when the two types of inputs are used together and in the right amounts will the task be
   accomplished most efficiently. This assumption parallels the assumption in consumer theory
   that consumers derive diminishing marginal utility from additional units of each good.

   Just as diminishing marginal utility is central to understanding consumer behavior,
   diminishing marginal returns is critical to understanding firm behavior.

8. **The firm can buy as many capital or labor inputs as it wants at fixed prices.**
   Just as we assumed consumers could buy as much of any good as they wanted at a fixed
   price, we assume the firm can do the same for its capital and labor purchases. This assumption can be justified in two ways. First, most firms are small relative to the markets
   for the inputs they use. Even the largest companies employ only a small fraction of an
   economy's workers. Second, as long as the markets that produce a firm's inputs are reasonably competitive, even the largest firms can likely acquire as much capital and labor
   as they desire at a fixed price.

9. **If there is a well-functioning capital market (e.g., banks and investors), the firm
   does not have a budget constraint.** As long as the firm can make profits, it will be able
   to obtain the resources necessary to acquire the capital and labor it needs to produce. If a
   firm doesn't have the cash necessary to finance its input expenditures, it can raise funds
   by issuing stock or by borrowing. Outside investors should be willing to finance a firm's
   expenditures if they expect it to be profitable. Notice that this assumption about a firm's
   production does not have a counterpart in consumer choice theory. Consumers always have
   a budget constraint, and it limits the maximum level of utility they can obtain.

You may have noticed that there are more simplifying assumptions for the production model than for the consumption model. This is because producer behavior is a bit
more complicated than consumer behavior. For example, we need to consider producer
behavior in two time frames, the short run and the long run. Although much of production theory resembles the consumer theory we covered in Chapter 4, the differences
are complex enough that we must be careful to simplify the model as much as possible.

application

Do Firms Really Always Minimize Costs?

One of our assumptions about firms' production behavior is that they seek to minimize
the total cost of producing their chosen output level. Sometimes there are limits to
firms' abilities to do this, however.

Economist James Schmitz points this out in a study of the iron ore industry in north-
ern Minnesota.[4] During the mid-20th century, this industry had a virtual monopoly on
supplying ore to Great Lakes steel mills because of its proximity to them. In the 1980s,
however, the steel mills became able to purchase iron ore from new, low-cost mines in
Brazil at a much lower price, even after including transportation costs.

---

[4] James A. Schmitz Jr., "What Determines Productivity? Lessons from the Dramatic Recovery of the
U.S. and Canadian Iron Ore Industries Following Their Early 1980s Crisis," *Journal of Political
Economy* 113, no. 3 (2005): 582–625.

How did the Minnesota iron ore producers respond to this entrance of foreign competition? They experienced a sudden increase in productivity—that is, a sudden reduction in the per-unit costs of producing their output. Schmitz shows that this cost decrease didn't arise from new technologies or higher-cost mines going out of business.

Instead, the lower costs resulted from simple changes in operations practices, such as allowing machine operators to do their own repair work. Previously, if a machine broke down, the mines' employment contracts required that even the simplest fixes be done by specified maintenance workers. Often, these workers would have to travel several miles to the worksite, causing idle machine time. Additionally, maintenance workers were assigned specific types of machines and parts. This meant that if a maintenance worker assigned to, say, shovels, was not available, a broken shovel would have to stay idle, even if a maintenance worker assigned to dump trucks (or any other machine besides shovels) could easily fix the problem.

Does this mean that the Minnesota firms weren't minimizing costs *before* competition from the Brazilian mines? In some sense, they weren't; they could have made these changes and substantially reduced their costs while still mining the same amount of ore. A broader interpretation might be that before competition from Brazil, labor was effectively more expensive for the mines. Workers were being "paid" a substantial amount in on-the-job leisure time ensured by their contracts. Labor was expensive enough that even though the firms' might have been minimizing costs *given the contracts that had already been signed*, there was a lot of potential for costs to go down if the contracts changed. This is exactly what happened: Once their jobs were in jeopardy, the workers agreed to more flexible work rules, reducing both their on-the-job leisure and their effective cost to the mines. As the Nobel Prize–winning economist John Hicks said, "The best of all monopoly profits is a quiet life." Once the iron ore industry became competitive, life wasn't so quiet for Minnesota's miners anymore. ■

Production Functions

A firm's task is to turn capital and labor inputs into outputs. A production function is a mathematical relationship that describes how much output can be made from different combinations of inputs.

As noted above, we simplify things in our model of production so that we can shrink the many outputs made and inputs used by real-world firms into something that we can get a better handle on. Namely, our firm makes one product as its output and uses two inputs, capital and labor, to do so. Capital includes the equipment and structures that firms use—an enormous range of inputs, from the machinery on assembly lines, to office buildings, to the iPhone that the CEO uses to keep abreast of what's happening at the firm while she's on the road. Labor includes the human inputs a firm uses, ranging from miners to computer programmers to summer interns and executive vice presidents. The production function summarizes how a firm transforms these capital and labor inputs into output. A production function is a formula that describes output (which we label Q for quantity) as a function of our two inputs, capital (K) and labor (L):

$$Q = f(K,L)$$

In this production function, f is a mathematical function that describes how capital and labor are combined to produce the output. Production functions can take a form such as $Q = 10K + 5L$ in which the inputs are separate, or $Q = K^{0.5}L^{0.5}$ in which the inputs are multiplied together. They can also take many other forms depending on the technology a firm uses to produce its output. The type of production function in which capital and labor are each raised to a power and then multiplied together (as in $Q = K^{0.5}L^{0.5}$ above) is known as a *Cobb–Douglas* production function. It is named after mathematician and economist Charles Cobb and economist (and later, U.S. Senator) Paul Douglas. The Cobb–Douglas production function is one of the most common types of production functions used by economists.

6.2 Production in the Short Run

We start by analyzing production in the short run because it is the simplest case. In our earlier discussion of the assumptions of this model, we defined the "short run" as the period during which a firm cannot change the amount of capital. While the capital stock is fixed, the firm can choose how much labor to hire to minimize its cost of making the output quantity. Table 6.1 shows some values of labor inputs and output quantities from a short-run production function. Here, we use the Cobb-Douglas production function of our earlier example and fix capital $(\overline{K})$ at four units, so the numbers in Table 6.1 correspond to the production function $Q = f(\overline{K}, L) = \overline{K}^{0.5}L^{0.5} = 4^{0.5}L^{0.5} = 2L^{0.5}$.

Figure 6.1 plots the short-run production function from Table 6.1. The plot contains the numbers in Table 6.1, but also shows output levels for all amounts of labor between 0 and 5 hours per week, as well as amounts of labor greater than 5 hours per week.

Even though capital is fixed, when the firm increases its labor inputs, its output rises. This reflects Assumption 6 above: More inputs mean more output. Notice, however, that the *rate* at which output increases slows as the firm hires more and more labor. This phenomenon of additional units of labor yielding less and less additional output reflects Assumption 7: The production function exhibits diminishing marginal returns to inputs. To see why there are diminishing marginal returns, we need to understand just what happens when one input increases while the other input remains fixed. This is what is meant by an input's *marginal product*.

Marginal Product

marginal product
The additional output that a firm can produce by using an additional unit of an input (holding use of the other input constant).

The incremental output that a firm can produce by using an additional unit of an input (holding use of the other input constant) is called the **marginal product.** In the short run, the marginal product that is most relevant is the marginal product of labor because we are assuming that capital is fixed. The marginal product of labor (MP_L) is the *change* in quantity (ΔQ) resulting from a one-unit *change* in labor inputs (ΔL):

$$MP_L = \Delta Q / \Delta L$$

The marginal product of labor for our short-run production function $Q = 4^{0.5}L^{0.5}$ is shown in the fourth column of Table 6.1. If a firm with this production function (in

Table 6.1   An Example of a Short-Run Production Function

Capital, K	Labor, L	Output, Q	Marginal Product of Labor, $MP_L = \frac{\Delta Q}{\Delta L}$	Average Product of Labor, $AP_L = \frac{Q}{L}$
4	0	0.00	—	—
4	1	2.00	2.00	2.00
4	2	2.83	0.83	1.42
4	3	3.46	0.63	1.15
4	4	4.00	0.54	1.00
4	5	4.47	0.47	0.89

which capital is fixed at four units) uses zero units of labor, it produces zero units of output. (Perhaps the firm can't make any output without anyone to run the machines.) If it hires one unit of labor to combine with the four units of capital, it can produce two units of output. Therefore, the marginal product of that first unit of labor is 2.00. With two units of labor (and the same four units of capital), the firm can produce 2.83 units of output, making the marginal product of the second unit of labor the change in output or $2.83 - 2.00 = 0.83$. With three units of labor, output rises by 0.63 to 3.46, so the marginal product of labor is 0.63, and so on.

This **diminishing marginal product** of labor—the reduction in the extra output obtained from adding more and more labor—is embodied in our Assumption 7 and is a common feature of production functions. This is why the production function curve in Figure 6.1 flattens at higher quantities of labor. A diminishing marginal product makes intuitive sense, too. If there is a fixed amount of capital, then every time you add a worker, each worker has less capital to use. If a coffee shop has one espresso machine and one worker, she has a machine at her disposal during her entire shift. If the coffee shop hires a second worker to work the same hours as the first, the two workers must share the machine. Because of this sharing, it's unlikely that the second worker will add as much production as the first worker. With three workers per shift and still only one machine, the situation gets worse. Adding a fourth worker will allow the firm to produce a tiny bit more output, but certainly, this fourth worker's marginal product will be smaller than that of the first (or, for that matter, the second and third) worker. The coffee shop's solution to this problem is to buy more espresso machines—that is, add more capital. We've assumed it can't do so in the short run, but it could (and would) do so in the long run. We look at what happens when the firm can change its capital level later in this chapter.

Keep in mind, however, that diminishing marginal returns do not have to occur all the time; they just need to occur eventually. A production function could have increasing marginal returns at low levels of labor before running into the problem of diminishing marginal product.

A Graphical Analysis of Marginal Product   We can plot the marginal product on a graph of the production function. Recall that the marginal product is the change in output quantity that comes from adding one additional unit of input: $MP_L = \Delta Q/\Delta L$. $\Delta Q/\Delta L$ is the slope of the short-run production function in Figure 6.1. Thus, the marginal product of labor at any given level of labor input is the slope of the production

diminishing marginal product
A feature of the production function; as a firm hires additional units of a given input, the marginal product of that input falls.

Figure 6.1   A Short-Run Production Function

This figure graphs the firm's continuous short-run production function using the values from Table 6.1. The production function's positive slope means that an increase in labor increases output. As the firm hires more labor, however, output increases at a decreasing rate and the slope flattens.

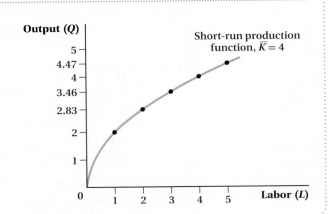

Figure 6.2   **Deriving the Marginal Product of Labor**

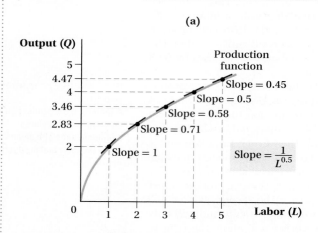

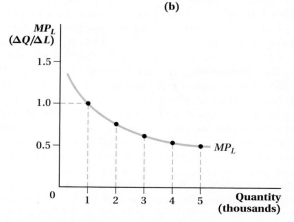

(a) The marginal product of labor is the slope of the production function. As the quantity of labor increases, the marginal product decreases, from $MP_L = 1$ when $L = 1$ to $MP_L = 0.45$ when $L = 5$ and the slope flattens.

(b) Using the production function in panel a, we can derive the marginal product of labor curve. The downward slope of the curve shows the diminishing marginal returns to labor.

function at that point. Panel a of Figure 6.2 shows how the MP_L can be derived from our production function. At $L = 1$, the slope of the production function (i.e., the slope of the line tangent to the production function at $L = 1$) is relatively steep. Adding additional labor at this point will increase output by a substantial amount. At $L = 4$, the slope is considerably flatter, and adding additional labor will boost output by a smaller increment than when $L = 1$. The marginal product of labor falls between $L = 1$ and $L = 4$, as we saw in Table 6.1. Panel b of Figure 6.2 shows the corresponding marginal-product-of-labor curve. Because this production function exhibits diminishing marginal returns at all levels of labor, the marginal product curve is downward-sloping.

A Mathematical Representation of Marginal Product   To find MP_L, we need to calculate the additional output obtained by adding an incremental unit of labor, holding capital constant. So let's compute the firm's increase in output when it uses $L + \Delta L$ units of labor instead of L units (holding capital constant). ΔL is the incremental unit of labor. Mathematically, MP_L is

$$MP_L = \frac{\Delta Q}{\Delta L} = \frac{f(\overline{K}, L + \Delta L) - f(\overline{K}, L)}{\Delta L}$$

Applying this to our short-run production function ($\overline{K}^{0.5} L^{0.5} = 4^{0.5} L^{0.5} = 2L^{0.5}$) gives

$$Q = f(\overline{K}, L)$$

$$MP_L = \frac{2(L + \Delta L)^{0.5} - 2L^{0.5}}{\Delta L}$$

The end-of-chapter appendix explores the Cobb-Douglas production function using calculus.

To consider what happens as we let ΔL get really tiny involves some calculus. If you don't know calculus, however, here is the marginal product formula for our Cobb–Douglas production function: $MP_L = \frac{1}{L^{0.5}}$. The MP_L values calculated using this formula are shown in Figure 6.2. (These values are slightly different from those in Table 6.1 because while the table sets $\Delta L = 1$, the formula allows the incremental unit to be much smaller. The economic idea behind both calculations is the same, however.)

Average Product

It's important to see that the *marginal* product is not the same as the *average* product. **Average product** is calculated by dividing the total quantity of output by the number of units of input used to produce that quantity. The average product of labor (AP_L), for example, is the quantity produced Q divided by the amount of labor L used to produce it:

average product
The quantity of output produced per unit of input.

$$AP_L = Q/L$$

The average product of labor for our short-run production function is shown in the last column of Table 6.1. Notice that the average product of labor falls as labor inputs increase.

6.1 figure it out

The short-run production function for a firm that produces pizzas is $Q = f(\overline{K}, L) = 15\overline{K}^{0.25}L^{0.75}$, where Q is the number of pizzas produced per hour, $\overline{K}$ is the number of ovens (which is fixed at 3 in the short run), and L is the number of workers employed.

a. Write an equation for the short-run production function for the firm showing output as a function of labor.

b. Calculate the total output produced per hour for $L = 0$, 1, 2, 3, 4, and 5.

c. Calculate the MP_L for $L = 1$ to $L = 5$. Is MP_L diminishing?

d. Calculate the AP_L for $L = 1$ to $L = 5$.

Solution:

a. To write the production function for the short run, we plug $\overline{K} = 3$ into the production function to create an equation that shows output as a function of labor:

$$Q = f(\overline{K}, L) = 15\overline{K}^{0.25}L^{0.75}$$
$$= 15(3^{0.25})L^{0.75} = 15(1.316)L^{0.75} = 19.74L^{0.75}$$

b. To calculate total output, we plug in the different values of L and solve for Q:

$L = 0$	$Q = 19.74(0)^{0.75} = 19.74(0) = 0$
$L = 1$	$Q = 19.74(1)^{0.75} = 19.74(1) = 19.74$
$L = 2$	$Q = 19.74(2)^{0.75} = 19.74(1.682) = 33.20$
$L = 3$	$Q = 19.74(3)^{0.75} = 19.74(2.280) = 45.01$
$L = 4$	$Q = 19.74(4)^{0.75} = 19.74(2.828) = 55.82$
$L = 5$	$Q = 19.74(5)^{0.75} = 19.74(3.344) = 66.01$

c. The marginal product of labor is the additional output generated by an additional unit of labor, holding capital constant. We can use our answer from (b) to calculate the marginal product of labor for each worker:

$L = 1$	$MP_L = 19.74 - 0 = 19.74$
$L = 2$	$MP_L = 33.20 - 19.74 = 13.46$
$L = 3$	$MP_L = 45.01 - 33.20 = 11.81$
$L = 4$	$MP_L = 55.82 - 45.01 = 10.81$
$L = 5$	$MP_L = 66.01 - 55.82 = 10.19$

Note that, because MP_L falls as L rises, there is a diminishing marginal product of labor. This implies that output rises at a decreasing rate when labor is added to the fixed level of capital.

d. The average product of labor is calculated by dividing total output (Q) by the quantity of labor input (L):

$L = 1$	$AP_L = 19.74/1 = 19.74$
$L = 2$	$AP_L = 33.20/2 = 16.60$
$L = 3$	$AP_L = 45.01/3 = 15.00$
$L = 4$	$AP_L = 55.82/4 = 13.96$
$L = 5$	$AP_L = 66.01/5 = 13.20$

This decline occurs because the marginal product of labor is less than the average product at each level of labor in the table, so each unit of labor added on the margin brings down labor's average product. The easiest way to see this is to consider your grades in a course. Suppose that your mid-semester average in a course is 80%. Now, you take an exam and score a 90%. Your average will rise because the score on the last exam taken (the *marginal* exam) is greater than your current average. On the other hand, if your next exam score is only 65%, your course average will fall, because the marginal score is lower than the average score.

 application

How Short Is the Short Run?

What sort of time period should we have in mind when thinking about the short-run production function? That is, how long do firms actually need to adjust their capital inputs? How long are they stuck with the capital they currently have? The answer depends on the firm and the industry. It depends on the specifics of the firm's costs of adjusting capital, which in turn are determined by the particular types of capital the firm uses, how large a change in capital inputs the firm wants to make, and the opportunity cost of management's time, among other factors.

Economists Russell Cooper and John Haltiwanger studied the capital adjustment/investment practices of thousands of U.S. manufacturing plants between 1972 and 1988. They found that about 1 of every 10 plants did not change its capital level at all over the course of a year.[5]

Cooper and Haltiwanger also found that when a plant did adjust its capital level, it usually made big changes. Naturally, plants with a larger gap between their actual and ideal capital levels made larger adjustments. (Cooper and Haltiwanger used economic theory to estimate what each factory's ideal capital level should be, based on the demand for the factory's product and on the factory's costs.) And once a big change was made, that plant was less likely to make another big change the next year. This pattern of investment "bursts" implies that once a factory changes its amount of capital, it tends to make the necessary adjustments all at once, rather than stringing out a large change over several years.

So, for Cooper and Haltiwanger's plants at least, the short run seems to range from a few months for factories that have a big desired change in capital to well over a year for those with only small desired changes. ∎

6.3 Production in the Long Run

In the long run, firms can change not only their labor inputs but also their capital. This difference gives them two important benefits. First, in the long run, a firm might be able to lessen the sting of diminishing marginal product. As we saw above, when capital is fixed, diminishing marginal product limits a firm's ability to produce additional output by using more and more labor. If additional capital can make each unit of labor more productive, then a firm could expand its output more by increasing capital and labor inputs *jointly*.

Think back to our example of the coffee shop. If the shop adds a second worker per shift when there is only one espresso machine, the firm will not gain much additional output because of the diminishing marginal product of labor. Hiring still another worker per shift will barely budge output at all. But if the firm bought another machine for each additional worker, output could increase with little drop in productivity. In this way, using more capital and labor at the same time allows the firm to avoid (at least in part) the effects of diminishing marginal products.

[5] Russell W. Cooper and John C. Haltiwanger, "On the Nature of Capital Adjustment Costs," *Review of Economic Studies* 73, no. 3 (2006): 611–633.

The second benefit of being able to adjust capital in the long run is that producers often have some ability to substitute capital for labor or vice versa. Firms can be more flexible in their production methods and in the ways they respond to changes in the relative prices of capital and labor. For example, as airline ticket agents became relatively more expensive and technological progress made automated check-in less so, airlines shifted much of their check-in operations from being labor-intensive (checking in with an agent at the counter) to being capital-intensive (checking in at an automated kiosk or even at home online).

The Long-Run Production Function

In a long-run production function, all inputs can be adjusted. The long-run production is the production function we first introduced in Section 6.2: $Q = f(K,L)$, but rather than having a fixed level of $\overline{K}$ and choosing L (as we did for the short run), now the firm can choose the levels of both inputs.

We can also illustrate the long-run production function in a table. Table 6.2 shows the relationship between output and inputs for our example production function $Q = K^{0.5}L^{0.5}$. The columns correspond to different amounts of labor. The rows denote different amounts of capital. The number in each cell is the quantity of output generated by the corresponding combination of inputs.

In the fourth row of the table, where the firm has four units of capital, the values exactly match the short-run production function values from Table 6.1. Table 6.2 adds to Table 6.1 other possible output quantities the firm could achieve once it can change its level of capital. One way to think about the long-run production function is as a combination of all the firm's possible short-run production functions, where each possible short-run function has a different fixed level of capital. Notice that for any given level of capital—that is, for any particular short-run production function—labor has a diminishing marginal product. For example, when capital is fixed at five units, the marginal product of labor of the first worker is 2.24, the MP_L of the second worker is 0.92 (= 3.16 − 2.24), the MP_L for the third worker is 0.71 (= 3.87 − 3.16), and so on.

Table 6.2 | **An Example of a Long-Run Production Function**

		Units of Labor, L				
		1	**2**	**3**	**4**	**5**
Units of Capital, K	**1**	1.00	1.41	1.73	2.00	2.24
	2	1.41	2.00	2.45	2.83	3.16
	3	1.73	2.45	3.00	3.46	3.87
	4	2.00	2.83	3.46	4.00	4.47
	5	2.24	3.16	3.87	4.47	5.00

6.4 The Firm's Cost-Minimization Problem

At the start of the chapter, we outlined a number of assumptions about a firm's production behavior. The third assumption is that the firm's goal is to minimize the cost of producing whatever quantity it chooses to make. (How a firm determines that quantity is the subject of Chapters 8–11.) The challenge of producing a specific amount of a particular good as inexpensively as possible is the firm's **cost-minimization** problem.

The firm's production decision is another *constrained optimization* problem. Remember from our discussion in Chapter 4 that these types of problems are ones in which an economic actor tries to optimize something while facing a constraint on her choices. Here, the firm's problem is a constrained *minimization* problem. The firm wants to minimize the total costs of its production. However, it must hold to a constraint in doing so: it must produce a particular quantity of output. That is, it can't minimize its costs just by refusing to produce as much as it would like (or refuse to produce anything, for that matter). In this section, we look at how a firm uses two concepts, isoquants (which tell the firm

cost minimization
A firm's goal of producing a specific quantity of output at minimum cost.

the quantity constraint it faces) and isocost lines (which tell the firm the various costs at which the firm can produce its quantity) to solve its constrained minimization problem.

Isoquants

When learning about the consumer's utility function in Chapter 4, we looked at three variables: the quantities of the two goods consumed and the consumer's utility. Each indifference curve showed all the combinations of the two goods consumed that allowed the consumer to achieve a particular utility level.

We can do the same thing with the firm's production function. We can plot as one curve all the possible combinations of capital and labor that can produce a given amount of output. Figure 6.3 does just that for the production function we have been using throughout the chapter; it displays the combinations of inputs that are necessary to produce one, two, and four units of output. These curves are known as **isoquants.** The word "isoquant" is derived from the Greek prefix *iso-*, which means "the same," and *quant*, which is a shortened version of the word "quantity."

Just as with indifference curves, isoquants further from the origin correspond to higher output levels (because more capital and labor lead to higher output), isoquants cannot cross (because if they did, the same quantities of inputs would yield two different quantities of output), and isoquants are convex to the origin (because using a mix of inputs generally lets a firm produce a greater quantity than it could by using an extreme amount of one input and a tiny amount of the other).

isoquant
A curve representing all the combinations of inputs that allow a firm to make a particular quantity of output.

The Marginal Rate of Technical Substitution   The slope of the isoquant plays a key role in the analysis of production decisions because it captures the tradeoff in the productive abilities of capital and labor. Look at the isoquant in Figure 6.4. At point A, the isoquant is steeply sloped, meaning that the firm can reduce the amount of capital it uses by a lot while increasing labor only a small amount, and still maintain the same level of output. In contrast, at point B, if the firm wants to reduce capital just a bit, it will have to increase labor a lot to keep output at the same level. Isoquants' curvature and convexity to the origin reflect the fact that the capital–labor tradeoff varies as the mix of the inputs changes.

marginal rate of technical substitution ($MRTS_{XY}$)
The rate at which the firm can trade input X for input Y, holding output constant.

The negative of the slope of the isoquant is called the **marginal rate of technical substitution** of one input (on the x-axis) for another (on the y-axis), or $\boldsymbol{MRTS_{XY}}$. It is the quantity change in input X necessary to keep output constant if the quantity of input Y changes. For the most part in this chapter, we will be interested in the $MRTS$ of labor for capital or $MRTS_{LK}$, which is the amount of labor needed to hold output constant if the quantity of capital used by the firm changes.

Figure 6.3   Isoquants

Each isoquant shows the possible combinations of labor (L) and capital (K) that produce the output (Q) levels 1, 2, and 4 units.

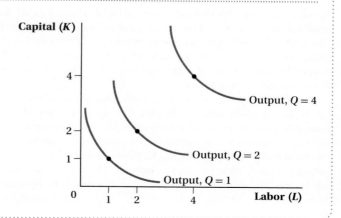

Figure 6.4 : **The Marginal Rate of Technical Substitution**

The negative slope of the isoquant is the marginal rate of technical substitution of labor L for capital K. At point A, the marginal product of labor is high relative to the marginal product of capital, and a relatively small decrease in labor would require a large quantity of capital to hold output constant. At point B, the marginal product of labor is low relative to the marginal product of capital, and a relatively small decrease in capital would require a large quantity of labor to hold output constant.

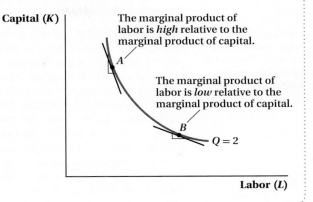

If we imagine moving just a little bit down and to the right along an isoquant, the change in output equals the marginal product of labor times the change in the units of labor due to the move, plus the marginal product of capital times the change in the amount of capital. (This change in capital is negative because we're taking away capital when we move down along the isoquant.) Because we're moving along an isoquant (for which output is held constant), though, this total change in output is zero. So we can write the total change as

$$\Delta Q = MP_L \times \Delta L + MP_K \times \Delta K = 0$$

If we rearrange this to find the slope of the isoquant, $\Delta K/\Delta L$, we have

$$MP_K \times \Delta K = -MP_L \times \Delta L$$

$$MP_K \times \frac{\Delta K}{\Delta L} = -MP_L$$

$$\frac{\Delta K}{\Delta L} = -\frac{MP_L}{MP_K}$$

$$MRTS_{LK} = -\frac{\Delta K}{\Delta L} = \frac{MP_L}{MP_K}$$

∂ The end-of-chapter appendix derives the relationship between the marginal rate of technical substitution and marginal products.

Therefore, the $MRTS_{LK}$ at any point on an isoquant tells you the relative marginal products of capital and labor at that point.

The concepts underlying the marginal rate of technical substitution are essentially identical to those of the marginal rate of substitution (MRS) for consumers, which we learned about in Chapter 4. The two are so closely tied together, in fact, that the names are essentially the same—the word "technical" is tacked on to distinguish the producer case. Both the $MRTS$ and MRS are about marginal tradeoffs. The MRS is about a consumer's willingness to trade one good for another while still obtaining the same utility level. The $MRTS$ is about a firm's ability to trade one input for another while still producing the same quantity of output. The shape of the curves in both cases tells you about the rate at which one good/input can be substituted for the other.

The nature of the marginal tradeoffs embodied in the MRS and $MRTS$ implies similar things about the shape of the curves from which they are derived. On the consumer side, indifference curves are convex to the origin because the MRS varies with the amount of each good the consumer is consuming. On the production side, isoquants are convex to the origin because the $MRTS$ varies with the amount of each input the firm uses to produce output. When the firm uses a lot of capital and just a little labor (point A in Figure 6.4), it can replace a lot of capital with a little more labor and still produce the same quantity of output. At this point, labor has a high marginal product relative to capital, and the firm's isoquant is steep. At point B, the firm uses a lot of labor and only a little capital, so capital has a relatively high marginal product and $MRTS_{LK}$ is small. A smaller $MRTS_{LK}$ means a flatter isoquant at that input mix.

Substitutability   How curved an isoquant is shows how easily firms can substitute one input for another in production. For isoquants that are almost straight, as in panel a of Figure 6.5, a firm can replace a unit of one input (capital, e.g.) with a particular amount of the second input (labor) without changing its output level, regardless of whether it is already using a lot or a little of capital. Stated in terms of the marginal rate of technical substitution, $MRTS_{LK}$ doesn't change much as the firm moves along the isoquant. In this case, the two inputs are close substitutes in the firm's production function, and the relative usefulness of either input for production won't vary much with how much of each input the firm is using.

Highly curved isoquants, such as those shown in panel b of Figure 6.5, mean that the $MRTS_{LK}$ changes a lot along the isoquant. In this case, the two inputs are poor substitutes. The relative usefulness of substituting one input for another in production depends a great deal on the amount of the input the firm is already using.

Perfect Substitutes and Perfect Complements in Production   In Chapter 4, we discussed the extreme cases of perfect substitutes and perfect complements in consumption. For perfect substitutes, indifference curves are straight lines; for perfect complements, the curves are "L"-shaped right angles. The same holds for inputs: It is possible for them to be perfect substitutes or perfect complements in production. Isoquants for these two cases are shown in Figure 6.6.

If inputs are perfect substitutes as in panel a, the $MRTS$ doesn't change at all with the amounts of the inputs used, and the isoquants are perfectly straight lines. This characteristic means the firm can freely substitute between inputs without suffering diminishing marginal returns. An example of a production function where labor and capital are perfect substitutes is $Q = f(K, L) = 10K + 5L$; two units of labor can always be substituted for one unit of capital without changing output, no matter how many units of either input the firm is already using. In this case, imagine that capital took

The online appendix explores the relationship between the production function and the shape of isoquants. (http://glsmicro.com/appendices)

Figure 6.5   The Shape of Isoquants Indicates the Substitutability of Inputs

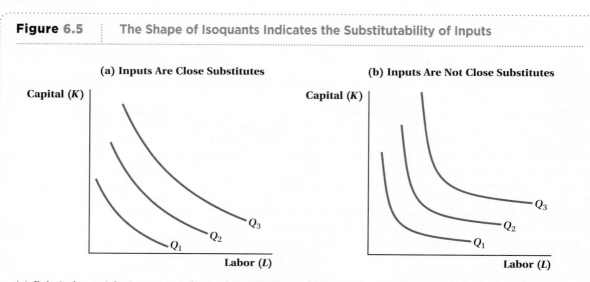

(a) Relatively straight isoquants indicate that $MRTS_{LK}$ does not vary much along the curve. Therefore, labor and capital are close substitutes for each other.

(b) Relatively curved isoquants indicate that $MRTS_{LK}$ varies greatly along the curve. Therefore, labor and capital are not close substitutes for each other.

Figure 6.6   **Perfect Substitutes and Perfect Complements in Production**

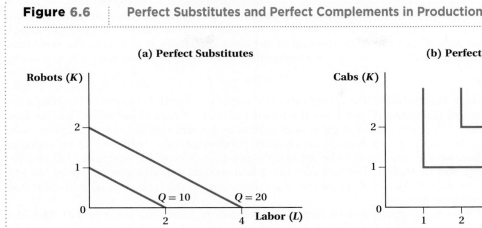

(a) Perfect Substitutes

Robots (*K*)

(b) Perfect Complements

Cabs (*K*)

(a) Robots *K* and labor *L* are perfect substitutes. The isoquants are straight lines, and the $MRTS_{LK}$ does not change along the isoquant. In this case, two humans can substitute for one robot.

(b) Cabs *K* and drivers *L* are perfect complements. The isoquants are L-shaped, and the optimal quantity (K, L) for each output *Q* is the corner of the isoquant. In this case, 1 cab with 1 driver produces $Q = 1$, while 2 cabs with 2 drivers produce $Q = 2$.

the form of a robot that behaved exactly like a human when doing a task, but did the work twice as quickly as a human. Here, the firm can always substitute one robot for two workers or vice versa, regardless of its current number of robots or workers. This is true because the marginal product of labor is 5 (holding *K* constant, a one-unit increase in *L* causes output to grow by 5). At the same time, holding *L* constant, a one-unit rise in *K* will increase output by 10 units, making the MP_K equal to 10. No matter what levels of *L* and *K* the firm chooses, $MRTS_{LK} = MP_L/MP_K = \frac{5}{10} = \frac{1}{2}$.

If inputs are perfect complements, isoquants have an "L" shape. This implies that using inputs in any ratio outside of a particular fixed proportion—that at the isoquants' corners—yields no additional output. Cabs and drivers on a given shift are fairly close to perfect complements in the production of cab rides. Anything other than a 1 to 1 ratio of cabs to drivers is unlikely to produce any additional cab rides. If a cab company has, say, 30 drivers and 1 cab, it will not be able to offer any more rides than if it had 1 driver and 1 cab. Nor could it offer more rides if it had 1 driver and 30 cabs. Therefore, the production function would be $Q = \min(L, K)$, where "min" indicates that output (Q) is determined by the minimum level of either labor (L) or capital (K). Of course, the cab company could offer more rides if it had 30 drivers *and* 30 cabs, because this would preserve the 1 to 1 driver-to-cab ratio.[6]

Isocost Lines

Up until this point in the chapter, we have focused on various aspects of the production function and how quantities of inputs are related to the quantity of output. These aspects play a crucial part in determining a firm's optimal production behavior, but the production function is only half of the story. As we discussed earlier, the firm's objective is to minimize its costs of producing a given quantity of output. While we've said a lot about how the firm's choices of inputs affect its output, we haven't talked about the costs of those choices. That's what we do in this section.

---

[6] There is nothing special about a 1 to 1 ratio. Inputs can be perfect complements at other ratios as well.

isocost line
A curve that shows all of the input combinations that yield the same cost.

The key concept that brings costs into the firm's decision is the **isocost line**. An isocost line connects all the combinations of capital and labor that the firm can purchase for a given total expenditure on inputs. As we saw earlier, *iso-* is a prefix meaning "the same," so "isocost" is a line that shows all of the input combinations that yield the same cost. Mathematically, the isocost line corresponding to a total expenditure level of C is given by

$$C = RK + WL,$$

where R is the price (the *rental rate*) per unit of capital, W is the price (the Wage) per unit of labor, and K and L are the number of units of capital and labor that the firm hires. It's best to think of the cost of capital as a rental rate in the same type of units as the wage (e.g., per hour, week, or year). Because capital is used over a long period of time, we can consider R to be not just the purchase price of the equipment but also the user cost of capital. The user cost takes into account capital's purchase price, as well as its rate of depreciation and the opportunity cost of the funds tied up in its purchase (foregone interest).

Figure 6.7 shows isocost lines corresponding to total cost levels of $50, $80, and $100, when the price of capital is $20 per unit and labor's price is $10 per unit. There are a few things to notice about the figure. First, isocost lines for higher total expenditure levels are further from the origin. This reflects the fact that, as a firm uses more inputs, its total expenditure on those inputs increases. Second, the isocost lines are parallel. They all have the same slope, regardless of what total cost level they represent. To see why they all have the same slope, let's first see what that slope represents.

We can rewrite the equation for the isocost line in slope-intercept form, so that the value on the vertical axis (capital) is expressed as a function of the value on the horizontal axis (labor):

$$C = RK + WL$$
$$RK = C - WL$$
$$K = \frac{C}{R} - \frac{W}{R}L$$

This means that the y-intercept of the isocost line is C/R, while the slope is the (negative of the) inputs' price ratio, $-W/R$.

Figure 6.7 : Isocost Lines

Each isocost line shows all bundles of inputs that have the same cost to the firm. As you move farther from the origin, the isocost lines represent higher total expenditures, from cost $C = \$50$ to $C = \$80$ to $C = \$100$. For wage $W = \$10$ and rental $R = \$20$, the slope of the isocost lines is $-W/R$, or $-\frac{1}{2}$. Therefore, for every one-unit increase in K, the firm has to give up two units of L, in order to keep cost constant.

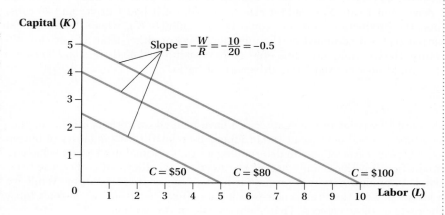

As is so often the case in economics, the slope tells us about tradeoffs at the margin. Here, the slope reflects the cost consequences of trading off or substituting one input for another. It indicates how much more of one input a firm could hire, without increasing overall expenditure on inputs, if it used less of the other input. If the isocost line's slope is steep, labor is relatively expensive compared to capital. If the firm wants to hire more labor without increasing its overall expenditure on inputs, it is going to have to use a lot less capital. (Or if you'd rather, if it chose to use less labor, it could hire a lot more capital without spending more on inputs overall.) If the price of labor is relatively cheap compared to capital, the isocost line will be relatively flat. This means the firm could hire a lot more labor and not have to give up much capital to do so without changing expenditures.

Because of our assumption (Assumption 8) that the firm can buy as much capital or labor as it wants at a fixed price per unit, the slopes of isocost lines are constant. That's why they are straight, parallel lines: Regardless of the overall cost level or the amount of each input the firm chooses, the relative tradeoff between the inputs in terms of total costs is always the same.

If these ideas seem familiar to you, it's because the isocost line is yet another concept that has an analogy in the consumer behavior that we studied in Chapter 4. There, we saw that a consumer's budget line expressed the relationship between the quantities of each good consumed and the consumer's total expenditure on those goods. Isocost lines capture the same idea, except with regard to firms and their input purchases. We saw that the negative of the slope of the consumer's budget constraint was equal to the price ratio of the two goods, just as the negative of the slope of the isocost line equals the price ratio of the firm's two inputs.

Isocost Lines and Input Price Changes   Just like budget lines for consumers, when relative prices change, the isocost line rotates. In our example, say labor's price (W) rose from $10 to $20. Now if the firm only hired labor, it would only be able to hire half as much. The line becomes steeper as in Figure 6.8. The isocost line rotates because its slope is $-W/R$. When W increases from $10 to $20, the slope changes from $-\frac{1}{2}$ to -1, and the isocost line rotates clockwise and becomes steeper.

Changes in the price of capital also rotate the isocost line. Figure 6.9 shows what happens to the $100 isocost line when the price of capital increases from $20 to $40 per unit, and the wage stays at $10 per unit of labor. If the firm hired only capital, it could afford half as much, so the slope flattens. A drop in the capital price would rotate the isocosts the other way.

Figure 6.8   When Labor Becomes More Expensive, the Isocost Line Becomes Steeper

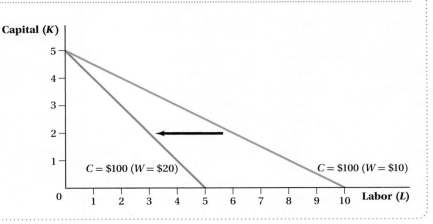

When the price of labor increases from $W = $10 to $W = $20 and the price of capital stays constant at $R = $20, the slope of the isocost changes from $-\frac{1}{2}$ to $-\frac{2}{2}$, or -1. The isocost line, therefore, becomes steeper, and the quantity of inputs the firm can buy for $100 decreases.

Figure 6.9 : When Capital Becomes More Expensive, the Isocost Line Becomes Flatter

When the price of capital increases from $R = \$20$ to $R = \$40$ and the price of labor stays constant at $W = \$10$, the slope of the isocost changes from $-\frac{1}{2}$ to $-\frac{1}{4}$. The quantity of inputs the firm can buy for $100 decreases and the isocost line becomes flatter.

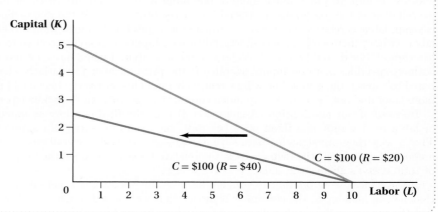

6.2 figure it out

Suppose that the wage rate is $10 per hour and the rental rate of capital is $25 per hour.

a. Write an equation for the isocost line for a firm.

b. Draw a graph (with labor on the horizontal axis and capital on the vertical axis) showing the isocost line for $C = \$800$. Indicate the horizontal and vertical intercepts along with the slope.

c. Suppose the price of capital falls to $20 per hour. Show what happens to the $C = \$800$ isocost line including any changes in intercepts and the slope.

Solution:

a. An isocost line always shows the total costs for the firm's two inputs in the form of $C = RK + WL$. Here, the wage rate (W) is $10 and the rental rate of capital (R) is $25, so the isocost line is $C = 10L + 25K$.

b. We can plot the isocost line for $C = \$800 = 10L + 25K$. One easy way to do this is to compute the horizontal and vertical intercepts. The horizontal intercept tells us the amount of labor the firm could hire for $800 if it only hired labor. Therefore, the horizontal intercept is $\$800/W = \$800/\$10 = 80$. The vertical intercept tells us how much capital the firm could hire for $800 if it were to use only capital. Thus, it is $\$800/R = \$800/\$25 = 32$. We can plot these points on the following graph and then draw a line connecting them. This is the $C = \$800$ isocost line labeled C_1.

We can calculate slope in several different ways. First, we can simply calculate the slope of the isocost line as drawn. Remember that the slope of a line is $\Delta Y/\Delta X$ (i.e., rise over run). Therefore, the slope is $\Delta Y/\Delta X = -\frac{32}{80} = -0.4$. We can also re-arrange our isocost line into slope-intercept form by isolating K:

$$800 = 10L + 25K$$
$$25K = 800 - 10L$$
$$K = (800/25) - (10/25)L = 32 - 0.4L$$

This equation tells us that the vertical intercept is 32 (which we calculated earlier) and -0.4 is the slope.

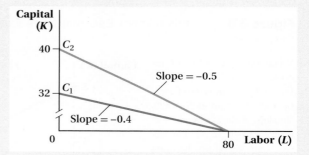

c. If R falls to $20, the horizontal intercept is unaffected. If the firm is only using labor, a change in the price of capital will have no impact. However, the vertical intercept rises to $\$800/R = \$800/\$20 = 40$ and the isocost line becomes steeper (C_2). The new slope is $-W/R = -\$10/\$20 = -0.5$.

Identifying Minimum Cost: Combining Isoquants and Isocost Lines

As we have discussed, a firm's goal is to produce its desired quantity of output at the minimum possible cost. In deciding how to achieve this goal, a firm must solve a cost-minimization problem: It must achieve an objective given a constraint. The objective is the firm's total cost of inputs, $RK + WL$. The firm chooses capital and labor inputs K and L to minimize these expenditures. What constrains the firm's cost-minimizing decision? The quantity of output the firm has chosen to produce. The firm must hire enough capital and labor inputs to produce a certain level of output. The production function relates input choices to the quantity of output, so we can sum up a firm's cost-minimization problem as follows: Choose K and L to minimize total costs, subject to the constraint that enough K and L must be chosen to produce a given quantity of output. (Remember that at this point in our analysis quantity has already been chosen. Now it's the firm's task to figure out how to optimally produce that quantity.)

Cost Minimization—A Graphical Approach

A graphical solution boils down to determining the right way to combine information about the firm's costs and the firm's production function. We have represented a firm's costs graphically using isocost lines. Isocost lines, however, don't convey any information about how much the firm can produce with a set of inputs. They only indicate how much each set of inputs costs. To represent the production function, we use isoquants. These tell us, for a given production function, how much capital and labor it takes to produce a fixed amount of output.

Before we work through a specific example, let's think about the logic of the firm's cost-minimization problem. The firm's objective is to minimize costs subject to the constraint that it has to produce a particular quantity of output, $\overline{Q}$. The cost-minimization part means the firm wants to be on an isocost line that is as close to the origin as possible, because isocost lines closer to the origin correspond to lower levels of expenditure. The output constraint means that the firm has to somehow end up on the isoquant that corresponds to $\overline{Q}$. Therefore, the firm's best choice is to be on the isocost line that is as close to the origin as possible but still provides enough capital and labor to allow the firm to produce $\overline{Q}$.

Figure 6.10 shows the isoquant for the firm's desired output quantity $\overline{Q}$. The firm wants to produce this quantity at minimum cost. How much capital and labor should it hire to do so? Suppose the firm is considering the level inputs shown at point A, which

---

Figure 6.10   Cost Minimization

The firm wants to minimize the cost to produce the quantity $Q = \overline{Q}$. Because A is on the isoquant, the firm can choose to use input combination A to produce $\overline{Q}$. However, A is not cost-minimizing because the firm can produce $\overline{Q}$ at a lower cost at any point below and to the left of the isocost C_A. Point B, located at the tangency between isocost C_B and the isoquant, is the firm's cost-minimizing capital and labor combination. Input combinations on C_C cost less than those on C_B but are too small to allow the firm to produce $\overline{Q}$.

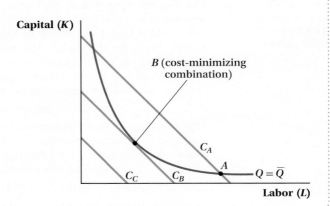

is on isocost line C_A. That point is on the $Q = \overline{Q}$ isoquant, so the firm will produce the desired level of output. However, there are many other input combinations on the $\overline{Q}$ isoquant that are below and to the left of C_A. These all would allow the firm to produce $\overline{Q}$ but at lower cost than input mix A. Only one input combination exists that is on the $\overline{Q}$ isoquant but for which there are no other input combinations that would allow the firm to produce the same quantity at lower cost. That combination is at point B, on isocost C_B. There are input combinations that involve lower costs than B—for example, any combination on isocost line C_C—but these input levels are all too small to allow the firm to produce $\overline{Q}$.

Point B has a special property. It is the point of tangency of the isocost line C_B to the $\overline{Q}$ isoquant. In other words, when the total costs of producing a given quantity are minimized, the isocost line is tangent to the isoquant.

With this tangency property, we once again see a similarity to optimal consumer behavior, which was also identified by a point of tangency. The parallels are particularly strong if we think about the expenditure-minimization interpretation of consumer behavior, where the consumer wants to choose a bundle of goods that minimizes the total expenditure required to achieve a given level of utility. Here, the firm wants to choose a set of inputs that minimizes the total cost of producing a given quantity of output.

Another important feature of the tangency result is that by definition, the isocost line and isoquant have the same slope at a tangency point. We know what these slopes are from our earlier discussion. The slope of the isocost line is the negative of the relative price of the inputs, $-W/R$. For the isoquant, the slope is the negative of the marginal rate of technical substitution ($MRTS_{LK}$), which is equal to the ratio of MP_L to MP_K. The tangency therefore implies that at the combination of inputs that minimizes the cost of producing a given quantity of output (like point B), the ratio of input prices equals the $MRTS$:

$$-\frac{W}{R} = -\frac{MP_L}{MP_K} \text{ or}$$

$$\frac{W}{R} = \frac{MP_L}{MP_K}$$

This condition has an important economic interpretation that might be easier to see if we rearrange the condition as follows:

$$\frac{W}{R} = \frac{MP_L}{MP_K}$$

$$MP_K \times W = MP_L \times R$$

$$\frac{MP_K}{R} = \frac{MP_L}{W}$$

∂ The end-of-chapter appendix uses calculus to solve the firm's cost-minimization problem.

The way we've written it, each side of this equation is the ratio of an input's marginal product to its price (capital on the left, labor on the right). One way to interpret these ratios is that they measure the marginal product per dollar spent on each input, or the input's "bang for the buck." Alternatively, we can think of each of these ratios as the firm's marginal benefit-to-cost ratio of hiring an input.

Why does cost minimization imply that each input's benefit-to-cost ratio is equal? Suppose the firm was producing an input bundle where this wasn't true. For example, if $\frac{MP_K}{R} > \frac{MP_L}{W}$, the firm's benefit-to-cost ratio for capital is higher than for labor. This would mean that the firm could replace some of its labor with capital while keeping its output quantity the same but reducing its total costs. Or if it wanted to, the firm could substitute capital for labor in a way that kept its total *costs* constant but raised its *output*. These options are possible because capital's marginal product per dollar is higher than labor's. If the sign of the inequality were reversed so $\frac{MP_K}{R} < \frac{MP_L}{W}$, the firm could reduce the costs of producing its current quantity (or raise its production without increasing costs) by substituting labor for capital. That's because, in this case, the marginal product per dollar spent is higher for labor. Only when the benefit-to-cost ratios of all the firm's inputs are the same is the firm unable to reduce the cost of producing its current quantity by changing its input levels.

Again, this logic parallels that from the consumer's optimal consumption choice in Chapter 4. The optimality condition for the consumer's expenditure-minimization problem was that the marginal rate of substitution between goods equals the goods' price ratio. Here, the analog to the *MRS* is the *MRTS* (the former being a ratio of marginal utilities, the latter a ratio of marginal products), and the price ratio is now the input price ratio. There is one place where the parallel between consumers and firms does *not* hold. The budget constraint, which plays a big role in the consumer's utility-maximization problem, doesn't really have a parallel in the firm's production problem. As we discuss in later chapters, firms' desires to maximize their profits lead to a particular quantity of output they want to produce. If for some reason they don't have enough resources to pay for the inputs necessary to produce this quantity, then someone should always be willing to lend them the difference, because the lender and the firm can split the extra profits that result from producing the profit-maximizing output, making both parties better off. This outcome means that with well-functioning capital markets, firms should never be limited to a fixed amount of total expenditure on inputs in the same way a consumer is constrained to spend no more than her income. That's the idea embodied in our Assumption 9.

Input Price Changes

We've established that the cost-minimizing input combination is at the point of tangency between an isocost line and the isoquant that corresponds to the output quantity the firm wants to produce. In other words, a firm is producing that level of output at the lowest cost when the marginal product per dollar spent is equal across all inputs. Given this result, a very useful question to ask is how changes in input prices affect the firm's optimal input mix. We analyze this question in the next sections.

6.3 figure it out

A firm is employing 100 workers ($W = \$15/\text{hour}$) and 50 units of capital ($R = \$30/\text{hour}$). At the firm's current input use, the marginal product of labor is 45 and the marginal product of capital is 60. Is the firm producing its current level of output at the minimum cost or is there a way for the firm to do better? Explain.

Solution:

The cost-minimizing input choice occurs when $MP_L/W = MP_K/R$. We need to determine if this is the case for this firm:

$$MP_L = 45 \text{ and } W = 15 \text{ so } MP_L/W = 45/15 = 3$$
$$MP_K = 60 \text{ and } R = 30 \text{ so } MP_K/R = 60/30 = 2$$

Therefore, $MP_L/W > MP_K/R$. The firm is not currently minimizing its cost.

Because $MP_L/W > MP_K/R$, \$1 spent on labor yields a greater marginal product (i.e., more output) than \$1 spent on capital. The firm would do better by reducing its use of capital and increasing its use of labor. Note that as the firm reduces capital, the marginal product of capital will rise. Likewise, as the firm hires additional labor, the marginal product of labor will fall. Ultimately, the firm will reach its cost-minimizing input choice where $MP_L/W = MP_K/R$.

A Graphical Representation of the Effects of an Input Price Change   We know that differences in input costs show up as differences in the slopes of the isocost lines. A higher relative cost of labor (from an increase in W, decrease in R, or both) makes isocost lines steeper. Decreases in labor's relative cost flatten them. A cost-minimizing firm wants to produce using the input combination where the slope of the isocost line equals the slope of the isoquant. This requirement means that when the inputs' relative price changes, the point of tangency between the isocost line (now with a new slope) and the isoquant must also change. Input prices cause the firm to move along the isoquant corresponding to the firm's desired output level to the input combination where an isocost line is tangent to the isoquant.

Figure 6.11 shows an example of this. The initial input price ratio gives the slope of isocost line C_1. The firm wants to produce the quantity $\overline{Q}$, so initially the cost-minimizing combination of inputs occurs at point A. Now suppose that labor becomes relatively more expensive (or equivalently, capital becomes less expensive). This change causes the isocost lines to become steeper. With the steeper isocost lines, the point of tangency shifts to point B. Therefore, the increase in the relative cost of labor causes the firm to shift to an input mix that has more capital and less labor than before.

The implication of this outcome makes sense: If a firm wants to minimize its production costs and a particular input becomes relatively more expensive, the firm will substitute away from the now relatively more expensive input and toward the relatively less expensive one.

This is why we sometimes observe very different production methods used to make the same or at least very similar products. For example, if you spend a growing season observing a typical rice-farming operation in Vietnam, you will see days where dozens of workers tend to a small paddy. Depending on the time of season, they might be planting, transplanting, or harvesting plants one-by-one. Whatever their particular task, they use only the most basic of tools. If you visit a rice farm in Texas, on the other hand, a typical day at work will involve a single farmer (and maybe a hired hand or two) driving large machines of various types. The farmer uses these machines to do the same tasks as the Vietnamese workers. A key reason for the differences in production methods is that the relative prices of capital and labor are very different in Vietnam and Texas. In Vietnam, labor is relatively cheap compared to capital. Therefore, the tangency of Vietnamese rice farms' isoquants and isocost lines is at a point such as point A in Figure 6.11. At point A, a lot of labor and only a little capital are used to grow rice. In Texas, on the other hand, labor is relatively expensive. This implies steeper isocost lines for Texas farms, making their cost-minimizing input mix much more capital-intensive, as at point B.

∂ The online appendix derives the firm's demands for capital and labor. (http://glsmicro.com/appendices)

Figure 6.11   **A Change in the Price of Labor Leads to a New Cost-Minimizing Input Choice**

When labor becomes relatively more expensive, the isocost line shifts from C_1 to C_2. With the steeper isocost line, the cost-minimizing input choice shifts from point A, with a high ratio of labor to capital, to point B, with a low ratio of labor to capital.

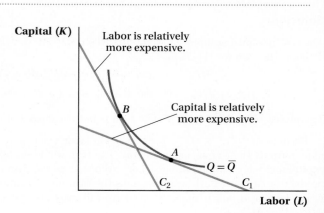

theory and data

Hospitals' Input Choices and Medicare Reimbursement Rules

Medicare is the government-paid medical insurance system for the elderly and disabled in the United States. It involves massive expenditures: $550 billion in 2011 (which works out to roughly $12,000 per beneficiary), accounting for about one-fifth of all health-related spending in the United States. Not surprisingly, then, Medicare is a huge source of revenues for producers of medical care like hospitals, physicians, and (due to the addition of the Medicare Part D drug benefit in 2006) pharmaceutical companies. This also means that when Medicare changes its rules about how it pays providers, such a change affects the way health care is produced.

In a 2008 study, economists Daron Acemoglu and Amy Finkelstein looked at how changes in Medicare payment structures affect health-care providers' input choices.[*] Medicare introduced what is called the Prospective Payment System (PPS) in 1983. The PPS changed how Medicare reimbursed hospitals for services they provided to Medicare patients. Before PPS, Medicare would simply reimburse a portion of a hospital's total costs (including both capital and labor costs), where the portion equaled the share of Medicare patient-days out of a hospital's total patient-days. That is, Medicare payments subsidized a hospital's expenditures on both capital and labor inputs.

The shift to PPS changed this reimbursement approach. Capital expenditures—building additions, renovations, and purchases of medical technologies—were rebated as before. But for everything else, PPS paid a flat rate based on the patient's diagnosis, regardless of the hospital's actual labor expenditures. So, for example, a cataract surgery would entitle the hospital to a pre-specified payment regardless of whether the hospital spent more or less on the labor inputs necessary to complete the patient's treatment. What PPS did, in effect, was change hospitals' relative prices of capital and labor inputs. Capital was priced as before, because PPS treated capital expenditures the same way as it always had. But now the hospital was completely responsible on the margin for any additional labor inputs. Rather than being reimbursed for any extra labor expenses as before, the hospital bore the full cost of any additional staffing time. Therefore, PPS raised the relative price of labor to hospitals, shifting the hospitals' isocost lines in the same way the lines shifted from C_1 to C_2 in Figure 6.11.

The prediction of our cost-minimization analysis is that hospitals would switch to more capital-intensive production because they now faced a higher relative price for labor (leading to steeper isocost lines). So, for example, whereas in the past a hospital might have admitted a patient with a minor head injury overnight for observation (hospital stays are labor-intensive), they would now take a CT scan of the patient's brain (using their newly purchased scanner) to verify that there is no significant damage, and send the patient home rather than admit her.

How can this prediction of our model be tested in the data? A straightforward way might be to look at hospitals' capital-to-labor ratios before and after PPS, and see if they increased. Acemoglu and Finkelstein did this and found that capital intensity, in fact, increased. The authors estimate that the average hospital saw a 10% increase in its capital-to-labor ratio within the first three years after the introduction of PPS. However, one might worry that capital-to-labor mixes change over time for other reasons. Perhaps, for example, wage levels have generally increased over time. It might just be coincidence that the average capital intensity in hospitals rose after PPS began.

To address this possible coincidence, Acemoglu and Finkelstein also conducted another more powerful test of the theory. Hospitals differ substantially in their share of patients who are on Medicare. Because PPS only applies to Medicare-related expenditures, the new payment structure should affect hospitals with a lot of Medicare patients more than it affects those with only a few. Expectedly, then, hospitals with a greater share of Medicare patients should have made larger shifts from labor to capital inputs.

[*] Daron Acemoglu and Amy Finkelstein, "Input and Technology Choices in Regulated Industries: Evidence from the Health Care Sector," *Journal of Political Economy* 116, no. 5 (2008): 837–880.

That is what happened. Capital-to-labor ratios went up overall after PPS, but hospitals with 75% Medicare patients moved to a capital-to-labor ratio that was, on average, about 13% higher than those with only 25% of their patients on Medicare.

Acemoglu and Finkelstein identified the specific types of capital inputs that hospitals bought more of. Hospitals with a large fraction of Medicare patients were more likely to adopt a number of advanced medical technologies like CT scanners, cardiac-care devices, and radiation-based cancer treatment equipment. The same hospitals were also more likely to decrease the average length of patient stays, a labor-intensive input into health-care production.

These results speak to the power of our model of firms' production behavior. Despite all the simplifications we made (our nine assumptions), the model seems to be a good predictor of actual firms' choices in the real world.

6.5 Returns to Scale

returns to scale
A change in the amount of output in response to a proportional increase or decrease in all of the inputs.

constant returns to scale
A production function for which changing all inputs by the same proportion changes the quantity of output by the same proportion.

increasing returns to scale
A production function for which changing all inputs by the same proportion changes output *more* than proportionately.

decreasing returns to scale
A production function for which changing all inputs by the same proportion changes output *less* than proportionately.

Economists use the term **returns to scale** to describe what happens to the amount of output in response to a proportional increase or decrease in all of the inputs.

A production function is said to have **constant returns to scale** if changing the amount of capital and labor by some multiple changes the quantity of output by exactly the same multiple. (For example, a doubling of capital and labor results in a doubling of output.) Our Cobb–Douglas production function $Q = K^{0.5}L^{0.5}$ has constant returns to scale. This is apparent in Table 6.2. When $L = K = 1$, $Q = 1$; when labor and capital are doubled to $L = K = 2$, then output doubles, too: $Q = 2$. If labor and capital are doubled again to $L = K = 4$, then $Q = 4$.

A production function has **increasing returns to scale** instead if changing all inputs by some multiple changes output *more* than proportionately. (Doubling capital and labor more than doubles output.) Finally, **decreasing returns to scale** exist if adjusting all inputs by the same multiple changes output by *less* than that multiple. (Output does not fully double when inputs are doubled.)

We assumed earlier in the chapter that inputs have diminishing returns—their marginal products fall as firms use more of them. So, how can returns to scale be constant or increasing when there are diminishing returns to inputs? The key difference between the two concepts is that marginal products refer to changes in *only one input while holding the other input constant*, but returns to scale is about changes in *all inputs at the same time*. In other words, diminishing marginal returns refers to short-run changes, while returns to scale is a long-run phenomenon because we are changing all inputs simultaneously.

Figure 6.12 on the next page demonstrates these returns to scale cases using isoquants. In the first panel, a doubling of inputs leads to the doubling of outputs, so the technology exhibits constant returns to scale. Similarly, the isoquants in panel b indicate increasing returns to scale, while decreasing returns to scale are shown in panel c.

Factors Affecting Returns to Scale

A number of aspects of a production technology determine a production function's returns to scale.

In some ways, it is natural for a production function to have constant returns to scale. If a production process can easily be replicated lock, stock, and barrel, output should expectedly grow proportionately with inputs. For example, if a firm has a factory that makes 1,000 cars a day using 3,000 units of labor and 4,000 units of capital, it seems reasonable that the firm could build an identical factory somewhere else (maybe even next door) and, having doubled all of its inputs, double its output. Adding a third identical factory and set of workers should again increase output commensurately, and so on.

Figure 6.12 Returns to Scale

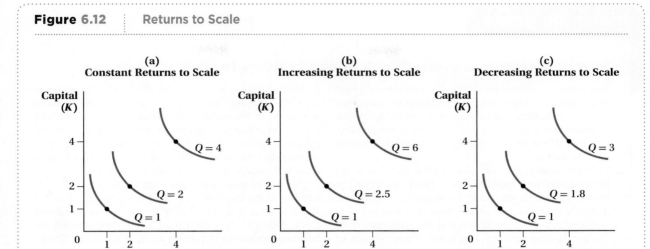

(a) A production function has constant returns to scale if changing the amount of capital and labor by some multiple changes the output by exactly the same multiple. When the input combination (L, K) doubles from $(1, 1)$ to $(2, 2)$, output doubles from $Q = 1$ to $Q = 2$.

(b) A production function has increasing returns to scale if changing the amount of capital and labor by some multiple changes the output by more than that multiple. When the

input combination (L, K) doubles from $(1, 1)$ to $(2, 2)$, output more than doubles from $Q = 1$ to $Q > 2.5$.

(c) A production function has decreasing returns to scale if changing the amount of capital and labor by some multiple changes the output by less than that multiple. When the input combination (L, K) doubles from $(1, 1)$ to $(2, 2)$, output less than doubles from $Q = 1$ to $Q = 1.8$.

But there are other influences than can push production functions toward increasing or decreasing returns to scale as well. For example, a common source of increasing returns to scale is **fixed costs.** These are payments to inputs that must be used no matter what the output quantity is, even if it is zero. (We talk more about fixed costs in Chapter 7.) If a certain quantity of inputs must be used before the firm can produce its first unit of output, increasing inputs after these fixed costs are paid will increase output more than proportionately. Consider the example of a firm that uses three inputs to earn its revenues: capital, labor, and a Web page. We assume the Web page input is a fixed cost, because the cost of its upkeep is basically the same whether the firm makes a lot of product or just a little. If the firm doubles its capital and labor inputs while keeping the same Web page, it will probably double its output. Therefore, the firm was able to double its output without having to double all its inputs. This is just another way of stating the definition of increasing returns to scale.

A firm can also experience increasing returns to scale if there is **learning by doing.** As a company makes more of a good, it tends to become more and more efficient at production. This sort of learning takes place with virtually any task that is repeated over and over (as you've probably learned from your own personal experience). If a firm gets better at producing the more output it makes, then it may be able to produce the second batch of output using fewer resources than it required for the first batch. That is, it will be able to double its output without having to double its inputs.

Decreasing returns to scale are possible but should be unlikely for the same reason that constant returns to scale are natural. If inputs are measured properly, and the firm has ample time to adjust all its inputs, the firm should be able to replicate its current production operation, allowing it to increase output by the same factor as inputs. Nevertheless, economists sometimes measure firms' production functions and find that

fixed cost
An input cost that does not vary with the amount of output.

learning by doing
The process by which a firm becomes more efficient at production as it produces more output.

How to determine a production function's returns to scale

A common question you will see on an intermediate micro exam is one that asks if a production function exhibits constant, increasing, or decreasing returns to scale. If you approach this question the right way, it is one of the easiest questions on which you will ever be tested.

Given a formula, first solve for the quantity when both capital and labor equal 1. Next, multiply the inputs by 2, and work out the quantity. If the total quantity doubles, the production function exhibits constant returns to scale. If it less than doubles, then the production function has diminishing returns to scale. More than doubles? You guessed it: increasing returns to scale.

Here is one last trick. If the production function is a Cobb–Douglas function, then all you need to do is add up all of the exponents on the inputs. If these add up to 1, then the production function exhibits constant returns to scale. If they sum to more than 1, it indicates increasing returns to scale, and if they add up to less than 1, it shows decreasing returns to scale.

Say you're given the production function $Q = K^{0.3}L^{0.8}$. Solving using the first method gives you $Q = 1$ when $K = 1$ and $L = 1$, and $Q = 2^{0.3}2^{0.8} = 2^{1.1}$ when $K = 2$ and $L = 2$. Since $2^{1.1}$ is greater than 2, this production function has increasing returns to scale. But this is a Cobb–Douglas function, so you could instead simply add the exponents ($0.3 + 0.8 = 1.1 > 1$) and find the same result.

they exhibit decreasing returns to scale. Most often, such a finding indicates that not all inputs are being fully measured. For instance, suppose a company builds a seemingly identical second factory with the same number of workers and capital as its first one, yet the second is less efficient. This might be because the second factory's manager is not as talented as the manager at the first, or because the company's productive corporate culture isn't as well established as at the original factory. Managerial talent and corporate culture are inputs to the firm's production, but are often too difficult to measure to include in standard labor and capital inputs measures. To have true decreasing returns to scale, the second factory would have to be less efficient even if the managerial talent and corporate culture were at the same level as at the first factory.

One reason a firm might have true decreasing returns to scale is regulatory burden. Many business regulations exempt small companies. As a result, as a company grows, it often has to comply with additional rules and regulations. Because the cost of complying with these regulations can be substantial, small firms that expand the scale of their operations above the threshold find themselves having to deal with a new set of costs now that they are no longer exempt.

6.4 figure it out

For each of the following production functions, determine if they exhibit constant, decreasing, or increasing returns to scale.

    a. $Q = 2K + 15L$

    b. $Q = \min(3K,\ 4L)$

    c. $Q = 15K^{0.5}L^{0.4}$

Solution:

The easiest way to determine the returns to scale for a production function is to simply plug in values for L and K, calculate Q, and then double the input levels to see what happens to output. If output exactly doubles, the production function exhibits constant returns to scale. If output rises by less than double, there are decreasing returns to scale. If output more than doubles, the production function has increasing returns to scale.

So, for each of these production functions, we will start with $K = L = 1$ and calculate Q and then perform the same exercise for $K = L = 2$. Note that K and L do not have to be equal for this method to work, but it does simplify the solution a bit.

a. If $L = 1$ and $K = 1$: $Q = 2K + 15L = 2(1) + 15(1) = 2 + 15 = 17$.

If $L = 2$ and $K = 2$: $Q = 2K + 15L = 2(2) + 15(2) = 4 + 30 = 34$.

Since output exactly doubles when inputs are doubled, the production function exhibits constant returns to scale.

b. If $L = 1$ and $K = 1$: $Q = \min(3K, 4L) = Q = \min(3(1), 4(1)) = \min(3, 4) = 3$.

If $L = 2$ and $K = 2$: $Q = \min(3K, 4L) = Q = \min(3(2), 4(2)) = \min(6, 8) = 6$.

Because output exactly doubles when inputs are doubled, the production function exhibits constant returns to scale.

c. If $L = 1$ and $K = 1$: $Q = 15K^{0.5}L^{0.4} = Q = 15(1)^{0.5}(1)^{0.4} = 15(1)(1) = 15$.

If $L = 2$ and $K = 2$: $Q = 15K^{0.5}L^{0.4} = Q = 15(2)^{0.5}(2)^{0.4} = 15(1.41)(1.31) = 27.71$.

Because output less than doubles when inputs are doubled, the production function exhibits decreasing returns to scale.

6.6 Technological Change

When economists try to measure production functions using data from firms' operations over time, they will often find that output rises in later periods even though the firms might still be using the same amount of inputs. The only way to explain this is that the production function must somehow be changing over time in a way that allows extra output to be obtained from a given amount of inputs. This shift in the production function is referred to as **total factor productivity growth** (or sometimes **technological change**).

We can adjust a production function to allow for technological change. There are many possible ways to do this, but a common and straightforward method is to suppose that the level of technology is a constant that multiplies the production function:

$$Q = Af(K, L)$$

where A is the level of total factor productivity, a parameter that affects how much output can be produced from a given set of inputs. Usually, we think of this as reflecting technological change. Increases in A mean that the amount of output obtainable from any given set of labor and capital inputs will increase as well.

How does this kind of technological change affect a firm's cost-minimization decisions? Consider the impact of a change in A on the components of the firm's cost-minimization problem above. First, the firm's isocost lines won't change. A is a feature of the production function, not the prices of inputs. Because A is part of the production function, though, it will affect the isoquants. An increase in A means that the same number of inputs will produce more output, so it also implies that the *same* output can be made with *fewer* inputs. Because an isoquant reflects the combinations of inputs that produce a given amount of output, higher values of A shift isoquants in (toward the origin).

total factor productivity growth (or technological change)
An improvement in technology that changes the firm's production function such that more output is obtained from the same amount of inputs.

Figure 6.13 : The Impact of Technological Change

An improvement in technology shifts the isoquant $Q_1 = \overline{Q}$ inward to $Q_2 = \overline{Q}$. The new cost-minimizing input combination (L_2, K_2) is located at the tangency between Q_2 and the isocost C_2. (L_2, K_2) uses fewer inputs and is, therefore, cheaper than the original cost-minimizing input combination (L_1, K_1) located at the tangency between Q_1 and the isocost C_1.

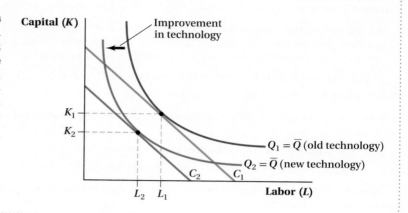

This is shown in Figure 6.13. Before, to produce $\overline{Q}$, the firm needed some combination of inputs on isoquant $Q_1 = \overline{Q}$. After technological change leads to an increase in A, the firm doesn't need to use as many inputs to produce $\overline{Q}$. Therefore, the isoquant for $\overline{Q}$ shifts in, to $Q_2 = \overline{Q}$.

If the firm's desired output remains $\overline{Q}$ after the technological change, then the firm's choice of inputs will be determined by the tangency of $Q_2 = \overline{Q}$ and its isocost lines, as in Figure 6.13. The initial cost-minimizing input combination (before the technological change) is where $Q_1 = \overline{Q}$ is tangent to isocost line C_1, that is, K_1 units of capital and L_1 units of labor. After the technological change, the optimal input combination becomes K_2 and L_2, where $Q_2 = \overline{Q}$ is tangent to isocost line C_2. Because the firm needs to use fewer inputs, technological change has reduced its costs of producing $\overline{Q}$.

For a vivid description of the power of technological change, see the Freakonomics study on pages 6-30 and 6-31.

🧩 application

Technological Change in U.S. Manufacturing

durable good
A good that has a long service life.

You might have noticed there's no shortage of talk about the shrinking (and in some more strident commentators' minds, impending disappearance) of the U.S. manufacturing sector. It's true that manufacturing employment has fallen—a lot. In 1994 there were 17 million manufacturing workers in the United States, about 18% of the total private sector workforce. Of these, 10 million workers were employed by companies manufacturing **durable goods**—goods that have long service lives, such as appliances, airplanes, cars, metal and wood products, and electrical equipment. By the end of 2011 there were only 11.8 million manufacturing workers, less than 11% of the private workforce, 7.4 million of whom were making durable goods. (This wasn't just due to the 2008–2009 recession, either. Manufacturing's share of employment had dropped steadily before 2008 as well.)

Given this, it might surprise you to find out that the total value of manufactured products made in the United States *increased* over the same period. Not by just a little, either. While the total inflation-adjusted output of private businesses grew by 53% between 1994 and 2010, the manufacturing sector's total output grew 49%, just about as fast. Furthermore, the total inflation-adjusted output of U.S. durable goods *more than doubled* over the period.

Figure 6.14 : U.S. Total Factor Productivity, 1994–2009

Data from the U.S. Bureau of Labor Statistics show that total factor productivity increased much more in the manufacturing industries than in the overall private business sector over the period 1994–2009. In particular, durable goods manufacturers saw a 37% increase in total factor productivity, enabling these firms to increase production while decreasing the number of laborers. As a result, unemployment rose even as output increased.

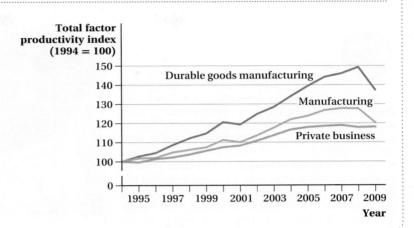

How is it possible for manufacturing employment to fall for an extended time while the sector's output grows just as fast as, or even considerably faster than, the rest of the economy? A partial answer to this question is that manufacturing firms shifted from using labor to using more capital inputs. But that's not the whole story. Much of the explanation lies in the fact that technological change was faster in manufacturing than in the rest of the economy, particularly in durable goods manufacturing.

Figure 6.14 shows the growth of technology (total factor productivity) for three segments of the U.S. economy. (These technology data were compiled by the U.S. Bureau of Labor Statistics.) The largest segment is the private business sector, which includes just about every producer in the economy outside of government bodies, including manufacturers. The second is the manufacturing sector, and the third isolates durable goods manufacturers specifically. The level of technology in each segment is given by an index, where the value of the index expresses the segment's total factor productivity level as a fraction of its value in 1994. So, for instance, an index value of 120 in a particular year means that the segment's total factor productivity is 20% higher than it was in 1994. This means that, given any fixed set of inputs, the segment's producers can make 20% more output than they could in 1994.

A comparison of the rates of technological change helps explain why manufacturing output could have gone up even as employment fell. Total factor productivity for the entire private business segment grew by about 18% during the period, meaning producers were able to make 18% more output from the same set of inputs in 2009 as they could in 1994. Manufacturers saw a somewhat greater 20% increase in total factor productivity during the period, and that includes a big slide during the recent recession that wasn't experienced by the economy as a whole. Before that slide, manufacturing total factor productivity had grown by over 25% since 1994. Durable goods manufacturers, in particular, saw a much stronger rate of technological change during the period. They were able to produce 37% more output in 2009 with the same inputs they used in 1994. This meant that they could use even fewer inputs than producers in other segments of the economy and still experience the same total output growth. This relative productivity growth, combined with the fact that they substituted more capital-intensive production, explains how they were able to double output over the period even while using less labor. ∎

freakonomics

Why Do Indian Fishermen Love Their Cell Phones So Much?

There are few products more cherished by American consumers than the cell phone. The modern smart phone is truly a technological wonder—used not just for phone calls and text, but also as a browser, calendar, GPS device, MP3 player, and video streamer. It's hard to imagine, as you lovingly caress your iPhone, that it was only a little over 25 years ago that the first cell phone, the Motorola DynaTAC 8000x, hit the consumer marketplace.[*] Weighing in at a hefty 1.75 pounds (almost six times the weight of the iPhone), it had a battery life of 60 minutes of use. All it did was make phone calls, and the sound quality was horrible. The price tag, adjusting for inflation: over $9,000. In the history of humankind, there are few examples of technological progress occurring as rapidly as has been the case with cell phones.

A local fisherman uses a mobile phone as he works Nariman Point in Mumbai, a commercial hub of India.

Prashanth Vishwanathan/Bloomberg via Getty Images

When economists talk about technological progress, they are referring to changes in the production function. Compared to thirty years ago, we've gotten much better at taking a set of inputs (e.g., plastic, silicon, metal, the time of engineers and factory workers, etc.) and turning them into cell phones.

Although it is natural to think of technological progress in terms of innovations in manufacturing, there are many other sources of such progress. Indeed, the cell phone is not just the beneficiary of technological progress—in some parts of the world, it is an important *source* of technological progress. Economist Robert Jensen has studied fishing villages in Kerala, a state on India's southern coast.[†] In the area observed, he looked at 15 markets where fishermen and consumers met to buy and sell the day's catch. If there were not enough buyers, the excess fish would go to waste because of the absence of refrigeration. If there were not enough sellers, some of the consumers went away empty-handed. Prices varied wildly in response to daily fluctuations in supply and demand, and up to 8% of fishermen had to let their fish go to waste because there was no demand.

Traditionally, fishermen would take their boats out to sea, make their catch, and face a guessing game as to which market to choose on a given day. Then cell phone coverage came to the area. Very quickly, fishermen adopted cell phones, which allowed them to call ahead to determine which market would offer them the best prices on their fish. Better information led to better matching of buyers and sellers. There were rarely wasted fish; in fact, Jensen found that after the complete adoption of cell phones, it became extremely rare for sellers not to find buyers for their fish. The figure presents evidence of just how profoundly cell phones affected this market. It shows the fluctuation in fish prices over time in three areas in Kerala. Each colored line in the graph represents prices at one particular market. The introduction of cell phones was staggered across regions, and the points at which cell phones became available are denoted by the vertical lines near week 20 for Region I, week 100 for Region II, and week 200 for Region III.

Before cell phones, prices in each region were extremely volatile. Sometimes prices were almost as high as 14 rupees per kilogram on one beach, whereas at another beach on the same day, the fish were basically given away for free. From day to day, it was difficult if

---

[*] The DynaTAC 8000x was the first cell phone available to the general public, but it was not the first cell phone produced or even to make a successful phone call. That distinction goes to an even heavier prototype in 1973.

[†] Robert Jensen, "The Digital Provide: Information (Technology), Market Performance, and Welfare in the South Indian Fisheries Sector," *The Quarterly Journal of Economics* 122, no. 3 (2007): 879–924. The figure is reproduced by permission of Oxford University Press and the kind permission of Professor Jensen.

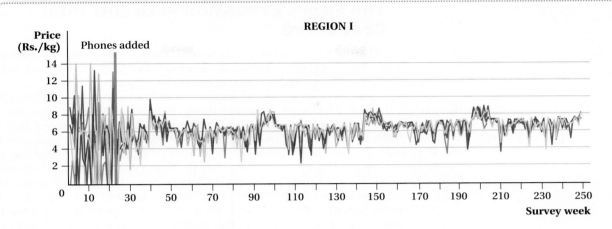

REGION I

Price (Rs./kg)

Phones added

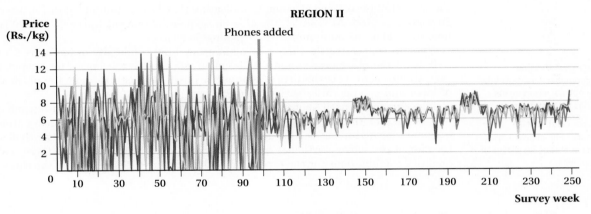

REGION II

Price (Rs./kg)

Phones added

Survey week

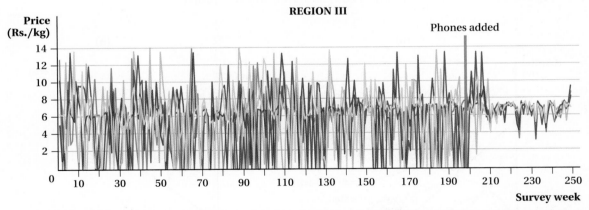

REGION III

Price (Rs./kg)

Phones added

Survey week

Each colored line shows the price of fish at a particular beach in each region. Before cell phones became available, prices were extremely volatile. After cell phones became available, as denoted by the vertical red lines, prices showed less variation.

not impossible to predict which market would have the best price. The impact of cell phone use on the market was seen as soon as cell phone service became available in each area, although as you might expect, it took a few weeks for people to learn how to adjust and figure out how best to use this new technology. Roughly 10 weeks after the introduction of cell phones into this industry, though, the variation in prices across beaches in each of the three regions on a given day had shrunk dramatically.

6.7 The Firm's Expansion Path and Total Cost Curve

We've seen so far how a firm minimizes its costs at the optimal production quantity. We can now use this information to illustrate how the firm's production choices and its total costs change as the optimal production quantity changes.

Panel a of Figure 6.15 shows sets of isoquants and isocost lines for a hypothetical firm, Ivor's Engines. The figure illustrates three isoquants and isocost lines, but remember that there are isoquants for every possible quantity level and isocost lines for every cost level. Recall that the combination of labor and capital that minimizes the cost of producing a given quantity of output is at the tangency of an isocost line and the isoquant corresponding to that output level. The figure shows three such tangencies. On the lower left, $Q = 10$ is the isoquant that corresponds to input combinations that allow Ivor's Engines to make 10 engines. This isoquant is tangent at point X to the $C = \$100$ isocost line, so $100 is the lowest cost at which Ivor can build 10 engines. The isoquant representing input combinations that produce 20 engines, $Q = 20$, is tangent to the $C = \$180$ isocost line at point Y, indicating that Ivor's minimum cost for producing 20 engines is $180. At point Z, the $Q = 30$ isoquant is tangent to the $C = \$300$ isocost line, so $300 is the minimum cost of making 30 engines.

The line connecting the three cost-minimizing input combinations in Figure 6.15a (as well as all the other cost-minimizing isoquant-isocost line tangencies for output levels that are not shown) is the firm's **expansion path.** It illustrates how the optimal mix of labor and capital varies with total output.

The expansion path shows the optimal input combinations at each output quantity. If we plot the total cost from the isocost line and the output quantity from the isoquants located along the expansion path, we have a **total cost curve** that shows the cost of producing particular quantities. Panel b of Figure 6.15 gives these cost and quantity combinations for the expansion path in Figure 6.15a, including the three cost-

expansion path
A curve that illustrates how the optimal mix of inputs varies with total output.

total cost curve
A curve that shows a firm's cost of producing particular quantities.

Figure 6.15 The Expansion Path and the Total Cost Curve

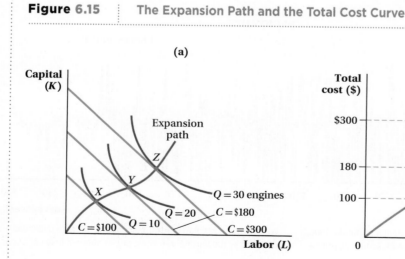

(a)

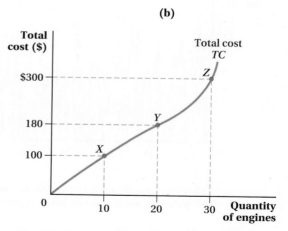

(b)

(a) The expansion path for Ivor's Engines maps the optimal input combinations for each quantity Q. Here, points X, Y, and Z are the cost-minimizing input combinations given output levels $Q = 10$, $Q = 20$, and $Q = 30$, respectively.

(b) The total cost curve for Ivor's Engines is constructed using the isocost lines from the expansion path in panel a. The cost-minimizing input combinations cost $100, $180, and $300 at output levels $Q = 10$, $Q = 20$, and $Q = 30$, respectively.

minimizing points at 10, 20, and 30 units of output. The total cost curve is another representation of the information revealed by the expansion path. Both the total cost curve and the expansion path show how, when the firm is minimizing its costs of producing any given quantity, the firm's minimized costs change when its output changes.

Note that the expansion path and the total cost curve that corresponds to it are for a given set of input prices (as reflected in the isocost lines) and a given production function (as reflected in the isoquants). As we saw earlier, if input prices or the production function changes, so will the cost-minimizing input combinations. Therefore, the expansion path and the total cost curve will change, too. In Chapter 7, we use the total cost curve—as derived from the expansion path—in our discussion of a firm's cost functions.

∂ The end-of-chapter appendix derives the firm's expansion path.

6.8 Conclusion

Much like the consumer from Chapter 4 minimizes her expenditures of achieving a given utility level, a firm minimizes its costs of producing a given quantity of a good. These optimal production decisions that a firm makes trace out its total cost curve, which shows the costs of producing a given quantity. In Chapter 7, we deepen our understanding of a firm's cost structure and delve into a discussion of the specific costs a firm faces. We'll see that a firm uses its knowledge of its cost structure to inform its cost-minimizing behavior.

Summary

1. In looking at a firm's **production** practices, we made several simplifying assumptions. Most importantly, we assume that **cost minimization**—minimizing the total cost of producing the firm's desired output quantity—is a key objective of any producer. [**Section 6.1**]

2. A **production function** relates the quantities of inputs that a producer uses to the quantity of output it obtains from them. Production functions typically have a mathematical representation in the form $Q = f(K,L)$. A commonly used production function is the Cobb–Douglas production function, which has the form $Q = K^{\alpha}L^{\beta}$, where α and β are constants. [**Section 6.1**]

3. In the short run, a firm's level of capital is fixed. Differences in output must be achieved by adjusting labor inputs alone. We looked at properties of the production function including an input's **marginal** and **average product** (we focused on labor in this case, because capital is fixed). We saw examples of **diminishing marginal products** for labor, where the incremental output obtained from using another unit of labor in production decreases. [**Section 6.2**]

4. The ability to adjust capital inputs, which firms enjoy in the long run, has two important implications. One is that the firm can alleviate diminishing marginal products of labor by increasing the amount of capital it uses at the same time. Second, it has an ability to substitute between capital and labor. [**Section 6.3**]

5. An isoquant curve shows all combinations of inputs that allow a firm to make a particular quantity of output. The curvature and slope of the isoquant represent the substitutability of the inputs in the production of the good. In particular, the negative slope of the isoquant is equal to the **marginal rate of technical substitution** of labor for capital. [**Section 6.4**]

6. An isocost line connects all the combinations of capital and labor that the firm can purchase for a given total expenditure on inputs. The relative costs of capital and labor determine the slope of the isocost line. [**Section 6.4**]

7. A firm aims to minimize its costs at any given level of output. The firm's cost-minimizing output occurs where the isocost line is tangent to the isoquant, or where the marginal rate of technical substitution is equal to the relative price of labor to capital. [**Section 6.4**]

8. **Returns to scale** is a property of production functions that describes how the level of output changes when all inputs are simultaneously changed by the same amount. Production functions can have returns to scale that are constant (if all inputs increase by a factor, output changes by the same factor), increasing (if all inputs increase by a factor, output changes by more than that factor), or decreasing (if all inputs increase by a factor, output changes by less than that factor). [**Section 6.5**]

9. When there is **technological change,** a production function changes over time so that a fixed

amount of inputs can produce more output. This is reflected by a shift of a production function's isoquants toward the origin. [**Section 6.6**]

10. A firm's cost curves are derived from its **expansion path,** which uses isoquants and isocost curves to show how its input choices change with output. The total cost curve relates the costs tied to the isocost lines and the quantities tied to the isoquants that intersect the expansion path. Productivity growth shifts total cost downward. [**Section 6.7**]

Review Questions

1. What are the differences between a firm's production in the short run and the long run?
2. What does a production function tell us?
3. Why is a firm's marginal product of labor more relevant than the marginal product of capital in the short run?
4. What does the diminishing marginal product of labor tell us about the relationship between labor inputs and marginal product?
5. How does the amount of output change as the isoquants are farther from the graph's origin? Why can't two isoquants cross?
6. What is the marginal rate of technical substitution? What does it imply about an isoquant's shape?
7. What does the curvature of an isoquant imply about the two inputs, capital and labor?
8. What is an isocost line? What does its slope tell us about the relative cost of labor and capital?
9. How will a firm react to an increase in the price of one input relative to another?
10. When is a production function said to have constant returns to scale, increasing returns to scale, or decreasing returns to scale?
11. How does technological change affect a firm's output?
12. What is an expansion path and how does it relate to a firm's total cost curve?

Problems (Solutions to problems marked * appear at the back of this book. Problems adapted to use calculus are available online at http://worthpublishers.com/GLS1e)

*1. Consider the production function presented in the table below:

		Labor (L)					
	0	**1**	**2**	**3**	**4**	**5**	**6**
Capital (K)	**1**	100	200	300	400	500	600
	2	200	400	600	800	1,000	1,200
	3	300	600	900	1,200	1,500	1,800
	4	400	800	1,200	1,600	2,000	2,400
	5	500	1,000	1,500	2,000	2,500	3,000
	6	600	1,200	1,800	2,400	3,000	3,600

a. If the firm decides to employ 6 units of capital and 1 worker, what is its output?
b. What other combinations of capital and labor could be used to produce the same level of output you found in (a)?
c. Plot the combinations you determined in (a) and (b) on a graph, with labor on the horizontal axis and capital on the vertical axis. Connect the dots to form the production isoquant corresponding to 600 units of output.

2. The table below represents the production function for Hawg Wild, a small catering company specializing in barbecued pork. The numbers in the cells represent the number of customers that can be served with various combinations of labor and capital.

		Labor (L)					
		1	**2**	**3**	**4**	**5**	**6**
Capital (K)	**1**	100	132	155	174	190	205
	2	152	200	235	264	289	310
	3	193	255	300	337	368	396
	4	230	303	357	400	437	470
	5	263	347	408	457	500	538
	6	293	387	455	510	558	600

a. Is this production function a short-run or long-run production function. How can you tell?
b. Suppose that Hawg Wild employs 5 units of capital and 2 workers. How many diners will be served?
c. Suppose that Hawg Wild employs 5 units of capital and 2 workers, but that the owner,

Billy Porcine, is considering adding his nephew to the payroll. What will the marginal product of Billy's nephew be?

d. Notice that when Hawg Wild uses 1 unit of capital, the marginal product of the fifth unit of labor is 16. But when Hawg Wild uses 5 units of capital, the marginal product of the fifth unit of labor is 43. Does this production function violate the law of diminishing marginal product of labor? Why or why not?

e. Suppose that Hawg Wild employs 5 units of capital and 2 workers, but that the owner, Billy Porcine, is considering adding another meat smoker to the kitchen (which will raise the amount of capital input to 6 units). What will the marginal product of the smoker be?

f. Hawg Wild employs 5 units of capital and 2 workers. Billy is considering the choice between hiring another worker or buying another smoker. If smokers cost $8 and workers $12, then at the margin, what is the most cost-effective choice for Billy to make?

3. Complete the table below:

Labor Input	Total Product	Marginal Product	Average Product
0	0	—	—
1		70	
2	135		
3			63
4		51	
5			60
6	366		

4. Suppose that a firm's production function is given by $Q = K^{0.33}L^{0.67}$, where $MP_K = 0.33K^{-0.67}L^{0.67}$ and $MP_L = 0.67K^{0.33}L^{-0.33}$.

a. As L increases, what happens to the marginal product of labor?

b. As K increases, what happens to the marginal product of labor?

c. Why would the MP_L change as K changes?

d. What happens to the marginal product of capital as K increases? As L increases?

5. Fetzer valves can be made in either China or the United States, but because labor in the United States is more skilled, on average, than labor in China, the production technologies differ. Consider the two production isoquants in the figure. Each represents either the production technol-

ogy for the United States or for China. Based on the $MRTS$, which production isoquant is more likely to represent the United States and which represents China? Explain.

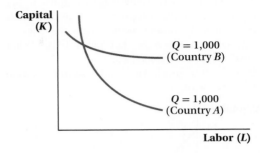

*6. Contrast the production functions given below:

a. Suppose that the production function faced by a 30-weight ball bearing producer is given by $Q = 4K^{0.5}L^{0.5}$, where $MP_K = 2K^{-0.5}L^{0.5}$ and $MP_L = 2K^{0.5}L^{-0.5}$. Do both labor and capital display diminishing marginal products? Does the production function display a diminishing marginal rate of technical substitution?

b. Suppose that the production function faced by a 40-weight ball bearing producer is given by $Q = 4KL$, where $MP_K = 4L$ and $MP_L = 4K$. Do both labor and capital display diminishing marginal products? Does the isoquant you drew in (a) display a diminishing marginal rate of technical substitution?

c. Compare your results. Must labor and capital display diminishing marginal products in order for the $MRTS$ to diminish?

*7. Suppose that Manny, Jack, and Moe can hire workers for $12 per hour, or can rent capital for $7 per hour.

a. Write an expression for Manny, Jack, and Moe's total cost as a function of how many workers they hire and how much capital they employ.

b. Assume that Manny, Jack, and Moe wish to hold their total costs to exactly $100. Use your answer from (a) to find the equation for an isocost line corresponding to exactly $100 of costs. Rearrange your equation to isolate capital.

c. Graph the equation for the isocost line, putting labor on the horizontal axis and capital on the vertical axis.

d. What is the vertical intercept of the line you drew? The horizontal intercept? What does each represent?

e. What is the slope of the line you drew? What does it represent?

f. Suppose that bargaining with the local labor union raises wages. Manny, Jack, and Moe must now pay $14 per hour. What happens to the isocost line corresponding to $100 of expenditure? Explain. Show the new isocost line on your graph.

8. A jeweler can potentially use two inputs in her handcrafted jewelry: copper or bronze. She finds that when she minimizes her costs, she uses either copper or bronze, but never both. What must her isoquants look like?

9. Consider the production and cost information depicted below:

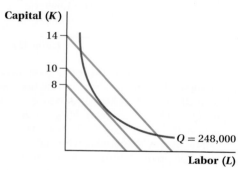

a. Suppose that capital can be hired for $24 per hour. Label each of the isocost lines with the appropriate total expenditure for the firm.

b. Suppose that labor can be hired for $36 per hour. Label the horizontal intercept of each isocost line, and determine the slope of each line.

c. Can the firm produce 248,000 units of output for exactly $336?

d. What is the minimum cost for which 248,000 units of output can be produced?

e. Suppose the firm is spending exactly $240 to make 248,000 units of output. If the marginal product of labor is 400 units of output, what must the marginal product of capital be?

10. Jake and Paul run a paper company. Each week they need to produce 1,000 reams of paper to ship to their customers. The paper plant's long-run production function is $Q = 4K^{0.75}L^{0.25}$, where Q is the number of reams produced, K is the quantity of capital rented, and L is the quantity of labor hired. For this production function, the $MP_L = K^{0.75}/L^{0.75}$ and the $MP_K = 3L^{0.25}/K^{0.25}$. The weekly cost function for the paper plant is $C = 10K + 2L$, where C is the total weekly cost.

a. What ratio of capital to labor minimizes Jake and Paul's total costs?

b. How much capital and labor will Jake and Paul need to rent and hire in order to produce 1,000 reams of paper each week?

c. How much will hiring these inputs cost them?

11. Use a diagram to explain the following: In the case of perfect substitutes, if the ratio of input prices equals the $MRTS$, will a unique solution to the firm's cost-minimization problem exist? In the case of perfect substitutes, if the ratio of input prices does not equal the $MRTS$, where will we find the solution to the firm's cost-minimization problem graphically?

12. Suppose that Gloucester Old Bank's customers can complete their transactions at a teller's window (involving labor) or at an ATM (involving capital). The production function for the bank's services is given as follows: $Q = 4K + 6L$, where Q is the number of customers served, K is the number of ATMs the bank has installed in town, and L is the number of tellers the bank has hired.

a. Suppose that Gloucester currently has 20 ATMs and 20 tellers. If 3 ATMs suddenly fail, how many additional tellers must the bank hire to maintain their original level of service?

b. Does your answer to (a) change if Gloucester originally only uses 17 ATMs? 30 ATMs?

c. What do production isoquants look like for Gloucester Old Bank? (*Hint*: Graph different combinations of tellers and ATMs that can serve an arbitrary number of customers, such as 200.)

d. How would you verbally describe the relationship between tellers and ATMs?

e. Suppose that installing and maintaining an ATM costs $20, and hiring a teller costs $32. What will happen to Gloucester's total number of customers served if it lays off 2 workers and installs 3 ATMs? What will happen to the bank's costs?

f. Using the idea developed in (e), if Gloucester Old Bank is interested in minimizing its costs, what strategy should it employ regarding its input mix?

13. Baldor, Inc. measures the marginal rate of technical substitution ($MRTS$) at $MP_L/MP_K = 3$. The prices of labor and capital faced by Baldor are such that currently $W/R = 4$.

a. Is Baldor minimizing its costs?

b. What can Baldor do to improve its situation?

*14. Suppose that the production function for iPods is $Q = 20K^{0.5}L^{0.5}$. The marginal product of labor is $10(K/L)^{0.5}$, and the marginal product of capital is $10(L/K)^{0.5}$.

a. Suppose that labor can be hired for $6, and capital can be hired for $9. When the firm is producing 49 units at lowest cost, what will the firm's marginal rate of technical substitution be?

b. Solve for the lowest-cost combination of labor and capital that will allow the firm to produce 49 iPods. Fractional units of labor and capital are certainly permissible.

c. What is the minimum cost of producing 49 iPods?

d. Suppose that the firm has exactly $300 to spend on producing iPods. What is the maximum number of iPods it can produce?

15. You are the CEO of large-scale corporate farms, and your managers run two farms in neighboring counties. Your chief financial officer reports that in both Rice and Reno counties, farm labor can be hired for $7.36 per hour, farm equipment can be rented for $433 per hour, and land can be rented for $50 per acre. She also reports that the $MRTS_{LK}$ in Rice county is higher than the $MRTS_{LK}$ in neighboring Reno county. Are you minimizing your costs? Explain.

16. With the production function $Q = 2 \min(K, L)$ and the cost function $C = 2K + 3L$, what combination of inputs minimizes costs for $Q = 10$? Show this solution graphically.

17. A young college student on a tight budget is campaigning for an open city council seat. A friend in her economics class estimates that voters are influenced by TV and newspaper ads according to the following function: Votes = $300TV^{0.6}NP^{0.2}$, where TV represents the number of television ads and NP represents the number of newspaper ads. Thus, the marginal product of a newspaper ad is $60TV^{0.6}NP^{-0.8}$ and the marginal product of a TV ad is $180TV^{-0.4}NP^{0.2}$. A local television ad costs $400, and a local newspaper ad costs $250. If the candidate needs 1,800 votes to win, what is the lowest-cost combination of newspaper and TV ads that will bring her victory?

*18. Mad Max's Road Warriors fix potholes in interstate highways. Max's road crews fill potholes using workers and shovels in 1 to 1 correspondence. A worker with 1 shovel can fill 10 potholes in a day. A worker with 2 shovels can still only fill 10 potholes, as can 2 workers with 1 shovel.

a. Draw the production isoquant corresponding to filling 30 potholes.

b. Assume that production displays constant returns to scale, and draw a few more isoquants.

c. If shovels rent for $5, and workers must be paid $25, draw several isocost lines.

d. If Mad Max has received a state contract to fill 30 potholes, what is the minimum cost at which it can fulfill the contract?

e. If the cost of renting a shovel suddenly rises from $5 to $6, what will happen to the composition of inputs that Mad Max uses to fill potholes? Why?

19. Determine whether each of the production functions below displays constant, increasing, or decreasing returns to scale:

a. $Q = 10K^{0.75}L^{0.25}$
b. $Q = (K^{0.75}L^{0.25})^2$
c. $Q = K^{0.75}L^{0.75}$
d. $Q = K^{0.25}L^{0.25}$
e. $Q = K + L + KL$
f. $Q = 2K^2 + 3L^2$
g. $Q = KL$
h. $Q = \min(3K, 2L)$

*20. Suppose that the production function for Alfred Barbuda, a producer of fine violins, is given by the following: $Q = 10K^{0.5}L^{0.5}$.

a. Suppose that Alfred is currently using 1 unit of capital. If he hires 4 workers, how many violins will they produce?

b. Suppose that Alfred is currently using not 1, but 2 units of capital. How many workers must he hire to match the level of production you found in (a)?

c. Rework your answer to (b), assuming that Alfred is currently using 4 units of capital.

d. Plot the combinations of labor and capital you found in (a–c) as a production isoquant.

e. (A test of your math skills) A change in capital technology alters Alfred's production function. Now Alfred's output is given by $Q = 10K^{0.7}L^{0.3}$. If Alfred employs 3 workers, how many machines will he have to use to achieve the production level you found in (a)? What happens to the isoquant you drew?

Chapter 6 Appendix:
The Calculus of Cost Minimization

In the appendix to Chapter 4, we saw that calculus makes solving the consumer's optimization problem easier. The benefits of using calculus also extend to the firm's constrained optimization problem, cost minimization. Cost minimization is analogous to expenditure minimization for the consumer, and the exercise of solving the producer's optimization problem will serve as a refresher in constrained optimization problems.

Marginal Product of Labor and Marginal Rate of Technical Substitution

To begin solving the firm's cost-minimization problem, we start with the Cobb–Douglas functional form (as we did in the Chapter 4 appendix). In this case, we use the production function that relates output Q to the amount of inputs capital K and labor L: $Q = AK^{\alpha}L^{1-\alpha}$, where $0 < \alpha < 1$, and where the parameter for total factor productivity, A, is greater than zero. We have been relying almost exclusively on the Cobb–Douglas functional form throughout our calculus discussions because this functional form corresponds closely with the assumptions we make about the consumer and the producer. In the context of the producer, the Cobb–Douglas production function satisfies all the assumptions we've made about capital, labor, and firm output, while still yielding simple formulas. In addition, we have chosen a Cobb–Douglas function with another unique property: Because the exponents on K and L (α, $1 - \alpha$) sum to 1, the production function exhibits constant returns to scale.

Before we jump into the producer's cost-minimization problem, let's confirm that the Cobb–Douglas production function satisfies the assumptions about the marginal products of labor and capital and the marginal rate of technical substitution (MRTS). Specifically, we need to show first that the marginal products of labor and capital are positive, and that they exhibit diminishing marginal returns. Next, we will confirm that the $MRTS$ is the ratio of the two marginal products.

Consider first the concept of the marginal product of capital, or how much extra output is produced by using an additional unit of capital. Mathematically, the marginal product of capital is the partial derivative of the production function with respect to capital. It's a partial derivative because we are holding the amount of labor constant. The marginal product of capital is

$$MP_K = \frac{\partial Q(K,L)}{\partial K} = \frac{\partial(AK^{\alpha}L^{1-\alpha})}{\partial K} = \alpha AK^{\alpha-1}L^{1-\alpha}$$

Similarly, the marginal product of labor is

$$MP_L = \frac{\partial Q(K,L)}{\partial L} = \frac{\partial(AK^{\alpha}L^{1-\alpha})}{\partial L} = (1 - \alpha)AK^{\alpha}L^{-\alpha}$$

Note that the marginal products above are positive whenever both capital and labor are greater than zero (any time output is greater than zero). In other words, the MP_L and MP_K of the Cobb–Douglas production function satisfy an important condition of production—that output increases as the firm uses more inputs.

We also need to show that the assumptions about the diminishing marginal returns of capital and labor hold true; that is, the marginal products of capital and labor decrease as the amount of that input increases, all else equal. To see this, take the second partial derivative of the production function with respect to each input. In other words, we are taking a partial derivative of each of the marginal products with respect to its input:

$$\frac{\partial^2 Q(K,L)}{\partial K^2} = \frac{\partial MP_K}{\partial K} = \frac{\partial(\alpha AK^{\alpha-1}L^{1-\alpha})}{\partial K} = \alpha(\alpha - 1)AK^{\alpha-2}L^{1-\alpha} = -\alpha(1-\alpha)AK^{\alpha-2}L^{1-\alpha}$$

$$\frac{\partial^2 Q(K,L)}{\partial L^2} = \frac{\partial MP_L}{\partial L} = \frac{\partial[(1-\alpha)AK^{\alpha}L^{-\alpha}]}{\partial L} = -\alpha(1-\alpha)AK^{\alpha}L^{-\alpha-1}$$

As long as K and L are both greater than zero (i.e., as long as the firm is producing output), both of these second derivatives are negative so the marginal product of each input decreases as the firm uses more of the input. Thus, the Cobb-Douglas production function meets our assumptions about diminishing marginal returns to both labor and capital.

We also know from the chapter that the marginal rate of technical substitution and the marginal products of capital and labor are interrelated. In particular, the $MRTS$ shows the change in labor necessary to keep output constant if the quantity of capital changes (or the change in capital necessary to keep output constant if the quantity of labor changes). The $MRTS$ equals the ratio of the two marginal products. To show this is true using calculus, first recognize that each isoquant represents some fixed level of output, say $\overline{Q}$, so that $Q = Q(K,L) = \overline{Q}$. Begin by totally differentiating the production function:

$$dQ = \frac{\partial Q(K,L)}{\partial K} dK + \frac{\partial Q(K,L)}{\partial L} dL$$

We know that dQ equals zero because the quantity is fixed at $\overline{Q}$:

$$dQ = \frac{\partial Q(K,L)}{\partial K} dK + \frac{\partial Q(K,L)}{\partial L} dL = 0$$

so that

$$\frac{\partial Q(K,L)}{\partial K} dK = -\frac{\partial Q(K,L)}{\partial L} dL$$

Now rearrange to get $-\dfrac{dK}{dL}$ on one side of the equation:

$$-\frac{dK}{dL} = \frac{\dfrac{\partial Q(K,L)}{\partial L}}{\dfrac{\partial Q(K,L)}{\partial K}} = \frac{MP_L}{MP_K}$$

The left-hand side of this equation is the negative of the slope of the isoquant, or the marginal rate of technical substitution.[1] Therefore,

$$MRTS_{LK} = \frac{MP_L}{MP_K}$$

In particular, we differentiate the Cobb–Douglas production function, $Q = AK^{\alpha}L^{1-\alpha}$, and set dQ equal to zero:

$$dQ = \frac{\partial Q(K,L)}{\partial K} dK + \frac{\partial Q(K,L)}{\partial L} dL = \alpha AK^{\alpha-1}L^{1-\alpha}dK + (1-\alpha)AK^{\alpha}L^{-\alpha}dL = 0$$

Again, rearrange to get $-\dfrac{dK}{dL}$ on one side of the equation:

$$MRTS_{LK} = -\frac{dK}{dL} = \frac{(1-\alpha)AK^{\alpha}L^{-\alpha}}{\alpha AK^{\alpha-1}L^{1-\alpha}} = \frac{MP_L}{MP_K}$$

which simplifies to

$$MRTS_{LK} = \frac{(1-\alpha)}{\alpha}\frac{K}{L}$$

Thus, we can see that the marginal rate of technical substitution equals the ratios of the marginal products for the Cobb–Douglas production function. This also shows that the

---

[1] Recall that isoquants have negative slopes; therefore, the negative of the slope of the isoquant, the $MRTS$, is positive.

$MRTS_{LK}$ decreases as the firm uses more labor and less capital, holding output constant, as we learned in the chapter. Using calculus makes it clear, however, that the rate at which labor and capital can be substituted is determined by α, the relative productivity of capital.

Cost Minimization Using Calculus

Now that we have verified the usefulness of the Cobb–Douglas function for modeling production, let's turn to the firm's cost-minimization problem. Once again, we are faced with a constrained optimization problem: The objective function is the cost of production, and the constraint is the level of output. The firm's goal is to spend the least amount of money to produce a specific amount of output. This is the producer's version of the consumer's expenditure-minimization problem.

As we saw with the consumer's problem, there are two approaches to solving the cost-minimization problem. The first is to apply the cost-minimization condition that we derived in the chapter. At the optimum, the marginal rate of technical substitution equals the ratio of the input prices, wages W and capital rental rate R. We just showed that the marginal rate of technical substitution is the ratio of the marginal products, so the cost-minimization condition is

$$MRTS_{LK} = \frac{MP_L}{MP_K} = \frac{W}{R}$$

For our Cobb–Douglas production function above, finding the optimum solution is easy using this relationship between the marginal rate of technical substitution and the input prices. We start by solving for K as a function of L using the equation for the marginal rate of technical substitution above:

$$\frac{MP_L}{MP_K} = \frac{(1-\alpha)}{\alpha}\frac{K}{L} = \frac{W}{R}$$

$$K = \left[\frac{\alpha}{(1-\alpha)}\frac{W}{R}\right]L$$

Next, plug K into the production constraint to solve for the optimum quantity of labor L^*:

$$\overline{Q} = AK^\alpha L^{1-\alpha} = A\left[\frac{\alpha}{(1-\alpha)}\frac{W}{R}L\right]^\alpha L^{1-\alpha}$$

$$\overline{Q} = A\left[\frac{\alpha}{(1-\alpha)}\frac{W}{R}\right]^\alpha L^\alpha L^{1-\alpha}$$

$$L^* = \left[\frac{(1-\alpha)}{\alpha}\frac{R}{W}\right]^\alpha \frac{\overline{Q}}{A}$$

Now solve for K^* by plugging L^* into the earlier expression for K as a function of L:

$$K^* = \left[\frac{\alpha}{(1-\alpha)}\frac{W}{R}\right]L^*$$

$$= \left[\frac{\alpha}{(1-\alpha)}\frac{W}{R}\right]\left[\frac{(1-\alpha)}{\alpha}\frac{R}{W}\right]^\alpha \frac{\overline{Q}}{A}$$

We can simplify this expression by inverting the term in the second set of brackets:

$$K^* = \left[\frac{\alpha}{(1-\alpha)}\frac{W}{R}\right]\left[\frac{\alpha}{(1-\alpha)}\frac{W}{R}\right]^{-\alpha} \frac{\overline{Q}}{A}$$

and combining the first and second terms:

$$K^* = \left[\frac{\alpha}{(1-\alpha)}\frac{W}{R}\right]^{1-\alpha} \frac{\overline{Q}}{A}$$

Thus, we have found that the cheapest way of producing $\overline{Q}$ units of output is to use $\left[\frac{\alpha}{(1-\alpha)}\frac{W}{R}\right]^{1-\alpha}\frac{\overline{Q}}{A}$ units of capital and $\left[\frac{(1-\alpha)}{\alpha}\frac{R}{W}\right]^\alpha\frac{\overline{Q}}{A}$ units of labor.

Now let's use a second approach to solve for the cost-minimizing bundle of capital and labor: the constrained optimization problem. In particular, the firm's objective, as before, is to minimize costs subject to its production function:

$$\min_{K,L} TC = RK + WL \text{ s.t. } \overline{Q} = AK^{\alpha}L^{1-\alpha}$$

Next, write this constrained optimization problem as a Lagrangian so that we can solve for the first-order conditions:

$$\min_{X,Y,\lambda} \mathcal{L}(K,L,\lambda) = RK + WL + \lambda(\overline{Q} - AK^{\alpha}L^{1-\alpha})$$

Now take the first-order conditions of the Lagrangian:

$$\frac{\partial \mathcal{L}}{\partial K} = R - \lambda(\alpha AK^{\alpha-1}L^{1-\alpha}) = 0$$

$$\frac{\partial \mathcal{L}}{\partial L} = W - \lambda[(1-\alpha)AK^{\alpha}L^{-\alpha}] = 0$$

$$\frac{\partial \mathcal{L}}{\partial \lambda} = \overline{Q} - AK^{\alpha}L^{1-\alpha} = 0$$

Notice that λ is in both of the first two conditions. Let's rearrange to solve for λ:

$$R = \lambda(\alpha AK^{\alpha-1}L^{1-\alpha})$$

$$\lambda = \frac{R}{\alpha AK^{\alpha-1}L^{1-\alpha}}$$

$$W = \lambda[(1-\alpha)AK^{\alpha}L^{-\alpha}]$$

$$\lambda = \frac{W}{(1-\alpha)AK^{\alpha}L^{-\alpha}}$$

Now set these two expressions for λ equal to one another:

$$\lambda = \frac{R}{\alpha AK^{\alpha-1}L^{1-\alpha}} = \frac{W}{(1-\alpha)AK^{\alpha}L^{-\alpha}}$$

How can we interpret λ in the context of the firm's cost-minimization problem? In general, the Lagrange multiplier is the value of relaxing the constraint by one unit. Here, the constraint is the quantity of output produced; if you increase the given output quantity by one unit, the total cost of production at the optimum increases by λ dollars. In other words, λ has a very particular economic interpretation: It is the marginal cost of production, or the extra cost of producing an additional unit of output when the firm is minimizing its costs. We can see that in our λs above: the cost of an additional unit of capital (or labor) divided by the additional output produced by that unit. In Chapter 7, we develop other ways to find marginal costs, but it's good to keep in mind that marginal cost *always* reflects the firm's cost-minimizing behavior.

We can get another perspective on cost minimization by inverting the expressions for λ:

$$\frac{\alpha AK^{\alpha-1}L^{1-\alpha}}{R} = \frac{(1-\alpha)AK^{\alpha}L^{-\alpha}}{W}$$

This relationship shows us precisely what we know is true at the optimum, that $\frac{MP_K}{R} = \frac{MP_L}{W}$, which we can rearrange to get the cost-minimization condition:

$$\frac{W}{R} = \frac{MP_L}{MP_K} = MRTS_{LK}$$

To solve for the optimal bundle of inputs that minimizes cost, we can first solve for K as a function of L:

$$\frac{K^{\alpha}}{K^{\alpha-1}} = \frac{W(\alpha L^{1-\alpha})}{(1-\alpha)RL^{-\alpha}}$$

$$K = \left[\frac{\alpha}{(1-\alpha)}\frac{W}{R}\right]L$$

Plug K as a function of L into the third first-order condition, the constraint:

$$\overline{Q} - AK^{\alpha}L^{1-\alpha} = \overline{Q} - A\left[\frac{\alpha}{(1-\alpha)}\frac{W}{R}L\right]^{\alpha}L^{1-\alpha} = 0$$

Now solve for the cost-minimizing quantity of labor, L^*:

$$A\left[\frac{\alpha}{(1-\alpha)}\frac{W}{R}\right]^{\alpha}L^{\alpha}L^{1-\alpha} = A\left[\frac{\alpha}{(1-\alpha)}\frac{W}{R}\right]^{\alpha}L = \overline{Q}$$

$$L^* = \left[\frac{\alpha}{(1-\alpha)}\frac{W}{R}\right]^{-\alpha}\frac{\overline{Q}}{A} = \left[\frac{(1-\alpha)}{\alpha}\frac{R}{W}\right]^{\alpha}\frac{\overline{Q}}{A}$$

Substitute L^* into our expression for K as a function of L:

$$K^* = \left[\frac{\alpha}{(1-\alpha)}\frac{W}{R}\right]L^* = \left[\frac{\alpha}{(1-\alpha)}\frac{W}{R}\right]\left[\frac{(1-\alpha)}{\alpha}\frac{R}{W}\right]^{\alpha}\frac{\overline{Q}}{A}$$

To simplify, invert the second term and combine:

$$K^* = \left[\frac{\alpha}{(1-\alpha)}\frac{W}{R}\right]\left[\frac{\alpha}{(1-\alpha)}\frac{W}{R}\right]^{-\alpha}\frac{\overline{Q}}{A} = \left[\frac{\alpha}{(1-\alpha)}\frac{W}{R}\right]^{1-\alpha}\frac{\overline{Q}}{A}$$

So using the Lagrangian, we arrive at the same optimal levels of labor and capital that we found using the cost-minimization condition:

$$L^* = \left[\frac{(1-\alpha)}{\alpha}\frac{R}{W}\right]^{\alpha}\frac{\overline{Q}}{A}$$

$$K^* = \left[\frac{\alpha}{(1-\alpha)}\frac{W}{R}\right]^{1-\alpha}\frac{\overline{Q}}{A}$$

6A.1 figure it out

A firm has the production function $Q = 20K^{0.2}L^{0.8}$, where Q measures output, K represents machine hours, and L measures labor hours. If the rental rate of capital is $R = \$15$, the wage rate is $W = \$10$, and the firm wants to produce 40,000 units of output, what is the cost-minimizing bundle of capital and labor?

Solution:

We could solve this problem using the cost-minimization condition. But let's solve it using the Lagrangian, so we can get more familiar with that process. First, we set up the firm's cost-minimization problem as

$$\min_{K,L} TC = 15K + 10L \text{ s.t. } 40{,}000 = 20K^{0.2}L^{0.8} \text{ or}$$

$$\min_{K,L,\lambda} \mathcal{L}(K,L,\lambda) = 15K + 10L + \lambda(40{,}000 - 20K^{0.2}L^{0.8})$$

Find the first-order conditions for the Lagrangian:

$$\frac{\partial \mathcal{L}}{\partial K} = 15 - \lambda(4K^{-0.8}L^{0.8}) = 0$$

$$\frac{\partial \mathcal{L}}{\partial L} = 10 - \lambda(16K^{0.2}L^{-0.2}) = 0$$

$$\frac{\partial \mathcal{L}}{\partial \lambda} = 40{,}000 - 20K^{0.2}L^{0.8} = 0$$

Solve for L as a function of K using the first two conditions:

$$\lambda = \frac{15}{4K^{-0.8}L^{0.8}} = \frac{10}{16K^{0.2}L^{-0.2}}$$

$$15(16K^{0.2}L^{-0.2}) = 10(4K^{-0.8}L^{0.8})$$

$$240(K^{0.2}K^{0.8}) = 40(L^{0.2}L^{0.8})$$

$$L = 6K$$

Now plug L into the third first-order condition and solve for the optimal number of labor and machine hours, L^* and K^*:

$$40{,}000 - 20K^{0.2}L^{0.8} = 0$$

$$20K^{0.2}(6K)^{0.8} = 40{,}000$$

$$20(6)^{0.8}K = 40{,}000$$

$$K^* \approx 477 \text{ machine hours}$$

$$L^* \approx 6(477) \approx 2{,}862 \text{ labor hours}$$

At the optimum, then, the firm will use approximately 477 machine hours and 2,862 labor hours to produce 40,000 units. But once again, the Lagrangian provides us with one additional piece of information: the value of λ, or marginal cost:

$$\lambda = \frac{15}{4K^{-0.8}L^{0.8}} = \frac{15}{4(477^{-0.8})(2{,}862^{0.8})} \approx \$0.89$$

Therefore, if the firm wants to produce just one more unit of output—its 40,001st unit of output, to be precise—it would have to spend an additional $0.89.

The Firm's Expansion Path

So far, we have only solved the firm's cost-minimization problem for a specific quantity. In other words, we've assumed that the firm knows how much output it wants to produce and then decides how best to produce that quantity at the lowest cost. But it might make sense to expand our thinking about how the firm makes its production decisions. In particular, what if a firm wants to know how its optimal input mix varies with its output quantity? This is the firm's expansion path, and it's something we found graphically in the chapter. Recall that an expansion path shows the cost-minimizing relationship between K and L for all possible levels of output. Let's now find the expansion path using calculus.

Consider again the firm with the familiar Cobb–Douglas production function, $Q = AK^{\alpha}L^{1-\alpha}$, and rental cost of capital and wage equal to R and W, respectively. First, write out the constrained optimization problem and the Lagrangian. Note that, unlike before, we are not going to assume that Q is a fixed level of output. In the expansion path, quantity is a variable, and that is reflected in the way we set up the constrained optimization problem below:

$$\min_{K,L} TC = RK + WL \text{ s.t. } Q = AK^{\alpha}L^{1-\alpha}$$

$$\min_{K,L,\lambda} \mathcal{L}(K,L,\lambda) = RK + WL + \lambda(Q - AK^{\alpha}L^{1-\alpha})$$

Take the first-order conditions for the Lagrangian:

$$\frac{\partial \mathcal{L}}{\partial K} = R - \lambda(\alpha AK^{\alpha-1}L^{1-\alpha}) = 0$$

$$\frac{\partial \mathcal{L}}{\partial L} = W - \lambda[(1 - \alpha)AK^{\alpha}L^{-\alpha}] = 0$$

$$\frac{\partial \mathcal{L}}{\partial \lambda} = Q - AK^{\alpha}L^{1-\alpha} = 0$$

As we saw earlier, solving the first two conditions gives us the optimal value of capital K^* as a function of L^*:

$$K^* = \left[\frac{\alpha}{(1-\alpha)}\frac{W}{R}\right]L^*$$

What does this tell us? Given a set of input prices, we now know the cost-minimizing amount of capital at every quantity of labor. The combination of labor and capital then determines the quantity of output. So, what have we found? The expansion path! We could also solve for the optimal amount of labor for every quantity of capital, but it's easier to graph the expansion path with K^* as a function of L^*. Notice that any Cobb–Douglas production function with exponents α and $(1-\alpha)$ generates a linear expansion path with slope

$$\frac{\alpha}{(1-\alpha)}\frac{W}{R}$$

This linear expansion path is yet *another* useful property of the Cobb–Douglas functional form.

6A.2 figure it out

Using the information from Figure It Out 6A.1, derive the firm's expansion path.

Solution:

Because we've already solved the expansion path for the generalized Cobb–Douglas production function, we can plug in the parameters from the firm's cost-minimization problem ($\alpha = 0.2$, $W = \$10$, $R = \$15$)

into the equation for the expansion path we found above:

$$K^* = \left[\frac{\alpha}{(1-\alpha)}\frac{W}{R}\right]L^* = \frac{0.2(10)}{0.8(15)}L^* = 0.167L^*$$

Therefore, when minimizing costs, this firm will always choose a combination of inputs in which there is 6 times as much labor as capital, no matter what its desired output is.

Problems

1. For the following production functions,
   - Find the marginal product of each input.
   - Determine whether the production function exhibits diminishing marginal returns to each input.
   - Find the marginal rate of technical substitution and discuss how $MRTS_{LK}$ changes as the firm uses more L, holding output constant.
   a. $Q(K,L) = 3K + 2L$
   b. $Q(K,L) = 10K^{0.5}L^{0.5}$
   c. $Q(K,L) = K^{0.25}L^{0.5}$

2. A more general form of the Cobb–Douglas production function is given by

   $$Q = AK^{\alpha}L^{\beta}$$

   where A, α, and β are positive constants.
   a. Solve for the marginal products of capital and labor.
   b. For what values of α and β will the production function exhibit diminishing marginal returns to capital and labor?
   c. Solve for the marginal rate of technical substitution.

3. Catalina Films produces video shorts using digital editing equipment (K) and editors (L). The firm has the production function $Q = 30K^{0.67}L^{0.33}$, where Q is the hours of edited footage. The wage is \$25, and the rental rate of capital is \$50. The firm wants to produce 3,000 units of output at the lowest possible cost.
   a. Write out the firm's constrained optimization problem.
   b. Write the cost-minimization problem as a Lagrangian.
   c. Use the Lagrangian to find the cost-minimizing quantities of capital and labor used to produce 3,000 units of output.
   d. What is the total cost of producing 3,000 units?
   e. How will total cost change if the firm produces an additional unit of output?

4. A firm has the production function $Q = K^{0.4}L^{0.6}$. The wage is \$60, and the rental rate of capital is \$20. Find the firm's long-run expansion path.

Costs

7

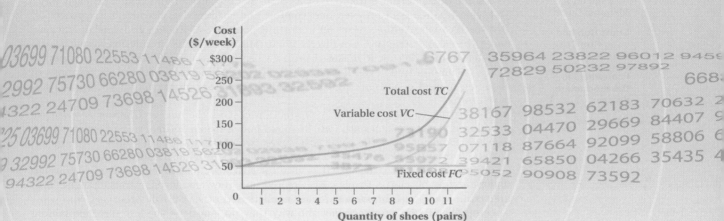

Cost ($/week)

$300
250
200
150
100
50
0

Total cost *TC*

Variable cost *VC*

Fixed cost *FC*

1 2 3 4 5 6 7 8 9 10 11

Quantity of shoes (pairs)

yanair is one of the largest and fastest-growing airlines in the world. It started flying in 1985 and, after an initial brush with financial problems in 1990, found its key to success: building a cost structure so low that its European customers, who were accustomed to dowdy and expensive national carriers, started flying Ryanair all over the continent. Ryanair's total passenger traffic increased almost 20-fold between 1997, when it launched its first routes outside Ireland and the United Kingdom, and 2011. In the five years from 2005 to 2010 alone, the number of passengers Ryanair carried grew by almost 38 million. To put that in perspective, this additional number of passengers equals about 7 months' worth of traffic for *all* airlines at London's busy Heathrow Airport.

Ryanair's cost-consciousness is famous. To save landing fees, it rarely flies to a city's main airport. Instead, it flies to secondary airports often located far away from the main city. (For example, its flights to Frankfurt, Germany, arrive at Frankfurt Hahn Airport, 78 miles [126 km] from Frankfurt's city center.) Its pilots are only allowed to load the legally mandated minimum requirement of fuel for each trip. The seats on its planes don't recline; the way Ryanair sees it, that's just a source of unnecessary maintenance costs. Nor do the seats have tray tables or seatback pockets—too much extra weight means extra fuel. Ryanair has discussed squeezing in 6 more seats on each plane—by getting rid of all but one of the plane's bathrooms. You better check yourself in for your flight online; it costs €40 (about $55 in 2011) to do it at the airport. (Ryanair doesn't like to employ a lot of desk agents.) To keep it simple, Ryanair only handles point-to-point itineraries. If you want to make a connection, you have to book two separate tickets. And if you miss your connection, even if you missed it because it was Ryanair's fault your first flight was late, you have to pay for a new ticket. This last rule might seem harsh until you realize that some of the airline's flights cost as little as €9 (a little more than $12) each way.

Flying Ryanair isn't for everyone; comfort and customer service aren't its specialties. But the Ryanair example raises an important point: Costs are key to firms' operations, and a firm's cost structure is a hugely important factor in its production decisions and in determining whether it makes a profit. Costs play a crucial part in determining a firm's optimal output level, how much the firm should grow or shrink in response to changing market conditions, and how easily it can start producing another product if it wants to.

We started to look at a firm's production cost at the end of Chapter 6 when we introduced the expansion path (which shows how a firm's optimal mix of inputs varies with total output) and the total cost curve (which shows a firm's cost of producing particular quantities of output). These two concepts provide the foundation for understanding a firm's cost structure. It is vital for a firm's management to have a thorough understanding of what a firm's costs are and how they change as output changes. This understanding is also important for economists and other outside observers who want to comprehend why producers act the way they do, and it is the key force explaining where supply curves come from (a topic we explore in Chapter 8). In this chapter, we examine the nature of a firm's costs by considering how a firm's production function and level of output determine its costs, given the prices of its inputs. We also consider how a firm's costs vary between the short run and the long run.

7.1 Costs That Matter for Decision Making: Opportunity Costs

accounting cost
The direct cost of operating a business, including costs for raw materials.

economic cost
The sum of a producer's accounting and opportunity costs.

opportunity cost
The value of what a producer gives up by using an input.

Economists think about cost differently than many others do. Most people are familiar with **accounting cost,** the direct cost of operating a business, including costs for raw materials, wages paid to workers, rent paid for office or retail space, and the like. **Economic cost**—the cost that economists pay attention to—includes accounting cost and something else: the producer's opportunity cost. **Opportunity cost** is what the producer gives up by using an input, whether that use is associated with an accounting cost or not. What the producer gives up is the return the input would earn in its next-best use: If a firm is using an input to do one thing, it is giving up the ability to use the input for something else. The lost value of this "something else" is the input's opportunity cost.

To operate its flight schedule, for example, Ryanair keeps on hand an inventory of fuel. You might think that because Ryanair has already paid for the fuel, there is no longer any cost associated with it. But that statement is based on the notion of accounting cost, not economic cost. If we think about the fuel's economic cost, then we quickly realize that it has an opportunity cost: Ryanair could sell the jet fuel to other companies instead of using the fuel itself. When might the airline choose to do this? Let's say the demand for its no-frills flights decreases (maybe a new, even lower cost airline enters the market). Now Ryanair makes fewer flights and is left with excess fuel. Savvy, cost-cutting company that it is, Ryanair isn't going to just sit on the excess fuel; it's going to sell the fuel, because Ryanair executives recognize opportunity cost.

It is important to understand the distinction between economic cost and accounting cost because production decisions are made, or at least *should* be made, based on economic cost, not accounting cost. Ryanair should use its jet fuel for flights only if that is the most profitable use for it. That is, the firm should consider its **economic profit** (total revenue minus economic cost) rather than its **accounting profit** (total revenue minus accounting cost).

When thinking about the most cost-effective use of its inputs, it doesn't matter if Ryanair's accounting profit is positive. If its *economic* cost is large enough, its economic profit may be negative. In this case, it may make more sense for the firm to have fewer flights and sell its excess fuel to another company. Making decisions about the use of inputs using only accounting cost can lead to profit-losing practices.

The recognition that a firm's decisions about production must be based on economic cost (which takes into account a firm's opportunity costs) underlies *everything* we discuss about costs in the rest of this chapter and throughout the remaining chapters of this book. Unless otherwise stated, when we talk about a firm's costs, we are talking about its economic costs.

economic profit
A firm's total revenue minus its economic cost.

accounting profit
A firm's total revenue minus its accounting cost.

 application

Making Big Money by *Not* Operating Your Business—a Lesson about Opportunity Cost

When electricity prices spiked in California in the summer of 2000, many businesses and homeowners winced as they saw their power bills rise to several multiples of their normal levels. However, one set of producers (besides the power generators) made out very well that summer: aluminum companies. Why was that? Because they decided to *not* make aluminum. This wasn't because their customers didn't want aluminum anymore. Instead, it was all about opportunity costs.

Aluminum smelting—the process through which metallic aluminum is extracted from ore—is done through electrolysis, which consumes massive amounts of electricity. Because of their need for a reliable supply of so much power, aluminum companies typically sign multiyear contracts with power generators that guarantee delivery of electricity at a price agreed upon in the contract.

The key to understanding why aluminum companies benefited so much from sky-high electricity prices, and why they acted as they did, is to recognize that the pre-specified prices in the aluminum companies' electricity supply contracts did *not* reflect the companies' true economic cost for electricity. By using that power to refine aluminum as they usually would, the firms would be giving up the ability to use that electricity for its next-best use. The value of this next-best use was the aluminum companies' opportunity cost of its electricity, which in this case was the price at which the aluminum smelters could sell that power back to the electrical grid.

During the price spike of 2000, this sell-back price was very high compared to the delivery price in the smelters' contracts. This meant that even though the contractual rate for the aluminum companies' electricity purchases hadn't changed, their economic costs of smelting aluminum, which included the opportunity cost of their electricity use, were extremely high.

How did they respond to these high economic costs? They stopped being aluminum companies and started being electricity companies. The firm Kaiser Aluminum, for example, shut down its plant and took the power that it had earlier contracted to obtain for $22.50 per megawatt-hour (MWh) and sold it back for $555 per MWh—or about 25 times what they paid! Kaiser made millions that year by *not* operating its plant. Kaiser's employees benefited from this recognition of opportunity costs, too: Under pressure from unions and local and federal politicians, the company continued to pay its employees full wages while the plant was shut down—and it still made a profit. ∎

7.1 figure it out

Cooke's Catering is owned by Daniel Cooke. For the past year, Cooke's Catering had the following statement of revenues and costs:

Revenues	$500,000
Supplies	$150,000
Electricity and water	$15,000
Employee salaries	$50,000
Dan's salary	$60,000

Dan has always had the option of closing his catering business and renting out his building for $100,000 per year. In addition, Dan currently has job offers from another catering company (offering a salary of $45,000 per year) and a high-end restaurant (at a salary of $75,000 per year). Dan can only work one job at any time.

    a. What is Cooke's Catering's accounting cost?

    b. What is Cooke's Catering's economic cost?

    c. What is Cooke's Catering's economic profit?

Solution:

    a. Accounting cost is the direct cost of operating a business. This includes supplies, utilities, and salaries:

$$\text{Accounting cost} = \$150,000 + \$15,000 + \$50,000 + \$60,000 = \$275,000$$

    b. Economic cost includes both accounting cost and the opportunity costs of owner-supplied resources. Dan's opportunity costs include the rent he could earn on his building ($100,000) and the opportunity cost of his time. Because Dan could give up the store and earn a higher salary at the restaurant, we need to take into account the difference in the salary he could earn ($75,000) and the salary he currently earns ($60,000). Note that his offer with the caterer is not relevant because opportunity cost measures the value of the next best alternative, which is working at the restaurant. Therefore, economic cost is Accounting cost + Opportunity costs:

$$\text{Economic cost} = \$275,000 + \$100,000 + \$15,000 = \$390,000$$

    c. Economic profit is equal to Total revenue − Economic cost = $500,000 − $390,000 = $110,000. Dan should continue to operate his catering business.

freakonomics

Paying for Papers: The Economics of Cheating

There's an old joke about an economics professor who got hauled into the dean's office after it was discovered that the professor had given the same exam to his students for four years in a row, not changing a single question. The dean admonished the professor, "If you never change the questions, the students can just memorize last year's solutions and get a perfect score!" Offended, the professor responded, "That's not true! The questions stay the same, but the answers change every year!" (Just to be clear, the professor had to have been a macroeconomist. In microeconomics, the answers rarely, if ever, change.)

Cheating by college students, like almost any human choice, can be understood using the tools of economics. The concept of opportunity cost is clearly central to the decision to cheat. Studying for exams, working through problem sets, and writing essays are all time-intensive activities. To carry out these tasks requires foregoing other activities, like going to parties, earning money at a part-time job, or even studying for another class. Of course, hiring *some-one else* to write your essay or complete your problem set also has costs, including financial costs. The person who writes your essay also has opportunity costs, so in order to be willing to do your work, he or she will usually need to be paid. In addition there are other costs, such as the possibly life-changing punishment you will receive if caught, the guilt you will feel over cheating, and your continuing ignorance because you have not actually learned the material.

As with so many other goods and services produced in the modern economy, techno-logical progress has radically changed the economics of cheating. Before the Internet, the supply of people who could help cheaters was local—typically, classmates who also had high opportunity costs—meaning that the price of forged essays was likely to be high. The covert nature of the market also made it difficult for buyers and sellers to coordinate.

The Internet changed all that. The first generation of Internet-based cheating took the form of pre-written essays that with few or no tweaks would fit a college assignment. Need a paper on Adam Smith's economic theories in *The Wealth of Nations*? How about the symbolism of Big Brother in George Orwell's *1984*? A simple Google search yields a host of pre-written options, ranging in cost from free to $50. Following this path, however, runs a high chance of getting caught. It didn't take long for services such as Turnitin.com, which scours Internet web pages for evidence of plagiarism, to become popular destinations for faculty members.

More sophisticated cheaters turn to essay-writing mills that resist automatic detection. In the modern essay mill, writers from around the world pound out papers for American college students for a per-page fee. These services cater to a wide swath of students, from community college freshmen to Ph.D. candidates, and each paper is written to the buyer's specifications. Just as many U.S. companies have found it profitable to outsource manu-facturing to developing countries, U.S. students have discovered there is no shortage of offshore workers willing to write essays.

As for the quality of the essays-for-hire, that may be another story. After all, whoever is writing that essay is willing to do the work for less money than you are. For example, if you offer someone $100 to write a paper for you, it must be worth at least that amount to not have to write it yourself. That implies, from an economic standpoint, the opportunity cost of the writer's time is lower than yours. This could possibly mean that the writer has lower-paying job opportunities as a result of having relatively low human capital.

Thinking like an economist may actually help you get a better paper delivered. Remem-ber that people, including illicit-paper writers, respond to incentives. So be sure to make it clear that if you get an A on the essay, a sizable bonus will be forthcoming . . . unless you are kicked out of school.

7.2 Costs That Do Not Matter for Decision Making: Sunk Costs

Unlike opportunity costs, which a firm must always consider when making production decisions, there are some costs that should never be taken into account when making such decisions.

In Chapter 6, we learned that some of a firm's costs are **fixed costs,** payments to inputs that must be used no matter what the output quantity is, even if it is zero. Suppose you own a restaurant. Some of your fixed costs would be rent (if you have

fixed cost
The cost of the firm's fixed inputs, independent of the quantity of the firm's output.

signed a lease), insurance, license fees, cookware, advertising expenses, and kitchen appliances such as the stovetop or a refrigerator. Now suppose your restaurant goes out of business. Even though you are no longer producing any output, you still must pay your fixed costs. However, you might be able to recover some of these. For example, you might sell the kitchen cookware and appliances, or you might also be able to sublet the building to another firm. Suppose that, instead of renting, you own the building and equipment. You can still probably recover some of your fixed cost by selling or renting these items to other firms. These types of fixed costs are sometimes said to be *avoidable* because the firm can take action so that it does not have to pay them if it stops operating.

Some fixed costs, however, are not avoidable. This type of cost is called a **sunk cost.** Once such a cost is paid by a firm, it can never be recovered. For your restaurant, for example, license fees and advertising costs are sunk. And if you've signed long-term rental agreements and are not allowed to sublet the building or equipment, you are on the hook for all the remaining rental payments even if you close the restaurant before the agreements expire. These remaining payments are sunk—you cannot recover them even by shutting down.

To sum up: If a fixed cost is avoidable, then it is not a sunk cost. If a firm cannot recover an expense even when shut down, then it is a sunk cost. The difference between sunk cost and avoidable fixed cost is crucial to the decisions a firm makes about how it will react if things begin to go south and the firm suffers a downturn in its business.

One part of a firm's cost that is sunk is the difference between what the firm still owes on its fixed capital inputs (such as the equipment and cookware at your restaurant) and what the firm can resell this capital for. This difference should be relatively small for restaurant equipment, for example, because most of it can be easily used by other restaurants—a grill is handy for almost any foodservice business—and there are active used equipment and rental markets that make it easy to find possible buyers.

Now suppose that your restaurant has a space theme, so every booth is shaped and painted as if it were the inside of a spaceship, and the tables look like control panels. Such booths, tables, and other items (menus, staff uniforms/spacesuits, etc.) tied specifically to your space-themed restaurant are not of much use to other restaurants, unless you happen to get lucky and find a similarly themed restaurant looking to expand. The cost of these booths and other space-themed equipment is likely to be sunk because you cannot recover it even if you shut down.

As you can see from this last example, whether capital can be used by another firm is an important determinant of sunk costs. Capital that is not very useful outside of its original application is called **specific capital.** Expenditures on buildings or machines that are very specific to a firm's operations are likely to be sunk, because the capital will have little value in another use.

Sunk Costs and Decisions

An important lesson about sunk costs is that once they are paid, *they should not affect current and future production decisions*. The reason for this is simple: Because they are lost no matter what action is chosen next, they cannot affect the relative costs and benefits of current and future production decisions.

For example, you've no doubt attended an event like a concert, sporting event, or show where you became bored well before the event ended. Should you have felt compelled to stay because you paid so much for the ticket? No. Once you are at the event, the ticket price is sunk—it's gone whether or not you decide to stay at the event. So, if you are asking yourself, "Should I stay or should I go?" (was it a Clash concert?), the ticket price shouldn't affect your answer. Whether the ticket price was $1 or $1,000, that cost is sunk and cannot be recovered whether you stay or leave. The only thing that you should consider in deciding to stay or go is whether you will have more fun

sunk cost
A cost that, once paid, the firm cannot recover.

specific capital
Capital that cannot be used outside of its original application.

doing something else (going for a walk, taking a nap, or calling a friend). If the alternative would be more entertaining, then you should go.

To put this in a production context, let's go back to our restaurant example. You, as the owner, are deciding between staying open for business or shutting down operations. Some of the restaurant's costs are sunk costs, including nonavoidable fixed costs and the possible losses you would incur if you had to resell capital for less than it is worth. These costs are not recoverable and must be paid whether the restaurant remains open or is shut down. In thinking about staying open for business, you know there will be some potential benefits (the money brought in from selling meals and drinks—your output), but there will also be definite costs (paying the waitstaff, purchasing ingredients, or turning on the heat or air conditioning). These benefits can be defined as the firm's **operating revenue,** while these costs are called **operating costs.** If you decide to shut down, you don't have to pay operating costs, but you also won't reap any benefit (operating revenue) either.

If business falls off, then, how should you decide whether to stay open for business or close the doors? Generally, the restaurant should stay open if the value of staying open is greater than the value of shutting down. But here's the important part: *Sunk costs should not enter into this decision.* You are going to lose your sunk costs whether you keep the restaurant open or not, so they are irrelevant to your decision about your restaurant's future. Therefore, the choice between staying open and shutting down depends *only* on whether the firm's expected revenues are greater than its expected operating costs. If it's going to cost you more to stay open than you'll bring in, you should close the restaurant. It doesn't matter if you are facing one dollar or one million dollars of sunk costs.

The Sunk Cost Fallacy   This stay-open or shut-down decision might sound simple enough. When faced with actual choices that involve sunk costs, however, people and firms sometimes have a difficult time making such decisions because they do not think properly about sunk costs. If they make the mistake of allowing sunk costs to affect their decisions, they commit what economists call the **sunk cost fallacy.** In making economic, finance, and life decisions, you want to avoid falling victim to this fallacy, but it's not hard to imagine scenarios where you might be tempted to do so.

Suppose, for example, that you are responsible for overseeing the construction of a new manufacturing facility for your firm. Construction has gone on for 3 years and has cost $300 million thus far (we'll assume this entire expenditure is sunk—the factory is specialized enough so that you can't sell it to another firm), and will need another 6 months and $50 million to complete. You then find out that a new and equally good production technology has just become available. Implementing this new technology would require an entirely different factory that will take only 6 months and $40 million to build. If you build this new factory, you can't use any part of the factory you are currently building. What should you do?

The correct answer is that you should stop the original building project and begin constructing the new factory. That's because the $300 million (and the prior 3 years) are sunk costs. They are lost whether you finish the first project or abandon it. The only comparison that should affect your decision, then, is between the relative benefits of finishing the first project and building an entirely new factory. Both will result in equally good production facilities in the same timeframe, but the new factory will cost only $40 million rather than the $50 million you would spend to complete the original factory. Thus, you should build the new factory. (This analysis assumes that the original building can be abandoned without incurring large costs—no more than $10 million.) Despite this logic, many people would be reluctant to let go of $300 million and 3 years of effort. The important point to realize is that the mere presence of this type of reluctance does not make it a good idea to give in to the temptation of the sunk cost fallacy.

operating revenue
The money a firm earns from selling its output.

operating cost
The cost a firm incurs in producing its output.

sunk cost fallacy
The mistake of letting sunk costs affect forward-looking decisions.

theory and data

Gym Memberships

"Should I stay or should I go?" applies to more than just a Clash concert, as economists Stefano DellaVigna and Ulrike Malmendier can attest to.* They studied consumers' actual behavior in buying—and using—gym memberships.

What they found probably won't surprise you: People are overly optimistic about how many times they'll go to the gym. Members who bought a membership that allowed unlimited visits ended up going to the gym just over four times per month on average, making their average cost per visit about $17. They did this even though the gym offered 10-visit passes for $100 (i.e., $10 per visit). This added up to an average overpayment for each member of about $600 over the course of their membership.

People often buy these memberships with the hope that such behavior will induce them to go to the gym more often. The fact that people then don't take full advantage of their memberships might, at first glance, seem like an irrational action. But the key point is that a gym membership is a sunk cost. In other words, when you're sitting on the couch watching TV and debating whether you should go work out, you're not going to consider how much you paid for your membership. It's sunk, after all. You will, on the other hand, consider the opportunity cost of going to the gym—maybe you'd rather spend more time studying economics, or more likely, watching your favorite show. Whatever the reason, the fact that your decision is based on opportunity cost, not sunk cost, makes it sound economics, even if it's not what your doctor would recommend.

*Stefano DellaVigna and Ulrike Malmendier, "Paying Not to Go to the Gym," *American Economic Review* 96, no. 3 (2006): 694–719.

 application

Why Do Film Studios Make Movies That They Know Will Lose Money?

Its losses on *Waterworld* made Universal Studios want to scream.

The feature film industry is a multibillion dollar enterprise. Blockbuster movies like *Avatar* or franchises like *Star Wars* and *Harry Potter* drive the industry. A single major blockbuster movie can cost hundreds of millions of dollars, but there are no guarantees that people will like it enough to make back the costs. It is a risky business.

Sometimes while filming a movie, things go so wrong that the studio making the movie knows that it will almost certainly lose money. Yet, filmmakers often finish these movies and release them. Why they do this can be explained by the existence of sunk costs and their irrelevance to decision making.

One of the most infamous movie productions ever was *Waterworld*. You have probably never seen it—not many people did. It was nominated for four "Razzies" ("saluting the worst that Hollywood has to offer that year"), including worst picture, worst actor, worst director, and worst supporting actor.

Waterworld is set in a future in which the ice caps have melted and water covers the earth. Kevin Costner stars as the Mariner, a mutant who can breathe under water. His job is to protect (from the evil Smokers) a young girl who has what may be a map of land tattooed on her back. The movie was filmed almost entirely on and under water.

Waterworld was released by Universal Studios in 1995, and at the time it was the most expensive movie ever made: It cost almost $175 million to produce even before the marketing and distribution expenses, basically ensuring a loss no matter how well it was received. It ended up grossing only $88 million in the United States and about twice that abroad. Because studios get to keep only a portion of the total ticket sales, experts presume it flopped terribly.

Let's think through Universal's decision to complete the movie and release it. At the outset, the studio expected the movie to bring in $150 million of revenue (a 50% cut of $300 million of global ticket sales), and the movie's budget was $100 million with 96 days of filming.[1] As filming began, about $16 million of the $100 million expected costs were sunk—including Kevin Costner's minimum guaranteed salary of $14 million.

Waterworld Economics as of June (in millions of dollars)

Expected Profit	Expected Revenue	Expected Additional Cost	Sunk Cost
+50	+150	-84	-16

Things started to go wrong quickly. The filming location in Kawaihae Harbor on the Big Island of Hawaii was so windy that scores of the crew became seasick each day. The medicines to alleviate the symptoms made them drowsy and impaired their ability to use cameras and other equipment. Several divers suffered decompression sickness and embolisms from being underwater for too long. There were rumors of contractual meal penalties exceeding $2.5 million because of so many overtime shoots, and a one-minute action scene in the movie ended up taking more than five weeks to film. Every additional day of filming added something like $350,000 to the film's cost. A few months into filming, the movie was expected to take 120 days and cost $140 million. Of the $140 million, about $100 million was sunk. But, the movie remained on path to turn a small profit.

Waterworld Economics as of September (in millions of dollars)

Expected Profit	Expected Revenue	Expected Additional Cost	Sunk Cost
+10	+150	-40	-100

Then the biggest accident struck. The "slave colony," a multi-ton part of a metal set located out in the harbor, sank 160 feet, and had to be hauled up at great expense. It took 21 days. At this late point in the filming, the expected total costs had now risen to $175 million, with fully $140 million of them already sunk (in some cases, quite literally) and $35 million still needed to complete the project.

Waterworld Economics as of December (in millions of dollars)

Expected Profit	Expected Revenue	Expected Additional Cost	Sunk Cost
-25	+150	-35	-140

By now, the studio had to know the movie would lose money. If the studio considered sunk costs in making its decision to keep going or close down the production, it would have definitely stopped production. However, that would have been a mistake. To see why, compare the tradeoffs the studio faced when weighing whether to stop filming or to finish the movie. If the studio went ahead and paid the additional $35 million of expected costs to complete the movie, it would earn an expected $150 million of revenue. Of course, it would lose the $140 million of sunk costs, but that would also be true if the studio canceled production instead. Canceling would allow the studio to avoid the

[1] Movie accounting is both secretive and notoriously "flexible," so we present a stylized version of the movie's economics. For more information on movie economics and to see some gory details about what went wrong in the filming and the various cost overruns, plus a fair amount of movie gossip, see Charles Fleming, "That Sinking Feeling," *Vanity Fair*, August 1, 1995; and "Fishtar? Why 'Waterworld,' with Costner in Fins, Is Costliest Film Ever," *Wall Street Journal*, January 31, 1996.

incremental $35 million cost, but it would forgo the $150 million in expected revenue. Looking forward and ignoring sunk costs as it should have, then, the studio faced a choice between an expected incremental gain of $115 million ($150 million in revenue − $35 million in costs) from finishing the movie and an expected incremental loss of $115 million ($35 million in saved costs − $150 in lost revenue) from halting production.

To be sure, if Kevin Costner and the makers of the movie had had a crystal ball in June to see what terrible events would transpire and the massive costs that were to come, the decision would have been different. But, that was before the costs were sunk. In June they could have halted production at a loss of only $16 million. Discovering the problems only after having sunk $140 million, on the other hand, meant that it made sense for the movie's producers to hold their noses, take the plunge, and hope that the expected gain would materialize. That's why copies of *Waterworld* still grace literally dozens of home movie collections today. ■

7.3 Costs and Cost Curves

We've seen that a firm considers its economic costs when making decisions about how much output to produce. Remember that the firm's economic costs include both accounting and opportunity costs so that the costs of all inputs are considered.

Economic analysis of costs divides costs into two basic types: fixed costs and variable costs. As we learned in Chapter 6, fixed costs (FC) are the costs of the firm that do not depend on how much output the firm produces. They must be paid even if the firm produces no output. **Variable costs** (VC) are costs that change as the firm changes its quantity of output. Every cost is either a fixed or variable cost, so a firm's **total cost** (TC) is the sum of its fixed and variable costs: $TC = FC + VC$.

Fixed Cost

BMW has an assembly plant in Spartanburg, South Carolina, where the company manufactures what it calls its Sport Activity series of SUVs. BMW has to pay for the building and its basic operating costs—electricity, heating fuel, security, and so on—whether it makes 0 cars per day, 1 car per day, or 1,000 cars per day. These basic costs, sometimes called *overhead*, are types of fixed costs.

We often think of fixed costs as being related primarily to capital inputs, but labor input costs can sometimes be fixed, too. For example, if BMW hires security guards to ensure that the plant is not broken into or vandalized, they work and have to be paid regardless of the factory's output. Thus, the security guards' wages are part of fixed cost. Furthermore, if the assembly line workers' contracts specify that they must be paid for a certain number of hours of work regardless of whether the plant is building cars or not, those workers' salaries would also be part of fixed cost because those costs don't vary by output level.

If fixed costs aren't sunk, they *can* be avoided, but only if the firm closes its business and exits the market completely. Exiting the market is different from producing zero output. If BMW stops production at the plant but keeps possession of the plant and its capital, it still has to pay fixed costs for its capital inputs. Even if it owns the capital, those inputs still have an opportunity cost that will be borne by the firm. To close its business completely, BMW would have to sell off its plant and all the capital within it. Only by selling off its capital can BMW avoid paying its fixed costs.

Variable Cost

Variable cost is the cost of all the inputs that change with a firm's level of output. When a firm needs more of an input to make more output, the payment for that input counts as a variable cost.

variable cost
The cost of inputs that vary with the quantity of the firm's output.

total cost
The sum of a firm's fixed and variable costs.

For every hamburger McDonald's makes, for example, it has to buy the ingredients. Payments for buns, ketchup, and beef are included in variable cost. Most labor costs are part of variable cost as well. When more workers are needed to make more hamburgers, when more doctors are needed to treat more patients, or when more programmers are needed to write more computer code, these additional workers' wages and salaries are added to variable cost. Some capital costs can also be variable. Suppose a construction firm occasionally rents a crane to build houses. If it has to rent more cranes when it builds more houses, the extra rental payments are included in variable cost. If it owns the cranes, and they wear out faster when they are used more often, this depreciation (the crane's loss in value through use) is part of variable cost as well, because the amount of depreciation depends on the firm's output.

Flexibility and Fixed versus Variable Costs

There is an important relationship between how easy it is for a firm to change how much of an input it uses and whether the cost of that input is considered part of fixed or variable cost. When a firm can easily adjust the levels of inputs it uses as output changes, the costs of these inputs are variable. When a firm cannot adjust how much of an input it buys as output varies, the input costs are fixed.

Time Horizon   The chief factor in determining the flexibility of input levels, and therefore whether the costs of the input are considered fixed or variable, is the time span over which the cost analysis is relevant.

Over very short time periods, many costs are fixed because a firm cannot adjust these input levels over short spans of time even if the firm's output level changes. As the time horizon lengthens, however, firms have greater abilities to change the levels of all inputs to accommodate output fluctuations. Given a long enough time span, all inputs are variable costs: There are no long-run fixed costs. This concept is very closely related to the distinction between short- and long-run production functions in Chapter 6, in which capital inputs are fixed in the short run and flexible in the long run.

Let's again suppose you run a small restaurant. On a given day, many of your costs are fixed: Regardless of how many customers come to eat, you are paying for the building, the kitchen equipment, and the dining tables. You've scheduled the cooks and waitstaff, so unless you can dismiss them early, you must pay them whether or not you are busy that day. About the only costs that are variable on an hour-to-hour basis are the food ingredients (if you make no omelets, you don't have to pay for more eggs) and the natural gas that heats the grill (if you don't have to turn the grill on to cook as much, you won't use as much gas).

Over a month, more of the restaurant's input costs become variable. You can schedule more workers on days that tend to be busy and fewer on slow days, for example. You can also choose hours of operation that exclude times which are sluggish, so that you only pay for full light and air conditioning when you are open and expect to be busy. All of those are variable costs now. But, you still have a one-year lease no matter what you produce, so that's a fixed cost.

Over longer horizons, even the building becomes a variable cost. If business isn't what you thought it would be when you first opened, you can terminate the lease (or sell the building if you own it). If business is great, you can build an addition. In the long run, all inputs are variable and so are the firm's costs.

Other Factors   Other features of input markets can sometimes also affect how easily firms may adjust their input levels, and thus determine their relative levels of fixed and variable costs.

One such factor is *the presence of active capital rental and resale markets*. These markets allow firms that need certain pieces of machinery or types of buildings only occasionally (like the construction firm above that sometimes needs a crane to build houses) to pay for the input just when it's needed to make more output. Without rental markets, firms would have to buy such inputs outright and make payments whether they use the inputs or not. By making capital inputs more flexible, rental markets shift capital costs from fixed to variable costs.

A great example of how rental markets have changed what costs are considered fixed and variable comes from the airline industry. In the past, airlines owned virtually all their planes. Today, however, about one-half of commercial jet aircraft worldwide are leased. Sometimes airlines lease planes directly from Airbus or Boeing, but more often they use specialized aircraft-leasing companies such as GE Capital Aviation Services or International Lease Finance Corporation. These leasing companies buy planes from manufacturers (over 30% of new aircraft are sold directly to specialized leasing companies) and then lease them out under contract to airlines needing extra capacity. If the capacity is no longer needed, the airline returns the plane to the leasing company, which typically then leases the plane to another airline that needs more capacity. These big leasing companies make the market for passenger airplanes very flexible, making it less likely that airlines will be stuck paying for planes when they have low demand. An active resale market for capital can function the same way as a rental. If you buy a textbook for $150, but there are students who will buy a used book from you at any time for $100, then it's as if you are renting the book for $50.

Labor contracts are another factor that affects the fixed versus variable nature of labor costs. Some contracts require that workers be paid a specified amount regardless of how much time they spend producing output. These payments are fixed costs. For example, U.S. automakers began running what were called "jobs banks" for their laid-off workers during the mid-1980s. These programs required that laid-off workers receive 95% of their regular salary, retain their health benefits, and continue to accrue pension benefits until they reach retirement age. (Jobs banks were a negotiated incentive for the United Auto Workers union—the UAW—to accept increased automation in factories.) Because of these contractual conditions, automakers' labor costs changed very little with their output. Jobs banks made autoworkers' pay a fixed cost; it was roughly the same whether or not the workers were building cars. In the face of declining sales, this high-fixed-cost structure was deadly for the automakers, and became one of many contributing factors to the Detroit Three's financial troubles from 2007 to 2009. The UAW, perhaps recognizing this, agreed to suspend the jobs bank program in late 2008. It wasn't enough, however: Chrysler and GM filed for bankruptcy in early 2009. In 2009 the federal government provided Chrysler and GM with $28.4 billion in loans. Part of the bailout agreement was a requirement for these firms to dramatically cut their fixed costs and restructure their businesses. In 2011 both firms were profitable for the first time in years.

Deriving Cost Curves

When producing output, firms face varying levels of the types of costs discussed above. The nature and size of a firm's costs are critically important in determining its profit-maximizing production behavior. To understand why firms act as they do, we have to recognize how their costs change with their production choices, and in particular with their choice of how much output to produce. The relationship between different types of costs and output is summarized in **cost curves.**

cost curve
The mathematical relationship between a firm's production costs and its output.

There are different types of cost curves depending on what kind of costs are being related to the firm's output. An example might be the most useful way to understand the different types of curves. Before we work through the example, however, it's important to note that both the costs and output quantities summarized by cost curves are measured over a particular time period. There can be hourly, daily, or yearly cost curves, for example. The specific period depends on the context, and as we discussed, what cost is fixed and what cost is variable depend on the time frame.

Consider the example of Fleet Foot (FF), a running shoe company. In the short run, FF uses fixed inputs (such as machinery) and variable inputs (such as labor and materials) to produce shoes. Table 7.1 shows the weekly costs for FF. These cost data are also shown graphically in Figure 7.1.

Table 7.1 | Fixed, Variable, and Total Cost for Fleet Foot

Output Quantity Q (Pairs of Shoes per Week)	Fixed Cost FC ($ per Week)	Variable Cost VC ($ per Week)	Total Cost TC ($ per Week)
0	50	0	50
1	50	10	60
2	50	17.5	67.5
3	50	22.5	72.5
4	50	25	75
5	50	30	80
6	50	37.5	87.5
7	50	47.5	97.5
8	50	60	110
9	50	75	125
10	50	100	150
11	50	150	200
12	50	225	275

Figure 7.1 | Fixed, Variable, and Total Costs

Plotting the values from Table 7.1 generates the total, fixed, and variable cost curves for Fleet Foot (FF). Because fixed cost is constant at $50 per week, the fixed cost curve is horizontal. The variable cost curve rises with output: At lower outputs, it increases with output at a diminishing rate, while at higher outputs, it begins to rise at an increasing rate. The total cost curve is the sum of the fixed and variable cost curves. It runs parallel to the variable cost curve and is greater than the variable cost curve by the amount of the fixed cost.

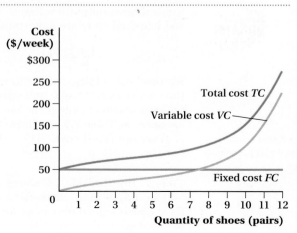

Fixed Cost Curve

Fixed cost does not vary with output, so it is constant and the fixed cost curve is horizontal. And because fixed cost must be paid in the short run even if the firm chooses to not produce anything, fixed cost is the same at $Q = 0$ as it is at every other level of output. As shown in Table 7.1, FF's fixed cost is $50 per week, so the fixed cost curve FC in Figure 7.1 is a horizontal line at $50.

Variable Cost Curve

Variable cost changes with the output level. Fleet Foot's variable cost rises as output increases because FF must buy a greater number of variable inputs. The relationship between the amount of variable inputs a firm must buy and its output means the slope of the VC curve is always positive. The shape of FF's particular VC curve in Figure 7.1 indicates that the *rate* at which FF's variable cost increases first falls and then rises with output. Specifically, the curve becomes flatter as weekly output quantities rise from 0 to 4 pairs of shoes, indicating that the additional cost of producing another pair of shoes is falling as FF makes more shoes. However, at quantities above 4 pairs per week, the VC curve's slope becomes steeper. This indicates that at these output levels, the additional cost of producing another pair of shoes is rising. We talk more about why this is the case later in the chapter.

Total Cost Curve

The total cost curve shows how a firm's total production cost changes with its level of output. Because all costs can be classified as either fixed or variable, the sum of these two components always equals total cost. In fact, as is clear in Figure 7.1, the total and variable cost curves have the same shapes and are parallel to one another, separated at every point by the amount of fixed cost. Note also that when output is zero, total cost isn't zero; it is $50. This is Fleet Foot's fixed cost, which must be paid in the short run even when the firm produces no output.

7.4 Average and Marginal Costs

Understanding the total cost curve (and its fixed and variable cost components) is an important part of analyzing firms' production behavior. To see why, we introduce two other cost concepts that play a key role in production decisions: average cost and marginal cost. In our Chapter 6 analysis of a firm's production decisions, we took the firm's desired output level as given. In the next few chapters, we will see that average and marginal costs are important in determining a firm's desired output level.

Average Cost Measures

Average cost is fairly straightforward. It's just cost divided by quantity. Since there are three costs (total, fixed, and variable), there are three kinds of average cost. Each of these measures examines the *per-unit* cost at that level of output. We compute these measures in Table 7.2 and illustrate them in Figure 7.2.

average fixed cost
A firm's fixed cost per unit of output.

Average fixed cost (AFC) is measured as fixed cost per unit of output, or

$$AFC = FC/Q$$

Column (6) of Table 7.2 shows average fixed cost AFC for Fleet Foot (FF). AFC falls as output rises. Since fixed cost doesn't change with the quantity of output, the fixed cost is spread over more and more units of output. The numerator (fixed cost) is constant while the denominator (quantity) rises, so average fixed cost becomes smaller and smaller as quantity goes up. Thus, as FF manufactures more running shoes, the average fixed cost it pays per pair of shoes declines.

Table 7.2 | **Costs for Fleet Foot**

(1)	(2)	(3)	(4)	(5)	(6)	(7)	(8)
Output Quantity Q	Fixed Cost FC	Variable Cost VC	Total Cost TC	Marginal Cost MC ($= \Delta TC/\Delta Q$) ($= \Delta VC/\Delta Q$)	Average Fixed Cost AFC ($= FC/Q$)	Average Variable Cost AVC ($= VC/Q$)	Average Total Cost ATC ($= TC/Q$)
0	50	0	50	—	—	—	—
1	50	10	60	10	50	10	60
2	50	17.5	67.5	7.5	25	8.75	33.75
3	50	22.5	72.5	5	16.67	7.5	24.17
4	50	25	75	2.5	12.5	6.25	18.75
5	50	30	80	5	10	6	16
6	50	37.5	87.5	7.5	8.33	6.25	14.58
7	50	47.5	97.5	10	7.14	6.79	13.93
8	50	60	110	12.5	6.25	7.5	13.75
9	50	75	125	15	5.56	8.33	13.89
10	50	100	150	25	5	10	15
11	50	150	200	50	4.55	13.64	18.18
12	50	225	275	75	4.17	18.75	22.92

Figure 7.2 | **Average Cost Curves**

We can construct the average fixed, average variable, and average total cost curves for Fleet Foot using the values from Table 7.2. As FF makes more pairs of shoes, the average fixed cost per pair decreases. The average variable cost initially decreases slightly and then increases after five pairs. Average total cost, the sum of average fixed and average variable costs, is U-shaped, and is separated from the average variable cost curve by the value of average fixed cost.

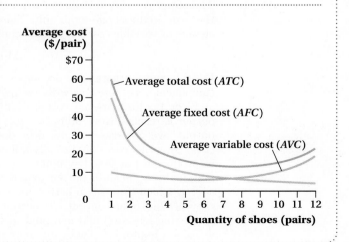

average variable cost
A firm's variable cost per unit of output.

Average variable cost measures the per-unit variable cost of production. It is calculated by dividing variable cost by the quantity of output:

$$AVC = VC/Q$$

Unlike average fixed cost, average variable cost can go up or down as quantity changes. In this case, it declines until five units are produced, after which it rises, leading to a U-shaped average variable cost curve.

average total cost
A firm's total cost per unit of output.

Average total cost is total cost TC per unit of output Q:

$$ATC = TC/Q$$

Average total cost for Fleet Foot is shown in the last column of Table 7.2. For FF, average total cost at first falls and then rises as output rises. Firms' average total costs often exhibit this sort of U-shaped pattern. To see why, first note that average total cost (ATC) is the sum of average fixed cost (AFC) and average variable cost (AVC):

$$ATC = TC/Q = (FC + VC)/Q$$
$$= FC/Q + VC/Q$$
$$= AFC + AVC$$

(This equation also implies that average fixed cost can be measured as the vertical distance between the average total cost curve and the average variable cost curve at any quantity.) Average total cost first falls as output rises because the dominant influence on average total cost is the rapidly declining average fixed cost. But as output continues to rise, average variable cost keeps increasing, first slowing the rate at which average total cost is falling and eventually causing average total cost to increase with output. These changes create a U-shaped average total cost curve.

Marginal Cost

marginal cost
The additional cost of producing an additional unit of output.

The other key cost concept is **marginal cost,** a measure of how much it costs a firm to produce one more unit of output:

$$MC = \Delta TC/\Delta Q$$

where ΔTC is the change in total cost and ΔQ is a one-unit change in output.

∂ The end-of-chapter appendix uses calculus to derive marginal costs from the total cost function.

Fleet Foot's marginal cost is shown in the fifth column of Table 7.2. It is the difference in total cost when output increases by one pair of shoes. But notice something else: Marginal cost also equals the difference in variable cost when one additional unit is produced. That's because, by definition, fixed cost does not change when output changes. Therefore, *fixed cost does not affect marginal cost*; only variable cost changes when the firm produces one more unit. This means marginal cost can also be defined as the change in variable cost from producing another unit of output:

$$MC = \Delta VC/\Delta Q \ (= \Delta TC/\Delta Q)$$

For this reason, there is no decomposition of marginal cost into fixed and variable cost components, as there was with average costs. Marginal cost is marginal variable cost.

Fleet Foot's marginal cost initially declines as output increases. After a certain output is reached (four units in Table 7.2), marginal cost begins to rise, and at higher output levels, it rises steeply. Why does marginal cost follow this pattern as quantity rises? Marginal cost may initially fall at low quantities because complications may arise in producing the first few units that can be remedied fairly quickly. Thus, declining marginal cost at lower output quantities could come from *learning by doing*, the process by which firms learn better, more efficient cost-lowering methods of production as they produce more output. As output continues to increase, however, these marginal cost reductions stop and marginal cost begins to increase with the quantity produced, as seen in Figure 7.3. There are many reasons why it becomes more and more expensive

Figure 7.3 Marginal Cost

Fleet Foot's marginal cost curve *MC* shows the additional cost of producing one more pair of shoes. It is U-shaped because average total cost decreases initially and then increases at higher output levels.

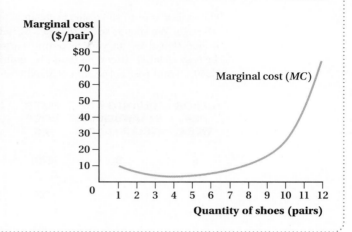

to make another unit as output rises: Decreasing returns to scale could kick in, capacity constraints may occur, inputs may become more expensive as the firm uses more of them, and so on.

Understanding the concept of marginal cost is critically important to firms' managers (and to your understanding of the next several chapters!). Marginal cost is one of the most central concepts in all of economics, and *it is the cost that matters for most of the key decisions a firm makes.*

7.2 figure it out

Fields Forever is a small farm that grows strawberries to sell at the local farmers' market. It produces strawberries using 5 acres of land that it rents for $200 per week. Fields Forever also hires labor at a price of $250 per week per worker. The table below shows how the output of strawberries (measured in truckloads) varies with the number of workers hired:

LABOR (WORKERS PER WEEK)	QUANTITY OF STRAWBERRIES (TRUCKLOADS PER WEEK)
0	0
1	1
3	2
7	3
12	4
18	5

Calculate the marginal cost of 1 to 5 truckloads of strawberries for Fields Forever.

Solution:

The easiest way to solve this problem is to add several columns to the table on the previous page. We should add fixed cost, variable cost, and total cost. Fixed cost is the cost of land that does not vary as output varies. Therefore, fixed cost is $200. Variable cost is the cost of labor. It can be found by multiplying the quantity of labor by the wage rate ($250). Total cost is the sum of fixed cost and variable cost.

LABOR PER WEEK	QUANTITY OF STRAWBERRIES (TRUCKLOADS)	FIXED COST, FC	VARIABLE COST, $VC = W \times L$	TOTAL COST, $TC = FC + VC$	MARGINAL COST, MC
0	0	$200	$250 \times 0 = \$0$	$200	—
1	1	200	$250 \times 1 = 250$	450	$250
3	2	200	$250 \times 3 = 750$	950	$500
7	3	200	$250 \times 7 = 1{,}750$	1,950	$1,000
12	4	200	$250 \times 12 = 3{,}000$	3,200	$1,250
18	5	200	$250 \times 18 = 4{,}500$	4,700	$1,500

Marginal cost is the change in total cost per unit increase in output, or $\Delta TC/\Delta Q$. When output rises from 0 units to 1 truckload of strawberries, total cost rises from $200 to $450. Therefore, the marginal cost of the first truckload of strawberries is $450 − $200 = $250. As output rises from 1 to 2 truckloads, total cost rises from $450 to $950, so the marginal cost is $950 − $450 = $500. When the third truckload is produced, total cost rises from $950 to $1,950 so marginal cost is $1,950 − $950 = $1,000. Production of the fourth truckload pushes total cost to $3,200, so the marginal cost of the fourth truckload is $3,200 − $1,950 = $1,250. When production rises from 4 to 5 truckloads, total cost rises from $3,200 to $4,700, so the marginal cost of the fifth truckload is $1,500.

We could have also calculated the marginal cost of each truckload by looking at only the change in variable cost (rather than the change in total cost). Because the amount of land is fixed, Fields Forever can only get more strawberries by hiring more labor and increasing its variable cost.

Relationships between Average and Marginal Costs

Because average cost and marginal cost are both derived from total cost, the two are directly related. If the marginal cost of output is less than the average cost at a particular quantity, producing an additional unit will reduce the average cost because the extra unit's cost is less than the average cost of making all the units before it. (This relationship is the same as that between the average and marginal products of labor we learned about in Chapter 6.) Suppose, for example, that a firm had produced nine units of output at an average cost of $100 per unit. If the marginal cost of the next unit is $90, the average cost will fall to ($900 + $90)/10 = $99, because the marginal cost of that extra unit is less than the average cost of the previous units.

This means that if the marginal cost curve is below an average cost curve for a particular quantity, average cost must be falling—that is, the average cost curve is downward-sloping. This is true whether we're talking about average total cost or average variable cost, because the marginal cost of producing another unit of output creates the same increment to both total and variable cost. This is also true even if, as is often the case, marginal costs are rising while they are below average costs. Producing another unit of output at a cost below the firm's current average will still bring down the average even if that marginal cost is rising with output. Just remember that the marginal cost curve is the cost at a specific output level—how much it costs to produce that specific unit—while average costs are averaging over all the previous units' costs, too.

This relationship is demonstrated in Figure 7.4, which shows an average total cost curve, an average variable cost curve, and a marginal cost curve all derived from a single total cost curve. At lower quantities, when the marginal cost curve is below the average cost curves, the average cost curves are downward-sloping.

When the marginal cost of the additional unit is above average cost, then producing it increases the average cost. Therefore, if the marginal cost curve is above an average cost curve at a quantity level, average cost is rising, and the average cost curve slopes up at that quantity. Again, this is true for both average total cost and average variable cost. This property explains why average variable cost curves and average total cost curves often have a U-shape. If marginal cost continues to increase as quantity increases, it eventually rises above average cost, and begins pulling up the average variable and average total cost curves.

The only point at which there is no change in average cost from producing one more unit occurs at the minimum point of the average variable and average total cost curves, where marginal and average cost are equal. These minimum points are indicated on Figure 7.4. (In the next chapter, we see that the point at which average and marginal costs are equal and average total cost is minimized has a special significance in competitive markets.)

∂ The online appendix derives the relationship between marginal and average costs. (http://glsmicro.com/appendices)

Figure 7.4   The Relationship between Average and Marginal Costs

When the marginal cost curve is below an average cost curve, the average cost curve is downward-sloping. At higher quantities, the marginal cost curve is above the average cost curve, and the average cost curve slopes upward. Therefore, the marginal cost curve intersects the average total and average variable cost curves at their minimums.

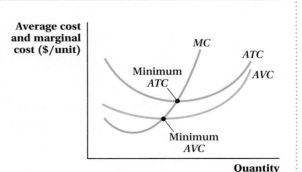

7.3 figure it out

Suppose a firm's total cost curve is $TC = 15Q^2 + 8Q + 45$, and $MC = 30Q + 8$.

a. Find the firm's fixed cost, variable cost, average total cost, and average variable cost.

b. Find the output level that minimizes average total cost.

c. Find the output level at which average variable cost is minimized.

Solution:

a. Fixed cost is a cost that does not vary as output changes. We can find FC by calculating total cost at zero units of output:

$$TC = 15(0)^2 + 8(0) + 45 = 45$$

Variable cost can be found by subtracting fixed cost from total cost:

$$VC = TC - FC = (15Q^2 + 8Q + 45) - 45 = 15Q^2 + 8Q$$

Notice that, as we have learned in the chapter, VC depends on output; as Q rises, VC rises.

Average total cost is total cost per unit or TC/Q:

$$ATC = \frac{TC}{Q} = \frac{15Q^2 + 8Q + 45}{Q}$$

$$= 15Q + 8 + \frac{45}{Q}$$

Average variable cost is variable cost per unit or VC/Q:

$$ATC = \frac{VC}{Q} = \frac{15Q^2 + 8Q}{Q}$$

$$= 15Q + 8$$

b. Minimum average total cost occurs when $ATC = MC$:

$$15Q + 8 + \frac{45}{Q} = 30Q + 8$$

$$15Q + \frac{45}{Q} = 30Q$$

$$\frac{45}{Q} = 15Q$$

$$15Q^2 = 45$$

$$Q^2 = 3$$

$$Q = \sqrt{3} = 1.732$$

c. Minimum average variable cost occurs where $AVC = MC$:

$$15Q + 8 = 30Q + 8$$

$$15Q = 0$$

$$Q = 0$$

7.5 Short-Run and Long-Run Cost Curves

Earlier in this chapter, we discussed how time horizons affect fixed and variable costs. Over longer periods of time, a firm has more ability to shift input levels in response to changes in desired output, making even "heavy-duty" capital inputs such as factories more flexible. In turn, this flexibility renders the firms' costs more variable and less fixed.

Recall from Chapter 6 that we defined the short-run production function as having a fixed level of capital, $\overline{K}$; that is, $Q = F(\overline{K}, L)$. In the long-run production function, $Q = F(K, L)$, capital can adjust. There is a related short-run versus long-run distinction in cost curves. Short-run cost curves relate a firm's production cost to its quantity of output when its level of capital is fixed. Long-run cost curves assume a firm's capital inputs can change just as its labor inputs can.

Short-Run Production and Total Cost Curves

A firm's **short-run total cost curve** shows the firm's total cost of producing different quantities of output when it is stuck at a particular level of capital $\overline{K}$. Just as there is a different short-run production function for every possible level of capital, so too is there a different short-run total cost curve for each capital level.

In Chapter 6, we saw that a firm's total cost curve (which relates cost and quantity of output) is related to its expansion path (which relates cost-minimizing input combinations to output). This relationship holds true in both the long run and the short run. However, in the short run, we must remember that a firm has only a fixed level of capital. Therefore, to examine how the firm minimizes its cost in the short run, we must examine the firm's expansion path given its fixed capital. Let's return to Ivor's Engines, the firm we looked at in Section 6.7. Figure 7.5 shows the same isoquants and

short-run total cost curve
The mathematical representation of a firm's total cost of producing different quantities of output at a fixed level of capital.

Figure 7.5 : **The Long-Run and Short-Run Expansion Path for Ivor's Engines**

Along Ivor's Engines long-run expansion path, the firm can change its level of capital. Along Ivor's short-run expansion path, capital is fixed at 6, and the expansion path is horizontal at $\overline{K} = 6$. Ivor's Engines can change its output quantity only by changing the quantity of labor used. At points X', Y, and Z', Ivor's Engines minimizes cost in the short run by using 5, 9, and 14 laborers to produce 10, 20, and 30 engines at a cost of \$120, \$180, and \$360, respectively. At $Q = 20$, the cost-minimizing capital and labor combination, Y, is the same in the long run and short run, and production cost is the same (\$180). At $Q = 10$ and $Q = 30$, production is more expensive in the short run than in the long run.

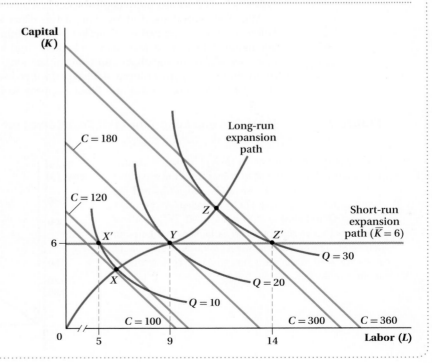

isocost lines we used to construct the long-run expansion path in Chapter 6. In the short run, Ivor's has a fixed capital level, and the expansion path is a horizontal line at that capital level. In the figure, we've assumed $\overline{K} = 6$. If the firm wants to adjust how much output it produces in the short run, it has to move along this line. It does so by changing its labor inputs, the only input it *can* change in the short run.

Suppose Ivor's Engines initially produces 20 units as shown by the isoquant $Q = 20$. Suppose also that the cost of producing 20 engines is minimized when 6 units of capital are employed. That is, the $Q = 20$ isoquant is tangent to the $C = \$180$ isocost line at point Y, when Ivor's capital inputs are 6. (We can justify this assumption by imagining that in the past, when it had the ability to change its capital input levels, Ivor's was making 20 engines and chose its optimal capital level accordingly.) The labor input level that minimizes the cost of producing 20 engines is $L = 9$ units.

To see the difference between short-run and long-run cost curves, compare the points on the isoquants on the short-run (fixed-capital) expansion path to those on the long-run (flexible-capital) expansion path. For an output level of 20 engines, these are the same (point Y) because we have assumed that a capital level of $K = 6$ was cost-minimizing for this quantity.

For the $Q = 30$ isoquant, however, the short-run and long-run input combinations are different. In the short run when capital is fixed at 6 units, if the firm wants to produce 30 units, it has to use the input combination at point Z', with 14 units of labor. But notice that Z' is outside (i.e., further from the origin than) the $C = \$300$ isocost line that is tangent to the long-run cost-minimizing input combination at point Z (which uses 11 units of labor). Instead, Z' is on the $C = \$360$ isocost line. In other words, it is more expensive for Ivor's Engines to produce 30 engines in the short run, when it cannot adjust its capital inputs. This is because it is forced to use more labor and less capital than it would if it could change all of its inputs freely.

The same property holds true if Ivor's wants to make 10 engines. When capital is fixed in the short run, the firm must use the input combination at point X' (with 5 units of labor). This point is on the $C = \$120$ isocost line, while the flexible-capital cost-minimizing input combination X is on the $C = \$100$ isocost line. So again, the firm's short-run total costs are higher than its long-run total costs. Here, it is because Ivor's is forced to use more capital than it would if it could adjust its capital inputs.

While we only looked at two quantities other than 20 engines, this general pattern holds at all other quantities. Whether Ivor's Engines wants to make more or fewer than 20 engines (the output level at which short- and long-run costs are the same), its total costs are higher in the short run than in the long run. Restricting the firm's ability to freely choose its capital input *necessarily* increases its costs, except when $Q = 20$ and the current level of capital and labor happens to be optimal.

∂ The end-of-chapter appendix uses calculus to derive short-run and long-run cost curves.

Figure 7.6 ┆ **Short-Run and Long-Run Total Cost Curves for Ivor's Engines**

The short-run total cost curve (TC_{SR}) for Ivor's Engines is constructed using the isocost lines from the expansion path in Figure 7.5. At Y, when $Q = 20$, TC_{SR} and the long-run total cost curve (TC_{LR}) overlap. At all other values of Q, including $Q = 10$ and $Q = 30$, TC_{SR} is above TC_{LR}, and short-run total cost is higher than long-run total cost. This is also true when $Q = 0$ since some input costs are fixed in the short run, while in the long run all inputs are flexible.

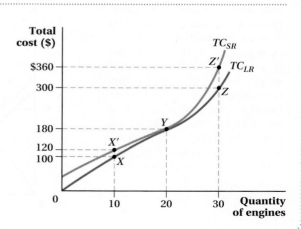

If we plot the total cost curves that correspond to these short- and long-run expansion paths, we arrive at Figure 7.6. The long-run total cost curve TC_{LR} is the same as when we assumed the firm was free to adjust all inputs to minimize costs. At $Q = 20$ engines, this curve and the short-run total cost curve TC_{SR} overlap because we assumed that capital was at the cost-minimizing capital level at this quantity. (We've labeled this point Y because it corresponds to the quantity and total cost combination at point Y in Figure 7.5.) For every other quantity, however, the short-run (fixed-capital) total cost curve is higher than the long-run (flexible-capital) total cost curve. Note that short-run total costs are positive when $Q = 0$ but zero in the long run. In other words, there are fixed costs in the short run but not in the long run when all inputs are flexible.

Short-Run versus Long-Run Average Total Cost Curves

From the total cost curves in Figure 7.6, we can construct Ivor's Engines long-run and short-run average total cost curves. These are shown in Figure 7.7. The long-run average total cost curve is ATC_{LR} and the short-run average total cost curve $ATC_{SR,20}$. (We add the "20" subscript to denote that the curve shows the firm's average total cost when its capital is fixed at a level that minimizes the costs of producing 20 units of output.)

As with the total cost curves, the short- and long-run average total cost curves overlap at $Q = 20$ engines, because that's where the firm's fixed capital level of 6 units is also cost-minimizing. Here, long-run and short-run average total costs are $180/20 = 9.

For all other output quantities, short-run average total cost is higher than long-run average total cost. Short-run total cost is higher than long-run total cost at every quantity level. Because average total cost divides these different total costs by the same quantity, average total cost must be higher in the short run, too. When Ivor's is making 30 engines with capital fixed at 6 units, its total costs are $360, and its short-run average total cost is $12 per unit. When it makes 10 engines, short-run average total cost is $120/10 = 12 per unit as well. These points on the short-run average total cost curve $ATC_{SR,20}$ are labeled Z' and X' to correspond to the analogous points on the short-run total cost curve in Figure 7.6. The long-run average total costs at 10 and 30 units are labeled Z and X, and these correspond to the similarly labeled points in Figure 7.6.

Up to this point, we've analyzed the distinction between long-run and short-run total and average total costs assuming that the short-run level of capital was fixed at 6 units, the level that minimized the cost of producing 20 engines. But suppose capital had been fixed at some other level instead. To be concrete, let's say it was fixed at 9 units of capital, the level that minimizes the cost of producing 30 engines. (This is the capital level at point Z in Figure 7.6.)

Figure 7.7   **Short-Run and Long-Run Average Total Cost Curves for Ivor's Engines**

The short-run average total cost curve ($ATC_{SR,20}$) and the long-run average total cost curve (ATC_{LR}) are constructed using TC_{SR} and TC_{LR} from Figure 7.6. At Y, when $Q = 20$ and the cost-minimizing amount of capital is 6 units, the ATC_{SR} and ATC_{LR} both equal $9. At all other values of Q, including $Q = 10$ and $Q = 30$, ATC_{SR} is above ATC_{LR}, and short-run average total cost is higher than long-run average total cost.

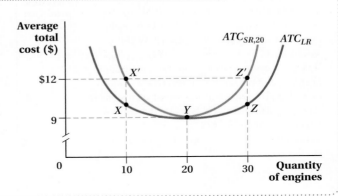

The analysis is exactly the same as above. The long-run total and average total cost curves don't change, because the firm will still choose the same capital inputs (resulting in the same costs) given its flexibility in the long run. However, the short-run cost curves change because the fixed level of capital has changed. By the same logic as above, the short-run total and average total cost curves will be above the corresponding long-run curves at every quantity except one. In this case, though, rather than overlapping at 20 units of output, it overlaps at $Q = 30$, because capital is now fixed at the cost-minimizing level for 30 engines. The logic behind why short-run total and average total costs are higher at every other quantity than 30 is the same: Not allowing the firm to change its capital with output raises the cost of producing any quantity except when the firm would have chosen that capital level anyway.

We can make the same comparisons with capital held fixed at 4 units, which minimizes the costs of producing 10 engines (corresponding to point X in Figure 7.6). Again, the same patterns hold. The short-run total and average total cost curves are higher at every quantity except $Q = 10$.

These other short-run average total cost curves are shown in Figure 7.8 along with $ATC_{SR,20}$ and the long-run average total cost curve ATC_{LR} from Figure 7.7. $ATC_{SR,10}$ and $ATC_{SR,30}$ show short-run average costs when the firm has a fixed capital level that minimizes the total costs of making 10 and 30 engines, respectively. As can be seen in Figure 7.8, the long-run average total cost curve connects the locations (only one per fixed capital level) at which the short-run average total cost curves touch the long-run curve. We could repeat our short-run analysis with capital held fixed at any level, and the short-run average total cost curve will always be higher than the long-run curve, except in one point. If we drew out every such short-run average total cost curve, they would trace the long-run average total cost curve just like the three we have shown in the figure. As economists say, the long-run average total cost curve is an "envelope" of short-run average total cost curves, because the long-run average total cost curve forms a boundary that envelops the entire set of possible short-run average total cost curves, as seen in Figure 7.8.

One interesting thing to notice about Figure 7.8 is that $ATC_{SR,10}$ and $ATC_{SR,30}$ do not touch ATC_{LR} at their lowest points. That's because even the output levels that minimize average total costs in the short run when capital is fixed (the low points on $ATC_{SR,10}$ and $ATC_{SR,30}$) can be produced more cheaply if capital inputs were flexible. In the one case where the short-run level of capital is fixed at the fully cost-minimizing level even if capital were flexible (the $ATC_{SR,20}$ curve), the two points are the same. For Ivor's Engines, this occurs at point Y, where output is 20 units.

Figure 7.8 | **The Long-Run Average Total Cost Curve Envelops the Short-Run Average Total Cost Curves**

$ATC_{SR,10}$ and $ATC_{SR,30}$ show short-run average costs when the firm has a fixed capital level that minimizes the total costs of making 10 and 30 engines, respectively. With, respectively, $\overline{K} = 4$ and $\overline{K} = 9$, $ATC_{SR,10}$ and $ATC_{SR,30}$ overlap ATC_{LR} at the cost-minimizing points X and Z, respectively. However, X and Z are not at the lowest points on $ATC_{SR,10}$ and $ATC_{SR,30}$ because the output levels that minimize $ATC_{SR,10}$ and $ATC_{SR,30}$ can be produced more cheaply if capital inputs are flexible.

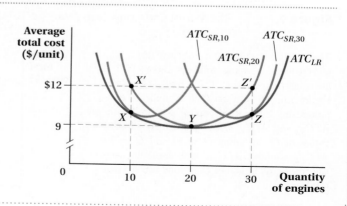

Steve and Sons Solar Panels has a production function represented by $Q = 4KL$, where the $MP_L = 4K$ and the $MP_K = 4L$. The current wage rate (W) is \$8 per hour, and the rental rate on capital (R) is \$10 per hour.

a. In the short run, the plant's capital stock is fixed at $K = 10$. What is the cost the firm faces if it wants to produce $Q = 200$ solar panels?

b. What will the firm wish to do in the long run to minimize the cost of producing $Q = 200$ solar panels? How much will the firm save? (*Hint*: You may have to review Chapter 6, to remember how a firm optimizes when both labor and capital are flexible.)

Solution:

a. If capital is fixed at $K = 10$ units, then the amount of labor needed to produce $Q = 200$ units of output is

$$Q = 4KL$$
$$200 = 4(10)L = 40L$$
$$L = 5$$

Steve and Sons would have to hire 5 units of labor. Total cost would be

$$TC = WL + RK = \$8(5) + \$10(10) = \$40 + \$100 = \$140$$

b. In Chapter 6, we learned that in the long run, a firm minimizes costs when it produces a quantity at which the marginal rate of technical substitution of labor for capital equals the ratio of the costs of labor (wage) and capital (rental rate): $MRTS_{LK} = W/R$. We know that

$$MRTS_{LK} = \frac{MP_L}{MP_K} = \frac{4K}{4L} = \frac{K}{L}$$
$$\frac{W}{R} = \frac{8}{10}$$

To minimize costs, the firm will set $MRTS_{LK} = W/R$:

$$10K = 8L$$
$$K = 0.8L$$

To produce $Q = 200$ units, we can substitute for K in the production function and solve for L:

$$Q = 200 = 4KL = 4(0.8L)(L)$$
$$200 = 3.2L^2$$
$$L^2 = 62.5$$
$$L = 7.91$$
$$K = 0.8L = (0.8)(7.91) = 6.33$$

To minimize cost, the firm will want to increase labor from 5 to 7.91 units and reduce capital from 10 to 6.33 units. Total cost will fall to

$$TC = WL + RK = \$8(7.91) + \$10(6.33) = \$63.28 + \$63.30 = \$126.58$$

Therefore, the firm will save $\$140 - \$126.58 = \$13.42$.

Short-Run versus Long-Run Marginal Cost Curves

Just as the short- and long-run average total cost curves are related to the total cost curve, so are marginal costs over the two time horizons. Long-run marginal cost is the additional cost of producing another unit when inputs are fully flexible.

Every short-run average total cost curve has a corresponding short-run marginal cost curve that shows how costly it is to build another unit of output when capital is fixed at some particular level. A short-run marginal cost curve always crosses its corresponding short-run average total cost curve at the minimum of the average total cost curve.

While a long-run average total cost curve is the envelope of all the short-run average total cost curves, this isn't true for short- and long-run marginal cost curves. Let's look at the relationship between the two step-by-step.

Figure 7.9 shows again the short- and long-run average total cost curves from Figure 7.8, and adds the short-run marginal cost curves corresponding to each short-run average total cost curve. ($MC_{SR,10}$ is the short-run marginal cost for $ATC_{SR,10}$, etc.)

How do we figure out what long-run marginal costs are? We know that in the short run with capital fixed, there is only one output level at which a firm would choose that same level of capital: the output at which the short-run average total cost curve touches the long-run average total cost curve. So, for example, if $Q = 10$, Ivor's Engines would choose a level of capital in the long run ($K = 4$) that is the same as that corresponding to short-run average total cost curve $ATC_{SR,10}$. Because the short- and long-run average total cost curves coincide at this quantity (but only at this quantity), so too do the short- and long-run marginal cost curves. In other words, because the firm would choose the same level of capital even if it were totally flexible, the long-run marginal cost *at this quantity* is the same as the short-run marginal cost on $MC_{SR,10}$. Therefore, to find the long-run marginal cost of producing 10 units, we can go up to the short-run marginal cost curve at $Q = 10$. This is point A in Figure 7.9 and represents the long-run marginal cost at an output level of 10 engines.

Likewise, the long-run marginal cost at $Q = 20$ is the value of $MC_{SR,20}$ when Ivor's Engines is making 20 engines. Therefore, long-run marginal cost at $Q = 20$ can be found at point Y in Figure 7.9 (this is the same point Y as in Figures 7.7 and 7.8). Repeating the logic, Ivor's long-run marginal cost for producing 30 engines equals the value of $MC_{SR,30}$ when output $Q = 30$, which is point B in the figure.

When we connect these long-run marginal cost points A, Y, and B, along with the similar points corresponding to every other output quantity, we trace out the long-run

Figure 7.9   Long-Run and Short-Run Marginal Costs

$MC_{SR,10}$, $MC_{SR,20}$, and $MC_{SR,30}$ are derived from $ATC_{SR,10}$, $ATC_{SR,20}$, and $ATC_{SR,30}$, respectively. The long-run marginal cost curve must intersect $MC_{SR,10}$, $MC_{SR,20}$, and $MC_{SR,30}$ at A, Y, and B, respectively, the points at which labor is cost-minimizing for $Q = 10$, $Q = 20$, and $Q = 30$ given, respectively, $\overline{K} = 4$, $\overline{K} = 6$ and $\overline{K} = 9$. Therefore, A, Y, and B are the long-run marginal costs for $Q = 10$, $Q = 20$, and $Q = 30$, respectively, and the long-run marginal cost curve MC_{LR} connects A, Y, and B.

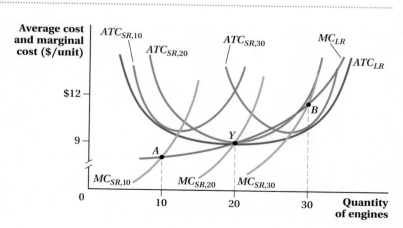

marginal cost curve MC_{LR}. Notice that, just as we have discussed, long-run marginal cost is below long-run average total cost when average total cost is falling (such as at point A), above long-run average total cost when average total cost is rising (such as at point B), and equal to long-run average total cost when average total cost is at its minimum (point Y).

7.6 Economies in the Production Process

Now that we have categorized the long-run average total cost, we want to examine how these average costs change as the firm size grows. Because all inputs are variable in the long run, we can consider how per-unit costs are affected as the firm alters its scale of operation. In other words, what happens to the firm's long-run average total cost as the firm increases all of its inputs by the same proportion?

Economies of Scale

We talked about returns to scale in Chapter 6. Remember that a production technology has increasing returns to scale if doubling all inputs leads to more than a doubling of output. If doubling all inputs exactly doubles output, returns to scale are constant, and if output less than doubles, there are decreasing returns to scale.

Economies of scale are the cost-based flip-side of returns to scale. Instead of looking at the way output changes in proportion to inputs, economies of scale look at the way cost changes in proportion to output. If doubling output causes cost to less than double, a firm has **economies of scale.** If doubling output causes cost to more than double, a firm has **diseconomies of scale.** If doubling output causes cost to double, a firm has **constant economies of scale.**

Because economies of scale imply that total cost increases less than proportionately with output, they also imply that long-run average total cost falls as output grows. That is, the long-run average total cost curve is downward-sloping when there are economies of scale because average total cost is total cost divided by output ($ATC = TC/Q$), and economies of scale imply the total cost rises at a slower rate than quantity. Similarly, diseconomies of scale imply an upward-sloping long-run average total cost curve because total cost rises more quickly than output. Constant economies of scale make the long-run average total cost curve flat.

Putting together these relationships, we can see what the typical U-shaped long-run average total cost curve implies about economies of scale. At low output levels (the left, downward-sloping part of the ATC curve where ATC is declining), total cost rises more slowly than output does. As a result, average total cost falls, and the firm has economies of scale.

At the very bottom of the average total cost curve where it is flat, average cost does not change, total cost rises proportionally with output, and marginal cost equals ATC. Here, therefore, average total cost increases at the same rate that output increases, and there are constant economies of scale.

At higher output levels (the right upward-sloping part of the ATC curve where ATC is rising), marginal cost is above average total cost, causing total cost to rise more quickly than output does. As a result, there are diseconomies of scale.

Economies of Scale versus Returns to Scale

Economies of scale and returns to scale are not the same thing. They are related—cost and the level of inputs move closely together—but there is a difference. Returns to scale describe how output changes when all inputs are increased by a common factor. But nothing says cost-minimizing firms must keep input ratios constant when they increase

economies of scale
Total cost rises at a slower rate than output rises.

diseconomies of scale
Total cost rises at a faster rate than output rises.

constant economies of scale
Total cost rises at the same rate as output rises.

7.5 figure it out

Suppose that the long-run total cost function for a firm is $LTC = 22,600Q - 300Q^2 + Q^3$ and its long-run marginal cost function is $LMC = 22,600 - 600Q + 3Q^2$. At what levels of output will the firm face economies of scale? Diseconomies of scale? (*Hint*: These cost functions yield a typical U-shaped long-run average cost curve.)

Solution:

If we can find the output that minimizes long-run average total cost, we can determine the output levels for which the firm faces economies and diseconomies of scale. We know that when $LMC < LATC$, long-run average total cost is falling and the firm experiences economies of scale. Likewise, when $LMC > LATC$, the long-run average total cost curve slopes up and the firm faces diseconomies of scale. So, if we can figure out where the minimum $LATC$ occurs, we can see where economies of scale end and diseconomies begin.

Minimum average cost occurs when $LMC = LATC$. But, we need to determine $LATC$ before we

begin. Long-run average total cost is long-run total cost divided by output:

$$LATC = \frac{LTC}{Q} = \frac{22,600Q - 300Q^2 + Q^3}{Q}$$

$$= 22,600 - 300Q + Q^2$$

Now, we need to set $LATC = LMC$ to find the quantity that minimizes $LATC$:

$$LATC = LMC$$
$$22,600 - 300Q + Q^2 = 22,600 - 600Q + 3Q^2$$
$$300Q = 2Q^2$$
$$300 = 2Q$$
$$Q = 150$$

Long-run average total cost is minimized and economies of scale are constant when the firm produces 150 units of output. Thus, at $Q < 150$, the firm faces economies of scale. At $Q > 150$, the firm faces diseconomies of scale. (You can prove this to yourself by substituting different quantities into the long-run average total cost equation and seeing if $LATC$ rises or falls as Q changes.)

output. So, the measure of economies of scale, which is about how total costs change with output, does not impose constant input ratios the way returns to scale does.

Because a firm can only reduce its cost more if it is able to change its input ratios when output changes, it can have economies of scale if it has constant or even decreasing returns to scale. That is, even though the firm might have a production function in which doubling inputs would exactly double output, it might be able to double output without doubling its total cost by changing the proportion in which it uses inputs. Therefore, increasing returns to scale imply economies of scale, but not necessarily the reverse.[2]

 **application**

Economies of Scale and Makin' Bacon

Examining the sizes of firms in an industry can often tell us about economies of scale. For example, U.S. Department of Agriculture economists James MacDonald and Michael Ollinger studied why meat-packing plants, and those that process pork in particular, have become so much larger in recent decades.[3] Plants that processed more

[2] The only case in which the two concepts are the same is when it happens to be optimal for the firm to hold input ratios constant as output increases. (This would show up as an expansion path that is a straight line extending out from the origin.) In this case, the firm gets no extra cost reduction from changing the proportions in which it uses its inputs as its output changes.

[3] James M. MacDonald and Michael E. Ollinger, "Scale Economies and Consolidation in Hog Slaughter," *American Journal of Agricultural Economics* 82, no. 2 (2000): 334–346.

than 1 million hogs per year accounted for 38% of the industry's output in 1977, but a whopping 87% of output only 15 years later. During the same period, one-third of the country's plants processing fewer than 50,000 hogs a year had shut down.

MacDonald and Ollinger hypothesized that the nature of scale economies in the industry had changed over that period. New technologies had reduced costs, especially at higher output levels. These new technologies could widen the output ranges over which processing plants experience economies of scale, allowing plants to become larger without increasing their average costs and, in fact, possibly decreasing average costs even further. We will see in later chapters that technologies that expand the downward-sloping portion of the average total cost curve can lead to higher optimal output levels.

To test their hypothesis, MacDonald and Ollinger needed to estimate the cost curves of pork-processing plants. Their task would have been easier if they had cost data from the same plant at different output levels, but they didn't. They only had annual data on plants' costs, and not many years of data for each plant. So, they used variation in output and cost levels *across* plants to measure the cost curves and assumed that every plant in the industry had the same cost curve—a bit of a stretch, perhaps, but probably a reasonable one given the standardized production methods.[4]

Figure 7.10 shows the long-run average total cost curves that MacDonald and Ollinger estimated from their data. Two long-run average total cost curves are shown: one for plants operating in 1977 and the other for plants operating in 1992. The figure also indicates the sizes at which the average-sized and 95th percentile plants operated in each year. (If the industry had 100 plants, the 95th percentile would be the fifth largest plant in the industry.) The curves show average total costs as an index, where costs are expressed as a percentage of average total costs for the average-sized plant in 1977.

The first thing to notice is that the industry definitely experienced total factor productivity growth; average total cost at all quantities fell over the 15 years. A plant in 1992 that was the same size as the average plant in 1977 had 4% lower average total cost than it had in 1977. Second, the cost decreases were larger for bigger plants. In 1977 the industry's largest plants (those around the 95th percentile) were operating at roughly the output quantity where economies of scale ended. This can be seen by the

Figure 7.10 | Average Total Cost Curves for Pork Processing Plants, 1977 and 1992

ATC_{1977} and ATC_{1992} are the long-run average total cost curves for pork processing plants in 1977 and 1992, respectively. Average total costs for both the average-sized plant and the 95th percentile plant were significantly lower in 1992 than in 1977. At the same time, the average-sized and 95th percentile plants grew in size. These findings support the idea that the cost structure and scale economies of the pork industry changed from 1977 to 1992.

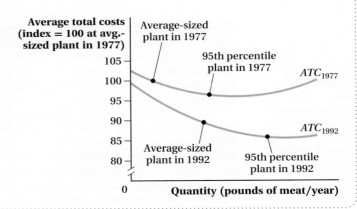

[4] The approach also raised the complication that input prices, which as we know from Chapter 6 affect plants' costs but are held constant when drawing a cost curve, likely varied across plants. MacDonald and Ollinger used statistical techniques to control for these differences and remove their influence from the estimated cost curves.

fact that they are located very near the bottom of the 1977 average total cost curve. But looking at the average total cost curve for 1992, we see that the *average-sized* plant in that year was just about as large as the 95th percentile plant in 1977, and its costs were still about 7% lower. Third, the average-sized plant in 1992 was still operating where there were substantial economies of scale. This is because new technologies had increased the range over which industry plants experienced scale economies. Industry plants became larger between 1977 and 1992 as a result. Fourth, not just the average, but the largest plants grew, too. The 95th percentile plant in 1992 was again operating near the output level where scale economies were exhausted, but this output level was much higher in 1992 than 1977. Had plants grown that large in 1977, they would have been operating on the upward-sloping part of the long-run average total cost curve, where there are diseconomies of scale.

Therefore, the results showed significant changes in the cost structure of these firms and the nature of scale economies. This may explain why so much production shifted to large plants in a relatively short period. ■

Economies of Scope

economies of scope
The simultaneous production of multiple products at a lower cost than if a firm made each product separately.

Many firms make more than one product. Just as economies of scale indicate how firms' costs vary with the quantity they produce, **economies of scope** indicate how firms' costs change when they make more than one product. Economies of scope exist when a producer can simultaneously make multiple products at a lower cost than if it made each product separately and then added up the costs.

To be more explicit, let's call a firm's cost of simultaneously producing Q_1 units of Good 1 and Q_2 units of Good 2 $TC(Q_1, Q_2)$. If the firm produces Q_1 units of Good 1 and nothing of Good 2, its cost is $TC(Q_1, 0)$. Similarly, if the firm produces Q_2 units of Good 2 and none of Good 1, its cost is $TC(0, Q_2)$. Under these definitions, the firm is considered to have economies of scope if $TC(Q_1, Q_2) < TC(Q_1, 0) + TC(0, Q_2)$. In other words, producing Q_1 and Q_2 together is cheaper than making each separately.

We can go beyond just knowing whether or not economies of scope exist, and actually quantify them in a way that allows us to compare scope economies across companies. We call this measure $SCOPE$, and it's the difference between the total costs of single-good production $[TC(Q_1, 0) + TC(0, Q_2)]$ and joint production $[TC(Q_1, Q_2)]$ as a fraction of the total costs of joint production. That is,

$$SCOPE = \frac{[TC(Q_1, 0) + TC(0, Q_2)] - TC(Q_1, Q_2)}{TC(Q_1, Q_2)}$$

If $SCOPE > 0$, the total cost of producing Goods 1 and 2 jointly is less than making the goods separately, so there are economies of scope. The greater $SCOPE$ is, the larger are the firm's cost savings from making multiple products. If $SCOPE = 0$, the costs are equivalent, and economies of scope are zero. And if $SCOPE < 0$, then it's actually cheaper to produce Q_1 and Q_2 separately. In other words, there are **diseconomies of scope.**

diseconomies of scope
The simultaneous production of multiple products at a higher cost than if a firm made each product separately.

There are two important things to remember about economies of scope. First, they are defined for a *particular* level of output of each good. Economies of scope might exist at one set of output levels—for example, 100 units of Good 1 and 150 units of Good 2—but not at a different pair, like 200 units of each, for instance. (The specificity of economies of scope to particular output levels is shared with economies of scale. As we discussed earlier in this section, for example, a U-shaped average total cost curve embodies changing scale economies over different output levels—positive economies at low output levels, negative ones at higher output.) Second, economies of scope do not have to be related to economies of scale. A firm can have one without the other or both at the same time. In fact, it gets a bit difficult to even define economies of scale once there are multiple outputs. We don't need to go into why this is so; it's enough to recognize that scale and scope economies are different things.

Why Economies of Scope Arise

There are many possible sources of scope economies. They depend on the flexibility of inputs and the inherent nature of the products.

A common source of economies of scope is when different parts of a common input can be applied to the production of the firm's different products. Take a cereal company that makes two cereals, bran bricks and wheat flakes. The firm needs wheat to produce either cereal. For bran bricks, it needs mostly the bran, the fibrous outer covering of the wheat kernel, but for wheat flakes, the firm needs the rest of the kernel. Therefore, there are natural cost savings from producing both cereals together. The wheat the firm buys can be split between the production of the two cereals. For example, if the firm makes only wheat flakes, the outer covering of the kernel of wheat might go to waste.

In oil refining, the inherent chemical properties of crude oil guarantee economies of scope. Crude oil is a collection of a number of very different hydrocarbon molecules; refining is the process of separating these molecules into useful products. It is physically impossible for a refining company to produce only gasoline (or kerosene, diesel, lubricants, or whatever petroleum product might be fetching the highest price at the time). While refiners have some limited ability to change the mix of products they can pull out of each barrel of crude oil, this comes at a loss of scope economies. That's why refineries always produce a number of petroleum compounds simultaneously.

The common input that creates scope economies does not have to be raw materials. For example, Google employees might be more productive using their knowledge about information collection and dissemination to produce multiple products (e.g., Google Earth, Google Docs, and Google+) than to produce just the main search engine.

7.7 Conclusion

We've covered all sorts of concepts about firms' costs in this chapter: opportunity costs, fixed costs, variable costs, sunk costs, marginal costs, average costs, long-run and short-run costs, economies of scale and scope, and more. That's a lot to keep straight, but the information we have covered here is important for understanding the constraints firms face when making production decisions. This information also allows us to connect what we learned in Chapter 6, which is how a firm optimally produces a *given* output quantity, to many of the analyses we do in Chapters 8–11, when we look at how firms decide what output quantity to produce in the first place, or even whether to produce at all.

Summary

1. Economic cost includes **accounting cost** plus the **opportunity cost** of inputs. Opportunity cost is the value of the input's next-best use. Decisions should be made taking opportunity costs into account—that is, on the basis of **economic cost,** not accounting cost. [**Section 7.1**]

2. **Sunk costs** are costs that can never be recovered even if the firm shuts down completely. Costs that are already sunk should not affect decisions going forward, because they have already been paid regardless of what choice is made in the present. [**Section 7.2**]

3. A firm's **total cost** can be split into fixed and variable components. **Fixed cost** does not change

when the firm's output does and must be paid even if output is zero. It can only be avoided by the firm completely shutting down and disposing of the inputs (an action that can be undertaken only in the long run). **Variable costs** are costs that change with the output level. [**Section 7.3**]

4. Cost curves relate a firm's cost to its output quantity. Because fixed cost doesn't change as output changes, fixed cost curves are horizontal, and **total cost curves** are parallel to **variable cost curves** (separated by the amount of fixed cost). [**Section 7.3**]

5. Two additional important cost concepts are **average** and **marginal costs.** Average cost at a

given output quantity equals the ratio of cost to output. **Average fixed cost** falls continuously as output increases. **Average variable cost** and **average total cost** tend to be U-shaped, falling initially, but then rising as output increases. Marginal cost is the additional cost of making one more unit of output. [**Section 7.4**]

6. In the short run, the firm's capital inputs are held constant along its expansion path, and all changes in output come from changing labor inputs. This means that, for all quantities except that quantity at which the fixed capital level is cost-minimizing, short-run total and average total costs must be higher than their long-run values. Every fixed capital level has its own short-run cost curves. The long-run average total cost curve is an "envelope" of all the short-run average total cost curves. Long-run marginal cost equals the short-run marginal costs at the quantities at which the fixed capital level is cost-minimizing. [**Section 7.5**]

7. **Economies of scale** describe the relative rate at which a firm's cost changes when its output changes. When cost increases at a slower rate than output, the firm has economies of scale. Average cost is falling and the long-run average total cost curve is downward-sloping when there are economies of scale. If cost increases at a faster rate than output, **diseconomies of scale** occur. Average total cost is rising and the long-run average total cost curve is upward-sloping in this case. If cost increases at the same rate as output, there are neither scale economies nor diseconomies, and long-run average total cost is constant. [**Section 7.6**]

8. **Economies of scope** describe how a firm's total cost changes with its product specialization. If producing two outputs jointly is cheaper than producing the same amount of the two outputs separately, then there are economies of scope. [**Section 7.6**]

Review Questions

1. What is the difference between a firm's accounting and economic costs? How do these costs relate to a firm's accounting and economic profits?
2. Define opportunity cost. How does a firm's opportunity cost relate to its economic cost?
3. What is the sunk cost fallacy?
4. Provide some examples of unavoidable fixed costs. How are these related to sunk costs? Describe why a firm should not consider sunk costs when making decisions.
5. Describe the relationship between fixed, variable, and total costs.
6. Why is a fixed cost curve horizontal? Why does a variable cost curve have a positive slope?

7. Name the three measures that examine a firm's per-unit cost at a given level of output.
8. Why does a firm's fixed cost not affect its marginal cost of producing an additional unit of a product?
9. Why is a firm's short-run total cost greater than its long-run total cost? Explain why this is also true for a firm's short-run and long-run *average* costs.
10. Describe the conditions under which a firm has economies of scale, diseconomies of scale, and constant economies of scale.
11. When does a producer face economies of scope? When does a producer face diseconomies of scope?

Problems (Solutions to problems marked * appear at the back of this book. Problems adapted to use calculus are available online at http://worthpublishers.com/GLS1e)

1. Jenny is considering starting a new business selling organic groceries. It would cost her $350,000 a year to rent store space and buy the groceries from a wholesaler, and she would have to quit her current job and give up a $70,000 annual salary.
   a. What is Jenny's opportunity cost of starting the business?
   b. If Jenny can make an accounting profit of $50,000 a year selling the organic groceries, should she start the business?

2. Casey is an expert poker player and can make $35 an hour playing poker online. On Saturday Casey goes to a local tournament with a $15 entry fee. He plays for four hours and wins first place, taking home the $150 prize. Did Casey make an economic profit at the tournament?

*3. Indicate whether the following statements are true or false, and then briefly explain your reasoning.
   a. It is possible for accounting and economic costs to be equal, but it is never possible for economic costs to be less than accounting costs.

b. It is possible for a firm to show an economic profit without showing an accounting profit.

4. Kyle recently opened a bar & grill. The costs associated with his new business are as follows:
   a. $300,000 to build the restaurant
   b. $30,000 for a liquor license
   c. $50,000 on furniture and kitchenware
   d. 2 cooks who will each be paid $5,000 per month
   e. 5 waiters who will each be paid $3 per hour plus tips

   Which of Kyle's costs are fixed, and which are variable? Explain.

*5. Amanda owns a toy manufacturing plant with the production function $Q = 100L - 3,000$, where L is hired labor hours. If the wage rate that Amanda pays her laborers is $7 per hour, what is her cost function?

6. A Toyota Camry costs $19,600 and has an average gas mileage of 27 mpg. A Toyota Prius costs $23,000 and has an average gas mileage of 50 mpg. Assuming gas costs $4 per gallon, generate total cost equations as a function of miles driven for each of these cars and identify the fixed and variable costs. How many miles do you have to drive before the two cars have the same total cost?

7. Philo T. Farmsworth is a corn farmer with a 40-acre tract of land. Each acre can produce 100 bushels of corn. The cost of planting the tract in corn is $20,000, and the cost of harvesting the corn is $10,000. In May, when corn is selling for $10 per bushel, Philo plants his crop. In September the price of corn has fallen to $2 per bushel. What should Philo do? Explain, assuming that there are no costs involved with bringing the corn to market to sell.

8. Complete the cost table below:

Quantity	Total Cost ($)	Average Total Cost ($)	Marginal Cost ($)
0	0	—	—
1	35		
2			25
3		28	
4	115		
5			40

*9. Consider the costs for Catherine's cupcake business:

Quantity (batches)	Fixed Cost ($)	Total Cost ($)
1	50	75
2	50	85
3	50	102
4	50	127
5	50	165
6	50	210

Re-create the above table with columns showing Catherine's variable cost, average total cost, average fixed cost, and average variable cost.

10. Daniel's Midland Archers (DMA) makes children's wooden practice arrows. Draw a set of representative short-run cost curves for DMA. Include average variable cost, average fixed cost, average total cost, and marginal cost.
    a. Suppose that Congress imposes a 39-cent excise tax on each children's wooden practice arrow DMA sells. Illustrate the effects of this tax on the cost curves of DMA. Which curves shift and which do not?
    b. Suppose that the city where DMA produces arrows increases the annual property tax on DMA's factory from $80,000 to $150,000. Illustrate the effects of this tax on the cost curves of DMA. Which curves shift and which do not?

11. Derive formulas for average fixed cost, average variable cost, average total cost, and marginal cost for the following cost function:

$$TC = 100 + 10Q$$

*12. Suppose a firm has the following production function: $Q = 2KL$. The marginal product of capital for this production function is $2L$, and the marginal product of labor is $2K$. If capital rents for $100 per unit per day, labor can be hired for $200 per unit per day, and the firm is minimizing costs,
    a. What is the total cost of producing q units of output?
    b. What is the average cost of producing q units of output?
    c. What is the marginal cost of producing q units of output?

13. You are the CEO of a major producer of funnel cakes. Your cost accountant has provided you with a table describing your cost structure, but you have inadvertently dripped cooking grease on it and most of the table is illegible. Reconstruct the table below, given the remaining legible numbers.

Q	TC	FC	VC	MC	AVC	AFC	ATC
0				—	—	—	—
1			17				
2				15			
3	101						
4					14.5		
5	122		67			11	
6							21

14. How does a firm's short-run ATC curve differ from its long-run ATC curve? Explain your answer.

*15. Suppose an increase in the minimum wage alters the cost of producing fast-food hamburgers. Show what happens to McDonald's long-run expansion path as a result of this wage increase.

16. Digging trenches requires two types of labor: unskilled labor (aka workers) and skilled labor (aka supervisors). Unskilled labor can be hired for $50 per day, and skilled labor can be hired for $100 per day. If, by hiring another unskilled laborer, K&B Construction Company can dig another 20 feet of trenches per day, and if by hiring another skilled laborer, it can dig another 30 feet of trenches per day, is K&B Construction Company minimizing its costs?

*17. A builder of custom motorcycles has a choice of operating out of one garage or two. When it operates out of one garage, its average total cost of production is given by $ATC_1 = Q^2 - 6Q + 14$. If it operates out of two garages, its average total cost of production is given by $ATC_2 = Q^2 - 10Q + 30$. What does this firm's $LATC$ look like? Can you describe it as a function?

18. Mike's Bicycle Factory builds specialty bicycles with the following long-run cost function: $TC = 2.5(Q^3)$. Plot Mike's ATC and MC curves for quantities 1 through 5.
    a. For which quantities does Mike's Bicycle Factory exhibit economies of scale?
    b. For which quantities does it exhibit diseconomies of scale?

*19. Suppose that a firm has the following Cobb–Douglas production function: $Q = 12K^{0.75}L^{0.25}$.
    a. What must its long-run total cost curve look like? Its long-run average total cost curve?
    b. How do your answers to part (a) change if the firm's production function is $Q = KL$?

20. In the short run, your firm can vary only the amount of labor it employs. Labor can be hired for $5 per unit, and your firm's fixed costs are $25. Your firm's short-run production function is given in the table below:

Labor Input	Output	Marginal Product of Labor	Average Product of Labor	Total Cost	Average Total Cost	Average Variable Cost	Marginal Cost
1	5						
2	12						
3	20						
4	28						
5	34						
6	39						
7	43						
8	46						
9	48						

a. Compute the marginal and average product of each worker. What shape does each take? When does the marginal product begin to fall? Average product?

b. Compute the total cost of producing each output level indicated in the table.

c. Compute the average total, average variable, and marginal cost at each level of output. When does marginal cost begin to rise? Average variable cost?

d. Is there a link between your answers to (a) and (c)?

Chapter 7 Appendix:
The Calculus of a Firm's Cost Structure

We saw in this chapter that firms face a multitude of costs—from opportunity costs and sunk costs to fixed and variable costs to marginal costs and more. These costs can be obtained directly from the firm's production function and its wage and rental rate for particular levels of output. But it is often helpful to have a more generalized form of a firm's costs that allows us to know its cost structure at any optimal input bundle. In this appendix, we use calculus to come up with total and marginal cost curves starting from the firm's production function.

Let's return to the firm with the Cobb–Douglas production function $Q = AK^{\alpha}L^{1-\alpha}$ with wages equal to W, the rental rate of capital equal to R, and the technology parameter A. Assume $0 < \alpha < 1$, and $A > 0$. The firm's total costs are

$$TC = RK + WL$$

This formula specifies the firm's total costs when the firm produces a specific quantity and, thus, knows its cost-minimizing bundle of capital and labor for that particular quantity. If the firm hasn't yet decided how much to produce, however, the firm would want to know its entire total cost curve—that is, what its total costs are at *any* quantity it chooses to produce. How can a firm find these costs? The firm wants to derive its total costs as a function of its demands for capital and labor. To do this, the firm first has to consider whether it is operating in the short or the long run. In the short run, capital is fixed at some level $\overline{K}$, and the firm's production function is $Q = A\overline{K}^{\alpha}L^{1-\alpha}$. Its demand for labor in the short run is then determined by how much capital the firm has. Finding the short-run demand for labor is as simple as solving for L in the production function:

$$L^{1-\alpha} = \frac{Q}{A\overline{K}^{\alpha}}$$

$$L = \left(\frac{Q}{A\overline{K}^{\alpha}}\right)^{\frac{1}{(1-\alpha)}}$$

Plugging this short-run demand for labor and the fixed amount of capital ($\overline{K}$) into the total cost equation, the firm faces short-run total cost:

$$TC_{SR} = R\overline{K} + WL$$

$$TC(Q)_{SR} = R\overline{K} + W\left(\frac{Q}{A\overline{K}^{\alpha}}\right)^{\frac{1}{(1-\alpha)}}$$

In the long run, the firm chooses the optimal amount of capital *and* labor, so its long-run demands for capital and labor look different. We know from the firm's cost-minimization problem in the Chapter 6 Appendix that at a fixed quantity $\overline{Q}$, the firm demands $L^* = \left[\frac{(1-\alpha)}{\alpha}\frac{R}{W}\right]^{\alpha}\frac{\overline{Q}}{A}$ and $K^* = \left[\frac{\alpha}{(1-\alpha)}\frac{W}{R}\right]^{1-\alpha}\frac{\overline{Q}}{A}$. At any level of Q, then, the firm demands $L^* = \left[\frac{(1-\alpha)}{\alpha}\frac{R}{W}\right]^{\alpha}\frac{Q}{A}$ and $K^* = \left[\frac{\alpha}{(1-\alpha)}\frac{W}{R}\right]^{1-\alpha}\frac{Q}{A}$, where Q is variable and not a fixed quantity.

These are the firm's long-run capital and labor demand curves. As with all demand curves, these are downward-sloping: As the wage (or rental rate) increases, the firm will want to purchase less labor (or capital), all else equal. Now that we have the firm's demands for both of its inputs, we can substitute them into the expression for total cost as a function of inputs to get the long-run total cost curve as a function of output:

$$TC_{LR} = RK + WL$$

$$TC(Q)_{LR} = R\left[\frac{\alpha}{(1-\alpha)}\frac{W}{R}\right]^{1-\alpha}\frac{Q}{A} + W\left[\frac{(1-\alpha)}{\alpha}\frac{R}{W}\right]^{\alpha}\frac{Q}{A}$$

Notice that total cost increases as output and the prices of inputs increase, but that total cost decreases as total factor productivity A increases.

We can now also find the firm's generalized marginal cost curve by taking the derivative of the total cost curve with respect to quantity Q. But be careful before you do this! We have to again consider whether the firm is operating in the short run or the long run. In the short run, the cost of capital is a fixed cost and will not show up in the firm's marginal cost curve. Short-run marginal cost is only a function of the change in labor costs:

$$MC(Q)_{SR} = \frac{dTC(Q)_{SR}}{dQ} = \frac{d}{dQ}\left[R\overline{K} + W\left(\frac{Q}{A\overline{K}^{\alpha}}\right)^{\frac{1}{(1-\alpha)}}\right]$$

$$= \frac{1}{(1-\alpha)}W\left(\frac{1}{A\overline{K}^{\alpha}}\right)^{\frac{1}{(1-\alpha)}}Q^{\frac{1}{(1-\alpha)}-1} = \frac{W}{(1-\alpha)}\left(\frac{1}{A\overline{K}^{\alpha}}\right)^{\frac{1}{(1-\alpha)}}Q^{\frac{\alpha}{(1-\alpha)}}$$

$$= \frac{W}{(1-\alpha)}\left(\frac{Q^{\alpha}}{A\overline{K}^{\alpha}}\right)^{\frac{1}{(1-\alpha)}}$$

As we would expect, marginal costs increase with output in the short run. Why? Because in the short run capital is fixed. The firm can only increase output by using more and more labor. However, the diminishing marginal product of labor means that each additional unit of labor is less productive and that the firm has to use increasingly more labor to produce an additional unit of output. As a result, the marginal cost of producing this extra unit of output increases as short-run production increases, all else equal.

In the long run, the firm can change both inputs, and its marginal cost curve reflects the firm's capital and labor demands. To get long-run marginal cost, take the derivative of long-run total cost with respect to Q:

$$MC(Q)_{LR} = \frac{dTC(Q)_{LR}}{dQ} = \frac{d}{dQ}\left[R\left[\frac{\alpha}{(1-\alpha)}\frac{W}{R}\right]^{1-\alpha}\frac{Q}{A} + W\left[\frac{(1-\alpha)}{\alpha}\frac{R}{W}\right]^{\alpha}\frac{Q}{A}\right]$$

$$= \frac{1}{A}\left[R\left[\frac{\alpha}{(1-\alpha)}\frac{W}{R}\right]^{1-\alpha} + W\left[\frac{(1-\alpha)}{\alpha}\frac{R}{W}\right]^{\alpha}\right]$$

Notice that this expression for marginal cost consists only of constants (A, α, W, and R). So, long-run marginal cost is constant for this production function. What is more, average total cost for this production function is exactly the same as marginal cost—you should be able to show this by dividing TC by Q. Both of these results (constant marginal cost and $MC = ATC$) are unique to firms with constant returns to scale. If these firms want to double output, they have to double labor and capital. This, in turn, doubles the firms' costs, leaving *average* total cost—total cost divided by total inputs—unchanged. If the firm does not face constant returns to scale, these results will not hold true. In particular, a firm with decreasing returns to scale would see increasing long-run marginal costs, while a firm with increasing returns to scale faces decreasing long-run marginal costs.

7A.1 figure it out

Let's revisit Figure It Out 7.4. Steve and Sons Solar Panels has a production function of $Q = 4KL$ and faces a wage rate of \$8 per hour and a rental rate of capital of \$10 per hour. Assume that, in the short run, capital is fixed at $\overline{K} = 10$.

a. Derive the short-run total cost curve for the firm. What is the short-run total cost of producing $Q = 200$ units?

b. Derive expressions for the firm's short-run average total cost, average fixed cost, average variable cost, and marginal cost.

c. Derive the long-run total cost curve for the firm. What is the long-run total cost of producing $Q = 200$ units?

d. Derive expressions for the firm's long-run average total cost and marginal cost.

Solution:

a. To get the short-run total cost function, we need to first find L as a function of Q. The short-run production function can be found by substituting $\overline{K} = 10$ into the production function:

$$Q = 4\overline{K}L = 4(10)(L) = 40L$$

Therefore, the firm's short run demand for labor is

$$L = 0.025Q$$

Now plug $\overline{K}$ and L into the total cost function:

$$TC_{SR} = R\overline{K} + WL = 10(10) + 8(0.025Q)$$
$$TC_{SR} = 100 + 0.2Q$$

This is the equation for the short-run total cost curve with fixed cost FC equal to 100 and variable cost VC equal to $0.2Q$. Notice that the fixed cost is just the total cost of capital, $R\overline{K} = 10(10) = \$100$. The short-run total cost of producing 200 units of output is

$$TC_{SR} = 100 + 0.2(200) = \$140$$

b. Average costs are a firm's costs divided by the quantity produced. Hence, the average total cost, average fixed cost, and average variable cost measures for this total cost function are

$$ATC_{SR} = \frac{TC}{Q} = \frac{100 + 0.2Q}{Q} = \frac{100}{Q} + 0.2$$

$$AFC_{SR} = \frac{FC}{Q} = \frac{100}{Q}$$

$$AVC_{SR} = \frac{VC}{Q} = \frac{0.2Q}{Q} = 0.2$$

Marginal cost is the derivative of total cost with respect to quantity, or

$$MC_{SR} = \frac{dTC}{dQ} = 0.2$$

Marginal cost for Steve and Sons is constant and equal to average variable cost in the short run because the marginal product of labor is constant when capital is fixed.

c. In the long run, Steve and Sons solves its cost-minimization problem:

$$\min_{K,L} TC = 10K + 8L \text{ s.t. } Q = 4KL \quad \text{or} \quad \min_{K,L,\lambda} \mathcal{L}(K,L,\lambda) = 10K + 8L + \lambda(Q - 4KL)$$

The first-order conditions are

$$\frac{\partial \mathcal{L}}{\partial K} = 10 - \lambda(4L) = 0$$

$$\frac{\partial \mathcal{L}}{\partial L} = 8 - \lambda(4K) = 0$$

$$\frac{\partial \mathcal{L}}{\partial \lambda} = Q - 4KL = 0$$

To find the optimal levels of labor and capital, we need to set the first two conditions equal to solve for K as a function of L:

$$\lambda = \frac{10}{4L} = \frac{8}{4K}$$

$$40K = 32L$$

$$K = 0.8L$$

To find the firm's long-run labor demand, we plug this expression for K as a function of L into the production function and solve for L:

$$Q = 4KL = 4(0.8L)L = 3.2L^2$$
$$L^2 = 0.31Q$$
$$L = 0.56Q^{0.5}$$

To find the firm's long-run demand for capital, we simply plug the labor demand into our expression for K as a function of L:

$$K = 0.8L = 0.8(0.56Q^{0.5})$$
$$= 0.45Q^{0.5}$$

The firm's long-run total cost function can be derived by plugging the firm's long-run input demands L and K into the long-run total cost function:

$$TC_{LR} = RK + WL = 10(0.45Q^{0.5}) + 8(0.56Q^{0.5})$$
$$= 8.98Q^{0.5}$$

Therefore, the cost for producing 200 units of output in the long run is

$$TC_{LR} = 8.98(200)^{0.5} \approx \$127$$

d. We can also find the long-run marginal and average total costs for this firm:

$$MC_{LR} = \frac{dTC}{dQ} = 4.49Q^{-0.5}$$

$$ATC_{LR} = \frac{TC}{Q} = \frac{8.98Q^{0.5}}{Q} = 8.98Q^{-0.5}$$

Notice that marginal cost in this case decreases as output increases. Furthermore, $MC < ATC$ for all levels of output. This is because Steve and Sons' production function, $Q = 4KL$, exhibits increasing returns to scale at all levels of output.

Problems

1. A firm has a production function of $Q = 0.25KL^{0.5}$, the rental rate of capital is $100, and the wage rate is $25. In the short run, $\overline{K}$ is fixed at 100 units.
    a. What is the short-run production function?
    b. What is the short-run demand for labor?
    c. What are the firm's short-run total cost and short-run marginal cost?
2. Margarita Robotics has a daily production function given by $Q = K^{0.5}L^{0.5}$, where K is the monthly number of hours of use for a precision lathe (capital) and L is the monthly number of machinist hours (labor). Suppose that each unit of capital costs $40, and each unit of labor costs $10.
    a. In the short run, $\overline{K}$ is fixed at 16,000 hours. What is the short-run demand for labor?
    b. Given that $\overline{K}$ is fixed at 16,000 hours, what are total cost, average total cost, average variable cost, and marginal cost in the short run?
    c. What are the long-run demands for capital and labor?
    d. Derive total cost, average cost, and marginal cost in the long run.
    e. How do Margarita Robotics' marginal and average costs change with increases in output? Explain.
3. A firm has a production function given by $Q = 10K^{0.25}L^{0.25}$. Suppose that each unit of capital costs R and each unit of labor costs W.
    a. Derive the long-run demands for capital and labor.
    b. Derive the total cost curve for this firm.
    c. Derive the long-run average and marginal cost curves.
    d. How do marginal and average costs change with increases in output? Explain.
    e. Confirm that the value of the Lagrange multiplier you get from the cost-minimization problem in part (a) is equal to the marginal cost curve you found in part (c).

Supply in a Competitive Market

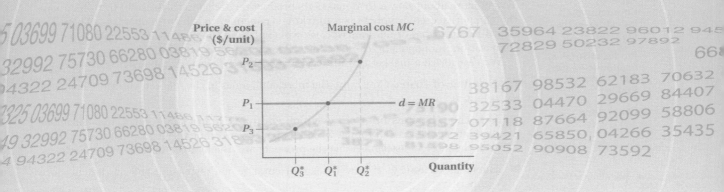

R aising chickens in urban areas is a new trend among fans of locally produced food. Suppose Ty is an aspiring urban farmer and has to decide on how many chickens to raise in his backyard. He might eat a few of the eggs and an occasional chicken himself, but he plans to sell most of his production at local markets. In essence, Ty is starting a firm, and he is facing the same production decisions any firm faces. How many chickens Ty raises isn't going to noticeably affect the total supply of eggs or chicken in the market. Not only do tens of thousands of people now raise chickens in their backyards, but there are also large farms that supply chickens to the market. How many chickens Ty raises *is* going to affect his profits, however. So, how does Ty—or any firm—make production decisions?

In Chapters 6 and 7, we learned how a firm chooses an input mix to minimize the cost of producing a particular amount of output and how this cost changes with the output level. In this chapter, we start exploring how a firm chooses how much output to make in the first place. In doing this, we move from talking about a firm's cost-minimizing behavior to a discussion of how a firm chooses an output level to maximize its profits. You will see that it gives us the supply curves we learned about in Chapters 2 and 3.

Although all firms use knowledge of marginal revenue, marginal costs, and prices to guide their actions, profit-maximizing behavior is different for different types of firms. We begin the chapter by explaining the different types of market structures within which firms operate and what competition truly means. Most of this chapter focuses on **perfect competition,** a market (or industry) with many firms producing an identical product with no barriers to entry, and explores how firms behave in a perfectly competitive industry to maximize their profits.

8.1 Market Structures and Perfect Competition in the Short Run

To say more about how a firm makes its production decisions, it is useful to think about the competitive environment, or **market structure,** in which it operates. There are four different types of markets that we will explore in the next several chapters: perfect competition, monopolistic competition, oligopoly, and monopoly.

We categorize a market or industry using three primary characteristics:

- **Number of firms.** Generally, the more companies in the market, the more competitive it is.

- **Whether the consumer cares which company made the good.** Can a consumer distinguish one firm's product from another, or are all of the goods identical? In general, the more indistinguishable the products are, the more competitive the market is.

- **Barriers to entry.** If new firms can enter a market easily, the market is more competitive.

Table 8.1 describes each market structure using these characteristics.

These three characteristics tell us a lot about the production decisions of firms in a given industry. For example, firms that can differentiate their products may be able to convince some consumers to pay a higher price for their products than for products made by their competitors. The ability to influence the price of their products has important implications for these firms' profit-maximizing decisions. Only firms in a perfectly competitive market have no influence on the price of their products; they take as given whatever price is determined by the forces of supply and demand at work in the wider market. A truly perfectly competitive market is rare, but it offers many useful lessons about how a market works, just as the supply and demand framework does. In this chapter, we focus on perfectly competitive markets. In Chapters 9 and 10, we look at monopoly and how monopolies can use different strategies to gain more profit, and in Chapter 11, we examine market structures that fall in between perfect competition and monopoly.

perfect competition
A market with many firms producing identical products and no barriers to entry.

market structure
The competitive environment in which firms operate.

Table 8.1 | **The Four Basic Market Structures**

	Perfect Competition	**Monopolistic Competition**	**Oligopoly**	**Monopoly**
Number of Firms	Many	Many	Few	One
Type of Products Sold	Identical	Differentiated	Identical or Differentiated	Unique
Barriers to Entry	None	None	Some	Many

Perfect Competition

What makes a market perfectly competitive? In Table 8.1, we saw that to be perfectly competitive, three conditions have to be satisfied. First, there need to be a large number of firms. If there are, then the impact that any one firm has on the market equilibrium price and output is small. Indeed, we assume that any one firm can change its behavior without the overall market equilibrium being affected at all.

The second requirement for perfect competition is that all firms produce an identical product. By identical, we don't just mean that all the firms make televisions or all the firms make smoothies. We mean the consumers view the output of the different producers as perfect substitutes; they do not care who made it. This might be more accurate for nails or gasoline or bananas, but is probably far from true for smart phones or automobiles.

Finally, for an industry to be perfectly competitive, there cannot be any barriers to entry. In other words, if someone decides she wants to start selling nails tomorrow, there is nothing that prevents her from doing so.

The key economic implication of these three assumptions (small firms, identical products, free entry) is that firms don't have a choice about what price to charge. If the firm charges a price above the market price, it will not sell any of its goods. (We'll show you the math behind this result later in this section.) And because we assume that the firm is small enough relative to the industry that it can sell as much output as it wants at the market price, it will never choose to charge a price below the market price. For that reason, economists call perfectly competitive firms *price takers*. The market price is determined solely by the forces of supply and demand, and the individual firm takes that price as a fact of its decision-making life.

The classic example of a firm operating in a perfectly competitive market is a farmer who produces a commodity crop, such as corn or soybeans. Because an individual farmer's output is tiny relative to total production for the entire market, the choice of how much to produce (or whether to produce at all) isn't going to create movements along the industry's demand curve. One farmer's decision to sell part or all of her soybean crop will not affect the price of soybeans. The *combined* effect of many soybean farmers' decisions *will* affect the market price, however, just as everyone in a city simultaneously turning on their faucets will cause water pressure throughout the city to drop. The key is that the city's water pressure won't fluctuate simply because one person decides to take a shower.

Note one important thing: Having a large number of firms in an industry does not automatically mean the industry is perfectly competitive. In the United States, for example, there are over 2,000 firms that sell ready-mixed concrete (the fluid form of concrete delivered to construction sites in the familiar barrel-backed mixer trucks). The output of any one of these firms is small relative to all the concrete sold in a year. Still, these firms are probably not price takers; they choose the prices they charge for their products.

How do these firms differ from soybean farmers? Why are they not price takers, too? Ready-mixed concrete firms have the ability to set their own prices for their output because, despite their small size relative to the overall market, their products are not homogeneous; perhaps most importantly, you can't ship concrete very far because it's heavy and perishable. So, the concrete of a firm in one town can't be substituted easily for that of a firm in another town (or even in some cases, a firm on the other end of the same town). This product differentiation makes the markets for these products noncompetitive and allows the concrete firms to have some market power—that is, to have some ability to set the price at which their product sells. On the other hand, the outputs of perfectly competitive firms are perceived by consumers to be exactly the same and perfect substitutes: a soybean is a soybean is a soybean. The identity of the soybean's producer doesn't matter.

If firms have to meet such strict criteria to be considered perfectly competitive, you might wonder why we devote so much time to understanding their production decisions. After all, if they're so rare in the real world, what's the point? There are several reasons why it's useful to start our study of market behavior with the perfectly competitive market.

First, it is the most straightforward. Because a perfectly competitive firm takes the market price as given, the only decision a firm must worry about to maximize profit is choosing the correct level of output. It doesn't need to think about what price to charge because the market takes care of that.

Second, there are a few perfectly competitive markets, and it's useful to know how they work (maybe you've dreamed of farming soybeans).

Third, there are many markets that are *close* to perfectly competitive. Perfect competition provides a fairly good idea about how these markets work.

Last, perfect competition is an important benchmark against which economists like to measure how efficient other markets are. Perfectly competitive markets are, in a specific sense, the most efficient markets there are (as we see later in this chapter). In competitive markets, goods sell at their marginal costs, firms produce at the minimum cost possible, and the combined producer and consumer surplus can't get any larger. Comparing a market to the outcome under perfect competition is a useful way to measure how efficient a market is.

The Demand Curve as Seen by a Price Taker

A perfectly competitive firm is a price taker. It must sell its output at whatever price is dictated by supply and demand forces in the market as a whole. The small size of each firm relative to the size of the total market also ensures that the perfectly competitive firm can sell as much output as it wants to at the market price.

Let's again think about our egg farmer Ty. The price for a dozen Grade-A large eggs is determined by the market forces of supply and demand. Panel a of Figure 8.1 shows the perfectly competitive market for Grade-A large eggs. Quantity demanded is equal to quantity supplied at the equilibrium market price of $1.25 per dozen.

As a producer in this market, Farmer Ty can sell all the eggs his hens can produce as long as he is willing to sell them at $1.25 per dozen. He can't sell them for more than that price because from a consumer's standpoint, a Grade-A large egg is a Grade-A large egg. If he insisted on charging $1.30 per dozen, consumers will just buy other producers' identical eggs at the market price of $1.25 per dozen, and Ty will end up selling nothing. At the same time, Ty has no incentive to lower his price below $1.25. He can already sell all the eggs he wants to at that price because his hens' output is such a tiny fraction of what is available on the market (you can see this by looking at the quantity axis for Ty's firm: he supplies dozens of eggs, while the market has *millions* of dozens of eggs)—he's not going to drive down the market price by selling a few more (or a few hundred more) dozen eggs.

This means the demand curve Ty (or any other egg farmer like him) faces personally is horizontal—that is, perfectly elastic—at a price of $1.25 (panel b of Figure 8.1). This logic holds for any firm in any perfectly competitive market: *The demand curve facing a firm in a perfectly competitive market is perfectly elastic at the market equilibrium price.*

8.2 Profit Maximization in a Perfectly Competitive Market

profit
The difference between a firm's revenue and its total cost.

We just saw that Ty—and, by extension, any perfectly competitive firm—sells at the price set by the market. Although perfectly competitive firms are price takers, they do have one decision to make: the quantity to supply. Economists usually assume firms choose their actions—like how much output to produce—to maximize profits. **Profit**

Figure 8.1 | **Market and Firm Demand in Perfect Competition**

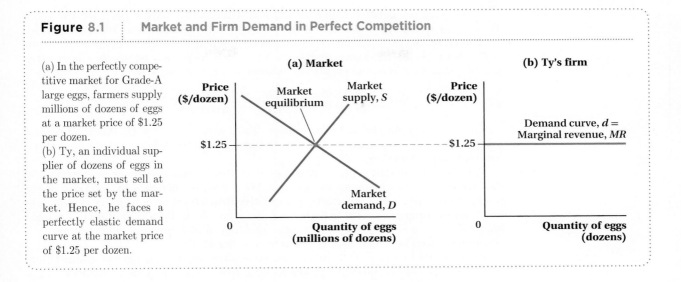

(a) In the perfectly competitive market for Grade-A large eggs, farmers supply millions of dozens of eggs at a market price of $1.25 per dozen.

(b) Ty, an individual supplier of dozens of eggs in the market, must sell at the price set by the market. Hence, he faces a perfectly elastic demand curve at the market price of $1.25 per dozen.

---

is the difference between a firm's revenue and its total cost. What does it mean to maximize profit? A firm does so by choosing the output level at which the gap between its total revenue and its total cost is largest. In this section, we will see that a perfectly competitive firm maximizes its profit when it produces the quantity of output at which the marginal cost of production equals the market price.

Total Revenue, Total Cost, and Profit Maximization

There are two basic elements to profit: revenue and cost. In general, these are both affected by a firm's decisions about how much output to produce and the price it will charge for its product. Because perfectly competitive firms cannot choose the market price, we only need to focus on the choice of output.

Mathematically, let's denote the profit a firm makes as π. The profit function is total revenue TR minus total cost TC (each of which is determined by the firm's output quantity):

$$\pi = TR - TC$$

To figure out the level of output that maximizes profit, we need to think about what happens to total cost and total revenue if the firm decides to produce one additional unit of output. Or, saying the same thing differently, we need to determine a firm's marginal cost and marginal revenue.

We know from Chapter 7 that marginal cost is the addition to total cost of producing one more unit of output:

$$MC = \Delta TC / \Delta Q$$

Marginal cost is always greater than zero—it takes more inputs to make more output.

Revenues are the other component of profits, and they are equal to a good's price times the quantity produced of the good. A firm's **marginal revenue** is the additional revenue it gets from selling one additional unit of output:

$$MR = \Delta TR / \Delta Q$$

marginal revenue
The additional revenue from selling one additional unit of output.

A perfectly competitive firm's marginal revenue is the market price for the good. To see why, remember that these firms can only sell their goods at the market price P. Therefore, the extra revenue they obtain from selling each additional unit of output is P. This is really important, and so we'll repeat it here: *In a perfectly competitive market, marginal revenue equals the market price; that is,* $MR = P$:

$$MR_{\text{Perfectly competitive}} = \frac{\Delta TR}{\Delta Q} = \frac{\Delta(P \times Q)}{\Delta Q} = P\frac{\Delta Q}{\Delta Q} = P$$

Think about what this outcome implies. Total revenue is $P \times Q$. When a firm is a price taker, P does not change no matter what happens to Q. For a price taker, P is a constant, not a function of Q.

This fact means that a perfectly competitive firm's total revenue is proportional to its output. If output increases by one unit, total revenue increases by the price of the product. For this reason, a perfectly competitive firm's total revenue curve is a straight line from the origin as shown in Figure 8.2. For example, if Ty sells another dozen eggs, his total revenue rises by the market price of $1.25. And if he keeps selling more, each additional dozen increases total revenue by another $1.25.

As we'll see in Chapter 9, in market structures other than perfect competition, price decreases as the quantity produced by a firm increases. This introduces an additional factor into our marginal revenue calculation for firms in those other types of markets. The price reduction doesn't happen in perfectly competitive markets because a firm does not affect the market price with its output choice. *Therefore, this case of marginal revenue equaling the market price is special*: It only applies to firms in perfectly competitive markets.

How a Perfectly Competitive Firm Maximizes Profit

Now that we're clear about marginal cost and marginal revenue, how does our firm maximize profit in a perfectly competitive market? We know that total cost is always going to rise when output increases (as shown in Figure 8.2)—that is, marginal cost is always positive. Similarly, we know that the firm's marginal revenue is constant at all quantities and equal to the good's market price. The key impact of changing output on the firm's profit depends on which of these marginal values is larger. If the market price (marginal revenue) is greater than the marginal cost of making another unit of output, then the firm can increase its profit by making and selling another unit, because revenues will go up more than costs. If the market price is less than the marginal cost,

---

Figure 8.2   Profit Maximization for a Perfectly Competitive Firm

Because a perfectly competitive firm faces a constant market price, its total revenue curve is a straight line from the origin with a slope equal to the marginal revenue, or the price. At the quantity Q^*, the slope of the total revenue curve (price) equals the slope of the total cost curve (marginal cost), and the firm is maximizing profit.

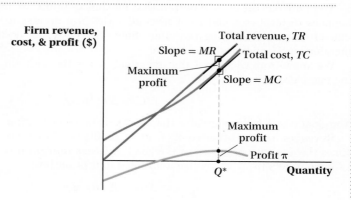

the firm should not make the extra unit. The firm will reduce its profit by doing so because while its revenues will rise, they won't rise as much as its costs. The quantity at which the opposing effects of marginal revenue and cost are balanced—that is, where the marginal revenue (price) from selling one more unit of output just equals the marginal cost of making another unit of output—is the point at which a firm maximizes its profit. This point occurs at Q^* in Figure 8.2. There, the slope of the total revenue curve (the marginal revenue—here, the market price) equals the slope of the total cost curve (the marginal cost at Q^*). In mathematical terms, the profit-maximizing level of output occurs where marginal revenue (here: price) equals marginal cost:

$$\frac{\Delta TR}{\Delta Q} = \frac{\Delta TC}{\Delta Q}$$

$$MR = P = MC$$

A firm should increase production as long as revenue increases by more than cost (i.e., when $MR = P > MC$). Conversely, a firm should decrease production if cost increases by more than revenue (i.e., when $MR = P < MC$).[1]

It should be clear from this discussion why cost plays such an important role in determining a firm's output (and this is true for a firm in any type of market structure): It is half of the firm's profit-maximization story. As cost changes, so does the firm's profit-maximizing output. In the next several chapters (which examine firms that are not perfectly competitive), we will learn how the firm's profit maximization is affected by the relationship between price and marginal revenue.

The analysis we've just completed shows that the output decision is fairly easy for the firm in a perfectly competitive market: It increases output until marginal cost is equal to the market price. If marginal cost rises with output—and we talked in Chapter 7 about the reasons why we might expect this—there will be a certain output level at which marginal cost rises to the market price. This is the profit-maximizing output level of a firm in perfect competition.

The $P = MC$ result is extremely useful because, by linking the market price to the firm's cost curve (or, more precisely, its marginal cost curve), we can determine how a competitive firm's output changes when the market price changes. Consider a firm with the marginal cost curve shown in Figure 8.3. If the market price is initially P_1,

> ∂ The appendix at the end of Chapter 9 uses calculus to solve the perfectly competitive firm's profit-maximization problem.

Figure 8.3   Profit Maximization for a Perfectly Competitive Firm Occurs Where $MR = P = MC$

At the initial market price P_1, the perfectly competitive firm is maximizing profit at Q_1^*, where $P = MC$. If price increases to P_2, the firm should increase output to Q_2^*. If, instead, price decreases to P_3, the firm is maximizing profit at Q_3^*.

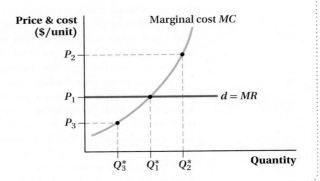

---

[1] Technically, we have to be a bit careful and say that $MR = P = MC$ implies profit maximization as long as marginal cost is rising at the quantity where that condition holds. If there were big economies of scale so that MC falls as output rises, the firm could make more profit by expanding output further.

then the firm's demand and marginal revenue curve is horizontal at that price. The firm will maximize profit by setting $MR = P_1 = MC$ and producing an output of Q_1^*. If the market price increases to P_2, the firm should increase its production to output Q_2^*. Why? Because the firm now faces a horizontal demand and marginal revenue curve at P_2, it should produce up to the point where marginal cost equals the market price. If price rises to P_2 and the firm continues to produce only Q_1, it could be selling those units between Q_1 and Q_2^* at a marginal revenue level (the new market price P_2) that is higher than its marginal costs. These extra sales would raise the firm's profit.

If the market price instead decreases from P_1 to P_3, the firm should reduce its quantity to Q_3^*, which has a lower marginal cost equal to P_3. If the firm does not make this change, it will be producing those units between Q_3^* and Q_1 at a loss because marginal revenue for those units would be lower than marginal cost.

 **application**

Do Firms Always Maximize Profits?

You've probably heard numerous stories of CEOs who spend firm money on lavish offices, parties, or other perks. Former Tyco CEO Dennis Kozlowski, for example, became famous for his extravagant profit-draining actions. He used $2 million of Tyco's money to throw his wife a birthday party in Italy and allegedly purchased a $6,000 shower curtain for his home. Kozlowski may have enjoyed his spending spree, but it certainly didn't benefit Tyco or its owners.

Given such stories, can we really assume that firms maximize profits? It is easiest to see why a small firm would want to maximize profits: Because the manager is usually the owner of the firm, maximizing the firm's profits directly affects her personally. But larger firms are typically run by people other than the owners. As a result, their managers may be tempted to engage in behavior that does not maximize profits. These profit-killing actions don't have to be as blatant as Kozlowski's. They can be subtle. A manager might want to raise short-run profit if her compensation package is based on it, at the expense of reductions in future profit. These missed profits could be recognized only after the manager has left the company—or never missed at all, because it can be difficult to tell what profits *should be*. Or, managers might undertake mergers and acquisitions that grow management's power but that cost the acquiring firm (and its shareholders) more than the acquisition is worth.

Although managers may sometimes take actions that aren't profit-maximizing, there are mechanisms in place to minimize the impact of such actions. These include boards of directors strong enough to confront management on the behalf of the shareholders, activist shareholders, a nosy financial press, and even the occasional academic economist, who takes it upon herself to look over the shoulders of firms' managers and scrutinize their behavior. These forces tend to push wayward managers back toward maximizing profits, as shareholders (the owners of the capital) would desire.

Perhaps more importantly, the competitive market itself pushes firms to maximize profit. Firms that maximize profits (or get as close to that as possible) will succeed where firms with profit-killing managers do not. Firms that maximize profits will attract additional capital more easily, have more money to invest, and take market share away from firms that fail to maximize profits. Firms that consistently fail to maximize profits will eventually be driven out of business by more profitable competitors.

If you're still unsure about the assumption of profit maximization, consider visiting Kozlowski at the Mid-State Correctional Facility in New York. As soon as Tyco's owners realized he wasn't maximizing profits, they took quick action. In 2005, Kozlowski was tried and convicted of grand larceny and conspiracy, falsifying business records, and violating business law. He'd probably be the first to tell you that owners go to great lengths to ensure that firms are profit-maximizing. ∎

Measuring a Firm's Profit

We've seen that a profit-maximizing firm in a perfectly competitive industry maximizes its profit by producing the quantity at which $P = MC$. But this doesn't tell us anything about the level of profit the firm is earning (or even if it is positive) at this point. To measure profit π, we subtract total cost (TC) from total revenue (TR):

$$\pi = TR - TC$$

Panel a of Figure 8.4 shows the firm's average total cost curve, its marginal cost curve, and its demand (marginal revenue) curve. The firm's total revenue equals the area of the rectangle with height P and base Q^*. Its total cost is the area of the rectangle with height ATC^* (ATC at the profit-maximizing level of output Q^*) and base Q^*. Because total revenue is greater than total cost at Q^*, the firm is earning a positive level of profit. Substituting the equations for TR and TC into the equation for profit, we see that

$$\pi = TR - TC$$
$$= (P \times Q) - (ATC \times Q)$$
$$= (P - ATC) \times Q$$

Therefore, the firm's profit can be seen in Figure 8.4 as the rectangle with height $(P - ATC^*)$ and base equal to the profit-maximizing quantity Q^*.

The profit equation tells us that profit $\pi = (P - ATC) \times Q$, and profit is positive only when $P > ATC^*$. If $P = ATC^*$, profit is zero, and when $P < ATC^*$, profit is negative. These scenarios are shown in panels b and c of Figure 8.4. Panel b shows that a firm earns zero profit when $P = ATC^* = MC$. In Chapter 7, we learned that $MC = ATC$ only when ATC is at its minimum. (Remember this fact! It will become very important to us toward the end of this chapter.) Panel c of Figure 8.4 shows a firm earning a negative profit because $P < ATC^*$. The obvious question is, why would a firm produce anything at a loss? We answer that question in the next section.

Figure 8.4   **Measuring Profit**

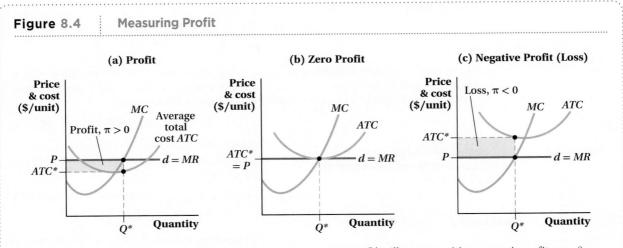

Given a firm's marginal cost curve MC, average total cost curve ATC, and market price P, the firm's profit can be measured by the area of the rectangle with length Q^* and height $(P - ATC^*)$.
(a) A firm facing a market price above its average total cost curve at Q^* will earn a positive economic profit, $\pi > 0$.
(b) A firm facing a market price equal to its average total cost at Q^* earns zero economic profit.
(c) A firm with average total cost above the market price, at Q^*, will earn negative economic profit (loss), $\pi < 0$.

8.1 figure it out

Suppose that consumers see haircuts as an undifferentiated good and that there are hundreds of barbershops in the market. The current market equilibrium price of a haircut is \$15. Bob's Barbershop has a daily short-run total cost given by $TC = 0.5Q^2$. The associated marginal cost curve is $MC = Q$.

a. How many haircuts should Bob give each day if he wants to maximize profit?

b. If the firm maximizes profit, how much profit will it earn each day?

Solution:

a. Firms in perfect competition maximize profit by producing the quantity for which $P = MC$:

$$P = MC$$
$$15 = Q$$

b. If Bob gives 15 haircuts and charges \$15 for each, the total revenue will be

$$TR = P \times Q$$
$$= \$15 \times 15 = \$225$$

We can use the firm's total cost function to find the total cost of producing 15 haircuts:

$$TC = 0.5Q^2 = 0.5(15)^2 = \$112.50$$

Since profit is $TR - TC$,

$$\pi = \$225 - \$112.50 = \$112.50 \text{ per day}$$

If Profit Is Negative, Should a Firm Shut Down? How does a perfectly competitive firm know if it is better off operating at a loss or shutting down and producing zero output? (Remember that shutting down in the short run is not the same thing as exiting the industry, because firms have some fixed costs they still must pay if they shut down in the short run.) The answer depends on the firm's costs and revenues under each scenario (continue to operate at a loss or shut down). Table 8.2 shows the information the firm needs to make its decision.

If the firm decides to shut down in the short run and produce nothing, it will have no revenue. Because it still must pay its fixed cost, we know that the firm's loss will exactly equal its fixed cost:

$$\pi_{\text{shut down}} = TR - TC = TR - (FC + VC)$$
$$= 0 - (FC + 0) = -FC$$

If the firm continues to operate at a loss in the short run, it will accumulate some revenue, but will have to pay both fixed and variable costs. The profit from operating is the difference between total revenue and fixed and variable costs:

$$\pi_{\text{operate}} = TR - TC = TR - FC - VC$$

What is the difference between these two scenarios? If you said, "revenue and variable cost," you are correct:

$$\pi_{\text{operate}} - \pi_{\text{shut down}} = TR - FC - VC - (-FC)$$
$$= TR - VC$$

Therefore, in the short-run a firm should operate as long as its revenue is greater than or equal to its *variable* cost, not its total cost ($TR \geq VC$). That's because fixed cost needs to be paid whether the plant operates or not, so it doesn't enter into the operate/shut-down decision. Making enough revenue to cover the firm's variable cost is sufficient to justify operating in the short run, even if

Table 8.2	Deciding Whether to Operate at a Loss or Shut Down in the Short Run	
	Shut Down	**Operate**
Revenue	None	Some (*TR*)
Cost	Fixed (*FC*)	Fixed (*FC*) + Variable (*VC*)
Loss	–*FC*	*TR* – *FC* – *VC*

Figure 8.5   **Deciding Whether to Operate or Shut Down in the Short Run**

At market price P, the firm earns a negative economic profit equal to the area of the rectangle with length Q^* and height $(P - ATC^*)$. Because price is above the firm's average variable cost AVC^* at the profit-maximizing quantity Q^*, however, the firm will continue to operate in the short run. That is because in doing so the firm can at least cover its variable cost.

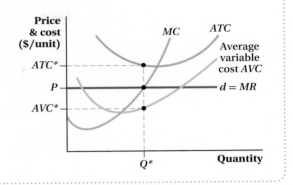

---

the firm can't cover all of its fixed cost. However, if the firm has total revenue that is lower than its variable cost ($TR < VC$), the firm should shut down. It can't cover its variable cost at this point and loses money on every unit it sells. The operate-or-shut-down decision can be summed up as follows:

$$\text{Operate if } TR \geq VC.$$

$$\text{Shut down if } TR < VC.$$

Figure 8.5 illustrates these rules. It shows a perfectly competitive firm's average total cost, average variable cost, marginal cost, and marginal revenue (market price) curves. In the case shown in the figure, the firm is losing money because $TR < TC$, but it continues to operate because $TR > VC$. How can we tell this from the figure? We know that TR is the area of a rectangle where P is the height and Q^* is the base ($TR = P \times Q$), and VC is the rectangle with height AVC^* (AVC at Q^*) and base Q^* ($VC = AVC \times Q$). Both TR and AVC contain Q^*, so this quantity cancels out and plays no role in the operate/shut-down decision. We can now rewrite our rules from above in terms of the market price P facing the firm and its average variable cost AVC^* at the profit-maximizing (or in this case loss-minimizing) quantity:

$$\text{Operate if } P \geq AVC^*.$$

$$\text{Shut down if } P < AVC^*.$$

Therefore, the firm should keep operating as long as the market price is at least as large as its average variable cost at the quantity where price equals its marginal cost. Keep in mind that these rules apply to all firms in all industries in any type of market structure.

8.2 figure it out

Cardboard boxes are produced in a perfectly competitive market. Each identical firm has a short-run total cost curve of $TC = 3Q^3 - 18Q^2 + 30Q + 50$, where Q is measured in thousands of boxes per week. The firm's associated marginal cost curve is $MC = 9Q^2 - 36Q + 30$. Calculate the price below which a firm in the market will not produce any output in the short run (the shut-down price).

Solution:

A firm will not produce any output in the short run at any price below its minimum AVC. How do we find the minimum AVC? We learned in Chapter 7 that AVC is minimized when $AVC = MC$. So, we need to start by figuring out the equation for the average variable cost curve and then solving it for the output that minimizes AVC.

AVC is equal to VC/Q. Remember that total cost is the sum of fixed cost and variable cost:

$$TC = FC + VC$$

Fixed cost is that part of total cost that does not vary with output (changes in Q have no effect on FC). Therefore, if $TC = 3Q^3 - 18Q^2 + 30Q + 50$, then FC must be 50. This means that $VC = 3Q^3 - 18Q^2 + 30Q$. Because $AVC = VC/Q$,

$$AVC = VC/Q = \frac{3Q^3 - 18Q^2 + 30Q}{Q} = 3Q^2 - 18Q + 30$$

Next, we find the output for which AVC is at its minimum by equating AVC and MC:

$$AVC = MC$$
$$3Q^2 - 18Q + 30 = 9Q^2 - 36Q + 30$$
$$18Q = 6Q^2$$
$$18 = 6Q$$
$$Q = 3$$

This means that AVC is at its minimum at an output of 3,000 cardboard boxes per week. To find the level of AVC at this output, we plug $Q = 3$ into the formula for AVC:

$$AVC = 3Q^2 - 18Q + 30$$
$$= 3(3)^2 - 18(3) + 30 = 27 - 54 + 30 = \$3$$

Therefore, the minimum price at which the firm should operate is \$3. If the price falls below \$3, the firm should shut down in the short run and only pay its fixed cost.

make the grade

A tale of three curves

One of the easiest ways to examine the diagrams of cost curves for a perfectly competitive firm is to remember that each of these cost curves tells only a part of the story.

What is the profit-maximizing output? The marginal cost curve: If you want to know the level of output that maximizes profit for any firm, you need to use the firm's marginal cost curve and equate marginal revenue and marginal cost. For a perfectly competitive firm *only,* you equate price and marginal cost because in perfect competition, marginal revenue is equal to price.

Is the firm earning a positive profit? The average total cost curve: Once you know the optimal level of output, you can use the average total cost curve to compare price and average total cost to determine whether a firm is earning a positive profit. Profit is measured as the rectangle with a base equal to output and a height equal to the difference between P and ATC at that quan-

tity of output. If a perfectly competitive firm is earning a positive profit, the story ends there. You don't even need to consider the firm's average variable cost curve.

Operate or shut down? The average variable cost curve: If a firm is earning a loss (negative profit) because its price is less than its average total cost, the decision of whether or not the firm should continue to operate in the short run depends entirely on the relationship between price and average variable cost. Look at the average variable cost curve to determine how these two variables compare at the profit-maximizing/loss-minimizing level of output. If price is greater, the firm should continue to operate; if average variable cost is greater, the firm should shut down.

Knowing which curve is used to answer these questions makes it easier to analyze complicated diagrams and answer questions for homework, quizzes, and exams. Remember that each curve has its own role and focus on that curve to simplify your analysis.

8.3 Perfect Competition in the Short Run

We've just learned that a perfectly competitive firm maximizes its profit where $MR = P = MC$, and that the firm will operate in the short run (even at an economic loss) as long as price is greater than or equal to average variable cost. We can now take our analysis one step further and derive the short-run supply curve for a perfectly competitive firm.

A Firm's Short-Run Supply Curve in a Perfectly Competitive Market

Because the supply curve shows the quantity supplied at any price, and the firm chooses to produce where $P = MC$, the short-run marginal cost curve must be the firm's short-run supply curve. There is one caveat: Only the portion of the marginal cost curve above the minimum average variable cost will be on the firm's supply curve. Why? Because at any price below the minimum average variable cost, the firm would shut down and its quantity supplied would be zero.

Figure 8.6 shows that the firm's short-run supply curve is the portion of its marginal cost curve MC that is at or above its average variable cost AVC, including the portion that is below its average total cost ATC. For prices below AVC, supply is zero, as shown in the figure. Keep in mind that we hold everything else constant except price and output when deriving the firm's supply curve.

Because of this relationship between marginal cost and the firm's short-run supply curve, anything that changes marginal cost will shift supply. As you may recall from Chapter 7, factors that shift the marginal cost curve include changes in input prices and technology. Fixed cost, on the other hand, does not affect a firm's marginal cost, and therefore changes in fixed cost do not shift the short-run supply curve. In the long run, as we know, no costs are fixed. Later in the chapter, we talk about how firms' long-run behavior in perfectly competitive markets differs from their short-run behavior.

Figure 8.6   The Perfectly Competitive Firm's Short-Run Supply Curve

Because a firm will only operate in the short run when the market price is above its average variable cost curve AVC, the perfectly competitive firm's short-run supply curve is the portion of the marginal cost curve MC above AVC. At prices below AVC, the firm shuts down, its quantity supplied is 0, and its supply curve is represented by the y-axis.

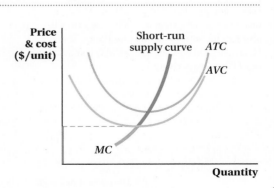

application

The Supply Curve of a Power Plant

In 2008 economists Ali Hortaçsu and Steven Puller published a detailed study of the Texas electricity industry.[2] Using data from this study, we can construct the supply curve for a single firm (Figure 8.7). This, along with the supply curves of the other firms in the industry, is a building block in the industry supply curve that we construct later in the chapter.

The first and most important step in deriving the firm's supply curve is to determine its marginal cost curve. In the electric power generation industry, marginal cost reflects the firm's cost of producing one more megawatt of electricity for another hour (this amount of energy, called a *megawatt-hour* [MWh], would power about 1,000 homes for an hour). This marginal cost comes from the firm's variable cost of running its generators at its various power plants—this includes the labor cost of operating and maintaining generators, the cost of environmental permits, and, most importantly, the cost of fuel.

Our firm has three power plants. Plant A uses coal to power its generator and has a capacity of 200 megawatts (MW); Plants B and C use natural gas and each has a capacity of 25 MW. Coal generators are generally cheaper to run than natural gas generators.

The marginal cost of running Plant A's coal generator is $18 per MWh and it is constant across the plant's production quantity up to 200 MW. The plant cannot produce quantities above this level, so the *plant's* marginal cost is, in effect, infinite at quantities greater than 200 MW. Plant B's natural-gas-fired generator has a constant marginal cost of $37 per MWh (up to its 25-MW capacity), and Plant C's natural gas generator has the highest constant marginal cost of $39 per MWh (up to its 25-MW capacity).

If the firm is generating 200 MW or less, only Plant A (its coal plant) will be on line (i.e., producing electricity), because that's the lowest-cost way of generating that quantity. Thus, the firm's marginal cost curve is flat at $18 per MWh for quantities from 0 to 200 MWh, as shown in Figure 8.7.

To generate quantities above 200 MWh, the firm has to use at least one of its other generators. If it wants to produce a quantity between 200 and 225 MWh, it only needs to run one of its natural gas plants, and it will put Plant B on line, the one with the smaller marginal cost of the two, $37 per MWh. Therefore at a quantity of 200 MWh, the firm's marginal cost curve jumps up to $37 per MWh. It stays at this level up to the quantity

Figure 8.7   The Marginal Cost Curve for an Electricity Firm (Firm 1)

A firm in the Texas electricity industry faces a stepwise marginal cost curve. When this firm supplies 200 MW or less, only its coal plant, Plant A, is on line, and its marginal cost is horizontal at $18 per MWh. At output quantities greater than 200 MW, the firm will also run its natural gas plants, Plants B and C, at marginal costs of $37 per MWh and $39 per MWh, respectively.

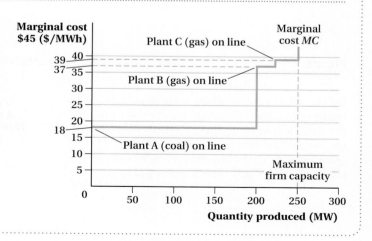

[2] Ali Hortaçsu and Steven Puller, "Understanding Strategic Bidding in Multi-Unit Auctions: A Case Study of the Texas Electricity Spot Market," *RAND Journal of Economics* 39, no. 1 (2008): 86–114.

of 225 MWh. To produce a quantity above 225 MWh, it needs to put Plant C on line, its natural gas generator with the $39 marginal cost, so the marginal cost curve jumps up to $39 per MWh. The firm's marginal cost remains at $39 per MWh up to the quantity of 250 MWh. At this point, the firm has exhausted its generating capacity and cannot produce any more electricity. Above 250 MWh, the firm's marginal costs effectively become infinite. Figure 8.7 reflects this as a vertical line extending off the graph at 250 MWh.

The portion of this marginal cost curve at or above the firm's average variable cost is its supply curve. We saw in Chapter 7 that a firm's total variable cost at any quantity is the sum of its marginal cost of producing each unit up to and including that quantity. Therefore, the firm's total variable cost of producing its first megawatt-hour is $18, and its average variable cost of producing that quantity is $18 per MWh. Its total variable cost of producing 2 megawatt-hours is $36, so its average variable cost is $36/2 = $18 per MWh. It's clear, therefore, that the average variable cost will be $18 per MWh at quantities up to 200 MWh. In other words, the marginal cost curve *is* the average variable cost curve up to that quantity. When marginal cost rises to $37 per MWh for the 201st megawatt-hour the firm produces, the *total* variable cost rises by $37 for 201 MWh, but the average variable cost only rises to ($18 × 200 MWh + $37)/201 MWh = $18.09 per MWh. By this logic, the firm's marginal cost curve will always be above its average variable cost curve at all quantities above 200 MWh. So, for this firm at least, its entire marginal cost curve is its supply curve. ∎

The Short-Run Supply Curve for a Perfectly Competitive Industry

We know that an individual firm in a perfectly competitive market cannot affect the price it receives for its output by changing the level of its output. What *does* determine the price in a perfectly competitive market? The *combined* output decisions of all the firms in the market: the industry supply curve. In this section, we look at how this combined output response is determined.

Before we begin, we must clarify what we mean by firms' "combined" decisions. What we do *not* mean is "coordinated." Firms in a perfectly competitive market do not gather at an annual convention to determine their output levels for the year, or have an industry newsletter or website that serves the same function. (Such a practice would typically get a firm's executives indicted for price fixing, in fact.) "Combined" here instead means aggregated—the total of all the individual firms' independent output decisions added together. An industry supply curve, then, indicates how much total output an industry supplies at any particular price.

It's easy to see how you can add up firms' short-run supply curves in an example. We assume that firms' combined output responses do not have any notable impact on *input* prices, so the industry short-run supply curve is the sum of firm-level short-run supply curves. Let's suppose that there are 100 firms in a perfectly competitive industry, each with the same short-run supply curve. Below a market price of $1 per unit, the firms do not operate because this is less than their average variable costs. For prices greater than or equal to $1 and less than $2, each firm supplies one unit of output. At any price equal to or above $2, each firm produces two units of output, but no more because of capacity limitations. (This is a ridiculously contrived example, but it keeps things simple enough so that we can concentrate on the concepts rather than the arithmetic.)

To derive the industry short-run supply curve from these firm supply curves, we add up the individual firm outputs at each possible market price. At prices below $1, the industry supplies no output, again because none of its firms can cover its average variable cost at those prices. When the price is between $1 and $2, the industry produces 100 units of output—1 unit from each of the 100 firms. When the price is at $2 or above, the industry quantity supplied is 200 units because each firm now makes 2 units. Therefore, the short-run supply curve for this industry is 0 units for prices below $1, 100 units for prices at or above $1 but below $2, and 200 units for prices $2 and higher.

The Short-Run Supply Curve: A Graphical Approach If we use a graphical approach to the short-run industry supply curve, the firms' supply curves would look as they do on the left-hand side of Figure 8.8. There, we've drawn the short-run supply curve that each of the industry's 100 firms share. To build the industry short-run supply curve, we horizontally add the firm's short-run supply curves: At any given price, we find the individual firms' outputs, add them up, and plot their sum to get the industry quantity supplied. These values yield the industry short-run supply curve on the right-hand side of the figure. Note how individual firms' supply curves are added up horizontally, not vertically, to obtain the industry supply curve, just as individual consumers' demand curves were horizontally added to obtain the market demand curve in Chapter 5.

In Figure 8.8, all industry firms have the same short-run supply curves (this is equivalent to saying they have the same cost curves). The analysis gets more complicated if firms in a perfectly competitive industry have different costs. In this case, the process for determining the industry supply curve is the same (we add up the supply curves of the individual firms), but there are additional ways in which the supply curves of individual firms can affect the shape of the industry supply curve.

To illustrate this point, let's now suppose that the industry (which still has 100 firms) has 50 firms with supply curves like those in Figure 8.8 and another 50 that have different supply curves. Let's say these other firms have higher costs and therefore will not produce any output at a market price less than $2. For prices greater than or equal to $2 and less than $3, they produce 1 unit of output, and at prices at or above $3, they produce 2 units. Now the industry supply curve is 0 units for prices under $1, because no firms can profitably produce below that price. For prices from $1 to just under $2, industry supply is 50 units; only the 50 low-cost firms can operate at these prices, and they produce 1 unit each. At prices at or above $2 and less than $3, the industry supplies 150 units: 100 units (50 firms times 2 units each) for the low-cost firms, and 1 unit for each of the 50 high-cost firms. At prices greater than or equal to $3, supply is 200 units, because all firms now produce 2 units of output.

In general, the industry supply curve is the horizontal sum of the supply curves of the individual firms within it. The examples above use very simple "step-type" firm-level supply curves, but conceptually there is little difference if the supply curves are

---

Figure 8.8   Deriving the Short-Run Industry Supply Curve When Firms Have the Same Costs

Supply$_{Firm}$ is the short-run supply curve of each firm in an industry with 100 firms. The short-run industry supply curve, Supply$_{Industry}$, is the horizontal sum of the individual firms' supply curves.

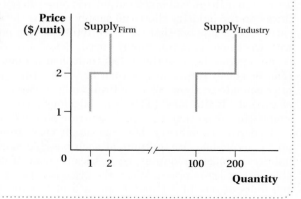

Figure 8.9   **Short-Run Industry Supply Curve When Firms Have Different Costs**

In a four-firm industry, in which each firm faces different costs, these cost differences are reflected in their individual supply curves ($S_{\text{Firm A}}$, $S_{\text{Firm B}}$, $S_{\text{Firm C}}$, and $S_{\text{Firm D}}$). The industry supply curve, S_{Industry}, is the horizontal sum of the four individual firms' supply curves. At prices between P_1 and P_2, only Firms A and B produce; at price P_2, Firm C also supplies its product on the market; and at price P_3, all four firms supply positive quantities.

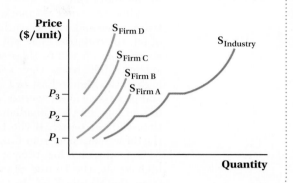

the more standard type that we're accustomed to. The firms' supply curves would look something like what we've drawn on the left-hand side of Figure 8.9. We're assuming there are four firms in the industry, with Firm A having the lowest costs, Firm B the next lowest, and so on. Again, the industry supply curve is the horizontal sum of the firms' supply curves. Only at prices above P_1 does any firm produce, so the industry supplies positive quantities only at price P_1 or higher. For prices between P_1 and P_2, the industry supply curve is the sum of Firm A and Firm B's supply curves. At P_2, Firm C starts producing. The industry supply curve shifts right by the quantity that C produces at P_2 when this happens, and Firm C's supply is also added to the industry supply curve above this price. Finally, Firm D starts producing at P_3, and again the industry supply curve shifts horizontally as this output is added.

These examples make an interesting point: Industry output increases as price increases for two reasons. One is that individual firms' supply curves are often upward-sloping—an individual firm will tend to produce more as the market price rises. The other comes from the fact that some firms might have higher costs than others, so they only begin operating at higher price levels.

 **application**

The Short-Run Supply of Crude Oil

U.S. politicians are constantly calling for the country to reduce its dependence on oil from the Middle East. About 25% of the oil the United States consumes comes from OPEC (the Organization of Petroleum Exporting Countries), and just under half of that (10% of U.S. consumption) is supplied by Middle Eastern countries who are members of OPEC. Many politicians take this to mean that reducing the country's dependence on Middle Eastern oil is simple: Cut consumption by 10%, and that will effectively eliminate imports from the Middle East. This will also increase the share of imported oil that comes from "friendlier" nations, such as Canada.

This type of logic ignores what we know about how perfectly competitive firms make production decisions. We've seen that a competitive firm's short-run supply curve is the portion of its marginal cost curve above its minimum average variable cost curve. If the market price dips below the price at the intersection between the marginal cost and average variable cost curves, then the firm will shut down in the short run.

While the crude oil market is not perfectly competitive, the same relationship between price and average variable cost holds for all firms. If we reduce our consumption of oil, the countries that will be hurt by a decrease in demand and the price drop that accompanies it will be those with the highest costs—those countries for which the market price falls below their average variable costs first. Where are oil production costs higher, the Middle East or Canada? You guessed it: Canada. Saudi Arabia can extract and process oil at an average variable cost of only a couple of dollars per barrel, but producers tapping the Canadian oil sands face much higher average variable costs, greater than $30 per barrel. If the United States reduces its oil consumption, we will reduce the oil we consume from Canada before we reduce oil consumed from Saudi Arabia.[3]

This outcome has been borne out historically. Today with oil prices at relatively high levels, the United States actually imports more oil from Canada than it does from the Middle East. In the late 1990s, on the other hand, when crude oil prices were at historic lows, only about 7% of U.S. oil consumption came from Canadian imports, while about 15% of consumption was imported from the Middle East. Thus, if we want to reduce our dependence on the Middle East, cutting back consumption a bit isn't the answer. ∎

Producer Surplus for a Competitive Firm

The intersection of the short-run industry supply curve and the market demand curve determines the market equilibrium price. Each perfectly competitive firm then takes this price as given and chooses the quantity of output at which it maximizes profit (and chooses whether to operate at all). We showed how we can measure a firm's short-run profit earlier. Equally important is producer surplus, which we first learned about in Chapter 3. Remember that producer surplus is the vertical difference between the market price and the supply curve, which we now know reflects firms' marginal costs.

At all but the lowest market price levels, firms will sell some units of output at a price above their marginal cost of production. In the Application on Texas electricity generation, for example, if the market price is at or above $37 per MWh, the firm would be able to sell the electricity generated by its coal plant at a marginal cost of $18 per MWh at a considerably higher price.

We can see this in a more general case in Figure 8.10, which shows the production decision of a particular firm. Profit maximization implies the firm will produce Q^*, the quantity where the firm's marginal cost equals the market price P. Notice that for all units the firm produces before Q^*, the firm's marginal cost of producing them is lower than the market price. The firm earns a markup for each of these units.

If we add up all these price-marginal cost markups across every unit of output the firm makes, we get the firm's producer surplus. This is equal to the shaded area in panel a of Figure 8.10. (If this isn't obvious to you, imagine slicing the shaded area into many tiny vertical slices, one for each unit of output. Each slice equals the difference between price and marginal cost for that unit of output. If we add up all the slices—i.e., sum the price-cost gaps for all the units of output—we get the firm's producer surplus.)

There's another way to compute producer surplus. First, remember from Chapter 7 that marginal cost involves only variable cost, not fixed cost. If we add up the firm's

[3] Austan Goolsbee, "Refined Thought: Dependency Paradox," *Fortune*, August 22, 2005. http://money.cnn.com/magazines/fortune/fortune_archive/2005/08/22/8270013/index.htm.

Figure 8.10   Producer Surplus for a Firm in Perfect Competition

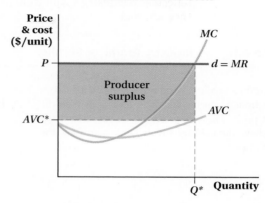

(a) Producer Surplus: Adding All of the Price-Marginal Cost Markups

(b) Producer Surplus: Total Revenue Minus Variable Costs

(a) At market price, a perfectly competitive firm produces Q^*. For each unit the firm produces below Q^*, the marginal cost MC is less than the market price, and the firm earns a producer surplus on that unit. As a result, total producer surplus is equal to the area below the demand curve and above MC.

(b) Producer surplus can also be calculated by a firm's total revenue minus its variable cost. A firm's total revenue is the entire rectangle with height P and length Q^*, and its variable cost is the rectangle with height AVC^* and length Q^*. Its producer surplus, therefore, is the area of the rectangle with height $(P - AVC^*)$ and length Q^*.

marginal cost for all the units of output it produces, we have its variable cost. And if we add up the firm's revenue for every unit of output it produces, we have its total revenue. That means the firm's total revenue minus its variable cost equals the sum of the price-marginal cost markups it earns on every unit it sells—that is, its producer surplus:

$$PS = TR - VC$$

In panel b of Figure 8.10, the firm's total revenue is the area of the rectangle with a height of P and a base of Q^*. Variable cost is output multiplied by average variable cost, so the firm's variable cost is the area of the rectangle with a base of Q^* and a height of AVC^* (AVC at the profit-maximizing level of output). The difference between these two areas is the shaded rectangle with base Q^* and height $(P - AVC^*)$. The area of this rectangle also equals the firm's producer surplus.

Producer Surplus and Profit

You're probably not going to be surprised when we tell you that producer surplus is closely related to profit. But it's really important to recognize that producer surplus is *not* the same thing as profit. The difference is that producer surplus includes no fixed costs, while profit does. In mathematical terms, $PS = TR - VC$ and $\pi = TR - VC - FC$.

A new firm may operate with profit less than zero. It will never operate with producer surplus less than zero because that means each unit is costing more to produce than it sells for, even without fixed costs.

Producer Surplus for a Competitive Industry

Producer surplus for an entire industry is the same idea as producer surplus for a firm. It is the area below the market price but above the short-run supply curve—now, however, it is the industry supply curve rather than the firm's (Figure 8.11). This surplus reflects the industry's gain from producing units at a lower cost than the price at which they are sold.

Figure 8.11   Industry Producer Surplus

An industry's producer surplus is the entire industry's surplus from producing units at a lower cost than the market price. This is represented by the shaded triangle above the industry supply curve and below the market price P.

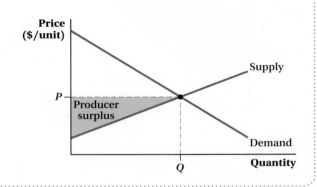

8.3 figure it out

Assume that the pickle industry is perfectly competitive and has 150 producers. One hundred of these producers are "high-cost" producers, each with a short-run supply curve given by $Q_{hc} = 4P$. Fifty of these producers are "low-cost" producers, with a short-run supply curve given by $Q_{lc} = 6P$. Quantities are measured in jars and prices are dollars per jar.

a. Derive the short-run industry supply curve for pickles.

b. If the market demand curve for jars of pickles is given by $Q^d = 6{,}000 - 300P$, what are the market equilibrium price and quantity of pickles?

c. At the price you found in part (b), how many pickles does each high-cost firm produce? Each low-cost firm?

d. At the price you found in part (b), determine the industry producer surplus.

Solution:

a. To derive the industry short-run supply curve, we need to sum each of the firm short-run supply curves horizontally. In other words, we need to add

each firm's quantity supplied at each price. Since there are 100 high-cost firms with identical supply curves, we can sum them simply by multiplying the firm supply curve by 100:

$$Q_{HC} = 100Q_{hc} = 100(4P) = 400P$$

Similarly, we can get the supply of the 50 low-cost firms by summing their individual supply curves or by multiplying the curve of one firm by 50 (since these 50 firms are assumed to have identical supply curves):

$$Q_{LC} = 50Q_{lc} = 50(6P) = 300P$$

The short-run industry supply curve is the sum of the supply by high-cost producers and the supply of low-cost producers:

$$Q^S = Q_{HC} + Q_{LC} = 400P + 300P = 700P$$

b. Market equilibrium occurs where quantity demanded is equal to quantity supplied:

$$Q^D = Q^S$$
$$6{,}000 - 300P = 700P$$
$$1{,}000P = 6{,}000$$
$$P = \$6$$

The equilibrium quantity can be found by substituting $P = \$6$ into either the market demand or supply equation:

$$Q^D = 6{,}000 - 300P \qquad Q^S = 700P$$
$$= 6{,}000 - 300(6) \qquad = 700(6)$$
$$= 4{,}200 \text{ jars} \qquad = 4{,}200 \text{ jars}$$

c. At a price of $6, each high-cost producer will produce $Q_{hc} = 4P = 4(6) = 24$, while each low-cost producer will produce $Q_{lc} = 6P = 6(6) = 36$ jars.

d. The easiest way to calculate industry producer surplus is to graph the industry supply curve. Producer surplus is the area below the market price but above the short-run industry supply curve. In the figure to the right, this is the triangle with a base

of 4,200 (the equilibrium quantity at a price of $6) and a height of $6:

$$PS = \frac{1}{2} \times \text{base} \times \text{height} = (0.5)(4{,}200)(\$6) = \$12{,}600$$

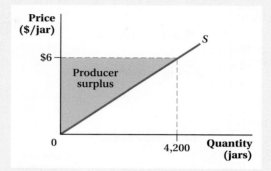

application

Short-Run Industry Supply and Producer Surplus in Electricity Generation

Let's suppose that Firm 1 from the Application on the Texas electricity industry earlier in this section is in an industry with two other firms. (In reality, the Texas electricity industry comprises many firms, but we have chosen three to make it less complicated.) Like Firm 1, Firm 2 has both coal and natural gas plants, and it relies on its relatively low-cost coal plant up to its production capacity of 675 MW. To produce quantities above that, Firm 2 needs to also operate its natural gas generators. Firm 3, on the other hand, has only natural gas generators, though each has a different marginal cost. The three panels of Figure 8.12 show each firm's marginal cost curve.

We can construct the industry marginal cost curve by finding the horizontal sum of the three firms' individual marginal cost curves. This is demonstrated in Figure 8.13. As was true for Firm 1's marginal cost curve, the industry will rely first on generators with relatively cheaper marginal costs. In other words, the industry will first use all available coal generators. For the first 675 MW, only Firm 2's coal plant operates, because it has the lowest marginal cost of all the industry's plants ($15 per MWh). If a higher quantity is produced, Firm 1 brings its 200-MW coal plant on line, raising the industry's marginal cost to $18 per MWh. At quantities above 875 MW (the combined capacity of the industry's coal-fired plants), Firm 3, which has the lowest-marginal-cost natural gas plant, at $23 per MWh, also starts generating power. Once that plant's 1500-MW capacity is used up—that is, when the industry is producing more than 2,375 MW—the industry marginal cost curve shifts up again as more plants are brought on line. Notice that this next step up in the industry marginal cost curve (to $24 per MWh) actually reflects the total production capacity of two plants, one each from Firms 2 and 3, because both these firms have generators that operate at this same marginal cost. The horizontal summation of the three firms' supply curves continues as the industry must bring additional plants on line to produce higher and higher quantities, and the industry marginal cost curve shifts up to reflect the higher marginal costs of operating these plants. Once the industry has exhausted its production capacity, just above 7,000 MWh, its

Figure 8.12 : **Differing Marginal Cost Curves across Electricity Producers**

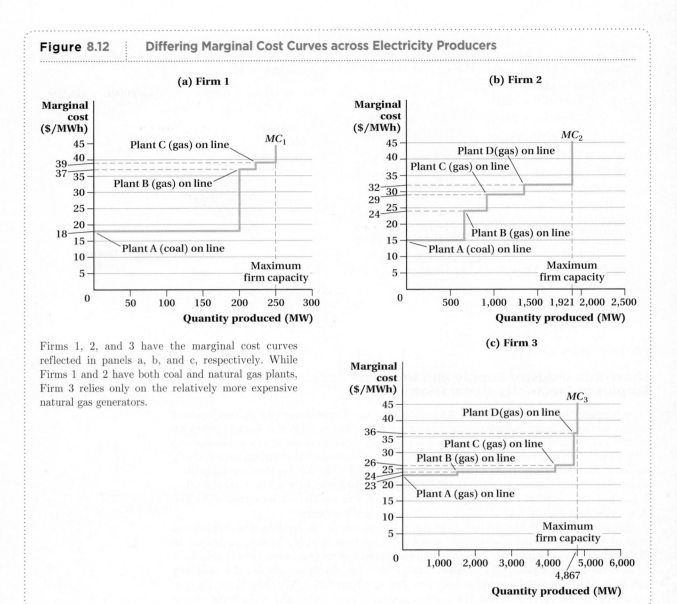

(a) Firm 1

(b) Firm 2

(c) Firm 3

Firms 1, 2, and 3 have the marginal cost curves reflected in panels a, b, and c, respectively. While Firms 1 and 2 have both coal and natural gas plants, Firm 3 relies only on the relatively more expensive natural gas generators.

marginal costs become infinite. This is reflected in the figure by the vertical marginal cost curve at that total capacity.

For all market prices at or above $18 per MWh, the industry is going to have at least one plant operating at a marginal cost that is below the market price. For example, if the market price were $23 per MWh, Firm 1 and 2's coal plants would both be operating at marginal costs that are smaller than the market price. In other words, price equals marginal cost only for the *marginal* plant—the last plant that needs to be brought on line to produce the industry quantity at that price. At a market price of $23 per MWh, the marginal plant is Firm 3's lowest-cost natural gas plant. The two coal plants therefore earn a markup above their marginal costs; they are able to sell their output at a price above their marginal cost of production. This markup is producer's surplus. ∎

Figure 8.13   **The Short-Run Supply of Electricity in Texas**

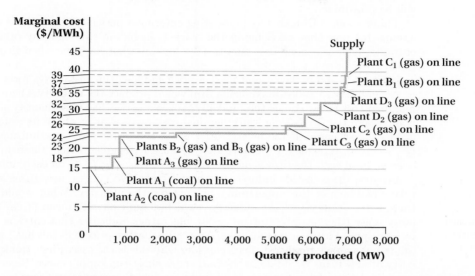

The short-run supply of electricity in Texas is the horizontal sum of the firms' marginal cost curves in Figure 8.12. When the market price is at least $15 per MWh, Firm 2 supplies electricity on the market. At prices at or above $18 per MWh, Firms 1 and 2 both supply on the market. At a market price of $23 per MWh, Firm 3 generates electricity using natural gas, and all three firms are suppliers on the electricity market.

8.4 Perfectly Competitive Industries in the Long Run

We already noted that there are differences between firms' short- and long-run supply curves. In the short run, a firm supplies output at the point where its short-run marginal cost equals the market price. This price can be below the firm's average total cost, but it must be at least as high as its short-run average variable cost. In other words, the firm must earn producer surplus, or else it shuts down. The short-run supply curve is therefore that portion of a firm's short-run marginal cost curve above its short-run average variable cost curve and zero otherwise.

In the long run, however, a firm produces where its *long-run* marginal cost equals the market price. Moreover, because all inputs and costs are variable in the long run, the firm's long-run supply curve is the part of its long-run marginal cost curve above its long-run average total cost curve ($LATC = LAVC$, because there are no fixed costs in the long run).

At the industry level, there are other distinctions between the short run and long run. The primary difference is that, in the long run, firms can enter and exit the industry. In the short run, the number of firms in the industry is assumed fixed, so only firms already in the market make production choices. This assumption makes sense; some inputs are fixed in the short run, making it difficult for new firms to start producing on a whim or for existing firms to avoid paying a fixed cost. In the long run, though, firms can enter or leave the industry in response to changes in profitability. In this section, we learn how this process works and what it implies about how competitive industries look in the long run.

Entry

Firms decide to enter or exit a market depending on whether they expect their action will be profitable.

Think about a firm that is considering entering a perfectly competitive market. We assume for now that all firms in the market, including this and any other potential entrants, have the same cost curves. (We look at what happens when firms have different costs later.)

Figure 8.14 shows the current market price and long-run cost curves for a typical firm in this industry. A profit-maximizing firm would produce the quantity where its long-run marginal cost curve equals the market price. We know that this quantity must be at a point where the firm's (long-run) marginal cost curve is at or above its (long-run) average total cost curve. If the market price is P_1, the firm's profit-maximizing quantity is Q^*, where LMC equals P_1. Notice that because P_1 is greater than the firm's minimum average total cost, the firm is making a profit of $(P_1 - LATC^*)$ on each unit of output.

Because firms in this industry are earning positive profits, new firms will want to take advantage of this opportunity by entering the industry. What would happen? If there is **free entry** into the industry—which doesn't have to mean "free" in the monetary sense (there can be startup costs), but rather, indicates that entry is not blocked by any special legal or technical barriers—the market price will fall until it equals the minimum average total cost. Let's consider why this is the case. First, think about what entry of new firms would do to the *industry's* short-run supply curve. Since this supply curve is derived from the sum of all industry firms' marginal cost curves, adding new firms would cause the industry to provide more output at any given price, as the supply from the new entrants is added to the industry total. In other words, entry shifts the short-run industry supply curve out from S_1 to S_2 (Figure 8.15). This outward shift lowers the market price from P_1 to P_2.

If P_2 is still above the minimum average total cost, an incentive remains for more firms to enter because they would be making profits by doing so. They would be making less profit than earlier entrants, but they're still better off entering the market than staying out. New entrants will shift the industry supply curve further out, lowering the market price even further.

This process continues until the last set of entrants drives down the market price to the minimum average total cost and there are no profits to be made by entering the industry. At this point, any potential entrant would be indifferent between entering

free entry
The ability of a firm to enter an industry without encountering legal or technical barriers.

Figure 8.14   **Positive Long-Run Profit**

In the long run, a perfectly competitive firm produces only when the market price is equal to or greater than its long-run average total cost $LATC^*$. Here, the firm produces Q^*, market price P_1 equals its long run marginal cost LMC, and its long-run economic profit equals $(P_1 - LATC^*)$ per unit.

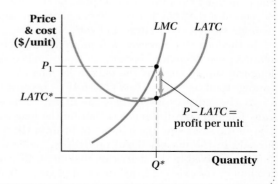

Figure 8.15 : **Entry of New Firms Increases Supply and Lowers Equilibrium Price**

When firms in an industry are earning positive economic profits, new firms will enter, shifting the short-run industry supply curve out from S_1 to S_2 and lowering the market price from P_1 to P_2.

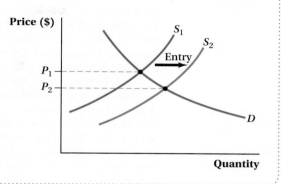

---

the industry and staying out, entry ceases, and the market is in **long-run competitive equilibrium.** The bottom line is that if there is free entry, the price in a perfectly competitive industry will be driven down toward the minimum average total cost of the industry's firms, and no firms will be making a profit.

This is an important idea and seems odd. How could they make no profit? And, if they make no profit, why bother? The answer is that in perfect competition, it's a tough world. You may have a good idea, but the profit you make only lasts until everyone else enters and copies it. One thing to remember about this no-profit condition is that it refers to *economic* profit, not accounting profit. It includes covering the opportunity cost of their time. It means business owners make only enough to stay in business—that is, to be no worse off than their outside option—and no more.

Exit

Now suppose the market price is *below* the minimum average total cost instead. No firms will enter the industry, because they would earn negative profits if they did. Further, firms already in the industry are making negative profits, so this market situation isn't sustainable. If there is **free exit** from the market, some of these firms will close up shop and leave the industry. Since we've assumed all firms in the market are the same, all firms are equally unprofitable and would prefer to exit. Which firms exit first? There are two ways to look at how firms make this decision. One is that there are a lucky few who figure out that they're losing money before the others, and they leave first. The other, probably more realistic possibility is that cost differences actually exist across firms, and the highest-cost firms exit first. (We'll talk more about this case below.)

This exit from the industry shifts its supply curve in, raising the market price. Just as entry continues until higher prices are driven down to the minimum average total cost, exit continues until the market price rises to minimum average total cost. At this point, exiting would not make any firms better off.

Free entry and exit are forces that push the market price in a perfectly competitive industry toward the long-run minimum average total cost. This outcome leads to two important characteristics of the long-run equilibrium in a perfectly competitive market. First, even though the industry's short-run supply curve is upward-sloping, the industry's *long-run* supply curve is horizontal at the long-run minimum average cost. Remember that a supply curve indicates the quantity supplied at every price. Long-run competitive equilibrium implies that firms produce where price is equal to minimum average total cost.

long-run competitive equilibrium
The point at which the market price is equal to the minimum average total cost and firms would gain no profits by entering the industry.

∂ The online appendix solves for the long-run competitive equilibrium. (http://glsmicro.com/appendices)

free exit
The ability of a firm to exit an industry without encountering legal or technical barriers.

Graphing the Industry Long-Run Supply Curve

Figure 8.16 shows how we can derive the industry long-run supply curve graphically. Suppose the industry (panel a) is currently in equilibrium at a price of P_1. Each firm takes the price as given and maximizes profit by producing where $P_1 = LMC$. Because price is also equal to long-run average total cost, the firm is earning zero profit. This means that firms have no incentive to enter or exit the market, so the industry is in long-run competitive equilibrium at P_1.

Now, suppose that the demand for the product rises as a result of a change in consumer tastes. This change increases the quantity demanded at each price and the demand curve shifts to D_2. Prices would rise temporarily to P_2. As a result, each firm would move upward along its supply curve and produce a higher quantity where $P_2 = LMC$. This increase in output would be reflected at the industry level as a increase in quantity to the level at the intersection of D_2 and S_1 in panel a. But even after this increase in output among existing industry firms, the market price is still above the firms' minimum $LATC$. As a result, new firms enter the market to take advantage of these economic profits. This shifts the industry quantity supplied at any given price, thereby shifting the short-run industry supply curve to the right. Eventually, the industry returns to long-run equilibrium when short-run supply shifts to S_2 and the market price falls back to long-run minimum average total cost (P_1). If we connect the two long-run equilibria, we have the industry's long-run supply curve S_{LR}, which is horizontal at P_1.

Figure 8.16   **Deriving the Long-Run Industry Supply Curve**

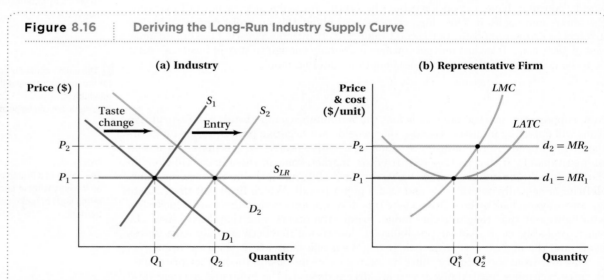

(a) The original long-run equilibrium for an industry is (P_1, Q_1) at the intersection between the long-run supply curve S_{LR} and the original demand curve D_1. After a change in tastes, demand increases to D_2, price increases to P_2, and firms earn positive economic profits in the short run. In the long run, new firms enter the industry, shifting the short-run supply curve to S_2 until it reaches the long-run equilibrium price P_1 at the new equilibrium quantity Q_2.

(b) At the long-run market price P_1, the representative firm earns zero economic profit and produces quantity Q_1^*. When market demand rises, the market price increases to P_2 and the firm's output increases to Q_2^*. At this combination, the firm earns positive economic profit. As entry into the industry occurs, the price falls back to P_1, and the firm reduces its output to Q_1^*. At this point, the firm earns zero economic profit.

theory and data

Entry and Exit at Work in Markets—Residential Real Estate

Residential real estate brokerage in the United States is a peculiar industry. For one thing, real estate agents' commissions are essentially the same everywhere, consistently hovering around 6% of the selling price, even though every city is a different market. Many have wondered whether that's from collusion among agents, but regardless of the reason, agents selling houses in, say, Boston, Massachusetts, charge essentially the same commission rate as those in Fargo, North Dakota.

Given that agents across the country get paid the same percentage of the sales price, it seems like it would be better to be an agent in a place with higher house prices, such as Boston or Los Angeles. With an average house selling for a little over $400,000 in Boston, real estate agents get around $24,000 per house. Compare this to the $12,000 they would make on a typical home in Fargo (average price $200,000). But it turns out that Boston agents pull in approximately the same average yearly salary as those in Fargo, despite the higher house prices. The same pattern holds across the United States: Regardless of house prices, agents' average salaries are roughly equal across cities.

Why do real estate agents everywhere end up making around the same yearly salary? Free entry. In a 2003 study, Chang-Tai Hsieh and Enrico Moretti look into just this phenomenon.[4] They find the key to explaining this pattern is that the typical Boston agent sells fewer homes over the course of the year than does the typical agent in Fargo. In other words, as housing prices increase, agents' productivity decreases, and the reduction in houses sold per year in high-house-price cities just about exactly counteracts the higher commission per house. So while average commissions *per house* might be twice as high in Boston as in Fargo, the typical Boston agent sells half the number of houses per year as the typical agent in Fargo. They end up making the same income.

Are the agents in Boston and other high-price real estate markets just being lazy? Hardly. This decrease in productivity is the result of free entry into the real estate market. It's not hard to become a real estate agent—spend maybe 30 to 90 hours in the classroom and pass a test, and you'll have your license. Therefore in cities with high housing costs (and high commissions per house sold), more people choose to become real estate agents. Having more agents means each agent sells fewer houses, on average. This drives down agents' average yearly salaries until they are on par with those for agents in other lower-cost cities.

Not only did Hsieh and Moretti find this pattern across cities with different average house prices, they found it *within* cities over time as well. When housing prices increased in a city, so did the number of agents seeking to sell those houses, keeping average agent salaries from rising along with house prices. If prices fell, the opposite happened: Agents left the market until the average productivity of those remaining rose to keep salaries at their original level. In this way, entry and exit into the market kept the long-run average price for agents (i.e., their salaries) more or less constant. So while the constant commission rate still marks residential real estate brokerage as a peculiar business, free entry into the business explains why average salaries are the same.

---

[4] Chang-Tai Hsieh and Enrico Moretti, "Can Free Entry Be Inefficient? Fixed Commissions and Social Waste in the Real Estate Industry," *Journal of Political Economy* 111, no. 5 (2003): 1076–1122.

freakonomics

The Not-So-Simple Economics of Blackmail

In 2006, a suspicious envelope arrived at Pepsi headquarters. The envelope wasn't laced with anthrax and didn't contain an explosive booby trap, but the contents *were* potentially deadly to Pepsi's main competitor, the Coca-Cola Corporation. The letter, sent by three Coke employees, offered to sell Coke's closely guarded secret recipe. No doubt, the value of the information to Pepsi would be massive. The letter writers would be rich beyond imagination. Or, at least that is what they must have thought. Instead, they found themselves behind bars, serving up to eight years on conspiracy charges after being caught in an FBI sting operation.

These three sketchy industrial spies (Edmund Duhaney, Joya Williams, and Ibrahim Dimson) appeared in an Atlanta court in 2006 for trying to sell confidential Coca-Cola Co. information to PepsiCo Inc.

While their fate must have come as a surprise to the formula stealers, if they had paid better attention in intermediate microeconomics, they might have ended up far better off.

The PepsiCo and Coca-Cola Corporations have been entrenched in the Cola Wars since at least the 1970s when Pepsi introduced the Pepsi Challenge in America's grocery stores and argued that soda drinkers prefer the taste of Pepsi in blind taste tests. Pepsi has won some victories (for instance, Coke's introduction of New Coke in 1985 is widely viewed as one of the worst marketing missteps in history), but mostly Coca-Cola has maintained the upper hand. Coke's U.S. market share today is around 40% compared to Pepsi's 30%.

In light of that fact, wouldn't Pepsi be desperate to weaken Coke by, say, buying Coke's secret formula and making it public? Most likely, the availability of the formula would cause dozens of new cola manufacturers to enter the market, making perfect substitutes for Coke, much like generic drug manufacturers enter the market when a prescription drug goes off patent. If all the Coke knockoffs tasted exactly like real Coke, and there were free entry, one might imagine that the market for the Coke version of cola would start to look a whole lot like perfect competition. The price of Coke would plunge. (In practice, it is unlikely that an exactly perfect-competition-like outcome would actually happen because so much of what buyers get when they purchase Coke is the mystique that comes from the advertising, but let's just ignore that for a second for the sake of argument.)

What would such a scenario do to Pepsi's profits? Coke and Pepsi are close substitutes. If the price of Coke falls, the demand for Pepsi falls, and along with it Pepsi's profits. A (near) perfectly competitive market for Coke would likely be disastrous for Pepsi, not the boon that the formula stealers imagined.

Thus, it is no surprise that the executives at Pepsi quickly delivered the letter offering to sell the secret formula to Coca-Cola, which then turned it over to the FBI. Unlike the criminals, the Pepsi execs must have been paying attention in their economics classes.

If the three renegade Coke employees had been better economists, what would they have done differently? For starters, they would have sent the letter not to Pepsi, but to a firm that was thinking of entering the cola market. A company like that might very well have put a great value on knowing Coke's formula and paid handsomely for it. So if you really want to begin a career of dastardly criminal enterprise, be sure to know your microeconomics or you may end up behind bars (where you belong!).

Adjustments between Long-Run Equilibria

In theory, the long-run implications of perfect competition are clear: a stable price, just high enough to cover firms' average total costs, with total industry quantity supplied adjusted by the free flow of firms in and out of the market. In reality, getting to the long run can take a long time. When changes in an industry's underlying demand or costs occur, some interesting things can happen while the industry transitions from the old long-run equilibrium to the new one.

A Demand Increase Suppose an industry is in long-run equilibrium when the demand for its product unexpectedly rises. As before, let's say this change in demand comes from a change in consumer tastes. That is, at any price, consumers now want to consume more of the product. This change shifts out the industry demand curve as we saw in Figure 8.16, which is replicated in panels a and b in Figure 8.17. In the short run, when entry is limited, the relevant industry supply curve is the short-run curve S_1. The initial short-term response to the demand increase is an increase in both equilibrium output and the market price as the industry moves up its short-run supply curve.

During this short-run response, firms earn positive economic profits and producer surplus. The market price, which was originally at the minimum long-run average total cost and therefore only just high enough for firms to earn zero economic profit, is now above this level.

Because price is above average cost, profit is positive and so new firms will enter the market. As firms enter, industry output increases at every price and the industry's short-run supply curve shifts out, from S_1 to S_2. With the demand curve now stable and fixed at its new level D_2, the supply shift raises industry output and lowers the market price, and consumers move along their demand curve. Entry continues until the price falls back to the minimum average cost level P_1. Total industry output Q_2 is higher in this new long-run equilibrium because the demand for the industry's product is higher than before, but the price is the same as that in the old long-run equilibrium. The horizontal line connecting the two long-run equilibria is the industry's long-run supply curve because it reflects the industry's supply response once free entry and exit are accounted for.

Figure 8.17   Long-Run Adjustments to an Increase in Demand in a Perfectly Competitive Industry

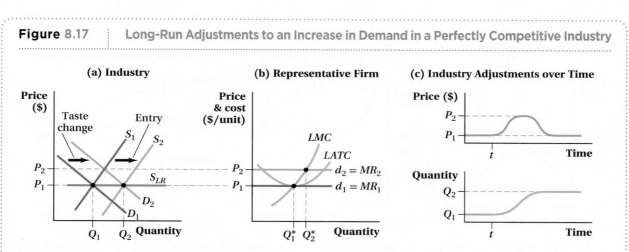

(a) As in Figure 8.16, an increase in demand will temporarily increase the market price from P_1 to P_2 and induce new firms to enter the market to capture the positive profits.

(b) An increase in demand leads to short-run economic profit for a perfectly competitive firm.

(c) An increase in demand leads to a short-run increase in price. Over time, new firms will enter the market, increasing equilibrium quantity to Q_2 and returning the market price to its long-run equilibrium P_1.

If we were to plot the industry's output and market prices over time during this adjustment between two long-run equilibria, we would see something like panel c of Figure 8.17. The industry is initially in equilibrium at quantity Q_1 and price P_1 (where P_1 equals the minimum long-run average total cost of industry firms). When demand shifts at time t, both quantity and price start to rise as the industry moves along its short-run supply curve. As entry begins, the industry's short-run supply curve shifts out, quantity continues to rise, and price falls. Eventually, price falls back to its original level P_1, while quantity rises to Q_2, the new equilibrium quantity.

The response to a decrease in demand for the industry's product would basically look the same, but with the direction of all the effects reversed: Demand falls, price and quantity fall along the initial supply curve, firms make negative profits, some firms leave the industry, supply decreases, Q falls, and prices rebound. When demand falls, exit from the industry is the force that brings price back (up) to the minimum long-run average total cost level.

A Cost Decrease   Now let's think about what happens if the costs faced by industry firms fell. This might occur because of a technological innovation or a permanent decrease in the cost of one of the industry's inputs. In either case, we assume that the cost reduction shifts down both the marginal and average total cost curves of industry firms.

Because of the decrease in marginal cost, every firm will want to supply more output at every given price, and each firm's short-run supply curve shifts out. The industry short-run supply curve also shifts out as a result.

These changes can be seen in Figure 8.18. Panel b shows what happens at the firm level. The firm initially has marginal and average total cost curves LMC_1 and $LATC_1$. In the initial long-run equilibrium, the market price P_1 equals the firm's minimum average total cost. Given these market conditions, the firm produces an output of Q_1^*. When costs fall, the firm's marginal and average total cost curves shift to LMC_2 and $LATC_2$. The original market price P_1 is now above the firm's average total cost.

∂ The online appendix shows the effects of demand and production costs on the long-run equilibrium. (http://glsmicro.com/appendices)

Figure 8.18   **Long-Run Adjustments to a Reduction in Costs in a Perfectly Competitive Industry**

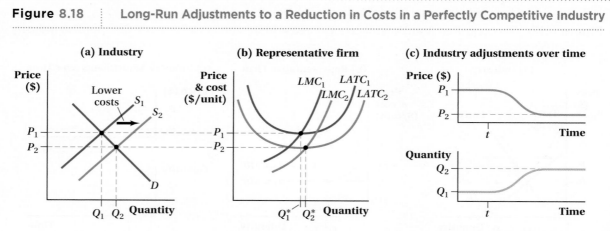

(a) A decrease in industrywide marginal costs leads to an increase in supply from S_1 to S_2. Industry quantity increases from Q_1 to Q_2, and the market price decreases from P_1 to P_2 in the long run.
(b) The decrease in industrywide marginal costs shifts the firm's long-run marginal cost from LMC_1 to LMC_2 and long-run average total cost from $LATC_1$ to $LATC_2$. In the long run, the firm increases output from Q_1^* to Q_2^*.
(c) An increase in supply leads to a long-run decrease in price from P_1 to P_2, and quantity increases from Q_1 to Q_2.

At the industry level (panel a), supply shifts out both because the lower costs mean existing firms in the industry have a higher optimal quantity, Q_2^*, and because the high price P_1 attracts new firms to enter the industry. This outward shift in supply raises the industry quantity supplied and lowers the market price. It continues until supply reaches S_2, at which point the market price has fallen to the new minimum average total cost level P_2.

If we plot the quantity and price changes over time in this case, as in panel c of Figure 8.18, we see that quantity rises and prices fall throughout the transition from the high-cost to the low-cost long-run equilibrium. Here, unlike the response to the demand shift, there is a permanent drop in the long-run price. This is because long-run costs have declined.

 application

The Increased Demand for Corn

The recent increase in the demand for corn driven by the U.S. ethanol boom provides a good opportunity to explore the predictions of our analysis. Small corn farmers operate in an essentially perfectly competitive market, so we can look at total corn output and its market price as reflecting perfectly competitive industry outcomes.

The ethanol boom arguably started with the passage of the Energy Policy Act of 2005, which both mandated increased biofuels (which include ethanol) consumption and raised ethanol subsidies. The number of ethanol plants in the United States grew from 81 in January 2005 to 204 by January 2011, and many existing plants expanded.[5] We can think of the Act as creating an outward shift in the demand for corn, which is the major input into ethanol production in the United States. Our analysis from above predicts that this would increase both corn output and prices in the short run.

Prices as high as an elephant's eye induce entry into corn production.

The data reflect this prediction. Estimated U.S. corn production in 2010 was 313 million metric tons, up about 10% from 2005. While quantities increased, prices rose even more steeply. At the Chicago Board of Trade, corn prices, which had hovered around a long-run average of between $2.50–3.00 per bushel for the decade prior to 2005, were over $6 per bushel in 2011.[6]

Our analysis also predicts that in the long run, prices that high should induce entry into corn production and eventually bring corn prices back down even as output continues to rise. Farms that once grew other crops will switch to corn production to take advantage of the new profit opportunities from growing corn. This shift in industry supply, if demand remains fixed (at its higher post-ethanol level), will increase quantity further and decrease price.

Time will tell if our prediction holds. There are a couple of reasons why it might not. First, further expansion of the ethanol industry (more plants have been planned but not yet built) will create further shifts in the demand curve. This could lead to still more short-run price increases and would delay the return of prices to their earlier levels. A

---

[5] Renewable Fuels Association, "Ethanol Industry Overview," Accessed March 28, 2012. http://www.ethanolrfa.org/pages/statistics#EIO.

[6] The production data here and the price data below are from the Feed Grains Database, U.S. Department of Agriculture.

second possibility is that growing corn has increasing costs in the long run. It might be, for example, that the growth in corn acreage drives up the demand and prices of the special equipment farmers use to plant, tend, and harvest corn or drives corn onto more and more marginal land.

Still, history offers a guide to the power of entry (plus some productivity improvement) to hold down prices. For example, there was a very substantial increase in grain prices in the 1970s. Corn prices rose to more than $3 per bushel in 1974 (this is almost $14 per bushel in 2011 dollars). Within three years, they had fallen back to $2 per bushel—still high compared to today, but a third lower than 1974—and over a longer period of time remained around the $2.50–3.00 per bushel mark (in 2011 dollars) all the way through 2005. Similar things happen in the oil market when prices rise—oil drillers scour the world for new reserves trying to enter the market. ■

8.4 figure it out

Suppose that the market for cantaloupes is currently in long-run competitive equilibrium at a price of $3 per melon. A listeria outbreak in cantaloupe crops leads to a sharp decline in the demand for cantaloupes.

a. In the short run, what will happen to the price of a cantaloupe? Explain and use a graph to illustrate your answer.

b. In the short run, how will firms respond to the change in price described in part (a)? What will happen to each producer's profit in the short run? Explain, using a diagram to illustrate your answer.

c. Given the situation described in (b), what can we expect to happen to the number of producers in the cantaloupe industry in the long run? Why?

d. What will the long-run price of a cantaloupe be?

Solution:

a. As we can see in panel a of the diagram below, a decline in the demand for cantaloupes will lead to a fall in the equilibrium market price of cantaloupes (from $3 to P_2).

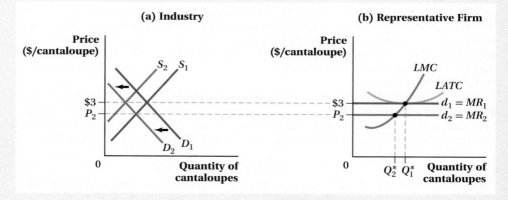

b. As shown in panel b, when price declines to P_2, each firm moves along its long-run marginal cost curve to determine its output, which falls from Q_1^* to Q_2^*. Remember that, before the decrease in demand, the industry was in long-run competitive equilibrium so that, at a price of $3 per cantaloupe, each firm was earning zero economic profit. Therefore, when price falls to P_2, it must be below the firm's average total cost. The drop in demand has led to an economic loss (or negative economic profit) for the firm.

c. If firms are incurring losses, we can expect some to exit the industry. Thus, the number of producers in the industry will fall, the quantity of cantaloupes will fall, and the price will rise.

d. The price of cantaloupes will continue to rise until it is once again at the minimum average total cost of $3. At this point, the industry is in long-run competitive equilibrium and firms have no incentive to enter or exit the industry.

Long-Run Supply in Constant-, Increasing-, and Decreasing-Cost Industries

We saw above that the long-run supply curve of a perfectly competitive industry is horizontal, at a price equal to the minimum average total cost of its producers. However, that analysis made an implicit assumption that firms' total cost curves didn't change when total industry output did. That is, we assumed that the industry is a **constant-cost industry.**

This might not always be the case. Firms in **increasing-cost industries** see their cost curves shift up when industry output increases. This might occur because the price of an input rises in response to the industry's higher demand for that input. Suppose an industry requires special capital equipment that is in limited supply. When there is an increase in the industry's output, firms compete for this scarce capital, pushing up its price. This means that, the higher industry output, the greater firms' average total costs, even in the long run. For this reason, the long-run supply curves of increasing-cost industries are upward-sloping. They're not as steeply sloped as the short-run supply curve for the industry, because they account for entry and exit, but they're not horizontal either.

Shifts from one long-run equilibrium to another in response to a demand shift are similar to the case above for a constant-cost industry. The only difference is that entry only brings price back down to the new, higher long-run average total cost level.

In **decreasing-cost industries,** firms' cost levels decline with increases in industry output. This might be because there are some increasing returns to scale at the industry level, or in the production of one or more of the industry's inputs. The long-run supply curves for these industries are downward-sloping. Again, the short-run transition between long-run equilibria when demand for the industry's product increases looks like the constant-industry case, but now entry continues past the point where the market price is driven down to the old long-run average cost level. Instead, entry continues until the price falls all the way to the new, lower minimum average total cost.

constant-cost industry
An industry whose firms' total costs do not change with total industry output.

increasing-cost industry
An industry whose firms' total costs increase with increases in industry output.

decreasing-cost industry
An industry whose firms' total costs decrease with increases in industry output.

8.5 Producer Surplus, Economic Rents, and Economic Profits

Our analysis of perfect competition has shown that in the long run, perfectly competitive firms earn no economic profit.

Cost Differences and Economic Rent in Perfect Competition

In looking at long-run outcomes in perfectly competitive markets, however, we've assumed that all firms in an industry had the same cost curves. This isn't very realistic, however. Firms differ in their production costs for many reasons: They might face different prices for their inputs; they might have various degrees of special know-how or other production abilities that make them more efficient; or they might be lucky through an accident of history to be blessed with a superior location or access to superior resources. When there are cost differences between firms in a perfectly competitive industry, the more efficient producers earn a special type of return called **economic rent.**

We saw in Section 8.3 that cost differences among firms is one of the reasons why industry marginal cost curves (and therefore their short-run supply curves) slope up. Higher-cost firms produce only when the market price is high.

To see what happens in the long run when firms have different cost curves, let's first think about how output quantities vary when firms' costs do. If all firms have the same cost, their marginal cost curves are the same. Therefore, their profit-maximizing outputs are the same, too: the quantity at which the market price equals (their common) marginal cost. But if firms have different marginal cost curves, their profit-maximizing outputs will differ as well.

Consider an example in which the factors that cause these firms' costs to differ are specific fixtures of the firm; that is, these costs can't be influenced by the firm's actions or sold to other firms. For instance, the factors might involve access to special technologies or a premium location. In any case, these factors affect only the cost structure of that particular firm. Figure 8.19 shows the long-run marginal cost curves for three firms. Firm 1 has a high marginal cost shown by curve LMC_1, Firm 2 has a moderate marginal cost LMC_2, and Firm 3 has a low marginal cost LMC_3. Each firm's marginal cost curve intersects the market price at a different quantity of output. Firm 1's profit-maximizing output is the smallest, Q_1^*. The next largest is Firm 2, which produces Q_2^*. Finally, Firm 3 produces the highest output Q_3^*. Therefore, higher-cost firms produce less, and lower-cost firms produce more, when firms have different costs. This negative

economic rent
Returns to specialized inputs above what firms paid for them.

Figure 8.19   **Firms with Different Long-Run Marginal Costs**

Firms in the same industry with differing long-run marginal costs will produce different quantities of output at the market price. Because each firm maximizes profit where $P = LMC$, low-cost producers will produce a greater quantity of output (Q_3^*) than high-cost producers (Q_1^*).

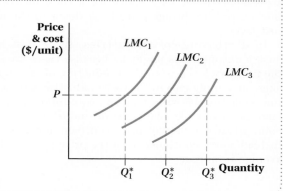

relationship between a firm's size (measured by its output) and its cost has been observed in many industries and countries.

Let's think for a minute about the industry's highest-cost firm. Suppose Firm 1 is this firm, and that the market price is above Firm 1's minimum average total cost. As we discussed above, if all producers have the same cost curve, a perfectly competitive market in which price is above the minimum average total cost will attract new entrants. These entrants shift the industry supply curve out and reduce the price until it equals the minimum average total cost. That's exactly what would happen here, too: If the market price is above Firm 1's minimum average total cost, the price is above all producers' minimum average total costs. Therefore, new firms will enter the market. If all these firms have lower costs than Firm 1, the industry supply curve will shift out until the price falls to the minimum average total cost of Firm 1.

If, on the other hand, some entrants have costs *above* Firm 1's cost, entry will occur until the supply curve shifts out only enough to lower the price to the minimum average total cost of the highest cost entrant.

In either case, the important thing to realize is that in a perfectly competitive market where firms have different costs, *the long-run market price equals the minimum average total cost of the highest-cost firm remaining in the industry.* That highest-cost firm makes zero profit and zero producer surplus. What about the other firms in the market? They have minimum average total costs that are lower than the minimum average total cost of the highest-cost firm, and therefore lower than the market price. They make a positive profit on every sale, and this profit is larger the lower their costs. It's just like what we saw in the earlier Application on electricity in Texas: the market price was determined by the marginal cost of the marginal producer, and the lower-cost generating plants could make extra producer surplus at that price. You might wonder why more firms with costs less than those of the highest-cost firm in the market don't enter. Well, they would, if they existed. By entering, they could make a positive margin over their average total cost on every sale. Furthermore, their entry could shift the industry supply curve out and drive down price enough so that the formerly highest-cost firm in the industry would no longer want to operate, because the long-run price would be below its minimum average total cost. Entry would occur, in fact, until there are no more firms left to enter that have costs below those of the industry's highest-cost firm. Note that if an existing low-cost firm can expand capacity at the existing low-cost level, that's a different form of entry but is entry nonetheless.

The long-run outcome in an industry in which firms have different costs occurs once all entry has stopped. All firms except the one with the highest cost sell their output at a price above their long-run average total costs, so they all earn producer surplus and economic rent. This surplus is tied to their special attributes that allow them to produce at a lower cost. As we said earlier, their lower cost could be the result of access to a special technology, better know-how of some sort or another, a better location, or a number of other possibilities. The greater this cost advantage is, the larger the producer surplus or economic rent.

Economic rents measure returns to specialized inputs above what the firms paid for them. Suppose a firm is a lower-cost firm because it was lucky enough to have hired a manager like Steve Jobs who was particularly smart and adept at efficiently running its production process. If the firm only needed to pay this manager the same salary as every other firm was paying its manager (or, at least not so much more as to wipe out the cost advantage of the manager's ability), *and* if there is a limited supply of similarly exceptional managers, the manager's human capital earns economic rent for the firm. If the firm is instead lower-cost because it has a favorable location that makes servicing customers easier, the location is the source of economic rent to the firm because not all firms can use that same location. What's important to recognize is that economic rents are determined by cost differences *relative* to other firms in the industry. That's because the profit earned by the scarce input depends on how much lower the firm's costs are than its competitors' costs. The larger the cost difference, the larger the rent.

Economic Profit ≠ Economic Rent   At this point, you might be a little confused: Earlier we said that perfectly competitive markets had zero economic profit in the long run, yet now we're saying that firms earn economic rents if they have different costs. Does the zero economic profit outcome only occur if all producers' costs are the same?

Firms in perfectly competitive industries make zero economic profit even if they have different costs. There is a distinction between economic profit and economic rent. Economic profit counts inputs' opportunity costs, and economic rent is included in the opportunity cost for inputs that earn them. This is because inputs that earn rents would still earn them if they were given to another firm. If we gave another firm the brilliant manager or better location discussed above, it would lower that firm's costs. That other firm would therefore be willing to pay more for that rent-earning input. This willingness to pay for the economic rent inherent to the input raises the opportunity cost of the input to the firm that currently owns it—by using the input, they're giving up the ability to sell it to another firm. Once this opportunity cost is subtracted from the firm's revenue, its economic profit is no higher than if the input earned no rent at all.

In practice, this is often hugely important. If one firm has lower costs because it has better programmers and engineers than a different firm, the wages paid to the scarce talent may very well end up absorbing the advantage. The rent in such a case goes to the owner of the scarce resource itself (the workers) rather than to the firm.

8.6 Conclusion

In this chapter, we learned about a firm's profit-maximizing behavior in a perfectly competitive industry. Perfectly competitive industries are characterized by having few barriers to entry, a large number of firms with identical products, and firms that are price takers. A perfectly competitive firm maximizes its profits by producing where the market price (the same as marginal revenue in a perfectly competitive market) is equal to its marginal costs. We saw that a firm's supply curve is the portion of its marginal cost curve at or above its average cost curve and that individual firms' supply curves combine to form the market supply curve.

In the real world, most firms have some influence over the market price, and although many industries approach perfect competition, truly perfectly competitive industries are rare. Even so, the profit-maximization framework we developed here will prove useful as a simple foundation on which to build analyses of more complicated market structures. We will start in Chapters 9 and 10 by looking at the type of firm that is most unlike the perfectly competitive firm—the monopoly that sells a unique product on the market. Firms in monopolistic competition and oligopolies share some characteristics with both monopolies and perfectly competitive firms. We examine those in Chapter 11.

Summary

1. An industry's **market structure** is characterized by the number of firms in the industry, the type of product sold, and the degree of barriers to entry. Given these criteria, there are four different types of market structures in an economy: perfect competition, monopolistic competition, oligopoly, and monopoly. **Perfectly competitive** industries have no barriers to entry and feature a large number of firms selling identical products. As a result of such character-

istics, these firms are price takers, facing horizontal demand curves equal to their marginal revenue curves. [**Section 8.1**]

2. A firm aims to maximize its **profits,** or the difference between its total revenue and its total costs. A perfectly competitive firm produces its profit-maximizing output when its **marginal revenue** equals the market price. [**Section 8.2**]

3. Because firms will operate in the short run only when price is greater than or equal to the firm's

average variable costs, a firm's short-run supply curve is the portion of its marginal cost curve at or above the average variable cost curve. For all prices below that, the firm's supply curve is vertical at the y-axis because quantity produced equals zero. [**Section 8.3**]

4. The industry supply curve is the horizontal sum of individual firms' supply curves; that is, the industry quantity supplied at any given price equals the sum of firms' quantities supplied at that price. Like a firm's supply curve, the industry supply curve generally slopes upward, but this may result from two factors. First, individual firms produce more as market prices rise; second, the quantity supplied by the industry will increase as firms operating with higher costs begin supplying at higher prices. [**Section 8.3**]

5. A firm's producer surplus is equal to its total revenue minus its variable cost, while a firm's profit is equal to its total revenue minus its *total* cost. Graphically, we can see both the firm's and industry's producer surpluses as the area below

the market price but above the firm's or industry's short-run supply curve. [**Section 8.4**]

6. When a perfectly competitive industry is in **long-run competitive equilibrium,** firms earn zero economic profits. This is because perfectly competitive industries have no barriers to entry: Firms have **free entry** and **free exit** into and out of the industry, and will choose to enter or exit an industry when it is profitable to do so. Over time, changes in demand or in costs will change the long-run equilibrium quantity supplied. For **constant-cost industries,** the long-run supply curve is horizontal, while **increasing-cost industries** and **decreasing-cost industries** result in upward- and downward-sloping supply curves, respectively. [**Section 8.4**]

7. While a perfectly competitive firm earns zero economic profits in the long run, it can earn positive **economic rents.** A firm earns positive rents when its costs are lower relative to those of other firms in the industry. [**Section 8.5**]

Review Questions

1. Economists categorize an industry by three criteria: the number of firms in the industry, the type of product sold, and barriers to entry. Using these three criteria, describe a perfectly competitive industry.

2. Why does a perfectly competitive firm face a horizontal demand curve?

3. Define a firm's profit.

4. What is the relationship between the market price and marginal cost when a perfectly competitive firm is maximizing its profit?

5. A firm operating at a loss will decide whether to shut down based on the relationship between the market price and the firm's average variable cost. When will a firm choose to operate? Why does a firm ignore its fixed cost when making this decision?

6. What is a perfectly competitive firm's short-run supply curve?

7. How do we use firms' short-run supply curves to create the industry short-run supply curve?

8. What happens to short-run industry supply when firms' fixed costs change?

9. Define producer surplus. What is the relationship between profit, producer surplus, and fixed costs?

10. Perfectly competitive industries have free entry and exit in the long run. When will firms decide to enter an industry? When will a firm exit an industry?

11. When do economists say that a market is in a long-run competitive equilibrium?

12. Economic rents are returns to scarce inputs above what firms paid for them. When will a firm earn economic rents?

13. Perfectly competitive firms earn zero economic profits in the long run. How can a firm earn zero economic profits and still yield positive economic rents?

Problems (Solutions to problems marked * appear at the back of this book. Problems adapted to use calculus are available online at http://worthpublishers.com/GLS1e)

*1. Nancy sells beeswax in a perfectly competitive market for $50 per pound. Nancy's fixed costs are $15, and Nancy is capable of producing up to 6 pounds of beeswax each year. Use that in-

formation to fill in the table below. (*Hint*: Total variable cost is simply the sum of the marginal costs up to any particular quantity of output!)

Quantity	Total Revenue	Fixed Cost	Variable Cost	Total Cost	Profit	Marginal Revenue	Marginal Cost
0	0	15				—	—
1							30
2							35
3							42
4							50
5							60
6							72

a. If Nancy is interested in maximizing her total revenue, how many pounds of beeswax should she produce?

b. What quantity of beeswax should Nancy produce in order to maximize her profit?

c. At the profit-maximizing level of output, how do marginal revenue and marginal cost compare?

d. Suppose that Nancy's fixed cost suddenly rises to $30. How should Nancy alter her production to account for this sudden increase in cost?

e. Suppose that the bee's union bargains for higher wages, making the marginal cost of producing beeswax rise by $8 at every level of output. How should Nancy alter her production to account for this sudden increase in cost?

*2. The graph below depicts the market for aloe vera gel. The left-hand panel depicts market demand and industry supply; the right-hand panel depicts the long-run cost curves for a representative firm in the industry.

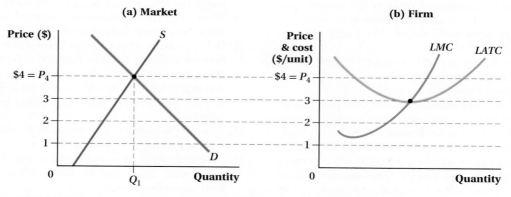

(a) Market   **(b) Firm**

a. Are the firms in the industry earning economic profits or losses? How can you tell?

b. The condition you indicated in (a) will result in entry or exit from the aloe vera gel industry. Indicate whether we will see entry or exit, and depict the effects of that movement in the diagram for the industry.

c. As a result of this change in the market, the price will change. Depict the effects of the price change on the representative firm in the right-hand panel.

d. At what price will entry/exit stop? Briefly explain why.

3. The egg industry is comprised of many firms producing an identical product. Demand and supply conditions are indicated in the left-hand panel of the figure below; the long-run cost curves of a representative egg producer are shown in the right-hand panel. Currently, the market price of eggs is $2 per dozen, and at that price consumers are purchasing 800,000 dozen eggs per day.

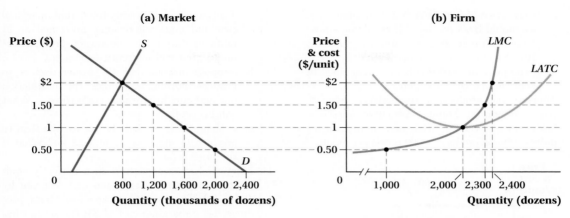

(a) Market   **(b) Firm**

a. Determine how many eggs each firm in the industry will produce if it wants to maximize profit.
b. How many firms are currently serving the industry?
c. In the long run, what will the equilibrium price of eggs be? Explain.
d. In the long run, how many eggs will the typical firm produce?
e. In the long run, how many firms will comprise the industry?

---

4. The diagram below depicts the revenues and costs of a firm producing vodka.

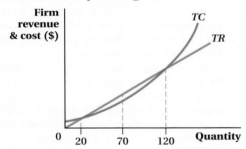

a. What will the firm's profit be if it decides to produce 20 units of output? 120 units?
b. Suppose the firm is producing 70 units of output and decides to cut output to 60. What will happen to the firm's profit as a result?
c. Suppose the firm is producing 70 units of output and decides to increase output to 80. What will happen to the firm's profit as a result?
d. At an output level of 70, draw a line tangent to the total cost curve. Does your line look similar to the total revenue curve? What does the slope of the total revenue curve indicate? What does the slope of the total cost curve indicate?
5. Josie's Pussycats sells ceramic kittens. The marginal cost of producing a particular kitten depends on how many kittens Josie produces, and is given by the formula $MC = 0.8Q$. Thus, the first kitten Josie produces has a marginal cost of $0.80, the second has a marginal cost of $1.60,

and so on. Assume that the ceramic kitten industry is perfectly competitive, and Josie can sell as many kittens as she likes at the market price of $16.
a. What is Josie's marginal revenue from selling another kitten? (Express your answer as an equation.)
b. Determine how many kittens Josie should produce if she wants to maximize profit. How much profit will she make at this output level? (Assume fixed costs are zero. It may help to draw a graph of Josie's marginal revenue and marginal cost.)
c. Suppose Josie is producing the quantity you found in (b). If she decides to produce one extra kitten, what will her profit be?
d. How does your answer to part (c) help explain why "bigger is not always better"?
6. Heloise and Abelard produce letters in a perfectly competitive industry. Heloise is much better at it than Abelard: On average, she can produce letters for half the cost of Abelard's. True or False: If Heloise and Abelard are both maximizing profit, the last letter that Heloise produces will cost half as much as the last letter written by Abelard. Explain your answer.
*7. Hack's Berries faces a short-run total cost of production given by $TC = Q^3 - 12Q^2 + 100Q + 1{,}000$.
a. What is the level of Hack's fixed cost?
b. What is Hack's short-run average variable cost of producing berries? (Express AVC as a function of Q.)

c. If the price of berries is $60, how many berries should Hack produce? How do you know? [*Hint*: You may want to carefully graph the *AVC* function you derived in part (b).]

d. If the price of berries is $73, should Hack be producing berries? Explain.

*8. Minnie is one producer in the perfectly competitive pearl industry. Minnie's cost curves are shown below. Pearls sell for $100, and in maximizing profits, Minnie produces 1,000 pearls per month.

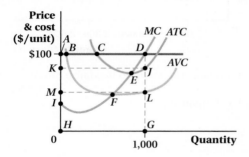

a. Find the area on the graph that illustrates the total revenue from selling 1,000 units at $100 each.

b. Find the area on the graph that indicates the variable cost of producing those 1,000 units.

c. Find the area on the graph that indicates the fixed cost of producing those 1,000 units.

d. Add together the two areas you found in (b) and (c) to show the total cost of producing those 1,000 units.

e. Subtract the total cost of producing those 1,000 units from the total revenue from selling those units to determine the firm's profit. Show the profit as an area on the graph.

9. True or False: "In the short run, if a firm is not earning a profit, it should shut down." Explain your answer.

10. Consider the diagram below that depicts the cost curves for a perfectly competitive firm. The market price (and marginal revenue) faced by this firm is $7.

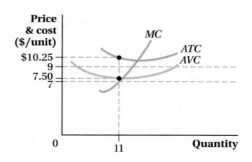

a. The owner of the firm finds that marginal cost and marginal revenue are equal at 11 units of output. If the owner produces 11 units, what will his profit or loss be?

b. Suppose instead that the owner decides to produce nothing—he idles the production line and cuts his variable costs to zero. What will his profit or loss be?

c. If the price is $7, is it better for the firm to produce 11 units, or nothing at all? What if the price is $9?

11. Marty sells flux capacitors in a perfectly competitive market. His marginal cost is given by $MC = Q$. Thus, the first capacitor Marty produces has a marginal cost of $1, the second has a marginal cost of $2, and so on.

a. Draw a diagram showing the marginal cost of each unit that Marty produces.

b. If flux capacitors sell for $2, determine the profit-maximizing quantity for Marty to produce.

c. Repeat part (b) for $3, $4, and $5.

d. The supply curve for a firm traces out the quantity that firm will produce and offer for sale at various prices. Assuming that the firm chooses the quantity that maximizes its profits [you solved for these in (b) and (c)], draw another diagram showing the supply curve for Marty's flux capacitors.

e. Compare the two diagrams you have drawn. What can you say about the supply curve for a competitive firm?

*12. Consider the following graph, which depicts the cost curves of a perfectly competitive seller of potatoes. Potatoes currently sell for $3 per pound.

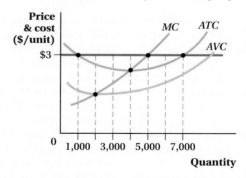

a. To maximize profit, how many pounds of potatoes should this seller produce?

Suppose that the potato grower's bank ratchets up the interest rate applicable to the grower's adjustable-rate mortgage loan. This increases the size of the potato grower's monthly mortgage payment.

b. Illustrate the change in the mortgage payment by shifting the appropriate cost curves.

c. Which curves shift? Which do not? Why?

d. How does the change in interest rates affect the grower's decision on how many potatoes to produce?

e. What happens to the potato grower's profit as a result of the increased interest rate?

f. How does the change in interest rates affect the shape and/or position of the grower's short-run supply curve?

13. The graphs below depict supply curves for John, Paul, and George, who are three producers in the perfectly competitive songwriting industry.

(a) John

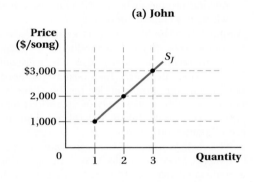

(b) Paul

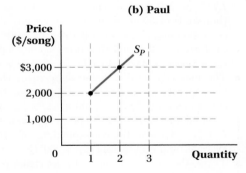

(c) George

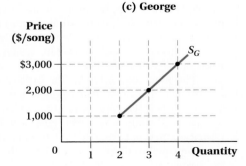

a. If the price of songs is $1,000, how many songs will John write? Paul? George? The three combined?

b. If the price of songs is $2,000, how many songs will John write? Paul? George? The three combined?

c. If the price of songs is $3,000, how many songs will John write? Paul? George? The three combined?

d. Assume that John, Paul, and George are the only three producers in the industry. Using your answers to (a–c), graph the short-run industry supply curve.

14. Consider Minnie the pearl producer with cost curves as shown below. Minnie produces 1,000 pearls when the price of pearls is $100.

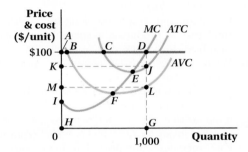

a. What is the area of producer surplus earned by Minnie if the price of pearls is $100?

b. Explain why areas ADI and $ADLM$ must be equal.

15. For the past nine months, Iliana has been producing artisanal ice creams from her small shop in Chicago. She's been just breaking even (earning zero economic profit) that entire time. This morning, the state Board of Health informed her that they are doubling the annual fee for the dairy license she operates under, retroactive to the beginning of her operations.

a. In the short run, how will this fee increase affect Iliana's output level? Her profit?

b. In the long run, how will this fee increase affect Iliana's output level?

c. Suppose that instead of doubling the annual fee for a license, the state Board of Health required Iliana to treat every pint of ice cream to prevent the growth of bacteria. How would this stipulation affect Iliana's production decision and profit in both the short and long run?

16. Martha is one producer in the perfectly competitive jelly industry. Last year, Martha and all of her competitors found themselves earning economic profits.

a. If entry and exit from the jelly industry are free, what do you expect to happen to the number of suppliers in the industry in the long run?

b. Because of the entry/exit you described in part (a), what do you expect to happen to the industry supply of jelly? Explain.

c. As a result of the supply change you described in part (b), what do you expect to happen to the price of jelly? Why?

d. As a result of the price change you indicated in part (c), how will Martha adjust her output?

*17. The canola oil industry is perfectly competitive. Every producer has the following long-run total cost function: $LTC = 2Q^3 - 15Q^2 + 40Q$, where Q is measured in tons of canola oil. The corresponding marginal cost function is given by $LMC = 6Q^2 - 30Q + 40$.

a. Calculate and graph the long-run average total cost of producing canola oil that each firm faces for values of Q from 1 to 10.

b. What will the long-run equilibrium price of canola oil be?

c. How many units of canola oil will each firm produce in the long run?

d. Suppose that the market demand for canola oil is given by $Q = 999 - 0.25P$. At the long-run equilibrium price, how many tons of canola oil will consumers demand?

e. Given your answer to (d), how many firms will exist when the industry is in long-run equilibrium?

18. Suppose that the restaurant industry is perfectly competitive. All producers have identical cost curves, and the industry is currently in long-run equilibrium, with each producer producing at its minimum long-run average total cost of $8.

a. If there is a sudden increase in demand for restaurant meals, what will happen to the price of restaurant meals? How will individual firms respond to the change in price? Will there be entry into or exit from the industry? Explain.

b. In the market as a whole, will the change in the equilibrium quantity be greater in the short run or the long run? Explain.

c. Will the change in output on the part of individual firms be greater in the short run or the long run? Explain and reconcile your answer with your answer to part (b).

19. Suppose that the market for eggs is initially in long-run equilibrium. One day, enterprising and profit-hungry egg farmer Atkins has the inspiration to fit his laying hens with rose-colored contact lenses. His inspiration is true genius—overnight his egg production rises and his costs fall.

a. Will farmer Atkins be able to leverage his inspiration into greater profit in the short run? Why?

b. Farmer Atkin's right-hand man, Abner, accidentally leaks news of the boss' inspiration at the local bar and grill. The next thing Farmer Atkins knows, he's being interviewed by Brian Williams for the NBC evening news. What short-run adjustments do you expect competing egg farmers to make as a result of this broadcast? What will happen to the profits of egg farms?

c. In the long run, what will happen to the price of eggs? What will happen to the profits of egg producers (including those of Farmer Atkins)?

d. Explain how, in the long run, competition coupled with the quest for profits ends up making producers better off only for a little while, but consumers better off forever.

20. Assume that the ice cream industry is perfectly competitive. Each firm producing ice cream must hire an operations manager. There are only 50 operations managers that display extraordinary talent for producing ice cream; there is a potentially unlimited supply of operations managers with average talent. Operations managers are all paid $200,000 per year.

- The long-run total cost (in thousands of dollars) faced by firms that hire operations managers with exceptional talent is given by $LTC_E = 200 + Q^2$, where Q is measured in thousands of 5-gallon tubs of ice cream. The corresponding marginal cost function is given by $LMC_E = 2Q$, and the corresponding long-run average total cost is $LATC_E = 200/Q + Q$.

- The long-run total cost faced by firms that hire operations managers with average talent is given by $LTC_A = 200 + 2Q^2$. The associated marginal cost function is given by $LMC_A = 4Q$, and the corresponding long-run average total cost is $LATC_A = 200/Q + 2Q$.

a. Derive the firm supply curve for ice cream producers with extraordinary operations managers.

b. Derive the firm supply curve for ice cream producers with average operations managers.

c. The minimum $LATC_A$ (for firms with average operations managers) is $40, achieved when those firms produce 10 units of output. The minimum $LATC_E$ (for firms with exceptional operations managers) is $28.28, achieved when those firms produce 14 units of output. Explain why, given only that information, it is not possible to determine the long-run equilibrium price of 5-gallon tubs of ice cream.

d. Referring to part (c), suppose that you know that the market demand for ice cream is given by $Q^d = 8,000 - 100P$. Explain why, in the long run, that demand will not be filled solely by firms with extraordinary managers. (*Hint*: Derive the industry supply of extraordinary producers and then use the demand curve to determine the equilibrium price. Can that price persist in the long run?)

e. In part (d), you explained why the supply side of the market will consist of both firms with extraordinary managers and firms with average managers. What will the long-run equilibrium price of ice cream be?

f. At the price you determined in part (e), all 50 firms with extraordinary managers will find remaining in the industry worthwhile. How many firms with average managers will also remain in the industry?

g. At the price you determined in part (e), how much profit will a firm with an average manager earn?

h. At the price you determined in part (e), how much profit will a firm with an extraordinary manager earn? How much economic rent will that talented manager generate for her firm?

Market Power and Monopoly

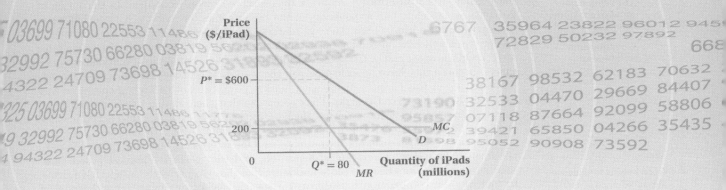

f you were in the market for a tablet computer in the spring of 2010, you had exactly one option: You could go for the iPad or, well, the iPad. It didn't even come in a choice of colors.

Apple couldn't have been happier. They had introduced a fantastically popular product, people were literally lined up ready to buy it, and the company was more or less the only game in town. Other technology companies were rushing their own tablets into production and distribution, but it would take time. It would probably also take considerable persuading to convince many wannabe iPad owners to give up their plans and buy a different product even if it were available.

This sort of situation doesn't fit the perfectly competitive model of a firm's supply behavior we covered in Chapter 8. In a perfectly competitive market, a firm's output is so small relative to the total market that its choice of whether or how much to produce does not have a noticeable impact on the total supply in the market. For this reason, a perfectly competitive firm takes the market price of its products as given when making its

market power
A firm's ability to influence the market price of its product.

monopoly
A market served by only one firm.

monopolist
The sole supplier and price setter of a good on the market.

profit-maximizing production choices. But that was not at all the case for Apple and the iPad in mid-2010. After all, Apple more or less *was* the market supply. By adjusting the number of iPads it produced for the market, it could cause movements along the market demand curve. If Apple produced only a few iPads, for example, the low quantity supplied would meet the demand curve at a high price, and quantity demanded would also be low. If it produced more, the quantity supplied would equal quantity demanded further down the demand curve, at a lower price. Therefore, Apple's choice of the quantity of iPads it supplied to the market gave it effective control over the price at which the iPad sold.

In this chapter, we start to look at firms' production choices when they have some ability to control the price at which their product sells. A firm that can influence the price its product sells for is said to have **market power**. The most extreme version of market power is a **monopoly**, a market that is served by only one firm. In the spring of 2010, Apple basically had a monopoly in the tablet computer market. A firm that has a monopoly (a **monopolist**) has the most market power; for a given market demand curve, its decision about how much to supply completely determines the market price (it's a price setter). On the other end of the spectrum, firms in perfectly competitive markets are price takers. Because they have no influence over the market price, they have no market power.

As we see in this chapter, firms with market power do not behave in the same way as perfectly competitive firms do. They recognize that their supply decisions will influence the price at which they can sell their output, so they take this into account when choosing how much to produce and sell. Perfectly competitive firms don't have this concern, so they make different output choices. One interesting outcome that we'll learn about is that market power can be measured, and that as firms' market power falls, their supply behaviors become more and more like those of perfectly competitive firms. In fact, perfect competition is really just a special case of our more general model of supply behavior: When market power falls all the way to zero, a firm with market power behaves exactly like a perfectly competitive firm.

9.1 Sources of Market Power

Some industries, like computer operating systems, airlines, and car manufacturers, for example, invariably end up with only a few companies having substantial market power. What differentiates these industries from perfectly competitive ones? How do firms in these industries gain the ability to influence the price at which they sell their goods? Where does their market power come from?

A key element of sustainable market power is that there must be something about the market that prevents competitors from entering it until the price is as low as it would be if the market were perfectly competitive. A firm with market power can generate a substantial amount of producer surplus and profit in a way that a competitive firm cannot. (Remember that producer surplus is the same thing as a firm's profit plus its fixed cost. In the long run, when fixed cost is zero, profit and producer surplus are equal.) As we saw in Chapter 8, however, that producer surplus should be an irresistible draw for other firms to enter the market and try to capture some of it. **Barriers to entry** are the factors that keep entrants out of a market despite the existence of a large producer surplus that comes from market power. The next few sections discuss the most important barriers to entry.

barriers to entry
Factors that prevent entry into markets with large producer surpluses.

natural monopoly
A market in which it is efficient for a single firm to produce the entire industry output.

Extreme Scale Economies: Natural Monopoly

The existence of a **natural monopoly** is one barrier to entry. A natural monopoly refers to a situation in which the cost curve of a firm in an industry exhibits economies of scale at any output level. In other words, the firm's long-run average total cost curve is always downward-sloping—the bigger the firm gets, the lower is its average total cost, even if it sells the entire market quantity itself.

In this type of situation, it is efficient (from a production standpoint) for society if a single firm produces the entire industry output; splitting output across more firms would raise the average total cost of production. Suppose a company could produce as large a quantity as it wants at a constant marginal cost of $10 per unit and has a fixed cost of $100. In this case, average total cost (total costs divided by output) declines across all quantities of output. In equation form,

$$TC = FC + VC = 100 + 10Q$$

so

$$ATC = \frac{TC}{Q} = \frac{100 + 10Q}{Q} = \frac{100}{Q} + 10$$

The larger the firm's quantity produced, Q, the lower is its average total cost. If all the firms in an industry have this same cost structure, the lowest-total-cost way to serve industry demand would be for one firm to produce everything. If more than one firm produces, the industry's average total cost of producing output rises because each firm that operates has to pay the fixed cost of $100 to produce anything at all. Having only one firm in the industry saves the replication of those fixed costs. That's why it is more cost-effective from society's perspective to have only one producer in the industry. Further, at a more practical level, it's difficult in these types of markets for new firms to enter and compete with the incumbent, because the incumbent's size usually gives it a cost advantage. Therefore, in markets with cost curves like this (high fixed cost and constant or slowly rising marginal cost), one firm will tend to become very large and dominate the industry with its low cost.

Many economists believe electricity transmission is a natural monopoly. The fixed cost of building a network of transmission lines, substations, meters, and so on, to supply homes and businesses is very large. Once the network is built, however, the marginal cost of delivering another kilowatt-hour of electricity is fairly close to constant. Therefore, we might expect a single firm to handle electrical transmission in a given market, and that is exactly what we often observe. If even just two competing firms operated in the transmission market in an area, there would be two sets of power lines running everywhere, and the fixed costs of the two firms would be huge. The additional cost of this second distribution network would be reflected in higher electricity prices.

Because electricity transmission companies are often natural monopolies, they are regulated by the government. Later in the chapter, we discuss why the government often regulates the behaviors of firms with market power whether their market power is the result of a natural monopoly or not. All that said, it is important to realize that even natural monopolies can disappear if demand changes sufficiently over time. Demand can rise so much that average total cost eventually rises enough to enable new firms to enter the market. This has been argued to have happened in a number of markets formerly believed to be natural monopolies, such as the markets for telephone and cable television service.

 **application**

Natural Monopoly in Satellite Radio

A real-life example of an industry that was probably a natural monopoly but consisted of two firms is satellite radio. Two companies, XM Radio and Sirius, launched satellites at a tremendous fixed cost and broadcast their own radio stations across the country. The advantage of satellite radio is that the quality of the audio is high, you can get the same stations in different markets if you are traveling, and you can access much more specialized channels (like the Bluegrass channel or the NASCAR channel) than you can from regular, over-the-air FM broadcasts. Customers pay a monthly subscription fee of about $20 per month.

The two services were quite similar technologically, so they tried to distinguish themselves from one another in customers' minds. XM signed an exclusive deal to carry all NFL football games on the radio, for example. Sirius signed deals to carry all MLB baseball games and to carry shock-jock Howard Stern (thus giving him wider latitude to be offensive than he had on regular radio).

It didn't work. Because the cost structure of a satellite radio company comprises a whopping fixed cost (building and launching the satellite) and a very low marginal cost, splitting the market meant that both companies operated at high levels of average total cost. They each incurred large losses as a result. The economics of the market said that two firms shouldn't exist, and the market finally realized this: In 2008 XM and Sirius merged to become one firm. ■

Switching Costs

A second common type of barrier to entry is the presence of consumer switching costs. If customers must give something up to switch to a competing product, this will tend to generate market power for the incumbent and make entry difficult. Think of a consumer who flies one airline regularly and has built up a preferred status level in the airline's frequent flyer program. Even if a competing airline comes into the market with lower prices, it may have a hard time getting that person to fly with it, because the customer might lose his privileged status (shorter lines, upgrades, no checked-bag fees, etc.) on his current carrier. This lost status is a switching cost that inhibits the consumer's ability to switch to a competitor, raising the incumbent airline's market power.

For some products, the switching cost comes from technology. For example, once you buy a DirecTV satellite dish and install it on your roof, the only way to switch to the DISH Network is to get a new satellite dish and converter box installed. Similarly, once you have typed in all your shipping information at Amazon or built up your reputation at eBay, you can't just transfer that information to a competitor. This also serves as a barrier to entry in the market for online retailers or auction sites.

For other products, switching costs arise from the costs of finding an alternative. If you have your car insurance with one company, it can be very time consuming to call around to different competitors to find out whether you could save money, and then fill out the paperwork required to actually switch.

Switching costs are not insurmountable barriers to entry. For example, some companies invest in trying to make comparing new options as easy as possible to convince people to swallow the switching costs and go with their (often) cheaper product. Progressive Insurance, for example, has a feature on its website that lets customers compare what their auto insurance premiums would be not just with Progressive, but with several of their competitors as well. But switching costs don't need to be insurmountable to be effective. To reduce the threat of competition and give the incumbent firm some market power, switching costs only need to be high enough to make entry costly, not impossible.

network good
A good whose value to each consumer increases with the number of other consumers of the product.

Perhaps the most extreme version of switching costs exists with a **network good:** a good whose value to each customer rises with the number of other consumers who use the product. With network goods, each new consumer creates a benefit for every other consumer of the good. Facebook is one example of a network good. If you are the only person in the world on Facebook, your account is not going to be much fun or very useful. If you're one of millions with accounts, however, now you're talking (. . . to each other).

The combination of large economies of scale (at or approaching natural monopoly levels) and network goods' attributes creates powerful entry barriers. Computer operating systems like Microsoft Windows are prone to become monopolies because they both have major economies of scale in production (software is a high-fixed-cost, low-marginal-cost business) and are network goods (people want to use a common operating system so that they can share software and file structure platforms).

Product Differentiation

Even if firms sell products that compete in the same market, all consumers might not see each firm's product as a perfect substitute for other firms' versions. For example, all bicycle makers operate in what could be thought of as the same market, but not every potential bike buyer will see a $500 Trek as exactly the same thing as a $500 Cannondale (or a $500 Giant, or . . .). That means firms can price slightly above their competition without losing all of their sales to their competitors. There is a segment of consumers who have a particular preference for one firm's product and will be willing to pay a premium (a limited premium, but a premium nonetheless) for it. This imperfect substitutability across varieties of a product is called **product differentiation,** and it is another source of market power. Product differentiation, which exists in one form or the other in most industries, prevents new firms from coming into the market and stealing most of the market demand just by pricing their product version a bit below the incumbents' prices. We discuss product differentiation in greater detail in Chapter 11.

product differentiation
Imperfect substitutability across varieties of a product.

Absolute Cost Advantages or Control of Key Inputs

Another common barrier to entry is a firm's absolute cost advantage over other firms in obtaining a key input. If a firm has control of a key input, that means it has some special asset that other firms do not have. For example, a key input might be a secret formula or a scarce resource. Controlling this input allows a firm to have costs lower than those of any competitor. To give an extreme example, suppose one firm owns the only oil well in existence and can prevent anyone else from drilling one. That would be a major advantage, because everyone else's cost of producing oil is infinite. The control of the input does not need to be that extreme, though. If a firm has one oil well whose production cost is substantially below that of everyone else's wells, that would be a cost advantage, too. These other firms would find it difficult to take business away from the low-production-cost firm, thus preserving its market power.

 **application**

Controlling a Key Input—The Troubled History of Fordlandia, Brazil

In the 1800s, there was no synthetic rubber. All rubber came from trees, and Brazil's rubber trees (*Hevea brasiliensis*) were the world's leading source. Rubber was one of Brazil's great exports.

In their natural state, the trees were often miles apart and hard to reach. In addition, because South American leaf-blight fungus (which attacked the trees in Brazil) could spread so easily from one tree to another, people could not plant the trees closer together. In 1876 an Englishman named Henry Wickham stole 70,000 rubber seeds for the British, who then planted them in concentrated plantations of many trees in what is now Malaysia. The innovation of planting the trees close together in a place without disease dramatically reduced the cost of harvesting rubber, gave

Rubber trees planted close together on a plantation in Malaysia.

Gavin Hellier/Alamy

the British an absolute cost advantage over everyone else in the rubber industry, and conferred market power on British rubber producers. By the early 1900s, Britain's plantations in Asia were meeting 95% of the world's demand for rubber. It was "the first worldwide monopoly of a strategic resource in human history."[1]

---

[1] Joe Jackson, *The Thief at the End of the World: Rubber, Power and the Seeds of Empire.* New York: Viking, 2008.

Colin McPherson/Corbis

Fordlandia ruins in Brazil.

In 1927 Henry Ford needed rubber for car tires and tried to copy the British. He set up a rubber plantation city in the Amazon called Fordlandia. Unfortunately, because Ford never consulted any experts on rubber trees, the Fordlandia plantation rapidly fell prey to the leaf-blight fungus, culture clash, social unrest, and other ills. Repeated efforts to start new plantations all failed. As a result, Ford was unable to imitate the success of the British, and no rubber from Fordlandia was ever used in a Ford car.

Britain's market power from the absolute cost advantage by controlling this key input (rubber plants not threatened by the fungus) survived until the development of cheap synthetic rubber after World War II. It's still true, though, that if you travel from Brazil to Malaysia, the Malaysian government requires you to walk through a fungicide treatment at the airport and irradiates your luggage with ultraviolet radiation to kill any South American leaf blight you might be harboring. ∎

Government Regulation

A final important form of entry barrier is government regulation. If you want to drive a cab in New York, you need to have a medallion (a chunk of metal that is actually riveted to a car's hood to show that the New York Taxi & Limousine Commission has granted the cab a license to operate). The number of medallions is fixed; currently, there are just over 13,000 available. If you want to enter this industry, you need to buy a medallion from its current owner, and you better start saving: Lately, medallion prices have been more than $700,000. That's a considerable entry barrier for a taxi driver. There are numerous other rules that prevent entry, such as licensing requirements in many occupations and industries.

Note, however, that some regulatory barriers are intentional and probably good, as we discuss later in the chapter when we consider government responses to monopoly. Examples include things like patents and copyrights, which explicitly give companies protection from entry by forbidding direct competitors.

Where There's a Will (and Producer Surplus), There's a Way

One important aspect to remember about barriers to entry is that they seldom last forever. If the producer surplus protected by entry barriers is large, competitors can often eventually find their way around even the most formidable barriers to entry. DuPont invented Nylon, the synthetic material, and patented it. In theory, this should have prevented entry. In reality, other companies figured out ways to develop competing, though not identical, synthetic fabrics that ultimately undermined the Nylon monopoly. Because there is no limit to the inventive capacity of the human mind, in the long run entrepreneurs and entrepreneurial firms will often find ingenious ways to encroach on other firms' protected positions.

9.2 Market Power and Marginal Revenue

Most firms have some sort of market power, even if they are not monopolists. We recognized this reality in Chapter 8 when we noted that truly perfectly competitive firms are rare—farmers who grow commodity crops and maybe a few other firms take prices as completely given, but they're the exception. The competitive market model is more of a useful starting point for studying market structures than it is a description of most product markets.

freakonomics

Why Drug Dealers Want Peace, Not War

When it comes to gaining market power, monopolists have been extremely creative in the strategies they employ: lobbying governments for privileged access to markets, temporarily pricing below marginal cost to keep out rivals, and artificially creating entry barriers, just to name a few.

But murder?

Can you imagine the CEO of Anheuser Busch InBev ordering a hit man to take out the board of directors of MillerCoors? No chance. Yet, not too long ago, when Prohibition laws made it illegal to produce and consume alcohol, such actions were commonplace among the "firms" that produced alcohol. For gangsters like Al Capone, violence was key to establishing and maintaining market power.

The crack cocaine trade offers a modern example of the same phenomenon. Because crack is illegal, crack markets function without legal property rights or binding contracts. Violence becomes a means of enforcing contracts and establishing market power. And because these gangsters are already working illegally, the costs of murder aren't nearly as high as in legal ventures. Researchers estimate that roughly one-third of *all* the homicides that occur in the United States—nearly 5,000 per year—are carried out by drug dealers fighting over property rights. But in a study based on the actual financial records of a Chicago gang over a three-year period, Steven Levitt and Sudhir Venkatesh showed that gang leaders try to avoid excessive use of violence. Why? Because it's bad for business! The shootings associated with a gang war scare away customers, reducing revenues by nearly 30%. During gang wars, the drug gang actually generated negative profits, on average.

Violence is one of the biggest costs of the illegal drug trade. Reducing this violence is one of the benefits touted by advocates of drug legalization. Simple economics suggests an alternative way to reduce the illegal drug trade and its effects. It is the high demand for drugs that makes drug sellers willing to take such extreme actions to establish market power. If the demand for illegal drugs were reduced, the ills associated with these markets would shrink, too. Several approaches along these lines have been tried—harsher punishments for users, education campaigns about drugs' health effects, and telling people to "Just Say No." These policies have met with mixed success, at best. Still, it's worth thinking about how to design better ways to reduce illegal drug demand, given the enormous benefits a sustained demand reduction would create.

What does it mean, practically speaking, for a firm to have market power? Suppose BMW quintupled production of all its vehicle models. We would expect the greater quantity of BMWs supplied to cause a movement down and along the demand curve to a new quantity at a lower price. Conversely, if BMW cut its production to one-fifth of its current level, we would expect BMW prices to rise. These outcomes mean that BMW should not act as if its production decisions don't affect its prices. That is, BMW is not a price taker because the price of its product depends on the quantity of cars it produces. It faces a downward-sloping demand curve: If BMW produces more cars, it will drive down the market price. If it produces fewer cars, it will increase price.

In fact, because BMW doesn't take its price as given, we could express the equivalent concept in terms of BMW choosing its price and letting the market determine the quantity it sells. That is, having market power means that if BMW sets a lower price for its cars, it will sell more of them, while if it raises prices, it will sell fewer. If a price-taking firm charges more than the market price, it will lose all its demand. But BMW won't. This is exactly the idea introduced in our earlier discussion of

Apple and the iPad. We can describe the firm's decision in terms of either choosing its profit-maximizing price or choosing its profit-maximizing level of output; either way, we (and the firm) get the same result.

Market Power and Monopoly

We made the argument that Apple was, effectively, a monopolist in the tablet computer market in the spring of 2010, but clearly we couldn't say the same about BMW. It competes against several other automakers in every market in which it operates. Why, then, do we talk about its price-setting ability the same way we talk about Apple in the tablet computer market? We do so because the basic lessons of this chapter apply whenever a firm has any market power, even if it isn't a monopolist. The key element of our analysis in this chapter is that a firm with market power faces a downward-sloping demand curve. In other words, its output level and price are interrelated. The firm cannot just sell whatever quantity it produces at a fixed market price that it takes as given, as a perfectly competitive firm can.

For a true monopolist, the firm's demand curve is exactly the market demand curve. But even if a firm is not a true monopolist, its demand curve still can slope downward. This condition exists in many market structures in which firms face competitors. As we will see in Chapter 11, two common types of these other market structures are **oligopoly,** in which a few competitors operate in a market, and **monopolistic competition,** in which there are many firms in the market but each firm's product is different enough that it faces a downward-sloping demand curve for the product it produces. The difference between monopoly and these other two cases is that in oligopoly and monopolistic competition, the particular shape of the demand curve faced by any given firm (even though it still slopes down) depends on the supply decisions of the *other* firms in the market. In a monopoly, there are no such interactions between firms. The monopoly's demand curve is the market demand, and that's that.

While we'll deal more extensively with the nature of interactions between firms in oligopoly and monopolistically competitive markets in Chapter 11, in this chapter we analyze how a firm in those kinds of markets chooses its production (or price) level *if it assumes that other firms will not change their behaviors in response to its choices.* Having made this assumption, as long as the firm's demand curve slopes downward, our analysis is the same whether this demand curve can be moved around by a competitor's actions (as in an oligopoly or monopolistically competitive market) or not (as in a monopoly). As a result, we sometimes interchange the terms "market power" and "monopoly power" even if the firm we are analyzing is not literally a monopolist. The point is that once the firm's demand curve is determined, its decision-making process is the same whether it is a monopoly, an oligopolistic firm, or a monopolistically competitive firm.[2]

oligopoly
Market structure in which a few competitors operate.

monopolistic competition
Market structure with a large number of firms selling differentiated products.

---

[2] This similarity between the supply behavior of a monopolist and nonmonopoly firms that face downward-sloping demand curves is very handy, because it is often difficult to say definitively whether a firm is a monopolist or not. A key element of defining monopoly is in deciding what the relevant market is. Your favorite hamburger place on the corner might be the only firm selling *those kinds of hamburgers* in *that location.* But you'd be hard pressed to call it a monopolist, even if you defined the market as narrowly as just "hamburger restaurants," and certainly not if you defined the market as including "places to eat." That's because you recognize that many of the restaurant's customers would be willing to substitute to other eateries, hamburger or otherwise, if the corner place significantly raised its prices. Even Apple, with iPads in 2010, wouldn't be a monopolist if we defined the market as "computing devices." Where to draw the boundaries of a market depends a lot on expected substitution patterns and can be tricky, but the nice thing is the gray area between monopoly and not-monopoly isn't that important to our analysis in this chapter. Again, what matters is that the firm faces a downward-sloping demand curve for any reason.

Marginal Revenue

The key to understanding how a firm with market power acts is to realize that, because it faces a downward-sloping demand curve, it can only sell more of its good by reducing its price. This one fact enters into every decision such firms make. As we learn later in the chapter, because firms with market power recognize the relationship between output and price, they will restrict output in a way that perfectly competitive firms won't. They do so to keep prices higher (and thereby make more money).

To see why these firms restrict output to keep their prices high, we need to remember the concept of a company's marginal revenue, the additional revenue a firm earns from selling one more unit. At first, that just sounds like the price of the product. And as we saw in Chapter 8, for a firm with no market power, this is exactly the case; the price is the marginal revenue. If a hotdog vendor walking the stands at a football game (a "firm" that can reasonably be thought of as a price taker) sells another hotdog, his total revenue goes up by whatever price he sells the hotdog for. The price doesn't depend on how many hot dogs he sells; he is a price taker. He could sell hundreds of hot dogs and it wouldn't change the market price, so his marginal revenue is just market price P.

But for a seller with market power, the concept of marginal revenue is more subtle. The extra revenue from selling another unit is no longer just the price. Yes, the firm can get the revenue from selling one more unit, but because the firm faces a downward-sloping demand curve, the more it chooses to sell, the lower the price will be for *all* units it sells, not just that one extra unit. (*Important note*: The firm is not allowed to charge different prices to different customers here. We deal with that scenario in Chapter 10.) This reduces the revenue the firm receives for the other units it sells. When computing the marginal revenue from selling that last unit, then, the firm must also subtract the loss it suffers on every other unit.

An example will clarify the firm's situation. Let's suppose that the firm in this case is Durkee-Mower, Inc., a Massachusetts firm that makes Marshmallow Fluff. Fluff has been around since 1920 and has a dominant position in the marshmallow creme market in the northeastern United States (you may have had some in a Fluffernutter sandwich, a s'more, or a Rice Krispies bar). This prominence in the market means that Durkee-Mower faces a downward-sloping demand curve for Fluff. If it makes more Fluff, its market price will fall, because the only way to get consumers to buy up the extra Fluff is to lower its price.

Table 9.1 shows how the quantity of Fluff produced this year varies with its price. As the quantity produced rises, the price falls because of the downward-sloping demand

Table 9.1   Marginal Revenue for Marshmallow Fluff

Quantity (millions of pounds) (Q)	Price ($ per pound) (P)	Total Revenue ($ millions) ($TR = P \times Q$)	Marginal Revenue ($ millions) ($MR = \frac{\Delta TR}{\Delta Q}$)
0	6	0	—
1	5	5	5
2	4	8	3
3	3	9	1
4	2	8	−1
5	1	5	−3

curve. The third column in Table 9.1 shows the total revenue for the year for each level of output. The marginal revenue of an additional unit of output (in this example, a unit is a million pounds) is shown in the last column. It equals the difference between total revenue at that level of output minus the total revenue had Durkee-Mower made one fewer unit.

If Durkee-Mower makes only 1 million pounds of Fluff, its price is $5 per pound, and its revenue is $5 million. Because total revenue would be zero if the firm didn't produce anything, the marginal revenue of the first million pounds is $5 million. If Durkee-Mower makes 2 million pounds of Fluff instead, the market price falls to $4 per pound—the lower price makes consumers willing to buy another million pounds of Fluff. Total revenue in this case is $8 million. Therefore, the marginal revenue of increasing output from 1 to 2 million pounds is $3 million, $3 per pound. Note that this is less than the $5 per pound price at a quantity of 1 million pounds. As we discussed earlier, the lower marginal revenue reflects the fact that a firm with market power must reduce the price of its product when it produces more. Therefore, the marginal revenue isn't just the price multiplied by one more unit of quantity (which would be $5 million in this case, or $5 per pound). It also includes the loss of revenue due to the fact that the firm now sells all units at a lower price. Because producing the extra million pounds drops price by $1 per pound, this portion of marginal revenue is equal to the quantity the firm now sells, 2 million pounds, times the drop in price, $1 per pound, or a loss of $2 million. The $3 million marginal revenue is therefore the gain from selling another unit at the old price, $5 million, minus the $2 million loss from the price reduction the extra output creates.

If Durkee-Mower produces 3 million pounds, the market price drops to $3 per pound. Total revenue at this quantity is therefore $9 million. The marginal revenue is now only $1 million. Again, this marginal revenue is less than the product of the market price and the extra quantity because producing more Fluff drives down the price that Durkee-Mower can charge for every unit it sells.

If the firm chooses to make still more Fluff, say, 4 million pounds, the market price drops further, to $2 per pound. Total revenue is now $8 million. That means in this case, Durkee-Mower has actually *reduced* its revenue (from $9 million to $8 million) by producing *more* Fluff. That is, the marginal revenue is now negative (−$1 million). In this case, the price-drop revenue loss due to the extra production outweighs the revenue gains from selling more units. If Durkee-Mower insists on making 5 million pounds, the price drops to $1 per pound and total revenue falls to $5 million. Again, the marginal revenue of this million-pound unit is negative, −$3 million, because the revenue loss due to price reductions outweighs the extra units sold.

Why Does the Price Have to Fall for Every Unit the Firm Sells?   One thing about marginal revenue that can be confusing for students at first glance is why the seller loses money on all of its sales if it decides to produce one more unit. For instance, in the Marshmallow Fluff example, why can't Durkee-Mower sell the first million pounds for $5 per pound, and then the second million pounds for $4 a pound, the third million for $3 a pound, and so on? That way the marginal revenue will always equal the price.

There are two reasons why the price drop applies to all units sold. The first is that we are not thinking of the firm's decision as being sequential. Durkee-Mower isn't deciding whether to sell a second million pounds after it has already sold its first million at $5 per pound. Instead, the firm is deciding whether to produce 1 million *or* 2 million pounds in this period. If it makes 1 million pounds, the price will be $5 per pound and revenue will be $5 million. If it instead produces 2 million pounds, each will be sold at a price of $4 per pound, and revenue will be $8 million. We are making the same assumption about the demand curve here that we have done throughout the book: The demand curve reflects demand during a given time period. All other issues of timing are ignored. Therefore, the demand curve reflects the quantity demanded *in this period* (a year in the Fluff example) at every price; whatever number of units the firm produces, they all sell at the same price.

The second reason why a price drop applies to all units sold is that we are assuming that, even within a particular time period, the market price has to be the same for *all* the units the firm sells. The firm can't sell the first unit to a consumer who has a high willingness to pay and the second unit to a consumer with a slightly lower willingness to pay. This is probably a realistic assumption in many markets, including the market for marshmallow creme. Grocery stores don't put multiple price tags on a given product. Imagine for a moment a scenario in which the price tag reads, "$5 if you really like Marshmallow Fluff, $4 if you like it, but not quite as much, and $1 if you don't really like Fluff but will buy it if it's cheap."

Marginal Revenue: A Graphical Approach   The idea that marginal revenue is different from the price is easy to see in a graph like Figure 9.1. On the downward-sloping demand curve, we can measure the total revenue TR (price × quantity) at two different points, x and y. At point x, the quantity sold is Q_1 and the price at which each unit is sold is P_1. The total revenue is price times quantity, seen in the figure as the rectangle $A + B$.

If the firm decides to produce more, say, by increasing output from Q_1 to Q_2, it will move to point y on the demand curve. The firm sells more units, but in doing so, the price falls to P_2. The new total revenue is $P_2 \times Q_2$ or the rectangle $B + C$. Therefore, the marginal revenue of this output increase is the new revenue minus the old revenue:

$$TR_2 = P_2 \times Q_2 = B + C$$

$$TR_1 = P_1 \times Q_1 = A + B$$

$$MR = TR_2 - TR_1$$

$$MR = (B + C) - (A + B) = C - A$$

The area C contains the extra revenue that comes from selling more goods at price P_2, but this alone is not the marginal revenue of the extra output. We must also subtract area A, the revenue the firm loses because it now sells all units (not just the marginal unit) for the lower price P_2 instead of P_1. In fact, if the price-lowering effect of increasing output is large enough, it is possible that marginal revenue could be less than zero. In other words, selling more product could actually end up reducing a firm's revenue.

Firms would like to sell different units at different prices if they could, charging high willingness-to-pay consumers a high price and low willingness-to-pay consumers a low price, because they could avoid the loss in marginal revenue caused by price falling for all their sales. This practice, called **price discrimination,** is possible in certain circumstances. We discuss them in Chapter 10.

price discrimination
Pricing strategy in which firms with market power charge different prices to customers based on their willingness to pay.

Figure 9.1   Understanding Marginal Revenue

For a firm with market power, the marginal revenue from producing an additional unit of a good is not equal to the good's price. When the firm decides to increase production from point x on the demand curve (quantity Q_1) to point y (Q_2), the price of the good decreases from P_1 to P_2. The firm's initial total revenue ($P_1 \times Q_1$) is equal to the area $A + B$. At the new production point, total revenue ($P_2 \times Q_2$) is equal to the area $B + C$. The firm's marginal revenue is the difference between the initial total revenue and the new total revenue, equal to $C - A$.

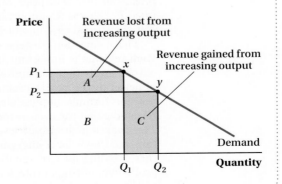

Marginal Revenue: A Mathematical Approach   We can compute a formula for a firm's marginal revenue using the logic we just discussed. As we saw, there are two effects of the firm selling an additional unit of output. Each of these will account for a component of the marginal revenue formula.

The first effect comes from the additional unit being sold at the market price P. In Figure 9.1, if we define $Q_2 - Q_1$ to be one unit, then this effect would be area C.

The second effect occurs because the additional unit drives down the market price for all the units the firm makes. To figure out how to express this component of marginal revenue, let's first label the change in price ΔP (so that, had the additional unit not been sold, the price would have been $P + \Delta P$). In Figure 9.1, we're looking at the effect of a decrease in price, so $\Delta P < 0$. Let's also label the quantity before adding the incremental unit of output as Q and the incremental output as ΔQ. The second component of marginal revenue is therefore $\left(\frac{\Delta P}{\Delta Q}\right) \times Q$, the change in price caused by selling the additional unit of revenue times the quantity sold before adding the incremental unit. In Figure 9.1, this is area A. Note that because price falls as quantity rises—remember, the firm faces a downward-sloping demand curve—the term $\Delta P / \Delta Q$ is negative. This conforms to our logic above that this second component of marginal revenue is negative. It is the loss in revenue resulting from having to sell the nonincremental units at a lower price.

Putting together these components, we have the formula for marginal revenue (MR) from producing an additional quantity (ΔQ) of output (notice that we add the two components together even though the second represents a loss in revenue because $\Delta P / \Delta Q$ is already negative):

$$MR = P + \left(\frac{\Delta P}{\Delta Q}\right) \times Q$$

∂ The end-of-chapter appendix derives a firm's marginal revenue using calculus.

This negative second component means that marginal revenue will always be less than the market price. If we map this equation into Figure 9.1, the first term is the additional revenue from selling an additional unit at price P (area C) and the second is area A.

Looking more closely at this formula reveals how the shape of the demand curve facing a firm affects its marginal revenue. The change in price corresponding to a change in quantity, $\Delta P / \Delta Q$, is a measure of how steep the demand curve is. When the demand curve is really steep, price falls a lot in response to an increase in output. $\Delta P / \Delta Q$ is a large negative number in this case. This will drive down MR and can even make it negative. On the other hand, when the demand curve is flatter, price is not very sensitive to quantity increases. In this case, because $\Delta P / \Delta Q$ is fairly small in magnitude, the first (positive) component P of marginal revenue plays a larger relative role, keeping marginal revenue from falling too much as output rises. In the special case of perfectly flat demand curves, $\Delta P / \Delta Q$ is zero, and therefore marginal revenue equals the market price of the good. We know from Chapter 8 that when a firm's marginal revenue equals price, the firm is a price taker: Whatever quantity it sells will be sold at the market price P. This is an important insight that we return to below: Perfect competition is just the special case in which the firm's demand curve is perfectly elastic, so $MR = P$.

This connection between the slope of the demand curve and the level of a firm's marginal revenue is important in understanding how firms with market power choose the output levels that maximize their profits. We study this profit-maximization problem in detail in the next section, but it's useful to reflect a bit now on what the marginal revenue formula implies about it. Firms that face steep demand curves obtain small revenue gains (or even revenue losses, if MR is negative) when they increase output. This makes high output levels less profitable. Firms facing flatter demand curves obtain relatively large marginal revenues when raising output. This contrast suggests that (holding all else equal) having a steeper demand curve tends to reduce a firm's profit-maximizing output level. In the next section, we see that this is exactly the case.

We can apply the marginal revenue formula to any demand curve. For nonlinear demand curves, the slope $\Delta P / \Delta Q$ is the slope of a line tangent to the demand curve at quantity Q. But the formula is especially easy for linear demand curves, because $\Delta P/\Delta Q$ is constant. For any linear (inverse) demand curve of the form $P = a - bQ$, where a (the vertical intercept of the demand curve) and b are constants, $\Delta P/\Delta Q = -b$. The inverse demand curve itself relates P (the other component of marginal revenue) to Q, so if we also plug $P = a - bQ$ and $\Delta P/\Delta Q = -b$ into the MR formula above, we arrive at an expression for the marginal revenue of any linear demand curve:

$$MR = P + \left(\frac{\Delta P}{\Delta Q}\right)Q$$

$$= (a - bQ) + (-b)Q = a - 2bQ$$

This formula shows that marginal revenue varies with the firm's output. This is true in this specific case of a linear demand curve, but it's important to recognize that it holds more generally. (The only exception to this outcome is for a perfectly competitive firm, for which marginal revenue is constant and equal to the market price for any production quantity.) Here, the marginal revenue curve looks a lot like the inverse demand curve. It has the same vertical intercept as the inverse demand curve, which is equal to a. (To see this, just plug $Q = 0$ into the demand and marginal revenue curves.) It also slopes down: A higher Q leads to lower marginal revenue. The only difference between the marginal revenue and demand curves is that the former is twice as steep: bQ in the inverse demand curve has been replaced with $2bQ$.[3]

The formula for MR doesn't just look a lot like an inverse demand curve, it is conceptually similar, too. Just as the inverse demand curve shows how the price changes with production levels, the marginal revenue formula shows how marginal revenue changes with production levels. Further connecting the two curves is the fact that both the market price and marginal revenue are measured in the same units—dollars per unit of the good, for example.

9.1 figure it out

Suppose the demand curve is $Q = 12.5 - 0.25P$.

   a. What is the marginal revenue curve that corresponds to this demand curve?

   b. Calculate marginal revenue when $Q = 6$. Calculate marginal revenue when $Q = 7$.

Solution:

   a. First, we need to solve for the inverse demand curve by rearranging the demand function so that price is on the left side by itself:

$$Q = 12.5 - 0.25P$$
$$0.25P = 12.5 - Q$$
$$P = 50 - 4Q$$

So, we know that the inverse demand curve is $P = 50 - 4Q$, with $a = 50$ and $b = 4$. Because $MR = a - 2bQ$, we know that $MR = 50 - 8Q$.

   b. We can plug these values into our MR equation to solve for marginal revenue:

When $Q = 6$, $MR = 50 - 8(6) = 50 - 48 = 2$.

When $Q = 7$, $MR = 50 - 8(7) = 50 - 56 = -6$.

Note that, as we discussed above, MR falls as Q rises and can even become negative.

---

[3] If you know calculus, you can see that the multiplier of 2 comes from the derivative of the total revenue function. For a linear inverse demand curve $P = a - bQ$, the total revenue curve (the firm's revenue as a function of its quantity produced) that corresponds to it is $P \times Q$, or $aQ - bQ^2$. To find marginal revenue, which is the additional revenue from an incremental increase in quantity, we take the derivative of this total revenue function with respect to Q. Doing so gives $MR = a - 2bQ$.

9.3 Profit Maximization for a Firm with Market Power

Now that we know how to compute marginal revenue, we can figure out the profit-maximizing output level for any firm with market power.

Many students' first instinct is to suppose that a firm with market power seeking to maximize its profit should sell until the marginal revenue falls to zero and then stop. After all, any more production after that would reduce revenues, and couldn't be profitable. That sort of production rule would, in fact, be correct if there was no cost of production. With production costs, however, it's not quite accurate. A firm with market power should pay attention to its marginal revenue, but one more piece of the puzzle is necessary to figure out the profit-maximizing output level.

How to Maximize Profit

In Chapter 8, we discussed the two basic elements of firm profit—revenue and cost—and how each of these is determined by the firm's choice of how much output to produce. We saw there that the profit-maximizing output was the one that set marginal revenue equal to marginal cost. We went on to show that marginal revenue for a perfectly competitive firm equals the market price, so maximizing profit meant producing the quantity at which price equals marginal cost. The logic behind this condition is that if price is above marginal cost, the perfectly competitive firm should produce more because the additional revenue it would earn exceeds the additional cost. If price is below marginal cost, it should cut back on production because it's losing money on those extra units.

The same underlying logic works for firms with market power except that *marginal revenue no longer equals price*. To maximize its profit, a firm should choose its quantity where its marginal revenue equals its marginal cost:

$$MR = MC$$

If marginal revenue is above marginal cost, a firm can produce more and earn more revenue than the extra cost of production, and increase its profit. If marginal revenue is below marginal cost, a firm can reduce its output, lose less revenue than it saves in cost, and again raise its profit. Only when these two marginal values are equal does changing output not increase profit.

Thus, we see that the monopolist and the perfectly competitive firm do exactly the same thing. They both produce at the level where $MR = MC$. It's just that marginal revenue no longer equals price for a firm with market power, and that explains why it behaves differently than a perfectly competitive firm.

The $MR = MC$ condition gives us the quantity that maximizes the firm's profit, but it also allows us to figure out the profit-maximizing price. The height of the demand curve at the profit-maximizing quantity Q^* tells us what market price will prevail for the firm's product if it produces that quantity.

For a firm with market power, we can think of the firm choosing a profit-maximizing quantity as equivalent to choosing a profit-maximizing price. The demand curve ties together price and quantity, so picking one implies the other. The monopolist can either produce the profit-maximizing quantity of output and let the market determine the price (which will be the profit-maximizing price), or it can set the profit-maximizing price and let the market determine the quantity (which will be the profit-maximizing quantity).

An important factor to remember is that even though firms with market power have an ability to set the price for their output, they (even monopolists) cannot profitably charge whatever price they want to. A firm with market power could *try* to keep raising its price (or equivalently, keep cutting its output), but if the firm raises the price by too much, its customers will stop buying—even if there are no other competitors.

∂ The end-of-chapter appendix uses calculus to solve the firm's profit-maximization problem.

For example, in 2010 the iPad dominated the market and Apple clearly had market power as a result. Does this mean Apple could have charged whatever price it wanted? Suppose Apple had charged $20,000 for each iPad. Just about everyone would have stopped buying it, even if it was the only tablet computer on earth. The vast majority of people would simply not find it worth having the iPad at that price. By raising the price for its product, even a monopolist can lose business, not to competitors, but by driving consumers out of the market altogether. The firm is limited by the demand for its product. Because the demand curve is downward-sloping, any rise in price is accompanied by a decline in quantity demanded. This sensitivity to price means that monopolists can't (or more precisely, wouldn't want to if they cared about profit) set sky-high prices. They'll charge a higher price than a more competitive firm, but the price won't be infinitely higher.

Profit Maximization with Market Power: A Graphical Approach

We can apply the exact logic of the previous analysis to graphically derive the profit-maximizing output and price of a firm with market power, given the firm's demand and marginal cost curves. Let's assume we are again looking at the market for iPads and that marginal cost is constant at $200. Specifically, we will follow these steps:

Step 1: **Derive the marginal revenue curve from the demand curve.** For a linear demand curve, this will be another straight line with the same vertical intercept that is twice as steep. In Figure 9.2, the marginal revenue curve is shown as MR.

Step 2: **Find the output quantity at which marginal revenue equals marginal cost.** This is the firm's profit-maximizing quantity of output. In Figure 9.2, Apple's profit-maximizing level of output is Q^*, or 80 million iPads.

Step 3: **Determine the profit-maximizing price by locating the point on the demand curve at the optimal quantity level.** To determine the price Apple should charge consumers to maximize its profit, we follow Q^* up to the demand curve and then read the price off the vertical axis. If Apple produces the profit-maximizing output level of 80 million, the market price will be $600. (Or equivalently, if Apple charges a price of $600, it will sell 80 million iPads.)

That's all there is to it. Once we have the firm's MR curve, we can use the profit-maximization rule $MR = MC$ to find the firm's optimal level of output and price.

Figure 9.2   :   **How a Firm with Market Power Maximizes Profit**

Apple will maximize its profit from the iPad by producing where $MR = MC$. Therefore, Apple will sell 80 million iPads at a price of $600 each, well above Apple's marginal cost of $200 per iPad.

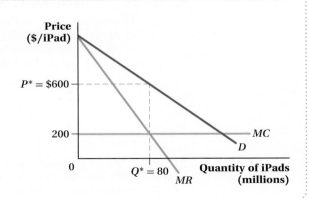

Profit Maximization with Market Power: A Mathematical Approach

We can also solve for the profit-maximizing quantity and price mathematically, given equations for the firm's demand and marginal cost curves. Again, we'll use the Apple iPad example.

Suppose Apple's marginal cost of producing iPads is constant at $200, and the demand curve for iPads (where Q is in millions and P in dollars) is $Q = 200 - 0.2P$. How much should Apple charge for iPads, and how many will it sell at that price? (Again, because of the equivalence of choosing price and choosing output level for firms with market power, we could ask how many iPads Apple should produce and at what price the iPads would sell, and the answer would be the same.)

We can figure this out using the same three-step process described above: Derive the marginal revenue curve, find the quantity at which the marginal revenue equals marginal cost, and then determine the profit-maximizing price by computing the price at that quantity on the demand curve.

Step 1: Derive the marginal revenue curve from the demand curve. Let's start by obtaining the inverse demand curve by rearranging the demand curve so that price is a function of quantity rather than the other way around:

$$Q = 200 - 0.2P$$

$$0.2P = 200 - Q$$

$$P = 1{,}000 - 5Q$$

This is a linear inverse demand curve of the form $P = a - bQ$, where $a = 1{,}000$ and $b = 5$. Earlier we learned that the marginal revenue curve for this type of demand curve is $MR = a - 2bQ$.[4] So for this demand curve, Apple's marginal revenue curve is

$$MR = 1{,}000 - 2(5Q) = 1{,}000 - 10Q$$

Step 2: Find the output quantity at which marginal revenue equals marginal cost. Apple's marginal cost is constant at $200, so we just set the marginal revenue curve equal to this value and solve for Q:

$$MR = MC$$

$$1{,}000 - 10Q = 200$$

$$800 = 10Q$$

$$Q^* = 80$$

So, Apple's profit-maximizing quantity of iPads is 80 million.

Step 3: Determine the profit-maximizing price by locating the point on the demand curve at the optimal quantity level. Find the profit-maximizing price by plugging the optimal quantity into the demand curve. This tells us at what price the optimal quantity (80 million iPads) will be sold:

$$P^* = 1{,}000 - 5Q^*$$

$$= 1{,}000 - 5(80)$$

$$= 1{,}000 - 400 = 600$$

---

[4] If we had a more complicated demand curve, we could compute the marginal revenue curve by using calculus. We would start with calculating total revenue by multiplying the inverse demand curve by Q. Then we would take the derivative with respect to Q to get the marginal revenue.

Given this demand curve and a constant marginal cost of $200 per iPad, then, Apple can maximize its profits by charging $600 per unit. It will sell 80 million iPads at this price. Notice that this price is well above Apple's marginal cost of $200, the price Apple would be charging in a perfectly competitive market. That's why firms like to have market power. The idea is simple: Reduce output. Raise prices. Make money.

9.2 figure it out

Babe's Bats (BB) sells baseball bats for children around the world. The firm faces a demand curve of $Q = 10 - 0.4P$, where Q is measured in thousands of bats and P is dollars per bat. BB has a marginal cost curve that is equal to $MC = 5Q$.

a. Solve for BB's profit-maximizing level of output. Show the firm's profit-maximization decision graphically.

b. What price will BB charge to maximize its profit?

Solution:

a. To solve this problem, we should follow the three-step procedure outlined in the text. First, we need to derive the marginal revenue curve for BB bats. Because the firm faces a linear demand curve, the easiest way to obtain the marginal revenue curve is to start by solving for the firm's inverse demand curve:

$$Q = 10 - 0.4P$$
$$0.4P = 10 - Q$$
$$P = 25 - 2.5Q$$

For this inverse demand curve, $a = 25$ and $b = 2.5$. Therefore, since $MR = a - 2bQ$, we know that BB's MR curve will be

$$MR = 25 - 2(2.5Q) = 25 - 5Q$$

To solve for the profit-maximizing level of output, we can follow the profit-maximization rule $MR = MC$:

$$MR = MC$$
$$25 - 5Q = 5Q$$
$$10Q = 25$$
$$Q^* = 2.5$$

Therefore, BB should produce 2,500 bats. This profit-maximization decision is shown in the figure below. Profit is maximized at the output level at which the marginal revenue and marginal cost curves intersect.

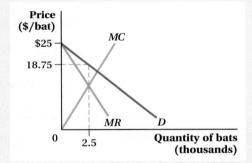

b. To find BB's optimal price, we plug its profit-maximizing level of output ($Q^* = 2.5$) into its inverse demand curve:

$$P^* = 25 - 2.5Q^*$$
$$= 25 - 2.5(2.5)$$
$$= 25 - 6.25 = 18.75$$

BB should charge a price of $18.75 per bat. This is also demonstrated on the figure by following $Q^* = 2.5$ up to the demand curve and over to the vertical axis.

A Markup Formula for Companies with Market Power: The Lerner Index

We can take the logic we've just learned even further to come up with a rule-of-thumb for pricing that firms can use to determine profit-maximizing prices and output levels.

Start with the definition of MR from above:

$$MR = P + \left(\frac{\Delta P}{\Delta Q}\right) \times Q$$

We know that the firm maximizes its profits by setting $MR = MC$, so plug that in:

$$MR = P + \left(\frac{\Delta P}{\Delta Q}\right) \times Q = MC$$

Now we'll use a math trick of multiplying the second term on the left side of the equation by P/P. This doesn't change the value of the equation, because multiplying by P/P is just another way of multiplying by 1. This changes our expression to

$$P + \left(\frac{\Delta P}{\Delta Q}\right) \times \left(\frac{P}{P}\right) \times Q = MC$$

or $\qquad P + \left(\frac{\Delta P}{\Delta Q} \times \frac{Q}{P}\right) \times P = MC$

If the section in parentheses looks familiar to you, it's because it is the inverse of the elasticity of demand. Remember in Chapter 2 that we defined the price elasticity of demand E^D as $\frac{\Delta Q/Q}{\Delta P/P}$ or $\frac{\Delta Q}{\Delta P} \times \frac{P}{Q}$. The inverse of this value is $\frac{1}{E^d} = \frac{\Delta P}{\Delta Q} \times \frac{Q}{P}$. Substituting the inverse elasticity into the profit-maximization condition gives us

$$P + \left(\frac{\Delta P}{\Delta Q} \times \frac{Q}{P}\right) \times P = MC$$

$$P + \frac{1}{E^d} \times P = MC$$

A final bit of algebraic rearranging gives

$$P - MC = -\left(\frac{1}{E^d}\right) \times P$$

or $\qquad \dfrac{P - MC}{P} = -\dfrac{1}{E^d}$

The left-hand side of this equation equals the firm's profit-maximizing **markup,** the percentage of the firm's price that is greater than (or "marked up" from) its marginal cost. What this equation indicates is that this markup should depend on the price elasticity of demand that the firm faces. Specifically, as demand becomes more elastic—that is, as E^D becomes more negative, or equivalently, larger in absolute value—the optimal markup as a fraction of price falls. (If you can't quite see this in the equation, notice that elastic demand means a large negative number for E^D is in the denominator, making the right-hand side of the equation small.) On the other hand, as demand becomes less elastic, E^D becomes smaller in absolute value, indicating that the markup should be a larger fraction of price.

If we stop to think about these implications for a minute, they make perfect sense. If demand is quite inelastic, consumers' purchases of the firm's product are not sensitive to changes in price. This makes it easier for the firm to increase its profit by raising its price—it will sell fewer units, but not too many fewer, and it will make a higher margin on every unit it does sell. This is exactly what the equation implies; the firm should mark up its price by a considerable amount over its marginal cost. A firm facing relatively elastic demand, on the other hand, will suffer a greater loss in quantity sold when it raises its price, making it less beneficial to charge a high markup over cost.

The measure of the markup given by the equation above has a special name: the **Lerner index** (after Abba Lerner, the economist who proposed it in 1934). As we just discussed, assuming the firm is trying to maximize its profit, the Lerner index tells us something about the nature of the demand curve facing the firm. When the index is high (i.e., when the markup accounts for a large fraction of the price), the demand for the firm's product is relatively inelastic. When the index is low, the firm faces relatively elastic demand. Because the ability to price above marginal cost is the definition of market power, the Lerner index is a measure of market power. The higher it is, the greater the firm's ability to price above its marginal cost.

The extreme case of perfectly elastic demand is interesting to study in terms of its implications for the Lerner index. When demand is perfectly elastic—the firm faces a horizontal demand curve and any effort to charge a price higher than the demand curve will result in a loss of all sales—then $E^d = -\infty$. As we see in the equation above, the Lerner index is equal to zero in this case. That means the markup is also zero; the firm sells at a price equal to marginal cost.

Another interesting case occurs when E^d is between 0 and −1—that is, when the firm faces a demand curve that is inelastic or unit elastic. In this case, the Lerner Index is greater than 1. But this would imply that $P - MC > P$, or $MC < 0$, and marginal cost can't be negative. Why does the optimal markup equation imply this nonsensical result? There is a mathematical answer that involves calculus, but there is an economic explanation as well. A firm should never operate at a point on its demand curve where demand is inelastic or unit elastic. (In the linear demand case, demand becomes less elastic as price falls.) To see why, let's think about what would happen if a firm was setting a price (or a quantity) that put it on an inelastic or unit elastic portion of its demand curve, and then decided to increase its price (or equivalently sell a smaller quantity). By definition, because demand is inelastic, whatever the percentage increase in price, the percentage drop in quantity will be smaller (or will exactly equal the percentage increase in price if demand is unit elastic). That means that the price increase will raise the firm's revenue (or not change it if demand is unit elastic). At the same time, because the firm is producing a smaller quantity, its total cost must fall, because cost curves always increase in quantity. So, the net effect of the price increase is to raise the firm's revenue (or keep it constant) while lowering its cost. In other words, the firm is guaranteed to raise profit by increasing prices as long as demand is inelastic. Therefore, it can't be profit maximizing to set a price where demand is inelastic.

The Lerner index can range anywhere from 0 (perfect competition) to 1 (perfectly inelastic demand). It is a summary of the amount of market power a firm has. In comparing degrees of market power across firms, the firm with the highest Lerner index has the most market power; the firm with the second-highest Lerner index has the second-most market power, and so on.

Measuring the Lerner Index   Firms with market power are keenly aware that their profit-maximizing markups are tied to the price elasticities they face. The difficulty from a practical standpoint, however, is that firms don't have a gauge from which they can simply read off a Lerner index to see what markup they should be charging. So, they can spend considerable effort trying to learn about the shape of the demand and marginal revenue curves they face, because that tells them about the price elasticity of demand of their customers.

Technologies that allow firms to change prices more frequently, and even offer different prices simultaneously to different consumers, have made firms' processes of feeling out their demand curves easier. This can lead to negative publicity, however. For example, Amazon got into a bit of trouble early in its history for conducting what it called a "pricing experiment" on its customers. Amazon was experimentally offering different prices to different customers for the same products, in an effort to measure the elasticity of demand by seeing how consumers' purchases responded to price changes. A customer sued when he discovered that when he removed the Amazon cookie from his computer, the price of the product he was shopping for dropped significantly. In the uproar that followed, people assumed that Amazon was price-discriminating, a practice we discuss in the next chapter. Amazon CEO Jeffrey Bezos apologized for the episode and indicated that there was no systematic price discrimination ongoing. He insisted that Amazon was simply randomizing prices to develop a better sense of demand in its market. This chapter shows exactly why Amazon might bother to do this. If a company has a good sense of the shape of its own demand curve, it can figure out the most profitable price to charge using the markup formula or the full monopoly pricing system.

application

Market Power versus Market Share

Guzzle & Nosh

Dr. Brown's Cel-Ray soda, a lock on its market since 1869.

Market power involves more than the size of a particular firm. For example, consider Dr. Brown's, a manufacturer of specialty sodas in the United States that produces a celery-flavored soda called Cel-Ray. Even though the sales of Coca-Cola are thousands of times larger than the sales of Cel-Ray, it turns out that Dr. Brown's has more market power than Coca-Cola by the economist's definition.

How can that be? The key factor to consider is the price elasticity of demand for the two products. Coca-Cola drinkers are, on average, fairly price-sensitive in the short run. The price elasticity of demand for a six-pack of Coke in a grocery store is around −4.1.[6] On the other hand, people who drink Cel-Ray must have a unique preference for the celery flavor. Whereas there are many substitutes for Coca-Cola, there really aren't many substitutes for Cel-Ray. Thus, Cel-Ray drinkers will likely be less price-sensitive than Coke drinkers. A reasonable guess at the price elasticity of demand for a six-pack of Cel-Ray is about −2.

If we use these two elasticities to measure the Lerner index for each product, we indeed see that Cel-Ray has more market power than Coke:

$$\text{Lerner index for Coke} = -\frac{1}{E^d} = -\frac{1}{-4.1} = 0.244$$

$$\text{Lerner index for Cel-Ray} = -\frac{1}{E^d} = -\frac{1}{-2} = 0.5$$

Therefore, Cel-Ray's profit-maximizing price is a higher markup over its marginal costs than Coke's profit-maximizing price. In other words, Coca-Cola's pricing behavior is actually closer to the pricing behavior of a competitive firm than Cel-Ray's. It is not the size of the market or the firm's market share that determines or measures market power, it is the firm's ability to price above its marginal cost. ∎

The Supply Relationship for a Firm with Market Power

We now know how to figure out the profit-maximizing quantity and price for a firm with market power, and we can do so for any given marginal cost and demand curves the firm might face. As you might imagine, we could sketch out all the combinations of the firm's profit-maximizing quantities and prices implied by any possible set of marginal cost and demand curves.

[6] Jean-Pierre Dube, "Product Differentiation and Mergers in the Carbonated Soft Drink Industry," *Journal of Economics and Management Strategy* 14, no. 4 (2005): 879–904.

This might sound a lot like a supply curve—it is, after all, a set of prices and the quantities produced. But it's not a supply curve. Firms with market power don't have supply curves, strictly speaking. Their profit-maximizing price and quantity combinations are not supply curves because those combinations depend on the demand curve the firm faces. As we saw in Chapter 8, supply curves exist completely independently of demand. They depend only on firms' marginal costs, because a perfectly competitive firm produces the quantity at which the market price (which the firm takes as given) equals its marginal cost. That's why a perfectly competitive firm's supply curve is a portion of its marginal cost curve, and a perfectly competitive industry's supply curve is the industry marginal cost curve. Neither of these supply curves is determined by anything having to do with demand; they are only about costs.

This strict relationship between costs and price isn't true for a firm with market power. Its optimal output level depends not only on the marginal cost curve, but also on the firm's marginal revenue curve (which is related to the demand curve). Put another way, a supply curve gives a one-to-one mapping between the price and a firm's output. But for a firm with market power, even holding constant its marginal cost curve, the firm could charge a high price at a given quantity if it faces a steeper demand curve or a lower price at the same quantity if it faced a flatter demand curve. Therefore, a simple mapping of price and quantity supplied is not possible for a firm with market power and there would be no supply curve.

9.4 How a Firm with Market Power Reacts to Market Changes

We now know how profit-maximizing firms with market power should make production and pricing decisions. We can use this behavior to think through the effects of various market changes, much as we did with supply and demand in the competitive setting. Even though firms with market power do not have a supply curve, we will see that in some ways they react similarly to competitive firms. There are some ways they can react, however, that are quite different.

Response to a Change in Marginal Cost

Let's first think about the effect of an increase in marginal cost. In the iPad example, marginal cost was constant at $200 and the inverse demand curve was $P = 1,000 - 5Q$ (where Q is in millions). Suppose there's a fire in the plant that manufactures the screen on the iPad, raising the marginal cost of the screen, and as a result, the marginal cost of the iPad increases from $200 to $250. What will happen in the market for iPads?

To determine the market impact of this increase in marginal cost, we follow the three-step method but with the new marginal cost curve:

Step 1: **Derive the marginal revenue curve.** The demand curve hasn't changed, so this is the same as before: $MR = 1,000 - 10Q$.

Step 2: **Find the quantity at which $MR = MC$.** The MC is now $250, so

$$1,000 - 10Q = 250$$

$$750 = 10Q$$

$$Q^* = 75$$

The new profit-maximizing quantity is 75 million units, down from 80 million.

Step 3: **Determine the profit-maximizing price using the optimal quantity and the demand curve.** The (inverse) demand curve is $P = 1,000 - 5Q$. Plugging in the new quantity, we have $P^* = 1,000 - 5(75) = \$625$. The new price will be $625, up from $600 before the fire.

Figure 9.3 How a Firm with Market Power Reacts to an Increase in Marginal Cost

If the marginal cost of producing an iPad rises from $200 to $250, Apple will decrease its output from 80 million to 75 million and the price of an iPad will rise from $600 to $625.

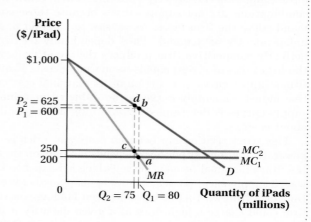

We illustrate the change from the initial equilibrium to the new one in Figure 9.3. The initial quantity of 80 million is set by $MR = MC_1$ ($200) at point a. This quantity corresponds to a price of $600, as indicated at point b. After the fire, the marginal cost curve shifts up to $250 ($MC_2$). Because the fire only affects the supply side of the market, the consumer's willingness to pay does not change, and the demand and marginal revenue curves do not shift. Now marginal revenue equals marginal cost at point c, at a quantity of 75 million. Following that quantity up to the demand curve (at point d), we can see that the price of an iPad will rise to $625.

A firm with market power responds to a cost shock in a way that is similar to a competitive firm's response. When marginal cost rises, price rises, and output falls. When marginal cost falls, price falls, and output rises.

But in competition, a change in marginal cost is fully reflected in the market price, because $P = MC$. That's not the case when the seller has market power. In the iPad example, the market price rose only $25 in response to a $50 increase in marginal cost. To maximize its profit, Apple does not want to pass along the full increase in its cost to its customers. The drop in quantity that results from the increase in cost is also smaller than the drop that would occur in a perfectly competitive market. Note, however, that the equilibrium quantity is still higher in a competitive market than one with market power, even after the cost increase. It's the *change* in Q that is smaller.

Response to a Change in Demand

Now suppose that instead of a cost shift, there is a parallel shift in the demand curve. Perhaps iPads become even more fashionable, increasing demand and shifting out the demand curve. Specifically, let's say the new inverse demand curve is $P = 1,400 - 5Q$. How would the market react to this change?

Again, we follow the three-step method. Because the demand curve has shifted in this case, the marginal revenue curve changes as well. The new demand curve is linear, so we know how to derive the marginal revenue curve; we double the number in front of the quantity in the inverse demand curve. So,

$$MR = 1,400 - 10Q$$

Setting this equal to the marginal cost (which we'll assume is back at its original level of \$200) implies:

$$1{,}400 - 10Q = 200$$

$$10Q = 1{,}200$$

$$Q = 120$$

The quantity produced after the demand shift is now 120 million units, up from 80 million. Finally, we find the new price by plugging this quantity into the inverse demand curve:

$$P = 1{,}400 - 5Q$$

$$= 1{,}400 - 5(120)$$

$$= 800$$

The new price is \$800, up from \$600 before the demand shift.

An outward demand shift leads to an increase in both quantity and price in a market where the seller has market power, the same direction as in perfect competition. But again, the size of the changes differs.

The Big Difference: Changing the Price Sensitivity of Customers

One type of market change to which firms with market power react very differently from competitive firms is a change in the price sensitivity of demand—in other words, making the demand curve steeper or flatter. Say a new competing tablet comes along so that consumers' demand for iPads becomes more price-sensitive but doesn't change the quantity demanded at the current price. With perfect competition, as in panel a of Figure 9.4, the

Figure 9.4   **Responses to a Rotation in the Demand Curve**

(a) Perfect competition

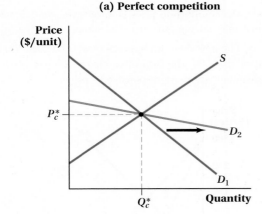

(b) Market power

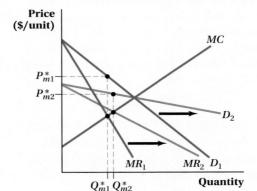

(a) For a perfectly competitive market, a rotation in the demand curve from D_1 to D_2 does not change the equilibrium quantity Q_c^* and price P_c^*.

(b) For a firm with market power, a rotation in the demand curve from D_1 to D_2 rotates the marginal revenue curve from MR_1 to MR_2. Prior to the rotation, the profit-maximizing quantity and price (Q_{m1}^*, P_{m1}^*) occurred where $MR_1 = MC$. After the rotation, the firm is profit-maximizing at a higher quantity and lower price (Q_{m2}^*, P_{m2}^*) where $MR_2 = MC$.

9.3 figure it out

The Power Tires Company has market power and faces the demand curve shown in the figure below. The firm's marginal cost curve is $MC = 30 + 3Q$.

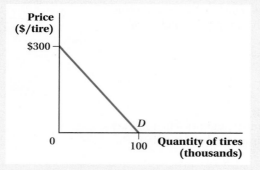

a. What is the firm's profit-maximizing output and price?

b. If the firm's demand changes to $P = 240 - 2Q$ while its marginal cost curve remains the same, what is the firm's profit-maximizing level of output and price? How does this compare to your answer for (a)?

c. Draw a diagram showing these two outcomes. Holding marginal cost equal, how does the shape of the demand curve affect the firm's ability to charge a high price?

Solution:

a. To solve for the firm's profit-maximizing level of output, we need to find the firm's marginal revenue curve. But, we only have a diagram of the demand curve. So, we will start by solving for the inverse demand function. The inverse demand function will typically have the form

$$P = a - bQ$$

where a is the vertical intercept and b is the absolute value of the slope ($= \left| \frac{\Delta P}{\Delta Q} \right|$). We can see from the figure of the demand curve that $a = 300$. In addition, we can calculate the absolute value of the slope of the demand curve as $\left| \frac{\Delta P}{\Delta Q} \right| = \left| \frac{-300}{100} \right| = 3$. Therefore, $b = 3$. This means that the demand for Power Tires is

$$P = 300 - 3Q$$

We know that the equation for marginal revenue (when demand is linear) is $P = a - 2bQ$. Therefore,

$$MR = 300 - 6Q$$

Setting marginal revenue equal to marginal cost, we find

$$MR = MC$$
$$300 - 6Q = 30 + 3Q$$
$$270 = 9Q$$
$$Q = 30$$

To find price, we substitute $Q = 30$ into the firm's demand equation:

$$P = 300 - 3Q$$
$$= 300 - 3(30) = 210$$

The firm should produce 30,000 tires and sell them at a price of $210.

b. If demand changes to $P = 240 - 2Q$, marginal revenue becomes $MR = 240 - 4Q$ because now $a = 240$ and $b = 2$. Setting $MR = MC$, we find

$$240 - 4Q = 30 + 3Q$$
$$210 = 7Q$$
$$Q = 30$$

Even with reduced demand, the firm should still produce 30 units if it wants to maximize profit. Substituting into the new demand curve, we can see that the price will be

$$P = 240 - 2Q$$
$$= 240 - 2(30) = 180$$

Here, the equilibrium price is lower even though the profit-maximizing output is the same.

c. The new diagram appears below. Because D_2 is flatter than D_1, the firm must charge a lower price. Consumers are more responsive to price.

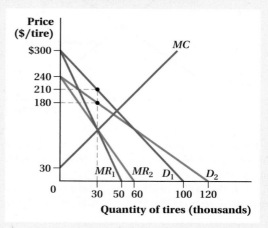

flattening of the demand curve does not change the point at which $P = MC$ (as embodied in the supply curve), so neither price nor quantity moves. The price sensitivity of consumers does not impact the sellers' output decisions as long as price is still equal to marginal cost.

Things are different, though, if the same demand curve rotation happens in a market in which there is a seller with market power. That's because with market power, the rotation in demand also moves the marginal revenue curve as shown in panel b of Figure 9.4. Even though the new demand curve D_2 crosses the marginal cost curve at the same quantity as the old demand curve, MR_2 intersects the marginal cost curve at a higher quantity than did MR_1 (Q^*_{m2} instead of Q^*_{m1}). Therefore, the firm's output rises as a result of the demand curve rotation and the price falls.

The opposite pattern holds when consumers become less price-sensitive and firms have market power: Output falls and price rises. Again, these changes wouldn't happen in perfect competition because suppliers' choices don't depend on the price sensitivity of demand.

9.5 The Winners and Losers from Market Power

Given that a firm with market power charges a price that is above its marginal cost, you might suspect that having market power is beneficial for firms, and it is. We see just exactly how beneficial it is in this section. We also see how market power affects consumers (*Hint*: badly). To do all this, we use the same tools we used to analyze competitive markets in Chapter 3—consumer and producer surplus. This approach allows us to directly compare markets in which firms have market power to those that are competitive.

Consumer and Producer Surplus under Market Power

Let's return to the Apple iPad example. Recall that Apple has a marginal cost of $200 and an inverse demand curve of $P = 1,000 - 5Q$ (where Q is in millions). This demand curve implied a marginal revenue curve $MR = 1,000 - 10Q$. We set that equal to marginal cost to solve for Q and found that to maximize profit, Apple should produce 80 million iPads and set its price at $600 per iPad.

We can compute the consumer and producer surplus when a firm has market power in the same way we computed these surpluses in a competitive market. The consumer surplus is the area under the demand curve and above the price. The producer surplus is the area below the price and above the marginal cost curve. At first glance, you might think this is different from producer surplus in a competitive market, which is the area below the price and above the supply curve. But remember that the supply curve in a perfectly competitive market is actually part of its marginal cost curve, so there is no difference in the case of market power.

We illustrate these surplus values in Figure 9.5. Apple's profit-maximizing price and quantity occur at point m. The consumer surplus is the triangle above the price $600 and below the demand curve. This area is labeled A. The producer surplus is the rectangle below $600 and above the marginal cost curve. It is labeled B.

We can compute these surplus values easily. The consumer surplus triangle has a base equal to the quantity sold and a height equal to the difference between the demand choke price and the market price. The demand choke price is especially easy to calculate from an inverse demand curve; you just plug in $Q = 0$ and solve for the price. In this case, it's $P_{DChoke} = 1,000 - 5(0) = 1,000$. So, the consumer surplus is

$$CS = \text{Triangle } A = \frac{1}{2} \times 80 \text{ million} \times (\$1,000 - \$600) = \$16 \text{ billion}$$

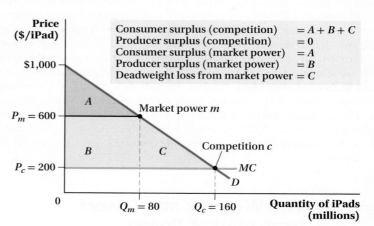

We can compute Apple's producer surplus, consumer surplus, and deadweight loss using the marginal cost curve, the demand curve, and the profit-maximizing output and price levels. Consumer surplus is the area of triangle A, equal to $\frac{1}{2} \times 80$ million $\times$ ($1,000 - $600) or $16 billion. The producer surplus, rectangle B, is (80 million) $\times$ ($600 - $200) or $32 billion. The deadweight loss is triangle C and can be calculated as $\frac{1}{2} \times$ (160 million − 80 million) $\times$ ($600 − $200) or $16 billion.

Figure 9.5 Surplus from the Apple iPad

The producer surplus is a rectangle with a base equal to the quantity sold and a height equal to the difference between the monopoly price and marginal cost. Therefore,

$$PS = \text{Rectangle } B = (80 \text{ million}) \times (\$600 - \$200) = \$32 \text{ billion}$$

So far, so good. Consumers earn $16 billion of consumer surplus from buying iPads, a fairly sizeable sum, and Apple does great, making $32 billion of surplus.

Consumer and Producer Surplus under Perfect Competition

Now let's think about how the market would look if Apple behaved like a competitive firm and priced at marginal cost. The price would be $200 because marginal cost is constant at $200. Plugging $200 into the demand curve equation yields a quantity of 160 million. Therefore, in the competitive equilibrium Apple would sell 160 million iPads at a price of $200 (point c in Figure 9.5). Note that because $P = MC$, Apple would earn zero producer surplus in a competitive market.

With competition, then, iPad prices would be lower, the quantity sold would be higher, and Apple would make a lot less money—producer surplus would fall by $32 billion. This competitive market outcome provides a way to see the standard result for markets in which firms have pricing power: A firm with market power reduces output and raises price relative to the perfectly competitive equilibrium, and by doing so, it raises producer surplus (and profit).

How does *consumer* surplus compare under market power and perfect competition? In Figure 9.5, consumer surplus under perfect competition is the entire triangular area $A + B + C$ below the demand curve and above the competitive price of $200. The triangle's base is the competitive quantity of 160 million and its height is the difference between the demand choke price of $1,000 and the competitive price. This means consumer surplus under perfect competition is

$$CS = \frac{1}{2} \times \text{Base} \times \text{Height} = \frac{1}{2} \times 160 \text{ million} \times (\$1,000 - 200) = \$64 \text{ billion}$$

Recall that when Apple exercises its market power, consumer surplus is $16 billion. So, consumers are much better off when there is competition. In this example, they have four times the consumer surplus under competition than with Apple having market power. On the other hand, by exploiting its market power, Apple would move from having no producer surplus to $32 billion of producer surplus. That's why firms want to use their market power whenever they can, even if it costs their customers a large amount of consumer surplus.

 **application**

Southwest Airlines

Southwest Airlines, the spunky low-cost carrier, has made a habit of entering the stronghold airports of incumbent carriers and driving down fares. One way to think about how this happens is that Southwest's arrival moves the airport from a situation in which incumbents have considerable market power to a situation that is closer to perfect competition.

The impact can be dramatic. Prices fall 25 to 50% on routes that Southwest starts to fly, and the number of passengers flying the route goes up substantially. It's probably no coincidence that among the 20 busiest airports in the United States, the four that saw the biggest drops in average fares from 2001 to 2011 were all airports at which Southwest began operating during that period. The lucky passengers were flying into and out of Denver (an average fare drop of 30% during the period), San Francisco (average drop of 17%), Philadelphia (average drop of 16%), and Boston (average drop of 15%). By the way, the fifth-largest fare drop occurred at New York's JFK airport, where Jet Blue, another low-cost airline patterned partially on the Southwest model, began operating in 2000.[7]

Passengers across the country have become familiar with these sorts of changes, which have become known as the "Southwest effect." As a result, many local governments and airport authorities have actively tried to recruit Southwest to come to or expand service in their city. We suspect you could hear a collective cheer coming from students at local schools in the cities where Southwest came to town. Thanks to competition from Southwest, their consumer surplus was going to rise—and their spring breaks in Florida were going to be more affordable. ■

The Deadweight Loss of Market Power

We've just seen how exercising market power can be great for firms and bad for consumers. Firms can earn considerably more producer surplus by restricting output and raising price, but this costs consumers a sizable chunk of their consumer surplus. That's not the only consequence of market power, though. Notice that, in the example above, the total surplus under market power is $48 billion ($16 billion consumer surplus + $32 billion producer surplus), which is smaller than the total surplus under competition of $64 billion. That missing $16 billion of surplus has been destroyed by the firm's exercise of market power. It's important to recognize that this loss is not surplus that is transferred from consumers to producers when producers restrict output and raise prices. No one gets it. It just disappears. In other words, it is the deadweight loss from market power.

The deadweight loss of market power can be seen in Figure 9.5. It is the area of triangle C whose base is the difference between the firm's output with market power and its output under perfect competition and whose height is the difference between the prices under market power (P_m) and competition (P_c). We know from our comparison of the total surplus of the market power and competitive cases above that this area is $16 billion. We can confirm that value by calculating the area of triangle C:

$$\text{DWL} = \frac{1}{2} \times (160 \text{ million} - 80 \text{ million}) \times (\$600 - \$200) = \$16 \text{ billion}$$

---

[7] These numbers were taken from data compiled by the Bureau of Transportation Statistics of the U.S. Department of Transportation.

The deadweight loss (DWL) is the inefficiency of market power. Note that this cost is exactly like the DWL from a tax or regulation we discussed in Chapter 3—a triangular area below the demand curve and above the marginal cost curve (supply curve, in Chapter 3). A firm with pricing power essentially puts a market power "tax" on consumers and keeps the revenue for itself. The DWL comes about because there are consumers in the market who are willing to buy the product (an iPad in this example) at a price above its cost of production, but can't because the firm has hiked up prices to increase its profit. Just as with the DWL from taxes and regulations, the size of the DWL from market power is related to the size of the difference between the monopoly and competitive output levels. The more the firm withholds output to maximize profits, the bigger is the efficiency loss.

> ∂ The online appendix uses integration to calculate producer surplus and dead-weight loss for monopolies. (http://glsmicro.com/appendices)

Differences in Producer Surplus for Different Firms

One more important point about the surplus implications of market power is how the slope of the demand curve influences the relative size of consumer and producer surplus in the market.

Consider two different markets, one with a relatively steep (inelastic) demand curve and one with a flatter (elastic) one. Each is served by a monopolist. To keep things easy to follow, imagine that both firms have the same constant marginal cost curves, and that it just so happens that each firm's profit-maximizing output is the same. We plot this case in Figure 9.6.

In the market in panel a of Figure 9.6, buyers aren't very price-sensitive, so the demand curve is steep. In the market in panel b, consumers are quite sensitive to prices, as reflected in the flatter demand curve. The marginal revenue curves in both markets are also shown in the figure. To maximize their profits, both firms choose quantity and price to set $MR = MC$. It is clear from looking at the figure that for the same-sized market (measured by the total quantity of the good that is produced, which we've set to be the same here), producer surplus is higher when the demand curve is steeper.

Figure 9.6　　**Gains from Market Power under Different Demand Curves**

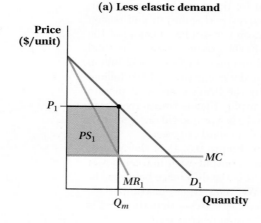
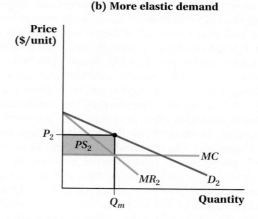

(a) When buyers are not very price-sensitive, the demand curve is steep. At $MR_1 = MC$ the producer supplies quantity Q_m at the relatively high price P_1, and generates the relatively large producer surplus PS_1.

(b) When buyers are price-sensitive, the demand curve is flat. At $MR_2 = MC$, the producer supplies quantity Q_m at the relatively low price P_2, and generates the relatively small producer surplus PS_2.

Let's return to our earlier problem regarding Babe's Bats (BB). Remember that BB faces an inverse demand curve of $P = 25 - 2.5Q$ and a marginal cost curve $MC = 5Q$. Calculate the deadweight loss from market power at the firm's profit-maximizing level of output.

Solution:

The easiest way to find deadweight loss is to use a diagram. Therefore, we should start by drawing a graph with demand, marginal revenue, and marginal cost:

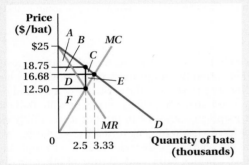

We know from our earlier problem that the profit-maximizing level of output is 2,500 bats sold at a price of $18.75.

To find the deadweight loss from market power, we need to consider the consumer and producer surplus and compare it with the competitive outcome. If BB participated in a competitive market, it would set price equal to marginal cost to determine its output:

$$P = MC$$
$$25 - 2.5Q = 5Q$$
$$25 = 7.5Q$$
$$Q = 3.33$$

Therefore, BB would sell 3,333 bats. Of course, the price will be lower at this level of output:

$$P = 25 - 2.5Q$$
$$= 25 - 2.5(3.33)$$
$$= 16.68$$

If the market were competitive, the bats would sell for $16.68 each. Consumer surplus would be areas $A + B + C$ (the area below the demand curve and above the competitive price), and producer surplus would be areas $D + E + F$ (the area below the competitive price but above the marginal cost curve). Total surplus would be areas $A + B + C + D + E + F$.

When BB exercises its market power, it reduces its output to 2,500 bats and increases its price to $18.75. In this situation, consumer surplus is only area A (the area below demand but above the monopoly price). Producer surplus is areas $B + D + F$ (the area below the monopoly price but above marginal cost). Total surplus under market power is $A + B + D + F$.

So, what happens to areas C and E? Area C was consumer surplus but no longer exists. Area E was producer surplus but also has disappeared. These areas are the deadweight loss from market power. We can calculate this area by measuring the area of the triangle that encompasses areas $C + E$. To do so, we have one more important calculation to make. We need to be able to calculate the height of the triangle, so we need to determine the marginal cost of producing 2,500 units:

$$MC = 5Q$$
$$= 5(2.5)$$
$$= 12.5$$

Now, we can calculate the area of the deadweight loss triangle:

$$\text{DWL} = \text{Areas } C + E = \frac{1}{2} \times \text{Base} \times \text{Height}$$

$$= \frac{1}{2} \times (3.33 - 2.5) \times (\$18.75 - \$12.50)$$

$$= \frac{1}{2} \times 0.83 \times \$6.25$$

$$= \$2.59375$$

Remember that the quantity is measured in thousands, so the deadweight loss is equal to $2,593.75.

That's because, as we pointed out earlier, a steeper demand curve raises the firm's profit-maximizing markup of price over marginal cost.

Firms with market power find it very lucrative to operate in markets in which consumers are relatively price-insensitive. If you're a consumer in that market, though, look out: Prices are going to be high.

9.6 Governments and Market Power: Regulation, Antitrust, and Innovation

We've seen the impact that market power can have on an industry—higher prices, smaller output, lower consumer surplus, and deadweight loss. The deadweight loss created by market power can justify government intervention in markets if such regulation can move the market toward a more competitive outcome and reduce deadweight loss. And, indeed, governments attempt to do this in several ways. Given this, it might be surprising that in certain markets the government actually encourages and protects market power, and that this too can be justified as a policy that benefits society as a whole. In this section, we explore several of the ways governments intervene in markets to either restrain or encourage market power.

Direct Price Regulation

When there is a concern that firms in an industry have too much market power, governments sometimes directly regulate prices. This often occurs in markets considered to be natural monopolies. If it appears that there is no way to prevent the existence of a natural monopoly because of the nature of the industry's cost structure, the government will often allow only a single firm to operate but will limit its pricing behavior to prevent it from fully exploiting its market power. Governments have used this argument to justify regulating, at various times, the prices of electricity, natural gas, gasoline, cable television, local telephone service, long-distance telephone service, airfares, trucking rates, and all sorts of other products.

To understand the logic behind these actions, consider a typical natural monopoly case as shown in Figure 9.7. Let's suppose it is the market for electricity distribution, which we argued earlier may, in fact, be a natural monopoly. With a demand curve of D, an unregulated electric company would produce at the point where marginal revenue equals marginal cost. This would lead to a price of P_m, substantially higher than the firm's marginal cost. The consumer surplus in this situation will be only the area A,

---

Figure 9.7 | **Government Regulation of a Natural Monopoly**

Before government regulation, the electric company produces at point m, where quantity is Q_m and price P_m is well above the firm's marginal cost curve. If the government sets a price cap at the level equal to the firm's marginal cost, the firm will produce at the perfectly competitive price (P_c) and quantity (Q_c). Consumer surplus under the regulation will expand from triangle A to the triangle $A + B + C$. However, since P_c falls below the firm's average total cost curve, the firm will be operating with negative profit, and the price cap is not a sustainable regulation.

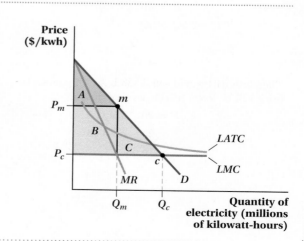

rather than the area $A + B + C$, as would be the case if prices were instead set at P_c, a level equal to the firm's marginal cost.

If the government imposes a price cap regulation such that the electric company cannot charge prices above P_c, output could equal its perfectly competitive level, and consumer surplus will equal area $A + B + C$. But there's a problem. P_c is below the firm's average total cost; if it sells every unit it produces at the regulated price, the firm will earn a negative profit, as it won't be able to cover its fixed cost. Therefore, a simple price regulation requiring competitive pricing is not a sustainable solution in regulating a natural monopoly. However, any regulation that would allow a price above marginal cost in order to allow the natural monopolist to recoup its fixed cost would also lead to a deadweight loss and less consumer surplus than the competitive case (though the deadweight loss may be smaller and the reduction in consumer surplus smaller than in the unregulated monopoly case).[8]

Aside from this problem, there are several other serious difficulties involved in using direct price regulations. First and foremost, only the company knows its true cost structure. Government regulators don't actually know what the firm's marginal cost is nor, for that matter, does the government actually know what the demand curve is. It's difficult to set the regulated price at the perfectly competitive level without knowing these two pieces of information. So, the regulator is left to estimate them. Further, the firm has an incentive to misrepresent the truth and make people believe its costs are higher than they really are, because this would justify a higher regulated price. In addition, companies that are regulated based on their cost often have no incentive to reduce their costs because the regulator would then reduce the regulated price, destroying any profit gained from the increase in efficiency.

Antitrust

Another approach governments use to address the effects of market power is **antitrust law** (sometimes called *competition law*, particularly outside the United States). Antitrust laws are meant to promote competition in a market by restricting firms from certain behaviors that may limit competition, especially if the firm is an established and substantial current player in the industry. In some cases, antitrust laws are used to prevent firms from merging with or acquiring other firms in order to stop them from becoming too dominant. Occasionally, these laws are even used to force the break-up of an established firm that is determined to have too much market power. Antitrust law tends to be strong and well enforced in wealthier countries, but is often much weaker elsewhere in the world.

antitrust law
Laws designed to promote competitive markets by restricting firms from behaviors that limit competition.

One of the strongest and most common prohibitions in antitrust law is the ban on collusion among competitors with regard to pricing and market allocation (agreements to divide up a market among firms). In the United States, for example, even discussing prices or market entry strategies with your competitors is a criminal act.

The antitrust authorities are also allowed to investigate whether a firm is monopolizing an industry unfairly and, if so, they can sue to change the behavior. There have been many such investigations in recent years—for example, those investigating Intel for its pricing of its CPUs to computer makers, American Express, Visa, and MasterCard for the rules they require merchants to follow when customers want to use credit cards to make purchases, and Realtors for the rules they set about who is allowed to list houses for sale.

The drawbacks of antitrust enforcement as a way of preventing market power have to do with the large potential costs and uncertainties involved. The government should not fight concentration that would increase efficiency and make consumers better off, but that's hard to measure directly.

---

[8] There is a way, at least theoretically, that regulation could achieve both the perfectly competitive outcome and allow the firm to pay its fixed costs. This would involve not just a per-unit price P_c, but also a lump-sum payment to the monopolist either from consumers or the government. Many regulated utilities have payment structures that try to replicate this in part, with a fixed monthly fee for service regardless of the quantity used plus an additional fee tied to the quantity the consumer purchases. However, these fee schedules are often only approximations to the true cost structure of the monopolist and can also be constrained by political considerations, so it is difficult to achieve perfectly competitive outcomes exactly.

Promoting Monopoly: Patents, Licenses, and Copyrights

Even as the government tries to limit market power through regulation and antitrust policy, it sometimes *encourages* monopolies and helps them legally enforce their market power by conferring patents, licenses, copyrights, trademarks, and other assorted legal rights to exercise market power.

Why would the government do this if it cares about consumers and competitive markets? Why give inventors a 20-year monopoly for their innovations in the form of a patent? Pharmaceutical companies, for example, receive patent-based monopolies on all sorts of medicines, which raise the prices people pay. Why license spectrum to radio stations and mobile phone companies, which prohibits others from broadcasting? Why give copyright owners of a book or movie 125 years of protection from anyone copying their works without getting approval and paying royalties? Michael Buffer, a professional boxing and wrestling ring announcer, has a trademark on his exhortation "Let's get ready to rumble!" The Transformers are similarly protected. You might like to pump up the crowd at a sales event or have a great idea for using the Transformers in your own movie, but the government has given Buffer and Hasbro the rights to determine how "Let's get ready to rumble!" and the Transformers will be used commercially.

Collectively, all of the monopolies created by the government add up to immense amounts of market power that inevitably lead to higher prices and lower quantities than would exist in a competitive market. The reason why it still might make sense for the government to do this is for the sake of encouraging innovation. Giving someone the exclusive right, at least temporarily, to the profits from innovation can provide a powerful incentive to create new things. Governments have decided that the consumer surplus created by these new goods can outweigh the deadweight loss from their producers having market power for a period of time. In some cases, innovation can be the upside of market power.

To see why, think about the market for a medical drug to cure the common cold, which affects hundreds of millions of people every year. There would certainly be demand for the product. We label that demand curve D in Figure 9.8.

Let's assume that the marginal cost of producing a dose of this medicine once it is discovered is constant at $5. (Once a drug is in production, the marginal cost of manufacturing it is very low. It doesn't cost much to make another pill or another dose of vaccine using a formula that's been developed and a production line that's already built.) The rest of the world would like the drug company that discovers the cure to act like a perfectly competitive firm and sell it at the marginal cost of $5 per dose, as at point c. This would create the largest possible consumer surplus of $A + B + C$.

Figure 9.8   :   Monopoly Power and Innovation

The government encourages innovation by giving companies monopolies on products. D represents the demand curve for the cure for the common cold. In a perfectly competitive market, the drug would be sold at a price equal to its marginal cost, $5, and consumer surplus would be $A + B + C$. However, at this price, the firm would be unable to recover the fixed cost of developing the drug and would choose not to invest in the cure for the common cold. By giving the firm a patent, the government allows it to recover the costs of innovation, and the firm produces at the monopoly price P_m and quantity Q_m. The consumer surplus is now the triangle A.

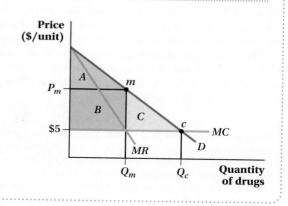

The problem is that selling the drug for $5 would leave the drug company with no producer surplus. Because the firm would need to expend massive amounts of fixed cost on discovering and developing the drug, it will not bother to do so if it immediately has to sell the drug at marginal cost. In other words, having to act like a perfectly competitive firm as soon as it develops this new drug would mean the firm won't want to actually develop the drug in the first place.

In theory, the government could try to subsidize the development cost (and it does subsidize many types of research and development), but all sorts of problems arise such as trying to figure out what will work, avoiding corruption, and so on.[9] Instead, the government makes a compromise. It promises the firm a monopoly on the drug if it develops it. The company realizes this means it can produce the quantity level Q_m (where $MR = MC$) and charge a price of P_m, giving it a producer surplus equal to area B from selling the drug. Therefore, as long as the firm expects the fixed cost of discovering the drug to be smaller than the producer surplus B, it will set out to discover the cure for the common cold. Ultimately, this benefits consumers by giving them a consumer surplus equal to area A. This is lower than the consumer surplus consumers would get in a competitive market $(A + B + C)$, but given that the firm would not have developed the drug in the first place if it had to charge a competitive price, consumers are better off with the more limited consumer surplus of A than none at all.

Overall, the economics of intellectual property protection suggest that it will tend to lead to innovations in just the types of goods that people like most. If a market for an innovation is large because there are a lot of consumers who would want to purchase it, that will tend to also make the monopoly profits in that market big. In addition, recall that in Chapter 3, we saw that goods with steeper demand curves tend to be those with the highest consumer surplus. Earlier in this chapter, we observed that the steeper demand curves are exactly the ones where monopoly profits are largest. So, a patent, license, or copyright that gives innovators a monopoly will tend to encourage innovation in exactly the types of goods that people value. The downside, of course, is that this will tend to lead to especially high prices as well.

 **application**

Internet File-Sharing and the Music Industry

Bands and record labels earn money from selling music. This is a risky business. Most of the costs associated with making a CD are development costs that must be paid up-front, before anyone knows how well the CD will sell. (The marginal cost of burning another disc is virtually zero.) And, in fact, most CDs aren't successful; by some reports, more than 90% of CDs released lose money. The few success stories have to cover the fixed costs for the losers.

Copyright law in the music industry is designed to encourage this risky creative activity by giving artists and record labels the exclusive right to sell their music. The market power generated is meant to allow them to cover their costs of development. But this system has been facing challenges. File-sharing sites that allow people to download music for free—violating the copyrights on the music in the process—started in 1999 and grew rapidly. By 2004 there were about 10 million simultaneous users of file-sharing systems. During the same time period, CD sales fell by about 20%. The argument made by the record industry was that if people stopped paying for music, essentially driving down price to the marginal cost of zero,

---

[9] Because drug development costs are fixed costs for pharmaceutical firms, such an approach is related to the fixed-cost transfer scheme we discussed for a natural monopoly. Again, these can theoretically reach an efficient market outcome, but there are many practical roadblocks to their successful implementation.

Table 9.2	Number of New Artists Releasing Albums by Genre, 1999 and 2004	
	1999	**2004**
Urban/Rap	1493	1297
Rock	1984	1919
Jazz	1453	1627
Country	644	904

music producers would no longer be able to cover the costs of developing new bands and new CDs. The implication was that, ultimately, consumers would be worse off. They would miss the consumer surplus they would have obtained from new music produced in a market where consumers actually paid for music.

Economists Julie Mortimer and Alan Sorensen explored whether this might be the case in a study of the music industry during the period when Internet file-sharing became prevalent.[10] They found that the number of new artists in rock and urban/rap, two music formats for which listeners are especially heavy users of the Internet, fell between 1999 and 2004. However, the number of new artists in jazz and in country, two genres with a smaller share of listeners who used file-sharing programs online, rose over this period. You can see the results from Mortimer's and Sorensen's study in Table 9.2.

These changes might be mere coincidence, but they are at least consistent with the idea that Internet file-sharing has reduced the amount of investment music producers put into new artists, because it reduces artists' and record labels' market power by undermining their copyright protection. Mortimer and Sorensen argue that the decrease in the demand for paid-for CDs has raised the incentive for bands to seek alternative ways to earn income from their art. Specifically, they document that artists are more likely to go on tour than they were before the rise of the file-sharing sites. ■

Patent Protection in Practice

A cure for the common cold is an example of a situation in which allowing monopoly power can make consumers better off. Intellectual property law raises many deeper issues, however. One issue is the optimal length of patents. A longer monopoly period will lead to a longer period during which consumer surplus is lower than it would be in a competitive market. On the other hand, it creates more producer surplus for innovators and could therefore induce more invention. But it's important to realize that to spur innovation, all the patent system needs to do is to protect enough producer surplus to pay for the innovation costs. Any additional market power beyond that will lead to a transfer of surplus from consumers to the firm without more innovation, and will involve deadweight loss, too. In the common cold example above, if the drug development costs are equal to B, then the amount B is all the producer surplus a patent would need to protect to convince the firm to develop the drug. If patents were lengthened and the amount of protected producer surplus were larger, the drug would still be invented, but consumers would pay higher prices (and consume lower quantities) for a longer period of time.

Another difficult question regards how substantial an innovation must be beyond existing goods in order to get a patent. If the government gives out patents for things that have already been invented, the only effect will be to create deadweight loss and transfer surplus from consumers to producers due to market power. Many people believe that the government has granted intellectual property rights too leniently, objecting to decisions like giving a patent to Amazon for any transaction involving one-click shopping (this happened in 1999 and the decision was reconfirmed in 2010); allowing MasterCard to trademark the term "priceless"; extending copyright to 125 years, much longer than the lifetime of any author; or letting biologist Craig Venter actually patent the human genes that his firm Celera Genomics

---

[10] Julie Holland Mortimer and Alan Sorensen, "Supply Responses to Digital Distribution: Recorded Music and Live Performances," Preliminary, December 29, 2005, cited by permission of the authors. http://www.aeaweb.org/assa/2006/0107_0800_0702.pdf.

mapped in its research. Someone was even granted a patent for a crustless peanut butter sandwich.

A further downside of patents, licenses, and other government-granted monopolies is that they can induce battles among firms to obtain market power that actually result in firms' squandering the producer surplus that the monopoly right would protect. Companies sometimes lobby to acquire a monopoly through expenditures on public relations, lawyers, advertising, and in situations with less scrupulous participants, even outright bribes. Much of that spending is just waste. All this useless spending is called **rent-seeking.** If this spending doesn't lead to more of the good being produced (someone is going to get the patent or license in any case) or to higher-quality output, it is just pure deadweight loss.

rent-seeking
A firm's attempts to gain government-granted monopoly power and, therefore, additional producer surplus.

theory and data

Determining a New Drug's Potential Market

Pfizer, the American pharmaceutical company, spent over $9 billion on research and development in 2010. To put that in perspective, that's nearly one-third of the federal government's budget for health research and development (R&D). The company's history of sizable investments like these in developing new drugs has certainly paid off, though—that same year, Pfizer pulled in nearly $68 billion in revenues. So how does a company like Pfizer know how to allocate its $9 billion dollar budget? Was it just good luck that led past research teams to pursue products as varied and popular as Chapstick and Xanax? Not really; you shouldn't be surprised to hear that firms do, in fact, use some basic market analysis to decide where to look for potential cash cows.

Pharmaceutical companies are willing to spend a lot on R&D in large part because the government grants them patents, thereby guaranteeing the companies' monopoly profits on new products. But while the promise of a patent certainly has spurred on Pfizer's R&D team, simply giving the firm a monopoly on a product isn't enough. The firm has to believe that when developing a new drug, the R&D costs will be offset by the good's potential revenues.

What do these companies look at to determine what products will sell? Economists Daron Acemoglu and Joshua Linn proposed that companies consider a drug's potential market size—in other words, what the future demand for a drug will likely be.[11] The age profile of the populations can be used as a rough estimate of market size for a given drug, since most drugs taken by the middle-aged are not prescribed to the elderly and vice versa. But Pfizer and its competitors don't just care about the *number* of people in a market; they also want to know how much money those people can fork over for pharmaceuticals. For this reason, Acemoglu and Linn looked at the share of income by age groups. As can be seen in Figure 9.9, the income share of people between the ages of 30 and 60 has steadily increased since 1970, and in 2000 it accounted for approximately 50% of income. Theoretically, then, Big Pharma should have diverted more of its funds to the development of drugs demanded by people aged 30 to 60 years old over the development of new pharmaceuticals for, say, glaucoma or vertigo, which are primarily consumed by older patients.

This is exactly what pharmaceutical companies have done. Acemoglu and Linn found that for every 1% increase in potential market size for a given drug type, development of new nongeneric drugs in that category increased around 4%. In other words, Big Pharma firms target their development toward products that offer the largest potential monopoly profits.

[11] Daron Acemoglu and Joshua Linn, "Market Size in Innovation: Theory and Evidence from the Pharmaceutical Industry," *The Quarterly Journal of Economics* 119, no. 3 (2004): 1049–1090.

Figure 9.9   Income Shares of People in Various Age Groups

The income share of people between the ages of 30 and 60 has steadily increased since 1970, and in 2000 it accounted for approximately 50% of income. Pharmaceutical companies devoted more of their drug development funds to drugs demanded by people of this age group.

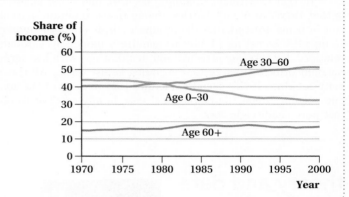

The pharmaceutical companies' actions make economic sense, but unfortunately leave a lot of drugs underfunded. Conditions such as Tourette syndrome or muscular dystrophy afflict a relatively small population and therefore have a small potential market size. For this reason, Congress passed the Orphan Drug Act, which offers tax credits and other economic incentives to companies that develop drugs for these "orphaned" diseases. Congress believed that to influence Big Pharma's R&D, you have to promise greater profits, and sometimes patents aren't enough.

9.7 Conclusion

Unlike the perfectly competitive firms of Chapter 8, firms with market power don't just choose the quantity they supply at some fixed price determined by the market. Monopolies and other types of firms with market power have the ability to influence the prices of their goods. As a result, they produce at the profit-maximizing quantity where $MR = MC$. This production level is lower than the quantity a perfectly competitive market would produce, leading to a higher market price, more producer surplus, less consumer surplus, and deadweight loss. To raise consumer surplus and reduce deadweight loss, governments often intervene through direct price regulation and antitrust laws to reduce firms' market power. On the other hand, governments also sometimes encourage market power to promote product innovation, such as through the issuance of patents, trademarks, and copyrights.

Even though the firms we've studied in this chapter have the ability to set the price of their products, they are still limited in one important aspect of pricing. In particular, we assumed that if a firm increased the quantity it produces, this would lead to a decrease in the price on *every* unit of the good sold. But what if a firm could sell its product at different prices to different types of consumers? We discuss this use of a firm's market power, a strategy broadly categorized as *price discrimination*, in Chapter 10.

Summary

1. Most firms have some **market power,** meaning that the firm's production decisions affect the market price of the good it sells. Firms maintain market power through **barriers to entry** into the market. These barriers include **natural monopolies,** switching costs, **product differentiation,** and absolute cost advantages of key inputs. [**Section 9.1**]

2. A **monopoly** is the sole supplier of a good in a market and represents the extreme case of a firm with complete market power. Monopolies and other firms with market power base their production decisions in part on their **marginal revenue,** the revenue from selling an additional unit of a good. Unlike perfectly competitive firms, these firms' marginal revenue falls as output rises. As a result, when a firm increases its production of a good, its marginal revenue falls, because it must sell all units of the good (not just the additional unit) at a lower price. [**Section 9.2**]

3. The profit-maximizing output level for a monopolist is found where marginal revenue equals marginal cost, $MR = MC$. A monopoly will charge a price above its marginal cost, meaning that the market price for a monopoly is higher than that for a perfectly competitive firm.

The **Lerner index** computes how much a firm should mark up its price; the more inelastic the demand for a product, the higher the firm's Lerner index and markup. [**Section 9.3**]

4. The changes in quantity supplied and price created by cost and demand shocks have the same direction, but different magnitudes, for firms with market power as for perfectly competitive firms. However, firms with market power respond differently to changes in consumers' price sensitivities—that is, rotations in the demand curve—than do perfectly competitive firms. [**Section 9.4**]

5. When a firm exercises its market power, it increases its producer surplus, decreases consumer surplus, and creates a deadweight loss. Producer surplus is greater when consumers are relatively price-insensitive and the demand curve is steep. [**Section 9.5**]

6. Governments often intervene to reduce the deadweight loss created by firms with market power. Direct price regulation and **antitrust laws** are aimed at reducing firms' market power. Conversely, governments also grant market power to firms through patents, copyrights, and other laws as a way of promoting innovation. [**Section 9.6**]

Review Questions

1. When does a firm have market power?
2. Name and describe three barriers to entry to a market.
3. What are the characteristics of a natural monopoly? Why is it efficient for society for a natural monopoly to produce all the output of an entire industry?
4. Describe the connection between the slope of the demand curve for a good and a firm's marginal revenue.
5. What is the profit-maximizing output level for a firm with market power?
6. Compare the consumer and producer surplus of perfectly competitive firms with that of firms with market power.
7. Why does the profit-maximizing strategy of a firm with market power create a deadweight loss?
8. Why do firms with market power have only demand—and not supply—curves?
9. Firms with market power respond differently to changes in consumers' price sensitivity than do perfectly competitive firms. Explain why this is true.
10. Name some regulations the government imposes on firms with market power.

Problems (Solutions to problems marked * appear at the back of this book. Problems adapted to use calculus are available online at http://worthpublishers.com/GLS1e)

1. People are always complaining about Facebook: It changed the way its news feed works, the privacy settings are awful, there are too many game notifications, and so on. Recognizing dissatisfaction with Facebook, Google tried three times to enter the social networking market, first with Buzz, then with Wave, and now with Google Plus. Users say that the Google Plus platform

is far superior to Facebook's, yet Google Plus appears to be failing. Explain why consumers might reject a superior product for an inferior one in a market like this.

2. Sally sells seashells by the seashore. When Sally prices her shells at $7 each, she sells 5 shells every day. When she prices her shells at $6, she sells 6.

a. What is Sally's total revenue when she chooses to sell 5 shells (by pricing at $7)?

b. What is Sally's total revenue when she chooses to sell 6 shells (by pricing at $6)?

c. What is the marginal revenue Sally receives from deciding to sell a 6th shell?

d. The 6th shell sells for a price of $6. Why is the marginal revenue from selling a 6th shell so much lower than $6?

3. Indicate whether the following statements are true or false, and then explain your answers:

a. The marginal revenue from selling another unit of eggs can never be higher than the price of eggs.

b. Because the price a seller charges is always greater than $0, the marginal revenue from selling another unit must also be greater than $0.

*4. Consider the demand curve for otter food shown below:

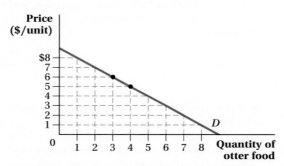

a. Indicate the area representing the total revenue Oscar the otter food seller would receive if he chose a price of $6.

b. On the same graph, indicate the area representing the total revenue Oscar the seller would receive if he chose a price of $5.

c. You should now have added two rectangles to your graph; however, because of some overlap, it actually appears that you've added three. One of the three is common to both scenarios above. The other two (smaller) rectangles are specific to scenario (a) or scenario (b). Label each rectangle with "A," "B," or "both" to indicate which rectangle each scenario belongs to.

d. Indicate what happens (gain or loss) to rectangle A as Oscar reduces his price from $6 to $5. Why?

e. Indicate what happens (gain or loss) to rectangle B as Oscar reduces his price from $6 to $5. Why?

f. Calculate the area of rectangle A and the area of rectangle B. Then, subtract the area of A from the area of B.

g. Calculate the marginal revenue Oscar receives when he sells a 4th unit. Does your answer agree with the number you calculated in (f)? Explain.

5. In Cleveland, Clive sells 15 cloves at a price of $5 each. If Clive lowers his price by 10%, to $4.50 per clove, he will sell 16, or 6.66% more. In Dallas, Della sells 15 cloves for $5 each. If Della lowers her price by 2%, to $4.90, she will sell 16 cloves, or 6.66% more.

a. Classify the demand curves that Clive and Della face as elastic or inelastic.

b. Determine the marginal revenue of the 16th unit for Clive. Then, compute the marginal revenue of the 16th unit for Della.

c. How does the marginal revenue received by a seller depend on the price elasticity of demand? Explain your answer.

*6. The demand for saffron is highly elastic. The demand for cigarettes is highly inelastic. The demand for peanut butter is unit-elastic.

a. If saffron producers reduce the price of saffron, what will happen to total revenue as a result? Will marginal revenue be positive, zero, or negative?

b. If cigarette makers reduce the price of cigarettes, what will happen to total revenue as a result? Will marginal revenue be positive, zero, or negative?

c. If peanut butter producers reduce the price of peanut butter, what will happen to total revenue as a result? Will marginal revenue be positive, zero, or negative?

7. In the chapter, we noted that the marginal revenue a seller receives can be expressed as $MR = P + (\Delta P/\Delta Q) \times Q$.

a. Using this formula as a starting point, show that marginal revenue can be expressed as $MR = P(1 + 1/E^D)$, where E^D is the price elasticity of demand.

b. Using your knowledge about the price elasticity of demand, explain why the marginal revenue a firm with market power receives must always be less than the price.

c. Using your knowledge of the price elasticity of demand, explain why the marginal revenue a perfectly competitive firm receives must be equal to the price.

*8. Consider the graph below, which illustrates the demand for Fluff. Fluff can be produced at a constant marginal and average total cost of $4 per case.

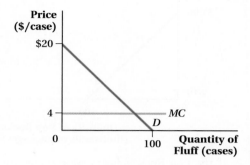

a. Draw in a carefully constructed marginal revenue curve.
b. Apply the $MR = MC$ rule to determine the profit-maximizing level of output. What price must the monopolist charge to maximize profit?
c. Calculate the profit earned by the monopolist.
d. The slope of the demand curve indicates that in order to sell one more unit, the price must fall by 20 cents. Verify that the seller cannot increase profit by reducing price and selling slightly more.
e. The slope of the demand curve indicates that if the price of Fluff increases by 20 cents, consumers will buy one less unit. Verify that the seller cannot increase profit by increasing price and selling slightly less.

*9. Irwin is a monopoly seller of specialty bearings. Consider the graph below, which illustrates the demand and marginal revenue curves for Irwin's 30-weight ball bearings, along with the marginal and average total costs of producing bearings:

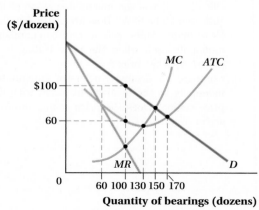

Quantity of bearings (dozens)

a. Find the monopolist's profit-maximizing level of output.

b. Determine the price the monopolist should charge to maximize profit.
c. Draw an appropriate rectangle on your graph to represent the total revenue the seller receives from selling the profit-maximizing quantity of bearings at the profit-maximizing price.
d. Draw an appropriate rectangle on your graph to represent the total cost of producing ball bearings.
e. The difference in the areas you drew in (c) and (d) represents profit. Calculate the profit Irwin earns from selling 30-weight ball bearings.

*10. Suppose that the demand for bentonite is given by $Q = 40 - 0.5P$, where Q is in tons of bentonite per day and P is the price per ton. Bentonite is produced by a monopolist at a constant marginal and average total cost of $10 per ton.
a. Derive the inverse demand and marginal revenue curves faced by the monopolist.
b. Equate marginal cost and marginal revenue to determine the profit-maximizing level of output.
c. Find the profit-maximizing price by plugging the ideal quantity back into the demand curve.
d. How would your answer change if marginal cost were instead given by $MC = 20 + Q$?

11. Suppose that econometricians at Hallmark Cards determine that the price elasticity of demand for greeting cards is −2.
a. If Hallmark's marginal cost of producing cards is constant and equal to $1.00, use the Lerner index to determine what price Hallmark should charge to maximize profit.
b. Suppose that Hallmark Cards wishes to know the price elasticity of demand faced by its archrival, American Greetings. Hallmark hires you to estimate it. Hallmark provides you with an educated guess concerning the marginal cost of producing a greeting card, which they estimate to be constant and equal to $1.22. A quick trip to the store tells you that American Greetings is selling its cards for an average of $3.25. Using these numbers and assuming that American Greetings is maximizing its profit, calculate the price elasticity of demand faced by American Greetings.

12. Many industrywide studies of the elasticity of demand for cigarettes (an industry dominated by a few firms with tremendous market power) indicate a price elasticity near −0.5. Yet, our study of market power tells us that a firm with

any market power at all should never operate
at a point on its demand curve where demand
is inelastic. How can you reconcile these apparently contradictory statements?

13. A monopolistic seller of fairy dust faces the
following inverse demand curve: $P = 100 - Q$,
where Q is smidgens of fairy dust per week.
Fairy dust can be produced at a constant marginal cost of $20 per smidgen.
   a. Graph this demand curve. Then, calculate the
      profit-maximizing price and quantity of fairy
      dust. Finally, calculate the seller's profit.
   b. A midsummer's druid festival greatly in-
      creases the demand for fairy dust, so that the
      price any particular consumer is willing to pay
      doubles. The inverse demand curve is now
      given by $P = 200 - 2Q$. Verify graphically
      that demand has increased and calculate the
      new profit-maximizing price and quantity.
   c. A tour bus full of druids took a wrong left
      turn at Albuquerque and showed up in town
      by accident. Now there are twice as many
      buyers at any price as there were before, and
      the inverse demand the seller faces is given
      by $P = 100 - 0.5Q$. Verify graphically that
      demand has increased and calculate the new
      profit-maximizing price and quantity.
   d. Suppose that the demand shift the seller faces
      is a parallel shift of the inverse demand curve
      such as $P = 150 - Q$. Verify graphically that
      demand has increased and calculate the new
      profit-maximizing price and quantity.
   e. What do your answers to (b), (c), and (d)
      indicate about how monopolistic suppliers re-
      spond to increases in demand?

14. Suppose that a monopolistic seller of designer
handbags faces the following inverse demand
curve: $P = 50 - 0.4Q$. The seller can produce
handbags for a constant marginal and average
total cost of $10.
   a. Calculate the profit-maximizing price for this
      seller.
   b. Suppose the government levies a $4 tax per
      unit on sellers of handbags. Calculate how
      this tax will affect the price the monopolist
      charges its customers.
   c. Who bears the burden of this tax?

15. Consider the market for Pop Rocks depicted in
the diagram below:

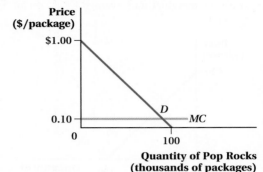

   a. If the Pop Rock industry were competitive,
      what would the competitive price and quan-
      tity be?
   b. If the Pop Rock industry were competitive,
      what would be the consumer and producer
      surpluses, respectively?
   c. Suppose that gangland figure Tommy Ver-
      cetti monopolizes the Pop Rock market.
      What price and quantity will he choose to
      maximize profit?
   d. Calculate the consumer and producer surplus
      of this Pop Rock monopoly.
   e. Compare your answers to (d) and (b). How
      big is the deadweight loss of monopoly?

*16. Suppose that a monopolistic seller of flux capaci-
tors faces the inverse demand curve $P = 40 - 0.5Q$,
and that the monopolist can produce flux capacitors at a constant marginal cost of $5.
   a. How many units will an unregulated monop-
      olist sell?
   b. Suppose that the government imposes a price
      ceiling of $6. What does this price ceiling do to
      the monopolist's marginal revenue curve? Spe-
      cifically, what is the marginal revenue of the
      10th unit? The 68th? How about the 69th?
   c. How many units will a profit-maximizing
      monopolist sell when the price ceiling is in
      place? At what price?
   d. Compare the deadweight loss of unregulated
      monopoly to the deadweight losses with the
      price ceiling. Does the price ceiling improve
      social welfare?

17. Consider a small, isolated town in which a brewery faces the following inverse demand: $P = 15 - 0.33Q$. The brewery can produce beer at a constant marginal and average total cost of $1 per bottle.
    a. Calculate the profit-maximizing price and quantity, as well as producer and consumer surplus and the deadweight loss from market power.
    b. If it were possible to organize the townsfolk, how much would they be willing to pay the brewery to sell beer at a price equal to its marginal cost?
    c. What is the minimum payment the brewery would be willing to accept to sell beer at a price equal to marginal cost?
    d. Is there potentially a bargain that can be struck between the townsfolk and brewery? What would the deadweight loss be if such a bargain were struck?
18. Consider the firm depicted in the diagram below.

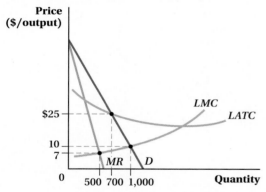

a. Is the firm a natural monopoly? How do you know?
b. Will this firm earn a profit if it is not subject to regulation? How do you know?
c. If the government requires the firm to charge no more than its marginal cost of production, how many units will be sold? At what price? What is the problem with the government capping prices at marginal cost?

d. Suppose the government allows firms to charge no more than their average total costs of production. How many units will this firm sell? At what price? What is the problem with capping prices at average total cost?
e. Evaluate the deadweight loss under each of the three pricing regimes above. Show each regime's deadweight loss as an area on the graph.

19. Five networks are vying to receive the pay-per-view broadcast rights to the World Series of Yahtzee. Each estimates that the inverse demand for watching this nail-biter of an event is given by $P = 100 - 0.01Q$. Each can provide the broadcast at a constant marginal cost of $1 per viewer.
    a. Calculate the deadweight loss of monopoly in the market for the televised Yahtzee tournament.
    b. Suppose that tournament Yahtzee's governing body plans to select one network at its discretion to air the tournament. How much will each network be willing to spend lobbying for the broadcast rights?
    c. Explain why, in this situation, the losses to society are much greater than just the deadweight losses of monopoly.
20. In the early days of navigation, sailors had a tough time figuring out exactly where they were. Pinpointing latitude was easy enough with a sextant, but because the earth was constantly spinning, pinpointing longitude by using celestial bodies was impossible. Anxious for a solution to this problem, the British government sponsored a contest with a prize of £20,000 (about $5 million in today's dollars) to the inventor who could devise a reliable method of calculating longitude. Once invented, the method would be made available to anybody who wanted to use it. Explain the advantages of such a system in maximizing social well-being relative to the traditional system of awarding patents.

Chapter 9 Appendix:
The Calculus of Profit Maximization

In Chapters 8 and 9, we saw that all firms—regardless of their degrees of market power—maximize their profits. In particular, the firm faces the optimization problem:

$$\max_{Q} \pi(Q) = TR(Q) - TC(Q)$$

This problem is relatively straightforward compared to the cost-minimization and utility-maximization problems we've focused on previously. Why? Look closely at the problem we wrote above, and you'll notice that there aren't any constraints on it. In fact, profit maximization is an *unconstrained* optimization problem and, as such, is much simpler to solve than the constrained optimization problems we've been dealing with so far.

What is more, the profit-maximization problem only has one choice variable, its output Q. Every other variable that factors into a firm's decisions—the quantities and prices of productive inputs, as well as the market price of the good—has already been accounted for in the equations for total revenue and total cost. How? First, total cost is determined only after a firm minimizes its costs, meaning it incorporates information about a firm's productive inputs. Next, consider total revenue, which is the product of price and quantity. For the perfectly competitive firm, price is constant, so given the market price, total revenue only varies with quantity. Firms with market power face variable prices, but we saw that those prices are a function of quantity sold. Therefore, total cost, total revenue, and—by extension—profit are all functions of quantity, holding all else constant.[1]

The Profit-Maximizing Condition

Let's begin by solving for the profit-maximizing condition. We take the first derivative of the profit-maximization problem above with respect to quantity Q to solve for the first-order condition:

$$\frac{d\pi}{dQ} = \frac{dTR}{dQ} - \frac{dTC}{dQ} = 0$$

$$\frac{dTR}{dQ} = \frac{dTC}{dQ}$$

$$MR = MC$$

What does this first-order condition tell us? As we saw in the chapter, *all* firms—firms with some market power, monopolists, and perfectly competitive firms inclusive—produce the profit-maximizing level of output when marginal revenue equals marginal cost.

We do need to check one more condition before considering this result conclusive. Producing where $MR = MC$ doesn't guarantee that the firm is maximizing its profit. It only guarantees that the profit function is at one extreme or another—the firm

---

[1] We could be very explicit about these functions and always write profit, total cost, and total revenue as $\pi(Q)$, $TR(Q)$, and $TC(Q)$; however, this becomes a little cumbersome. So in this appendix, we'll just write π, TR, and TC and remind you now and then that each is a function of Q.

could actually be minimizing its profit instead of maximizing it! To make sure we avoid this pitfall, we need to confirm that the second derivative of the profit function is negative:

$$\frac{d^2\pi}{dQ^2} = \frac{d^2(TR - TC)}{dQ^2} = \frac{d^2TR}{dQ^2} - \frac{d^2TC}{dQ^2} = \frac{dMR}{dQ} - \frac{dMC}{dQ} < 0$$

When will $\frac{dMR}{dQ} - \frac{dMC}{dQ} < 0$? This condition holds when

$$\frac{dMR}{dQ} < \frac{dMC}{dQ}$$

or when the *change* in marginal cost exceeds the *change* in marginal revenue. We have seen that marginal cost generally increases with output, while marginal revenue either is constant (for a price taker like the firms we saw in Chapter 8) or decreases as the quantity produced rises (for firms with market power, as we observed in Chapter 9). Therefore, this second-order condition generally is met because

$$\frac{dMR}{dQ} \leq 0 < \frac{dMC}{dQ}$$

The firm has to be careful about assuming this, however. If marginal cost is declining (which can be true of a firm with increasing returns to scale over the range that it is producing), we need to confirm that marginal revenue is decreasing at a faster rate than marginal cost:

$$\left|\frac{dMR}{dQ}\right| > \left|\frac{dMC}{dQ}\right|$$

If this condition does not hold for a firm experiencing increasing returns to scale, the firm is not maximizing its profit. In this context, the firm could increase its profit by producing more output because the decrease in total cost from the additional output would be greater than the decrease in total revenue.

Marginal Revenue

We know that all firms maximize profits when marginal revenue equals marginal cost. But what exactly is the marginal revenue of a firm? As we did in the past two chapters, we want to derive the relationship between marginal revenue and price. We'll do this first for firms in general and then look specifically at the case of a perfectly competitive firm.

We will start with the expression for total revenue:

$$TR = PQ$$

Note that, in general, price P is not fixed, but is instead a function of the quantity the firm produces.[2] To find marginal revenue, we take the derivative of the total revenue function with respect to Q using the product rule:

$$\frac{dTR}{dQ} = \frac{dPQ}{dQ} = P\frac{dQ}{dQ} + Q\frac{dP}{dQ}$$

Equivalently,

$$MR = P + Q\frac{dP}{dQ}$$

What does this tell us about the relationship between marginal revenue and price? Because a firm with market power faces a downward-sloping demand curve, the good's price *decreases* as the quantity produced increases. Mathematically, $\frac{dP}{dQ} < 0$.

---

[2] The one exception to the general rule that price is a function of output that we've seen so far is for firms in a perfectly competitive market—price takers. We'll come back to this special case shortly.

Therefore, for a firm with market power,

$$MR < P$$

We can also see this result logically. P is the gain from selling an additional unit of the good at the new price. $Q\frac{dP}{dQ}$ is the loss from lowering the price on all previous units in order to sell the increased quantity. Therefore, the revenue from selling an additional unit of the good is less than the good's market price, because for every gain in revenue (P), there is a corresponding loss ($Q\frac{dP}{dQ}$).

Let's work through a generic example to clarify this. Suppose a firm has the inverse demand curve $P = a - bQ$. (We discussed this particular inverse demand curve in footnote 3 in Chapter 9, but we'll go into more detail here.) To find marginal revenue, we first determine total revenue by multiplying P by Q:

$$TR = PQ = (a - bQ)Q = aQ - bQ^2$$

Now, we can take the derivative of total revenue to get marginal revenue:

$$MR = \frac{dTR}{dQ} = \frac{d(aQ - bQ^2)}{dQ} = a - 2bQ$$

As you can see, the marginal revenue curve derived from a linear demand curve is itself linear. It also has the same price intercept (in this case, a) and is twice as steep as the demand curve. As a result, it's clear that

$$a - 2bQ < a - bQ \text{ or}$$

$$MR < P$$

But what about the special case of the perfectly competitive firm? Unlike firms with market power, perfectly competitive firms are price takers that face horizontal demand curves. We know from above that the marginal revenue for any firm is

$$MR = P + Q\frac{dP}{dQ}$$

For a perfectly competitive firm, price remains fixed with changes in quantity, meaning $\frac{dP}{dQ} = 0$. Thus, $MR = P$ for all quantities of output.

Therefore, the profit-maximizing condition for the perfectly competitive firm is

$$MR = P = MC$$

This unique relationship is precisely what we showed in Chapter 8.[3]

9A.1 figure it out

Let's reconsider the solution to Figure It Out 9.2 and use the calculus approach we learned above. Babe's Bats (BB) faces a demand curve of $Q = 10 - 0.4P$ and a total cost curve of $TC = 2.5Q^2$. BB's output, Q, is measured in thousands of baseball bats, and P in dollars per bat.

a. Solve for BB's profit-maximizing level of output using calculus.

b. What price will BB charge to maximize its profit?

---

[3] We can also show the relationship between price, marginal revenue, and marginal cost for the perfectly competitive firm by starting from profit maximization. For the perfectly competitive firm, $\pi = PQ - TC$. Taking the first-order condition with respect to Q gives us $P - MC = 0$ or $P = MC$ because price is independent of the quantity produced.

Solution:

a. First, we need to set up Babe's profit-maximization problem:

$$\max_{Q} \pi = TR - TC = PQ - TC$$

Because Babe's Bats has some market power, its choice of Q affects the price. So, we need to use the demand curve for BB's bats to solve for price as a function of quantity, or the firm's inverse demand curve:

$$Q = 10 - 0.4P$$
$$0.4P = 10 - Q$$
$$P = 25 - 2.5Q$$

Substituting this expression for P and the total cost curve into the profit function, we find

$$\pi = TR - TC = PQ - TC$$
$$= (25 - 2.5Q)Q - 2.5Q^2$$
$$= 25Q - 2.5Q^2 - 2.5Q^2 = 25Q - 5Q^2$$

So, the firm's profit-maximization problem is

$$\max_{Q} \pi = 25Q - 5Q^2$$

The first-order condition for this problem is

$$\frac{d\pi}{dQ} = \frac{d(25Q - 5Q^2)}{dQ} = 0$$
$$25 - 10Q = 0$$
$$10Q = 25$$
$$Q^* = 2.5 \text{ or } 2,500 \text{ bats}$$

b. Now we need to plug Q^* from (a) into the inverse demand curve to obtain the profit-maximizing price:

$$P^* = 25 - 2.5Q = 25 - 2.5(2.5) = \$18.75 \text{ per bat}$$

Babe's Bats is maximizing its profit when it sells 2,500 baseball bats at a price of $18.75 per bat. A shortcut to solving is to begin with the profit-maximizing condition $MR = MC$, as we did in the chapter. In general, beginning with the profit-maximizing condition is easiest for firms with linear demand curves and simple cost functions. However, some firms have more complicated demand curves and total cost functions. For these firms, solving the profit-maximization problem directly using calculus may save you some work.

Now that we've worked through the calculus of profit maximization for a firm with market power, let's look at an example for a perfectly competitive firm.

9A.2 figure it out

Let's return to Figure It Out 8.1 and to Bob's Barbershop, the perfectly competitive firm with a daily total cost of $TC = 0.5Q^2$. Assume that the market price of a haircut is $15.

a. How many haircuts should Bob give each day if he wants to maximize his profit?

b. If the firm maximizes profit, how much profit will it earn each day?

Solution:

a. Bob's problem is to choose the quantity of haircuts that will maximize his profit or

$$\max_{Q} \pi = TR - TC = PQ - TC = 15Q - 0.5Q^2$$

Solving for the first-order condition gives

$$\frac{d\pi}{dQ} = \frac{d(15Q - 0.5Q^2)}{dQ} = 0$$
$$15 - Q = 0$$
$$Q^* = 15 \text{ haircuts}$$

Let's confirm that this is the same result that we get from choosing the quantity where $P = MC$. In the chapter, the question provided you with the marginal cost, but now we can solve for it by taking the first derivative of the total cost curve with respect to quantity, the firm's choice variable:

$$MC = \frac{dTC}{dQ} = \frac{d0.5Q^2}{dQ}$$
$$= 2(0.5Q) = Q$$

Now finding Bob's optimal quantity of haircuts per day is easy:

$$P = MC$$
$$P = Q$$
$$Q^* = 15 \text{ haircuts}$$

b. At 15 haircuts per day, Bob will earn

$$\pi = TR - TC = PQ - 0.5Q^2$$
$$= 15(15) - 0.5(15)^2 = \$225 - \$112.50 = \$112.50 \text{ per day}$$

Problems

1. Find marginal revenue for the firms that face the following demand curves:
   a. $Q = 1{,}000 - 5P$
   b. $Q = 100P^{-2}$

2. Suppose a firm faces demand of $Q = 300 - 2P$ and has a total cost curve of $TC = 75Q + Q^2$.
   a. What is the firm's marginal revenue?
   b. What is the firm's marginal cost?
   c. Find the firm's profit-maximizing quantity where $MR = MC$.
   d. Find the firm's profit-maximizing price and profit.

3. Suppose that American Borax is a monopolist and that the worldwide demand for borax is $Q = 100 - P$ where Q is tons of borax and P is the price per ton. The total cost function for American Borax is $TC = 10Q + 0.5Q^2$.
   a. Write out the firm's total revenue as a function of Q.
   b. What is the profit function for American Borax?
   c. Find the firm's profit-maximizing quantity by applying calculus to the profit function.
   d. Find American Borax's profit-maximizing price and profit.

4. Suppose a firm faces the inverse demand curve $P = 600Q^{-0.5}$. The firm has the total cost curve $TC = 1{,}000 + 0.5Q^{1.5}$. Find the firm's profit-maximizing output, price, and profit.

5. Consider a firm in a perfectly competitive market with total costs given by
   $$TC = Q^3 - 15Q^2 + 100Q + 30$$
   a. What is this firm's marginal cost function? Over what range of output are the firm's marginal costs decreasing? Increasing?
   b. Suppose that the market price is $52. What is this firm's profit-maximizing level of output? How do you know this is the profit-maximizing output? How much profit does this firm earn by producing the profit-maximizing output?

Market Power and Pricing Strategies

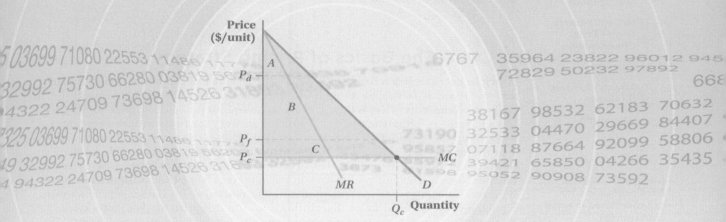

You've no doubt noticed many places where you can receive price discounts if you show your student ID. Commonly discounted goods include movie admissions, clothing at the campus bookstore, gym memberships, train fare, and even computer equipment.

It's nice of these sellers to give you a price break while you're getting your education. School isn't cheap, and every little bit helps. The sellers' generosity must say something about the value that they put on everyone receiving a good education. Right?

Not really. The main motivation behind such student discounts isn't altruism. Instead, it is almost surely the sellers' attempt to extract more producer surplus from the market than they would otherwise. That's not to say you're worse off because they've offered these discounts; in fact, they make it more likely you will be able to consume goods that would otherwise be too expensive for you. But there's something in it for the sellers, too—these discounts increase their producer surplus and improve their bottom lines.

pricing strategy
A firm's method of pricing its product based on market characteristics.

price discrimination
The practice of charging different prices to different customers for the same product.

How, exactly, does offering student discounts raise a seller's producer surplus? From our study of market power in Chapter 9, we know that when a firm can influence its own price, it makes a higher profit than a perfectly competitive (i.e., price-taking) company. The market power pricing rule we came up with, however, required the firm to charge the same price to all customers. In this chapter, we see that if a firm can charge different prices to different groups of customers (e.g., students and nonstudents), it can raise surplus and profit above those earned by a standard monopolist charging every customer the same price. There are many ways in which firms with market power can charge different prices for the same good. This chapter explores the most common of these strategies and looks at how they affect producers and consumers in the market.

10.1 The Basics of Pricing Strategy

A **pricing strategy** is a firm's plan for setting the price of its product given the market conditions it faces and its desire to maximize profit. The pricing strategy for a perfectly competitive firm is that it charges the equilibrium market price for its product and earns no economic profit. The pricing strategy for firms with market power is more complex. A firm with market power that charges one price to all its customers sets the market price according to the quantity of output it chooses to produce to maximize its profit. (Remember that firms operating in markets with barriers to entry are able to earn economic profits even in the long run.) Some firms with market power, however, can charge different prices to different customers for the same product using a pricing strategy called **price discrimination.** If a firm with market power can price discriminate, it can earn greater economic profit than a single-price monopoly.

It is important to understand that price discrimination is not the same phenomenon as the existence of different prices for different goods. Price differences can occur across similar products even in a competitive market if the marginal costs of producing the products are different. For example, if the marginal cost of washing SUVs at the car wash is higher than that of washing Mini Coopers because SUVs are bigger, car washes might charge more to wash SUVs. Price discrimination is something different. It implies the use of market power to charge higher prices for the same product to those consumers who are willing to pay more for it. Price variations due to price discrimination do not reflect differences in marginal costs; they exist simply because the firm with market power has the ability to charge different prices for the same product.

There are several pricing strategies a company can use depending on its circumstances. These range from *direct price discrimination* to *indirect price discrimination* to *bundling* to *two-part tariffs* and beyond. The motivation for these strategies is straightforward: A company with market power charges a higher price for the units of output that provide consumers with greater consumer surplus. By adjusting the price, a firm extracts more producer surplus from each transaction.

When Can a Firm Pursue a Pricing Strategy?

All the pricing strategies we discuss in this chapter start from two key requirements:

Requirement 1: The firm must have market power. A company must have market power to price discriminate. It's that simple. If the firm you have in mind does not have market power, you are in the wrong chapter of the book. You should be in Chapter 8 on perfect competition. Without market power, a firm can't choose its price at all, much less choose to charge different prices to different consumers or use more advanced pricing strategies.

Requirement 2: The firm must prevent resale and arbitrage. To take advantage of advanced pricing strategies, a firm must be able to prevent its customers from reselling its product among themselves. Otherwise, the customers able to buy units at a low price could purchase a large number of units and resell them to other customers who would otherwise have had to buy the product from the firm at a higher price. The practice of taking advantage of price differences for a product by buying at a lower price and reselling at a higher price is called **arbitrage.**

The ability to engage in arbitrage makes all customers better off. The low-price customers make a profit on resale, and the high-price consumers can buy the product at a lower price than the firm would charge. The firm isn't better off, though. It is effectively shut out from directly selling to any consumers except those who want to buy at the lowest price. Because it would then be selling at only one price, however, the firm would be back in the traditional situation for a firm with market power described in Chapter 9: It should produce the quantity at which marginal revenue equals marginal cost and charge the price at which buyers would consume that quantity (and therefore not worry about resellers).

If a firm meets these two requirements, it can attempt to implement more profitable pricing strategies. Figure 10.1 provides an overview of these strategies.

arbitrage
The practice of reselling a product at a price higher than its original selling price.

Figure 10.1   **An Overview of Pricing Strategies**

A firm's optimal pricing strategy is determined by characteristics of the firm, its product, and its consumers. In particular, a firm takes into account its degree of market power, whether the product can be resold, and its knowledge of its customers' demand for the product.

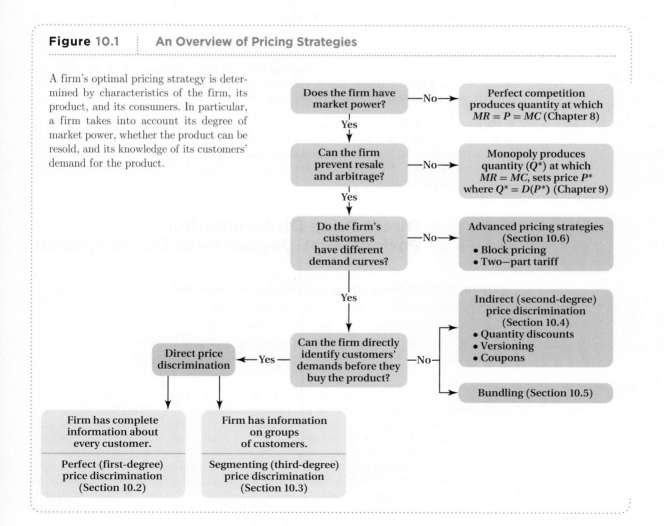

Strategies for Customers with Different Demands The first pricing strategies we look at involve price discrimination. For price discrimination to be an option, a firm needs to have different types of customers with different price sensitivities of demand. The exact kind of price discrimination the firm should use depends on the kind of information the firm has.

1. **Can a firm identify its customers' demands before they buy?** If the firm has complete, detailed information about each customer's own demand curve before she buys the product, it can practice *perfect price discrimination* and charge every customer a different price. If information about its customers is less detailed, a firm may be able to discriminate by customer group, as in third-degree price discrimination. The key to these kinds of price discrimination is that a firm must be able to directly identify different customers or groups of customers (as can a store that requires students to show IDs when making purchases) and charge different prices to each customer or group of customers.

2. **Can a firm identify its customers' differing demands only after they make a purchase?** If a firm cannot identify different types of consumers *before* they make their purchases, it can try more indirect price discrimination, which involves offering different pricing packages and then identifying the customer's type from the pricing package she chooses. These pricing packages can take the form of quantity discounts, different versions of the product at different prices, or (under the right conditions) bundling together different products.

Do a Firm's Customers Have the Same Demand Curves? There is still another set of pricing strategies that a firm can use even if its consumers have the same demand curves. These strategies involve offering different unit prices to the same customer for different quantities purchased or charging lump-sum fees on top of per-unit prices.

We explore all these strategies in the remainder of this chapter. To help clarify a firm's decision, each pricing strategy section has a When to Use It feature that explains what a firm needs to know about its market and customers to use a given pricing strategy most effectively. By using the best strategy, the firm can extract the most producer surplus from the market.

10.2 Direct Price Discrimination I: Perfect/First-Degree Price Discrimination

When to Use It Perfect/First-Degree Price Discrimination

1. The firm has market power and can prevent resale.
2. The firm's customers have different demand curves.
3. The firm has complete information about *every* customer and can identify each one's demand before purchase.

Let's start our study of pricing strategies by looking at a firm that has market power, can prevent resale, and knows that its consumers differ in their willingness to pay and therefore have different demand curves. To choose a price discrimination strategy that will allow the firm to reap the greatest benefits of these three characteristics, the firm must first ask itself whether it can directly identify what type of demand its customers have *before* they purchase the product, or whether it can determine this only *after* they buy the product. That is, do the buyers have some identifiable characteristic that allows the firm to observe their sensitivity to price and willingness to pay for the firm's product? If they do, the company can directly identify its customers' demands beforehand

and increase its producer surplus by using **direct price discrimination,** that is, by charging different prices to different customers based on something that a firm can observe directly about its customers' identities. If it can know its consumers' demands only *after* they buy the product, then the firm has to use *indirect price discrimination,* which we discuss later in the chapter.

Let's first consider the possibilities for a firm that has so much information about its customers before they buy that it knows each individual buyer's demand curve and can charge each buyer a different price equal to the buyer's willingness to pay. This type of direct price discrimination is known as **perfect price discrimination** or **first-degree price discrimination.**

Suppose a firm faces a market demand curve like the one labeled D in Figure 10.2. Panel a shows the outcomes for a perfectly competitive firm and a monopolistic firm. We know from Chapter 8 that in a perfectly competitive market, the equilibrium price (which is the same as MR in that case) equals marginal cost MC and the firm produces quantity Q_c. Consumer surplus is the area under the demand curve and above the price, $A + B + C$. Because we assume that marginal cost is constant, there is no producer surplus.

In Chapter 9, we saw that a firm with market power facing demand curve D and with no ability to prevent resale produces the quantity where its marginal cost equals its

direct price discrimination
A pricing strategy in which firms charge different prices to different customers based on observable characteristics of the customers.

perfect price discrimination (first-degree price discrimination)
A type of direct price discrimination in which a firm charges each customer exactly his willingness to pay.

Figure 10.2   Perfect (First-Degree) Price Discrimination

(a) Perfect competition and monopoly

Consumer surplus (competition)	$= A + B + C$
Producer surplus (competition)	$= 0$
Consumer surplus (market power)	$= A$
Producer surplus (market power)	$= B$
Deadweight loss from market power	$= C$

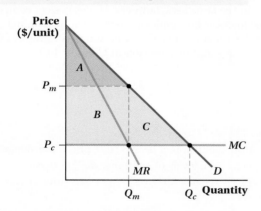

(b) Perfect price discrimination

Consumer surplus	$= 0$
Producer surplus	$= A + B + C$
Deadweight loss from market power	$= 0$

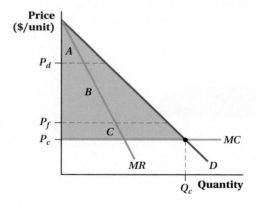

(a) A competitive market will set price equal to marginal cost, producing Q_c and selling at a price of P_c. Consumers will receive a consumer surplus equal to $A + B + C$ and the firm will earn zero producer surplus. A single-price monopoly will sell quantity Q_m at a price of P_m and receive a producer surplus equal to B. Consumers will receive consumer surplus equal to A and the deadweight loss from market power will be area C.

(b) If a firm with market power can identify each customer's demand curve, then it will charge each customer her willingness to pay and capture the entire surplus, $A + B + C$. For example, the firm will charge a customer willing to pay P_d exactly the price P_d and a customer willing to pay P_f the price P_f. The firm will sell up to the quantity Q_c, the perfectly competitive quantity where $P_c = MC$. There is no deadweight loss when a firm practices perfect price discrimination.

marginal revenue, Q_m, and sets the price P_m for that quantity from its demand curve. It charges this single price to everyone in the market. This market power pricing has three outcomes relative to the competitive pricing: (1) There is now a producer surplus equal to the rectangle B (far better from the firm's perspective than the competitive outcome, no producer surplus); (2) there is now a deadweight loss equal to the triangle C, because quantity is below its competitive level; and (3) consumer surplus is reduced to area A.

If, however, the firm with market power can prevent resale and directly identify each and every customer's demand curve (panel b), the outcome is very different. In this case, the firm can charge every customer her willingness to pay for every unit (or, to guarantee she'd take the deal, just a bit below this level). This is perfect price discrimination, and the benefit to the firm is tremendous. For any unit of output where a customer's willingness to pay is greater than the firm's marginal cost of producing it, the firm captures the whole amount of available surplus. So, for example, a customer accounting for the portion of the demand curve at P_d pays that relatively high price, while another at P_f pays that relatively low price. In these and all other cases, even though the prices are different, customers pay the most they are willing to pay, and the firm gets the entire surplus (the area below demand and above marginal cost).

After all such transactions, the firm will have sold a quantity of Q_c to various consumers at different prices depending on each buyer's willingness to pay. (Because the firm can prevent resale, customers aren't able to buy the product from another customer for a lower price than the firm offers.) The producer surplus the firm earns as a result equals the entire surplus in the market $(A + B + C)$. This is the maximum amount of surplus that can be made from the market because no consumer will pay more than his or her willingness to pay (that rules out the area above the demand curve) and the firm must pay its costs (that eliminates the area below the marginal cost curve). It's good to be a firm that can perfectly price discriminate.

Another interesting feature of perfect price discrimination is that, unlike the single-price market power outcome, there is no deadweight loss! It is efficient: No potential surplus is lost from a reduction in the equilibrium quantity. The quantity sold (Q_c) is the same quantity that would be sold if the market were perfectly competitive. Who *keeps* the market surplus is very different in the two cases, however: Under perfect competition, the entire surplus goes to the consumers, while under perfect price discrimination, the entire surplus goes to the producer. Efficiency is not the same thing as fairness. (We will further discuss issues of market efficiency and distribution in Chapter 14.)

∂ The online appendix demonstrates efficiency for firms that practice perfect price discrimination. (http://glsmicro.com/appendices)

10.1 figure it out

A firm with market power faces an inverse demand curve for its product of $P = 100 - 10Q$. Assume that the firm faces a marginal cost curve of $MC = 10 + 10Q$.

a. If the firm cannot price discriminate, what is the profit-maximizing level of output and price?

b. If the firm cannot price discriminate, what are the levels of consumer and producer surplus in the market, assuming the firm maximizes its profit? Calculate the deadweight loss from market power.

c. If the firm has the ability to practice perfect price discrimination, what is the firm's output?

d. If the firm practices perfect price discrimination, what are the levels of consumer and producer surplus? What is the deadweight loss from market power?

Solution:

a. If the firm cannot price discriminate, it maximizes profit by producing where $MR = MC$. If the inverse demand function is $P = 100 - 10Q$, then the marginal revenue must be $MR = 100 - 20Q$. (Remember that, for any linear inverse demand function $P = a - bQ$, marginal revenue is $MR = a - 2bQ$.)

Setting $MR = MC$, we obtain

$$100 - 20Q = 10 + 10Q$$
$$90 = 30Q$$
$$Q = 3$$

To find the optimal price, we plug $Q = 3$ into the inverse demand equation:

$$P = 100 - 10Q$$
$$= 100 - 10(3)$$
$$= 100 - 30$$
$$= 70$$

The firm sells 3 units at a price of $70 each.

b. To find consumer and producer surplus, we need to start with a diagram showing the demand, marginal revenue, and marginal cost curves:

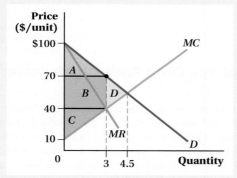

Consumer surplus is the area above price and below demand (area A). Producer surplus is the area above marginal cost but below the price (area $B + C$). (Note that we could just label these two areas as a large trapezoid, but it is easier to remember the formulas for the area of a rectangle and a triangle!) We can calculate the areas:

$$\text{Area } A = \frac{1}{2} \text{ base} \times \text{height}$$
$$= \frac{1}{2} \times 3 \times (\$100 - \$70)$$
$$= 0.5(3)(\$30)$$
$$= \$45$$

Consumer surplus is $45.

$$\text{Area } B = \text{base} \times \text{height}$$

To get the height of areas B and C, we need the MC of producing a quantity of 3:
$MC = 10 + 10Q = 10 + 10(3) = \$40$. So,

$$\text{Area } B = 3 \times (\$70 - \$40)$$
$$= 3(\$30)$$
$$= \$90$$

$$\text{Area } C = \frac{1}{2} \times \text{base} \times \text{height}$$
$$= \frac{1}{2} \times 3 \times (\$40 - \$10)$$
$$= 0.5(3)(\$30)$$
$$= \$45$$

So, Producer surplus = Area B + Area C = $90 + $45 = $135.

The deadweight loss from market power is the loss in surplus that occurs because the market is not producing the competitive quantity. To calculate the competitive quantity, we set $P = MC$:

$$100 - 10Q = 10 + 10Q$$
$$90 = 20Q$$
$$Q = 4.5$$

The deadweight loss can be seen on the diagram as area D:

$$\text{Area } D = \frac{1}{2} \times \text{base} \times \text{height}$$
$$= \frac{1}{2} \times (4.5 - 3) \times (\$70 - \$40)$$
$$= 0.5(1.5)(\$30)$$
$$= \$22.50$$

The deadweight loss from market power is $22.50.

c. If the firm practices perfect price discrimination, it will produce where $P = MC$. As we saw in part (b) above, this means that the firm will produce 4.5 units.

d. If the firm practices perfect price discrimination, consumer surplus will be zero because every consumer will be charged a price equal to his willingness to pay. Producer surplus will be the full area between the demand curve and the marginal cost curve (area $A + B + C + D$):

$$\text{Producer surplus} = \text{area } A + \text{area } B + \text{area } C + \text{area } D$$
$$= \$45 + \$90 + \$45 + \$22.50$$
$$= \$202.50$$

There is no deadweight loss when the firm perfectly price discriminates. The competitive output level is achieved ($Q = 4.5$). Producers end up with the entire surplus available in the market.

Examples of Perfect Price Discrimination

Actual cases of died-in-the-wool perfect price discrimination are rare. What firm really knows every single customer's willingness to pay for its product? There are instances, though, where sellers charge many, many different prices for the same product. Two classic examples are cars and college education.

When people walk into a car dealership, the salesperson sizes them up and eventually begins negotiating over price. While the dealer doesn't have *complete* information about each customer's willingness to pay, haggling differently with every customer is a lot like perfect price discrimination—the auto dealer is trying to simultaneously learn about the customer's valuation of the car and arrive at a price as close as possible to that level. That's why you should think twice when you go to buy a car and the salesman asks you, "How much are you looking to spend on a car?" That's an invitation for you to give up your consumer surplus.

Likewise, families applying for college financial aid are required to submit complete information about their assets and income along with the student's assets and income. From this information, the school has an almost perfect understanding of each student's willingness to pay. This allows schools to produce an individually tailored financial aid plan. But that is another way of saying that they charge a different tuition price to each student, depending on how much they think the student can afford.

 application

How Priceline Learned That You Can't Price Discriminate without Market Power

Priceline is the online travel service known in part for originating the "name your own price" model of online sales. The initial idea was that people would go to Priceline's site and enter what they were willing to pay for an airplane ticket—for example, $300 for a round-trip from Los Angeles to Boston on April 10th. Priceline would then see if there were any airlines willing to supply the ticket to Priceline for less than that. If so, Priceline would charge the customer's credit card $300 and issue the ticket, earning the difference as profit.

The idea was that by asking each person what she was willing to pay, Priceline could engage in something like perfect price discrimination and therefore make a lot of money. We can think of its original business model in terms of Figure 10.3. Priceline figured that, with a marginal cost of tickets of MC and travelers' willingness to pay (demand curve) at D, it stood to earn producer surplus approximately equal to the area $A + B$. The stock market liked this model, too: Within three years of starting up its Web site, the company was valued at $13 billion, more than several of the major airlines combined.

There was a serious problem in Priceline's approach, however. Priceline wanted to price discriminate, but it didn't really have market power in the travel agency industry. There are thousands of offline travel agencies; several other major online travel firms like Orbitz, Travelocity, and Expedia; and airlines sell a lot of tickets directly from their own Web sites. We know from what we've just learned that a company can't price-discriminate if it doesn't have market power. Priceline learned this lesson the hard way.

Priceline's problem was that, because travelers could also get fares at low prices directly from other travel sites, they wouldn't offer their true willingness to pay from their demand curves. Instead, customers would only offer to buy tickets at a lower price than they could buy them elsewhere.

Priceline's market demand curve was therefore not the consumer's demand curve D, but rather a curve strictly below the market price of tickets at other sites. In the figure, the outside price occurs at P_{out}. So, the actual demand curve facing Priceline was not

---

Figure 10.3 | **Perfect Price Discrimination without Market Power: What Went Wrong with Naming Your Own Price**

With market power, Priceline could use perfect price discrimination to capture the entire surplus above MC but below D, the area $A + B$. However, because it does not have market power, Priceline's demand curve D_{act} is below demand curve D. Using perfect price discrimination, Priceline can only capture B, the area above MC but below D_{act}.

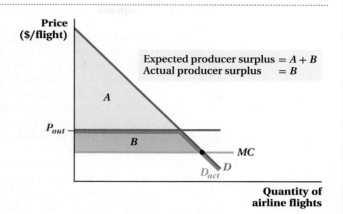

Expected producer surplus $= A + B$
Actual producer surplus $= B$

D but D_{act} instead. This kind of price discrimination doesn't make large profits. It left Priceline with a surplus of only B, the small area below the actual demand curve and above marginal cost. Indeed, this demand curve left Priceline with less producer surplus than that earned by other travel sites (which were charging prices at or above P_{out}).

Realizing this, Priceline eventually deemphasized the "name your own price" business model and expanded into the conventionally priced online travel business. It has so far succeeded—its stock market valuation was back up to over $20 billion in 2011 after falling all the way to $225 million in 2000. It had a tough road back. The moral of the story is, as always: Remember your economics. ∎

10.3 Direct Price Discrimination II: Segmenting/ Third-Degree Price Discrimination

When to Use It Segmenting/Third-Degree Price Discrimination

1. The firm has market power and can prevent resale.
2. The firm's customers have different demand curves.
3. The firm can directly identify specific *groups* of customers with different price sensitivities (but not the demand of every individual customer) before purchase.

Because it's rare for a firm to have the kind of comprehensive information about customers that it needs to practice perfect price discrimination, a firm can't generally capture *all* of the market surplus using price discrimination. But it can still earn more profit than a regular monopoly by using a pricing strategy called **segmenting** (or **third-degree price discrimination**), charging different prices to different groups (segments) of customers based on the identifiable attributes of those groups.[1]

segmenting (third-degree price discrimination)
A type of direct price discrimination in which a firm charges different prices to different groups of customers.

---

[1] While third-degree discrimination sounds like a variant of first-degree discrimination, the truth is that these names were somewhat arbitrarily coined by economist E. H. Chamberlin back in the 1930s.

For this kind of pricing strategy to work, the company must be able to directly identify *groups* of customers—students, for example—who have systematically different demands than other buyers. This group-level demand identification is typically much easier to determine than figuring out every individual customer's willingness to pay.

Think about a company that sells a clothing line emblazoned with the logo of a local university. If the company knows that students typically don't have a lot of money and tend to be bargain hunters while their parents or the faculty are less price-sensitive, the firm will want to charge students a lower price for clothing and parents or faculty a higher price. To do this, the company needs to be able to identify the groups directly. It must be able to tell before the sale which customers are students and which are parents or faculty, as well as prevent parents and faculty from pretending to be students to get the discount. One way the company can do this is to make showing a student ID a condition of the lower price.

As with all forms of price discrimination, however, the company must be able to prevent resale. They can't sell school sweatshirts at a student discount just to have the students then turn around and sell them to visiting parents or faculty for less than the higher price these groups would be charged. As a practical matter, if such resales became a problem, the company could institute a quota that would limit the number of sweatshirts a student could buy. Limiting resale is critical to price discrimination.

How many of these triathletes had to travel to Cozumel to compete?

The Benefits of Segmenting: A Graphical Approach

If a firm is able to engage in segmenting, how different should the prices be across the groups, and how much does the company stand to gain by price discriminating compared to the standard one-price monopoly strategy?

To answer these questions, let's consider an example with two consumer groups, the market for entry into the prestigious Ironman 70.3 Cozumel Triathlon. This triathlon is a race that comprises a 1.2-mile swim, a 56-mile bike ride, and a 13.1-mile run. It may seem like a masochistic pursuit, but people pay serious money to enter this race.

There are two kinds of people who want to enter the Ironman Cozumel: people who live in and around Cozumel, and people who fly in from somewhere else. The two groups' demand curves for entering the race are shown in Figure 10.4. Panel a shows the demand (D_T) for the participants traveling to Cozumel for the competition. The travelers mostly come from the United States; have high incomes and expensive triathlon equipment; and will have to pay for a plane ticket, a hotel room, food, and a rental car. They don't care if the price of their registration for the race is a bit higher, because it's a small share of the total cost to them. In other words, the demand curve for the traveling participants is fairly inelastic.

Panel b of the figure shows the local group's demand curve, D_L. The local residents' demand is more price-sensitive because they have many other activities they can pursue if the price of entering the race is too high. Thus, their demand curve is flatter and more elastic.

Preventing resale won't be a problem for the firm organizing the race as long as it can tell which athletes are from out of town and which are not. This is easy because out-of-town athletes have to pay their entrance fees with some form of identification

Figure 10.4   **Segmenting Entry Fees at the Ironman 70.3 Cozumel Triathlon**

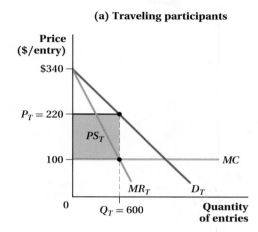

(a) Traveling participants

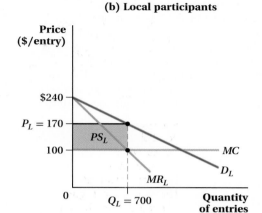

(b) Local participants

(a) The Ironman 70.3 Cozumel Triathlon segments its participants into two groups, traveling and local participants. Traveling participants are relatively insensitive to price and have an inelastic demand curve D_T. The number of traveling participants will be $Q_T = 600$, and each will pay a registration fee of $P_T = \$220/\text{entry}$. Producer surplus, PS_T, will be relatively large.

(b) Local participants have a relatively elastic demand curve D_L. A greater number of locals will register for the triathlon ($Q_L = 700$) at a lower price ($P_L = \$170/\text{entry}$). Producer surplus for locals, PS_L, is relatively small.

that gives their address, and they have to prove who they are when claiming their bib numbers on race day.

The fundamental economic idea of segmenting is simple. If a firm can directly identify groups that have different demands and charge different prices to each, it can essentially treat each group as a separate market. The firm then sets its profit-maximizing quantity for each one of these "markets" where $MR = MC$ and sets the corresponding single-price profit-maximizing price according to each market's demand curve.

Let's see how the organizers of the Ironman Cozumel competition follow the segmenting strategy. The organizers have identified these two different demand curves and treat each as a separate market. From the demand curve of out-of-town entrants (travelers) D_T, the organizers compute marginal revenue, labeled MR_T in panel a of Figure 10.4. Then from the point at which MR_T equals marginal cost MC, the organizers determine the optimal quantity of entries to sell to out-of-towners ($Q_T = 600$). At that quantity, the entry fee is $P_T = \$220$.

The organizers go through the same process for the local entrants. These entrants' demand curve D_L in panel b implies a marginal revenue curve MR_L. The optimal number of entries for the organizer to offer to locals is $Q_L = 700$, the quantity at which marginal revenue from locals equals marginal cost. (The marginal cost is the same for either type of racer. It amounts, basically, to the cost of a bib, some extra Gatorade, some water, a finisher's medal, and a race T-shirt.) The price, determined from the locals' demand curve, is $P_L = \$170$, significantly lower than the $220 price for traveling entrants.

Figure 10.5 | **Single-Price Monopolist at the Ironman 70.3 Cozumel Triathlon**

A single-price monopolist faces the kinked demand curve D, equal to the horizontal sum of the demand curves for travelers and local participants. The race organizer will sell 1,300 entries at a price of $186.67, between the two prices ($170 and $225) charged when the market is segmented. The resulting producer surplus, rectangle A, is smaller than the producer surplus under market segmentation.

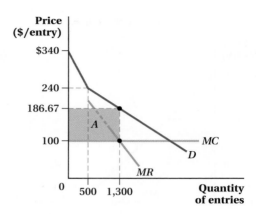

That's all there is to the strategy. As long as a seller can keep people from sneaking into the lower-price group or keep those in the lower-price group from reselling to the higher-price group, it can use segmenting to treat each group like a separate market and set the monopoly price for each market.

A firm following this pricing strategy will not earn as much producer surplus as one using perfect price discrimination (which would allow it to take the entire surplus from the market). However, it will earn more surplus than if it acted like a regular monopoly and charged the same price to everyone, because the strategy gives the firm some ability to charge a higher price to consumers with relatively inelastic demand and lower prices to consumers with relatively elastic demand.

Figure 10.5 shows the total Ironman Cozumel demand and marginal revenue that would face a monopolist forced to set only a single price. As in Chapter 5, we calculate the market demand as the horizontal sum of the participants' demand curves—in this case, the sum of the traveling and local participants' demands. This results in a kink in the market demand curve at $240, the demand choke price for local participants. At prices above $240, no locals purchase tickets, so the market demand curve is just the traveling racers' demand curve.

A single-price monopolist race organizer sets the quantity of entries where its marginal cost equals marginal revenue, and charges the price corresponding to the total market demand curve. This quantity, 1,300 racers, is shown in Figure 10.5, and the corresponding price is $186.67 per entry. Notice how this price falls between the two prices ($170 and $225) that the organizers charge the segments when price-discriminating. Although it might not be obvious from looking at the figure, the producer surplus for the single-price monopolist is considerably smaller than the surplus the monopolist would earn by segmenting the market. (We see that this is indeed the case when we calculate the benefits from segmenting in the next section.)

The Benefits of Segmenting: A Mathematical Approach

To do the same analysis of segmenting using mathematics, we start with the two distinct demand curves for the Ironman Cozumel. The demand curve of the traveling participants is given by $Q_T = 1{,}700 - 5P_T$, and the locals' demand curve is $Q_L = 2{,}400 - 10P_L$.

Note that, in accordance with our story, the locals' quantity demanded is more sensitive to price than the travelers' quantity demanded: A \$1 increase in the entry fee reduces the number of local entrants by 10, while it only decreases the number of traveling entrants by 5. We assume the marginal cost to the organizer of adding another triathlete to the race is a constant \$100, no matter how many entrants there are.

The mathematical analysis of segmenting is done using the same steps as in the graphical analysis above. If the race organizers can identify the separate groups and prevent resale, they can compute the marginal revenue curves for each segment and solve for the monopoly prices separately for each group.

We can follow the methods discussed in Chapter 9 to find the marginal revenue curves from linear demand curves. First, we determine the inverse demand curves by rearranging the demand function to express price in terms of quantity demanded. Doing so gives us the following equations:

$$
\begin{array}{cc}
\textbf{For travelers:} & \textbf{For locals:} \\
Q_T = 1{,}700 - 5P_T & Q_L = 2{,}400 - 10P_L \\
5P_T = 1{,}700 - Q_T & 10P_L = 2{,}400 - Q_L \\
P_T = 340 - 0.2Q_T & P_L = 240 - 0.1Q_L
\end{array}
$$

Next, we know that the marginal revenue curve will look like the inverse demand curve, but the coefficient on quantity will be twice as large. The marginal revenue curves for the two segments are

$$
\textbf{For travelers:} \qquad \textbf{For locals:}
$$
$$
MR_T = 340 - 0.4Q_T \quad \text{and} \quad MR_L = 240 - 0.2Q_L
$$

The organizers want to sell the quantities at which marginal cost (\$100, the same for both groups of triathletes) equals its marginal revenue. Setting each marginal revenue equation above equal to marginal cost tells us the optimal number of entrants from each group:

$$
\begin{array}{cc}
\textbf{For travelers:} & \textbf{For locals:} \\
MR_T = MC & MR_L = MC \\
340 - 0.4Q_T = 100 & 240 - 0.2Q_L = 100 \\
240 = 0.4Q_T & 140 = 0.2Q_L \\
Q_T = 600 & Q_L = 700
\end{array}
$$

The last step is to find the entry fees that correspond to these quantities by plugging the quantities back into the inverse demand curve:

$$
\begin{array}{cc}
\textbf{For travelers:} & \textbf{For locals:} \\
P_T = 340 - 0.2Q_T & P_L = 240 - 0.1Q_L \\
= 340 - 0.2(600) & = 240 - 0.1(700) \\
= 340 - 120 & = 240 - 70 \\
= \$220 & = \$170
\end{array}
$$

Therefore, in a segmentation strategy, the race organizers sell 600 entries to out-of-towners for \$220 each and 700 entries to locals at \$170 each.

The total producer surplus the organizers earn is the difference between the price and the marginal cost for each segment times the number of entries sold to that segment. In Figure 10.4, those surpluses are rectangles PS_T for the segment of nonlocal triathletes and PS_L for the local triathletes. Using the results we computed above, we have

$$
\begin{array}{cc}
\textbf{For travelers:} & \textbf{For locals:} \\
PS_T = (220 - 100) \times 600 & PS_L = (170 - 100) \times 700 \\
= 120(600) & = 70(700) \\
= \$72{,}000 & = \$49{,}000
\end{array}
$$

for a combined producer surplus of \$121,000 to the race organizer.

In our graphical analysis, we contended that the price-discriminating monopolist earns more producer surplus than the single-price monopolist. This makes intuitive sense, because a firm that segments the market can charge higher prices to more price-inelastic customers and capture more of their consumer surplus. But how can we show this algebraically?

First, we can see that the marginal cost curve intersects demand at the part of the demand curve below the kink—the portion of the demand curve that is the sum of the local and nonlocal demand:

$$Q = 1{,}700 - 5P + 2{,}400 - 10P = 4{,}100 - 15P$$

The inverse demand curve at this intersection is then $P = \frac{4{,}100}{15} - \frac{Q}{15}$, and the marginal revenue curve has twice the slope, or $MR = \frac{4{,}100}{15} - \frac{2Q}{15}$. We set MR equal to the marginal cost to solve for the optimal number of participants under the single-pricing strategy:

$$\frac{4{,}100}{15} - \frac{2Q}{15} = 100$$

$$4{,}100 - 2Q = 1{,}500$$

$$Q = 1{,}300$$

Note that 1,300 is exactly the sum of the local and traveling participants under the previous pricing system. Single-price monopolists and those who segment differ in the prices they set, but not always in the quantity they provide. That doesn't mean the firm would be selling to the same group of individuals, however. The new price will be lower than the segmented price for travelers (inducing more to buy than in the segmented case) and higher than the segmented price for locals (excluding some locals from buying). Just what is the price in this instance? Plug the quantity into the inverse demand curve:

$$P = \frac{4{,}100}{15} - \frac{1{,}300}{15} = \$186.67$$

Thus, although locals face a slightly higher price, the travelers get a bargain relative to the segmented outcome.

To calculate the producer surplus, we find the area of the rectangle A in Figure 10.5:

$$PS = (186.67 - 100) \times 1{,}300$$

$$= 86.67(1{,}300) = \$112{,}671$$

If the monopolist organizers segment the market for triathlon entries, they earn $121,000 in producer surplus; if they must charge a single price, they earn $112,671. Just by segmenting the market, the monopolist organizers can increase their producer surplus by $8,329, or about 7%.

How Much Should Each Segment Be Charged?

Because the standard market power pricing rule applies in each segment, it also means that the Lerner index, the basic markup formula we derived in Chapter 9, applies in each market. Recall that this formula relates the price elasticity of demand to the markup of price over marginal cost:

$$\frac{(P - MC)}{P} = -\frac{1}{E^D}$$

If the firm sells the same good to both segments of the market, the marginal cost of producing for each segment is the same. In this case, the only reason to charge different prices to customers in different segments is because they have different demand elasticities. To see what the Lerner index implies for the ratio of the prices in the two segments (label them 1 and 2), first solve the Lerner index for price in each segment:

$$\frac{(P_1 - MC)}{P_1} = -\frac{1}{E_1^D}$$

$$P_1 - MC = -\frac{1}{E_1^D} \times P_1$$

$$P_1 + \left(\frac{1}{E_1^D} \times P_1\right) = MC$$

$$P_1\left(1 + \frac{1}{E_1^D}\right) = MC$$

$$P_1\left(\frac{E_1^D}{E_1^D} + \frac{1}{E_1^D}\right) = MC$$

$$P_1 = \left(\frac{E_1^D}{1 + E_1^D}\right) \times MC$$

Likewise,

$$P_2 = \left(\frac{E_2^D}{1 + E_2^D}\right) \times MC$$

Now, we can compute the ratio of these prices:

$$\frac{P_1}{P_2} = \frac{[E_1^D/(1 + E_1^D)] \times MC}{[E_2^D/(1 + E_2^D)] \times MC}$$

$$= \frac{[E_1^D/(1 + E_1^D)]}{[E_2^D/(1 + E_2^D)]}$$

As the demand in Segment 1 becomes less elastic relative to Segment 2 (i.e., E_1^D becomes smaller than E_2^D in absolute value), the ratio P_1/P_2 will rise. That is, the greater the difference in price sensitivities between the segments, the greater should be the ratio in their prices.

Returning to our Ironman Cozumel example, suppose we know that the elasticity of demand for travelers is −1.83 and the elasticity for locals is −2.43.[2] We can immediately determine what the ratio of prices should be by plugging these elasticities into the formula:

$$\frac{P_1}{P_2} = \frac{\dfrac{-1.83}{-1.83 + 1}}{\dfrac{-2.43}{-2.43 + 1}} = \frac{\dfrac{-1.83}{-0.83}}{\dfrac{-2.43}{-1.43}} = \frac{2.2}{1.7} = 1.29$$

In other words, the race organizer should set the price travelers face to be almost 1.3 times (i.e., 30% higher than) the price for locals. This is in fact the ratio between the $220 and $170 optimal entry fees we computed earlier.

---

[2] If you remember the calculation of elasticity from Chapter 2, you can verify these values.

make the grade

Is it really price discrimination?

We mentioned this before, but it bears repeating: Always be careful about the distinction between *price discrimination,* when firms charge different prices for the same product, and *price differences.* It's often surprisingly hard to tell them apart. Prices can differ across different customer groups if a firm with market power price discriminates, but prices can also differ across the groups if the marginal cost of supplying the groups differs, even in a perfectly competitive market.

For example, a bottle of Coca-Cola, which is basically just carbonated water plus syrup, is often less expensive than a bottle of carbonated water alone. Perhaps this price difference reflects price discrimination because the kinds of people who buy bottled water are less price-sensitive than the people who buy soda. But maybe the cost of bottling fancy carbonated water is greater than the cost of bottling soft drinks (a lot more people buy soda than carbonated water and there might be some economies of scale, for example). You can't tell just from the prices.

The only way to tell the difference between price discrimination and price differences due to costs in competitive markets (without actually being able to observe the firm's marginal cost) is to find something that changes the price elasticity of demand without changing the cost. Price discrimination implies that a firm with market power sets its price based on the elasticity of demand and the marginal cost of producing. Price in a competitive market depends only on marginal cost. (This is related to the distinction we discussed in Chapter 9 about how firms with market power react differently than competitive firms to rotations in demand.)

10.2 figure it out

You manage a hair salon that has two locations: one in a large city in Ohio with several competing salons, and another in a small city in Pennsylvania with less competition. In Ohio, your customer's price elasticity of demand is −3, while for your Pennsylvania customers it is −2. Assume that the marginal cost of producing a haircut is $30 regardless of location.

a. What are your salon's optimal markups and prices in each location?

b. Why do they differ?

Solution:

a. The Lerner index provides us with a formula for seeing the relationship between pricing and the price elasticity of demand:

$$\frac{(P - MC)}{P} = -\frac{1}{E^D}$$

Substituting for marginal cost (= $30) and the price elasticity of demand for Ohio customers (= −3), we get

$$\frac{(P - \$30)}{P} = \frac{1}{-(-3)}$$
$$P = 3(P - \$30)$$
$$2P = \$90$$
$$P = \$45$$

Repeating the same steps for Pennsylvania gives

$$\frac{(P - \$30)}{P} = \frac{1}{-(-2)}$$
$$P = 2(P - \$30)$$
$$P = \$60$$

Customers in Ohio will be charged a price of $45 per haircut, while those in Pennsylvania will be charged a price of $60 per haircut.

b. Because demand is relatively more elastic in Ohio than in Pennsylvania (the absolute value of the price elasticity of demand is greater), customers in Ohio are more price-sensitive. Therefore, they will be charged a lower price.

Ways to Directly Segment Customers

There are many ways firms directly identify customer segments for the purposes of price discrimination. Here are some of the most common ones.

By Customer Characteristics Firms sometimes price according to customer characteristics such as age (e.g., senior citizen discounts at the movies or child discounts at a hotel), gender, or whether the customer is a student or local resident. The basic idea remains to identify the more price-sensitive customers and charge them less. Firms need to be careful when pricing based on consumer characteristics in certain countries because in some cases this may be prohibited by laws against discrimination based on age, gender, race, physical disabilities, and so on.

Segmenting can even be based on the user's species. Doctors and veterinarians sometimes use the same medicines. Drug makers recognize that Grandma's willingness to pay for the arthritis medication Lodine probably well exceeds someone's willingness to purchase Lodine for her arthritic dog Rover (and not only because Grandma's savings are larger than Rover's collection of buried rawhides). This difference in willingness to pay probably explains why a congressional investigation found that the price of Lodine for humans was almost three times higher than for dogs. Indeed, it determined that manufacturers priced almost every comparable medication significantly higher for people than for animals.[3]

freakonomics

Victoria's Not-So-Secret Price Discrimination

Sometimes price discrimination can end up being costly not just to consumers, but also to producers. In 1996 Denise Katzman of New York City sued Victoria's Secret for gender discrimination and asked for millions of dollars in damages. In alleging gender discrimination, Katzman didn't object to the catalog's pages of scantily clad women. Rather, she pointed to the promotional coupon on the catalog's back page.

The problem? While Ms. Katzman's catalog offered her $10 off an order of $75, an almost identical catalog for a male friend offered $25 off the same amount. Was her catalog out of date? Nope. The folks at Victoria's Secret were just engaging in a little "naked" price discrimination.

Although the company kept its reasons for the different promotions a secret, we can speculate on why it might employ such price discrimination using our economics reasoning. We know that price discrimination occurs when a company uses its market power to charge higher prices to people who are willing to pay more. In this case, Victoria's Secret recognized that its practice of sending out catalogs gave it the opportunity to segment its customers and advertise different prices to different types of customers. Women might be willing to purchase $75 of fancy underwear for a price of $65, but men are probably not as willing to shell out that kind of money for underwear for their wives or girlfriends. They might only pay $50 for the same order. Because most people don't end up reading through their friends' catalogs, this form of price discrimination could easily go undetected.

Ms. Katzman never did collect her millions in damages, however. Neither did fellow New Yorker Roy Den Hollander who in 2007 brought suit against bars that sponsor Ladies' Nights, which Hollander termed "invidious." He lost his suit, and bars everywhere continue to advertise gender-based price discrimination with weekly Ladies' Nights.

[3] http://lobby.la.psu.edu/010_Insuring_the_Uninsured/Congressional_Statements/House/H_Thurman_031600.htm

Customer characteristics can also apply to firms or other corporate organizations in business-to-business transactions. Academic journals, for example, know that individuals are much more price sensitive to subscription prices than libraries, so the publishers charge significantly more for institutional subscriptions than for individual ones. Elsevier, for example, one of the largest publishers of academic journals, charges individuals $112 for a year's subscription to the *International Journal of Industrial Organization* (don't all rush to order it at once), but the publisher charges libraries $1,720 for the same subscription.

By Past Purchase Behavior Consumers reveal a lot about their willingness to pay when they buy other products, and many sellers use that information to segment customers. In industries like auto insurance or direct-broadcast satellite TV, where people don't like switching companies once they decide on a provider, existing customers tend to be less price-sensitive than potential new customers. As a result, it is common for firms in these industries to give special discounts to new customers, such as reduced premiums during the first policy period or the first three months of a subscription free. These are ways to price discriminate based on whether the customer has bought the product before.

For some other products, the price sensitivity of new customers is *lower* than that of past purchasers. For example, it is notoriously difficult to convince people to upgrade their software to a new version. When Microsoft releases a new version of Windows, the price of upgrading an older version is typically much lower than buying the new version outright. With this low price, Microsoft is trying to entice the more price-sensitive customers to purchase the new version.

By Location Customers living in one area may have a hard time getting to another to take advantage of a lower price, or they might not even have knowledge of the prices in other locations. This often allows sellers to charge different prices in different locations, depending on the price sensitivity of local demand.

Over Time One way to price discriminate in certain markets is to take advantage of the different kinds of people who buy a product at different times. When a new generation of computer CPUs first hits the market, for example, the new CPUs usually sell at a substantial premium, sometimes hundreds of dollars more than the last generation's chips. Yet only a few months later, they are available for a fraction of their original price. Maybe marginal cost fell that much, you say? Perhaps. But how about movies in first-run theaters that cost $10 but then cost only $4 when the same movie runs at a discount movie house several weeks later? Or hardcover books that cost $26.95 while their paperback versions cost only $10.95, when the actual difference in production cost is only about a dollar? These are all cases in which the kinds of people who want the latest, greatest, most current version of a product—PC gamers, big movie fans, and active readers—tend to be less sensitive to price than the folks who enter the market later.

In other cases, demand can become less price-sensitive (more inelastic) over time, and price discrimination will lead to price increases over time. Many goods and services that have initially uncertain quality have this feature. For example, tickets to a new play or musical that hasn't been reviewed are often relatively inexpensive. But once local reviewers have given the play a "thumbs up," demand can become much more inelastic and the producers raise the price accordingly.

In either situation, a firm that prices the same good differently in two different time periods applies the basic segmentation rules and uses the standard monopoly pricing rule as it applies to the state of demand in each period.

However, there is one complication in pricing across time that is worth keeping in mind. Technically, pricing across time is only segmenting if the seller *directly* assigns customers to a given time period. That is, in segmentation strategies, the seller is effectively saying, "You buyers over here, this is your price. You buyers over there, you have a different price." Buyers are stuck paying the price designated for their group (assuming again as we have throughout this chapter that the seller can prevent resale). With time-based segmentation, however, if customers are forward-looking, meaning that they consider what the seller might do in the future even as they decide whether to buy today, then the seller is *not* actually directly segmenting its customers. The seller cannot prevent its customers from changing groups; the buyers choose when to buy. So, for example, if buyers believe that the seller is charging a high price today but will reduce the price in the future, they might consider waiting to purchase, even if they had the type of relatively inelastic demand that the seller was trying to take advantage of with the high current price. In cases like this, the seller needs to consider how the different prices it plans to charge over time will affect the consumer's decision of when to buy.

For instance, Intel might want to initially price its fast new CPU at an extremely high level to take advantage of a segment of high-horsepower PC gamers with really inelastic demand, while making deep discounts thereafter. But if gamers realize Intel is likely to do this, they might be willing to trade off waiting to purchase the new CPU in exchange for enjoying the deep discount. This potential response will limit Intel's ability to segment the market in the first place. It could lead to Intel having to charge a lower initial price than it would have otherwise, and perhaps also reduce the discount applied to that price later.

The more forward-looking consumers are, the more segmenting across time actually becomes something known as indirect price discrimination, the pricing strategy we discuss next.

theory and data

Segmenting by Location in the European Market for Cars

Car manufacturers like Volkswagen and BMW who do a lot of business in Europe sell the same car in many different countries. The customers in these countries have very different incomes and tastes in cars. Because the automakers in this market likely have some market power, this is an excellent opportunity for segmenting *if* the automakers can prevent their customers in one country from selling to those in another. Manufacturers could then segment their customers by country, selling the same car at different prices in each country using the price discrimination methods we've been discussing. This practice would allow these manufacturers to earn higher profits and more producer surplus than they could by selling their cars at the same price everywhere.

A VW Golf bought in Hannover, Germany costs more than the same car bought in Portugal or Greece.

It turns out the auto companies have many options for preventing resale across countries. First, they can print all manuals and documents only in the country's language. Swedish drivers don't want manuals in Greek, and vice versa. Second, they can forbid servicing a car in a country other than the one in which it was purchased. No one wants to get towed to Romania when their car experiences problems in Spain. Third, they can punish dealers who sell cars to people from a different country.

Economists Pinelopi Goldberg and Frank Verboven gathered evidence on car prices in Europe to investigate this issue.[*] They found that the price of the same car could vary substantially across countries. For example, in 2003, the price of a VW Golf in Germany was 10% higher than in Portugal and almost 25% more expensive than in Greece.

Goldberg and Verboven concluded that some of the price differences across countries in Europe arose from differences in the taxation of autos, but that much of the price

---

[*] Pinelopi K. Goldberg and Frank Verboven, "Cross-Country Price Dispersion in the Euro Era: A Case Study of the European Car Market," *Economic Policy* 19, no. 40 (October 2004): 483–521.

difference was due to basic direct price discrimination by segmenting. The auto firms were varying their markups depending on the conditions of local demand. The VW Golf pricing patterns are consistent with the theory that demand in Germany is less elastic than in Portugal or Greece, so VW charged its German customers more.

Goldberg and Verboven had some good news for European consumers (especially those in high-demand countries), though. They uncovered clear evidence that, as Europe has become more economically integrated, it has been much more difficult for car sellers to prevent resale or arbitrage across boundaries and the price differences have narrowed.

10.4 Indirect/Second-Degree Price Discrimination

> **When to Use It** Indirect/Second-Degree Price Discrimination
>
> 1. The firm has market power and can prevent resale.
> 2. The firm's customers have different demand curves.
> 3. The firm cannot directly identify which customers have which type of demand before purchase.

indirect price discrimination (second-degree price discrimination)
A pricing strategy in which customers pick among a variety of pricing options offered by the firm.

We've seen how firms with market power can use direct price discrimination to increase their producer surplus above the amount they could earn by charging only a single price. The key is to charge higher prices to customers with relatively inelastic demand and lower prices to those with more elastic demand. However, being able to directly observe a customer's demand type before purchase (as required with direct price discrimination) is often difficult. A firm might know that its customers have different price sensitivities, but it may not be able to tell to which group any particular customer belongs.

Even without this knowledge, a firm can still earn extra producer surplus through price discrimination by using a pricing strategy called **indirect price discrimination,** also known as **second-degree price discrimination.** In this pricing strategy, a firm gives its customers various pricing choices and allows the customers to choose among them.

There are many different kinds of indirect price discrimination techniques a company can use. The principle that underlies all of them, however, is the need to set up the pricing options to convince customers to pick the "right" choice; that is, to purchase the option meant for their group rather than another option for a different group. For example, airlines choose ticket rules and prices so that business travelers with inelastic demand pay more, on average, for their tickets than leisure travelers with relatively more elastic demand. At the same time, however, the airline wants to keep business travelers from deciding that tickets meant for them are too expensive and instead buying up cheaper tickets intended for leisure travelers.

Indirect Price Discrimination through Quantity Discounts

quantity discount
The practice of charging a lower per-unit price to customers who buy larger quantities.

The most basic type of indirect price discrimination is the **quantity discount,** a pricing strategy in which customers who buy larger quantities of a good pay a lower per-unit price. For quantity discounting to work, customers who purchase larger quantities of a product need to have relatively more elastic demands than consumers who buy smaller quantities. If the consumers in the market do not have these elasticity characteristics, the firm would be trying to find a way to raise prices on the people who buy greater quantities, the opposite of a quantity discount.

To illustrate the idea, let's say there are two types of customers of the online brokerage house E*TRADE. One type of customer is not very interested in trading stocks. Because of this, these customers don't have a big incentive to shop across different online trading houses in search of lower commission rates (the fees they pay a brokerage firm to facilitate a trade). Thus, their demands are relatively inelastic with respect to the commission charged. The demand curve for uninterested traders is D_u in panel a of Figure 10.6. The other type of customer is obsessed with trading stocks. Because these individuals trade many times each day, they are very sensitive to the commission rate. Thus, their demands are relatively elastic with respect to the commission. The demand curve for these obsessed traders is shown as D_o in panel b. The marginal revenue curves for each group are MR_u and MR_o, respectively. The marginal cost is the same for both groups.

E*TRADE would like to charge higher commissions to the uninterested traders with an inelastic demand than it charges the obsessed traders with the more elastic demand. This third-degree price discrimination (segmenting) would bring E*TRADE more producer surplus, but the company cannot pursue this strategy because it cannot tell which type of trader each person is when she signs up for an account. What E*TRADE *does* know, however, is what the demand curves of the two groups look like, even if it can't identify to which group any given trader belongs. Based on the demand curve D_u, for example, E*TRADE would want to set its standard profit-maximizing quantity and price (commission per trade) for uninterested traders where MR_u equals MC: For Q_u trades per month, E*TRADE would charge uninterested traders $30 per trade. For obsessed traders, E*TRADE would like to follow the same procedure and charge them a price of $9 per trade; at that commission, the obsessed traders would make Q_o trades per month.

Figure 10.6   **Quantity Discounts at E*TRADE**

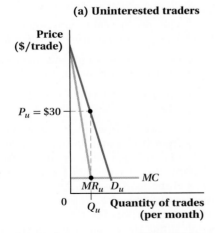
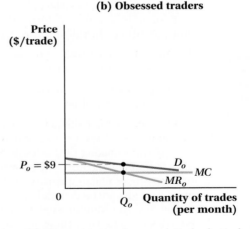

(a) Uninterested traders

Price ($/trade)

$P_u = \$30$

MR_u D_u MC

0 Q_u **Quantity of trades (per month)**

(b) Obsessed traders

Price ($/trade)

$P_o = \$9$

D_o MC MR_o

0 Q_o **Quantity of trades (per month)**

(a) The online brokerage company E*TRADE has two types of customers: uninterested traders and obsessed traders. Uninterested traders have a relatively inelastic demand curve D_u. E*TRADE would like to charge uninterested traders the profit-maximizing commission rate $P_u = \$30$ per trade and sell quantity Q_u trades per month.

(b) Obsessed traders have a relatively elastic demand curve D_o. E*TRADE would like to charge them the lower commission rate $P_o = \$9$ per trade. Although E*TRADE cannot directly identify which group any particular trader belongs to, it can set different prices for the two groups using a quantity discount by requiring traders to make at least Q_o trades per month to get a reduced commission rate.

If E*TRADE could segment the market, it would charge each group P_u and P_o per trade, and at those prices, each group would make Q_u and Q_o trades per month. However, E*TRADE can't directly assign different commission rates to different traders. And it can't just offer new customers a choice of whether to pay \$30 or \$9 commissions no matter how much or little they trade because every customer would choose the cheaper option. What can E*TRADE do to take as much of each trader's surplus for itself? Rather than offer all customers a \$9 per trade commission, E*TRADE can tie that commission rate to a requirement that the customer make at least Q_o trades per month. For customers who do not want to make at least Q_o trades per month, E*TRADE can offer a \$30 per trade commission plan that allows them to trade as little or much as they'd like in one month.

The idea behind this strategy is that an obsessed trader, who demands a high quantity of trades and has a more elastic demand, will choose the \$9 plan that requires a purchase of at least Q_o trades each month. An uninterested trader, on the other hand, will choose the \$30 per trade plan. In other words, traders from both groups will sort themselves into the price and quantity combinations designed for them, even though E*TRADE cannot directly identify either type. This is the essence of any kind of successful indirect price discrimination strategy: The firm must set its prices so that a customer doesn't try to fake her demand type and buy the package meant for another customer type. We discuss this requirement for the successful implementation of all indirect price discrimination (including quantity discounts) next.

Incentive Compatibility

The plan to charge uninterested traders a higher commission than obsessed traders is logical, but for such a plan to work well and allow E*TRADE to reap the maximum producer surplus available to it, E*TRADE needs to make sure that the uninterested trader won't want to switch from her \$30/Q_u package to the \$9/Q_o package designed for the obsessed traders. That is, the \$9 commission deal can't be so good that the uninterested trader will make extra trades just to obtain the lower price. E*TRADE has to be sure that the uninterested trader's consumer surplus is bigger with the \$30 per trade package than with the \$9 package that requires a purchase of at least Q_o trades. The offers need to be internally consistent so that each type of buyer actually chooses the offer designed for it.

Economists have a term for this type of internal consistency: **incentive compatibility.** In this example, the two packages are incentive compatible if:

incentive compatibility
The requirement under an indirect price discrimination strategy that the price offered to each consumer group is chosen by that group.

1. An uninterested trader prefers the \$30 package over the \$9 package (and she will make this choice if the \$30 package gives her greater consumer surplus than the \$9 package).

2. An obsessed trader prefers the \$9 package because it offers her more consumer surplus than the \$30 package.

Let's see whether this set of offers is incentive compatible. First, we need to show that the uninterested trader's consumer surplus from trades at \$30 each is greater than her surplus from making Q_o trades at \$9 each. Finding the consumer surplus from the first offer is familiar territory. As shown in Figure 10.7, at a price of \$30 per trade, an uninterested trader makes quantity Q_u trades, and the consumer surplus is the area under the uninterested trader's demand curve and above the \$30 price. This is triangle A in panel a.

Finding the uninterested trader's consumer surplus for the \$9 package offer is a bit trickier. The first thing we need to do is put the \$9 package's price and quantity combination in the diagram showing the demand for trades of an uninterested trader. Call this point X, as shown in panel a. Notice that point X lies *above* the uninterested trader's demand curve. That means if an uninterested trader were to make trade number Q_o (at a commission of \$9), she would actually lose consumer surplus by doing so. At a price of \$9, an uninterested trader really only wishes to purchase Q_{max} trades, the quantity demanded at that price.

The fact that Q_{max} is less than Q_o implies that the uninterested trader's willingness to pay for the trades between Q_{max} and Q_o is lower than the \$9 she would have to pay

Figure 10.7   Incentive Compatibility

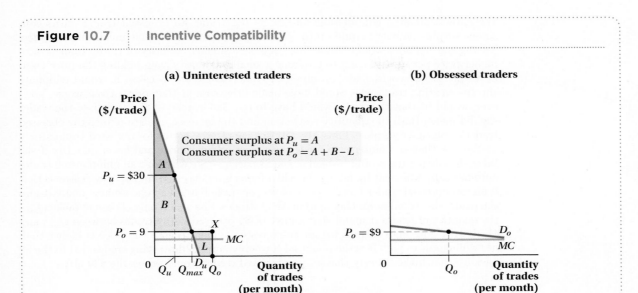

(a) Before charging a quantity discount to obsessed traders, E*TRADE needs to ensure that its pricing strategy is incentive compatible. At $P_u = \$30$ per trade, uninterested traders make Q_u trades and receive surplus A. At the quantity and price offered to obsessed traders (Q_o, P_o), their surplus is reduced by area L but increases by area B. Uninterested traders will choose to pay $30 per trade if area B is greater than area L.
(b) Under the pricing policy for uninterested traders, obsessed traders would have to pay both a higher price ($P_u = \$30 > P_u = \$9$) and make fewer trades per month ($Q_o > Q_u$). Therefore, the quantity discount is incentive-compatible for these traders.

for them. In fact, all trades for which her demand curve (which indicates her willingness to pay) lies below $9 will result in a loss of consumer surplus. In panel a, these surplus-destroying trades are those between Q_{max} and Q_o, and the total consumer surplus lost is the area labeled L. (The demand curve just runs along the horizontal axis once it hits the axis, because willingness to pay for higher quantities is zero.) That area is the downside for an uninterested trader accepting the lower-commission offer. There is an upside, however. The first Q_{max} trades she conducts create consumer surplus, area $A + B$ in the figure. This consumer surplus is quite a bit larger than her surplus under the $30 per trade offer (area A) because the price is so much lower. The net consumer surplus an uninterested trader gets from taking the $9 package offer is therefore area A + area B – area L.

Comparing the uninterested trader's consumer surpluses from the two offers, we can now see that she will choose the $30 per trade offer over the $9 package offer if

$$\text{area } A > \text{area } A + \text{area } B - \text{area } L$$

$$0 > \text{area } B - \text{area } L$$

$$\text{area } B < \text{area } L$$

That is, an uninterested trader will take the offer designed for her ($30 per trade) if the extra consumer surplus she would obtain from the lower commission rate (area B) is smaller than the loss she suffers from having to buy a larger quantity than she would have otherwise at the lower offered price (area L).

For uninterested traders, we have outlined under what conditions the offers are incentive compatible. Will an obsessed trader choose the $9 package meant for her?

We know that at a commission rate of $9 per trade, an obsessed trader earns consumer surplus on every trade up to Q_o; she is happy to trade that much at that price. Taking the $30 offer would require her to make a smaller quantity of trades than Q_o at a higher price per unit. Having to consume a smaller quantity even holding the price fixed at $9 per trade would make an obsessed trader worse off, because it would eliminate surplus-creating trades she would have made otherwise at that price. Even worse, however, would be that the trader would have to pay $30 instead of $9 for each of the trades she did make. Both the quantity restriction and the increase in price reduce the obsessed trader's consumer surplus. Thus, the $9 package offer is better for obsessed traders.

We saw that an uninterested trader also faces a higher price and lower quantity if she takes the $30 per trade offer instead of the $9 package. So, why isn't an uninterested trader automatically worse off by taking the $30 offer as is an obsessed trader? The reason is that if an uninterested trader faced a price of $9 per trade but got to choose how many trades she made, she would never choose to make Q_o trades. She would only choose to make Q_{max}, the quantity of trades demanded at a price of $9 per trade. Any trades between Q_{max} and Q_o destroy consumer surplus for an uninterested trader because the price is higher than her willingness to pay. It is the potential consumer surplus-destroying trades tied to the $9 package that make it likely that an uninterested trader would prefer the $30 offer.

10.3 figure it out

Suppose you are a pricing analyst for MegaDat Corporation, a firm that recently developed a new software program for data analysis. You have two types of clients who use your product. Type A's inverse demand for your software is $P = 120 - 10Q$, where Q represents users and P is in dollars per user. Type B's inverse demand is $P = 60 - 2Q$. Assume that your firm faces a constant marginal cost of $20 per user to install and set up this software.

a. If you can tell which type of buyer is buying the product before a purchase is made, what prices will you charge each type?

b. Suppose instead that you cannot tell which type of buyer the client is until after the purchase. Suggest a possible way to use quantity discounts to have buyers self-select into the pricing scheme set up for them.

c. Determine whether the pricing scheme you determined in part (b) is incentive-compatible.

Solution:

a. To maximize profit, set $MR = MC$ for each type. Therefore, we first need to solve for the marginal revenue curves for each type. Because we have linear inverse demand curves, we know that the MR curves will have the same vertical intercept but twice

the slope. This means that $MR = 120 - 20Q$ for Type A buyers and $MR = 60 - 4Q$ for Type B buyers. Now set $MR = MC$ to find the profit-maximizing quantity for each type:

For Type A:	For Type B:
$120 - 20Q_A = 20$	$60 - 4Q_B = 20$
$20Q_A = 100$	$4Q_B = 40$
$Q_A = 5$	$Q_B = 10$

At these quantities, the prices will be

For Type A:	For Type B:
$P_A = 120 - 10Q_A$	$P_B = 60 - 2Q_B$
$= 120 - 10(5)$	$= 60 - 2(10)$
$= \$70$	$= \$40$

b. The firm could charge $70 per user for a package where the buyer can purchase any quantity she wishes and a price of $40 for any buyer willing to purchase 10 or more units.

c. This plan is incentive-compatible for Type B users. They are willing to continue to purchase $Q = 10$ at a price of $40 each.

For a Type A consumer, we need to consider the amount of consumer surplus she receives under each scheme. We can do this with the help of a diagram showing the Type A demand curve and the two prices, $70 and $40.

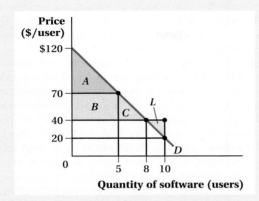

At a price of $70, a Type A buyer would choose to purchase 5 units. Consumer surplus would equal area A, the area below the demand curve but above price.

If a Type A buyer were to opt to purchase the other package (10 units at a price of $40 each), her consumer surplus would be the area above the price and below demand (areas $A + B + C$), but she would also lose consumer surplus because she would be buying units that she values less than the price of $40. This would be area L in the diagram.

Thus, opting for the quantity discount would change the Type A buyer's consumer surplus by area B + area C − area L. The $40 10-unit package would be incentive-compatible only if area $L >$ area B + area C. Let's calculate those values:

$$\text{Area } B = \text{base} \times \text{height}$$
$$= (5)(\$70 - \$40)$$
$$= (5)(\$30)$$
$$= \$150$$

To calculate area C, we need to determine the base of the triangle. This means that we need to know the quantity at which the Type A buyer's willingness to pay is exactly $40:

$$P = 120 - 10Q$$
$$40 = 120 - 10Q$$
$$10Q = 80$$
$$Q = 8$$
$$\text{Area } C = \frac{1}{2} \times \text{base} \times \text{height}$$
$$= (0.5)(8 - 5)(\$70 - \$40)$$
$$= (0.5)(3)(\$30)$$
$$= \$45$$

Therefore, area B + area C = $150 + $45 = $195.

To calculate area L, we need to be able to determine the height of the triangle. To do so, we need the price at which a Type A buyer would be willing to purchase $Q = 10$ units:

$$P = 120 - 10Q$$
$$= 120 - 10(10)$$
$$= 120 - 100$$
$$= \$20$$
$$\text{Area } L = \frac{1}{2} \times \text{base} \times \text{height}$$
$$= (0.5)(10 - 8)(\$40 - \$20)$$
$$= (0.5)(2)(\$20)$$
$$= \$20$$

So, we know that area B + area C = $150 + $45 = $195 and area L = $20.

Because area A + area $B >$ area L, the $40 10-unit pricing scheme is not incentive-compatible for Type A buyers. These buyers will want to receive the quantity discount and will purchase 10 units at a price of $40 each. Thus, this pricing scheme would not be successful at making the buyers self-select into the pricing scheme established for their types.

Indirect Price Discrimination through Versioning

Airline tickets are a classic example of what we call **versioning**—offering a range of products that are all varieties of the same core product. Airlines have a group of business travel customers who are not very sensitive to prices and a group of leisure travelers who are highly sensitive to price. Airlines want to charge different prices to the two passenger groups, but they can't tell who is flying on business when a customer buys a ticket. So, the airlines instead offer different versions of the product (tickets on a given flight) available at different prices. The cheaper version, with many restrictions, is intended for leisure travelers who buy generally well in advance of the travel date, stay over a Saturday night, and book a round-trip flight. The more expensive version has fewer restrictions and is intended

versioning
A pricing strategy in which the firm offers different product options designed to attract different types of consumers.

for business travelers who generally don't like spending a weekend away from home, often need to buy their tickets at the last minute, and may choose to purchase a one-way flight for each segment to provide them with added flexibility. By offering two versions of tickets for a given flight, the airline attempts to make the two types of customers sort themselves (and by doing so, the airline captures more producer surplus).

For this scheme to work, the airlines need to make sure the prices of each version are incentive compatible. If the airline sets the prices for each group based on the markup formula it would use with direct price discrimination, the restricted-travel version might be too cheap relative to the ticket with fewer restrictions. In this case, business travelers might actually bite the bullet and start planning trips earlier or stay at their destination over the weekend. In some cases, business travelers might try to skirt the rules altogether. For example, it's possible to avoid the Saturday stay requirement by buying what is known as "back-to-back" tickets. For example, a business traveler wishing to fly from Philadelphia to Orlando and back for a Wednesday meeting might buy one Philadelphia-Orlando round-trip with a departure on Wednesday morning and a return on Sunday, and an Orlando-Philadelphia round-trip with a Wednesday evening departure and a Sunday return. The traveler would only use the first leg of each trip. As you might expect, this kind of behavior is intensely hated by the airlines, which try to forbid it in every way they can, but, basically, it's just the market's normal response to indirect price discrimination.

Versioning and Price-Cost Margins   With versioning, the different versions' marginal costs do not need to be the same. All that is necessary for versioning to work is for the markup of price over marginal cost to be bigger for the versions bought by customers with less elastic demand.

Consider the example of an automaker like Toyota, which sells a lot of midsize sedans. Some of Toyota's buyers in this segment will not be very price-sensitive. Maybe they are status-conscious, or just have a particular taste for cars with many fancy features. Others will be more price-sensitive. If Toyota could tell which type of customer was which when they walked through the door, Toyota could just use direct price discrimination and charge different prices according to the strategy we discussed in Section 10.3. In reality, however, it's not always easy to tell what type of customer comes through the door at any particular time. So, Toyota uses indirect price discrimination and designs two different versions of the car that it can sell at different markups, hoping to induce buyers to segment themselves based on their sensitivity to price and tastes for features.

For example, Toyota makes the Camry, one of the highest-selling cars in the world. It sells, nicely equipped, for about $25,000 in the United States. But Toyota also makes the Lexus ES 350, which is built on the same platform and in the same plant as the Camry. It is similar in many ways to the Camry but is more luxurious. Think of the ES 350 as being a Camry but with a sun roof, dual-zone climate control, a GPS navigation system, xenon headlights, and a premium stereo system. The ES 350 sells for around $38,000.

While a sunroof, xenon headlights, and all those extra options raise Toyota's marginal cost of producing an ES 350, it's unlikely that this increase in marginal cost would amount to $13,000 per car. Toyota charges more than the cost difference because the different versions split its customers into groups based on their price sensitivities. The Lexus group has less elastic demand, so Toyota's markup over marginal cost can be higher, just like the Saturday-night stay splits an airline's customers into leisure and business travelers.

To be incentive compatible, Toyota can't make the deal for the cheap version so good that it convinces the luxury customers to purchase Camrys instead. Quantitatively, think of it the following way. Suppose there are just two types of customers whose willingness to pay for each car is listed in Table 10.1.

Table 10.1	Consumer Valuations for Camrys and ES 350s	
	Toyota Camry	**Lexus ES 350**
Budget consumer	$27,000	$30,000
Luxury consumer	$28,000	$42,000

Notice that both consumers believe the Lexus is worth more than the Camry. It's not that Toyota has made a version that one group likes and the other doesn't. The budget consumers value a Lexus more than a Toyota, but not very much more: $30,000 versus $27,000. The luxury consumers, however, value the ES 350 *a lot* more than the Camry: $42,000 versus $28,000.

If Toyota prices the Camry at $25,000 and the Lexus ES 350 at $38,000, the budget consumers get $2,000 of consumer surplus from buying the Camry and –$8,000 from buying the Lexus (it costs more than they value it), so they will buy the Camry. The luxury consumers get $3,000 of surplus from buying the Camry and $4,000 from the Lexus, so they go with the Lexus. Each group chooses the version designed to take advantage of the nature of their demand curves. That means these prices are incentive compatible.

What would happen if Toyota priced the Lexus at $40,000 rather than $38,000? The budget consumers would still buy the Camry. Now, however, the status consumers would get more consumer surplus from buying the Camry ($3,000) than from buying the Lexus ($2,000), so they would also decide to buy the Camry. That $2,000 price increase for the Lexus would cause Toyota to lose $13,000 (losing a sale of a $38,000 Lexus at the old price for a $25,000 Camry instead) for each luxury consumer. (Or worse: The luxury consumers might go buy another automaker's luxury car.) By charging the group with the less elastic demand too high a price, Toyota would not be setting incentive-compatible prices and its attempt at indirect price discrimination would fail.

One detail that is important to note is that it is not the mere existence of customers with inelastic demand that allows Toyota (or any other firm) to indirectly price-discriminate with versioning. What is required is that *differences* exist in demand elasticities across customer groups. If different consumer groups had the same price elasticities of demand, even if relatively inelastic, then designing versions specifically for each group will not help a firm price discriminate. Automakers offer cars with different paint colors, for example, but there is rarely price discrimination based on paint color because the price sensitivities of people who like blue cars and silver cars are no different.

There is virtually no limit to the kinds of versioning a company can implement to get its customers to self-select into groups based on their price sensitivities. Now that you understand this kind of price discrimination, you will start to see it everywhere you look. Some firms offer "enhanced" features, such as the way Intuit does with its TurboTax software. It has a bare-bones version that is actually free online, versions with special Q&A features, and a small business application package that includes the ability to handle more complex structures like partnerships. The marginal cost difference between editions is trivial, but by offering "bells and whistles" versions, Intuit is able to get the less price-sensitive business customers to pay more.

Indirect Price Discrimination through Coupons

Coupons are also a form of indirect price discrimination. Retailers would like to charge shoppers who have less elastic demands more for products while setting a lower price for consumers who are more sensitive to price. Again, however, they have no way of directly identifying and separating these different groups when they buy, so they have to get the groups to do it themselves. Coupons are the device they use to do so.

The key to the way coupons work is that the trouble of using coupons—searching for the right site or deal online, combing through junk mail, or searching through newspaper inserts—is more likely to be borne by consumers who have more elastic demand. Because both the willingness to do the work clipping the coupons and the willingness to shop around for cheaper groceries are determined by the consumers' perceived value of time, coupon clipping and the price elasticity of demand are likely to be correlated. That way, the people who actually end up getting a price discount from a coupon are those consumers with more elastic demand—exactly the group to whom the retailers would like to offer lower prices. The shoppers who are less sensitive to price end up paying the higher, undiscounted price.

That's why coupons usually aren't right next to (or especially already attached to) the items to which they apply. If they were, it would be easy for even the shoppers with less elastic demand to use them, and everyone would receive the discount. The fact that firms require consumers to expend a little effort to use a coupon is not coincidence; it is exactly the point. Mail-in rebates work on the same principle: Only those consumers willing to go through the trouble of filling out the form and sending it in—presumably the most price-sensitive ones—will receive the discount.[4]

10.5 Bundling

When to Use It Bundling

1. A firm has market power and can prevent resale.
2. A firm sells a second product and consumers' demand for that product is negatively correlated with their demand for the first product.

bundling
A pricing strategy in which the firm sells two or more products together at a single price.

Another indirect price discrimination strategy that firms with market power can use to increase their producer surplus over the standard monopoly pricing surplus is called **bundling.** This strategy involves putting together two or more products that a firm produces and selling them as a single package with its own price.

When you subscribe to cable or satellite television, for example, you are buying a bundled good. You pay a single monthly fee for service, and the cable or satellite company delivers a number of networks together. You don't pick and choose every channel individually. For your $45 per month, you get, say, 90 channels rather than paying $6 per month for ESPN, $4 a month for MTV, and so on.

Sometimes, things can be bundled just because people really prefer buying things together. Think about a pair of basketball shoes. Although shoemakers could sell shoes individually, there really isn't much demand for single shoes or for mixing a Nike basketball shoe for the left foot with an Under Armour shoe for the right. People want to buy both shoes together. This sort of bundling, which occurs because the goods are strong complements to one another (i.e., one good raises the marginal utility of the other), is not a price discrimination strategy. Nike and Under Armour would bundle their left and right shoes together even if they operated in a perfectly competitive market.

In this chapter, we're interested in ways that companies can use bundling as a way to price discriminate. To explain how bundling can be a strategic pricing decision, it is vital that we first clear up an extremely common misconception. Bundling will generally *not* allow a company with market power in one product to leverage its market power into a second product. To illustrate what we mean, let's look at a specific example.

Take a cable company providing TV channels to your home. To make it easy, let's say there are only two cable networks: ESPN and the soap opera network SOAPnet (ESPN is among the most watched cable networks, and SOAPnet is not). Why would the cable company force you to buy both as a bundle for some price rather than just sell them separately?

At first glance, people tend to think it's a way for the cable company to leverage market power/high demand for ESPN to force people to pay more for the lesser product (SOAPnet). But this "forcing it down their throat" argument usually does not make sense. To see why, suppose there are two customers (Jack and Dakota) in the market.

---

[4] That said, there is occasionally a coupon right next to (or even attached to) an item. In this case, the point of the coupon is not to price discriminate as much as it is to advertise. It's essentially a little sign that says, "Buy me . . . I'm cheaper than usual."

Both like ESPN a lot and SOAPnet less, as reflected in Table 10.2. Jack values ESPN at $9 per month and Dakota values it at $10 per month. Jack values SOAPnet at $1 per month, while Dakota values it at $1.50. For simplicity, let's assume the marginal cost of supplying the networks is zero.

Does the cable company raise its producer surplus by bundling the prized ESPN with SOAPnet? If it sells the channels separately, it would have to price each channel at the lower of the two customers' valuations for each channel ($9.00 for ESPN and $1.00 for SOAPnet). Otherwise, the company would sell to only the one customer and would lose the revenue from the other.[5] Thus, it sells ESPN for $9 per month and SOAPnet for $1 per month, earning a total surplus of $20 per month $(2 \times \$9) + (2 \times \$1)$ from selling the channels separately.

Table 10.2	Positively Correlated Valuations per Subscriber-Month		
	ESPN	**SOAPnet**	**Bundle**
Jack	$9.00	$1.00	$10.00
Dakota	$10.00	$1.50	$11.50

Now suppose the cable company sells the channels as a bundle. The combined value the customers put on the bundle ($10.00 per month for Jack and $11.50 for Dakota) means the company will again set the price at the lower valuation so it won't lose half of the market. It therefore prices the bundle at $10 and sells it to both customers. This yields a surplus of $(2 \times \$10)$, or $20 per month, the same amount it earned selling the networks separately. Bundling has not raised the firm's surplus.

Furthermore, if the company combines ESPN with something customers don't actually want at all (say, e.g., that the valuation on SOAPnet was zero or even negative), then the amount that customers would be willing to pay for that network plus ESPN would be that much lower. As a general matter, then, a company can't make extra money by attaching a highly desired product to an undesired one.

How should a firm bundle products to make more producer surplus? Suppose that, instead of the valuations being what they are in Table 10.2, the two valuations for SOAPnet are switched. Both customers value ESPN far more, but now Jack has a higher valuation for SOAPnet ($1.50 per month) than does Dakota ($1.00). The key thing that has changed, as will become clear in a minute, is that *the willingness to pay for the two goods is now negatively correlated across the consumers*. This means that one of the customers has a higher willingness to pay for one channel than the other customer, but a lower willingness to pay for the other channel. In our example, Jack has lower willingness to pay for ESPN than Dakota but greater demand for SOAPnet, as shown in Table 10.3.

With this change, the firm receives more producer surplus using the bundling strategy. If the cable company sells the channels separately, the calculation is the same as before: ESPN for $9 per month, SOAPnet for $1, and earns a total of $20 of surplus per month. If the firm bundles the channels, however, it can sell the package to both customers for $10.50 per month. This earns the company $(2 \times \$10.50)$ or $21 of producer surplus per month, more than the $20 per month from selling the channels separately.

The reason why bundling works in the second scenario is the negative correlation between the two customers' willingness to pay, which occurs because Dakota values one part of the bundle (ESPN) more than Jack, while Jack values SOAPnet more than Dakota. If the cable company wants to sell to the entire market, it can only set a price equal to the smaller of the two customers' willingness to pay, whether pricing separately or as a bundle. In the first example with positively correlated demand (when Dakota had a higher willingness to pay for both channels), the

Table 10.3	Negatively Correlated Valuations per Subscriber-Month		
	ESPN	**SOAPnet**	**Bundle**
Jack	$9.00	$1.50	$10.50
Dakota	$10.00	$1.00	$11.00

---

[5] In reality, most network owners like Disney, which owns ESPN and SOAPnet, do not own the cable company, so they actually bundle the channels they sell to the cable company that then passes along that bundle to you. The point is the same, however.

lower of the customers' valuations for the bundle ($10 per subscriber for Jack) is smaller by $1.50 than the larger valuation ($11.50 per month for Dakota) because it reflects Jack's lower valuations for both channels. Therefore, if the cable company wants to sell the channels as a bundle, it must offer Dakota a discount that embodies the fact that Jack has a lower willingness to pay for both channels. As a result, the cable company does no better than having sold the channels separately.

With a negative correlation of demands across customers, there is less variation (only $0.50) in each customer's willingness to pay for the bundle: $10.50 per month for Jack and $11.00 per month for Dakota. This reduced variation means the cable company doesn't need to give as large a discount to Dakota to sell to both customers. Bundling has reduced the difference in total willingness to pay across the customers. What's important is that the smaller of the two combined valuations is larger when the channel demands are negatively correlated. Jack will pay $10.50 instead of only $10, which allows the company to raise its price. In this way, bundling allows sellers to "smooth out" variations in customers' demands, raises the prices sellers can charge for their bundled products, and increases the amount of surplus they can extract.

Mixed Bundling

The previous example shows why a firm might choose to sell two products as a bundle instead of separately. Sometimes, however, firms simultaneously offer the products separately *and* as a bundle and then let the consumer choose which to buy. This indirect pricing strategy is called **mixed bundling.** The Extra Value Meals at McDonald's include a sandwich, fries, and a drink at one price. McDonald's also offers these three things individually. This is where mixed bundling acts as a form of indirect price discrimination because the firm offers different choices and lets customers sort themselves in ways that increase producer surplus.

Mixed bundling is a lot like the bundling strategy we've just discussed (offering only the bundle is often called **pure bundling**). It is useful in the same type of situations, but is better than pure bundling when the marginal cost of producing some of the components is high enough that it makes sense to let some customers opt out of buying the entire bundle.

Returning to our cable network example, let's suppose there are four customers and that they value the networks according to Table 10.4. The willingness to pay is negatively correlated across the networks, so we know bundling can work as a pricing strategy.

Now suppose instead of marginal costs being zero, the marginal cost of supplying ESPN is $6.00 per month and SOAPnet is $1.00 per month. Therefore, the marginal cost of producing the bundled package is $7.00. If the cable company sells the bundle for $12.15 (the minimum valuation of the bundle across the customers), it will sell the bundle to all four customers. Subtracting costs, this will net a per-customer producer surplus of $5.15 per month for a total of (4 × $5.15), or $20.60.

But look more closely at Penny and Sheldon. Their relative values for the two channels are extreme. Penny really values ESPN and barely values SOAPnet, while the opposite is true for Sheldon. And crucially, the value they put on one of these channels is *below* the marginal cost of supplying it: SOAPnet for Penny and ESPN for Sheldon. As we will see, in these cases it makes sense for the cable company to try to split these customers off from the bundle, because it does not want to supply channels to customers who value them at less than the cost of providing them.

mixed bundling
A type of bundling in which the firm simultaneously offers consumers the choice of buying two or more products separately or as a bundle.

pure bundling
A type of bundling in which the firm offers the products only as a bundle.

Table 10.4   **Negatively Correlated Valuations When the Marginal Cost Exceeds the Valuation for Some Customers**

	ESPN (*MC* = $6)	SOAPnet (*MC* = $1)	Bundle (*MC* = $7)
Penny	$12.00	$0.50	$12.50
Leonard	$11.00	$1.15	$12.15
Raj	$9.00	$3.15	$12.15
Sheldon	$5.00	$7.75	$12.75

Figuring out the right mixed bundling strategy is slightly complicated because of incentive compatibility, so we'll take it one step at a time. Given the issues we just discussed, the cable company would like to end up selling the bundle to Leonard and Raj, only ESPN to Penny, and only SOAPnet to Sheldon. Because both Leonard and Raj value the bundle at $12.15 per month, that's a reasonable starting point for thinking about the price of the bundle. If this is the price of the bundle, however, the company can't charge Sheldon his full $7.75 valuation for SOAPnet. If it tried to, Sheldon would choose the bundle instead because it would give him 60 cents more consumer surplus ($12.75 – $12.15) than if he bought only SOAPnet (consumer surplus of zero if priced at $7.75). A price of $7.75 for SOAPnet is therefore not incentive compatible. To set an incentive-compatible price for SOAPnet, the cable company has to leave Sheldon with at least 60 cents of consumer surplus per month. Thus, the incentive-compatible price for the purchase of SOAPnet alone would be $7.75 – $0.60, or $7.15 per month. And because Leonard and Raj value SOAPnet at less than $7.15, both will buy the bundle rather than take the SOAPnet-only option, so incentive compatibility holds in the other direction, too.

We can do the same type of calculations with ESPN and Penny. The cable company can't charge $12.00 for ESPN alone, because Penny would opt for the bundle to get 35 cents ($12.50 – $12.15) of consumer surplus rather than zero from buying ESPN at $12.00. So, the company has to leave Penny with at least 35 cents of surplus from buying just ESPN. The highest price that will achieve this is $12.00 – $0.35, or $11.65. Again, offering this option won't move Leonard and Raj away from the bundle, because both value ESPN at less than $11.65.

So with those three prices—ESPN alone for $11.65, SOAPnet alone for $7.15, and the bundle for $12.15—the cable company will sell two bundles (to Leonard and Raj) to earn a producer surplus (subtracting out the marginal costs) of $5.15 per month for each bundle. Additionally, it will sell ESPN alone to Penny to earn a surplus of $11.65 – $6.00 = $5.65 and SOAPnet alone to Sheldon for a surplus of $7.15 – $1.00 = $6.15. The total monthly producer surplus from using mixed bundling is therefore (2 × $5.15) + $5.65 + $6.15 = $22.10. That is more than the $20.60 per month the cable company would make by using pure bundling.

Producer surplus has increased because the cable company has saved itself the trouble of delivering a product to a customer who values it at less than it costs to produce.

10.4 figure it out

Fit Club, Inc. is a health club that offers two types of equipment: weight machines and a swimming pool. There are currently three customers (Abe, Betty, and Chris), whose willingness to pay for using each type of equipment per month is listed in the table below:

	Willingness to Pay (per month)	
	WEIGHT MACHINES	INDOOR POOL
Abe	$60	$50
Betty	$50	$125
Chris	$25	$140

The weight room and the swimming pool each have a constant marginal cost of $20 per month. In the case of the pool, the marginal cost is the price of the water and chemicals used, while the marginal cost of the weight machines is the cost of cleaning and maintaining them. Each customer is considering monthly access to each type of equipment, and the firm has to decide what type of membership package to offer the customers.

a What price will the firm charge for each product if it wishes to sell a health club membership to all three customers? What is the firm's producer surplus if it sells separate access to the weight room and the pool room at these prices?

b. What price will the firm charge for a bundle of access to both the weight room and the swimming pool if it wishes to sell the bundle to all three customers? How much producer surplus will Fit Club, Inc. earn in this case?

c. Suppose the firm is considering offering its customers a choice to either purchase access to the weight room and the swimming pool separately at a price of $60 for the weight machine and $140 for the pool, or to purchase a bundle at a price of $175. Which option will each customer choose? How much producer surplus will Fit Club, Inc. earn in this situation?

Solution:

a. To sell access to the weight machines to all three customers, the health club must charge a price no greater than $25, the lowest willingness to pay of the customers (Chris). For the same reason, the price for the pool will be $50.

At these prices, the firm's producer surplus for its sales of access to the weight machines will be

$$\text{Producer surplus for weight machine} = (\text{Price} - \text{marginal cost}) \times \text{quantity}$$
$$= (\$25 - \$20) \times 3$$
$$= (\$5)(3) = \$15$$

For access to the pool, producer surplus will be

$$\text{Producer surplus for the pool} = (\$50 - \$20) \times 3$$
$$= (\$30)(3) = \$90$$

Total producer surplus will be $15 + $90 = $105.

b. To determine the price of the bundle, we need to calculate each buyer's willingness to pay for the bundle. This is done simply by summing the customers' willingness to pay for each product as shown in the table below:

	Willingness to Pay (per month)		
	WEIGHT MACHINES	**INDOOR POOL**	**BUNDLE**
Abe	$60	$50	= $60 + $50 = $110
Betty	$50	$125	= $50 + $125 = $175
Chris	$25	$140	= $25 + $140 = $165

So, the maximum price the health club can charge for its bundle (and still sell to all three buyers) is $110. It will sell 3 bundles at this price. Therefore, its producer surplus will be

$$\text{Producer surplus for bundle} = (\text{price} - \text{marginal cost}) \times \text{quantity}$$
$$= (\$110 - \$40) \times 3$$
$$= (\$70)(3) = \$210$$

c. We need to compare each buyer's willingness to pay to the prices set for purchasing access to each room separately and the price of the bundle.

Abe will only purchase a weight machine membership. His willingness to pay for the pool is below the price of $140. The same is true for the bundle, which he values only at $110. Therefore, the health club will only sell Abe access to the weight machines.

Betty will not be willing to buy either membership separately, because her willingness to pay for each is below the set price. However, Betty's willingness to pay for the bundle ($175) is exactly equal to the price, so she will purchase the bundle.

Chris will only purchase access to the indoor pool. His willingness to pay for weight machines is only $25, far below the price of $60. Likewise, Chris is willing to pay at most $165 for the bundle. Thus, the health club will only be able to sell pool access to Chris.

Total producer surplus will therefore be:

$$\text{Producer surplus for weight machines} = (\text{price} - \text{marginal cost}) \times \text{quantity}$$
$$= (\$60 - \$20) \times 1$$
$$= \$40$$
$$\text{Producer surplus for the pool} = (\$140 - \$20) \times 1$$
$$= \$120$$
$$\text{Producer surplus for bundle} = (\$175 - \$40) \times 1$$
$$= \$135$$

Total producer surplus when the health club offers customers a choice of bundling or separate prices is $40 + $120 + $135 = $295.

10.6 Advanced Pricing Strategies

> **When to Use It** Block Pricing and Two-Part Tariffs
>
> 1. The firm has market power and can prevent resale.
> 2. The firm's customers may have either identical or different demand curves.

In the previous sections, we analyzed pricing strategies based on price discrimination, the ability of a firm to charge more for units of output sold to those willing to pay more and, as a result, extract producer surplus by departing from the single-price monopoly pricing discussed in Chapter 9. In this section, we look at how firms with market power can achieve that goal not by charging a given price per unit, but by varying unit prices offered to the same customer or charging lump-sum fees on top of per-unit prices. We start with a return to our discussion of quantity discounts.

Block Pricing

We call the strategy in which a firm reduces the price of a good if the customer buys more of it **block pricing.** You see this sort of thing all the time. Buying a single 12-oz can of Pepsi might cost $1, but a six-pack of 12-oz cans costs only $2.99. However, unlike indirect price discrimination (such as quantity discounts), block pricing does not require that buyers have different demand curves and price sensitivities. All buyers of Pepsi may, in fact, have the same demand curve, but Pepsi could still gain producer surplus from providing buyers with an option to buy a larger quantity of soda at a lower price.

Consider Figure 10.8, which shows a demand curve for Walmart's photo holiday cards. Here, we assume this is the demand curve of just one customer (or we could suppose all customers have this same demand curve), so the firm is not trying to price-discriminate across customers with different types of demand, as would be the case if Walmart offers quantity discounts. If Walmart follows the pricing rule for firms with market power in Chapter 9, it will pick the quantity at which marginal revenue equals marginal cost and charge a price equal to the height of the demand curve at that quantity. In the figure, the monopoly quantity is 100 cards and the price is 25 cents per card. Walmart's producer surplus from pricing at that point equals the area of rectangle A.

If Walmart can prevent resale, however, it doesn't have to charge a single price. Suppose it offers the first 100 holiday cards for sale at 25 cents each, but then allows a consumer to buy as many as 25 more cards (numbers 101–125) at a lower per-unit price of 20 cents each. The customer will take advantage of this offer because the incremental purchase at the lower price yields an additional consumer surplus equal to the area of triangle B. Walmart is better off, too, because it adds an additional amount of producer surplus equal to the area of rectangle C.

Walmart could keep offering discounted prices on larger quantities. For example, it could offer the next 50 cards, up to the 175th photo card, for 10 cents each. Again, the consumer will take the deal because the consumer surplus from that block of cards (area D in the figure) is positive. Walmart also comes out ahead because it earns producer surplus E. Note that the price strategy we just described could also be expressed in the following way: 100 units are $25, 125 units are $30, and 175 units are $35. Even if all customers have this same demand, all will opt to purchase 175 cards at a price of $35 and Walmart still increases its producer surplus. (This is why block pricing is different

---

Figure 10.8 : **Block Pricing**

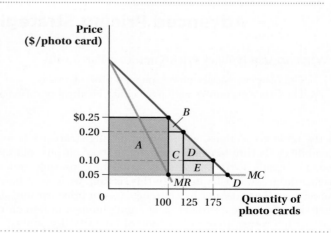

D is the demand curve of an individual consumer of Walmart's photo cards. Under monopoly pricing, Walmart sells at the point on the demand curve corresponding to the quantity where $MR = MC$ ($Q = 100$ photo cards, $P = \$0.25$ per card). When Walmart can prevent resale, it can use a block pricing strategy instead. It could still sell the first 100 at a price of $0.25 per card, while charging a lower price of $0.20 each for the next 25 photos purchased (for a total quantity of 125 cards) and $0.10 each for the next 50 cards (for a total of 175 cards). Producer surplus increases from area A to $A + C$ to $A + C + E$, respectively, and consumer surplus increases by area B and areas $B + D$, respectively.

from the quantity discounts we saw when discussing indirect price discrimination. Here, no customer sorting needs to occur for Walmart to gain producer surplus.)

A block-pricing strategy like this raises more producer surplus for a firm than does the conventional single-price monopoly strategy because it allows a firm to better match the prices of different quantities of its output to consumers' valuations of those quantities. For the first set of units that customers buy—the units for which customers have a high willingness to pay—the firm charges a relatively high price. With block pricing, the firm doesn't have to completely give up selling a large number of units by charging that initial high price. Block pricing lets it sell additional units of its product, those for which consumers have lower willingness to pay, at lower prices.

This example shows how block pricing can work for even a single customer type, though if there were lots of identical customers, the firm would need to be able to prevent resale to avoid being undercut by its own customers.

Two-Part Tariffs

Another pricing strategy available to firms with market power and identical consumers is the **two-part tariff,** a pricing strategy in which a firm breaks the payments for a product into two parts. One component is a standard per-unit price. The second is a fixed fee that must be paid to buy any amount of the product at all, no matter how large or how small.

For example, a lot of mobile phone "unlimited service" calling plans have this structure. You might pay, say, $50 a month for service and then be able to make as many calls as you would like at no additional cost. Here, the fixed fee portion of the two-part tariff is $50 and the per-unit price is zero (though for other markets and products, the per-unit price is often positive). A video game system such as Microsoft's XBox is like a two-part tariff, too. Here, the cost of the console itself is the fixed fee and the cost of the individual games represents the per-unit price.

To see why using a two-part tariff can be advantageous for a firm with market power, consider the market in Figure 10.9. It shows the demand for mobile phone service offered by the firm, the marginal revenue curve corresponding to demand, and the firm's constant marginal cost.

The firm's conventional single-price monopoly profit-maximizing quantity is found where marginal revenue equals marginal cost. The quantity at which this condition holds is 300 minutes per month, and the price at which consumers are willing to

> **two-part tariff**
> A pricing strategy in which the payment has two components, a per-unit price and a fixed fee.

Figure 10.9   **Two-Part Tariff**

As a single-price monopoly, a mobile phone service will sell 300 minutes of mobile service per month at a price of $0.10 per minute. Using a two-part tariff, however, the firm can increase its producer surplus from rectangle B to the triangle $A + B + C$. To do this, it will charge the per-unit price of $0.05 per minute, where $D = MC$, and set a fixed fee equal to the consumer's surplus at this quantity, the area $A + B + C$. Under this pricing scheme, the firm will sell 600 minutes of mobile service per month.

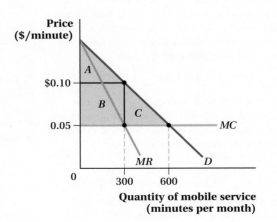

purchase that quantity is 10 cents per minute. At the price of 10 cents per minute, the consumer surplus is area A and the firm's producer surplus is rectangle B.

Now suppose instead that the firm uses the following two-part tariff pricing structure. First, it reduces the per-unit price all the way to marginal cost, 5 cents. This change increases the number of units it sells from 300 minutes to 600, but drives per-unit profit to zero. However, the firm knows that each customer will buy a quantity of 600 minutes per month of air time at this price and have a consumer surplus equal to area $A + B + C$ as a result. Knowing that this consumer surplus represents the willingness of the consumers to pay above the market price, the firm will set a fixed fee to try to capture that consumer surplus. Therefore, the firm decides to set the fixed-fee portion of the two-part tariff equal to $A + B + C$. This fee is not per minute; it's a one time per month fee for any consumer who wants to buy *any* number of units at 5 cents per minute.

What happens under this two-part tariff pricing structure? At a unit price of 5 cents per minute, the consumer buys 600 minutes of air time. This part of the price structure doesn't make the phone company any money, because its marginal cost of delivering service is also 5 cents per minute. However, the company is also charging the fixed fee $A + B + C$. And importantly, the consumer is willing to pay that, because if she uses 600 minutes of air time, she will enjoy consumer surplus equal to the same area. The company has set the size of the fixed fee so that the consumer is no worse off (and actually it could make her strictly better off if it charged just a touch less than $A + B + C$) than if she bought nothing. By using a two-part tariff, the firm captures the *entire* surplus in the market for itself, as opposed to only area B under standard market power pricing.

Again, if you spread this insight to a market with many identical customers, the ability to prevent resale would be crucial for making the pricing strategy work. If the phone company couldn't prevent resale, one customer could pay the fixed fee, buy up a huge amount of minutes at marginal cost, sell off these extra minutes at a small markup to other consumers who did not pay the fixed fee, and make lots of money. For example, if the consumer could rig her phone so other people would pay her 6 cents per minute to make calls on it when she wasn't using the phone, this would defeat the company's strategy.

10.5 figure it out

You have been hired as an intern at the Golden Eagle Country Club Golf Course. You have been assigned the task of creating the pricing scheme for the golf course, which typically charges an annual membership fee and a per-use cost to its customers. Each of your customers is estimated to have the following demand curve for rounds of golf per year:

$$Q = 300 - 5P$$

If Golden Eagle can provide rounds of golf at a constant marginal cost of $50 and charges that amount per round of golf, what is the most that members would be willing to pay for the annual membership fee?

Solution:

This pricing scheme, with an annual membership fee and a per-unit price, is a two-part tariff. If the

price per round of golf is set at $P = \$50$, then each member will want to play

$$Q = 300 - 5P$$
$$= 300 - 5(50)$$
$$= 300 - 250$$
$$= 50 \text{ rounds per year}$$

With this knowledge, we can determine the maximum annual membership fee each customer is willing to pay. This will be equal to the amount of consumer surplus the customer will get from playing 50 rounds of golf each year at a price of $50 per round.

To calculate consumer surplus, it is easiest to draw a diagram, plot the demand curve, and find the area of consumer surplus. To simplify matters, let's rearrange the demand function into an inverse demand function:

$$Q = 300 - 5P$$
$$5P = 300 - Q$$
$$P = 60 - 0.2Q$$

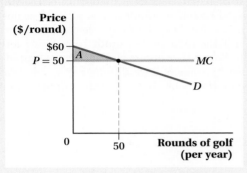

The vertical intercept is 60 and the consumer surplus is the area below the demand curve and above the price of $50, area A. We can calculate the area of triangle A:

$$\text{Area of } A = \frac{1}{2} \times \text{base} \times \text{height}$$

$$= \frac{1}{2} \times 50 \times (\$60 - \$50) = 0.5(50)(\$10)$$

$$= \$250$$

If the golf course set the price of a round of golf at $50, the consumer would purchase 50 rounds per year. This gives the golfer a consumer surplus equal to $250. Therefore, customers would be willing to pay up to $250 for an annual membership.

Being able to capture the entire surplus in the market is great if you're running a firm, but it's important to realize that a firm can attain this extreme result only if its customers have the same demand curve. The problem is much more complicated when there are customers with different demand curves.

For this more advanced two-part tariff pricing case, think about a firm that faces two kinds of customers whose demand curves for the firm's product are shown in Figure 10.10. Panel a shows the demand curve of the firm's relatively low-demand

---

Figure 10.10   **Two-Part Tariff with Different Customer Demands**

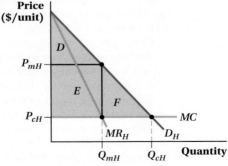

(a) For low-demand customers, the firm would want to sell a quantity of Q_{cL}, charge a per-unit price of P_{cL} and a fixed fee equal to the consumer surplus $A + B + C$. Since this is much lower than the consumer surplus for high-demand customers ($D + E + F$ in panel b), such a pricing strategy will leave a lot of surplus to the high-demand customers in the market.

(b) For high-demand customers, the firm would want to sell a quantity of Q_{cH}, and charge a per-unit price of P_{cH} and a fixed fee equal to $D + E + F$. Since this fixed fee is higher than the consumer surplus for low-demand customers, low-demand customers won't buy anything.

customers, while panel b shows the demand of the firm's relatively high-demand customers. If the firm tries to use a two-part tariff where it sets the unit price at marginal cost MC and the fixed fee at $A + B + C$, it will capture all of the surplus from the relatively low-demand customers in panel a but leave a lot of surplus to the relatively high-demand customers in panel b, because area $A + B + C$ is much smaller than area $D + E + F$. If the firm instead sets the fee at $D + E + F$ to capture the surplus of the high-demand customers, low-demand customers won't buy at all. This is not necessarily better than the first strategy. If the firm has a lot of low-demand customers, this could be a big loss for the firm, even if the reduction in profit from losing any given low-demand customer might be small. So, neither approach is perfect. Computing the profit-maximizing two-part tariff when consumers have different demands is a mathematical challenge beyond the scope of this book, but it usually entails a unit price above the firm's marginal cost.

10.7 Conclusion

We explored a number of different ways in which firms with market power, under the right conditions, can increase the producer surplus they earn above and beyond the surplus they can earn by following the standard, one-price market power pricing rule we focused on in Chapter 9. These pricing strategies are all around us; after learning about them in this chapter, you will start to recognize them in practice. You may also find yourself wondering why a particular firm isn't using one of these strategies. Just remember that certain conditions must be met for the price discrimination to work.

These various pricing strategies work in different ways, but there are some common threads. First, none will work unless the firm has market power. Therefore, any firm operating in a perfectly competitive market cannot use these strategies because it is a price taker. Second, the firm must prevent resale. Without the ability to prevent resale, doing anything besides the single-price monopoly pricing in Chapter 9 is futile. Third, while price discrimination strategies differ in the specifics of their mechanisms and the types of markets in which they are applicable, all of these methods work on the basic principle that the firm can make more producer surplus if it can adjust the price it charges so that consumers end up paying higher prices for those units of its output that provide them with greater consumer surplus. Price discrimination also works by charging higher prices to consumers with less elastic demand and lower prices to consumers with more elastic demand.

Other pricing strategies, such as block pricing and two-part tariffs, can be used even in markets where all consumers have the same demand. These strategies work by allowing consumers to buy relatively large quantities at a low price on the margin, but then grab back producer surplus for the firm through higher up-front payments.

In the next chapter, we examine firms with degrees of market power that fall between perfect competition and monopoly. We will find that these firms' decisions are not made in a vacuum (where they only consider their own costs and their customers' demands), but are also based on the decisions made by other firms in the same market. Although many may choose to follow the pricing strategies discussed in this chapter, each firm has to take into account how its competitors may react to such a move before determining if the strategy increases its producer surplus.

Summary

1. By using **pricing strategies,** a firm with market power can extract more producer surplus from a market than it can from following the monopoly pricing rule of Chapter 9 (where the firm produces the quantity at which marginal revenue equals marginal cost, and then charges the price at which buyers would consume that quantity). It can only do so, however, if the situation satisfies certain criteria. A crucial factor is that in addition to market power, the firm has to be able to prevent resale among customers. If the firm can prevent resale, the amount of information it has on its customers determines what kind of pricing strategy it can follow. [**Section 10.1**]

2. When customers differ and the firm has sufficient information about its customers' demands to charge every person a different price, **perfect** or **first-degree price discrimination** is possible. This **direct price discrimination** strategy allows the firm to capture the entire surplus in the market for itself. It is very rare to have this kind of information, however. [**Section 10.2**]

3. If the firm has different types of customers and can directly identify at least two groups whose price elasticities of demand differ, it can charge different prices to the two groups and earn more producer surplus. The profit-maximizing direct price discrimination strategy in this case is to follow the single-price monopoly pricing rule separately for each group. There are many ways to directly separate customers, including customer characteristics, geography, past purchase behavior, the timing of the purchase, and so on, a practice known as **segmenting,** or **third-degree price discrimination.** [**Section 10.3**]

4. If the company knows that there are different types of customers but cannot directly identify which group a customer belongs to before the purchase, it must rely on **indirect (second-degree) price discrimination.** This involves designing choices that induce customers to sort themselves into groups. **Quantity discounts** can be used if customers who demand a higher quantity also have a more elastic demand. **Versioning** a product can also work. The key additional requirement for indirect price discrimination is that the pricing structure has to be **incentive compatible,** meaning that each consumer group wants to take the offer designed specifically for them. [**Section 10.4**]

5. If a company sells multiple products and consumers' demands for the products are negatively correlated, it can sell the products together as a bundle and increase producer surplus beyond what it could earn by selling the products separately. Sometimes, particularly if the marginal cost of producing one of the products exceeds the value that a customer places on that product, the company may be better off using **mixed bundling,** which gives customers the choice of buying individual products at high prices or a bundle of products at a discount. [**Section 10.5**]

6. Even when there are not different types of customers, a firm can use advanced pricing strategies like **block pricing** (a discount for buying extra quantity) or a **two-part tariff** (a fixed fee paid up-front in addition to a price per unit of the good) as a way to capture more producer surplus than it could earn with standard monopoly pricing. However, each of these strategies is much more complicated to implement when there are many consumers with different demand curves. [**Section 10.6**]

Review Questions

1. What are the two requirements of price discrimination?
2. Why is producer surplus maximized under perfect price discrimination?
3. What are the two types of direct price discrimination?
4. What are some ways that a firm can segment its customers?
5. Contrast direct price discrimination and indirect price discrimination.
6. What is incentive compatibility? Why is it necessary for an indirect price discrimination strategy to be incentive compatible?
7. Provide an example of product versioning.
8. What are the differences between the following three pricing strategies: block pricing, segmenting, and quantity discounts?
9. What is the difference between mixed bundling and pure bundling?
10. What are the two component prices of a two-part tariff?

Problems (Solutions to problems marked * appear at the back of this book. Problems adapted to use calculus are available online at http://worthpublishers.com/GLS1e)

*1. Consider the demand for schnitzel in the diagram below. Suppose that there is a single seller of schnitzel, who acts as a single-price monopolist.

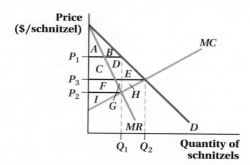

a. Indicate the profit-maximizing price and quantity.

b. List the areas of consumer and producer surplus.

c. Suppose the seller begins perfectly price discriminating. How many schnitzels will she sell?

d. What happens to areas A and B when the seller begins perfectly price discriminating?

e. What happens to areas E and H when the seller begins perfectly price discriminating?

2. Indicate whether the following statement is true or false, and explain your answer: Because the potential profit from perfect price discrimination is always higher than the potential profit from third-degree price discrimination (segmenting), firms that practice third-degree price discrimination must not be maximizing profit.

3. There are seven consumers, each of whom is hungry for exactly one Butterfinger. The consumers' maximum willingness to pay is given in the table below:

Consumer (age, gender)	Maximum Willingness to Pay
Marge (34, female)	$2
Homer (38, male)	4
Lisa (6, female)	5
Maggie (2, female)	6
Ned (46, male)	1
Krusty (55, male)	3
Bart (9, male)	7

a. Given that each consumer wants one and only one Butterfinger, draw the demand curve for Butterfingers.

b. If Butterfingers are priced at $7, only one will be sold. Who buys that Butterfinger? Label the point at $7 on the demand curve with the name of that buyer.

c. If Butterfingers are priced at $6, a second buyer will be priced into the market. Who is that buyer? Label the point at $6 on the demand curve with the name of that buyer.

d. Continue to label each point on the demand curve with the name of the buyer represented by that point.

e. Suppose that you are a monopoly seller of Butterfingers, which you can produce at a constant marginal and average total cost of $2. Suppose you charge every customer the same price for Butterfingers. What price should you set to maximize your profit? How many Butterfingers will you sell? Calculate your profit. Calculate the consumer surplus received by the buyers. Calculate the deadweight loss.

f. Suppose that every customer that comes into your Butterfinger store has their maximum willingness to pay displayed in neon on their foreheads. You decide to use this information to increase your profit by practicing first-degree price discrimination. How many Butterfingers will you sell? Calculate your profit. Calculate the consumer surplus received by the buyers. Calculate the deadweight loss.

g. Where does the consumer surplus go when you begin price discriminating?

h. What happens to the deadweight loss?

4. Consider the problem faced by the Butterfinger seller in Problem 3.

a. Assume that the seller is able to prevent resale between customers. In the real world, why is the seller *still* unlikely to be able to perfectly price discriminate?

b. Because of the reason you just indicated, the Butterfinger seller decides to segment her customers into two groups, each of which will be charged a different price. In order to maximize profit, should the seller sort by gender or by age?

c. Based on your answer to (b), determine who is in each group, and indicate (1) the price the seller should set for each group, (2) the total profit received by the seller, (3) total consumer surplus, and (4) the deadweight loss.

d. Is this pricing strategy (segmenting) more profitable to the seller than perfectly price discriminating? Is this pricing strategy more profitable than charging every consumer the same price?

e. What happens to consumer surplus and deadweight loss when a single-price monopolist begins segmenting in this way?

*5. Promoters of a major college basketball tournament estimate that the demand for tickets on the part of adults is given by $Q_{ad} = 5{,}000 - 10P$, and that the demand for tickets on the part of students is given by $Q_{st} = 10{,}000 - 100P$. The promoters wish to segment the market and charge adults and students different prices. They estimate that the marginal and average total cost of seating an additional spectator is constant at $10.

a. For each segment (adults and students), find the inverse demand and marginal revenue functions.

b. Equate marginal revenue and marginal cost. Determine the profit-maximizing quantity for each segment.

c. Plug the quantities you found in (b) into the respective inverse demand curves to find the profit-maximizing price for each segment. Who pays more, adults or students?

d. Determine the profit generated by each segment, and add them together to find the promoter's total profit.

e. How would your answers change if the arena where the event was to take place had only 5,000 seats?

6. In Problem 5, you found the profit that a promoter of a major college basketball tournament would earn if he were to segment the market into adults and students. Suppose that the promoter's CEO decides that price discrimination presents a poor public image, and announces that everybody will be charged the same price. His resident economist (you) is tasked with figuring out what that price should be.

a. Find the total demand for tickets by adding the demand curves of adults and students.

b. Derive the inverse demand curve for tickets, as well as the associated marginal revenue curve associated with that demand.

c. Find the profit-maximizing quantity of tickets and the corresponding price.

d. Determine the promoter's profit.

e. Compare the promoter's profit when he tries to price for the entire market, to his profit when he simply charges the adult price from the previous problem. Is it better for the promoter to price for the entire market and almost fill the arena, or to price for adults only and have a lot of empty seats?

7. You are the owner of a nail salon. Your female customer's price elasticity of demand for manicures is −2.5; your male customer's price elasticity of demand for manicures is −1.2. The marginal cost of manicuring a customer's nails is $12.

a. If you segment the market by gender, what price should you charge women? What price should you charge men?

b. Explain intuitively why you should charge each group a different price.

8. Movie theaters often charge substantially less for afternoon showings than for evening showings. Explain how theaters use time of day to segment their customers into low-elasticity and high-elasticity groups.

*9. Owners of a movie theater have determined that the elasticity of demand for movie tickets equals −2.0 for students and −1.5 for adults.

a. If the owners of the theater decide to segment the market, who should be charged a higher price, students or adults? Use your knowledge of microeconomic theory to explain why.

b. Use the Lerner index as described in the text to determine the ratio of prices. In percentage terms, how big a price premium should be charged to the group that pays the higher price?

10. Owners of a Florida restaurant estimate that the elasticity of demand for meals is −1.5 for senior citizens and −1.33 for everyone else.

a. Given this information, how big (in percentage terms) should the senior citizen discount be?

b. Suppose that the restaurant owners discover that seniors tend to demand more attention from their waiters and send back more food as unsatisfactory, to the extent that the marginal cost of serving a senior is twice as high as serving an adult. Accounting for these costs, how large should the senior citizen discount be? (*Hint*: Refer back to the example in the text, but don't cancel out marginal costs!)

c. Were your results in part (b) surprising? Explain them, intuitively.

11. A local golf course's hired-gun econometrician has determined that there are two types of golfers, frequent and infrequent. Frequent golfers' annual demand for rounds of golf is given by $Q_f = 24 - 0.3P$, where P is the price of a round of golf. In contrast, infrequent golfers' annual demand for rounds of golf is given by $Q_i = 10 - 0.1P$. The marginal and average total cost of providing a round of golf is $20.

a. If the golf course could tell a frequent golfer from an infrequent golfer, what price would it charge each type? How many times would each type golf? How much profit would the golf course generate?

The greens manager has difficulty telling frequent from infrequent golfers, so she decides to use second-degree price discrimination (quantity discounts) to make different types of golfers self-select into the most profitable pricing scheme. The course sets a price for individual rounds of golf, but also offers a quantity discount for members willing to buy a rather large quantity of rounds in advance. The course's owners hope that frequent golfers will self-select into the discounted plan, and that infrequent golfers will choose to buy individual rounds.

b. What price should the golf course set for individual rounds of golf? Why?

c. If the course wishes to maximize profit, what price and minimum quantity should it establish for the discounted plan?

d. Which plan will generate the greatest consumer surplus for frequent golfers, the individual-round plan or the discount plan? Illustrate your answer by showing and measuring the areas of surplus on frequent golfers' inverse demand curves.

e. Which plan will generate the greatest consumer surplus for infrequent golfers, the individual-round plan or the discount plan? Illustrate your answer by showing the areas of surplus on infrequent golfers' inverse demand curves.

f. Based on your answers to (d) and (e), will the plan be successful in making golfers self-select into the most profitable plan for the golf course?

g. Suppose that each type of golfer came to the course with the word "frequent" or "infrequent" tattooed on his or her forehead. Is this information of any value to the golf course owner? (In other words, can the owner earn any more profits by segmenting than it did with its quantity discount plan?)

12. Many textbooks are now available in two versions, a high-priced "domestic" version and a low-priced "international" version. Each version generally contains exactly the same text, but slightly altered homework problems.

a. Why would a textbook publisher go to the trouble to produce two versions of the same text?

b. Discuss whether the publisher's strategy would be more effective if it made the alterations secret, or if it announced them boldly.

c. The production of international versions of textbooks was concurrent with the explosion of the Internet. Explain why this is likely to be more than just a coincidence.

*13. Rockway & Daughters Piano Co. wishes to sell a piano to everyone. But some consumers are budget-conscious, and others are not, and unfortunately, Rockway cannot tell which is which. So, Rockway produces a premium line of pianos that it markets under the Rockway name, and a similar line of pianos that it markets under the Dundee name. While the cost of producing these pianos is quite similar, all consumers agree that Rockway pianos are of higher quality than Dundee pianos, and would be willing to pay more for a Rockway. Budget-conscious consumers feel that Dundee pianos are worth $6,000, and Rockways are worth $8,000. Performance artists believe that Dundee pianos are worth $7,000 and Rockways are worth $12,000.

a. Suppose Rockway & Daughters prices its Dundee pianos at $5,000 and its Rockway pianos at $10,500. Are these prices incentive compatible—that is, will more price-conscious consumers purchase the Dundee line, while more performance-oriented players choose the Rockway? Explain.

b. How much must Rockway & Daughters reduce the price of its Rockway line in order to achieve incentive compatibility?

c. Suppose instead that Rockway & Daughters tries to achieve incentive compatibility by raising the price of its Dundee line. Can it do so? And if so, how?

14. London's Market Bar has a unique pricing system where a computer sets the price based on demand. When demand picks up, the computer begins to gradually reduce prices. This pricing strategy is puzzling to those who have studied supply and demand. Celene Berman, the assistant manager, says a group of "young city-boy types" recently kept asking why prices "were going the wrong way around." Explain, using your knowledge of block pricing, why the owner's strategy of reducing prices as sales increase might actually lead to increased profit for the bar.

*15. Microsoft sells two types of office software, a word processor it calls Word, and a spreadsheet it calls Excel. Both can be produced at zero marginal cost. There are two types of consumers for these products, who exist in roughly equal proportions in the population: authors, who are willing to pay $120 for Word and $40 for Excel, and economists, who are willing to pay $50 for Word and $150 for Excel.

a. Ideally, Microsoft would like to charge authors more for Word and economists more for Excel. Why would it be difficult for Microsoft to do this?

b. Suppose that Microsoft execs decide to sell Word and Excel separately. What price should Microsoft set for Word? (*Hint*: Is it better to sell only to authors, or to try to sell to both authors and economists?) What price should Microsoft set for Excel? What will Microsoft's profit be from a representative group of one author and one economist?

c. Suppose that Microsoft decides to bundle together Word and Excel in a package called Office, and not offer them individually. What price should Microsoft set for the package? Why? How much profit will Microsoft generate from a representative group of one author and one economist?

d. Does bundling allow Microsoft to generate higher profit than selling Word and Excel separately?

16. Three consumers, John, Kate, and Lester, are in the market for two goods, dates and eggs. Their willingness to pay for dates and eggs is given in the table below:

	Dates (1 package)	Eggs (1 dozen)
John	$0.60	$2.00
Kate	$1.30	$1.30
Lester	$2.00	$0.60

a. If you are a local farmer who can produce dates and eggs for free, what is the optimal price for dates and eggs if you price them individually? How much profit will you generate?

b. If you bundle dates and eggs together, what price should you set for a bundle containing one package of dates and a dozen eggs? How much profit will you generate?

c. Is there any advantage to mixed bundling in this case? Why or why not?

d. Suppose that the cost of producing dates and eggs rises to $1.00 per package and $1.00 per dozen, respectively. Now is there any advantage to mixed bundling? Why or why not? Explain your answer with a numerical illustration.

e. What accounts for the change in optimal strategy when costs change?

*17. Elaine makes delicious cupcakes that she mails to customers across the country. Her cupcakes are so delicious that she has a great degree of pricing power. Elaine's customers have identical demands for cupcakes. A representative customer's demand is shown in the diagram below. Elaine can make a cupcake for a constant marginal and average total cost of $0.50.

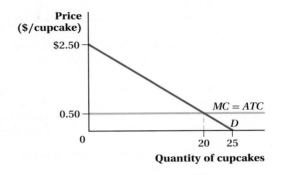

a. If Elaine is an ordinary monopolist, what price should she charge for cupcakes? How many will each customer order? How much profit will Elaine earn? How much consumer surplus will the buyer get?

b. Suppose that Elaine decides to offer a quantity discount according to the following terms: The first 10 cupcakes can be bought for $1.50 each; any cupcake over 10 will be offered at a discounted price. What discount price will maximize Elaine's profit from this pricing scheme? (*Hint*: Draw a new demand curve for Elaine's customers' demand, but since her customers have already purchased 10, begin your demand curve at the 11th unit. Alternatively, shift the vertical axis to the right by 10 units.)

c. How many cupcakes will customers order at full price? How many at the discounted price?

d. What will Elaine's profit be? How does this scheme compare to the profit she earned as an ordinary monopolist?

e. Suppose that Elaine gets super-greedy and decides to implement a three-tiered pricing system. What three prices should she choose to maximize her profit? At what quantities will the price points change? What will her profit be?

f. Suppose Elaine decides to charge $2.40 for the first cupcake, $2.30 for the second, and so on. How many cupcakes will she sell, and what will her profit be?

g. What happens to consumer surplus as Elaine adds more price points? Where does it go?

18. Consider the demand for cupcakes in Problem 17. Suppose Elaine decides to sell cupcakes only in packages of 20.

a. How much would customers be willing to pay to obtain a 20-pack of Elaine's cupcakes? (*Hint*: Remember that the value of each cupcake is given by the corresponding point on the demand curve. Add up those values for cupcakes 1–20.)

b. How much profit will Elaine earn from each customer?

c. How does the profit from this scheme compare to the profit Elaine earned in part (f) of Problem 17?

19. Many gyms offer a mixed two-part tariff pricing scheme. One can join the gym and then have daily access at a very low cost (often, free); alternatively, one can choose not to join and pay a higher daily fee (perhaps $10 or $15). Explain the rationale for this dual pricing scheme. What must be true of the gym's customers' demands?

20. SmacFone is a major provider of pay-by-the-minute, no contract cellphones that are very popular with ordinary consumers. They are also quite popular with drug dealers, who appreciate the anonymity that such phones provide. The demand curves for talking minutes that SmacFone faces from each type of customer are given in the diagrams below. SmacFone's marginal and average total cost of service is 5 cents per minute.

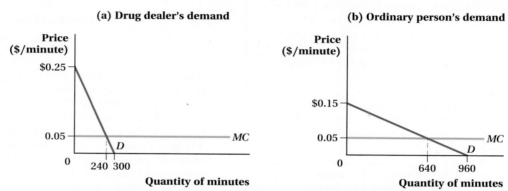

a. Determine the profit-maximizing price and quantity that SmacFone would like to charge each type of consumer, and show it on the appropriate graph. Then, determine the potential profit that SmacFone could generate from each segment.

Because SmacFone cannot tell whether a new customer is an ordinary person or a drug dealer, it decides to use second-degree price discrimination to separate consumers. SmacFone sets a Plan A price of 15 cents per minute, but offers a special Plan B price of 10 cents per minute if a customer purchases 320 or more minutes.

b. Determine how much consumer surplus ordinary consumers would receive under Plans A and B. Which plan should ordinary consumers choose if they are trying to maximize their surplus?

c. Determine how much consumer surplus drug dealers would receive under Plans A and B. Which plan should drug dealers choose if they are trying to maximize their surplus?

d. Is the pricing scheme SmacFone derived incentive compatible? (In other words, will the plan successfully direct drug dealers to Plan A and ordinary consumers to Plan B?) How much profit will SmacFone generate with this set of plans?

Imperfect Competition

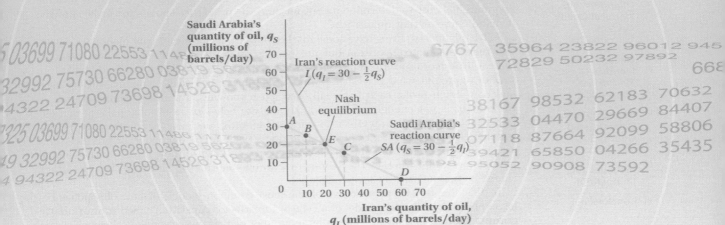

Saudi Arabia's quantity of oil, q_S (millions of barrels/day)

Iran's reaction curve
$I(q_I = 30 - \frac{1}{2}q_S)$

Nash equilibrium

Saudi Arabia's reaction curve
$SA(q_S = 30 - \frac{1}{2}q_I)$

Iran's quantity of oil, q_I (millions of barrels/day)

I n previous chapters, we studied the two ends of the market power spectrum: perfect competition and monopoly. In perfect competition, a firm has no market power because it is only one of many producers in the market, the price is driven down to marginal cost, and output is relatively high. In a monopoly, one firm has complete market power because it is the only producer of a good in the market, price is greater than marginal cost, and output is lower. We also learned about the many pricing strategies that firms with market power can use to earn greater economic profit.

Between these two ends of the spectrum are lots of industries, most of them perhaps, that are neither perfectly competitive nor monopolistic. Coke and Pepsi dominate the cola market. Nintendo, Sony, and Microsoft dominate video games. These companies compete but are hardly the personification of perfect competition. Yet they aren't stand-alone monopolies either. The industry structure between perfect competition and monopoly is known as **imperfect competition.**

This chapter introduces that important but sometimes complicated market structure. We begin by looking at several types of **oligopoly,** a market structure characterized by competition among a small number of firms. Because there are many possible ways in which oligopolistic firms compete, there is no single model of oligopoly that is applicable to every situation. One theme of this chapter is that having a few competitors in an industry—rather than many or only one—can lead to multiple possible price and output outcomes. Several kinds of price and quantity outcomes *could* occur in an oligopoly, depending on the market circumstances. This isn't the case with perfect competition or monopoly. With perfect competition, price equals marginal cost and the market's output equals the point on the market demand curve at that price/cost level. With a monopoly (ignoring price discrimination), the firm equates marginal revenue and marginal cost to determine its output, and the price corresponds to the level of the demand curve at that quantity.

With oligopolies, firms have some market power but not necessarily monopoly power, and there is some competition but not perfect competition. This means that we need to be a little more specific about aspects of the particular market we're studying before we can figure out what prices they will charge, how much each company will produce, and how much profit each firm will earn. Just knowing how many companies are in the market is not enough information to analyze behavior in an oligopolistic market. Other factors that have an effect on price and quantity decisions in an oligopoly include whether the companies make identical products (as in an oil oligopoly) or products that are slightly different from one another (like Coke and Pepsi), how intensely the companies compete, and whether they compete with one another by choosing the prices they charge or the quantities they produce.

In this chapter, we present five of the most common models of how oligopolies behave, plus one additional model of a type of imperfect competition called **monopolistic competition,** a market in which a large number of firms have some market power but each makes zero economic profit in the long run. Whenever you have this many models as possible explanations for market behavior, it's important to figure out which one is appropriate for a specific case. This decision isn't always obvious in practice, so we discuss some ideas for determining which model is most appropriate for various real-world situations.

11.1 What Does Equilibrium Mean in an Oligopoly?

Before we introduce the many oligopoly models, we need to lay some groundwork. Specifically, we have to expand on our idea of what equilibrium is. The concept of equilibrium in perfect competition and in monopoly is easy. It means a price at which the quantity of the good demanded by consumers equals the quantity of the good supplied by producers. That is, the market "clears." The market is stable at such a point: There are no shortages or surpluses, and consumers and producers do not want to change their decisions.

The problem with applying that idea of equilibrium to an oligopolistic industry is that each company's action influences what the other companies want to do. To achieve an outcome in which no firm wants to change its decision requires determining more than just a price and quantity for the industry as a whole.

An equilibrium in an oligopoly starts with the same idea as in perfect competition or monopoly: The market clears. But it adds the requirement that no company wants to change its behavior (its own price or quantity) once it knows what other companies are doing. In other words, each company must be doing as well as it can *conditional* on what the other companies are doing. Oligopoly equilibrium has to be stable not only in equating the total quantities supplied and demanded, but also in remaining stable among the individual producers in the market.

imperfect competition
Market structures with characteristics between those of perfect competition and monopoly.

oligopoly
Competition between a small number of firms.

monopolistic competition
A type of imperfect competition with a large number of firms in which each firm has some market power but makes zero economic profit in the long run.

This idea of equilibrium—that each firm is doing its best conditional on the actions taken by other firms—is called a **Nash equilibrium.** It is named after Nobel Laureate John Nash who was the subject of the award-winning book and movie titled *A Beautiful Mind*. The Nash equilibrium concept is even more central in the next chapter when we study game theory that further explores strategic interaction among firms. For our purposes in this chapter, however, the following example will help clarify what is and what is not a Nash equilibrium in an oligopoly.

> **Nash equilibrium**
> An equilibrium in which each firm is doing the best it can conditional on the actions taken by its competitors.

 application

An Example of Nash Equilibrium: Marketing Movies

Major computer-animated movies like Disney's *Cars 2* or DreamWorks's *Kung Fu Panda 2* are amazingly expensive to make. Paying for the computer rendering, the animators, the actors—these things add up. *Cars 2* and *Kung Fu Panda 2* each cost almost $175 million to produce. But on top of these production costs, Disney and DreamWorks each then had to pay another $75 million or so for advertising. In other words, they spent the equivalent of almost half the production cost trying to get people to watch their movie.

Let's suppose Disney and DreamWorks are the only two movie companies that make animated feature films, and that their advertising influences people's choices of what movie to see. However, advertising doesn't increase the overall number of movies people see, just which movie they watch. From Disney's or DreamWorks' point of view, then, advertising can convince a moviegoer to see its movie instead of the competition's, but advertising is not going to bring people into theaters who wouldn't have gone otherwise.

Now suppose both studios plan to make the next installments in these series, *Kung Fu Panda 3* and *Cars 3*, and release them on the same summer weekend. Further, we assume that the cost of production is still $175 million and the cost of advertising is $75 million. If both studios advertise and compete with one another, their marketing efforts will cancel out. As a result, the two will split the market, and each will bring in, let's say, $400 million of revenue. Subtracting the $175 million production cost and the $75 million advertising cost, that leaves $150 million of profit to each studio.

If, on the other hand, the studios could somehow agree not to advertise at all, they would again split the market, but this time each would save the $75 million in advertising costs. The studio profits in this case would be greater at $225 million each.

Disney and DreamWorks would prefer the second, higher-profit outcome. The problem is that, due to the nature of advertising's influence on moviegoers, if only one studio advertises and the other doesn't, then the studio that advertises will get a larger share of the audience and the other one will be left with less. Suppose, for example, that the studio engaged in advertising would earn $700 million of revenue, and the other would earn only $100 million. The firm advertising its film therefore earns a profit of $450 million ($700 million of revenue minus the $175 million production cost and the $75 million in advertising). The other studio, the one that doesn't advertise, *loses* $75 million ($100 million of revenue minus the $175 million production cost).

Table 11.1 lays out these scenarios. The table's four cells correspond to the four possible profit outcomes if each firm pursues the strategy described at the top of each column and the start of each row: Both firms advertise (upper left), neither firm advertises (lower right), DreamWorks advertises and Disney doesn't (upper right), or vice versa (lower left). Profit is measured in millions of dollars.

Table 11.1   An Advertising Game*

		Disney	
		Advertise	**Don't Advertise**
DreamWorks	**Advertise**	150 , 150	450 , −75
	Don't Advertise	−75 , 450	225 , 225

*Outcomes are measured in millions of dollars of profit.

The number before the comma in each cell is DreamWorks' profit if both studios take the actions that correspond to that cell. The number after the comma is Disney's profit.

Look at the table and think about where equilibrium might occur in this industry. At first glance, you might expect that, because they could maximize their joint profits by agreeing not to advertise, the studios should just collaborate and earn $225 million each. This is not a Nash equilibrium, however. Here's why: Suppose a studio used this reasoning and actually held off from advertising because it believed its profit would be higher. Once the first studio decides not to advertise, however, the other studio has a strong incentive to advertise. The other studio can now earn far more profit by advertising than by going along with the don't-advertise plan. Recall that Nash equilibrium means that both companies are doing the best they can, *given what the other is doing*. Because one studio can earn a higher profit by advertising when the other doesn't, agreeing not to advertise is not a Nash equilibrium.

To make this concrete, let's say Disney has decided not to advertise. Looking at the profits in Table 11.1, you can see that if DreamWorks goes along, it will earn $225 million in profit. If it instead abandons the agreement and chooses to advertise, however, it will earn $450 million. Clearly, DreamWorks will do the latter. You can also see in the table that it works the other way, too: If DreamWorks chooses not to advertise, Disney does better by advertising (also earning $450 million instead of $225 million).

Therefore, any agreement to hold off from advertising is not stable because both parties have an incentive to cheat on it. Even if one of them sticks to the agreement, the other will earn more profit by backing out of it. Because each studio will earn higher profit by advertising when the other does not, an outcome in which neither studio advertises cannot be a Nash equilibrium. Agreeing not to advertise is not a Nash equilibrium.

Our analysis so far has established that if one studio *doesn't* advertise, the other studio wants to advertise. What is a studio's optimal action if the other studio *does* advertise? The answer may be found in Table 11.1. If Disney advertises, DreamWorks earns $150 million by advertising and loses $75 million by not advertising. A similar situation holds for Disney's best response to DreamWorks. Therefore, advertising is each studio's best response to the other's choice to advertise.

We have just shown that choosing to advertise is a studio's best course of action regardless of whether the other studio advertises or not. Because this is true for both Disney *and* DreamWorks, the only Nash equilibrium in this case is for both studios to advertise. It is stable because each company is doing the best it can given what the other is doing.

Notice that this is true even though it means the studios' profits in the Nash equilibrium will be $150 million each—lower than the $225 million each would earn if they could both hold off from advertising. Situations like these, in which the Nash equilibrium is an outcome that is somehow worse for all involved than another (unstable) outcome, are known as **prisoner's dilemmas** in game theory. We will look at such situations in more detail in the next few sections and in the next chapter. ∎

prisoner's dilemma
A situation in which the Nash equilibrium outcome is worse for all involved than another (unstable) outcome.

11.2 Oligopoly with Identical Goods: Collusion and Cartels

Model Assumptions Collusion and Cartels

- Firms make identical products.
- Industry firms agree to coordinate their quantity and pricing decisions, and no firm deviates from the agreement even if breaking it is in the firm's best self-interest.

In the next several sections, we examine several models of imperfect competition. They give very different answers about the way in which firms make decisions, so it's important to know which model is the right one to use. Each section will have a box that lists the conditions an industry must meet for that model to apply. In the first model, all the firms in an oligopoly coordinate their production and pricing decisions to collectively act as a monopoly would. They then split the monopoly profit among themselves.

This type of oligopoly behavior is known as **collusion** and the organization formed when firms collude is often called a **cartel.** (Sometimes the term "cartel" is reserved for joint monopoly behavior when the firms involved have a public agreement, while "collusion" is used to refer to this behavior when it is done in secret. Both describe the same economic behavior, however.)

If the companies in an oligopoly can successfully collude, figuring out the oligopoly equilibrium is easy. The firms act collectively as a single monopolist would, and the industry equilibrium is the monopoly equilibrium (output is the level for which $MR = MC$ and the price is determined by the demand curve as we saw in Chapter 9).[1] Don't try this at home, though. Cartels and collusion violate the law in most every country of the world, and in the United States, it is a criminal offense that has landed many executives in prison. We discussed in Chapter 9 that governments pass and aggressively enforce antitrust laws because of monopolies' potential to harm consumers. That doesn't mean collusion doesn't happen, but it explains why it's often done in secret. This secrecy can make the instability problem we discuss next—which would exist even if collusion were legal—worse.

cartel or collusion
Oligopoly behavior in which firms coordinate and collectively act as a monopoly to gain monopoly profits.

The Instability of Collusion and Cartels

The firms in an oligopoly would love to collude because they can earn more profit; Adam Smith, the eighteenth-century philosophy professor and one of the fathers of the discipline of economics, recognized this. He wrote in *The Wealth of Nations*, "People of the same trade seldom meet together, even for merriment and diversion, but the conversation ends in a conspiracy against the public, or in some contrivance to raise prices."

But colluding is not easy. It turns out that each member of a cartel has strong incentives not to go along. Although firms in a market might be able to come to some initial agreement over a bargaining table, collusion turns out to be very unstable.

Think about a situation in which there are two firms, Firm A and Firm B, in an industry trying to collude. To keep things simple, suppose both firms have the same constant marginal cost c. If the two firms can act collectively as a monopolist, we can follow the monopoly method from Chapter 9 to figure out the market equilibrium. We know that each firm will operate where marginal revenue equals marginal cost. The problem is that each will want to increase its output at the other's expense.

Suppose the inverse market demand curve for their product is $P = a - bQ$, where P is the price per unit and Q is the quantity produced. We know from Section 9.2 that the marginal revenue curve corresponding to this linear inverse demand curve is $MR = a - 2bQ$. The firms will produce a quantity that sets this equal to their marginal cost c:

$$MR = MC$$
$$a - 2bQ = c$$

Solving this equation for Q gives $Q = (a - c)/2b$. This is the industry's output when its firms collude to act like a monopolist. If we plug this back into the demand curve equation, we find the market price at this quantity: $P = (a + c)/2$.

This is the industry's *total* production in the collusive monopoly outcome. Any combination of the individual firms' outputs that adds to this total will result in the

---

[1] While figuring out the market equilibrium price, total quantity, and total profits in a cartel is easy, it's not always easy (either for economists studying cartels or the firms in the cartels themselves) to determine how the cartel's quantity and profits will be divided among its members. We discuss this later in the section.

monopoly price and profit. Of course, the firms have to decide how to split this profit. A reasonable assumption is that because they both have the same costs, they'll each produce half of the output, $Q/2 = (a - c)/4b$, and split the monopoly profit equally. That's what we assume here. (Later in this section, we discuss why collusion is even more unstable when firms have different costs.)

Cartel Instability: A Mathematical Analysis   To see why collusion is unstable, let's work though an example with specific numbers. Suppose the inverse demand curve is $P = 20 - Q$ and $MC = \$4$. Setting $MR = MC$, as above, the total industry output in a collusive equilibrium will be $Q = 8$ units, and the monopoly price will be $P = \$12$. Assuming that Firms A and B split production evenly, each makes 4 units under collusion. This outcome is shown in Figure 11.1.

Collusion and cartels fall apart for the same reason that Disney and DreamWorks can't agree to stop advertising in our earlier example. It's in each company's interest to expand its output once it knows the other company is restricting output. Each company has the incentive to cheat on the collusive agreement. In other words, collusion is not a Nash equilibrium.

To see why, think about either company's output choice in our example. Will Firm A want to stick with the output of 4 (half the monopoly output of 8) if Firm B agrees to produce 4? If Firm A decides to increase its output to 5 instead of 4, then the total quantity produced would increase to 9. This higher output level lowers the price from $12 to $11 (the demand curve in Figure 11.1, like most demand curves, shows that a higher quantity lowers price).

Once Firm A cheats and increases its output, the industry is no longer at the monopoly quantity and price level, and total industry profit will fall because of overproduction. Total profit drops from $Q \times (P - c) = 8 \times (12 - 4) = \$64$ at the monopoly/cartel level down to $9 \times (11 - 4) = \$63$ after Firm A increases its output on the sly.

Although the profit of the industry as a whole falls, Firm A, the company that violates the agreement, succeeds by earning more. Its profit under collusion was $32 (half of the monopoly profits of $64). But now its profit is higher: $5 \times (11 - 4) = \$35$. The extra sales from increasing production more than make up for the lower prices caused by the increase in production.

Remember that a Nash equilibrium requires each firm to be doing the best it can given what the other firm is doing. This example clearly shows that one firm *can* do

---

Figure 11.1   Cartel Instability

A cartel would like to operate as a monopoly, restricting output to 8 (where $MR = MC$) and selling each unit at a price of $12 for an industry profit of $(\$12 - \$4) \times 8 = \$64$. If production and profit are shared equally between two firms, each firm earns a profit of $(\$12 - \$4) \times 4 = \$32$. However, Firm A may earn a greater profit by cheating on the agreement and producing another unit, which raises total output in the market and lowers price to $11 per unit. At this price and output, Firm A earns a profit of $(\$11 - \$4) \times 5 = \$35$. So, both firms can earn a profit by cheating, and collusion is not stable.

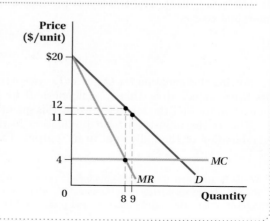

better by violating the collusive agreement if the other firm continues to uphold it, so collusion is not a Nash equilibrium. In fact, the cheating firm can do better still by producing more than 5 units. If one firm sticks to the collusive agreement and makes 4 units, the profit-maximizing output for the other firm is 6 units. At this quantity, the price is $20 - (4 + 6) = \$10$, and the cheating firm's profit is $6 \times (10 - 4) = \$36$. (Test this out for yourself. Notice that the cheating firm's profit only starts to fall if it produces 7 or more units.)

Because both firms face the same incentive—both can do better by cheating if the other one continues to abide by the collusive agreement—collusion is extremely difficult to sustain.

Increasing the Number of Firms in the Cartel   This example was for a two-firm cartel. If there are more firms, the difficulties of holding an agreement together get even worse. When a cartel has many firms, each stands to gain more by cheating on the agreement. Consider the above example again, but now with four firms instead of two. In a collusive agreement, each firm would make 2 units (one-fourth of the total quantity of 8) and earn \$16 (one-fourth of the monopoly profit of \$64). Suppose three of the firms are abiding by the cartel agreement and making 2 units but the fourth decides to cheat and make 3. Price would again fall to \$11. The company that cheated on the agreement would earn a profit of $3 \times (11 - 4) = \$21$. The \$5 increase in profit from cheating here is even larger than the \$3 increase when there were only two firms. Would the cheater want to increase production beyond 3 units? Yes. In fact, if the other firms remain at the collusive output (2 units per firm), the cheater will increase its profit by producing both a 4th and a 5th unit. However, producing a 6th unit would reduce the cheater's profit. (To see this, consider the prices that would occur when total output is 8, 9, and 10 units and calculate the cheating firm's profits at those prices.) Because profit falls when the cheating firm produces 6 units, its profit-maximizing output will be 5 units.

This outcome implies that the profit-maximizing output level for the cheating firm (5 units) is also larger relative to the collusive quantity (2 units per firm) when there are more firms. With two firms, the cheater's profit-maximizing output (6 units) was only 2 units more than the collusive quantity (4 units per firm). With four firms, the cheater's profit-maximizing output (5 units) is 3 units more than the collusive quantity (2 units). Cheating becomes more pervasive (and more rewarding) as the number of firms in the cartel grows.

Besides raising the value to cheating, having more firms in a cartel also reduces the damages suffered by any firm that continues to abide by the collusive agreement. This is because the profit losses caused by the cheating will be spread across more firms. This factor further contributes to the difficulty of maintaining collusion when more firms are involved.

This cheating problem is familiar to cartels everywhere. Each firm in the cartel wants every *other* firm to collude, thereby raising the market price, while it steals away business from everyone else by producing more output, thus lowering the market price. Because every firm in a cartel has this same incentive to cheat, it's difficult to persuade anyone to collude in the first place.

 **application**

OPEC and the Control of Oil

The Organization of Petroleum Exporting Countries (OPEC) is an example of a cartel that has a lot of difficulty coordinating the actions of all 12 of its members to keep the price of its good, oil, high. First of all, OPEC nations wouldn't be monopolists even if they could coordinate their actions, because they don't control

---

Figure 11.2 | OPEC's Actual Production versus Quota

OPEC's member nations regularly produce higher quantities than their agreed upon quotas, a symptom of the cartel's instability.

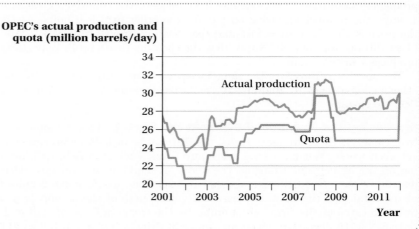

---

all of the world's supply of oil. About half of the world's current oil production and a substantial portion of its proven reserves are in non-OPEC nations.[2] Oil producers in those non-OPEC counties are happy to let OPEC try to collude, because if OPEC is successful, it raises the price at which these other countries can sell their oil, but the non-OPEC countries don't have to abide by the cartel restrictions and can sell as much oil as they like. So right away, there's a problem: OPEC can't keep all of the gains from its collusion.

On top of that, OPEC has trouble keeping itself together because of a cartel's natural instability. The cartel meets monthly to assign production quotas for each member. Frequently, however, the members choose not to abide by the agreement and over-pump oil. And in this case, "frequently" more or less means all the time. Figure 11.2 shows OPEC's production quota agreements compared to its actual production during the 2001–2012 period.[3] Actual production never matches the agreed upon numbers. Member countries always pump more, just as economics tells you will happen. Each member has a great temptation to overproduce given the cartel setup. The exception to this outcome is Saudi Arabia, which often produces *less* than its allocation from the collusive agreement (at a considerable cost to Saudi profit) to keep some semblance of collusive discipline. Otherwise, OPEC might completely disintegrate into a free-for-all production frenzy.

So next time you pay $60 to fill your gas tank, go ahead and get mad! But don't just blame it on OPEC. They don't have their act together often enough to actually make your gas prices high. ■

---

[2] See http://www.nationmaster.com/graph/ene_oil_res-energy-oil-reserves
and http://www.nationmaster.com/graph/ene_oil_pro-energy-oil-production for details.

[3] OPEC's actual production data are from the U.S. Energy Information Administration's *International Petroleum Monthly*. Quota data are taken from the OPEC Statistical Bulletin. Both series have been adjusted to remove Iraq (which OPEC exempted from quotas during the period) as well as the entry of Ecuador and Angola into OPEC in 2008, and Indonesia's departure in 2009.

Suppose that Squeaky Clean and Biobase are the only two producers of chlorine for swimming pools. The inverse market demand for chlorine is $P = 32 - 2Q$, where Q is measured in tons and P is dollars per ton. Assume that chlorine can be produced by either firm at a constant marginal cost of $16 per ton and there are no fixed costs.

    a. If the two firms collude and act like a monopoly, agreeing to evenly split the market, how much will each firm produce and what will the price of a ton of chlorine be? How much profit will each firm earn?

    b. Does Squeaky Clean have an incentive to cheat on this agreement by producing an additional ton of chlorine? Explain.

    c. Does Squeaky Clean's decision to cheat affect Biobase's profit? Explain.

    d. Suppose that both firms agree to each produce 1 ton more than they were producing in part (a). How much profit will each firm earn? Does Squeaky Clean now have an incentive to cheat on this agreement by producing another ton of chlorine? Explain.

Solution:

    a. If the firms agree to act like a monopoly, they will set $MR = MC$ to solve for the profit-maximizing output:

$$MR = MC$$
$$32 - 4Q = 16$$
$$4Q = 16$$

$Q = 4$ and each firm will produce 2 tons. To find the price, we substitute the market quantity ($Q = 4$) into the inverse demand equation:

$$P = 32 - 2Q = 32 - 2(4) = \$24 \text{ per ton}$$

Each firm will earn a profit of ($24 – $16) × 2 = $16.

    b. If Squeaky Clean cheats and produces 3 tons, Q rises to 5 and price falls to $22. Squeaky Clean's profit will be equal to ($22 – $16) × 3 = $18. Therefore, Squeaky Clean does have an incentive to cheat on the agreement because its profit would rise.

    c. If Squeaky Clean cheats, the price in the market falls to $22. This reduces Biobase's profit, which is now ($22 – $16) × 2 = $12.

    d. If both firms agree to limit production to 3 tons, $Q = 6$ and $P = \$20$. Therefore, each firm earns a profit of ($20 – $16) × 3 = $12. If Squeaky Clean tries to produce 4 tons of chlorine, Q rises to 7 and P falls to $18. Therefore, Squeaky Clean's profit will be ($18 – $16) × 4 = $8. Thus, Squeaky Clean does not have an incentive to cheat on this agreement because its profit would fall.

What Makes Collusion Easier?

Although collusion isn't an especially stable form of oligopoly, there are some conditions that make it more likely to succeed.

    The first thing an aspiring cartel needs is a way to detect and punish cheaters. We just saw that companies in a cartel have the private incentive to produce more output (or charge a lower price) than the collusive level. If the other firms in a cartel have no way of knowing when a member cheats—and no form of punishment to inflict when they discover someone is cheating—there is zero chance that any agreement will hold. That's why collusion is more likely to work when firms can closely observe the transaction quantities and prices of other firms. Such transparency limits the ability of potential cheaters to cut secret, lower-price deals with customers. If a firm cheats, the cartel needs to have some way to enforce the agreement or punish the cheater. Because collusion is generally illegal, the cartel can't really take the cheaters to court but it might be able to take other actions that reduce the profits of firms that stray from the agreement, such as shutting them out of a share of future cartel profits.

Second, a cartel may find it easier to succeed if there is little variation in marginal costs across its members. To maximize profit, a monopoly (or a cartel trying to act like a monopoly) wants to use the lowest-cost production method. This desire complicates any scheme to share the monopoly profit among the cartel members and leaves open more opportunities to cheat. Within OPEC, for example, Saudi Arabia can pump its oil out of the ground for about $4 a barrel, while in Nigeria it costs about $20 per barrel to do so. How can OPEC explain to Nigeria that the most efficient production strategy would be to sell only Saudi Arabian oil and none from Nigeria?

Third, cartels are more stable when firms take the long view and care more about the future. Think of staying in a cartel (i.e., choosing not to cheat on a collusive agreement) as trading off a short-term opportunity cost to earn a long-term gain. The short-term opportunity cost is giving up the higher profit a firm could obtain by cheating on the agreement. The long-term benefit is that, if the cartel can avoid dissolving into competition, it stands to make monopoly profits. The more the firm values those future monopoly profits relative to the quick hit of additional profit from cheating, the more they will abide by the collusive agreement. Impatient companies, like those in danger of bankruptcy and therefore in desperate need of profit today, are more likely to cheat.

 **application**

The Indianapolis Concrete Cartel

In 2006 and 2007 the U.S. Department of Justice busted up a long-lived ready-mixed concrete cartel in the Indianapolis Metro and Southwest Indiana areas. The case ended up being one of the largest domestic price-fixing prosecutions in the history of the United States. Millions of dollars in fines were levied, and ten executives were given prison sentences.[4]

The Indianapolis cartel struggled with instability issues. Despite the fact that price-fixing conversations had gone on "for as long as anyone could remember," the cartel members were constantly dealing with cheating by members and struggling for ways to punish firms that deviated from agreements. They also had to figure out how to handle a financially struggling firm that was desperate for revenue and perhaps willing to slash prices to get it.

The group held regular meetings at local restaurants or hotels (paying cash for conference rooms to avoid leaving a paper trail) to try to adjust the agreement to current market conditions. Executives monitored agreements by anonymously gathering price quotes from their competitors over the phone. If a violation occurred, the cartel would issue threats, though it's unclear exactly what was threatened and how many threats were actually carried out. If violations were widespread enough, the ringleaders would call an emergency meeting at the local Cracker Barrel restaurant.

These efforts met with mixed success. Sometimes cheating would overwhelm their effort to hold to an agreement. Firms were reluctant to give up the customers they had gained by undercutting the other cartel members. Still, the cartel was on occasion able to maintain enough discipline to inflate prices by an amount estimated to be as much as 17% above their noncollusive level.

Everything began to fall apart when the cartel tried to deal too aggressively with a noncooperative manager from a firm that was not part of the cartel. After repeated attempts to cajole the manager into joining the scheme, the cartel members started

[4] Much of the material for this box was taken from: Kevin Corcoran, "The Big Fix," *The Indianapolis Star*, (May 6, 2007): A1, A22-A23.

complaining about various aspects of his performance to his corporate bosses. Feeling backed into a corner, the manager went to the FBI and informed them of the cartel's operations. By the time criminal proceedings ended a few years later, many careers had been destroyed and several of the cartel companies had been liquidated or bought out. ■

freakonomics

How the Government Lost the Fight against Big Tobacco

Things were looking grim for tobacco companies in 1997. The Big Four—an oligopoly consisting of Philip Morris, Reynolds, Brown and Williamson, and Lorillard—were in serious financial trouble. Smoking had been in decline for decades. Even more worrisome were the many health-based lawsuits that had been brought against the companies. Philip Morris, home of the Marlboro Man, alone faced over 500 litigation cases. All four companies were on thin financial ice.

So you would think that when the government started to threaten further legislation on cigarette sales, the companies would have been frightened. Instead, tobacco executives secretly licked their chops. They were fairly sure they could trick government officials into helping, not hurting, them. Turns out that in some ways the executives were right.

After prolonged negotiations, state governments and the tobacco companies signed what became known as the Tobacco Settlement. The final deal involved a $368.5 billion payment from tobacco companies to the states over twenty-five years, seemingly a huge blow to the tobacco companies.

In reality, however, the tobacco companies didn't pay for the settlement. Smokers did. The revenue from the settlement came in the form of a per-pack cigarette tax. But as we know from our discussion of tax incidence in Chapter 3, when consumer demand is very inelastic (as is likely the case with an addictive good like cigarettes), the consumers bear most of the tax. In addition, the settlement gave companies protection from future litigation.

On top of all these goodies, the settlement included features that helped the tobacco companies solidify their status as a tight-knit oligopoly and, arguably, made it easier for them to collude on prices. For example, the settlement created enormous barriers for new entrants seeking to enter into the market and effectively guaranteed existing Big Four tobacco companies a minimum market share over a wide range of possible market prices. Both of these features reduced competition overall in the market, making it easier for the Big Four to raise their prices without fear of losing market share.

So what could the government have done? Jeremy Bulow and Paul Klemperer, two economists who closely documented the tobacco settlement saga, had a novel suggestion for the government: Buy out the companies and run the cigarette industry itself.[5] Their argument was that this would have been cheaper than the settlement proved to be and would have given the government the freedom to run the tobacco industry the way it wanted. But would a buyout lessen the impact of the government's anti-smoking campaigns, causing many to turn again to smoking? Not according to Bulow and Klemperer, who write, "If there is one thing government monopolies are traditionally good at, . . . it is deglamorizing their products and making them as consumer-unfriendly as possible."

---

[5] Jeremy Bulow and Paul Klemperer, "The Tobacco Deal," *Brookings Papers on Economic Activity* (1998): 323–394.

11.3 Oligopoly with Identical Goods: Bertrand Competition

> **Model Assumptions** Bertrand Competition with Identical Goods
> - Firms sell identical products
> - The firms compete by choosing the price at which they sell their products.
> - The firms set their prices simultaneously.

In the previous section, we learned that the collusion/cartel model of oligopoly in which firms behave like a monopoly is unlikely to hold in reality. If firms don't (or can't) cooperate to act as a single monopolist would, we need a model in which they compete directly against one another. The first such model is as simple as it gets: Firms sell the same product, and consumers compare prices and buy the product with the lowest price. Economists call this structure **Bertrand competition,** after Joseph Bertrand, the nineteenth-century French mathematician and economist who first wrote about it. When firms are selling identical products, as we're assuming here, Bertrand oligopoly has a particularly simple equilibrium and it's just like perfect competition. Later in the chapter, we see how things change if firms sell products that are not identical.

Bertrand competition
Oligopoly model in which each firm chooses the price of its product.

Setting Up the Bertrand Model

To set up this model, let's suppose there is a market with only two companies in it. They sell the same product and have the same marginal cost. For example, suppose there are only two stores in a city, a Walmart and a Target, and these stores are located next to one another. They both sell Sony PlayStations. Each firm's marginal cost is $150 per console. This includes the wholesale price the firm has to pay Sony as well as miscellaneous selling costs such as stocking the consoles on shelves, checking customers out, and so on.

We make one further assumption: Consumers don't view either store differently in terms of service, atmosphere, and the like. This assumption isn't completely realistic, but it preserves our assumption that the firms are selling the same product. If consumers did value these things separately from the video games, then in a way the products would no longer be identical and we would need to model the firms' behavior using the model of differentiated products discussed later in the chapter.

With only two companies in a market, it might seem as if there would be a lot of market power and high markups over cost. But suppose the customers in this market have a simple demand rule: They buy the PlayStation from the store that sells it at the lowest price. If both stores charge the same price, consumers flip a coin to determine where they buy. This rule means, in effect, that the store charging the lower price will get all the demand for PlayStations in the market. If both stores charge the same price, each store gets half of the demand.

Suppose the total demand in the market is for Q consoles. Let's denote Walmart's price as P_W and Target's price P_T. The two stores then face the following demand curves:

Demand for PlayStations at Walmart:

$$Q, \quad \text{if } P_W < P_T$$

$$\frac{Q}{2}, \quad \text{if } P_W = P_T$$

$$0, \quad \text{if } P_W > P_T.$$

Demand for PlayStations at Target:

$$Q, \quad \text{if } P_T < P_W$$

$$\frac{Q}{2}, \quad \text{if } P_T = P_W$$

$$0, \quad \text{if } P_T > P_W.$$

Each store chooses its price to maximize its profit, realizing that it will sell the number of units according to the demand curves above. We've assumed the total number of consoles sold, Q, doesn't depend on the price charged. The price only affects which store people buy from. (We could alternatively have allowed Q to depend on the lowest price charged; all of the key results discussed below would remain the same.)

Nash Equilibrium of a Bertrand Oligopoly

Remember that in a Nash equilibrium, each firm is doing the best it can given whatever the other firm is doing. So to find the equilibrium of this Bertrand model, let's first think about Target's best response to Walmart's actions. (We could do this in the other order if we wanted.) If Target believes Walmart will charge a price P_W for PlayStations, Target will sell nothing if it sets its price above P_W, so we can probably rule that out as a profit-maximizing strategy. Target is left with two options: Match Walmart's price and sell $Q/2$ units, or undercut Walmart and sell Q. Because all it has to do is undercut Walmart by *any* amount, dropping its price just below P_W will only reduce its per-unit margin by a tiny amount, but the store will double its sales because it will take the whole market.

As an example, suppose $Q = 1,000$ and Target thinks Walmart will charge $P_W = \$175$. If Target also charges $P_T = \$175$, it will sell 500 PlayStations at a profit of \$25 each (the \$175 price minus the \$150 marginal cost). That's a total profit of \$12,500. But if Target charges \$174.99, it will sell 1,000 PlayStations at a profit of \$24.99 each. This is a profit of \$24,990—almost double what it was at \$175. Target has a strong incentive to undercut Walmart's expected price.

Of course, things are the same from Walmart's perspective: It has the same incentive to undercut whatever price it thinks Target will choose. If it believes Target is going to charge $P_T = \$174.99$ for a PlayStation, Walmart could price its consoles at \$174.98 and gain back the entire market. But then Target would have the incentive to undercut *this* expected price, and so on.

This incentive for undercutting would only stop once the price each store expects the other to charge falls to the level of the stores' marginal costs (\$150). At that point, cutting prices further would let a store gain the entire market, but that store would be selling every PlayStation at a loss (try to make that up on increased volume!).

The equilibrium of this Bertrand oligopoly occurs when each store charges a price equal to its marginal cost—\$150 in this example. Each obtains half of the market share, and each store earns zero economic profit. The stores would like to make more, but if either firm raises its price above marginal cost by even the smallest amount, the other firm has a strong incentive to undercut it. And dropping prices below marginal cost would only cause the stores to suffer losses. So the outcome isn't the most preferable outcome for the firms, but neither firm can do better by unilaterally changing its price. This is the definition of a Nash equilibrium.

In the identical-good Bertrand oligopoly, one firm cannot increase its profit by raising its price *if* the other firm still charges a price equal to its marginal cost. If the firms could somehow figure out a way to coordinate changes in their actions so that they both raised prices together, they would raise their profits. However, the problem with this strategy, as we saw earlier, is that collusion is unstable. Once the firms are charging prices above marginal cost, a firm can raise its profits by unilaterally changing its action and lowering its price just slightly.

The Bertrand model of oligopoly shows you that even with a small number of firms, competition can still be extremely intense. *In fact, the market outcome of Bertrand competition with identical goods is the same as that in a perfectly competitive market: Price equals marginal cost.* This super-competitiveness occurs because either firm can steal the whole market away from the other by dropping price only slightly. The strong incentive to undercut the price leads both firms to drop their prices to marginal cost.

This example had only two firms, but the result would be the same if there were more. The intuition is the same: Every firm's price-cutting motive is so strong that the only equilibrium is for them to all charge a price equal to marginal cost, leading them to split the market evenly.[6]

theory and data

Computer Parts I

Bertrand markets with identical goods turn out to have a simple equilibrium solution, but the conditions present in the model are rare in the real world. One actual market that comes fairly close to these conditions is an online market for computer chips, which was the focus of the study by Glenn Ellison and Sara Ellison that we discussed briefly in Chapter 2.* In this market, high-tech customers who like to build their own computers shop for CPUs and memory chips using an online price search engine that tracks down and lists the products of various electronic parts retailers. The photo shows an example of the array of options available to a customer shopping in this market for a particular CPU.

The search engine lists choices by ascending price. A search for this particular CPU at this site yields 20 pages of listings. But as you can see, the chips are all similar. Chances are if you were a buyer, you probably aren't going to bother going through each and every page. These are basically identical products.

In addition, in this market, most consumers seem to simply buy the cheapest product available, just as in the Bertrand model. As we discussed in Chapter 2, Ellison and Ellison measured the price elasticity of demand for chips like these to be around −25, so pricing just 1% above its competitors decreases a company's sales by 25%.

Demand this responsive to changes in prices is fairly close to what we just described for a Bertrand oligopoly with identical products. Even a small price cut below that of a competitor will

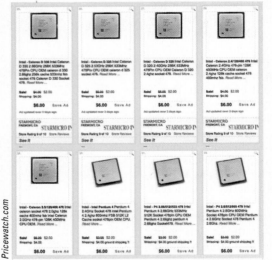

An online search engine lists an array of CPUs from various retailers at different prices.

Pricewatch.com

---

* Glenn Ellison and Sara Ellison, "Search, Obfuscation, and Price Elasticities on the Internet," *Econometrica* 77, no. 2, (2009): 427-452.

[6] This again assumes all firms in the market have the same marginal cost. If firms have different marginal costs in an identical-product Bertrand oligopoly, then the equilibrium is for the lowest-cost firm (or firms, if there are more than one with the same, lowest-in-market costs) to charge a price just under the *second-lowest* cost in the market. At any price higher than that, the lowest-cost firm(s) will have to split the demand with other firms without holding any pricing advantage (the other firms can now undercut). But there's no reason to charge any less than that amount, either. It would only reduce profit without resulting in any additional sales. Therefore in equilibrium, the lowest-cost firm(s) sell(s) at a price just below the second-lowest cost level, split demand (if more than one firm has this lowest cost), and earn(s) positive profit because it (they, if more than one) earn(s) a profit margin on every sale.

bring in a large number of extra sales. At the same time, though, pricing higher than another firm will result in the firm losing a lot of sales.

  The identical-product Bertrand model predicts that this price elasticity of demand will lead to an equilibrium where firms charge a price equal to their marginal cost. This outcome is close to what Ellison and Ellison found in the computer parts market they studied. First, prices didn't vary too much across retailers. Second, after collecting a significant amount of information to estimate the CPU retailers' marginal costs, Ellison and Ellison determined that the lowest-priced products were being sold at prices that approximately equaled the retailers' marginal costs.

11.4 Oligopoly with Identical Goods: Cournot Competition

Model Assumptions Cournot Competition with Identical Goods

- Firms sell identical products.
- Firms compete by choosing a quantity to produce.
- All goods sell for the same price—the market price, which is determined by the sum of the quantities produced by all the firms in the market.
- Firms choose quantities simultaneously.

When firms sell identical goods, the Bertrand competition model results in the same equilibrium that we find in a perfectly competitive market, where price equals marginal cost. Because consumers care only about the price of the good (since the product is identical across firms), each firm faces a demand that is perfectly elastic. Any increase in a firm's price results in it losing all of its market share. The demand for the product will go to the firm offering the lowest price.

  But what if firms face capacity constraints, and thus a limit on how much demand they can fill in the short run? With this restriction, if a firm undercuts another's price, it can only steal as many customers as it has available capacity and this capacity is probably not the size of the whole market.

  In this model, there won't be as much pressure for a firm to respond to price cuts because each firm will not lose all of its customers even if it keeps its price higher than that of a competitor. In fact, if the capacity of the low-price company is small enough, its competitor may not feel the need to cut prices much at all. This avoids the price-cutting spiral we saw in the Bertrand model.

  In this situation, the critical issue is for a firm to determine how much capacity it has and thus what quantity it can produce.

Setting Up the Cournot Model

We raise the idea of capacity constraints to motivate another major oligopoly model, **Cournot competition** (named after its first modeler, Augustin Cournot—yet another nineteenth-century French mathematician and economist).

  In Cournot competition, firms produce identical goods and choose a quantity to produce rather than a price at which to sell the good. Individual firms do not control the price of their goods as they do in the Bertrand model. First, all firms in the industry decide how much they will produce; then based on the quantity produced by all firms, the market demand curve determines the price at which all firms' output will sell. In Chapter 9, we learned that when dealing with a monopolist, the price-quantity outcome is the same whether a firm sets the price of its product or the number of units of output

Cournot competition
Oligopoly model in which each firm chooses its production quantity.

it produces. In an oligopoly, however, the market outcome differs depending on whether the firm chooses to set its price or its quantity.

To be more specific, let's say there are two firms in a Cournot oligopoly, Firm 1 and Firm 2. (There can be more; we keep it at two to simplify our analysis.) Each has a constant marginal cost of c, and both firms independently and simultaneously choose their production quantities q_1 and q_2. The good's inverse demand curve is

$$P = a - bQ$$

where Q is the *total* quantity produced in the market. Therefore, $Q = q_1 + q_2$.

Firm 1's profit π_1 is the quantity q_1 it produces times the difference between the market price P and its production costs c, or

$$\pi_1 = q_1 \times (P - c)$$

Substituting the inverse demand equation for P, we find that

$$\pi_1 = q_1 \times [a - b(q_1 + q_2) - c]$$

Similarly, Firm 2's profits are given by the equation

$$\pi_2 = q_2 \times [a - b(q_1 + q_2) - c]$$

These two profit equations make clear that the firms in this oligopoly strategically interact. Firm 1's profit is not just a function of its own quantity choice q_1, but also of its competitor's quantity q_2. Likewise, Firm 2's profit is affected by Firm 1's output choice. The logic is that each firm's production choice, through its influence on the market price P, affects the other firm's profit.

An example of an industry that is like the Cournot model is the crude oil industry. Crude oil is a commodity; consumers are indifferent about oil from different sources. The price of oil is set on a worldwide market, and it depends on the total amount of oil supplied at a given time. Therefore, it's realistic to assume that oil producers, even those such as Saudi Arabia or Iran with large oil reserves, do not choose the price of their outputs. They just choose how much to produce. (As we discussed beforehand, OPEC chooses production quantity targets, not prices.) Oil traders observe these production decisions for all oil producers, and they bid oil's market price up or down depending on how the total quantity produced (the market supply) compares to current demand. This price-setting process derives from the demand curve that connects total output to a market price.

Equilibrium in a Cournot Oligopoly

Finding the equilibrium for a Cournot oligopoly will be easier to follow using an example. Suppose for simplicity that only two countries pump oil, Saudi Arabia and Iran. Both have a marginal cost of production of $20 per barrel. Also assume that the inverse demand curve for oil is $P = 200 - 3Q$, where P is in dollars per barrel and Q is in millions of barrels per day.

Finding the equilibrium for the Cournot model is similar to doing so for a monopoly, but with the one change noted above: The market quantity Q is the sum of the quantities produced in Saudi Arabia q_S and Iran q_I, rather than just the monopolist's output: $Q = q_S + q_I$. After recognizing this difference, we follow the same steps we used to solve for a monopoly's profit-maximizing output. That is, we find each country's marginal revenue curve, and then find the quantity at which marginal revenue equals marginal cost.

Let's examine Saudi Arabia's profit maximization first. As we learned in Section 9.2, we can more easily find a firm's marginal revenue curve by starting with its inverse demand curve. Therefore, we start by writing the inverse demand curve equation in terms of the quantity choices of each country:

$$P = 200 - 3Q = 200 - 3(q_S + q_I) = 200 - 3q_S - 3q_I$$

Because the slope of the marginal revenue curve is twice the slope of the inverse demand function, Saudi Arabia's marginal revenue curve is[7]

$$MR = 200 - 6q_S - 3q_I$$

Saudi Arabia maximizes profit when it produces the quantity at which its marginal revenue equals its marginal cost:

$$200 - 6q_S - 3q_I = 20$$

We can solve this equation for Saudi Arabia's profit-maximizing output:

$$q_S = 30 - 0.5q_I$$

This outcome differs from the monopoly outcome: If Saudi Arabia were a monopoly, setting marginal revenue equal to marginal cost would result in a single quantity Q because its quantity supplied q_S would be the market quantity supplied Q. In this example, however, Saudi Arabia's profit-maximizing output depends on the competitor's output q_I. Similarly, Iran's profit-maximizing q_I depends on q_S because it faces the same market demand curve and has the same marginal cost:

$$q_I = 30 - 0.5q_S$$

This result shows that one country's output choice effectively decreases the demand for the other country's output. That is, the demand curve for one country's output is shifted in by the amount of the other country's output. If the Saudis expect Iran to produce, say, 10 million barrels per day (bpd), then Saudi Arabia would effectively be facing the demand curve

$$P = 200 - 3q_S - 3q_I = 200 - 3q_S - 3(10) = 170 - 3q_S$$

If it expected Iran to pump out 20 million bpd, Saudi Arabia would face the demand curve

$$P = 200 - 3q_S - 3(20) = 140 - 3q_S$$

This demand that is left over to one country (or more generally, firm), taking the other country's output choice as given, is called the **residual demand curve.** We just derived Saudi Arabia's residual demand curves for two of Iran's different production choices, 10 and 20 million bpd.

In effect, a firm in a Cournot oligopoly acts like a monopolist, but one that faces its residual demand curve rather than the market demand curve. The residual demand curve, like any regular demand curve, has a corresponding marginal revenue curve (it's called . . . wait for it . . . the **residual marginal revenue curve**). The firm produces the quantity at which its residual marginal revenue equals its marginal cost. That's why Saudi Arabia's optimal quantity is the one that sets $200 - 6q_S - 3q_I = 20$. The left-hand side of this equation is Saudi Arabia's residual marginal revenue (expressed in terms of any expected Iranian output level q_I). The right-hand side is its marginal cost.

How does the profit-maximizing output of one country change with the other country's expected production? In other words, what role do strategic interactions play in a Cournot oligopoly? This can be seen in Figure 11.3, which shows Saudi Arabia's residual demand, residual marginal revenue, and marginal cost curves. (The Iranian case would be the same, just with the two countries' labels switched.) The residual demand RD_S^1 and residual marginal revenue RMR_S^1 curves correspond to an Iranian output level of 10 million bpd. In other words, if Saudi Arabia expects Iran to produce 10 million bpd, Saudi Arabia's optimal output quantity is 25 million bpd. If it expects Iran to produce 30 million bpd, Saudi Arabia's residual demand and marginal revenue curves shift in

residual demand curve
In Cournot competition, the demand remaining for a firm's output given competitor firms' production quantities.

residual marginal revenue curve
A marginal revenue curve corresponding to a residual demand curve.

---

[7] The inverse demand curve for Saudi Arabia is plotted in a diagram with quantity, q_S, on the horizontal axis and price on the vertical axis. The slope is $\Delta P/\Delta q_S = 3$. This means that only the coefficient on q_S is used to determine the slope of the marginal revenue curve. The slope of the marginal revenue curve is $\Delta MR/\Delta q_S = 6$.

Figure 11.3   Optimal Quantity Choices

Saudi Arabia's optimal production quantity is dependent on Iran's production quantity. If the Iranian output level is 10 million bpd, Saudi Arabia's optimal output is 25 million bpd, where its residual marginal revenue curve intersects its marginal cost. If Iranian output increases to 30 million bpd, Saudi Arabia's residual demand and residual marginal revenue curves shift to RD_S^2 and RMR_S^2. As a result, Saudi Arabia's optimum output decreases to 15 million bpd.

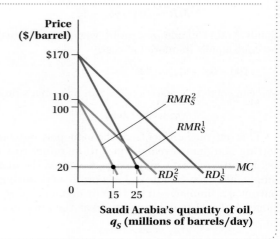

---

to RD_S^2 and RMR_S^2, to $P = 110 - 3q_S$ and $MR = 110 - 6q_S$, respectively. The Saudis' optimal quantity then falls to 15 million bpd. At Iranian output levels higher than 30 million bpd, Saudi Arabia's residual demand and marginal revenue curves would shift in further and its optimal quantity would fall.

It's clear that each competitor's profit-maximizing output depends on the other's, and in an opposite direction: If a firm expects its competitor to produce more, it should reduce its production. Although this kind of interaction seems to create a hopeless chicken-and-egg problem, we can still pin down the specific production quantities for each country if we return to the concept of Nash equilibrium: Each producer does the best it can, taking the other producer's action as given.

To see what that implies for a Cournot oligopoly, note that the equation for each country's profit-maximizing output is described given the particular output choice of the other country. The equation for q_S gives Saudi Arabia's best response to any production level q_I that Iran might choose. Likewise, the q_I equation gives Iran's best response to any Saudi production decision. In other words, when both equations hold simultaneously, each country is doing the best it can given the other country's action. So, the Nash equilibrium is the combination of outputs that make both equations hold.

Cournot Equilibrium: A Graphical Approach   We can show this graphically in Figure 11.4. Saudi Arabia's output is on the vertical axis and Iran's output is on the horizontal axis. The curves illustrated are **reaction curves.** A reaction curve shows the best production response a country (or firm, in a more general oligopoly context) can make given the other country's/firm's action. Because both reaction curves are downward-sloping, a firm's optimal output falls as the other producer's output rises.

Reaction curve SA shows Saudi Arabia's best response to any production choice of Iran—it shows the points at which $q_S = 30 - 0.5q_I$. If it expects Iran to produce no oil ($q_I = 0$), for example, the profit-maximizing Saudi response is to produce $q_S = 30$ million bpd. This combination is at point A. The optimal q_S falls as Iranian production rises. If Iran produces $q_I = 10$, then Saudi Arabia maximizes its profit by producing $q_S = 30 - 0.5(10) = 25$ million bpd (point B). If $q_I = 30$, then the optimal q_S is 15 million bpd (point C). Saudi Arabia's optimal production continues to fall as Iran's production rises until it hits zero at $q_I = 60$ million bpd (point D). At any q_I greater than 60 million bpd, the market price is below \$20 per barrel (see the demand curve). Because this price is below the marginal cost of production, it wouldn't be profitable for Saudi Arabia to pump any oil if Iran produced 60 million bpd.

reaction curve
A function that relates a firm's best response to its competitor's possible actions. In Cournot competition, this is the firm's best production response to its competitor's possible quantity choices.

Figure 11.4   **Reaction Curves and Cournot Equilibrium**

A reaction curve represents a firm's optimal production response given its competitor's production quantity. SA and I are the reaction curves for Saudi Arabia and Iran, respectively. At point E, where Iran and Saudi Arabia each produce 20 bpd ($q_I = q_S = 20$), the market has reached a Nash equilibrium. Here, the two countries are simultaneously producing optimally given the other's actions.

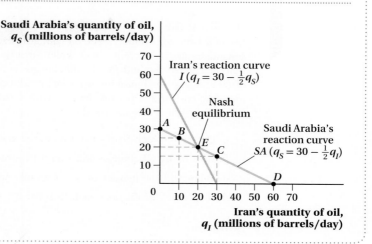

Line I is the corresponding reaction curve for Iran's profit-maximizing quantity $q_I = 30 - 0.5q_S$. It's essentially the same as SA, except with the axes flipped. Just as Saudi Arabia's profit-maximizing output falls with Iran's production choice, Iran's optimal production decreases with expected Saudi production q_S. The optimal q_I is 30 million bpd if $q_S = 0$, and it falls toward 0 as q_S rises toward 60 million bpd.

Each country realizes that its actions affect the desired actions of its competitor, which in turn affect its own optimal action, and so on. This back-and-forth strategic interaction is captured in firms' reaction curves, and is why the equilibrium is found where reaction curves intersect. The intersection of the two reaction curves at point E shows the quantities at which both competitors are simultaneously producing optimally given the other's actions. That is, point E is the Nash equilibrium of the Cournot oligopoly—the mutual best response. If one country is producing at point E, the other country would only reduce its profits by unilaterally producing at some other point. At this equilibrium, each country produces 20 million bpd, and total output is 40 million bpd.

Cournot Equilibrium: A Mathematical Approach   In addition to finding the Cournot equilibrium graphically, we can solve for it algebraically by solving for the output levels that equate the two reaction curves. One way to do this is to substitute one equation into the other to get rid of one quantity variable and solve for the remaining one. For example, if we substitute Iran's reaction curve into Saudi Arabia's reaction curve for q_I, we find

$$q_S = 30 - 0.5q_I = 30 - 0.5(30 - 0.5q_S)$$
$$= 30 - 15 + 0.25q_S$$
$$0.75q_S = 15$$
$$q_S = 20$$

∂ The online appendix finds the equilibrium for Cournot competition using calculus. (http://glsmicro.com/appendices)

Thus, the equilibrium output for Saudi Arabia is 20 million bpd. If we substitute this value back into Iran's reaction curve, we find that $q_I = 30 - 0.5q_S = 30 - 0.5(20) = 20$. Iran's optimal production is also 20 million bpd. Equilibrium point E in Figure 11.4 has the coordinates (20, 20), and total industry output is 40 million bpd.

The equilibrium price of oil at this point can be found by plugging these production decisions into the inverse market demand curve. Doing so gives $P = 200 - 3(q_S + q_I) = 200 - 3(20 + 20) = \$80$ per barrel. Each country's profit is 20 million bpd × ($80 - $20) = $1,200 million = $1.2 billion per day, so the industry's total profit is $2.4 billion per day.

11.2 figure it out

OilPro and GreaseTech are the only two firms who provide oil changes in a local market in a Cournot duopoly. The oil changes performed by the two firms are identical, and consumers are indifferent about which firm they will purchase an oil change from. The market inverse demand for the oil changes is $P = 100 - 2Q$, where Q is the total number of oil changes (in thousands per year) produced by the two firms, $q_O + q_G$. OilPro has a marginal cost of $12 per oil change, while GreaseTech has a marginal cost of $20. Assume that neither firm has any fixed cost.

    a. Determine each firm's reaction curve and graph it.

    b. How many oil changes will each firm produce in Cournot equilibrium?

    c. What will the market price for an oil change be?

    d. How much profit does each firm earn?

Solution:

a. Start by substituting $Q = q_O + q_G$ into the market inverse demand curve:
$$P = 100 - 2Q = 100 - 2(q_O + q_G) = 100 - 2q_O - 2q_G$$

From this inverse demand cure, we can derive each firm's marginal revenue curve:
$$MR_O = 100 - 4q_O - 2q_G$$
$$MR_G = 100 - 2q_O - 4q_G$$

Each firm will set its marginal revenue equal to its marginal cost to maximize profit. From this, we can obtain each firm's reaction curve:
$$MR_O = 100 - 4q_O - 2q_G = 12$$
$$4q_O = 88 - 2q_G$$
$$q_O = 22 - 0.5q_G$$
$$MR_G = 100 - 2q_O - 4q_G = 20$$
$$4q_G = 80 - 2q_O$$
$$q_G = 20 - 0.5q_O$$

These reaction curves are shown in the figure below.

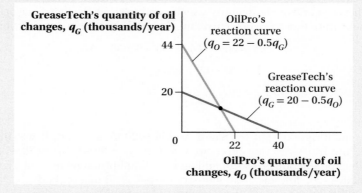

b. To solve for equilibrium, we need to substitute one firm's reaction curve into the reaction curve for the other firm:

$$q_O = 22 - 0.5q_G$$
$$q_O = 22 - 0.5(20 - 0.5q_O) = 22 - 10 + 0.25q_O = 12 + 0.25q_O$$
$$0.75q_O = 12$$
$$q_O = 16$$
$$q_G = 20 - 0.5q_O = 20 - 0.5(16) = 20 - 8 = 12$$

Therefore, OilPro produces 16,000 oil changes per year, while GreaseTech produces 12,000.

c. We can use the market inverse demand curve to determine the market price:

$$P = 100 - 2Q = 100 - 2(q_O + q_G) = 100 - 2(16 + 12) = 100 - 56 = 44$$

The price will be $44 per oil change.

d. OilPro sells 16,000 oil changes at a price of $44 for a total revenue $TR = $ 16,000 × $44 = $704,000. Total cost $TC = $ 16,000 × $12 = $192,000. Therefore, profit for OilPro is $\pi = $ $704,000 − $192,000 = $512,000.

GreaseTech sells 12,000 oil changes at a price of $44 for a total revenue of $TR = $ 12,000 × $44 = $528,000. Total cost $TC = $ 12,000 × $20 = $240,000. Thus, GreaseTech's profit is $\pi = $ $528,000 − $240,000 = $288,000.

Note that the firm with the lower marginal cost produces more output and earns a greater profit.

Comparing Cournot to Collusion and to Bertrand Oligopoly

Let's compare this equilibrium in a Cournot oligopoly ($Q = 40$ million bpd at $P = \$80$) and profit ($2.4 billion per day) to the outcomes in other oligopoly models we've analyzed. These results are described in Table 11.2.

Collusion   Let's first suppose Saudi Arabia and Iran can actually get their acts together and collude to act like a monopolist. In that case, they would treat their separate production decisions q_I and q_S as a single total output $Q = q_S + q_I$. Following the normal marginal-revenue-equals-marginal-cost procedure, we would find that $Q = 30$ million bpd. Presumably, the two countries would split this output evenly at 15 million bpd because they have the same marginal costs. This is less

Table 11.2   **Comparing Equilibria across Oligopolies**

Oligopoly Structure	Total Output (million bpd)	Price ($ per barrel)	Industry Profit (per day)
Collusion	30	$110	$2.7 billion
Bertrand (identical products)	60	20	0
Cournot	40	80	2.4 billion

than the total Cournot oligopoly production of 40 million bpd that we just derived. Furthermore, because monopoly production is lower, the price is higher, too: Plugging this monopoly quantity into the demand curve, price becomes $P = 200 - 3(30) = \$110$ per barrel. We also know that total industry profit must be higher in the collusive monopoly outcome. In this case, it's 30 million bpd × ($110 − $20) = $2.7 billion per day (or $1.35 billion for each country). This total is $300 million per day higher than the Cournot competition outcome. At the collusive monopoly equilibrium, output is lower than at the Cournot equilibrium, and price and profit are higher.

Bertrand Oligopoly with Identical Products   Next, let's consider the Nash equilibrium in the Bertrand case with identical products. This is easy: We know that price will equal marginal cost, so $P = \$20$. Total demand at this price is determined by plugging $20 into the demand curve: $P = 20 = 200 − 3Q$, or $Q = 60$ million bpd. The two countries would split this demand equally, with each selling 30 million bpd. Because they both sell at a price equal to their marginal cost, each country earns zero profit. At the Bertrand equilibrium, output quantity is higher than at the Cournot equilibrium, price is lower, and there is no profit.

Summary   To summarize, then, in terms of total industry output, the lowest is the collusive monopoly outcome, followed by Cournot, then Bertrand:

$$Q_m < Q_c < Q_b$$

The order is the opposite for prices, with Bertrand prices the lowest and the collusive price the highest:

$$P_b < P_c < P_m$$

Similarly, profit is lowest in the Bertrand case (at zero), highest under collusion, with Cournot in the middle:

$$\pi_b = 0 < \pi_c < \pi_m$$

Therefore, the Cournot oligopoly outcome is something between those for monopoly and Bertrand oligopoly (for which the outcome is equivalent to perfect competition). And, unlike the collusive and Bertrand outcomes, the price and output in the Cournot equilibrium depend on the number of firms in the industry.

What Happens If There Are More Than Two Firms in a Cournot Oligopoly?

These intermediate outcomes are for a market with two firms. If there are more than two firms in a Cournot oligopoly, the total quantity, profits, and price remain between the monopoly and perfectly competitive extremes. However, the more firms there are, the closer these outcomes get to the perfectly competitive case with price equaling marginal cost and economic profits being zero. Having more competitors means that any single firm's supply decision becomes a smaller and smaller part of the total market. Its output choice therefore impacts the market price less and less. With a very large number of firms in the market, a producer essentially becomes a price taker. It therefore behaves like a firm in a perfectly competitive industry, producing where the market price equals its marginal cost. Most Cournot markets are not at this limit, so price is usually above marginal cost, but for intermediate cases, more firms in a Cournot oligopoly lead to lower prices, higher total output, and lower average firm profits.

Cournot versus Bertrand: Extensions

The fact that the intensity of competition changes with the number of firms in the market is a nice feature of the Cournot model. This prediction is more in line with many people's intuitive view of oligopoly than the Bertrand model's prediction that anything more than a single firm leads to a perfectly competitive outcome. The downside of the Cournot framework is that it's a bit more of a stretch than usual to assume that companies can only compete in their quantity choices and have no ability to charge different prices. How many oligopolies could that describe? Oil seems a very special case, but is it?

Economists David Kreps and José A. Scheinkman examined this assumption in more detail. They proved an important result (though it's too mathematically advanced to detail here) that helps expand the applicability of the Cournot model.[8] Kreps and Scheinkman showed that under certain conditions, even if firms actually set their prices instead of quantities, the industry equilibrium looks like the Cournot outcome. The key added element in Kreps's and Scheinkman's Cournot story is that firms must first choose their production capacity before they set their prices. The firms are then constrained to produce at or below that capacity level once they make their price decisions.

As an example of a market described by the Cournot model, imagine that a few real estate developers in a college town build student apartments that are identical in quality and size. Once these developers build their apartment buildings, they can charge whatever price the market will bear for the apartments, but their choice of prices will be constrained by the number of apartments they have all built. If, for some reason, the developers want to charge a ridiculously low rent of, say, $50 per month, they would probably not be able to satisfy all of the quantity demanded at that low price because they only have a fixed number of apartments to rent. If the developers first choose the number of apartments in their buildings and then sell their fixed capacity at whatever prices they choose, Kreps and Scheinkman show that the equilibrium price and quantity (which, as it turns out, will equal the developers' capacity choice in this case) will be like a Cournot oligopoly.

This result means that in industries in which there are large costs of investing in capacity so that firms don't change their capacity very often, the Cournot model will probably be a good predictor of market outcomes even if firms choose their prices in the short run. (In the long run, the firms could both change their capacity by building more apartment buildings and change the prices they choose.)

11.5 Oligopoly with Identical Goods: Stackelberg Competition

Model Assumptions   Stackelberg Competition with Identical Goods

- Firms sell identical products.
- Firms compete by choosing a quantity to produce.
- All goods sell for the same price (which is determined by the sum total of quantities produced by all the firms combined).
- Firms do *not* choose quantities simultaneously. One firm chooses its quantity first. The next firm observes this and then chooses its quantity.

The Cournot model gave us a way to analyze oligopolistic markets that are somewhere between collusion/monopoly and Bertrand/perfect competition. As in most oligopoly models, equilibrium in the Cournot model came from firms rationally thinking through how other firms in the market are likely to behave in response to their production decisions.

---

[8] David M. Kreps and José A. Scheinkman, "Quantity Precommitment and Bertrand Competition Yield Cournot Outcomes," *The Bell Journal of Economics* 14, no. 2, (1983): 326-337.

Importantly, the Cournot model also relies on another assumption whose implications we didn't think about in much detail, namely, that the firms choose simultaneously. That is, each firm chooses its optimal quantity based on what the firm believes its competitor(s) *might* do. If it expects its competitor(s) to produce some other quantity, its own optimal action changes—that was the logic of the reaction curve.

If you think about it, though, each company has an incentive to try to choose its output level first and force its competitors to be the one who has to react. The first firm to make its decision could increase its output and say "Oops, I have already made more than Cournot says I am supposed to produce. What are you going to do about it?" Because the competitor's reaction curve slopes downward in this case, the competitor, seeing the high quantity the original firm is producing, would want to reduce its output. Therefore, there is a **first-mover advantage** in this market.

An oligopoly model in which firms move sequentially—first one, then another, then (if there are more than two firms) another, and so on, is called **Stackelberg competition.** (Heinrich Freiherr von Stackelberg was an early-twentieth-century German economist who first analyzed this type of oligopoly.) The firm that moves first is sometimes called the Stackelberg leader. To see how sequential competition changes things, let's revisit our oil producers, Saudi Arabia and Iran.

In that example, the market inverse demand for oil was $P = 200 - 3Q$, and both countries had a constant marginal cost of $20 per barrel. Each firm produced where marginal revenue equaled marginal cost:

$$MR_S = 200 - 6q_S - 3q_I = 20$$

$$MR_I = 200 - 6q_I - 3q_S = 20$$

In Cournot competition, we rearranged this equation to solve for each country's reaction curve:

$$q_S = 30 - 0.5q_I$$

$$q_I = 30 - 0.5q_S$$

We know that this formula gives the best output a country can choose, taking as given the other country's output level. Plugging one reaction curve into the other gave us the Nash equilibrium, in which each country produced 20 million bpd at a market price of $80 per barrel.

Stackelberg Competition and the First-Mover Advantage

Now suppose Saudi Arabia is a Stackelberg leader: It chooses its quantity first. What will Saudi Arabia do with this first-mover advantage?

Iran's incentives remain unchanged. It still has the same reaction curve, and the reaction curve continues to show Iran's best response to any choice by Saudi Arabia. In Stackelberg competition, however, Iran will know with certainty what Saudi Arabia's production decision is before it makes its own. Iran reacts optimally to any production choice that Saudi Arabia makes by plugging this value for q_S into its reaction function. Importantly, *Saudi Arabia realizes Iran will do this before it makes its first move.*

Because Saudi Arabia knows that Iran's output is going to be a function of whatever Saudi Arabia chooses first, the Saudis want to take that impact into account when they make their *initial* production decision. In this way, Saudi Arabia can take advantage of being the first-mover. To do so, it plugs Iran's best response (which it knows from previous experience) into its own demand and marginal revenue curve equations. The fact that the Saudi marginal revenue curve changes means that Saudi Arabia will no longer have the same reaction curve it had in the Cournot model. In that model, Saudi Arabia faced the demand curve

$$P = 200 - 3(q_S + q_I)$$

first-mover advantage
In Stackelberg competition, the advantage gained by the initial firm in setting its production quantity.

Stackelberg competition
Oligopoly model in which firms make production decisions sequentially.

Now that it is a first-mover in a Stackelberg oligopoly, Saudi Arabia's demand is

$$P = 200 - 3q_S + 3q_I = 200 - 3q_S - 3(30 - 0.5q_S) = 200 - 3q_S - 90 + 1.5q_S$$

Do you see what happened? We substituted Iran's reaction function ($q_I = 30 - 0.5q_S$) directly into the Saudi demand curve. We did this because Saudi Arabia recognizes that, by going first, its output choice affects its demand (and therefore its marginal revenue) both directly and indirectly through its effect on Iran's production decision. The direct effect is captured by the term $-3q_S$ in the equation; this effect is the same as in the Cournot model. The indirect effect comes from the impact of Saudi Arabia's output choice on Iran's production response. This is embodied in the equation's second q_S term ($1.5q_S$).

We can further simplify this demand curve:

$$P = 110 - 1.5q_S$$

We know from Chapter 9 that Saudi Arabia's marginal revenue curve is then $MR_S = 110 - 3q_S$. Setting this equal to marginal cost ($20 per barrel) and solving for q_S give Saudi Arabia's profit-maximizing output in this Stackelberg oliopoly:

$$MR_S = 110 - 3q_S = 20$$

$$3q_S = 90$$

$$q_S = 30$$

As the first-mover, Saudi Arabia finds it optimal to produce 30 million bpd, 10 million more than the Cournot oligopoly output (20 million bpd).

Next, we have to see how Saudi Arabia's decision affects Iran's optimal production level. To do that, we plug Saudi Arabia's output level into Iran's reaction curve:

$$q_I = 30 - 0.5q_S = 30 - 0.5(30) = 15$$

Iran now produces 15 million bpd, rather than 20 as in the Cournot case. By moving first, Saudi Arabia gets the jump on Iran, leaving Iran no choice but to drop its output level from 20 to 15 million bpd.

Therefore, total production is 45 million bpd in the Stackelberg case. This is more than the output produced in the Cournot oligopoly (40 million). And, because production is higher, the market price must be lower under sequential production decisions than under Cournot's simultaneous-decision framework. Specifically, the price is $200 - 3(30 + 15) = \$65$ per barrel (instead of the Cournot equilibrium price of $80).

What happens to profit? For Saudi Arabia, profit is $30 \times (65 - 20) = \$1,350$ million/day. This is $150 million more than its $1,200 million/day profit in the (simultaneous-move) Cournot oligopoly. Such an outcome shows us the advantage of being the first-mover. Iran, on the other hand, makes a profit of only $15 \times (65 - 20) = \$675$ million per day, well below its Cournot profit level of $1,200 million per day. In the next chapter on game theory, we discuss the role of first-mover advantage in strategic decision making in more detail. For now, we can already see why firms might want to come into a market early, and try to make their production decisions before other firms have a chance.

Although it's somewhat abstract and mathematical, the idea of Stackelberg competition in which one firm moves first and obtains an advantage that leads later firms to adjust their strategy and reduce their output is very true to life. The market for touch-screen smartphones like the iPhone is a good example of this sort of competition. Apple released the iPhone before any other firm had a smartphone to market. Apple signed up a large number of customers before the competitors' phones were released and those competitors then had to choose their production plans with the full knowledge that Apple's quantity was already high.

11.3 figure it out

Consider again the case of the two oil change producers OilPro and GreaseTech from Figure It Out 11.2. Recall that the market inverse demand for the oil changes is $P = 100 - 2Q$, where Q is the total number of oil changes (in thousands per year) produced by the two firms, $q_O + q_G$. OilPro has a marginal cost of \$12 per oil change, while GreaseTech has a marginal cost of \$20.

a. Suppose this market is a Stackelberg oligopoly and OilPro is the first mover. How much does each firm produce? What will the market price of an oil change be? How much profit does each firm earn?

b. Now suppose that GreaseTech is the first-mover in this Stackelberg oligopoly. How much will each firm produce and what will the market price be? How much profit does each firm earn?

Solution:

a. We need to start by reconsidering the demand for OilPro's product. It is going to move first and we assume that it knows from previous experience that GreaseTech's output is a function of OilPro's output. Thus, we need to substitute GreaseTech's reaction curve, from the figure in the prior Figure It Out (11.2), into the market inverse demand curve to solve for the inverse demand for OilPro.

GreaseTech's reaction curve is $q_G = 20 - 0.5q_O$. Substituting this into the inverse market demand curve, we get

$$P = 100 - 2Q = 100 - 2(q_O + q_G) = 100 - 2q_O - 2q_G$$
$$= 100 - 2q_O - 2(20 - 0.5q_O) = 100 - 2q_O - 40 + q_O = 60 - q_O$$

So, the inverse demand curve for OilPro oil changes is $P = 60 - q_O$. This means that the marginal revenue curve for OilPro is

$$MR_O = 60 - 2q_O$$

Setting $MR = MC$ will provide us with OilPro's profit-maximizing output:

$$MR_O = 60 - 2q_O = 12$$
$$2q_O = 48$$
$$q_O = 24$$

Now that we know q_O, we can substitute it into GreaseTech's reaction curve to find q_G:

$$q_G = 20 - 0.5q_O = 20 - 0.5(24) = 20 - 12 = 8$$

OilPro will produce 24,000 oil changes, while GreaseTech will only produce 8,000. Using the inverse market demand, we can determine the market price:

$$P = 100 - 2(q_O + q_G) = 100 - 2(32) = 100 - 64 = \$36$$

OilPro's profit will be $\pi_O = (\$36 - \$12) \times 24{,}000 = \$576{,}000$. GreaseTech's profit will be $\pi_G = (\$36 - \$20) \times 8{,}000 = \$128{,}000$.

b. If GreaseTech is the first-mover, we can use OilPro's reaction curve (from the figure in the prior Figure It Out (11.2)) to find the inverse market demand for GreaseTech.

OilPro's reaction curve is $q_O = 22 - 0.5q_G$. Substituting into the market inverse demand, we get

$$P = 100 - 2q_O - 2q_G = 100 - 2(22 - 0.5q_G) - 2q_G = 100 - 44 + q_G - 2q_G$$
$$= 56 - q_G$$

This is the inverse demand for GreaseTech's oil changes. Its marginal revenue is therefore

$$MR_G = 56 - 2q_G.$$

Setting $MR = MC$, we can see that

$$MR_G = 56 - 2q_G = 20$$
$$2q_G = 36$$
$$q_G = 18$$

To find OilPro's output, we substitute q_G into OilPro's reaction curve:

$$q_O = 22 - 0.5q_G = 22 - 0.5(18) = 22 - 9 = 13$$

So, when GreaseTech is the first-mover, OilPro only produces 13,000 oil changes, while GreaseTech produces 18,000. We can determine the price using the inverse market demand:

$$P = 100 - 2(Q_O + Q_G) = 100 - 2(31) = \$38$$

GreaseTech's profit will be $\pi_G = (\$38 - \$20) \times 18,000 = \$324,000$. OilPro's profit will be $\pi_O = (\$38 - \$12) \times 13,000 = \$338,000$.

11.6 Oligopoly with Differentiated Goods: Bertrand Competition

Model Assumptions Bertrand Competition with Differentiated Goods

- Firms do *not* sell identical products. They sell differentiated products, meaning consumers do not view them as perfect substitutes.
- Each firm chooses the prices at which it sells its product.
- Firms set prices simultaneously.

Every model of imperfect competition that we've looked at so far—collusion, Bertrand, Cournot, and Stackelberg—has assumed that the industry's producers all sell the same product. Often, however, a more realistic description of an industry is a set of firms that make similar but not identical products. When consumers buy a car, breakfast cereal, pest-control services, or one of many other products, they must choose between competing versions of the product, each with its own unique features, produced by a small number of companies. A market in which multiple varieties of a common product type are available is called a **differentiated product market.**

How can we analyze a "market" when the products aren't the same? Shouldn't each product be considered to exist in its own separate market? Not always—it is often

differentiated product market
Market with multiple varieties of a common product.

possible to treat the products as interacting in a single market. The key is to explicitly account for the way consumers are willing to substitute among the products.

To see how a Bertrand oligopoly works with differentiated products, think back to the Bertrand model we studied in Section 11.3. There, two companies (Walmart and Target in our example) competed by setting prices for an identical product (the Sony PlayStation). Now, however, instead of thinking of the firms' products as identical as we did in Section 11.3, we assume that consumers view the products as being somewhat distinct. Maybe this is because, even though a PlayStation console is the same regardless of where customers buy it, the stores have different locations and customers care about travel costs. Or, perhaps the stores have different atmospheres or return policies or credit card programs that matter to certain customers. The specific source of the product distinction isn't important. Regardless of its source, this differentiation helps the stores exert more market power and earn more profit. When products were identical, the incentive to undercut price was so intense that firms competed the market price right down to marginal cost and earned zero economic profit as a result. That is not the outcome in the differentiated-product Bertrand model, as we see in the following example.

Equilibrium in a Differentiated-Products Bertrand Market

Suppose there are two main manufacturers of snowboards, Burton and K2. Because many snowboarders view the two companies' products as similar but not identical, if either firm cuts its prices, it will gain market share from the other. But because the firms' products aren't *perfect* substitutes, the price-cutting company won't take all of the business away from the other company just because it sets its price a bit lower. Some people are still going to prefer the competitor's product, even at a higher price.

This product differentiation means that each firm faces its own demand curve, and each product's price has a different effect on each firm's demand curve. So, Burton's demand curve might be

$$q_B = 900 - 2p_B + p_K$$

As you can see, the quantity of boards Burton sells goes down when it raises the price it charges for its own boards, p_B. On the other hand, Burton's quantity demanded goes up when K2 raises its price, p_K. In this example, we've assumed that Burton's demand is more sensitive to changes in its own price than to changes in K2's price. (For every one dollar change in p_B, there is a two-unit decrease in quantity demanded; this ratio is 1 to 1—and positive—for changes in p_K.) This is a realistic assumption in many markets.

K2 has a demand curve that looks similar, but with the roles of the two firms' prices reversed:

$$q_K = 900 - 2p_K + p_B$$

The responses of each company's quantity demanded to price changes reflect consumers' willingness to substitute across varieties of the indus-

There is profit to be made from consumers' perceived differences between the Burton snowboard on the left and the K2 snowboard on the right.

try's product. But this substitution is of limited magnitude; a firm can't take over the entire market with a 1 cent price cut, as it can in the identical-products Bertrand model.

To determine the equilibrium in a Bertrand oligopoly model with differentiated products, we follow the same steps we used for all the other models. We assume each company sets its price to maximize its profit, taking the prices of its competitors as given. That is, we look for a Nash equilibrium. To make things simple, we assume that both firms have a marginal cost of zero.[9]

Burton's total revenue is

$$TR_B = p_B \times q_B = p_B \times (900 - 2p_B + p_K)$$

Notice that we've written total revenue in terms of Burton's price, rather than its quantity. This is because in a Bertrand oligopoly, Burton chooses the price it will charge rather than how much it will produce. Writing total revenue in price terms lets us derive the marginal revenue curve in price terms as well. Namely, marginal revenue is

$$MR_B = 900 - 4p_B + p_K$$

We can solve for Burton's profit-maximizing price through the usual step of setting this marginal revenue equal to the marginal cost, zero in this case. Doing so and rearranging give

$$MR_B = 900 - 4p_B + p_K = 0$$

$$4p_B = 900 + p_K$$

$$p_B = 225 + 0.25p_K$$

Notice how this again gives a firm's (Burton's) optimal action as a function of the other firm's action (K2's). In other words, this equation describes Burton's reaction curve. But here, the actions are price choices rather than quantity choices as in the Cournot model.

K2 has a reaction curve, too. It looks similar, but is a little different than Burton's because K2's demand curve is slightly different. Going through the same steps as above, we have

$$MR_K = 900 - 4p_K + p_B = 0$$

$$4p_K = 900 + p_B$$

$$p_K = 225 + 0.25p_B$$

An interesting detail to note about these reaction curves in the Bertrand differentiated-product model is that a firm's optimal price *increases* when its competitor's price increases. If Burton thinks K2 will charge a higher price, for example, Burton wants to raise its price. That is, the reaction curves are upward-sloping. This is the opposite of the quantity reaction curves in the Cournot model (review Figure 11.4). There, a firm's optimal response to a competitor's output change is to do the opposite: If a firm expects its competitor to produce more, then it should produce less.

---

[9] We assume zero marginal cost in this example because the concept of marginal cost is a little different when firms choose prices rather than quantities. Remember that marginal cost is the change in total cost driven by changing output by one unit: $MC = \Delta TC / \Delta q$. As in all other market structures, a firm in a differentiated-product Bertrand oligopoly maximizes profit by setting its marginal revenue equal to its marginal cost. But the expression for marginal revenue in a Bertrand setup is the change in revenue resulting from small *price* changes, or $MR = \Delta TR / \Delta P$, rather than from small *quantity* changes, or $MR = \Delta TR / \Delta q$. Therefore, the profit-maximizing price in a differentiated-product Bertrand oligopoly sets this price-based marginal revenue equal to a price-based marginal cost: $\Delta TR / \Delta P = \Delta TC / \Delta P$. We could go through some extra algebra to tie the two together—there is an equilibrium with nonzero marginal costs in the example—but it's easier for our purposes here to just assume marginal costs are zero.

Differentiated Bertrand Equilibrium: A Graphical Approach   Figure 11.5 plots Burton and K2's reaction curves. The vertical axis shows Burton's optimal profit-maximizing price; the horizontal axis represents K2's optimal profit-maximizing price. The positive slope of Burton's reaction curve indicates that Burton's profit-maximizing price rises when K2 charges more. The positive slope of K2's reaction curve indicates that K2's profit-maximizing price rises when Burton charges more. If Burton expects K2 to charge $100, then Burton should price its boards at $250 (point A). If instead Burton believes K2 will price at $200, then it should price at $275 (point B). A K2 price of $400 will make Burton's optimal response $325 (point C), and so on. K2's reaction curve works the same way.

The point where the two reaction curves cross, E, is the Nash equilibrium. There, both firms are doing as well as they can given the other's actions. If either were to decide on its own to change its price, that firm's profit would decline.

Differentiated Bertrand Equilibrium: A Mathematical Approach   We can algebraically solve for this Nash equilibrium as we did in the Cournot model—by finding the point at which the reaction curve equations equal one another. Mechanically, that means we substitute one reaction curve into the other, solve for one firm's optimal price, and then use that price to solve for the other firm's optimal price.

First, we plug K2's reaction curve into Burton's and solve for Burton's equilibrium price:

$$p_B = 225 + 0.25p_K$$
$$p_B = 225 + 0.25 \times (225 + 0.25p_B)$$
$$p_B = 225 + 56.25 + 0.0625p_B$$
$$0.9375p_B = 281.25$$
$$p_B = 300$$

Substituting this price into K2's reaction curve gives its equilibrium price:

$$p_K = 225 + 0.25p_B = 225 + (0.25 \times 300) = 225 + 75 = 300$$

At equilibrium both firms charge the same price, $300. This isn't too surprising. After all, the two firms face similar-looking demand curves and have the same (zero) marginal costs. Interestingly, *that* particular implication of the identical-products Bertrand oligopoly that we looked at in Section 11.3 (that both firms charge the same price in equilibrium) holds here. The difference is that the price no longer equals

⟲ The online appendix finds the equilibrium for differentiated Bertrand competition using calculus. (http://glsmicro.com/appendices)

Figure 11.5   :   **Nash Equilibrium in a Bertrand Market**

This shows Burton and K2's reaction curves. At point E, when each sells 600 snowboards at a market price of $300 per snowboard, the market is at a Nash equilibrium, and the two companies are producing optimally.

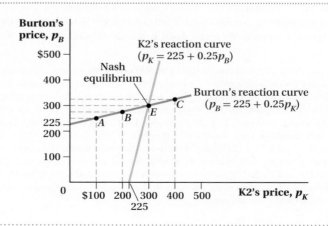

marginal cost. Instead, equilibrium prices are above marginal cost ($300 is certainly more than zero!).

To figure out the quantity each firm sells, we plug each firm's price into its demand curve equation. Burton's quantity demanded is $q_B = 900 - 2(300) + 300 = 600$ boards. K2 sells $q_K = 900 - 2(300) + 300 = 600$ boards also. Again, the fact that both firms sell the same quantity is not surprising because they have similar demand curves and charge the same price. Total industry production is therefore 1,200 boards, which is two-thirds of what it would be if both firms charged their marginal costs (each firm in that case would make 900 boards, meaning total production of 1,800 boards). In the Bertrand model where the firms produce differentiated products, each firm earns a profit of $600 \times (300 - 0) = \$180,000$.

11.4 figure it out

Consider our example of the two snowboard manufacturers, Burton and K2. We just determined that at the Nash equilibrium for these two firms, each firm produced 600 snowboards at a price of $300 per board. Now let's suppose that Burton launches a successful advertising campaign to convince snowboarders that its product is superior to K2's so that the demand for Burton snowboards rises to $q_B = 1,000 - 1.5p_B + 1.5p_K$, while the demand for K2 boards falls to $q_K = 800 - 2p_K + 0.5p_B$. (For simplicity, assume that the marginal cost is still zero for both firms.)

a. Derive each firm's reaction curve.

b. What happens to each firm's optimal price?

c. What happens to each firm's optimal output?

d. Draw the reaction curves in a diagram and indicate the equilibrium.

Solution:

a. To determine the firms' reaction curves, we first need to solve for each firm's marginal revenue curve:

$$MR_B = 1,000 - 3p_B + 1.5p_K$$
$$MR_K = 800 - 4p_K + 0.5p_B$$

By setting each firm's marginal cost equal to marginal revenue, we can find the firm's reaction curve:

$$MR_B = 1,000 - 3p_B + 1.5p_K = 0$$
$$3p_B = 1,000 + 1.5p_K$$
$$p_B = 333.33 + 0.5p_K$$
$$MR_K = 800 - 4p_K + 0.5p_B = 0$$
$$4p_K = 800 + 0.5p_B$$
$$p_K = 200 + 0.125p_B$$

b. We can solve for the equilibrium by substituting one firm's reaction curve into the other's:

$$p_B = 333.33 + 0.5p_K$$
$$p_B = 333.33 + 0.5(200 + 0.125p_B) = 333.33 + 100 + 0.0625p_B$$
$$p_B = 433.33 + 0.0625p_B$$
$$0.9375p_B = 433.33$$
$$p_B = \$462.22$$

We can then substitute p_B back into the reaction function for K2 to get the K2 price:

$$p_K = 200 + 0.125p_B$$
$$= 200 + 0.125(462.22) = 200 + 57.78 = \$257.78$$

So, the successful advertising campaign means that Burton can increase its price from the original equilibrium price of \$300 (which we determined in our initial analysis of this market) to \$462.22, while K2 will have to lower its own price from \$300 to \$257.78.

c. To find each firm's optimal output, we need to substitute the firms' prices into the inverse demand curves for each firm's product. For Burton,

$$q_B = 1,000 - 1.5p_B + 1.5p_K = 1,000 - 1.5(462.22) + 1.5(257.78)$$
$$= 1,000 - 693.33 + 386.67 = 693.34$$

For K2,

$$q_K = 800 - 2p_K + 0.5p_B = 800 - 2(257.78) + 0.5(462.22) = 800 - 515.56 + 231.11 = 515.55$$

Burton now produces more snowboards (693.34 instead of 600), while K2 produces fewer (515.55 instead of 600).

d. The reaction curves are shown in the diagram below:

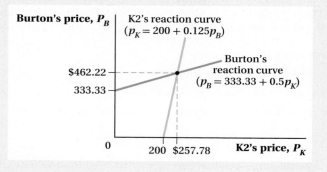

theory and data

Computer Parts II—Differentiation Out of Desperation

The computer chip retailers in the Ellison and Ellison study discussed in the Theory and Data application in Section 11.3 operated in what was essentially a Bertrand market with identical goods. As a result, they charged prices equal to their marginal costs. At prices that low, they were making little profit and struggling to cover their fixed costs.

This intense competition made such firms desperate to move away from the strictures of this kind of market. Ellison and Ellison documented how some computer parts retailers used a little economic know-how to get away with setting their prices above marginal cost. Those firms realized that the key to getting more producer surplus was to differentiate their products, thus shifting the structure of competition from a Bertrand oligopoly with identical products to one with differentiated products.

Just how could these firms differentiate what were otherwise identical computer chips? They couldn't do this the way K2 and Burton can with the snowboards they sell, by varying designs, materials, and so on. So they turned to slightly more, well, creative methods— methods that Ellison and Ellison categorized as "obfuscation."

Ellison and Ellison found that online firms rely on two primary means of obfuscation. In the first, the firm lists a cheap but inferior product that the price search engine displays at the beginning of its listings. Customers click on this product and are redirected to the firm's website, where the company then offers a more expensive product upgrade. Once one firm undercuts its competitors with this "loss leader" strategy, all firms will list similarly cheap products or risk having their product listing buried deep in the last pages of the listings. As a result, it becomes more time-consuming for the customer to compare the prices of the product "upgrades," and the firm can charge a price higher than marginal cost without the risk of being priced out.

Another common strategy is the use of product add-ons. As with the first method, firms list artificially cheap products that bait consumers into visiting the firm website. This time, instead of upgraded products, customers are offered product add-ons, such as additional screws to fasten the chip to the circuit board or a snazzy mouse pad. Often, these products are added on automatically; that is, to purchase only the original product, the consumer has to unselect a number of additional products. Although the product the consumer initially selected may be selling at or even below marginal cost, the add-ons often sell at inflated prices—the mouse pad one online firm offered Ellison and Ellison cost nearly $12. This practice allows the firm to sell the entire bundle of products at a price above marginal cost.

Obfuscation methods such as these are part of the reason the Bertrand model with identical products that we first studied is so unusual in the real world. Even products that aren't obviously differentiable can be made to stand out through some clever strategies by the firms. Given that firms selling such products would otherwise expect to earn something close to nothing, they have a massive incentive to figure out differentiation strategies, and thus try to reduce competition.

11.7 Monopolistic Competition

> **Model Assumptions** Monopolistic Competition
>
> - Industry firms sell differentiated products that consumers do not view as perfect substitutes.
> - Other firms' choices affect a firm's residual demand curve, but the firm ignores any strategic interactions between its own quantity or price choice and its competitors'.
> - There is free entry into the market.

In the models we've studied so far, we haven't considered the possibility that other firms might want to enter markets in which firms are earning positive economic profits. Presumably, there are other firms that would like a piece of that action. If there are no barriers to entering a market such as the snowboard market, an additional firm will cause Burton and K2's profits to decline. We saw in the Cournot model that adding more firms to the industry drove the equilibrium closer to perfect competition. In this section, we look at our last model of imperfect competition, and see what happens when there is entry into a market with differentiated products. **Monopolistic competition** is a market structure characterized by many firms selling a differentiated product with no barriers to entry. This term might sound like an oxymoron—competitive monopoly?—and in a way it is, but the term reflects the basic tension between market power and competitive forces that exists in these types of markets.

Every firm in a monopolistically competitive industry faces a downward-sloping demand curve, so it has some market power and every firm follows the monopoly pricing rule. That's where the "monopolistic" comes from. What is *competitive* about such

monopolistic competition
A market structure characterized by many firms selling a differentiated product with no barriers to entry.

markets is that there are no restrictions on entry as exist in monopoly markets—any number of firms can come into the industry at any time. This means that the firms in a monopolistically competitive industry, despite having market power, earn zero economic profit. (If they were making a profit, more firms would enter to acquire some of this profit. Entry only stops when profit is driven to zero for every firm in the market.)

Many markets are monopolistically competitive. For example, there are hundreds of fast-food restaurants in Chicago and probably a similar number in every other major city in the United States. There are some differences between them, but basically people view such restaurants as largely interchangeable. Because travel is costly, though, each restaurant has a bit of market power in its local neighborhood. So, a restaurant does have some ability to set its own prices. At the same time, however, there's little to stop a new restaurant from opening. If people in a neighborhood become more enthralled with eating out, an existing restaurant might be able to raise its prices and earn economic profit for a brief period, but if the demand increase is expected to be anything more than temporary, we would likely see a new restaurant (or restaurants) opening up to grab some of that profit.

Keep in mind that, while monopolistic competition is categorized as "imperfect competition" along with oligopoly, there are differences between these two market structures. One is that oligopoly markets have barriers to entry, while monopolistically competitive markets do not. However, the key distinction between oligopoly and monopolistic competition is the assumption about strategic interaction. In an oligopoly, firms know that their production decisions affect their competitors' optimal choices, and all oligopolistic firms take this feedback effect into account when making their decisions. On the other hand, in monopolistic competition firms do not worry about the production decisions of their competitors because the impact of any competitor on another is assumed to be too small for these firms to be concerned about.

Equilibrium in Monopolistically Competitive Markets

To analyze monopolistically competitive markets, let's look at a single company with market power—say for a moment that, for some reason, a city has only one fast-food burger restaurant. In this city, this restaurant has a monopoly on fast-food burgers. The firm faces a downward-sloping demand curve for meals served per day, as in Figure 11.6. We'll label this demand D_{ONE} (for one firm). The figure also shows the

---

Figure 11.6   **Demand and Cost Curves for a Monopoly**

A monopolist restaurant has demand D_{ONE}, marginal revenue MR_{ONE}, average total cost ATC, and marginal cost MC. The restaurant produces where marginal revenue equals marginal cost, at quantity Q^*_{ONE}. The restaurant's profit, represented by the shaded rectangle, is the difference between the firm's price P^*_{ONE} and average total cost ATC^* multiplied by Q^*_{ONE}.

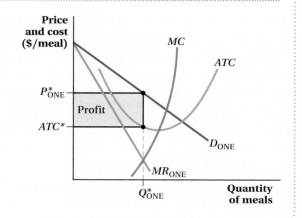

marginal revenue curve that corresponds to this demand, as well as shows the firm's average total and marginal cost curves.

Because the restaurant in Figure 11.6 is a monopolist, it produces where its marginal revenue equals marginal cost, Q^*_{ONE}. The price it charges is P^*_{ONE}. In addition to the marginal cost of production, however, the restaurant has to pay fixed cost equal to F (this fixed cost is the reason why the firm's average total cost curve is U-shaped). The monopolist restaurant's profit is shown by the shaded rectangle: the difference between the price and the average total cost at the quantity produced, multiplied by that quantity. Because average total cost includes both variable and fixed costs, the average total cost at Q^*_{ONE}—that is, ATC^*—fully reflects all of the firm's production costs.

So far, this market is just like a regular monopoly. But now suppose a restaurateur notices that this firm is making an economic profit and decides to open a second, slightly different fast-food restaurant in the city. The new restaurant may differ in location, type of food served, anything that differentiates it from the existing restaurant.

The key to understanding what happens in monopolistically competitive markets is to recognize what happens to the demand curve(s) of the market's existing firm(s) when another firm enters. We know that when there are more substitutes for a good available, the demand curve for the initial good becomes more elastic (less steep). Having another restaurant open up means that more substitution possibilities now exist for consumers. Instead of there being one firm with a demand curve, as in Figure 11.6, the entry of a second firm means that each restaurant now has a demand curve that is a bit flatter than the monopolist firm's demand curve. And, because the demand is being split across two firms, not only is the monopolist firm's demand curve flatter, but it has shifted in as well. Figure 11.7 shows this change from one to two firms, as the initial (monopolist) firm's demand curve (now it is a residual demand curve) shifts from D_{ONE} to D_{TWO}. Notice how D_{TWO} is both flatter than and to the left of D_{ONE}. The marginal revenue curves also shift accordingly. (The figure illustrates only what's going on for one of the two firms in the market; the picture is exactly the same for the other firm.)

Even after entry, however, both firms are essentially monopolists over their own residual demand curves. Each individual firm's demand curve reflects the fact that (1) it is splitting the market with another firm and (2) the presence of a substitute product makes the firm's demand more elastic. The competitor's presence *is* accounted

---

Figure 11.7   **The Effect of Firm Entry on Demand for a Monopolistically Competitive Firm**

When a second restaurant enters the market, the original restaurant's demand curve shifts left from D_{ONE} to the more elastic residual demand curve D_{TWO}, and the marginal revenue curve MR_{ONE} shifts to MR_{TWO}. The restaurant now sells quantity Q^*_{TWO} at price P^*_{TWO} and earns profit represented by the shaded rectangle.

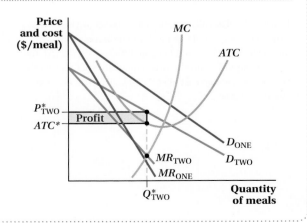

for, but it is incorporated in the firm's residual demand curve. In monopolistic competition, the firm takes this residual demand as given. This is different from the oligopoly models we covered, in which firms realize that their actions affect the desired actions of their competitors, which in turn affect their own optimal action, and so on. This strategic interaction is captured in firms' reaction curves. A monopolistically competitive firm, on the other hand, acts like it is in its own little monopoly world, even though its competitors' actions affect the residual demand it faces. This assumption about monopolistically competitive firms' ignorance of strategic interactions is more likely to hold in industries where there are a large number of firms selling related but differentiated products.

Assuming the two firms have identical residual demand curves, both produce the quantity Q_{TWO}^* at which marginal revenue equals marginal cost and charge the profit-maximizing price P_{TWO}^* at that quantity. Each firm earns the profit given by the shaded rectangle in the figure.

Because two firms in the market make positive economic profit, we should expect still more firms to enter. Each new firm that enters will further shift any individual company's demand curve to the left and make it more elastic (flatter).

Entry will cease only when industry firms are no longer making any economic profit. Once that point is reached, the market will be described by Figure 11.8. When there are N firms in the market, each firm's residual demand curve eventually shifts back to D_N. Faced with this demand curve, the firm produces the quantity Q_N^* at which marginal revenue equals marginal cost, charges a price of P_N^* and earns zero economic profit.

Why does economic profit equal zero at this point? Look at where the firm's average total cost curve is relative to its demand curve. The two curves are tangent at Q_N^* and P_N^*. If price equals average total cost, profit is zero. The firm is just covering its costs of operation (variable and fixed) at this point.

Here's an important point about monopolistically competitive markets: Even though entry occurs until profits are zero, the entry process does not ultimately lead to a perfectly competitive outcome in which price equals marginal cost. Firms in a monopolistically competitive market face a downward-sloping demand curve, so marginal revenue is always less than price. At the profit-maximizing output, marginal cost will equal marginal revenue, which means that marginal cost will also be less than price. Free entry ensures that this markup over marginal cost is just enough to cover the firm's fixed cost, and no more.

Figure 11.8   Long-Run Equilibrium for a Monopolistically Competitive Market

In a monopolistically competitive market with N firms, firms face long-run demand D_N, marginal revenue MR_N, marginal costs MC, and average total cost ATC. At the long-run equilibrium, the firm's quantity is Q_N^*, price P_N^* is equal to average cost ATC^*, and each firm earns zero economic profit.

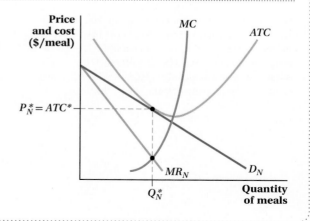

Sticky Stuff produces cases of taffy in a monopolistically competitive market. The inverse demand curve for its product is $P = 50 - Q$, where Q is in thousands of cases per year and P is dollars per case.

Sticky Stuff can produce each case of taffy at a constant marginal cost of $10 per case and has no fixed cost. Its total cost curve is therefore $TC = 10Q$.

a. To maximize profit, how many cases of taffy should Sticky Stuff produce each month?

b. What price will Sticky Stuff charge for a case of taffy?

c. How much profit will Sticky Stuff earn each year?

d. In reality, firms in monopolistic competition generally face fixed costs in the short run. Given the information above, what would Sticky Stuff's fixed costs have to be in order for this industry to be in long-run equilibrium? Explain.

Solution:

a. Sticky Stuff maximizes its profit by producing where $MR = MC$. Since the demand curve is linear, we know from Chapter 9 that the MR curve will be linear with twice the slope. Therefore, $MR = 50 - 2Q$. Setting $MR = MC$, we get

$$50 - 2Q = 10$$
$$Q = 20$$

Sticky Stuff should produce 20,000 cases of taffy each year.

b. We can find the price Sticky Stuff will charge by substituting the quantity into the demand curve:

$$P = 50 - Q = 50 - 20 = \$30 \text{ per case}$$

c. Total revenue for Sticky Stuff will be $TR = P \times Q = \$30 \times 20{,}000 = \$600{,}000$. Total cost will be $TC = 10Q = (10 \times 20{,}000) = \$200{,}000$. Therefore, Sticky Stuff will earn an annual profit of $\pi = TR - TC = \$600{,}000 - \$200{,}000 = \$400{,}000$.

d. Long-run equilibrium occurs when firms have no incentive to enter or exit. Therefore, firms must be earning zero economic profit. From (c), we know that Sticky Stuff is earning a profit of $400,000. In order for its profit to be zero, Sticky Stuff must face annual fixed cost equal to $400,000.

11.8 Conclusion

In this chapter, we've looked at multiple models of imperfect competition—that middle ground between perfect competition (which we studied in Chapter 8) and monopoly (which we studied in Chapter 9). We started with the reminder that the number of firms in a market is only one of many factors that can determine market prices, quantities, and producer profits. So, it's no surprise that there are different models of imperfect competition, each of which has different predictions about market outcomes. Which model is the most applicable to any market situation requires some judgment on the part of the economist. Are the products essentially identical, or slightly or completely differentiated? Are the firms setting prices or quantities? Are firms making their choices simultaneously or in sequence? Are there barriers to entry or is entry into the market free? These and other questions need to be considered when choosing the imperfect competition model most applicable to the industry being analyzed. In the next chapter, we examine how individuals and firms may act strategically to achieve a greater outcome (such as increased utility or higher profits).

Summary

1. In oligopolistic markets, each firm makes production decisions conditional on its competitors' actions. The resulting market equilibrium is known as a **Nash equilibrium,** one of the cornerstones of economic game theory. A Nash equilibrium occurs when each firm is doing its best given the actions of other firms. [**Section 11.1**]

2. Oligopolistic firms may be able to form cartels, in which all participating firms coordinate their production decisions and act collectively as a monopoly. The resulting market quantity and price are equal to those from a monopoly, and industry profit is maximized. While collusive behavior allows firms to capture monopoly profits, **collusion** and **cartels** are rarely stable because every firm has the incentive to increase its own profit by producing more (pricing lower). [**Section 11.2**]

3. In **Bertrand competition,** products are identical and firms compete on price. Each firm simultaneously sets the price of its good, and consumers then choose to purchase all of the quantity demanded from whichever firm has the lowest price, even if the price is only one penny lower. The Bertrand model shows that only two firms need to be in a market to achieve the perfectly competitive market outcome where price equals marginal cost. This result arises because firms in these situations have such a strong incentive to try to undercut the prices of their rivals. Market output is equal to the competitive level of output and firm profits are zero. [**Section 11.3**]

4. In contrast to firms in Bertrand competition, firms in **Cournot competition** simultaneously choose the quantity of a good to produce, and not the price at which the good sells. The Cournot equilibrium price is generally above the price in Bertrand competition, but below the monopoly price. The Cournot output is less than the Bertrand level of output, but greater than the output generated by a cartel. Firms in a Cournot oligopoly earn greater profits than those in the Bertrand model, but less than the monopoly profit. [**Section 11.4**]

5. In **Stackelberg competition,** firms make production decisions sequentially. Because the first firm in an industry can make production decisions independently of other firms and may be able to capture larger profits, a **first-mover advantage** exists for these firms. [**Section 11.5**]

6. In the Bertrand model with differentiated products, consumers in these markets are willing to substitute across goods, but do not consider them identical, or perfect substitutes. As a result, small differences in prices do not lead to all demand being satisfied by the producer with the lowest price (as in the Bertrand oligopoly with identical products). [**Section 11.6**]

7. **Monopolistic competition** is a market structure in which firms sell differentiated products, and firms have some characteristics of both monopolies and perfectly competitive firms. Because there are no barriers to entry in a monopolistically competitive market, economic profit is driven to zero through the entry of firms. [**Section 11.7**]

Review Questions

1. Name some different forms of imperfect competition.
2. Define Nash equilibrium. Why do firms in oligopoly situations reach Nash equilibria?
3. Why are collusions and cartels often unstable?
4. What is the market equilibrium in Bertrand competition with identical goods?
5. Contrast Bertrand and Cournot competition. Why do they reach different market equilibria?
6. What does the residual demand curve tell us about a firm's output in Cournot competition?
7. How can reaction curves be used to find a firm's equilibrium in Cournot competition?
8. What causes the first-mover advantage in Stackelberg competition?
9. Contrast the market equilibria in Betrand competition with identical products and with differentiated products.
10. What are the characteristics of a monopolistically competitive firm?
11. When will firms enter a monopolistically competitive industry? At what point will firms stop entering a monopolistically competitive industry?
12. Why do firms in monopolistic competition not reach the perfectly competitive equilibrium?

Problems (Solutions to problems marked * appear at the back of this book. Problems adapted to use calculus are available online at http://worthpublishers.com/GLS1e)

*1. Because cooking soufflés is incredibly difficult, the supply of soufflés in a small French town is controlled by two bakers, Gaston and Pierre. The demand for soufflés is given by $P = 30 - 2Q$, and the marginal and average total cost of producing soufflés is $6. Because baking a soufflé requires a great deal of work and preparation, each morning Gaston and Pierre make a binding decision about how many soufflés to bake.

a. Suppose that Pierre and Gaston agree to collude, evenly splitting the output a monopolist would make and charging the monopoly price.

 i. Derive the equation for the monopolist's marginal revenue curve.

 ii. Determine the profit-maximizing collective output for the cartel.

 iii. Determine the price Pierre and Gaston will be able to charge.

 iv. Determine profits for Pierre and Gaston individually, as well as for the cartel as a whole.

b. Suppose that Pierre cheats on the cartel agreement by baking one extra soufflé each morning.

 i. What does the extra production do to the price of soufflés in the marketplace?

 ii. Calculate Pierre's profit. How much did he gain by cheating?

 iii. Calculate Gaston's profit. How much did Pierre's cheating cost him?

 iv. How much potential profit does the group lose as a result of Pierre's cheating?

c. Suppose that Gaston, fed up with Pierre's behavior, also begins baking one extra soufflé each morning.

 i. How does the extra production affect the price of soufflés in the marketplace?

 ii. Calculate Gaston's profit. How much did he gain by cheating?

 iii. Calculate Pierre's profit. How much did Gaston's cheating cost him?

 iv. How much potential profit does the group lose as a result of Pierre's and Gaston's cheating?

 v. Demonstrate that it is in neither Pierre's nor Gaston's best interest to cheat further on their agreement.

2. Suppose in the previous problem that Gaston can produce soufflés at a constant marginal cost of $5, but Pierre produces soufflés for $7. Together, they collude to produce three units each.

a. How much profit will each producer earn? What will be the total profit of the cartel?

b. Gaston observes that he is a more efficient producer than Pierre, and suggests that if they are going to produce six units, the cartel's interests are better served if Gaston produces all of the soufflés.

 i. If Gaston produces and sells all of the soufflés and Pierre produces nothing, what happens to the profit of the cartel?

 ii. Is Pierre likely to agree not to produce any soufflés?

 iii. Suppose Gaston offers to pay Pierre not to produce any soufflés. How much would Gaston potentially be willing to offer? What is the minimum offer that Pierre should accept?

 iv. Suppose that the deal in part (iii) is reached for Pierre's minimum price. What happens to Pierre's profit if he cheats on his agreement with Gaston and increases his output from zero soufflés to one? What happens to Gaston's profit?

 v. Compare Pierre's incentive to cheat under this arrangement with the incentive that exists when they split production equally. Also compare Gaston's vulnerability to Pierre's cheating under both arrangements. Why might this cartel choose to use the less-profitable method of each member producing three units to the potentially more-profitable method of having Gaston produce everything?

3. Suppose that the inverse market demand for pumpkins is given by $P = \$10 - 0.05Q$. Pumpkins can be grown by anybody at a constant marginal cost of $1.

a. If there are lots of pumpkin growers in town so that the pumpkin industry is competitive, how many pumpkins will be sold, and what price will they sell for?

b. Suppose that a freak weather event wipes out the pumpkins of all but two producers, Linus and Lucy. Both Linus and Lucy have produced bumper crops, and have more than enough pumpkins available to satisfy the demand at even a zero price. If Linus and Lucy collude to generate monopoly profits, how many pumpkins will they sell, and what price will they sell for?

c. Suppose that the predominant form of competition in the pumpkin industry is price competition. In other words, suppose that Linus and Lucy are Bertrand competitors.

What will be the final price of pumpkins in this market—in other words, what is the Bertrand equilibrium price?

d. At the Bertrand equilibrium price, what will be the final quantity of pumpkins sold by both Linus and Lucy individually, and for the industry as a whole? How profitable will Linus and Lucy be?

e. Would the results you found in parts (c) and (d) be likely to hold if Linus let it be known that his pumpkins were the most orange in town, and Lucy let it be known that hers were the tastiest? Explain.

4. Suppose that three grocery stores sell Bubba's Gourmet Red Beans and Rice. Bullseye market is able to acquire, stock, and market them for $2.00 per package. OKMart can acquire, stock, and market them for $1.98 per package. SamsMart can acquire, stock, and market them for $1.96 per package.

a. If the three competitors are located in close proximity to one another, so that the cost of going to a different store to purchase red beans and rice is negligible, and if the market for prepackaged gourmet red beans and rice is characterized by Bertrand competition, what will the prevailing market price be?

b. Where will customers buy their red beans and rice? Bullseye, OKMart, or SamsMart? What does your answer suggest about the potential rewards to small improvements in efficiency via cost-cutting?

c. Suppose that each day, equal numbers of customers begin their shopping at each of the three stores. If the cost of going to a different store to purchase red beans and rice is 2 cents, is the Bertrand result likely to hold in this case? Where will customers purchase red beans and rice? Where will they not purchase them?

5. Suppose that two firms are Cournot competitors. Industry demand is given by $P = 200 - q_1 - q_2$, where q_1 is the output of Firm 1 and q_2 is the output of Firm 2. Both Firm 1 and Firm 2 face constant marginal and average total costs of $20.

a. Solve for the Cournot price, quantity, and firm profits.

b. Firm 1 is considering investing in costly technology that will enable it to reduce its costs to $15 per unit. How much should Firm 1 be willing to pay if such an investment can guarantee that Firm 2 will not be able to acquire it?

c. How does your answer to (b) change if Firm 1 knows the technology is available to Firm 2?

*6. Jack and Annie are the only sellers of otters in a three-state area. The inverse market demand for otters is given by $P = 100 - 0.5Q$, where Q = the total quantity offered for sale in the marketplace. Specifically, $Q = q_J + q_A$, where q_J is the amount of otters offered for sale by Jack and q_A is the amount offered for sale by Annie. Both Jack and Annie can produce otters at a constant marginal and average total cost of $20.

a. Graph the market demand curve. What would be the prevailing price and quantity if this industry were controlled by a monopolist?

b. Suppose that Jack, an excellent mathematician (but perhaps not quite as brilliant an economist), solves part (a). Being a very egalitarian sort, Jack announces that he will bring half of the monopoly quantity to market each day.

i. The market inverse demand for otters is given by $P = 100 - 0.5(q_J + q_A)$. Plug in Jack's announced output for q_A to solve for the residual demand curve faced by Annie.

ii. Solve for, and graph, the residual marginal revenue curve faced by Annie.

iii. Given Annie's otter production cost of $20, how many units should Annie bring to market to maximize her profit?

c. Given your answers to (b), what will the industry quantity and final price of otters be? How much profit will Annie earn? Jack?

d. Suppose that Jack observes Annie's output from part (b), and decides to change his own.

i. Solve for, and graph, the residual demand curve faced by Jack.

ii. Solve for, and graph, the residual marginal revenue curve faced by Jack.

iii. Given Jack's otter production cost of $20, how many units should he bring to market to maximize his profit?

iv. What will the industry quantity and final price of otters be? How much profit will Annie earn? Jack?

e. Is the outcome you found in part (d) an equilibrium outcome? How do you know?

*7. The platypus is a shy and secretive animal that does not breed well in captivity. But two breeders, Sydney and Adelaide, have discovered the secret to platypus fertility and have effectively cornered the market. Zoos across the globe come to them to purchase their output; the world inverse demand for baby platypuses is given by $P = 1,000 - 2Q$, where Q is the combined output of Sydney (q_S) and Adelaide (q_A).

a. Sydney wishes to produce the profit-maximizing quantity of baby platypus. Given Adelaide's choice of output, q_A, write an equation for the residual demand faced by Sydney.

b. Derive Sydney's residual marginal revenue curve.

c. Assume that the marginal and average total cost of raising a baby platypus to an age at which it can be sold is $200. Derive Sydney's reaction function.

d. Repeat steps (a), (b), and (c) to find Adelaide's reaction function to Sydney's output choice.

e. Solve for Sydney's profit-maximizing level of output and Adelaide's profit-maximizing level of output.

f. Determine industry output, the price of platypus, and the profits of both Sydney and Adelaide.

g. If Adelaide were hit by a bus on her way home from work, and Sydney were to become a monopolist, what would happen to industry quantity, price, and profit?

8. Suppose that there are two producers of prokrypton-B, a rare mineral capable of incapacitating aliens from distant planets. Governments across the globe are interested in purchasing defensive stores of the rare mineral. The market demand for prokrypton-B is given by $P = 200 - 0.2Q$, where Q is the collective output of the industry, in tons; q_A is the output of Firm A; and q_B is the output of Firm B. Assume that each firm produces prokrypton-B at a marginal cost of $10 per ton.

a. Derive each firm's reaction function.

b. Solve for the equilibrium quantity of each firm, as well as industry output.

c. Solve for the market price of prokrypton-B.

d. Solve for the profit earned by each firm.

e. Suppose that a labor dispute drives Firm B's cost to $12 per ton.

   i. What happens to the output of each firm as a result?

   ii. What happens to the market price of prokrypton-B?

   iii. What happens to the profit of each firm?

9. Suppose that the market demand for concrete is given by the equation $P = 300 - \frac{1}{3}Q$, where Q is the total quantity, in yards, supplied by three existing firms. Assume that the three firms are identical, and that the marginal and average cost of producing a cubic yard of concrete is exactly $30.

a. Derive reaction curves for Firm 1, Firm 2, and Firm 3.

b. By repeated substitution, find the output of each firm.

c. Solve for the market price, firm profits, and industry profits.

d. How would the price, quantity, and industry profit change if one of the firms were to exit the industry?

10. Consider the demand for boccie balls shown in the diagram below. Demand is given by $P = 80 - Q$. Boccie balls can be produced at a constant marginal and average total cost of $20.

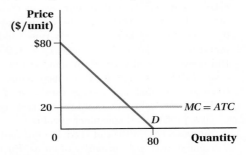

a. If the boccie ball industry were perfectly competitive, what quantity would be sold, and what price would prevail in the market?

b. Suppose that the boccie ball industry were a monopoly. Draw in a marginal revenue curve and determine the profit-maximizing quantity.

   i. Divide the monopoly (one-firm) quantity by the competitive quantity to determine the proportion of competitive output that a monopolist provides. Present your answer in reduced fractional form.

   ii. Determine the price, and draw a dot on the demand curve indicating the monopolist's price and quantity.

c. Suppose the boccie ball industry were a Cournot duopoly (two-firm), with two firms. Use the procedures developed in this chapter to determine the industry output.

   i. Divide the duopoly quantity by the competitive quantity to determine the proportion of competitive output that a duopoly provides. Present your answer in reduced fractional form.

   ii. Determine the price, and draw a dot on the demand curve indicating the duopoly's price and quantity.

d. Hypothesize as to the fraction of competitive output that would be sold if the boccie ball industry had three identical Cournot competitors. Then check your answer.

e. In general, what fraction of the competitive output level will be brought to market if there are N identical firms in the industry?

f. What happens to the quantity sold as more competitors are added to the industry? The price? What happens to consumer surplus and deadweight loss? Does this provide support for the government's desire to ensure competitive industries rather than monopolies or small oligopolies?

11. Two organic emu ranchers, Bill and Ted, serve a small metropolitan market. Bill and Ted are Cournot competitors, making a conscious decision each year regarding how many emus to breed. The price they can charge depends on how many emus they collectively raise, and demand in this market is given by $Q = 150 - P$. Bill raises emus at a constant marginal and average total cost of \$10; Ted raises emus at a constant marginal and average total cost of \$20.

a. Find the Cournot equilibrium price, quantity, profits, and consumer surplus.

b. Suppose that Bill and Ted merge, and become a monopoly provider of emus. Further, suppose that Ted adopts Bill's production techniques. Find the monopoly price, quantity, profits, and consumer surplus.

c. Suppose that instead of merging, Bill considers buying Ted's operation for cash. How much should Bill be willing to offer Ted to purchase his emu ranch? (Assume that the combined firms are only going to operate for one period.)

d. Has the combination of the two ranches discussed above been good for society or bad for society? Discuss how the forces of monopoly power and increased efficiency tend to push social well-being in opposite directions.

12. Suppose that in a particular market, the inverse demanded for hasenpfeffer is given by $P = 100 - Q$. The market is served by two Cournot competitors, Hansel and Gretel, whose quantities are denoted q_H and q_G, respectively. Both competitors can produce hasenpfeffer at a constant marginal and average total cost of \$10.

a. Find the Cournot equilibrium output and price.

b. Suppose that demand doubles so that at each price, twice as many servings are demanded as before. Specifically, $P = 100 - 0.5Q$. What happens to the Cournot price and quantity as a result of the increase in demand?

c. Suppose that the original demand doubles, but in a different way, so that each customer is willing to pay twice as much as before to obtain hasenpfeffer. Specifically, $P = 200 - 2Q$.

What happens to the Cournot price and quantity as a result of the increase in demand?

d. Would your answers to (b) and (c) remain the same if Hansel and Gretel were Bertrand competitors rather than Cournot competitors?

*13. The market for nutmeg is controlled by two small island economies, Penang and Grenada. The market demand for bottled nutmeg is given by $P = 100 - q_P - q_G$, where q_P is the quantity Penang produces and q_G is the quantity Grenada produces. Both Grenada and Penang produce nutmeg at a constant marginal and average cost of \$20 per bottle.

a. Verify that the reaction function for Grenada is given by $q_G = 40 - 0.5q_P$. Then verify that the reaction function for Penang is given by $q_P = 40 - 0.5q_G$.

b. Find the Cournot equilibrium quantity for each island. Then solve for the market price of nutmeg and for each firm's profit.

c. Suppose that Grenada transforms the nature of competition to Stackelberg competition by announcing its production targets publicly in an attempt to seize a first-mover advantage.

   i. Grenada must first decide how much to produce, and to do this, it needs to know the demand conditions it faces. Substitute Penang's reaction function into the market demand curve to find the demand faced by Grenada.

   ii. Based on your answer to the problem above, find the marginal revenue curve faced by Grenada.

   iii. Equate marginal revenue with marginal cost to find Grenada's output.

   iv. Plug Grenada's output into Penang's reaction function to determine Penang's output.

   v. Plug the combined output of Grenada and Penang into the market demand curve to determine the price. How do the industry quantity and price compare to those under Cournot competition?

   vi. Determine profits in Grenada and Penang. How do the profits of each compare to profits under Cournot competition? Is there an advantage to being the first-mover?

14. Consider the Cournot-Stackelberg competing islands of Penang and Grenada discussed in the previous problem. What will happen to Grenada's and Penang's output if:

a. Grenada's cost of production decreases to \$16, while Penang's stays at \$20. Explain.

b. Penang's cost of production decreases to \$16, while Grenada's stays at \$20. Explain.

*15. The market for cellular service is dominated by two sellers, AT&T and Verizon. AT&T and Verizon are Bertrand competitors, but because the services offered by those two sellers are not identical, customers have some degree of preference that makes them slightly resistant to switching from one to another. The demand for AT&T services is given by $q_A = 1{,}000 - 3p_A + 2p_V$, where q_A is the number of customers in a particular service area, p_A is the price of AT&T service, and p_V is the price of Verizon service. The demand for Verizon services is given by $q_V = 1{,}000 - 3p_V + 2p_A$. Assume that both sellers can produce cellular service at zero marginal cost.

   a. Derive AT&T's reaction curve. Your answer should express p_A as a function of p_V. If Verizon raises its price by \$9, how should AT&T respond to that price increase?

   b. Derive Verizon's reaction curve. Your answer should express p_V as a function of p_A.

   c. Solve for the price AT&T should charge to maximize profit.

   d. Solve for the price Verizon should charge to maximize its profit.

   e. Determine the quantity each seller will sell. Then calculate its profits, assuming that its marginal and average total costs are zero.

16. Internet users in a small Colorado town can access the Web in two ways: via their television cable or via a digital subscriber line (DSL) from their telephone company. The cable and telephone companies are Bertrand competitors, but because changing providers is slightly costly (waiting for the cable repairman can eat up at least small amounts of time!), customers have some slight resistance to switching from one to another. The demand for cable Internet services is given by $q_C = 100 - 3p_C + 2p_T$, where q_C is the number of cable Internet subscribers in town, p_C is the monthly price of cable Internet service, and p_T is the price of a DSL line from the telephone company. The demand for DSL Internet service is similarly given by $q_T = 100 - 3p_T + 2p_C$. Assume that both sellers can produce broadband service at zero marginal cost.

   a. Derive reaction functions that show the price each competitor should charge in response to the price charged by the other.

   b. Solve for each competitor's price, quantity, and profit, assuming that average total costs are zero.

   c. Suppose that the cable company begins to offer slightly faster service than the telephone company, which alters demands for the two products. Now $q_C = 100 - 2p_C + 3p_T$ and $q_T = 100 - 4p_T + p_C$. Show what effect this increase in service has on the prices and profit of each competitor.

17. Consider two Bertrand competitors in the market for brie, François and Babette. The cheeses of François and Babette are differentiated, with the demand for François' cheese given by $q_F = 30 - p_F + p_B$, where q_F is the quantity François sells, p_F is the price François charges, and p_B is the price charged by Babette. The demand for Babette's cheese is similarly given as $q_B = 30 - p_B + p_F$.

   a. Find the Bertrand equilibrium prices and quantities for these two competitors.

   b. Now consider a situation in which François sets his price first, and Babette responds. Follow procedures similar to those you used for Stackelberg quantity competition to solve for François' profit-maximizing price, quantity, and profit.

   c. Solve for Babette's profit-maximizing price, quantity, and profit.

   d. Was François' attempt to seize the first-mover advantage worthwhile?

18. Consider a monopolistically competitive industry. A graph of demand and cost conditions for a typical firm is depicted in the diagram below.

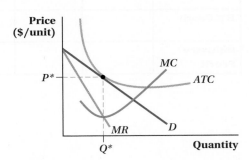

   a. Is this firm generating producer surplus? Is this firm earning a profit? How can you reconcile your answers?

   b. Do you expect any entry into or exit from this industry to occur? Explain.

   c. Suppose that the government reduces annual licensing fees, causing the fixed cost of the typical firm to fall. Make appropriate shifts of all curves that might be affected. What happens to producer surplus? What happens to profit? Do you expect the fall in fixed costs to cause entry into or exit from this industry? Explain.

d. Shift the demand and marginal revenue curves to reflect the entry/exit you indicated in (c). Find the new equilibrium.

e. Continue to reduce fixed cost. What happens to the demand curve as fixed cost continues to fall? What happens to producer surplus and profit?

f. Find the equilibrium as fixed cost falls to zero.

19. When competition between firms is based on quantities (Cournot competition), the reaction functions we derive tell us that when Firm A increases its output, Firm B's best response is to cut its own. However, when competition between firms is based on price (Bertrand competition), reaction functions tell us that Firm B's response to a cut in Firm A's price (which will lead to an increase in the quantity A sells) should be a corresponding cut in B's price (and a corresponding increase in its own output). Reconcile these two results.

*20. Suppose that the market demand for rose hips is given by $P = 100 - Q$. There are two firms, A and B, producing rose hips, each at a constant marginal and average total cost of $5. Fill in the table below for each market structure.

	Collusive Monopoly	Cournot Oligopoly	Bertrand Oligopoly	Stackelberg Oligopoly (A is first-mover)
A's Quantity				
B's Quantity				
Industry Quantity				
Price				
A's Profit				
B's Profit				
Industry Profit				

Game Theory

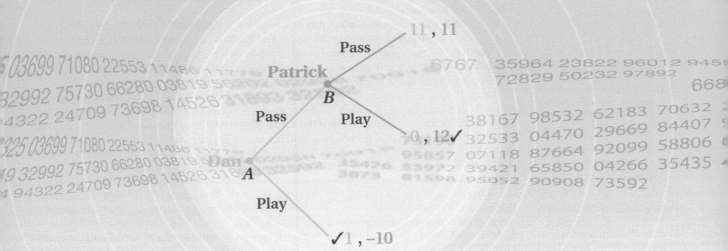

When Amazon first came out with its eBook reader, the Amazon Kindle, it priced the books at $9.99, which was below the royalties that the company had to pay the publishers for the books. It was widely cited that Amazon was going to lose money on the books in order to sell more Kindle devices at high profit margins. Soon after that, however, Apple released the iPad equipped with its own eBook reader as well as many other capabilities. Competition between the devices drove Amazon to cut the price of its Kindle significantly. Soon after that, Amazon created a Kindle App for the iPad that allowed iPad users to purchase and read their Kindle books on their Apple devices. Then, to compete directly with Apple's iPad, Amazon released its own tablet device, the Kindle Fire, at a price lower than the iPad. Each of these moves entailed strategic considerations by Apple and Amazon that involved thinking through the likely moves and countermoves their competitor would undertake.

In the previous chapter, we looked at various ways in which firms make price and quantity decisions in industries in which they have some market power but also face some competition. We discussed how market equilibrium in these situations requires

game theory
The study of strategic interactions among two or more economic actors.

strategic decision
An action made based on the anticipation of others' actions.

simultaneous game
A game in which participants choose their actions simultaneously without knowing their opponents' strategies.

repeated games
A series of simultaneous games among the same set of economic actors.

sequential game
Economic game in which players take consecutive turns.

more than quantity supplied equaling quantity demanded. Each individual firm must also be unwilling to change its price or output decisions once it knows its competitors' price or output decisions. In other words, the point at which quantity demanded equals quantity supplied must also be a Nash equilibrium.

The firm interactions we covered in the last chapter, just like the interactions between Amazon and Apple, are more complicated than those in perfectly competitive or monopolistic markets. These market structures involve many possible market outcomes because of strategic interactions between imperfectly competitive firms. Each firm's actions affect not only its own payoff but also the other firms' payoffs. Because every firm takes this interconnectedness into account when planning what to do, decision making can become quite complex.

Being able to understand what might happen when economic actors interact strategically, as they do in oligopoly markets, is the purpose of **game theory,** the focus of this chapter. Game theory studies behavior when several players are making **strategic decisions**—that is, their actions affect others, others' actions affect them, and they are trying to anticipate the actions of others.

Game theory applies to *real* games, too. Playing chess well involves choosing your moves based on how you believe your opponent will respond. In poker, if you raise the bet, you're thinking about whether the other players believe you have good cards and will therefore fold, or believe you are bluffing and will call your bet. In this chapter, we learn that game theory can be used to better understand all kinds of economic decisions, such as when movies are released, what products companies choose to produce, how to deter the entry of competitors, and many others. Truth be told, we already used a fair amount of game theory in the previous chapter. The oligopoly models—collusion, Bertrand, Cournot, Stackelberg, and differentiated-product Bertrand—are all specific applications of game theory.

In this chapter, we study three basic categories of games. First are **simultaneous games,** in which participants have to choose their strategies at the same time without knowing what strategies their opponents are pursuing. Examples of simultaneous games include Chapter 11's Cournot and Bertrand models, in which firms choose quantities or prices simultaneously. Next, we look at **repeated games** in which the players play the same simultaneous game over and over. Our discussion in Chapter 11 about how collusion could be stable in some circumstances even though every colluding firm has an incentive to cheat on the agreement can be explained by considering the collusive model as a repeated game. Finally, we look at **sequential games,** in which one firm moves first and the next firm gets to see what the first mover did. These games are like the Stackelberg oligopoly we analyzed in Chapter 11.

Being comfortable with these three basic types of game structures will give us an extremely useful tool for understanding many economic scenarios. That said, though, there are many other, more advanced areas of game theory we won't cover in this chapter. For example, a very important area of game theory studies situations in which some players have information that other players do not. These are known as games with asymmetric information; we discuss the role of asymmetric information in economic decision making in Chapter 15. Another set of games we won't cover are *cooperative games*, in which players are able to make binding commitments to one another and can form coalitions that play as a single unit. We instead focus on *noncooperative games*, in which it's every player for herself, a more accurate reflection of the nature of most games between firms and, often, consumers as well.

Several themes emerge as we apply game theory to understand the strategic interactions producers and consumers engage in every day. First, understanding game theory is all about being able to see the world through the eyes of the other guy. A player must anticipate what her opponents will do and plan for it. A second theme is that much of game theory (at least the kind we study in this chapter) rests on the view that opponents are rational; that is, they know what's good for them. If that isn't true (and who hasn't had to deal with some irrational bozo, on occasion?), what a player should do may vary quite a lot from the standard game theoretical approach.

A final theme evokes something we discussed while analyzing oligopoly in Chapter 11. How you set up the rules of the game—who gets to move first, or who starts with what—can make a very big difference in the outcomes that game theory predicts.

12.1 What Is a Game?

Every game, no matter how simple or complex, shares three common elements: players, strategies, and payoffs. We describe what each of these concepts means in the context of game theory to lay the groundwork for our analysis in the rest of the chapter.

The **players** in a game are the decision makers. They face situations in which outcomes they care about are affected both by their own choices and by the choices of others. Players in economic games can be firms (and their managers), consumers, workers, or many other entities. Regardless of their role, however, by definition, all players make choices.

A **strategy** is a player's plan of action for a game. Generally, the strategy a player chooses to pursue depends on the anticipated actions of other players. That is, the strategy a player chooses depends on what strategies she *thinks* her competitors will use.

Strategies can be simple, such as "I'll redesign my product this year no matter what my competitor does," or more complex, such as "If the other firm has kept its price high for the last three periods, I'll set a high price this period. Otherwise, I will keep prices low for the next two periods, and try to take some market share from my competitors." In fact, instead of being dependent on the actions of an opponent, a strategy can even be random: "I'll flip a coin. If it comes up heads, I'll charge a low price, and if it comes up tails, I'll charge a high price."

Payoffs are the outcomes the players receive from playing the game. For consumers, the payoff may be measured in terms of utility or consumer surplus. For firms, payoffs generally represent producer surplus or profits. Most of the time, one player's payoff depends on the strategies that both the player and her opponents choose. The fact that the players' actions affect each other's payoffs and that they know about this effect ahead of time is what makes game theory *game* theory. When only the player's own choices affect her payoffs, that is called a *single-agent problem*. A monopolist choosing an output level given the demand and marginal cost curves it faces or the consumers' utility-maximization problem are examples of single-agent problems. Once a player's actions are affected by others' choices, however, it's a game. The player now has an incentive to understand what motivates her opposing players. The better she can understand her opponent's motivation, the better the choices she can make in response.

These are the three common elements of games, and you need to understand them to be able to predict the likely outcomes of strategic interactions. But a key to forming those predictions—that is, to pinning down a game's equilibrium outcome—is to understand how players' strategies intertwine. The next section deepens our knowledge of strategies before we move on to analyzing various types of games.

Dominant and Dominated Strategies

Predicting behavior in games is about finding a player's **optimal strategy**—the action that has the highest expected payoff. This can be difficult because a particular strategy may be optimal for a player if her opponent chooses one action, but not optimal if her opponent chooses another action (this is another way of saying her optimal strategy must be a best response to the other player's chosen strategy). Some situations, though, don't entail that level of complexity; we start by talking about those simpler situations.

player
A participant in an economic game, who must decide on actions based on the actions of others.

strategy
The plan of action that a player takes in an economic game.

payoff
The outcome a player receives from playing the game.

optimal strategy
The action that has the highest expected payoff.

Table 12.1   An Advertising Game*

		Disney	
		Advertise	Don't Advertise
DreamWorks	Advertise	150 , 150	450 , –75
	Don't Advertise	–75 , 450	225 , 225

Outcomes are measured in millions of dollars of profit.

dominant strategy
A winning strategy for a player, regardless of her opponents' strategies.

dominated strategy
A losing strategy for a player, regardless of her opponents' strategies.

payoff matrix
A table that lists the players, strategies, and payoffs of an economic game.

If a strategy is always the best thing for a player to do no matter what the other players do, it is called a **dominant strategy.** Strategies that are never the right thing to do are called **dominated strategies.**

Let's think back to our example from the last chapter of the advertising decisions of DreamWorks and Disney with regard to their animated movies. We made a box that listed each company's strategy and the subsequent payoffs in millions of dollars of profit to each company. This box, called a **payoff matrix,** is shown in Table 12.1 (which is a reprint of Table 11.1). The first (left) payoff always belongs to the row player; the second (right) payoff always belongs to the column player. Thus, DreamWorks' choices are shown on the left (the rows of the payoff matrix) and its payoffs are listed in red, before the comma. Disney's choices are listed along the top of the table (the columns of the payoff matrix) and its payoffs are in blue, after the comma.

In Chapter 11, we saw that this game is a prisoner's dilemma: Even though DreamWorks and Disney could both make higher profits if they agreed not to advertise, each had such a strong individual incentive to advertise that they both ended up committing to a full advertising budget.

The expression "prisoner's dilemma" comes from the classic example often used to introduce people to the concept behind this type of game. In the example, two suspected conspirators are brought in by the police and interviewed in separate rooms. If neither confesses, the district attorney will only have enough evidence to convict them on a lesser charge, and they will quickly go free. If both confess, they will be convicted of a serious crime and severely punished. If one confesses but not the other, the one who confesses will get a lighter sentence for cooperating, and the other will receive an especially harsh sentence. While clearly the prisoners would be best off if they could coordinate on remaining silent, the payoff structure of the game is set up so that each has the unilateral incentive to confess. This makes the game's Nash equilibrium a very unappealing one (at least to the suspects): Both confess and receive severe sentences. Here, DreamWorks and Disney are the prisoners and advertising is akin to confessing.

The reason for this outcome is that in this game, the "Advertise" strategy is a dominant strategy for both companies. That is, DreamWorks makes more profit by advertising *Kung Fu Panda 3* whether Disney advertises *Cars 3* or not. If Disney does not advertise, DreamWorks earns $450 million if it advertises instead of $225 million if it doesn't. If Disney *does* advertise, DreamWorks earns $150 million if it also advertises, but loses $75 million if it doesn't. If we do a similar analysis for Disney's response to DreamWorks' advertising decisions, we arrive at the same result.

On the other side of the coin, the "Don't Advertise" strategy is never the best thing to do. In other words, it is a dominated strategy because "Advertise" is a dominant strategy. (When one strategy is dominant, all other strategies must be dominated.) There is never a situation in which Disney's or DreamWorks' payoffs are larger from choosing "Don't Advertise" than from choosing "Advertise."

The notion of dominated strategies is useful for finding the equilibrium in a game. Because a dominated strategy is not a player's best choice under any circumstances, it makes no sense for a player to ever choose such a strategy. So, the first thing to do when analyzing any game is to go through the payoff matrix and eliminate all the dominated strategies as possible equilibrium outcomes for *all* players. In the game in Table 12.1, this process eliminates the "Don't Advertise" row for DreamWorks because DreamWorks can always achieve a higher payoff from advertising, so it will not select this strategy. Likewise, we want to eliminate the "Don't Advertise" column for Disney for the same reason. Note that not every game has dominated strategies. If a game has dominated strategies, however, as does this DreamWorks-Disney game, it is much easier to find the game's equilibrium outcome once the dominated strategies have been ruled out as possibilities.

After crossing out this row and column, a look at the remaining square shows there's only one possible strategy for rational players to pursue: Both DreamWorks and Disney end up advertising and earning $150 million each. Notice that we are sure of this outcome even though both companies must make their decisions simultaneously; that is, they do not know what action the other company will take before making their own choices.

12.2 Nash Equilibrium in One-Period Games

In Chapter 11, we had to expand the concept of equilibrium to apply it to market outcomes in oligopolistic industries. Because each oligopolistic firm's price and quantity decisions influence those of its competitor, equilibrium in oligopolies requires more than just an equilibrium price and quantity for the industry as a whole. The market stability equilibrium *also* requires that no firm in the industry wants to change its decision *given* the choices its competitors are making.

A Nash equilibrium is a natural concept for determining the likely outcome of a game. In a Nash equilibrium, no player wants to unilaterally change her strategy given whatever strategies the other players are choosing. That is, the players are all doing the best they can, given the others' actions.

When there are a lot of dominated strategies in a game, as in the DreamWorks-Disney example above, finding a Nash equilibrium can be fairly easy. However, in most games eliminating dominated strategies alone won't completely pin down Nash equilibria. That's because the conditions that must hold in a Nash equilibrium are not as stringent as those that define dominant and dominated strategies. A dominant strategy is *always* the best thing for a player to do, no matter what an opponent does. But a Nash equilibrium only requires that an action is the best thing a player can do *given the action the opponent happens to be taking.* Therefore, a game can have a Nash equilibrium even if it has no dominated or dominant strategies. Finding the equilibrium in these more general cases can still be straightforward if there aren't too many players or possible actions.

The first step to finding a Nash equilibrium in any game is to lay out the game's players, strategies, and the payoffs that result from every possible combination of strategies. Such is what Table 12.1 does for the DreamWorks-Disney game. This particular way of organizing the economic content of a game—that is, by putting each player's payoffs into a matrix based on the strategies chosen by the players—is called the **normal form.** Putting a game into normal form makes it easier to determine what its equilibria are (or if there is any equilibrium at all).

normal form
The common organization of an economic game into its players, strategies, and the payoffs in a payoff matrix.

Let's do an example with a new game. Two competing magazines, *I'm Famous Weekly* and *Look at Me! Magazine*, are each considering what to use as the cover story for its next issue. They each have the same two choices, which we'll label reality show (RS) and celebrity interview (CI). We assume that neither magazine can observe its competitor's cover choice until it's on the newsstands, so both magazines must make their choices simultaneously. In addition, we assume some readers only like stories about reality shows, others only like celebrity interviews, and the readers who prefer celebrity interviews outnumber those who like reality show articles. If a magazine is the only one offering a particular type of story, it will get all of those readers. If both offer the same story, they will split those readers between them, but *Famous* will receive a larger share than *Me!* because a majority of readers prefer *Famous*, all else equal.

The profits (in thousands of dollars) that each magazine earns depend on its own choice for a cover story as well as its competitor's choice. These choices and their payoffs are shown in Table 12.2. As before, the red number before the comma

Table 12.2 | **Choosing a Cover Story***

		Look at Me! Magazine's Cover Story	
		Reality Show (RS)	**Celebrity Interview (CI)**
I'm Famous Weekly's Cover Story	**Reality Show (RS)**	300 , 0	400 , 400 ✓
	Celebrity Interview (CI)	✓ 500 , 300 ✓	✓ 450 , 200

*Payoffs are measured in thousands of dollars of profit.

in each cell is the payoff to *I'm Famous Weekly*, and the blue number after the comma is the payoff to *Look at Me! Magazine*.

To zero in on the game's Nash equilibrium, let's first consider *Famous*' best responses to *Me!*'s possible actions. If *Me!* chooses an RS cover story (left column), then *Famous*' best action is to choose a CI cover. This is because it will earn a $500,000 payoff by choosing CI but only $300,000 by choosing RS. To keep track of this best response, we'll put a check next to *Famous*' payoff in the bottom left cell. If *Me!* runs a CI cover, *Famous*' best response is still to choose CI because it earns $450,000 instead of $400,000. Because this is *Famous*' best response in this situation, we put another check next to the $450. We can see that choosing a celebrity interview as its cover strategy is a dominant strategy for *Famous*; no matter what *Me!* does, *Famous* makes more money by going with the CI cover.

Now let's do the same exercise for *Me!*. If *Famous* chooses a reality show cover, then *Me!* should choose a celebrity interview cover, because it will make $400,000 of profit rather than $0. We put a check next to the $400 payoff in the upper-right cell to indicate that this is a best response for *Me!*. However, if *Famous* chooses a CI cover, *Me!* is better off choosing an RS cover. It will make $300,000 instead of $200,000 by doing so, because it will have the reality show readers all to itself rather than splitting the set of celebrity interview fans. Another check goes next to the $300 payoff for *Me!* in the lower-left corner.

Looking at the pattern of checks (i.e., the pattern of best-response strategies), we can see a couple of things right away. First, *Famous* will choose a celebrity interview for its cover because this is a dominant strategy. Why? Remember that a dominant strategy is the best strategy for a player to follow no matter what the other player does. Because choosing a celebrity interview cover results in higher payoffs (profits) for *Famous* no matter what *Me!* does (look at the check marks for *Famous*' payoffs in Table 12.2), the celebrity interview is a dominant strategy for *Famous*. And, because a reality show cover is never the best option for *Famous*, RS is a dominated strategy.

Me! Magazine, on the other hand, has no dominant strategy: If *Famous* chooses a CI cover, *Me!* will earn a higher profit by choosing a reality show cover. If *Famous* instead chooses an RS cover, then *Me!* is better off choosing CI. Thus, *Me!*'s best strategy changes with the choice made by *Famous*; no one strategy is best under all circumstances, so *Me!* has no dominant strategy. It also has no dominated strategy because both strategies (RG and CI) can each be a best strategy for *Me!*, depending on *Famous*' action.

Second, even though we can't eliminate all but one possible outcome by getting rid of dominated strategies, there is still a Nash equilibrium to the game. In fact, we can see that *Famous* choosing a CI cover story and *Me!* choosing an RS cover are a mutual best response—both players have checks by their payoffs in this cell. Therefore, this is a Nash equilibrium. As is true of Nash equilibria in general, even if you gave either magazine the ability to unilaterally change its strategy choice, once one magazine knew what the other was doing, it wouldn't want to switch because doing so would only reduce its profit. That stability is a primary reason why the Nash equilibrium is useful for predicting the outcomes of games.

The check method

Solving games can be challenging and complicated. But there are ways to simplify games that will make you a Nash equilibrium expert in no time!

To begin, always look at each player's decision-making process separately. Suppose you are trying to solve a game with two players, "Row" and "Column," each of whom can take one of two actions: "A" or "B."

Let's start by considering how Row should form her strategy:

■ First, ask, *"If Column chooses action A, what is the best action for Row to take?"* Then place a check mark next to the payoff for that action for Row. Row's payoffs should always be to the left of the comma in payoff matrices.

■ Next, ask, *"If Column chooses action B, what is the best action for Row to take?"* Then place a check mark next to that option.

Second, repeat the exercise from Column's perspective:

■ First, ask, *"If Row chooses A, what is the best action for Column to take?"* Check mark that payoff. (Remember that Column's payoffs should always be to the right of the comma in payoff matrices.)

■ Next, ask, *"If Row chooses B, what is the best action for Column to take?"* Another check mark.

Once you have finished looking at the game from both players' perspectives, look at all of the boxes in the payoff matrix. Do any have two check marks? If so, those are Nash equilibria. However, if none have double check marks, then the game does not have a Nash equilibrium (at least in pure strategies, covered later in this section).

The following sample game illustrates this method at work. (We print the payoff matrix in black ink rather than red and blue, so you can see what a matrix will look like on an assignment or exam.)

First, we look at Row's choices. If Column chooses action A, Row is better off choosing A (100 > 50). If Column chooses action B, Row is once again better off choosing action A (125 > 75). Therefore, we place check marks next to both of Row's payoffs from choosing A.

Next, we look at Column's choices. If Row chooses action A, Column is better off choosing B (100 > 50). If Row chooses action B, however, Column is better off choosing A (100 > 75). We place check marks next to these payoffs.

Note that there is only one box in the payoff matrix in which two check marks appear: Row selecting A and Column choosing B. This is the Nash equilibrium of the game.

You can also use this method to look for dominant and dominated strategies for each player. A dominant strategy is a strategy that is best for a player *no matter what action the other player takes*. Consider Row's decision we described above. If her answer to both questions is the same (always choose action A no matter what action Column takes or always choose B no matter what action Column takes), that strategy is a dominant strategy. You can then cross out the alternative (dominated) strategy, allowing you to reduce the game to fewer options. Then, repeat the process for Column. Crossing out can only occur when there are dominated strategies. When using the check method, dominated strategies are indicated by rows or columns without any check marks.

Remember that following dominant strategies will lead to a Nash equilibrium but not all Nash equilibria involve dominant strategies. Here is an easy way to tell the difference (again using our example from above):

Row: *"Column, I don't care what you do!* **No matter what action you take,** *I am always better off choosing action A."* (In other words, Row has a dominant strategy.)

Column: *"Row, your choice influences my best option.* **Given that you are choosing action A,** *I am better off choosing action B."* (Column has no dominant strategy, but choosing B when Row chooses A is the best response.)

Practice these steps, and game theory will no longer be a mystery to you!

		Column	
		A	B
Row	A	✓ 100 , 50	✓ 125 , 100 ✓
	B	50 , 100 ✓	75 , 75

12.1 figure it out

Two grocery stores in a small city are considering ways to update their stores. Each store can build a new store, remodel its existing store, or leave its store in its current condition. The game is shown below. Food4U's payoffs are listed before the comma and Grocery Mart's after. Payoffs listed are the stores' annual profits in thousands of dollars.

		Grocery Mart		
		Build New Store	**Remodel Existing Store**	**Leave Store As Is**
Food4U	**Build New Store**	200 , 200	300 , 400	400 , 150
	Remodel Existing Store	400 , 300	450 , 450	300 , 175
	Leave Store As Is	150 , 300	175 , 350	350 , 300

a. Are there any dominant strategies for either Food4U or Grocery Mart? Explain.

b. Are there any dominated strategies for either Food4U or Grocery Mart? Explain.

c. Solve for any Nash equilibria.

Solution:

a. A dominant strategy is a strategy that is best for a player no matter what strategy its opponent follows. Let's begin with the decision for Food4U. If it believes that Grocery Mart will build a new store, Food4U will remodel its existing store ($400,000 > other payoffs when Grocery Mart builds a new store). If Food4U believes that Grocery Mart will remodel its existing store, it will also remodel its existing store ($450,000 > other payoffs). But, if Food4U believes that Grocery Mart will leave its store as it currently stands, Food4U will build a new store ($400,000 > other payoffs). Because no strategy is the best to follow no matter what Grocery Mart does, Food4U does not have a dominant strategy.

Now, let's examine the decision for Grocery Mart. If Grocery Mart believes that Food4U will build a new store, its best strategy would be to remodel its existing store ($400,000 > other payoffs). If Grocery Mart thinks that Food4U will remodel its store, Grocery Mart's best strategy is to also remodel its own store ($450,000 > other payoffs). And, if Grocery Mart believes that Food4U will leave its own store as it is, Grocery Mart will still want to remodel its own store ($350,000 > other payoffs). Therefore, remodeling its store is a dominant strategy for Grocery Mart because it is the best strategy for Grocery Mart to follow regardless of the strategy Food4U chooses.

b. When Food4U believes that Grocery Mart will either build a new store or remodel its current store, Food4U's best strategy is to remodel its own store. When Food4U believes that Grocery Mart will leave its own store in its current state, Food4U is better off by building a new store. This means that under no circumstances is it better for Food4U to leave its store as is. Thus, "Leave Store As Is" is a dominated strategy for Food4U. Because "Remodel Existing Store" is a dominant strategy for Grocery Mart, the other two strategies must be dominated strategies.

c. Using the check method (shown in the table below), we can see that the Nash equilibrium occurs when Food4U and Grocery Mart both remodel their stores. This makes sense because "Remodel Existing Store" is a dominant strategy for Grocery Mart, and when Grocery Mart remodels its store, Food4U is also better off remodeling its own store.

		Grocery Mart		
		Build New Store	Remodel Existing Store	Leave Store As Is
Food4U	Build New Store	200 , 200	300 , 400 ✓	✓ 400 , 150
	Remodel Existing Store	✓ 400 , 300	✓ 450 , 450 ✓	300 , 175
	Leave Store As Is	150 , 300	175 , 350 ✓	350 , 300

Multiple Equilibria

Predicting likely outcomes of a game can be fairly easy when there's only one Nash equilibrium, as there is with prisoners' dilemmas or with the magazine cover story game we just analyzed. Because of the mutual-best-response logic of the Nash equilibrium, it's likely that the players will end up following the Nash equilibrium strategies. But things can get a lot tougher to figure out if there is more than one Nash equilibrium. And, games with multiple Nash equilibria aren't at all unusual.

Let's revisit DreamWorks and Disney, but this time we look at their choice of when to release their next movies. Suppose that both companies currently have animated movies ready for distribution, so now they must decide when these movies should open in theaters around the country.

Both companies want to take advantage of certain periods of the year when people have especially high demand for watching movies. We'll simplify things by saying the companies basically have three periods from which to choose their opening date. One is the Memorial Day weekend (which we'll call May). This has traditionally been a big movie-going time of the year and, as such, is an appealing option for an opening date. The second possibility is the time around Christmas and New Year's (which we'll call December). This is also typically a high-demand period of the year, though not quite as high as Memorial Day. Finally, there is mid-March, usually a low-demand period.

DreamWorks and Disney both understand these demand patterns. And if either were a monopolist, it could easily rank its opening date choices: May is best, then December, then March. But they're not monopolists. Their profits from choosing a particular opening date will depend on the *other* company's choice as well. This is, then, a game theory problem. The two companies realize that if they both choose the same opening date, it will be a relative disaster. They'll split the animated feature market down the middle rather than having the whole market to themselves (though at different times in the year).

Table 12.3   Selecting a Release Date*

Disney's Opening Date Choice

		May	December	March
Dream-Works' Opening Date Choice	**May**	50 , 50	✓ 300 , 200 ✓	✓ 300 , 100
	December	✓ 200 , 300 ✓	0 , 0	200 , 100
	March	100 , 300 ✓	100 , 200	−50 , −50

*Payoffs are measured in millions of dollars of profit.

So how will DreamWorks and Disney balance these opposing considerations? Table 12.3 shows the specifics of the game they are playing, including the payouts that both companies would receive for any possible set of opening date strategies.

If either company chooses a May opening when the other does not, the May opener makes $300 million. If either company opens by itself in December, its movie will make $200 million. Finally, if either company has a March opener to itself, it makes $100 million.

If both companies open their movies in the same month, however, neither fares so well. In fact, we assume they'll earn lower profit regardless of the opening date (although they'll lose more if they open during worse times of the year). If they both choose to open in May, they make only $50 million each. If both movies open in December, each company earns zero profit. And if both firms opt to open in March, they will each incur a $50 million loss.

What is the Nash equilibrium for this game? To find out, we apply our check method to mark each player's best-response strategies. First, let's do it for DreamWorks. If Disney chooses a May opening date, DreamWorks' best response is to choose a December opening ($200 million > $100 million > $50 million). If Disney chooses December, then May is DreamWorks' best response. May is also DreamWorks' best response if Disney chooses a March opening date. We've put checks next to the payoffs for all of DreamWorks' best responses. (Remember that DreamWorks' numbers are in red and to the left of the comma.)

Everything for Disney's optimal responses is just a mirror image, so we can check off its best responses in the same manner. If DreamWorks chooses a May opening date, Disney should choose December ($200 million is its largest payoff possible). If DreamWorks chooses either a March or December opening date, Disney earns more profit by choosing May ($300 million is its largest payoff possible).

Now we've identified each firm's best responses to any possible strategy its competitor might pursue. One thing to notice is that a March opening is a dominated strategy for both players. That is, it is *never* optimal to open in March regardless of what the competitor might do. So we can cross out any outcomes that involve either firm opening in March. That simplifies the game to the four squares in the upper left of the game table. These are shown by themselves in Table 12.4.

Look at the mutual best responses, where there are two checks in the same box. There are two of them. Either DreamWorks picks December and Disney chooses May, or the other way around. Both outcomes are Nash equilibria of the game. This game shows the difficulty of predicting the outcome of games with multiple equilibria. We can narrow

Table 12.4   Selecting a Release Date (Simplified Game)*

Disney's Opening Date Choice

		May	December
Dream-Works' Opening Date Choice	**May**	50 , 50	✓ 300 , 200 ✓
	December	✓ 200 , 300 ✓	0 , 0

*Payoffs are measured in millions of dollars of profit.

down the possibilities—no rational company would choose a March date, for example, and both companies would avoid opening their movies on the same weekend—but we cannot say precisely what the one outcome will be. We know that one company would likely pick May and the other December, but given the information in the table, we have no basis to determine what company chooses which date.

Later in the chapter, we see that changes in the structure of the game, such as changes in the sequence of moves or modest shifts in payouts, can lead to different outcomes than the multiple Nash equilibria shown here. For the time being, however, we've gone as far as game theory can take us with this game.

Mixed Strategies

We have been focusing on games in which a player makes a choice between different actions, choosing the specific strategy that maximizes her payoff. This type of strategy is known as a **pure strategy.** However, it may not always be in the player's best interest to follow a pure strategy. In some situations, it may be best for the player to choose her actions randomly from the set of pure strategies available to her. This type of strategy is called a **mixed strategy.**

As an example of a game that can be played using a mixed strategy, think of a soccer game in which a player is taking a penalty kick. You've probably seen this on TV, or perhaps done it yourself on the field. The kicker faces the goalie, alone, and kicks the ball from close range. The distance is so close, in fact, that the goalie just dives to one side or the other and prays that it's the right way. It turns out that penalty kicks can be analyzed using game theory. There are players (the kicker and the goalie), with each having a set of strategy choices ("kick left" or "kick right" for the kicker, "dive left" or "dive right" for the goalie), and payoffs that depend on the chosen strategies of both players. This game is shown in Table 12.5.

Let's assume we're considering a pivotal penalty kick: If the goalie picks the same side as the kicker, the goalie's team wins, and if the players choose opposite sides, the kicker's team wins. We can assign payoffs of 1 to the winner and 0 to the loser. That's what is shown in the table. Note that, because the kicker and goalie face each other, a kicker choosing to kick to the right will hope that the goalie dives to the left—that is, the goalie's *own* right. To avoid confusion, we set up the table so a dive by the goalie toward where the kicker kicks the ball is considered to be the same direction choice—that is, both choose right or both choose left.

Let's use our check method again. The kicker always wants to do the opposite of what the goalie does. If the goalie chooses left, the kicker's best response is to choose right. If the goalie dives right, the kicker wants to kick left. However, the goalie always wants to match the kicker's choice: If the kicker chooses left, the goalie's best response is to go left and go right if the kicker chooses right. Putting checks by all these responses gives us the situation in the table.

Notice what has happened: *There is no box with two checks in it.* That's because no set of strategies exists such that both players simultaneously choose the best response to the other's choice. Our check method therefore doesn't indicate any pure-strategy Nash equilibrium to the game, at least in the way we have been defining a Nash equilibrium. In pure strategies, a Nash equilibrium always has two checks in a box.

It turns out that there actually *is* a Nash equilibrium to this game, but it is not one in pure strategies in which each player chooses a single action. All the games we've analyzed so far have had at least one (and sometimes more) pure-strategy equilibria,

pure strategy
A strategy in which the player chooses a particular action with certainty.

mixed strategy
A strategy in which the player randomizes her actions.

Table 12.5 | **A Mixed-Strategy Game: Penalty Kicks in Soccer**

		Goalie	
		Left	Right
Kicker	Left	0,1 ✓	✓ 1,0
	Right	✓ 1,0	0,1 ✓

such as both firms choosing to advertise, magazines selecting different cover stories, or film studios ensuring their films are not released at the same time.

The Nash equilibrium that exists in the penalty-kicks game involves *randomizing* across different strategies, that is, sometimes choosing one option (kick right) and at other times choosing another (kick left). Suppose the kicker, rather than simply choosing left or right as a strategy to follow all of the time, formed a strategy like "I will kick right 80% of the time and kick left 20% of the time." The goalie could have a similar strategy of diving one way or the other with a set probability. These randomized actions are mixed strategies. In mixed strategies, the randomization pattern (whether the probability mix is 80/20, 50/50, or anything else) is itself a strategy, just as kicking left for certain is a strategy.

Although the 80/20 right/left strategy example above is a mixed strategy, it is not a Nash equilibrium strategy. Think about it: If the kicker is going right 80% of the time, then the goalie's best response is to always go right. But the kicker's best response to a goalie diving right every time is to kick *left* all of the time. But if the kicker always goes left, the goalie also wants to go left all the time!

The only mixed-strategy Nash equilibrium in this game is for both the kicker and goalie to go left and right exactly half of the time. If the kicker kicks to the right half of the time and to the left the other half, the goalie gets the same payoff whether she jumps left or right, so she is happy to randomize between the two. And if the goalie splits 50/50, the same is true of the kicker. Therefore, this is a mutual best response.

The strange thing about a mixed-strategy Nash equilibrium is that, given that they are using the optimal probabilities, both players are indifferent between the actions they randomize over. If they weren't indifferent, they would prefer to play a pure strategy, where they would kick (dive) one direction all of the time. To arrive at a mixed-strategy equilibrium, each player needs to pick the probability of taking each action so that the player's *opponent* is indifferent between her own actions. By choosing a 50/50 split between kicking right and left, the kicker leaves the goalie equally well off whether she chooses to dive left or dive right. As a result, there is no way for the goalie herself to do better than dive right 50% of the time and dive left 50% of the time. This is one of the most confusing and counterintuitive results in all of economics, so if it seems bizarre, you are not alone in thinking so.

By the way, there was one more Nash equilibrium in the DreamWorks-Disney opening date game we analyzed earlier in Tables 12.3 and 12.4. We had two Nash equilibria for that game: (December, May) and (May, December). Because these equilibria involved each of the studios following a specified strategy, these were pure-strategy equilibria. But there is also a mixed-strategy equilibrium in that game. If both DreamWorks and Disney randomly choose with 50% probability between December and May openings—a coin flip, just like the kicker/goalie game above—that would be a Nash equilibrium. If each knows the other is randomizing, they will do the best they can by randomizing as well.

∂ The online appendix solves for mixed strategy equilibria. (http://glsmicro.com/appendices)

![puzzle] application

Random Mixed Strategies in Soccer

One of this book's authors, Steven Levitt, researched whether soccer players used mixed strategies when they take penalty kicks. Along with his coauthors Pierre-Andre Chiappori and Tim Groseclose, Levitt collected data on all the penalty kicks during a three-year period in the French and Italian elite soccer leagues.[1]

---

[1] Pierre-Andre Chiappori, Tim Groseclose, and Steven Levitt, "Testing Mixed-Strategy Equilibria When Players Are Heterogeneous: The Case of Penalty Kicks on Soccer." *American Economic Review* 92, no. 4 (September 2002): 1138–1151.

They classified kickers' and goalies' choices into one of three strategies: left, right, and center. This is a bit more complicated than our earlier left/right example, but the logic of the analysis is the same: The Nash equilibrium theory says that kickers and goalies should randomize across the choices in a way that makes the observed success rates of any direction choice the same.

This is just what Levitt, Chiappori, and Groseclose found in the actual data. The kickers and goalies seem to randomize their choices almost perfectly. The success rate was basically identical no matter which way they went. Chalk up a victory for game theory! It predicted very well the behavior of these players—who certainly had a lot at stake in the games they were playing and therefore had great incentive to optimize their behavior.

This kicker and goalie are playing more than one kind of game.

The funny side story of this research involves one hapless player who didn't quite figure out how randomized strategies work. When we talk about mixed strategies involving randomizing across strategies with certain probabilities, we mean *randomizing*. It's more than just making sure that one-third of the kicks occur in each direction, because you also need to make sure that a given strategy does not depend on the strategy the kicker chose before (for the same reason that a coin which always comes up heads, tails, heads, tails, heads, tails, and so on would be highly suspect even though each outcome happens 50% of the time).

Evidently, truly randomizing was too difficult for this player. So, he followed a set pattern for his kicks: first left, then center, then right, then back to left, and so on. He figured that mixing equally across the three choices would be enough to make goalies randomize in response. But it didn't take too long for the goalies to figure out his system. They started blocking virtually all of his kicks. This player may not know microeconomics, but he still learned (the hard way) that in soccer, there is no pure-strategy Nash equilibrium. ■

The Maximin Strategy (Or: What If My Opponent Is an Idiot?)

In game theory, the idea of Nash equilibrium is based on players rationally considering all the possible payoffs and coldly calculating their optimal best responses to their opponent's choices. You can probably imagine, then, that the notion of players making systematic errors (errors that are nonrandom and occur over and over again in the same direction) poses a big problem for predicting the outcomes of games by looking for Nash equilibria. If a player cannot trust her opponents to at least do what's in their own (the opponents') best interests, how should she act?

In Chapter 17, we look at some of the new economic research on behavioral economics, the branch of economics that argues people don't always behave rationally and, not being machines, often make various systematic errors in judgment.

We have a lot to say about irrationality in Chapter 17, but now is a good time to bring up a type of strategy known in game theory as the **maximin strategy** (short for "maximize the minimum"). Maximin is a conservative strategy because the player is not going for the highest payoff, but is instead choosing a strategy to minimize losses. Therefore, maximin can be useful in games in which one or more players might be irrational. The idea of the maximin strategy (and the origin of its name) is that a player takes actions that minimize the damage to her in the worst-case scenario—maximizing her minimum payoff. In other words, if an opponent chooses the exact strategy that would punish a player as much as possible (even if it hurts the opponent, too), in what way can the player respond that will minimize her damage? A maximin strategy limits

maximin strategy
A strategy in which the player minimizes her exposure to loss.

<table>
<tr><td rowspan="2">**Table 12.6**</td><td colspan="2">**Choosing a Cover Story Using a Maximin Strategy***</td></tr>
</table>

		Look at Me! Magazine's Cover Story	
		RS	**CI**
I'm Famous Weekly's Cover Story	**RS**	300 , 0	400 , 400 ✓
	CI	✓ 500 , 300 ✓	✓ 450 , 200

*Payoffs are measured in thousands of dollars of profit.

a game's downside; instead of looking for the best outcome given an opponent's actions, the player just tries to minimize her exposure to losses.

Let's go back to our earlier example in which two magazines are choosing a cover story for their next issue. We saw that a celebrity interview (CI) cover story was a dominant strategy for *I'm Famous Weekly*, and that the Nash equilibrium had *Look at Me! Magazine* going with a reality show (RS) cover as a best response. The payoffs are shown in Table 12.6 (which is the same as Table 12.2).

But suppose for a minute that *Me!*'s management believes its competitor isn't just *Famous* but also dumb, so dumb that it can't even tell that CI is its dominant strategy. If the *Famous* editorial board goes with the reality show cover (because they're irrational, confused, or in a hurry), it would be disastrous for *Me! Magazine* to proceed with an RS cover: Its profit would be zero. (Remember that both magazines are making these cover story decisions simultaneously.) If *Me!* goes with a CI cover instead, the worst it can do is make $200,000 if *Famous* opts for a CI cover (as it rationally should) and the best it can do is $400,000 if *Famous* acts irrationally and does an RS cover.

If *Me!* is risk-averse enough, it will choose to go with a celebrity interview cover even though the Nash equilibrium outcome has it producing a reality show gossip cover. This choice (choosing a CI cover) is a maximin strategy for *Me!*: It chooses the strategy that maximizes its minimum possible outcome, by raising it from $0 under RS to $200,000 under CI. The outcome of the game in this case is not a Nash equilibrium or a profit-maximizing equilibrium, however. *Me!* could do better (earning $300,000) by unilaterally changing its cover from CI to RS *if it knew for sure* that *Famous* was going to choose CI. *Me!* is giving up that best response in order to avoid what it considers to be a potential disaster should *Famous* be too dumb to do the rational thing.

Something that's interesting to note about this sort of situation is that a firm might realize it can influence its competitor's behavior by seeming to be crazy. The mere threat of irrational behavior—if it's credible enough—can be used in some cases to manipulate an opponent's actions in a player's favor.

 application

Fun in the Sun: Wine Making for Irrational Billionaires

Ah, owning a vineyard—the sun, the hills, the natural beauty. Sniffing wine out of one of those big glasses while sitting in Tuscany or Napa Valley, talking about vintages and "hints of chocolate and black currants" have an appeal to rich people throughout the world. So much so, in fact, that it seems just about every wealthy celebrity who retires decides to go into wine making. Examples include movie maker Francis Ford Coppola, tire magnates Leonard and Brooks Firestone, golfer Greg Norman, and many others.

If you simplify the business of wine making, you can think of two basic types of product: high-end wine and cheap (jug) wine. A guy who has made lots of money, say, running a successful tire company is probably not better equipped to make high-end wine than a big wine maker with extensive experience like Gallo. From a pure profit perspective, the payoffs from which wine the celebrity and Gallo choose to make might look something like those shown in Table 12.7.

If both the celebrity and Gallo decide to produce the same type of wine, Gallo will make a larger profit because of its relative expertise. In fact, the celebrity might be expected to lose money if both make high-end wine because the market is a bit smaller and the costs are higher. Both Gallo and the celebrity will be profitable if they make different types of wine, but with the one serving the larger, lower-cost jug wine market making higher profit.

Let's look at the players' best responses, shown by the checks. We can see that the Nash equilibrium

Table 12.7	Choosing a Wine to Produce*	
	Celebrity's Wine-Making Choice	
	High End	**Cheap**
Gallo's Wine-Making Choice High End	5 , −10	✓ 60 , 15 ✓
Cheap	✓ 50 , 5	30 , 10 ✓

*Payoffs are measured in thousands of dollars of profit per acre of vineyard.

has Gallo making high-end wine and the celebrity making cheap wine. In fact, making high-end wine is a dominated strategy for the celebrity: No matter what type of wine Gallo chooses to make, the celebrity's profit is higher by producing cheap wine.

If the celebrities think like game theorists, they'll realize this. So, Gallo ought to be able to count on celebrities making cheap wine, in which case Gallo should make high-end wine, right? Well, the problem is that these celebrities may not act rationally to maximize their profits. Or, to be more generous, their wine-making dream is driven by something besides profit. Almost always, celebrities will try to make high-end, award-winning wines (the kind they are accustomed to drinking, naturally), and they are willing to give up a lot of money in lost profit for this bragging right.

If Gallo suspects that the celebrities might be committed to producing high-end wine because of irrationality or motives other than profit, it might make sense for Gallo to go with a maximin strategy. In this case, that would be to produce cheap wine. The worst it could do in this case is make $30,000 per acre. If Gallo made high-end wines instead, its profit could fall as low as $5,000 per acre if the celebrity also chooses to produce the "good stuff."

This example comes straight from microeconomic research done by Fiona Scott Morton and Joel Podolny.[2] Their study of the wine industry documents an extremely large amount of entry into the high-end market segment—presumably from rich amateur vintners wanting to impress—despite extremely low profits in that segment. It makes sense, then, that the big wine makers place their main focus on mass market wines instead. They can avoid competition with wineries that simply don't care about losing money. Sometimes the toughest competitor may be the one who doesn't care about losing. ∎

12.3 Repeated Games

You now know how to find the Nash equilibrium (or equilibria) in a game in which the players make simultaneous moves. One of the examples we went over was the prisoner's dilemma facing DreamWorks and Disney in choosing whether to advertise (Table 12.1). Both firms would be better off if they could coordinate so that neither company advertises, but each firm has the individual incentive to advertise, so the firms are stuck making lower profits than they would if they could coordinate their decisions.

---

[2] Fiona M. Scott Morton and Joel M. Podolny, "Love or Money? The Effects of Owner Motivation in the California Wine Industry," *Journal of Industrial Economics* 50 (December 2002): 431–456.

Now consider a perfectly sensible question: Would it matter if these firms played this prisoner's dilemma game twice in a row? The basic problem in a prisoner's dilemma is that neither firm has the individual incentive to cooperate with the other, even though both would be better off if they could jointly agree to do so. It seems reasonable that if players know they are going to end up in the same situation again (and perhaps again and again), they might have a better chance of coordinating their actions in a mutually beneficial way. In this section, we examine this very issue and learn how to analyze repeated games that are more general than prisoner's dilemmas.

Finitely Repeated Games

When a simultaneous game is played repeatedly, players' strategies consist of actions taken during each repetition. If a game is played twice, players' strategies will involve what they do in both Periods 1 and 2. Players can even develop fancy strategies that change the second-period decision depending on what happens in the first.

So, how would we analyze the DreamWorks-Disney prisoner's dilemma if it is played twice—first for one pair of movies (*Kung Fu Panda 3* vs. *Cars 3*), and then for a second pair (*Kung Fu Panda 4* vs. *Cars 4*)? Would this lead to an outcome in which neither firm advertises?

backward induction
The process of solving a multistep game by first solving the last step and then working backward.

To answer this question, we first have to figure out how to think about games that are played more than once. The way to do this—not only for repeated prisoner's dilemmas like the one here, but also for any game with multiple rounds of play—is to use **backward induction** and solve the game from the end. Once you determine what happens in the last period of the game, you next ask what players would do in the period before the final one, given that they know how all the other players will act in the last period. (They know this because they can analyze the game's last period just as you can.) You repeat this process for as many steps as there are in a game, working backward one step at a time, until you can solve for the outcome in the first period. At that stage, you'll have figured out the players' optimal strategies at all points in the game.

In our example game here, there are only two periods or steps, so backward induction is fairly easy. First, we know that whatever might happen in the first period, the second period is the end of the interaction. So, when the two players get to the second and final period, they will be facing a one-shot prisoner's dilemma.

Unfortunately for the firms, the fact that the final period is a one-shot prisoner's dilemma means that, despite our speculation that it might be possible, cooperation in both periods (or either period, for that matter) is *not* a Nash equilibrium. Here's why. Suppose DreamWorks knows for sure that Disney will agree not to advertise in both periods. DreamWorks' best response in the last period, because it's just a one-shot prisoner's dilemma, is to cheat on the agreement and advertise. (After all, Disney can't do anything to punish them for cheating. It's the end of their interaction.) The logic works in reverse, too: Disney will also advertise in the second period.

Now you can probably see how things will unravel. Both players realize *in the first period* that they will both end up cheating in the second. It's going to be every firm for itself. But if they know this is how things will go down, what's the point of cooperating (by not advertising) in the first period? If a studio violates the first-period agreement and advertises, there can't be any special punishment in Period 2—it already knows what's going to happen. So, the first period becomes essentially another one-shot prisoner's dilemma, and we know the outcome of that from our discussion above: Both players cheat (advertise).

There goes that idea: As long as everyone knows when the game will end, repeated play doesn't help players solve their cooperation problems in prisoner's dilemmas. In every period, the Nash equilibrium remains the same as it was in the one-period setup.

Adding more periods won't matter, either. Even if the game is repeated 50 times (finishing with *Kung Fu Panda 53* vs. *Cars 53*), the 50th and final period will still be a one-shot game in which both firms go with their dominant strategies and advertise. In the 49th period, the firms realize that period 50 will be a cheatfest, so Period 49 becomes a one-shot game in which both firms advertise. The logic continues (and any nonadvertising agreements unravel) all the way back to the first period.

Not every game played across multiple periods is a repeated prisoner's dilemma like this one. But the use of backward induction is a standard technique that can be applied to determine equilibria in other types of multiple-period games. We look at examples of multiple-period games later in the chapter.

Infinitely Repeated Games

It turns out the prisoner's dilemma conundrum isn't completely hopeless. There is a possible way out (or, more specifically, a possible way to cooperate). The problem with the repeated game scenario that we just discussed is that everyone knows when the last period is, so they know that all players will cheat in the last period. This knowledge causes everything before the last period to unravel. But what if the players didn't know for sure when the last period was? Or if the players thought of themselves as playing the game over and over, forever?

The first thing you have to do in this seemingly odd game is specify a strategy for every period. This could become massively complex, given all the different orders in which a player could take actions. To make things easy, let's consider the following simple strategy. DreamWorks does not advertise in the first period and will afterward continue not to advertise as long as Disney doesn't break the agreement and advertise. If Disney ever advertises, though, DreamWorks abandons the deal and advertises from that point forward, forever. Disney's strategy is the mirror image of this: Don't advertise at first and stick to the agreement as long as DreamWorks doesn't advertise, but switch to advertising from then on if DreamWorks ever advertises.

Is this set of strategies a Nash equilibrium when the game is played forever, or perhaps more realistically, where the game could end in any particular period, but the players never know when exactly the last period will come?

Since there is no final period in this game that the players can predict precisely, we can't use backward induction. The way to think about Nash equilibria in this case is to weigh what a player could gain at any given point from trying something different from her current strategy. The logic of this approach comes straight from the definition of a Nash equilibrium: A player is doing as well as possible given the actions of the other players. If we can show that *any* change of strategy would make the player worse off, we know that sticking with the current strategy is a best response. If we can show this same thing for all of the players, we know the strategies result in a Nash equilibrium.

Let's try that here. Suppose DreamWorks decides to break with the cooperative don't-advertise strategy and starts advertising even though Disney hasn't advertised. We know that DreamWorks will experience a short-term gain in this period because even though DreamWorks advertises, Disney does not—remember, we're holding the actions of the other player fixed, so Disney will be playing the cooperative strategy of not advertising. This strategy is shown in the upper-right payoff box of Table 12.8 (a reprint of Table 12.1): DreamWorks will make $450 million this period and Disney will lose $75 million.

DreamWorks pays a price for its cheating ways, however. When it violates the agreement, it destroys any chance that Disney will cooperate in the future. Having chosen to advertise in some period, DreamWorks will have to duke it out with Disney from that point forward. Both firms will advertise all future films, and each studio will earn $150 million each time the game is played.

Table 12.8	**The Single-Period Payoffs of an Infinitely Repeated Advertising Game***

		Disney	
		Advertise	**Don't Advertise**
DreamWorks	**Advertise**	150 , 150	450 , −75
	Don't Advertise	−75 , 450	225 , 225

*Payoffs are measured in millions of dollars of profit.

What is DreamWorks' payoff from cheating? It earns \$450 million in the current period. In the next and every following period, it earns \$150 million. Let's allow for a firm to care somewhat less about future payoffs than current payoffs. We embody this discounting of the future with the variable d. (We will discuss the origin and impact of the discount rate and how to compute a "present value" for future payments in Chapter 13.) This variable is a number between 0 and 1, and it shows what a payoff in the next period is worth in the current period. That is, the firm views \$1 in the next period as being worth \$$d$ today. If $d = 0$, the player doesn't care at all about the future: Any payoff in the next period (or following periods) is considered worthless today. If $d = 1$, the player makes no distinction between future payoffs and today's payoffs; they are all equally valuable. A higher d means the player cares more about the future, making the value of future payments greater.[3]

Let's write down DreamWorks' payoff if it decides to break from the don't-advertise strategy and advertise in the current period:

Payoff from breaking away:

$$450 + d \times (150) + d^2 \times (150) + d^3 \times (150) + \ldots$$

Notice how payoffs further in the future are discounted more and more, because d is a per-period discount. What we have to do is compare this to the payoff DreamWorks receives by sticking with the don't-advertise strategy and earning \$225 million in this and every future period:

Payoff from sticking with the don't-advertise strategy:

$$225 + d \times (225) + d^2 \times (225) + d^3 \times (225) + \ldots$$

The analysis is the same for Disney's choice of adhering to the don't-advertise strategy or reneging and surprise advertising in one period. If we can show that the payoff from sticking with the strategy is greater than the payoff from breaking away, we know that the outcome of pursuing the cooperative, don't-advertise strategy is a Nash equilibrium. This is true if

$$225 + d \times (225) + d^2 \times (225) + d^3 \times (225) + \ldots > 450 + d \times (150) + d^2 \times (150) + d^3 \times (150) + \ldots$$

$$75 \times (d + d^2 + d^3 + \ldots) > 225$$

$$(d + d^2 + d^3 + \ldots) > 3$$

To solve for d, we can use a simple math trick, $d + d^2 + d^3 + \ldots = d/(1 - d)$ for any d between zero and one ($0 \leq d < 1$), and substitute it into the equation above:

$$\frac{d}{(1 - d)} > 3, \quad d > 0.75$$

What does this mean? As long as DreamWorks and Disney care enough about the future—as long as they view \$1 in the next period to be worth at least as much as \$0.75 in this period—they can earn higher expected profits by cooperating and not advertising than they could by unilaterally deviating and advertising today, setting off a cheating battle forever after. In other words, both firms cooperating (i.e., not advertising) is a Nash equilibrium in this game.

This "caring about the future" condition makes sense. Choosing to cooperate is about skipping a big payoff (profit) right now that the firm could earn by cheating on the

---

[3] When a game might end in any given period with some probability p, and that's the reason why the players don't care as much about the future, then we can think of $d = 1 - p$. The larger the chance that the game ends after today, the less the players care about future payoffs.

agreement in order to get a stream of higher payoffs (profits) in the future by cooperating. The more players care about the future—the larger d is—the more willing they are to sustain those future cooperative payouts. If this isn't quite clear to you, suppose $d = 0$, meaning that neither DreamWorks nor Disney cares about future payoffs at all. Then the only relevant payoffs for both firms are those of the one-period prisoner's dilemma, and we know in such a case that advertising is a dominant strategy for both firms. There's no reason to cooperate when you don't care about the future, which is where the benefit from cooperating is earned.

By the way, the strategy we analyzed here—in which the players cooperate as long as they both cooperate, but stop cooperating forever if one player cheats—is called the **grim trigger strategy** (or **grim reaper strategy**). Like a visit from the grim reaper, the punishment for deviating from cooperation, never cooperating again, is permanent for both players. In an alternative strategy, known as **tit-for-tat,** players initially cooperate and then do exactly whatever their opponent has done in the prior period. If the opponent cooperated last period, then the player cooperates this period. If the opponent cheated instead, then the player cheats until her opponent cooperates again (allowing the player to punish the opponent's cheating for one period in the process). The outcome of the tit-for-tat strategy is a little more complicated to work through than that of the grim trigger strategy, but a tit-for-tat strategy can also support cooperation as a Nash equilibrium in an infinitely repeated game if firms care sufficiently about the future. Tit-for-tat is also appealing because it closely matches the types of actions we often see in the real world. For example, gas stations situated across the road from one another will often engage in price wars in which each reduction in price by one station is quickly matched by the other. This situation is like the noncooperative breakdown in a repeated prisoner's dilemma—both stations would prefer coordinating on higher prices, but each has the incentive to cut price to sell a higher quantity. However, quite often if one station relents and actually raises its price in an attempt to start cooperating, the other station will follow suit rather than insisting on the grim strategy of keeping prices low forever.

Now we've identified the factors that can make coordination in a prisoner's dilemma a Nash equilibrium: The players cannot determine when the game will end, and the players have to care sufficiently about future payoffs.

grim trigger strategy (or grim reaper strategy)
A strategy in which cooperative play ends permanently when one player cheats.

tit-for-tat
A strategy in which the player mimics her opponent's prior-period action in each round; for example, the player cheats when her opponent cheated in the preceding round, and cooperates when her opponent cooperated in the previous round.

12.2 figure it out

Suppose that two motorcycle manufacturers, Honda and Suzuki, are considering offering 10-year full coverage warranties for their new motorcycles. Although the warranties are expensive to offer, it could be disastrous for one firm if it does not offer a warranty while its competitor does. Let's assume the payoffs for the firms are as follows (profits are in millions of dollars, with Honda's profits in red before the comma and Suzuki's in blue after it):

a. If the game is played once, what is the outcome?

b. Suppose the game is repeated three times. Will the outcome change from your answer in (a)? Explain.

c. Now, suppose the game is infinitely repeated and

		Suzuki	
		Offer Warranty	Don't Offer Warranty
Honda	Offer Warranty	20 , 20	120 , 10
	Don't Offer Warranty	10 , 120	50 , 50

Suzuki and Honda have formed an agreement to not offer warranties to their customers. Each firm plans the use of a grim trigger strategy to encourage compliance with the agreement. At what level of d would Honda be indifferent about keeping the agreement vs. cheating on it? Explain.

Solution:

a. We can use the check method to solve for the Nash equilibrium in a one-time game:

		Suzuki	
		Offer Warranty	Don't Offer Warranty
Honda	Offer Warranty	✓ 20 , 20 ✓	✓ 120 , 10
	Don't Offer Warranty	10 , 120 ✓	50 , 50

The Nash equilibrium occurs when both firms offer a warranty. Note that this is not the best cooperative outcome for the game, but it is the only stable equilibrium.

b. If the game is played for three periods, there would be no change in the players' behavior. In the third period, both firms would offer warranties because that is the Nash equilibrium. Knowing this and using backward induction, players will opt to offer warranties in both the second and the first periods as well.

c. Honda's expected payoff from cheating and offering a warranty would be the 120 million from the first period (when cheating) and 20 million for each period after that (because Suzuki will also start offering warranties):

$$\text{Expected payoff from cheating} = 120 + d \times (20) + d^2 \times (20) + d^3 \times (20) + \ldots$$

Honda's expected payoff from following the agreement is earning 50 million each period throughout time:

$$\text{Expected payoff from following agreement} = 50 + d \times (50) + d^2 \times (50) + d^3 \times (50) + \ldots$$

Therefore, Honda will be indifferent between these two options when the payoff streams are equal:

$$120 + d \times (20) + d^2 \times (20) + d^3 \times (20) + \ldots = 50 + d \times (50) + d^2 \times (50) + d^3 \times (50) + \ldots$$

$$d \times (30) + d^2 \times (30) + d^3 \times (30) + \ldots = 70$$

$$d + d^2 + d^3 + \ldots = \frac{7}{3}$$

Because $d + d^2 + d^3 + \ldots = \dfrac{d}{(1-d)}$ for any $0 \leq d < 1$:

$$\frac{d}{(1-d)} = \frac{7}{3}$$

$$d = 0.7$$

Therefore, Honda will be indifferent between following the agreement or cheating if $d = 0.7$.

Multiple Equilibria in Infinitely Repeated Games   The weird thing about infinitely repeated games is that there are usually a whole range of possible Nash equilibria. Suppose DreamWorks and Disney are playing tit-for-tat strategies in the game above. We mentioned that following this strategy can sustain cooperation, period-after-period, in equilibrium. But suppose for some reason, every once in a while, one of the firms advertises. The competitors might go through a cycle of punishment as a result, but with tit-for-tat it's possible that the two studios could return to cooperation afterward. Thus, an equilibrium with cooperation part of the time, but not all of the time, also exists. In fact, any outcome that is at least as good for the players as the one-shot cheating payoff has the potential to work as an equilibrium in this infinitely repeated game. The idea that many equilibria exist in repeated games and that anything that meets a minimum threshold could, in principle, work as a Nash equilibrium is known as the Folk Theorem. The Folk Theorem holds even in much more complicated games than we will cover in this book.

12.4 Sequential Games

There are many situations in which players do not have to make their moves at the same time, as we've been assuming so far. Instead, they take actions in turn. One player moves first, and the other observes this action before making her decision. Games with this structure are known as **sequential games.**

The normal-form matrix that we've been using for simultaneous games doesn't work for sequential games, because it does not provide us with a way to keep the timing of actions separate from the choice of actions. Instead, we plot sequential games in what's called the **extensive form** or a **decision tree** (Figure 12.1). The sequence of the game flows from left to right. Each node in an extensive form game represents a choice, and the player listed at that node is the one choosing what action to take. The payoffs to every possible sequence of strategies are listed at the far right.

Figure 12.1 revisits the DreamWorks-Disney release date game we presented earlier in Table 12.3 (which we repeat on the next page as Table 12.9 for convenience) as a

sequential games
Games where one player moves first and other players observe this action before making their decisions.

extensive form or **decision tree**
Representation of a sequential game that shows both the choice and timing of players' actions.

Figure 12.1 | **Decision Tree for Choosing a Release Date**

In this sequential game, DreamWorks chooses a release date first at node *A*. If DreamWorks chooses a May release date, Disney will choose a December release date at node *B*; if DreamWorks chooses December or March, Disney will choose May at nodes *C* and *D*, respectively. Unlike the simultaneous game outcome in Table 12.4, the companies reach a single Nash equilibrium at node *B*. Here, DreamWorks releases *Kung Fu Panda 3* in May, and Disney releases *Cars 3* in December.

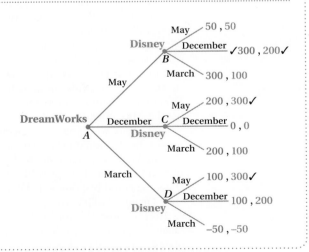

Table 12.9   **Selecting a Release Date***

		Disney's Opening Date Choice		
		May	**December**	**March**
Dream-Works' Opening Date Choice	**May**	50 , 50	✓ 300 , 200 ✓	✓ 300 , 100
	December	✓ 200 , 300 ✓	0 , 0	200 , 100
	March	100 , 300 ✓	100 , 200	−50 , −50

*Payoffs are measured in millions of dollars of profit.

game in which both firms make their decisions at the same time. Now we assume that Dream-Works finishes *Kung Fu Panda 3* first and gets to choose a release date before Disney chooses one for *Cars 3*.

The leftmost node (*A*) in the decision tree represents Dream-Works' opening date choice. Once it has decided, then Disney can choose. If DreamWorks chooses a May opening date, then Disney makes its choice from node *B*. If DreamWorks instead chooses December, then Disney decides from node *C*. For a DreamWorks opening choice of March, Disney responds from node *D*.

Depending on two firms' choices, the firms earn the payoffs listed on the far right. [As in the normal form game, the first number listed in each pair (red) is DreamWorks' profit, and the second number (blue) is Disney's profit.] If you look at these payoffs for a minute, you can see that we've just transformed the normal form game payoffs in Table 12.9 into extensive form for this sequential game. When one firm moves first, however, as DreamWorks does here, the outcome of the game is completely different. When the game was a simultaneous-move game, we found that there were two pure strategy Nash equilibria: (1) DreamWorks releases in May for a profit of $300 million, and Disney releases in December for a profit of $200 million and (2) DreamWorks releases in December for a profit of $200 million, and Disney releases in May for a profit of $300 million. What do you think will happen in a sequential game?

Just as we did in the repeated simultaneous games in Section 12.3, we use backward induction to find Nash equilibria in sequential games. Suppose DreamWorks picks May. That puts us at node *B* in the game tree, and Disney must now choose an opening date in response. If Disney also chooses May, it will make $50 million. If it chooses December, its profit will be $200 million. If it chooses March, it will earn $100 million. Therefore, the best response Disney can make is to choose December, and we put a check next to Disney's December payout in the figure.

Now suppose DreamWorks picks a December opening instead, putting the game at node *C*. Going through the same process, we see that if Disney chooses May, it earns $300 million. It now makes zero profit by going with December and earns $100 million with a March opening. Disney's best response to DreamWorks' December is to open in May, so we check this choice.

Finally, if DreamWorks chooses to open its film in March (node *D*), Disney will open in May. It earns $300 million by doing so instead of earning only $200 million with a December opening and losing $50 million with a March opening. Again, we put a check by the May opening choice.

Now that we know how Disney will respond in the last stage for all possible first moves by DreamWorks, we can work backward to figure out exactly what choice DreamWorks will make at the first node (*A*). DreamWorks understands how Disney will respond to each of its possible strategy choices and can make its own decision based on these expected responses. If DreamWorks chooses a May opening, for example, it knows that Disney maximizes its own profit by choosing a December opening.

Here is how DreamWorks looks at its choice in the first stage. If it chooses May, Disney will open in December, and DreamWorks earns $300 million. If DreamWorks opens in December, Disney will respond by opening in May, and DreamWorks will earn $200 million. Finally, DreamWorks earns $100 million with a March opening because

Disney will respond with a May opening. It is clear that DreamWorks' highest payout, $300 million, occurs when it chooses a May opening date, and we put a check next to that payoff.

That's it; we've pinned down the equilibrium of the sequential game. *Kung Fu Panda 3* opens in May and *Cars 3* opens in December. DreamWorks earns $300 million in profit and Disney makes $200 million. In the simultaneous-move game, we had multiple equilibria; either firm could open in May and the other in December. But when the firms act sequentially, the firm that chooses first gets the lucrative May slot. The sequential structure eliminates the multiple equilibria problem that can occur with simultaneous games. The outcome is still a Nash equilibrium, though. Taking the other player's action as given, each player is doing the best it can once its turn rolls around.

Note that we just arbitrarily picked DreamWorks as the first-mover in playing this game. If we look at the structure of the game's payouts for a minute, it should be apparent that if Disney were able to choose first, the equilibrium would be reversed: Disney would open in May (earning $300 million) and DreamWorks would open in December (earning $200 million). This outcome raises a few questions. What factors would determine which firm is the first-mover in the real world? If it wasn't clear who would make the first move in a sequential game, could a firm just be the first to *threaten* to open in May and gain the first-mover advantage? Also, is moving first always an advantage in a sequential game? We look at these sorts of questions in the next section.

make the grade

Backward induction and trimming trees

Solving sequential games requires you to work backward, using a technique that game theorists call *backward induction*. It may seem a little strange to start with the second player when you know that the second player must wait until the first player makes her move. After all, the whole point of a sequential game is that the *order* of plays is important, and often the first player has a first-mover advantage. So, why would we start solving the game from the end and work backward?

Remember that we assume all players know the strategies available to every player in the game and the payoffs that accompany every possible outcome. Before Player 1 decides her strategy, she must consider what Player 2 is likely to do. After all, Player 1's payoff is determined both by her choice and that of her opponent. When we are solving the game, we want to think like the players. Therefore, to determine the best strategy for Player 1 to use, we must first examine what Player 2 is likely to do given every possible choice that Player 1 might choose. While it seems like we are acting as if Player 2 is moving first, in reality we are just putting ourselves in Player 1's shoes as she considers her best strategy, and that begins with predicting Player 2's moves.

There is another useful step, called "trimming the branches," that you can take to simplify sequen-

tial games. (This term comes from the idea that the extensive form of a game is often referred to as a "decision tree.") Trimming the branches is very similar to removing dominated strategies in a normal-form game. Basically, this method allows you to narrow the solution options by eliminating any branches that represent any actions that Player 2 would never take.

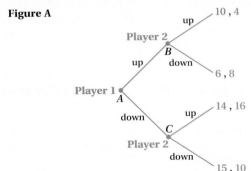

Figure A

We can use backward induction to solve the game shown in Figure A. Remember, we are trying to think like Player 1—who is moving first—in considering what Player 2 will do. Look at node *B*, where Player 1 has selected "up." What will Player 2 do? He will choose "down," because his payoff is greater. Not only can we add a check mark to that payoff, but we can also eliminate "up" as an option at node *B* (because Player 2 will not choose it). Therefore, we can trim (mark out) that branch as shown in Figure B. Now, consider what Player 2 will do if Player 1 chooses "down" (node *C*). Here, Player 2 will choose "up," so we can put a check mark next to that payoff and mark out the "down" branch at node *C*.

Figure B

$$10, 4$$

Player 2 — *B*

up — down

$$6, 8\checkmark$$

Player 1 • *A*

down — up

$$\checkmark14, 16\checkmark$$

C

Player 2

down

$$15, 10$$

The final step we must take is choosing Player 1's best strategy. She knows that, given Player 2's expected moves, she is only left with two options (those not trimmed from the tree): Choose "up" and earn a payoff of 6 or choose "down" and earn a payoff of 14. Therefore, she will choose "down" and we can place a check mark by her payoff.

Backward induction and trimming the tree greatly simplify even the most complex sequential games. The trick is to place yourself in the first player's shoes by considering the actions that will be chosen by the second (third, fourth, etc.) player. Sometimes it is beneficial to do things backward!

Another Sequential Game

Let's close this section by considering another sequential game. Here's how it works.

Suppose that Dan and Patrick are two contestants on a game show called "Play or Pass." They flip a coin to decide who goes first, and Dan wins. The rules are simple: Dan decides if he wants to play or pass. If Dan chooses "Play," the game ends and he receives a payoff of 1, and Patrick receives a payoff of −10. However, if Dan chooses "Pass," then Patrick gets a turn. If Patrick chooses "Play," he receives a payoff of 12 and Dan receives a payoff of 0. If Patrick chooses "Pass," however, both players receive a payoff of 11. This sequential game is shown in Figure 12.2. Dan's decision occurs at node *A*, and Patrick's at node *B*.

Before we solve for the equilibrium of this game, let's look at all the possible payoffs. One outcome—which occurs if both Dan and Patrick call "Pass"—results in high payoffs for both players, with each getting 11. The other two outcomes are lopsided:

Figure 12.2   Sequential Play or Pass Game

In the play or pass game, Dan must first decide whether to play or pass (node *A*). If Dan decides to play, he earns a payoff of 1 and Patrick loses 10. If Dan chooses to pass, Patrick will choose to play at node *B*, yielding Dan a payoff of zero and Patrick a payoff of 12. Therefore at the Nash equilibrium, Dan will play and earn 1.

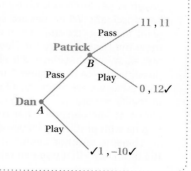

$$11, 11$$

Pass

Patrick

B

Pass — Play

$$0, 12\checkmark$$

Dan •

A

Play

$$\checkmark1, -10\checkmark$$

If Dan calls "Play" immediately, the game ends with him earning a payoff of 1 and Patrick losing 10. If Dan instead calls "Pass" and Patrick responds with "Play," the game ends with Patrick earning 12 and Dan obtaining nothing. You might think that a game structure like this gives the players a strong incentive to get to the pass/pass outcome, so that both can receive a positive payoff. Let's use backward induction to see if this prediction is correct.

At node B, Patrick can call "Play" and earn 12 or call "Pass" and earn 11. Because the higher payoff comes from choosing "Play," Patrick will choose that. Knowing that Patrick will choose "Play" if he gets a turn, Dan will call "Play" at node A and earn 1. (If for some reason Dan calls "Pass," he knows he will earn a payoff of 0.) Faced with this choice, it's clear that Dan does better by calling "Play" and ending the game right off the bat. Therefore, the equilibrium payoffs are 1 for Dan and −10 for Patrick.

This equilibrium probably wasn't obvious to you just from our initial look at the game's structure and payoffs. The example shows how backward induction can provide help beyond intuition alone when determining the outcomes of sequential games. The example also demonstrates the value of behaviors that players might take to change the structure of a game in a favorable way. We talk about these sorts of behaviors in the next section.

12.3 figure it out

Two firms, GamesRUs (GRU) and PlayThings Incorporated (PTI), are considering a new television advertising campaign for their Christmas gift registries. Because television advertising is expensive, each firm earns greater profit ($50 million) when it does not advertise. If both choose to advertise, very few new customers are gained and each firm earns only $30 million profit. However, if one firm advertises while the other does not, the firm choosing to advertise gets the majority of customers, earning a profit of $70 million, while its competitor only earns $20 million profit.

a. Create a table showing the normal form of this game.

b. List all Nash equilibria.

c. If this game is played sequentially and GRU makes its decision before PTI, what will the outcome be?

d. Is there a first-mover advantage in this case? Explain.

Solution:

a. The normal form is shown below (payoffs are in millions of dollars with GRU's profits before the comma and PTI's after):

		PTI	
		Advertise	Don't Advertise
GRU	Advertise	30 , 30	70 , 20
	Don't Advertise	20 , 70	50 , 50

b. We can use the check method to determine the Nash equilibria. If GRU believes that PTI will advertise, its best move is to also advertise ($30 million > $20 million). If GRU believes that PTI will not advertise, its best move is to advertise ($70 million > $50 million). Therefore, advertising is a dominant strategy for GamesRUs because it is the best strategy no matter what strategy PlayThings Inc. follows. Note, too, that because PTI's payoffs are the same as those of GRU's, advertising is also a dominant strategy for PTI. Therefore, we end up with the following:

		PTI	
		Advertise	**Don't Advertise**
GRU	**Advertise**	✓ 30 , 30 ✓	✓ 70 , 20
	Don't Advertise	20 , 70 ✓	50 , 50

Because advertising is a dominant strategy for both firms, the outcome of this game is found in the upper-left portion of the payoff matrix and each firm earns a profit of $30 million. This is the Nash equilibrium because neither firm has an incentive to change its strategy given the strategy of the other.

c. The extensive form of this game (with GamesRUs moving first) is shown in the figure at right:

Using backward induction, we can see that, when GRU chooses to advertise, PTI will also choose to advertise (because $30 million > $20 million). If GRU chooses not to advertise, PTI will still choose to advertise (because $70 million > $50 million). Therefore, if GRU understands how PTI will respond to its strategy, it will also choose to advertise (because $30 million > $20 million).

d. No first-mover advantage exists in this case because both firms have dominant strategies. A dominant strategy is the best strategy to follow *no matter what your opponent does*. Therefore, it is irrelevant if one firm makes its decision before the other firm; each firm will always choose its dominant strategy: to advertise.

12.5 Strategic Moves, Credibility, and Commitment

There's something not very satisfying about the equilibrium of the play or pass bargaining game. There was a big payoff for both players (11, 11) available later in the game, yet because each player followed his own self-interest, the equilibrium ended up with one player receiving something small (Dan earned a payoff of 1) and the other really getting hurt (Patrick lost 10). With this kind of result from the quick-exit equilibrium, you might think that both players would have an incentive to get around it.

In this section, we discuss ways in which players can avoid such poor outcomes in certain kinds of sequential games. The key is for players to use **strategic moves.** These are defined by Nobel Laureate Thomas Schelling in his wonderful book *The Strategy of Conflict* as actions taken early in a game to influence the ultimate outcome in a way that benefits the player.[4] Examples of such actions include side payments, promises, and threats, and their purpose is to alter the payoffs of a game to change its outcome in a way that is favorable for the player taking the action.

> **strategic move**
> An action taken early in a game that favorably influences the ultimate outcome of the game.

Side Payments

One of the simplest types of strategic behavior is a **side payment,** a promise of a payment from one player to an opposing player conditional on the choice the opponent makes. A side payment is, in essence, a type of bribe aimed at compelling the opponent to choose the strategy that is in the player's best interest.

> **side payment**
> A type of bribe that influences the outcome of a strategic game.

Let's think about side payments in the context of the "Play or Pass" game. What's the essence of the problem? Dan chooses to play right away in the game because he knows that if he doesn't, Patrick's best choice is to choose "Play" and leave him, Dan, with nothing. But note how much Patrick's "best" choice hurts him: Because "Play" is Patrick's best choice at node B, Dan has no choice but to choose to play at node A, end the game early, and cause Patrick to lose 10. This poor outcome for Patrick could be avoided if Patrick was able to convince Dan that he will choose "Pass" at node B if given the opportunity to do so (i.e., if Dan will not immediately end the game at node A by choosing to play). Moreover, Dan would *like* to be convinced that Patrick will choose "Pass" at node B because then Dan would earn 11 rather than the measly 1 he receives at the Nash equilibrium.

How might Dan get Patrick to commit to choosing "Pass" at node B? A side payment can achieve this. Suppose Dan, instead of choosing to play right away, ending the game, and receiving a payoff of 1, makes the following take-it-or-leave-it offer to Patrick: "If you promise to choose to pass if I choose to pass, I'll give you a payment of 2. That way, you will definitely earn 13: your payoff at node B from choosing 'Pass,' plus my payment to you of 2. If you refuse this offer and stick with choosing 'Play' at node B, you will force me to choose to play, and you will lose 10."

How does this side payment of 2 affect the game's outcome? As Figure 12.3 shows, Patrick's payoff from "Pass" at node B is now 13 instead of 11. Because this is more

---

Figure 12.3   :   **A Side Payment Can Alter the Nash Equilibrium**

In the original sequential play or pass game (Figure 12.2), Dan chose to play and received a payoff of 1. If Dan instead offers Patrick a side payment of 2 if Patrick will pass when it is his turn, the equilibrium changes. Now when Dan passes to Patrick, Patrick will also choose to pass. At the new Nash equilibrium, Dan and Patrick earn payoffs of 9 and 13 (respectively), more than they would have earned without the side payment.

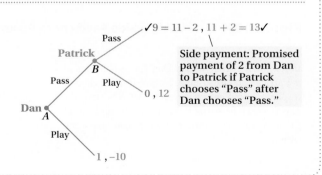

[4] Strategic behavior is an incredibly rich area of study in microeconomics; we simply don't have the room to do a full overview in this book. We will touch on a few of the more common concepts and leave it to you to dig further through one of the many books on the topic if you're interested.

than he would get by choosing to play, he'll now want to choose to pass instead. Dan is just fine with this: He gets a payoff of 9 (the original payoff of 11 minus the side payment of 2), which is a lot better than the 1 he would have received by choosing to play.

Effective use of side payments, then, can alter the game in beneficial ways for both players. In this game, the players have figured out how to take some of the extra payment they receive in the coordinated outcome and split it in a way that creates incentives for them to coordinate.

Somewhat amazingly, just having the *ability* to make side payments can sometimes work, even if no money ever changes hands. Suppose, for example, that Patrick proposes the side payment this time. Before the game starts, he promises Dan that if he (Patrick) chooses to play at node B, he will give Dan a payment of 2 as a punishment to himself for hurting Dan. This promised punishment reduces Patrick's payoffs from "Play" at node B from 12 to 10 (Figure 12.4) and changes his node B best option from "Play" to "Pass." Realizing that the side payment punishment makes Patrick's best option to pass, Dan now faces the following node A options: Choose to play and receive 1, or choose to pass and receive 11. Dan now chooses "Pass." Patrick responds by choosing to pass at node B, and both earn 11.

Note that no side payment actually needs to be made: The punished option (Patrick choosing to play) is not chosen because the punishment makes "Pass" the better choice for Patrick. This promised punishment encourages Dan to choose "Pass" at node A because it eliminates Dan's worry about what Patrick will do at node B. With the punishment in place, Patrick is better off by also selecting to pass.

In fact, if Patrick wants to send a *really* strong message, he could promise to pay Dan the full payment of 12 if he (Patrick) chooses "Play," or an even bigger amount. The key is that the side payment must be large enough to make "Play" a lower-paying choice than "Pass" for Patrick.

Commitment

Side payments might not always work. In our play or pass game, we assumed that Dan and Patrick would have no difficulty in sticking to the choice encouraged by the promised side payment, but that's not always the case. In real life, a player might have incentives to renege on side-payment agreements. By their very nature, side payments may often be secret. Players may find it difficult (or completely undesirable) to ask a court to enforce these types of contracts. Therefore, firms often use other strategic moves to try to achieve better game outcomes.

Figure 12.4 | **Using a Side Payment as Punishment for Noncooperation**

Here, Patrick offers to pay Dan 2 as a punishment if Patrick chooses to play. Now if Patrick chooses to play, he will earn a payoff of 10, less than the payoff of 11 he earns if he passes. Therefore, at the new Nash equilibrium, both players pass and earn a payoff of 11.

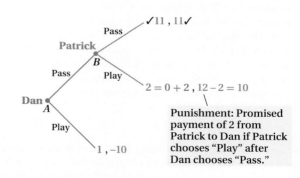

Let's think about this some more by returning once again to the simultaneous-game version of the movie-release-date problem for DreamWorks and Disney. In this version, we drop the March choice because it is a dominated strategy, so in Table 12.10, we're looking again at the game from Table 12.4.

Each studio would like to signal convincingly that it is releasing its movie in May to force its competitor into a December release. At the same time, the studios need to be careful to not *both* choose a May release. In Section 12.4, we saw that if one of the companies can move first, then it will take advantage of its first-mover status and choose May, forcing the other to open in December. But what if the game is a simultaneous-move game? Is there a way a firm can gain this sort of first-mover advantage?

One possible approach to gaining first-mover advantage might be for one studio to issue a strong threat: "We're going to release our movie in May regardless of when we think you're going to release yours." By doing this, the threat-issuing firm hopes its opponent, worried about making only the tiny profit that would come with a simultaneous opening, will relent and open in December. But simply threatening to open in May doesn't change the fact that if the other firm actually *does* open in May, the firm making the threat would want to switch to December if given the opportunity. In other words, "opening in May no matter what" is a **noncredible threat,** meaning that it is not rational for the player to actually carry out the threat should the situation actually occur (for instance, if the other studio also chooses May). No one will believe a studio threatening to open in May no matter what because it doesn't make rational sense for the firm to make that choice: Opening in May is not a best response when the other studio chooses May.

The key to making a successful strategic move toward an exclusive May opening is a **credible commitment,** a choice (or a restriction of choices) that guarantees a player will take a particular future action if certain conditions occur that transform the game. A firm not only needs to threaten to open in May, it also needs to take actions ahead of time that would make it costly for it to *not* do so and thus signal to the firm's opponent that the firm will carry out its threat.

Suppose DreamWorks funds an early national advertising campaign for *Kung Fu Panda 3* with "Opening This May" all over the ads and leaks word to the media during production that it expects the film to be a "summer blockbuster." Suppose DreamWorks even signs contracts for distribution that incorporate huge penalty payments to theaters if the movie does not arrive on screens in May. Or perhaps DreamWorks creates copies of the movie that will disintegrate after the summer so that *Kung Fu Panda 3* can never be viewed again (yes, this is a stretch, but we are making the point of what counts as a credible move).

Each of these actions gives DreamWorks a way to credibly commit to a May opening and thus change its payoffs. If the payoff changes from this commitment are large enough, DreamWorks can alter the basic structure of the game. As long as DreamWorks makes less than $50 million if it opens in December, opening in May will become a dominant strategy for DreamWorks, as you can see in Table 12.11. Suppose that DreamWorks makes commitments that will cost it

noncredible threat
A threat made in a game that is not rational for the player to follow through on, and as such is an empty threat.

credible commitment
A choice or a restriction of choices that guarantees a player will take a particular future action if certain conditions occur.

Table 12.10   **Selecting a Release Date**

		Disney's Opening Date Choice	
		May	**December**
Dream-Works' Opening Date Choice	**May**	50 , 50	✓ 300 , 200 ✓
	December	✓ 200 , 300 ✓	0 , 0

*Payoffs are measured in millions of dollars of profit.

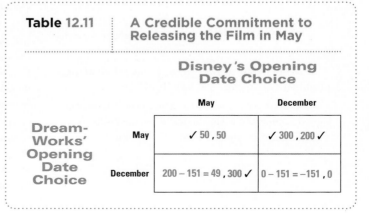

Table 12.11   **A Credible Commitment to Releasing the Film in May**

		Disney's Opening Date Choice	
		May	**December**
Dream-Works' Opening Date Choice	**May**	✓ 50 , 50	✓ 300 , 200 ✓
	December	200 − 151 = 49 , 300 ✓	0 − 151 = −151 , 0

$151 million if *Kung Fu Panda 3* opens in December. Subtracting 151 from DreamWorks' payoffs in the "December" row changes its payoffs to 49 in the lower left and −151 in the lower right. Now, no matter what Disney does, DreamWorks is better off if it chooses May.

Once DreamWorks has made its threat to open in May credible, Disney's best response is to choose a December release date. Therefore, DreamWorks has achieved what it wanted (forcing Disney to choose a December opening) by *limiting* its own options ahead of time. By making a December choice so unappealing as to be impossible, DreamWorks effectively commits itself to take its threatened action (opening in May).

What is so compelling about this strategic move is that on its face it looks irrational. Imagine explaining to your boss that she should make the movie disintegrate after the summer. "You took microeconomics for *that*?!" you hear, as security escorts you to your desk to box up your possessions. But, by taking these seemingly detrimental actions, you have actually helped the studio earn $100 million more profit ($300 million instead of $200 million) than it may have earned without them (because the studio could have ended up with a December opening while its competitor chose May). "Nicely done, kid," your boss says as you move into a corner office.

12.4 figure it out

MagicPill Inc. has developed a new wonder drug for curing obesity that has been approved by the Food and Drug Administration. If the drug is released for sale, a competitor, GenDrug, will attempt to copy the formula and steal all of MagicPill's customers by offering the wonder drug at a lower price. (Assume there are no patent laws at this time.) The extensive form of the game is shown below (payoffs represent profits in millions of dollars):

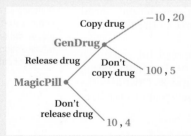

a. Should MagicPill release this new wonder drug for sale? Explain.

b. Would your answer to (a) change if GenDrug promised not to copy the new drug? Explain.

c. Would your answer to (a) change if GenDrug signed a contract with MagicPill promising to pay $10 million if it copies the drug? Explain.

d. How would your answer to (a) change if patent laws protect MagicPill's exclusive right to produce its new wonder drug?

Solution:

a. No, MagicPill will not release the drug. Using backward induction, we can see that if the drug is released, GenDrug will choose to copy it (because it can earn $20 million profit rather than $5 million). Knowing this, MagicPill is better off not releasing the drug (because it can earn $10 million rather than losing $10 million).

b. No. GenDrug's promise would not be credible. The incentive ($15 million additional profit) is large enough that MagicPill cannot believe the promise by GenDrug.

c. No. The payment of $10 million by GenDrug will not change GenDrug's incentive for copying the drug ($20 million − $10 million > $5 million). Furthermore, the payment of $10 million would not be enough to induce MagicPill to release the drug (− $10 million + $10 million < $10 million).

d. Yes. If the patent prohibited GenDrug from copying the wonder drug, we can ignore the "Copy Drug" option in the game. In this case, Magic Pill will want to release the drug because $100 million > $10 million.

🧩 application

Dr. Strangelove and the Perils of Secrecy

Stanley Kubrick's classic 1964 black comedy *Dr. Strangelove or*: *How I Learned to Stop Worrying and Love the Bomb* is set in the midst of the Cold War and the nuclear arms race between the United States and the Soviet Union.

In real life, the military consulted extensively with game theorists in the realm of nuclear deterrence. For example, two Nobel Laureate game theorists mentioned in this chapter, John Nash and Thomas Schelling, worked for a time at RAND Corporation analyzing various facets of the Cold War conflict.

The movie mocks the game theory basis of nuclear deterrence. In the movie, a rogue U.S. general, convinced that water fluoridation is a Communist conspiracy to "sap and impurify all of our precious bodily fluids," orders his bomber squadron to launch a nuclear attack on the Soviets. The president orders his top commander to stop the bombers, but the commander says it's impossible; to establish a credible commitment to fight back against a Soviet attack, the bombers cannot be recalled once they pass the point of no return. The president calls the Soviet premier to plead with him not to respond with a massive retaliation, but discovers that, unfortunately, the Soviets have recently installed a doomsday machine that automatically responds to any attack by launching a world-destroying nuclear barrage. Further, the doomsday machine has been programmed to consider any attempt to shut it down as sabotage, thereby also triggering an automatic launch. The Soviets believed this was the only way the machine would act as a credible commitment to respond to an attack.

Oddly, however, the Soviets had kept the machine a secret for six months. The president's game theory advisor, Dr. Strangelove (thought by some to be a parody of John von Neumann, one of the inventors of game theory), asks the Soviet ambassador incredulously, "The whole point of the doomsday machine is lost if you keep it a secret! WHY DIDN'T YOU TELL THE WORLD, EH?" The ambassador answers, "It was to be announced at the Party congress on Monday. As you know, the premier loves surprises."

We're not sure this is the message that Stanley Kubrick wanted to deliver by making this movie, but it's still right: If you have a doomsday machine, make it credible, and ANNOUNCE IT! ∎

Entry Deterrence: Credibility Applied

One of the most common applications of strategic moves in microeconomics relates to deterring firms from entering an industry.

We have seen repeatedly throughout the past several chapters that firms can earn much higher profit levels if they are able to prevent other firms from entering their market. Preventing entry isn't always easy, though. One reason, as with DreamWorks' threat to open in May no matter what, is the issue of credibility.

Think of the iPad as if it were the only tablet on the market and Apple as a monopolist (it wasn't far from it in the beginning). Now suppose another company comes along—Amazon, say—that threatens to enter the market with its own tablet computer.

We can think of this as a sequential game. The extensive form of the game is shown in Figure 12.5. The payoffs are profits in billions of dollars.

First, Amazon decides whether to enter the market. If it doesn't enter, the game is over. Amazon earns a profit of zero and Apple earns the monopoly profit of $2 billion (Amazon's payoffs are listed in red, first in every payoff pair). If Amazon enters the market, however, then Apple must decide how to react. If Apple fights Amazon's entry by starting a price war, Amazon will lose $0.5 billion and Apple will earn only $0.8 billion. If Apple doesn't fight, Amazon will earn $0.5 billion and Apple $1 billion—less than the monopoly profit, but more than it would by engaging in a price war.

Figure 12.5 : **An Entry Game***

Amazon uses backward induction to decide whether to enter the tablet market currently dominated by Apple. If Amazon chooses to enter the market, Apple's optimum strategy is to not fight a price war and Amazon earns $0.5 billion in profit, higher than the zero profit it earns when it doesn't enter the market. Because Amazon knows that Apple's threat to enter a price war is not credible, Amazon will enter the tablet market.

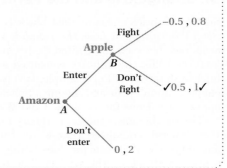

* Payoffs are in billions of dollars of profit.

It might seem as though Apple could crush a new entrant like the Amazon Kindle Fire anytime it wants by just promising to start a price war. If so, Amazon will lose money if it enters. Therefore, Amazon should look ahead and realize what Apple wants to do, leading Amazon to the conclusion that it's better if it doesn't enter, right?

Not so fast. Amazon will consider the credibility of a price-war threat. Why should it believe that Apple will start a price war just because Apple says it will? Look what a price war does to Apple: If Amazon enters, Apple earns only $0.8 billion by fighting but earns $1 billion by going along. Because Amazon knows this, Apple's threat is not credible. By using backward induction, then, Amazon realizes its choices are between entering and earning $0.5 billion (knowing Apple will back down) or not entering and earning nothing. Amazon will therefore call Apple's bluff and enter, and Apple won't fight when it does.

From our previous discussion, we know that the only way Apple can deter entry is by initiating a strategic move that somehow makes the threat to fight credible. One classic maneuver discussed by business strategists is the use of excess capacity. Under this strategy, the incumbent (Apple) builds all the capacity it would need *if* Amazon were to enter and there was a price war—remember that with low prices, quantity sold would go up significantly. The strategy is to build this capacity *before* entry ever occurs.

This strategy wouldn't affect Apple's payoffs much in the event of an actual price war, because it's going to be fully utilizing the capacity it has already built. But the fact that Apple has so much capacity also tends to reduce its price (and profits) if it remains a monopolist, or if Amazon enters and Apple rolls over (since its output would be greater because of its capacity). This output effect of the extra capacity occurs because it greatly lowers Apple's marginal cost, causing its optimal price to fall. A closely related interpretation of this effect is that if the two firms operate in a Cournot oligopoly, Apple's extra capacity is used to raise its output, thus lowering the market price.

Let's suppose Apple invests in extra capacity at an earlier date, and this investment lowers its profit to $1.2 billion in the monopoly case with no entry (because the extra factory capacity sits idle) and to $0.6 billion if Amazon enters and Apple chooses not to fight. This investment would change the game tree from the one shown in Figure 12.5 to the one in Figure 12.6 because Apple's threat to fight is now credible.

The strategic use of overcapacity affects the game's payoffs in an advantageous way for Apple. Now, if Amazon enters, Apple makes more profit by fighting ($0.8 billion) than not ($0.6 billion). Amazon realizes that Apple will definitely fight and chooses to not enter, because zero profit is better than incurring a half billion dollar loss (–$0.5 billion). Apple remains a monopolist, earning $1.2 billion instead of the $1 billion it would have made as a duopolist in the original equilibrium (Figure 12.5). Apple has therefore made its threat to start a price war credible by making a strategic move (early capacity investment choices).

Again, strategic considerations have made seemingly irrational actions beneficial. Imagine trying to explain this strategy to the boss:

Figure 12.6 : **Excess Capacity to Create a Credible Threat**

To lend credibility to its threat of a price war, Apple invests in extra capacity before Amazon decides whether to enter the tablet market. Apple's profit as a monopolist decreases to \$1.2 billion, a profit that is still higher than Apple's equilibrium payoff in Figure 12.5. With this credible threat, however, if Amazon chooses to enter the market, Apple will choose to fight, earning \$0.8 billion. Because Amazon will lose \$0.5 billion under this strategy, Amazon will choose not to enter the market.

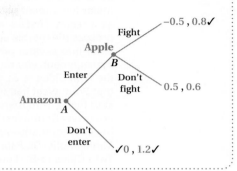

"We need to build a series of factories that we will never use to create massive excess capacity for making iPads."

"Wait, what? Why would we pay for factories we don't need?" the boss asks.

"So we can credibly prove that our profit will be lower if Amazon enters the market and we don't try to stop them," you say.

Somewhere in the accounting department, someone reads this plan and feels his blood pressure rise. "Now the economist wants us to pay for factories that we won't even use!" But, she's absolutely right—those unused factories will make the company an extra \$200 million in profit.

theory and data

Incumbent Airlines' Responses to Threatened Entry by Southwest

While economists rightfully pay a lot of attention to theories about strategic behavior in response to entry threats, actually testing these theories is difficult. By nature, most market data are about firms already operating in a market. But entry threats come from firms that aren't yet in a market. Rarely can economists actually pin down data that measure this potential for entry before it ever happens.

Two of the authors (Austan Goolsbee and Chad Syverson)[*] figured out a way around this problem in a study testing for strategic behavior among incumbents in the passenger airline industry. Goolsbee and Syverson measured how incumbents responded when Southwest Airlines threatened to offer service on the incumbents' routes. They measured this strategic response by tracking what happened to incumbents' fares, passenger traffic, and capacity when Southwest Airlines loomed as a potential competitor.

How can one measure the threat of entry in this industry before actual entry ever occurs? The secret is in understanding the way Southwest expands its route network. When Southwest begins operating in a new airport (and it has entered a lot of new airports during the past 20 years), it does not immediately offer service from that new airport to every other airport in its route network. Instead, it ramps up its operations at the new airport over time. It begins by offering service between the new airport and only a handful of other airports in the Southwest network. It then gradually adds flights to more destinations from the new airport, connecting more of the dots in its network. It's this practice of gradually rolling out routes that allows one to observe entry threats before entry actually occurs. Once Southwest has started operating in that new airport, even if it hasn't started flying a particular route yet, it's much more likely to do so soon.

---

[*] Austan Goolsbee and Chad Syverson, "How Do Incumbents Respond to the Threat of Entry? Evidence from the Major Airlines." *Quarterly Journal of Economics* 123, no. 4 (2008): 1611–1633.

An example of this principle in action occurred in March 2009, when Southwest began operations at the Minneapolis–St. Paul airport. Southwest's service to and from the Twin Cities began with nonstop flights to just one location: Chicago Midway. Delta airlines—a major incumbent on the Twin Cities-to-Midway route—had a new competitor to deal with as a result. That's a case of Southwest actually entering a market. But the route-rollout process meant this actual entry on one route was accompanied by Southwest threatening entry into several other routes to other cities in its network. For example, if you're Delta management, you recognize that even though Southwest hasn't actually started flying from the Twin Cities to St. Louis (another route on which you are the primary incumbent), now that Southwest has operations in the Twin Cities, it's much more likely that Southwest will start flying from there to St. Louis. Similarly, if you're in the boardroom at US Airways, you now view Southwest's entry into the Twin Cities-to-Phoenix route—one in which you are a major incumbent—as much more likely than before. In this way, Southwest's start at the Minneapolis–St. Paul airport in March 2009 coincided with entry threats felt by Delta on its Twin Cities-to-St. Louis route and US Airways on its Twin Cities-to-Phoenix route. Similar entry threats were noticed by other incumbent airlines on their own routes to Minneapolis–St. Paul. Therefore, if incumbents on these routes were going to make any strategic moves in response to this threatened entry, they should have done so around this time.

Goolsbee and Syverson tested for strategic behavior by looking at how incumbents like Delta and US Airways behaved on hundreds of routes like these that Southwest similarly threatened to enter as it expanded into roughly 20 new airports over a 12-year period.

The data indicate that incumbents did indeed engage in strategic behavior on routes when Southwest loomed as a potential competitor. Table 12.12 illustrates how incumbents' average fares changed on threatened routes around the time Southwest entered the new airport. It shows incumbents' average fares on threatened routes relative to what they were on those same routes more than two years before Southwest entered the new airport.

By the quarter Southwest entered the new airport, incumbents had dropped their fares by 17% on the routes that Southwest threatened. Incumbents continued to drop fares after Southwest was in the new airport, on average, to levels 21% below their prior levels. This is a fairly substantial fare cut. It can be compared to the total 28% fare cut (again, relative to fares more than two years prior) that incumbents made when Southwest finally did enter those routes it was threatening. In other words, about two-thirds of incumbents' total pricing response to competition from Southwest occurred before Southwest actually started flying on their routes.

Goolsbee and Syverson hypothesized that these strategic responses to threatened entry were attempts by the incumbent airlines to build up loyalty among their flyers on the threatened routes, especially highly valuable frequent-flyer/business customers. This would make it more difficult for Southwest to steal those customers away if and when it began flying the route. This motive is consistent with the finding in the data that incumbents dropped fares more on threatened routes that were likely to have had a smaller share of leisure flyers. Certainly, it's true that flyers responded to these preemptive price cuts. Incumbents saw increased passenger traffic on the threatened routes when they dropped their fares.

One interesting thing to note is that the incumbents actually began cutting prices before Southwest started operating in the new

Table 12.12	Incumbent Airlines' Responses to Southwest's Threat of Entry
Period	**Relative Fare Change**
2+ years before Southwest starts operating at the new airport	0
1–2 years before Southwest starts operating at the new airport	–6%
Less than 1 year before Southwest starts operating at the new airport	–12%
Quarter Southwest starts operating at the new airport	–17%
After Southwest has begun operating at the new airport, but before it has started flying the route	–21%
After Southwest has begun operating at the new airport, and it has started flying the route	–28%

airport—by 12% in the prior year, for example. This makes sense when you think about when incumbents would actually recognize an entry threat. Southwest doesn't just show up one day at a new airport saying, "We've got a plane parked outside. . . . Who wants to buy a ticket?" They have to lease gates, hire staff, and (of course) sell tickets before ever starting operations at a new airport. This process can take over a year. Incumbents therefore know Southwest is coming and can respond strategically before Southwest actually starts operating in the new airport.

However, in many cases Southwest was simply a tide that the incumbents weren't going to be able to stop, no matter how aggressively they responded to the entry threat. That is, in fact, what happened to Delta and US Airways in Minneapolis–St. Paul. Southwest now flies from the Twin Cities to both St. Louis and Phoenix (among other destinations). But don't think this necessarily means the incumbents' efforts were futile. By cutting fares early, they may have been able to keep business flyers whom they otherwise would have lost to Southwest. While the incumbents would have preferred that Southwest had never shown up, they may have been making the best of a tough competitive situation.

Reputation

One last example of a strategic behavior a player might undertake to deter the entry of a rival is to establish a stellar reputation in a given market. Reputations themselves can be sources of commitment to a game-playing strategy.

Suppose Apple is facing potential entry not just by Amazon, but by scores of potential tablet makers. Apple could benefit from establishing a reputation for aggressively fighting any entry in any market. If Apple *didn't* fight the entry by Amazon, such behavior may leave them open to even more new entrants into the tablet market such as HP or ASUS. Thus, Apple may incur the costs of fighting Amazon (even though doing so could harm its current profit) in order to promote its reputation as a fighter to deter future entrants. In this case, its desire to establish and then preserve a tough reputation becomes a commitment device itself.

Tobacco companies tried this strategy in their response to lawsuits by their former (and sometimes still current) customers. These suits were often for relatively small sums of money. Many of the suing smokers probably figured they could get the tobacco companies to settle the cases, essentially paying them off to avoid the high costs of a full trial.

But the companies realized that settling one case would only encourage more lawsuits. Other smokers would observe the settlement and file suit in hopes of obtaining their own. While going to trial in any one case would be a money-loser for the tobacco companies, settling could open the door to perhaps billions of dollars in future settlement costs.

The companies therefore tried to establish a reputation for fighting any lawsuit with everything they had. They might pay millions in legal fees to fight even a $1,000 lawsuit. While this practice might seem irrational at first glance, the hope was that developing such a reputation would effectively commit them to fight any suit in the future, thereby cutting off the "entry" of new plaintiffs before they even filed papers.

Ultimately, though, the cigarette companies' strategy fell apart. The lawsuits grew so numerous and so massive that the companies reached a multi-billion dollar settlement with the federal government and numerous state governments, the Tobacco Master Settlement Agreement, to shield them from further lawsuits.

Even a reputation for being crazy can be valuable. Return to the case of Apple facing entry by Amazon. Suppose Apple could convince Amazon that, regardless of the profit implications, it was just crazy enough to ignite a self-destructive price war for tablets, no matter what Amazon does. This could work to Apple's advantage. If Apple were so combative as to actually *enjoy* fighting for its own sake—even if it's costly in profit terms—it might be able to convince a rational potential entrant like Amazon to stay out of the market. In the spirit of our earlier discussion of the maximin strategy, Amazon might find that avoiding a vicious price war with a rabid competitor is a lower-risk option than hoping for a rational response to its entry.

freakonomics

How Game Theory Just Might Save Your Life

It doesn't get much worse than this. In 2007, Eric Damfreville and Celine Cordelier were bloodied, bruised, and blindfolded, their hands and feet bound. Until the previous day, Eric and Celine had been French aid workers in Afghanistan. Now they were hostages, kidnapped by the Taliban. Based on past history, there was no reason to be optimistic. Taliban hostages are typically held for months or even years. There was a good chance they would be killed unless a large ransom was paid.

You might expect that the French government acted swiftly to pay the ransom and get back its citizens. After all, a ransom demand of a few million euros, while a large sum to the kidnappers, is a drop in the bucket for the French government to pay. But France, like most countries, has a long-held policy of not paying ransoms to terrorists. The game theory behind this stance is simple. When a country rewards one kidnapper with a ransom, it encourages others to enter the kidnapping market. A government's commitment to a blanket policy against ransoms reduces the *total* number of kidnappings, but makes being kidnapped worse for those who actually are taken hostage.

But Eric and Celine's kidnappers didn't ask the French government for a ransom. Instead, the kidnappers' demands were political: Withdraw your troops from Afghanistan, and we'll release the hostages.

Then President Nicolas Sarkozy quickly agreed to the terms, and Eric and Celine went free.

The media reaction was swift and negative. Reporters condemned Sarkozy for both negotiating with terrorists and changing his country's military strategy in the process.

But Sarkozy, it turned out, understood game theory a lot better than the Taliban kidnappers. As soon as the hostages were released, the kidnappers lost all of their bargaining power. While breaking his promise might be politically costly if it had been made to the United States government or to French voters, no one cared if he double-crossed the Taliban. Shortly after the hostages returned home, Sarkozy announced that France was raising its military commitment in Afghanistan by almost 50%.

One thing is for sure: Eric and Celine are very grateful that the Taliban aren't better economists.

12.6 Conclusion

Thinking through your opponent's likely responses before you make your decisions remains the essence of strategic thinking and the basis of game theory. Game theory gives us a formal way to think about how companies and people should act in these environments. To figure out the equilibrium in an oligopolistic market in which firms must interact strategically with each other, we need to understand the exact rules of the game (Who are the players? What are their payoffs? Are they making decisions simultaneously or sequentially?). Once we understand the game and how it's being played, we can figure out what the equilibrium should be. It's more difficult to predict outcomes in markets with small numbers of players who interact strategically, but it is important and—as the example of the iPad and the Kindle Fire indicate—very common in the real world.

Even in situations in which people choose their actions strategically there are often some obvious equilibria that the games will gravitate toward. These can vary a lot depending on whether the games involve repeated interactions or if the decisions become sequential and one player moves followed by the other one, and so on.

As long as you (or a firm or a government) are thinking about how your opponent will react when you are making your decisions, you are using game theory. It will not only improve your chess game, it will make you a better economist.

Summary

1. **Game theory** is the study of what happens when economic actors—like the firms and consumers we've studied up until this point—behave strategically. Every game features three key elements: **players, strategies,** and **payoffs. Dominant strategies** are always the best action for players to take regardless of their opponents' actions, while **dominated strategies** are never the best action. Identifying any dominant and dominated strategies in a game makes solving for the Nash equilibria easier. [**Section 12.1**]

2. In **simultaneous-move games,** a player must choose her strategy without first knowing her opponent's choice. The mutual-best-response concept of Nash equilibrium is a natural way to predict the outcomes of such games. Depending on the particular structure of the strategies and payoffs, games can have one, multiple, or even **mixed-strategy** Nash equilibria. Players may also vary their strategies if faced with an irrational or erratic opponent. In addition, players may be interested in using a **maximin strategy** to minimize their losses in a game. [**Section 12.2**]

3. The outcome of a one-shot simultaneous game differs from the outcome of a **repeated** simultaneous game. **Backward induction** is used to find the equilibria of multistage games. When applied to a repeated prisoner's dilemma, backward induction reveals that cooperation is still not an equilibrium when a repeated game has a known final stage (regardless of how many stages there are). However, when the actors play an infinite game or do not know with certainty which is the final round, cooperation can be an equilibrium. [**Section 12.3**]

4. In **sequential games,** players take actions in turn, meaning that one player sees the other's action before choosing her own strategy. As with other multistage games, backward induction can be used to find the equilibria of sequential games. [**Section 12.4**]

5. Players often use strategic moves to ensure that their later outcomes are favorable. Economic actors may strategically use **side payments, credible commitments,** and **reputation. Entry deterrence** is one of the most common applications of strategic moves in microeconomic analysis. [**Section 12.5**]

Review Questions

1. What are the three common elements of an economic game?
2. What differentiates game theory from single-agent problems?
3. How does the existence of multiple Nash equilibria complicate the solution to an economic game?
4. How can a payoff matrix be used to find a player's optimal strategy?
5. Why might a player pursue a mixed strategy?
6. Why is the maximin strategy considered a conservative strategy?
7. Define backward induction. How can backward induction be used to solve a strategic game?
8. Compare the grim trigger and tit-for-tat strategies.
9. Why do we use decision trees—instead of normal-form matrices—to solve sequential games?
10. How can side payments be beneficial to both players in a two-player game?
11. Describe the relationship between credibility and entry deterrence to a market.
12. What are some ways in which a company uses its reputation to its advantage?

Problems (Solutions to problems marked * appear at the back of this book. Problems adapted to use calculus are available online at http://worthpublishers.com/GLS1e)

*1. Consider the game below:

		Duvall		
		Stop	**Drop**	**Roll**
Earl	**Hammer**	4 , 14	9 , 6	5 , 3
	Anvil	8 , 2	6 , 12	1 , 7
	Stirrup	11 , 5	16 , 3	9 , 8

a. Who are the players in this game?
b. What strategies are available to Duvall?
c. If Earl plays Hammer and Duvall plays Roll, then what is Earl's payoff?
d. If Earl plays Stirrup and Duvall plays Drop, what is Duvall's payoff?

2. For each player in the following games, find the dominant strategy, if any.

a.

		Coyote	
		Anvil	**Dynamite**
Roadrunner	**Beep**	6 , 2	4 , 5
	Run	7 , 3	6 , 8

b.

		Bart	
		Pout	**Whine**
Maggie	**Lay Finger on Butterfinger**	6 , 8	11 , 3
	Ignore Butterfinger	2 , 6	9 , 5

c.

		Martha	
		Red	**White**
Julia	**Steak**	5 , 2	8 , 4
	Chicken	6 , 1	7 , 3

*3. For each of the following games, use dominance to find the Nash equilibrium. Each game contains only one Nash equilibrium.

a.

		MacBeth	
		Clean Spot	**Listen to Wife**
MacDuff	**Slay King**	10 , 2	8 , 4
	Roll Head	6 , 4	4 , 5

b.

		Ferris	
		Twist	**Shout**
Elvis	**Bump**	4 , 8	6 , 6
	Grind	2 , 4	4 , 3

c.

		Eagle	
		Take It Easy	**Take It to the Limit**
Matthew	**Get Under Table**	5 , 3	3 , 2
	Stand Up	3 , 5	14 , 4

*4. Use best-response analysis (the check method) to find the Nash equilibrium or equilibria (if any) in each of the following games.

a.

		Fred	
		Opera	**Bowling**
Wilma	**Opera**	5 , 2	0 , 0
	Bowling	0 , 0	2 , 5

b.

		Chuck	
		Straight	**Swerve**
Ren	**Straight**	0 , 0	3 , 1
	Swerve	1 , 3	2 , 2

5. Consider the game below:

		Ethel	
		Left	Right
Fred	Up	100 , 50	130 , 8
	Down	150 , 6	−10,000 , 4

a. What is the Nash equilibrium in this game?

b. Explain why this game might reasonably end up at a non-equilibrium outcome. Whose play is likely to be responsible for that happening?

6. You and a classmate (let's call him Dave) discover that your economics teacher has been secretly talking about notions such as "love," "fairness," and "decency." Desperate to preserve his reputation in the community of economists, he tries to buy your silence in the following way. "You two sit silently at a table. I'll put down a hundred-dollar bill. You can take the bill, or pass the decision to Dave. Before Dave decides, I'll put another hundred-dollar bill on the table. If he passes, I'll add yet another bill to the table and you can have another turn. The game will end when someone takes the money, or when the $500 in my wallet is gone, whichever comes first." You both agree to keep quiet about your instructor's transgressions for the chance to play the game, and as your teacher indicated, you get the first turn.

a. Suppose that each of you has passed twice, and your instructor has just put the last $100 bill on the table. It is your turn: What should you do?

b. Suppose that you have passed twice, and Dave has passed once. Your instructor has just put the fourth $100 bill on the table. What should Dave do: Take the money or pass? Why?

c. Suppose that you and Dave have each passed once. Your instructor has just put the third $100 bill on the table. What should you do: Take the money or pass? Why?

d. Suppose that you have passed once. Your instructor has just put the second $100 bill on the table. What should Dave do: Take the money or pass? Why?

e. Your instructor has just laid the first $100 bill on the table. It is your turn. Should you take the money or pass? Why?

f. What is the likely outcome of this game? Does your instructor pay the entire $500 for your silence?

7. Consider the situation the economics professor faces in Problem 6, but now let's suppose that Dave makes you the following offer: "Let's really soak this guy. I'll pass on turns 2 and 4 if you'll go halves on the 500 bucks with me." Should this offer fundamentally alter the outcome of the game? (*Hint*: Think about this problem using backward induction!)

8. Two oligopolistic aluminum manufacturers are engaged in bitter competition with one another. The biggest firm, Big Aluminum Giant (BAG), is deciding whether to expand capacity or hold the line. The smallest firm, Little Aluminum Giant (LAG), is also considering expansion. The table below shows payoffs for the firms under various scenarios:

		BAG	
		Don't Expand	Expand
LAG	Don't Expand	3 , 4	2 , 3
	Expand	4 , 2	1 , 1

a. What is the Nash equilibrium outcome in this game of capacity expansion? Why? How does dominance play a role in arriving at your answer?

b. Suppose the game is played sequentially, with BAG moving first. What is BAG's best strategy? Does it lead to the same equilibrium you found in the simultaneous game?

9. Each day, you and a friend play odds/evens to see who gets the last doughnut. On command, you each extend either one or two fingers. If the sum of the fingers is odd, you get the doughnut. If the sum of the fingers is even, your friend gets the doughnut.

a. Let the payoffs from winning be 1, and from losing, 0. Fill in the payoff matrix below:

		You	
		One Finger	Two Fingers
Friend	One Finger		
	Two Fingers		

b. Find the pure-strategy Nash equilibria in this game, if any.

c. If you always play one finger, how will your friend respond? How much can you expect to win, on average?

d. If you always play two fingers, how will your friend respond? How much can you expect to win, on average?

e. If you mix one finger and two fingers 50:50, and your friend does the same, what fraction of the time will you emerge victorious? How much can you expect to win, on average? Does mixing give you a higher average payout than playing a pure strategy?

f. Suppose your day-by-day mixture is as follows: 1, 2, 1, 2, 1, 2, 1, 2. Will your 50:50 mixture give you a higher payout than playing a pure strategy? Why or why not?

g. Economist Avinash Dixit claims that there is no better way to surprise your opponent than to surprise yourself. Suggest an easy way to randomize your play that gives you a 50:50 mix overall, but that does so in an unpredictable fashion.

*10. Your little twin sisters (whom you lovingly refer to as Thing 1 and Thing 2) are driving you crazy! You've baked them a lovely birthday cake, but they won't stop fighting over who gets the biggest slice. To settle the dispute, you draw on a time-honored ritual: You ask Thing 1 to cut the cake, and Thing 2 to choose which piece she wants.

a. Draw the extensive form of this game. Let Thing 1's strategies be "Cut Evenly" or "Cut Unevenly"; depending on what's on the platter, Thing 2's strategies might include "Take Big Slice," "Take Small Slice," or "Take Equal Slice." Assign payoffs to Thing 1 and Thing 2 that grow with the size of the slice they receive.

b. Use backward induction to find the equilibrium outcome for this game. Is the equilibrium consistent with your experience?

c. After the rules are announced, Thing 2 says, "It's not fair! I want to be the one who gets to cut the cake, not the one that chooses the slice!" Is Thing 2's complaint valid—in other words, is there a first-mover advantage in this game?

11. Crazy Eddie and Loopy Larry are two electronics merchants, who sell plasma TVs at either a high price or a low price. If they both charge a high price, they will each earn high profits. If one charges a high price while the other charges a low price, the low-price seller will get all the business and earn a huge profit. If they both charge low prices, their customers get great deals and the merchants each earn a modest profit.

a. Draw the extensive form of the game between Crazy Eddie and Loopy Larry. Assume that Crazy Eddie moves first and can choose a high price or a low price. Loopy Larry then follows with a high price or a low price.

b. Find the equilibrium outcome in the battle between Crazy Eddie and Loopy Larry.

c. In a series of wild TV commercials, Crazy Eddie announces, "Crazy Eddie will not be undersold! Find a better price, and I will match it!" Loopy Larry responds with the same offer. Redraw the game these two cutthroat competitors play, but give each player the chance to match his competitor's price if he prices high and his competitor prices low.

d. Find the equilibrium outcome in the battle between Crazy Eddie and Loopy Larry. Has the price-matching guarantee been good for consumers? Is price-matching indicative of intense competition?

12. After years of training, Sara has landed a contract playing professional lacrosse. Eager to leverage her pro status by bringing in endorsements, she asks Jenny MacGuire to be her personal manager. Jenny has offered Sara a choice of two payment plans. Sara can engage Jenny's services for a flat fee of $100,000. Alternatively, Sara can pay Jenny 15% of all endorsement revenue.

Sara estimates that if Jenny expends modest effort ($20,000 worth) in her job, she will generate $600,000 in endorsement revenue for Sara. But if Jenny expends high effort ($50,000 worth), she'll bring in $1 million in endorsements. On the day Sara and Jenny are to sign their agreement, Jenny tells Sara, "I am 100% dedicated to you, and will always work as hard as humanly possible on your behalf no matter what payment plan you choose."

a. Sara has a choice of payment plans; Jenny has a choice of effort levels. Determine the relevant payouts for all of the possible outcomes, and draw the extensive form of the game Sara and Jenny are playing.

b. Find the equilibrium outcome to this game. Will Sara choose the flat fee or the 15% plan? Will Jenny expend modest effort or high effort?

c. Is Jenny's promise believable?

d. Discuss the implications of the type of payment scheme on the incentives and payoffs each player faces. Then, extend your analysis by discussing paying workers an annual salary vs. paying them a certain amount for each finished product they produce (called "piece-rate compensation").

13. Abel, Brenda, and Charlene are members of the Human Resources Management club at their university. The club plans to bring a motivational speaker to campus with money earned selling doughnuts at the local farmers' market.

If the club sells doughnuts on three weekends, it will be able to afford a terrific speaker and Abel, Brenda, and Charlene will each get 100 units of happiness. If the club sells doughnuts on two weekends, it will be able to afford an above-average speaker that brings each member 70 units of happiness. If the club sells doughnuts on just one weekend, it will be able to bring in their college's personnel director to speak and each member will receive 25 units of happiness. If the club doesn't sell doughnuts at all, nobody will receive anything.

Abel is scheduled to sell doughnuts the first weekend, Brenda the second, and Charlene the third, after which the farmers' market closes down for winter. Working at the farmers' market costs the worker 40 units of happiness.

On the scheduled day, each worker must choose between staffing the doughnut stand or sleeping in.

a. Draw the extensive form of this game, with Abel moving first, Brenda second, and Charlene third.

b. Solve for the equilibrium outcome of this game. What does each player do? What kind of speaker does the club bring in?

c. Is there an advantage to being the first mover in this game? Explain why or why not.

14. Bonnie and Clyde are players in a classical prisoner's dilemma. Captured by police, they are separated and each is offered the following deal: If nobody talks, there is enough evidence to convict them on a lesser charge, and each will get 3 years in jail. If one sells out the other on the primary charge, the one that talked will serve 1 year and the one that didn't will serve 20 years. If they both sell out the other, they will each serve 10 years. Payoffs for this scenario are presented below:

		Clyde	
		Confess	**Don't Confess**
Bonnie	**Confess**	10 years , 10 years	1 year , 20 years
	Don't Confess	20 years , 1 year	3 years , 3 years

a. What is the Nash equilibrium in this prisoner's dilemma game? Is the outcome a great one for either player?

b. Suppose that, in the squad car on the way to the station, Bonnie tells Clyde, "If you rat me out, I'll have my peeps break your kneecaps." Assuming that Clyde is indifferent between spending 7 years in prison and having his kneecaps broken, redraw the payoffs in the game to reflect Bonnie's strategic move.

c. How does Bonnie's strategic threat alter the outcome of the game? Explain.

d. Suppose Clyde knows that Bonnie is a sadist, who would willingly pay a year in jail for the pleasure of breaking his kneecaps no matter what Clyde does. Will Bonnie's threat alter the outcome of the game? Explain.

*15. In a dry, dusty desert town, only two people (Antoinette and August) have water wells. Each day, they begin their morning by pumping water, which they then bring to the town square to sell. Pumping water costs them essentially nothing, but time is such that each can afford to make only one trip to the town center, which means that they must decide how much to pump at the start of each day.

The townsfolk's demand for water is given in the table below:

Price	$12	$11	$10	$9	$8	$7	$6	$5	$4	$3	$2	$1	$0
Q (gallons)	0	10	20	30	40	50	60	70	80	90	100	110	120

Suppose for simplicity that Antoinette and August are limited to pumping either 20, 30, 40, or 50 gallons of water each.

a. Verify that the payoffs in the game table on the next page, which reflect the profits Antoinette and August earn, are accurate. Fill in any missing values. Remember that the market price is determined by total production, but that each producer's profit is determined by how much each chooses to produce.

		August			
		20	**30**	**40**	**50**
Antoinette	**20**	$160 , $160	$140 , $210	$120 , $240	$100 , $250
	30	$210 , ?	$180 , $180	$150 , ?	$120 , ?
	40	$240 , $120	? , $150	$160 , $160	$120 , $150
	50	? , $100	$200 , $120	$150 , $120	? , ?

b. Suppose that Antoinette and August agree to collude and restrict their combined output to maximize their joint profits. They agree to divide production and profits equally. Referring to the payoff matrix above, how many gallons will they agree to produce in total? How many gallons of the total market supply will each supply? How much profit will each earn?

c. Does Antoinette have any incentive to cheat on this collusive arrangement? Does August? If so, how will such cheating manifest itself?

d. What is the Nash equilibrium in this game? Is the Nash equilibrium an ideal outcome for our two water producers?

e. How does the game Antoinette and August are playing resemble a prisoner's dilemma game?

16. Assume that two clothing manufacturers, Lands' End and L.L. Bean, market their goods strictly by mail order. Each produces an essentially identical field coat. The cost of producing such a coat is exactly $100. Because the field coats are perfect substitutes, customers will flock to the seller that offers the lowest price. If both firms offer identical prices, each receives half the customers.

For simplicity, assume that the two firms have the choice of pricing at whole-dollar prices of $103, $102, or $101. Market demand at $103 is 100 coats; at $102, 110 coats, and at $101, 120 coats. The profit each firm would earn at various prices is shown in the payoff matrix below:

		L.L. Bean		
		$103	**$102**	**$101**
Lands' End	**$103**	$150 , $150	$0 , $220	$0 , $120
	$102	$220 , $0	$110 , $110	$0 , $120
	$101	$120 , $0	$120 , $0	$60 , $60

a. What is the equilibrium outcome of the game Lands' End and L.L. Bean are playing?

b. Is collusion between Lands' End and L.L. Bean likely to last?

c. If Lands' End and L.L. Bean were allowed to quote prices in cents rather than whole dollars, what would the likely outcome of this game be?

d. Suppose that in hopes of raising prices above equilibrium, L.L. Bean decides to announce the price for its field coat early in the summer. Will that strategic move be successful for L.L. Bean? Why or why not?

17. There are two ice cream vendors, Ben and Jerry, on a crowded strip of beach. There are five permissible locations for ice cream vendors to locate, cleverly named positions 1, 2, 3, 4, and 5. Position 1 is at the far north end of the beach, Position 5 at the far south end, and Position 3 in the middle, while Positions 2 and 4 are midway between their respective neighbors. Each location may accommodate more than one vendor. There are 1,000 beachgoers scattered uniformly across the beach (200 at each position) who will buy from the closest vendor.

a. Fill in the payoff matrix on the next page, with payouts reflecting the number of customers each vendor receives. (Example: If Ben is at Position 1 and Jerry is at Position 4, Ben will get 400 beachgoers at locations 1 and 2, and Jerry will get 600 of the beachgoers at Positions 3, 4, and 5.)

		Jerry				
		Position 1	**Position 2**	**Position 3**	**Position 4**	**Position 5**
	Position 1					
	Position 2					
Ben	**Position 3**					
	Position 4					
	Position 5					

b. Find the Nash equilibrium or equilibria in this game. Where are Ben and Jerry likely to end up locating?

18. You are one of two member nations of OOEC: the Organization of Otter Exporting Countries, a cartel designed to artificially restrict otter output in an attempt to generate monopoly profits. Demand conditions are such that various combinations of output yield the profits in the payoff matrix below:

		Other Country	
		Produce 1,000 Otters	**Produce 2,000 Otters**
Your Country	**Produce 1,000 Otters**	$500 , $500	$250 , $700
	Produce 2,000 Otters	$700 , $250	$400 , $400

a. If your country is able to successfully collude with the other country, how many otters will each country produce, and how much profit will each earn?

b. What is the equilibrium outcome in this game if it is only played once? Is the equilibrium outcome a good one for your country?

*19. Refer to Problem 18. It seems realistic to assume that the game could continue indefinitely—after all, the world will need otters 50 years from now just as badly as it does today. But time is money, so a dollar of profit a year from now is only valued as much as d received today, where d (the discount rate) is some amount less than $1.

Assume that you adopt a grim trigger strategy whereby your country pledges to produce 1,000 otters as long as the other country produces 1,000 otters. But should the other country ever produce 2,000 otters, you will respond by producing 2,000 otters, forever and ever. After you announce your strategy, the other country pledges to abide by the grim trigger strategy.

a. What stream of profits will you generate if both countries adopt such a grim strategy? (Don't forget to discount each year's future profits by the appropriate multiple of d.) Express your answer as a sum.

b. Suppose your country decides to take advantage of the other country's pledge to reduce output by expanding your own output in the first year. What stream of profits can you expect to generate? Again, be sure to discount appropriately, and express your answer as a sum.

c. Suppose $d = 0.5$. Are you better off cheating on your agreement, or abiding by it? How does your answer change if $d = 0.99$? What about $d = 0.01$?

d. At what level of d are you indifferent between cheating on or abiding by the agreement?

20. In the 1960s, tobacco producers engaged in fierce battles for market share. The major weapon in that war was advertising—advertising that was designed not to attract new smokers, but to lure smokers away from competing brands. Consider the following scenario: There are two tobacco sellers, Phillip and R. J., each of whom can choose to advertise on TV (at a cost of $20 million) or not. There are $100 million of pre-advertising profits available to the two firms. If they both adopt the same budget, they will split the market evenly. If one chooses a high budget while the other chooses low, the high-budget firm will steal

half the other's customers and capture $75 million of pre-advertising profit; the other will earn $25 million. The firms' net profits (after advertising expenses are considered) are illustrated in the payoff matrix below:

		R. J. Advertise	R. J. Don't Advertise
Phillip	**Advertise**	$30 , $30	$55 , $25
	Don't Advertise	$25 , $55	$50 , $50

a. Verify that the payoffs in the table reflect the story told above.
b. What is the Nash equilibrium in this game? Is the equilibrium outcome a good one for anybody?
c. Suppose that Phillip and R. J. promise one another that they will not advertise. Is such a promise credible? Explain.
d. In 1971 the federal government banned cigarette advertising on TV. Initially, tobacco companies protested vehemently. Referring to the game table above, discuss whether Big Tobacco's protests were genuine.

Investment, Time, and Insurance

13

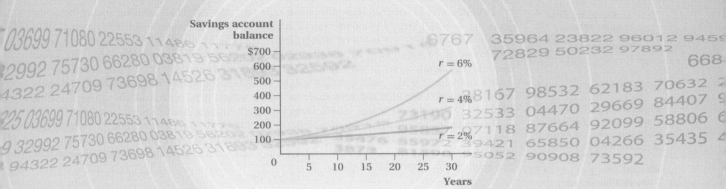

A t the end of May 2012, the *Dragon C2* spacecraft made history by docking with the International Space Station. This was the first time a private company, rather than a government, was able to launch a craft into orbit and dock it with the station. SpaceX, the company that built both the *Dragon* and its launch vehicle, the *Falcon 9* rocket, had spent a reported $1.2 billion to achieve this milestone. The mission's success led NASA to award over $1 billion in contracts to SpaceX to conduct additional missions. While the first *Dragon* mission only carried cargo, SpaceX designed the craft to carry people and hopes to one day lead missions that will take astronauts to the station.

The economics behind SpaceX's initial decision to design and build the *Dragon* and *Falcon* contain two interesting features that have been missing from our analyses to this point. The first is the element of *time*. SpaceX was formed in 2002, 10 years before the mission that in many ways it was founded to achieve. It had to spend vast sums of money developing its products before it would ever expect to receive payback for

investment
The purchase of capital in the present with the intent of reaping future benefits.

insurance
A payment from one economic actor to another with the aim of reducing the risk facing the payer.

them. The second additional feature is *uncertainty*. No one at SpaceX knew for sure in 2002 whether the mission would eventually be successful from either a technical or financial point of view. (Indeed, many outside observers were doubtful even at the beginning of 2012.) Yet over the 10-year span between the founding of the company and the successful mission of the *Falcon* and the *Dragon*, SpaceX managers had to make hugely consequential decisions without a sure sense of how things would turn out.

The decisions SpaceX faced, and the inherent elements of time and uncertainty they involved, are actually like many decisions that firms and consumers face every day. In this chapter, we explore economic decisions involving time and uncertainty. We pay particular attention to two types of decisions, those involving investment and insurance.

Investment is the purchase of capital now with the intent of reaping future benefits from it. A retail firm's construction of a new store is an example of investment. The firm pays the up-front costs of design, construction, shelf-stocking, and training new employees in order to earn future profits from sales over the store's lifetime.[1] We learn how payoffs that occur at different times can be valued on an equal basis, and discuss how to account for the riskiness that might be associated with future payoffs from capital investment. We also see how interest rates, which play a critical role in evaluating capital investment decisions, are determined in the investment capital market.

Insurance can be thought of as one economic actor paying another to reduce the economic risk facing the payer. Consumers and firms buy all types of insurance to reduce the risks they face. We explore why they are willing to do so and how much they are willing to pay to reduce risks.

13.1 Present Discounted Value Analysis

Decisions about actions and transactions involving costs and benefits that occur at different times are a bit more complex to evaluate than those that involve costs and benefits occurring at the same time.

When everything happens at once, comparing costs and benefits is straightforward; if an action's benefits outweigh its costs, then do it. But now, consider a capital investment decision that involves a $1,000 cost in the present and pays off $1,200 in five years. Is this investment a good idea? If the $1,200 were to be paid tomorrow or next week, the choice would be obvious. If you have to wait five years for the payoff, however, the choice is not obvious. Maybe you could get a higher return by saving the money instead, or maybe you'll need the funds for something else that comes up along the way. The decision would be even more complex if the costs and benefits were paid out and received in different amounts in different periods. Suppose an investment involved costs of $500 now, and again one and two years from now, and paid benefits of $400 one, two, three, and four years from now. How can you evaluate that choice? And what if those future benefits are *uncertain* and may not be paid because the outcome of the investment is *risky*?

Because the costs and benefits of all the decisions we've analyzed up to now have occurred at the same time, we need some new tools to evaluate the types of decisions

---

[1] The words "investment" and "investing" are often used in casual conversation to describe individuals and firms saving money through banks, brokers, and other financial institutions. This isn't exactly what economists usually mean when they use these words; the economic definition implies the purchase of some sort of capital with the hope of a future payoff. As we see later in the chapter, however, savings and investment (by the economic definition) are, in fact, linked. This connection results from the functioning of capital markets. Essentially, savers provide funds that investors use to purchase capital. The investors compensate the savers by paying back some of the investment's returns.

that have costs and benefits that occur over time. The first tool we introduce in this section is the concept of **present discounted value (PDV),** a mathematical concept that allows consumers and producers to compare costs and benefits over time in a way that puts all present and future financial values on equal footing.

Interest Rates

Interest rates and rates of return play a key role in present discounted value analysis. You've almost surely dealt with these concepts in your personal finances (savings accounts, car loans, student loans, mutual fund or stock holdings, etc.), but it's worth a quick review to set up our present discounted value analysis.

Interest is a periodic payment made by individuals or firms that depends on the value of the assets the interest payments are tied to. The value of the assets is called the **principal.** The **interest rate** is the amount of interest paid, expressed as a fraction of the principal. Interest rates are quoted on a per-period basis: yearly, monthly, or even daily, so the payment of interest is a "flow payment," paid out per unit of time. For example, if a savings account has $100 in it (the principal here) at a 4% annual interest rate, it pays $4 of interest at the end of the year. That is, $I = A \times r$, where I is the amount of interest paid, A the principal (think "A" for assets), and r the interest rate.

When interest paid in one period is added to the principal, and the interest rate in the next period is applied to the sum, this is called **compounding** or **compound interest.** Suppose our savings account pays a 4% interest rate that is compounded annually. An initial principal deposit of $100 earns $4 interest after one year. If the account holder keeps this interest in the account, the principal becomes $104. The interest in the second period is computed based on this new principal, making it $104 \times 0.04 = $4.16. Notice how this interest payment is slightly more than the first-period's interest payment. That's because the interest rate has been applied to a higher principal level. The third period interest is $108.16 \times 0.04 = $4.33, raising the principal to $112.49 after three periods. If the account holder leaves the account untouched, this process continues. Principal growth accelerates over time because the interest rate keeps getting applied to larger and larger principals.

It's fairly easy to figure out how the compounding process works in general. Let's say we were given an initial principal amount A. With an interest rate r, our principal after one time period would be $A + (A \times r) = A \times (1 + r)$. (In the example above, $A = \$100$ and $r = 0.04$.) After two periods, the principal would grow to

$$A \times (1 + r) \times (1 + r) = A \times (1 + r)^2$$

After three periods, the principal would become

$$A \times (1 + r)^2 \times (1 + r) = A \times (1 + r)^3$$

Repeating this type of calculation shows that the value of the account after t periods, V_t, will be

$$V_t = A \times (1 + r)^t$$

Figure 13.1 uses this formula to plot how an initial principal amount of $100 would grow over 30 years. It shows three cases. The bottom line traces the account balance growth when the interest rate is 2%, the middle line shows the case of a 4% interest rate, and the top line assumes a 6% rate. Higher interest rates lead to faster growth—no surprise there. Each of the lines has the same basic shape, however, with the lines growing steeper as time goes on. This is because the compounding process—in which present-period interest is computed on not just the last period's principal but also on the interest it earned—accelerates the growth of the account balance. (The increasing steepness is a bit subtle in the lowest interest rate case, but it's still present.)

present discounted value (PDV)
The value of a future payment in terms of equivalent present-period dollars.

interest
A periodic payment tied to an amount of assets borrowed or lent.

principal
The amount of assets on which interest payments are made.

interest rate
Interest expressed as a fraction of the principal.

compounding or **compound interest**
A calculation of interest based on the sum of the original principal and the interest paid over past periods.

Figure 13.1 | **Compound Interest**

Compounding is used to plot the growth of an initial principal amount of $100 over 30 years at interest rates of 2%, 4%, and 6%. While higher interest rates lead to faster growth, each of the lines has the same basic shape and becomes steeper over time.

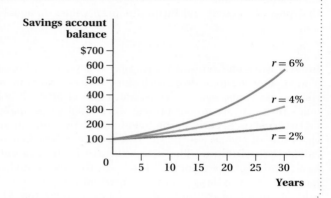

Notice that because of compounding, the same gap in interest rate levels can imply very different balances after extended periods. With a 2% interest rate, for example, the balance after 30 years is $100 \times (1.02)^{30} = \$181.14$. With a 4% interest rate, it's $100 \times (1.04)^{30} = \$324.34$, or $143.20 higher. But, with a 6% interest rate, the 30th-year balance is $574.35, or $250.01 higher than the 4% case.

Also, because of compounding, the number of periods it takes the balance to double is less than you might think. Many people would guess that with a 4% interest rate, it might take 25 years for the $100 initial principal to grow to $200. But, that's not the case; it happens instead in the 18th year because you earn more than $4 per year in interest as the account compounds in size. For a 6% rate, the balance goes above $200 in the 12th year. And it takes about 35 years with a 2% rate, rather than 50.

The "Rule of 72"

There's a handy rule-of-thumb for approximating how long it will take for a balance growing at any constant interest rate to double. It's referred to as the "Rule of 72." To use it, simply divide 72 by the per-period interest rate. The quotient will be the approximate number of periods until the balance doubles.[2]

An account compounding at 4% per year should double every $72/4 = 18$ years, just as we saw in our example above. It should take about $72/6 = 12$ years for a sum to double at a 6% rate, and $72/2 = 36$ years for the principal to double at the 2% rate. These numbers are close to what we found in our example.

Present Discounted Value

As we discussed in the chapter's introduction, a fundamental feature of capital investment decisions is that their costs and benefits are incurred and earned at different times. Typically, investment decisions involve spending money in the present to earn

---

[2] Some people use the "Rule of 70" instead; it works the same way. The Rule of 70 is slightly more accurate, but the Rule of 72 is often used for convenience, because so many numbers divide into it evenly. For you math fans out there, the reason the Rule of 72 (or 70) works is that the size of initial value A growing at a constant rate r over a time period t is $X = Ae^{rt}$. If we replace X with $2A$ (to represent a doubling of the initial value) and take the natural log of both sides of the equation, we have $rt = \ln 2$. Since $\ln 2 \approx 0.70$, substituting and solving give $t \approx 0.70/r$ (that's why the Rule of 70 is a slightly better approximation).

benefits in later periods. Adding up an investment project's benefits and subtracting its costs while ignoring when they occur would be easy, but doesn't make much sense. This method would imply, for example, that a project costing $1,000 today and paying $1,001 in 50 years would be worthwhile. It's doubtful anyone would find that project sensible—and *not* because inflation makes $1,001 worth less in real terms. Even without any inflation, it still would not make sense, as we will explain shortly. What we need is a way to adjust expenditures and payoffs that happen at different times so that they can be compared on an apples-to-apples basis. Present discounted value (PDV) analysis (sometimes called just present value analysis) uses the concepts of interest rates and compounding that we just discussed, but in reverse. Here's how.

In the previous section, we figured out how large an initial principal value would grow to be if compounded at a given interest rate. Present discounted value flips this calculation on its head. It takes a future dollar value and asks how large the initial principal would have to be today in order to grow at a given interest rate to that future value. For example, let's say we wanted to know the present value of a $104.00 payment one year from now at an interest rate of 4%. At 4% interest, the principal today must be $100; at 4%, the $100 will grow to $104 in one year. So, at 4% interest, the PDV of $104 next year, its value in today's dollars, is $100. The $104 in the future and the $100 in the present are worth the same amount because $100 today can be used to create $104 in one year at the given rate of interest (4%).

Discounting can also be used to compare payments that happen more than one period apart. For example, again assuming a 4% interest rate, the PDV of $108.16 in two years (what we saw above would be the account balance after two years) is $100. The PDV of $112.49 in three years at 4% is also $100.

Present discounted values use interest rates and compounding to compare payments happening at different times. The idea is to appropriately discount future values so that they can be put in terms of equivalent present-period dollars. This lets us compare an investment's costs and benefits, regardless of when they are paid, on an equal footing. Once we've done that, we can ask whether a particular investment is a good idea or compare a number of different investment choices to see which is best.

Remember in our examples above that the growth of the account balance depended on the interest rate. Just as the interest rate affects the relative sizes of the initial principal and future account balances, it also operates in reverse to affect the PDV of a given future value. Consider the case of a $104 payment that will occur in one year. We know that this payment's PDV is $100 at a 4% rate, but what if the interest rate were different? Suppose it was 6%. To find the PDV in this case, we have to find what initial principal would grow at a 6% rate to be exactly $104 after one year. This is easy using the formula we derived above. In this case,

$$A \times (1 + r) = A \times (1 + 0.06) = \$104$$

$$A = \frac{\$104}{1.06} = \$98.11$$

This means that the PDV of $104 is $98.11 when the interest rate is 6%. If we did the same exercise with a 2% interest rate, we would find that the PDV of $104 at this rate is $101.96.

It's important to notice from these examples that the PDV of a given future value is *always* inversely related to the interest rate. That is, the higher the interest rate, the smaller the initial principal needs to be to grow to the same future value. Therefore, a particular future-period payment has a lower PDV when the interest rate is higher.

All we had to do to compute the PDVs above was reverse the equation for the future account balance under compounding. We solved for the initial principal that would be needed to grow to that future value. That's what a present discounted value is. We saw above that any initial principal A growing at interest rate r for t periods will grow to a value of

$$V_t = A \times (1 + r)^t$$

A PDV reinterprets V_t as the future payment that needs to be expressed in present-value terms. A, as the initial principal, is the PDV. That is,

$$PDV = \frac{V_t}{(1 + r)^t}$$

We can use this equation to find the present discounted value of any payment V_t that occurs t periods in the future. This equation plays a central role in much of what we do in this chapter. Knowing how to calculate PDV is practical, too. If you go to buy a car and the salesperson tells you that you can either buy the car for some price or lease it for $2,000 down and $500 per month, you need to figure out the PDV of the payments to determine which option is the better deal.

The present value equation has some important implications. First, PDVs are proportional to the future value being discounted. If V_t were twice as high, its PDV would be, too.

Second, just as we noted above, higher interest rates imply lower PDVs for fixed values of V_t and t. The intuition is that higher interest rates reduce the initial value necessary to grow to future value V_t.[3]

Finally, the PDV of any particular value V_t is smaller the further into the future that it occurs. The PDV of $104 one year from now is greater than the PDV of $104 in two years, which is itself greater than the PDV of $104 three years from now, and so on.

Present Discounted Value of Payment Streams   We just saw how we can find the PDV of a payment that occurs at one particular moment in the future. It's easy to extend this method to *payment streams*—collections of payments that happen at different times. To compute the PDV of an entire stream, we apply the present value discounting equation to each of the stream's elements and then add them together.

Suppose you earn a scholarship that will pay you $1,000 in each of four installments: The first installment arrives today, and then the next three come one, two, and three years from today. The PDV of the scholarship is the sum of the PDVs of each installment. So, for any generic annual interest rate r, the scholarship's PDV is

$$PDV = \$1,000 + \frac{\$1,000}{(1 + r)} + \frac{\$1,000}{(1 + r)^2} + \frac{\$1,000}{(1 + r)^3}$$

The first $1,000 payment is not discounted because it occurs in the present period. (This is what the PDV formula implies, too. If $t = 0$—that is, the payment happens 0 periods from now, or today—then the denominator of the first installment in the PDV equation is 1.) The second installment is discounted by $(1 + r)$, because it occurs in one year (we left the $t = 1$ implicit in that term). The third installment, which happens in two years, is discounted by $(1 + r)^2$. The final installment is discounted by $(1 + r)^3$ because that payment doesn't come for three years.

The interest rate affects the PDV of a stream of payments in the same way that it affects a single payment. For $r = 0.04$ (a 4% interest rate), for example, the scholarship's $PDV = \$1,000 + \$961.54 + \$924.55 + \$889.00 = \$3,775.09$. This present value is less than the simple $4,000 sum of the payments because of discounting. Payments in the future are not equivalent to the same dollar-sized payment in the present. For $r = 0.06$, the scholarship's PDV is lower, at $3,673.01. For $r = 0.02$, the PDV is higher, $3,883.88.

---

[3] An important detail when calculating PDVs is to make sure the interest rate r matches the period t. That is, if t is expressed in years, annual interest rates should be used. If t is instead, say, months, then monthly interest rates should be used (and if necessary, converted from whatever time basis they were originally expressed in).

Special Cases of PDVs   There are some commonplace payment stream patterns that have general PDV formulas that are worth learning. One is a constant payment that is made for a set number of periods. For example, a car loan might require a payment of $400 per month for 60 months. Fixed-rate mortgages also have this type of payment pattern. Let's call the regular per-period payment M. The PDV of a set of regular payments M made for T periods (starting one period from now) is

$$PDV = \frac{M}{(1 + r)} + \frac{M}{(1 + r)^2} + \cdots + \frac{M}{(1 + r)^T} = M \times \Sigma_{t=1}^{T} \frac{1}{(1 + r)^t}$$

If we simplify the series of terms with $1/(1 + r)^t$ for various t, we end up with

$$PDV = \left(\frac{M}{r}\right) \times \left[1 - \left(\frac{1}{(1 + r)^T}\right)\right]$$

The PDV of this stream of payments is proportional to the regular payment M. That means if you borrow twice as much at the same terms (interest rate and repayment length), your regular payment will be twice as high. The payment stream's PDV is negatively related to the interest rate, but not proportionately. Specifically, changes in r have the largest effect on the PDV at low interest rates; their influence declines in size as r climbs. Finally, the PDV of the payment stream grows with T. This is no surprise; the longer the payments last, the greater the total value of those payments. This formula also shows the familiar tradeoff facing many borrowers: When borrowing a fixed amount of money (i.e., a given PDV), a borrower can often lower his payment M by agreeing to a longer payback term T.

An interesting special case of this formula occurs when T goes to infinity, meaning a payment of M every period, forever. (This type of arrangement is called a *perpetuity*.) The PDV of this perpetual stream can be expressed as

$$PDV = \frac{M}{(1 + r)} + \frac{M}{(1 + r)^2} + \frac{M}{(1 + r)^3} + \cdots$$

This may look like it's infinitely large, but it's not because the $(1 + r)^t$ values in the denominator grow fast enough with time that the PDV of payments in the far distant future is basically worth zero. You can see the result of this property by plugging a large number for T into the PDV formula. For instance, if the final payment occurs 500 years from now, this makes the expression $(1 + r)^{500}$ in the denominator very large. With an interest rate of 4%, you would divide the 500th-year payment by more than 325 million to compute its value in today's terms. Its PDV is therefore basically zero.

When T goes to infinity, the PDV formula above simplifies to

$$PDV = \frac{M}{r}$$

This says that the PDV of any regular payment occurring forever equals the payment divided by the interest rate. If the interest rate is 5%, the PDV of a payment M is 20 times the payment ($\frac{M}{0.05} = 20 \times M$). If the interest rate is 10%, the PDV is $10 \times M$; for $r = 2\%$, the PDV is $50 \times M$.

While you may believe that the idea of a payment occurring infinitely seems unrealistic, there are actually a few investment choices or financial instruments that pay off forever. One of the best known is a type of bond, called a consol, issued by the government of the United Kingdom. Consols pay a constant interest payment forever to whoever holds the bond. The fact that these bonds don't have infinite prices when traded on financial markets proves that even infinite payment streams have finite present values because of discounting.

British government debt aside, the perpetuity PDV formula is most useful as a shorthand way to approximate PDVs. It's not easy to compute the PDVs of even steady payment streams in your head, but if you can assume the payments continue forever, an approximation is easy. This approximation is an upper bound: Any other type of payment stream would end at some period $T < \infty$, so the perpetuity PDV approximation is always higher than the true value.

To see an example of this, suppose you are talking to a friend who is thinking about buying a business. He is confident the business can earn a profit of $100,000 per year for the foreseeable future. The business is being sold for $1.2 million. If the interest rate is 10% (and expected to stay at or near that level), would you advise him to buy? Not at that price: Even if the business paid that $100,000 profit forever, the PDV of the business is only

$$PDV = \frac{M}{r}$$

$$= \frac{\$100,000}{0.10}$$

$$= \$1 \text{ million}$$

The business's earnings can't justify the $1.2 million asking price. On the other hand, if the interest rate is 5%, then the PDV of the business would be $100,000/0.05 = $2 million, which would make the $1.2 million price worth considering.

 application

The Present Discounted Value of Bonds

bond
Financial instrument that indicates the issuer is indebted to the purchaser.

face value or **par value**
The principal that the bond issuer pays interest on.

coupon rate
The rate of the regular periodic amount paid out to bondholders.

coupon payments
Set of scheduled interest payments that recur over a bond's entire life.

maturity
The length of a bond's life.

A **bond** is a financial instrument that indicates the issuer (usually, a government or a corporation) is indebted to the purchaser of the bond (the bondholder). It's basically a tradable IOU. The principal that the issuer pays interest on is a bond's **face value** (also called the **par value**). The **coupon rate** is the rate of interest applied to this principal, and the **coupon payments** are the set of scheduled interest payments that recur over the bond's entire life. Each coupon payment equals the bond's face value times its coupon rate.[4] A bond's **maturity** is the time between when the bond is issued and when the borrower pays the face value to the bondholder. At the end of this period, a bond is said to have "matured." Maturities vary greatly across different types of bonds, ranging from as short as weeks to months, to as long as decades (or, in the case of consols, forever). Coupon payments are made over the entire life of the bond, so the maturity determines how many coupon payments are made.[5]

There are active financial markets in which bonds are traded (the total value of all outstanding bonds in the world is in the tens of trillions of dollars). What determines the price of a bond in these markets? At its heart, a bond is a payment stream that the issuer (the firm or government) promises to pay the bearer (the bondholder). Not surprisingly, then, the PDV of a bond's payment stream is closely related to its market price. This is true not just when the bond is initially issued, but also when it is traded in financial markets after the issuer has already started making payments. In the latter case, the PDV of the remaining payments is tied to the bond's price. (There are many

---

[4] The word "coupon" originates from traditional-style paper bonds, which had a strip of coupons attached to them that the bondholder would tear off when the periodic payment was due and send to the bond issuer for payment.

[5] Some bonds do not have coupon payments at all; that is, their coupon rate is zero. You may have heard of this type before—they are called *zero-coupon bonds*. The only payment a zero-coupon bond makes to the bondholder is its face value at maturity. Since this payment occurs in later periods and is therefore discounted, the PDV of a zero-coupon bond is less than its face value.

other factors, such as the risk associated with the issuer, that determine a bond's price. We discuss risk later in this chapter.)

Let's see how to determine a bond's PDV by considering a hypothetical corporate bond that has the following attributes: a $1,000 face value, a 10% annual coupon rate, and a 5-year maturity.

To find the coupon payments, we multiply the face value by the coupon rate. Therefore, the coupon payments are $1,000 $\times$ 0.10 = $100 each. These will be made once every year throughout the lifetime of the bond. (Real bonds usually make coupon payments twice a year, but to keep things simple, we assume only a single payment each year.)

In addition to the coupon payments, the other component of a bond's payoffs to its bearer is its face-value redemption at maturity. The bearer of this bond will be paid $1,000 five years from the bond's original issuance.

Putting this all together, the PDV of the bond at the time it is issued is

$$PDV = \frac{\$100}{(1+r)} + \frac{\$100}{(1+r)^2} + \frac{\$100}{(1+r)^3} + \frac{\$100}{(1+r)^4} + \frac{\$100}{(1+r)^5} + \frac{\$1,000}{(1+r)^5}$$

The first five terms are the coupon payments; the final term is the face-value redemption.

Notice that this PDV depends on the interest rate just like all PDVs. Because a higher interest rate means the bond's future payments to the bondholder are discounted more steeply, the bond's PDV is negatively related to the interest rate. Furthermore, the interest rate r used to compute the PDV, which can and does change with financial market conditions, generally does *not* equal the coupon rate, which is fixed for the life of the bond. This implies that all else equal, as r rises, the price of a bond—what an investor is willing to pay for the PDV of the payments tied to the bond—will fall.

The price that a bond fetches when it is sold in financial markets determines what is called the bond's **yield** (or sometimes, the **yield to maturity**). A bond's yield turns the PDV equation for a bond on its head and asks, "What would the interest rate have to be to make the bond's PDV equal to its market price?" You can think of this question as determining the implicit interest rate the bond must pay to make a buyer willing to hold the bond at its market price.

Suppose that the hypothetical bond we discussed above was being traded in the financial markets at a price of $963. The bond's yield would be the value of r that solves

$$\$963 = \frac{\$100}{(1+r)} + \frac{\$100}{(1+r)^2} + \cdots + \frac{\$100}{(1+r)^5} + \frac{\$1,000}{(1+r)^5}$$

There's no easy way to algebraically back out what r is in this equation, but r can be found numerically by using a spreadsheet. The solution is $r = 0.11$—that is, the bond's yield is 11%. If the market price were lower, say, $894.48, then the bond's yield would be 13%. Therefore, yields are also inversely related to the bond's market price. Because every possible market price corresponds to a unique value of yield, a yield is another way of stating what the price of a bond is. And that's often how the prices of bonds are reported by the financial press—as yields.

There's one other interesting feature of yields. Suppose the market price were exactly equal to the bond's face (or par) value, $1,000. Solving for the yield would indicate that the yield is 10%, or the same as the coupon rate. This isn't a coincidence; any bond's yield equals its coupon rate if its price is its face value. A bond with its price equal to its face value (and therefore a yield equal to its coupon rate) is said to be **at par.** A bond with a price less than its face value is said to be selling **below par.** As we saw in our examples above, bonds selling below par have yields higher than their coupon rates. Those selling at prices above face value—that is, **above par**—have yields below their coupon rates. ■

yield or **yield to maturity**
The interest rate that makes a bond's present discounted value equal to its current market price.

at par
Description of a bond whose price equals its face value, or whose yield equals its coupon rate.

below par
Description of a bond with a price less than its face value, or whose yield is greater than its coupon rate.

above par
Description of a bond with a price above its face value, or whose yield is less than its coupon rate.

13.1 figure it out

Suppose that Emmy is going to turn 21 exactly one year from today, and she wants to throw a spectacular party. Emmy would like to have $1,000 to spend, and wants to set aside enough money today to fund her $1,000 party in a year.

a. If interest rates are 6%, how much does Emmy have to set aside today?

b. If interest rates are 9%, how much does Emmy have to set aside today?

c. What happens to the amount she needs to set aside as interest rates change? Explain.

Solution:

a. We can use the present discounted value PDV formula to determine the amount that Emmy needs

to set aside today to have $1,000 one year from now if the interest rate is 6%:

$$PDV = \frac{V}{(1 + r)} = \frac{\$1,000}{1 + 0.06} = \frac{\$1,000}{1.06} = \$943.40$$

b. If the interest rate rises to 9%, Emmy will need to set aside

$$PDV = \frac{V}{(1 + r)} = \frac{\$1,000}{1 + 0.09} = \frac{\$1,000}{1.09} = \$917.43$$

to fund her party.

c. As the interest rate rises, the present value of $1,000 falls. This is because Emmy's current funds will grow more quickly at a higher interest rate. Therefore, she will not need to set as much aside to fund her party.

13.2 Evaluating Investment Choices

Now that we've covered the basics of present discounted value analysis, we'll discuss how to apply that framework to evaluate investment choices.

Net Present Value

In Section 13.1, all the payments had the same sign. That is, the individual payments have all been considered proceeds for whoever owns the payment stream. But, there are many cases in which some payments are benefits and others are costs. Investment projects, for example, usually have up-front costs and don't pay benefits until sometime in the future. We can incorporate costs and benefits into a single present discounted value fairly easily: Payments that are benefits enter into the PDV calculation with positive signs, while costs have negative signs. The individual terms of the payment stream are still added up to get the PDV. Now, however, those costs reduce the PDV because they have a negative sign.

Let's suppose you often have to make copies and are considering buying your own desktop copier to save the hassle and cost of going to the local copy center. You have found a desktop unit that costs $500, and you expect to be able to use it for the next three years. (For simplicity, we assume that paper, toner, and electricity don't cost anything.) You figure out that over the course of a year, a desktop unit will save you $200 in time, effort, and money compared to using the copy store. Thus, there are three $200 benefit payments: one a year from now, another in two years, and a third in three years. (For simplicity, we assume that the $200 benefit comes in one payment at the end of the year.) The payoff structure of the copier purchase is shown in Table 13.1. Should you buy the desktop copier or continue using the copy center?

The first thing to do is figure out the present discounted value of the copier investment. Applying the PDV formula, we have

$$PDV = -\$500 + \frac{\$200}{(1 + r)} + \frac{\$200}{(1 + r)^2} + \frac{\$200}{(1 + r)^3}$$

The first term is the cost of buying the copier. It happens in the present period, so it is not discounted. Because it is a cost to the decision maker rather than a benefit, it is negative. The other terms account for the future benefits of buying the copier. They have positive signs and are discounted based on how far into the future they occur.

As we have seen in our examples, the PDV of this potential investment also depends on the interest rate. If $r = 4\%$, the PDV of buying the copier is \$55.02:

$$PDV = -\$500 + \frac{\$200}{(1 + r)} + \frac{\$200}{(1 + r)^2} + \frac{\$200}{(1 + r)^3}$$

$$= -\$500 + \frac{\$200}{(1 + 0.04)} + \frac{\$200}{(1 + 0.04)^2} + \frac{\$200}{(1 + 0.04)^3}$$

$$= -\$500 + \$192.31 + \$184.91 + \$177.80 = \$55.02$$

This positive number implies that at a 4% interest rate, the copier's future benefits outweigh its costs in present value terms, so buying the copier is a worthwhile idea. If the interest rate is 2% instead, the net PDV is larger: \$76.78, an even stronger case for buying the copier. However, if r is higher than 4%, the PDV is less than \$55.02. In fact, if r is high enough, the net PDV will be negative. At a 10% interest rate, for example, the PDV is −\$2.63; that is, buying the copier creates a *loss* of \$2.63 in present value terms. At an interest rate of 10%, the present value of the copier's future benefits does not make up for its up-front costs. Figure 13.2 plots the PDV of this example investment versus r. You can see that the copier's PDV becomes negative at an interest rate just below 10%, at 9.7% to be exact, and continues to drop at higher interest rates.

Using PDV to evaluate the return of a proposed investment (as we just did in our copier example) is sometimes called **net present value (NPV) analysis,** a method of evaluating investment projects that uses present discounted value to put all of an investment project's future cost and benefit flows on a common basis so they can be

net present value (NPV) analysis
The use of the present discounted value to evaluate the expected long-term return on an investment.

Table 13.1	Payoff Structure of the Copier Purchase

Period	Costs	Benefits
0	\$500	\$0
1	0	200
2	0	200
3	0	200

Figure 13.2   The PDV of a Copier Purchase

The present discounted value (PDV) of an investment in a desktop copier is plotted against the interest rate r. In this case, investing in a desktop copier yields positive returns up until $r = 9.7\%$. At interest rates higher than 9.7%, you should continue to make copies at the local office supply store rather than purchasing your own desktop copier.

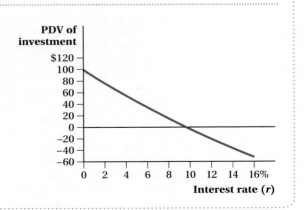

compared apples-to-apples. If the PDV of a project's benefits outweighs the PDV of its costs, the project's NPV (the sum of these PDVs) will be positive, and the investment is a worthwhile undertaking. If the PDVs of the costs are greater than the benefits, the project's NPV will be negative, and the investment is not worthwhile.

We can extend the NPV analysis method to more complex costs and benefits payment streams. Costs incurred in the future rather than the present have negative signs and are discounted just like any other payments. Because costs and benefits that occur in the same period are discounted equally, they can first be combined into a *net* benefit for each period. If costs outweigh benefits, the net benefit is negative; if benefits outweigh costs, the net benefit is positive. Once the PDVs of all net benefits are computed, they are added together to obtain the net present value.

This procedure gives us the generic formula for computing the NPV of any investment decision. Label the periods spanned by the investment project $0, 1, 2, \ldots, T$, where 0 is the current period and T is the last period in which any costs or benefits associated with the project occur. $B_0, B_1, \ldots, B_T$ are the investment's benefits in the respective periods and $C_0, C_1, \ldots, C_T$ are the costs. The NPV formula is

$$NPV = (B_0 - C_0) + \frac{(B_1 - C_1)}{(1 + r)} + \frac{(B_2 - C_2)}{(1 + r)^2} + \cdots + \frac{(B_T - C_T)}{(1 + r)^T}$$

where $B_t - C_t$ is the net benefit in any particular period t. In our desktop copier example above, $T = 3$, $B_0 = \$0$, $B_1 = B_2 = B_3 = \$200$, $C_0 = \$500$, and $C_1 = C_2 = C_3 = \$0$:

$$NPV = (B_0 - C_0) + \frac{(B_1 - C_1)}{(1 + r)} + \frac{(B_2 - C_2)}{(1 + r)^2} + \cdots + \frac{(B_T - C_T)}{(1 + r)^T}$$

$$= (0 - \$500) + \frac{(\$200 - 0)}{(1 + 0.04)} + \frac{(\$200 - 0)}{(1 + 0.04)^2} + \frac{(\$200 - 0)}{(1 + 0.04)^3}$$

$$= -\$500 + \$192.31 + \$184.91 + \$177.80 = \$55.02$$

The NPV formula is extremely useful and can be used to evaluate all sorts of investment decisions regardless of the timing of their positive or negative payouts.

The Key Role of Interest Rates in Determining NPV

For payment streams with both positive and negative terms, the value of the interest rate r can determine whether the net present value NPV is positive or negative. This is because the interest rate, through its discounting role, determines how important future payoffs are relative to those occurring nearer to the present time period. As r rises, more distant payoffs become relatively less important. Mathematically speaking, this is because the term $(1 + r)^t$ in the denominator grows larger with t.

This characteristic means that investment projects tend to become less appealing in NPV terms when the interest rate is higher. Investment projects typically have up-front costs with their benefits realized later on. Higher interest rates reduce the present discounted value of those future benefits relative to the investment's current and earlier costs, driving down the investment's NPV.

It's easy to see the economic intuition behind this result if you recognize that the interest rate can be thought of as the opportunity cost of investing. Consider households or firms that are deciding whether to put financial capital toward a potential investment project. They face a choice. They can invest and earn the investment's returns, or they could instead lend their funds on the financial market to other investors implementing their own projects. A household could do this by holding assets in, say, a mutual fund rather than building an addition to their house. Firms can also use financial markets to offer their uncommitted funds to others. (We talk more about the capital financial markets where these transactions occur at the end of the chapter.) If the firm or household chooses to undertake an investment project, it is giving up the return it could have made by lending to others through the financial market. What is that return? The interest rate r. That's why r captures the opportunity cost of investing. The higher the market interest rate is, therefore, the more a household or firm gives up by investing. NPV analysis, by putting all payments on a common present-value basis using the market interest rate, implicitly accounts for this opportunity cost. The higher opportunity costs of investment implied by higher interest rates are the reason why investments with a typical "up-front-costs-for-future-returns" payment stream pattern have NPVs that fall as interest rates rise.

application

Replacing Planes

In the mid-1990s, Northwest Airlines (bought in 2008 by Delta Airlines) was considering replacing its roughly 150 DC-9 aircraft. These planes were the workhorses of Northwest's route network, accounting for a large share of the total flights the airline flew. They were also some of the oldest planes in its fleet.[6]

Management had two options. It could buy replacement planes at $35 million each, or it could renovate and update the old planes' cabins at a cost of $7 million each and delay having to purchase new planes for another 12 years. There was a tradeoff involved with keeping the old planes, however: They had higher operating costs primarily because they were less fuel-efficient. Specifically, an old plane cost $1.5 million a year more to operate than a new one would. What should management do?

Let's start the analysis by laying out the payment flows involved. If Northwest opts to buy new planes, it has to pay $35 million per plane immediately and operating costs C per year thereafter.

If Northwest does not buy the new planes, it pays $7 million immediately to refurbish each DC-9. For the next 12 years, Northwest has to pay the DC-9's higher annual operating costs of C + $1.5 million. At the end of the 12th year, Northwest must buy new planes, which we'll assume still cost $35 million each. After that point, Northwest's expenditures are C, the same as they would have been if it had bought the new planes immediately. The costs are C because Northwest no longer has to pay the additional $1.5 million per year it costs to operate the older planes.

Northwest has to decide which of these cost streams would be smallest. Table 13.2 shows the difference

Table 13.2 | **Cost Profiles for Northwest Airlines' Investment Decisions**

Year	Costs If New Plane Bought ($ millions per plane)	Costs If Old Plane Kept ($ millions per plane)	Net Cost Difference If New Plane Bought ($ millions per plane)
0	−$35	−$7	−$28
1	−C	−(C + $1.5)	1.5
2	−C	−(C + 1.5)	1.5
...	...	...	...
11	−C	−(C + 1.5)	1.5
12	−C	−(C + 1.5 + 35)	36.5
13	−C	−C	0
14	−C	−C	0
...	...	...	...

[6] This example is based on an actual decision Northwest faced at the time. We picked the dollar values in the example to be realistic, but we don't know what Northwest actually paid. Furthermore, to keep things simple, we've ignored many other aspects of the plane-replacement problem that matter in real life, such as flyers' willingness to pay to fly on newer aircraft, the interactions between Northwest's plane choice and its contracts with its unions, and so on.

Table 13.3 Northwest Airlines' NPV of Buying New Planes

Year	Buying New Plane ($ millions)	Buying New Plane, Growing Costs ($ millions)	Buying New Plane, Lower r ($ millions)
0	−28.0	−28.0	−28.0
1	1.39	1.39	1.44
2	1.29	1.41	1.39
3	1.19	1.44	1.33
4	1.10	1.47	1.28
5	1.02	1.49	1.23
6	0.95	1.52	1.19
7	0.88	1.55	1.14
8	0.81	1.58	1.10
9	0.75	1.61	1.05
10	0.69	1.64	1.01
11	0.64	1.67	0.97
12	14.49	15.60	22.80
13	0	0	0
...	...	...	...
NPV =	$−2.80	$4.37	$7.94

between the two payment streams over the relevant horizon.

Looking at the difference in costs makes it clear that buying the new planes is an investment: Northwest pays an up-front cost (the $28 million difference between the purchase cost and the refurbishment cost), but it saves the additional operating costs of $1.5 million per year and the $35 million cost of purchasing a new plane after each refurbished plane is retired after 12 years. Following the 12th year, Northwest has new planes and no longer any additional operating costs. The question for management is whether this investment is worth it.

Suppose the interest rate Northwest faces is 8%. We first compute the PDV of each year's net payment as shown in the third column of Table 13.2. These PDVs are given in the first column of Table 13.3. Their sum is the per-plane NPV of buying new planes right away. The fact that the sum is −$2.8 million indicates that buying new planes causes a net *loss* to Northwest of $2.8 million per plane. In other words, in net present value terms, Northwest's additional cost of buying the new planes immediately at $35 million each instead of refurbishing the old ones for $7 million each is too high relative to the money the airline would save in lower operating costs and by being able to put off buying new planes for another 12 years. Therefore, Northwest should choose to keep the DC-9s in its fleet for the time being; otherwise, the airline is setting itself up for a net loss of $2.8 million per plane.

This is what Northwest chose to do; refurbished DC-9s were still flying Northwest routes over a decade later. Under what circumstances might Northwest have found it beneficial to replace the DC-9s? We consider two such cases: operating costs that increase by 10 per year and a lower interest rate.

Suppose Northwest anticipates that the additional operating cost of the DC-9s is going to increase by 10% per year (so it's $1.5 million in the first year, $1.65 million in the second, etc.), perhaps because it expects fuel prices or maintenance costs to rise. The NPV analysis for this case is shown in Column 2 of Table 13.3. Notice how the present value of the operating cost difference actually rises over time rather than falls. This is because the 10% cost growth rate is higher than the 8% interest rate. With growing operating costs, the NPV of purchasing a new plane is now positive ($4.37 million), implying that Northwest should replace the DC-9s immediately. This makes sense: If the DC-9s are becoming more costly over time, this raises the return of replacing them earlier.

As a final case, let's suppose again that the operating cost difference is fixed at $1.5 million per year, but that Northwest faces a lower interest rate of 4%. This lower interest rate means that the future cost savings won't be discounted as much, nor will the savings from not having to purchase new planes 12 years from now. Both of these factors raise the value of buying the new planes right away, and that's exactly what we see in Column 3 of Table 13.3. The NPV of purchasing now is $7.94 million per plane. Had either of these situations held at the time the decision had to be made, Northwest would have been more likely to replace its DC-9 fleet. ∎

NPVs versus Payback Periods

You've probably heard investment evaluations couched in terms of **payback periods,** the time it takes for an investment's initial costs to be recouped in future benefits. For our desktop copier example above, the payback period is three years. The total benefits obtained after two years ($200 + $200 = $400) are less than the $500 up-front cost, but the $600 in total benefits recovered after three years are greater.

Payback periods are extremely easy to compute; that's the advantage of using them to evaluate investment choices. Their disadvantage is that they don't take into account the idea of discounting future money by an interest rate. They treat future payments as equivalent to current payments in dollar terms, even though that's not the case (unless the interest rate is zero). The desktop copier, for example, would be considered worthwhile in payback period terms as long as three years is an acceptable period to the person deciding about the investment. At high enough interest rates, however, the project will have a negative NPV. You would do better by not buying the copier and earning interest on the $500 instead. If you had used the payback period method as an evaluation standard when interest rates are high, you would mistakenly buy the copier. For this reason, while payback periods are a handy "first-pass" way to think about investments, they aren't as good as NPV methods and can, in fact, lead to some wrong decisions.

payback period
The length of time required for an investment's initial costs to be recouped in future benefits without discounting future flows.

13.2 figure it out

Marty owns a travel agency and is considering the purchase of a flux capacitor. Owning the capacitor will enable Marty to earn $100,000 per year selling trips through time. Marty plans to hold on to the capacitor for three years. He estimates that at the end of three years, he will be able to resell the flux capacitor for $250,000.

a. If the flux capacitor is priced at $475,000, and interest rates are 7%, calculate the net present value of the investment.

b. Is the flux capacitor a wise investment for Marty? Explain.

Solution:

a. Net present value is the present value of the benefits minus the present value of the costs for each period. We must account for three factors in this calculation: the price Marty must pay initially, the revenue he earns each of the three periods, and the amount he will receive from selling the capacitor at the end of the three years. Therefore,

$$NPV = -\$475,000 + \frac{\$100,000}{1.07} + \frac{\$100,000}{(1.07)^2} + \frac{\$100,000}{(1.07)^3} + \frac{\$250,000}{(1.07)^3}$$

Note that the cost of $475,000 is occurring now so it is not discounted (and it enters the equation with a minus sign), while the benefits (the annual revenue and the sale price) occur in the future and thus must be discounted.

Calculating, we get

$$NPV = -\$475,000 + \$93,457.94 + \$87,343.87 + \$81,629.79 + \$204,074.47 = -\$8,493.93$$

b. No, this is not a wise investment for Marty because the NPV is negative.

13.3 The Correct Interest Rate to Use, and Capital Markets

In everything we've done to this point, we've talked about "the" interest rate r. But real financial markets have many different interest rates. Which one should investors use to evaluate net present values?

Nominal versus Real Interest Rates

Because investments' costs and benefits occur at different times, price inflation can affect the net value of an investment, a fact we've ignored so far. When prices change over time, they create their own discounting effect: A future payment doesn't have the same purchasing power as an equal-sized payment in the present. If there is inflation (rising prices), a future payment of $1,000 will buy fewer goods and services than a payment of $1,000 today. The further the payment is in the future, the more prices will likely have increased, and the larger is this purchasing power gap. Because firms and households care about real purchasing power, they need to adjust for these gaps when evaluating investments.

Economists account for inflation in these situations by drawing a distinction between nominal and real interest rates. **Nominal interest rates** are rates of return expressed only in currency values without regard for how much purchasing power those values hold. **Real interest rates** (also called *inflation-adjusted interest rates*) express rates of return in terms of purchasing power, the amount of goods and services that the payment can purchase. If the growth rate in the price level has reduced a future payment's purchasing power because a dollar buys less in the future than it does in the present, real interest rates take that into account.

As long as inflation rates aren't wildly high, the basic rule is that the real interest rate, r, is approximately the nominal interest rate, i, minus the inflation rate, π:[7]

$$r \approx i - \pi$$

Once we have computed the real interest rate, we use it as the interest rate r in PDV and NPV calculations. This will automatically take into account the discounting effects of price changes over the lifetime of the investment as well as the other reasons future payments are discounted.

nominal interest rate
Rate of return expressed in raw currency values.

real interest rate
Rate of return expressed in terms of purchasing power.

Other Rate Adjustments

We've established that individuals making investment decisions should base their NPV calculation on the real interest rate. And, we know that the real interest rate is the difference between the nominal interest rate and the inflation rate. But, what is the appropriate nominal interest rate to use in this calculation?

To answer this question, it's helpful to recall that the interest rate captures the opportunity cost of investing. It is an opportunity cost because resources used to purchase capital cannot be otherwise saved to earn interest. NPV analysis asks whether an investment's future payoffs are worth the current costs by comparing those future payoffs to what would have been earned by simply saving the funds and earning inter-

---

[7] This became known as the Fisher rule, in honor of the early-twentieth-century Yale economist Irving Fisher. It derives from the fact that any principal amount A earning a nominal interest rate of i will be worth $A \times (1 + i)$ in non-inflation-adjusted terms. If the inflation rate over the period is π, then money that could buy A worth of goods at the beginning of the period can buy $A/(1 + \pi)$ at the end of the period. So, the real value of the principal at the end is $A \times (1 + i)/(1 + \pi)$. The real interest rate is the percentage change in purchasing power over the initial principal's purchasing power: $r = [(A(1 + i)/(1 + \pi)) - A]/A = (1 + i)/(1 + \pi) - 1 = (i - \pi)/(1 + \pi)$. If π isn't very high, that's approximately equal to $i - \pi$.

est. Discounting future flows in an NPV analysis puts them on comparable terms with the possible interest earned on savings.

This means that the interest rate used to compute NPVs should be the alternative rate of return that is forgone if the investment is made. If a firm is considering whether or not to build a new store, for example, it is in essence deciding between building the store or instead saving the funds in the financial market and earning the market rate. If the NPV of the project computed using that market rate is positive, then building the store is preferable to earning the financial market return. If it's negative, however, the firm should skip building the store and save its money in the market instead. (At the end of the chapter, we discuss how the interest rate should be modified to take into account the uncertainty inherent in risky investments.)

Capital Markets and the Determination of the Market Interest Rate

It's important to realize that even though individuals take their interest rate as given when discounting future payoffs to put them in PDV terms, interest rates themselves are prices determined in capital markets. As prices in other markets do, interest rates adjust to equate the quantity supplied with the quantity demanded. The good whose supply and demand are being priced out by the interest rate is capital. Therefore, changes in interest rates that we observe reflect movements in the supply of, or demand for, capital.[8]

The demanders of capital are firms and households making investment decisions like the ones we've been discussing in this chapter. If these decision makers decide to implement the potential investment projects they are considering, they will need the capital to do so.

Capital demand, like any demand curve, is downward-sloping. The quantity of capital demanded falls when the interest rate rises because, as we learned earlier, higher interest rates reduce the NPV of investments as future payoffs become smaller in present value terms relative to the up-front costs. So, investment projects that would have had positive NPVs at lower interest rates—whether they are firms' expansion plans or households' education or home renovation plans—become unprofitable at higher interest rates. This drives down the quantity of investment capital demanded by households and firms.

The supply of capital comes from those looking to lend funds to those who want to make investments. Such lenders can include people who save their money in a bank that, in turn, lends it to demanders of capital, or it can include institutions that lend directly to companies or governments by buying bonds. The interest rate is the price borrowers pay to borrow capital and the price savers receive for lending (supplying) their capital. The capital supply curves slope upward because higher interest rates raise the return to lending and thus increase the quantity of capital supplied.

Figure 13.3 shows the supply and demand curves for the capital market. The equilibrium interest rate equates the total amount of capital demanded by firms and households with worthwhile investment projects and the total amount of capital supplied by firms and households that would rather lend than directly invest their funds.

---

[8] You can interpret "capital" in this section in either one of two ways. One interpretation is as financial capital—the funds that are available for or spent on a household or business investments. The second interpretation is as an input to production, such as physical capital (stores, factories, tractors, etc.) or human capital (education and job training). Both are equivalent for our purposes here because financial capital is used to purchase productive capital for investment. For example, a firm's demand for the capital it uses to make its products creates an equivalent demand for the financial capital it needs to buy that productive capital.

Figure 13.3 : **Supply and Demand in the Market for Capital**

(a) Market equilibrium

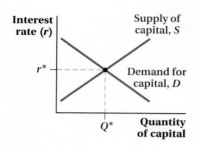

(b) New technology

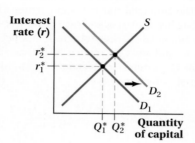

(c) Lower preference for saving

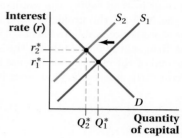

(a) As with all other economic markets, the capital market determines the equilibrium price and quantity of capital. Here, the equilibrium interest rate r^* and quantity of capital Q^* are at the intersection of supply S and demand D of capital. (b) When a new technology is introduced that raises firms' expected future payoffs from an investment, the demand for capital shifts out from D_1 to D_2. As a re-sult, the equilibrium interest rate rises from r_1^* to r_2^*, and quantity increases from Q_1^* to Q_2^*. (c) When preferences change in a way that reduces households' saving, the capital supply curve shifts inward from S_1 to S_2. This raises the equilibrium interest rate from r_1^* to r_2^*. Quantity decreases from Q_1^* to Q_2^*.

Shifts in either the supply or demand of capital alter the equilibrium interest rate. Suppose a new technology raises firms' projections for the future payoffs associated with its investments, for example. In panel b, this change increases the demand for capital at each interest rate, and shifts the demand for capital from D_1 to D_2. The equilibrium interest rate increases to r_2^*, as does the quantity of capital invested (to Q_2^*). In panel c, tighter monetary policy by the economy's central bank (the Federal Reserve in the United States) or a change in household preferences that reduces their rate of saving will decrease the capital supply and shift the supply curve to the left from S_1 to S_2. Just as with the outward demand shift, this decrease in supply raises the interest rate. However, in this scenario, the quantity of capital declines.

The changes to the interest rate that emanate from the capital market influence the interest rates that those facing investment choices use in their NPV analyses, so they have significant effects in the economy.

13.3 figure it out

Suppose that the demand for capital is $Q^D = 44 - 9r$, where r is the interest rate (expressed as a percentage) and Q is the quantity of capital (measured in millions of dollars). The supply of capital is $Q^S = -20 + 7r$.

a. Calculate the market equilibrium interest rate and quantity of capital.

b. Suppose that business confidence increases and more firms seek to expand their factories. Use a diagram to show what would happen to the equilibrium interest rate and quantity of capital.

Solution:

a. Market equilibrium occurs when the quantity of capital demanded equals the quantity of capital supplied:

$$Q^D = Q^S$$
$$44 - 9r = -20 + 7r$$
$$16r = 64$$
$$r^* = 4$$

$$Q^D = 44 - 9r = 44 - 9(4) = 44 - 36 = 8$$
$$Q^S = -20 + 7r = -20 + 7(4) = -20 + 28 = 8$$

The equilibrium interest rate is 4%, and the equilibrium level of capital is $8 million.

b. If business confidence increases and more firms seek to expand their factories, the demand for capital will rise. This rise will lead to an increase in both the equilibrium interest rate and the equilibrium quantity of capital, as shown in the diagram to the right.

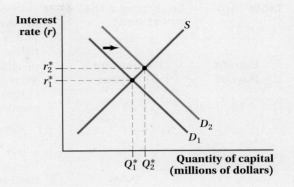

13.4 Evaluating Risky Investments

We now understand how to analyze investment choices using net present value analysis, and we have developed a sense of how the interest rate used in NPV analysis is determined. The analysis and the choice seem to provide very clear and certain answers about what investments should and should not be made. There is one crucial feature of these decisions we've ignored until now: What if things don't work out as we expect them to? What if instead of paying out a positive benefit in every period, the investment sometimes does not pay a benefit at all, or worse, ends up never paying a benefit? In real life, firms and consumers face a lot of uncertainty when making investment decisions. In this section, we discuss the ways to analyze NPVs while taking those uncertainties into account, including situations in which investors have the option of waiting to gather more information before deciding to invest.

NPV with Uncertainty: Expected Value

The basic way to incorporate risk into NPV investment analysis is to compute NPV as an *expected value*, that is, by weighting each payoff by the probability that it happens. Any risky payout can be described as a combination of two things: the different payouts that could possibly happen, and the probability of each possible outcome occurring.

Consider an example of a risky investment that will pay an uncertain benefit in one year. Table 13.4 shows the possible benefits along with the probabilities of their occurrence. Looking at these possible outcomes, we see that the investment could perform poorly and earn no return with a fairly small probability (0.2, or 20%), do very well and deliver a $2 million payout with a small probability (0.2), or, most likely, yield a modest $1 million payout with higher probability (0.6).[9]

---

[9] Many factors can affect these probabilities in actual investment choices. Sometimes probabilities are objectively defined; that is, they are verifiably exact. An example is the outcome of flipping a coin: Everyone knows there is exactly a 50% chance of either a head or tail. Another example is a state lottery game that promises 10% of all cards are winners. You know that 1 out of every 10 cards will be a winner. In most real-world investment scenarios, however, probabilities are not objective, but subjective. That is, they are determined by the decision maker's judgment rather than set in stone by the fact that a coin only has two sides or that an accounting firm has verified the lottery's procedures. With subjective probabilities, knowing which factors affect the possible outcomes helps a decision maker. We're not going to worry about the distinction between the two types of probabilities here—we keep it simple and assume all the probabilities we discuss are objectively defined—but it's worth remembering the difference in practical situations.

Table 13.4	Analyzing a Risky Investment

Benefit Payout	Probability of Payout
$0	0.2
$1 million	0.6
$2 million	0.2

To have some way to compare this uncertain payout to other risky outcomes, we need some common basis of comparison. We use the concept of **expected value** to do so. The expected value of any uncertain outcome (e.g., a payment—whether it is positive or negative doesn't matter) is the sum of the product of each possible outcome/payment and the probability of that outcome/payment. (Equivalently, it is the probability-weighted average outcome.) In general terms, for an uncertain outcome with N possible payments,

$$\text{Expected value} = (p_1 \times M_1) + (p_2 \times M_2) + \cdots + (p_N \times M_N)$$

where p_1, p_2, ... are, respectively, the probabilities of Payments 1, 2, and so on, and M_1, M_2, ... are the payments themselves. So, in our example investment above, the expected benefit payout is

$$\text{Expected benefit payout} = (0.2 \times \$0) + (0.6 \times \$1 \text{ million}) + (0.2 \times \$2 \text{ million})$$
$$= \$0 + \$0.6 \text{ million} + \$0.4 \text{ million}$$
$$= \$1 \text{ million}$$

expected value
The probability-weighted average payout.

For payment flows that are guaranteed—that is, for which there is no uncertainty—computing expected value is especially easy. Because the payment is certain, its probability is 1 (or 100% if you prefer). Therefore, the expected value is just 1 times the guaranteed payment, or the guaranteed payment itself. For example, an investment with a $1 million guaranteed payout has an expected payout value of $1 million.

Using expected value, then, all of the NPV calculations hold up exactly the same way as before, but you just need to multiply outcomes by their probabilities.

Risk and the Option Value of Waiting

Evaluating an investment using expected value provides a natural way to incorporate risk into the NPV calculation. One way risk can influence decisions is by creating an incentive to postpone investments and gather more information. This incentive, known as the **option value of waiting,** arises if waiting will resolve some of the uncertainty about the investment before deciding whether to go forward with the investment. (The name refers to the fact that an investor's option to postpone an investment decision is conceptually related to financial options—contracts that give someone the right, but not the obligation, to buy or sell an item.)

option value of waiting
The value created if an investor can postpone his investment decision until the uncertainty about an investment's returns is wholly or partially resolved.

Let's use an example to see how this operates. It's 2007 and you want to get a high-definition DVD player. You can choose between Blu-ray and HD DVD systems. They are in the middle of what economists call a "standards war": It's likely only one format will succeed in becoming the standard platform in the market, with the other probably dying off. The battle is expected to be settled by 2008, one year later. So, if you buy the wrong player, within a year you won't be able to purchase any movies for it. If you choose correctly, everything will be fine.

Let's attach some numbers to see how this uncertainty affects the NPV and the option value of buying a player. Suppose the interest rate is 5%, Blu-ray machines cost $450, and HD DVD players cost $400. Furthermore, each type of player gives its owner $50 per year of value forever if there are movies available and $0 if not (i.e., if the player's format has lost the standards war). Given this information, the value of a Blu-ray DVD player in the first year is −$450 + $50 = −$400. For every year following that, it offers a $50 benefit. Using the formula we discussed above, the total PDV of this infinite stream of $50 benefits is $50/0.05 = $1,000. The HD DVD player has a first-year value of −$400 + $50 = −$350 and a per-year $50 benefit after that. The PDV of the HD DVD's infinite stream of $50 benefits is also $1,000.

Finally, suppose analysts believe that Blu-ray (which maintained a small market lead at the time) has a 75% chance of winning the standards war and HD DVD has a 25% chance.

Now we have everything we need to compute the net present value or NPV of buying each player in 2007. If you purchase a Blu-ray, the first year's payouts include the price you pay for the machine ($450) and the $50 benefit you receive from it for that year. After that, starting in 2008, there is a 75% chance Blu-ray will win the standards war and you will receive a $50 annual benefit forever ($PDV = \$1,000$). On the other hand, there is a 25% chance HD DVD will win the standards war and your Blu-ray will become worthless. Therefore, the NPV of buying the Blu-ray in 2007 is

$$Blu\text{-}ray\ NPV_{2007} = (-\$450 + \$50) + 0.75 \times (\$1,000/1.05) + 0.25 \times (\$0/1.05)$$

$$= -\$400 + 0.75 \times \$952.38 + 0.25 \times \$0$$

$$= -\$400 + \$714.29 + \$0 = \$314.29$$

Notice that this NPV calculation is an *expected* value—we've weighted each cost and benefit by the probability that it occurs. The payments in the first year, the $450 outlay to buy the player and the $50 benefit you receive from it, are guaranteed, so they are multiplied by 1. For future payouts, we multiply the $1,000 PDV benefit stream received if Blu-ray wins the standards war by the 75% probability that Blu-ray does, in fact, win the war. Similarly, we multiply the $0 benefit stream that occurs if Blu-ray loses by the 25% chance that this outcome occurs. Both of these future benefit streams effectively occur one year in the future, so we must also discount their value by $1 + r$, or 1.05 in this case. Given all this, the NPV of buying the Blu-ray DVD player is $314.29.

We calculate the NPV of buying the HD DVD player in the same way. The differences are that the price of the HD player is only $400 and the probabilities are reversed. There is only a 25% chance that HD DVD becomes the standard in 2008 and you receive the $1,000 PDV of future benefits. There is a 75% chance it loses and future benefits are zero:

$$HD\ DVD\ NPV_{2007} = (-\$400 + \$50) + 0.25 \times (\$1,000/1.05) + 0.75 \times (\$0/1.05)$$

$$= -\$350 + 0.25 \times \$952.38 + 0.75 \times \$0$$

$$= -\$350 + \$238.10 + \$0 = -\$111.90$$

The NPV of buying the HD DVD player is −$111.90.

So, we see that the NPV of buying the Blu-ray is $314.29, while the NPV of buying the HD DVD is negative, −$111.90. These calculations indicate that if you *had* to choose your player in 2007, you would buy a Blu-ray.

But, what if you could wait a year before deciding whether to buy? You could find out which platform wins the standards war and then buy that one, sure that you'll have a supply of movies available (and the $1,000 of benefit they give you) in the future. To find the value of waiting, we need to compute the NPV of that plan in 2007. Why 2007, even though following through with the plan means you wouldn't actually buy anything until 2008? Because we need to compare the NPVs of this wait-until-2008 plan on an even basis to the NPVs of buying in 2007 that we calculated above.

This wait-until-2008 NPV, NPV_{o2008} (the "o" indicates the option value of waiting), is:

$$NPV_{o2008} = 0.75 \times (-\$400/1.05) + 0.75 \times (\$1,000/1.05^2) + 0.25 \times (-\$350/1.05) + 0.25 \times (\$1,000/1.05^2)$$

$$= 0.75 \times (-\$380.95) + 0.75 \times (\$907.03) + 0.25 \times (-\$333.33) + 0.25 \times (\$907.03)$$

$$= -\$285.71 + \$680.27 - \$83.33 + \$226.76 = \$537.98$$

Here, in the 75% chance Blu-ray wins the standards war, you buy that type of machine. It delivers a net benefit of −$400 in 2008 (its $450 cost plus its $50 benefit) and gives you a $50 per year benefit forever after (PDV = $1,000). From the perspective of 2007, however, the first of these payment flows occur one year in the future and therefore must be discounted by 1.05, and the second payment occurs in two years and must be discounted by 1.05^2. If HD DVD wins, which happens with a 25% chance, you buy that type of machine instead in 2008, earning a −$350 the first year and the $1,000 lifetime benefit after that. When we add together all of these probability-weighted costs and benefits, we end up with the wait-until-2008 plan having a NPV of $537.98.

So, while the NPV of buying the Blu-ray in 2007 was positive ($314.29), waiting one more year before buying has an even higher NPV ($537.98). Where does this extra value come from? Waiting eliminates the chance that you buy a standards-war-losing video player that ends up providing no future benefit. By not buying until 2008, you *guarantee* yourself the $1,000 PDV of future benefits of the player, rather than rolling the dice and hoping you happen to choose the right format. This ability to choose after you see what happens is what creates the option value of waiting; you can eliminate the worst possible outcomes that could have happened had you made your investment earlier. There is a cost to waiting, however: You delay any benefit of the investment in a player by a year. (This is fully taken into account in the calculations because we computed NPV_{o2008} from the perspective of 2007, thereby accounting for the lost $50 in benefits that buying a player early would have provided.) But in this case, at least, the amount of uncertainty is great enough that it's very valuable to wait to eliminate it. The option value of waiting is the difference between the NPV of the wait-until-2008 policy and the NPV of buying a Blu-ray now: $537.98 − $314.29 = $233.69.

Option values of waiting arise in many real-world investment decisions because uncertainty is so common. Recognizing the value that waiting creates can be one of the most important considerations in evaluating investment options.

13.4 figure it out

Alex is a house flipper: He buys old houses that appear to be bargains, rehabs them, and then puts them back on the market for resale. Alex recently discovered a lovely Victorian home that he is considering for rehab. There is a 0.2 probability that Alex will lose 10% on the deal, a 0.7 probability that he will gain 8% on the deal, and a 0.1 probability that he will gain 20%.

a. Calculate Alex's expected return from the project.

b. Suppose that, in a different neighborhood, there is a bungalow selling for the same price. Alex estimates that there is a 0.3 probability that he will gain 3%, a 0.5 probability that he will gain 5.8%, and a 0.2 probability that he will gain 9%. Calculate Alex's expected return from this project.

c. Assume that Alex has only enough money to flip one house. If he bases his decision solely on expected return, is it clear which project Alex will prefer? If not, is there an additional factor that might tip the balance?

Solution:

a. Remember that Expected value = $(p_1 \times M_1) + (p_2 \times M_2) + (p_3 \times M_3)$. Substituting the numbers for the Victorian, we find

Expected return = $(0.2 \times -10) + (0.7 \times 8) + (0.1 \times 20) = -2 + 5.6 + 2 = 5.6\%$

b. Substituting the numbers for the bungalow, we find

Expected return $= (0.3 \times 3) + (0.5 \times 5.8) + (0.2 \times 9) = 0.9 + 2.9 + 1.8 = 5.6\%$

c. The expected return for the two investments is the same. If this is the only basis of comparison, neither the Victorian nor the bungalow is obviously superior. However, there is no chance he will lose money on the bungalow, while he faces a 0.2 probability of experiencing a 10% loss on the Victorian. Some investors (perhaps including Alex) may be willing to give up a small chance at a higher return if they know that the worst outcome is less costly, as is the case with the bungalow. This preference is characteristic of *risk aversion*, which we discuss more below.

13.5 Uncertainty, Risk, and Insurance

Expected value gives us a way to think about risks in the context of investment. But, as we see in this section, when we use expected value analysis, we are implicitly assuming that people aren't especially afraid of risk. In expected value terms, a 10% chance of $10 million is worth just as much as having $1 million for sure. We explore what happens when people do not like taking risks and see why insurance is valuable to these people. In addition, we learn how risk changes investment decisions.

Expected Income, Expected Utility, and the Risk Premium

To understand what we mean by people not liking risk, think about a person and the utility he gets from consuming the goods he can buy with his income. Our analysis in Chapter 4 explains what bundle of goods a person picks given the goods' prices and the person's income, but when trying to figure out consumers' distastes for risk, we don't need to keep track of exactly what goods are in that bundle. All we need to know is the total amount of utility this person enjoys at any given income level.

We plot the relationship between utility and income for a particular individual, Adam, in Figure 13.4. Adam's income is shown on the horizontal axis, and his utility from consuming the goods he buys with that income level is on the vertical axis. Utility rises with income, as we would expect, because the more income he has, the more stuff he can buy. However, the curve becomes less steep as his income rises. That is, Adam has diminishing marginal utility of income. The bump in utility he would enjoy from an increase in income of, say, $10,000 to $15,000 is more than the extra utility he'd experience from moving from an income of $1,000,000 to $1,005,000. It turns out that if diminishing marginal utility holds, Adam will be sensitive to risk and willing to pay to eliminate or reduce uncertainty.

To make the relationship between risk and diminishing marginal utility as clear as possible, let's consider a specific example. Suppose most of Adam's income comes from a retail shop he owns, and that the only important uncertainty his business faces is whether the store burns down in an overnight fire. A fire will destroy the building's inventory as well as its usefulness as a place to sell products, causing Adam's income to take a big hit.

We assume the utility, U, Adam enjoys from goods purchased with his income is given by the function

$$U = \sqrt{I}$$

Figure 13.4 | A Risk-Averse Individual Will Pay to Avoid Risk

Adam faces a 50% probability of an income of $100,000 (point B) and a 50% probability of an income of $36,000 (point A). Therefore, his expected income is $68,000 and his expected utility is 8 (point C). A certain income of $64,000 also gives Adam a utility of 8 (point E). Because Adam is risk-averse, he is willing to give up as much as $4,000 in expected income (the distance from point C to point E) to have a certain income of $64,000 instead of his uncertain income.

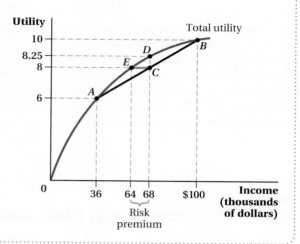

where I is Adam's income in thousands of dollars. This utility function is plotted in Figure 13.4, and it clearly exhibits diminishing marginal utility of income.

Now suppose that Adam's income is $100,000 in a year there is no fire and only $36,000 if there is a fire. The utility levels corresponding to these incomes are shown as points B and A, respectively, in Figure 13.4. With $100,000 in income, Adam's utility is $U = \sqrt{100} = 10$; with $36,000 in income, it's $U = \sqrt{36} = 6$.

Let's say the probability that there is a fire (this is where the uncertainty comes from) is 50%—unrealistically high, but useful for keeping the math simple. A lower, more realistic probability would not change the basic idea of this analysis.

Following a basic expected value calculation, we first compute Adam's expected income for the year. There's a 50% chance his store burns down, making his income $36,000. There's a 50% chance that no fire happens and his income is $100,000. Applying the formula for computing expected values, we find that Adam's expected income is $68,000:

$$\text{Expected income} = (0.5 \times \$36,000) + (0.5 \times \$100,000)$$

$$= \$18,000 + \$50,000$$

$$= \$68,000$$

Similarly, we can compute his expected utility:

$$\text{Expected utility} = (0.5 \times 6) + (0.5 \times 10)$$

$$= 3 + 5$$

$$= 8$$

We plot these expected income and utility levels at point C. Notice how this point is halfway along the straight line connecting A and B, the income-utility combinations in the fire and no-fire cases. This isn't a coincidence. Adam's expected income and utility values will be somewhere on that same line for *any* probability of a fire. Where exactly on the line the point will be depends on the probability that each event (fire or no fire) occurs. The higher the probability of a fire, the closer Adam's expected income and utility will be to the fire income-utility point A. (If a fire happens 100% of the time, point A is the expected income and utility.) If the probability of a fire is instead very low, Adam's expected income and utility will be near point B. The expected values shown at point C happen to be at the halfway point on the AB line because the fire and no-fire outcomes each have a 50% chance of happening.

Notice another important thing about point C: It's at an expected utility level, 8, that is below Adam's utility function at that same income level. According to Adam's utility function, an income level of $68,000 lets him achieve a utility of $U = \sqrt{68} = 8.25$, as shown at point D in Figure 13.4. What this means is that the same expected income, $68,000, can give Adam different levels of expected utility depending on the riskiness of the underlying income levels on which the expectation is based. Due to the chance of fire, Adam's income is uncertain and his $68,000 in expected income delivers an expected utility of 8. But, if his income is *guaranteed* to be $68,000, even though his expected income of $68,000 has not changed, his expected utility would be 8.25. In other words, the very uncertainty about what his income will be reduces Adam's expected utility. If a person prefers having a guaranteed amount to having a risky but equivalent-in-expected-value amount, we say the person is **risk-averse.** Uncertainty reduces the utility of a risk-averse person like Adam.

A related way to see how uncertainty reduces expected utility is to ask what guaranteed income would offer Adam the same expected utility level as his uncertain income. That equivalent income level, sometimes referred to as the **certainty equivalent,** is shown at point E in Figure 13.4. The certainty equivalent in this example is $64,000, because $U = \sqrt{64} = 8$. Adam derives the same expected utility from a guaranteed $64,000 income as he does from having a 50% chance of a $36,000 income and a 50% chance of a $100,000 income. Another way to put this is that Adam is willing to give up $4,000 in expected income ($68,000 − $64,000) in exchange for eliminating his income uncertainty. This income difference is called the **risk premium**—it's the extra amount of expected income (here, $4,000) Adam must receive to make him as well off when his income is uncertain as when it is guaranteed.

Notice how these relationships we've just pointed out—that for risk-averse individuals, expected utility falls as a given expected income becomes more uncertain, and that risk-averse individuals are willing to give up expected income to reduce uncertainty—are, graphically speaking, a consequence of the diminishing marginal utility of income. That is, the fact that point C (or any point on the AB line) is below the income-utility curve is a direct consequence of the fact that there is diminishing marginal utility of income. Diminishing marginal utility causes this curve to be concave as income rises, ensuring that any uncertain combination of income-utility outcomes will have an expected utility below that of an equivalent expected income that is guaranteed.

Insurance Markets

A world full of uncertainties and risk-averse people creates demand for insurance. We all understand the basic concept of insurance from our everyday lives, but economists define it specifically as when one economic actor pays another to reduce the payer's economic risk. The details of the insurance-risk aversion connection are important to understand, and we'll go through them in a minute, but the basic idea is fairly simple. If someone is risk-averse, he will pay to have his risks reduced. That's what insurance does: It reduces risk by paying a claim to the policyholder to make him better off when things would otherwise be bad (his car is stolen, he becomes sick and needs to pay a lot of medical bills, etc.). In exchange for this, the policyholder pays a premium to the insurer and makes do with a little less income (by the amount of the premium) when times are good to protect himself against the possibility of bad outcomes.

The Value of Insurance   The loss in expected utility Adam experiences due to the uncertainty of his income and his willingness to give up some expected income to reduce this loss suggest a way to make him better off. Suppose someone or some company offers him an insurance contract to reduce his uncertainty and that it involves the following arrangement. If Adam's store burns down, the insurer will pay him a sum of money. This will reduce his losses in the bad situation. In exchange, Adam makes a

risk-averse
Suffering an expected utility loss from uncertainty, or equivalently, being willing to pay to have that risk reduced.

certainty equivalent
The guaranteed income level at which an individual would receive the same expected utility level as from an uncertain income.

risk premium
The compensation an individual would require to bear risk without suffering a loss in expected utility.

payment to the insurer—a policy premium—if there isn't a fire. This premium reduces his income in a good situation; there's no fire, but Adam has to do without the money he pays for the premium. By reducing Adam's uncertainty, the insurance contract raises Adam's expected utility for any given expected income level. Note that the arrangement does not raise Adam's expected utility by increasing his expected income; in fact, the insurance policy could very well reduce his expected income. Nevertheless, he benefits because less uncertainty translates into greater expected utility.

We can see this benefit more explicitly in some examples. A straightforward policy would have the insurer pay Adam $32,000 if a fire destroys his store while having Adam pay the insurer a $32,000 premium if there is no fire. Under such a policy, Adam's income is $68,000 regardless of whether a fire occurs. If there's a fire, his income is $36,000 and his payout from the insurer is $32,000, and $36,000 + $32,000 = $68,000; if no fire occurs, his income is $100,000 and his insurance premium is $32,000, and $100,000 − $32,000 = $68,000. As we saw above, that guaranteed income of $68,000 yields Adam an expected utility of 8.25, greater than the expected utility of 8 he would receive without an insurance policy and the same *expected* income of $68,000. This policy offers what is sometimes called **complete insurance** or **full insurance:** All uncertainty has been eliminated for Adam; he ends up equally well off no matter what event happens (fire or no fire). Even partial insurance is valuable, however. Suppose that the policy instead pays Adam $20,000 if there is a fire in exchange for a $20,000 premium in the case of no fire. This makes his income $36,000 + $20,000 = $56,000 in the case of a fire and $100,000 − $20,000 = $80,000 if no fire occurs. This policy keeps Adam's expected income at $68,000 ($0.5 \times \$56,000 + 0.5 \times \$80,000 = \$68,000$), but gives him an expected utility of 8.21 ($0.5 \times \sqrt{56} + 0.5 \times \sqrt{80} = 3.74 + 4.47 = 8.21$). While this is less than the expected utility of 8.25 from having a guaranteed $68,000 in income, it is higher than Adam's expected utility of 8 without a policy.

Insurance is a good deal for Adam, but what's in it for the insurer? An insurance policy basically shifts Adam's risk to the insurer: The insurer does not know for certain what its profit from the policy will be. However, insurers don't typically suffer a loss as a result of this transfer because they issue a large number of policies like Adam's. By adding together all these risks from all the policies they issue, insurers greatly reduce the uncertainty of their profits.

To see why adding risks together helps an insurer, suppose that an insurer has sold policies to thousands of people exactly like Adam, each of whom owns a store that delivers income to the storeowner but also has a 50% chance of burning down. Although it is very uncertain if any particular store is going to burn down, because the insurer covers thousands of such stores, in a given year that insurer can expect almost exactly half of its covered stores to burn down. Thus, rather than having very high uncertainty over the claims it will have to pay, the insurer actually has low uncertainty. The insurer doesn't make big profits half the time and lose big money the other half; instead, it knows it's going to almost surely have to pay claims on about half its stores while collecting premiums from the other half. This **diversification**—reducing risk by combining uncertain outcomes—is one of the key functions of insurance markets. An important part of making diversification work is that risks being added together must be at least partially unrelated. If instead they were highly correlated with one another—for instance, if all the insured stores were tightly packed together in the same location so that if one burned down, they all would—the insurer couldn't diversify away the risk. Half the time no stores would burn down, and half the time all the stores would burn down. The insurer would be left with a risk just as uncertain as Adam's, but only bigger.

Insurers can benefit from offering to take away policyholder's risks in another way. Remember that risk aversion creates a willingness to pay to remove or reduce risk. Insurers can design policies to capture some of this value. Both of the example policies we discussed above have the same expected profit for the insurer: zero. The payment the insurer makes to Adam in case of a fire equals the policy premium he pays in the absence of a fire, and both outcomes happen with equal probability. (For example,

complete insurance or full insurance
An insurance policy that leaves the insured individual equally well off regardless of the outcome.

diversification
A strategy to reduce risk by combining uncertain outcomes.

0.5 × –$32,000 + 0.5 × $32,000 = –$16,000 + $16,000 = $0.) When the expected net payments of an insurance policy are zero—that is, when the expected premiums equal the expected payouts—a policy is said to be **actuarially fair.**

But, we've just seen how insurance has value for consumers like Adam; insurers try to design policies to capture some of this value. Consider the following policy: The insurer pays Adam $20,000 if there is a fire, while Adam pays a $24,000 premium if no fire occurs. Adam's expected utility under this policy is 8.10 ($0.5 × \sqrt{56} + 0.5 × \sqrt{76} = 8.10$). The policy raises his expected utility relative to the level it would be without the policy. Adam's expected income under the policy is (0.5 × $56,000) + (0.5 × $76,000) = $66,000. This is $2,000 less than his expected income of $68,000 without the policy, but Adam is willing to give up this $2,000 because his expected utility is higher with the policy than without it. As we saw above, in fact, Adam is willing to give up as much as $4,000 in expected income to purchase a policy that would remove all of his income uncertainty.

From the insurer's point of view, Adam's $2,000 drop in expected income is its expected profit from the policy: There is a 50% chance it will have to pay Adam $20,000 and a 50% chance it will not have to pay Adam anything, but will earn a $24,000 premium, yielding an expected profit of (0.5 × $24,000) – (0.5 × $20,000) = $2,000. While this outcome from Adam's policy is highly uncertain, again, if the insurer sells thousands of such policies to unrelated risks, it can expect to earn profits of nearly $2,000 per policy without much uncertainty around that total.

Why would the insurer design a policy that only has an expected profit of $2,000 when Adam would give up as much as $4,000 in expected income for insurance? Well, the insurer would charge $4,000 if it could. Whether it can charge the higher premium depends on how competitive the insurance market is. The more competitive the market is, the more the terms of policies will be tilted in the favor of policyholders and toward being actuarially fair.

theory and data

The Insurance Value of Medicare

The Medicare program, which provides insurance coverage to almost every person over age 65 in the United States, came into being in 1965. It was the largest expansion of health insurance coverage of the twentieth century. A study by economists Amy Finkelstein and Robin McKnight of the program's effects over the decade following its introduction showed, rather startlingly, that it had virtually no impact on the mortality of the elderly.[10] Given the program's size, evidence that it did not improve mortality rates among the elderly seems fairly discouraging.

Finkelstein and McKnight documented, however, that although it did not improve survival rates, Medicare did dramatically reduce the out-of-pocket expenses for elderly people who became really sick. Folks in the top quartile of medical expenses saw their out-of-pocket costs fall by about 40%. Finkelstein and McKnight performed a basic calculation using standard utility theory to show that the ability to avoid such large negative shocks is an especially important form of insurance for risk-averse individuals. In fact, they estimated that the insurance value of Medicare in reducing people's exposure to risk was worth two-fifths of the entire cost of the Medicare program. When people are risk-averse, insurance can be worth a lot.

[10] Amy Finkelstein and Robin McKnight, "What Did Medicare Do? The Initial Impact of Medicare on Mortality and Out of Pocket Medical Spending," *Journal of Public Economics* 92, no. 7 (2008): 1644–1668.

The Degree of Risk Aversion

Given the connection between diminishing marginal utility of income (reflected in how curved the utility-income relationship is) and risk aversion, it should be clear that the greater the curve in a consumer's utility function, the more risk-averse he is.

Figure 13.5 demonstrates this in an example. The figure's two panels show portions of the utility-income functions for two consumers with different degrees of curvature. The consumer in the left panel (a) has relatively little curvature; his marginal utility of income drops relatively slowly as his income rises. The consumer in the right panel (b) has a relatively large amount of curvature because his marginal utility of income falls quickly as his income rises.

Suppose that these consumers faced a situation like Adam's, with a 50% chance of a $36,000 income and a 50% chance of a $100,000 income. The utility-income points corresponding to these outcomes are shown at points A and B in both panels. The consumers' expected incomes and utilities again occur at the midpoints of the AB lines, point C in each panel. The figure also shows the certainty equivalents for the consumers, point E.

The horizontal distances between points C and E in each panel—that is, the expected income consumers are willing to give up in order to have their risky expected incomes at point C replaced by the guaranteed income at point E—are the consumers' respective risk premia. Notice how the risk premium of the more risk-averse consumer in the right panel is larger than that for the less risk-averse consumer. This reflects the fact that the degree of a consumer's risk aversion is tied to the curvature in his utility function (or equivalently, the rate at which his marginal utility of income falls as his income grows). When there is more curvature, the expected utility loss due to any given amount of income uncertainty is larger. Consumers with highly curved utility functions have a greater willingness to pay to have risk reduced.

Figure 13.5   Utility Functions and Risk Aversion

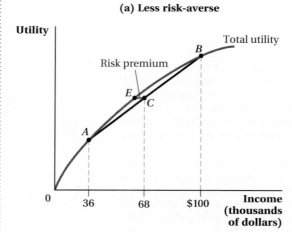
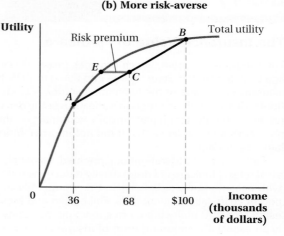

The degree of risk aversion can be seen in the curvature of the utility curve. A consumer who is less risk-averse (panel a) has a utility function that is fairly straight, while a consumer who is more risk-averse (panel b) has a utility function that is highly curved. The risk premium that each consumer is willing to pay (distance CE) varies with his degree of risk aversion. The greater the level of risk aversion, the more curvature of the utility function, and the larger the risk premium.

If the curve stays straight, we call the consumers *risk-neutral*. If it curves up (which can happen), then we say that person is *risk-loving*. A risk-lover would actually pay money to have a chance to gamble on a big payoff rather than take the certainty equivalent.

Risk Aversion and Investment Decisions

In our earlier analysis of firms' investment choices, we handled uncertainty by computing expected values. However, this approach to uncertainty implicitly assumes risk-neutrality. In this framework, a risk-neutral firm is indifferent between an investment that returns a net benefit of $0 with a 50% probability and $10 million with a 50% probability, and another investment that has a guaranteed net benefit of $5 million. Both projects have expected net benefits of $5 million.

If investors are instead risk-averse, they need to adjust their comparisons for the riskiness created by the uncertainty of future payoffs. One approach to doing so is to build a risk adjustment into the interest rate itself. For projects with payoffs that are certain under any possible circumstance, the **risk-free interest rate** can be used to compute NPVs. This interest rate is defined as the rate that any asset paying a guaranteed return would pay. For risky projects, though, a risk-averse investor will require more than the risk-free rate if he is to invest in a project, just as a consumer requires a higher expected income to be willing to accept a riskier income scenario relative to a guaranteed income. This additional required expected return is akin to the risk premium we defined in the insurance discussion. The size of the rate-of-return risk premium is tied to the amount of risk inherent in the investment: A project with modest risk must pay a modest risk premium to make risk-averse investors willing to undertake it, while a riskier project requires a larger risk premium. Exactly how to do risk-sensitive discounting for the NPVs of risky projects is a central part of the analysis in the study of finance, and we'll leave the issue to that field. Nevertheless, while the calculations can get rather complicated, the idea is easy to understand.

> **risk-free interest rate**
> Rate of return on an investment that any asset paying a guaranteed return would pay.

freakonomics

Apocalypse Now: How Much Will We Pay to Prevent Disaster?

A tsunami rumbles down the streets of Manhattan. People in India scramble to find enough blankets and coats after a massive blizzard. Tornadoes wreak havoc in Los Angeles. Sure, such freaks of nature are probably impossible, but they make for fun movies.

Even if we're unlikely to see a tornado in L.A. any time soon, real threats of catastrophe are always lurking just around the corner. Economics gives us a way to think about these horrendous scenarios. We can estimate what it would be worth to society to prevent a catastrophe. Or, to put it more personally: How much should *you* personally be willing to pay to ward off disaster?

In the 2004 catastrophe movie *The Day After Tomorrow*, New York City was hit by a giant tsunami that froze solid. How much would society be willing to pay to avoid this situation?

Let's consider, for instance, a particular disaster scenario, like a large asteroid hitting the earth. Assume that such an event happens once every 1,000 years at random, and when it occurs, there is a 1% chance you will be killed. So per year, the likelihood you will die from such a catastrophe is 1 in 100,000.

How much is it worth to you to permanently eliminate that risk? In a recent paper, economists Gary Becker, Kevin Murphy, and Robert Topel tried to answer this question.[11] Their conclusions will probably surprise you. Using standard assumptions, they found that you should be willing to pay 4.5% of your annual income to make such a threat go away. Remember, this is only a *1%* chance of death every *1,000* years, so 4.5% of current earnings seems impossibly large. But by their calculation, it isn't. If the catastrophe meant a 1% chance of death every 100 years (instead of every 1,000 years), their calculations say we should be willing to pay 36% of this year's income to permanently eliminate the threat!

There are a number of reasons why the amount is so large. First, death is permanent and really bad for utility—now and in the future. Second, people are risk-averse, so the utility function is concave. This means that big negative shocks to utility are very costly, and there is no bigger negative shock than getting killed. Third, they assume that income grows over time so future utility (assuming no catastrophe) will usually be even higher than today. We are willing to pay a big share of today's income to safeguard our ever-larger future incomes.

These calculations are only useful if a catastrophe of this magnitude is possible. But, could this scenario ever occur outside of a Hollywood studio? The answer is yes, at least according to economist Martin Weitzman.[12] Using a variety of climate models, he estimates a 1% chance of an increase of more than 20 degrees Celsius (36 degrees Fahrenheit) in the earth's average temperature. It's not clear what would happen if temperatures shot up more than 20 degrees, but it wouldn't be good—Weitzman characterizes this as a "mega-catastrophe," at the very least causing mass species extinctions.

Before you try to start a moon colony or something, however, remember that scientists are discovering all kinds of ways to curb climate change, and advances in other areas—such as medicine—are also reducing the chances of an untimely death.[13] When it comes to maximizing future utility, brilliant scientists are probably our best hope. So, if you know any really smart economics majors, try to convince them to double major in a hard science!

---

[11] Gary S. Becker, Kevin M. Murphy, and Robert H. Topel, "On the Economics of Climate Policy," *The B.E. Journal of Economic Analysis & Policy* 10, no. 2 (2010): article 19.

[12] Martin Weitzman, "On Modeling and Interpreting the Economics of Catastrophic Climate Change," *The Review of Economics and Statistics* 91, no. 1 (2009): 1–19.

[13] Steven D. Levitt and Stephen J. Dubner, *SuperFreakonomics,* New York: Harper Collins, 2009.

13.5 figure it out

The Hotel California faces a risk that it will suffer a fire causing a $200 million loss with a probability of 0.02. The owner of the firm, Don Glenn, has a utility function of $U = W^{0.5}$, where W is the owner's wealth (as measured by the value of the hotel in millions of dollars). Suppose that the initial value of the hotel is $225 million ($W = 225$).

a. What is Don Glenn's expected loss?

b. What is Don Glenn's expected utility?

c. What is Don Glenn's risk premium?

Solution:

a. The expected loss is calculated by multiplying the probability of a loss by its dollar amount:

$$\text{Expected loss} = 0.02 \times \$200 \text{ million} = \$4 \text{ million}$$

Another way to calculate the same thing is to compute Don Glenn's expected wealth and subtract it from his wealth if there were no fire:

$$\text{Expected wealth} = (0.98 \times \$225 \text{ million}) + (0.02 \times \$25 \text{ million})$$
$$= \$220.5 \text{ million} + \$0.5 \text{ million} = \$221 \text{ million}$$

Therefore his expected loss is $225 million – $221 million = $4 million.

b. Without a loss, Don has $225 million. With a loss, he has $225 million – $200 million = $25 million. His utility without a loss (when $W = 225$) is $U = W^{0.5} = (225)^{0.5} = 15$. His utility with a loss (when $W = 25$) is $U = W^{0.5} = (25)^{0.5} = 5$.

Because a 0.02 probability of a fire exists, there is a 0.98 probability that no fire will occur. Therefore, Don Glenn's expected utility is

$$\text{Expected utility} = (0.98 \times 15) + (0.02 \times 5) = 14.7 + 0.1 = 14.8$$

c. With no insurance, Don Glenn has an *expected* utility of 14.8. There is a guaranteed wealth level that would deliver a certain utility of 14.8, however. If an insurance policy could guarantee him that wealth level or higher, Don Glenn would be willing to purchase it. Therefore we must first determine how much guaranteed wealth would offer him a utility level of 14.8:

$$U = W^{0.5} = 14.8$$
$$W = (14.8)^2 = 219.04$$

Therefore, a certain wealth of $219.04 million would provide Don Glenn with a guaranteed utility of 14.8.

From part (a) above, his expected wealth without insurance is $221 million. But he's willing to accept a guaranteed income of only $219.04 million to ensure he receives the same expected utility as in the case without insurance. Therefore the risk premium is $221 million – $219.04 million = $1.96 million.

13.6 Conclusion

Deciding how to invest and whether to invest remains one of the central issues of any business and a great many individual decisions, too. To make such decisions rationally, there must be a way to compare future payoffs to current costs, and to make that comparison, you need to use the interest rate and discounting.

When investments are risky, there is an additional layer of complication that requires you to know how to quantify risks and compare payoffs and costs. Given the way most people value income, individuals are often especially sensitive to risks and that characteristic is the foundation of most insurance markets.

We've only scratched the surface of these issues here. If we've piqued your interest, the field of finance spends much effort wrestling with the issue of how time and uncertainty shape various markets.

Summary

1. Using **compound interest rates, present discounted value (PDV)** allows consumers to compare the costs and benefits of an investment over time in a consistent way by putting the future benefits of a given investment into its present-day dollar value. [**Section 13.1**]

2. **Net present value (NPV)** analysis incorporates the PDVs of both the costs and benefits of an investment to arrive at a summary measure of the investment's return. The concept of a **payback period,** the length of time before an investment's initial costs are recouped in future benefits, provides another way of determining the net benefits of a given investment. The weakness of payback periods is that, unlike NPV analysis, they do not discount future cash flows. [**Section 13.2**]

3. The **real interest rate** captures the difference between an investment's **nominal interest rate** expressed in currency values and the inflation rate. The equilibrium interest rate, as with any good's price, equates the quantities supplied and demanded of a good, which in this case is capital. [**Section 13.3**]

4. Investing can be a risky and uncertain undertaking. Evaluating investments using **expected value**— or the expected outcome of an investment— is one way to include risk in NPV analysis. For risky investments, there is often an **option value of waiting,** that is, waiting to invest may eliminate some of the uncertainty. [**Section 13.4**]

5. A **risk-averse** person gains more utility from a set amount of income than from the equivalent amount in expected value from an uncertain income. Because it reduces the policyholder's risk, **insurance** increases the individual's expected utility. Through practices such as **diversification** and by designing policies to capture some of the policy's value to the consumer, insurers also benefit from selling insurance policies. [**Section 13.5**]

Review Questions

1. Provide an example of an investment.
2. What is the benefit of using present discounted value analysis?
3. How can you calculate the interest rate associated with a given set of assets?
4. Describe the two main parts that make up a bond's payment stream.
5. When will an investment's net present value be positive? Given its sign, should you invest in this project?
6. What advantage does net present value analysis have over the use of payback periods to evaluate investment decisions?
7. What is the approximate relationship between an investment's nominal interest rate and its real interest rate?
8. How is the equilibrium interest rate determined in the market for capital? Who are the suppliers and demanders of capital?
9. How can expected value be used to evaluate risky investments?
10. What is the value of insurance to a risk-averse consumer?
11. Why do we consider diversification a key function of insurance markets?
12. Define the risk-free interest rate. How does it relate to the interest rate on a risky investment?

Problems (Solutions to problems marked * appear at the back of this book. Problems adapted to use calculus are available online at http://worthpublishers.com/GLS1e)

*1. You are a bunny rancher.
   a. Suppose that you have 100 bunnies, and that because of your successful animal husbandry, your stock of bunnies grows by 20% each year. How many bunnies will you have at the end of this year?
   b. Suppose that you have 120 bunnies, and that because of your successful animal husbandry, your stock of bunnies grows by 20% each year. How many bunnies will you have at the end of this year?

c. Suppose that you have 100 bunnies, and that because of your successful animal husbandry, your stock of bunnies grows by 20% over the course of each year. How many bunnies will you have at the end of two years?

d. Suppose that you have 100 bunnies, and that your bunny stock grows by 20% per year. How many bunnies will you have at the end of 10 years?

2. Imagine that you have $100 of ill-gotten gains stashed in an offshore bank account. Lest the IRS get too nosey, you plan to leave that account idle until your retirement in 45 years.

a. If your bank pays you 3% annual interest, what will your account balance be upon retirement?

b. If your bank pays you 6% interest, what will your account balance be upon retirement?

c. Does doubling the interest rate double your accumulated balance at retirement? More than double it? Less? Explain your answer.

3. Suppose that when you were one year old, your grandmother gave you a shiny silver dollar. Your parents put that silver dollar in a savings account with a guaranteed 9% interest rate, and then promptly forgot about it.

a. Use the Rule of 72 to *estimate* how much that account will grow to by the time you are 65.

b. Calculate *exactly* how much you will have in that account using the formula for compound interest.

c. How close are your answers to (a) and (b)?

4. On your 20th birthday, a dear aunt sends you a lovely card and an IOU for $1,000, to be paid on your 21st birthday. Eager to lay your hands on the cash (after all, the Spice Girls only have a reunion tour every decade or so), you try to sell your aunt's IOU to your sister.

a. If interest rates are 6%, what is the most your sister should be willing to pay for the IOU?

b. If interest rates are 9%, what is the most your sister should be willing to pay for the IOU?

c. Does the value of your aunt's promise go up when interest rates rise? Explain why or why not.

*5. You are writing the great American novel, and have signed a contract with the world's most prestigious publisher. To keep you on schedule, the publisher promises you a $100,000 bonus when the first draft is complete, and another $100,000 following revisions. You believe that you can write the first draft in a year, and have the revisions done at the end of a second year.

a. If interest rates are 5%, what is the value today of the publisher's future payments?

b. Suppose the publisher offers you $80,000 after the first draft and $125,000 following revisions. Is this a better deal than the original offer?

6. A state lottery makes the following announcement: "Frederick Carbuncle has just won $100 million! We'll pay Frederick $10 million each year for the next 10 years!"

a. Has Frederick really won $100 million? Explain.

b. Many state lotteries allow winners to choose a single payment instead of a series of annual payments. "We'll offer you the present value of your annual payments, Frederick," the lottery commissioner says. "And because we're feeling generous, we'll use a really high interest rate when we calculate how much that prize will be. Congratulations, Fred!" Comment on the generosity of the lottery commissioner.

7. You have just purchased a Kia with a $20,000 price tag. The dealer offers to let you pay for your car in five equal annual installments, with the first payment due in a year.

a. If the dealer finances your purchase at an interest rate of 10%, how much will your annual payment be?

b. How much would your payment be if you had purchased a $40,000 Camry instead of a $20,000 Kia?

c. How much would your payment be if you arranged to pay in 10 annual installments instead of 5? Does your payment fall in half? Why or why not?

d. How much would your payment fall if you paid $10,000 down at the time of purchase?

8. Many college graduates feel as if their student loan payments drag on forever. Suppose that the government offers the following arrangement: It will pay for your college in its entirety, and in return you will make annual payments until the end of time.

a. Suppose the government asks for $6,000 each year for all of eternity. If interest rates currently sit at 4%, what is the present value of the payments you will make?

b. Your college charges $140,000 for four years of quality education. Should you take the government up on its offer to pay for your college? What if your college charged $160,000?

9. As a New Year's gift to yourself, you buy your roommate's 1976 Ford Pinto. She has given you

the option of two payment plans. Under Plan A, you pay $500 now, plus $500 at the beginning of each of the next two years. Under Plan B, you would pay nothing down, but $800 at the beginning of each of the next two years.

a. Calculate the present value of each plan's payments if interest rates are 10%. Should you choose Plan A or Plan B?

b. Recalculate the present value of each plan's payments using a 20% interest rate. Should you choose Plan A or Plan B?

c. Explain why your answers to (a) and (b) differ.

*10. Consider the following two bonds: a Treasury bill that will pay you $1,000 in 1 year, and a zero-coupon Treasury bond that will pay you $1,000 in 30 years.

a. Calculate the value of each of these bonds today if interest rates are 4%.

b. Suppose interest rates rise to 8%. What will happen to the price of each bond?

c. Suppose you believe that interest rates are due to rise. Where would you prefer to have your life savings invested, Treasury bills or zero-coupon Treasury bonds? Why?

11. Ralph is considering purchasing an ostrich, which he can graze for free in his backyard. Once the ostrich reaches maturity (in exactly three years), Ralph will be able to sell it for $2,000. The ostrich costs $1,500.

a. Suppose that interest rates are 8%. Calculate the net present value of the ostrich investment. Does the NPV indicate that Ralph should buy the ostrich?

b. Suppose that Ralph passes on the ostrich deal, and invests $1,500 in his next-best opportunity: a safe government bond yielding 8%. How much money will he have at the end of three years? Is this outcome better or worse than buying the ostrich?

c. Calculate the net present value of the ostrich if interest rates are 11%. Does the NPV method indicate that Ralph should buy the ostrich?

d. If Ralph passes on the ostrich deal, and invests in a government bond yielding 11%, how much money will he have at the end of three years? Is this outcome better or worse than buying the ostrich?

e. Based on your answers to (b) and (d), how well does the NPV method capture the concept of opportunity cost?

*12. Marian currently makes $40,000 a year as a librarian. She is considering a career change: For a current expenditure of $30,000, she can obtain her florist's license and become a flower arranger. If she makes that career change, her earnings will rise to $48,000 per year. Marian has five years left to work before retirement (you may safely assume that she gets paid once at the end of each year).

a. Calculate the net present value of Marian's investment in floriculture if interest rates are 10%.

b. Assume that in terms of job satisfaction, floriculture and librarianship are identical. Should Marian change careers?

c. Compare the present value of Marian's earnings as a librarian to the present value of Marian's earnings as a florist. Is the difference large enough to justify spending $30,000?

d. Does the method you used in part (a) give an identical answer to the method you used in part (c)? Explain.

13. You are currently driving a gas-guzzling Oldsmobuick that you expect to be able to drive for the next five years. A recent spike in gas prices to $5 per gallon has you considering a trade to a fuel-efficient hybrid Prius. Your Oldsmobuick has no resale value, and gets 15 miles per gallon. A new Prius costs $25,000, and gets 45 miles per gallon. You drive 10,000 miles each year.

a. Calculate your annual fuel expenditures for the Prius and the Oldsmobuick.

b. Calculate the present value of your costs if you continue to drive the Oldsmobuick for another five years. Assume that you purchase a new Prius at the end of the fifth year, and that a Prius still costs $25,000. Also assume that fuel is paid for at the end of each year. (Carry out your cost calculations for only five years.)

c. Calculate the present value of your costs if you purchase a new Prius today. Again, carry out your cost calculations for only five years.

d. Based on your answers to (b) and (c), should you buy a Prius now, or should you wait for five years?

e. Would your answer change if your Oldsmobuick got 30 miles per gallon instead of 15?

14. You have $832.66 in a savings account that offers a 5.25% interest rate.

a. If you leave your money in that account for 20 years, how much will you have in the account?

b. Suppose that inflation is expected to run at 3.25% for the next 20 years. Use the real interest rate to calculate the inflation-adjusted amount your account will contain at the end of the 20-year period.

c. The amount you calculated in (b) is smaller than the amount you calculated in (a). Explain exactly what the amount you calculated in (b) tells you, and why the difference arises.

15. Mel is a risk-neutral investor concerned about the future availability of gas. He is considering purchasing a gallon of gas today and placing it in storage for 10 years as a hedge against future gas price increases.

   a. If today's price of gas is $4.00 per gallon, and the future price of gas is $6.00 per gallon, is placing a gallon of gas in storage a good idea? Assume that the market interest rate is 4%.

   b. Suppose that Mel is uncertain of the future price of gas. He estimates that there is a 0.1 probability that gas will continue to sell for $4.00 per gallon, a 0.4 probability that gas will sell for $5 per gallon, and a 0.5 probability that gas will sell for $6.80 per gallon. Should Mel place a gallon of gas in storage today? Will your answer be the same if Mel is risk-averse?

16. You are romantically interested in Chris, but have always wanted to date the president of the Economics Club. As it turns out, Chris is battling Pat for control of the Econ Club. That battle should be decided in a year, and you estimate the odds of Chris winning at 60%. Attracting Chris and kindling a relationship will involve $1,000 of effort on your part; if Chris wins the presidency, you will receive benefits worth $2,200 (assume you receive these benefits one year after beginning the relationship). If Chris loses the election, you receive nothing.

   a. Calculate the net present value of building a relationship with Chris today. Notice that the costs of kindling a relationship today are certain, but the benefits are uncertain.

   b. Considering only your answer to (a), should you initiate a relationship with Chris at this time? Assume you are risk-neutral in formulating your answer.

   c. Calculate the net present value of waiting until the presidency is decided to build a relationship with Chris. Note that both the costs and benefits of kindling a relationship are uncertain at this point, but that the two will be certain in one year.

   d. Based on your answers to both (a) and (c), should you initiate a relationship with Chris today, or should you wait to initiate the relationship until the presidency is determined?

*17. You are considering the purchase of an old fire station, which you plan to convert to an indoor playground. The fire station can be purchased for $200,000, and the playground will generate lifetime profits (excluding the cost of the building) of $700,000. (Assume that those profits are all realized one year after opening.) However, there is a 20% chance that the city council will rezone the district to exclude establishments such as yours; a hearing is scheduled for the coming year, and if your building is rezoned, your profit will be zero. Assume that there is no other building currently under consideration.

   a. Calculate the net present value of opening the playground today. Note that the cost of purchasing the building today is certain, but the benefits are uncertain.

   b. Calculate the net present value today of opening the playground in one year, after the zoning issues have been decided. Note that both the costs and benefits of opening the playground are uncertain today, but will be certain in one year.

   c. Based on your answers to (a) and (b), should you open the playground today, or should you wait until the zoning commission reaches its decision?

18. Using diagrams of the market for capital, determine the effect of the following events on market interest rates:

   a. Consumers increase their saving rate.

   b. Advances in nanotechnology reduce firms' costs and increase estimates of future profits.

   c. Congress eliminates the tax deductibility of contributions to 401k savings plans.

   d. The Federal Reserve floods banks with new money.

   e. Banks tighten lending standards.

*19. Speedy Steve is a traveling salesman. His utility function is given by $U = I^{0.5}$, where U is his utility and I is his income. Steve's income is $900 each week, but if Steve is caught speeding while making his rounds, he will receive a hefty fine. There is a 50% chance he will be caught speeding in any given week, and pay a fine of $500.

   a. Calculate Steve's expected income and expected utility.

   b. Suppose that Steve's boss offers him a position in online sales that eliminates the risk of being caught speeding. What salary would provide Steve with the same utility he expected to receive as a traveling salesman?

   c. Suppose instead that Steve was given the opportunity to purchase speeding ticket insurance that would pay all of his fines. What is the most Steve would be willing to pay to obtain this insurance? Explain how you arrived at this number.

d. If the company issuing the insurance referred to in (c) convinces Steve to pay the amount you indicated, will the insurer earn a profit? If so, how much profit will it earn?

20. Danielle is a farmer, with a utility function of $U = I^{0.5}$, where U is Danielle's utility and I is her income. If the weather is good, she will earn $100,000. If there is a hailstorm, she will earn only $50,000. The probability of a hailstorm in any given year is 30%.

a. What is Danielle's expected income if she is uninsured? Her expected utility?

b. Suppose a crop insurer makes the following offer to Danielle: In years when there is no hailstorm, Danielle pays the insurer $16,000. In years when there is a hailstorm, the insurer pays Danielle $34,000. What is Danielle's expected income? Her expected utility?

c. Comment on the following statement referring to your answers to parts (a) and (b): "The insurance agreement in (b) reduces Danielle's expected income. Therefore, it must make her worse off."

d. Suppose instead the insurer offers Danielle the following: In years when there is no hailstorm, Danielle pays the insurer $10,000; in years when there is a hailstorm, the insurer pays Danielle $20,000. How does Danielle's expected income and expected utility compare to the uninsured outcome in (a) and the insured outcome in (b)?

General Equilibrium 14

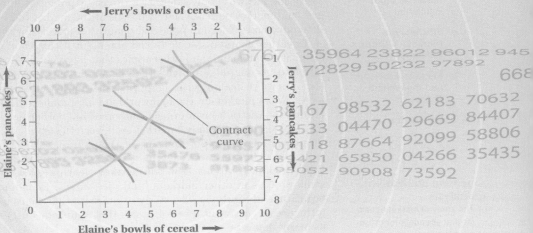

In the early 2000s, China, India, and other emerging market countries in Asia began growing dramatically. With that growth came an unquenchable demand for all sorts of commodities and raw materials such as iron ore and natural gas. Perhaps no country on earth benefitted more from this growth than Australia. Australia is blessed with amazing amounts of natural resources that it mines and exports. The growth in Asia has meant a big increase in demand for Australian commodities and, with this, a sizable increase in the profits and income the nation earns.

Yet looking beyond the lucrative expanding market for its commodities, Australia also experienced some problems. While companies and workers in Australia's mining sector reaped a big windfall as demand rose for Australia's exported natural resources, this drove up the cost of living for everyone else. Some other sectors of the Australian economy, such as manufacturing, actually suffered from the boom. They've had to raise wages to keep from losing their workers to the mining sector—wage increases not matched by increases in the manufacturers' own productivity levels. The resulting higher

general equilibrium analysis
The study of market behavior that accounts for cross-market influences and is concerned with conditions present when all markets are simultaneously in equilibrium.

partial equilibrium analysis
Determination of the equilibrium in a particular market that assumes there are no cross-market spillovers.

input costs made Australian-made goods more expensive and made it more difficult for Australian firms to compete against other countries' exports.

This tendency of countries experiencing big natural resource booms to suffer a weakening of their manufacturing base because of the resulting higher costs is known to economists as "Dutch disease," named after an episode in the Netherlands in the 1960s when newly discovered natural gas deposits drove up wages in the Netherlands and the value of its currency.

Dutch disease is a perfect example of the ways in which one market can have an impact on a completely different market. Throughout most of this textbook, we've examined how markets function in isolation. Each market has its own demand side that reflects consumers' tastes and its own supply side that is driven by producers' input costs, production technologies, and market power. These two sides of the market combine in a self-contained unit to determine an equilibrium price and quantity primarily for that one market.

In earlier chapters, we've talked about substitutes and complements, the cross-price elasticity of demand, and other topics that have involved the interaction of markets for different goods, but we have largely ignored how other markets might indirectly affect the ones we're dealing with. Ignoring cross-market effects simplifies our analysis, but at a cost. Most markets in the real world are interconnected. What happens in one (such as mining in Australia) can impact outcomes in another (such as Australian manufacturing). In some cases, across-market spillover effects can be so large that ignoring them means we miss an important part of the picture.

In this chapter, we're going to stop ignoring these across-market effects and think explicitly about how the market-clearing process in one market affects the same process in other markets (and vice versa). Economists refer to this as **general equilibrium analysis,** the study of markets that takes into account all cross-market influences to arrive at a set of prices that simultaneously equates supply and demand in many markets.

General equilibrium holds when all markets are in equilibrium at the same time. Taking explicit account of the way each market operates on its own while recognizing the influences of market spillovers is the key to understanding general equilibrium effects. What we've been doing up to this point is called **partial equilibrium analysis,** the determination of equilibrium in a particular market while assuming that it is not affected by spillovers from any other market. General equilibrium analysis is more complicated because there are more "moving parts" to keep track of. You might think it's fairly unlikely that all those markets could manage to achieve equilibrium at the same time, but one of the most fundamental results of microeconomic theory proves that it can all come together under the right circumstances.

General equilibrium analysis also deals with conceptual questions about how well markets allocate goods. It asks whether market outcomes in general equilibrium are desirable. Now, defining "desirable" can be a sticky issue, so economists are a little more specific about the standards that well-functioning markets are held to. We discuss in this chapter what these standards are and investigate what must be true for markets to meet them.

14.1 General Equilibrium Effects in Action

General equilibrium economic analysis has two parts. One part describes the mechanics of market interactions, and illustrates how various market features affect the size and direction of equilibrium effects. This branch of general equilibrium analysis describes markets *as they are*. The other part asks whether economy-wide market equilibria are efficient or equitable (and explains how to define those terms). You could say this type of analysis focuses on markets *as they ought to be*. People will never fully agree on how markets ought to behave, but general equilibrium analysis at least gives us a way to describe how it can work.

These two approaches use somewhat different frameworks for thinking about general equilibrium, and are in some respects independent of each other. Later in the chapter, we look at how the second approach works. In this section, we discuss the first approach and learn how general equilibrium effects work in markets and what market features influence these mechanisms.

An Overview of General Equilibrium Effects

The Energy Policy Act of 2005 set mandates to encourage the use of renewable fuels, including biofuels like ethanol, in the United States. It required that at least 4 billion gallons be used in 2006, 4.7 billion gallons in 2007, and 7.5 billion gallons by 2012. All of these amounts were likely to be well above the quantities a freely operating market would provide. For various technological and cost reasons, virtually the entire mandate was met with the use of corn-based ethanol. From an economic perspective, then, the Act increased the demand for corn and shifted the demand curve for corn outward.

Recall that in the Chapter 8 Application "The Increased Demand for Corn" (p. 333), we analyzed how this might affect the equilibrium price and quantity in the corn market. The increase in demand should drive up prices and induce more production: Corn producers would plant more, and wheat, soybean, or rice farmers would switch some of their production to corn. The increase in demand moves the market up its supply curve (because marginal costs rise with the added production), and raises the equilibrium price and quantity of corn. These predictions of the theory are consistent with what happened following the passage of the Act: Corn production grew over 10% between 2005 and 2010, and prices more than doubled.[1]

Can the use of corn to make biofuel lead to an increase in the price of wheat?

Yet, corn wasn't the only commodity crop that saw large price increases during this same period. Wheat and rice prices grew by two-thirds, and soybean prices doubled. General equilibrium suggests that the price increases in these markets might be related, even though the other crops had no direct role in meeting the renewable fuels mandate. An increase in the price of corn increases the demand for corn substitutes (such as wheat, rice, and soybeans).

These cross-market effects don't stop there. Higher corn demand also increases the demand for the inputs farmers use to produce it. Those inputs may have upward-sloping supply curves of their own, so the increased demand for corn may also drive up the prices of farm machinery, fertilizer, or farmland. That's what happened in real life, too: Between 2005 and 2010, the prices of agricultural chemicals and the average value of an acre of cropland rose over one-third.[2] Furthermore, the increased demand for substitutes like wheat also helped drive up the cost of the inputs used to make the substitutes.

---

[1] Production data may be found in the U.S. Department of Agriculture *Corn Yearbook* and *Wheat Yearbook*. Price data for corn and the other crops discussed below are from the Chicago Board of Trade.

[2] Agricultural chemical price data are from the U.S. Bureau of Labor Statistics, and cropland values from the U.S. Department of Agriculture.

All these spillover effects on other markets bounce back and affect the corn market itself. Figure 14.1 demonstrates how this feedback might work. Panel a shows the corn market. Before the renewable fuels mandate, the market is in equilibrium with demand curve D_{c1} and supply curve S_{c1}, and the equilibrium quantity and price are Q_{c1} and P_{c1}. The direct effect of the mandate is to increase the demand for corn from D_{c1} to D_{c2}. In a partial equilibrium analysis, we'd expect this to increase the quantity and price of corn to Q_{c2} and P_{c2}, respectively, and we'd be done.

A general equilibrium analysis, however, recognizes that because wheat and corn are substitutes, an increase in the demand for corn will affect the wheat market as shown in panel b. Before the mandate, wheat supply and demand are at S_{w1} and D_{w1}. The higher corn price caused by the renewable fuels mandate causes people to shift, say, from corn-based breakfast cereals to wheat-based cereals, thus increasing the demand for wheat from D_{w1} to D_{w2}, and raising wheat quantities and prices to Q_{w2} and P_{w2}.

Now, because wheat is a substitute for corn, higher wheat prices cause the demand for corn to increase, and there is a secondary outward shift in corn demand, from D_{c2} to D_{c3}. This raises the quantity and price of corn to Q_{c3} and P_{c3}. Higher corn prices, in turn, shift out wheat demand *again*, from D_{w2} to D_{w3}, raising wheat quantity and price to Q_{w3} and P_{w3}, and so on.

This feedback eventually slows down and stops. The size of the secondary feedback effect is smaller than the initial demand shift from D_{c1} to D_{c2}, the third shift is smaller than the second, and so on until the markets settle at a stable point. In the corn and wheat markets in Figure 14.1, the final demand curves after all the feedback effects are shown by D_{cF} for corn and D_{wF} for wheat.

Figure 14.1   **General Equilibrium Effects in Corn and Wheat Markets**

(a) Corn market

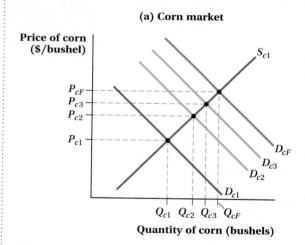

(b) Wheat market

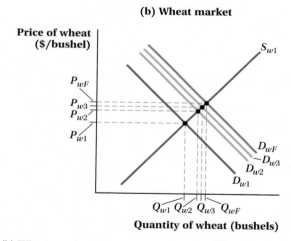

(a) Before the renewable fuels mandate, the corn market is in equilibrium at (Q_{c1}, P_{c1}), where the initial demand curve D_{c1} and supply curve S_{c1} intersect. The direct effect of the renewable fuels mandate shifts demand out to D_{c2}. Because the mandate also increases the price of wheat, however, the demand for corn continues to shift out until general equilibrium is reached at (Q_{cF}, P_{cF}), where D_{cF} intersects S_{c1}.

(b) Wheat, a substitute good for corn, is at an initial equilibrium of (Q_{w1}, P_{w1}), where the initial demand curve D_{w1} and supply curve S_{w1} intersect. When the renewable fuels mandate increases corn prices, the demand for wheat increases to D_{w2}. The subsequent increases in corn prices continue to shift out the demand for wheat until general equilibrium is reached at (Q_{wF}, P_{wF}), where D_{wF} intersects S_{w1}.

Therefore, the general equilibrium effect of the renewable fuels mandate in the corn market is to increase quantity from Q_{c1} to Q_{cF} and price from P_{c1} to P_{cF}. These changes are considerably larger than the quantity and price increases to Q_{c2} and P_{c2} that a partial equilibrium analysis implies. When the links between two markets are strong, as they are between corn and wheat, the gap between the partial and general equilibrium outcomes in the corn market is larger. Moreover, in a partial equilibrium analysis, the effect of the fuels mandate on wheat quantities and prices, which increase from Q_{w1} and P_{w1} to Q_{wF} and P_{wF}, is completely ignored.

We can also analyze the supply-side/input links between industries, such as the spillovers created when two markets use common inputs. (We examine this case in detail in a later quantitative section.) In this case, higher corn demand causes the supply of wheat to fall because farmers shift some of their production from wheat to corn. This decrease in supply shifts the supply of wheat inward, and with no change in wheat demand (we ignore demand spillovers like those we just discussed to focus on supply-side links), the equilibrium quantity of wheat falls and its price rises. This is demonstrated in Figure 14.2.

The decrease in wheat supply from S_{w1} to S_{w2} and the resulting increase in its price feed back, in turn, to the corn market and shift the supply of corn from S_{c1} to S_{c2} because this raises the price of inputs into corn production.

Now that we have an overview of how general equilibrium works, the next two subsections put actual numbers to the two cases we've just discussed to make the process of determining general equilibrium effects more explicit.

Figure 14.2 : **Supply-Side Input Links across Industries**

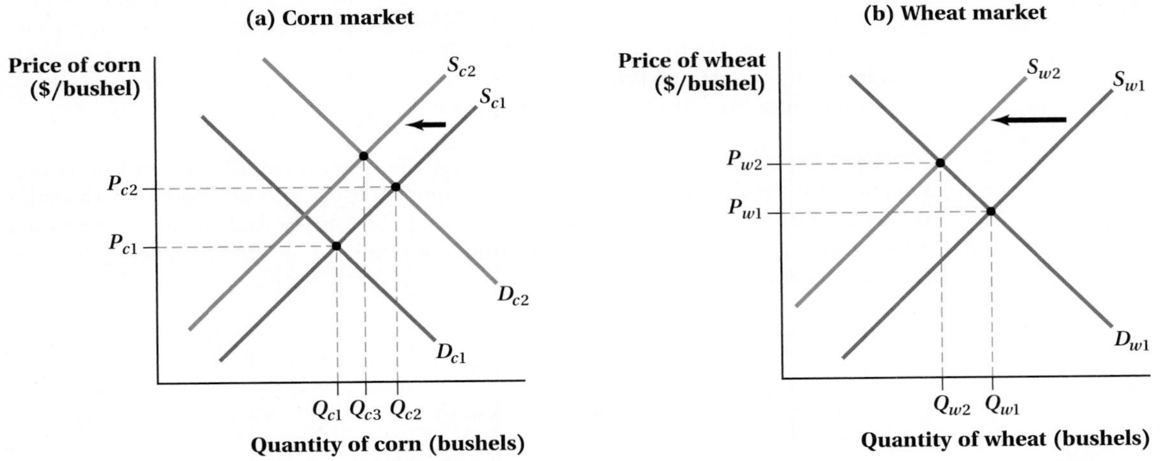

(a) Corn market

(b) Wheat market

(a) The increase in the demand for corn shifts demand from D_{c1} to D_{c2}. As a result, the quantity of corn increases from Q_{c1} to Q_{c2}, and the price of corn increases from P_{c1} to P_{c2}. (b) The increased demand for corn causes farmers to shift some of their production from wheat to corn. Consequently, the supply of wheat shifts in from S_{w1} to S_{w2}. The quantity of wheat decreases from Q_{w1} to Q_{w2}, and the price of wheat increases from P_{w1} to P_{w2}. The resulting increase in the wheat price feeds back in turn to the corn market, shifting the supply of corn from S_{c1} to S_{c2} because of increases in the price of inputs into corn production.

Quantitative General Equilibrium: The Corn Example with Demand-Side Market Links

Let's put some specific numbers on the types of processes discussed above to get a better feel for analyzing general equilibrium effects. To simplify our analysis, we assume that wheat and corn are the only two goods in the world. In this world, general equilibrium is the set of wheat and corn prices that simultaneously equate supply and demand in both markets.

We consider two numerical examples. In this section, we look at the cross-market general equilibrium effects that arise because of demand-side links between the wheat and corn markets (i.e., because consumers' preferences for wheat and corn are interrelated). In the next section, we look at how supply-side links between the markets (the production of wheat and corn is interrelated) drive the general equilibrium effects.

Let's suppose the supply of wheat is $Q_w^s = P_w$, where Q_w^s is the quantity of wheat supplied (in millions of bushels) and P_w is the price of wheat (in dollars per bushel). This supply curve has the typical upward slope: The quantity of wheat supplied increases as wheat prices rise. Similarly, corn supply is $Q_c^s = P_c$, where Q_c^s is the quantity of corn supplied (in millions of bushels) and P_c is the price of corn (in dollars per bushel). This supply curve also slopes upward; the quantity of corn supplied increases as corn prices rise.

Now let's say wheat demand is given by the equation $Q_w^d = 20 - P_w + P_c$. This equation tells us that, as with a standard demand curve, the quantity of wheat demanded decreases as wheat prices rise. But notice that the quantity of wheat demanded is also affected by corn prices P_c: When they increase, so does Q_w^d. This second effect reflects the fact that wheat is a substitute for corn. Therefore, higher corn prices cause consumers to shift some grain purchases toward wheat. This raises the quantity of wheat demanded at any given wheat price and shifts out the wheat demand curve. We assume corn demand is given by the equation $Q_c^d = 20 - P_c + P_w$. Thus, corn is a substitute for wheat; higher wheat prices shift out the demand for corn.

The fact that wheat and corn are substitutes for each other in this example is what creates general equilibrium effects. If we had assumed that wheat demand and corn demand were only a function of their own prices (while keeping the same supply curves that we assumed above), no cross-market effects would occur. Changes in wheat prices wouldn't shift the demand for corn, and vice versa. As a result, there would be no general equilibrium impact of one market's price on the other.

Finding Equilibrium Prices Describing the general equilibrium in this two-good economy requires figuring out what prices equate supply and demand in both markets. We start with the wheat market. Substituting the supply and demand curves above into the partial equilibrium condition that the quantity of wheat supplied must equal the quantity demanded, we have

$$Q_w^s = Q_w^d$$
$$P_w = 20 - P_w + P_c$$

We can rearrange this equation to express the equilibrium wheat price in terms of the price of corn:

$$P_w = 10 + \frac{P_c}{2}$$

Repeating the same steps for corn (equating the quantity supplied and demanded and solving for the corn price in terms of the wheat price) gives

$$P_c = 10 + \frac{P_w}{2}$$

These equations look similar to each other because we set up the example so that the two markets have identically shaped supply and demand curves.

The two equations for wheat and corn prices make clear that each market's equilibrium price depends on the other's. This is the essence of general equilibrium. We can find the prices that put both markets in equilibrium by substituting $P_c = 10 + \dfrac{P_w}{2}$ for P_c in $P_w = 10 + \dfrac{P_c}{2}$ and solving for P_w:

$$P_w = 10 + \frac{P_c}{2}$$

$$= 10 + \frac{\left(10 + \dfrac{P_w}{2}\right)}{2}$$

$$\frac{3P_w}{4} = 15$$

$$P_w = \$20$$

The general equilibrium price for wheat, then, is \$20 per bushel.

To find corn prices in general equilibrium, we substitute the wheat price $P_w = 20$ into the equation for the price of corn:

$$P_c = 10 + \frac{P_w}{2}$$

$$= 10 + \frac{20}{2} = \$20$$

Corn prices are also \$20 per bushel. That corn and wheat prices are the same is a special case, once again, because we assumed the two markets have identically shaped supply and demand curves.

Finding Equilibrium Quantities   Given the equilibrium prices of \$20 per bushel, we can calculate the general equilibrium quantities of wheat and corn by substituting $P_w = 20$ and $P_c = 20$ into the supply or demand curve equations for wheat and corn:

	For wheat:	For corn:
Supply	$Q_w^s = P_w$	$Q_c^s = P_c$
	$Q_w^s = 20$	$Q_c^s = 20$
Demand	$Q_w^d = 20 - P_w + P_c$	$Q_c^d = 20 - P_c + P_w$
	$Q_w^d = 20 - 20 + 20$	$Q_c^d = 20 - 20 + 20$
	$Q_w^d = 20$	$Q_c^d = 20$
Equilibrium Q	$Q_w^s = Q_w^d = Q_w = 20$	$Q_c^s = Q_c^d = Q_c = 20$

The general equilibrium quantities for wheat and corn are therefore both 20 million bushels.

This is the initial general equilibrium in the economy (akin to quantities and prices Q_{c1}, Q_{w1}, P_{c1}, and P_{w1} in our example in the previous section).

General Equilibrium Effects   Now let's look at how an isolated change in one market can create general equilibrium effects in the other. Suppose the renewable fuels mandate increases the demand for corn by 12 million bushels at any given set of corn and wheat prices. As a result, the demand curve for corn becomes

$$Q_c^d = 32 - P_c + P_w$$

This is reflected in the shift of corn demand from D_{c1} to D_{c2} in Figure 14.3.

We know that prices have to change—if they stayed at \$20, the quantity of corn demanded would be 32 million bushels but the quantity supplied only 20 million bushels. To find out what the new general equilibrium price is in the corn market, we have to repeat our steps above using the new corn demand curve.

Figure 14.3 | **The Effects of a Renewable Fuels Mandate on the Markets for Corn and Wheat**

(a) Corn market

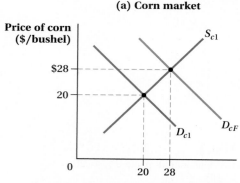

(b) Wheat market

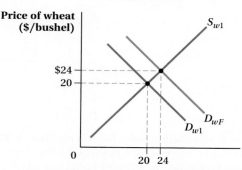

(a) Before the renewable fuels mandate, the corn market supplies 20 million bushels of corn at a price of $20 per bushel, where D_{c1} intersects S_{c1}. When the demand for corn shifts out to D_{cF}, corn's price increases to $28 per bushel, and its quantity increases to 28 million bushels.

(b) Wheat, a substitute good for corn, is at an initial equilibrium of 20 million bushels at $20 per bushel, where

initial demand curve D_{w1} and supply curve S_{w1} intersect. When the renewable fuels mandate increases corn prices, the demand for wheat increases to D_{wF}. The wheat market now supplies 24 million bushels of wheat at a price of $24 per bushel, where D_{w2} intersects S_{w1}.

Because the supply and demand curves for wheat are not directly changed by the mandate, the equation for the price of wheat in terms of corn remains the same ($P_w = 10 + \dfrac{P_c}{2}$). But, the equation for the equilibrium price of corn, which was $P_c = 10 + \dfrac{P_w}{2}$, changes because of the new corn demand curve. Setting $Q_c^s = Q_c^d$, we now have

$$P_c = 32 - P_c + P_w$$
$$= 16 + \frac{P_w}{2}$$

Again, we can solve for the general equilibrium wheat price by plugging one price equation into the other. This gives

$$P_w = 10 + \frac{P_c}{2}$$
$$= 10 + \frac{\left(16 + \dfrac{P_w}{2}\right)}{2}$$
$$\frac{3}{4}P_w = 18$$
$$P_w = \$24$$

The price of wheat is now $24 per bushel. Substituting this price back into the new price of corn equation shows that the new equilibrium corn price is $P_c = 16 + \dfrac{24}{2} = \$28$ per bushel. We then plug these prices into the supply or demand curves to obtain the new general equilibrium quantities:

$$Q_c^d = 32 - 28 + 24 = 28 \text{ million bushels of corn and}$$
$$Q_s^d = 20 - 24 + 28 = 24 \text{ million bushels of wheat}$$

Summing Up   We've just seen how an increase in the demand for corn leads not only to higher corn prices and quantities, as we would expect from a partial equilibrium analysis that just looks at what happens in the corn market, but also to higher wheat prices and quantities. Not surprisingly, the price increase is greater for corn (an \$8 per bushel, or 40% increase) than for wheat (a \$4 per bushel, or 20% increase). Notice how wheat prices rose even though the initial change in the economy—the increase in corn demand—did not directly affect the wheat supply and demand curves. The general equilibrium effect works instead through prices of substitute goods and was not included in our previous analyses of markets.

14.1 figure it out

Whiskey and rye are substitutes. Suppose that the demand for whiskey is given by $Q_w = 20 - P_w + 0.5P_r$, and that the demand for rye is given by $Q_r = 20 - P_r + 0.5P_w$, where Q_w and Q_r are measured in millions of barrels and P_w and P_r are the prices per barrel. The supplies of whiskey and rye are given by $Q_w = P_w$, and $Q_r = P_r$, respectively.

a. Solve for the general equilibrium prices and quantities of whiskey and rye. Then, determine the equilibrium quantities.

b. Suppose that the demand for whiskey falls by five units at every price so that $Q_w = 15 - P_w + 0.5P_r$. Calculate the new general equilibrium prices and quantities of whiskey and rye.

Solution:

a. We first need to solve for the price of whiskey as a function of rye by setting quantity demanded and quantity supplied equal in the whiskey market:

$$20 - P_w + 0.5P_r = P_w$$
$$2P_w = 20 + 0.5P_r$$
$$P_w = 10 + 0.25P_r$$

Then, we follow the same step for the rye market so that we have the price of rye expressed as a function of the price of whiskey:

$$20 - P_r + 0.5P_w = P_r$$
$$2P_r = 20 + 0.5P_w$$
$$P_r = 10 + 0.25P_w$$

To solve for P_w, we can substitute in the equation we just derived for P_r:

$$P_w = 10 + 0.25P_r = 10 + 0.25[10 + 0.25P_w] = 10 + 2.5 + 0.0625P_w$$
$$0.9375P_w = 12.5$$
$$P_w = \$13.33$$

This means that P_r is

$$P_r = 10 + 0.25P_w = 10 + 0.25(13.33) = 10 + 3.33 = \$13.33$$

Because $Q_w = P_w$ and $Q_r = P_r$, $Q_w = 13.33$ million barrels and $Q_r = 13.33$ million barrels.

b. When the demand for whiskey falls, both the markets for whiskey and rye will be affected. We will need to follow the same steps used in part (a) to solve for the new equilibrium prices and quantities.

First, we solve for the price of whiskey as a function of the price of rye:

$$15 - P_w + 0.5P_r = P_w$$
$$2P_w = 15 + 0.5P_r$$
$$P_w = 7.5 + 0.25P_r$$

Because the supply and demand for rye are not affected initially, we know from part (a) that

$$P_r = 10 + 0.25P_w$$

Therefore, we can substitute P_r into the equation for P_w:

$$P_w = 7.5 + 0.25P_r = 7.5 + 0.25[10 + 0.25P_w] = 7.5 + 2.5 + 0.0625P_w$$
$$0.9375P_w = 10$$
$$P_w = 10.67$$

Substituting for P_w and solving for P_r, we get

$$P_r = 10 + 0.25P_w = 10 + 0.25(10.67) = 10 + 2.67 = 12.67$$

Because $Q_w = P_w$ and $Q_r = P_r$, $Q_w = 10.67$ million barrels and $Q_r = 12.67$ million barrels.

theory and data

The General Equilibrium of Carmageddon

In July 2011 residents of metropolitan Los Angeles prepared for disaster. Residents stocked up on food so they wouldn't have to leave their houses for the weekend. Hospitals put into effect emergency procedures to ensure they would have enough staff. Local news stations planned for live coverage.

The city wasn't preparing for a massive flood or military attack. Instead, they were getting ready for "Carmageddon," a weekend-long construction project during which the 405, one of the main freeways connecting Los Angeles to outlying areas, would be closed.

The city government hoped that when the project was finished, it would lessen congestion and commute times on the notoriously busy Los Angeles freeways. To this end, officials planned to build an additional lane, and add a carpool lane to encourage people to share their commutes with coworkers. How successful were these measures? Was Carmageddon worth all of the hassle?

It's too early to tell for Los Angeles—some aspects of the construction project are still under way—but a recent paper by economists Gilles Duranton and Matthew Turner suggests that the construction project is not likely to make much difference to commuters because of general equilibrium effects.[3]

Over the past 20 years, as the U.S. roadway system expanded, the average number of cars on the road in metropolitan areas nearly doubled. Using this fact as a jumping-off point, Duranton and Turner examined more closely the effects of increasing the number of highways and major roadways on traffic in urban areas. In particular, the researchers looked at the effect of the number of lane-kilometers in an area on vehicle-kilometers traveled. Lane-kilometers are the product of a road's length and its number of lanes, capturing the road's total vehicle-carrying capacity. Vehicle-kilometers are the product of the number of vehicles on the road and the average distance a vehicle travels.

What they found would probably shock the Angelenos: The elasticity between vehicle-kilometers traveled and lane-kilometers is approximately 1.03. That is, for every increase in roads' traffic-carrying capacity, there was a *one-for-one* increase in how much people drove. So, for example, if the 405 expansion added 10% to the highway's ability to handle traffic, you could expect the number of cars on that stretch of highway to grow by 10%, too. Thus, even as measures are taken to improve congestion, the traffic commuters face seems to hold steady.[4]

Why doesn't the density of cars on the road decrease as the number of roads increase? When Los Angeles builds a highway to improve traffic, the city is relying on a partial equilibrium analysis. Unfortunately, this problem involves general equilibrium effects—an increase in roadways in an area has effects beyond those predicted by partial equilibrium analysis. The Duranton and Turner study documents that expanding the supply of roadways encourages more businesses and people to move to the area and farther out from downtown. This resulting increase in drivers' demand for roadways continues until traffic in the area converges to its "natural" steady level.

These findings indicate that Los Angeles gridlock is unlikely to be improved by highway expansion. But, there was one unexpected benefit of Carmageddon on area traffic: Because most people stayed home that weekend, those who did take to the roads faced practically empty roadways for a couple of days.

[3] Gilles Duranton and Matthew A. Turner, "The Fundamental Law of Road Congestion: Evidence from US Cities," *American Economic Review* 101, no. 6 (October 2011): 2616–2652.

[4] For a look at a different approach to reducing congestion, see the Application "Would Higher Driving Taxes Make Us Happier Drivers?" on pages 657–658.

Quantitative General Equilibrium: The Corn Example with Supply-Side Market Links

In the example just covered, the link between the corn and wheat markets was on the demand side. The two products were substitutes, so the change in one good's price affected the demand for the other. Supply-side links can create general equilibrium effects as well. Corn production and wheat production, for example, use common inputs (fertilizer, land, and for that matter, farmers).

Again, let's start with some specific and simple forms for the supply and demand curves. Suppose the demand curve for wheat is $Q_w^d = 20 - P_w$ and the demand curve for corn is $Q_c^d = 20 - P_c$. Notice that the demand-side links between the markets are now gone. Only a good's *own* price affects its quantity demanded. We are looking at a situation in which there is no demand-side interaction between markets, only supply-side interactions.

The supply curves are now $Q_w^s = 2P_w - P_c$ for wheat and $Q_c^s = 2P_c - P_w$ for corn. You can see the connections between the two markets in these new supply curve equations. The quantity supplied of each good increases as its own price increases and decreases as the other good's price increases. This relationship captures the notion that when one good's price increases, production shifts toward that good, allocating scarce resources away from production of the other good (such as replanting wheat fields as corn fields).

We can solve for the general equilibrium prices and quantities using the same steps we followed in the demand-side market links analysis. (Here, we skip some of the details because we've already done these types of calculations.) Setting $Q_w^s = Q_w^d$ and solving for the price of wheat in terms of the corn price give

$$P_w = \frac{20}{3} + \frac{P_c}{3}$$

Again, the symmetry of how we've set up these markets will result in a similar solution for corn prices: $P_c = \frac{20}{3} + \frac{P_w}{3}$. If we solve this system of equations, we find that $P_w = \$10$ per bushel and $P_c = \$10$ per bushel. If we substitute these prices into the supply and demand curves, we find that the quantities of both wheat and corn in this general equilibrium are 10 million bushels.

Now again suppose there is a 12 million bushel increase in the quantity demanded of corn at all prices because of the renewable fuels mandate, so that $Q_c^d = 32 - P_c$. The equation expressing the wheat price as a function of the corn price is the same as above $(P_w = \frac{20}{3} + \frac{P_c}{3})$ because the supply and demand curves for wheat are not directly affected. The equation for the price of corn changes, though. It's now $P_c = \frac{32}{3} + \frac{P_w}{3}$. When we solve this equation and the one for wheat prices above, we find that $P_w = \$11.50$ and $P_c = \$14.50$ per bushel. Plugging these prices into the supply or demand curves shows that the equilibrium wheat quantity is 8.5 million bushels and the equilibrium quantity of corn is 17.5 million bushels.

Summing Up   Once again, an increase in corn demand leads to increases in both corn and wheat prices in general equilibrium. This is true whether the links are supply-side interactions between markets as here or demand-side links as in the previous example.

In this case, the cross-market effect is driven by supply-side links: Higher corn prices move production from wheat to corn, thus decreasing the quantity of wheat supplied at every price, and shifting in wheat's supply curve. Because the demand curve for wheat does not change, wheat prices rise. Also, just as in the case of demand-side links, the price increase is larger for the good receiving the direct demand shift (corn).

However, notice that these similarities do not necessarily mean that demand-side market links create the same general equilibrium effects as supply-side connections. While the prices of all goods go up in both cases, their implications for quantities differ. In the demand-side link case above, the general equilibrium quantities of both goods increased in response to the demand shift for corn. In the supply-side case we just discussed, though, while equilibrium corn quantities rose, wheat quantities fell.

The quantity results are different because with the demand-side connection between the two markets, the increase in the demand for corn also increased the demand for wheat. Because the supply curves in both markets were fixed, these increases in demand led to increases in both quantities. With supply-side connections, however, the increased demand for corn resulted in a decrease in the supply of wheat, lowering its equilibrium quantity. These opposing predictions about the quantity changes in the wheat market give us a way to test whether the general equilibrium corn and wheat price increases are caused by demand-side or supply-side across-market effects. If the two goods are substitutes, then demand-side linkages imply that wheat *quantities* rise in response to the increased corn demand. If wheat quantities fall, on the other hand, this suggests supply-side links are more important.[5]

---

[5] A full analysis would test between the two possibilities while controlling for other influences on the amount of wheat and corn production, but a look at the raw numbers is still instructive. U.S. corn acreage increased 8% between 2005 and 2010, while wheat acreage fell by about 6% over the same period. This is consistent with the observed higher wheat prices resulting more from supply-side than demand-side spillovers.

freakonomics

Where Have All the Good Teachers Gone?

Teachers, on average, don't seem as great today as they used to be. There are still a lot of fantastic K–12 teachers out there—you probably know some of them. But, if you take an average teacher in 1960 and match them against an average teacher from 2010, the 1960s teacher comes out ahead on many dimensions as well as in various student performance measures.[*]

Why has teacher quality declined? What changed between 1960 and today that has been so detrimental to students? Actually, it was most likely the birth control pill.

Oral contraceptives don't have side effects that make teachers less effective (we hope the FDA would issue a report if they did). Instead, the introduction of the pill had general equilibrium effects that spread beyond just the contraceptive market. At the most fundamental level, it changed the marriage market, which in turn affected the job market by expanding the set of careers women could pursue.

Oral birth control allowed women—and men—to better control their fertility. For women, this meant that large investments in schooling made more sense, because they didn't have to worry as much about an unexpected pregnancy disrupting their plans. Consequently, more and more women entered graduate and professional programs, training for jobs in medicine, law, and business. In 1970, 9.1% of physicians were women.[†] Today, 32.3% of all physicians and surgeons are women, and more than half of the students in medical schools are female.[‡] Similarly, only 5.1% of lawyers and judges were women in 1970; in 2010, women made up over 30% of lawyers and the majority of current law students.

What do these statistics have to do with the decline in teacher quality? Let's consider the general equilibrium effects of the pill to deduce what the majority of the women in medicine, law, and business today might have been doing prior to 1960. First, these women expected to get married at a younger age, quite possibly right out of college. As a result, they would be more likely to have chosen a career that required at most a four-year degree. They'd probably also want a job that offered generous maternity leave (or at least one that was easy to leave when they started to bear children). And, last, they'd want a job that was intellectual. What career fits all these criteria? Teaching! In fact, in 1960, of employed college-educated women in their early thirties, nearly 50% were teachers.[§]

Is it bad that teacher quality has declined? We want good teachers, but we also want good doctors! And the women who choose law or medicine over teaching probably view themselves as better off—after all, they could still have chosen teaching but elected not to. If we decide we need better teachers, microeconomics offers a fairly simple solution to the problem of teacher quality: Increase wages and more people will opt for a career in the classroom over one in the courtroom.

[*] John H. Bishop, "Is the Test Score Decline Responsible for the Productivity Growth Decline?" *American Economic Review* 79, no. 1 (March 1989): 178–197.

[†] Claudia Goldin and Lawrence F. Katz, "The Power of the Pill: Oral Contraceptives and Women's Career and Marriage Decisions," *Journal of Political Economy* 110, no. 4 (August 2002): 730–770.

[‡] Bureau of Labor Statistics, *Household Data Annual Averages*, 2010.

[§] Claudia Goldin, Lawrence F. Katz, and Iliana Kuziemko, "The Homecoming of American College Women: The Reversal of the College Gender Gap," *Journal of Economic Perspectives* 20, no. 4 (Fall 2006): 133–156.

application

General Equilibrium Interaction of Cities' Housing and Labor Markets

In our earlier examples, we saw that general equilibrium effects can show up when a price change in one market shifts supply or demand curves in other markets. But, general equilibrium effects can affect the slopes of supply and demand curves, too.

Recent research by economist Raven Saks documented an example of this.[6] Saks looked at how the labor markets in major cities responded to increased demand for labor by local firms. (This outward shift in labor demand is typically caused by heightened demand for the products of firms that operate in the area.) A partial equilibrium analysis of the effect of a labor demand shift in the city follows. In the short run, as firms experience increased demand for their products, their demand for labor increases and the labor demand curve shifts to the right from DL_1 to DL_2 (Figure 14.4a). Given an upward-sloping short-run labor supply curve SL_{SR}, this increase in demand leads to an increase in both employment and wages, as seen in the movement from equilibrium A to B.

The short-run labor supply curve slopes up because the wage must rise to induce the existing local labor force to work more. But over time, higher wages in the city will also cause workers in other cities to move in. This ability of workers to migrate across cities in response to wage changes means the long-run labor supply curve is more elastic

Figure 14.4 | Interaction between Labor and Housing Markets

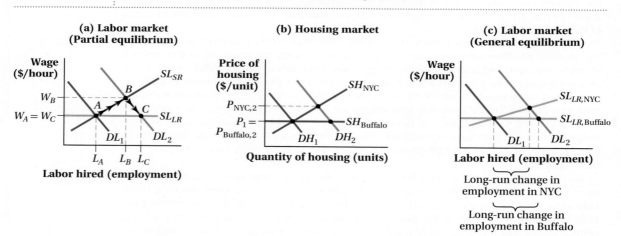

(a) An increase in the demand for labor by local firms shifts demand from DL_1 to DL_2, resulting in a short-run increase in employment and wages from L_A to L_B and W_A to W_B, respectively. In the long run, workers from other cities migrate to the area. As a result, the long-run supply curve SL_{LR} is relatively elastic, and the quantity of labor supplied increases to L_C, pushing down wages to their original level at $W_C = W_A$. (b) The influx of new workers has general equilibrium effects that extend beyond the labor market. As a result of the migration to the city, demand for housing DH_1 shifts out to DH_2. In a market such as Buffalo where the supply of housing ($SH_{Buffalo}$)

is relatively elastic, housing prices stay constant at $P_1 = P_{Buffalo,2}$. In New York City, the relatively inelastic supply of housing (SH_{NYC}) means that housing prices will rise to $P_{NYC,2}$. (c) New York City's relatively steeper long-run labor supply curve ($SL_{LR,NYC}$) reflects the increase in housing prices seen in panel b, while Buffalo's long-run labor supply curve ($SL_{LR,Buffalo}$) is similar to the flat supply curve in panel a. Because of the effects of the housing market on the labor market, Buffalo will experience a greater increase in employment and a smaller increase in wages than New York City.

[6] Raven E. Saks, "Job Creation and Housing Construction: Constraints on Metropolitan Area Employment Growth," *Journal of Urban Economics* 64, no. 1 (July 2008): 178–195.

(flatter) than the short-run labor supply curve. This long-run supply curve is labeled SL_{LR} in panel a. (We've assumed for now that the migration response is significant enough that the long-run supply curve is perfectly elastic—that's why the curve is flat—though we'll see in a minute this may not be true in general equilibrium.)

The long-run migration response moves the equilibrium down the new labor demand curve from point B to point C, increasing employment further as wages fall to their original level. Once the wage equals its original level, new workers stop moving to the city, employment growth stops, and the long-run labor market equilibrium is at point C. The increase in the quantity of labor demand from L_A to L_C is therefore the city's long-run total employment response to the shift in labor demand.

Saks' research suggested the story is more complex than this, however. General equilibrium effects arising from links between the labor and housing markets also influence the size of the long-run employment response. This is because the influx of new workers into the city due to the increase in demand in the labor market also increases demand in the local housing market. This demand shift is shown in panel b of Figure 14.4 as movement in the housing demand curve from DH_1 to DH_2. In cities with steep housing supply curves, like New York City (we discuss what determines the steepness of cities' housing supply curves below), worker migration drives up housing prices. This increase in housing prices is seen in panel b. When the housing demand curve shifts, the market moves up along New York's housing supply curve SH_{NYC}, and the price rises from P_1 to $P_{NYC,2}$. In cities with more elastic supply, like Buffalo, house prices rise less or may not increase at all. In panel b, Buffalo's housing supply curve is $SH_{Buffalo}$; there is no equilibrium price change in response to the demand shift, so $P_1 = P_{Buffalo,2}$.

Any price effect in the housing market has, in turn, its own impact on the labor market. Higher housing prices counteract wage increases driven by the shift in labor demand. To spur a given amount of migration, then, wages have to rise more in cities with steeper housing supply curves, because they have to make up for the higher home prices new workers in the city face. This means that markets like New York City with steeper long-run housing supply curves have steeper long-run labor supply curves, too. Similarly, markets like Buffalo with flatter housing supply curves have flatter long-run labor supply curves. This long-run response reflects the general equilibrium connection between the local housing and labor markets. So while Buffalo's labor supply curve looks something like SL_{LR} in panel a of Figure 14.4, New York City's is steeper. Panel c of Figure 14.4 plots these two long-run labor supply curves against the initial labor demand shift. As we can see, the demand shift leads to a smaller long-run increase in total employment in more inelastic housing supply markets like New York than in more elastic housing supply markets like Buffalo.

Saks tested the hypothesis that the total employment effect of labor demand shifts in general equilibrium depends on the steepness of cities' housing supply curves. She compared employment responses to labor demand shifts in cities with different housing supply elasticities. Although she could not measure housing supply curves directly, she showed that metropolitan areas with more legal restrictions on building (and therefore likely with steeper housing supply curves, because such restrictions make it more expensive to increase the quantity of housing supplied) had smaller long-run employment responses to equal-sized labor demand shifts. A 1% outward shift in labor demand (i.e., one that would increase local firms' labor demand by 1% at any given wage) in cities with few building restrictions like Nashville, Tennessee, or Bloomington-Normal, Illinois, led to a long-run employment increase of about 1%. In restrictive cities like New York and San Francisco, however, a 1% increase in labor demand led to long-run employment increases that were one-third smaller. ■

14.2 General Equilibrium: Equity and Efficiency

The second branch of general equilibrium analysis deals with conceptual—some might even say philosophical—questions of how well markets allocate goods. That is, it asks whether market outcomes in general equilibrium are in any sense desirable. Defining "desirable" can be a sticky issue, however, so economists are a little more specific about the standards for well-functioning markets. In this section, we talk about what these standards are, and whether markets can meet them.

Standards for Measuring Market Performance: Social Welfare Functions

social welfare function
Mathematical function that combines individuals' utility levels into a single measure of society's total utility level.

One way economists often try to think about the overall desirability of market outcomes is to use a **social welfare function,** a mathematical function that combines the utility levels of the individuals in a society to obtain a single overall measure of an economy's performance. That way, various market outcomes (i.e., distributions of utilities across all individuals in the economy) can be compared to one another. If one outcome has a higher value than another according to the social welfare function, the higher-valued outcome is considered more desirable.

The ranking of various market outcomes depends on the particular form of the social welfare function one chooses to use to evaluate outcomes in the first place. For example, a function that explicitly penalizes inequalities in individuals' utility levels will rank certain market outcomes very differently than a function that ranks outcomes based only on average utility levels. Choosing a social welfare function to evaluate outcomes is therefore a bit of a philosophical exercise; it depends on one's notion of what sort of outcomes are desirable in the first place. Thus, social welfare functions can be thought of as ways to rank economic outcomes once one has already decided what features of the outcomes (such as the amount of inequality or whether particular groups of individuals have systematically higher or lower utilities) are desirable. Social welfare functions are much less useful for deciding whether inequality is inherently bad, and how bad it is if so. The functions embody these views, but they don't reveal their accuracy or lack thereof.

Given the subjectivity of social welfare function choice, economists have not decided on any hard-and-fast rules about the particular form a social welfare function should take. However, some versions are more commonly used than others because they're easy to work with or because they succinctly capture elements of various philosophies about what is desirable in terms of the distribution of utilities across individuals.

The Utilitarian Social Welfare Function One common type of social welfare function adds together the utility levels u of everyone in the economy, with equal weight given to each person:

$$W = u_1 + u_2 + \cdots + u_N$$

utilitarian social welfare function
Mathematical function that computes society's welfare as the sum of every individual's welfare.

where W is the value of the social welfare function, the grand total of all utility in a society. The subscripts denote individuals; there are a total of N people in this economy. This **utilitarian social welfare function** says that society's welfare is the sum total of every individual's welfare. That seems easy enough. But, note that a utilitarian society will be one with relatively little concern about how equally utility is distributed among individuals. Raising anyone's utility a given amount has the same total welfare effect for society regardless of how well off that person already was. In fact, a utilitarian function would say there's no harm in driving any particular individual's utility down to zero as long as someone else experiences an equal-sized utility gain, even if that person is already better off than everyone else in the economy.

Rawlsian social welfare function
Mathematical function that computes society's welfare as the welfare of the worst-off individual.

The Rawlsian and Egalitarian Social Welfare Functions The utilitarian social welfare function's relative indifference to utility inequality has led people to propose the use of other social welfare functions.

One proposed function assumes that social welfare is determined literally by how the worst-off member of society does. The **Rawlsian social welfare function** is named for political philosopher John Rawls, who argued on social justice grounds that a society should strive to maximize the utility of its worst-off member. In mathematical terms, the Rawlsian social welfare function says that

$$W = \min[u_1, u_2, \ldots, u_N]$$

In words, society's welfare W is the minimum of all the utilities in society. Only the utility of the least well-off individual matters; the utility levels of all other individuals in the society do not matter at all. The Rawlsian utility function is an extreme example of an **egalitarian** welfare function. In an ideal egalitarian society, every individual is equally well off, and any departures from total equality cannot increase social welfare.

egalitarian
Belief that the ideal society is one in which each individual is equally well off.

The Drawbacks of Social Welfare Functions   Although social welfare functions can be useful, they can be difficult to use as practical standards for evaluating market outcomes, especially because different functions may give such varied answers about what makes for desirable outcomes. For example, think about how differently a utilitarian society and an egalitarian society would think about taxing the rich to give to the poor. As we mentioned above, how one would evaluate the result of such policies is going to depend on subjective judgments about how worthwhile inequality reductions are in the first place.

Furthermore, even if everyone agreed on the type of social welfare function to use, combining individuals' utility levels mathematically—which is the point of a social welfare function—is conceptually dicey, as we discussed in Chapter 4. A social welfare function can give different total welfare values to the *same* sets of consumption bundles, depending on the individual utility functions one chooses. This makes it even more difficult to compare economic outcomes.

14.2 figure it out

Arnold, Bruce, and Sylvester are residents of a tiny commune in Peru. Arnold currently has a utility level (U_A) of 55 utils; Bruce's utility, U_B, is 35 utils; and Sylvester's utility, U_S, is 10 utils. Angelina, the benevolent ruler of the commune, is considering enacting a new policy that will increase Arnold's utility by 10 utils and decrease Sylvester's by 5.

a. If Angelina believes the social welfare function is given by $W = U_A + U_B + U_S$, should she enact the change?

b. If Angelina believes the social welfare function is given by $W = \min[U_A, U_B, U_S]$, should she enact the change?

c. If Angelina believes the social welfare function is given by $W = U_A \times U_B \times U_S$, should she enact the change?

Solution:

a. To determine if Angelina should enact the policy, we must calculate the social welfare before and after the change.

Before:

$$W = U_A + U_B + U_S = 55 + 35 + 10 = 100$$

After:

$$W = U_A + U_B + U_S = 65 + 35 + 5 = 105$$

Because welfare is increased after the change, Angelina should enact the policy.

b. Before:

$$W = \min(U_A, U_B, U_S) = \min(55, 35, 10) = 10$$

After:

$$W = \min(U_A, U_B, U_S) = \min(65, 35, 5) = 5$$

In this case, Angelina should not enact the new policy because welfare is reduced.

c. Before:

$$W = U_A \times U_B \times U_S = 55 \times 35 \times 10 = 19{,}250$$

After:

$$W = U_A \times U_B \times U_S = 65 \times 35 \times 5 = 11{,}375$$

Again, because welfare falls as a result of the new policy, Angelina should not enact it.

Standards for Measuring Market Performance: Pareto Efficiency

The difficulties with trying to use social welfare functions to evaluate how well markets are working have led economists to use a different criterion that everyone can understand and agree on: Pareto efficiency.

Pareto efficiency
An economic allocation of goods in which the goods cannot be reallocated without making at least one individual worse off.

Pareto efficiency holds in an economy if no one can be made better off without making someone else worse off. Here's an example of what it implies. In one small economy, Larry has a laptop, Moe has a TV, and Curly has a used Oldsmobile Cutlass Supreme. If there is no way to reshuffle the goods among the three guys that makes no one worse off and at least one person better off, then the economy is Pareto-efficient. If a reshuffling of the goods could make one or more better off without making anyone worse off, then the economy isn't Pareto-efficient. So, for example, if Larry would happily swap his laptop for Curly's Cutlass Supreme and Curly would also like to make this swap, then the initial allocation of goods wasn't Pareto-efficient. These sorts of trades are not possible in a Pareto-efficient allocation because one person will not be willing to participate. Under Pareto efficiency, *someone* would be made worse off by any rearrangement of goods, whether it's a simple two-person, two-good swap, or something a lot more complicated.[7]

What this means for general equilibrium is that a Pareto-efficient economy should not have a lot of something for nothing—what economists call "free lunches" or "$20 bills lying on the sidewalk" (figuratively or literally). In this way, Pareto efficiency is a fairly intuitive concept of efficiency.

Another important feature of Pareto efficiency is that it doesn't have to be fair or equitable, or maximize some social welfare function. Pareto-efficient allocations can result in large differences in individuals' utility levels. In fact, as long as marginal utilities are positive, giving one person everything in the economy and everyone else nothing is Pareto-efficient! Any rearrangement of goods from this allocation requires taking something away from the person with everything. Because marginal utilities are positive, this reallocation makes that person worse off, violating the Pareto efficiency condition.

That's why it is important to remember that Pareto efficiency is a weak standard to hold markets to. We might find a Pareto-efficient outcome (sometimes called a Pareto equilibrium) that is unappealing from the perspective of equality. Still, it is a useful benchmark, because we are interested in knowing whether voluntary trade in markets can somehow eliminate any free lunches that might exist in an initial distribution of resources.

Looking for Pareto Efficiency in Markets

Now that we've defined Pareto efficiency as a standard to measure market outcomes, let's see how market outcomes compare to Pareto-efficient outcomes. This is an extremely important question to economists: Markets are the most common way for the world to allocate billions of goods to billions of people. We would like to know, for lack of a better phrase, whether markets are any good at this. But to answer this question, we need to compare market equilibria to certain standards such as Pareto efficiency.

We start by giving away the ending: Under a certain set of assumptions about the market environment, market outcomes *are* Pareto-efficient. Economists had speculated about this possibility for as long as there have been economists. Adam Smith's famous notion of an *invisible hand* (the unseen force in markets that tends to create socially beneficial results even though market participants act only in their individual best

---

[7] Note that this doesn't mean *no one* could be made better off by a reshuffling of goods from a Pareto-efficient allocation outcome. In fact, it's likely an individual or set of individuals would be made better off. But, this would come at the expense of others.

interests) essentially made the point that market outcomes can be efficient. It wasn't until the mid-twentieth century, however, that the Pareto efficiency result was proven mathematically. (The highly technical proof is beyond the scope of this chapter, but we'll cover the economic intuition behind it later.)

The market efficiency result is a big reason why economists tend to look favorably on markets: Markets have a natural tendency to arrive at efficient outcomes under a certain set of assumptions. (You are already familiar with some of these assumptions, such as perfect competition and price-taking behavior among suppliers and consumers.) The chances that *all* of these assumptions actually hold in any real-world market are small, however, so real markets may not be completely Pareto-efficient.

If real markets aren't completely efficient, why do economists still seem to favor market solutions, probably much more often than the general public? It's because the market efficiency proof shows exactly what must hold for markets to be efficient. That is, whatever makes markets work or fail isn't mysterious. We *know* what things gum up the works and often this suggests what kinds of policies would remove the gum.

Therefore, economists of most political orientations tend to think that markets have the potential to create the greatest amount of benefits for the greatest number of people. What they are more likely to disagree on is how much intervention (such as government actions to reduce market power) is necessary to make markets run smoothly.

Efficiency in Markets—Three Requirements

Now it's time to look at the details of what must be true if markets are operating efficiently. There are three basic conditions that must hold in an efficient economy:

1. **Exchange efficiency.** For exchange efficiency to hold, the allocation of a set of goods across people must be Pareto-efficient: No consumer can be made better off in her consumption without making someone worse off. The term *exchange* comes from the fact that we don't worry about what products are made or how, or who buys them. We just pretend we give a collection of items to people and let them trade (exchange) things if they want to.

2. **Input efficiency.** For input efficiency to hold, inputs must be allocated to producing the goods in the economy in such a way that making a higher quantity of one good means a smaller quantity must be made of at least one other good.

3. **Output efficiency.** The first two conditions take the set of goods produced in the economy as a predetermined starting point, and then evaluate efficiency in how they are allocated among consumers (exchange efficiency) and producers (input efficiency). Output efficiency deals with *which* goods are produced and in what quantities. For output efficiency to hold, the mix and amount of goods that the economy produces cannot be changed without making some consumer or producer worse off.

We study each of these three conditions separately, in detail, below, and then show how they are interrelated in an efficient general equilibrium.

exchange efficiency
A Pareto-efficient allocation of a set of goods across consumers.

input efficiency
A Pareto-efficient allocation of inputs across producers.

output efficiency
A mix of outputs that simultaneously supports exchange and input efficiency.

14.3 Efficiency in Markets: Exchange Efficiency

Before we begin our examination of the various aspects of an efficient general equilibrium with a discussion of *exchange efficiency*, we introduce an extremely handy tool for analyzing market efficiency, the **Edgeworth box.** The box is named after the Irish economist Francis Edgeworth, and it illustrates an economy with two consumers and two goods (or, alternatively, two producers and two inputs). This simple set-up demonstrates almost all the concepts we need to understand market efficiency.

Edgeworth box
Graph of an economy with two economic actors and two goods that is used to analyze market efficiency.

The Edgeworth Box

Suppose there are two consumers—we'll call them Jerry and Elaine—each of whom has his or her own preference for two goods, bowls of cereal and pancakes. Let's also suppose that there are a total of 10 bowls of cereal and 8 pancakes that can be split between them. We want to figure out in what Pareto-efficient ways we can distribute these goods between Jerry and Elaine.

To do this analysis, we use an Edgeworth box. An Edgeworth box utilizes the fact that when there is a fixed total number of goods to be split between two individuals, giving one more unit of a good to one person necessarily means the other person gets one fewer unit. In our case, for example, if Elaine gets one more bowl of cereal, Jerry must get one fewer. A point within or on the sides of the Edgeworth box shows the distribution of two goods (like cereal and pancakes) between two people (like Jerry and Elaine).

Figure 14.5 illustrates how the Edgeworth box works in our example. The horizontal sides of the box measure 10 bowls of cereal; the vertical sides measure 8 pancakes. The lower-left-hand corner represents one consumer (we'll say Elaine here, though we could just as easily have picked Jerry) who receives zero units of both goods. If we give Elaine one more bowl of cereal, we move her allocation one unit to the right. If we give her one more pancake, we move Elaine's allocation one unit up.

The upper-right-hand corner represents Jerry when he receives zero units of both goods. Note that if Jerry receives no goods, Elaine receives all of both goods—10 bowls of cereal and 8 pancakes. If we give Jerry one more bowl of cereal, his allocation moves one unit to the left (one less bowl for Elaine). If we give him one more pancake, Jerry moves down one unit (one less pancake for Elaine).

To get accustomed to working with the Edgeworth box, let's do some quick examples. Consider an initial allocation at point A in Figure 14.5. At point A, Elaine has 3 bowls of cereal and 6 pancakes, and Jerry has the rest of the goods, 7 bowls of cereal and 2 pancakes. If we change the allocation by giving Elaine another bowl of cereal and taking one from Jerry, we are at point B; Elaine has 4 bowls of cereal and 6 pancakes and Jerry has 6 bowls of cereal and 2 pancakes. If we change the allocation from point B by taking away a pancake from Elaine and giving it to Jerry, we move to point C (Elaine has 4 bowls of cereal and 5 pancakes and Jerry has 6 bowls of cereal and 3 pancakes). Any change in the allocation that moves one of the consumers in a

---

Figure 14.5 | **A Consumption Edgeworth Box**

This Edgeworth box plots specific allocations of cereal (10 bowls total, shown on the horizontal axes) and pancakes (8 total, shown on the vertical axes) between two consumers, Jerry and Elaine. If Jerry consumes 7 bowls of cereal and 2 pancakes, Elaine consumes 3 bowls of cereal and 6 pancakes (point A). If Jerry consumes one fewer bowl of cereal at point B, then Elaine's consumption of cereal increases by 1 bowl to 4 bowls of cereal. At point C, Jerry now eats one more pancake, decreasing Elaine's consumption of pancakes by 1 pancake to 5 pancakes.

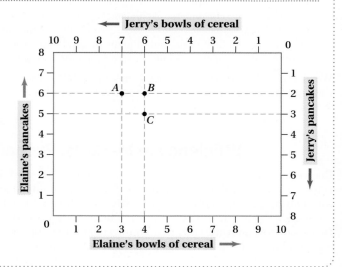

certain direction will move the other consumer by the same amount but in the opposite direction. As a result, the Edgeworth box allows us to see simultaneously the effects of changes in goods allocations on both consumers.

Gains from Trade in the Edgeworth Box

To analyze whether allocations are efficient, we need to know about consumers' preferences. In Chapter 4, we learned that indifference curves represent consumers' preferences. To see the gains from trade, we add Elaine's and Jerry's indifference curves to the Edgeworth Box (Figure 14.6).

Elaine's preferences for bowls of cereal and pancakes are represented by indifference curves U_{E1}, U_{E2}, U_{E3}, and so on. Each shows combinations of cereal and pancakes that make Elaine equally well off. Indifference curves further away from Elaine's origin depict more of each good, and so represent higher utility levels. Jerry's preferences are represented by indifference curves U_{J1}, U_{J2}, U_{J3}, and so on. Jerry's indifference curves may look odd, but when you remember that Jerry's origin is in the upper right corner, then they look like all other indifference curves: bowed toward the origin. Indifference curves further away from Jerry's origin show higher utility levels.

Now that we've laid out Jerry and Elaine's preferences, how can we use them to determine what an efficient allocation of the two goods would be? We start at an arbitrary allocation, point A, and ask if we can reshuffle who gets what *and* make both Elaine and Jerry better off by doing so. (Remember the definition of Pareto efficiency: There is no possible way to reallocate who gets what without making at least one individual worse off than before.) At allocation A, such a reshuffling is possible. Let's see why.

Elaine and Jerry each have indifference curves that pass through point A, U_{E3} and U_{J3}. We know from our analysis in Chapter 4 that any allocation giving Elaine quantities of cereal and pancakes that are above and to the right of U_{E3} will give her a higher utility than at point A. Similarly, any allocation that raises Jerry's utility will be below and to the left of U_{J3}. Knowing this, we can figure out the allocations that make *both* Elaine and Jerry better off, or at least make one of them better off without making the other worse off. These are the allocations in the shaded area in Figure 14.6. Any distribution of goods in this area must be on indifference curves (not drawn to keep the graph uncluttered) that correspond to higher utility levels for both Elaine and Jerry.

Figure 14.6   Edgeworth Box with Two Sets of Indifference Curves

By including Jerry's and Elaine's indifference curves, we can determine the efficient allocation of bowls of cereal and pancakes. Point A is an inefficient allocation because any point in the shaded area, including point C, will yield both Jerry and Elaine higher utilities.

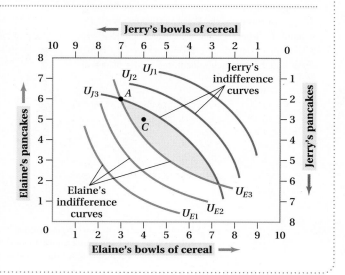

Any change that moves the allocation of goods from A to somewhere in the shaded area makes both Elaine and Jerry better off. For example, if we gave one of Jerry's bowls of cereal to Elaine and one of Elaine's pancakes to Jerry, we'd be at point C inside the shaded area, and Jerry and Elaine would both have higher utility levels than at the initial allocation (point A).

Remember that a Pareto-efficient allocation is one that, if changed in any way, would make at least one person worse off. Because there is a set of allocations that would make both Jerry and Elaine better off (the shaded area), point A cannot be Pareto-efficient. (Reallocations that make at least one person better off without making anyone worse off are sometimes referred to as *Pareto-improving reallocations* or just *Pareto improvements*.) Jerry and Elaine, if given allocation A, would *both* be willing to make the trade: Elaine could give a pancake to Jerry in exchange for a bowl of cereal.[8]

If the existence of a shaded area like that in Figure 14.6 means an allocation isn't Pareto-efficient, you might think that only allocations *without* shaded areas *are* Pareto-efficient, and you'd be right. What exactly would this sort of allocation look like? To see, let's think about another allocation that is inside the shaded area, point C.

Although C gives both Jerry and Elaine higher utility levels than A, there are still mutually beneficial trades that can be made. These can be seen in Figure 14.7. For example, indifference curves U_{E4} and U_{J4} are Elaine and Jerry's indifference curves that pass through C. The area that U_{E4} and U_{J4} enclose are cereal and pancake allocations that would make both Elaine and Jerry better off than they are with allocation C. Therefore, allocation C can't be Pareto-efficient either. But, notice that this area is smaller than the corresponding area for allocation A. We seem to be closing in on Pareto efficiency.

To find a Pareto-efficient allocation, we need to locate one where there is no area between Jerry and Elaine's indifference curves. When will this hold? When we reach indifference curves for Elaine and Jerry that meet at a single point, point D in Figure 14.7. Notice that Elaine and Jerry's indifference curves that pass through this

---

Figure 14.7   **Closing in on Pareto Efficiency for Elaine and Jerry**

A Pareto-efficient allocation of pancakes and bowls of cereal occurs at a tangency between Jerry's and Elaine's indifference curves, where Jerry's marginal rate of substitution MRS_{cp} equals Elaine's MRS_{cp}. In this case, the Pareto-efficient allocation is point D, where Elaine's indifference curve U_{E5} is tangent to Jerry's indifference curve U_{J5}. Here, Jerry and Elaine each consume 5 bowls of cereal and 4 pancakes.

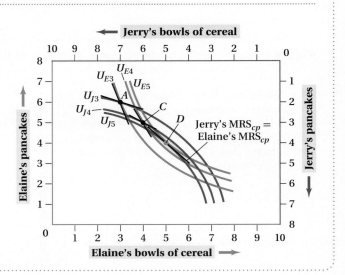

---

[8] While we've only drawn a two-consumer, two-good case in Figure 14.6, these concepts extend to any number of people consuming allocations of any number of goods. It's just that we haven't figured out how to draw in 4-, 5-, or higher-dimensional hyperspace yet. We're working on it, though; wish us luck.

point, U_{E5} and U_{J5}, are tangent to each other. Also notice that we can't change the allocation even slightly without making either Jerry or Elaine worse off by going below and to the left of U_{E5}, or above and to the right of U_{J5}. Allocation D, therefore, is Pareto-efficient.

We've shown that exchange efficiency is achieved when two consumers' indifference curves are tangent. Only at such a tangency are there no mutually beneficial gains from trade. This tangency condition offers an interpretation for what must be true for exchange efficiency to hold. Recall from Chapter 4 that the slope of an indifference curve at any point reflects the marginal rate of substitution (MRS) between goods at that point. That means at a common tangency like point D, the slopes of both Jerry and Elaine's indifference curves are the same. (Remember, the slope of a curve at a particular point equals the slope of a line tangent to the curve at that point.) Thus, at point D, Jerry and Elaine have the same MRS between cereal and pancakes. At any point that *isn't* a Pareto-efficient allocation, consumers have different MRS for the goods. At points A and C in Figure 14.7, the difference in the slopes of Elaine and Jerry's indifference curves is clear.

To understand why the MRSs need to be equal, think for a moment about what it would mean if they weren't. One consumer would have a higher marginal utility from consuming one of the goods than the other consumer would. For the other good, the order of the two consumers' marginal utilities would be switched. When marginal utilities for the same good are unequal across consumers, each could give a unit of her low-marginal-utility good to the other. She would be getting rid of what is, for her, a relatively low-value item, but she would receive in return the good for which she has a higher marginal utility. The same would be true of the consumer receiving the unit, so both individuals would be better off. Only when marginal utility ratios are equal across the two consumers—that is, when exchange efficiency has been achieved—would there not be a mutual benefit from trade.

In allocation A in Figure 14.7, Elaine would be willing to trade 3 pancakes for 1 bowl of cereal. That is, her MRS_{cp} (marginal rate of substitution of cereal for pancakes) and the absolute value of the slope of her indifference curve is 3. Jerry would trade 3 bowls of cereal for 1 pancake, or equivalently, one-third of a pancake for a bowl of cereal. So, Jerry's $MRS_{cp} = 1/3$. Elaine therefore has a relatively high marginal utility from cereal at allocation A; she'd be willing to give up 3 pancakes to get 1 bowl. Jerry feels the opposite. He would enjoy another pancake so much he would be willing to part with 3 bowls of cereal for it. Clearly, both would benefit from making a trade here. Jerry could give Elaine a bowl of cereal (which he doesn't value much, relatively speaking) in exchange for a pancake (which he does). Elaine would be happy to accept that trade, and they would end up at allocation C, which we know Elaine and Jerry like better than A. In fact, any trade where Jerry gives Elaine a bowl of cereal in exchange for anywhere between one-third and 3 pancakes will make Jerry and Elaine better off. Mutually beneficial trade between Elaine and Jerry could continue like this until allocation D is reached. Only at that point, when their marginal rates of substitution are equal, would neither want to trade. Further exchange would necessarily make one of them worse off than at D, where their MRSs are equal.

Prices and the Allocation of Goods   Up to this point, we've talked about the allocation of goods as if magical economists shuffle goods among consumers. In reality, prices determine how goods are distributed in markets. Consumers choose how much of each good to consume given the prices they face. In Chapter 4, we learned that a utility-maximizing individual consumes the product bundle at which her MRS between goods equals the ratio of those goods' prices. (This optimal consumption bundle is located where the indifference curve is tangent to the budget line.)

In Elaine and Jerry's case, then, we know that they will both consume amounts where $MRS_{cp} = \dfrac{P_c}{P_p}$. We also just saw that Elaine and Jerry's MRS_{cp} will be equal in a

Pareto-efficient allocation. Thus, it must be that Pareto efficiency in a market implies

$$\text{Elaine's } MRS_{cp} = \text{Jerry's } MRS_{cp} = \frac{P_c}{P_p}$$

In other words, an efficient market will result in the goods' price ratio equaling consumers' marginal rates of substitution for those goods.

If an initial allocation is not efficient, consumers will be willing to sell their allocated goods that (for them) have marginal utilities below the market price. They could then use the proceeds to buy high-marginal-utility goods. There will be individuals whose relative marginal utilities for those goods are the reverse and who will be willing to be on the other side of those transactions. In this way, we don't need magical economists to reshuffle goods among people to get everyone's MRS to match. Prices will lead people to do it themselves.

The Consumption Contract Curve   The key condition of exchange efficiency that consumers' marginal rates of substitution are equal—that is, their indifference curves are tangent to one another—is true at more than one location in the Edgeworth box. In Figure 14.8, we've drawn a more extensive set of Elaine and Jerry's indifference curves, showing several tangencies. If we connect these tangencies and all those in between (remember, there are indifference curves running through every point in the box), *every* allocation on the line is Pareto-efficient—they all meet the equal-MRS test. This line, called the **consumption contract curve,** shows all possible Pareto-efficient allocations between two consumers buying two goods.

Looking at the contract curve emphasizes the distinction between efficiency and equity that we mentioned earlier. While all allocations along the contract curve are efficient, they have very different implications for Jerry and Elaine's respective utility levels. Some—those toward the lower-left corner of the Edgeworth box—imply low utility for Elaine and high utility for Jerry. Those toward the upper right, on the other hand, will be good for Elaine and relatively bad for Jerry.[9]

consumption contract curve
Curve that shows all possible Pareto-efficient allocations of goods across consumers.

Figure 14.8   A Consumption Contract Curve

The consumption contract curve connects every point of tangency between Jerry's and Elaine's indifference curves for bowls of cereal and pancakes. Each point on the contract curve represents a Pareto-efficient allocation of bowls of cereal and pancakes between Jerry and Elaine.

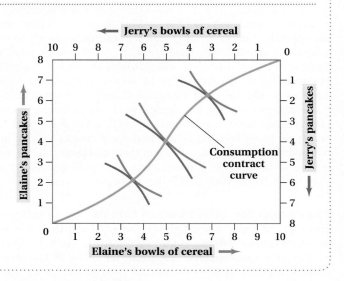

---

[9] In fact, the lower-left and upper-right corners of the Edgeworth box—the actual origins themselves—can also be on the contract curve. At either origin, either Elaine or Jerry will be consuming everything, and the other will be consuming nothing. If Elaine and Jerry's marginal utilities of a good are always positive, there is no way that a good can be moved from one of them to the other without making the one who was consuming everything worse off. Allocations where one person gets everything and everyone else receives nothing can be Pareto-efficient.

Consider the Edgeworth box below (Figure A), which depicts the amount of soda and pizza available to two consumers, Thelma and Lou.

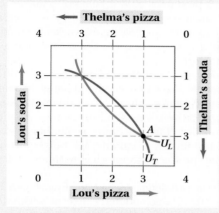

Figure A

a. Suppose that Thelma and Lou are initially at point A. How much soda does each have? How many slices of pizza?

b. Suppose that Thelma and Lou's child Ted takes 2 pieces of pizza from Lou and gives them to Thelma, then takes 2 sodas from Thelma and gives them to Lou. Find and plot the new allocation in the Edgeworth box. Label the allocation with a large "B." Does such a reallocation represent a Pareto improvement? Explain your answer.

c. Suppose that Ted had reallocated 1 piece of pizza and 1 soda instead of 2 of each. Would such a reallocation represent a Pareto improvement? Explain your answer, using indifference curves to illustrate it.

Solution:

a. At point A, Thelma has 3 sodas and Lou has 1 soda. Thelma has 1 slice of pizza, while Lou has 3 slices of pizza.

b. If Ted takes 2 slices of pizza from Lou and gives them to Thelma, Lou will end up with 1 slice, while Thelma will have 3. If Ted takes 2 sodas from Thelma and gives them to Lou, Thelma will be left with 1 soda and Lou will have 3 sodas. This allocation can be represented at point B in Figure B. A Pareto improvement occurs when at least one individual is made better off without making anyone worse off.

Because point B is on the same indifference curves as point A, neither Thelma nor Lou is better off. Therefore, this is not a Pareto improvement.

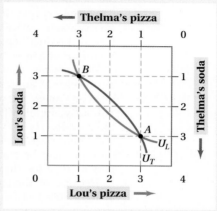

Figure B

c. If Ted takes 1 slice of pizza from Lou and gives it to Thelma, both Lou and Thelma will end up with 2 slices each. If Ted also takes 1 soda from Thelma and gives it to Lou, both Thelma and Lou will be left with 2 sodas each. This allocation can be represented by point C in Figure C. A Pareto improvement occurs when at least one person is made better off without harming another person. In this case, point C is on a higher indifference curve for both Thelma and Lou, implying that they are both better off with this new allocation. Therefore, it is a Pareto improvement. Moreover, as drawn below, the allocation at point C is also Pareto efficient.

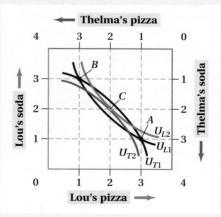

Figure C

14.4 Efficiency in Markets: Input Efficiency

Exchange efficiency shows what conditions must hold on the demand side of a market for the market to be efficient. Efficiency is also important on the production side of the economy, especially the efficiency with which inputs are allocated across the production of various goods and services. An input can be used to make one product or another, but not both simultaneously. So, which product should it be used to make? That is, how do we answer questions such as how much steel should be used to make cars instead of smartphones (or TVs, or surgical instruments), or how many workers should make each type of product? Questions like these are at the heart of the second market efficiency condition of general equilibrium, *input efficiency*.

It turns out that a lot of the tools we used to analyze exchange efficiency are also useful in analyzing input efficiency. We saw that in exchange efficiency, goods are consumed where consumers' indifference curves are tangent to one another. Similarly, input efficiency requires an allocation of inputs across producers where their *isoquants* are tangent to each other. The reasoning is similar to the exchange efficiency case. At locations where producers' isoquants are tangent to each other, no input can be transferred from one producer to another without at least one experiencing a loss in output.

Because of the similarity of the two problems, we use an Edgeworth box for our analysis. It's just like the one we used for Elaine and Jerry, except with two producers instead of two consumers. And rather than allocating two goods between consumers, we look at how two inputs are allocated between the producers.

Figure 14.9 shows how 20 units of labor (horizontal axes) and 12 units of capital (vertical axes) are allocated between Cereal, Inc. (CI) and Pancake, Inc. (PI). CI's origin, which denotes where it is using zero units of capital and labor, is at the lower-left-hand corner of the box. Increases in CI's use of inputs are represented by movement to the right (labor) and up (capital). CI's isoquants—Q_{C1}, Q_{C2}, Q_{C3}, and so on—show the combinations of labor and capital that produce a given amount of output. PI's origin,

---

Figure 14.9   A Production Edgeworth Box

An Edgeworth box can be used to determine the efficient input allocation between two firms. In this case, Cereal, Inc.'s and Pancake, Inc.'s labor inputs are on the horizontal axes and their capital inputs are shown on the vertical axes. Q_{C1}, Q_{C2}, and Q_{C3} are examples of Cereal, Inc.'s isoquants, and Q_{P1}, Q_{P2}, and Q_{P3} are examples of Pancake, Inc.'s isoquants.

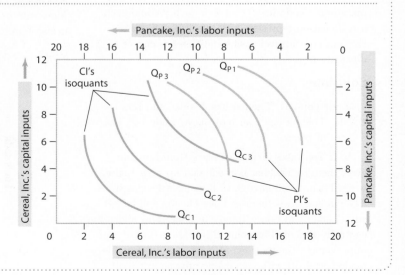

which denotes where it is using zero units of capital and labor, is at the upper-right-hand corner of the box. Increases in PI's use of inputs are represented by movements to the left (labor) and down (capital). PI's isoquants—Q_{P1}, Q_{P2}, Q_{P3}, and so on—show the combinations of labor and capital that produce a given amount of output.

The connection between the analysis of Elaine and Jerry's consumption bundles and the analysis of Cereal, Inc.'s and Pancake, Inc.'s input use is direct. CI's isoquants look "normal." PI's isoquants also look normal if we remember that we're looking at them from the upper-right origin. Start at an arbitrary allocation of inputs between the two firms, point F in Figure 14.10. At this point, CI is using 14 units of labor and 4 units of capital, which means that PI is using 6 units of labor and 8 units of capital. CI's isoquant Q_{C1} and PI's isoquant Q_{P1} pass through point F and enclose an area. If they use input combinations in this highlighted area, both firms can make more output than they can with input allocation F. Because both firms can make more output with the same total inputs, F cannot be a Pareto-efficient allocation of inputs.

At input allocation G, where CI's and PI's isoquants Q_{C2} and Q_{P2} are tangent, there is no way to move labor and capital from one firm to the other and raise output for at least one of the firms without reducing the other firm's output. Therefore, G is a Pareto-efficient allocation of inputs. This tangency condition also indicates that firms experience no mutually beneficial gain from trading inputs with each other.

There are more similarities between input and exchange efficiency. Exchange efficiency implies that consumers' marginal rates of substitution—the slopes of their indifference curves—are equal. Input efficiency implies equal slopes of producers' isoquants. As you may recall from Chapter 6, this slope is called the marginal rate of technical substitution ($MRTS$), the ratio of inputs' marginal products. For example, the $MRTS$ between labor and capital is the ratio of the marginal product of labor to the marginal product of capital, $MRTS_{LK} = \dfrac{MP_L}{MP_K}$. In our example, input efficiency requires that

$$\text{CI's } MRTS_{LK} = \text{PI's } MRTS_{LK} = \frac{MP_L^{\text{CI}}}{MP_K^{\text{CI}}} = \frac{MP_L^{\text{PI}}}{MP_K^{\text{PI}}}$$

Figure 14.10   **Edgeworth Box with Two Sets of Isoquants**

A Pareto-efficient allocation of capital and labor inputs occurs at a tangency between Cereal, Inc.'s and Pancake, Inc.'s isoquants, where Cereal, Inc.'s marginal rate of technical substitution ($MRTS_{LK}$) equals Pancake, Inc.'s $MRTS_{LK}$. Point F shows a possible allocation of labor and capital between Cereal, Inc. and Pancake, Inc. Because it lies on the intersection of isoquants Q_{C1} and Q_{P1}—and not at the tangency—F is an inefficient allocation. G, which is located at the tangency between Q_{C2} and Q_{P2}, is a Pareto-efficient input allocation.

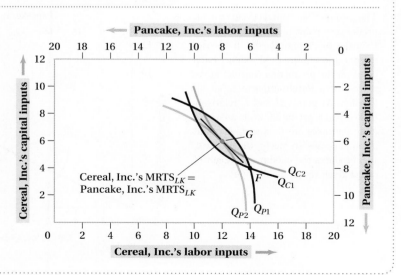

We can see this common $MRTS_{LK}$ slope in Figure 14.10.

We also learned in Chapter 6 that cost-minimizing firms set their $MRTS$ equal to the ratio of the input prices (wages and rental rates in the cases of labor and capital). Putting this all together, input efficiency implies

$$\text{CI's } MRTS_{LK} = \text{PI's } MRTS_{LK} = \frac{MP_L^{CI}}{MP_K^{CI}} = \frac{MP_L^{PI}}{MP_K^{PI}} = \frac{W}{R}$$

where W is the wage rate and R the capital rental rate.

Finally, a similarity exists between input and exchange efficiency in terms of the set of efficient allocations. In the exchange efficiency case, the collection of efficient goods allocations, the contract curve, connects all common tangencies of the consumers' indifference curves. The **production contract curve** connects all common tangencies of producers' isoquants and contains all efficient allocations of inputs across producers (Figure 14.11).

Just as different locations on the contract curve can imply very different total utility levels for Elaine and Jerry, different locations on the production contract curve correspond to disparate production quantities of cereal and pancakes. In the lower left, Cereal, Inc. uses few inputs and relatively little cereal is made, while many pancakes are produced. The opposite is true in the upper-right corner where a lot of cereal and few pancakes are produced.

production contract curve
Curve that shows all Pareto-efficient allocations of inputs across producers.

The Production Possibilities Frontier

The production contract curve generates a useful idea. Think about what various input allocations across the two firms imply about the tradeoffs between the *output* of either good. Imagine running along the production contract curve from the lower-left corner in Figure 14.11 to the upper-right corner, but instead of thinking about what each point corresponds to in terms of inputs, consider what each point means for cereal and pancake output.

Figure 14.11 A Production Contract Curve

The production contract curve connects every point of tangency between Pancake Inc.'s and Cereal, Inc.'s isoquants for capital and labor. Each point on the production contract curve represents a Pareto-efficient input allocation. At points H and I, relatively little cereal is produced, while relatively more pancakes are produced. At point J, no pancakes are made, while Cereal, Inc. produces the maximum amount of cereal given the available inputs.

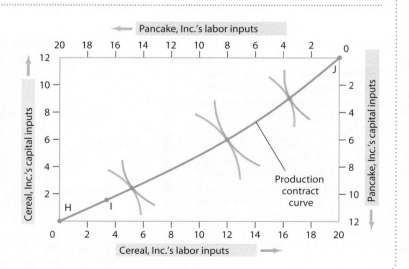

At the very lower-left-hand corner, no inputs are used to make cereal, so cereal production is zero. Pancake output, however, is maximized at this location. This combination is plotted as point H on Figure 14.12. (For comparison, we've labeled the corresponding input combination in Figure 14.11.) Pancake production is positive; cereal output is zero.

Now move up and to the right along the production contract curve to input allocation I in Figure 14.11. This move shifts inputs from pancake to cereal production. The corresponding effect on output is traced by the movement from point H to point I in Figure 14.12. Cereal output increases while pancake output falls. As we continue in the same direction along the production contract curve, cereal production rises further as pancake production drops more. When we reach the upper-right-hand corner of the Edgeworth box, cereal output is maximized, and pancake output is zero (point J).

We just traced out all the possible combinations of the cereal and pancakes that could be made if inputs are allocated efficiently across producers. The level of output for any particular good will depend on how many inputs are applied to its production, but whatever level this is, as long as the input allocation is on the production contract curve, efficiency tells us we cannot increase the output of the other good without decreasing the output of the first. The curve that connects these possible output combinations, curve HJ in Figure 14.12, is called the **production possibilities frontier (PPF)**. Again, we see that efficiency doesn't necessarily imply equality. Depending on the location on the production possibilities frontier, the two goods in this example can be made efficiently in very different proportions.

Inefficient input allocations will lead to cereal and pancake outputs that are inside the PPF. For example, the inefficient input allocation given by point F in Figure 14.10 might correspond to the output combination at point F in Figure 14.12. At point F, more of both goods could be made with the same total amount of inputs. The possible combinations of outputs that would be an improvement over point F (and that are attainable given the total amount of inputs available) are those contained within the wedge-shaped area in Figure 14.12. This area corresponds to the outputs that could be made by input combinations within the shaded area between Q_{C1} and Q_{P1} in Figure 14.10. Points on the PPF curve itself, rather than inside it, correspond to the outputs produced by efficient combinations of inputs along the production contract curve. For example, Point G in Figure 14.12 shows the output that corresponds to the efficient input allocation G in Figure 14.10.

production possibilities frontier (PPF)
Curve that connects all possible efficient output combinations of two goods.

Figure 14.12 | A Production Possibilities Frontier

The production possibilities frontier (PPF) plots all possible output combinations of cereal and pancakes that are made if inputs are allocated efficiently. Points H, I, G, and J all lead to efficient outputs. Point F, which lies within the PPF, results from an inefficient allocation of inputs across producers.

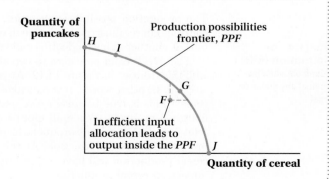

14.4 figure it out

Suppose that there are 10 units of capital available in a small economy and 20 units of labor. Those inputs can be used to produce food and clothing.

a. If the $MRTS_{LK}$ in the clothing industry is 4, and the $MRTS_{LK}$ in the food industry is 3, is the economy productively efficient? Explain your answer.

b. If you indicated in part (a) that the economy was not productively efficient, suggest a reallocation of labor and capital that will lead to a Pareto improvement.

Solution:

a. Production efficiency requires that the $MRTS$ between labor and capital be equal across industries.

Therefore, the economy is not productively efficient because the $MRTS_{LK}$ for clothing is greater than $MRTS_{LK}$ for food.

b. To become equal, $MRTS_{LK}$ in the clothing industry must fall, while the $MRTS_{LK}$ in the food industry must rise. This means that the clothing industry should use more labor and less capital, while the reverse is true for the food industry. As the clothing industry uses more labor and less capital, the MP_L will fall and the MP_K will rise, decreasing the $MRTS_{LK}$. Likewise, as the food industry uses less labor and more capital, the MP_L will rise and the MP_K will fall, increasing $MRTS_{LK}$. This Pareto improvement will move the economy toward productive efficiency.

14.5 Efficiency in Markets: Output Efficiency

We've described what must be true if exchange and input efficiency hold, and we've seen a lot of parallels between the two cases: common tangencies, consumer and production contract curves, and so on. While we've drawn analogies, however, we haven't discussed whether there is any direct connection between the two types of efficiency.

If we think about it for a minute, though, a connection must exist. Inputs are used to make goods that are consumed, after all. There should be a link between the efficient allocation of inputs for making different outputs and the efficient allocation of these outputs across consumers. The link is *output efficiency*, which involves the choice of how many units of each product the economy should make. Understanding the requirements for output efficiency requires grasping the inherent tradeoff between the production of various goods. We describe this tradeoff first, and then show how it ties together the three efficiency conditions.

The Marginal Rate of Transformation

marginal rate of transformation (MRT)
The tradeoff between the production of any goods on the market.

The production possibilities frontier, which we showed was related to the production contract curve, illustrates how much of one output must be given up to obtain one more unit of another. This tradeoff is called the **marginal rate of transformation (MRT)**.

The *MRT* from pancakes to cereal, for example, is the slope of the production possibilities frontier in Figure 14.12. At point H, the frontier is relatively flat, so the *MRT* is small. In other words, few pancakes have to be given up to produce one more bowl of cereal. This is true because we've assumed (realistically) that inputs have diminishing marginal products. When all inputs are being used to make pancakes, the inputs have relatively low marginal products in pancake production, but relatively large marginal products in cereal production. At this point, shifting just a few inputs from pancake to cereal production will have a tiny impact on total pancake production but a noticeable impact on cereal production.

The opposite is true near point J. There, the inputs' marginal products in pancake production are high and are low in cereal production. The MRT from pancakes to cereal is therefore very high. Intermediate MRT levels exist at points toward the middle of the production possibilities frontier, like G.

This logic shows how the marginal rate of transformation is related to inputs' marginal products. We can pin down this relationship with the following thought experiment. Suppose we want to increase cereal production. To do so, we take one unit of labor, a worker, say, who was making pancakes at Pancake, Inc., and instead have her start working at Cereal, Inc. How much pancake output have we given up by making this shift? The marginal product of labor at Pancake, Inc., is MP_L^{PI}. How much cereal output have we gained? The marginal product of labor at Cereal, Inc., MP_L^{CI}. The ratio of these two values—the amount of pancakes that must be given up to obtain more cereal—is the definition of the marginal rate of transformation MRT. Therefore,

$$MRT_{PC} = \frac{MP_L^{\text{PI}}}{MP_L^{\text{CI}}}$$

That is, the marginal rate of transformation from pancakes to cereal is the ratio of labor's marginal product in pancake production to its marginal product in cereal production.

Similarly, moving a unit of capital from Pancake, Inc. to Cereal, Inc. will lead to the conclusion that the MRT is also the ratio of capital's marginal products at the two firms:

$$MRT_{PC} = \frac{MP_K^{\text{PI}}}{MP_K^{\text{CI}}}$$

We can see this equivalence another way. First, remember two things from above: The production contract curve connects all equal-marginal-rate-of-technical-substitution points, and every point on the production contract curve corresponds to a point on the production possibilities frontier. Therefore, it must be the case that firms' marginal rates of technical substitution are equal at any point on the frontier. Next, realize that because the $MRTS$ is the ratio of the marginal products of inputs, $\frac{MP_L^{\text{PI}}}{MP_K^{\text{PI}}} = \frac{MP_L^{\text{CI}}}{MP_K^{\text{CI}}}$ at every point on the PPF. We can rearrange this equation to show that on the PPF, $\frac{MP_L^{\text{PI}}}{MP_L^{\text{CI}}} = \frac{MP_K^{\text{PI}}}{MP_K^{\text{CI}}}$. That is, the ratios of an input's marginal product across firms are the same for all inputs on the PPF, which is the same as saying that the MRT on the PPF is related to inputs' marginal products.

We've defined the marginal rate of transformation MRT and shown that it is related to inputs' marginal products, and through these marginal products, the MRT is related to firms' marginal rates of technical substitution. What role do these equivalencies play in linking exchange and input efficiency?

Let's suppose that the consumption and production sides of the market have independently come to efficient allocations. To give a specific example, say Elaine and Jerry are at an exchange-efficient allocation on the contract curve where the marginal rate of substitution between pancakes and cereal is 1.5: Each is willing to give up one-and-a-half pancakes to have one more bowl of cereal. (Equivalently, each would have to be given one-and-a-half pancakes to make up for the loss of 1 bowl of cereal.)

Suppose, as well, that the economy's production side has arrived at an efficient input allocation on the production possibilities frontier—where the marginal rate of transformation from pancakes to cereal is 1. That is, 1 pancake of output must be given up to make another bowl of cereal.

These outcomes result in a mismatch between consumers' willingness to substitute one good for the other and firms' abilities to switch from producing one to the other. To *consume* one more bowl of cereal, Elaine and Jerry are both willing to give up 1.5 pancakes for 1 bowl of cereal. But to *produce* one more bowl of cereal, society needs to only give up 1 pancake for 1 bowl of cereal. So, this economy has a disconnect between the production- and consumption-side tradeoffs. Because Elaine and Jerry's relative preferences for cereal are stronger than the relative costs of making cereal, we would want to allocate additional inputs toward cereal making. This example shows that exchange and input efficiency can exist together, but there is a missing link that keeps the economy from being completely efficient.

This missing link between efficiency on the consumption and production sides of the economy is *output efficiency*. This exists when the tradeoffs on the consumption and production sides of an economy are equal. The tradeoff on the consumption side is the marginal rate of substitution. The tradeoff on the production side is the marginal rate of transformation. Output efficiency therefore requires $MRS = MRT$. In our example above, if Elaine and Jerry were at an efficient allocation where their common MRS was equal to the MRT, then output efficiency would exist.

Figure 14.13 shows the production possibilities frontier from Figure 14.12 with a consumer's indifference curves plotted with it. It doesn't really matter whose indifference curves we plot—Jerry's or Elaine's—because exchange efficiency means they both have the same MRS. That is, their indifference curves have the same slope at all efficient allocations.

The outcome in the example above, where Elaine and Jerry's MRS is 1.5, and the MRT is 1, is shown at point M. Exchange efficiency holds at this point because Elaine and Jerry have the same MRS. Input efficiency also holds because the output combination is on the production possibilities frontier. But, output efficiency does not hold because the indifference curve U_M that goes through output combination M cuts inside the PPF. This configuration makes two important facts hold. First, output combinations above and to the right of U_M are preferable to those on U_M. Second, any output combination on or inside the PPF is feasible—that is, it can be produced with the available input. Thus, U_M and the PPF border a set of output combinations that are both (1) preferred to M and (2) possible to produce. This cannot be an efficient outcome because we can make Elaine and Jerry better off without using more inputs.

Figure 14.13 ⋮ **Achieving Output Efficiency**

Output efficiency occurs at the tangency between the consumers' indifference curves and the production possibilities frontier, where the marginal rate of substitution MRS equals the marginal rate of transformation MRT. Point M shows a possible output combination of pancakes and cereal. Because it lies on the intersection of the PPF and the indifference curve U_M—and not at the tangency—M is an inefficient output combination. N, which is located at the tangency between the PPF and U_N where $MRS = MRT$ = 1.25, is an efficient output allocation.

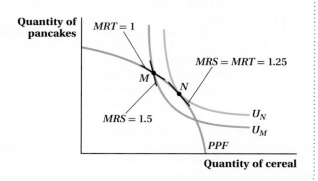

How do we reach an efficient outcome? By shifting some production from pancakes to cereal until output combination N is reached. At this combination, the indifference curve U_N is tangent to the PPF. Therefore, $MRS = MRT$ (we've assumed both are 1.25 in the figure), and we arrive at output efficiency. We know this is the efficient output mix because no other feasible output combination exists that would give Elaine and Jerry higher utility. Thus, output efficiency is also marked by a tangency condition.

Another way to think about the $MRT = MRS$ condition is as a statement of that classic principle of economic optimality, that marginal benefits should equal marginal costs. As we discussed earlier, the MRS between goods equals the goods' price ratio. Under perfect competition, as we saw in Chapter 8, a profit-maximizing firm will produce a quantity at which its marginal cost equals the good's price. For complete efficiency to hold in our cereal and pancakes example, the marginal rate of substitution must equal not only the ratio of the goods' prices but also the ratio of the goods' marginal costs of production: $MRS_{CP} = \dfrac{P_{CL}}{P_{PL}} = \dfrac{MC_{CL}}{MC_{PL}}$. Because the marginal cost of production equals the price of an input divided by the marginal product of that input (essentially, it's how much you have to spend on an extra amount of input to raise output by one unit), $MC_C = \dfrac{W}{MP_L^C}$ and $MC_P = \dfrac{W}{MP_L^P}$. Therefore, $\dfrac{MC_C}{MC_P} = \dfrac{MP_L^P}{MP_L^C}$. Earlier, we showed that this ratio of the marginal products of labor is also equal to the MRT. (We would arrive at the same answer if we used the marginal products of capital because these ratios are equivalent.) Saying that output efficiency implies $MRT = MRS$ is the same as saying that it equates the ratio of consumers' marginal utilities of goods to the marginal costs of producing those goods.

14.5 figure it out

In Ecoland, producers make both televisions and clocks. At current production levels, the marginal cost of producing a clock is $50 and the marginal cost of producing a television is $150.

    a. How many clocks must Ecoland give up if it wishes to produce another television?

    b. What is the marginal rate of transformation from clocks to televisions in Ecoland?

    c. At current production levels, consumers are willing to give up 2 clocks to obtain another television. Is Ecoland achieving output efficiency? Explain.

Solution:

    a. Because the marginal cost of producing a television is three times that of producing a clock, Ecoland must give up 3 clocks for each television it produces.

    b. The marginal rate of transformation (MRT) measures how much of one output must be given up to obtain one more unit of another. Therefore, the MRT from clocks to televisions is 3.

    c. Because consumers are only willing to trade 2 clocks for a television, the marginal rate of substitution (MRS) is 2. However, output efficiency requires that $MRS = MRT$. Therefore, Ecoland is not achieving output efficiency.

14.6 Markets, Efficiency, and the Welfare Theorems

The links between the marginal rate of transformation, marginal rate of substitution, and input and output prices have implications for the ability of markets to create efficient outcomes.

In our discussions of exchange, input, and output efficiencies, we acted as if it would be easy to shift input and output allocations through some basic interventions. But, the examples were by nature oversimplified—two inputs, two outputs, two firms, and two consumers. We also had, by virtue of constructing the example ourselves, full knowledge of firms' production functions and consumers' utility functions.

The real economy is vastly more complicated on every front. Trying to centrally coordinate the allocations of inputs to production and consumption bundles to consumers, while also getting the optimal output mix, would be astronomically difficult. Whenever central coordination has been tried on a large scale, as in Communist economies during the twentieth century, it failed quite spectacularly.

Do the harsh realities of this complexity mean that our Pareto-efficient outcomes are only theoretical fantasies? Perhaps not. As we suggested earlier in discussing the relationship between exchange efficiency and utility-maximizing behavior, markets and prices might achieve efficiency even in the absence of an all-knowing, omnipotent economic controller.

In the section on exchange efficiency, we learned that if consumers maximize their utility (taking goods' prices as given), they will end up with the same marginal rates of substitution. Markets can meet the exchange efficiency condition in this way.

On the production side, for any given set of input prices, profit-maximizing firms will choose their input mix so that their marginal rate of technical substitution ($MRTS$) equals the input price ratio. This outcome equates firms' $MRTS$ levels, the condition for input efficiency.

Prices, then, create two of the three efficiency conditions. The final link, output efficiency, ties these two conditions together. One way to think about output efficiency's $MRS = MRT$ condition is that it sets the ratio of goods' prices equal to their marginal costs of production. If the goods are produced by a perfectly competitive industry, price will equal marginal cost. Therefore, the price and cost ratios are equal, satisfying output efficiency while preserving input and exchange efficiency. Decentralized, competitive markets can achieve all three efficiency conditions.

This is the ending we gave away at the start of our discussion of efficiency—markets can create efficient outcomes, even in the absence of interventions and forced allocations, by letting prices do the work: Input prices equate marginal rates of technical substitution in production, and output prices lead to the optimal output mix among producers and cause consumers to equate their marginal rates of substitution. The result, that perfectly competitive markets in general equilibrium distribute resources in a Pareto-efficient way, is called the **First Welfare Theorem.** It formalized Adam Smith's notion of the "invisible hand."

First Welfare Theorem
Theorem stating that perfectly competitive markets in general equilibrium distribute resources in a Pareto-efficient way.

The First Welfare Theorem comes with a lot of conditions. A big one is that firms and consumers take as given all the prices of goods and inputs. In other words, there is no market power. Market power prevents markets from reaching an efficient outcome because the output price ratio, which is now set by producers rather than taken as given, no longer needs to equal the marginal cost ratio. As a result, market power supports markups that drive a wedge between the two ratios and create output inefficiency. If firms or individuals have market power in buying goods, this, too, will create inefficiencies.

The First Welfare Theorem relies on other assumptions we shouldn't ignore. These include the absence of *asymmetric information*, *externalities*, and *public goods*. We discuss exactly what these are and why they can lead to market failures in Chapters 15 and 16.

application

Output Efficiency among Manufacturing Firms in India

We learned how the output-efficient product mix reflects both cost (marginal rate of transformation or MRT) and demand (marginal rate of substitution or MRS) factors, and how well-functioning markets can lead firms to produce that optimal mix. In reality, those cost and demand factors are constantly changing. When changes occur, prices in competitive markets should change accordingly and spur firms to switch to the new optimal product mix.

Economists have documented a lot of evidence that firms, when choosing what products to make, do respond to market signals. In a 2010 study, however, a group of economists found that these sorts of product mix shifts are slower and less frequent among firms in India than in other economies.[10] As a result, India may lag behind other countries in output efficiency.

The study looks at the products made by over 4,000 Indian manufacturing firms and tracks their production of about 2,000 separate products. (To give you an idea of the level of detail this involves, example products from the iron and steel industry include welded steel tubular poles, stranded wire, and malleable iron castings.) Some of the firms made only one product, but many manufactured multiple products.

The results show an interesting contrast. In some ways, Indian firms' production choices look a lot like those in more developed countries. Bigger firms, on average, make a larger variety of products than smaller firms, for example. And when firms grow, they often do it by adding products. However, the results also show that overall product turnover—the frequency with which firms add new products or drop old ones—is significantly lower in India. For example, this "product churn" rate is less than two-thirds that computed using comparable U.S. data. What's particularly interesting is that this lower product turnover does not seem to occur because Indian firms are less likely to start making new products. Instead, they are less likely to drop old ones.

What might this result say about output efficiency in India? As costs and tastes change, the efficient quantity of certain products will rise while others will fall. If markets are working well, prices should change to reflect the new costs and tastes, and firms should respond to these price changes by shifting what they manufacture. More firms will begin making products whose markets are growing. Those making products for which the markets are shrinking will shut down or cut back on the manufacture of such products. This shift allows the inputs used to make those dying products to be put toward making ascending products instead. (Or, it might also be that a product itself isn't dying, but there is a cost change that makes particular firms much less capable of manufacturing the product than before. In this case, those firms can shut down those product lines and allow more able firms to pick up the lost production.)

In India, firms appear reluctant to stop manufacturing products whose consumption levels (and likely profitability) are shrinking. Too many resources are devoted to making low-marginal-utility goods, upsetting the $MRT = MRS$ condition and output efficiency.

Why isn't the market in India output-efficient? The study's authors speculate that the tight regulations on when and how firms can change the level and location of employment (part of the extensive Indian regulatory structure often referred to as the "license raj") make it costly for firms to shut down existing production lines, even if they are making a faltering product or one that is a bad match for their abilities. As a result, the product mix becomes skewed away from the efficient combination and firms make too many things that people don't value very much. ∎

---

[10] Pinelopi K. Goldberg, Amit K. Khandelwal, Nina Pavcnik, and Petia Topalova, "Multiproduct Firms and Product Turnover in the Developing World: Evidence from India," *Review of Economics and Statistics* 92, no. 4 (November 2010): 1042–1049.

As we come to the end of our analysis of the general equilibrium efficiency, remember: Efficiency does not imply equality nor does it have to match anyone's concept of fairness. Efficient markets can (and do) lead to unequal outcomes. Does this mean that any effort to increase equity will necessarily harm efficiency? In theory, no. In practice, however, the answer is often yes.

It is theoretically possible to change how equitable market outcomes are while still ensuring that the outcome is efficient. This result is a prediction of the **Second Welfare Theorem.** This theorem says that (under the same assumptions made for the First Welfare Theorem) any Pareto-efficient equilibrium can be achieved by choosing the right initial allocation of goods. What this means is that, if we want efficient outcomes that are also equitable (by whatever standard we judge this), we can get to those outcomes by being careful about how we initially allocate goods and inputs across consumers and producers. Imagine, for example, shuffling the allocation of goods among consumers along the contract curve from an undesirable unequal market outcome to whatever particular point we feel is most equitable. By doing that, we're changing the allocation in a way that preserves efficiency while moving toward what we believe is a more equal outcome.[11] We could also do similar reshufflings in the input market and along the production possibilities frontier, preserving overall efficiency while obtaining a particular outcome we prefer.

Achieving this goal is not easy. First, there is the practical issue of how society could gather enough information about preferences and production technologies to know what the exact transfers should be. Second, the necessary reallocations would have to be what are called **lump-sum transfers,** transfers to or from an individual where the size of the transfer cannot be affected in any way by the individual's choices. These are the sort of reach-in-and-reshuffle reallocations we imagined the magical economist undertaking in our earlier discussions. In reality, lump-sum transfers are almost never used (and we could probably drop the "almost") because it is difficult to legislate taxes or subsidies that bear absolutely no relation to people's actions.[12]

In reality, governments must try to achieve equity through transfers (taxes and subsidies) that depend on individuals' actions, such as taxes on income and payroll (which depend on how much you work), sales (how much you buy), and property (how valuable your home is), and subsidies like social security payments (which depend on how much you worked in the past and currently), Medicare (how many health services you consume), and so on. The problem is that these kinds of transfers change the relative prices of the actions or goods that are taxed or subsidized. This creates wedges between the costs of goods and services and the post-tax or post-subsidy prices that consumers face, creating losses in efficiency (just as market power does).

This doesn't mean seeking more equitable outcomes is wrong. It just says that there will likely be some inefficiency introduced when trying to promote it.

Second Welfare Theorem
Theorem stating that any given Pareto-efficient allocation in a perfectly competitive market is a general equilibrium outcome for some initial allocation.

lump-sum transfer
Transfer to or from an individual for which the size is unaffected by the individual's choices.

---

[11] Even this precise placement isn't necessary. What is required is that our intervention puts the allocation somewhere on the line that is tangent to consumers' indifference curves at an equitable efficient point. Trade among consumers at the market price (as those with low-marginal-product goods trade with others for high-marginal-product goods) will move any initial allocation on this line to the efficient point.

[12] Lump-sum taxes are also treacherous for politicians. People tend to really despise lump-sum taxes, probably because they feel (correctly) that there is nothing they can do to mitigate the burden of the tax. Indeed, capitation taxes (sometimes called "head taxes")—which are levied on each person regardless of her actions or status—are banned by the U.S. Constitution. Margaret Thatcher's ouster as the United Kingdom's prime minister was in a large part driven by negative popular reaction toward her party's institution of a local tax system that approximated a lump-sum tax structure.

14.7 Conclusion

In this chapter, we saw that all markets are interconnected: What happens in any given individual market affects countless other markets. Take a simple trip to the grocery store to purchase chocolate chip cookie dough ice cream. Before that single container of ice cream could make it into your hands, a Wisconsin dairy farmer milked cows, Brazilian sugar cane was processed and distributed, and the cacao plant was harvested. And that's just three of the many markets that contributed to the production of the ice cream. Many more markets—such as the market that produced the ice cream packaging—were also involved. This coming together of individual markets to produce a single good, and how they jointly influence one another, is one example of general equilibrium in action.

General equilibrium allows us to consider a wide variety of concepts that partial equilibrium cannot address. Issues about the desirability of economic outcomes can be explored using the conditions for exchange, input, and output efficiencies. If certain conditions are met, we saw that the free market will generate an efficient market without any intervention. In reality, however, these conditions are often not met. We've already extensively discussed in Chapters 9–11 one of these breaks in conditions, market power. In Chapters 15 and 16, we look at more ways in which market failures can lead to inefficient outcomes.

Summary

1. In this chapter, we've stepped outside our normal approach of looking at markets in isolation and have instead specifically contemplated how markets are interrelated. This recognition of markets' interrelatedness and explicit accounting for its effects is called **general equilibrium analysis.** It focuses on what is necessary for all markets to be in equilibrium simultaneously and what happens when they are. [**Section 14.1**]

2. General equilibrium analysis allows us to consider fundamental questions about whether market outcomes are desirable. Social welfare functions (functions that summarize the utility levels of every individual in society) are one tool that economists use to make such judgments, but they have several drawbacks. As a result, economists often instead focus on Pareto efficiency as a criterion. A market is **Pareto-efficient** if resources cannot be reallocated without making at least one person worse off. Individual markets must have three types of efficiencies to create economy-wide efficiencies: **exchange efficiency, input efficiency,** and **output efficiency.** [**Section 14.2**]

3. **Edgeworth boxes** display a simple model economy with two consumers and two goods, and allow for an analysis of exchange efficiency. A Pareto-efficient allocation occurs at the tangency point between two consumers' indifference curves. The **consumption contract curve** represents all such Pareto-efficient allocations between any two individuals' consumption of two goods. [**Section 14.3**]

4. Input efficiency considers the production side of the economy, and occurs where two firms' isoquants are tangent, or where the firms' marginal rates of technical substitution are equal. The **production contract curve** maps out these efficient allocations across two producers, while the **production possibilities frontier (PPF)** looks at the possible output combinations of two goods given efficient production. [**Section 14.4**]

5. Output efficiency links the concepts of exchange and input efficiency, and exists when the tradeoffs on the consumption and production side of the economy are equal. The tradeoff between the production of any two goods is the **marginal rate of transformation (MRT),** equal to the slope of the production possibilities frontier. When the marginal rate of transformation equals the marginal rate of substitution (the consumption tradeoff), a market has achieved output efficiency. [**Section 14.5**]

6. Under certain conditions, markets can lead to efficiency without any interventions being necessary. The **First Welfare Theorem** shows

how markets can result in Pareto-efficient distributions of goods. The **Second Welfare Theorem** states that every Pareto-efficient allocation is a general equilibrium outcome for some initial allocation. While the conditions that lead to market efficiency may not always hold in the real world, the market efficiency result is nevertheless a powerful finding that strengthens our understanding of both market efficiencies and market failures. [**Section 14.6**]

Review Questions

1. Describe the two branches of general equilibrium analysis.
2. Social welfare functions combine the utility levels of everyone in society into a single index. List three types of social welfare functions and discuss what they mean.
3. How do economists generally define efficiency in a market?
4. What are the three requirements of an efficient market?
5. What can the Edgeworth box be used to examine? What does an Edgeworth box plot?
6. What is the relationship between consumers' marginal rates of substitution and the goods' prices in an efficient market? How can this relationship be seen in an Edgeworth box?
7. How does the consumption contract curve relate to Pareto efficiency?
8. What does input efficiency imply about the relationship between the marginal rate of technical substitution and input prices? How can this relationship be seen in an Edgeworth box?
9. How does the production contract curve relate to Pareto efficiency?
10. How does the production possibilities frontier relate to the marginal rate of transformation?
11. What conditions are required for the First Welfare Theorem to hold?
12. What does the Second Welfare Theorem predict?

Problems (Solutions to problems marked * appear at the back of this book. Problems adapted to use calculus are available online at http://worthpublishers.com/GLS1e)

1. Peanut butter has always been thought to be a delicious, wholesome food. That is, until the FDA releases its Food Defect Guidelines that set maximum allowable amounts of rodent excreta that may be present in every jar (surprisingly, the maximum is not zero!). Following this release, the demand for peanut butter falls.
   a. What is the immediate effect on the price of peanut butter and the quantity consumed?
   b. Peanut butter and jelly are complements. What is the residual effect on the price of jelly?
   c. What effect does the change in the price of jelly you indicated in part (b) have on the demand for peanut butter?
   d. Does the demand effect you indicated in part (c) tend to push peanut butter prices and quantities back toward their original values, or farther away from them?
*2. Following a renewable fuels mandate in 2005, the demand for yellow corn, the key ingredient in ethanol, skyrocketed.

   a. What is the immediate effect of the increase in demand on the price and quantity of yellow corn?
   b. Yellow corn and white corn (the key ingredient in corn tortillas) are substitutes in production. As a result of the changes in the market for yellow corn, what happens to the supply of white corn?
   c. How does the changing supply of white corn affect its market price?
   d. As the price of white corn changes, what effect does that change have on the supply of yellow corn? Indicate the likely effects on both the price and quantity of yellow corn produced.
   e. Does the change in the price of white corn tend to push yellow corn prices and quantities back toward their initial values, or farther away from them?
*3. The following statements describe supply and demand conditions in the markets for cheese and wine, respectively.

- The demand for cheese is given by $Q_c^d = 30 - P_c - P_w$, where Q_c^d is the quantity of cheese demanded each week in ounces, P_c is the price of a pound of cheese, and P_w is the price of a bottle of wine.
- The demand for wine is given by $Q_w^d = 30 - P_c - P_w$.
- The supply of cheese is given by $Q_c^s = P_c$.
- The supply of wine is given by $Q_w^s = P_w$.

a. Are wine and cheese linked on the supply side of the market, or on the demand side?

b. Equate supply and demand in the cheese market, and simplify to express the price of cheese as a function of the price of wine.

c. Equate supply and demand in the wine market, and simplify to express the price of wine as a function of the price of cheese.

d. Substitute the expression for the price of wine you found in (c) into the equation you found in (b) to solve for the price of cheese.

e. Plug the price you calculated in (d) into the expression you derived in (c) to solve for the price of wine.

f. Plug the prices of wine and cheese you found in (d) and (e) back into either the supply or demand functions for wine and cheese to find the equilibrium quantities of wine and cheese that will be sold.

4. Consider the wine and cheese problem you solved in Problem 3. Suppose the demand for wine changes so that at every price, 10 fewer bottles are demanded.

a. Hold the price of cheese constant, and calculate the partial equilibrium effects of the change in the demand for wine. What happens to the price? What happens to the quantity?

b. Plug the new price of wine into the demand for cheese. Does the shock to the wine market cause the demand for cheese to increase or decrease?

c. Calculate the effect of the change in demand for cheese on the price of cheese and the quantity of cheese sold.

d. Plug the new price of cheese into the demand for wine. Does it cause the demand for wine to increase or decrease? Does the wine market get pushed farther from its initial equilibrium, or back toward it? How will these changes in the wine market feed back into the cheese market?

e. Following the steps taken in Problem 3, but using the new cheese demand function, solve for the new general equilibrium price and quantity of both wine and cheese.

f. How does the final general equilibrium price and quantity of wine you calculated in (e) compare to the partial equilibrium effects you calculated in part (a)?

5. Suppose that lettuce and tomatoes are goods that are related on the demand side of the market, and that both markets are in equilibrium. George and Janet are analyzing the effect of an increase in the demand for tomatoes. George is using a partial equilibrium framework, and Janet is using a general equilibrium framework.

a. True or False: George will predict a larger increase in the price of tomatoes than Janet will. Explain.

b. True or False: George will predict a larger increase in the quantity of tomatoes sold than Janet will. Explain.

c. True or False: The answers to parts (a) and (b) depend on whether lettuce and tomatoes are complements or substitutes. Explain.

6. In the central United States, farm ground is devoted to corn and beans as far as the eye can see. The supply of beans (in millions of bushels) is given by $Q_b^s = 2P_b - P_c$. The supply of corn is given by $Q_c^s = 2P_c - P_b$. Let the demand for beans be given by $Q_b^d = 30 - P_b$, and the demand for corn be given by $Q_c^d = 30 - P_c$.

a. Solve the general equilibrium price and quantity of both beans and corn. (*Hint*: If you have trouble with this step, follow the procedures outlined in Problem 3.)

b. Suppose there is a shock to bean demand, so that the quantity demanded at each price increases by 8 million bushels. The new demand for beans can be written as $Q_b^d = 38 - P_b$. Solve for the new general equilibrium price and quantity of beans and corn.

c. What happens to the price of beans and the quantity sold as a result of the demand increase?

d. What happens to the price of corn and quantity sold as a result of the increase in the demand for beans? Explain.

7. You are a USDA pork analyst, charged with keeping up to date on developments in the market for "the other white meat." Recently, the demand for beef decreased.

a. Explain how pork and beef might be linked on the demand side of the market.

b. Explain how pork and beef might be linked on the supply side of the market.

c. You notice that within a few months, the overall quantity of pork being sold increases. Is this fact consistent with a demand-side link between beef and pork, or a supply-side link?

8. Bob, Carol, and Ted are residents of a tiny commune in darkest Peru. Bob currently has a utility level (U_b) of 55 utils, Carol's utility (U_c) is 35 utils, and Ted's utility (U_t) is 10 utils. Alice, the benevolent ruler of the commune, has discovered a policy that will allow her to redistribute utility between any two people she chooses in a util-to-util transfer.

   a. If Alice believes the social welfare function is given by $W = \min(U_b, U_c, U_t)$,

      i. Recommend a transfer that will improve social welfare, if any such transfers are possible.

      ii. What is the highest level of welfare that the commune can achieve, and how must utility be divided among Bob, Carol, and Ted?

   b. If Alice believes the social welfare function is given by $W = U_b + U_c + U_t$,

      i. Recommend a transfer that will improve social welfare, if any such transfers are possible.

      ii. What is the highest level of welfare that the commune can achieve, and how must utility be divided among Bob, Carol, and Ted?

   c. If Alice believes the social welfare function is given by $W = U_b \times U_c \times U_t$,

      i. Recommend a transfer that will improve social welfare, if any such transfers are possible.

      ii. What is the highest level of welfare that the commune can achieve, and how must utility be divided among Bob, Carol, and Ted?

9. Al has found $1,000 and has decided to divide it between his children, Bud and Kelly.

   a. If Al believes that a fair division means giving equal amounts of cash to everyone, how much should he give to Bud and Kelly?

   b. Suppose that Bud is rich and Kelly is poor. Assume that the marginal utility provided by a dollar declines the richer you are. If Al wishes to ensure that his gift provides the greatest possible collective happiness to his children, how should he divide the cash?

   c. Suppose that Bud is rich and Kelly is poor. Assume that the marginal utility provided by a dollar declines the richer you are. If Al is concerned with distributing equal happiness to Bud and Kelly, how should he divide the cash?

   d. How do each of your answers to (a), (b), and (c) align with some notion of fairness?

10. Abel, Baker, and Charlie are identical triplets with identical tastes. The utility they get from consuming various amounts of bacon, eggs, and cheese is summarized in the following table:

# of Units Consumed	Utility from Bacon	Utility from Eggs	Utility from Cheese
1	100	60	80
2	155	110	135
3	175	150	183
5	190	180	210
5	200	200	225

Thus, if Abel has 4 pieces of bacon and 3 eggs, his total utility will be 190 + 150, or 340.

   a. Suppose that Abel initially has 5 pieces of bacon, Baker has 5 eggs, and Charlie has 5 pieces of cheese. Assuming that bacon, eggs, and cheese all trade one-for-one in the marketplace, suggest a series of Pareto-improving trades that will raise everyone's overall utility.

   b. What allocation does each end up with when all gains are exhausted?

   c. Show that once all gains are exhausted, if we force Abel to trade any of his goods for any of Baker's goods, neither will be made better off, and at least one will be made worse off.

*11. Consider the Edgeworth box diagram below, which illustrates the amount of peaches and cream in the refrigerator of Billy Joe and Bobby Sue.

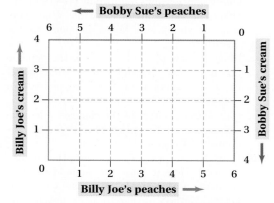

   a. How many peaches do Billy Joe and Bobby Sue have in their fridge?

   b. How much cream do Billy Joe and Bobby Sue have in their fridge?

   c. Suppose that Billy Joe pulls 5 peaches and 1 pint of cream out of the fridge, and says, "You can have the rest" to Bobby Sue. Illustrate this allocation of peaches and cream by placing a point in the Edgeworth box. Label the point "A."

d. Bobby Sue pulls the remaining peaches and cream out of the refrigerator, and comments, "Hey—I'm a bit long on cream and short on peaches here. Give me a couple of your peaches and take one of my creams." Represent this reallocation of peaches and cream by placing a second point in the Edgeworth box. Label the point "B."

e. Billy Joe happens to find a couple of extra peaches behind last night's gnocchi leftovers, and proudly proclaims, "Finders keepers!" Represent the effects of Billy Joe's discovery by altering your Edgeworth box. Assume that Bobby Sue acknowledges and respects the "finders, keepers" rule.

12. Consider the Edgeworth box below, which represents the amount of tea and crumpets available to Eliza and Henry.

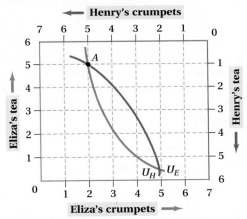

a. Suppose that Eliza and Henry are currently at point *A*. How many servings of tea and how many crumpets are each enjoying?

b. Suppose that while Eliza is using the powder room, Henry takes 4 cups of tea from Eliza. Feeling guilty, he leaves 2 of his crumpets on her nightstand before hastily making his exit. Show that this reallocation of tea and crumpets is a Pareto improvement.

c. Show that if Henry had left only 1 crumpet on Eliza's nightstand, the reallocation would not have represented a Pareto improvement.

13. Johnny and June are divorcing and must divide their music collection, which contains two types of music: country and folk. A mediator suggests an initial division of the collection. Given the initial division, Johnny's *MRS* between folk and country is 3, and June's *MRS* is 1.

a. Use an Edgeworth box to show that the allocation of music is inefficient. Be sure to draw indifference curves for both Johnny and June, and to show their respective marginal rates of substitution at the initial allocation.

b. Suggest a general reallocation that could potentially make both parties better off. Explain who would have to give up folk music and who would have to give up country.

c. After some reallocation, Johnny's *MRS* and June's *MRS* are equal. Show that the allocation is Pareto-efficient.

14. Consider the following Edgeworth box diagram that illustrates the preferences of Ed and Peggy for fish and chips.

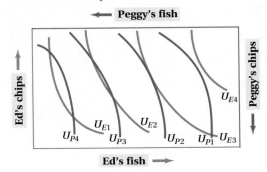

Draw the consumption contract curve corresponding to these preferences. (*Hint*: You may need to add some indifference curves to the diagram.)

*15. Chris and Pat like both beer and pizza. Chris views pizza and beer as perfect one-to-one substitutes. Pat believes that beer and pizza are perfect complements, and always consumes them in one-to-one proportions.

a. Construct an Edgeworth box for Chris and Pat.

b. Derive the contract curve for Chris and Pat. What shape will it take?

16. Bill and Ted like apples and oranges. Bill is always willing to substitute 1 apple for 1 orange. Ted is always willing to substitute 1 apple for 2 oranges.

a. Assume that there are 10 apples and 10 oranges to split between Bill and Ted. Construct an appropriately sized Edgeworth box for them.

b. Draw indifference curves for both Bill and Ted in your Edgeworth box. Draw Bill's indifference curves with thick lines, and Ted's with thin lines. (*Hint*: Remember that both Bill and Ted believe that apples and oranges are perfect substitutes!)

c. Demonstrate that any initial allocation of apples and oranges in which Bill and Ted each have some apples and some oranges is Pareto-inefficient.

d. Find a few Pareto-efficient allocations; then shade the consumption contract curve. (*Hint*: You showed in part (c) that both parties having both goods couldn't be efficient!)

*17. The Edgeworth box below shows how castaways Tom and Hank are allocating labor and capital to the production of two goods, food and clothing.

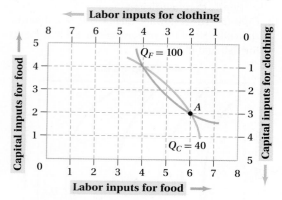

The economy is currently at point *A*.

a. How many units of labor and capital are being used in the production of each good?

b. How many units of food are being produced? Clothing?

c. Suggest a simple reallocation of labor and capital between food and clothing that will enable Tom and Hank to enjoy more food and clothing than they currently produce.

18. On a small tropical island, two firms draw on the same supply of labor and capital. The first firm produces fish, and in the fishing industry the marginal product of labor is 8 and the marginal product of capital is 5. The second firm produces coconut, and in the coconut industry the marginal product of labor is 64 and the marginal product of capital is 32.

a. Show that the allocation of labor and capital between the two industries is inefficient.

b. Suggest a reallocation of labor and capital that will enable the island to produce more fish and coconuts without using more resources.

*19. Consider the production contract curve in the graph below which illustrates efficient allocations of labor and capital to the production of two goods, guns and roses.

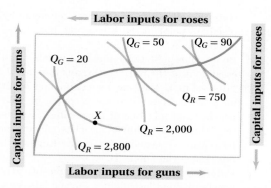

a. Use the information in the production contract curve to draw the production possibilities frontier for guns and roses. Put roses on the horizontal axis and guns on the vertical axis. Assume that when all resources are devoted to gun production, 100 guns can be produced; when all resources are devoted to rose production, 3,000 roses can be grown.

b. Locate point *X* in the Edgeworth box. Draw a corresponding point *X* on your production possibilities frontier. Be as accurate as possible in locating this point.

20. Consider the production possibilities frontier depicted below, which shows the different combinations of guns and roses an economy can produce when it uses all its inputs efficiently.

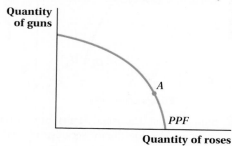

a. If the *MRT* at point *A* is 2.0, and the marginal product of labor in the gun industry is 12, what must the marginal product of labor be in the rose industry?

b. If, at point *A*, the marginal product of capital in the gun industry is 6, what must the marginal product of capital in the rose industry be?

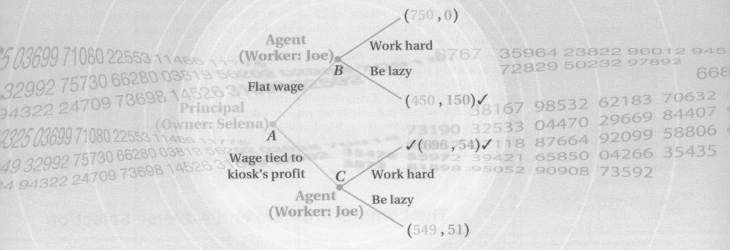

There's a good chance you've been in the market for a used car (and if you haven't yet shopped for a used car, chances are you will soon!). About 35 million used cars and small trucks are sold each year in the United States, far more than the roughly 12 million new vehicles that are sold.[1] One of the concerns you probably had was the quality of the car you were considering for purchase. A number of worries may have run through your head. If you dealt with an individual seller, you may have wondered why that person decided to sell the car. Did he expect it to break down soon? Had it already started to give him problems that he knows about but that can't be seen from casual observation? If you bought from a dealership, you may have wondered where it got the car. Was it a rental before, abused by a series of uncaring, non-owner drivers who drove it over railroad tracks at 60 miles per hour? Was it repossessed from an owner who couldn't afford to make the payments, much less keep up with its maintenance? Would the dealer honor the warranty if problems later developed?

[1] U.S. Department of Transportation. *National Transportation Statistics 2012.*

The analyses we've done to this point don't fully capture the economics of such a situation and many others like it. That's because in all the topics and issues we've analyzed throughout the book, we assumed that economic decision makers know everything relevant about the markets in which they operate. In our models thus far, consumers know all the attributes of the goods they are buying and how intensively they will use them. Likewise, firms know how hard their employees will work, or how talented they are at their jobs. That is, they've described markets with **complete information**—all market participants know everything important for making economic decisions.

In the real world, however, information is neither free nor commonly shared among all parties in a transaction. Economists need an extra set of tools to understand what happens in these types of situations, and in this chapter we discuss these tools. Specifically, we look at markets in which one party knows more than the other about the goods or services being traded. Economists' term for this imbalance in knowledge is **asymmetric information**.[2]

Asymmetric information can have a profound impact on markets—an impact that is, from a social standpoint, quite negative. If the information gaps are large enough, in fact, it is theoretically possible for a market to *completely shut down* even if everyone could benefit from trade if it occurred! Interestingly, the people who suffer from such market failure include not only those with an information disadvantage, but also those who hold the extra information. We'll explain why below. Given that asymmetric information can destroy the large gains in consumer and producer surplus that occur from markets, it's not surprising that many institutions have arisen to mitigate such effects. We talk about these institutions in this chapter as well.

complete information
Situation in which all participants in an economic transaction know the relevant information.

asymmetric information
A situation in which there is an imbalance of information across participants in an economic transaction.

lemons problem
An asymmetric information problem that occurs when a seller knows more about the quality of the good he is selling than does the buyer.

15.1 The Lemons Problem and Adverse Selection

A common manifestation of asymmetric information in markets is the **lemons problem.** This problem exists when the sellers know more about the quality of a good they are selling than the buyer does. The used car example in the introduction is one such case. It is, in fact, the origin of the problem's name, because poor-quality cars are sometimes referred to as "lemons." The issue was first formalized by the economist George Akerlof in 1970.[3]

To see how damaging the lemons problem can be to markets, consider the following example. (It is clearly simplistic, but this makes clearer what the effect is, the way it works, and why it can cause such difficulties.) Suppose there are two types of used cars: good ones (we'll call them "plums") and bad ones ("lemons"). Half of used cars are plums, and the other half are lemons. Potential buyers value plums at $10,000, but lemons have no value to them. Sellers value plums at $8,000 and also have no value for lemons.

Observable Quality

Let's start by thinking about this market if the quality of cars were observable to both the sellers (the current owners of the cars) and the buyers. Because sellers value plums at only $8,000 and buyers value them at $10,000, the half of used cars that are of good

---

[2] Economic situations with *symmetric information*—meaning that all participants in a transaction share the same knowledge—include both cases of complete information as well as cases in which market participants don't have full knowledge, but they are *equally* ignorant.

[3] George Akerlof, "The Market for 'Lemons': Quality Uncertainty and the Market Mechanism," *The Quarterly Journal of Economics* 84, no. 3 (August 1970): 488–500. Akerlof earned the right to name the problem—he actually called it the "Lemons Principle"—by virtue of being the first to formalize it. It is good that he chose the name as modestly as he did; it's easier to remember how to correctly spell "lemons" than "Akerlof."

quality will sell at prices between $8,000 and $10,000. (Any price in this range will suffice.) Both parties are better off because of the trade. Buyers value the cars more than their former owners did, and the cars are sold at a price that makes both the buyer and seller no worse off than had no trade occurred (in fact, at least one of them *must* be better off). Lemons have no value to either their current owners or potential buyers. Therefore, no lemons will be sold, and no one is better or worse off for it.

Thus, the outcome when quality is fully observable to everyone is that buyers and sellers in the market are at least as well off—and many are better off—because of the transactions in the used car market. This is the way in which well-functioning markets work and raise the welfare of the markets' participants.

Unobservable Quality

Now let's consider what would happen under asymmetric information, when sellers know if their cars are plums or lemons, but buyers do not. (It's easy to imagine that car owners know more about the quality of their own cars than do potential buyers. They've been operating them firsthand and have experienced all of the cars' functional problems.) All that buyers know is that half of used cars available for sale are plums and half are lemons. They therefore recognize that the probability any particular car is of good quality is 50%.

What is the most that a buyer would now be willing to pay for a used car? Since he values a plum at $10,000 and a lemon at $0, and a car has a 50% chance of being either, the most a buyer would be willing to pay for a used car is ($10,000 × 0.50) + ($0 × 0.50) = $5,000. Anything more than that and he will be worse off in expectation: Any one car only has an expected value of $5,000.

Now, let's think about the owner of a plum who is considering whether to sell it. This seller values his car at $8,000. But, he recognizes that, because buyers can't know for sure whether or not his car is a plum, he could never get more than $5,000 by selling it. As a result, the seller doesn't offer his quality car for sale. Of course, an owner of a lemon *would* be more than willing to sell his car at $5,000—he has no value for his lemon car, after all. But, here's the problem: Buyers, who are not naïve, recognize that the owners of good cars don't want to sell when the most buyers would pay for a car is $5,000. Therefore, any used car available for sale *must* be a lemon. Since buyers have no value for lemons, they are not willing to buy any used car that is actually offered for sale at any price.

Now the tragedy of the lemons problem is apparent. We have a situation in which we know that if information were equally known by both buyers and sellers, there would be a large set of used car sales that would make people better off (because buyers value the plum cars more than their former owners did). But when there are information asymmetries, no sales take place. There is *no* market. All those potential gains from exchange are destroyed because one side knows more than the other.

Adverse Selection

This example brings up two important points about asymmetric information and the lemons problem. The first is that the existence of quality differences is not, by itself, the cause of difficulties. If there were complete information in the market and the quality of products were common knowledge, higher-quality products would have higher prices and lower-quality products would have lower prices. (Here, those prices would be between $8,000 and $10,000 for high-quality cars and $0 for lemons.) Those consumers with a high valuation for quality will pay a premium for it, and those who place less importance on quality can buy the cheaper (monetarily and figuratively) versions if they wish. But, there's no unnecessary reduction in exchange in this case: Every buyer who is willing to pay more for a good than it is worth to the seller will be able to buy it. In other words, the market is efficiently allocating goods.

The lemons problem arises when information about quality is not known by both buyer and seller. This asymmetry gums up the works because it leads to poor-quality goods being disproportionately put on sale. That is, the average quality of items *that are offered for sale* is lower than the average quality of all such items, *including those not for sale*. This is exactly what happened in the simple example above: The average value of used cars to buyers was $5,000, but the average value of those actually offered for sale was $0. This prevents trades from happening that otherwise would if information were equally distributed.

When there are stronger incentives for "bad" types of a product to be involved in a transaction than "good" types of the product, we call that **adverse selection** (so named because the selection of types into the market tilts adversely toward those of bad quality). In our used car case, lemons are the "bad" types. They are disproportionately likely to be put up for sale because buyers can't tell the difference between lemons and good cars. This makes the price buyers are willing to pay for a used car of uncertain quality too low to induce owners of good cars to sell. The sellers who *are* willing to offer their cars for sale at this price must therefore be lemon owners. (Adverse selection on the buy side of the market can also cause problems. We'll see that below in our discussion of the insurance market.)

The second important point in this example is that information asymmetry harms not only those with less information, but also those who have *more* information. Both sides lose because information asymmetries keep sales from taking place that would have benefited both buyers and sellers. In our example, buyers and owners of good used cars suffer because they miss out on trades that would happen if each side knew the car's quality. Paradoxically, rather than their information edge being an advantage for the sellers, it is a hindrance.

Could sellers get around this problem by telling potential buyers that their car is indeed a plum? Wouldn't this get rid of the information asymmetry and regain the benefits of exchange? Unfortunately, no. The problem is that lemon sellers have an incentive to lie about the quality of their cars. These sellers will try to pass their cars off as plums (being truthful can't improve the value of their car in buyers' eyes, but perhaps a sale might go through if they lie). If buyers recognize this incentive to lie, simply stating one's car is a plum won't be informative about its true quality. Without additional information, a buyer wouldn't be able to tell a plum *seller* (claiming a high-quality car) from a lemon *seller* (also claiming a high-quality car) any better than he can tell a plum from a lemon. However, there are ways that sellers of good cars can credibly convey this information to buyers. We will discuss them further below.

The specific example we ran through above was, as we said, purposely simplistic. Lemons problems usually don't completely destroy markets. After all, we see plenty of cars purchased in the used car market in the real world. However, adverse selection can still reduce trade to a level below what is economically efficient. The vicious cycle of uncertain quality still reduces buyers' willingness to pay, leading in turn to low-quality cars being disproportionately offered for sale, further reducing buyers' willingness to pay and exacerbating adverse selection, and on and on. In our simple example, this feedback process was so strong that buyers were unwilling to pay for *any* car brought to market, since it was sure to be a lemon. But, real-world factors usually slow down the adverse-selection feedback before it completely spins the market into oblivion.

For example, in reality there is a much broader distribution of quality among used cars than the two-type distribution in our example. Furthermore, buyers and sellers don't all have the same value for each type. These factors tend to diminish the disastrous effect of information asymmetries on markets. There will be disproportionately more "worse" types offered for sale, and the amount of trade will still be inefficiently low, but cars will be bought and sold.

---

adverse selection
A situation in which market characteristics lead to more low-quality goods and fewer high-quality goods being put on the market.

Adverse selection is why, when considering buying a used car, you are likely to have the type of concerns about quality discussed in the introduction to this chapter. You recognize, for example, that the late-model Kia you are considering is likely to be of lower quality than the average late-model Kia, because owners satisfied with their current Kias are less likely to put them on the market. This holds down your willingness to pay for such cars, reinforcing in turn the reluctance of owners of good-quality Kias to sell them.

Other Examples of the Lemons Problem

Potential lemons problems abound in the economy. We've discussed the canonical example—used cars—but "lemons" can exist in any market where the quality of a product is better known by the seller than by the buyer. Used goods other than cars are obvious examples. Online sales might be especially vulnerable to lemons issues: Transactions are not face-to-face, and potential buyers typically cannot physically inspect the product beforehand.

Adverse selection is common in services and factor (input) markets, too. People seeking to remodel their homes often confront the lemons problem, for example. It is difficult to judge the quality of workmanship one could expect from a tradesperson. This concern might make homeowners reluctant to offer adequate compensation to contractors who bid on a job. But, this reluctance would, in turn, reduce the likelihood of a high-quality (but expensive) contractor taking the job, making it instead more likely that a contractor who would take a job at this lower pay level is incompetent.

In input markets, lemons problems can show up in used capital sales. Trucks, machine tools, and even buildings are often bought from sellers who know more about their quality than buyers. Labor markets can have their own adverse selection issues. Suppose workers differ in, and know, their "quality"—which could be their willingness to work hard, their honesty, or their knowledge of the tasks necessary for the job. If an employer could readily observe the quality type of any worker, it could pay him his marginal product (which will be higher for higher-quality workers), and everything would be fine. But, if the employer can't easily tell good workers from bad, it will only be willing to offer a wage equal to an average of the marginal products of the different worker types. This result can make higher-quality workers less likely to apply for a job, and lower-quality workers will be adversely selected in the applicant pool.

Institutions That Mitigate Lemons Problems

Because lemons problems can destroy so much economic value by keeping beneficial exchanges from happening, many institutions in real-world markets have been set up to lessen information asymmetries, if not eliminate them altogether. We'll again start with the example of the used car market, but the lessons we draw from this can be much more general. Many of the mechanisms that work to reduce adverse selection in the used car market act similarly in many other markets. We'll talk about a few specific cases later on.

Institutions and market mechanisms that address asymmetric information in the used car market basically work in one of three ways. One set acts to solve the asymmetric information problem directly, by giving buyers the ability to observe a car's quality before any transaction. The second set of institutions works by punishing sellers who try to sell cars they know are lemons but still pass them off as higher quality. The third set reduces adverse selection by increasing the number of high-quality used cars brought to market. Note that the second and third sets of mechanisms don't allow buyers to observe car qualities directly. Instead, the second set creates incentives for sellers to be truthful about quality, even if it's still not observable before the transaction. The third set increases the average quality of used cars offered for sale by creating incentives for owners to put good-quality used cars on the market. We'll discuss some examples of each type of mechanism in this section.

Reducing Asymmetric Information Directly There are several ways potential buyers can learn about the quality of a used car. Buyers can have a trusted mechanic who is not affiliated with the seller check out the car before agreeing to purchase it, for example. Owners can make their cars' ownership and maintenance records available. (Remember our earlier discussion about why sellers may take the initiative to close the information gap, even though they know more about quality than buyers. Both parties lose—even the one with more information—when the lemons problem keeps mutually beneficial exchanges from happening.)

Some companies have made a successful business model out of reducing information asymmetries. Autocheck and Carfax specialize in providing information about used cars. Customers can type a car's unique Vehicle Information Number into either company's Web site and immediately see the ownership history of the car, and sometimes the maintenance records, too. This is valuable information for buyers, but again sellers also benefit from the service. In fact, a large fraction of Autocheck and Carfax searches are paid for not by buyers, but instead by auto dealers who have bought subscriptions that allow their customers to do background searches on cars the buyers are considering.

Incentives for Truthful Quality Reporting The second set of institutions reduces the lemons problem by making it costly for sellers to be dishonest about their cars' quality. These mechanisms can work even if they don't actually give the buyer all the information about the car that the seller knows.

A classic example of this type of mechanism is reputation, a potential buyer's perception of a seller. Businesses that operate honestly (by selling good-quality cars or, when selling lower-quality cars, by disclosing this and selling at an appropriately discounted price) will develop a reputation for doing so. This makes consumers more likely to do business with them. Dishonest dealers, on the other hand, will suffer when word gets out about their practices. There are, of course, limits to reputation. The stereotypical checkered-blazer used car salesman seen in the movies and on TV, while an obvious caricature, probably didn't arise out of the blue. Reputation incentives work best when a business expects to operate for a long time, because a good reputation pays off in increased business in the future. A "fly-by-night" seller may be willing to cheat to make a quick buck today, knowing he will have moved on to something else before his loss of reputation would really matter.

Warranties also reduce adverse selection. High-quality car sellers can communicate the value of their cars to buyers by offering to fix any problems that occur within a reasonable amount of time after the sale or even return the buyer's money if he is unsatisfied. Just as with reputation, warranties don't solve the lemons problem by getting rid of the asymmetric information. They instead give sellers an incentive to be truthful about the quality of their cars. It's expensive—too expensive—for a seller to offer a warranty on a car he knows is a lemon. The seller has, as they say, "put his money where his mouth is." Recognizing this, if a buyer sees that a car will be sold under warranty, he can reasonably infer that it is a higher-quality car. Cars without warranties are likely to be lower-quality. (And that's fine, again as long as the price reflects their lower-quality levels.)[4]

---

[4] The fact that warranties are relatively less expensive to offer for good cars rather than bad ones, and therefore act as an effective way for buyers to distinguish between otherwise unobservable quality, means that warranties are what economists call *signals*. Signals are a particular type of solution to asymmetric information problems that we discuss in more detail later in the chapter.

Well-designed legislation and regulation can also counteract adverse selection. Most states have "lemon laws." As the name suggests, these laws focus on conditions that must be met in auto sales. The laws essentially mandate short-term warranties for dealer-sold used cars under a specified age and mileage limits. While enforcement costs can limit their power, these warranty mandates help keep low-quality cars out of the part of the market covered by lemon laws. Note that it is not a good idea to keep low-quality used cars from being sold altogether. There are people who would prefer them given their budgets and tastes as long as these cars are priced appropriately. Again, what's important is not that low-quality cars are removed from the market, but rather that all potential buyers recognize them as such.

Increasing the Average Quality of Cars Placed on the Market   The lemons problem can be mitigated if something reduces adverse selection. Bringing more plums onto the market, even if the quality of individual cars is still unobservable, would achieve this. Raising the average quality of cars available increases buyers' willingness to pay for used cars. This increase in demand further encourages owners of higher-quality used cars to sell. In the end, the amount of trade in the market rises, making both buyers and sellers better off.

Leasing programs are one way to make this happen. With a lease, a buyer or "lessee" takes ownership of a car for a set period of time, with the option to return the car to the seller (the "lessor") at the end of the contract period. By encouraging the return of vehicles at a predetermined date regardless of their quality, leasing increases the number of higher-quality cars on the used car market and reduces adverse selection.

Beyond Used Cars   These examples show that the lemons problem, while potentially very damaging to markets, also offers powerful incentives for people and firms to take actions that limit its reach. The examples discussed all involve the used car market, but it is easy to find similarly structured mechanisms working in other markets with asymmetric information.

For instance, we see similar institutions at work in our home repair services and labor market examples discussed earlier. In home repair, referral networks enable homeowners to learn more about contractors' performance and specialties before they hire them. Angie's List is a company that compiles grades on contractors from their previous clients. Homeowners can use these grades when considering which contractor to hire. (Plain evidence of such information's value is the fact that over half a million people have purchased memberships allowing them to view these grades.) Angie's List and other business rating organizations like the Better Business Bureau also enhance the benefits to contractors of preserving a good reputation.

Referrals and reputations also play an obvious role in labor markets. You normally list references on your résumé. Firms often check with these references and previous employers about a potential employee's performance. Other institutions—schools, trades associations, and so on—act as third parties that certify competence at various tasks. There are even "warranties" of sorts in labor markets. Employees are often hired on a provisional basis at pay rates below their position's typical pay, or they work for some period as a probationary employee, a status that makes it easier for the firm to break off employment. These types of arrangements let firms "try out" a worker at relatively low cost before committing to a longer-term agreement.

These examples are good news. Even though the lemons problem can be potentially very damaging, it has spurred the creation of market institutions that moderate its impact. In some cases, these institutions are so effective that they remove completely the effects of information asymmetries on the number of trades that take place. Nevertheless, it's important to remember that this doesn't mean the lemons problem doesn't influence those markets or their participants. Buyers are still going to be concerned about the quality of the used car they are considering, for instance. It's just that the buyers will be better able to obtain a good sense of the car's quality before purchase.

15.1 figure it out

Suppose that consumers value a high-quality used laptop computer at a price of $400, while they value a low-quality used laptop at $100. The supply of high-quality laptops is $Q_H = P_H - 100$, while the supply of low-quality laptops is $Q_L = 2P_L - 50$. Potential buyers cannot tell the difference between high-quality and low-quality laptops when purchasing one.

a. Assume that buyers believe there is a 50% probability that a used laptop will be of high quality. What would be the price that buyers are willing to pay for any used laptop?

b. If the price determined in (a) is offered in the market for used laptops, how many high-quality laptops will be made available in the market? How many low-quality laptops will be available in the market? Are buyers correct in their assumption that 50% of the used laptops available for sale are of high quality? Explain.

c. What would you expect to happen over time as information about the true odds of buying a high-quality used laptop becomes known? Explain.

Solution:

a. If buyers expect that 50% of the used laptops available are of high quality (meaning that the other 50% are of low quality), then the expected value of a laptop is equal to

$$0.50 \times \$400 + 0.50 \times \$100 = \$200 + \$50 = \$250$$

Therefore, $250 would be the most that buyers are willing to pay for a used laptop.

b. If the price of a used laptop is $250, then the quantity supplied of high-quality laptops is $Q_H = P_H - 100 = 250 - 100 = 150$. The quantity supplied of low-quality used laptops is $Q_L = 2P_L - 50 = 2(250) - 50 = 500 - 50 = 450$.

Therefore, there will be 600 used laptops for sale (150 of high quality and 450 of low quality). The probability of buying a used laptop of high quality is not 50%, but actually equal to 150/600 = 0.25 or 25%. Because of asymmetric information, buyers are not willing to pay a very high price for a used laptop. Therefore, the owners of high-quality laptops will be reluctant to sell them, while the owners of low-quality laptops will be eager to sell them. This changes the proportion available in the market.

c. Over time, buyers will adjust their expected value of used laptops. This will further reduce the price buyers are willing to pay. Owners of high-quality used laptops will be even less inclined to sell them, reducing even more the proportion of high-quality used laptops available. Ultimately, it is possible that the market could end up with only low-quality used laptops available.

 **application**

Reputations in Collectibles Sales

Collectibles like coins, stamps, and antiques have inherent lemons problems. The subtlest of differences, at least as perceived by experts, can cause otherwise similar items to vary greatly in quality and resale value. Expert dealers can use their superior knowledge about what affects the quality of such goods to take advantage of less knowledgeable buyers. Some recent research has looked closely at how reputation mechanisms reduce this sort of asymmetric information problem in collectibles markets.

Luís Cabral and Ali Hortaçsu investigated a key reputation mechanism on eBay: feedback scores.[5] Buyers and sellers on eBay can comment on and rate (positive, negative, or neutral) their interactions. Ratings histories allow buyers and sellers to build reputations for fair dealing by engaging in a number of transactions where the other party is satisfied (and willing to state this). Dishonest actions like misrepresenting a product's quality can be reported to discourage others from dealing with the scofflaw.

Cabral and Hortaçsu looked specifically at the impact of sellers' ratings in a sample of collectibles markets. They measured how changes in sellers' ratings impact future sales and find stark effects consistent with large reputation costs. For example, there is a "steep first step" when a seller loses what was up to that point a spotless rating history. Sellers averaged sales growth rates of 7% in the week prior to their first negative rating, but their sales fell 7% the week after. Additional negative ratings had smaller impacts on sales, but this isn't much of a consolation to sellers: Negative ratings are also more frequent after a seller's first.

Losing one's reputation is also correlated with leaving the market: Seller exits are often preceded by a burst of negative ratings. The direction of cause-and-effect isn't clear here. Maybe sellers who lose their reputations can no longer make enough sales to stay profitable. On the other hand, if a seller knows he is going out of business for some reason, he has little incentive to preserve a reputation—he's not going to be around for it to pay off. This leads to shady deals to earn short-run profits instead. (Maybe something similar explains why negative ratings occur more frequently after sellers receive their first negative rating.) Whatever the direction of causation, the results leave no doubt that sellers in it for the long haul are likely to have higher feedback scores.

In a different study, John List showed that reputation's ability to shrink the lemons problem is more powerful when it is paired with verification from third-party experts.[6] In a series of experiments at sports memorabilia shows, List had research assistants approach sellers to offer randomly determined dollar amounts for specified items such as particular players' baseball cards. These items vary in quality depending on minor differences in the sharpness of their corners, glossiness, and the centering of their printing. Nonexperts would have a difficult time telling the difference between subtle gradations in quality, even though the distinction could mean a three- to four-fold difference in the item's value.

The items that List's subjects offered to buy were not quality-rated by professional collectibles rating companies. This presented dealers with a chance to overrepresent the true quality of the items they sold. If the dealers believed the buyers weren't sophisticated enough to make subtle quality distinctions, they might be successful in claiming the items were worth more than their true market value. (It was also helpful that the dealers did not know they were participating in an experiment.)

After the purchases were made, List had the offered items professionally graded to determine their true quality level. If reputation were important to dealers, they would likely respond to higher dollar offers by giving the purchaser a higher-quality card. Not doing so and having the buyer find this out later (perhaps when he or she tried to resell the item) could damage the sellers' ability to conduct future business. If reputation were unimportant, on the other hand, dealers should give the purchaser the lowest-quality card they possibly could, regardless of the price offer.

List's results showed an interesting split. Dealers who reported (on a survey taken after the experiment was finished) that they were locally based or otherwise frequented

[5] Luís Cabral and Ali Hortaçsu, "The Dynamics of Seller Reputation: Evidence from eBay," *Journal of Industrial Economics* 58, no. 1 (March 2010): 54–78.

[6] John List, "The Behavioralist Meets the Market: Measuring Social Preferences and Reputation Effects in Actual Transactions," *Journal of Political Economy* 114, no. 1 (February 2006): 1–37.

the particular show where the experiment was conducted did, in fact, give higher-quality cards to buyers making higher offers. On the other hand, nonlocal dealers who weren't regular attendees of the show gave buyers uniformly low-quality cards. This makes sense: Building a reputation involves giving up short-term gains (not pulling a fast one on an unsuspecting buyer) in exchange for future rewards (increased business due to the status of being an honest dealer). This tradeoff is worth it for sellers who expect to interact repeatedly with the same set of consumers. On the other hand, sellers who won't be around later to "cash in" on their reputations have little incentive to build one in the first place.

The importance of third-party quality verification was seen when List looked at delivered qualities of a particular product (ticket stubs) that ratings companies had just started grading. At shows taking place before grading was available, all dealers—*even local dealers*—delivered low-quality goods. After verification was available, however, local dealers shifted to delivering higher-quality stubs to buyers who offered more money. Nonlocal dealers, as in the other case, kept selling lemons.

Verification and reputation therefore work hand-in-hand to reduce lemons problems. This makes a lot of intuitive sense: If you never know you've been ripped off, how can the seller's reputation suffer? Keep this in mind next time you're at a flea market. And, make sure you look for the local dealers. ■

Adverse Selection When the Buyer Has More Information: Insurance Markets

In all of the lemons-problem situations we've discussed so far, the seller has had more information about the quality of the good or service than the buyer. But, information asymmetries where buyers know more than sellers can cause problems, too. Insurance markets are an important case in point.

What do buyers know more about than sellers in insurance markets? Buyers know more about their risk of needing to make claims on their insurance policies. Think about what insurance is: a good that compensates a policyholder when particular events occur. Depending on the type of insurance, these events could involve the policyholder getting sick, being in a car accident, having a tree fall on his house, or even death. Individuals expecting such events to be more likely will obviously assign a greater value to being insured. If you realized that you will need expensive braces, for example, you would greatly value dental insurance because it would help pay for your expensive orthodontia.

This means that buyers are adversely selected in insurance markets. From the standpoint of insurance companies, potential customers differ in "quality" because they have different likelihoods of making claims on their policies. (The expected sizes of their claims can be different, too.) Risky or simply bad drivers are more likely to make claims on their auto insurance policies; unhealthy individuals are more likely to make health insurance claims.

Just as with the "seller-side" lemons problems discussed earlier, mere quality variation is not a problem in and of itself. If insurance companies could easily observe potential policyholders' inherent riskiness, they could simply charge policy premiums commensurate with that risk. Customers likely to make more frequent or larger claims would pay higher premiums. There would be no economic efficiency loss in this world: Risky customers would obviously prefer to pay lower rates, but they would at least be able to find coverage. The higher premiums would compensate their insurers for the higher expected payouts the insurers would have to make on the policies.

The adverse selection problem occurs when the customer knows more about their expected claim behavior than insurers do. Insurance companies realize that the riskiest customers will be those most likely seeking to buy insurance, and will buy more insurance than low-risk individuals. They, after all, have the most to gain from being insured. If the insurance companies can't tell the good risks (those customers unlikely to make many claims) from the bad, though, they have to charge premiums high enough to account for the large fraction of riskier customers.

This starts the vicious cycle again: The high premiums price some low-risk customers out of the insurance market. These low-risk buyers don't want to pay high premiums for a policy they are relatively unlikely to need. This, in turn, makes the high-risk individuals an even greater share of those seeking insurance. This necessitates that the insurance company charge an even higher premium, and so on. In a worst-case scenario, this can result in the destruction of the market like the used car example discussed above.

Adverse selection on the buyer side of a market can therefore be as damaging as adverse selection on the seller side. And just as in the cases above, the party with more information can be hurt just as much as the party with less information. In particular, low-risk insurance customers could lose the ability to buy insurance if they cannot convince insurers that they are, in fact, less risky. At the same time, insurance companies suffer from adverse selection because it makes it more difficult for them to write policies for a consumer segment that they would very much prefer to insure, if they could see everyone's true risk type. (There's another asymmetric information problem in insurance markets when insurers cannot observe all of the actions of their policyholders: Once someone is insured against a particular event, he or she is less likely to take steps to prevent that event from occurring. Someone who has auto insurance may not drive as carefully, for example. This type of problem is called *moral hazard*. We discuss moral hazard problems more extensively later in the chapter.)

Mitigating Adverse Selection in Insurance

Just as we saw in the markets with seller-side lemons problems, many market institutions have arisen to mitigate adverse selection in insurance.

Group Policies   One example is the writing of group insurance policies. These are general policies written for members of a specified group, often defined as employees of particular firms. Most people obtain their health insurance this way, for example. Why does group insurance help with adverse selection? By tying insurance to employment status, the insurance company removes much of the link between individuals' riskiness and their insurance purchases. That is, it pools together a wider range of risk types. The good risks are added to the bad, reducing the correlation between individuals seeking to buy health insurance and their chances of falling ill. This is in many ways similar to the way in which leasing reduces the lemons problem in the used car market by breaking the tie between a car's quality and its likelihood of being resold. (It also doesn't hurt, from the insurance company's perspective, that unhealthy people are less likely to be employed. This, too, reduces adverse selection.)

Screening   A second adverse selection reduction tactic is screening. Insurance companies vet potential customers for the likelihood of their submitting claims by observing as many risk factors as possible. People seeking life insurance, for example, typically have to complete a medical questionnaire and submit to blood and urine tests, and sometimes a full medical exam. Having a risk factor present doesn't necessarily mean that a potential policyholder will be denied coverage. Once his risk is known by both the buyer and seller, the customer might still be offered coverage, but he would have to pay higher premiums that match his riskiness. For example, life insurance premiums are higher for smokers, diabetics, or those with high blood pressure. Screening for risk factors isn't constrained to direct influences on expected claims. If you have purchased auto insurance, in addition to asking questions about your driving habits and running a records check for moving violations and accidents, the insurer may have asked you to supply an academic transcript to take advantage of a good-student discount. Even though academic performance is not directly related to driving, good academic performance is historically linked in the data to lower accident rates. The insurer wants to account for as many observable risk factors as possible and adjust premiums to these factors accordingly. (Of course, all of these relationships between observable risk factors and actual policy claims hold *on average*, not individual-by-individual.)

Denying Coverage Insurers can also try to head off adverse selection directly by outright denying coverage to individuals with certain risk factors. Health insurance policies will not cover conditions that already existed at the time the policy was purchased. If you could buy insurance *after* you became ill, many people would not buy it beforehand. Insurers would pay out massive claims while receiving little premium revenues. If it's prevalent enough, no one—healthy or unhealthy—might be able to obtain coverage.

This problem explains the economics behind the "mandate" rules in the Affordable Care Act (aka Obamacare) and the Massachusetts health care insurance law on which it was patterned. Both policies have provisions that forbid health insurers from denying anyone coverage, but also mandate that everyone must buy health insurance. While controversial, the mandates help solve what could otherwise be extreme adverse selection problems. The mandate is a lot like a government-driven form of the benefits from group insurance we discussed above. Requiring everyone to buy insurance solves the adverse selection problem by eliminating adverse selection entirely. Under a mandate, the average insurance customer must have the average insurance risk in the population. It's the same reason that states require all drivers to get auto insurance.

Summing Up These mechanisms and others like them moderate adverse selection in insurance markets. The mechanisms exist for the same reason that the seller-side mechanisms discussed earlier arose: In the absence of such mechanisms, asymmetric information between parties in the market could destroy considerable gains from exchange. By and large, the mechanisms have kept insurance markets functioning well, from property and casualty (e.g., home and auto) insurance to life and disability insurance. Whether they have worked as well in health insurance markets has been a focus of serious policy debate, however. We're not going to delve much deeper into that issue here—that's a whole other course. But our discussion should make you familiar enough with the underlying issues to be able to understand and knowledgeably participate in the debate yourself.

 **application**

Adverse Selection and Compulsory Insurance

Amy Finkelstein and James Poterba measured the extent of adverse selection in annuity markets in the United Kingdom.[7] Annuities are insurance products whereby, in exchange for a lump-sum upfront premium, the policyholder receives a guaranteed stream of payments—for example, on a monthly basis—for a set period of time. This period, set at the time of purchase, can vary from several years to the remainder of the policyholder's life. An example annuity might take the form of a 65-year-old male paying a £50,000 upfront premium for a guaranteed monthly payment of £400 as long as he lives.

The potential for adverse selection in annuities derives from the fact that the insurer's obligation to make the payments ends at the policyholder's death, even if it occurs before the end of the policy's established term. If policy buyers have better information than these insurance companies about the policyholders' expected remaining lifetimes (as they may well, since these individuals likely have private information about their

---

[7] Amy Finkelstein and James Poterba, "Selection Effects in the United Kingdom Individual Annuities Market," *Economic Journal* 112, no. 476 (January 2002): 28–50.

own health), disproportionately long-lived (healthy) individuals will buy the largest-valued and longest-termed annuities.

An interesting feature of the annuity market in the United Kingdom is that both compulsory and voluntary markets coexist. The compulsory market arose because holders of certain retirement accounts are required by law to buy an annuity with a fraction of their retirement account balances when they stop working. The voluntary market allows others who wish to buy additional annuities to do so. By comparing these two groups, Finkelstein and Poterba tested whether compulsory insurance reduces adverse selection in this market.

The authors found evidence of adverse selection in both the compulsory and non-compulsory annuity markets. Adverse selection exists even in the compulsory market because once people have annuitized the legally required fraction of their retirement funds, they have the option of putting additional money from their accounts into an annuity. And, as we would expect, healthier people annuitized a larger fraction of their retirement accounts. Similar patterns held within the voluntary annuity market.

Our discussion above suggests that adverse selection should be even worse in the voluntary than in the compulsory market. This was, in fact, seen in the data. Retirees buying voluntary annuities lived longer on average than those buying in the compulsory market. For example, 48% of 65-year-old males in the compulsory market lived at least until age 82, while 56% of 65-year-old males in the voluntary market survived that long. The compulsory market, by forcing all individuals to buy an annuity and not just those with long expected lifetimes, removed some of the opportunity for adverse selection to happen. ■

15.2 Moral Hazard

Another information asymmetry that can cause problems in insurance markets is moral hazard. In this section, we discuss moral hazard's impact on insurance markets and on other markets as well.

Moral hazard exists when the information gap involves the inability of one party in an economic transaction to observe another party's behavior. That last word—"behavior"—is important. Moral hazard is about how one party *acts* once an economic relationship has been entered into; that is, after an insurance policy has been sold, a contract has been signed, an employee has been hired, and so on.

moral hazard
A situation that arises when one party in an economic transaction cannot observe the other party's behavior.

A stark example of a moral hazard problem is outright fraud. Suppose you pay a mechanic to fix a problem with your car, and he, in turn, pockets the money without making any substantive repairs, with the hope that you will be unable to detect this. That is fraud supported by unobservable action. You either literally cannot see whether the work has been done—for instance, whether he actually replaced the valves in the engine or not—or you don't know enough about cars to be able to tell the difference. It's difficult to rely simply on the car's performance to determine the quality of the work, or whether anything was done at all. A lack of improvement in the car's performance might indicate nothing was done, but there are also genuine reasons why no performance improvement might be observed even if the mechanic did the work as specified.

Fraud aside, numerous moral hazard situations are less overtly malicious but still potentially very damaging to well-functioning markets. Insurance markets again offer many such cases. We talked about adverse selection in insurance, which deals with the unobservable riskiness of people seeking insurance coverage. Therefore, adverse selection is a concern to insurers before a policy is ever written. Moral hazard is different. Moral hazard has to do with the effect that insurance coverage has on individuals' behaviors: specifically, that they will make fewer efforts to avoid having to make claims once they are already covered. Moral hazard is therefore a concern to insurers after a policy has been purchased.

An Example of Extreme Moral Hazard

An example will make this clear. (It's slightly ridiculous in order to exaggerate the point, but it shares many characteristics with other moral hazard situations in insurance.) Suppose movie producers could buy "box office insurance" that guaranteed them a specified gross revenue for a particular film if box office receipts did not reach this level. Producers wanting more coverage—that is, a higher minimum revenue guarantee—could obtain it for a higher premium.

Such policies could potentially be very valuable economically. Movie revenues are very volatile and unpredictable. Producers might prefer to have a more certain income flow for planning purposes among many other reasons. Insurance companies could find selling such policies appealing in principle as well: If the insurers spread their risk over enough movies, they could earn enough premium revenue from the successful movies that didn't need to cash in their policies to both pay claims on disappointing movies and make a profit.

There's a potential adverse selection problem here: Producers of lower-quality movies are more likely to want to buy this type of policy. But, let's ignore that for the moment. Even if adverse selection weren't a problem, moral hazard would be. To see why, consider the decisions a producer faces once he is covered by such an insurance policy. Suppose the movie hadn't yet been shot when the policy was purchased. What incentive would the producer now have to make a film that audiences found appealing? The producer is guaranteed the insured gross revenue, no matter what. Therefore, the producer's optimal response is to make as low-cost a film as possible. The film could be of a test pattern, with one copy distributed to one theater for one night. The producer will have spent virtually nothing on the film but will have earned a guaranteed amount of revenue. Even if the insurance contract was signed after filming, the producer would still have no incentive to spend resources marketing it.

Again, this is a somewhat absurd example to make a point, but these forces operate in many markets. Figure 15.1 shows one way to think about how moral hazard works more generally. This figure plots a potential policyholder's marginal benefit and the marginal cost of taking actions that increase the chance of a "good" outcome occurring.

Figure 15.1   **Moral Hazard in the Insurance Market**

In a market without insurance, a potential policyholder would take actions to improve the potential for a good outcome up until A^*, where the marginal benefit of further action, MB, equals the marginal cost of further action, MC. If instead the policy offers full insurance, MB shifts to MB_{FI}, and the policyholder does not take any action (makes zero effort) to make the good outcome more likely. If the policy offers partial insurance, MB shifts to MB_{PI}, and the policyholder takes action level A^*_{PI}.

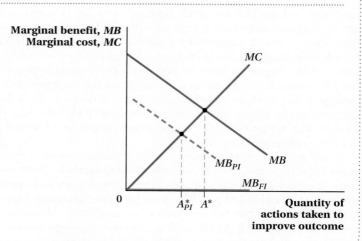

What we mean by "good" outcomes depends on the particular situation. This could include a movie doing well at the box office, a driver not getting in an accident, a person not falling into ill health, and so on. Importantly, however, actions that raise the likelihood of such good outcomes are not costless to the potential policyholder. Those actions may involve financial cost, such as hiring a decent cast and crew and designing a solid marketing plan for a movie, and almost always involve effort, such as driving with care and resisting the temptation to text friends while behind the wheel, and eating well and exercising regularly. The cost in terms of money and effort of taking a bit more of these sorts of actions is shown in Figure 15.1 as marginal cost MC. We assume this marginal cost rises with the amount of actions already taken. This assumption is realistic; making initial efforts to put together a decent movie or to not drive recklessly is probably not too difficult and thus not too costly, but after having implemented the easier actions, taking further actions to improve outcomes becomes increasingly arduous and costly.

The benefit of such actions is the gain that the potential policyholder obtains when a good outcome occurs. Thus, the marginal benefit of the actions is the incremental increase in the good outcome (or the probability of the outcome) that taking further action creates. In Figure 15.1, these marginal benefits are shown as MB. We assume they decrease as the amount of action taken increases, because it's likely that the initial actions taken to create a good outcome (which, remember, we have assumed are not too difficult or costly) go a reasonable distance to make it likely that the movie is a success, that a driver doesn't get in an accident, or that a person is healthy. As more actions are taken to ensure a good outcome, however, the smaller the impact that each additional action has.

In a market with no insurance, the potential policyholder would take actions up to point A^*. Here, his marginal benefit of taking further action just equals his marginal cost of doing so; taking any more or less action than this level would only reduce his net benefit. Action levels less than A^* would decrease his expected benefit more than it saves him in cost. Actions beyond A^* would cost more than they are worth in benefit.

Now suppose he obtains insurance against bad outcomes. If the movie is a flop, he gets in a car accident, or needs medical care due to unhealthy behavior, the policy will kick in. If the policy offers *full insurance*—that is, the policy pays off enough so that the policyholder is just as well off as he would have been had the good outcome occurred instead of the bad one—then there is *no* marginal benefit to taking any actions that make the good outcome more likely. The policyholder is going to be just as well off regardless of what outcome happens. In this case, the marginal benefit curve shifts to MB_{FI} (for full insurance) in Figure 15.1. This curve lies along the horizontal axis because with full insurance there is no marginal benefit to taking actions that make the good outcome more likely. In this case, even the simplest, most basic actions involve a marginal cost greater than their marginal benefit, so it is optimal for the policyholder to take no action that would make the good outcome more likely. This outcome is terrible for the insurer, because it makes it much more probable that the insurer will have to pay a claim on the policy.

Even without full insurance, the existence of a policy that pays off in case of a bad outcome will reduce the policyholder's marginal benefit of taking actions to make good outcomes more likely—whatever payouts the insurance company makes mean that any bad outcome won't be as bad as it would have been without the insurance. In situations of *partial insurance*, the marginal benefit curve might shift to something like MB_{PI} in Figure 15.1. In this case, the policyholder still takes actions to raise the likelihood of a good outcome occurring, but takes fewer actions than he would have if he had no insurance. Specifically, he takes action level A^*_{PI}, where his marginal cost equals his now lower marginal benefit of action. Therefore, bad outcomes are more likely than they would have been if he weren't insured.

These cases exemplify the moral hazard problem in insurance: Being insured against a bad outcome actually leads the insured party to act (or not act) in ways that increase the probability of the bad outcome. If the loss associated with having a low-performing box office film is removed by insurance, for example, the policyholder has no motive to prevent a lousy box office gross from happening. Or, if you know your car repairs will be paid at least partially if you get in an accident, you may be less careful when driving. These actions leave the insurer stuck with a higher likelihood of having to pay a claim.

The role of information asymmetries in the moral hazard problem involves the insurer's inability to observe and verify the actions of the policyholder. If the insurer could specify that the policyholder take certain actions and be able to observe that the policyholder follows through, moral hazard becomes less of a problem (more on this in the next section). An insurance company underwriting a movie's box office receipts, for example, might specify certain production requirements: cast and crew members, minimum budget, running length, marketing expenditures, and so on. But as a practical matter, it is impossible to observe and verify every single action taken by a producer that affects a movie's revenue. Thus, there will always be some moral hazard problem. Because such a large fraction of producers' actions are unverifiable, the problem is so difficult that it would likely destroy the market for box office insurance altogether.

15.2 figure it out

Anastasia and Katherine own a café. Because of their equipment and business, they run a risk of loss due to small kitchen fires. This risk can be mitigated by taking precautions such as purchasing fire extinguishers or by increasing the training and awareness of the café's employees. Assume that the marginal cost of these precautions can be represented by $MC = 80 + 8A$, where A is equal to the actions taken to mitigate the risk of a fire. Likewise, the marginal benefit of these precautions is $MB = 100 - 2A$.

a. If the café has no insurance, what would be the optimal level of precautions for Anastasia and Katherine to take?

b. Suppose the café has insurance that reduces the marginal benefit of taking precautions to $MB = 90 - 4A$. What happens to the optimal level of precautions? Explain why this is the case.

Solution:

a. With no insurance, the optimal level of precautionary actions would occur where $MB = MC$:

$$100 - 2A = 80 + 8A$$
$$10A = 20$$
$$A = 2$$

b. Once the insurance is in place, the marginal benefit of taking precautions falls to $MB = 90 - 4A$. The optimal level of precautions also falls:

$$MB = MC$$
$$90 - 4A = 80 + 8A$$
$$12A = 10$$
$$A = 0.83$$

The optimal level of precautionary actions falls when insurance is available. If a fire occurs, the café's owners will experience a smaller loss as a result of the insurance coverage. Therefore, the owners' incentives to try to prevent a loss are reduced.

Examples of Moral Hazard in Insurance Markets

Destroyed markets aside, moral hazard is still an issue in existing insurance markets. Many have argued that the National Flood Insurance Program encourages homeowners to build—and sometimes *rebuild*—too close to water. This program is administered by the U.S. government. It covers damages to homes caused by flooding (private insurance rarely covers such losses). The program's provisions do not do a good job of matching premiums to risk, however. Even policyholders with large prior claims can re-obtain coverage relatively cheaply. As you might expect, knowing one's beach house will be fully insured in case of a storm surge doesn't do much to discourage the construction of beach houses in vulnerable locations. There are several cases where benefits were paid out on properties that had been destroyed by storms multiple times, and then rebuilt each time in the same location. A Government Accountability Office report in 2010 calculated that 1% of the properties covered by the program had experienced repetitive losses, accounting for 25 to 30% of total claim costs.[8]

Auto insurers are always concerned about their policyholders' unobserved driving habits. Insurance is usually priced by the period (per six-month term) rather than the intensity of driving. Sometimes rough premium adjustments for mileage are made, but they are based on the policyholders' reported "typical" mileage numbers, not actual use. Additionally, there is no adjustment for aggressive driving, like jackrabbit starts and stops or tailgating, which are associated with the increased probability of being in an accident. Once covered, then, the driver doesn't bear the full marginal cost he imposes on the insurance company when driving more miles or more aggressively. Drivers therefore have too little incentive to avoid actions that raise the likelihood of their being in an accident. (The standard structure of auto insurance policies may be changing, however; see the Application "Usage-Based Auto Insurance" later in this chapter.)

Unemployment insurance, while offering some financial relief to workers who have lost their jobs by partially replacing their lost wages, can also reduce unemployed individuals' incentives to look for work. While unemployment benefits are tied to the recipient actively looking for work, the agencies that administer the program cannot fully observe recipients' true efforts to find employment. The intensity of the job search and the individual's effort in interviews are clearly difficult to monitor.

Moral Hazard outside Insurance Markets

Moral hazard problems aren't restricted to insurance markets. They can arise between lenders and borrowers in financial markets. Lenders often loan funds to borrowers to use for a particular purpose. Suppose a borrower asks for a loan to invest in new equipment for his business. Once he has the money, however, he may find expenditures on other items more appealing. Perhaps an office suite with fancy antique furniture would suit him well. If the borrower uses the loan to buy cheap used equipment so that he can spend the rest on the office suite, and the lender can't fully observe how the funds are used, a moral hazard problem exists. By spending part of the loan on an unproductive office suite and shortchanging expenditures on productive capital, the borrower reduces the probability that he will be able to repay the loan. This is bad news for the lender. It results from the lender's inability to observe exactly how the borrower uses the loaned funds.

Discussions about policy responses to the recent financial crisis have involved moral hazard concerns. Governments around the world have bailed out banks and other financial institutions in an effort to stave off a collapse of the financial system. There is concern, however, that such policies could backfire by encouraging overly risky behavior by banks in the future. This criticism is based on moral hazard arguments. Specifically, a bailout keeps institutions that played too fast and loose in the run-up to the crisis from bearing the full cost of their bad decisions. If the bailouts cause banks to expect similar rescue actions should another collapse happen in the future (perhaps because the banks perceive themselves as "too big to fail"), they may again take overly risky actions. After all, if their bets do not pay off, the banks will probably be covered anyway. This scenario, while taking place outside the insurance market, is in many ways similar to the moral hazard problem facing insurers. Here, taxpayers are the insurance

[8] Government Accountability Office, "National Flood Insurance Program: Actions to Address Repetitive Loss Properties," Statement of William O. Jenkins Jr., March 2004.

company. If financial institutions know they will be bailed out by the government if things go badly, they are in essence insured against such outcomes. They therefore take fewer actions to avoid bad outcomes (such as engaging in less risky behavior) as a result.

Unobserved actions play an important role in labor markets, too. Employers cannot typically observe all the actions of their employees. Employees may wish to engage in work-time activities that they find enjoyable but that are not in the firm's best interest. (Playing computer solitaire, surfing the Internet, and talking with co-workers about the big game last weekend are just some examples.) This presents employers with the difficulty of figuring out how to induce employees to do their jobs even when some of the workers' activities cannot be monitored. These employer-employee relationships apply at all ends of the manager-worker hierarchy: from those between foreman and line workers to those between shareholders and the firm's CEO. There is actually a special class of economic analyses—called *principal-agent relationships*—that deal with these sorts of issues. They are important enough that we discuss them separately later in the chapter.

Mitigating Moral Hazard

Just as with adverse selection and the lemons problem, many market mechanisms have developed to reduce moral hazard. One possibility for insurance markets that we hinted at above is the insurer's specifying certain actions that must be taken by the policyholder as a condition of coverage. This is often followed up by the insurer verifying that the actions have, in fact, been taken. For example, commercial property insurance companies may require smoke detectors and firefighting equipment to be installed and maintained in buildings they insure. These insurers may then send inspectors to verify compliance with such regulations. Auto insurance companies sometimes exclude coverage for personal vehicles if they are used for business purposes (a practice that suggests unusually intense use or frequent driving by those outside the insured's family). Many life insurance policies include an exemption from paying benefits if the policyholder commits suicide within two years of purchase.

These approaches seek to head off moral hazard problems directly, by specifying and monitoring what the policyholder does. That is, these methods recognize that while the actions of the policyholder might not be perfectly observable, key behaviors that greatly impact the insurer's payoff can be specified by contract (assuming that the insurer maintains the ability to monitor and verify the policyholder's actions).

A related, more-carrot-and-less-stick approach is for insurers to structure policy contracts to give policyholders incentives to take actions that reduce risk. This is a common practice. Homeowners typically get a break on their policies if they install smoke detectors, dead-bolt locks, or modernize their electrical system. Life insurance policy rates drop for those who quit smoking. Auto insurance policies offer discounts to drivers who maintain a clean driving record. Insurers can also reduce moral hazard by structuring policies that align policyholders' incentives with those of the insurer. This is done by giving insured individuals some "skin in the game." That is, devices are used to directly tie together the policyholders' and the insurer's payoffs. There are several ways this can be done. These devices—deductibles, copayments, and coinsurance—are all quite common; each is probably familiar to you.

Deductibles are the portion of claims that the policyholder must pay out of his own pocket. A person with a $500 deductible on his auto insurance, who causes an accident leading to damage of $5,000, will only obtain $4,500 from the insurer for repairs. By imposing some cost of claims directly on the policyholder, the insurer gives him an incentive to take actions that reduce the likelihood of claims. Copayments work similarly. These are payments (most commonly applied in health insurance markets) that the policyholder must dole out whenever making a claim. A $5 fee you have to pay for each prescription you obtain through a prescription drug plan, for example, is a common type of copayment. In coinsurance, the responsibility for paying claims is split between the insurer and the policyholder on a set schedule. Many traditional health insurance policies, for instance, pay 80% of the cost of services. The policyholder remains responsible for the other 20%. The purpose of each of these three devices is to give a policyholder some incentive to reduce the size or likelihood of his claims.

These and other practices reduce the impact of moral hazard on insurance markets, preserving much of the economic gains from their existence. It's important to remember, however, that even when damped by these institutions, moral hazard can still affect the structure of the markets in which it is a factor.

🧩 application

Usage-Based Auto Insurance

As we discussed above, the typical structure of car insurance policies leads to moral hazard problems. Insurance is priced by the time period, and premiums are weakly (if at all) related to the actual intensity or riskiness of driving within the coverage period. Policyholders therefore don't fully pay for the extra risk their insurers bear when they drive many miles or drive aggressively. As a result, they have too little incentive to take risk-reducing actions.

The solution to this problem is conceptually clear: Insurers should monitor their policyholders' actual driving behavior and adjust premiums based on the observed actions. Particularly heavy or risky driving during the coverage period should cost more.

This solution has not been widely implemented, however, because of the practical difficulties in monitoring drivers' habits. It would be impossibly expensive for your auto insurer to, for example, pay a monitor to sit in your back seat and record your routines as you drove around.

Things may be changing, though. Technological advances have reduced the barriers to such monitoring. Small electronic devices that interface directly with cars' onboard computers can now gather data on miles driven, acceleration and deceleration rates, and the times of day at which the wheels were rolling. Auto insurers have started to experiment with these technologies. For example, U.K. insurer Norwich Union offers Pay As You Drive™. Under this coverage, drivers' premiums are adjusted for the actual mileage and the time of day they drive. (As you might guess, late night to early morning is the highest-risk, and therefore most expensive, driving period.) U.S. insurer Progressive has launched a similar program with its Snapshot® option. Drivers earn discounts off the standard premium if they drive fewer miles at the right times of day or if they can reduce hard accelerations and stops.

Such policies, called usage-based insurance (UBI), are at this point still optional. Drivers do not have to submit to monitoring and can instead stick with standard contracts. The fact that UBI is optional creates an adverse selection issue in standard policies: Car owners who know they are heavy or aggressive drivers will systematically avoid UBI policies. As such policies become more commonplace, this could result in standard policies becoming significantly more expensive, because the drivers opting into standard policies will be systematically riskier. This would further induce safer drivers to choose UBI, exacerbating the adverse selection problem. ∎

15.3 Asymmetric Information in Principal–Agent Relationships

Principal–agent relationships are a common set of economic transactions involving asymmetric information. They exist whenever one party (the principal) hires another (the agent) to perform some task, and the principal has an asymmetric information problem because he cannot fully observe the agent's actions (or, sometimes, the

principal–agent relationships
Economic transactions that feature information asymmetry between a principal and his hired agent, whose actions the principal cannot fully observe.

information the agent possesses). When this information asymmetry is combined with the fact that the principal's and agent's individual self-interests are usually not perfectly aligned, things become interesting.

There are many, many examples of principal-agent relationships. One of the most common, and the one on which we focus in this section, is between an employer and employee. An employer would like the employee to perform certain tasks. The employee likes to be paid for working, but might not prefer to work as hard or work at the same tasks as the employer would like him to.

The divergence in an employer's preferences (let's call our employer Yvonne) and those of her employee (let's call her Jean) is not in and of itself a problem. The two could write an employment contract with Jean's pay contingent on her completing a set of tasks or conveying certain information specified by Yvonne. Jean would then have strong incentives to do as Yvonne wished, and Yvonne would have to compensate Jean enough for her to be willing to complete the requested actions. The problem lies in the fact that, because of the information asymmetry, the principal (Yvonne) can't ever know for sure if the agent (Jean) has done what she requested. Yvonne must instead infer the adequacy of Jean's responses as best as she can, using only imperfect information about Jean's job performance. For example, Yvonne can't just observe sales and know exactly how hard Jean worked. Maybe Jean didn't work hard, but other things caused sales to be high. Or, maybe Jean did work hard but other factors caused sales to be low. Yvonne can't know for sure. While sales are likely to be correlated with Jean's effort, they are also influenced by unrelated factors. This makes sales an imperfect measure for Yvonne to gauge Jean's actual level of effort.

This logic carries over to other types of principal-agent relationships. A company's shareholders—the principals in this case—want the CEO and management team (the agents) to take actions that maximize the market value of the company. But, management might want instead to use company resources to pay for personal perks, like fancy corporate dining rooms, unneeded corporate jets, and extravagant personal travel. If it's not clear whether such expenses are justified—fancy dining rooms might help close big deals and corporate jets do save time, for example—shareholders can't be certain that management is or isn't acting fully in the shareholders' interests.

The moral hazard problems facing insurers and their policyholders can also be cast as principal-agent relationships. Insurance companies (the principals) want policyholders (agents) to take actions to reduce risks. Because insurance companies typically can't observe all these actions, a principal–agent problem exists.

What can the principals do in these situations? The principals know how they would like their agents to act. The problem is that the principals cannot fully observe what the agents do. Otherwise, the principals could simply make the agents' payoffs conditional on taking the desired actions. Instead, the principals must somehow set up incentives to make it in the agents' *own best interests* to take the actions that the principals desire.

Principal–Agent and Moral Hazard: An Example

Let's consider a simple example. Suppose that the daily profit of a small mobile phone kiosk in the local mall is higher when the kiosk's employee, Joe, works harder. (We'll assume for simplicity that Joe is the only employee.) Joe can work hard, in which case the kiosk's daily profit is $1,000 with 80% probability and $500 with 20% probability. (The latter might happen if overall traffic at the mall falls for some reason.) Alternatively, Joe could laze about by staring blankly at passersby or texting his friends. If Joe does so, the probability of the kiosk's profit will be reversed: There will be 20% probability of a profit of $1,000 and 80% probability of $500. Joe doesn't like to work hard; he has to be paid at least $150 before he's willing to do so. Otherwise, he's going to text his friends all day.

How should the kiosk's owner (Selena, the principal) structure Joe's (the agent's) compensation? Remember, the root of the principal–agent problem is that the owner can't perfectly observe the employee's effort. Perhaps it's too costly for Selena to monitor the kiosk all day long, or maybe Joe's effort involves some dimension that is not readily apparent to Selena for some other reason. Otherwise, Selena could simply require Joe to work hard, and pay him $150 if he does. Joe will be willing to accept this deal because he is being paid enough to compensate him for his cost of effort. Selena also likes this deal because inducing Joe to work hard raises her expected profit from $600 ($0.2 \times \$1,000 + 0.8 \times \$500$) to $900 ($0.8 \times \$1,000 + 0.2 \times \$500$), a $300 increase, but it only costs Selena at most $150 in wages.

When Joe's effort is unobservable, however, his pay cannot be based on how hard he works. And, simply offering Joe a flat wage of $150 isn't a solution either. Because he faces a cost of working hard but would take home the same pay regardless of whether he exerts any effort, he would choose to be lazy. This is clearly undesirable to Selena, who would pay $150 in wages but only earn the low expected profit of $600 rather than $900. When effort is unobservable, therefore, simply offering enough pay to compensate Joe for his effort does not actually lead to him working hard.

What Selena *can* do, however, is tie Joe's pay to something she knows is related to Joe's effort: namely, the kiosk's profit. Because Joe can affect the likelihood that profits (and therefore his wages) are high by working hard, this offers him an incentive to exert effort. Of course, the extra wages he expects to earn working hard have to be high enough to compensate him for that extra effort.

Suppose Selena offers the following deal: Joe is paid $250 if the kiosk's profits are high (i.e., $1,000) and $0 if profits are low ($500). What sort of behavior would this lead to? Think about Joe's tradeoffs. If he works hard, he has an 80% chance of earning $250 and a 20% chance of earning nothing. His expected earnings are $200 ($0.8 \times 250 + 0.2 \times 0$). However, he also suffers an effort cost of $150, so his net gain from working hard is $50. If Joe chooses to be lazy, he will have an 80% chance of earning nothing and a 20% chance of earning $250, yielding expected earnings of $50. By being lazy, Joe pays no effort cost, so his net gain from being lazy is also $50. Under this compensation plan, then, Joe is indifferent between working hard and being lazy. Therefore, raising Joe's pay just a little bit (say, to $255) in the case of a high profit will make him prefer working hard over being lazy.

Does Selena also prefer this new plan? We already know that if Joe works hard, the kiosk's expected profit will be $300 higher. Selena expects to pay Joe $204 ($0.8 \times 255 + 0.2 \times 0$) if he works hard. Thus, the new compensation scheme is worthwhile from Selena's perspective, because by giving Joe the incentive to work hard, it raises her expected profit net of wages by $96.

Selena (the principal) can, in fact, give Joe (the agent) incentives to work hard. The key is to pay him much more when observable events occur that are correlated with his unobservable effort (i.e., when profit is high because Joe works hard). By tying the agent's compensation to outcomes that the principal likes, the principal aligns the agent's incentives on the margin with her own.

The Principal–Agent Relationship as a Game

This example, as with more general principal–agent problems, can also be thought of as a sequential game (see Chapter 12). The first mover in a principal–agent game is the principal, and the strategy he chooses is the agent's compensation structure. Given the principal's chosen compensation structure, the agent then chooses his strategy, which we can think of as effort or, more generally, any action that improves the principal's payoff. Taking this action may be costly for the agent, however, and the principal does not directly observe it. Payoffs are realized for both players based on the action chosen by the *agent*.

Figure 15.2 shows the game tree for the interaction between the mobile phone kiosk owner, Selena, and her employee, Joe. Selena moves first; she has the choice of paying Joe a flat wage of $150 that doesn't depend on the kiosk's profit or a wage that is tied to the kiosk's profit: $255 if profit is high and $0 if it is low. Once the compensation structure is chosen, Joe then chooses his effort level: high or low. Given this choice, Selena and Joe earn their expected payoffs.

As with any sequential game, we can find the equilibrium using backward induction. Suppose Selena chooses the flat $150 pay structure. If Joe works hard, Selena's expected payoff is $750 (the $900 profit from the kiosk minus the $150 wage she pays Joe), and Joe's payoff is $0 (his $150 wage minus his $150 effort cost of working hard). If Joe chooses to be lazy, Selena's expected payoff is $450 ($600 kiosk profit minus wages of $150), while Joe's payoff is $150 (his wage alone, because he has no cost of effort). Selena prefers Joe to work hard, but Joe's payoff is greater from being lazy. As a result, Joe chooses to be lazy under this compensation plan.

Now suppose Selena chooses to link Joe's pay to the kiosk's profit: Joe receives $255 for high profit and $0 for low profit. Joe works hard in this case, Selena's expected payoff is $696 ($900 in expected kiosk profit minus the expected $204 in pay to Joe), and Joe's expected payoff is $54 (his $204 expected wage minus his $150 effort cost of working hard). If Joe chooses to be lazy, Selena's expected payoff is $549 ($600 kiosk profit minus wages of $51), while Joe's expected payoff is $51. Joe's expected payoff from working hard is higher in this scenario, so he makes the extra effort and raises the kiosk's expected profit.

Now that we've solved for the last stage of the game, we can figure out Selena's equilibrium action in the first stage. If she chooses the flat $150 pay structure, Joe doesn't work hard and her expected payoff is $450. If Selena chooses to link pay to the kiosk's performance ($255 for high profit and $0 for low profit), then Joe works hard and her expected payoff is $696. Therefore, Selena's optimal action in the first stage is to choose the performance-linked pay structure.

That's the equilibrium of this principal–agent game: Selena chooses a pay structure that links Joe's compensation to an observable outcome, the kiosk's profits, that is correlated with Joe's unobservable effort. In response to this choice, Joe exerts the amount of effort the owner desires.

Again, what Selena would *really* prefer is to monitor Joe's effort directly, specify that he works hard as a condition of employment, and pay a flat wage of $150 to compensate Joe for working hard. In this case, Selena's expected payoff would be $750, higher than in the equilibrium above. Selena can't do this, however, because she is unable to continuously monitor Joe's effort. As a result of the principal–agent problem, Selena is left with the second-best outcome, a $696 expected payoff.

Figure 15.2   **The Principal–Agent Problem as a Sequential Game**

In a game between a mobile phone kiosk owner, Selena, and her employee, Joe, Selena has the first move. If Selena chooses to pay a flat $150, the interests of Joe and Selena do not align. Joe earns more by being lazy ($150 compared to a payoff of $0 if he works hard, because of his cost of effort). Selena prefers that he works hard, so that she earns $750 compared to $450 if Joe is lazy. If Selena chooses to link Joe's pay to the kiosk's profit, Joe's and Selena's interests align. Now, Joe will choose to work hard, earning him $54 and Selena $696. As a result, Selena chooses to link Joe's pay to the kiosk's profit.

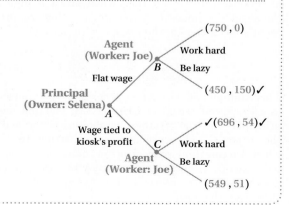

freakonomics

Yo-ho-ho and . . . Fair Treatment for All?

Pirates of the seventeenth and eighteenth centuries were a nasty bunch. They terrorized women and children, forced enemies to walk the plank, and would cut off a person's finger to acquire the gold ring he was wearing. They were the epitome of lawlessness.

At least that is what the pirates wanted people to believe.

It turns out pirates were running a smear campaign against themselves—one happily promulgated by many journalists, novelists, and current-day movie makers. By spreading stories about themselves as murderous criminals, the pirates were able to plunder without having to resort to violence very often. Blackbeard, for instance, became infamous for allegedly cutting off the ring finger of an uncooperative passenger—all because he wanted the passenger's gold ring. After that incident, Blackbeard and his crew could use the violent story—instead of violence itself—to get what they wanted in future expeditions.

No principal–agent problems for this crew.

Walt Disney/Stephen Vaughn/The Kobal Collection

As economist Peter T. Leeson[9] has shown, these terrorists of the sea had a surprising set of rules aboard ship that outlawed womanizing, drinking, brawling, and gambling. There were also clear rules about how the bounty would be shared. And, believe it or not, captains were democratically elected.

Ironically, pirate ships on the whole were more peaceful than the company-run merchant ships they were attacking, and for sound economic reasons. Merchant ships had absentee owners who preferred to stay back home in Europe rather than spend months enduring the cruelties of life at sea. The ship captains were given full, autocratic power over their sailors, as well as enforcers and weapons to make sure their orders were followed. The captains were rewarded if they got their cargo quickly and safely back to port. How happy the sailors were was not particularly important to the owners of the ships. The threat of mutiny was often in the air.

In contrast to merchant ships, pirate organizations did not have a principal–agent problem. All members of the pirate organization were on board the ship and there was no asymmetric information. Pirates elected their captains to lead in times of battle and could depose the captain if he abused his powers. To further ensure fair treatment by the captain, pirate organizations also had a quartermaster who was in charge of allocating provisions and dividing the loot among the crew members. Compensation details were also worked out. Above and beyond the normal pay, a pirate was awarded pay for carpentry work, loss of limb, and other services to the buccaneering cause. In essence, a pirate organization was a democratic one, run with a system of checks and balances.

So, why don't screenwriters and directors depict pirate life as it was? That's not a very hard question. How many people do you think would pay to come and watch a subdued Johnny Depp sitting down to hammer out the details of a pirate constitution with his moralistic co-pirates? Even economists would stay home.

[9] Peter T. Leeson, "An-*arggh*-chy: The Law and Economics of Pirate Organization," *Journal of Political Economy* 115, no. 6 (2007): 1049–1094.

More General Principal–Agent Relationships

The Selena–Joe example is simple: It has only two outcomes (high or low profits) and two choices for the agent (high or low effort). However, its insights hold in more general settings with multiple possible outcomes and a range of agent choices. The optimal compensation structure fully aligns the marginal incentives of the agent with those of the principal. In other words, principals want to design compensation structures that make agents face the same incentives the principals would face if they were making the agents' choices for them. When this is not the case, the principals' and agents' incentives are misaligned and can lead to inefficient outcomes.

You might wonder, if principal–agent situations are so common, especially in employment relationships, why pay-for-performance (or maybe pay-for-outcome is more accurate) isn't the norm. Certainly, many people in sales professions have their pay tied directly to outcomes related to their performance through commissions. Some workers also get paid piece rates, where they are paid a set amount per unit of work they complete (per dress sewn, e.g.). But, many people are paid a fixed hourly wage or even an annual salary. Does this mean that there is no principal–agent dynamic involved in those jobs? Well, there might be less of an issue, but other "levers" are available to tie job outcomes to compensation. Annual bonuses, promotions, stock options, deferred compensation, and threats of being fired all serve as ways that employers can give workers the incentives to perform as the employer wishes. So when you are looking for evidence of principal-agent relationships, be sure to consider the full range of tools the principal has available to induce the agent to behave in a way (unobservable by the principal) that results in the best outcome for the principal.

theory and data

The Principal–Agent Problem in Residential Real Estate Transactions

Home sellers face an asymmetric information problem when they hire a real estate agent. An agent typically knows more about the state of the housing market than does a home seller. Indeed, the agent's extra information is one of the reasons why people want to hire a real estate agent.

In addition to this information gap, contracts in the industry typically give agents very weak marginal incentives to get the highest price for the houses they sell. Most agents are paid a commission that is a small fraction of the selling price of the home. Typically, the total commission on a sale is around 6%, but after the buyer's agent and the brokerage for which the agent works receive their shares of the commission, the seller's agent takes home only about 1.5% of the sales price.

You might think that having compensation tied to the outcome the seller would desire (a higher sales price) fits the optimal principal-agent compensation plans we just discussed, but this is true only to a limited extent. The problem is that the agent's incentive to get a higher price for his client *on the margin* is far less than the homeowner's. By taking actions that raise the sales price by $1,000, the agent would only earn an extra $15, while the owner would earn $940. The owner's marginal incentives are over 60 times larger than the agent's.

The combination of the information gap and the misaligned incentives can create distortions, as two of this book's authors (Steven Levitt and Chad Syverson) point out in their study of real estate transactions.[10] Because agents bear much of the cost of selling a house

[10] Levitt, Steven D. and Chad Syverson, "Market Distortions When Agents Are Better Informed: The Value of Information in Real Estate Transactions," *Review of Economics and Statistics* 90, no. 4 (November 2008): 599–611.

(hosting open houses, buying ads, showing the home to potential buyers, etc.), but gain much less from a higher price, the agents have an incentive to convince the homeowner to sell faster at a lower price. For example, while most homeowners would wait two extra weeks if they could get an offer that is $10,000 higher (that's worth an extra $9,400 to the sellers), agents may not be willing to pay two extra weeks' worth of selling costs for an incremental commission increase of only $150. And, because sellers know less than agents about the likely offers forthcoming on their houses, sellers are susceptible to being convinced to quickly accept a lower offer.

The test of this theory compares house-sales outcomes in the typical principal–agent setting described above to those that happen when the real estate agent *is* the home-owner. In the second case, the principal and agent are the *same person*, so there is no principal-agent problem. By comparing the two outcomes, Levitt and Syverson measured the distortions created by the asymmetric information and misaligned incentives in the principal-agent relationship between the seller and the real estate agent.

The results confirm the predictions above. When real estate agents sell their own houses, they keep their homes on the market longer and sell them for a higher price than comparable non-agent-owned homes. (In fact, agents earn, on average, an extra 3.7% in terms of sales price and wait 10 days longer to do so.) This suggests that agents are able to convince sellers to accept early offers that they themselves take a pass on. Furthermore, when the information gap between agents and sellers is smaller—and therefore the principal-agent distortions are expectedly smallest—there are smaller differences in outcomes across agent-owned and non-agent-owned homes. For example, agent-owners on blocks of very similar houses (e.g., tract homes) have sales price and time-on-market differences that are close to those of non-agent-sellers on the same block. Presumably, this is because when all houses in a neighborhood are similar, everyone has a good idea of what his own house is worth. On blocks with very different house types and styles, however, the agent-owner gap is larger, an outcome consistent with agents having a larger information advantage in these areas.

15.3 figure it out

Pablo is a struggling artist who wants to rent an apartment from Donald. Pablo loves to draw, so much so that he often draws on any surface he can find, including walls. In fact, Pablo would get $300 in utility from being able to draw his artwork on the walls in his apartment. On the other hand, Donald would like Pablo to leave the apartment walls clean and free of any marks. If Pablo draws his art on the walls, it will cost Donald $500 to have the apartment repainted. Therefore, Donald is considering charging Pablo a damage deposit of $500.

a. Explain why this situation could be considered a principal–agent problem. Who is the principal? Who is the agent?

b. Draw the extensive form of this principal–agent problem and use backward induction to solve for the Nash equilibrium.

Solution:

a. Donald is the principal and Pablo is the agent. Donald would like Pablo to treat the apartment the same way he (Donald) would. However, Donald cannot be at the apartment to monitor Pablo's behavior all of the time. Therefore, a principal–agent problem exists. Donald's and Pablo's interests do not coincide.

b. The extensive form of this principal–agent problem is shown in the illustration on the next page. We can use backward induction to solve the game. If no damage deposit is charged, Pablo will want to paint on the walls because $300 > $0. If Donald charges a damage deposit, Pablo will leave the walls untouched because $0 > -$200. Given this information, we can see that Donald will charge the

$500 damage deposit (because $0 > -$500). Thus, the Nash equilibrium is that Donald will charge the $500 damage deposit and Pablo will leave the walls untouched.

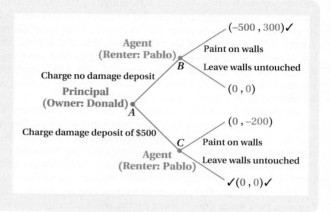

15.4 Signaling to Solve Asymmetric Information Problems

We talked earlier in the chapter about ways that sellers of high-quality goods can convince buyers of this fact. One involved offering warranties. The notion was that, since low-quality products are especially expensive to warranty (because they break more often), the very fact that a seller offers a warranty suggests that he or she is likely selling a high-quality product.

It turns out this basic idea applies across many economic settings, enough, in fact, to have its own name: **signaling.** Signaling lets one party in a transaction communicate to another party something that is otherwise not immediately observable. It's one way in which asymmetric information problems can be solved in markets.

Signaling was first formalized by economist Michael Spence in the early 1970s.[11] The basic idea of signaling is that there is some action, the "signal," that conveys otherwise unknown information about the signal sender. For the signal to be meaningful—that is, for the receiver to actually be able to learn something about the signal sender—the net economic benefit of sending the signal must vary across different "types" of senders. That is, sending the signal must be less costly for some types of senders than others. In the warranty example, sending the signal of providing a warranty is less costly for producers of high-quality products than for producers of low-quality products. This difference makes it more likely that high-quality products will have a warranty, allowing consumers to infer something about a product's quality, which would be otherwise unobservable at the time of purchase.

The Classic Signaling Example: Education

Signaling can have surprisingly powerful effects. Even if a signal is inherently worthless—that is, if the action itself has no economic consequence of its own other than as a signal—the information it conveys can completely determine equilibrium prices and quantities. To see how this might be possible, let's consider *the* classic signaling example: the correlation between more schooling and higher wages. To be concrete, we focus specifically on the well-documented fact that college graduates earn more, on average, than workers with only high school diplomas.

Suppose that going to college does *absolutely nothing* to improve your productivity on a job. (This is not what labor economists who have studied the issue have found, but it's a good assumption to make if we want to see how powerful signaling can be.)

signaling
A solution to the problem of asymmetric information in which the knowledgeable party alerts the other party to an unobservable characteristic of the good.

[11] Michael Spence, "Job Market Signaling," *Quarterly Journal of Economics* 87, no. 3 (1973): 355–374.

Let's assume that productivity is a function of personal organization, perseverance, and the abilities to concentrate on the task at hand and learn new things quickly. Employers would like to find workers with these qualities. They want to hire more productive workers and are willing to pay them more. But, the problem of asymmetric information gets in the way. Employers cannot easily discern through a quick interview or by looking at a résumé if a potential employee has these characteristics.

Highly productive workers would like to convince potential employers they would be good hires. But, how can applicants do this? Simply saying, "Hey, I'm very productive" is cheap talk. Less productive workers will say the same thing. Productive workers need some sort of "expensive talk" instead. That's what a college degree offers. Why? College is costly, and, importantly, it's more costly for some than others. It's costly in a monetary sense, but also in a much broader sense. Finishing a degree takes a lot of effort. To be able to expend the necessary effort, a student has to have certain qualities, like being organized, a willingness to persevere, and the abilities to concentrate on the task at hand and learn new things quickly.

The very same attributes that make a worker productive also make it easier for him to finish college. College is hard, but people without those attributes find it extremely hard. If you are a productive worker, therefore, a good way to demonstrate this to employers is by completing a college degree. You have made a costly choice that indicates something about your qualities that would otherwise be difficult to observe. That is, you have sent a **signal.** Here, the signal is aimed at employers with the intent of demonstrating your productivity.

signal
A costly action taken by an economic actor to indicate something that would otherwise be difficult to observe.

The signal in this example won't be meaningful if unproductive workers also receive college degrees. Employers could no longer use the completion of a degree to distinguish highly productive workers from less productive ones. This is why it's important that the signal is more costly for low-productivity workers to send (by finishing college). If the cost gap is large enough (we'll describe in a minute how large that gap has to be), low-productivity workers won't obtain college degrees.

When more productive workers finish college and less productive workers don't, employers can tell the difference between them. These employers are willing to pay the college graduates more, because they are more productive. We end up with the empirical fact we talked about earlier: College graduates earn more pay.

Remember the assumption we made at the start of this example: College has *no* inherent effect on workers' productivity levels. Despite this, we've shown that college graduates can end up being paid more. That's because a college degree, in its role as a signal, allows employers to figure out which workers are productive and which are not.

Signaling: A Mathematical Approach Let's use some specific numbers to make this result clearer. Suppose there are two types of workers, high-productivity and low-productivity. Each year of higher education costs high-productivity workers $25,000. This includes the monetary cost equivalent of going to class, finishing assignments, studying for exams, and so on. For low-productivity workers, each year of higher education costs $50,000 because of the higher cost of effort they face when attending school. Therefore, we can write the total costs of going to college as

$$C_H = \$25,000y$$

$$C_L = \$50,000y$$

where y is years in college, and C_H and C_L are the costs of attending school for high- and low-productivity workers, respectively.

Let's suppose that, over the course of a worker's lifetime, a high-productivity worker produces $250,000 worth of value for employers, while a low-productivity worker produces $125,000 of value. Because of the production of this extra value, employers are willing to pay high-productivity workers up to $125,000 more in wages.[12]

[12] Wages will be exactly $125,000 more if there is enough competition among firms for workers. For simplicity, we assume that outcome holds here, but it isn't necessary to make signaling work.

To be willing to pay high-productivity workers more, however, employers need to be able to tell them apart from low-productivity workers. Let's suppose for a moment that employers use completion of a college degree as a way to do that. That is, employers pay workers for whom $y \geq 4$ extra wages to the tune of $125,000 over the course of their lifetime. For employers to use this payment strategy, it must be true that only high-productivity workers finish college. Otherwise, employers would face the prospect of paying extra wages to workers who weren't creating the extra value to justify the higher wage.

Do only high-productivity workers finish college? Let's consider the cost and benefit of completing four years of college for each type of worker. For high-productivity workers, finishing college—that is, receiving at least $y = 4$ years of higher education—costs $100,000:

$$C_H = \$25{,}000y = \$25{,}000 \times 4 = \$100{,}000$$

Low-productivity workers face a larger cost of finishing college, $200,000:

$$C_L = \$50{,}000y = \$50{,}000 \times 4 = \$200{,}000$$

The benefit to each worker of finishing college is actually the same. Employers pay a total premium of $B = \$125{,}000$ in wages for completion of a college degree. Remember, because employers can't tell directly how productive a worker is, they are trying to rely on college completion to make the distinction.

Therefore, the net benefit (NB) to completing college for high-productivity workers is

$$NB_H = B - C_H = \$125{,}000 - \$100{,}000 = \$25{,}000$$

while for low-productivity workers, it is

$$NB_L = B - C_L = \$125{,}000 - \$200{,}000 = -\$75{,}000$$

High-productivity workers are $25,000 better off if they finish college, so they do. Low-productivity workers are actually worse off because of the higher cost of finishing for them. They will choose not to finish college. (In fact, they won't attend any college, because no wage premium is paid for any $y < 4$. Only some college study would impose costs on low-productivity workers without providing any benefit.)

Signaling: A Graphical Approach With this example, we've shown that the employers' strategy makes sense. They pay a wage premium to college graduates on the expectation that they will be high-productivity workers, even though the employers can't observe productivity directly. Their expectation turns out to be correct because low-productivity workers aren't willing to pay the extra costs that completing college requires of them.

This outcome can be seen in Figure 15.3, which shows workers' costs and benefits of college as a function of the number of years in college. Low-productivity workers' costs are shown by curve C_L; they increase $50,000 for every year of schooling. High-productivity workers' costs are shown by curve C_H. They are lower because these workers only pay a total cost of $25,000 per year. The wage premium (benefit) of college to both types of workers is shown by curve B. Workers with fewer than four years of college receive no wage premium. Those with four or more years, however, earn a premium of $125,000, which is why the wage premium jumps from 0 to $125,000 at $y = 4$.

For low-productivity workers, no amount of college creates a positive net benefit. Going for fewer than four years offers no wage premium but imposes costs. Attendance for exactly four years results in a wage premium of $125,000, but this isn't worth the $200,000 cost. And, more than four years only raises costs further without any additional wage premium. For high-productivity workers, however, four years of college do make sense. The four years cost them $100,000, but earn them a wage premium of $125,000, leading to a $25,000 net benefit. In this example, in fact, high-productivity workers don't just have

The benefits of a signal of education on the job market are shown using the relative costs and benefits of a four-year degree to low-productivity and high-productivity workers. Low-productivity workers' costs increase by \$50,000 for every year of college, as shown by C_L. High-productivity workers' costs, represented by C_H, are lower at \$25,000 per year. At four years of college, the wage premium jumps from \$0 to \$125,000. In this market, high-productivity workers will attend exactly four years of college because the benefits of college outweigh the costs. Low-productivity workers will not attend college because the costs of education outweigh the benefits.

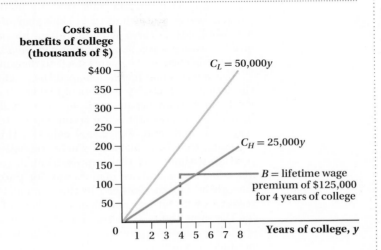

an incentive to finish college, they have an incentive to finish it in only four years, as more schooling creates extra costs without the benefit of extra pay.

This example demonstrates the potential power of signaling. Here, something that has no real benefit to society (because we assumed the education does not enhance worker productivity) is actually used to determine how much income each worker earns. The productive workers pay to go to college, but society gets nothing economically useful in return. A college degree doesn't make these workers *more* productive, because they were already more productive before attending college. Yet, using a degree as a signal allows productive workers to indicate their productivity to employers so these workers are paid more. However, four years of college are a rather expensive signal! If these workers could somehow find a cheaper way to signal their greater productivity, society would be better off.

Economists sometimes use "money burning" as a shorthand phrase to refer to the wasteful expenditure of resources for the purposes of sending a signal. In fact, *literally* burning money can itself be a signal in some cases. Suppose wealth were imperfectly observable (perhaps it's difficult to show people all your assets at once or to convince them of their value), and that a person wished to signal his wealth to another. He could do so by starting a cash bonfire. While burning money is obviously costly, it is less costly—relatively speaking—for wealthier people. Therefore, wealthy individuals could show that they are rich by demonstrating that they literally have money to burn.

Education and Productivity As we said, economists have found a lot of evidence that, in reality, college (and more years of education in general) does have positive effects on actual on-the-job productivity. Students aren't wasting all their tuition and effort just to prove that they will make good employees. There is some evidence, however, that *part* of the wage differences between workers with different education levels comes from signaling effects. For example, evidence exists of what is called the "sheepskin effect"—students with four years of college and a degree to show for it earn higher wages than students who have also finished four years of college but who did not receive a degree because they were just short of some graduation requirement. If time in school is what confers skills that are useful in the labor force, and employers pay workers based on which of those skills they observe in workers, then whether a student actually holds a degree shouldn't affect his pay. The fact that having the degree does affect a worker's pay suggests that signaling is at work; employers are, in part, relying on the existence of the degree itself to determine how much to pay workers.

This sheepskin effect has shaped the recent debate about college costs and whether the actual productivity benefits of higher education are overstated. After all, if tuition levels double not because college has actually made graduates more productive but instead because students are trying harder to signal their abilities by going to highly regarded (and more expensive) colleges, this situation is like an arms race among students, that is, a situation where competitors just try to stay ahead of their competition without any real improvement in rank. (The term is often used in military discussions as countries manufacture or purchase more and more weapons to try to stay ahead of one another.) In this example, students are spending large amounts of resources without any real change in their job market prospects because they're sending the same signal as before, but it's now more expensive. In addition, the increased spending does not provide any additional benefits to society in the form of more productive workers.

The evidence also suggests, however, that signaling effects are largest right after a worker is hired and quickly disappear thereafter. This isn't surprising; after employees work for a while, firms can directly observe their actual productivities. The employees' wages respond in turn. More productive workers—whether they have finished college or not—end up being paid more. Less productive workers—again, college graduates or not—earn lower pay. Because the employees' performances have directly revealed information about their productivities, the signal is no longer necessary.

To sum up, there are two reasons why schooling is important and increases wages: (1) because it raises productivity and (2) because it works as a signal that the person is more productive. While both matter in the labor market, the evidence suggests that Reason 1 plays a bigger role in explaining the relationship between income and schooling than does Reason 2.

Other Signals

Signaling is present in all sorts of economic situations beyond our example. As we mentioned earlier, for instance, warranties signal that a good is of high quality.

Buying an engagement ring for a fiancée can signal one's commitment to getting married. If, as sometimes happens, the woman keeps the ring should the wedding be called off, only men expecting the wedding to very likely occur will be willing to pay for the ring. The ring, as with attending college and offering warranties, allows men to substitute "expensive talk" regarding their (imperfectly observed) true feelings for what would otherwise be cheap talk.

The choices people make about the products they use or the ways in which they live their lives can be signals. They may want to inform family, friends, neighbors, or even strangers about some aspect of their personalities that would otherwise be difficult to convey. Some monks take vows of poverty. This, in part, signals their devotion to the Divine. (Whether they are signaling their devotion to other people or their deity is unclear.) Dressing up to go to work can be a signal of one's commitment to and seriousness about a job. Consumption patterns can be used to signal income or wealth to one's social network.

These examples only scratch the surface of the wide span of signaling that occurs in our society. They also indicate both the frequency of asymmetric information in economic interactions as well as the power signaling can have to reduce it.

 **application**

Advertising as a Signal of Quality

Firms use advertising to send all kinds of messages about their products: newer, cheaper, cooler—you name it, there's an ad saying it. But many economists argue that sometimes the message about the product isn't what's *in* the ad; instead, it's that the ad *exists* at all. In other words, the mere fact that a company advertises a product sends a signal that there is something desirable about that product.

The argument for advertising as a signal goes something like this. Advertising is costly, but it's really costly for unsuccessful, unprofitable companies. Why would a company be unsuccessful? Because it makes products that consumers don't like. So, the only firms that can afford to advertise are those that make things that consumers want to buy. By advertising, companies are effectively saying to consumers, "Our product is so excellent and will make us so much profit that we can afford to spend all this money advertising it. Companies that make lousy products aren't able to do that." All that's needed for this signaling effect to work is for the company to spend money on advertising. The ad doesn't need to offer any particular information at all about the product.

Perhaps one of the best examples of an "all-signal, no information" ad was E*TRADE's Super Bowl ad in 2000. The Super Bowl has the highest advertising rates in the entire TV world. The E*TRADE ad opens with two oddly dressed men sitting in lawn chairs in an open garage. Between them, a chimpanzee in an E*TRADE T-shirt stands on a bucket, dancing to the tune of "La Cucaracha" as the men (try to) clap to the beat. After 25 seconds, the screen goes dark and shows the line, "We just wasted 2 million bucks. What are you doing with your money?"

The ad was widely considered to be a success. Evidently millions of people thought, "That must be some kind of trading firm if they can afford to waste their money on Super Bowl ads like that." Signal sent; signal delivered.

15.4 figure it out

Last year, Used Cars"R"Us sold very few cars and ended up with a large economic loss. The owner, Geoffrey, has developed two strategies to help the dealership sell more vehicles in the coming year by signaling that it deals in only high-quality used vehicles:

- Change the name of the dealership to Quality Used Cars"R"Us.
- Offer a 60-day bumper-to-bumper warranty for every car sold.

Which of these two strategies is the best signal of high quality? Explain.

Solution:

To be a good signal of quality, a signal must be cheaper for high-quality producers and more expensive for low-quality producers. Therefore, the best signal is the 60-day warranty. If the cars sold at Used Cars"R"Us are truly of high quality, the warranty will not be very expensive for the dealership to offer. On the other hand, if Used Cars"R"Us only sold lemons, the warranty would be very expensive and negate the benefit of increased sales. Thus, consumers can be more confident that a dealership offering a warranty has higher-quality products than those that do not.

The change of the name of the dealership would just be "cheap talk." Any dealership can alter its name, and the cost of doing so will not vary across high-quality sellers and low-quality sellers.

15.5 Conclusion

In this chapter, we've studied markets in which asymmetric information exists—one party knows more than the other about the goods or services being traded. We saw that asymmetric information can have big impacts on how well markets operate. Under complete information, for example, buyers and sellers in a market engage in mutually beneficial exchanges and partake of the economic surplus created by these exchanges. In the extreme, asymmetric information can cause markets to seize up completely, because buyers and sellers are so afraid of making a decision with a poor economic outcome for them. Such a freeze on market exchanges harms not just the parties with the information disadvantage but also those with the advantage. This potential for economic harm explains why so many economic institutions have come about to reduce the effects of information asymmetries.

We've looked at numerous examples of ways that asymmetric information can show up in markets: adverse selection, moral hazard, and principal-agent problems, and we've discussed the steps consumers and firms take to try to reduce their impact. We covered a lot of ground, but it's important to remember that we really only scratched the surface of this very interesting area of economics.

In the next chapter, we study more ways that the canonical markets we studied in the earlier parts of this book may fail to deliver outcomes that are socially optimal. Specifically, we investigate the roles of externalities and public goods.

Summary

1. The **lemons problem,** a common feature of markets like the used car market, exists when the seller knows more about the quality of a good than does the buyer. The existence of lemons on the market results in **adverse selection** into the market; low-quality goods are more likely to be put on the market than high-quality goods because consumers cannot differentiate between the two types of goods before buying them. The same type of adverse selection problem occurs in markets in which buyers have more information than sellers, such as the insurance market. [**Section 15.1**]

2. When one party in an economic transaction cannot observe the *behavior* of the other party, **moral hazard** arises. Moral hazard is especially common in insurance markets, because once insured against a bad outcome, the insured party is more likely to act in ways that increase the probability of that bad outcome. Clauses that specify the actions that must be taken by a policyholder in order to be covered are designed to mitigate moral hazard. [**Section 15.2**]

3. Information asymmetry in the workplace and other economic arenas can lead to **principal–agent problems**. In this case, the principal hires an agent whose actions the principal cannot fully observe. To ensure that the agent acts in the principal's best interest, the principal must create incentive structures which align the interests of the agent with the principal's own best interests. [**Section 15.3**]

4. One way to solve information asymmetry is through the use of **signaling,** in which one party in a transaction communicates information that is not immediately observable. A common example of signaling is education, which enables employers to distinguish relatively high-productivity workers from low-productivity workers. [**Section 15.4**]

Review Questions

1. Contrast market situations with complete and asymmetric information. What is an example of a market with complete information?

2. What characteristics of a market can create the lemons problem?

3. Define adverse selection. Why does the lemons problem result in adverse selection?

4. How can warranties reduce the lemons problem in an economic market?

5. How can insurance companies mitigate the problems of adverse selection?

6. What is moral hazard? Describe the example of moral hazard in the insurance market.

7. How can insurance providers use incentives to reduce moral hazard in the insurance market?

8. What market characteristics can create problems in a principal–agent relationship?

9. How can principals reduce the problems associated with principal–agent relationships?

10. How can signaling be used to reduce asymmetric information in a market?

11. How can education be used as a signal in the job market?

12. Name two examples of signals other than education. How do these examples reduce asymmetric information?

....

Problems (Solutions to problems marked * appear at the back of this book. Problems adapted to use calculus are available online at http://worthpublishers.com/GLS1e)

1. Consider the market for used cars shown in the figure below. The top panel (a) shows the market for low-quality cars (lemons); the bottom panel (b) shows the market for high-quality cars (plums). If all buyers and sellers had full information about the quality of automobiles being offered for sale, lemons would sell for $8,000 and plums would sell for $16,000.

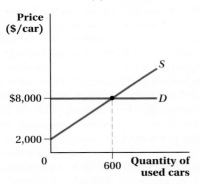

(a) Lemons

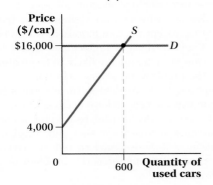

(b) Plums

   a. Suppose that buyers recognize that the chance of getting a lemon is 50%, but are unable to tell whether a car is a lemon or a plum. What is the expected value of a used car to a buyer?

   b. If the market works to the extent that prices reflect the expected value of a used car, how many high-quality automobiles will be offered for sale at the price determined in (a)? How many low-quality automobiles will be offered for sale? Of the automobiles offered for sale, what is the proportion of low-quality automobiles?

   c. Compared to a market with perfect information, what kind of deadweight loss does the information loss generate in the market for high-quality used cars? Is there a deadweight loss in the market for lemons, too?

2. In Problem 1, we discovered that imperfect information about the quality of used cars caused fewer plums and more lemons to be offered for sale. Thinking in discrete steps,

   a. How does this revision of the expected value affect the proportion of lemons to plums offered for sale by sellers?

   b. How does the change in the proportion of lemons to plums affect buyers' willingness to pay for a used car?

   c. How does the changing market price (buyers' willingness to pay) affect the quantity of plums and the quantity of lemons offered for sale?

   d. Briefly describe the logical conclusion of this feedback process.

*3. In an isolated town, there are two distinct markets for cars. Buyers will pay up to $12,000 for a high-quality car or $8,000 for a low-quality car. There are 100 high-quality cars for sale, and the sellers have a minimum acceptable price of $11,000. There are also 100 low-quality cars for sale at a minimum acceptable price of $5,000. The supply of automobiles is perfectly inelastic above the reservation price.

   a. If there is perfect information, how many high-quality and how many low-quality cars will be sold?

   b. Suppose that the quality of a car is known to the seller, but not to the buyer. What price will prevail in the marketplace if buyers correctly estimate the chance of acquiring a low-quality car at 50%? What happens to the number of high-quality cars for sale at that price?

c. After sellers make all adjustments, what will the equilibrium price of cars be? What proportion of those cars will be high-quality cars?

d. What happens to your answers to (a), (b), and (c) if sellers of high-quality cars have a reservation price of $9,500 instead of $11,000?

4. In the 1960s Yale University began offering students an alternative to taking out student loans. Instead, students could attend Yale in exchange for a specified percentage of their earnings over a significant length of time. Yale used historical data to determine the percentage so that the program would pay for itself—large payments from high earners would offset the smaller payments from low earners.

a. If you were planning on becoming a Wall Street financier, would you be more likely to take out loans or enroll in the Yale program? Why?

b. If you were planning on becoming a missionary, would you be more likely to take out loans or enroll in the Yale program? Why?

c. The tuition program turned out to be a financial disaster for Yale. Do your answers to (a) and (b) shed light on why? Explain.

d. What kind of information problem did the Yale program suffer from?

5. Toyota regularly takes its own cars in trade for new models. It then subjects them to a rigorous inspection process, fixing defects as it goes, and offers them for sale with an extended warranty. Explain how these procedures help Toyota deal with the adverse selection problem.

*6. A few years ago, a new online insurer appeared. Found at www.ticketfree.org, the insurer offered, for a price, up to $500 of coverage against speeding tickets.

a. Who has more valuable information in this potential transaction, the buyer of speeding ticket insurance or the seller?

b. Explain why the existence of information asymmetries creates an adverse selection problem in the market for speeding ticket insurance.

c. What is likely to happen to the behavior of both faster and slower drivers once they have

purchased speeding ticket insurance? What is this kind of problem called?

d. Ticketfree.org is no longer in operation. Use your answers to (b) and (c) to explain why.

7. To assist in ensuring adequate and affordable health care for all, the federal government has mandated that health insurers provide health insurance to all, regardless of their physical condition. Insurers may not reject coverage for preexisting health problems.

a. Explain why this mandate, standing alone, creates tremendous potential for adverse selection problems.

b. A second part of recent health care reforms is a mandate that every person must either obtain insurance through his employer or through the private market. Explain how this mandate reduces (i) adverse selection problems in general and (ii) the adverse selection problems discussed in part (a) in particular.

8. Many health and casualty insurance policies require policyholders to pay a certain amount (called a deductible) for claims before the insurer itself will begin to pay.

a. Explain how the existence of a deductible reduces the problems of moral hazard.

b. Often, insurers will let policyholders choose a low deductible, or will offer them a larger deductible in exchange for a substantial reduction in the premium. Explain how this two-tiered system helps insurers deal with the problem of adverse selection.

9. After a probationary period of six years, during which they teach, research, and serve on committees, university professors who meet acceptable standards are given tenure. Tenure offers these professors tremendous job security.

a. Explain why a tenure system makes universities susceptible to a moral hazard problem.

b. Explain why the problems of moral hazard caused by tenure are likely to be greater than the problems of adverse selection.

10. Suppose that, to deal with adverse selection problems, a new federal lemons law requires all used car dealerships to provide a one-year warranty for each car they sell. Explain how this new law, designed to reduce adverse selection, might increase the problem of moral hazard.

*11. Harry is dating Sally. Because he is devastated at the thought of being dumped, he spends considerable resources making himself attractive to her: expensive haircuts, ballroom dancing classes, a gym membership, and so on. Harry's marginal cost of making himself attractive to Sally is given by *MC* in the graph below. Sally, of course, appreciates his efforts: The marginal benefit Harry receives from his efforts (which account for the probability of being dumped) is shown as *MB*.

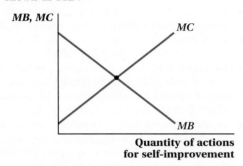

**Quantity of actions
for self-improvement**

a. On the graph, determine the optimal amount of resources Harry should expend making himself more attractive to Sally.
b. Harry marries Sally. The marriage contract raises the cost of exiting a relationship, and thus, for any given level of Harry's expenditure, Sally is less likely to dump Harry. Illustrate the effects of the marriage contract in the accompanying graph by shifting the appropriate curve in the appropriate direction.
c. "Harry has really let himself go since we got married. He burps too much, seldom shaves, and never takes out the trash." Is this commonly heard statement consistent with the illustration you have drawn?
d. What kind of problem does this illustrate: adverse selection or moral hazard?
e. A "covenant marriage" is one that is virtually impossible to exit for a given period of time. Illustrate the effects of a covenant marriage on your graph, and comment on the predictions your graph holds for the quality of relationships fostered by covenant marriages.
12. Consider the graph in the next column, which demonstrates the costs and benefits of theft-proofing one's home. The marginal costs increase as more precaution is taken: It's cheap to install good locks, but more difficult to install invisible laser intruder-detection systems. The marginal benefit declines as more precaution is taken: If I am a burglar, adding a guard dog isn't going to provide much deterrence if you already have an electric fence and 30 locks on each door and window.

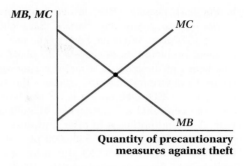

**Quantity of precautionary
measures against theft**

a. Determine the optimal amount of precaution the homeowner would take if theft insurance were unavailable.
b. Suppose that the homeowner can obtain an insurance policy that covers half of any losses he might suffer. Assuming that the marginal benefit curve represents dollar losses to the homeowner, shift the marginal benefit curve an appropriate distance and determine what happens to the homeowner's optimal amount of care.
c. Suppose that the insurance company decides to institute a deductible: The homeowner pays the first $1,000 of losses, and after that the insurance company splits the losses with the homeowner 50-50. Shift the marginal benefit curve by an appropriate amount (be sure to indicate the magnitude of the shift in an appropriate fashion). What effect does the deductible have on the precautions taken by the homeowner?
*13. After years of training, Sara has landed a contract playing professional lacrosse. Eager to leverage her pro status by bringing in endorsements, she asks Jenny MacGuire to be her personal manager. Jenny has offered Sara a choice of two payment plans. Sara can engage Jenny's services for a flat fee of $100,000. Alternatively, Sara can pay Jenny 15% of all endorsement revenue.

Sara estimates that if Jenny expends modest effort ($20,000 worth) in her job, she will generate $600,000 in endorsement revenue for Sara. But if Jenny expends high effort ($50,000 worth), she'll bring in $1 million in endorsements.

a. Suppose Sara agrees to the flat-rate plan. What can Sara expect to receive if Jenny expends modest effort? If Jenny expends high effort? What can Jenny expect to receive in either case? Explain the associated principal-agent problem. Who is the principal? Who is the agent?

b. For both possible effort levels, determine the rewards to Jenny and Sara if Sara chooses the 15% plan. What happens to the principal-agent problem if Sara chooses this plan?

14. The board of directors of a major corporation is trying to determine how to structure the salary of the new CEO. One option is for the board to offer the new CEO a flat salary of $1 million per year. A second option is to offer a profit-sharing plan with a base salary of $200,000 plus 10% of the firm's profit. If the CEO puts a lot of effort into the job, she will generate a $10 million profit for the firm. If the CEO exerts modest effort, the corporation will earn $7 million in profit. Expending a lot of effort costs the CEO $500,000; expending modest effort costs her $300,000.

   a. Draw the extensive-form game tree for the game played between the board and the CEO. Assume that the board moves first, choosing the type of salary offer. Assume that the CEO moves second, choosing her effort level. Be sure to enumerate payoffs to the board (and the shareholders they represent) and the CEO.

   b. What is the equilibrium outcome for this game? What kind of contract should the board offer? What level of effort should the CEO choose?

15. Consider the questions faced by the board and the CEO in Problem 14. Assume that, as before, expending modest effort costs the CEO $300,000. But, assume now that expending high effort costs the CEO $750,000.

   a. Draw the extensive form for this game and find the equilibrium. Does the change in the cost of high effort alter the outcome? Explain.

   b. Demonstrate that the directors cannot improve their outcome by changing the base salary in the profit-sharing plan.

   c. What is the minimum share of the firm's profit that will induce the CEO to expend high effort?

16. You have decided to produce a line of moisture-wicking skateboarding clothes. You're a wonderful designer, but a lousy tailor, and as a result, you decide to hire your roommate (who is a wonderful seamstress) to produce the clothes for you. Is it better for you to pay your roommate by the hour or to pay by the garment? Explain.

17. Princess Buttercup has a multitude of potential suitors. She wishes to separate them into two groups—those who are truly interested in her hand in marriage, and those who are only interested because she's convenient, pretty, and rich. Let's call these two groups "interested" and "nonchalant," respectively. In an attempt to separate the two groups, Princess Buttercup devises a plan under which potential suitors must slay dragons before coming to the castle to court her.

   • Those who slay the requisite number of dragons, $\overline{D}$, will be allowed to court her.

   • Those who do not slay the requisite number of dragons will only be allowed to court Buttercup's ugly half-sister, Princess Poison Ivy.

   • To a member of either group, the benefit to courting Princess Buttercup is equal to $1,000.

   • To a member of either group, the benefit to courting Princess Poison Ivy is $64.

   • To a member of the "interested" group, who pursue their goal with unbridled passion, the cost of passing Buttercup's test is given as D^2, where D is the number of dragons slain.

   • To a member of the "nonchalant" group, who pursue their goal halfheartedly, the cost of passing Buttercup's test is given as D^3, where D is the number of dragons slain.

   a. Princess Buttercup wants to sort the interested suitors from the nonchalant suitors. What is the *minimum* number of dragons Princess Buttercup can ask potential suitors to slay if she wants them to separate into groups? (You can round to an appropriate integer.)

   b. Suppose that Princess Buttercup asks suitors to slay *three fewer* dragons than you indicated in your answer to (a). Why will asking suitors to slay this many dragons not help Princess Buttercup filter out the nonchalant suitors?

   c. What is the *maximum* number of dragons Princess Buttercup can ask potential suitors to slay if she wants to be able to distinguish between interested and nonchalant suitors? (Again, you may round your answer to an appropriate integer.)

   d. Suppose that Princess Buttercup asks potential suitors to slay *three more* dragons than you indicated in your answer to (c). Why will asking suitors to slay this many dragons not help Princess Buttercup filter out the nonchalant suitors?

   e. Suppose that Princess Buttercup has appropriately set the number of dragons, filtered out the nonchalant suitors, and from the pool of interested suitors chosen her prince. Now, she wishes to see if her prince wants her because of love, or whether her prince is only interested given her vast fortune. What modern American legal device might Princess Buttercup use as a screening tactic to discover the true answer? Explain your response.

*18. Suppose that there are two types of workers in the world: Charlie Hustles, who are high-productivity workers, and Lazy Susans, who are low-productivity workers. The market would pay $70,000 (this and all numbers in this question are in present value terms) to hire a Charlie Hustle, but only $20,000 to hire a Lazy Susan. The problem, of course, is that a firm cannot tell on sight whether a job applicant is a Charlie or a Susan. One way to attempt to separate the Chucks and the Suzies is to require a college degree. It is easy for a Charlie Hustle to obtain a degree (the degree takes four years to complete and costs $40,000 in total). It is harder for a Lazy Susan to obtain a degree (six years and a cost of $60,000). Assume that a college education adds nothing to either worker's productivity.

a. If the company, operating blindly with no degree requirements, were to pay an average wage of $45,000, what would most of its applicants look like?

b. Suppose that the company announces that it will pay $70,000 to those with college degrees, and $20,000 to those without. What is the net benefit of a college education to a Charlie? To a Susan? Does the degree requirement allow the firm to filter out low-quality applicants?

c. Suppose that a new federal subsidy to assist low-productivity workers reduces the cost of obtaining a degree to $46,000. What is the net benefit of a college education to a Charlie? To a Susan? Does the degree requirement allow the firm to filter out low-quality applicants?

d. In light of your answers to (b) and (c), discuss the following assertion: *To be effective, a signal must be costly, but it must be more costly for a low-productivity applicant.*

e. Colleges and universities have been accused of practicing grade inflation. In fact, some colleges have actually outlawed awarding a grade of "F." Given your answer to (d), discuss the impact of this practice on the signaling value of a college diploma. Is this practice good for students? Does your answer depend on the quality of the student? Explain.

*19. Peacocks, with their fabulous tails, live wild in the jungle. There, a tail is a detriment—it slows the birds in flight, and presents an excellent handle for a predator to grab hold of. Nevertheless, males continue to grow them because peahens love bling, and the more, the better.

a. Explain the value of a long tail as a signal, focusing on the general principle that signals must be costly to a strong bird, but even more costly to a weak bird.

b. Peahens would receive the same information if all peacocks cut their tails in half. In light of this truth, explain why the signal is socially costly.

c. Suppose all male peacocks agreed to cut their tails in half. Explain why such an agreement is unlikely to last, and why the disintegration of the agreement makes all peacocks worse off.

20. In the late 1800s "wildcat banks," which were easy to charter and largely unregulated, sprang up across the American West. Some new banks chose to operate out of simple and inexpensive wooden structures, but others built elaborate buildings out of stone, with lots of gilding and other adornment.

a. Explain how the variety of building types that sprung up can be attributed, at least in part, to the potential for moral hazard.

b. Explain how the building choices of bankers in late 1800s America illustrate the inherent wastefulness of signaling.

Externalities and Public Goods

16

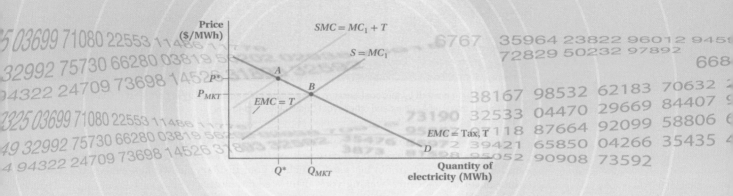

For people living in most major cities in the United States, air pollution is a fact of life. Ozone, particulates, and general "crud" in the air result from economic activities such as driving cars and operating power plants and factories. This pollution imposes a significant cost on the health of people who must live with it. Some studies estimate the damages in terms of health costs at more than $100 billion per year.[1]

Over the past 40+ years, the United States has sought to reduce pollutants released into its air by setting limits on the amounts of pollution generated by cars and by various industries. In recent years, however, the baseline level of pollution on the West Coast (the level that would exist if there were NO domestic polluters) has risen significantly. Experts believe that much of the increase in baseline pollution results from polluted air that originates in coal-burning power plants in Asia (primarily China), blows across the Pacific on the jet stream, and settles on the West Coast of the United States.

[1] Nicholas Z. Muller, Robert Mendelsohn, and William Nordhaus, "Environmental Accounting for Pollution in the United States Economy," *American Economic Review* 101, no. 5 (August 2011): 1649–1675.

Imaginechina via AP Images/steinphoto/iStockphoto

The pollution emitted by this coal-burning power plant in Changchun City in northeast China ends up in the air over Los Angeles and other West Coast cities and towns.

People in the suburbs often experience another type of pollution. For example, suppose your neighbor hires a lawn care service (with its assorted mowers, weed wackers, and leaf blowers) to groom her yard. Much to your dismay, the workers arrive at 7 A.M. on a Saturday morning, waking you out of a sound sleep.

In both of these examples, a transaction takes place between two parties (the power-producing plants and their customers, the lawn service and your neighbor), and they each get something out of it (money, electric power, a neat lawn). But, they are not the only ones who get something out of the transactions: Inhabitants of the U.S. West Coast experience increased air pollution, and you lose a good morning's sleep.

These last two outcomes are not just inconveniences or bad luck—they are evidence of a market failure. As we learned in Chapter 3, markets are efficient when all transactions that positively benefit society take place. It is this condition—that transactions make *society* better off, not just the parties directly involved in a transaction—that is not satisfied in the power plant and lawn service transactions. The power plant and lawn service look at their costs and set their prices just as the production and cost chapters would advise them to. And when the firms and their customers enter into a transaction, all participants take into account the costs and benefits from the transaction. What they *don't* consider are the costs their transactions impose on West Coasters and suburbanites. An efficient market would take those costs into account, but because West Coasters and the suburbanites are not part of the transaction, such costs do not enter into the firms' cost calculations and output decisions.

In Chapter 15, we saw that an imbalance of information between the participants in a transaction can lead to an inefficient market outcome (the production and consumption of too much or too little of a good), which reduces welfare by decreasing the surplus available to consumers and producers in a market. Asymmetric information is one source of the market failures we observe in an economy. In this chapter, we look at two other sources of market failures: *externalities* (such as the increased pollution and noise in our examples) and *public goods* (which we discuss in detail in the chapter). In addition to looking at why and how the existence of externalities and public goods cause market failures, we examine government policies implemented with the hope that they will encourage the production of surplus-maximizing quantities of various goods and thus eliminate market failures.

16.1 Externalities

As we learned in the introduction, **externalities** exist whenever economic transactions impact third parties not directly involved in the transaction. **Negative externalities** (such as increased West Coast pollution and rude awakenings) impose costs on other people or firms. **Positive externalities** benefit third parties who are not directly involved in a transaction. A classic example of a positive externality involves bees. The bees in a beekeeper's hives not only produce honey for the beekeeper to sell but also help pollinate the crops and flowers on neighboring properties, a beneficial service for which the neighbors often do not pay the beekeeper.

A free market usually does not produce the optimal quantity of a good when an externality is present. Instead, the market will produce too much of those goods with negative externalities and not enough of the goods with positive externalities.

Why Things Go Wrong: The Economic Inefficiencies from Externalities

Externalities create inefficient outcomes because society's overall benefit or cost from a transaction is different from the private benefit or cost to the consumer and producer involved in the same transaction. Private cost and benefit are the variables we normally consider when analyzing a market. **External marginal cost** is the cost imposed on a third party when an additional unit of a good is produced or consumed, and **external marginal benefit** is the benefit conferred on a third party when an additional unit of a good is produced or consumed.

When there are no externalities in a market, society's cost and benefit and private cost and benefit are the same, and no external marginal costs or benefits exist. When there are externalities, the **social cost** (the cost to society as a whole) is the private cost plus the external cost, and the **social benefit** (the benefit to society as a whole) is the private benefit plus the external benefit. As we see in the next sections, incorporating social cost and benefit alters our analysis of market outcomes, including the optimal quantities and prices.

Negative Externalities: Too Much of a Bad Thing

To begin our study of negative externalities, let's look at the air pollution created by fossil-fuel-fired power plants when they generate electricity (Figure 16.1). Firms in a competitive industry decide how many megawatt hours (MWh) to produce by following the basic method presented in Chapter 8: Their optimal output is found at the point where price P (which equals marginal revenue and is represented by the demand curve in a competitive market) equals the industry's marginal cost (MC_I).[2] Note, however, that this marginal cost is *private* marginal cost. It is not *social* marginal cost because it does not include any external costs that the industry's output imposes on other people. The industry produces Q_{MKT} MWh of electricity and the equilibrium market price per MWh is P_{MKT}.

Now let's assume that as the industry produces Q_{MKT}, it also produces particulates, ozone, and other pollutants that cause health and environmental damage to others. To make things easier, we assume that the per-unit external marginal cost of pollution

---

externality
A cost or benefit that affects a third party not directly involved in an economic transaction.

negative externality
A cost imposed on a third party not directly involved in an economic transaction.

positive externality
A benefit conferred on a third party not directly involved in an economic transaction.

external marginal cost
The cost imposed on a third party when an additional unit of a good is produced or consumed.

external marginal benefit
The benefit conferred on a third party when an additional unit of a good is produced or consumed.

social cost
The cost of an economic transaction to society, equal to the private cost plus the external cost.

social benefit
The benefit of an economic transaction to society, equal to the private benefit plus the external benefit.

---

[2] Of course, power plants do not produce in a perfectly competitive market. We could do this exercise for a single firm with market power following the normal monopoly rule of setting output at the level for which marginal revenue equals marginal cost. Here, too, the external marginal cost would not be included in the firm's decision, leading to an inefficient level of output. Assuming a competitive industry makes the analysis simpler, though, so we will stick with that.

is constant and fixed at EMC.[3] External marginal cost is summarized by EMC in Figure 16.1.

To obtain the social marginal cost, we add together MC_I and EMC and come up with the curve SMC. Once the cost of the externality is taken into account, we see that society as a whole has a higher marginal cost of producing electricity than does the industry (the SMC curve is above the MC_I curve). With all costs fully accounted for, total surplus is maximized at Q^* and price P^*, where price (demand) equals social marginal cost. Because we've now included the cost of the externality, the price is higher than that in the market equilibrium, and the quantity produced is lower. When the production of a good creates a negative externality and its external cost is ignored by producers, the market produces a greater level of output than is socially optimal.

The pollution externality and the market inefficiency it creates arise because the power companies in the industry do not pay pollution costs. They pay only private production costs, such as expenditures for fuel, labor, physical capital, and so on. They completely ignore the external costs that society must bear because of the pollution the industry generates. (In the real world, power companies can be required to pay these external costs. We discuss how this is accomplished later in the chapter.)

As a result, market output is greater than the efficient level of output when negative externalities are present. The true, full marginal cost of electricity production includes both the power companies' private marginal cost *and* the external marginal cost of their pollution. If the firms in the industry had to pay both of these costs, the industry would choose to generate a smaller quantity of electricity.

Exactly where does the inefficiency come from? At point A, every person who buys electricity values it at least as much as it costs society to produce the electricity (including the pollution costs). The industry produces at point B, however, and the portion of the demand curve between points A and B represents consumers who value the electricity they want to purchase less than it costs society to produce. They buy the electricity only because the market price is so low. If the price reflected the true cost of the product, these consumers would not buy this electricity.

The size of the inefficiency depends on how many people buy electricity who otherwise wouldn't if the price represented the true social cost. This is reflected in the difference between Q^* and Q_{MKT}. The size of the inefficiency also depends on the discrepancy between the cost to society of producing the good and the benefit consumers obtain

---

Figure 16.1   Negative Externalities in a Competitive Electricity Market

The social marginal cost of electricity (SMC) equals the industry's private marginal cost (MC_I) plus the external marginal cost (EMC). The socially optimal quantity of electricity, Q^*, is found at point A, the intersection of the social marginal cost curve SMC and D. In a competitive market, however, production occurs at point B (Q_{MKT}, P_{MKT}), where $MC_I = S = D$. Because the industry does not take into account the external marginal cost (EMC), it produces a quantity of electricity Q_{MKT} that is higher than the socially optimal quantity (Q^*). This results in a deadweight loss equal to the shaded triangle.

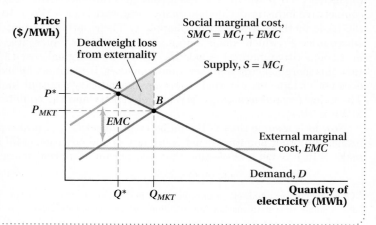

---

[3] In reality, external marginal cost can rise or fall as Q rises; the analysis is the same.

from it. We see this part of the loss in the size of the vertical gap between the social marginal cost curve SMC and the demand curve D: The larger this gap, the further the market outcome is from the socially optimal one.

When we put together the differences in quantity produced and in cost and benefit, we can determine the exact size of the inefficiency arising from the externality. It is the triangular area between SMC and demand D and between units Q^* and Q_{MKT}. This area shows by how much society's cost of producing the excess units of electricity (reflected in the SMC curve) exceeds the consumers' benefit from buying these units (reflected in the D curve). The triangle is the sum of the loss from each unit for which society's costs are greater than the consumers' benefits.

This triangle looks like the deadweight loss triangles we've seen before because it *is* a deadweight loss triangle. This deadweight loss is the reduction in social welfare that results from resources being used to produce goods for which costs exceed benefits.

There are many examples of negative externalities in the world. They range from huge issues in the realms of businesses and governments (Asian pollution) to smaller irritations in our everyday lives (noisy lawn mowers).

- When British Petroleum decided to take a risk and skimp on safety on its oil rigs in the Gulf of Mexico, it saved some private cost but did not take into account the damage a spill would cause to the environment and to other industries in the region if things went wrong. Things certainly did go wrong in 2010.

- Small private jets in the United States generally pay significantly lower landing fees than large commercial airplanes do, but they crowd the airspace and lead to flight delays for others. Because the private jets do not have to pay the full cost of their flights (such as the higher costs of congestion), this is a negative externality.

- When individuals decide not to get vaccinated (or decide not to vaccinate their children) against the measles, they and their children become carriers who can give the disease to others. When doctors overprescribe antibiotics for patients, bacteria develop resistance to the medicine. Because both these actions impose costs on third parties, they have negative externalities.

- When you go to a ball game and the woman in front of you is wearing a big hat that blocks your view, she is not including the external marginal cost in her decision to wear the hat.

Remember that, without incorporating external cost into production decisions, firms will supply too much of goods that have negative externalities and sell them for too low a price.

16.1 figure it out

Assume that notebook paper is sold in a perfectly competitive industry. The industry short-run supply curve (or marginal cost curve) is $P = MC = 2Q$, where Q is measured in millions of reams per year. The inverse demand for notebook paper is $P = 40 - 8Q$.

a. Find the equilibrium market price and quantity sold.

b. Suppose that, in their production processes, paper manufacturers have been dumping waste in nearby streams. The external marginal cost is estimated to be $0.50 for each ream produced. Calculate the socially optimal level of output and price for the paper industry.

Solution:

a. First, rearrange the inverse supply and demand equations to put them in terms of quantity supplied and quantity demanded:

$$P = 2Q \qquad\qquad P = 40 - 8Q$$
$$Q^S = 0.5P \qquad\qquad 8Q = 40 - P$$
$$\qquad\qquad\qquad Q^D = 5 - 0.125P$$

Market equilibrium occurs where $Q^D = Q^S$:

$$0.5P = 5 - 0.125P$$
$$0.625P = 5$$
$$P = \$8$$

When $P = \$8$,

$$Q^S = 0.5P = 0.5(8) = 4$$
$$Q^D = 5 - 0.125P = 5 - 0.125(8) = 5 - 1 = 4$$

Paper will sell for \$8 per ream and 4 million reams will be sold each year.

b. The social marginal cost is equal to the industry marginal cost plus the external marginal cost:

$$SMC = MC + EMC$$
$$= 2Q + 0.50$$

To find the socially optimal price and quantity, we equate the social marginal cost with the inverse demand:

$$2Q + 0.50 = 40 - 8Q$$
$$10Q = 39.50$$
$$Q^* = 3.95$$

The socially optimal level of output is 3.95 million reams of paper each year.

The socially optimal price can be found by substituting the optimal quantity into either the social marginal cost or inverse demand curves:

$$P^* = 2Q + 0.50 = 2(3.95) + 0.50 = \$7.90 + 0.50 = \$8.40$$
$$= 40 - 8Q = 40 - 8(3.95) = 40 - 31.60 = \$8.40$$

Therefore, the socially optimal price is \$8.40 per ream.

Positive Externalities: Not Enough of a Good Thing

A positive externality exists when economic activity has a spillover benefit enjoyed by third parties who are not directly engaged in the activity. Just as negative externalities create a gap between private marginal cost and social marginal cost (equal to the external marginal cost), positive externalities create a gap between the private benefit (as summarized by the demand curve) and the social benefit. The social benefit is represented by the social demand curve, which is the sum of the buyers' private benefit (the demand curve) and the external marginal benefit.

We can explore positive externalities by looking at the decision on how many years of education to obtain. There is a benefit to getting more education, and we express that in a demand curve. There is also a cost (sometimes a huge cost!) to spending more years in school that includes not only tuition, books, and supplies, but also the opportunity cost of not being able to take a job that pays a salary while you are in school (which is often even more expensive than the tuition). Evidence does exist, however, that when more people in a city or a country acquire more years of education, the pay and job prospects of other people living in their area rise. One possible explanation for this link is that the more education you have, the more likely you are to start companies and hire other people. If true, there is a positive externality from your decision to spend additional years in school because the social benefit of that longer education is greater than the private benefit. It should come as no surprise then that in a circumstance like this, the free market will lead people to purchase fewer years of education than would be socially optimal.

To see why, let's consider the market for college degrees that is represented in Figure 16.2. In our analysis, we assume that all college degrees are of equal value. Again, to keep our analysis simple, we assume a perfectly competitive market.[4]

The number of students getting a college degree will be at the point where the private marginal benefit of the college degree (measured by the demand curve) equals the marginal cost of obtaining the degree (point B). Left to its own devices, then, the free-market equilibrium occurs where Q_{MKT} college degrees are produced and consumed, and the price of a college degree is P_{MKT} (where $MC = P = MR$ for a competitive market).

The external marginal benefit EMB from each person getting a college degree is shown by the EMB curve.[5] The social demand curve SD is the private marginal benefit (demand curve) plus the external marginal benefit. SD measures the marginal benefit of college degrees to society as a whole rather than only to the students. In Figure 16.2, $SD = D + EMB$.

The socially optimal number of college degrees occurs at point A, the intersection of the marginal cost curve and the social demand curve SD. At this point, Q^* degrees are awarded at a price of P^*. In the free-market outcome (point B), however, the quantity of degrees Q_{MKT} is too low and creates a deadweight loss equal to the shaded triangle in Figure 16.2. For all of the potential degrees between Q_{MKT} and Q^*, the social demand curve lies above the marginal cost curve, but the private demand curve is below

---

Figure 16.2   :   **Positive Externalities in the Market for College Degrees**

The social demand for college degrees (SD) equals the private marginal benefit curve (D) plus the external marginal benefit (EMB). The socially optimal number of college degrees, Q^*, is found at point A, the intersection of the marginal cost curve $S = MC_I$ and SD. In an unregulated market for college degrees, production occurs at point B (Q_{MKT}, P_{MKT}), where $D = S = MC_I$. Because the market does not take into account the external marginal benefit (EMB), it ends up producing fewer college degrees Q_{MKT} than the socially optimal quantity (Q^*), resulting in a deadweight loss equal to the shaded triangle.

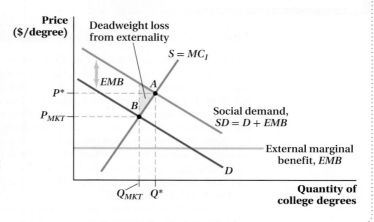

---

[4] It wouldn't make much difference to the results if we looked at differentiated markets and added market power. It would just be more complicated because we would have to keep track of marginal revenue curves for suppliers with market power and the cross-price elasticities of demand for different types of education.

[5] Again, for convenience, we assume that the EMB is flat—the same external marginal benefit per additional college degree—but it could be rising or falling with the number of degrees awarded without significantly altering the analysis.

marginal cost. As a result, some people choose not to seek degrees even though society as a whole would prefer that they did. Those potential students do not consider the external marginal benefit when deciding to obtain a college degree—for them, the private benefit is not great enough to convince them that a college degree is worth it, even though the social benefit actually makes getting that degree optimal from a societal standpoint. The bottom line is that when a good has a positive externality associated with it, the market will likely provide too little of the good because the external marginal benefit is ignored.

Later in the chapter, we talk in detail about how governments try to encourage greater production and consumption in markets with positive externalities. For now, we just note that states and countries tend to subsidize college education to persuade their citizens to get more education than they would choose to acquire on their own.

Another classic example of positive externalities includes the research and development (R&D) undertaken by companies in many industries. These firms spend money to come up with new and better products, but often the discoveries they make help other firms improve their own products and come up with new ideas. Apple created the iOS operating system for iPhones and iPads through their own R&D and, in turn, this creation enabled app developers to create programs they could sell for a profit. For example, the Finnish firm Rovio Mobile (a computer game development firm) came up with the program Angry Birds, which has been downloaded more than 1 billion times. Without Apple's R&D, Rovio would not have been able to profit like this.

Because Apple does not fully take account of the social demand curve when producing its R&D, it likely produces less R&D than society would like it to. The same is true for scientific research of many kinds, especially basic science research. Firms won't produce enough R&D if they can't fully recover or capture the social benefits of the R&D production.

Positive externalities are also attached to activities that make things safer for others or that improve the value of other people's property. Thus, companies that spend money on cyber security help make the Internet safer for everyone, and people who invest in the appearance of their homes raise property values for the whole neighborhood.

theory and data

The Positive Externality of LoJack

LoJack is a radio transmitter that a car owner can have installed on her vehicle to make recovery easy if the car is stolen. Because thieves can't tell which cars have LoJack (it normally is installed out of sight), it does not directly deter theft of the cars on which it is installed. However, LoJack's introduction and diffusion into a city can reduce overall car theft rates because with more LoJacks hidden away in cars throughout the city, car thieves are much more likely to be caught if they do steal a car.

These factors imply that the social benefit of installing LoJack is likely to be large relative to the private benefit. Most of its theft-deterring properties apply to *all* cars, not just those that have LoJack installed. In fact, the primary private benefit to the LoJack buyer is not theft deterrence, but that once the car is stolen, it is more likely to be recovered quickly and with minimal damage.

Because the crime-fighting nature of LoJack is a positive externality, car owners don't reap much of the benefits they create for society when they install a LoJack unit on their cars. As a result, the actual number of installed LoJack devices in a private market is likely to be below the optimal level.

Ian Ayres and Steven Levitt measured the size of the LoJack externality in a joint study.[6] They estimated the private benefit of installing LoJack by multiplying the probability that

---

[6] Ian Ayres and Steven D. Levitt, "Measuring Positive Externalities from Unobservable Victim Precaution: An Empirical Analysis of Lojack," *Quarterly Journal of Economics* 113, no. 1 (February 1998): 43–77.

Figure 16.3 : Positive External Benefits in the Market for LoJack

In the market for LoJack, the private benefit of LoJack is approximately $150 per device, while the external marginal benefit is over $1,300 per device. The socially optimal production level (Q^*, P^*) occurs at the intersection of the social demand curve (SD) and supply $S = MC_I$, and is well above the free-market production level $(Q_{MKT} = 5\%$ of vehicles, $150).$

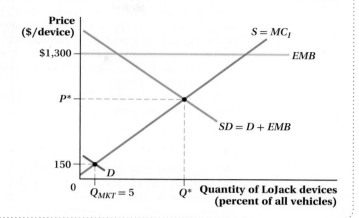

---

a car in their data would be stolen times the savings in damages that a quick LoJack-aided recovery confers. They estimated the private benefit to be about $150. This is the equilibrium price in Figure 16.3, which shows the market for LoJack devices. Note that the free-market output was only about 5% of all vehicles at the time of the study.

They estimated a much larger social benefit. By examining LoJack installations and car theft patterns within and across cities, Ayres and Levitt estimated that having LoJack in an additional 1% of cars in a market can lead to as much as a 20% decline in auto thefts. (Interestingly, there was also some evidence that car thieves in markets with high LoJack installation rates switched to stealing older cars, because most LoJacks are installed on newer cars.) Ayres and Levitt's numbers implied that every three additional LoJacks resulted in one fewer stolen car.

Based on the average amount of damages people and insurance companies pay to repair or replace a stolen car ($4,000 at the time of the study according to reports in the National Crime Victimization Survey), Ayres and Levitt estimated that the external benefit from a LoJack was greater than $1,300 (= $4,000/3). This is the value of the *EMB* in Figure 16.3.

Thus, given the positive externality of LoJack, someone who installs a unit on her car enjoys a private marginal benefit that is only about one-tenth of the external marginal benefit ($150 versus $1,300). Therefore, the social value of LoJack devices (as represented by the *SD* curve) lies far above the private value (demand) curve. Because the LoJack owners do not reap all the benefits from installing the device, far fewer people buy LoJacks than society would like, and the market ends up at an equilibrium quantity of LoJack units that is far below the socially optimal level Q^*.

16.2 Fixing Externalities

Left to its own devices, a free market produces more than (with negative externalities) or less than (with positive externalities) the optimal welfare-maximizing quantity. As a result, the market generates deadweight losses when a good has negative or positive externalities.

Is society doomed to live with this inefficiency? No. Just as we saw in Chapter 15 that asymmetric information's potential welfare losses offer powerful incentives to create institutions that remedy them, the same is true for externalities. Governments or the economic actors involved in transactions with externalities may implement one of several market interventions that can reduce the inefficiencies externalities create.

Externality fixes come in two basic types: those that work through their effect on price and those that work through their effect on quantity. Both types try to steer the market away from the inefficient outcome of the private market (in which only private marginal costs and benefits are considered) toward the more efficient outcome (in which social marginal costs and benefits are considered). The price approach pushes prices to reflect the true social costs and benefits. The quantity approach pushes quantities toward efficient levels.

Because many real-world solutions to externalities occur to try to correct for the ill effects of pollution, we focus on that particular negative externality throughout this section.

The Efficient Level of Pollution

Before considering how to correct for an externality, we need to consider how the government chooses its efficiency target. The goal is to set the level of total pollution allowable at its efficient level. The **efficient level of pollution** is the level of emissions necessary to produce the efficient quantity of the good tied to the externality. Therefore, the total amount of emissions allowable is set at the level that allows the market for the good to produce the quantity at which demand equals marginal social cost.

We can also think about the efficient amount of pollution (or any negative externality) as the level that balances its costs and benefits. Pollution's costs—the health implications and such—are easy enough to grasp. Pollution's benefits derive from the fact that some pollution is a necessary by-product of the production of many goods. If we completely ban pollution, we also ban the production of all these goods. This outcome would surely create a loss for society. The benefit of pollution reflects the benefit of these goods. (It is for this reason that market efficiency does not generally mean that the level of a negative externality must be driven to zero.)

We can see how the efficient level of pollution is determined in Figure 16.4. In reality, it is likely that the marginal cost of pollution (*MCP*) rises with the level of pollution. The additional damages of a bit more pollution are relatively modest at low levels, but the types and severity of the damage usually grow as pollution increases. This is reflected in the shape of curve *MCP* in Figure 16.4.

The marginal benefit of pollution (*MBP*), on the other hand, is likely to be high at low levels because *some* positive level of pollution is necessary to make many goods. But, the marginal benefit will tend to fall as pollution output increases (and as output of the good increases). At higher output levels of pollution (and the good), production

efficient level of pollution
The level of emissions necessary to produce the efficient quantity of the good tied to the externality.

Figure 16.4   The Efficient Level of Pollution

The efficient level of pollution (*POLL**) occurs where the marginal cost of pollution *MCP* equals the marginal benefit or marginal abatement cost of pollution ($MBP = MAC = P^*_{POLL}$).

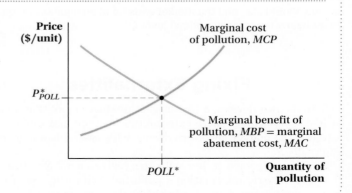

technologies can become more flexible so that less pollution is produced at higher quantities of the good's output. Also, because demand curves slope down, the price at which an industry can sell its marginal unit of output falls, which, in turn, makes pollution less valuable on the margin. These factors are reflected in curve MBP in Figure 16.4.

There is a different way to think about the marginal benefit curve MBP that allows us to consider how much it would cost a firm to reduce the level of pollution it creates. Just as the MBP curve shows the marginal benefit from pollution, it also reflects the flip-side: the marginal cost of *cutting* pollution, also called *pollution abatement*. After all, every unit of pollution a producer cuts entails a lost marginal benefit: the loss of the sale of the extra product that could have been made using that extra unit of pollution. As more cuts in the amount of pollution are made (that is, as we move from right to left along the horizontal axis in the figure), the marginal cost of cutting pollution rises. Therefore, MBP also reflects the marginal cost of cutting pollution, which economists often call the **marginal abatement cost (MAC).** This is shown in Figure 16.4 by indicating that MBP and MAC are equal, allowing us to view this curve in either way.

The efficient level of pollution is, not surprisingly, where its marginal benefit equals its marginal cost, or $POLL^*$ in Figure 16.4. The logic is the same as we've seen before: If something's marginal benefit is higher than its marginal cost, more of it should be produced; if its marginal cost is greater than its marginal benefit, less of it should be produced. Net benefits are maximized where the next unit equates the two marginal effects.

If we want to think of the marginal benefit curve as being the marginal abatement cost curve instead, we can interpret optimal pollution in terms of emissions cuts. Emissions should be cut whenever the marginal cost of doing so (as reflected by the MAC curve) is less than the reduced harm (as reflected by MCP). This will be true at any pollution levels greater than $POLL^*$. On the other hand, if marginal abatement costs are greater than the marginal cost of the pollution, which will be the case at pollution levels less than $POLL^*$, then pollution cuts should be scaled back. These considerations are balanced at the optimal pollution level $POLL^*$.

The optimal "price" of pollution is equal to the marginal cost of pollution (and marginal benefit) at the optimal quantity, or P^*_{POLL} in Figure 16.4. If pollution were tradable (which, as we see later, it can be), at P^*_{POLL} polluters would be willing to purchase the right to pollute up to the level $POLL^*$. For levels of pollution below $POLL^*$, the price P^*_{POLL} is lower than the value from being able to pollute more (measured by the marginal benefit of pollution). At the same time, those harmed by pollution would still be willing to sell an amount of pollution rights equal to $POLL^*$, because at this price they are being more than compensated for the harm they suffer ($P^*_{POLL} > MCP$).

In principle, the efficient level of pollution can be obtained equally well through either price or quantity mechanisms. If regulators could impose the socially optimal price in a market, for instance, the quantity (of either the good or the externality) at that price would also be at its optimal level. Similarly, if regulators could specify the socially optimal quantity, the price at that quantity would be the optimal price. In practice, however, we will see that one approach may be easier than the other to enact, depending on the nature of the externality and the information available to regulators.

marginal abatement cost (MAC)
The cost of reducing emissions by one unit.

Using Prices to Fix Externalities

One way to view the failure of the free market in the presence of externalities is that the market participants do not consider the correct, society-wide costs and benefits when they make their decisions. If prices can be modified so that the private cost matches the social cost or the private benefit matches the social benefit, then producers and consumers would make the "right" choice, the choice that results in a welfare-maximizing price and quantity.

For goods tied to negative externalities, price-based mechanisms apply additional costs by making firms or consumers pay an extra amount for each unit of the good they produce or consume. This causes them to cut back on production or consumption, bringing down the market quantity toward the efficient level.

For goods associated with positive externalities, additional demand can be added by paying firms for producing (or buyers for purchasing) each unit of output. This, in essence, raises the demand curve faced by the producers, spurring them to increase output. Therefore, the price received by the seller and the amount of output produced will become equal to their efficient levels.

Pigouvian Taxes   One of the most common types of price-modification policy used to address negative externalities is a **Pigouvian tax.**[7] This type of tax (named after the British economist Arthur Pigou who pioneered the idea in 1920) raises a good's price to take into account the external marginal costs imposed by a negative externality.[8]

Pigouvian tax
A tax imposed on an activity that creates a negative externality.

Let's look at how a Pigouvian tax works. Suppose that coal-burning power plants emit pollution that dirties the air of surrounding communities and imposes health costs on the people living in those areas. A Pigouvian tax on electricity generated by these plants would bring equilibrium in the electricity market toward an efficient level of output and price (Figure 16.5).

Because the electricity industry's private marginal costs MC_I are not the same as the social marginal costs SMC, overproduction results: The power company generates Q_{MKT} when the optimal quantity is Q^*.

Now, let's say that a government could impose a tax T per MWh on electricity production equal to the external marginal cost EMC of pollution. This would increase the private marginal cost of supplying energy, and shift MC_I up to $MC_I + T$. Because $T = EMC$, the industry's marginal cost curve is now the same as the social marginal cost curve SMC. The old marginal cost curve MC_I intersected the demand curve at the price P_{MKT}. At that price, the industry's output was Q_{MKT}. If the size of the tax is chosen so that the tax-inclusive marginal cost curve $MC_I + T$ intersects the demand curve at the efficient price P^*, the industry's output falls to the efficient quantity Q^*.

The Pigouvian tax raises the electricity industry's marginal cost by an amount equal to the external damages its production causes. This exactly aligns the industry's private incentives with society's. In effect, the Pigouvian tax "internalizes" the pollution externality. That is, it forces the industry to take into account the external damage of its operations when it decides how much electricity to generate. This process results in the efficient market outcome.

Figure 16.5   :   A Pigouvian Tax Corrects for a Negative Externality

In an unregulated market, the power industry overproduces quantity Q_{MKT} at price P_{MKT} (point B). A Pigouvian tax (T) equal to the external marginal cost EMC shifts the supply curve (S) up from marginal cost $S = MC_I$ to the social marginal cost curve (SMC). Now, the industry produces at point A, where SMC intersects demand (D), and supplies the socially efficient quantity Q^* MWh at price P^*.

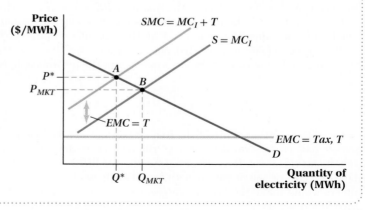

---

[7] Governments at all levels use different types of taxes and subsidies. Only those that are designed to address externalities are called Pigouvian.

[8] Arthur C. Pigou, *The Economics of Welfare*, London: Macmillan, 1920.

In reality, there are all kinds of Pigouvian taxes. One of the rationales for placing taxes on cigarettes and alcohol and for the recent calls for imposing taxes on soda arises from the external costs (from second-hand smoke, drunk driving, obesity, health expenses, etc.) that consumers of these goods do not otherwise bear.

Another example of a Pigouvian tax comes from the European Union. In 2012 the EU made an effort to curb greenhouse gas pollution and global warming by imposing a carbon emissions fee on international airline flights. This fee would force the airlines to account for the high amounts of greenhouse gas emissions made by large commercial aircraft. The effectiveness of this fee was lessened, however, because several nations including India and China refused to require their airlines to pay the fee.

 application

Reducing Spam

Nearly 80% of the e-mails sent in the world are unwanted spam.[9] Spam is an economic bad—something you'd rather consume less of—and there are many negative externalities associated with it. All of this junk e-mail wastes your time, clogs e-mail inboxes, and can eat up valuable bandwidth and make the Internet slower. When deciding to send junk e-mail, the senders do not take into account the costs it imposes on the recipients or other Internet users.

Private citizens and U.S. lawmakers have been trying to put a stop to spam for years. They've discussed establishing a national anti-spam registry and penalties for violating spam regulations, mechanisms to make filtering programs more efficient, and ways to improve recipients' ability to ignore the unwanted messages.

Because spam imposes a negative externality, one approach to deal with it would be to impose a Pigouvian tax on e-mail. Indeed, the United Nations proposed such a tax in 1999 when it argued for a 1/100th of a cent tax per outgoing e-mail. For the ordinary e-mailer or worksite, a tax that low would amount to basically nothing and wouldn't greatly affect e-mailing behavior. For spam e-mail services, however, who regularly send millions of e-mails daily, the tax would translate into a sizable cost. Send 10 e-mails in a day, and you're out only one-tenth of a penny. Send 10 million? The spamming firm now owes $1,000 for something that previously was essentially free. In this way, the proposed tax would function as a Pigouvian tax on spammers, causing them to internalize the negative externality of spam.

Despite being an economically sound proposition, the idea of the spam tax quickly went nowhere. People objected to the idea of a world government enforcing anything and doubted that officials would be able to figure out who the senders were and make them pay their taxes.

A tax on spam e-mail may be a bit outmoded now anyway. Junk e-mail is so ubiquitous that you probably barely notice it, even as you click "delete" on yet another message hawking diet pills. Spam filters have improved, too; they now can automatically divert a greater fraction of spam e-mails to the junk folder. Never ones to lose out on a business opportunity, however, spammers have begun to take advantage of other cheap technologies. Spam text messaging, in particular, is on the rise—from 2.2 billion total spam texts to U.S. numbers in 2009 to more than twice that at 4.5 billion in 2011.[10]

Spammers have even started turning to Facebook. They shouldn't become too reliant on social networking sites like Facebook, though. Because Facebook owns its entire network, it is much easier for it to internalize the externality of spam—perhaps through a tax or fee of its own—than it is for the government. ∎

---

[9] Symantec, Message Labs Intelligence Report, 2011. http://www.symantec.com/about/news/release/article.jsp?prid=20110426_01.

[10] Will Oremus, "Hell Phone: Is There Any Way to Stop the Scourge of Text Message Spam?" *Slate*, April 13, 2012.

Pigouvian subsidy

A subsidy paid for an activity that creates a positive externality.

Pigouvian Subsidy   When there is a positive externality, a **Pigouvian subsidy** can be used to decrease a good's price (paid by the buyer) to take into account the external marginal benefits. The subsidy raises the effective price (the market price plus the subsidy) at which producers can sell their products, thus making it profit-maximizing for them to increase their outputs to the socially optimal level. In the market for college degrees (presented again in Figure 16.6), the private market would produce only Q_{MKT} degrees if left to its own devices. However, if the government institutes a subsidy of Sub per student (exactly equal to the EMB), the demand for college degrees rises to $D + Sub$, which also happens to be the social demand curve. Output in the market rises to Q^*, the socially optimal level of output.

There are many types of actual subsidies that are at least supposed to be based on Pigouvian principles. Tax credits for education or to buy hybrid cars and fuel-efficient home appliances are examples of Pigouvian subsidies.

One practical problem facing Pigouvian taxes and subsidies is how to figure out their correct size. Realistically, it's difficult to estimate the exact external marginal cost of carbon pollution or the exact external marginal benefit from more college degrees, so setting the correct rate for the Pigouvian tax or subsidy is also difficult. If a government sets the Pigouvian tax or subsidy at the incorrect level, the market price and quantity will still be inefficient. We discuss this problem more below.

Figure 16.6   **A Pigouvian Subsidy Corrects for a Positive Externality**

In an unregulated market, colleges underproduce the quantity of college degrees (Q_{MKT}) at price P_{MKT} (point B). A Pigouvian subsidy (Sub) equal to external marginal benefit (EMB) shifts demand (D) out to social demand (SD). Now, the college market produces where supply (S) intersects SD, and supplies the socially efficient quantity of college degrees (Q^*) at price P^* (point A).

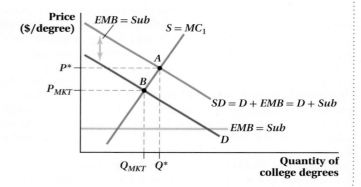

16.2 figure it out

Refer to Figure It Out 16.1 on page 647. Suppose the government places a $0.50 tax on each ream of paper sold.

  a. What price would buyers pay and what price would sellers receive (net of the tax)?

  b. How many reams of paper would be sold?

Solution:

  a. To solve this problem, we can use the method we learned in Chapter 3 where we consider that the price paid by buyers, P^B, is equal to the price received by sellers, P^S, plus the tax: $P^B = P^S + T$. Therefore, $P^B = P^S + 0.50$. We can rewrite the demand curve and the supply curve (the industry marginal cost curve) from Figure It Out 16.1:

$$Q^D = 5 - 0.125P^B \quad \text{and} \quad Q^S = 0.5P^S$$

Because $P^B = P^S + 0.50$, we can substitute this expression into the demand curve for P^B:
$$Q^D = 5 - 0.125P^B = 5 - 0.125(P^S + 0.50) = 5 - 0.125P^S - 0.0625 = 4.9375 - 0.125P^S$$

Now that the supply and demand equations are both written in terms of P^S, we can solve $Q^D = Q^S$:
$$4.9375 - 0.125P^S = 0.5P^S$$
$$0.625P^S = 4.9375$$
$$P^S = \$7.90$$
$$P^B = P^S + 0.50 = \$7.90 + \$0.50 = \$8.40$$

Note that this is the socially optimal price we found in Figure It Out 16.1.

To solve for the quantity sold, we can substitute the buyer's price ($P^B = \$8.40$) into the demand curve or the seller's price ($P^S = \$7.90$) into the supply curve:
$$Q^D = 5 - 0.125P^B = 5 - 0.125(8.4) = 5 - 1.05 = 3.95$$
$$Q^S = 0.5P^S = 0.5(7.9) = 3.95$$

This is the socially optimal quantity.

 **application**

Would Higher Driving Taxes Make Us Happier Drivers?

Imagine you were the only driver on the road. You could go fast, ignore stop lights and stop signs, and make left turns without first checking for oncoming traffic—all with no worry that you'd hit another car. Having other drivers on the road creates enormous negative externalities. In 2011 *TIME Magazine* reported that road congestion costs Americans nearly \$90 billion a year in fuel costs and lost productivity.[11] That doesn't even account for the fender benders and other accidents generated by having other cars on the road. Most mistakes that drivers make, such as swerving out of a lane or running a stop sign, only cause a crash if there is another car present to hit.

In 2003 London Mayor Ken Livingstone looked at the externalities associated with driving in his city and decided they were way too high. Over 1 million people commuted into the city center during the peak morning rush hour alone. While the city offered public transit, too few people used it. As a result, commuting on the roadways in London—for all commuters, including drivers, bus riders, and bicyclists—was painfully slow and dangerous.

Mayor Livingstone used economics to try to solve the problem by instituting a Pigouvian tax on drivers. Starting in 2003, drivers entering London's central district faced a £5 toll. Estimates made before the fee was levied suggested that Londoners would pay about £286 million in tolls but would see about £331 million in savings in time and vehicle operation costs. In the first year of the tax, congestion was reduced by an estimated 30%. Cars were travelling at speeds unheard of since the 1960s—nearly 11 miles per hour, up from 8 miles per hour prior to the tax. Londoners hope that over time the toll will also reduce air pollution.

[11] Mike Billips, "Congestion Pricing: To Skip Traffic, Atlanta Says Pay Up," *TIME Magazine*, January 23, 2011.

The biggest benefit of fewer cars on the road, surprisingly, might not be less congestion or less pollution. In fact, economists Aaron Edlin and Pinar Karaca-Mandic calculate that by far the best reason to tax driving is that fewer cars on the road lead to fewer car crashes.[12] Edlin and Karaca-Mandic estimate that every extra driver on the road raises insurance costs for other drivers by a combined $2,000; in other words, my driving imposes a $2,000 externality on other drivers. After the toll, London saw car crashes in the city drop by about 25%.

Tolls are one way to deal with an automobile externality; gasoline taxes are another. When the gas tax is raised, the price of gas increases and people choose to drive less often. Edlin and Karaca-Mandic find that the appropriate gasoline tax to offset the externality of car crashes would be at least $1 per gallon. In addition to making the roads safer, a tax of this size would generate around $220 billion annually in revenue for governments. ■

Quantity Mechanisms to Reduce Externalities

Quantity-based interventions have the same goal as price-based mechanisms: to move a market with externalities toward the efficient outcome. They just use a different lever.

quota
A regulation mandating that the production or consumption of a certain quantity of a good or externality be limited (negative externality) or required (positive externality).

Quotas   The simplest of the quantity-based approaches is to set a **quota,** a mandated limit on the quantity of a good or an externality a producer can make or a consumer can buy (if the externality is negative), or a required quantity of a good or an externality a producer must make or a consumer must purchase (if the externality is positive). By regulating output, the amount of the externality associated with producing this output is also regulated. When negative externalities are present, the quantity restriction must be set below the free-market equilibrium quantity (which, as we saw earlier, is too large in a free market). The optimal quantity restriction would be set at the lower, efficient quantity. Quantity can also be controlled with licensing, where only a particular amount of an activity (production or consumption) is allowed by authorities.

In Figure 16.7, we look once again at the market for electricity production and see that the pollution externality leads to excessive production at Q_{MKT} and an inefficient market outcome. Suppose that the government enacts a law mandating that the production of electricity can be no greater than Q^*. With this law in place, the private MC_I curve becomes vertical at that quantity level. The private MC_I curve now intersects the demand curve at point A and the private decision matches the socially efficient one.

Figure 16.7   **The Effects of a Quota on a Market with a Negative Externality**

In an unregulated market, the power industry overproduces the quantity of electricity (Q_{MKT}) at price P_{MKT} (point B). When the government enacts a quota limiting production to Q^*, the private marginal cost curve MC_I becomes vertical at Q^*, intersecting the social marginal cost SMC and demand D at the socially optimal quantity Q^* and price P^* (point A).

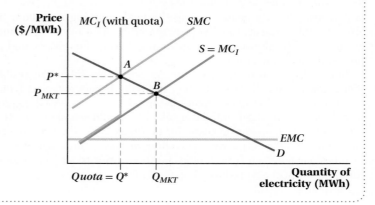

[12] Aaron Edlin and Pinar Karaca-Mandic, "The Accident Externality from Driving," *Journal of Political Economy* 114, no. 5 (2006): 931–955.

Examples of quotas used in actual practice include restrictions on the amount of pollution factories can emit and the amount of noise neighbors can make. Similarly, hunting and fishing licenses limit the number of fish or animals a person can take because of the negative externality that overfishing and overhunting exert on other fishers and hunters currently and in the future.

We see fewer real-world mandates for positive externalities. Such quotas require people to supply or purchase a minimum quantity that is higher than the free-market equilibrium output. For example, people are required by law to attend school until age 16 in most states. Vaccines for infectious diseases are often mandated by law, as is the purchase of auto liability insurance for drivers. Each of these is a quantity-based way to promote more of an activity that has a positive externality on others.

Practically speaking, however, the use of quotas creates complications. First, as with setting Pigouvian taxes, it is difficult to determine what the socially optimal amount of the quotas actually should be.

A second difficulty with quotas is that the government often wants to influence the total amount of an externality produced by an industry, but can only set quotas on a firm-by-firm basis. For example, it might be much more expensive to reduce pollution emitted from old power plants and much cheaper to reduce pollution from newer plants. Under these conditions, enacting a rule that says each plant must hit the same target level will not be the most cost-effective way to accomplish the goal of less pollution. (In the next section, we discuss how giving out permits and allowing permit holders to buy and sell the permits can solve this complication.)

Third is the question of the distribution of costs and benefits. A Pigouvian tax, for example, generates revenues for the government (or creates costs for the government in the case of subsidies). With quotas and mandates, the benefits or costs are left with the market participants. With licensing, the government receives some revenue, while market participants incur some cost but also reap some benefits.

Government Provision of a Good   Another type of quantity intervention in the case of positive externalities occurs when the government actually provides the product itself. Basic scientific research has a large positive externality and little private sponsorship, so the federal government subsidizes it through tax credits and research funding. Governments also perform research directly, as does the United States at the National Institutes of Health and a system of federal labs around the country.

Price-Based versus Quantity-Based Interventions with Uncertainty

We saw above that, as a matter of principle, quantity and price mechanisms can be equally effective at addressing externalities. In reality, though, there are situations in which one type of market intervention might be preferred to the other.

A particularly important situation in which one mechanism might be preferred to the other is when the optimal level of the externality is not fully known. The importance of uncertainty in dealing with externalities was first pointed out by American economist Martin Weitzman in 1974.[13]

Such uncertainty is a realistic possibility. The marginal benefits and the marginal costs of pollution are difficult to measure and often shift with changes in technologies, input costs, and new discoveries about how damaging pollution is to human health. As a result, efforts to intervene in markets with externalities are generally inexact and any Pigouvian taxes or quantity mandates that regulators set are not exactly right. Not being exactly right is always costly, but it can be even more costly if the wrong intervention is used.

---

[13] Martin Weitzman, "Prices vs. Quantities," *The Review of Economic Studies* 41, no. 4 (1974): 477–491.

Let's look at Figure 16.8, which illustrates the marginal cost and marginal benefit of water pollution caused by fertilizer runoff from farms (measured in parts per million, or milligrams per liter of water). The marginal cost of water pollution is shown by the MCP curve. The marginal benefit of pollution and the marginal cost of removing this pollution are shown by the $MBP = MAC$ curve. In Figure 16.8, the efficient quantity of runoff pollution in the market $POLL^*$ is found where the marginal benefit of pollution is exactly equal to the marginal cost of pollution (point A).

Before we examine how uncertainty can affect the ability of a regulation to move the market to its efficient level of pollution, let's remind ourselves of how to measure the deadweight loss that occurs when the pollution level is not at the efficient level. The deadweight loss equals the area between the marginal benefit of pollution (or alternatively, the marginal abatement costs) and the marginal cost of pollution for each of the units of pollution between the efficient level of pollution and the current level of pollution.

If the level of pollution is too high (to the right of $POLL^*$), the pollution costs society more (as seen by the MCP curve) than its value (in terms of output produced along with the pollution, reflected in the MBP curve). Conversely, when the level of pollution is inefficiently low (the level lies to the left of $POLL^*$), there are units of pollution that provide greater value (in terms of the output that would be produced along with the pollution) than their cost.

Now suppose the regulator does not know exactly what farmers' marginal abatement costs are. This implies that the regulator is unsure about the true marginal benefits of the water pollution. Can we say whether the regulator would be better off choosing a quantity- or price-based mechanism to reduce the pollution to its efficient level?

For example, suppose the regulator mistakenly estimates farmers' marginal abatement costs as being lower than they really are, shown by curve $MBP_e = MAC_e$ in Figure 16.8. If these were the true abatement costs, the optimal level of pollution would be $POLL_B$ because the marginal cost of pollution is equal to the estimated marginal benefit of pollution at point B. The regulator could achieve a pollution level of $POLL_B$ in two ways: by limiting the quantity of fertilizer used so that total runoff pollution is $POLL_B$, or by setting a tax on runoff at price T.

If the regulator uses a quantity mechanism, the amount of pollution will be limited to $POLL_B$, lower than the socially optimal level $POLL^*$. In this case, the deadweight loss from incorrectly mandating the quantity is the triangle X in Figure 16.8. This area reflects the pollution for which the true marginal benefit is higher than the marginal cost to society. This pollution does not occur, however, because of the quantity restriction at the wrong pollution level.

Figure 16.8   **When Quantity Mechanisms Are Preferable to Price Mechanisms**

$MBP = MAC$ and MCP are the marginal benefit (marginal abatement cost) and marginal cost of pollution curves for farmers' fertilizer use. The efficient level of water pollution is quantity $POLL^*$ of fertilizer runoff. If government regulators incorrectly estimate farmers' marginal abatement costs at $MAC_e < MAC$, the quantity-based intervention would reduce pollution to $POLL_B < POLL^*$, while the Pigouvian tax would increase pollution to $POLL_C > POLL^*$. Because MAC is flat relative to MCP, the quantity-based intervention is preferable to the price mechanism, as seen by comparing the resulting deadweight losses from the two interventions ($X < Y$).

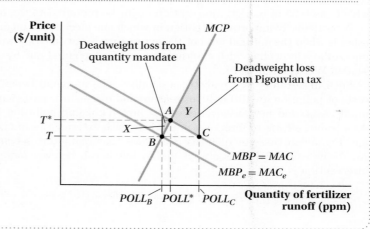

If the regulator instead uses a Pigouvian tax equal to T, farmers will reduce their fertilizer use until their marginal abatement cost equals the tax (at point C). Additional cuts in the level of pollution beyond this point would be more expensive (in terms of forgone output) than simply paying the pollution tax. So, this incorrect tax (due to the misestimate of marginal abatement costs) results in the farmers polluting an amount, $POLL_C$, that is much greater than the optimal level. The deadweight loss from this mistake by the regulator is area Y. Comparing area Y (caused by setting the wrong price) to the deadweight loss of area X (caused by setting the wrong quantity), it's clear that setting the wrong tax creates a much bigger loss, even though both the quantity restriction and tax were not far from their optimal values in absolute terms. Note that the optimal tax level would be T^*, which would result in the efficient level of pollution $POLL^*$.

This result—that price-based mechanisms led to larger inefficiency losses—is *not* a consequence of the regulator believing that abatement costs were lower than they actually were. If the regulator were instead mistaken in the other direction—that is, it thought abatement costs were higher than they really were—we'd find the same thing. (Though in that case, pollution will be above the optimal level under a quantity-based intervention and below it with a Pigouvian tax.)

The reason why the deadweight losses are so much larger with price mechanisms results from the way we set up the example. We've drawn the marginal abatement curve as relatively flat and the marginal cost of pollution curve as relatively steep. The flat MAC curve implies that farmers' abatement choices are very sensitive to the price of abatement (in other words, the tax), so being just a little wrong on setting a Pigouvian tax leads to wild swings in the amount of pollution the farmers create. These large swings, in turn, cause big inefficiency losses because the marginal cost of pollution is so sensitive to the amount of pollution (as shown by the steep MCP curve). Therefore, when faced with cases in which farmers' abatement choices are sensitive to a tax and the marginal cost of pollution is likely to rise rapidly with pollution, regulators should favor quantity-based interventions. That way, if they're wrong about how much tweaking the market needs, damages will be limited.

Given this result, you might suspect that if the situation were reversed, and the marginal abatement cost curves were fairly steep and the marginal cost of pollution curve were relatively flat, price mechanisms would cause fewer inefficiency losses than quantity-based interventions. You'd be right. This case is shown in Figure 16.9.

In Figure 16.9, the optimal level of pollution from fertilizer runoff is where the marginal cost of pollution is equal to the marginal benefit of pollution (or marginal abatement cost). This can be seen at point A, with an efficient level of pollution $POLL^*$. Once again, suppose the regulator believes that farmers' abatement costs are lower than they really

---

Figure 16.9   **When Price Mechanisms Are Preferable to Quantity Mechanisms**

If government regulators incorrectly estimate farmers' marginal abatement costs at $MAC_e < MAC$, the quantity-based intervention would reduce pollution to $POLL_B < POLL^*$, while the Pigouvian tax would increase pollution to $POLL_C > POLL^*$. Because MAC is steep relative to the marginal cost of pollution MCP, the price mechanism is preferable to the quantity mechanism, as seen by comparing the resulting deadweight losses from the two interventions ($Y > X$).

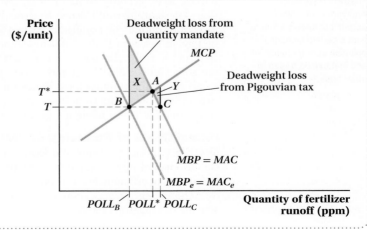

are, shown by curve $MBP_e = MAC_e$. If regulators use a quantity-based intervention, they will set the quantity mandate at $POLL_B$, pollution will be $POLL_B$ instead of $POLL^*$, and area X will be the deadweight loss from inefficiency. If a Pigouvian tax is used instead, regulators will set it at T. Farmers will produce a quantity of pollution $POLL_C$, and the deadweight loss from the inefficient level of pollution is area Y.

Figure 16.9 makes it apparent that when the marginal abatement cost curve is steep relative to the marginal cost of pollution curve, mistakes in setting Pigouvian taxes are less costly than those in setting quantity mandates. The relative insensitivity of abatement to the level of the tax means that being a little wrong about the optimal tax won't have much effect on the actual level of pollution. But, setting the wrong quantity will be very costly. Regulations that force producers to undertake unnecessarily high abatement will be expensive relative to the marginal costs of pollution it saves. Similarly, mandating too little abatement will mean that some pollution cuts with benefits that would far outweigh their costs won't be made.

Therefore, when regulators are uncertain about the optimal level of an externality, the choice of quantity- or price-based market interventions should depend on what the regulator perceives are the relative sensitivities of the marginal cost of pollution and the marginal abatement cost (or marginal benefit of pollution). In reality, the marginal abatement cost is not likely to be rising at a constant rate for all levels of pollution. Instead, the marginal abatement cost curve is probably relatively flat at low levels of abatement (because many cuts can be made cheaply) but then quite steep as more cuts are made. This implies that at low levels of regulation, quantity mechanisms might be favored. On the other hand, if previous regulations have already wrung out many of the easiest, least costly pollution cuts, the marginal abatement cost curve is likely to be steeper, making pollution taxes the more preferable mechanism for controlling the externality.

In extreme cases, it would be clear which mechanism to use. If you knew for certain that a quantity of radiation greater than a particular level (say, $\overline{POLL}$) would mean the death of everyone in the world, then you would be far better off imposing a quantity rule to prevent reaching that level rather than relying on a tax whose impact on quantity is uncertain.

A Market-Oriented Approach to Reducing Externalities: Tradable Permits Markets

Trying to mandate the total externality in a market by restricting each firm's quantity or determining the correct amount of tax involves a lot of effort. Worse, it may lead to costly errors. If producers differ in their costs of changing output levels, it would be optimal for firms that could do this more cheaply to make a larger share of the necessary quantity adjustments. But, it can be very difficult for a regulator to know what each firm's costs are and set quantity restrictions or taxes appropriately.

tradable permit
A government-issued permit that allows a firm to emit a certain amount of pollution during production and that can be traded to other firms.

In these cases, it might be preferable to allow firms to jointly determine how best to reduce an externality to its optimal level. **Tradable permits** for pollution can achieve this. These are permits issued to firms by the government that allow the holder to emit a certain amount of pollution. After the permits are allocated among firms, they may be traded between firms, allowing some firms to emit a greater amount of a pollutant than other firms. In essence, a market for pollution emissions develops. Such systems are sometimes called "cap-and-trade" programs for this reason: The government sets a cap on pollution emissions, issues an amount of permits equal to this cap, and then firms trade the rights to pollute among them. For example, the United States regulates sulfur dioxide (SO_2) using a system of tradable permits.

Firms' Costs of Reducing Emissions   Suppose there are only two firms in the electricity industry, Acme and Best. The amount of pollutants that each would emit in the absence of any externality remedy is 40 tons, or 80 tons total for the industry. We presume the efficient level of pollution for the industry is 50 tons.

Achieving efficiency therefore requires reducing emissions by a total of 30 tons. Any scheme of emissions reduction across the two firms that adds to 30 tons will work. But, if the two firms differ in their costs of cutting emissions, all these schemes are not made equal. Let's see why.

Suppose Best uses a newer, more flexible technology than Acme. This allows it to switch to less-polluting inputs at lower cost, which means that Best faces a lower marginal abatement cost, the additional cost of reducing an additional unit of emissions. Let's assume that the marginal abatement cost for Acme is $MAC_A = 2e_A$, where e_A measures the number of tons of emissions cut by Acme. Best, which has the more flexible technology, has marginal abatement cost $MAC_B = e_B$ per ton, where e_B measures the number of tons of emissions reduced by Best. Notice that, for both firms, we assume that the more the firm cuts emissions, the more expensive it is to cut an additional ton. This seems reasonable. Firms can often reduce emissions fairly easily at first by making small changes to their production process. Larger cuts, however, involve more complicated and costly adjustments.

The lowest-cost way for society to achieve the 30-ton emissions cut is to split the cut across the two firms in a way that equalizes the two firms' marginal abatement costs. Why? Because if these marginal abatement costs are not equalized, Acme could save more by increasing emissions than it would cost Best to decrease them by the same amount. This change in emissions levels would keep total emissions constant at 50 tons but save money. Therefore, the cheapest way to achieve the 30-ton drop in emissions is to make sure $MAC_A = MAC_B$, or $2e_A = e_B$. Because total emissions reduced must be equal to 30 or $e_A + e_B = 30$, we can solve for e_A and e_B:

$$2e_A = e_B$$

$$2e_A = 30 - e_A$$

$$3e_A = 30$$

$$e_A = 10$$

$$e_B = 2e_A = 20$$

That is, Acme should cut 10 tons of emissions and Best should cut 20 tons. At these levels, the marginal abatement cost for each firm of reducing one more ton of emissions is the same and equal to $20.

It's not surprising that cost minimization implies that Best, which faces lower marginal abatement costs, cuts emissions more. But, it's difficult in the real world to know how expensive abatement is for each firm. (Plus if you ask them, they may well lie anyway. Firms want to make abatement seem more expensive for them than it really is, so that their competitors pay the costs of cutting emissions instead.) This is the problem with firm-by-firm output quotas. With imperfect information about firms' marginal abatement costs, firm-by-firm mandates would end up being the lowest-cost combination only through luck. Mistakes would lead to unnecessarily costly emissions cuts.

Tradable Permits Markets to the Rescue   A tradable permits market allows the emissions cut to be achieved at the lowest cost while sparing the regulator the trouble of determining how these cuts should be apportioned across firms. We know the regulator can achieve the efficient *total* level of emissions by issuing only 50 permits to the industry, where each permit allows the firm that owns it to emit 1 ton of pollutant. But, why would a permits market achieve this efficient level of pollution at the lowest possible cost?

Suppose, for example, that both firms are given twenty-five 1-ton permits initially. Remember that the market equilibrium has each firm emitting 40 tons, and that total emissions must be cut by 30 tons (from 80 to 50). Therefore, if no permits are traded, each firm would have to cut emissions by 15 tons. The firms can do better, however. If Acme (the firm with higher abatement costs) could reduce emissions by only 14 tons instead of 15, it would save $MAC_A = 2e_A = 2(\$15) = \$30$, its marginal cost of cutting the 15th ton. Best, on the other hand, could increase abatement to 16 tons for an additional cost of only $MAC_B = e_B = \$16$. So, Best could offer to sell one of its permits to Acme for any price between \$16 and \$30, and Acme would accept the offer. Acme then pollutes a little bit more, Best a little less, and both firms are better off.

If we continue this logic, one permit at a time, we will see that Acme will be willing to buy permits from Best as long as (1) there is a gap between the firms' marginal abatement costs, and (2) the permit price is within this gap. Permit trading will stop once the firms' marginal abatement costs are equalized. As we saw earlier, this occurs when Acme cuts 10 tons of emissions (and emits 30 tons) and Best cuts 20 tons (and emits 20 tons). The equilibrium permit price—the price that leads to this allocation of permits—will be \$20, the firms' equivalent marginal abatement costs at these levels. At this permit price and these emissions levels, neither firm will want to trade any more.

While the example starts with a particular initial permit allocation, 25 tons for each firm, the outcome wouldn't change for a different allocation. Suppose all 50 permits are initially allocated to Acme. Even in the absence of a permit market, Acme only wants to emit 40 tons, so it could certainly sell at least 10 permits to Best. As long as the price is less than Best's marginal abatement costs, Best will buy the permits. That means Best will buy the first permit at any price less than \$40 (without any permits, it would have to cut all 40 tons of pollution that it would normally produce), and it would be willing to pay up to \$31 for the 10th permit (with this many permits, it saves having to cut the 31st ton). But, Acme can still do better by selling even more permits to Best. If it sells an 11th permit, Acme would have to cut emissions to 39 tons, paying an extra 2(\$1) = \$2 in costs to abate its first ton, but Best would be willing to pay up to \$30 for that permit. We can apply this logic repeatedly to show that permit trading would continue until Acme has 30 permits and Best has 20, and the market-clearing permit price is \$20. Therefore this new allocation, as with any other possible allocation, leads to the same result as before.

Allowing the firms to trade permits achieves the total emissions cuts necessary for efficiency at the lowest possible cost, and it does so without the regulator having to determine which firm cuts how much. This works because trading permits allows firms that face lower abatement costs to shoulder more of the emissions-cutting burden, while giving them a way to be compensated for their additional abatement costs. High-abatement-cost firms prefer to buy these permits because it's cheaper for them than cutting emissions directly.

16.3 figure it out

Global Package Service (GPS) and Mail & Parcel Service (MAPS) are the only two cargo airlines using a small regional airport. Unfortunately, the jets used by GPS and MAPS inflict noise pollution on a nearby town. At their current production levels, GPS creates 600 decibel-hours of noise each day, while MAPS creates 750 decibel-hours of noise each day. Government regulators would like to lower the total noise pollution in the area to its optimal level of 1,000 decibel-hours. GPS faces a total abatement cost of $TAC_G = 20d_G + 2d_G^2$ and a marginal abatement cost of $MAC_G = 20 + 4d_G$, where d_G is the number of decibel-hours of noise pollution abated by GPS. The planes used by MAPS have older technology, so its total abatement cost and marginal abatement cost are greater: $TAC_M = 40d_M + 3d_M^2$ and $MAC_M = 40 + 6d_M$, where d_M is the number of decibel-hours of noise pollution abated by MAPS.

a. Suppose that regulators implement a quantity regulation and divide the optimal level of noise pollution equally between the firms, allowing each firm to produce only 500 decibel-hours of noise. How many decibel-hours of noise pollution will each firm have to cut?

b. How much will this cut in jet noise cost each firm? What is the total cost of reducing the noise pollution to its optimal level?

c. Now, suppose that government regulators create one thousand 1-decibel-hour permits and divide them equally between the two firms, allowing the firms to trade with one another. How many decibel-hours of noise pollution does MAPS cut? How many decibel-hours of noise pollution does GPS cut? What is the price of a permit?

d. What is the total cost of reducing the noise pollution to its optimal level under the system of tradable permits? How does this compare with the cost of quantity regulation you determined in part (b)?

Solution:

a. If regulators require each firm to cut its noise pollution to 500 decibel-hours, GPS will have to cut 100 decibel-hours (= 600 − 500) and MAPS will have to cut 250 decibel-hours (= 750 − 500).

b. The total cost of abatement for GPS is $TAC_G = 20d_G + 2d_G^2$. Because $d_G = 100$,
$$TAC_G = 20(100) + 2(100)^2 = 2,000 + 20,000 = \$22,000$$

The total cost of abatement for MAPS is $TAC_M = 40d_M + 3d_M^2$. Because $d_M = 250$,
$$TAC_M = 40(250) + 3(250)^2 = 10,000 + 187,500 = \$197,500$$

Therefore, the total cost of the regulation would be $22,000 + $197,500 = $219,500.

c. Under a system of tradable permits, GPS and MAPS will end up splitting the reduction in noise pollution in the most efficient way. This occurs when $MAC_G = MAC_M$ or when
$$20 + 4d_G = 40 + 6d_M$$

Therefore, we need to solve for d_G and d_M, remembering that $d_G + d_M$ must add to 350 (the total reduction in noise pollution required). Therefore, $d_G = 350 - d_M$. Substituting into the expression above, we get
$$20 + 4d_G = 40 + 6d_M$$
$$20 + 4(350 - d_M) = 40 + 6d_M$$
$$20 + 1,400 - 4d_M = 40 + 6d_M$$
$$10d_M = 1,380$$
$$d_M = 138$$

Therefore, $d_G = 350 - 138 = 212$. GPS will reduce its noise pollution by 212 decibel-hours to a level of 388 decibel-hours (= 600 − 212), while MAPS will reduce its noise pollution by 138 decibel-hours to a level of 612 (= 750 − 138). Total noise pollution will be at the optimal level of 1,000 decibel-hours (= 388 + 612). If each firm is initially given five hundred 1-decibel-hour permits, GPS will sell 112 permits (= 500 − 388) to MAPS.

The price of a permit will be equal to $MAC_G = MAC_M$:
$$\text{Price} = 20 + 4(212) = 40 + 6(138) = \$868$$

Each permit will sell for $868.

d. Under the system of tradable permits, the total cost of abatement for GPS is $TAC_G = 20d_G + 2d_G^2$. Because $d_M = 212$,
$$TAC_G = 20(212) + 2(212)^2 = 4,240 + 89,888 = \$94,128$$

The total cost of abatement for MAPS is $TAC_M = 40d_M + 3d_M^2$. Because $d_M = 138$,
$$TAC_M = 40(138) + 3(138)^2 = 5,520 + 57,132 = \$62,652$$

Therefore, the total cost of the regulation would be $94,128 + $62,652 = $156,780. This is much smaller than the cost of quantity regulation, which was $219,500.

Note that both firms end up better off as well. GPS actually makes money off the new regulation by selling its permits. Its total revenue from the sale of the permits is equal to (number of permits) × (price of permit), or 112 × $868 = $97,216. This is larger than GPS' cost of abatement, leaving them with extra funds in the amount of $3,088 (= $97,216 − $94,128). On the other hand, MAPS pays $97,216 for the permits and also faces $62,652 in abatement costs for a total cost of $159,868. This is far lower than the cost that MAPS faced under the quantity regulation described in part (b), which was $197,500.

16.3   Further Topics in Externalities and Their Remedies

tragedy of the commons

The phenomenon that a common resource is used more intensively than it would be if it were privately owned.

In this section, we look at two special topics. First, we explore a classic form of negative externality known as the **tragedy of the commons** which occurs when many people share access to an open resource. Second, we show how externalities, including the tragedy of the commons, can sometimes be solved by the market players themselves (including the third parties affected by the externality) without any government intervention. This type of solution can occur if property rights are clear and if the parties to the transaction are free to negotiate with each other.

The Tragedy of the Commons

A special, and often quite damaging type of externality, called the tragedy of the commons, occurs when anyone can use a **common resource** without restraint. By common resource, we mean any property that allows free access to all individuals who want to use it but whose value to any one individual is affected by the number of people using it. The concept of the "tragedy" comes from the dilemma that common resources create: Because everyone has free access, the resource is used more intensively than it would if it were privately owned. This leads to a decline in the value of the resource for everyone.

common resource

An economic good that all individuals can access freely and whose value to the individual consumer decreases as others use it.

A reservoir of water, fishing grounds in oceans, public forests, public airwaves, and even public restrooms are all examples of common resources. The key element is that anyone can use or take from the common resource and those who use it cannot be monitored easily. This anyone-can-access characteristic of a common resource is called **nonexcludability** because people cannot be excluded from consuming it. Because access to the resource is shared by all comers, common resources are also called *common-pool* or *common-property resources*.

nonexcludability

A defining property of a common resource, that consumers cannot be prevented from consuming the good.

The problem with common resources is that no single user takes into account the negative externality she imposes on others by using the common resource, leading everyone to consume too much of it. The externality involved with a common resource arises because of the combination of open access and depletion through use. When deciding how much of the common resource to consume, everyone considers only her own cost of use. But, this use depletes the resource for all other users. Because individuals don't consider the cost they impose on others when making their decisions about how much of the common resource to consume, they end up using too much of the resource. And, because everyone accessing the resource creates this same externality with her own use, the total utilization of the resource is above the socially optimal amount. This outcome is analogous to the market quantity being higher than the efficient level in our earlier negative externality examples. Without controls, too much water is extracted from aquifers, fishing grounds are overfished, too many trees are cut on public lands, too many communications devices jam the airways, and so on.

The Petrified Forest National Park in Arizona, for example, is a surreal landscape full of fallen ancient trees that have been petrified into rock. It is a common resource for everyone to enjoy, yet many visitors steal pieces of petrified wood to keep as a souvenir. The parks service estimates that it loses about 12 tons per year in theft. Each thief thinks, "I can take just a small piece . . . it won't make any difference," and doesn't take into account that removal of that one piece reduces the value of the park for others. Without controls—park ranger patrols, heavy fines and punishments, and so on—this attitude would easily lead to a dwindling of the resource. This happened to the original Plymouth Rock, in Massachusetts, the supposed landing spot of the Mayflower immigrants in 1620. So many people chipped off pieces of the rock that by 1835 it had dwindled to less than half its original size and had to be moved behind a fence to prevent it from disappearing completely.

In some cases, the consequences of this overuse can be severe: Instead of preserving a sustainable fishing stock, for example, overfishing can easily drive an entire population of fish to extinction. It's not that fishers prefer to drive their prey to extinction; in fact, they prefer to have a steady supply available. But, the overfishing happens because of the externality and the open access to the fishing stock.

Remedies for the Tragedy of the Commons   Because the tragedy of the commons is just a special form of negative externality, any of the solutions we described in the previous section can be used to try to fix it, and they are in fact employed in many actual situations. For example, governments use price-based mechanisms (Pigouvian taxes) to charge individuals for the external damage they do to the common resource, or they charge a fee for each unit of the common resource an individual consumes (such as an entrance fee to a national park). Governments also set quantity restrictions (quotas) on the rate at which common resources can be extracted, such as limits on the amount of fishing, hunting, or logging, for example. These interventions can be used by governments or other organized public or private regulatory bodies. In fact, as we see later, users of common resources have incentives to join together to self-regulate use of the resource.

Another way to fix the tragedy of the commons externality involves defining property rights and facilitating negotiation among those who share the common resource. For the airwaves, for example, the government auctions off spectrum and says that whoever buys the spectrum is the only one allowed to broadcast at that frequency. Granting sole control of one part of the resource to one party eliminates the negative externality. The person in control gets all the benefit and pays all the cost of using the resource, so she doesn't have an incentive to overuse it.

The Coase Theorem: Free Markets Fixing Externalities on Their Own

Sometimes, government does not need to step in with taxes, subsidies, or quotas to force consumers and producers to solve an externality problem and arrive at an efficient market price and quantity. In fact, under certain circumstances, individuals can address and solve the externality themselves. The reason this may be possible lies at the heart of the **Coase theorem,** which states that parties can reach the optimal level of an externality if they can costlessly negotiate with one another, regardless of the allocation of property rights. The Coase theorem was developed by Nobel Prize-winning economist Ronald Coase in 1960.[14]

As an example of how individuals can solve an externality problem on their own, let's take a look at the market for Internet domain names. Early in the history of the Internet in the United States, domain names were not automatically included in trademarks. Madonna, for example, has trademarked her name, which gives her the right to stop people from calling themselves Madonna, from releasing albums under that name, from selling merchandise with the name "Madonna" on it, and so on. However, the trademark for her name did not automatically give her the right to the Internet domain name www.Madonna.com. Instead, businessman Don Parisi engaged in *cybersquatting*; he bought the domain name in 1998 for $20,000, and proceeded to post pornography and ads on his site. Buying up and using domain names in ways that damage a third party is a classic negative externality. Madonna fought Parisi for the right to her name, and in 2000 the World Intellectual Property Organization ruled in Madonna's favor. Similar confusions and arguments exist today over the names people use on Facebook, Twitter, and Tumblr.

At first glance, it seems that whether individuals or companies have the legal right to enforce trademarks over domain names or Twitter handles would make a big difference in whether rogue operators will buy the names of famous people. In other words, we might expect that if there is no law for preventing cybersquatting, there will be more of

Coase theorem
Theorem that states that costless negotiation among market participants will lead to the efficient market outcome regardless of who holds legal property rights.

---

[14] Ronald Coase, "The Problem of Social Cost," *Journal of Law and Economics* 3 (1960): 1–44.

it. But, the Coase theorem tells us that in many situations it doesn't actually matter to whom the law gives the legal rights. The market participants should negotiate and reach deals that will yield the correct outcome regardless of the initial allocation of rights.

To understand why and under what conditions this negotiation can take place, let's look at another domain-name dispute from the early 2000s. The 1970s British progressive rock band Jethro Tull has sold more than 60 million albums (enough to allow it to squeak in as one of the 100 best-selling recording artists of all time). Early in the cybersquatting battles, a man named Denny Hammerton of Minneola, Florida, bought the Internet domain www.JethroTull.com and informed the band that he would sell it to them for $13,000.

The Coase theorem tells us that it's not whether the law says bands automatically have the rights to URLs with their name that determines if Jethro Tull will end up controlling its own domain name. Instead, the determining factor is whether the external cost the band incurs from someone else owning it (in other words, the value Jethro Tull places on owning that domain name) is greater than the value the cybersquatter places on owning it. If Jethro Tull values it more highly, then the band should be willing to pay more than anyone else to get control of the domain name. If, for example, Jethro Tull places a value of $14,000 on controlling this URL, then it would pay Mr. Hammerton the $13,000 he requested, and Jethro Tull would end up with the domain. This would be the efficient outcome: Jethro Tull places a higher value on the resource (in this case, the

Rock group Jethro Tull (seen here performing in the 1970s) faced a negative externality when a cyber-squatter bought up their domain name on the Internet for his own purposes.

Gijsbert Hanekroot/Redferns/Getty Images

domain name) than does Mr. Hammerton, so the domain goes to its highest valued use. No law granting property rights to Jethro Tull is necessary to achieve this outcome; negotiation among the affected parties is sufficient.

Suppose instead that Jethro Tull only suffers a negative externality of $10,000 from Mr. Hammerton's ownership (i.e., the band values the domain at $10,000). In this case, the domain name would remain with Mr. Hammerton. This is now the efficient outcome because Mr. Hammerton places a greater value on the domain than does Jethro Tull. Again, the parties involved reach an efficient outcome without a law assigning specific property rights over URLs; only negotiation is necessary.

These examples show that when negative externalities are present, the third party incurring an external cost may be willing to pay those generating the externality to stop. (Of course, this will only occur when the external cost borne by the third party is greater than the value of the externality to those generating it.) Likewise, those generating an externality may pay for the right to impose external costs on third parties. These payments allow the efficient outcome to be reached through negotiation.

Do property rights matter at all, according to the Coase theorem? Yes—they affect who pays whom in order to reach the efficient outcome. Suppose again that Jethro Tull values the domain name at $14,000, while Mr. Hammerton values it at $13,000. These values tell us that the efficient outcome will be for Jethro Tull to own this domain name, regardless of which party initially owns the property rights. But, whether Jethro Tull will actually have to pay for the domain *does* depend on how the property rights are assigned. If the law says that Jethro Tull's trademark should also apply to its domain, then Jethro Tull ends up with the domain and no money exchanges hands. However, if the trademark doesn't apply, then Jethro Tull will pay Mr. Hammerton between $13,000 and $14,000 for the domain. Either way, the efficient outcome is reached, but in the first case Jethro Tull doesn't have to pay Mr. Hammerton anything, and in the second case the band must fork over the cash.

If we altered our example a bit, we could come up with a scenario whereby Mr. Hammerton actually pays Jethro Tull for the domain. For example, suppose that Jethro Tull values the domain at only $10,000 and the property rights are such that Jethro Tull's trademark gives the band ownership of that domain. Here, the efficient outcome would be for Mr. Hammerton to own the domain, since he values it more highly. Therefore, Mr. Hammerton will pay Jethro Tull between $10,000 and $13,000 for the domain. Again, the efficient outcome can be reached through bargaining; it does not matter where the initial property rights lie. Only the direction of payments is affected by the property rights.

How did things work out for Jethro Tull and Mr. Hammerton? In 2000 the World Intellectual Property Organization ruled that Jethro Tull had the rights to the domain name. We can assume that the band valued the domain name more than Mr. Hammerton, because Mr. Hammerton did not negotiate to buy it back from Jethro Tull.

We want to be careful not to oversimplify this negotiation process. Caution must be exercised about relying too much on Coase-type negotiations to sort out externality problems and thus eliminate concern about the distribution of property rights. The assumption that the parties involved (those creating the externality and those suffering from it) can bargain costlessly is critically important. If making deals is costly—if, for instance, lawyers become involved in negotiating the dispute—the Coase theorem doesn't have to apply. It can also be difficult to organize such a negotiation when there are multiple parties involved; for example, it would not be easy to get millions of people living on the West Coast of North America to agree on a contract to pay factories in China to stop burning dirty coal. The Coase theorem says that it doesn't matter whether the law gives the factories the right to pollute as much as they want or requires them to obtain the permission of all breathers of air before they can burn their coal. However, when negotiating costs are daunting, the Coase theorem will fail and governments or laws may be the only way that an externality can be addressed.[15]

16.4 figure it out

Green Acres Fertilizer Company is located near Barney's Dry Cleaning Service. In its production process, Green Acres emits noxious odors that are absorbed by the clothing that Barney is cleaning. The result is that Barney has lost many customers over time. Barney estimates that the odors cost his business $10,000 per year. Green Acres can eliminate its odors by altering its production process at a cost of $12,000 per year.

a. If Green Acres has the right to emit the odors, what will the socially optimal outcome be? How will it be reached? Will any money change hands?

b If Barney has the right to odor-free air, what will the socially optimal outcome be? How will it be reached? Will any money change hands?

Solution:

a. The socially optimal outcome will occur when Green Acres emits the odor. The cost of eliminating the emissions ($12,000 per year) is greater than the external cost of the odor ($10,000 per year). If Green Acres has the right to emit the odors, it will continue to do so. Barney does not value clean air enough to purchase that right from Green Acres, so no money will change hands.

b. The socially optimal outcome will still be for Green Acres to emit the odor. The optimal outcome is determined by the relative values that Green Acres and Barney place on the resource (air). Because Green Acres values the air more highly, it should use the resource and emit the odor. However, because Barney has a right to odor-free air, Green Acres will have to purchase the right to emit odors from him. Assuming that this transaction can be done costlessly, Green Acres will have to pay Barney between $10,000 and $12,000 for that right.

[15] Asymmetric information can also cause problems for the predictions of the Coase theorem. If negotiating parties have private information about their valuations of an externality (or its absence), they won't be anxious to share them with the other negotiating parties. As we saw in Chapter 15, if information asymmetries are bad enough, negotiations might break down, even if an agreement would be efficient under full information.

 **application**

The Tragedy of the Commons Meets the Coase Theorem in the Texas Oil Fields

Gary Libecap and Steven Wiggins have documented that, in real life, if bargaining costs are low enough, common resource users can solve their own tragedy of the commons problem, just as the Coase theorem predicts.[16] They have also shown that when bargaining becomes too costly, negotiations break down, as expected.

Their study looks at oil drillers in Texas during the 1920s when people rushed in to extract newly discovered oil. Oil deposits are common resources that are normally spread over a large area, crossing many different owners' land. One drilling company, even if it owned the land surrounding its wells, had a hard time restricting all other firms' access to that pool of oil. Therefore, access to the oil deposit was not completely controlled by any single owner.

Because drillers pulled oil from common deposits, any one firm's drilling reduced the oil available to other nearby firms. As with all tragedies of the commons, this situation gave each firm an incentive to drill too many wells and to pump oil as quickly as possible, reducing the overall value of the deposit for all firms in the process. Extracting oil too quickly leaves behind pockets of oil that can only be recovered at high cost and, in some cases, not at all. Fast extraction also raises every firm's operating costs because each firm is working at capacity (leading to increased breakdowns and accidents), and each also has to build storage facilities for all of the oil it is pumping out of the ground.

The Coase theorem predicts that the firms accessing a common field should be able to solve these problems through negotiation. In principle, they could agree to reduce the overall extraction rate to maximize the joint value of the oil deposit, and then apportion this value among themselves. (Which firms would receive the largest value shares would depend on their relative bargaining positions, which are affected by legal property rights and other factors.) Practically speaking, however, bargaining can be very difficult. Some oil fields had dozens of firms with extraction rights. Bargaining to a mutually acceptable agreement in these cases could be costly.

The study clearly backed up the Coase theorem predictions: In oil fields where only a few firms held big majorities of the extraction rights—and therefore where bargaining should be easiest—firms quickly signed contracts that regulated extraction rates. The larger firms had the most to gain from preserving the field's total value, because they would receive a larger share of this benefit.

In fields with many different owners, however, the firms usually could not successfully agree to any private contracts. Even when extraction-limiting contracts *were* reached, firms with smaller extraction capacities were more likely to cheat on the agreements than larger ones. This finding is not surprising because the small firms have the least to gain by going along with the agreements and the most to gain by cheating to secure more of the resource than they would get under a deal. ■

The Coase Theorem and Tradable Permits Markets

One area in which the Coase theorem has impacted the real world is in the design of government strategies to combat pollution. As we demonstrated earlier in the chapter, tradable permits can move a market with a negative externality to the socially optimal outcome, often at a lower cost than quantity mechanisms such as quotas.

---

[16] Gary D. Libecap and Steven N. Wiggins, "Contractual Responses to the Common Pool: Prorationing of Crude Oil Production," *American Economic Review* 74, no. 1 (March 1984): 87–98.

The Coase theorem says that it shouldn't matter who gets the right to pollute (i.e., the quota allotments) as long as the firms are allowed to trade freely and bargaining costs are low. Thus, the government can reach an efficient amount of pollution by setting up a market for tradable permits.

By enabling trades, the market for permits allows the reduction in emissions to be achieved efficiently while sparing the government the trouble of determining how the reductions in the externality should be apportioned across firms. The government can achieve the efficient *total* level of emissions by issuing the optimal number of permits to the firms in an industry and allowing them to trade among themselves to reach the right outcome. Firms that face lower abatement costs will reduce emissions more. It gives them a way, through permit sales, to be compensated for their additional abatement costs. High-abatement-cost firms, at the same time, prefer to buy these permits because it's cheaper for them than cutting emissions directly.

Externalities, uncorrected, cause markets to be inefficient. But, tradable permit markets *create a new market* for the externality itself. Externalities are essentially extra, unpriced "products" tied to market transactions. Polluters don't consider the external costs of their emissions because they don't have to pay those costs. But, by creating a market for pollution, tradable permit markets actually put a price on pollution itself. Because the permit market makes polluting firms face this price, polluters have to consider the social implications of their production activity. Price mechanisms (such as Pigouvian taxes) that are used to address externalities serve the same purpose: They put a price on an externality that normally doesn't have one, causing market participants to be aware of the externality's effects.

We can therefore think of externalities as resulting from missing markets. The fundamental problem is that, in the absence of intervention, there is no way to do for externalities what markets do for regular goods: Provide a value for their costs and benefits to society through the price mechanism. The Coase theorem basically implies that, if you can create a market for the externality, the market's supply-and-demand mechanism will lead to the efficient outcome.

16.4 Public Goods

So far in this chapter, we have looked at market failures in which markets end up with an inefficient level of output as a result of externalities or unclear property rights. There is another type of good for which markets can fail to deliver the socially optimal level of output. **Public goods** are goods (such as national defense, a fireworks display, or clean air) that are accessible to anyone who wants to consume them and that remain just as valuable to the consumer even as other people consume them. For example, when you watch a fireworks display from your backyard, it makes no difference if you are the only person watching the display or if all of your neighbors are watching the fireworks, too. And, the individuals putting on the fireworks display can't stop people from watching it, even if they wanted to. As a result, public goods have distinctive properties that make it difficult for markets to deliver them at efficient levels. Note that a public good is *not* necessarily provided by a government, although governments often provide public goods because private markets may provide too little of the goods, or even any amount of the good at all.

Public goods are similar in some ways to positive externalities: They provide external benefits to individuals other than those who purchase them. For example, if you host a fireworks display, you may not consider the benefits received by your neighbors when making your purchases. This leads to an output that is smaller than is socially optimal because the full benefits of the fireworks display are not considered. Put simply, if the true social benefits were taken into account, there would be more (and perhaps more elaborate) fireworks displays.

public good
A good that is accessible to anyone who wants to consume it, and that remains just as valuable to a consumer even as other people consume it.

Table 16.1   Examples of Goods by Characteristics

	Excludable *Individuals can be kept from consuming.*	**Nonexcludable** *Individuals cannot be kept from consuming.*
Rival *One individual's consumption affects another's consumption.*	**Private good:** taco, gasoline, paper	**Common resource:** shared property, fisheries, interstate highways
Nonrival *One individual's consumption has no effect on another's consumption.*	**Club good:** Satellite TV services, private park, movie	**Public good:** fireworks display, mosquito abatement, national defense

nonrival
Defining property of a public good that describes how one individual's consumption of the good does not diminish another consumer's enjoyment of the same good.

private good
A good that is rival (one person's consumption affects the ability of another to consume it) and excludable (individuals can be prevented from consuming it).

club good
A good that is nonrival and excludable.

In the discussion of the tragedy of the commons, we learned that some goods are *nonexcludable*, which means all people who want to use the good have access to it—they cannot be prevented from using the good. This is true for public goods as well. However, public goods are not only nonexcludable but also **nonrival,** meaning that one person's consumption of the good does not diminish another consumer's enjoyment of the *same good.* (A different way to think of a good being nonrival is that the marginal cost of providing the good to yet another consumer is zero.)

For example, a TV weather forecast is a nonrival good because the value of the forecast to a consumer is unaffected by the number of individuals also watching the same forecast. The fact that your neighbor watches the forecast (or hears it on the radio, or reads it online or in a newspaper) does not in any way diminish or eliminate the utility you derive from watching the same forecast. Any good that many people can consume independently without using it up or degrading it is a nonrival good. In contrast, if a consumer buys a rival (regular) good, then someone else cannot buy that exact good. For example, if you are eating a taco, another person cannot eat that same taco. Because the taco is also excludable (a person can be kept from consuming it), it is a **private good.** Table 16.1 shows the different types of goods that exist categorized by rivalry and excludability.

■ An example of a rival, excludable good is a gallon of gasoline. Because the gasoline is rival, another person can't consume the exact same gallon you bought. And, once you consume the gasoline, it is no longer available for anyone else to consume. Gasoline is also excludable because producers can keep you from consuming the gasoline unless you purchase it.

■ An example of a rival, nonexcludable good is a common resource such as the stock of a particular fish, like sturgeon in the Caspian Sea (which are a valuable source of caviar). This good is rival because fish that are caught by one boat cannot be caught by another. However, this good is nonexcludable because it is virtually impossible to stop someone from fishing if she wants to.

■ An example of a nonrival good that is excludable is a satellite TV broadcast of a football game. This good is nonrival because anyone can receive the satellite transmission without taking away the ability of other consumers to watch. However, this good is excludable because consumers must pay a subscription fee to receive the show's unscrambled signal. Nonrival, excludable goods are sometimes referred to as **club goods.**

■ An example of a nonrival, nonexcludable good is mosquito abatement, which is often performed by spraying public waterways with pesticides. This good is nonrival because one person's enjoyment of a mosquito-free environment does not impact another person's enjoyment of the same. And, because getting rid of mosquitos helps everyone regardless of who paid for it, mosquito abatement is also nonexcludable.

The Optimal Level of Public Goods

Before we can see why markets provide inefficient levels of public goods, we have to define what the efficient level of output is for these types of goods. It's a little different from the efficiency conditions we've discussed before.

Efficiency generally occurs when a market produces the quantity for which the marginal cost of producing the good just equals the marginal benefit society receives from the good. For a competitive market without externalities, that quantity is also where quantity supplied equals quantity demanded. As we saw earlier in this chapter, in markets with externalities present, we need to be sure that all external costs and benefits are considered when determining the efficient output. Efficiency in these markets thus occurs at the output for which social demand (which measures social marginal benefit) is equal to social marginal cost.

With public goods, the marginal benefit from the good is not the benefit for just one consumer because more than one person can consume the good simultaneously. A public good is nonrival, so to value the good, we have to add the marginal benefits of everyone who consumes it. Put differently, a public good's **total marginal benefit** curve is the *vertical* sum of the marginal benefit curves of all its many consumers. This total marginal benefit (MB_T) is what equals marginal cost when a public good is being provided at its optimal level. In equation form, the total marginal benefit is written

$$MB_T = \Sigma MB_i$$

total marginal benefit
The vertical sum of the marginal benefit curves of all of a public good's consumers.

The summation symbol Σ denotes that the good's marginal benefits are added over all consumers (whom we've indexed with i) of that good.

There is no "sum of marginal costs" condition because the cost of producing a public good is just like the cost of producing any other good. While a public good is simultaneously consumed, there is nothing in its definition that implies it is simultaneously produced. Whether made by an individual, a firm, or a government, the marginal cost of a good is the same no matter if that good is a public or standard private good.

Figure 16.10 shows the public goods efficiency condition for a simple example in which the public good is consumed by two people. The marginal benefit curves of each person are illustrated in the figure as MB_1 and MB_2. The total marginal benefit of the public good, shown as curve MB_T, is the vertical sum of the individual marginal benefit curves. MC is the marginal cost of producing the good.

Figure 16.10   **Efficiency in the Market for a Public Good**

The two consumers of a public good have marginal benefit curves MB_1 and MB_2. At the efficient point, both consumers consume Q^*_{Pub} of the public good, where their total marginal benefit curve (MB_T) intersects the marginal cost curve (MC). If the two consumers privately bought the good, each would consume less than the optimal level at quantities Q_1 and Q_2, where MB_1 and MB_2 each intersect MC.

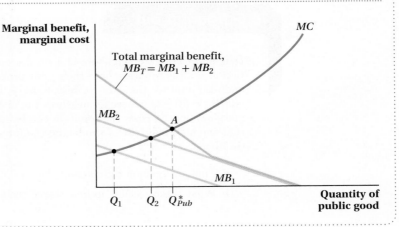

Efficiency requires that the public good be provided at point A where $MB_T = MC$, with a quantity of Q^*_{Pub}. It's important to realize that this is the quantity of the public good that *both* individuals consume. Because it is nonrival, they don't have to split Q^*_{Pub} between them. They consume Q^*_{Pub} units of the good simultaneously.

Why isn't this efficiency condition achieved in the private market? For the same reasons we saw in markets with externalities, the free market is going to encounter a problem providing the right level of public goods. The market facilitates private exchanges until a good's *private* marginal cost equals individuals' *private* marginal benefits. However, that is not where the *combined* marginal benefits of multiple consumers equal the good's marginal cost. If individuals could buy the public good themselves at marginal cost, each would buy the quantity at which *her own* marginal benefit equals its marginal cost. Looking at Figure 16.10 again, Person 1 would buy Q_1, where $MB_1 = MC$. Similarly, Person 2 would buy Q_2.

Therefore, although both individuals would be willing to pay for some quantity of the public good, neither would by herself pay for the efficient quantity because her individual marginal benefit is less than the joint marginal benefit. The inefficiency arises in a way that is similar to how inefficiency arises with a positive externality: Individuals paying privately for a public good don't consider everyone else's benefit from the good. This is one reason why private markets fail to produce the efficient quantity of public goods. Left to their own devices, private markets don't supply enough national defense, mosquito abatement, clean air, fireworks displays, and the like.

In addition to not taking into account the total marginal benefit of the good and thus having less of it available than is socially optimal, the **free-rider problem** is another source of inefficiency in the markets for public goods. A free-rider is someone who enjoys a good or service without paying for it. For example, electronics manufacturers, shoe manufacturers, and car manufacturers want people to be able to try out their products before purchase, and there are sellers that provide those services. In many cases, however, online retailers, who don't have to provide (or pay for) try-out and other services, can offer much lower prices than "brick-and-mortar" stores. The online retailers are free-riding on the services provided by the brick-and-mortar stores. The problem with this is that if enough people try out a product in a retail store and then go online to buy it at a lower price, offline retailers will stop providing try-out services. The free market ends up generating too little of the try-out information (which benefits consumers and producers) because it has become a public good.

free-rider problem
A source of inefficiency resulting from individuals consuming a public good or service without paying for it.

16.5 figure it out

Dale and Casey are neighbors in a rural area. They are considering the joint installation of a large fountain near their joint property line so that each can enjoy its beauty and also improve the value of his property. Dale's marginal benefit from the fountain is $MB_D = 70 - Q$, where Q measures the diameter of the fountain (in feet). Casey's marginal benefit from the fountain can be represented as $MB_C = 40 - 2Q$. Assume that the marginal cost of producing the fountain is constant and equal to $80 per foot (in diameter).

a. Find an equation to represent the total marginal benefit of the fountain.

b. What is the socially optimal size of the fountain?

c. Show that if either Dale or Casey had to build a fountain by themselves, neither would find even the smallest fountain worth building.

Solution:

a. The total marginal benefit is the vertical summation of Dale's and Casey's individual marginal benefit curves:

$$MB_T = MB_D + MB_C = (70 - Q) + (40 - 2Q) = 110 - 3Q$$

b. The socially optimal size of the fountain occurs where MB_T equals the marginal cost of producing the fountain:

$$MB_T = MC$$
$$110 - 3Q = 80$$
$$3Q = 30$$
$$Q = 10$$

The optimal size of the fountain is 10 feet in diameter.

c. Dale's marginal benefit is $MB_D = 70 - Q$. If the smallest possible fountain was zero feet in diameter ($Q = 0$), Dale's marginal benefit would only be $70, while the marginal cost would be $80. Therefore, Dale would not find even the smallest fountain to be worth the cost. Likewise, the marginal benefit of a zero-foot fountain for Casey will be $MB_C = 40 - 2Q = 40, which is also less than the $80 marginal cost.

Solving the Free-Rider Problem

A common solution to the free-rider problem in the fireworks case, the online retailer case, and in paying for public goods more generally is for an entity like the government or the manufacturer to compel people to pay their share through a tax or a retailer fee. This is why the most expensive and broad-scoped public goods such as national defense, "rule-of-law" goods (e.g., court systems, police services), and national transportation infrastructure—items for which free-riding might be the most severe—are paid for through taxation.[17]

Other solutions are also possible. Beneficiaries of a public good can form an organization that compels members to pay their share of the public good's costs. The tricky issue in such situations is convincing potential members to *voluntarily* form a group that will *compel* them to pay for something they'd rather not pay for at all. Condo owners, for example, often form a condo association to pay for maintaining a pool and other common areas because free-rider problems will develop among the owners if they don't.

---

[17] Note that the government, having raised the necessary revenues through taxes to pay for the public good, does not necessarily need to itself produce the public good to achieve efficiency. In principle, the government could use the tax receipts to pay private entities to provide the public good. The U.S. interstate highway system, for example, was paid for with public funds but built by private contractors. Still, governments often both fund and directly provide the public good because of scale efficiencies or other reasons.

As economist Mancur Olson pointed out in 1965, the likelihood of solving the free-rider problem depends on how large the public good's benefits are per potential member of the group that would enjoy the good.[18] If each potential member's gain from cooperative action—her benefit from having the efficient level of the public good available—would be large, it is more likely that a cooperative group will form. When the benefit-per-potential-member ratio is low, group-forming success is less likely. Because each member of the group only benefits a little from the public good, less is lost trying to free-ride. The incentive to free-ride makes it difficult to hold any possible group together. (This is a lot like the logic we discussed in Chapter 11 about why it's easier for a small number of firms to form a stable cartel than it is for a large number of firms to do the same thing.)

It's important to realize that the benefit per member of a public good might not be closely correlated with the *total* benefit of the good. It's quite possible that a public good that would offer an enormous total benefit may not end up being provided because the size of its potential group is also really large, making the average benefit per person too small to overcome free-riding. At the same time, a public good with a much smaller total benefit might be provided if it benefits only a select group who enjoy a large benefit per member. This effect is a possible explanation why special interest groups can successfully lobby for programs that jointly benefit their members despite imposing a much larger collective cost on everyone else. Each member of the special interest group enjoys large gains by paying lobbyists to put forward the group's agenda and encourage legislators to vote favorably for its programs. The lobbying can be thought of as a public good for the members. Even though the program imposes a very large collective cost on everyone outside the special interest group, the cost borne by any one person is too small to overcome free-riding, and no one mounts a concerted effort to stop the legislation.

For example, suppose that there are four large steel manufacturers in the United States, and each is on the verge of bankruptcy. The CEO for one of these firms comes up with the idea of lobbying the government for financial support to keep her firm from bankruptcy and she convinces the other firms to do the same. The four firms band together and hire a lobbyist to help the firms plead their case to legislators. The lobbyist argues that, without federal support, these manufacturers will have to close their doors, leading to serious problems for the U.S. economy. The legislators vote to provide $800 million to the firms ($200 million to each firm).

This large potential gain per member from cooperating increases the likelihood that interest group members will work collectively without free-riding. Even when the costs of the special interest programs are much larger for everyone else than are the programs' benefits to the special interest group, opposition may not form if these enormous costs are spread over a larger population. In our example, the $800 million will be paid by the hundreds of millions of taxpayers in the United States (maybe $4 to $6 per taxpayer). Fighting the program would be greatly jointly beneficial for those bearing the costs, but if each individual's share of the program's imposed cost is relatively small, he or she may prefer to free-ride on the efforts of others. If everyone makes this choice, opposition to special interests will be weak, even though opponents would have much to gain from stopping the special interests' programs.

[18] Mancur Olson, *The Logic of Collective Action: Public Goods and the Theory of Groups*, Cambridge, MA: Harvard University Press, 1965.

freakonomics

Is Fire Protection a Public Good?

In September 2010 a small trash fire sparked a fire at a house just outside of South Fulton, Tennessee. Firefighters rushed to the scene. But instead of putting out the blaze, the firefighters stood by and simply let the house burn to the ground.[*]

Why didn't they do anything? To understand why, we have first to understand how the South Fulton fire department is funded. Residents in the city of South Fulton pay taxes to fund the fire department, so the city itself has fire coverage. It's inefficient for the rural areas outside South Fulton to have their own fire department. So, the South

South Fulton, Tennessee, firefighters allowed this man's home to burn down to prevent rural areas from free-riding on South Fulton's fire protection services.

Fulton fire department offers fire coverage—for a $75 yearly fee per household—to these surrounding areas. The South Fulton government can't force the people in the outlying areas to pay; it's up to the rural homeowners to voluntarily cough up the $75. As you can imagine, many of them do not pay. "After all," they figure, "What's the chance my house will catch fire? And if it does catch fire, will the fire department actually just let it burn? No way."

It turns out, however, that South Fulton Fire Chief David Wilds thinks like an economist. To the noneconomist, it might seem that the neighborly thing to do would be to fight any rural house fire, regardless of the fee. But, the local fire chief recognized an important fact: Without the enforced yearly fee, firefighting is a nonexcludable good; that is, no individual or family could be kept from enjoying the fire protection. The time and effort the fire department put into preventing fires, fighting those that do arise, and watchfully waiting when there isn't a fire benefit everyone in an area, whether it's their house on fire or not.

Homeowners would like to enjoy the benefits of this nonexcludable good but only actually pay if and when their house catches on fire. (This is also related to the adverse selection problem in insurance markets we discussed in Chapter 15.) That sort of payment arrangement wouldn't provide much of a budget for the fire department to work with, however. So, the department requires all rural homeowners to pay their fire coverage service fee ahead of time if they want the fire department to answer their calls.

We know why the firefighters didn't put out the blaze—it's a matter of public goods. But why did they bother showing up at all? The answer also involves the public good aspect of firefighting. The firefighters had an obligation to these homeowners' neighbors who *had* paid the fee. That's why they were there, watching the house burn down, but prepared to put out any fire that crossed the border to the neighbors' yards. And, in fact, firefighters did stop the fire from crossing into a neighboring yard while ignoring the still roaring fire on the original property.

The strong economic rationale behind this fire department's policy doesn't mean it hasn't taken a lot of heat for its decision. Letting the house burn garnered Fire Chief Wilds national attention, and the media did not appreciate the economic logic of his decision. In response to this public uproar, it only stands to reason that Wilds would succumb to political pressure and abandon the policy. If you think that's what happened, then you underestimated Wilds. Just a little over a year later, he allowed another house to burn to the ground, ensuring his spot in the Freakonomics Hall of Fame.

---

[*] "No Pay, No Spray: Firefighters Let Home Burn," October 6, 2010, msnbc.com and "Firefighters Let Home Burn over $75 Fee—Again," April 20, 2012, msnbc.com.

16.5 Conclusion

Throughout the book, we have seen that an economy relies on free, competitive markets to provide optimal outcomes for producers and consumers: Firms produce and consumers buy up to the point at which the marginal benefit of the product equals the marginal cost of producing it. When there are externalities or public goods involved, however, this process doesn't work.

When one economic actor's purchase or production decision imposes costs or benefits on other economic actors that are not included in the transaction, these imposed costs and benefits are not taken into account by the decision maker, and free-market outcomes can lead the economy far away from its optimum. There will be too many products with negative externalities and too few products with positive externalities. Common resources and public goods are a bit different from externalities, but the markets for them show many of the same pathologies: overconsumption (of common resources) and underprovision (of public goods).

There are many ways to mitigate or even get rid of the problems associated with market failures. Governments can impose Pigouvian taxes or subsidies on markets with externalities to bring the private costs and benefits in line with the true costs and benefits to society. For common resource and public goods problems, governments can impose quantity restrictions or mandates or even provide a product themselves. However, governments aren't the only entities that may correct for these market failures. The Coase theorem indicates that, if negotiation costs are low enough, the private sector may itself come up with a closer-to-optimal solution.

The key to this chapter is understanding why some markets may not always work as efficiently as the standard economic models predict. In the last chapter of this book, we examine situations in which economic actors (consumers and producers) may not appear to be the rational, utility- and profit-maximizing agents we have modeled throughout this text.

Summary

1. **Externalities** impose costs or benefits on a third party not directly involved in an economic transaction. Without market intervention, both **negative** and **positive externalities** result in inefficient market outcomes. In an efficient market, firms produce where the market demand for the good equals the social marginal cost. [**Section 16.1**]

2. Regulators can use quantity- or price-based interventions to fix externalities and push the market equilibrium toward the efficient outcome. **Pigouvian taxes** (or **subsidies**) are a tax (or subsidy) on the production or consumption of a good. The simplest form of a quantity-based intervention is a **quota.** Whether a price-based intervention like a Pigouvian tax or a quantity-based intervention like a quota should be used depends on the relative steepness of the **marginal abatement** and **external marginal cost** curves. [**Section 16.2**]

3. The **tragedy of the commons** affects common-pool resources, which are used more intensively than users would prefer if they could coordinate their actions. The **Coase theorem** predicts that in the absence of transaction costs, negotiation among economic actors will lead to efficient outcomes regardless of who holds the property rights, and is used as the basis for a frequently used strategy to combat pollution: the use of **tradable permits. [Section 16.3]**

4. All **public goods** are characterized by two properties. First, public goods are **nonrival,** meaning one consumer's enjoyment of the good does not diminish another's enjoyment of it. Second, public goods are **nonexcludable,** that is, once a public good is on the market, it is impossible to prevent people from consuming it. Because of these two properties, public goods create a **free-rider problem** in which consumers want to freely consume, or free-ride, the public good that others have provided. [**Section 16.4**]

Review Questions

1. Contrast negative and positive externalities. Provide an example of each type of externality.
2. Why does an unregulated market overproduce goods with negative externalities?
3. How can the external marginal benefit and external marginal cost curves be used to find the efficient level of an externality?
4. Why are the marginal benefit and marginal abatement cost of pollution considered equivalent?
5. How do regulators use Pigouvian taxes to produce efficient outcomes?
6. Describe how tradable pollution permits can be used to address pollution.

7. Compare and contrast Pigouvian taxes and quantity-based solutions to externalities. What are some of the advantages and disadvantages of each?
8. What types of solutions can address the tragedy of the commons?
9. What is the main prediction of the Coase theorem?
10. What are the two defining properties of public goods?
11. When is a public good being produced efficiently?
12. Why does the free-rider problem arise?

Problems (Solutions to problems marked * appear at the back of this book. Problems adapted to use calculus are available online at http://worthpublishers.com/GLS1e)

*1. Kansas City is famous for its barbeque. But, good barbeque comes at a cost: Pit masters have to bear the costs of producing slow-roasted pulled pork and beef briskets. There is also an external cost: Every time a pit master roasts another rack of ribs, it offends the sensibilities of nearby animal lovers. Consider the graphical representation of a typical pit master in the competitive BBQ industry below:

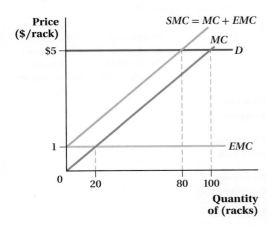

a. What is the market price of barbeque?
b. How much psychic damage (external cost) do animal lovers suffer for each rack roasted?
c. If our pit master accounts only for her private costs, how many racks will she roast? How much total damage will animal lovers suffer?

d. If our pit master feels sympathy for animal lovers and wholly considers their feelings in her decision about how many racks to produce, how many racks will she roast?
e. Does the decision to consider animal lovers' feelings eliminate the damage they suffer from transactions in the rib market?
f. Cutting output *below* the level you determined in (d) clearly benefits animal lovers. Who is hurt by such a decision? Explain why such an output cut would not be Pareto efficient, that is, there is another allocation that would make someone better off without making anyone worse off.

2. Jill sells bouquets of flowers that she grows in her backyard. Jill's marginal cost of producing bouquets is given by $MC = 0.25Q$, where Q is the number of bouquets she makes. Jill can sell all the bouquets she wishes at the local farmers' market for $6 per bouquet. Unfortunately, Jill's floriculture aggravates the allergies of her next-door neighbor, Cooper: Every bouquet that Jill grows produces 50 cents' worth of sneezes.
a. Jill wants to maximize her profit. Determine the profit-maximizing quantity of bouquets.
b. Assume that Jill produces the quantity of bouquets you determined in (a). Add up the cost of the last bouquet to Jill and the cost that bouquet imposes on Cooper, and compare your answer to the $6 worth of benefit the last bouquet creates for the buyer. Is producing the last bouquet a good thing for society?

c. From society's standpoint, is Jill overproducing or underproducing bouquets?

d. Suppose that Jill marries Cooper. Determine the social marginal cost of producing bouquets by adding the 50 cents' worth of damage each bouquet causes Cooper to Jill's private marginal cost. Express your answer as an equation.

e. Determine how many bouquets Jill should produce if she fully considers the costs she imposes on her new husband. Explain why it makes a difference if Cooper is just a neighbor or is Jill's husband.

3. Suppose that the inverse demand for marching band music is given by $P = \$1{,}000 - Q$. Because marching bands across the world produce music of sufficient quality at increasing marginal cost, the industry marginal cost is given by $MC = 0.75Q$. Unfortunately, marching band music is not produced in a vacuum: People near marching bands become increasingly aggravated the more music they hear. At the industry level, the external marginal cost is given by $EMC = 0.25Q$.

   a. Graph the demand, marginal cost, and external marginal cost functions.
   b. If marching bands do not consider the external marginal costs they impose on others, how many songs will be played?
   i.   Calculate the total consumer surplus.
   ii. Calculate the total producer surplus.
   iii. Calculate the total surplus to market participants.
   iv. Calculate the total damage to those harmed. (*Hint*: This damage can be represented as the area under the *EMC* curve. It's up to you to figure out why!)
   v.   Subtract the damage to those harmed from total surplus to market participants to determine the net value created for society by marching band music.
   c. Determine social marginal cost.
   d. Determine the quantity of marching band music that would be produced if marching bands were forced to consider the costs they imposed on others.
   e. What happens to the price of marching band music if the bands were forced to consider the external marginal costs?
   f. As you did in (b), calculate consumer surplus, producer surplus, and total damage. (Be sure to remember that producer surplus is the area between *private* marginal cost and the price!) Compared to your answers in (b),

   i.   What happens to the total surplus received by market participants when external marginal costs are considered?
   ii. What happens to the damage created by marching band music?
   iii. What happens to the net value created for society by marching band music?

*4. Gasoline brings great benefit to those who buy it, but burning it also creates external costs. Consider the graph below, which shows the demand for gasoline, the private marginal cost of producing gasoline, and the social marginal cost of producing gasoline.

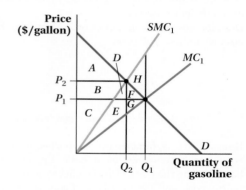

   a. Suppose that buyers and producers of gasoline do not consider the external marginal costs they impose on others. Determine the equilibrium quantity and price; then use the letters in the diagram to fill in the appropriate spaces in the table below:

	External Marginal Costs Not Considered	External Marginal Costs Considered
Consumer Surplus		
Producer Surplus		
External Damage (–)		
Total net value to society		

   b. Suppose that conscientious sellers, out of the sheer goodness of their hearts, decide to incorporate external marginal costs into their production decisions. Determine the new quantity (*Hint*: Use the social marginal cost curve) and price, then use the letters in the diagram to fill in the appropriate spaces in the table on the previous page. (Be sure to remember that producer surplus is the area above *private* marginal cost and below the price, out to the relevant quantity.)

c. Producers rarely do something out of the goodness of their hearts, and are likely to consider only their private marginal costs. Compare total surplus in both cases to determine the deadweight loss of the externality when external marginal costs are not considered.

5. The private demand for drive-in movies is given by $P = 20 - 0.1Q$. The industry marginal cost of showing drive-in movies is given by $MC = 0.1Q$.

a. Graph the private demand and marginal cost curves, and determine the price and quantity of movies that will be shown.

b. Drive-in movies can be viewed imperfectly from outside the fence. The external marginal benefits received by such viewers are given by $EMB = 2 - 0.01Q$. Graph the external marginal benefit curve, and then use that information to graph the social demand curve.

c. Suppose that all drive-in movies are nationalized and shown for the public good. The Movie Czar chooses the price and quantity of movies that bring the greatest benefit net of costs to all viewers, regardless of the vantage point from which they view the movie. Determine the optimal price and quantity of drive-in movies.

d. Indicate the deadweight loss created by the positive externality as an area on your graph, and calculate its value. (*Hint*: You'll need to determine how much external marginal benefit the very last unit of output created when drive-ins were privately run.)

e. Can government-run movies potentially improve on the private market outcome when a positive externality exists?

6. Suppose that growing flowers produces both a positive externality (people in the neighborhood get to view the flowers) and a negative externality (the flowers aggravate peoples' allergies).

a. True or false, and explain your answer (using a diagram): We can say for sure that too many flowers are being produced.

b. True or false, and explain your answer (using a diagram): We can say for sure that the market price of flowers is too high.

*7. The inverse demand for leather is given by $P = 50 - 0.5Q$. The industry supply of leather is determined by its marginal cost: $MC = 0.45Q$. Unfortunately, the production of leather causes noxious chemical residue to leach into groundwater supplies. The external marginal cost caused by these residues grows with the amount of output, and is measured as $EMC = 0.05Q$.

a. Suppose that the government wishes to reduce the externality to efficient levels by imposing a restriction on quantity (a quota). What maximum level of output should it set for leather production? What price would prevail in the marketplace once this quota is in place?

b. Suppose that the government wishes to reduce the externality to efficient levels by levying a tax on leather production. How high would that tax need to be? What is the resulting net price paid by buyers once the tax is in place? How much leather is bought and sold with the tax in place?

8. Two pink slime producers, XL and IPSP, are located in an otherwise pastoral mountain town. Each producer emits 30 tons of ammonium hydroxide into the atmosphere each year. City planners wish to cut the level of ammonium hydroxide pollution to 50 tons overall.

a. Alfred B. Packer steps forward with the following suggestion. "Make each firm cut emissions by 5 tons. That seems fair, doesn't it?" Do you agree? Explain your answer.

b. Suppose that XL and IPSP are both capable of reducing emissions by 5 tons, but that it costs XL $50, and IPSP $100, to clean up each ton of emissions. Comment on the fairness of Packer's proposal in light of this additional information.

c. If you were the "King of the World" and hoped to clean up the ammonium hydroxide at the lowest possible cost, how would you split the burden of the cleanup between XL and IPSP?

d. Suppose the city goes to a tradable permits system for reducing ammonium hydroxide emissions. It prints 50 permits, each of which gives the bearer the right to emit 1 ton of ammonium hydroxide. It then distributes 25 permits each to XL and IPSP, and informs both that they are free to buy and sell the permits to each other.

i. When permits are traded, who will be the likely buyer of permits, and who will be the likely seller? Explain.

ii. What is the lowest price that you expect pollution permits to sell for?

iii. What is the highest price you expect pollution permits to sell for?

iv. When trade is complete, how many permits do you expect to see sold?

v. Under the tradable permits system, how much of the cleanup does XL end up being responsible for? How does this outcome compare to your answer to (c)?

9. Suppose that Penn Products and Teller Industries are both emitting 30 metric tons of perfluorocarbons (PFCs) into the atmosphere. Regulators wish to reduce emissions to 40 metric tons overall, and plan to achieve this with a system of tradable permits. Penn's marginal abatement costs are given by $MAC_P = 5e_P$, where e_P is the number of metric tons of emissions that Penn is cutting. Thus, the cost of cleaning up the first metric ton is $5, the second ton costs $10 to clean up, and so on. Teller's marginal abatement costs are given by $MAC_T = 7.5e_T$, where e_T is the number of metric tons of emissions that Teller cuts.

a. The lowest-cost way to reduce emissions is found when both firms' marginal abatement costs are equalized. Equate Penn's and Teller's marginal abatement costs, and solve for e_P in terms of e_T. For each metric ton that Teller cuts, how many tons should Penn cut?

b. Because 20 metric tons are to be cut, we know that $e_P + e_T = 20$. Use your answer for (a) to solve for e_T. How many metric tons will Teller be responsible for cleaning up if the cleanup is done efficiently? How about Penn?

c. Calculate the cost of Teller's share of the cleanup. Do the same for Penn, and then compute the total cost of reducing PFC emissions by 20 metric tons.

d. Suppose that Teller cleans up one metric ton less, and Penn cleans up one more ton. Recompute the total cost of the cleanup to determine if the outcome you found in (c) was efficient. Then, double check your work by reversing the situation: Let Teller clean up one additional metric ton, and Penn one fewer ton.

e. If government regulators give Penn and Teller each their own twenty 1-ton pollution permits and allow them to trade, how many permits will end up trading hands, and what price will a permit sell for?

10. Consider the market for smelted kryptonite depicted below. A by-product of kryptonite smelt-

ing is the release of clouds of toxic blackish-yellow smoke. Each ton of toxic smoke emitted causes nearby residents' health-care expenditures to rise; the external marginal costs associated with the toxic exhaust are depicted as EMC on the graph:

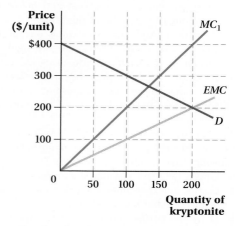

a. On the diagram, *carefully* graph the social marginal cost curve associated with the kryptonite industry. Precision matters!

b. Without any environmental regulation, how much kryptonite is produced?

c. From society's standpoint, how much kryptonite should be produced?

d. Regulators can achieve the efficient level of kryptonite production by imposing a tax on kryptonite production. To achieve the efficient level of production, how big should that tax be?

e. Draw an industry supply curve that reflects the tax you determined in part (d). Show that private producers, forced to internalize their externality by the tax, produce the socially optimal amount.

f. Could the same result have been achieved by assessing a tax on the buyers of kryptonite? If so, how much would that tax need to be?

*11. In Paris, hundreds of small bakeries produce bread for sale to their customers at a marginal cost of $MC = 2 + 0.1Q$. The inverse demand for bread is given by $P = 10 - 0.1Q$, where P is in euros per loaf and Q is loaves per hour. The baking of bread also creates a positive externality: There is nothing quite like the smell of fresh-baked bread. Tourists and residents receive external marginal benefits given by $EMB = 2 - 0.02Q$.

a. Find the quantity of bread produced in Paris in the absence of any government intervention.

b. To achieve the socially optimal output, government can use a price-based intervention. Determine the ideal measure for government to use to achieve this goal. Specify both the type of policy and its magnitude.

12. Consider the diagram below, which depicts the external marginal cost of pollution by each ton of sulfur dioxide emitted by power plants, and the marginal abatement cost of eliminating that pollution.

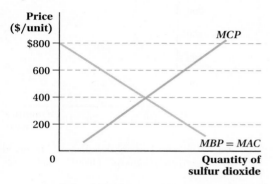

a. Explain why the marginal abatement cost (or marginal benefit of pollution) curve slopes downward.

b. Find the efficient level of pollution and indicate it on your graph.

c. Firms, which care little about the damage imposed on people hundreds or thousands of miles away, have little incentive to produce the optimal amount of pollution on their own. Explain how, if regulators tax the producer $400 for each ton of pollutant emitted, power producers will have an incentive to cut emissions to exactly the socially optimal level.

d. Explain why a tax of $600 for each ton of pollutant emitted is too high a tax, and $200 per ton is too low a tax.

13. Brimstone is a caustic by-product of the production of fairy dust. The external marginal cost caused by inhalers of brimstone is indicated in the graph at right as MCP. The marginal abatement costs to fairy dust producers ($MBP = MAC$) are indicated as well. Suppose that regulators overestimate the damage that brimstone causes; their best guess of the harm is shown as MCP_e.

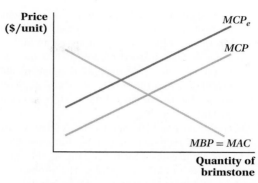

a. Show (graphically) that if regulators attempt to achieve what they believe to be an efficient amount of brimstone, it doesn't matter whether they attempt to limit the quantity of brimstone, or set what they believe to be an efficient tax.

b. Show graphically that the elasticities of the marginal abatement cost and marginal cost of pollution are irrelevant to the choice of a quantity or price intervention.

c. Show that the results you demonstrated in (a) and (b) also hold if regulators *underestimate* the amount of marginal pollution cost brimstone causes.

*14. Al regularly rehearses accordion music on his back deck with members of his musical troupe, the Starland Polka Band. Practicing on his deck saves him the $500 per year it would take to rent a rehearsal space. Unfortunately, practicing on his deck keeps his neighbor, Marcy, awake at night. The value of Marcy's lost sleep is $600 per year.

a. Is it efficient for Al to rehearse on his back deck? Explain your answer.

b. If the law says that it is illegal for Al to rehearse on his back deck, will Al end up practicing there? What might Marcy do to try to stop him?

c. Suppose that the law says it is legal for Al to rehearse on his back deck.

   i. How much is Marcy willing to pay to get him to stop?

   ii. What is the minimum amount of money Al is willing to accept in exchange for his silence?

   iii. If possible, craft a bargain between Marcy and Al that results in his silence. Show that the bargain (if possible) makes both parties better off.

d. Given your answers to (b) and (c), does the outcome of this conflict depend on the law? Is the outcome consistent with your answer to (a)?

e. Suppose that instead of doing $600 damage to one neighbor, Al does $1 damage to 600 neighbors. Are those 600 neighbors as likely to be able to convince him to stop as easily as Marcy can? Explain.

15. Assume that everyone agrees that global warming is both real and caused by humans. Give two major reasons why bargaining in the spirit of Coase is unlikely to resolve the problem of excess carbon emissions.

*16. Two dairy farmers, Ben and Jerry, share a common pasture. Each has a choice of grazing 1 or 2 cows on the pasture. If 2 cows graze on the pasture, each will give 1,000 gallons of milk each year, which may be sold for $1 each at the local farmers' market. If 3 cows graze on the pasture, the grass will be thinner and each will give 750 gallons of milk. If 4 cows graze on the pasture, the grass will have little chance to recover and each cow will only give 400 gallons of milk.

a. What is the efficient number of cows to keep on the common pasture—2, 3, or 4? Explain.

b. If Jerry keeps 1 cow in the pasture, how many should Ben keep? (Assume that the only thing that concerns Ben is revenue received at the farmers' market.)

c. If Jerry keeps 2 cows in the pasture, how many should Ben keep?

d. Repeat your analysis for Jerry. What outcome are we likely to see—2, 3, or 4 cows in the pasture?

e. What strategies might be useful in preventing overgrazing on the commons?

17. Classify each of the following goods using these terms: nonrival, nonexcludable, private good, public good, and common resource.

a. Hamburger   e. Park
b. Lighthouse   f. Broadcast television
c. Flood control   g. Cellular telephone service
d. Swimming pool   h. Computer software

18. Using the appropriate terminology, explain why public radio stations, which rely on contributions from listeners, always seem to be in financial jeopardy.

19. A home-team baseball victory produces benefits for residents (in terms of hometown pride) that is both nonrival and nonexcludable. The graph below depicts the marginal benefits that Beatrice, Edward, and Charlotte (the residents of a very tiny town indeed) receive from home-team wins. The graph also depicts the marginal costs of achieving each victory.

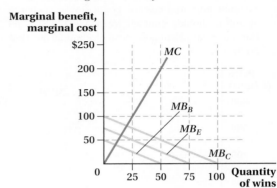

a. Draw the total marginal benefit received by hometown residents. Graph your result carefully.

b. Determine the socially optimal number of wins. Indicate this amount on your graph.

20. There are two consumers of mosquito abatement, a public good. Dash's benefit from mosquito abatement is given by $MB_D = 100 - Q$, where Q is the quantity of mosquito abatement. Lilly's benefit is given by $MB_L = 60 - Q$.

a. Calculate the total marginal benefit, MB_T.

b. Suppose that mosquito abatement can be provided at a marginal cost of $MC = 2Q$. Find the optimal level of mosquito abatement.

c. How much benefit do Dash and Lilly enjoy at the optimal level of mosquito abatement? (Assume Dash and Lilly do not have to bear any of the cost personally, but that abatement is provided by the government at no direct cost to the recipient.)

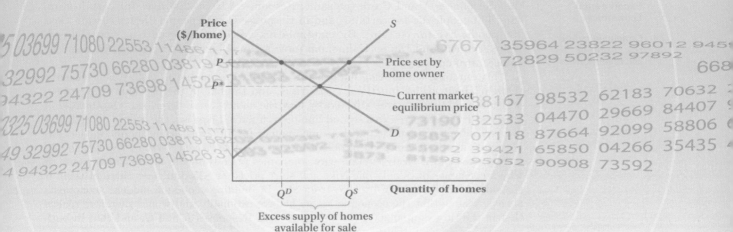

imagine you run the Centers for Disease Control and Prevention (CDC) located in Atlanta, Georgia. Your job is to keep America safe. Suddenly, an unusual flu-like disease breaks out in Florida. Your best scientists estimate that 600 Americans will die from the disease if no government action is taken. You are given a choice between two programs to address this crisis.

■ Program 1 offers two possible responses to the crisis, each of which costs the same. Because of resource constraints, you can choose only one. Response A will save 200 people. Response B is risky. It has a one-third chance to save all 600 people but a two-thirds chance to save no one. Which do you pick?

■ Program 2 also offers two possible responses, each of which costs the same. Again, you can choose only one. With Response C, 400 people will die for certain. With Response D, there is a one-third chance that no one will die and a two-thirds chance that everyone will die. Again, ask yourself, what would you choose?

Did you choose Response A for Program 1 and Response C for Program 2? You should have, because both responses are the same; they are only described differently. In either case, 200 people live and 400 people die with certainty. Similarly, Responses B and D are the same, but worded differently. With each response, there is a one-third chance to save everyone and a two-thirds chance to save no one.

In a famous study, economic researchers asked people what response they would pick.[1] With Program 1, 72% of the people chose Response A: Better to save 200 lives for certain with this option than gamble on saving more lives and risk saving no one with Response B. But when offered Program 2, 78% of the same people picked Response D. Their reasoning? How can you pick a response (C) in which 400 people die for sure when you can take a chance to save everyone? Remember that Responses A and C are the same: Response A saves 200 lives for certain (and thus 400 people die for certain), and in Response C, 400 people die for certain (and 200 people live for certain). By manipulating how these alternatives were framed, Amos Tversky and Daniel Kahneman (now a Nobel laureate) were able to alter the choices dramatically.

This outcome should not happen in a standard economic model. When we have thought about utility functions, costs, risks, and the like in the previous 16 chapters, decision making was never affected by how the choices were described. One bundle of goods is either preferred to a second bundle or it isn't. Likewise, the cost of a particular level of output is calculated in the same manner for all levels. An economic model cannot explain why framing the problem in terms of lives saved versus lives lost should matter. Nor can it easily explain why companies price things in 99-cent increments or why a consumer buys only one Nike golf shirt priced at $25, but buys three of them if the shirt is marked down by 50% from $50. In building economic models, economists always assume that the economic actors behave rationally and would therefore realize that in the flu example 200 lives are saved with Responses A and C, and that in both cases the price of the shirt is $25.

In recent years, economists have increasingly come to accept the fact that, as great a job as standard economic models do in explaining the ways of the world, they sometimes fail badly when human psychology plays a role in people's decision making.

The nature of these models' failures matters. If people and firms sometimes make mistakes and act differently from the perfectly rational, self-interested agents that underlie the analysis in our previous chapters and if those mistakes are random (i.e., they do not occur with any predictable pattern), then the standard economic models may be flawed but still the best thing we have. If the mistakes of the model are *systematic*, that is, if people repeatedly act differently from the model in predictable ways, then the flaws are much more serious. It is this systematic departure from rational economic decision making that motivates the rising prominence of **behavioral economics,** the branch of economics that incorporates insights from human psychology into models of economic behavior.

behavioral economics
Branch of economics that incorporates insights from human psychology into models of economic behavior.

Like the field of behavioral economics itself, this chapter is a bit different from the conventional microeconomics we've presented in the 16 preceding chapters. Instead of laying out specific models and showing you how to solve and apply them, this chapter examines some of the ways that economists and psychologists have expanded traditional economic models in an effort to better explain real-world behaviors. The first half of this chapter presents an overview of some of the key psychological biases and mistakes people make that have emerged from behavioral economics research and why they pose a problem for traditional models. In addition, we learn how fully rational, self-interested market participants can take advantage of such biases in a well-functioning market. These biases include the susceptibility to framing (the bias we saw earlier in the disease example), overconfidence, being overly oriented to the present, the inability to ignore sunk costs, and other economic sins.

---

[1] Amos Tversky and Daniel Kahneman, "The Framing of Decisions and the Psychology of Choice," *Science* 211, no. 4481 (1981): 453–458.

We then discuss the new ways economists have begun to test these behavioral economic models using actual experiments rather than traditional statistical methods like econometrics. We conclude the chapter and the book with a discussion of what behavioral economics means for the future of microeconomics. By the end, you should have a balanced picture of the role of economic decision makers and their behavior, and the strengths (and weaknesses) of microeconomics.

17.1 When Human Beings Fail to Act the Way Economic Models Predict

The actors who populate the economic models we have seen in this book worry about one thing and one thing only: getting the most they can for themselves. Firms maximize profit; consumers maximize utility. They make rational tradeoffs that involve complicated sets of choices and require an impressive degree of computational ability.

Critics of the "normal" economic models have mockingly used the term *Homo economicus* to describe the species of creature that inhabits the economic world. They envision *Homo economicus* to be like a regular human being (*Homo sapiens*) except that he is able to solve any complicated economic problem, always knows *exactly* what he wants and how to get it, and *never* make any mistakes. In other words, *Homo economicus* doesn't seem much like *Homo sapiens* at all.

In this section, we explore five of the most important ways in which behavioral economics says *Homo economicus* differs from *Homo sapiens*.[2]

Systematic Bias 1: Overconfidence

One psychological bias that behavioral economists say real people suffer from is **overconfidence.** When individuals believe their skill level and judgment are better than they truly are, or when they expect that outcomes that are better for them are more likely to happen than they truly are, they will systematically make mistakes in a rational economic model which assumes people have realistic expectations and base decisions strictly on the facts.

When asked in surveys, the typical adult says that he is a better than average driver, and 93% of American college students say that they are above average drivers. It turns out that in their own minds, most people believe they are outstanding on many different dimensions, not just behind the wheel. Other studies have found that people overestimate their intelligence, sense of humor, and many other factors. On at least one Internet dating site, 77% of listed individuals (about equal fractions for men and women) rated themselves as having either "very good" or "above average" physical attractiveness. In fairness, perhaps they don't believe their attractiveness is superior but are just saying this so they can get a first date and then wow their companions with their smarts and sense of humor.

Two economic settings in which overconfidence clearly plays an important role are the stock markets and futures markets. Every time someone makes a trade in one of these markets—selling 100 shares of Google, say, or a thousand barrels of oil—there must be another trader willing to take the other side of the transaction and buy the shares. The buyer must believe the value will rise, the seller that it won't. One of them is wrong. If the person on one side of the trade believes that the other has better information or better judgment, he probably won't want to make the trade. But, if each trader thinks he is smarter than everyone else, he will want to make more trades.

Likewise, company managers confident in their own abilities will be inclined to make bigger investments and take more risks on the overconfident view that they will succeed.

overconfidence
A belief that skill and judgment are better than they truly are, or that better outcomes are more likely to happen than their true probability.

---

[2] If you get interested in behavioral economics, the books *Nudge* by Richard Thaler and Cass Sunstein and *Thinking, Fast and Slow* by Daniel Kahneman give thorough overviews of the field.

How Economic Markets Take Advantage of Overconfident People

Having a psychological bias opens a person up to being taken advantage of in the marketplace by more rational players. The health club industry keenly understands and takes advantage of people who suffer from overconfidence bias. When individuals sign up for a health club, they tend to be far too optimistic about the prospects of sticking to their exercise goals; they use the health club much less, on average, than they expect to at the outset. Aware of this, health clubs tailor their offerings to exploit such overoptimism. For example, suppose individuals who work out frequently are willing to pay $100 a month for a health club membership, but a membership is only worth $20 a month for those who work out infrequently. Having just made a New Year's resolution to be more fit in the upcoming year, overly optimistic consumers believe they will go to the gym frequently over the next year. And, indeed, some people will stick to their resolution for the entire year. Most, however, will be heavy users of the gym for only a few months.

In light of this, rational health club owners detected a business strategy. They could have priced their product the way most goods are priced: per unit like a gallon of milk or a ticket to the movie. But health clubs don't price that way—they don't usually allow customers to pay, say, $10 for each visit to the club. Instead, health clubs usually require customers to sign a long-term contract that involves a big up-front payment, sometimes with a very short trial period.

If every customer overconfidently believes he will be a heavy gym user after a week of working out, he might be willing to make an up-front payment of $1,200 for an annual membership that allows him unlimited use of the gym for a year. That type of contract extracts a lot more revenue from overly optimistic consumers than charging them per visit. Consumers may be willing to pay huge up-front fees even though they would have been better off paying even very high prices per trip to the gym because of how infrequently they end up going. Behavioral economics researchers have documented exactly this situation for health club businesses.[3]

Systematic Bias 2: Self-Control Problems and Hyperbolic Discounting

Another psychological bias highlighted by behavioral economics is people's strong desire to have things NOW and the difficulties that poses for self-control. We discussed discounting the future in Chapter 13, where we learned about net present value, and in Chapter 12's discussion of repeated games. In those discussions, we used a simple discounting framework in which people discount the future by a set percentage each period, such as 10% per year (that is, they viewed a payment of $1 a year from today as equivalent to $0.90 today). Behavioral economists argue that although people may think that way about decisions well into the future, they seem to value the here and now by much more than the basic discount rate would suggest. This behavior is called **hyperbolic discounting**—where people tend to prefer immediate payoffs to later payoffs, even if the later payoff is much greater.

hyperbolic discounting
Tendency of people to place much greater importance on the immediate present than even the near future when making economic decisions.

The best way to understand this is to think about a person deciding to buy a Ronco Juicer As Seen on TV. It costs either $300 up-front or four (easy) monthly payments of $90 each. Either way, Ronco sends the juicer to the consumer upon purchase; there's no four-month delay if you chose the installment payment plan. A fully rational consumer (one who conforms to economic models' assumptions of rationality) buying the juicer would do a net present value calculation discounting at a discount rate of, say, 5% per month (this is really high but it makes our point easier to see than if we use a lower discount rate). The cost of the juicer in one payment is $300. The four undiscounted payments of $90 total $360, but the NPV of the four payments is $90/(1.05) + 90/(1.05)^2 + 90/(1.05)^3 + 90/(1.05)^4 = \$319.13$. Because the NPV of the four payments ($319.13) is higher than the up-front cost ($300), the consumer should pay for the juicer in full upon purchase.

---

[3] Stefano DellaVigna and Ulrike Malmendier, "Paying Not to Go to the Gym," *American Economic Review* 96, no. 3 (2006): 694–719.

However, because hyperbolic discounters really, really value things that happen now, they have a huge discount rate between now and even the near future. Another way to say this is they need to earn a much higher interest rate to make it worth their while to postpone their instant gratification. In our example, let's say our hyperbolic discounting consumer discounts the first month at 25%, and the remaining three months at 5%. The calculation then involves a NPV of $90/(1.25) + 90/(1.25)(1.05) + 90/(1.25)(1.05)^2 + 90/(1.25)(1.05)^3 = \$268.08$, less than the \$300 upfront cost. Someone who really wants things now will therefore opt for the installment plan because it allows him to have the juicer and keep more of his money today. The hyperbolic discounter's very high discount rate in the first period makes paying the full \$300 immediately very painful because he wants to have that money available to buy other things (that he also wants NOW).

One of the problems that hyperbolic-discounting consumers introduce into normal economic models of consumer decisions like savings and investment choices is that their decisions stop being **time-consistent.** That is, consumers today will specify their preferred actions now, next year, the year after that, but then when they get to *next* year (year 2), they won't want to stick with the plan they set up. When a decision is a year off in the distance, waiting an extra day seems like no big deal. But after a year passes, so now that same wait is between today and tomorrow, the waiting feels much more costly. What people *think* they will do two years from now, and what they *actually* do, no longer match up, even if the world two years from now ends up being exactly how they imagined it.

When people are not time-consistent, analyzing their behavior becomes quite complicated. The person you are today is different from the person you will be tomorrow, and that fact turns self-control issues into a game theory battle between two different people. The "*today* you" wants to save a lot of money next year, but "*next year* you" would rather spend the money and put off saving one more year. If you understand that you are like this, "today you" (who wants to save next year) can take an action that commits your future self (who, next year, wants to spend) to save. You could sign up with your employer to automatically take money out of your salary for a retirement account starting next year. You could also write out a check to an organization you do not like and hand it to a friend who promises to mail it to the organization if you don't follow your plan (and who will rip up the check if you do). People use less extreme versions of these sorts of commitment devices all the time. Smokers might throw away their cigarettes or dieters their ice cream so their future self won't be tempted.

How Economic Markets Take Advantage of People with Self-Control Problems   Because hyperbolic discounters put too much weight on the present, they make choices they often regret in the long run, such as not studying hard enough for their final exam in economics, having unprotected sex, or not saving enough for the future.

Clever marketers often try to take advantage of people's propensity to impulsiveness. Furniture stores let you sit on the futon and offer "no money down" purchases that end up costing more over time. During the housing bubble of the 2000s, many people refinanced their mortgages but with the added kicker that the bank allowed them to take a significant amount of cash out of the home, thus increasing the debt on the house until it equaled the entire value of the house. Some banks went even further, allowing homeowners to go "underwater": that is, take out enough cash to raise their debt above their houses' values, hoping or assuming that house values would continue to rise. Credit card companies are some of the most adept at tempting hyperbolic discounters. They send out offers of 0% interest for the first 30 days, low minimum payments on your monthly bill, and "free" balance transfers from other cards. In each case, the cards make it as easy as possible for consumers to obtain money or reduce the costs of borrowing right now in exchange for higher costs they will have to pay in the future.

As you might imagine, if you build an economic model in which some people or firms are hyperbolic discounters who put great weight on the present and others are fully

time-consistent
Consistencies in a consumer's economic preferences in a given economic transaction, whether the economic transaction is far off or imminent.

rational economic agents who discount at "normal" rates, after a while, the rational discounters end up with all the money (because they are patient and keep building up their savings year after year), and those who "want it now" end up broke (because they want everything right away and spend all their money each year). So, if you believe you are prone to impulsive hyperbolic discounting behavior, watch out. Try to find ways to stick to your plans and avoid temptations.

Systematic Bias 3: Falling Prey to Framing

Another systematic bias in decision making is that people often make incompatible (and thus irrational) decisions depending on how a decision or problem is framed. The disease treatment program example at the opening of the chapter was a case in point, but there are many types of framing biases.

endowment effect
The phenomenon where simply possessing a good makes it more valuable; that is, the possessor must be paid more to give up the good than he would have paid to buy it in the first place.

One is the **endowment effect,** which occurs when the pain a person suffers when giving up something they already have is greater than the pleasure they gained in acquiring it. An example will clarify how the endowment effect works. Suppose a professor decides to give every student in his class a gift. He gives coffee mugs to half of the students in the class and chocolate bars to the other half. The gifts are of equal average value and distributed randomly, so some students who prefer candy will end up with mugs and vice versa. Conventional economic models tell us that allowing the students to trade in a free market will increase total welfare (we discussed this, for example, in Chapter 14). Because there are an equal number of identically valuable gifts and because they were randomly assigned, something like half the students should want to swap gifts (because we expect half the students to prefer candy and half to prefer mugs).

When researchers have tested this and similar scenarios in real life, however, that's not what happened. When behavioral economist Richard Thaler tried this exact experiment, only 15% of students (instead of around 50% as the theory predicts) were willing to trade what they had been given initially, regardless of what item that was. As soon as the students received the mug or the candy, they felt it was more valuable to them. Indeed, when asked if they would sell the coffee mug back to the experimenter at the retail price, many people refused to do so, even though they had never chosen in the past to buy such a coffee mug at the store. (Presumably, having passed on the mug at the store means they valued the mug less than its retail price.) Their perception of the utility they would obtain from the mug had been altered by their ownership of the mug. That is the endowment effect.

loss aversion
A type of framing bias in which a consumer chooses a reference point around which losses hurt much more than gains feel good.

The endowment effect is a special case of a broader pattern of behavior known as **loss aversion.** A loss averse person has a reference point in mind that takes on special significance. He might choose this reference point based on any one of a number of reasons depending on the setting, such as how much he paid for a good the last time he bought it, how much income he thinks his neighbor earns, or the number of points he scored in yesterday's basketball game. Whatever the reference point is based upon, loss aversion implies that falling below that point (which is perceived by the person as suffering a loss) hurts worse than rising above it (perceived as a gain) feels good. So, for instance, if a restaurant raises prices and the consumer's reference point is what he paid for the meal last time, he suffers a large drop in utility relative to how good he feels when the restaurant lowers its prices by the same amount.

This is not true for the consumers we model elsewhere in the book; they just care about the bundle of goods they are able to buy. A small price increase lowers those consumers' utility levels by essentially the same amount as a small price reduction increases their utility levels. What makes loss aversion different is that consumers' choices depend on where they start. When a loss averse person is just above the reference point, he is likely to act as if he is very risk averse. But if he is just a little below the reference point, he may very well act like he's risk loving in order to try to get back to the reference point.

We will see a particularly relevant example of this behavior in the housing market in the next section, where homeowners seem to use the price at which they originally purchased a house as a reference point when trying to sell their houses. This leads these homeowners to suffer from the sunk cost fallacy.

Another framing bias is **anchoring.** People tend to base their decisions on the pieces of information they are given. When asked what percentage of countries in the United Nations were in Africa, for example, people responded with a smaller number on average if the question were "Is it more than 10%?" rather than "Is it more than 65%?"[4] In a market transaction, anchoring bias means that a consumer's willingness to pay for a kayak, say, is higher if he first sees several high-priced items that frame the kayak purchase and raise his willingness to pay. Thus, the presentation of the products and their prices influences a consumer's choice, whereas conventional demand theory says that the willingness to pay comes straight from the consumer's tastes. Framing and labeling are not supposed to matter.

A final form of framing bias is **mental accounting,** which occurs when individuals divide their current and future assets into separate, nontransferable portions. In traditional consumer behavior theory, a consumer makes rational decisions about savings or about buying various products based on his income, on prices, and on other factors that are part of his utility function. In contrast to this rational consumer, some behavioral economists claim that people make mental accounts in which they divide up their money and their purchases. Instead of considering "savings" as one big category, for example, people keep mental accounts for college money, vacation money, and retirement money, and act as if moving funds between these accounts is difficult or impossible. For consumption, they may have mental accounts for monthly spending on gasoline, clothing, and food instead of one account for "consumption."

Mental accounting can also apply to different sources of income. If a person finds a $20 bill on the floor and goes out and spends this windfall but saves most of a $20 tip he receives at work, he is thinking like a mental accountant. The standard economic model would say that a $20 bonus is a $20 bonus. It doesn't matter whether it came from the floor or from a grateful customer.

How Markets Take Advantage of People Who Fall Prey to Framing   The number of ways a clever marketer can use a person's framing bias to make money is almost unlimited. Some cynics might even say that knowing how to do this is the very *definition* of clever marketing.

To take advantage of people with the endowment effect bias, a firm might offer a money-back guarantee. Before buying a product, the fully rational consumer isn't always sure whether he will like it, so the option to return it and get his money back has value—the guarantee makes it more likely that he will buy the product to try it out. After buying the product, though, a customer with an endowment bias will experience an exaggerated increase in the product's value to him, so he will be very unlikely to return it for a refund, even if he is not fully satisfied.[5]

To take advantage of people with an anchoring bias, a firm might artificially inflate the base price of a good and then advertise a "50 percent off" sale. By anchoring in the

anchoring
A type of framing bias in which a person's decision is influenced by specific pieces of information given.

mental accounting
A type of framing bias in which people divide their current and future assets into separate, nontransferable portions, instead of basing purchasing decisions on their assets as a whole.

---

[4] Amos Tversky and Daniel Kahneman, "Judgment under Uncertainty: Heuristics and Biases," *Science* 185 no. 4157 (1974): 1124-1130.

[5] Note that there are other explanations for why producers give money-back guarantees that don't rely at all on behavioral economics. When there is asymmetric information (Chapter 15), a producer who makes a high-quality good can use a money-back guarantee to signal that the good is of high quality. It is more costly for a company that makes low-quality goods to offer a money-back guarantee, because more consumers will return the low-quality good, so providing the guarantee up-front is a credible sign that this product is indeed well made. Contrasting views of economic behavior like this lie at the heart of the vigorous debate over behavioral economics among economists.

consumer's mind the idea that the good is worth the original inflated price, the half-price good looks like a bargain, even though the "50 percent off" price is what the good normally would have sold for anyway.

A buyer who is a mental accountant must beware of the tactic often used by salespeople in car showrooms across the world: "How much do you want to pay for a car?" Once you put an amount of money into a mental account, you can be fairly sure that a smart seller will find a way to withdraw it for you.

Systematic Bias 4: Paying Attention to Sunk Costs

One of the most important themes in economic decision making is that sunk costs do not matter when making a decision. The money is already spent and it cannot be recovered, so it shouldn't matter for the decision. Rational decision makers think at the margin and only consider opportunity costs. (To review these ideas, see Chapter 7.)

sunk cost fallacy
The mistake of allowing sunk costs to affect decisions.

In reality, however, behavioral economists say that people seem quite influenced by sunk costs when making decisions. A classic example of the **sunk cost fallacy** comes from an experiment published in 1985 by psychologists Hal Arkes and Catherine Blumer.[6] In 1985, the researchers worked out a deal with the Ohio University theater so that when a person arrived at the ticket window and asked to buy a season ticket (for 10 plays), the buyer was randomly assigned a price for the season ticket. A third of the buyers paid the full price of $15 per play for the season ticket. A second group paid $13 per season ticket, and a third group got the season ticket for just $8.

Given that the ticket holders all had tickets in hand on the morning of a performance, we should be able to assume that how much people paid for the tickets had no bearing on the level of the marginal benefit from attending the plays. The price of the ticket was a sunk cost, and the marginal cost of attending was just the value of their time. No matter what the purchasers had paid for the ticket, the opportunity cost of attending the play was the same; there was no additional expense. And yet, in the first half of the season, the people who had paid full price attended about 25% more of the plays than did the groups that received discounts. Behavioral economists argued it was because the high-price group felt a greater obligation to attend so that they could get their money's worth from the tickets. This result illustrates that people just can't seem to ignore sunk costs, even though they rationally should.[7]

Companies and governments have made similar sunk cost mistakes. One example involves the development of the Concorde supersonic jet, which was jointly developed by the British and French governments. The joint venture began in the early 1960s, amidst great optimism. Plans went quickly awry, however. Ultimately, development costs ended up being six times higher than projected, cost overruns that were anticipated far in advance. By virtually all accounts, the right course of action would have been to stop the project, but the governments forged ahead because there was "too much invested to quit," as described in Allan Teger's 1980 book on the subject.[8] Ultimately, only 20 of the airplanes were ever made, and the last plane was taken out of service in 2003.

[6] Hal R. Arkes and Catherine Blumer, "The Psychology of Sunk Cost," *Organizational Behavior and Human Decision Processes* 35, no. 1 (1985): 124–140.

[7] It is worth noting that the standard economic model better predicts the theatergoers' behavior in the second half of the season than in the first half. In the second half of the season, there were no differences in attendance according to the price paid for the tickets, so any sunk cost fallacy effect disappeared. Indeed, all three groups appear to have figured out that they just don't like going to the theater that much: Attendance fell to about two plays in the second half of the season, regardless of the price paid for the tickets.

[8] Allan I. Teger, *Too Much Invested to Quit*, Oxford: Pergamon Press, 1980.

application

Sunk Cost Bias and the Breakdown of the Housing Market

For most people, buying a home represents the largest investment they will make in their lives. Of all the situations in which one might expect people to adhere to rational economic decision making, you would think that the purchase of a house would rank near the top of the list because there is so much money involved.

However, the results of a study by economists David Genesove and Christopher Mayer suggest the sunk cost fallacy may be alive and well in people's housing decisions.[9] In particular, home sellers appear to have a strong aversion to selling their homes for less than the prices they paid for them, a finding that illustrates both loss aversion and a sunk cost bias.

The price that an owner paid for the house is irrelevant to the price for which he should sell it. What a house is worth is dictated by *current* market conditions—the supply and demand for houses. The market doesn't care what anyone paid for a house 10 years ago.

What happens if sellers fall prey to the sunk cost bias and refuse to sell their houses at a nominal loss, even in a down market? These sellers will end up pricing their houses above prevailing market prices. As we learned way back in Chapter 2 (and as Figure 17.1 demonstrates), when price is set above the market equilibrium price, the quantity sold (demanded), Q^D, is below the equilibrium quantity, and there is an excess supply of homes available in the market, $Q^S - Q^D$.

In downtown Boston in the 1990s, this is exactly what happened. Condo prices fell by about 40% in the recession in the early part of the decade, but few condo owners were willing to sell at these extremely low market prices. In fact, the average asking price was about 35% above the expected market value. As evidence that this gap was caused by the sunk cost fallacy, the bigger the loss an owner faced, the *higher* he set his asking price, holding everything else constant.[10]

Figure 17.1   **Excess Supply in the Market for Homes**

Homeowners looking to sell in 1990s Boston fell prey to the sunk cost fallacy. These homeowners set house prices at $P > P^*$. As a result, only Q^D houses on the market sold—far fewer than the Q^* houses that would have sold at the market equilibrium. Consequently, there was an excess supply of houses equal to $Q^S - Q^D$.

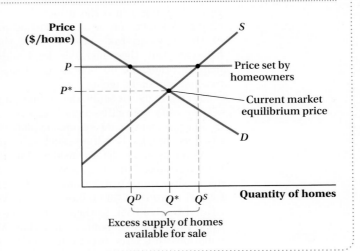

---

[9] David Genesove and Christopher Mayer, "Loss Aversion and Seller Behavior: Evidence from the Housing Market," *Quarterly Journal of Economics* 116, no. 4 (November 2001): 1233–1260.

[10] Note that this was true for all sellers, not just those whose mortgages were "underwater," meaning prices had fallen so much that the homeowner's debt exceeded the entire value of the property. In such cases, a sale would require the homeowner to come up with additional cash to pay off the mortgage.

As you would expect when people hold out for above-market-prices, these properties mostly just sat on the market. Fewer than one-third of listed units sold within 180 days. Half the normal number of condos per year ended up selling. Homeowners just wouldn't sell their condos for less than they paid for them. People effectively locked themselves into their homes, unwilling to move if they had to take a nominal loss. This attitude imposed real costs on the condo owners: They couldn't move to a different home even though they wanted to (perhaps because their family size changed, they took a job in a different location, or experienced a change in income).

This situation happened many years ago, but the same issue has arisen again at an even larger scale in the wake of the housing bubble that burst in the mid-2000s. Millions of people have seen the value of their homes fall to less than the amount they paid for them. ■

How Markets Take Advantage of Loss-Averse People Attentive to Sunk Costs   At the most basic level, the market will leave the losses and the carrying costs in the hands of the people who are suffering from the sunk cost fallacy. In the housing market application, for example, it's the stubborn homeowners with losses who suffer: They're stuck because no one will buy their overpriced houses. Market participants who do not suffer from the sunk cost bias can end up benefitting from the mistakes of people who do. Again, in the context of the housing example, the fact that biased homeowners are trying to sell houses at prices that are too high opens the door for rational sellers to undercut them.

Systematic Bias 5: Generosity and Selflessness

Economic models are premised on the belief that consumers and firms act in rational self-interest. Perhaps one of the most basic challenges to this assumption is that people often engage in nonmaximizing acts of generosity, selflessness, and **altruism**— acts for which the welfare of others is the primary concern. For example, parents sacrifice for their children; volunteers work long, hard hours for various causes; military personnel fight for their country; and so on. Economists have tried to incorporate this behavior into standard models by adding the taste for generosity (called the "warm glow of giving") into the utility function or by letting a parent's utility depend not only on his own consumption but also on his children's consumption. These are some of the ways to take into account the generosity bias when modeling consumer behavior. But, these methods don't address the fundamental issue that, by frequently helping others at no benefit to themselves, people don't always appear to act as rational economic agents.

Interestingly (or sadly, depending on your perspective), in the debate to explain acts of generosity and selflessness, many economists have detected the aroma of self-interest or other conventional economic explanations for behaviors that might otherwise be classified as completely selfless, such as charitable giving.

As an example, let's consider alumni donations to colleges and universities in the United States. Alumni generosity accounts for a tremendous amount of the budget of many educational institutions. The Council for Aid to Education reports that donations totaled more than $30 billion in 2011. We normally think that alumni donors are motivated to give back to their institutions in thanks for what those schools did for their lives. But, when economists Jonathan Meer and Harvey Rosen began to examine the donations to a large private university, contributions looked a bit less selfless than at first glance.[11] Alumni with children were dramatically more likely to give than alumni

altruism
Acts motivated primarily by a concern for the welfare of others.

---

[11] Jonathan Meer and Harvey S. Rosen, "Altruism and the Child Cycle of Alumni Donations," *American Economic Journal: Economic Policy* 1, no. 1 (2009): 258–286.

without them. The donations increased significantly when the child reached age 14 and continued to increase through the period when the child applied to college. By age 18 or 19, if the alum's child is admitted to the same college, donations were more than 10 times higher than for alumni without children. For an alumnus whose child applied but was rejected by the college, donations fell precipitously and were no higher than donations from alumni without children. Therefore the seemingly selfless behavior of donating to a nonprofit university seems instead to be directly influenced by the self-interest of getting one's child into a good school.

Another look at generosity may be found in a study by John List, Stefano DellaVigna, and Ulrike Malmendier.[12] They sent out volunteers to knock on doors and solicit charitable contributions. Many people gave donations, consistent with altruism. But in one part of the experiment, List and his cohorts asked their solicitors to first put flyers on the front doors of those houses they intended to visit, to let the occupants know that someone would be coming by the next day at a specific time to solicit contributions. If the residents were indeed altruistic, one would expect them to make a special effort to be home to contribute to the charity. Instead, List, DellaVigna, and Malmendier found just the opposite. When warned that the solicitors were coming, many people made a point of not being home or else refused to open the door even though they would have likely given a contribution to someone who showed up at their door unannounced. In this experiment, people seemed mainly to contribute not out of altruism, but because of the social pressure associated with not wanting to look selfish when asked for a small donation.

Because economic models assume that rational decision makers are self-interested, the overall subject of charitable giving and generosity poses a systematic puzzle to standard economic models. These examples demonstrate, however, that in many circumstances there still seems to be an important role for self-interest in people's behavior.

17.2 Does Behavioral Economics Mean Everything We've Learned Is Useless?

At this point, you may be wondering why you bothered reading 16 chapters on economic models only to find out that behavioral economics says people don't actually behave the way the models predict they would. And, it may seem that we could have simply avoided studying difficult models and theories that don't work and instead just read a book on behavioral economics.

Although these qualms seem reasonable, they are not correct. First of all, the behavioral anomalies we've discussed in this chapter do not invalidate the economic models you've learned. They show us that some people, under certain circumstances, act in a way that the basic models might miss. But, the foundational models you have learned actually do a remarkably good job of describing how the economic world works *most* of the time. When describing something as complex as human behavior, that is still an important advance.

Second, in many areas in which behavioral economics seems to give a different answer, simple adjustments to the basic economic model often provide perfectly viable alternative explanations. As an example, think about behaviors that the basic, rational consumer decision-making model might have a hard time explaining, such as people becoming addicted to things that are bad for them like smoking cigarettes. Yet,

---

[12] John List, Stefano DellaVigna, and Ulrike Malmendier, "Testing for Altruism and Social Pressure in Charitable Giving," *Quarterly Journal of Economics* 121, no.1 (2012): 1–56.

Nobel laureate Gary Becker has developed conventional economic models to explain such seemingly irrational behaviors. His "rational addiction" model (developed with Kevin Murphy) is just a variant of the consumer behavior theory we studied in Chapters 4 and 5.[13] In it, consumers think about the lifetime costs of becoming addicted and balance that against the utility they get from smoking, knowing that starting now will make it hard to stop in the future. This theory can explain why addiction rates respond to prices, for example, in a better way than an explanation based on the belief that people become addicted because they just can't help themselves.

Becker and Murphy have also developed a theory of discrimination. This theory puts hatred into racists' utility functions so that they pay for their prejudice just as they would have to pay for other goods. A business owner might pay, for example, in the form of lower profits and lower output due to hiring less talented and qualified employees instead of talented and more qualified minority applicants.

Third, as we emphasized in the previous section, people and firms that have systematic biases tend to lose out to people in the marketplace who are not biased. Markets can weed out systematic biases, and economic actors that participate repeatedly in markets often recognize and adjust for their behavioral biases or just exit the marketplace completely. Once biased participants are gone, remaining participants exhibit less irrationality than might a random survey respondent.

It is important for economists and businesses to test how people behave as thoroughly as they can. This desire to better understand the behavior of consumers, customers, suppliers, and producers has led to the rise of another new field of economics: experimental methods.

17.3 Testing Economic Theories with Data: Experimental Economics

The unorthodox results emanating from behavioral economics research in recent years have placed even more significance on the issue of how economists can test which models are correct. All economic models generate predictions that, in principle, can be tested and compared. Some predictions are fairly basic, such as the prediction from demand theory that demand curves slope downward. This sounds like just about the easiest thing to test in the world. But, real-world complications often get in the way of testing even the most basic predictions from the models. Even if you had data on the prices and quantities of, say, chicken nuggets across different cities, you couldn't really say that supply-and-demand theory predicts that the markets with higher prices will have lower quantities demanded. The theory predicts that *holding all else equal*, when prices are higher, consumers will want less of a good. A comparison of two markets only sheds light on this question if all else is equal between the two markets, and in the real world, that's a big "if."

econometrics
Field that develops and uses mathematical and statistical techniques to test economic theory.

To get around the problem of messiness in the real world, economists have developed a large number of data, statistical, and analytical techniques to help test economic theories—techniques such as how to use shifts in a market's supply curve to statistically trace out its associated demand curve and so on. These techniques are part of the field of **econometrics,** the use of mathematics and statistics to describe numerical relationships between key economic variables. Even the best econometric techniques still rely on some strong assumptions to get around the potential complications of the real world, to say nothing of the messiness inherent in most data.

experimental economics
Branch of economics that relies on experiments to illuminate economic behavior.

Dissatisfied with empirical data methods like econometrics, some economists have turned to **experimental economics,** in which they can hold everything else equal and directly test economic hypotheses by conducting explicit experiments.

[13] Gary S. Becker and Kevin M. Murphy, "A Theory of Rational Addiction," *Journal of Political Economy* 96, no. 4 (August 1988): 675–700.

Lab Experiments

Lab experiments allow an economist to control all aspects of a test and explain precisely what was done. Typically, the experimenter has groups of subjects take part in the same activity, but with one element of the activity altered for one group. For instance, to test if demand curves slope downward, an experimenter might bring students into a lab, give them each $30, and then randomly assign each of them to one of three groups. Each group would then be given the chance to buy coffee mugs embossed with their school's mascot, but one group would face a price of $3 per mug, the second $5 per mug, and the third $10 per mug. Everything but the price is the same in this experiment, so a comparison of the quantities purchased by the groups traces out a demand curve and allows the experimenter to test whether it slopes downward (which, fortunately for economics, the experiments overwhelmingly verify).

Randomized experiments that randomly assign participants to a treatment group allow researchers to test for influences such as mental accounting errors, overconfidence, the endowment effect, and the various biases we talked about earlier in the chapter.

As helpful as economic laboratory experiments are, they are not without shortcomings or controversy. Economic experiments suffer from some important weaknesses that are missing in most scientific applications of the experimental method. First, unlike chemical compounds or lab mice, humans know that when they participate in an experiment, their behavior is being watched. Not surprisingly, critics point to the fact that participants in economic experiments tend to act differently as a result. One factor that tends to distort participants' behavior is that subjects in lab experiments exhibit a strong tendency to act in a manner that they believe will please or impress the experimenter or the other participants. For example, college students repeatedly make choices in experiments that are more socially desirable, cooperative, or morally "proper" and shy away from things that make them look selfish or that simply maximize their personal gains in the experiment. This distortion leads some to question whether lab experiments really tell us about people's behavior in actual markets and whether the experiments truly show that individuals make systematic mistakes in their decision making.

A second issue with the typical lab experiment is that the stakes of the experiment are often much different than in real life. It doesn't take much money to entice undergraduates to participate in experiments, which is fortunate because research budgets are usually small. Consequently, the stakes at risk in the typical economics lab experiment are low. Low stakes make it less costly for participants to act in ways that are against their own self-interest. Further, sometimes experiments involve really complex or tedious tasks that hardly seem worth doing for so little, whereas in the real world, if you could make a million dollars completing some tedious calculations, you would be much more likely to complete them.

A third issue with lab experiments is that students are often asked to do tasks in the lab that are foreign to them, such as participating in auctions with randomized and strange rules like requiring the top two bidders to pay but with only the highest bidder receiving the prize. One might expect students to do poorly at this task compared to experts who have studied and practiced such tasks, or even people who can do a Web search to learn how to effectively participate in an auction or who can call a more auction-savvy friend for advice.

Finally, although an experimenter can control the experiment, he cannot control the personal baggage brought by the participants. For instance, experimenters often design experiments as one-shot games so that the choice made by a lab subject should be dictated exclusively by the direct payoff and not by any future considerations. But in real life, people do not seem to be able to assume away their cultural norms. The Freakonomics box on the next page describes how differently people from varying cultures play the same lab games, highlighting the difficulties of designing experiments that truly hold everything else equal.

lab experiment
Test of an economic theory in a laboratory setting.

freakonomics

Going to the Ends of the World (Literally) to Test Economic Theory

The great majority of economics lab experiments are done with college students. This is a perfect example of the principles of economics at work: Students are plentiful and willing to participate in experiments for low wages. This makes it cheap and easy to run experiments on campus, and economic researchers have responded by running lots of these experiments. When researchers have looked beyond students to other subject pools like CEOs, professional soccer players, and dealers at flea markets, the results have generally been similar to those obtained from students. It is also the case that Americans and Europeans tend to make similar choices in many lab experiments.

The fact that lab results are robust (i.e., they hold up) across different groups of subjects is good news for lab experiments because it means that what we find in one particular experiment is more likely to generalize to other settings. Researchers can conduct experiments using students and be reasonably confident that, if they replicate the study using stay-at-home moms or movie stars, the results will be similar.

One characteristic that is shared by virtually all of the subjects who have been part of experiments, however, is their *culture*. Americans, whether they are college students, CEOs, or pro athletes, have grown up with a shared culture. European culture differs from American culture, but both of them are closer to each other than to many non-Western cultures. Do the lab experiments on economic behavior yield similar results when conducted in other places?

The Lamalera cooperate in whaling and in games while the Hadza, a hunting and gathering tribe, display more self-interest and less cooperation in games.

A collaborative team of economists and anthropologists set out to answer this question.* The team gathered together anthropologists who had spent their careers living with and studying indigenous societies in many different parts of the world. These were small-scale societies that have virtually no contact with the modern world. These groups included hunter-gatherers in Tanzania, nomadic herders in Mongolia, and whale hunters in Indonesia. The anthropologists learned how to carry out these experimental games and then scattered to the far reaches of the world to conduct them. The results obtained from these different groups were all over the map. Some groups behaved more like *Homo economicus* than Westerners; others deviated even further from economic predictions than had American college students. Members of some cultures exhibited remarkable altruism, whereas others were the epitome of selfishness.

And yet, from this wild mish-mash of findings, a simple yet profound pattern emerged: How people played these experimental games was systematically related to the norms that existed in their cultures. For instance, the Lamalera of east Indonesia subsist by hunting whales, an activity that requires high degrees of cooperation across large numbers of hunters to succeed. Not surprisingly, the Lamalera played the games in a cooperative way, with players frequently passing up chances to act in a way that would benefit them to the detriment of the other players.

In contrast, the Hadza, hunters and gatherers in Tanzania, were very self-interested and uncooperative toward one another. It is said that the Hadza abandoned traditional garb for

*Joseph Henrich, Robert Boyd, Samuel Bowles, Colin Camerer, Ernst Fehr, Herbert Gintis, and Richard McElreath. "In Search of Homo Economicus: Behavioral Experiments in 15 Small-Scale Societies," *American Economic Review Papers and Proceedings* 91, no. 2 (2001): 73–78.

Western-style blue jeans because the deep pockets of the jeans allowed them to more effectively hide the spoils of their hunting and gathering from the prying eyes of their neighbors. The Hadza in the lab experiments did not cooperate much with the other players and instead looked out for themselves.

Perhaps the most remarkable example of culture permeating the lab came from the Au and Gnau peoples of Papua New Guinea. When playing a lab game that involved splitting a pie between themselves and another player, the Au and Gnau often offered the bigger slice of the pie to their opponent (something that virtually never happens with American students), and the opponent frequently refused to accept this bigger slice (again, not likely with the American students). It turns out that the Au and Gnau are competitive gift-giving societies in which accepting a gift today obligates the recipient to provide a more generous gift to the giver in the future. Thus, a gift is a mixed blessing in this culture. Even though the lab experiment was explicitly described as a one-shot game and played anonymously so there was no chance that the recipient of the big slice of the experimental pie could be obligated to make a more generous repayment in the future, the Au and Gnau apparently brought such powerful cultural norms into the lab that they participated in the experiment as if it were a typical, real-life gift exchange.

These experiments teach us an important lesson about lab experiments. Although it might seem as if the experimenter gets to choose the game that is played and the context of the experiment, in practice, experimental subjects bring their own contexts with them when they enter the lab. In particular, when people enter a lab, they are not able to instantly abandon life lessons about what society expects and the rules of thumb that serve them well in the real world.

Despite the potential pitfalls of lab experiments, they remain a useful economic tool. After all, the analysis of nonexperimental data suffers from many shortcomings as well. But, be wary of thinking that what happens in the lab will automatically happen in real markets. Instead, when faced with data generated from a lab experiment, consider the various biases we've discussed and contemplate how they might distort any interpretation of the lab results.

Natural Experiments and Field Experiments

Responding to some of the criticisms of lab experiments, economists have begun to use experiments in the real world instead of the lab to test their theories, in the hope that they can merge some of the control features of lab experiments with the real stakes and context of the marketplace.

One type of real-world experiment is known as a **natural experiment.** A natural experiment is a situation in which, by chance, something happens that allows the researcher to learn about an economic question of interest. When the United States passed the Clean Air Act and its amendments, for example, it set up pollution thresholds for counties in the United States. If a county had a pollution level above the threshold, it faced stringent anti-pollution requirements. If the county fell below the threshold, even by a small amount, the anti-pollution requirements did not apply. For counties just a tiny bit above and just a tiny bit below the threshold, the Clean Air Act provided a natural experiment on the impact of environmental regulation and researchers documented effects on pollution, industrial activity, health, infant mortality, and so on. An obvious problem with natural experiments is that they are hard to find. A second weakness is that it is not always straightforward to generalize from a specific natural experiment to other settings of economic interest.

The other type of real-world experiment is the **field experiment.** A field experiment uses randomization, just as in the lab, but is carried out in real-world settings, ideally

natural experiment
A randomization or near-randomization that arises by happenstance.

field experiment
Research method in which randomizations are carried out in real-world settings.

using research subjects who are making decisions as part of their everyday lives, unaware that they are part of an experiment. Consequently, it is possible to make strong inferences about behavior from field experiments without having to worry about how the artificiality of the lab might be distorting the results. The study we discussed in the previous section in which researchers sent volunteers to people's homes to ask for donations is a classic type of field experiment.

Clever firms have long engaged in field experiments, and you have unknowingly been part of these experiments throughout your life. Often when you receive a catalog or a credit card offer in the mail, the firm sending it is actually conducting a field experiment, by changing around the order in which the goods are presented for some customers, altering the descriptions of goods to see which lead to more sales, and perhaps playing with the prices offered to different recipients. Economists have increasingly turned to field experiments to answer questions as diverse as whether paying high-school students for good grades leads to better outcomes, the best way to incentivize people to lose weight, and which movies will be box-office hits.

17.4 Conclusions and the Future of Microeconomics

In this chapter, we have addressed a group of topics collectively known as *behavioral economics*. The claims and predictions of behavioral economics often contradict the findings of the economic models we learned in the earlier chapters of this book. Behavioral economics describes economic decision makers (firms, consumers, governments) that make systematic and fundamental errors based on psychological biases—propensity to overconfidence, mental accounting, susceptibility to framing, sunk cost fallacies, and others. The actions predicted by behavioral economics leave biased agents open to being taken advantage of by all sorts of rational economic actors, as we have also tried to emphasize. But in some sense, the behavioral economics ideas we studied in this chapter provide a critique of the traditional microeconomics we outlined in the previous 16 chapters.

With that critique has come a renewed emphasis on how we test theories. The use of data to test economic theories is the realm of econometrics, and a full discussion of econometric techniques is beyond the scope of this book. We have, however, introduced some of the new ways in which economists and companies go about testing economic theories outside of econometrics by using experiments in the lab and in the field. The results from those experiments sometimes suggest the importance of behavioral economics critiques and sometimes seem to verify the usefulness of the main economic models we've studied.

We, the authors, strongly believe in the importance and insight of microeconomics. We recognize that the traditional models, while extremely powerful, are far from perfect. The goal of every economist should be to understand actual economic behavior. If that means discovering where the limits of our discipline lie, then we should commit to finding those limits.

In the end, microeconomics remains one of the most useful and most important contributions humanity has ever created. What you have learned about the subject in this course can serve you extremely well in life if you will let it.[14] One cannot help but be struck by the thought that if the rest of the world knew as much about economics as you now do after completing microeconomics, we would all be a lot better off.

The goal of academics is to disseminate that knowledge through teaching and writing. You can help spread that knowledge through your actions. We hope you have enjoyed the ride and that you will use what you've learned for the rest of your life.

---

[14] Thus, we suggest keeping your book for future reference! Of course, you'll have to analyze that suggestion using your skills of economic analysis and consider the incentives of all parties involved.

Summary

1. The traditional economic models of the previous chapters assume that economic actors such as consumers and firms are fully rational, self-interested, maximize their well-being, and don't make systematic errors. **Behavioral economics** argues that the conventional models do not take into account psychological biases in human behavior, and that these systematic biases affect the decisions made by parties in an economic transaction. Such biases include **overconfidence, time inconsistency,** susceptibility to framing, attention to sunk cost, and possibly **altruistic** behavior. [Section 17.1]

2. Even if we accept the existence of systematic human psychological biases, the fundamental microeconomics of the preceding chapters is still incredibly valuable and relevant to the real world. Markets tend to take advantage of people suffering from psychological biases and drive them out (or take their money). [Section 17.2]

3. Economists have moved into a new realm of testing economic theories using **lab** and **field experiments** rather than purely **econometric** data analyses. Experiments allow economists to test only the economic theory of interest, holding all else equal. [Section 17.3]

4. Microeconomics is, perhaps, the most important and useful thing you will ever learn in your life. [Section 17.4]

Review Questions

1. Characterize *Homo economicus*. How does he differ from a regular human being?
2. Define overconfidence.
3. What does hyperbolic discounting lead consumers to prefer?
4. Why is time consistency important in economic models?
5. How does the endowment effect contradict aspects of conventional economic theory?
6. What is the importance of the reference point in loss aversion?
7. Describe one example of anchoring.
8. How does mental accounting affect individuals' consumption decisions?
9. How do economists attempt to account for altruism in economic models?
10. What tends to happen to irrational or biased actors in the market system?
11. Lab experiments allow economists to test economic theory while holding all other variables constant. What are some downfalls of lab experiments?
12. Contrast natural and field experiments. What are some advantages of each?

Problems (Solutions to problems marked * appear at the back of this book. Problems adapted to use calculus are available online at http://worthpublishers.com/GLS1e)

1. AJ pays full price to view *Batman: The 20th Iteration* at the multiplex. After three minutes of viewing, he realizes that the movie is worse than anything he could be watching on TV at home. Yet, he stays to the end, "... because I paid $9 for the ticket." What behavioral bias has AJ fallen victim to? Explain.

2. Connor and Marie are in a relationship with one another, a relationship punctuated by constant bickering and mistrust. "Connor," Marie's friends tell her, "is a jerk. Why on earth don't you leave him?" To which Marie responds, "Silly, we've been together for 9 years! I can't just throw away those years!" Explain how Marie has fallen victim to the sunk cost bias.

3. Lots of people pay high fees to join a gym in early January, and then fail to work out more than a few times. Does this evidence provide support for or against the sunk cost bias? Explain your reasoning.

*4. In a recent survey, two-thirds of respondents indicated that they were not saving enough for retirement. What behavioral bias can explain the willingness of individuals to knowingly underfund their future standard of living? Explain.

*5. Economist Dean Karlan has opened stickk.com, a nonprofit entity that he calls a "commitment store." Individuals attempting to achieve a goal (to lose weight, to quit smoking, to write daily in a journal, etc.) authorize stickk.com to charge them a prespecified amount if they fail to reach their goal (as determined by a third-party referee).

a. What behavioral bias is stickk.com designed to help overcome?

b. Should they fail, subscribers are given the option of donating the fees to a charity they support or to an organization that they despise. Why might allowing the subscribers to direct their losses to a favorite charity weaken their resolve?

6. You are considering becoming a hedge-fund manager, and will make your living by charging your clients a fee for managing their money. You are considering two payment schemes: a "no-load" scheme whereby you charge each client an annual fee that is a relatively high percentage of the amount of money you manage for them, or a "front-load" scheme in which you charge investors a very large one-time fee for each dollar they invest, followed by a very low annual fee.

a. If your investors are overconfident in your ability to generate abnormally high returns, which scheme can potentially generate the highest profit for you? Explain.

b. If your investors are a group of very conservative pessimists, which scheme can potentially generate the highest profit for you? Explain.

*7. You are a personnel manager at a ball-bearing factory. You are considering two schemes to motivate your employees during a period of particularly brisk business. In Scheme A, you tell your employees, "If you increase your output by 10%, I will give you a $500 bonus at the end of the month." In Scheme B, you tell your employees, "I am giving you a $500 bonus. But if you do not achieve 10% growth by the end of the month, I will withdraw it."

a. If your employees are completely rational, will they be motivated more by Scheme A, Scheme B, or will both schemes motivate them equally?

b. If your employees are swayed by the endowment effect, which scheme is likely to be most effective in motivating them? Explain your answer.

c. Discuss the interplay of the endowment effect and framing bias inherent in this problem.

8. Where are you more likely to see racial discrimination: in the highly competitive financial services industry, or in the tobacco industry (where four firms control about 99% of the market share)? Explain your answer, drawing on your knowledge of market structures from Chapters 8, 9, and 11.

9. "The most heartfelt gifts are anonymous ones." Explain this statement, drawing on your knowledge of utility functions that account for behavioral traits.

10. Consider the Ultimatum Game, a two-player game often played in experimental economics labs. In the Ultimatum Game, one player is given an amount of money and then instructed to give some arbitrary portion of it to an anonymous second player. The second player has the option of accepting the offer or rejecting it. If the second player rejects the offer, neither player gets anything.

a. According to traditional economic theory (which assumes that individuals are self-interested utility maximizers), what should the first player offer the second?

b. What does traditional economic theory suggest the second player should be willing to accept?

c. In experimental settings, the first player often offers the anonymous second player about 50% of the initial amount. Is this result consistent with theory? Can we easily attribute this anomaly to something other than an innate sense of fairness? Explain.

11. Consider the Dictator Game, a two-player game often played in experimental economics labs. In the Dictator game, one player (the Dictator) is given an amount of money and then instructed to give some arbitrary portion of it to an anonymous second player. The second player must accept whatever the first player offers, if anything.

a. According to traditional economic theory, what should the first player offer the second?

b. In experimental settings, the average offer given to the second player is about 30% of the initial amount. Explain how such an offer might not be motivated by an innate sense of fairness.

Math Review Appendix

Section 1: Math concepts and basic skills

There is no doubt that economics is about ideas. These economic ideas can be conveyed in a variety of languages—from words to the use of algebraic equations and graphs. We've used all these methods in the text, and the appendices scattered throughout the book and online add yet a third language: calculus.

Sometimes it's easier to express and understand economic ideas using mathematical symbols rather than words. The material we present here reviews the algebra and geometry concepts we use in the text, as well as the calculus that the material in the appendices relies on. You have likely encountered most of these concepts and techniques before in your high school or college algebra or calculus classes, but we compile them here in a way that is most relevant to your study of economics. We will begin with a discussion of lines and curves, which are crucial to economic ideas such as utility and income, among others, and will set the foundation for the rest of our review.

Lines and Curves Functions describe the relationships between input variables and outputs, and may be written generically as $y = f(x)$, where x is some input and y the output. One function crucial to our study is that of the line, which we commonly write in the form $y = mx + b$, and which we've graphed on the x-y plane—the Cartesian plane—in Figure A.1 below. As in our generic function, x and y are inputs and outputs, respectively.

We can learn a lot from this functional form of the line, which is known as the *slope-intercept* form for reasons that will soon become clear. The line's slope, m, describes the change in y from a given change in x, and can be written mathematically as

$$m = \frac{\Delta y}{\Delta x} = \frac{y_2 - y_1}{x_2 - x_1}$$

where Δ represents the change in a variable, and (x_1, y_1) and (x_2, y_2) are two points on the line.

Figure A.1 Slope and Intercept of a Line

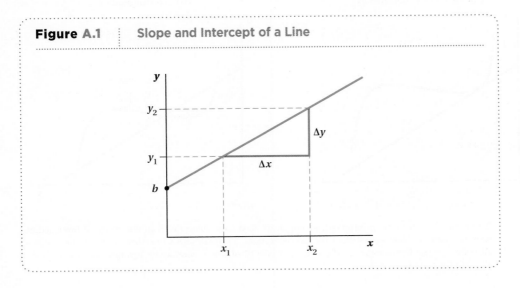

The slope tells us two important pieces of information about the line. First, it describes how flat or steep the line is. In other words, we can answer the question: If x increases by one unit, by how much does y change? The slope also tells us whether the relationship between x and y is negative or positive. An upward-sloping line, as in Figure A.1, has a positive slope, meaning that when x increases, so does y. A negative slope indicates that an increase in x results in a decrease in y, creating a downward-sloping line. A flat, horizontal line has a slope equal to zero; as x changes, there is no corresponding change in y. On a vertical line, x doesn't change at all, even as y increases or decreases. As a result, we describe a vertical line's slope—which is equal to infinity—as undefined.

The form $y = mx + b$ holds one final piece of information about the line: b, or the y-intercept. You can clearly see this in Figure A.1—it's where the line intersects the y-axis. In this case, the y-intercept is positive, but the line could also have a negative intercept and intersect the y-axis below the x-axis, or have a y-intercept equal to zero.[1]

We have described the equation for the line using the slope-intercept form, but a line can be expressed in any way that demonstrates the relationship between the input x and its output y. You might also see a line written in the standard form of a line, $mx - y = -b$, or even as $x = \dfrac{(y - b)}{m}$. In fact, we'll see that last form a lot throughout our study of economics: It's how we typically write supply and demand functions.

By definition, the slope of a straight line is constant; the slope will be the same no matter where you measure the change in x and y. But, the relationship between x and y may be more complicated. In contrast to the line, a curve can have different slopes at different points along it. Because a curve can have an almost infinite number of shapes and curvatures, there are no standard functional forms for curves.

Tangency The point at which a given line and curve just touch—without intersecting or overlapping—is the tangent point. It describes the point at which the slope of the line is equal to the slope at the particular point on the curve. This concept of tangency is particularly useful in the study of microeconomics, which relies on tangencies in optimization problems such as profit and utility maximization.

Graphically, a tangent point is easy to see. Point A in panel a of Figure A.2 is a tangent point between the curve and a line. How can we tell this is a tangency? At A, the

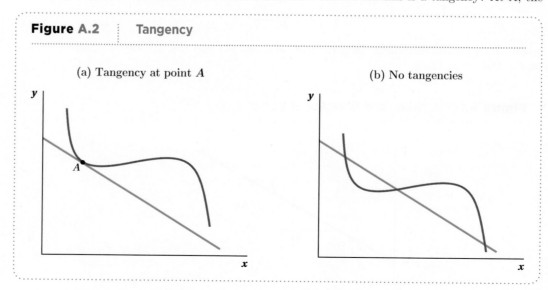

Figure A.2 Tangency

(a) Tangency at point A

(b) No tangencies

---

[1] A line may also have no y-intercept, although we won't see these much in our study of intermediate microeconomics. This occurs when the line is vertical. Vertical lines will either intersect the y-axis at all points (if the line is equal to the y-axis, or $x = 0$) or, more commonly, not intersect the y-axis at all (say, for the line $x = 2$ or $x = -4$).

A line has a slope of –2 and an intercept of 10.

   a. Write the line in slope-intercept form.

   b. Graph the line on a Cartesian plane.

   c. Draw a curve tangent to the line.

Solution:

   a. The slope-intercept form of a line can be expressed as $y = mx + b$, where m is the slope and b is the intercept. The slope-intercept form corresponding to $m = -2$ and $b = 10$ therefore is $y = -2x + 10$.

   b. To graph the equation $y = -2x + 10$ on the Cartesian plane, we can calculate the coordinates of the intercepts and connect these points. Because the equation is in slope-intercept form, we already know that the intercept along the y-axis occurs at point (0, 10). (Another way to solve for this is to plug $x = 0$ into the equation for the line. Note that when $x = 0$, $y = -2(0) + 10 = 10$.)

   To get the x-axis intercept, we can substitute $y = 0$ into the equation for the line: $0 = -2x + 10$. Rearranging this equation, we see that $2x = 10$ or $x = 5$. We therefore know that (5, 0) is another point along this line. Next, we connect these points to illustrate the line in the x-y plane.

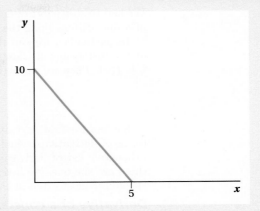

   c. A curved line tangent to the line $y = -2x + 10$ is included in the figure below. Note that, for this example, the tangency occurs at only one point on the line we graphed in the previous part of this problem. We could have drawn a curve that is tangent to the line at more than one point.

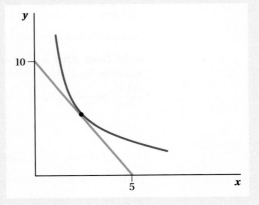

curve just touches the line without crossing it. In this case, this is the only point at which the slope of the curve equals the slope of the line, and is therefore tangent to the line.

   Not all lines and curves are tangent to each other. Panel b illustrates an example of a curve and a line that, while intersecting, have no tangencies.

Section 2: Calculus review

The basic algebraic concepts we just reviewed are used throughout the book. We'll turn now to calculus, which we use in the appendices to further our understanding of economic concepts. If you've taken calculus before, this section will be purely review. If you haven't taken calculus, you might be able to pick up a few tricks. This section is *not* a substitute for a background in calculus. If you want to apply calculus to economics, it's important to start with the solid foundation that an entry-level course in calculus provides.

First Derivatives We have already seen that slopes are incredibly important to our study of economics. We can find the slope of a line using the formula $m = \frac{\Delta y}{\Delta x} = \frac{y_2 - y_1}{x_2 - x_1}$. We had to stop short of describing the slope of a curve, since a curve's slope, unlike that of a line, differs along the curve. This is where calculus can help us.

In particular, we can describe the slope of a curve (or a line) using a *derivative*, or the instantaneous rate of change of a function at a given point. Take the function $y = f(x)$. Then we can write the derivative in the equivalent forms

$$f'(x) = \frac{df(x)}{dx} = \frac{dy}{dx}$$

Solving for first derivatives is easiest to demonstrate using examples of a few basic forms of derivatives, which we outline below. The rules we present are by no means an exhaustive list of derivatives rules. For that, you should consult a calculus text. But, these are the ones we'll rely on in the calculus appendices, and which you'll probably encounter most often in the context of economics.

Derivative of a constant: Take the function $f(x) = c$, where c is a constant. Then $\frac{df(x)}{dx} = 0$. Why? We know that a line of this form is horizontal at $y = c$. Since a horizontal line has a slope equal to zero, its derivative must also equal zero.

Power rule for derivatives: Perhaps the rule that we will most often rely on is the power rule. Given a function $f(x) = cx^\alpha$, where c is again some constant, the derivative takes the form $\frac{df(x)}{dx} = c\alpha x^{\alpha-1}$. In words, you multiply x by its exponent and subtract one from the exponent you began with to find the derivative. This is perhaps best illustrated with an example. Take $f(x) = 3x^4$. Then, $\frac{df(x)}{dx} = 3(4)x^{4-1} = 12x^3$.

Addition and subtraction rules for derivatives: We can rely on the rules above to find the derivatives for equations of the form $f(x) = g(x) + h(x)$. To solve for $\frac{df(x)}{dx}$, simply take the derivative of $g(x)$ and $h(x)$ separately:

$$\frac{df(x)}{dx} = \frac{dg(x)}{dx} + \frac{dh(x)}{dx}$$

As before, let's illustrate this with a simple example. Take the function $f(x) = x^2 + 10$. Then, $\frac{df(x)}{dx} = \frac{d(x^2)}{dx} + \frac{d(10)}{dx} = 2x + 0 = 2x$.

Note that this rule applies whether you are adding or subtracting, since subtraction is simply the addition of a negative number. In other words, if $f(x) = g(x) - h(x)$, $\frac{df(x)}{dx} = \frac{dg(x)}{dx} - \frac{dh(x)}{dx}$.

Second Derivatives We've found the derivative of a function, but sometimes we need to find the derivative of the derivative, or the *second* derivative:

$$f''(x) = \frac{d^2f(x)}{dx^2} = \frac{d^2y}{dx^2}$$

What does the second derivative tell us about a function? While the first derivative describes the slope of a function, the second derivative describes a function's curvature. A function's curvature is said to be convex (as shown in Figure A.3, panel a) or concave (panel b). Note that a function may be convex over some values of x, and concave over others, such as in panel c.

Figure A.3 Convexity and Concavity

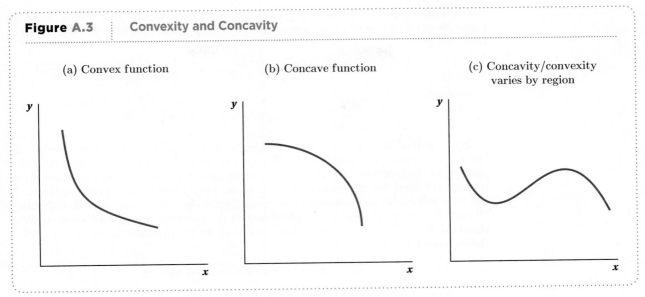

(a) Convex function

(b) Concave function

(c) Concavity/convexity varies by region

Over some range of x, a curve is said to be convex if the second derivative with respect to x is greater than zero, meaning that

$$\frac{d^2f(x)}{dx^2} > 0$$

It is concave when

$$\frac{d^2f(x)}{dx^2} < 0$$

These two rules we've presented may seem to be a bit of hand-waving, but the intuition behind them is clear. Consider first the meaning of a function's first derivative: A positive (or negative) first derivative indicates that a function is increasing (or decreasing) over that region. Similarly then, the second derivative tells us whether the slope, as measured by its first derivative, is increasing or decreasing over that region. A positive second derivative indicates that the slope increases with higher values of x (panel a), which we call *convexity*; a negative second derivative means that the slope decreases with higher values of x (panel b), which we call *concavity*.[2]

Partial Derivatives Above we found first and second derivatives for single-variable equations. Sometimes, however, we will need to find the slopes or curvatures of a multi-variable equation. In this case, we apply partial derivatives.

Consider the function $z = f(x, y)$ where x and y are both inputs into the function that maps output z. Given this function, we can now find two partial first derivatives: the first derivative of z with respect to x, or $f_x(x, y) = \dfrac{\partial f(x, y)}{\partial x} = \dfrac{\partial z}{\partial x}$, and the first derivative of z with respect to y, or $f_y(x, y) = \dfrac{\partial f(x, y)}{\partial y} = \dfrac{\partial z}{\partial y}$.

Calculating partial derivatives is actually quite simple when you know how to calculate a standard derivative. To find $\dfrac{\partial f(x, y)}{\partial x}$, you simply take the first derivative of

---

[2] Note that in panel a, the slope is increasing since it is becoming less negative as we move to the right. Similarly, the slope in panel b is decreasing since it is becoming more negative as we move to the right.

$f(x, y)$ with respect to x, holding y constant. Let's demonstrate this with a standard Cobb–Douglas equation[3] of the form $f(x, y) = x^\alpha y^{1-\alpha}$. Using the power rule for derivatives, we get

$$\frac{\partial f(x, y)}{\partial x} = \alpha x^{\alpha-1} y^{1-\alpha}$$

Similarly,

$$\frac{\partial f(x, y)}{\partial y} = (1 - \alpha)x^\alpha y^{1-\alpha-1} = (1 - \alpha)x^\alpha y^{-\alpha}$$

These partial derivatives isolate the slopes (or rates of change of the function) in the x and y directions, respectively. What if we want to describe the curvatures of a multi-variable function? To do this, we rely on second partial derivatives. It's a bit of a tongue-twister, but it's easiest to think about second partial derivatives in comparison to standard second derivatives: Second partial derivatives are partial derivatives of partial derivatives, just as standard second derivatives are standard derivatives of standard derivatives. For the function $z = f(x, y)$, we are primarily interested in finding the curvature in two directions:

$$f_{xx}(x, y) = \frac{\partial^2 f(x, y)}{\partial x^2} = \frac{\partial^2 z}{\partial x^2} \text{ and}$$

$$f_{yy}(x, y) = \frac{\partial^2 f(x, y)}{\partial y^2} = \frac{\partial^2 z}{\partial y^2}$$

Using the Cobb–Douglas function from above, we get

$$\frac{\partial^2 f(x, y)}{\partial x^2} = \alpha(\alpha - 1)x^{\alpha-2} y^{1-\alpha}$$

$$\frac{\partial^2 f(x, y)}{\partial y^2} = -\alpha(1 - \alpha)x^\alpha y^{-\alpha-1}$$

There is actually, in this case, another type of second partial derivative that we could calculate. Known as a cross partial derivative, it calculates the first partial derivative with respect to x, and the second partial derivative with respect to y, or vice versa:

$$f_{xy}(x, y) = \frac{\partial^2 f(x, y)}{\partial x \partial y} = \frac{\partial^2 z}{\partial x \partial y} \text{ and}$$

$$f_{yx}(x, y) = \frac{\partial^2 f(x, y)}{\partial y \partial x} = \frac{\partial^2 z}{\partial y \partial x}$$

While it is useful to be aware of these cross partial derivatives, we will not rely on them for the analyses in this book.

One application of partial derivatives that we will use, however, is total differentiation. Total differentiation gives us the *total* change in a function, or the combined change in both the x and y directions. This comes up often in our study of economics: Sometimes we need to describe movements along a curve when two variables change simultaneously, as do a firm's capital K and labor L inputs in Chapter 6. To totally differentiate a multi-variable function, we solve

$$df(x, y) = \frac{\partial f(x, y)}{\partial x}dx + \frac{\partial f(x, y)}{\partial y}dy$$

[3] You will see Cobb–Douglas functions a lot in your study of economics—it is one of the most common functional forms for a variety of economics concepts, including utility and production functions. We won't go into much detail about its properties here, but it is useful to see basic calculus techniques applied to this very common set of functions. In the calculus appendices, we'll assume $0 < \alpha < 1$ for the purposes of solving economics problems. But to solve first and second partial derivatives, we don't actually need to make this assumption, and so we don't make it here. The exponent α could be negative or positive, fractional or a whole number, and the rules we present here still apply.

Let's break down what each part of this equation tells us. The two partial derivatives $\left(\dfrac{\partial f(x,\,y)}{\partial x}\ \text{and}\ \dfrac{\partial f(x,\,y)}{\partial y}\right)$ indicate the *rate* of change in the x and y directions, respectively. Likewise, dx and dy are the changes in x and y. Combining these as we do in the equation above gives us the *total* change of the function with respect to all variables.

Unconstrained Optimization Problem

In many ways, what we have been building up to in this math review is the last mathematical concept we will look at here: basic, or unconstrained, optimization. (For a consideration of *constrained* optimization, see the Appendix to Chapter 4.) In solving an optimization problem, we will rely on the derivative techniques we have learned thus far.

Begin with a function of the form $y = f(x)$. We will first solve for what is known as the first-order condition. To do this, we set the first derivative equal to zero:

$$\frac{df(x)}{dx} = 0$$

What does this tell us? Remember first that $\dfrac{df(x)}{dx}$ is the slope of the function $f(x)$, examples of which are shown in Figure A.4. When this slope is zero, the line tangent to the curve is horizontal. This means that the curve must be at either a maximum (panel a) or a minimum (panel b).

We actually don't yet know whether the first-order condition we found has given us a maximum or a minimum. We just know that we have found an optimum. To learn whether we have maximized or minimized the function, we need to return to our second piece of derivative knowledge: second derivatives. Specifically, we need to take the second derivative of the function, and test whether it is negative or positive:

When $\dfrac{d^2 f(x)}{dx^2} < 0$, the curve is concave, and the point is a maximum.

When $\dfrac{d^2 f(x)}{dx^2} > 0$, the curve is convex, and the point is a minimum.

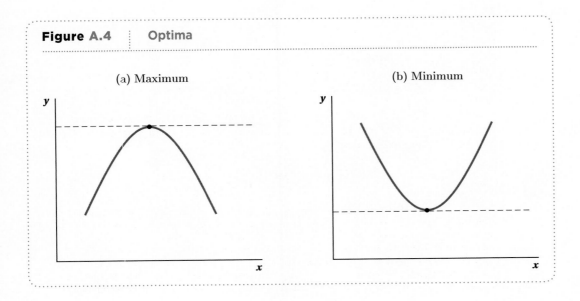

Figure A.4   Optima

(a) Maximum

(b) Minimum

A.2 figure it out

Optimize the function of one variable $y = 5x^2 - 100x$. Use the second derivative to determine if the point is a maximum or a minimum.

Solution:

First, solve for the first-order condition by setting the first derivative equal to zero. In this case,

$$\frac{df(x)}{dx} = \frac{d(5x^2 - 100x)}{dx} = 5(2)x^{2-1} - 100 = 10x - 100 = 0$$

Solve for x to find the optimum:

$$10x - 100 = 0$$

$$x = 10$$

Again, the first-order condition only tells us that we have optimized the function. To tell if this is a maximum or a minimum, we take the second derivative:

$$\frac{d^2f(x)}{dx^2} = \frac{d(10x - 100)}{dx} = 10 > 0$$

Because $\dfrac{d^2f(x)}{dx^2} > 0$, we see that this is a minimum.

Solutions to Review Questions

CHAPTER 1

1. Microeconomics looks at the specific economic actions of consumers and producers, while macroeconomics is a broader examination of the combined economic behavior of all consumers and producers in an economy.
2. Most of you make multiple consumption decisions each day, from the coffee you buy in the morning to the classes, textbooks, and notebooks you purchase for your education.
3. Consumption and production decisions interconnect to determine the market price and supply. This is because producers produce the goods and services that consumers consume.
4. Microeconomics relies on tools for graphs and mathematics in addition to empirical methods to explore microeconomic theories and phenomena.
5. Computers have made using empirical analysis easier and faster. In economic terms, the relative price of empirical analysis has decreased.

CHAPTER 2

1. The supply and demand model assumes that (a) supply and demand are in a single market, (b) all goods in the market are identical, (c) all goods sell for the same price and everyone in the market has the same information, and (d) there are many consumers and producers in the market.
2. A complement is a good that is purchased and used *in combination with* another good. A substitute is a good that can be used *in place of* another good.
3. We assume that there is no change in any other factors that may also affect how much of a good a consumer buys. The downward slope reflects the fact that consumers demand less of a good as its price increases.
4. A change in quantity demanded is a movement along the demand curve that occurs because of a change in the good's own price, while a change in demand reflects a shift of the entire demand curve caused by a change in a determinant of demand other than the good's price.
5. The upward slope of the supply curve reflects the fact that holding all else equal, producers supply more of a good as its price increases.

6. An inverse supply curve writes the equation for a supply curve as price as a function of quantity supplied. Economists use the inverse supply curve to make the supply choke price more explicit.
7. A change in quantity supplied is a movement along the supply curve that occurs because of a change in the good's own price, while a change in supply reflects a shift of the entire supply curve caused by a change in a determinant of supply other than the good's price.
8. The market equilibrium occurs at the intersection of supply and demand curves for a good. At equilibrium, the quantity supplied by producers equals the quantity demanded by consumers.
9. When the market price is too low, there is excess demand (shortage) for a good because consumers demand more of the good than producers are willing to supply at the relatively low price.
10. A demand shift causes equilibrium price and quantity to change in the same direction. More specifically, an outward shift in demand increases both price and quantity, while an inward shift in demand decreases price and quantity.
11. A supply shift causes equilibrium price and quantity to change in opposite directions. More specifically, an outward shift in supply decreases price but increases quantity; an inward shift in supply increases price but decreases quantity.
12. When both supply and demand shift, the direction of change in either quantity or price is determined by the relative magnitudes and directions of the shifts.
13. If supply and demand both increase, quantity increases; if both supply and demand decrease, quantity decreases. The effect on price is unknown: It depends on the relative magnitudes of the supply and demand shifts.
14. The slope of a supply or demand curve relates changes in the level of prices to changes in the level of quantity demanded or supplied. Elasticity represents the *responsiveness* of quantities to prices. More specifically, we express elasticity as the percentage change in quantity for a given percentage change in price.
15. The magnitude of each is as follows: inelastic $E < 1$, elastic $E > 1$, unit-elastic $E = 1$, perfectly elastic $E = 0$, and perfectly inelastic $E = \infty$.
16. Total expenditure and total revenue are both equal to price times quantity.

17. The price elasticity of demand reveals whether total expenditures will increase or decrease with prices. In particular, total expenditures increase with prices if demand is inelastic, decrease with prices if demand is elastic, and stay constant if demand is unit-elastic.

18. Normal goods have positive income elasticities; luxury goods have income elasticities greater than 1; and inferior goods have negative income elasticities.

19. When a good has a positive cross-price elasticity with another good, that good is a substitute for the other good. When a good has a negative cross-price elasticity with another good, that good is a complement for the other good.

CHAPTER 3

1. Consumer surplus is the difference between the price consumers would be willing to pay for a good and the price they actually have to pay. Producer surplus is the difference between the price at which producers would be willing to sell their good or service and the price they actually receive.

2. The demand choke price is the price at which quantity demanded is reduced to zero. Consumer surplus is equal to the area of the triangle with its base equal to the quantity sold and its height the difference between the market price and the demand choke price.

3. The supply choke price is the price at which quantity supplied is reduced to zero. Producer surplus is equal to the area of the triangle with its base equal to the quantity sold and its height the difference between the market price and the supply choke price.

4. An inward shift of the supply curve reduces consumer surplus and has an ambiguous effect on producer surplus. An outward shift of the supply curve increases consumer surplus, while also having an ambiguous effect on producer surplus.

5. An inward shift of the demand curve reduces producer surplus and has an ambiguous effect on consumer surplus. An outward shift of the demand curve increases producer surplus, while also having an ambiguous effect on consumer surplus.

6. A price ceiling sets the highest price that can be paid legally for a good. If this price is set below the equilibrium price, consumers will demand more of the good than producers are willing to supply, resulting in excess demand for the good.

7. A price floor sets the lowest price that can be paid legally for a good. If this price is set above the equilibrium price, producers will supply more of the good than consumers are willing to buy, resulting in excess supply for the good.

8. Deadweight loss is the reduction in total surplus that results from a market inefficiency. A large price elasticity indicates that supply or demand is sensitive to price. As a result, the resulting deadweight loss in a market with a large price elasticity will be relatively large.

9. A nonbinding price ceiling is set at a level above equilibrium price, and a nonbinding price floor is set at a level below equilibrium price.

10. A quota directly regulates the *quantity* of a good or service that can be provided unlike a price floor or price ceiling that directly regulates the *price* of a good or service.

11. Crowding out is a reduction in private economic activity that occurs because the government increases its presence in the market.

12. Crowding out does not depend on the elasticity of supply because we have assumed that government supply is not affected by market price. The elasticity of demand does affect the relative size of crowding out; a market with a relatively inelastic demand will see a large reduction in price due to government supply, resulting in many private businesses being crowded out of the market.

13. A tax causes quantity to decrease and the price that consumers pay to increase. A tax wedge occurs because the price suppliers receive for the good is lower than the price consumers pay by the amount of the tax.

14. The tax wedge reduces both consumer and producer surplus in the market, creating the deadweight loss of a tax.

15. The tax incidence is who—the producers or consumers—actually bears the burden of a tax. The tax incidence is determined by the elasticity of supply and demand.

16. A subsidy is the opposite of a tax—it is a payment by the government to a buyer or seller of a good or service.

17. A subsidy increases both producer and consumer surplus.

18. In a market with a subsidy, more people purchase the good or service than would have in the competitive market. The resulting deadweight loss derives from these people who would not have purchased the good in the competitive market.

CHAPTER 4

1. Completeness and rankability mean that consumers can make comparisons across all consumption bundles. "More is better" describes the assumption that for most goods, consuming more of the good benefits the consumer. Transitivity implies that if a consumer prefers good A to good B and good B to good C, then the consumer also prefers good A to good C. Finally, consumers prefer variety meaning that the more a consumer has of a particular good, the less she is willing to give up something else to get more of that good.

2. Utility provides a measure of how satisfied a consumer is with a consumption bundle. The utility function describes the relationship between a consumer's satisfaction level, or utility, and what the consumer actually consumes.

3. An indifference curve shows the combination of all the different consumption bundles at a given utility level. In other words, given a utility level, it shows all the consumption bundles among which a consumer is indifferent.

4. The marginal rate of substitution of X for Y reveals the willingness of a consumer to give up good X for good Y while still being left equally well off.

5. The negative of the slope of the indifference curve is equal to the consumer's MRS_{XY}, or how much of good X he is willing to give up to receive more of good Y. As you move along a consumer's indifference curve in the standard case, the curvature of the indifference curve reflects the change in the consumer's relative preferences for the two goods. In particular, as the consumer gains more of good X, she is willing to give up less of good Y—a characteristic of the indifference curve that stems from our assumption that consumers prefer variety.

6. Indifference curves that are relatively steep indicate that the consumer is willing to give up a large quantity of good Y to get another unit of good X. Relatively flat indifference curves imply that the consumer would require a large increase in good X to be willing to give up a unit of good Y.

7. Perfect substitutes are goods that a consumer can trade for another good, in fixed units, and receive identical levels of utility. Indifference curves for perfect substitutes are straight lines.

8. Perfect complements are goods whose utility levels depend on being used in fixed proportion with one another. Indifference curves for perfect complements are L-shaped.

9. Consumers make utility-maximizing decisions based on the goods' prices and the consumers' incomes.

10. We make three assumptions before defining the economic model that incorporates a consumer's budget constraint: (a) Each good has a fixed price and unlimited quantity, (b) the consumer's income is fixed, and (c) the consumer cannot save or borrow.

11. A consumer's budget constraint is the curve that describes the entire set of consumption bundles a consumer can purchase when spending his entire income.

12. The slope of the budget constraint is equal to the negative of the ratio of the two prices, $-P_x/P_y$. Any nonproportional change in the goods' prices would affect the slope.

13. The consumer's optimal, or utility-maximizing, consumption bundle occurs at the point of tangency between his budget constraint and his indifference curve.

14. At the point of tangency between the consumer's budget constraint and her indifference curve, the ratio of the goods' marginal utilities equals the ratio of the goods' prices.

15. Using the utility-maximization approach, we search for the indifference curve that maximizes utility, given a set budget constraint. Under expenditure minimization, we search for the budget line that minimizes expenditure, given a set utility level. Both methods arrive at the same optimal budget constraint if we pick the same utility level for expenditure minimization as what is reached in the utility-maximization problem.

CHAPTER 5

1. The income effect describes the change in a consumer's consumption choice given a change in the purchasing power of the consumer's income. In describing this change, we hold the goods' prices fixed.

2. We characterize a good as normal when consumption of the good rises with income. Luxury goods are a class of normal goods whose income elasticity is greater than 1. In contrast to normal goods, the consumption of an inferior good decreases when income rises.

3. The income expansion path connects the optimal bundles of two goods for one consumer, while the Engel curve shows the relationship between the quantity of a good consumed and a consumer's income. While both the Engel curve and the income expansion path contain the

same information, the income expansion path allows us to understand how *two* goods' relative quantities change with income. The Engel curve isolates the impact of income changes on the consumption of a single good.

4. Holding the consumer's income constant, we can draw his demand curve by connecting the utility-maximizing quantities of a good at different prices of the good. When the price of a good increases, the consumer's demand for the good decreases, creating a downward-sloping demand curve.

5. The demand for pizza will shift in response to changes in the consumer's income or preferences, as well as the price of other goods. Three possibilities of shifts in the demand for pizza are listed below:

   a. **Increase in the consumer's income:** If pizza is a normal good, then an increase in the consumer's income will shift out his demand for pizza.

   b. **Decrease in the consumer's relative preference for pizza:** If the consumer's relative preference for pizza decreases—say, he starts preferring the substitute good, Chinese take-out—then his demand for pizza will shift in.

   e. **Increase in the price of another good:** If the price of a good such as Chinese take-out increases, then the consumer's demand for pizza will shift out. If the price of a complement of a good—like the beverage the consumer prefers to have with his pizza—increases, then the consumer's demand for pizza will shift in.

6. Both the income and substitution effect stem from a change in the prices of two goods. While the substitution effect is the change in a consumer's consumption choices that results from a change in the *relative prices* of the two goods, the income effect describes the change resulting from the consumer's *purchasing power*.

7. We can isolate income and substitution effects using three basic steps. Take a consumer with initial utility-maximizing bundle A.

   a. A change in the goods' prices rotates the budget constraint. The new optimal bundle (B) is at the tangency of the new budget constraint to a new indifference curve.

   b. The line that is parallel to the new budget constraint but tangent to the original indifference curve gives you point A'. The substitution effect is the movement from A to A'.

   c. The income effect is the movement from A' to the new optimal bundle B.

8. The direction of the substitution effect is the same for both normal and inferior goods, but the income effect differs between the two types of goods. If a normal good's price decreases, the change in consumption due to the income effect is an increase in consumption of the good. If an inferior good's price decreases, the change in consumption due to the income effect is a decrease in consumption of the good.

9. A Giffen good is a good for which price and quantity demanded are positively related. In other words, if the price of the good decreases, the consumer demands *less*—not more—of the good.

10. A complement is a good that is purchased and used in combination with another good. A substitute is a good that can be used in place of another good.

11. When the price of a good's substitute rises, the demand for the good increases, meaning substitutes have a positive cross-price elasticity of demand. Complements have a negative cross-price elasticity of demand; when the price of a good's complement rises, the demand for the good decreases.

12. The shape of the indifference curve reveals information about the degree of two goods' substitutability. The less curved the indifference curve, the more substitutable the two goods are.

13. The market demand is the horizontal sum of all individuals' demand curves for a good.

14. For a given change in price, the change in quantity demanded by the market as a whole must be at least as great as the change in quantity demanded by an individual consumer. As a result, the market demand curve must be at least as flat as an individual's demand curve.

CHAPTER 6

1. In the short run, a firm's capital is fixed, while in the long run, a firm can change its quantities of both labor *and* capital inputs.

2. A production function shows the relationship between a firm's inputs (capital and labor) and its output quantity.

3. Because capital is fixed in the short run, the firm's marginal product of labor is most relevant to its production decisions.

4. Firms experience a diminishing marginal product of labor—as a firm hires additional units of labor, the marginal product of labor falls, meaning that less output can be produced for an additional unit of input. This can be seen in

the gradual flattening of the graph of the firm's production function.

5. A producer's isoquants share many of the same characteristics as a consumer's indifference curves. Isoquants farther from the origin are associated with higher output levels. Isoquants cannot cross because if two isoquants did, it would imply that the same quantities of inputs yield two different quantities of output.

6. The marginal rate of technical substitution is the rate at which the firm can trade one input (X) for another (Y) holding output constant, and is equal to the marginal product of input X over the marginal product of input Y. For the standard case, the $MRTS$ implies a curved isoquant. As you move down and to the right along the isoquant, the marginal product of labor becomes low relative to the marginal rate of capital.

7. The curvature of the isoquant demonstrates the degree of substitutability between capital and labor. A nearly straight isoquant implies that the $MRTS$ is nearly constant along the isoquant, implying that the two inputs are close substitutes for each other in the production process. A more curved isoquant indicates that capital and labor are poor substitutes for each other in the production process.

8. An isocost line is the curve that shows all the input combinations that yield the same cost. Since the slope of the isocost line is the negative ratio of wages to the capital rental rate, $-W/R$, we can use the slope to determine the cost tradeoff of substituting labor for capital (or vice versa).

9. In reaction to an increase in the price of one input (say, labor), the firm will substitute away from units of that input to another (in this case, capital) *in the long run*.

10. Returns to scale refer to the change in the amount of output in response to a proportional change in all the inputs. Constant returns to scale indicate that a proportional change in all inputs changes the quantity of output by that same proportion. Increasing returns to scale means that a proportional change in all inputs changes the quantity of output more than proportionately. Finally, decreasing returns to scale imply that a proportional change in all inputs changes the quantity of output less than proportionately.

11. Technological change, A, enters the production function as a scale factor: $Q = Af(K, L)$. This type of technological change implies that after an improvement in technology, the firm produces extra output using the same level of productive inputs as prior to the change.

12. The expansion path plots the optimal input combinations for each output quantity. The total cost curve plots the output quantities from the expansion path against the total cost of the productive inputs.

CHAPTER 7

1. Accounting costs include the direct costs of operating a business, while a firm's economic costs are its accounting costs plus its opportunity costs. A firm can calculate its profits in one of two ways: as accounting profits equal to its total revenue minus its accounting costs, or as economic profits equal to its total revenue minus its economic costs.

2. Opportunity cost is the value of what a producer gives up by using an input. A firm's opportunity costs are what differentiate the calculation of its accounting costs from that of its economic costs. Specifically, opportunity costs are included in economic cost but not in accounting cost.

3. A firm that lets its sunk costs affect its operating decisions has committed the sunk cost fallacy. In the forward-looking perspective, firms—and people—shouldn't allow costs that have already been paid and cannot be recovered to affect their decisions in the present.

4. Fixed costs include expenditures on overhead such as the cost of the building or plant and utility bills. Once paid, these types of expenditures become sunk costs, but a firm *can* avoid them by closing up shop and shutting down. Once they are sunk costs, however, the firm shouldn't take them into consideration when making production decisions. That would be committing the sunk cost fallacy, as we saw in Question 3 above.

5. A firm's total cost is equal to the sum of its fixed and variable costs.

6. A firm's fixed costs are constant no matter what its output level is, resulting in a horizontal fixed cost curve. The variable cost curve is positively sloped—as production increases, the associated variable costs increase.

7. Average fixed, average variable, and average total cost curves calculate a firm's fixed, variable, and total costs as costs per unit.

8. Since a firm's fixed cost does not vary with the level of output, fixed cost does not affect its marginal cost of producing an additional unit of output. That marginal cost is dependent only on the firm's variable cost.

9. In the short run, a firm has fixed costs on capital, while in the long run, the firm can vary

both its capital and labor inputs. As a result, short-run total cost may be greater than long-run total cost. Since average cost is calculated as the total cost per unit of output, the same relationship holds true for a firm's short-run and long-run average costs.

10. Economies of scale look at the way a firm's costs increase with output. A firm with economies of scale has costs that increase at a slower rate than the increase in output. With diseconomies of scale, the firm's costs increase at a faster rate than the increase in output. Constant economies of scale indicate that the firm's costs increase at the same rate as the increase in output.

11. Economies of scope look at how a firm's costs change when it produces more than one product. Economies of scope exist when a firm can produce more than one product simultaneously at a lower cost than producing the products separately. Diseconomies of scope indicate that a firm produces more than one product simultaneously at a higher cost than producing the products separately.

CHAPTER 8

1. A perfectly competitive industry has no barriers to entry, and features many firms selling identical products.

2. Perfectly competitive firms are price takers. As a result, the demand curve facing a perfectly competitive firm is horizontal; no matter what quantity the firm produces, the market price at which the firm sells its product stays constant.

3. A firm's profit is the difference between its revenue and its total cost.

4. At its profit-maximizing output, the perfectly competitive firm's marginal cost equals the market price.

5. A firm will stay in operation so long as the market price is at least as large as the firm's average variable cost at its profit-maximizing level. In the short run, fixed costs need to be paid whether the firm stays in operation or not; because of this, the firm's fixed costs will not enter into its operating decisions.

6. The portion of the short-run marginal cost curve above the minimum average variable cost is the perfectly competitive firm's supply curve. At any price below the minimum average variable price, the firm shuts down, and supply goes to zero.

7. The short-run industry supply is the horizontal sum of the short-run supply curve of all individual firms in the industry. This industry supply curve represents the combined decisions of all firms in the industry.

8. In the short run, fixed costs do not affect firms' operating decisions, and any changes in fixed costs do not affect the short-run industry supply.

9. Producer surplus is the aggregation of price-marginal cost markups across every unit of output that the firm makes, or the revenue a firm makes above and beyond its variable cost. A firm's profit is its producer surplus minus its fixed cost.

10. Firms enter a perfectly competitive industry when the market price is above minimum long-run average total cost, or when firms in the industry earn positive economic profits. Conversely, a firm exits the industry when the market price is below minimum long-run average total cost, or when the firm earns negative economic profits.

11. Long-run competitive equilibrium occurs when price is equal to the firm's minimum average total cost. In other words, in the long run, there is no entry or exit into the industry, and firms earn zero economic profits.

12. A firm earns economic rents when it has lower costs than other firms in its industry.

13. Economic profits incorporate a firm's opportunity costs. Once opportunity costs are included, all firms—even those earning positive economic rents—earn zero economic profits in perfect competition.

CHAPTER 9

1. A firm that can influence the price at which it sells its product holds market power.

2. Industries with market power have barriers to entry that prevent new firms from entering the market:
   a. Natural monopolies—or markets in which it is efficient for a single firm to produce the entire industry output—serve as effective barriers to entry to other firms.
   b. A switching cost makes it less likely a consumer will switch from one business or product to another, since the consumer will have to give up something in order to make the switch.
   c. Differentiation among products creates an imperfect substitutability across otherwise similar products. As a result, new entrants to the market cannot gain customers simply by selling their product at a lower price.

d. A firm's control of key inputs (absolute cost advantage) also will prevent entry into the market.

3. Natural monopolies face economies of scale at all output levels. This means that the larger the firm is, the lower its average total costs. Splitting industry output among different firms would increase average total costs, making it most efficient for one firm to produce the entire industry output.

4. Just as the demand curve shows the relationship between a good's price and its quantity, the marginal revenue curve shows the relationship between a good's marginal revenue and its quantity. The marginal revenue curve of a linear demand curve is also very similar to a demand curve on other dimensions: Its vertical intercept is identical, and its slope is twice the slope of the demand curve.

5. A profit-maximizing firm produces where marginal revenue equals marginal cost.

6. A perfectly competitive firm faces a market price equal to its marginal cost, and thus does not earn producer surplus. A firm with market power is able to price above its marginal cost; as a result, it earns producer surplus, at the expense of some of the consumer surplus that would benefit buyers under perfect competition.

7. The deadweight loss represents the inefficiency of market power: There are consumers who demand the product at a price above its marginal cost but below the higher price set by the firm with market power. The resulting loss in surplus from these consumers who do not purchase the product under monopoly is the deadweight loss.

8. Firms with market power face a set of profit-maximizing prices and quantity combinations, but these combinations do not, strictly speaking, form a supply curve. These price-quantity combinations depend on the firm's demand curve, while a supply curve by its formal definition exists independent of its associated demand curve.

9. In perfect competition, suppliers' production decisions are independent of the price sensitivity of demand. This is not true for decisions made by firms with market power. A change in the price sensitivity of demand rotates the demand curve, thereby rotating the firm's marginal revenue curve. The firm's profit-maximizing price-quantity combination is now at the intersection of the new marginal revenue curve and the marginal cost curve.

10. Governments use a variety of regulations to restrict market power and decrease deadweight loss, including:

a. Direct price regulations that set the price that a firm may charge in a market.

b. Antitrust laws that restrict firms from behaviors that limit competition in a market.

CHAPTER 10

1. In order for a firm to price-discriminate, it must have market power and be able to prevent resale or arbitrage of its product.

2. Under perfect price discrimination, the producer charges each individual customer the price equal to his willingness to pay for the product. As a result, the producer captures all available surplus of the market, maximizing his producer surplus.

3. Direct price discrimination encompasses two types of price discrimination. We discussed the first—perfect or first-degree price discrimination—in our answer to Question 2 above. The second, segmenting or third-degree price discrimination, is the practice of charging different prices to different groups of customers based on identifiable group characteristics.

4. Segmenting may be based on one of a variety of characteristics, including customer characteristics such as age or gender, past purchasing behavior, location, and overtime.

5. Direct price discrimination hinges on the firm's ability to distinguish customers' demand for the product before purchase. In indirect price discrimination, the firm doesn't have this knowledge; instead, it allows customers to choose among a variety of offered prices, effectively having customers sort themselves into groups based on their demand for the product.

6. Incentive compatibility dictates that the price offered to each consumer group must be chosen by that group. Without incentive compatibility, the firm using indirect price discrimination will not be maximizing its producer surplus.

7. A firm that offers different product options designed to attract different types of customers is using yet another pricing strategy—versioning. An airline that offers business class and coach tickets, for example, is betting on versioning to maximize its producer surplus.

8. When segmenting, the firm uses its knowledge of characteristics of specific groups of customers to charge different prices to the groups. Quantity discounting is a form of indirect price discrimination in which firms charge a lower per-unit price to customers who buy larger quantities.

Similar to a quantity discount, block pricing reduces the price of a good when the customer buys more of the good. Unlike both segmenting and quantity discounts, however, block pricing does not depend on customers having different demand curves and price sensitivities; the firm still earns surplus by offering all customers the option of purchasing a greater quantity at a lower price.

9. A firm that uses mixed bundling offers consumers the choice of buying two or more products separately or as a bundle, while pure bundling is a type of bundling in which the firm offers the products only as a bundle.

10. A firm using a two-part tariff breaks the product's price into two components: the standard per-unit price and a fixed fee that must be paid to buy any amount of the product at all.

CHAPTER 11

1. Imperfectly competitive markets have characteristics between those of perfectly competitive and monopolistic markets. Oligopolies and monopolistic competition are two examples of imperfectly competitive markets.

2. Nash equilibrium is an equilibrium in which each firm does the best it can conditional on the actions its competitors take. Since oligopolies are in a stable equilibrium where no firm wants to change its behavior when it learns of its competitors' market behavior, we say that oligopolies reach a Nash equilibrium.

3. A member of a cartel often has a strong incentive to cheat on its collusive agreement to gain more of the market and thus increase its profit. As a result, cartels are extremely instable.

4. The market outcome of Bertrand competition is identical to that of perfect competition: At equilibrium, price equals marginal cost and quantity equals the competitive market quantity. This is because all firms have a strong incentive to continue to cut prices to gain more of the market. Firms will continue to slash prices until all firms charge a price equal to the marginal cost of production.

5. Firms in Bertrand competition set their *prices* simultaneously. In contrast, firms in Cournot competition choose *quantities* simultaneously, and sell their products at the same market price. As a result, the equilibrium in Bertrand competition is the result of price cutting; as we saw in Question 4, this outcome is equivalent to the perfectly competitive equilibrium. The Cournot

equilibrium is based on quantity decisions, and firms in Cournot competition are in equilibrium at the point where their reaction curves intersect.

6. The residual demand curve gives the demand remaining for a firm's output given its competitor firms' outputs.

7. In Cournot competition, the reaction curve shows a firm's best production response to its competitor's possible quantity choices. The Cournot equilibrium occurs at the intersection of the two firms' reaction curves.

8. Unlike in Cournot competition, firms in Stackleberg competition do not choose quantities simultaneously but instead choose sequentially. As a result, the firm that chooses first has the first-mover advantage. This first mover decides the optimal quantity it should produce, and all other firms in the market must react to the first firm's quantity choice.

9. Firms in a Bertrand market with differentiated products hold some market power. As a result, they can price above the perfectly competitive market price that Bertrand oligopolies with identical products face in equilibrium.

10. Three primary characteristics mark a monopolistically competitive firm:
   a. Firms sell differentiated products that consumers do not consider perfect substitutes.
   b. Other firms' choices affect a firm's residual demand curve. However, the firm makes production decisions ignoring the interactions between its own quantity or price choice and its competitors'.
   c. As with a perfectly competitive market, there is free entry into the market.

11. Firms will enter a monopolistically competitive market when firms in the market earn positive economic profits. Entry will continue until economic profits are driven to zero.

12. Firms in monopolistic competition are not price takers, but instead face a downward-sloping demand curve. As a result, a monopolistically competitive firm charges a price above its marginal revenue (and, likewise, its marginal cost), and the market never reaches the perfectly competitive equilibrium.

CHAPTER 12

1. All economic games have three common elements:
   a. Players, or the decision makers in a game
   b. Strategies, or a player's plan of action in a game
   c. Payoffs, or the outcome of a game

2. Unlike single-agent problems, game theory is concerned with situations in which a player's actions affect his opponents' choices and payoffs, and not just her own.

3. In games with multiple Nash equilibria, just as with all games with Nash equilibria, firms' best responses depend on competitor firms' decisions. As a result, we can narrow down the possible outcomes but cannot determine the final outcome of the game prior to its being played.

4. The payoff matrix incorporates information about all three elements of a game—its players, their possible strategies, and the associated payoffs—and therefore can be used to eliminate dominant strategies as possible equilibrium outcomes and to find the players' mutual best responses or the strategy that will lead to the Nash equilibrium or equilibria.

5. In some situations, it may be best for the player to choose actions randomly from the set of available pure strategies and therefore to pursue a mixed strategy. One example would be in a game in which a pure strategy does not lead to a mutual best response (i.e., two checks using the check-box method).

6. A player using a maximin strategy is not going for the greatest payoff, but rather is choosing the conservative strategy of minimizing her losses.

7. Backward induction allows us to consider all steps in a multistep game. To use backward induction, we solve first for the game's final step, and then proceed backward.

8. A player using a grim trigger strategy cooperates with her opponent so long as his opponent is also cooperative. If her opponent cheats, the player permanently ends the game. In tit for tat, the player instead mimics her opponent's actions. When the opponent cooperates, so does she; when the opponent cheats, the player cheats in the next period.

9. Unlike a normal-form matrix, a decision tree incorporates information about the timing of decisions, a piece of information that is key to the outcome of a sequential game.

10. In some games, a player may offer a side payment to his opponent. This payment is designed to ensure the opponent chooses the strategy optimal to the player, and provides both with a greater outcome than they would receive in a game without side payments.

11. Entry deterrence relies on credibility. Without it, the claim a firm makes about its actions once new firms enter is simply an empty threat. With credible commitment, a firm's threat can deter entrance, and allows the firm to earn greater profits than it would in a market with more firms.

12. A reputation—for fighting lawsuits, for aggressively competing against new entrants, or for being unpredictable or crazy, among other actions—signals a commitment to a game-playing strategy, and can prevent new entrants to the market, as well as affect other market behaviors of competitors.

CHAPTER 13

1. Investment is defined as the purchase of capital now with the intent of reaping future benefits from that capital. Examples of investment include the purchase of stocks and bonds, as well as economic transactions such as a retail firm's investment in a new store or a manufacturing company's purchase of a new production technology.

2. Present discounted value (PDV) analysis uses interest rates and compounding to put all payments in terms of equivalent present-period dollars. The advantage of PDV analysis is that it enables us to compare payments that occur across different time periods.

3. The interest rate is calculated as the interest paid on assets as a fraction of the principal, or size of the assets.

4. A typical bond consists of a regular periodic payment that recurs over the bond's entire life, or until the bond has matured. This is calculated as the bond's coupon rate multiplied by the second part of a bond's payment stream—its face value. A bond's face value is the lump-sum payment paid out to the bondholder when a bond matures.

5. An investment's net present value will be positive when the PDV of its benefits outweighs the PDV of its costs. This suggests that the investment is worthwhile.

6. While payback periods are a relatively simple way to compare an investment's initial costs to its future benefits, they do not discount an investment's future payouts by an interest rate. As a result, payback period analysis is less reliable than NPV analysis, which considers the *present-day value* costs and benefits of an investment.

7. An investment's nominal interest rate expresses rates of return in raw currency values, while the real interest rate expresses rates of return in terms of purchasing power. The real interest

rate approximately equals the nominal interest rate minus the inflation rate.

8. The equilibrium interest rate, like any market price, occurs at the intersection of the supply and demand of capital. In the market for capital, the demand for capital consists of firms and households making investment decisions, and the suppliers of capital, or investors, are people with the funds available to make investments.

9. Expected value takes into account the uncertainty associated with an investment by using the probability that an investment payout will occur. More specifically, it is equal to the sum of the product of each possible payout and the probability that such a payout will occur.

10. Insurance benefits a risk-averse consumer because it reduces the uncertainty associated with a given investment or situation. This reduction in uncertainty increases the policyholder's expected utility.

11. Because insurance companies insure many consumers, the companies can rely on diversification to reduce their own risk, as well as to earn net profits on their insurance policies. Diversification reduces the risk to an insurer by combining uncertain (and unrelated) outcomes across all policyholders. As a result, the insurer will most likely only have to pay claims on a portion of its insurance policies, while collecting premiums from all those remaining.

12. The risk-free interest rate is the rate that any asset paying a guaranteed return would pay. For risky investments, risk-averse investors demand interest rates that are higher than the risk-free rate.

CHAPTER 14

1. General equilibrium analysis describes economic markets in two distinct ways. The first describes economic markets as they are in the real world. The second branch of general equilibrium analysis aims to describe markets as they ought to exist, and attempts to define what constitutes an efficient or equitable market.

2. We looked at three types of social welfare functions: utilitarian, Rawlsian, and egalitarian. A utilitarian social welfare function is simply the total sum of every individual's welfare. In the Rawlsian worldview, social welfare is determined by the utility of the worst-off individual and therefore the social welfare function is equal to the minimum utility level across individuals. The egalitarian social welfare function posits that the ideal society is one in which every individual is equally well off.

3. Most economists consider a market's efficiency using the concept of Pareto efficiency. A Pareto-efficient allocation is one in which you could not reallocate the goods without making at least one individual worse off than before.

4. In order for an economy to be considered efficient, it must exhibit exchange, input, and output efficiency.

5. The Edgeworth box can be used to examine market efficiency, including exchange, input, and output efficiency. It plots the allocation of two goods (products or inputs) between two economic actors (either consumers or firms).

6. Two goods are allocated efficiently when the consumers' marginal rates of substitution are equal to the ratio of the goods' prices. A Pareto-efficient allocation can be found at the tangency between the two consumers' indifference curves.

7. The contract curve is the line that shows the collection of all possible Pareto-efficient allocations.

8. An economy exhibits input efficiency when the two firms' marginal rates of technical substitution equal the ratio of the wage rate to the capital rental rate. An efficient input allocation can be found at the tangency between the two firms' isoquants.

9. Similar to the contract curve for consumers, the production contract curve is the line that shows the collection of all possible Pareto-efficient input allocations.

10. The marginal rate of transformation is the tradeoff between how much of one output must be given up to gain an additional unit of the other output. This can be seen on the production possibilities frontier—which connects all possible Pareto-efficient output combinations—as the slope of the production possibilities frontier at a given point.

11. The First Welfare Theorem relies on many conditions that often do not hold in the real world. The first assumption is that firms operate in a perfectly competitive market. The theorem also relies on the absence of market power and of several concepts explored in the next chapter—asymmetric information, externalities, and public goods.

12. The Second Welfare Theorem predicts that every Pareto-efficient allocation is a general equilibrium outcome for some initial allocation.

CHAPTER 15

1. In a market with complete information—such as a perfectly competitive market—all parties in an economic transaction know the relevant information. Markets with asymmetric informa-

tion are perhaps more common. These are markets in which one party knows more than the other party in the economic transaction.

2. The lemons problem arises in markets in which the seller knows more about the quality of the good than does the buyer.

3. Adverse selection is the offering of a disproportionately high number of low-quality to high-quality goods on the market. In a market with the lemons problem, buyers cannot tell the difference between low- and high-quality goods prior to purchase, and the price they are willing to pay for high-quality goods is below the price at which sellers are willing to part with high-quality goods; therefore, adverse selection results.

4. Warranties serve as a signal to potential buyers that a product is of relatively high quality. This is because the seller of a low-quality good isn't going to offer a warranty—it's too expensive for him to offer a warranty on a product he knows is a lemon.

5. In the insurance market, buyers (potential insurance holders) know more about their likelihood to file claims than do the insurance companies. A variety of solutions to this asymmetric information problem that results in adverse selection of buyers into the insurance market include:

   a. Group policies, which pool together a group of people with a wide array of risks

   b. Screening, which vets potential insurance holders for the likelihood that they will file claims

   c. Denying coverage, such as what happens to people with preexisting health conditions in the health insurance market

6. Moral hazard arises when one party in an economic transaction cannot observe the other party's behavior. Moral hazard is a particular problem in insurance markets where policyholders, once insured, make fewer efforts to avoid the bad outcomes that insurance will now cover.

7. Insurance companies take a range of actions to mitigate moral hazard. They may specify certain actions that a policyholder must take in order to be covered, such as installing smoke detectors. Practices such as good driver policies give policyholders incentives to take actions to reduce risk. Lastly, deductibles, copayments, and coinsurance directly connect the policyholder's payoff to the insurer's payoff.

8. Two main market characteristics combine to create principal-agent problems. First, the principal (e.g., employer) must be unable to fully observe the agent's (e.g., employee's) actions.

Second, the self-interests of the principal and agent must not align.

9. Principals want to align their agents' incentives with their own. To do so, principals can compensate agents in such a way that they face the same incentives the principals would face if they were making the agents' choices for them. Payment structures such as commissions, piece rates, and annual bonuses are designed with this goal in mind.

10. Signaling is a situation in which a knowledgeable party communicates an unobservable characteristic to the other party. This communication of information can resolve the asymmetric information problem in many markets.

11. In the classic signaling model, education is a costly action that has no impact on an individual's productivity yet can reveal information about that worker to potential employers. Because it is too costly for low-productivity workers to pursue, only high-productivity workers obtain a degree. On the job market, that degree serves as a signal of the individual's productivity to potential employers.

12. Signals may be used in all facets of life. Purchasing an engagement ring would signal your commitment to marriage. Parking an expensive car in your driveway would let your neighbors know of your wealth. And, wearing a nice suit to work gives your employer an idea of just how seriously you take your job.

CHAPTER 16

1. Negative externalities, like pollution, impose costs on third parties not directly involved in the economic transaction. Positive externalities confer benefits on third parties. Factors such as education and increased immunizations provide benefits to people beyond those directly involved.

2. In an unregulated market, firms pay only the private cost of the good. For a good with a negative externality, this private cost does not equal the social cost of the good, since the external marginal cost of the good is positive. As a result, firms face lower costs than the social cost and overproduce the good.

3. The efficient production level of an externality occurs at the intersection between the social marginal cost curve (equal to the private marginal costs plus external marginal costs) and the social demand curve (equal to the private marginal benefits plus external marginal benefits).

4. The marginal benefit of pollution curve allows us to consider how much it would cost a firm

to reduce the level of pollution it creates and therefore is equivalent to the marginal cost of cutting pollution, also known as the marginal abatement cost.

5. A Pigouvian tax is a tax that equals the external marginal cost imposed by an externality. This tax rate shifts marginal costs up to the social marginal cost, resulting in efficient production on the market.

6. The holder of a government-issued tradable permit has two options: The firm may emit a certain level of pollution allowed by the permit, or the firm may trade its permit to another firm in the industry. By restricting the number of tradable permits issued, the government puts a cap on the amount of pollution that a given industry can produce. At the same time, since permits may be traded, the policy allows pollution across individual firms to vary and effectively creates a market for pollution.

7. In a market in which the optimal level of the externality is known, a price-based mechanism such as a Pigouvian tax or a quantity-based mechanism such as a quota or tradable permits market will produce the same efficient result. But when the optimal level is unknown, a deadweight loss is produced. Depending on market characteristics, a Pigouvian tax or a quantity-based mechanism will prove more optimal. In particular, the deadweight loss from regulation is minimized in a market with a relatively flat marginal abatement cost curve when a quantity regulation is imposed. A Pigouvian tax is more optimal in a market with a relatively steep marginal abatement cost curve.

8. The tragedy of the commons is the phenomenon whereby anyone can use a common resource without restraint. As a result, that common resource is used more intensely than it would if it were privately held. As with other negative externalities, Pigouvian taxes or quantity-based mechanisms are one set of solutions to the tragedy of the commons. Another solution is to grant property rights to an individual, transforming the resource from one that is commonly held to one that is privately held.

9. The Coase theorem predicts that economic parties will reach the optimal level of an externality if they can costlessly negotiate with one another, regardless of who holds the property rights.

10. Public goods are nonexcludable and nonrival. This means that anyone can access and use the good (nonexcludable), and that any one person's consumption of the good does not diminish another consumer's enjoyment of it (nonrival).

11. When produced efficiently, a public good's total marginal benefit—the vertically combined marginal benefit curves of all its individual consumers—equals its marginal cost.

12. A free-rider is an individual who uses a good or service without paying for it. Since a public good is nonexcludable and nonrival, the free-rider problem arises.

CHAPTER 17

1. *Homo economicus*, unlike the typical human, follows the principles and predictions of economics exactly. He knows what he wants and how to get it, and can solve any and every economic problem he faces (no matter how complicated) with no mistakes.

2. Overconfidence—a trait that afflicts the average human but not *Homo economicus*—is a person's belief that his skill level or judgment is better than it actually is.

3. Hyperbolic discounting leads consumers to prefer payoffs in the present to future payoffs, even if the future payoff is of greater monetary value.

4. A *time-inconsistent* person's actions differ across time. The choice he makes today is different from the choice he makes in the future and that fact makes self-control issues like a game theory battle between two different people. As a result, it is difficult to analyze his behavior using traditional economic theory and models.

5. The endowment effect states that an individual's perception of the value of an object is altered by owning the good. In other words, the pain a person suffers from giving up the object is greater than the pleasure he experienced when receiving it—a fact not taken into consideration in traditional economic models.

6. Nominal loss aversion refers specifically to the instance when individuals care about the nominal—not inflation-adjusted—value of their loss, whereas loss aversion in the standard economic model assumes that consumers respond to real variables.

7. Anchoring is the tendency to base a decision on the specific pieces of information that were given. As one possible example, a shopper who first looks at high-end designer dresses may be more likely to pay a high price for the dress she eventually purchases than the person who first checks out the bargain rack.

8. Mental accounting describes a bias in which individuals divide their current and future assets into separate, nontransferable portions. Mentally apportioning income into separate purchasing

and saving categories may affect how much a person spends and what he spends it on.

9. Economists account for the "warm glow" of altruism by incorporating generosity into the utility function, or allowing a person's utility to depend on not only his own consumption but also the consumption of other people, such as his children.

10. Irrational or biased actors tend to lose out to more rational, economically sound market participants. As a result, people who exhibit economic biases are often weeded out of the market.

11. Laboratories differ from real life in several key ways that make lab experiments potentially problematic. First, individuals' behaviors tend to change when they know they are being watched by an experimenter. Second, the stakes of economic games played in the lab are much lower than those played in real life. In addition, participants are often asked to perform tasks in the lab that are foreign to them, and in real life, people do not assume away their cultural norms. Even so, lab experiments allow experimental economists to test and gain insights into many economic theories.

12. A natural experiment is a situation in which, by chance, something happens that allows the researcher to learn about an economic question. A field experiment uses randomization, just as in the lab, but is carried out in real-world settings. Both natural and field experiments allow economists to examine economic actors in their natural environments, and field experiments, like lab experiments, give economists a degree of control over the way in which the theory is tested.

Solutions to Select End-of-Chapter Problems

CHAPTER 2

2. a. The demand curve for organic carrots when $P_C = 5$ and $I = 10$ becomes

$$Q_O^D = 75 - 5P_O + 5 + (2 \times 10) = 100 - 5P_O$$

In other words,

$$5P_O = 100 - Q_O^D$$

$$P_O = 20 - \frac{1}{5}Q_O^D$$

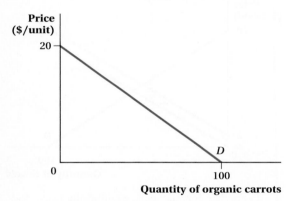

Price ($/unit)

Quantity of organic carrots

b. For $P_O = 10$, the quantity demanded is

$$Q_O^D = 100 - (5 \times 10) = 50$$

c. When $P_O = 5$, the quantity demanded of organic carrots is

$$Q_O^D = 100 - (5 \times 5) = 75$$

d. Suppose $P_O = 10$ and $P_C = 15$, and $I = 10$; then

$$Q_O^D = 75 - 5P_O + 15 + (2 \times 10) =$$
$$75 - (5 \times 10) + 15 + (2 \times 10) = 60$$

Thus, there has been a change in the quantity demanded due to the change in the price of conventional carrots, which leads to an outward shift in the demand curve for organic carrots. The new function represented by D_2 is

$$Q_O^D = 75 - 5P_O + 15 + (2 \times 10) = 110 - 5P_O$$

$$\rightarrow P_O = 22 - \frac{1}{5}Q_O^D$$

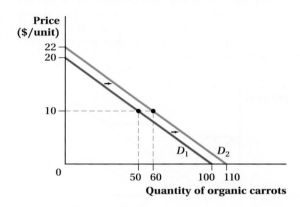

Price ($/unit)

Quantity of organic carrots

e. When the price of conventional carrots increases, the demand for organic carrots shifts, which leads to an increase in the quantity demanded for organic carrots at the original price.

f. An increase in income shifts out the demand curve for organic carrots. Hence, as the average consumer income increases, the quantity demanded of organic carrots increases. Such an observation is consistent with the definition of a normal good.

3. a. Since tea and coffee are the classic examples of substitutes, as the price of tea increases, the demand for coffee is likely to increase.

b. An increase in the price of doughnuts decreases the quantity demanded of doughnuts. Because doughnuts and coffee are complements, this will likely decrease the demand for coffee.

c. A decrease in the price of coffee will decrease the quantity demanded of coffee via a movement along the demand curve.

d. The Surgeon General's announcement will likely increase the number of people who are interested in drinking coffee and, thus, increase the demand for coffee.

e. Heavy rain will decrease the supply of coffee. This can be shown as an inward shift of the supply curve. As a result, the equilibrium price increases and the equilibrium quantity decreases. This adjustment is accomplished via a movement along the demand curve.

6. The hard freeze causes the supply curve to shift in. On the other hand, the information released by the *Journal of the American Medical Association* shifts the demand curve out.

   In this particular scenario, both events will tend to increase the price of orange juice, assuming that the supply and demand curves are not special cases in terms of elasticity. Yet, the effect on quantity of orange juice sold is ambiguous as it depends on the magnitude of the shifts in the two curves.

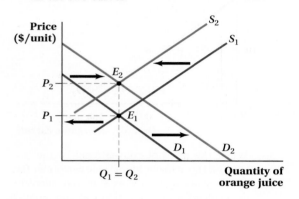

10. a. The inverse supply is

$$P = \frac{Q^S}{10}$$

whereas the inverse demand is

$$P = 20 - \frac{1}{5}Q^D$$

The graph is shown below.

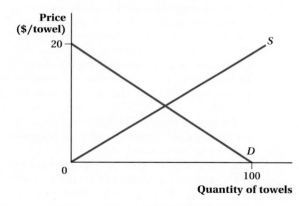

b. Define Q_E and P_E as equilibrium quantity and price, respectively. In equilibrium, price is such that demand is equal to supply. Therefore in equilibrium,

$$\frac{Q^S}{10} = 20 - \frac{Q^D}{5}$$

$$\frac{Q_E}{10} = 20 - \frac{Q_E}{5}$$

$$Q_E = 200 - 2Q_E$$

$$3Q_E = 200$$

$$Q_E = \frac{200}{3} = 66\frac{2}{3}$$

The equilibrium price is then

$$P_E = \frac{Q_E}{10} = \frac{\frac{200}{3}}{10} = \frac{20}{3} = 6\frac{2}{3}$$

c. The new supply function is

$$Q^S = 10P - 20$$

Hence, the new inverse supply function is

$$P = \frac{1}{10}Q^S + 2$$

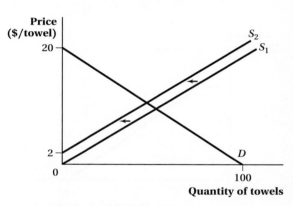

d. Solving for the new equilibrium price and quantity, we get

$$\frac{Q^S}{10} + 2 = 20 - \frac{Q^D}{5}$$

$$\frac{Q_E}{10} + 2 = 20 - \frac{Q_E}{5}$$

$$Q_E + 20 = 200 - 2Q_E$$

$$3Q_E = 180$$

$$Q_E = 60$$

The equilibrium price is now

$$P_E = \frac{Q_E}{10} + 2 = \frac{60}{10} + 2 = 8$$

13. a. In equilibrium, $Q^S = Q^D$ so that

$$Q^D = 100 - P = -20 + 2P = Q^S$$

$$100 - P = -20 + 2P$$

$$P_E = 40$$

The equilibrium price for pillows is 40.

b. The equilibrium quantity is

$$Q_E = 100 - P_E = 60$$

c. The equilibrium quantity using the supply equation is

$$Q^S = -20 + 2P_E = 60 = Q_E$$

Hence, $Q^S = Q^D = Q_E$, just like what was obtained in (b).

d. The elasticity of supply or demand can be calculated using the expression

$$E = \frac{1}{\text{slope of the inverse demand curve}} \times \frac{P}{Q}$$

Note that $P = 40$ and $Q = 60$ at the equilibrium point. The slope of the demand curve is -1, so that

$$E_D = \frac{1}{-1} \times \frac{40}{60} = -\frac{2}{3}$$

whereas the slope of our supply curve is 0.5, so that

$$E_S = \frac{1}{0.5} \times \frac{40}{60} = \frac{4}{3}$$

The elasticity of demand lies within the interval $-1 < E_D < 0$. Hence, the demand is inelastic. The coefficient of elasticity of supply is elastic. Out of the two, the supply is more elastic.

e. Inverting the demand function, we get

$$Q^D = 100 - P$$
$$P = 100 - Q^D$$

Inverting the supply function yields

$$Q^S = -20 + 2P$$
$$P = 0.5Q^S + 10$$

At the equilibrium, we get

$$100 - Q^D = \frac{Q^S}{2} + 10$$
$$100 - Q_E = \frac{1}{2}Q_E + 10$$
$$\frac{3}{2}Q_E = 90$$
$$Q_E = 60$$
$$P_E = 100 - Q_E = 40$$

Therefore, the equilibrium point coincides with our previous answer. Since the equilibrium point is the same and since the slopes of both curves are also unchanged, the elasticities will correspond to the previously derived coefficients in part (d).

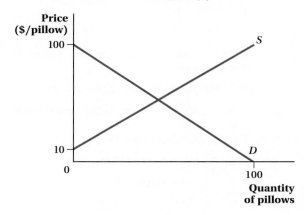

18. a. Consider increasing frog's legs from 1 to 3; that is, by 200%. On the other hand, the price decreases from $3 to $1; that is, by 200%. Hence, the price elasticity of demand is

$$E_D = \frac{\%\Delta Q^D}{\%\Delta P} = \frac{200\%}{-200\%} = -1$$

The demand curve is unit-elastic.

b. The revenue function is given by

$$P \times Q = P \times \frac{3}{P} = 3$$

so it does not matter how many frog's legs are sold. As long as the quantity is positive, the revenue is $3.

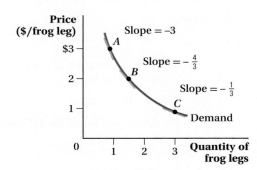

CHAPTER 3

7. a. Solving for the equilibrium price and quantity, we get

$$Q^S = 30P - 2{,}000 = 6{,}000 - 20P = Q^D$$

$$50P = 8{,}000$$

$$P^* = \$160$$

Thus, the equilibrium price is $160. The equilibrium quantity is

$$30P - 2{,}000 = 30 \times 160 - 2{,}000 = 2{,}800$$

Hence, 2,800 divers are being served each year.

b. The demand choke price is

$$Q^D = 6{,}000 - 20P$$

$$0 = 6{,}000 - 20P$$

$$P = \$300$$

Thus, the consumer surplus is

$$\frac{1}{2} \times (2{,}800 - 0) \times (\$300 - \$160) = \$196{,}000$$

c. The supply choke price is

$$Q^S = 30P - 2{,}000$$

$$0 = 30P - 2{,}000$$

$$P \approx \$66.67$$

Thus, the producer surplus is

$$\frac{1}{2} \times (2{,}800 - 0) \times (\$160 - \$66.67) \approx \$130{,}662$$

d. The new demand function is $Q^D = 7{,}000 - 20P$. The new equilibrium price is

$$Q^S = 30P - 2{,}000 = 7{,}000 - 20P = Q^D$$

$$50P = 9{,}000$$

$$P^* = \$180$$

Thus, the new equilibrium price is $180. The new equilibrium quantity is

$$30 \times 180 - 2{,}000 = 3{,}400$$

Hence, 3,400 divers are being served each year.

The new demand choke price is

$$0 = 7{,}000 - 20P$$

$$P = \$350$$

The new consumer surplus is

$$\frac{1}{2} \times (3{,}400 - 0) \times (\$350 - \$180) = \$289{,}000$$

The new producer surplus is

$$\frac{1}{2} \times (3{,}400 - 0) \times (\$180 - \$66.67) \approx \$192{,}661$$

e. The consumers are better off, as the consumer surplus increases by

$$\$289{,}000 - \$196{,}000 = \$93{,}000$$

10. a. The cost to consumers in lost surplus is

Areas A and $B = (0.5 - 0) \times (\$4 - \$3) +$

$$\frac{1}{2} \times (1 - 0.5) \times (\$4 - \$3) = \$0.75$$

Since the quantity is measured in millions of pounds, the cost to consumers is $750,000.

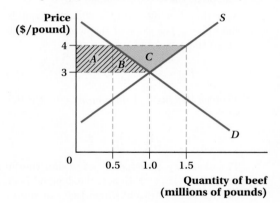

b. The cost to taxpayers is

$$(1.5 - 0.5) \times \$4 = \$4$$

Therefore, the cost to taxpayers is $4,000,000.

c. The gain in producer surplus is

Areas A, B, and $C =$ Cost to consumers $+$

$$\frac{1}{2} \times (1.5 - 0.5) \times (\$4 - \$3) = \$1.25$$

Thus, producers gain $1,250,000.

d. The loss to society is

$$\$4{,}000{,}000 + \$750{,}000 - \$1{,}250{,}000 = \$3{,}500{,}000$$

e. The gain of producers from the scheme is $1,250,000. Therefore, compensating the producers marginally above their gain should suffice. It costs consumers and taxpayers collectively $2.2 million instead of $4.75 million; the scheme is better for all parties concerned.

11. The price increases from P^* to P_{Quota}. The producer surplus before the introduction of the quota was represented by areas D and E. After the quota, the producer surplus is areas B and D. The overall effect on the producer surplus

is ambiguous and depends on the elasticities of supply and demand. The consumer surplus before the introduction of the quota was areas $A + B + C$. After the quota, the consumer surplus shrunk to area A. The deadweight loss is areas $C + E$.

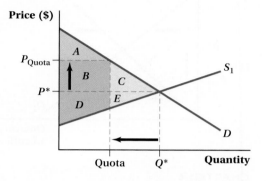

15. a. The inverse demand function is

$$Q^D = 20 - 2P$$

$$P = 10 - 0.5Q^D$$

The inverse supply curve is

$$Q^S = 4P - 10$$

$$P = 2.5 + 0.25Q^S$$

The equilibrium price is

$$Q^D = 20 - 2P = 4P - 10 = Q^S$$

$$6P = 30$$

$$P^* = \$5$$

The equilibrium quantity is

$$20 - (2 \times 5) = 10 \text{ gallons of ice cream}$$

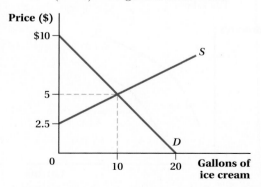

b. The demand curve shifts inward by the amount of the tax. See the graph that follows.

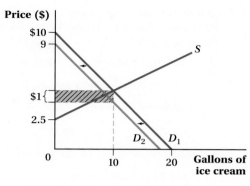

c. The buyers face a new price $P_S + \text{TAX}$, and sellers sell at P_S:

$$Q^D = 20 - 2 \times (P_S + 1) = 4P_S - 10 = Q^S$$

$$6P_S = 28$$

$$P_S \approx 4.67$$

Hence, buyers pay \$5.67 and sellers sell at \$4.67.

The quantity sold is

$$4 \times 4.67 - 10 = 8.68$$

d. After the \$1 tax, buyers pay \$5.67 for a gallon of ice cream. After the buyers send in the tax, the sellers only end up with \$4.67 per gallon sold. Therefore, of the \$1 going to the government, approximately 67% of it is coming out of consumers' pockets because their price went up by 67 cents per gallon. The price realized by the suppliers goes down by approximately 33 cents per gallon. The incidence of this tax is 67% on the buyers and 33% on the seller. Hence, buyers bear a proportionately greater burden of the tax. This happens when demand is relatively inelastic when compared to supply, which in this case is relatively elastic.

e. Before the tax, the demand choke price is \$10 per gallon of ice cream. Hence, the consumer surplus is

$$\frac{1}{2} \times (10 - 0) \times (\$10 - \$5) = \$25$$

After the tax, the demand choke price is \$9 per gallon of ice cream. Hence, the consumer surplus is

$$\frac{1}{2} \times (8.68 - 0) \times (\$10 - \$5.67) \approx \$18.79$$

Or if you reduce the choke price and use the gross price of \$4.67, the consumer surplus is still

$$\frac{1}{2} \times (8.68 - 0) \times (\$9 - \$4.67) \approx \$18.79$$

f. Before the tax, the supply choke price is $2.50 per gallon of ice cream. Hence, the producer surplus is

$$\frac{1}{2} \times (10 - 0) \times (\$5 - \$2.50) \approx \$12.50$$

After the tax, the producer surplus is

$$\frac{1}{2} \times (8.68 - 0) \times (\$4.67 - \$2.50) =$$

$$0.5 \times 8.68 \times \$2.17 \approx \$9.42.$$

g. The tax revenue raised by the government is

$$\$1 \times 8.68 \approx \$8.68$$

h. The tax creates the deadweight loss of

$$0.5 \times 1 \times \$1.33 \approx \$0.67$$

17. A per-unit tax shifts the supply curve in. The price goes up and the quantity sold goes down. The consumer surplus before the tax is areas $A + B + C + D$. The consumer surplus after the tax is area A. The producer surplus before the tax is areas $E + F + G + H$. The producer surplus after the tax is F. The deadweight loss is $D + G$. The tax revenue is areas $B + C + E + H$. Suppliers bear the larger burden of this tax.

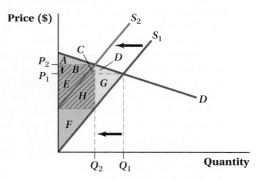

19. a. The equilibrium price of coffee would go down.
    b. The equilibrium quantity of coffee depends on the elasticities of supply and demand; therefore, the change can occur in any direction.
    c. In the first scheme, the subsidization has an effect on the equilibrium price and quantity of coffee after the introduction of the tax. In particular, the subsidization will decrease the equilibrium price and increase the equilibrium quantity of coffee. In the second scheme, after the introduction of the tax, splitting

the revenue among coffee vendors does not cause any change to the equilibrium price and quantity.

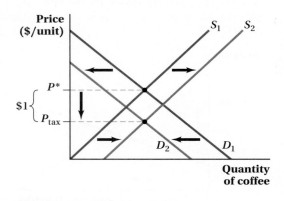

CHAPTER 4

4. In the figures that follow, bundles along the indifference curve labeled U_2 are strictly preferred to bundles along the indifference curve U_1.
   a. Both pencils and pens are goods for Paul.

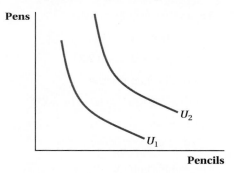

   b. Carrots are a good and broccoli is a bad for Rhonda.

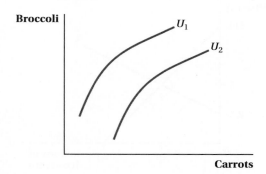

c. Hip-hop is a good, heavy metal is a neutral.

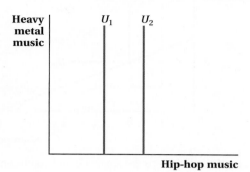

d. Dress shirts and cufflinks are perfect complements.

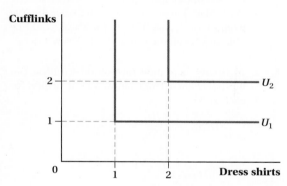

5. A and B are two bundles on the same indifference curve, U_1, so any bundle that lies along the straight line joining A and B will lie on a higher indifference curve. Bundle C, consisting of 3 peaches and 2 apples, is such a bundle so John will choose bundle C over bundle A.

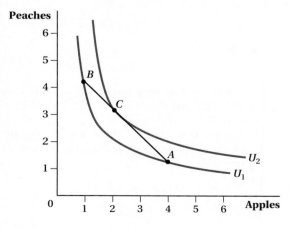

7. a.

$$U(1, 2) = (1)(2) = 2$$
$$U(2, 1) = (2)(1) = 2$$
$$U(5, 2) = (5)(2) = 10$$

b.

Bundle	Quantity of X	Quantity of Y	Utility
A	2	2	4
B	10	0	0
C	1	5	5
D	3	2	6
E	2	3	6

From the table, $U(D) = U(E) > U(C) > U(A) > U(B)$ and we have the ranking ($>$ denotes strictly preferred, $\sim$ denotes indifferent)

$$D \sim E > C > A > B$$

c.

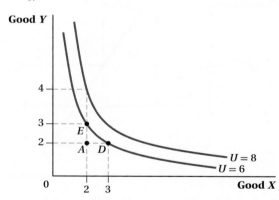

The "more is better" assumption is satisfied.

d.

Bundle	Quantity of X	Quantity of Y	MU_X	MU_Y
F	1	2	2	1
G	2	2	2	2
H	1	3	3	1

e. Comparing bundle F and G, $MU_X = 2$ for both bundles. MU_X is constant.

15. a.

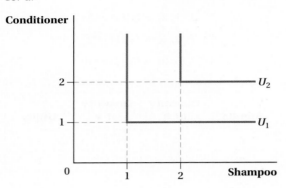

b. Mitzi's budget constraint is

$$4S + 2C = 12$$

Since Mitzi likes to consume the two goods, shampoo and conditioner, in a 1 to 1 ratio, she can purchase together 1 unit of each for a total of $2 + $4 = $6. With $I = 12 of income, Mitzi can afford 2 units of each.

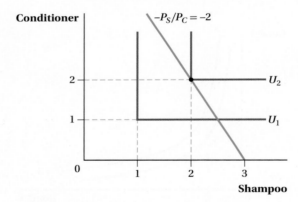

c. When there is a change in prices so that $P_S + 2 and $P_C = 4, the new budget constraint for Mitzi will be $2S + 4C = 12$. The slope of the budget constraint is now $-\dfrac{P_S}{P_C} = -\dfrac{1}{2}$, but the total cost of a unit of each good (Mitzi's ideal consumption ratio) is still $6, so she can afford to purchase 2 units of each good.

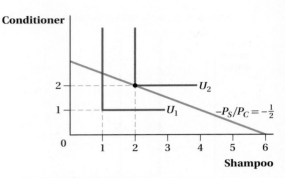

d. If Mitzi likes to use shampoo and conditioner in the ratio 2 to 1, then under the original prices, a bundle consisting of $S = 2$ and $C = 1$ would have cost $2(4) + 1(2) = 10. With the change in prices, the same bundle would cost $2(2) + 1(4) = 8. Mitzi would be able to consume more under the new prices.

17. a. Anthony's marginal rate of substitution can be determined from his marginal utility for each good:

$$MRS_{LG} = \frac{MU_L}{MU_G} = \frac{0.5L^{-0.5}G^{0.5}}{0.5L^{0.5}G^{-0.5}}$$

$$= \frac{G}{L} = \frac{2}{1}$$

$$G^* = 2L^*$$

Anthony's optimal bundle must also lie on his budget constraint, $2L + G = 30$. Substituting the relation from the tangency condition gives

$$2L^* + 2L^* = 30$$

$$4L^* = 30$$

$$L^* = 7.5$$

and

$$G^* = 15$$

The optimal consumption bundle is $(L^*, G^*) = (7.5, 15)$, and this will give Anthony utility $U = (7.5)^{0.5}(15)^{0.5} = 10.6$.

b. If there is a doubling in the price of guitar picks to $P_G = 2, then from the tangency condition:

$$MRS_{LG} = \frac{P_L}{P_G}$$

$$\frac{G}{L} = \frac{2}{2}$$

$$G^* = L^*$$

Anthony will want to consume the two goods in equal quantities. In order to maintain utility at $U = 10.6$

$$U(L,G) = L^{0.5}G^{0.5}$$

$$10.6 = L^{0.5}G^{0.5}$$

with $G^* = L^* = k$

$$10.6 = k^{0.5}k^{0.5}$$

$$10.6 = k$$

Anthony will consume the bundle $(L^*, G^*) = (10.6, 10.6)$, which at the new price for guitar picks will cost

$$(2)(10.6) + (2)(10.6) = \$42.40$$

Anthony will require income $I' = \$42.40$ in order to maintain the same level of utility.

18. a. Indifference curves:

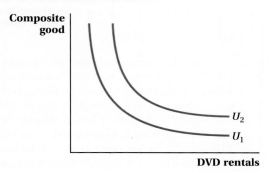

b. À la carte plan:

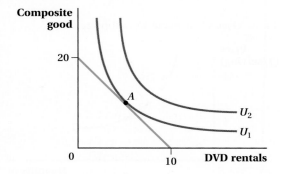

c. Flat-fee plan:

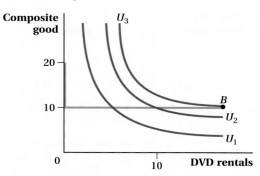

d. The consumer will rent more movies under the flat $10 fee.

e. The consumer's marginal rate of substitution will be lower under the flat $10 fee.

f. Under the flat $10 fee, the consumer is more likely to view many films, even those that are low quality, because the relative price of an additional movie is zero.

CHAPTER 5

3. a.

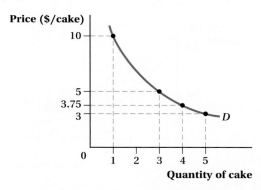

b. When the price of cakes decreases from $10 to $5, the two effects are equivalent. On the other hand, when the price of cakes decreases from $5 to $3.75 and from $3.75 to $3, the dominant effect is the income effect.

c. As the indifference curves become flatter, Andrew's preferences change in that he demands fewer cupcakes relative to cakes (than before) at every price. Hence, the demand curve for cakes will shift up.

5. a.

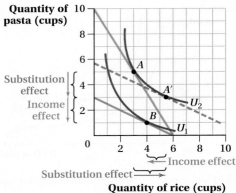

Quantity of pasta (cups)

Substitution effect

Income effect

Income effect

Substitution effect

Quantity of rice (cups)

b. The two effects seem to be equivalent in magnitude for pasta with a decrease of 2 cups of pasta for each effect. As far as rice, the substitution effect dominates the income effect; in particular, the substitution effect increases by 2 cups of rice, whereas the income effect decreases by 1 cup of rice.

11. a. When the price of a movie ticket is $10, Tyler sees 6 movies in the theater.

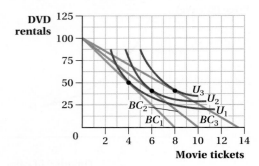

b. Refer to part (e).
c. When the price of a movie ticket is $12.50, Tyler sees 4 movies in the theater.
d. When the price of a movie ticket is $7.50, Tyler sees 8 movies in the theater.

e.

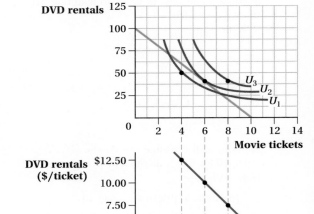

DVD rentals

Movie tickets

DVD rentals ($/ticket)

Quantity of movie tickets

13. a. Carmen's indifference curves are straight, parallel lines. For her, watching a movie and seeing a basketball game are perfect substitutes. Carmen's utility function can be described as $U = X + 2Y$, where X denotes the basketball games and Y denotes the movies.
b. The optimal consumption bundle is to buy 5 basketball games in order to reach the highest feasible utility curve U_4, given the budget constraint.

14. a. Gaston's demand for red beans

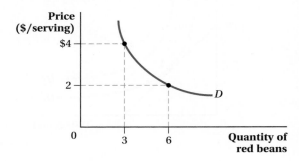

Price ($/serving)

Quantity of red beans

b.

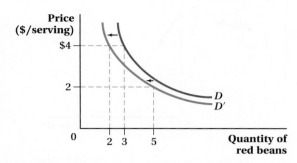

c. When the price of rice increases to $3, the demand for red beans decreases.
d. The changes in prices and quantities are consistent with the definition of complements.

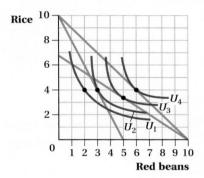

20. a. The implication of the optimal bundle is that Yoshi's income is at least $600. In addition, assuming well-behaved indifference curves implies that Yoshi's income is greater than $600. As a result of the tax and the rebate, the intercepts in the two axes change. The intercept of the horizontal axis, after the tax and the rebate, lies to the left of $Y/3$. The intercept of the vertical axis, after the tax and the rebate, lies above Y. The graph is indicated at the top of the next column. As shown, Yoshi's consumption of soda will decrease and his consumption of the composite good will increase.

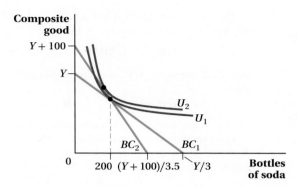

b. Yoshi will be better off as his optimal bundle lies on a higher indifference curve than before.
c. Since Yoshi cuts back on soda, the government raises less than $100 in revenue. At the same time, the government spends $100 subsidizing Yoshi. The government is therefore worse off.

CHAPTER 6

1. a. The firm's output is 600.
   b. Output of 600 can also be achieved with either 3 units of capital and 2 units of labor, 2 units of capital and 3 units of labor, or 1 unit of capital and 6 units of labor.
   c.

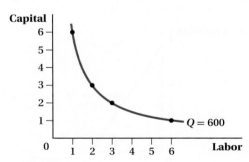

6. a. Labor and capital display diminishing marginal products:

$$MP_K = 2\left(\frac{L}{K}\right)^{0.5}$$

As K increases, MP_K decreases. Similarly,

$$MP_L = 2\left(\frac{K}{L}\right)^{0.5}$$

MP_L is a decreasing function of L. The production function displays a diminishing marginal rate of technical substitution, since

$$MRTS = \frac{MP_L}{MP_K} = \frac{K}{L}$$

Consequently, as L increases, $MRTS$ decreases.

b. In this case, labor and capital do not display diminishing marginal returns. Since

$$MP_K = 4L$$

then as K increases, MP_K remains unchanged. Since

$$MP_L = 4K$$

then as L increases, MP_L remains unchanged.

The production function indeed displays a diminishing marginal rate of technical substitution. Because

$$MRTS = \frac{MP_L}{MP_K} = \frac{K}{L}$$

then as L increases, $MRTS$ decreases. Notice that the $MRTS$ for this production function is identical to the $MRTS$ of the prior function.

c. Labor and capital do not need to display diminishing marginal products in order for the $MRTS$ to diminish.

7. a. The cost function is

$$\$12 \times L + \$7 \times K$$

b.

$$\$100 = \$12 \times L + \$7 \times K$$

$$K = \frac{100}{7} - \frac{12}{7}L$$

c. **Capital (K)**

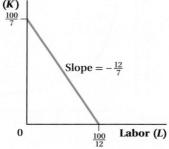

Slope $= -\frac{12}{7}$

d. The vertical intercept indicates the quantity of capital that can be rented with $100 if no labor is hired. The horizontal intercept indicates the quantity of labor that can be hired with $100 if no capital is rented.

e. The slope is the (negative) ratio of the price of labor (wage) and the rental price of capital. The isocost line has a slope of $-\frac{12}{7}$.

f. In this case, the isocost function rotates inward as shown:

$$K = \frac{100}{7} - 2L$$

Capital (K)

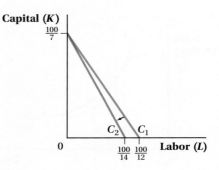

The new isocost line is steeper; the slope is -2.

14. a. The firm's marginal rate of technical substitution is

$$MRTS = \frac{w}{r} = \frac{6}{9} = \frac{2}{3}$$

b.

$$MRTS = \frac{MP_L}{MP_K} = \frac{10\left(\frac{K}{L}\right)^{0.5}}{10\left(\frac{L}{K}\right)^{0.5}} = \frac{2}{3}$$

$$\frac{K}{L} = \frac{2}{3}$$

Using the production function, we get

$$Q = 20K^{0.5}L^{0.5} = 49$$

$$20\left(\frac{2}{3}L\right)^{0.5}L^{0.5} = 49$$

$$L \approx 3$$

Since $K = \frac{2}{3}L$, $K = 2$.

c. The minimum cost of producing 49 iPods is

$$\$6 \times 3 + \$9 \times 2 = \$36$$

d. From the cost function

$$300 = 6L + 9K = 6 \times \frac{3}{2}K + 9K = 18K$$

$$K = \frac{50}{3}. \text{ Hence,}$$

$$L = 25$$

Thus, the maximum number of iPods it can produce is

$$20K^{0.5}L^{0.5} = 20 \times \left(\frac{50}{3}\right)^{0.5} \times 25^{0.5} \approx 408$$

18. a.

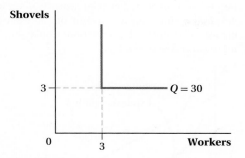

b.

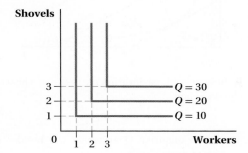

c.

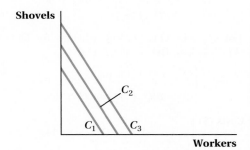

d. The minimum cost at which Mad Max can fulfill the contract is

$$3 \times \$5 + 3 \times \$25 = \$90$$

e. The composition of inputs will not change as Mad Max still needs to have an equal number of workers and shovels.

20. a. With 1 unit of capital and 4 units of labor, Alfred produces

$$10K^{0.5}L^{0.5} = 10 \times 1 \times 2 = 20$$

b. With 2 units of capital,

$$20 = 10 \times 2^{0.5}L^{0.5}$$

$$L = 2$$

Thus, Alfred must hire 2 workers.

c. With 4 units of capital,

$$20 = 10 \times 4^{0.5}L^{0.5}$$

$$L = 1$$

Thus, Alfred must hire 1 worker.

d.

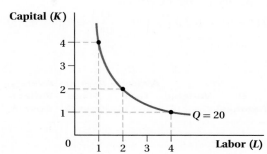

e. The new production function is

$$10K^{-0.7}L^{0.3}$$

To achieve the same level of production with 3 workers,

$$20 = 10K^{-0.7}3^{0.3}$$

$$K \approx 1.681$$

The isoquant curve becomes more flat since, to maintain the level of production, more labor is required to substitute 1 unit of capital.

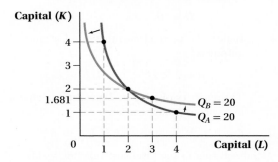

CHAPTER 7

3. a. True. Economic costs include both, accounting costs and the opportunity cost. Conditional on the opportunity cost equalling zero, accounting and economic costs may be equal, but since the opportunity cost cannot be negative, the economic costs are at least as high as the accounting costs.

b. No, it is not possible. The economic profit is the total revenue minus the economic cost, whereas the accounting profit is the total revenue minus the accounting costs. Since economic cost is at least as large as the accounting cost, it is not possible to make an economic profit without making an accounting profit.

5. If Q is assumed to be the production per hour, Amanda's cost function is

$$TC = \$7 \times L = \$7 \times \left(30 + \frac{Q}{100}\right) = 210 + 0.07Q$$

per hour.

9.

Q (batches)	Variable Cost ($)	Average Total Cost ($)	Average Fixed Cost ($)	Average Variable Cost ($)
1	25	75	50	25
2	35	42.5	25	17.5
3	52	34	16.67	17.33
4	77	31.75	12.5	19.25
5	115	33	10	23
6	160	35	8.33	26.67

12. a. Using the optimality condition, we get

$$\frac{MP_L}{MP_K} = \frac{2K}{2L} = \frac{\$200}{\$100} = \frac{W}{r}$$

$$K = 2L$$

Hence, the production function of q units of output is

$$q = 2 \times 2L \times L = 4L^2$$

The quantity of labor and quantity of capital in terms of production are

$$L = 0.5\sqrt{q} \text{ and } q = 2KL = KK = K^2$$

Substituting in the total cost function yields

$$\$100K + \$200L = \$200\sqrt{q}$$

b. The average cost of producing q units of output is

$$\frac{TC}{q} = \frac{200q^{0.5}}{q} = \frac{200}{q^{0.5}} = \frac{\$200}{\sqrt{q}}$$

c. The marginal cost is

$$\frac{\$100}{\sqrt{q}}$$

15. Since labor becomes more expensive, the isocost lines will rotate clockwise (from the blue lines to the red ones).

The long-run expansion path (which shows points of tangency between isocost lines and isoquants) shifts up as a result of the wage increase. The optimal production would employ more capital and less labor.

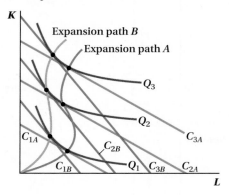

17. A builder will be indifferent between the two choices when

$$ATC_1 = ATC_2$$

Thus, the quantity Q at which the builder of custom motorcycles is different is

$$Q^2 - 6Q + 14 = Q^2 - 10Q + 30$$
$$Q = 4$$

For $Q < 4$, ATC_1 is less, whereas for $Q > 4$, ATC_2 is less. Hence, the $LATC$ is

$$\begin{cases} Q^2 - 6Q + 14, \text{ for } Q \leq 4 \\ Q^2 - 10Q + 30, \text{ for } Q > 4 \end{cases}$$

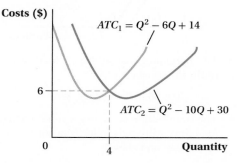

19. a. This Cobb–Douglas production function exhibits constant returns to scale. Hence, the long-run average cost curve is horizontal, whereas the long-run total cost curve is a straight upward-sloping line.

b. Now the production function exhibits increasing returns to scale. The long-run average cost curve is downward-sloping and the total cost curve's slope is positive, but as output increases, the slope declines.

CHAPTER 8

1. a. Nancy should produce 6 pounds of beeswax to maximize profit.
   b. Nancy's maximum profit is $28; she should produce 4 pounds of beeswax to generate that profit.
   c. Marginal revenue and marginal cost are equal.
   d. The marginal cost does not change, so the profit-maximizing quantity stays the same.
   e. Nancy maximizes profit by producing 3 pounds of beeswax.

Quantity	Total Revenue	Fixed Cost	Variable Cost	Total Cost	Profit	Marginal Revenue	Marginal Cost
0	0	15	0	15	−15	—	—
1	50	15	38	53	−3	50	38
2	100	15	81	96	4	50	43
3	150	15	131	146	4	50	50
4	200	15	189	204	−4	50	58
5	250	15	257	272	−22	50	68
6	300	15	337	352	−52	50	80

2. a. The market equilibrium price shown in panel (a) is $4.

   Firms earn economic profit equal to

   $$\pi = (P_4 - P_{LATC}) \times Q > 0$$

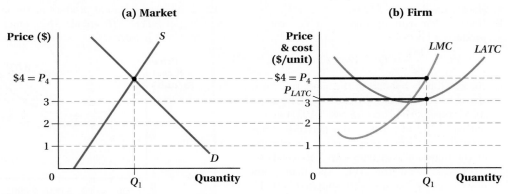

   That is, the profit-maximizing firm will produce Q units, and at that quantity, price is greater than average total cost.

   b. The condition indicated in (a) will result in more firms entering the aloe vera gel industry. This will shift the supply curve out, decreasing the market equilibrium price and increasing the equilibrium quantity.

(a) Market

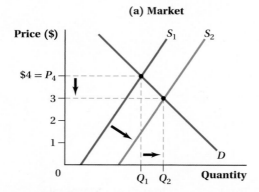

c. The price will decrease. As the price falls, each firm will reduce output and profit will shrink.

d. At a price of $3, the entry will stop; otherwise, the representative firm would experience an economic loss.

(b) Firm

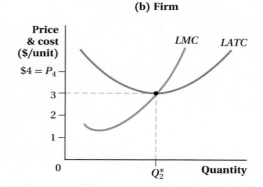

7. a. Hack's fixed cost is $1,000.

   b. Hack's short-run average variable cost of producing berries is

   $$AVC = \frac{VC}{Q} = Q^2 - 12Q + 100$$

   c. Hack will only operate in the short run when the market price is greater than or equal to its average variable cost curve (AVC) at the optimal level of output; the perfectly competitive short-run supply curve is the portion of the marginal cost curve MC above AVC. At prices below the AVC, the firm shuts down; that is, the quantity supplied is 0. To find the minimum price at which Hack is willing to produce, we equalize the marginal cost with the average variable cost so that

   $$Q^2 - 12Q + 100 = 3Q^2 - 24Q + 100$$

   $$2Q(Q - 6) = 0$$

   $$Q = 6$$

   The AVC at $Q = 6$ is

$$AVC = 6^2 - 12 \times 6 + 100 = \$64$$

Thus, if the price is $60, then Hack will not produce any berries, since that price lies below the minimum point of the AVC curve.

   d. Yes. A price of $73 is above the $64 threshold, so Hack should produce a positive number of berries. However, that is only the case for the short run. Since Hack is earning a negative profit once fixed cost is taken into account, he should shut down in the long run.

8. a. The rectangle $ADGH$ represents the total revenue when selling 1,000 units at $100 each.

   b. The variable cost at 1,000 units is represented by the area $MLGH$.

   c. The fixed cost of producing 1,000 units is equal to the area $KJLM$.

   d. The total cost of producing 1,000 units is shown by the area $KJGH$.

   e. The profit from producing 1,000 units is represented by the $ADJK$ area.

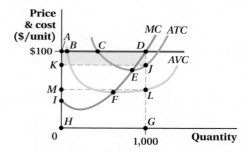

12. a. The seller should produce at the level of output where MR equals MC, which occurs at 5,000 potatoes.

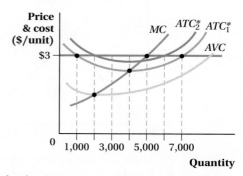

   b. An increase in the mortgage payment increases the fixed cost of production, shifting the average total cost curve up.

   c. Only the average total cost curve shifts. The average variable cost curve remains unchanged since the mortgage payment does not alter the variable cost. Similarly, the marginal cost curve is not affected by the increase in the fixed cost.

d. The change in interest rates has no effect on the producer's decision of how many potatoes to produce in the short run because MC does not shift. (However, if the increased interest rate will increase the total cost of production above total revenue, leading to a negative economic profit, then the potato grower would shut down in the long run.)

e. The potato grower's profit decreases. The total revenue remains unchanged but the total cost of production increases as a result of the increase in fixed cost.

f. The grower's short run supply is the MC curve above AVC. Since neither the MC curve nor the AVC curve shifted, the short run supply curve is unaffected.

17. a. The long-run average total cost of producing canola oil is

$$LATC = \frac{LTC}{Q} = Q^2 - 15Q + 40$$

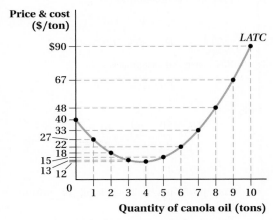

b. The long-run equilibrium price of canola oil is approximately $12, which is the minimum of the $LATC$ curve.

c. Each firm will produce the quantity of canola oil that corresponds to the minimum point on the $LATC$ curve, that is, 4 tons of canola oil.

d. Using the demand function, we get

$$Q^D = 999 - 0.25P = 999 - 0.25 \times 12 = 996$$

At the long-run equilibrium price, consumers will demand approximately 996 tons of canola oil.

e. Since each representative firm supplies 4 tons of canola oil, the number of suppliers in the long-run equilibrium will be

$$\frac{996}{4} = 249$$

CHAPTER 9

4. a., b. and c.

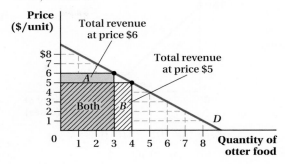

d. As Oscar reduces his price from $6 to $5, the rectangle A represents the loss. This is the revenue lost from decreasing the price.

e. As Oscar reduces his price from $6 to $5, the rectangle B represents the gain. This is the revenue gained from decreasing the price and selling more units.

f. The area of rectangle A is

$$(\$6 - \$5) \times 3 = \$3$$

The area of rectangle B is

$$\$5 \times (4 - 3) = \$5$$

Subtracting area A from area B, we obtain $5 - $3 = $2.

g. The marginal revenue from selling a 4th unit is

$$MR = TR_B - TR_A = (\$5 \times 4) - (\$6 \times 3) = \$2$$

Therefore, the result corresponds to the value obtained in (f).

6. a. The total revenue will increase and the marginal revenue will be positive.

b. The total revenue will decrease and the marginal revenue will be negative.

c. The total revenue will not change and the marginal revenue will be zero.

8. a. The inverse demand function is

$$P = 20 - 0.2Q$$

Thus, the total revenue is

$$TR = P \times Q = 20Q - 0.2Q^2$$

Hence, the marginal revenue can be represented by

$$MR = 20 - 0.4Q$$

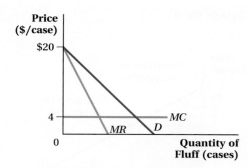

b. Applying the $MR = MC$ rule, we get

$$20 - 0.4Q = 4$$
$$Q = 40$$

The profit-maximizing level of output is 40. The price that the monopolist must charge to maximize profit is

$$P = 20 - (0.2 \times 40) = \$12$$

c. The profit earned by the monopolist is

$$\pi = TR - TC = (\$12 \times 40) - (\$4 \times 40) = \$320$$

d. Suppose that the seller decreases the price by 20 cents to sell one more unit of the good. The profit becomes

$$\pi = TR - TC = (\$11.80 \times 41) - (\$4 \times 41) = \$483.8 - \$164 = \$319.8$$

e. Suppose that the seller increases the price by 20 cents and sells one less unit of the good. The profit becomes

$$\pi = TR - TC = (\$12.20 \times 39) - (\$4 \times 39) = \$319.8$$

9. a. The monopolist will maximize its profit by producing the level of output at which $MR = MC$, that is, 100 dozen bearings.
   b. The monopolist should charge \$100 per dozen to maximize profit.
   c.

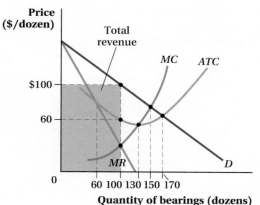

d.

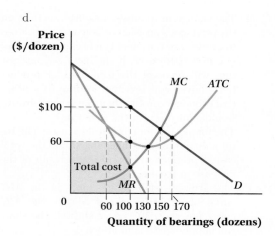

e. The profit is

$$\pi = TR - TC = (100 \times \$100) - (100 \times \$60) = \$4,000$$

10. a. The inverse demand curve is

$$Q = 40 - 0.5P$$
$$P = 80 - 2Q$$

The marginal revenue is

$$MR = 80 - 4Q$$

b.
$$MR = 80 - 4Q = 10 = MC$$
$$4Q = 70$$
$$Q = 17.5$$

The profit-maximizing level of output is 17.5 tons of bentonite.

c. The profit-maximizing price is

$$17.5 = 40 - 0.5P$$
$$0.5P = 40 - 17.5$$
$$P = \$45$$

d. If the marginal cost is $20 + Q$, the profit-maximizing quantity is

$$MR = 80 - 4Q = 20 + Q = MC$$
$$5Q = 60$$
$$Q = 12$$

The profit-maximizing price is

$$12 = 40 - 0.5P$$
$$P = \$56$$

16. a. The marginal revenue is $40 - Q$:

$$MR = 40 - Q = 5 = MC$$
$$Q = 35$$

The unregulated monopolist will sell 35 flux capacitors.

b. The price ceiling is also the marginal revenue for the first 68 units; that is, $MR = 6$ because consumers are willing to pay $6 or more. However, selling the 69th unit requires reducing the price to $5.50. Thus, the total revenue from selling 68 units is $6 \times 68 = \$408$, and the total revenue from selling 69 units is $\$5.50 \times 69 = \$379.50$. Therefore, the marginal revenue of the 69th unit is $-\$28.50$.

c. The monopolist will sell the first 68 units at a price of $6, since the marginal revenue exceeds the marginal cost. The monopolist will not sell the 69th unit because the marginal cost is greater than the marginal revenue.

d. As shown in the diagrams below, the price ceiling indeed reduces the deadweight loss.

Case 1: Unregulated Monopoly

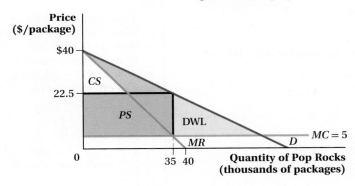

Case 2: Price Ceiling

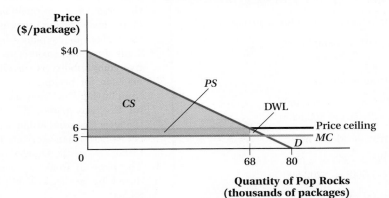

CHAPTER 10

1. a. The profit-maximizing price is P_1 and quantity Q_1.
   b. The consumer surplus is A and B. The producer surplus is C, D, F, G, and I.
   c. The seller will sell Q_2 schnitzels.
   d. Once the seller begins to perfectly price-discriminate, areas A and B, the original consumer surplus, becomes part of the new producer surplus.
   e. Areas E and H are no longer the deadweight loss, but become part of the producer surplus.

5. a. The inverse demand for adults is

$$P = 500 - 0.1Q$$

   Hence, the marginal revenue is

$$500 - 0.2Q$$

   The inverse demand for students is

$$P = 100 - 0.01Q$$

   Hence, the marginal revenue is

$$100 - 0.02Q$$

   b. The profit-maximizing quantity for adults is

$$500 - 0.2Q = 10$$
$$Q = 2,450$$

   The profit-maximizing quantity for students is

$$100 - 0.02Q = 10$$
$$Q = 4,500$$

   c. The profit-maximizing price for adults is

$$500 - (0.1 \times 2,450) = \$255$$

   The profit-maximizing price for students is

$$100 - (0.01 \times 4,500) = \$55$$

   Adults pay more.
   d. The profit from adults is

$$TR - TC = (\$255 \times 2,450) - (\$10 \times 2,450) = \$600,250$$

   The profit from students is

$$TR - TC = (\$55 \times 4,500) - (\$0 \times 4,500) = \$202,500$$

   Hence, the total profit is \$802,750.

e. Given that the capacity is 5,000, continue to sell 2,450 tickets to adults at \$255, which maximizes profit in that segment. Sell the remaining 2,550 tickets for as much as the student segment will bear, \$74.50. So, students should pay \$74.50 = 100 − (0.01 × 2,550). The total profit in this case would be \$164,475 + \$600,250 = \$764,725.

9. a. From the Lerner index,

$$\frac{(P - MC)}{P} = \frac{1}{-E^D}$$

   the price for students is

$$\frac{(P - MC)}{P} = \frac{1}{2}$$
$$P = 2P - 2MC$$
$$= 2MC$$

   The price for adults is

$$\frac{(P - MC)}{P} = \frac{1}{1.5}$$
$$P = 1.5P - 1.5MC$$
$$= 3MC$$

   Thus, adults should be charged a higher price. From microeconomic theory, adults have a more inelastic demand for theater tickets when compared to students, so they should be charged more.
   b. The ratio of prices is

$$\frac{P_{\text{Student}}}{P_{\text{Adult}}} = \frac{2}{3}$$

   Rearranging the above, we obtain $P_{\text{Adult}} = 1.5P_{\text{Student}}$. Therefore, adults are charged 50% more than students.

13. a. The price-conscious consumers will buy the Dundee pianos because their valuation exceeds the price of lower-quality pianos; the price of Rockway pianos exceeds the valuation of the higher-quality pianos by these customers. Thus, for budget-conscious customers, incentive compatibility is sustained. However, the net gain for performance-oriented consumers from buying Dundee pianos is \$2,000, whereas for Rockway pianos it is \$1,500. Therefore, the incentive compatibility condition is violated, as performance-oriented consumers would rather choose the Dundee pianos.
    b. The price of Rockway pianos should be reduced by at least \$500, but by less than \$3,500.

c. Yes, incentive compatibility can be achieved by raising the price of Dundee pianos from $5,000 to at least $5,501 (but not higher than $6,000). Then, budget-conscious consumers will still buy Dundee pianos and performance-oriented professionals will choose the Rockway pianos.

15. a. It may be difficult for Microsoft to be able to observe a customer's demand type before purchase.

b. Word should cost $120, so that only authors buy it, and Excel should cost $150, so that only economists purchase it. The profit is $120 + $150 = $270, since ATC and MC are zero. To sell Word to both groups, the price must equal the maximum willingness to pay of the group which values Word lower; that is, $50. Hence, Word would be sold to both groups and the profit would be $50 + $50 = $100; that is, $20 less than if the price were set at $120. Similarly for Excel, if the price were set at $40, so that both groups would be willing to buy it, the profit would be $80 instead of $150.

c. The price for Microsoft Office should be $160, so that both groups, authors and economists, would be willing to buy the product.

d. The profit from selling the bundled Office to a representative group of one author and one economist is $320. Compared to the $270 profit available from selling Word and Excel separately [see part (a)], bundling generates higher profit.

17. a. The inverse demand function is $P = 2.5 - 0.1Q$. Thus, the marginal revenue is

$$2.5 - 0.2Q$$

The profit-maximizing quantity is

$$MR = 2.5 - 0.2Q = 0.5 = MC$$

$$Q = 10$$

The profit-maximizing price is

$$2.5 - (0.1 \times 10) = \$1.50$$

The profit from the representative customer is

$$TR - TC = (P - ATC) \times Q =$$
$$(\$1.50 - \$0.50) \times 10 = \$10$$

The consumer surplus is area A.

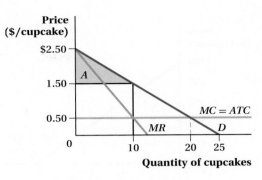

Thus, the consumer surplus is

$$\frac{1}{2} \times (\$2.50 - \$1.50) \times 10 = \$5$$

b. and c. The demand function does not change. Consider the "discounted" part of the demand function.

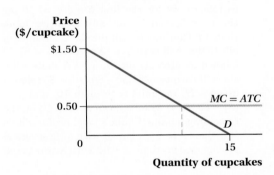

The new inverse demand function is $P = 1.5 - 0.1Q$.

Thus, the marginal revenue is

$$1.5 - 0.2Q$$

The profit-maximizing quantity is

$$MR = 1.5 - 0.2Q = 0.5 = MC$$

$$Q = 5$$

The profit-maximizing price is

$$1.5 - (0.1 \times 5) = \$1$$

At full price, each consumer will order 10 cupcakes and at the discounted price 5 cupcakes.

d. The profit from this two-tiered pricing plan is

$$\$10 + (\$1 - \$0.50) \times 5 = \$12.50$$

Having introduced the discounted price for cupcakes, Elaine has increased her profit by $2.5.

e.

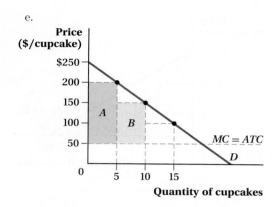

To implement a three-tiered pricing system, simply split the demand curve above marginal cost into four equal parts, as shown in the graph above. Elaine will set the price points as follows: $2 for the first 5 units, $1.50 for the next 5, and $1 for any quantity more than 10. Consumers will purchase 15 units in all. Elaine will earn $5 \times (\$2 - \$0.50) = \$7.50$ (shown as area A) on the first 5 units sold; she will earn $5 \times (\$1.50 - \$0.50) = \$5$ (shown as area B) on units 6 through 10, and $5 \times (\$1 - \$0.50) = \$2.50$ (shown as area C) on the remaining 5 units. Elaine's total profit will be $15. She earns more profit with a three-tiered pricing system than she did with a two-tiered system.

f. Elaine is essentially adopting a 20-tiered pricing system. She will sell one cupcake at $2.40, the next at $2.30, and so on, working her way down the customer's demand curve one unit at a time. She will stop cutting the price when it dips below her cost of production: In total, she will sell 20 cupcakes and the price of the last cupcake will be $0.50.
Accounting for her cost of production, she will earn a profit of $1.90 + $1.80 + \cdots + $0.10 + $0. This all adds up to $19.00 profit.

g. The consumer surplus decreases and is captured as profit by Elaine. The pricing strategy should eliminate all deadweight loss as well, captured as profit by Elaine.

CHAPTER 11

1. a.
   i. The marginal revenue is $MR = 30 - 4Q$.
   ii. The profit-maximizing collective output for the cartel solves the condition $MR = MC$; that is,

$$30 - 4Q = 6$$
$$4Q = 24$$
$$Q = 6$$

   iii. The price Pierre and Gaston will be able to charge is

$$P = 30 - 2Q = 30 - (2 \times 6) = \$18$$

   iv. Pierre and Gaston split the output equally; hence, each of them gets

$$TR - TC = (\$18 - \$6) \times 3 = \$36$$

The profit for the cartel is $72.

b.
   i. The extra production of soufflés decreases the price in the marketplace; that is,

$$P = 30 - 2Q = 30 - (2 \times 7) = \$16$$

   ii. Pierre's profit is now

$$TR - TC = (\$16 - \$6) \times 4 = \$40$$

Hence, Pierre gained $4 by cheating.
   iii. Gaston's profit is now

$$TR - TC = (\$16 - \$6) \times 3 = \$30$$

Hence, Gaston lost $6.
   iv. The profits are now $40 + $30 = $70. Therefore, as a result of Pierre's cheating, the group loses $2 of potential profit.

c.
   i. The extra production of soufflés decreases the price further in the marketplace; that is,

$$P = 30 - 2Q = 30 - 2(8) = \$14$$

   ii. Gaston's profit is now

$$TR - TC = (\$14 - \$6) \times 4 = \$32$$

Hence, Gaston gains $2 compared to the previous scenario.
   iii. Pierre's profit is now

$$TR - TC = (\$14 - \$6)4 = \$32$$

Hence, Pierre loses $8 compared to the previous scenario.
   iv. The group's profits are $32 + $32 = $64. Therefore, they lose in total $8 of potential profit.
   v. If they decide to continue cheating, the price of soufflés will decrease, which will result in a reduction of profit for both individuals. More specifically, if one cheats

further, the total output rises to 9. The price becomes

$$P = 30 - 2Q = 30 - 2(9) = \$12$$

The profit for the cheater is now

$$TR - TC = (\$12 - \$6) \times 5 = \$30$$

Hence, neither Pierre nor Gaston has an incentive to cheat as the cheater's profit falls from $32 to $30.

6. a

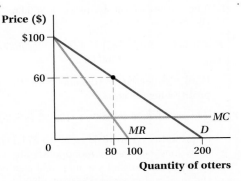

The profit-maximizing quantity for a monopolist is

$$MR = 100 - Q = 20 = MC$$

$$Q = 80$$

Thus, the price is
$$P = 100 - 0.5Q = 100 - 0.5 \times 80 = \$60$$

b.

  i.
$$P = 100 - 0.5(q_J + q_A) = 100 - 0.5(40 + q_A)$$
$$= 80 - 0.5q_A$$

  ii. The residual marginal revenue for Annie is

$$MR = 80 - q_A$$

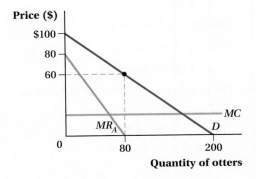

iii. In order to maximize profit, the quantity of otters Annie brings to the market is

$$MR_A = 80 - q_A = 20 = MC$$

$$q_A = 60$$

c. The quantity produced by both of them is 100. Therefore, the final price of otters is

$$P = 100 - 0.5Q = 100 - 0.5 \times 100 = \$50$$

Annie's profit is

$$TR - TC = (\$50 - \$20) \times 60 = \$1,800$$

Jack's profit is

$$TR - TC = (\$50 - \$20) \times 40 = \$1,200$$

d.

  i.   The residual demand curve for Jack is

$$P = 100 - 0.5(q_J + q_A) = 100 - 0.5(q_J + 60)$$
$$= 70 - 0.5q_J$$

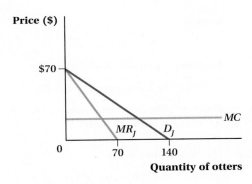

ii. The residual marginal revenue for Jack is

$$MR_J = 70 - q_J$$

iii. In order to maximize the profit, Jack should produce the quantity that satisfies the $MC = MR$ condition, that is,

$$MR_J = 70 - q_J = 20 = MC$$

$$q_J = 50$$

iv. The total quantity produced is 110. The final price of otters is

$$P = 100 - 0.5Q = 100 - 0.5 \times 110 = \$45$$

Annie's profit is

$$TR - TC = (\$45 - \$20) \times 60 = \$1,500$$

Jack's profit is

$$TR - TC = (\$45 - \$20) \times 50 = \$1,250$$

e. Solving for the Cournot equilibrium, we get

$$P = 100 - 0.5(q_J + q_A)$$

The marginal revenue for Jack is

$$MR_J = 100 - q_J - 0.5q_A$$

In equilibrium, $MC = MR$. Hence,

$$MR_J = 100 - q_J - 0.5q_A = 20 = MC$$

$$q_J = 80 - 0.5q_A$$

Similarly, for Annie

$$MR_A = 100 - 0.5q_J - q_A$$

And

$$q_A = 80 - 0.5q_J$$

Thus,

$$q_J = 80 - 0.5(80 - 0.5q_J)$$

$$= 53.33$$

Likewise,

$$q_A = 53.33$$

Therefore, in equilibrium the price is

$$P = 100 - 0.5(q_J + q_A) = \$46.66$$

Therefore, the outcome found in part (d) is not an equilibrium outcome.

7. a. The inverse demand is

$$P = 1,000 - 2(q_s + q_A)$$

The residual demand faced by Sydney is

$$P = (1,000 - 2q_A) - 2q_s$$

b. The residual marginal revenue is

$$MR_S = (1,000 - 2q_A) - 4q_s$$

c.

$$MR_S = 1,000 - 2q_A - 4q_s = 200 = MC$$

$$q_S = 200 - 0.5q_A$$

d. The residual marginal revenue for Adelaide is

$$MR_A = 1,000 - 4q_A - 2q_s$$

Thus,

$$MR_A = 1,000 - 4q_A - 2q_S = 200 = MC$$

$$q_A = 200 - 0.5q_S$$

e. The profit-maximizing level of output for Sydney is

$$q_S = 200 - 0.5q_A = 200 - 0.5(200 - 0.5q_S)$$
$$= 100 + 0.25q_S$$

$$= 133.33$$

The profit-maximizing level of output for Adelaide is

$$q_A = 200 - 0.5q_S = 200 - 0.5(133.33) = 133.33$$

f. The output of the industry is 266.66. Thus, the price is

$$P = 1,000 - 2(q_S + q_A) = 1,000 - 2(266.66)$$
$$= \$466.66$$

Both Sydney and Adelaide earn the same profit, which is equal to

$$TR - TC = (\$466.66 - \$200) \times 133.33 \approx \$35,556$$

Total industry profit is equal to $71,111.11.

g. If Sydney becomes a monopolist, she would set the price so that the marginal cost equals the marginal revenue, that is,

$$MR = 1,000 - 4Q = 200 = MC$$

$$Q = 200$$

The price is

$$P = 1,000 - 2Q = 1,000 - 2 \times 200 = \$600$$

The profit is now

$$TR - TC = (\$600 - \$200) \times 200 = \$80,000$$

Therefore, the quantity sold decreases, price increases, and so does the profit for the industry as a whole.

13. a. The reaction function for Grenada is

$$MR_G = 100 - q_P - 2q_G = 20 = MC$$

$$q_G = 40 = 0.5q_P$$

The reaction function for Penang is

$$MR_P = 100 - 2q_P - q_G = 20 = MC$$

$$q_P = 40 - 0.5q_G$$

b. The equilibrium quantity for Grenada is

$$q_G = 40 - 0.5q_P = 40 - 0.5(40 - 0.5q_G)$$
$$= 20 + 0.25q_G$$

$$= 26.67$$

The equilibrium quantity for Penang is

$$q_P = 40 - 0.5q_G = 40 - (0.5 \times 26.67) = 26.67$$

The market price is then

$$P = 100 - q_P - q_G = \$46.67$$

The profit for Grenada is

$$TR_G - TC_G = (\$46.67 - \$20) \times 26.67 = \$711.11$$

The profit for Penang is

$$TR_P - TC_P = (\$46.67 - \$20) \times 26.67 = \$711.11$$

c.

i. The demand faced by Grenada is

$$P = 100 - q_P - q_G = 100 - (40 - 0.5q_G) - q_G$$
$$= 60 - 0.5q_G$$

ii. The marginal revenue for Grenada is

$$MR_G = 60 - q_G$$

iii. Grenada's output is

$$MR_G = 60 - q_G = 20 = MC$$

$$q_G = 40$$

iv. Penang's output is

$$q_P = 40 - 0.5q_G = 40 - (0.5 \times \mathbf{40}) = 20$$

The price is

$$P = 100 - q_P - q_G = 100 - 20 - 40 = \$40$$

The industry quantity is greater compared to the Cournot competition, and the price is lower.

vi. The profit for Grenada is

$$TR_G - TC_G = (\$40 - \$20) \times 40 = \$800$$

The profit for Penang is

$$TR_P - TC_P = (\$40 - \$20) \times 20 = \$400$$

Grenada's profit is greater in the Stackelberg competition, whereas the profit for Penang is smaller in the Stackelberg competition. Therefore, the first-mover is better off.

15. a. AT&T total revenue is

$$TR_{AT\&T} = p_A \times q_A = p_A(1,000 - 3p_A + 2p_V)$$

The marginal revenue is

$$MR_{AT\&T} = 1,000 - 6p_A + 2p_V$$

Setting the marginal revenue equal to the marginal cost gives

$$MR_{AT\&T} = 1,000 - 6p_A + 2p_V = 0 = MC$$

$$p_A = 166\frac{2}{3} + \frac{1}{3}p_V$$

If Verizon increases its price by $9, AT&T increases its price by $3.

b. The total revenue for Verizon is

$$TR_V = p_V \times q_V = p_V(1,000 - 3p_V + 2p_A)$$

The marginal revenue is

$$MR_V = 1,000 - 6p_V + 2p_A$$

Setting the marginal revenue equal to the marginal cost gives

$$MR_V = 1,000 - 6p_V + 2p_A = 0 = MC$$

$$p_V = 166\frac{2}{3} + \frac{1}{3}p_A$$

c. The price that AT&T will charge is

$$p_A = 166\frac{2}{3} + \frac{1}{3}p_V = 166\frac{2}{3} + \frac{1}{3}\left(166\frac{2}{3} + \frac{1}{3}p_A\right)$$

$$= \frac{2,000}{9} + \frac{1}{9}p_A$$

$$= \$250$$

d. The price that Verizon will charge is

$$p_V = 166\frac{2}{3} + \frac{1}{3}p_A = \$250$$

e. AT&T will sell

$$q_A = 1,000 - 3p_A + 2p_V = 1,000 - 750 + 500 = 750$$

Verizon will sell exactly the same quantity, that is,

$$q_V = 1,000 - 3p_V + 2p_A = 1,000 - 750 + 500 = 750$$

Each firm sells the same quantity of output at the same price; hence, both will make the same profit, which equals

$$TR - TC = (\$250 \times 750) - 0 = \$187,500$$

20.

	Collusive Monopoly	Cournot Oligopoly	Bertrand Oligopoly	Stackelberg Oligopoly (A is first-mover)
A's Quantity	23.75	31.67	47.50	47.50
B's Quantity	23.75	31.67	47.50	23.75
Industry Quantity	47.50	63.33	95	71.25
Price	$52.50	$36.67	$5	$28.75
A's Profit	$1,128.13	$1,002.70	$0	$1,128.13
B's Profit	$1,128.13	$1,002.70	$0	$564.06
Industry Profit	$2,256.25	$2,005.40	$0	$1,692.19

The Collusive Monopoly Case

Firms produce exactly the same output and sell it at the price where $MC = MR$, that is,

$$MR = 100 - 2Q = 5 = MC$$

$$Q = 47.50$$

Thus, each firm produces 23.75 units of output. The monopolistic price is

$$P = 100 - Q = \$52.50$$

Both Firm A and Firm B generate the same profit, which is equal to

$$TR - TC = (\$52.50 - \$5) \times 23.75 = \$1,128.13$$

The profit for the industry is $2,256.25.

The Cournot Oligopoly Case

The inverse demand function is

$$P = 100 - q_A - q_B$$

The residual marginal revenue for Firm $i = \{A, B\}$ is

$$MR = 100 - 2q_A - q_B$$

Therefore, the reaction function for Firm i is

$$100 - 2q_A - q_B = 5$$

$$q_A = 47.5 - 0.5q_B$$

Therefore, the output produced by Firm A and Firm B is

$$q_1 = 47.5 - 0.5q_2 = 47.5 - 0.5(47.5 - 0.5q_1)$$
$$= 23.75 + 0.25q_1$$

$$q_A = 31.67 = q_B$$

The output for the industry is 63.33. The price is

$$P = 100 - q_A - q_B = \$36.67$$

Both firms earn the same profit, which is equal to

$$TR - TC = (\$36.67 - \$5) \times 31.67 = \$1,002.70$$

Hence, the profit for the industry is

$$\$1,002.70 \times 2 = \$2,005.40$$

The Bertrand Oligopoly Case

Both firms will sell the product at the marginal cost of $5 and each will produce exactly the same quantity, that is,

$$5 = 100 - 2q_i$$

$$q_i = 47.50$$

Since firms sell output at the marginal cost, each firm's profit is $0; thus, the industry profit is also equal to $0.

The Stackelberg Oligopoly Case

The reaction function for Firm B is

$$100 - q_A - 2q_B = 5$$

$$q_B = 47.5 - 0.5q_A$$

Assuming that Firm A is the first-mover, the inverse demand function faced by Firm A is

$$P = 100 - q_A - q_B = 100 - q_A - 47.5 + 0.5q_A$$
$$= 52.5 - 0.5q_A$$

Equating the marginal revenue with marginal cost, the quantity produced by Firm A is

$$MR = 52.5 - q_A = 5$$

$$q_A = 47.50$$

Thus, Firm B produces

$$q_B = 47.5 - 0.5q_A = 47.5 - 0.5 \times 47.5 = 23.75$$

The industry quantity is 71.25. The price is

$$P = 100 - q_A - q_B = \$28.75$$

Firm A generates a profit of

$$TR_A - TC_A = (\$28.75 - \$5) \times 47.50 = \$1,128.13$$

Firm B generates a profit of

$$TR_B - TC_B = (\$28.75 - \$5) \times 23.75 = \$564.06$$

Thus, the industry's profit is $1,692.19.

CHAPTER 12

1. a. The players are Duvall and Earl.
   b. Duvall's strategies are Stop, Drop, and Roll.
   c. If Earl plays Hammer and Duvall plays Roll, Earl's payoff is 5.
   d. If Earl plays Stirrup and Duval plays Drop, Duvall's payoff is 3.

3. a. Both players have dominant strategies. MacDuff's dominant strategy is Slay King. McBeth's dominant strategy is Listen to Wife. Therefore, by dominance, the Nash equilibrium of this game is (8, 4) or (Slay King, Listen to Wife).
   b. Both players have dominant strategies. The dominant strategy for Elvis is Bump. Ferris' dominant strategy is Twist. Therefore, by dominance, the Nash equilibrium for this game is (4, 8) or (Bump, Twist).
   c. Only Eagle has a dominant strategy in this game, namely Take It Easy. Given that Eagle will always play Take It Easy, the best choice for Matthew is Get Under Table. Therefore, by dominance, the Nash equilibrium in this game is (5, 3) or (Get Under Table, Take It Easy).

4. a. When Wilma chooses Opera, Fred's best response is to also choose Opera. When Wilma chooses Bowling, Fred's best response is to also choose Bowling. Similarly, when Fred chooses Opera, Wilma should also choose Opera, and when Fred chooses Bowling, so should Wilma. Therefore, there are two Nash equilibria, (Opera, Opera) and (Bowling, Bowling).
   b. When Ren chooses Straight, Chuck's best response is to choose Swerve. When Ren chooses Swerve, Chuck should choose Straight. If Chuck chooses Straight, Ren should play Swerve, and when Chuck chooses Swerve, Ren should play Straight. Therefore, there are two Nash equilibria, (Swerve, Straight) and (Straight, Swerve).

10. a.

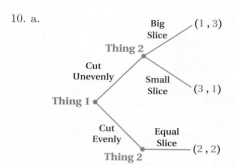

b. The equilibrium outcome for this game is (2, 2) or (Cut Evenly, Equal Slice), so Thing 1 and Thing 2 take equal slices. The reason is that in the case of an uneven split, the second-mover will always choose the larger piece. Thus, the first-mover knows that she will end up with a smaller piece if she doesn't cut evenly. Therefore, her best move is to cut the cake evenly. This is consistent with my experience.

c. Given the discussion in (b), the equilibrium outcome of this game will always be for the cutter to cut even slices, no matter who is the first-mover. Therefore, there is no first-mover advantage here.

15. a. The payoffs are accurate. For example, if we assume August and Antoinette sell 20 gallons each, they sell 40 gallons in total and the market price is \$8 per gallon. Hence, each of them earns \$160. The same verification can be done for any other.

			August			
			20	**30**	**40**	**50**
Antoinette		**20**	\$160 , \$160	\$140 , \$210	\$120 , \$240	\$100 , \$250
		30	\$210 , **\$140**	\$180 , \$180	\$150 , **\$200**	\$120 , **\$200**
		40	\$240 , \$120	**\$200** , \$150	\$160 , \$160	\$120 , \$150
		50	**\$250** , \$100	\$200 , \$120	\$150 , \$120	**\$100** , **\$100**

b. To maximize joint profits, August and Antoinette will produce 60 gallons of water altogether. Hence, each produces 30 gallons of water (50% of the market supply) and earns \$180.

c. Yes, if either August or Antoinette increases production by 10 gallons, the profit of the cheater increases by \$20. However, the profit of the noncheater decreases by \$30, and the profits to the group as a whole decline.

d. There are three Nash equilibria in this game. The equilibria are (50, 30), (30, 50) and (20, 20). None of the equilibria is ideal for the group, as total group profits are less than if both agree to restrict output to 30 gallons.

e. Both players' dominant strategy is to cheat (confess), which corresponds to the dominant strategy equilibrium from the prisoner's dilemma game.

19. a. The sum should equal

$$500 + d \times 500 + d^2 \times 500 + \cdots$$

b. The sum should equal

$$700 + d \times 400 + d^2 \times 400 + \cdots$$

c. If $d = 0.5$, the sum from part (a) is equal to

$$500 + d \times 500 + d^2 \times 500 + \cdots = 500 + \left(\frac{500d}{1-d}\right)$$
$$= \left(\frac{500}{1-d}\right) = \$1,000$$

If you decided to cheat, you would get

$$700 + d \times 400 + d^2 \times 400 + \cdots = 700 + \left(\frac{400d}{1-d}\right)$$
$$= 700 + 400 = \$1,100$$

Thus, when $d = 0.5$, you should cheat. If $d = 0.99$, plugging 0.99 into the calculations above, we see that abiding gives us a payout of $50,000; cheating yields a payout of $40,300. Therefore, you should abide. If $d = 0.01$, abiding gives a payout of $505.05; cheating yields a payout of $704.04. You should cheat.

d. Setting both sums from parts (a) and (b) equal to each other, we get

$$500 + d \times 500 + d^2 \times 500 + \cdots = 700 + d \times 400 + d^2 \times 400 + \cdots$$

$$\frac{500}{1-d} = 700 + \frac{400}{1-d^1}$$

$$500 = 700(1-d) + 400d$$

$$d = \frac{2}{3}$$

At $d = \frac{2}{3}$, you are indifferent between cheating or abiding by the agreement.

CHAPTER 13

1. a. At the end of this year, I would have

$$100 + (100 \times 0.2) = 100 \times (1 + 0.2) = 100 \times 1.2 = 120 \text{ bunnies}$$

b. At the end of this year, I would have $120 + (120 \times 0.2) = 120 \times (1 + 0.2) = 120 \times 1.2 = 144$ bunnies.

c. At the end of two years, I would have 144 bunnies, that is, 120 bunnies at the end of the first year and 144 at the end of the second year.

d. At the end of 10 years, I would have

$$100 \times (1 + 0.2)^{10} \approx 619 \text{ bunnies}$$

5. a. The value of the publisher's future payments is

$$\frac{\$100,000}{1.05} + \frac{\$100,000}{1.05^2} = \$185,941$$

b. Considering the second offer, the value becomes

$$\frac{\$80,000}{1.05} + \frac{\$125,000}{1.05^2} \approx \$189,569$$

Hence, this is a better deal than the original one as $189,569 > $185,941. The net present value of the loss in payments of the first year (20,000/1.05) is more than compensated for by the net present value increase in payments offered in the second year (25,000/1.05²).

10. a. The value of the Treasury bill today is

$$\frac{\$1,000}{1.04} \approx \$961.54$$

The value of the zero-coupon Treasury bond today is

$$\frac{\$1,000}{1.04^{30}} \approx \$308.32$$

b. The current price of each bond will decrease. The price of the Treasury bill and the zero-coupon Treasury bond would be, respectively,

$$\frac{\$1,000}{1.08} \approx \$925.93$$

$$\frac{\$1,000}{1.08^{30}} \approx \$99.38$$

c. If the interest rates rise to 8%, the bill will lose a small fraction of its value, but the bond will lose $\frac{2}{3}$ of its value. You would prefer to have invested in Treasury bills because the net present value of the amount you "overpaid" given the now higher interest rates would be lower.

12. a. The net present value of Marian's investment is

$$-\$30,000 + \frac{\$8,000}{1 + 0.10} + \cdots + \frac{\$8,000}{(1 + 0.10)^5} =$$

$$-\$30,000 + \$30,326.29 = \$326.29$$

b. The net present value of Marian's investment is $326.29.

   Therefore, Marian should change careers.

c. The present value of Marian's earnings as a librarian is

$$\frac{\$40,000}{1 + 0.10} + \cdots + \frac{\$40,000}{(1 + 0.10)^5} = \$151,631.47$$

   The present value of Marian's earnings as a florist is

$$\frac{\$48,000}{1 + 0.10} + \cdots + \frac{\$48,000}{(1 + 0.10)^5} = \$181,958$$

   The difference of $181,957.76 − $151,631.47 = $30,326.29 is large enough to justify spending the $30,000.

d. The methods used in parts (a) and (c) give precisely the same answer, $326.29:

$$\frac{\$48,000}{1 + 0.10} + \cdots + \frac{\$48,000}{(1 + 0.10)^5} - \frac{\$40,000}{1 + 0.10} + \cdots$$
$$+ \frac{\$40,000}{(1 + 0.10)^5} - \$30,000$$
$$= -\$30,000 + \frac{\$8,000}{1 + 0.10} + \cdots + \frac{\$8,000}{(1 + 0.10)^5}$$
$$= \$326.29$$

17. a. The NPV is

$$-\$200,000 + 0.80 \times \frac{\$700,000}{(1 + 0.10)} + 0.20$$
$$\times \frac{\$0}{(1 + 0.10)} = -\$200,000 + \frac{\$560,000}{(1.10)} =$$
$$\$309,090.91$$

b. The net present value today of opening the playground in one year is

$$\frac{-\$200,000}{1.10} + \frac{\$700,000}{(1 + 0.10)^2} = \$396,694.21$$

c. The NPV in part (b) is greater than the NPV in (a). Therefore, you should wait until the zoning commission reaches its decision.

19. a. Steve's expected income is

$$\$900 - 0.50 \times \$500 = \$650$$

   His expected utility can be found as follows. Half the time, he will receive $900^{0.5}$ or 30. The other half of the time, he will receive $400^{0.5}$ or 20:

$$U = 0.5 \times 30 + 0.5 \times 20 = 25$$

b. A salary of $625 would provide Steve with the same utility he expected to receive as a traveling salesman because $625^{0.5} = 25$.

c. Steve gets exactly the same utility from a risk-free $625 a week as he does from a risky job where his earnings average $650. Given that he is paying $250 to the traffic court each week anyway, he would be willing to pay an extra $25 in weekly earnings to avoid the uncertainty. Therefore, he should be willing to pay $275 for speeding ticket insurance.

d. The insurance would break even if the insurer charges Steve $250 each week. If the insurer can charge him the $275 he is willing to pay, it will earn a $25 profit.

CHAPTER 14

2. a. The price and quantity of yellow corn increase.

b. The supply of white corn decreases because farmers shift some of their production from white corn to yellow corn.

c. The market price of white corn increases.

d. As a result of the increase in the price of white corn, the supply of yellow corn decreases as the farmers now shift some of their production back toward white corn. The price of yellow corn increases and the quantity decreases.

e. The increase in the price of white corn tends to push yellow corn prices further away from its initial value (as both shift, the increase in demand and the decrease in the supply of yellow corn push prices upward, whereas the quantity is pushed back toward its initial value).

3. a. Wine and cheese are linked on the demand side of the market.

b. $Q_c^d = 30 - P_c - P_w = P_c = Q_c^s$
   $P_c = 15 - 0.5P_w$

c. $Q_w^d = 30 - P_c - P_w = P_w = Q_w^s$
   $P_w = 15 - 0.5P_c$

d. $P_c = 15 - 0.5P_w = 15 - 0.5(15 - 0.5P_c)$
   $\qquad\qquad = 7.5 + 0.25P_c$

   $0.75P_c = 7.5$
   $\quad P_c = \$10$

e. $P_w = 15 - 0.5P_c = 15 - 0.5 \times 10 = \$10$

f. $Q_w = 30 - P_c - P_w = 30 - 10 - 10 = 10$

   $Q_c = 30 - P_c - P_w = 30 - 10 - 10 = 10$

11. a. They have 6 peaches in their fridge.

b. They have 4 pints of cream in their fridge.

c. and d.

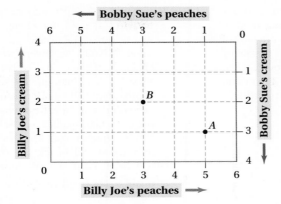

e. Suppose Billy Joe happens to find 2 extra peaches and is permitted to keep them.

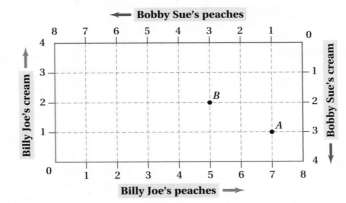

15. a. and b.

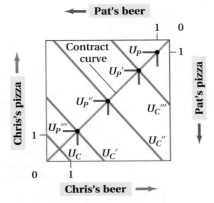

The contract curve will be at a 45-degree line.

17. a. There are six labor inputs for food and two for clothing. There are two capital inputs for food and three for clothing.

b. 100 units of food and 40 units of clothing are being produced.

c. Suppose that one less unit of labor and one additional unit of capital are being used in the food production. Hence, one more unit of labor and one less unit of capital are being used for clothing. This reallocation will enable Tom and Hank to enjoy more food and clothing than they are currently producing.

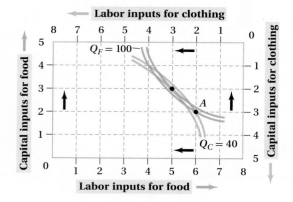

19. a. and b.

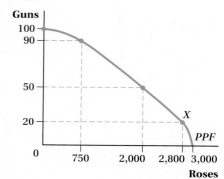

CHAPTER 15

3. a. If there is perfect information, 100 high-quality cars and 100 low-quality cars will be sold.

   b. If the quality of the car is not known to the buyer, the expected price of a used car to a buyer is

   $$\$12,000 \times 0.5 + \$8,000 \times 0.5 = \$10,000$$

   No high-quality cars will be offered for sale at that price as it is below the minimum acceptable price of $11,000.

   c. No high-quality cars will be offered for sale and the equilibrium price will range between $5,000 and $8,000 depending on the negotiation skills of buyers and sellers of low-quality cars.

d. If there is perfect information, the answer to part (a) does not change. Similarly, the market price for a used car will remain the same, $10,000, as buyers' valuation has not changed. Given the reservation price of $9,500 of the high-quality sellers, 100 high-quality cars will be offered for sale as the expected price for a car exceeds the reservation price of high-quality car sellers. Moreover, 100 low-quality cars are also offered for sale at $10,000. All in all, the equilibrium price will be $10,000 and the proportion of high-quality cars to all cars will be $\frac{1}{2}$.

6. a. The buyer has more valuable information as he knows his driving type.

   b. Buyers are aware if they are likely to be caught for speeding. Thus, those choosing to enroll in the coverage are the speedy drivers. Those who do not exceed the speed limit will not buy the coverage. Hence, this asymmetric information creates an adverse selection problem in the market.

   c. Both types will be less careful and drive faster once they buy coverage. This kind of behavioral response is called moral hazard.

   d. The insurance was most likely overwhelmingly purchased by those drivers who were inclined to speed. Thus, revenues earned from insurance premiums were likely insufficient to offset the costs of paying out claims.

11. a

   MB, MC

   MC

   Optimal amount of resources

   MB

   Quantity of actions for self-improvement

   b. There is a shift-in of the marginal benefit curve (to the left), which leads to a smaller optimal quantity of actions for self-improvement.

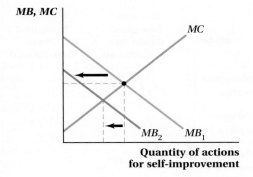

**Quantity of actions
for self-improvement**

c. Yes, it is consistent with the illustration. The quantity of actions for self-improvement decreased.

d. It is a moral hazard problem, as Harry's behavior is likely to change with the change in incentives.

e. The marginal benefit curve is a horizontal line with an optimal amount of actions for self-improvement at 0.

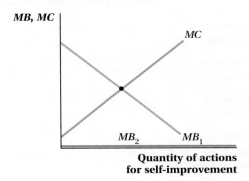

**Quantity of actions
for self-improvement**

13. a. If Jenny expends modest effort, Sara can expect to receive $600,000 in revenue, but will spend $100,000 on Jenny's services, for a net of $500,000. If Jenny expends high effort, Sara can expect to receive $1 million in revenue, but will spend $100,000 on Jenny's services, for a net of $900,000.

   If Jenny expends modest effort, she will be paid $100,000 while expending $20,000 of effort, for a net of $80,000. If Jenny expends high effort, she will be paid $100,000 while expending $50,000 of effort, for a net of $50,000. Here, Sara is the principal and Jenny is her agent. The problem is that Jenny expending high effort is in Sara's best interest, but Jenny expending modest effort is in Jenny's best interest.

   b. Under the 15% plan, if Jenny expends modest effort, Sara can expect to receive $600,000

in revenue, but will spend $90,000 on Jenny's services, for a net of $510,000. If Jenny expends high effort, Sara can expect to receive $1 million in revenue, but will spend $150,000 on Jenny's services, for a net of $850,000.

   If Jenny expends modest effort, she will be paid $90,000 while expending $20,000 of effort, for a net of $70,000. If Jenny expends high effort, she will be paid $150,000 while expending $50,000 of effort, for a net of $100,000.

   The 15% payment scheme makes the principal agent problem disappear: expending high is not only in Sara's best interest, but it is also in Jenny's.

18. a. If the company were to pay an average wage of $45,000, most of its applicants would look like Lazy Susan.

   b. The market is willing to pay $70,000 to those who signal ability through a college degree. Otherwise, the pay offered will be $20,000 now that this requirement is in place. Thus, the net benefit of obtaining a degree is the $50,000 difference minus the cost of a degree. For Charlie Hustle, this difference is +$10,000 ($50K minus $40K). For Lazy Susan, the net benefit is –$10,000 ($50K minus $60K).

   Therefore, the degree requirement does permit the firm to separate the two groups of applicants.

   c. The net benefit to a college education to a Charlie remains unchanged, whereas the net benefit to a Susan now becomes $50,000 – $46,000 = $4,000. In this case, the net benefit for both types of applicants is positive. Therefore, the degree requirement is not sufficient anymore to allow the firm to filter out low-quality applicants.

   d. The assertion is correct. Obtaining the signal to low-productivity applicants must be more costly; otherwise, the filtering will not be possible.

   e. Grade inflation is definitely a bad practice for students as it bridges the qualitative differences among students in a way that makes it almost impossible to differentiate the level and potential of students. A B or a B+ student who is pushed in the A range prevents the appropriate sorting and inhibits the efficient functioning of merit. This is bad for high-quality students who would like to distinguish themselves. It also is bad for both types of students because this signal then becomes an "arms race" (as explained in the chapter) of who will be able to (get into and) graduate from the most prestigious (most expensive) institutions of higher learning.

19. a. The signal is costly to both types of birds because it represents an expense in terms of being slower in flight and thus susceptible to predators. However, it is even more expensive to a weak bird given that he is already more likely to fall victim to a predator's attack.

b. If the same signal could be achieved at a lower cost (represented by the lower danger of being caught by predators when the tails are half as long), then any growing of tails longer than that is just a waste of resources from society's point of view.

c. Such agreement is unlikely to last as peacocks have an incentive to cheat and grow their tails in order to signal greater attractiveness to peahens. Therefore, the scheme would break apart, which would result in peacocks growing their tails long. Such a signal would be costly as peacocks would be slower in flight and more susceptible to predators.

CHAPTER 16

1. a. The market price is $5, where marginal benefit equals marginal cost.

b. The external cost is $1 regardless of the number of racks roasted.

c. The intersection of the marginal benefit curve (demand) and the marginal cost curve determines the number of racks. Thus, 100 racks will be roasted. Animal lovers will suffer damage of $1 for each rack, for a total damage of $100.

d. Incorporating the external costs would lead the pit master to produce 80 racks.

e. The total damage suffered by animal lovers will be $80. Some of the damage is eliminated, but not all.

f. Cutting the level of output further would hurt the pit master, who would be foregoing profits. Such a cut is not Pareto optimal, because although the output cut would reduce damage to the animal lovers by $1 per rack roasted, below 80 units any output cut will cost the pit master more than $1 in lost profit.

4. a. The equilibrium price is P_1 and quantity is Q_1.

	External Marginal Costs Not Considered	External Marginal Costs Considered
Consumer Surplus	$A + B + D + F$	
Producer Surplus	$C + E + G$	
External Damage (−)	$D + E + F + G + H$	
Total net value to society	$A + B + C − H$	

b. The new quantity is Q_2 and price is P_2.

	External Marginal Costs Not Considered	External Marginal Costs Considered
Consumer Surplus	$A + B + D + F$	A
Producer Surplus	$C + E + G$	$B + C + D + E$
External Damage (−)	$D + E + F + G + H$	$D + E$
Total net value to society	$A + B + C − H$	$A + B + C$

c. As indicated in the table above, when external costs are ignored by producers, total net value is lower by area H. Thus, H is the deadweight loss.

7. a. The SMC is $MC + EMC = 0.45Q + 0.05Q = 0.5Q$. The efficient output level can be found where $MB = SMC$:

$$50 − 0.5Q = 0.5Q$$
$$Q^* = 50$$

Thus, government should set the quota at 50 units. The price that prevails in the marketplace once this quota is in place is

$$P = 50 − 0.5Q^* = 50 − 0.5 \times 50 = \$25$$

b. At the efficient level of production, $Q^* = 50$, the external damage can be calculated as $.05Q$, or $2.50. If government imposes a

$2.50 tax on producers, their private marginal costs will be given as

$$MC = 0.45Q + 2.50$$

Producers will find the profit-maximizing level of output where $MB = MC$, or where

$$50 - 0.5Q = 0.45Q + 2.50$$

Solving, we get 50 units for Q, the profit-maximizing level of output. The prevailing market price can be found by substituting $Q = 50$ into the MB curve:

$$P = 50 - 0.5(50) = \$25$$

Buyers will pay $25. Sellers will receive that amount less the tax, or $22.50.

11. a. Without any government intervention, the quantity of bread produced is

$$P = 10 - 0.1Q = 2 + 0.1Q = MC$$
$$0.2Q = 8$$
$$Q = 40$$

b. Ideally, society would like producers to consider all of the benefits their activity creates, both internal and external. Thus, the total social benefit is given as

$$P + EMB = 10 - 0.1Q + 2 - 0.02Q = 12 - 0.12Q$$

So, the magnitude of a price-based intervention is

$$12 - 0.12Q = 2 + 0.1Q = MC$$
$$0.22Q = 10$$
$$Q \approx 45.45$$

Producers are under-producing relative to the welfare-maximizing quantity of 45.45. The government can use a price-based intervention to encourage them to produce more. In this case, the appropriate intervention is to subsidize production. At the ideal quantity, bread baking creates an external marginal benefit of

$$EMB = 2 - 0.02(45.45) = \$1.09$$

If the government offers producers a subsidy of $1.09 per loaf, producers' marginal cost becomes

$$MC = 2 + 0.1Q - 1.09$$

Equating MC and MB yields

$$2 + 0.1Q - 1.09 = 10 - 0.1Q$$
$$Q = 45.45$$

A subsidy of $1.09 encourages producers to produce the socially optimal amount.

14. a. No. Rehearsing on the deck brings Al $500 of benefits, but costs Marcy $600 in lost sleep. Society loses $100 of welfare as a result of Al's rehearsals.

b. If rehearsals are illegal, Marcy can simply call the police to put an end to Al's rehearsals. No rehearsals will take place.

c. i. Marcy is willing to pay Al up to $600 per year to rehearse elsewhere.

ii. The minimum amount of money that Al is willing to accept is $500.

iii. Let us assume that Marcy pays Al $550 for silence. Al is better off taking the offer, as he gains $50 (= $550 − $500) and Marcy is better off paying him as $600 − $550 = $50.

d. The outcome does not depend on the law. When rehearsing is illegal, Marcy calls the police. When rehearsing is legal, Marcy pays Al to rehearse elsewhere. No matter what the law states, society gets the same efficient outcome. It will be more difficult for the neighbors to organize and to gather the amount that would compensate Al for the rent. Neighbors will try to avoid chipping in and free-ride. Thus, even though it is not efficient for Al to rehearse on his back deck, that may be the outcome for society.

16. a.

Number of cows	2	3	4
Total gallons of milk each year	2,000	2,250	1,600

The efficient number of cows is 3.

b. If Ben keeps 1 cow, that cow will produce 1,000 gallons of milk and Ben will earn $1,000. If Ben keeps 2 cows, each will produce 750 gallons of milk and Ben will earn $1,500. Ben will keep 2 cows.

c. If Ben keeps 1 cow, that cow will produce 750 gallons of milk and Ben will earn $750. If Ben keeps 2 cows, each will produce 400 gallons of milk and Ben will earn $800. Ben will keep 2 cows.

d. Following similar reasoning, Jerry's best choice is to keep 2 cows regardless of how many cows Ben grazes. So, both Ben and Jerry will keep 2 cows on the pasture. Relative to what is socially ideal (3 cows), Ben and

Jerry keep too many cows and the pasture is overgrazed.

e. It could be useful to restrict the number of cattle grazed on some specific area or to charge a tax for grazing. An alternative would be to sell the pasture to Ben or Jerry, who will then have a private incentive to graze the socially ideal number of cows.

CHAPTER 17

4. This behavioral bias is known as the hyperbolic discounting bias. People place relatively more importance on current time periods rather than future periods when making economic decisions; that is, people choose to consume more today than save for retirement.

5. a. The site stickk.com helps individuals to overcome the hyperbolic discounting problem that leads to time inconsistency. Having specified their goals, individuals have an incentive to consistently achieve them in order to avoid incurring the penalty.

b. If we assume that individuals are altruistic or generous, or exhibit warm glow, failing to meet their goals does not cost them as much since the fee is donated to an organization they hold in high regard. It is, therefore, more likely that individuals will "stick" to their commitment if they identify a charity they despise, since they will be more inclined to work hard to avoid the cost (ill-feeling) of having to contribute to it.

7. a. Assuming completely rational employees, both schemes would motivate them equally because their expected value is identical.

b. Scheme B is likely to be more effective in the presence of the endowment effect; that is, employees will lose more utility from having the $500 withdrawn than they would gain from receiving Scheme A's $500 bonus. Naturally, they would be inclined to work hard to achieve it in this case, so as to not lose what they believe they already own.

c. The offers under Schemes A and B are essentially identical: Meet the 10% increase, you are $500 richer; fail to meet the 10% increase and you get nothing. Employees prefer Scheme A in terms of framing because most people are inclined to opt for scenarios that are framed as rewards rather than punishments. However, it would be more profitable for you and your factory to utilize Scheme B if you had reason to expect that the employees will be swayed by the endowment effect.

References

Acemoglu, Daron and Amy Finkelstein. "Input and Technology Choices in Regulated Industries: Evidence from the Health Care Sector." *Journal of Political Economy* 116, no. 5 (2008): 837–880.

Acemoglu, Daron and Joshua Linn. "Market Size in Innovation: Theory and Evidence from the Pharmaceutical Industry." *The Quarterly Journal of Economics* 119, no. 3 (2004): 1049–1090.

Akerlof, George. "The Market for 'Lemons': Quality Uncertainty and the Market Mechanism." *Quarterly Journal of Economics* 84, no. 3 (August 1970): 488–500.

Arkes, Hal R. and Catherine Blumer. "The Psychology of Sunk Cost." *Organizational Behavior and Human Decision Processes* 35 (1985): 124–140.

Ayres, Ian and Steven D. Levitt. "Measuring Positive Externalities from Unobservable Victim Precaution: An Empirical Analysis of Lojack." *Quarterly Journal of Economics* 113, no. 1 (February 1998): 43–77.

Becker, Gary S. and Kevin M. Murphy. "A Theory of Rational Addiction." *Journal of Political Economy* 96, no. 4 (August 1988): 675–700.

Becker, Gary S., Kevin M. Murphy, and Robert H. Topel. "On the Economics of Climate Policy." *The B.E. Journal of Economic Analysis & Policy* 10, no. 2 (2010): article 19.

Billips, Mike. "Congestion Pricing: To Skip Traffic, Atlanta Says Pay Up." *TIME Magazine*, January 23, 2011.

Bishop, John H. "Is the Test Score Decline Responsible for the Productivity Growth Decline?" *American Economic Review* 79, no. 1 (1989): 178–197.

Black, Dan A., Seth Sanders, and Lowell Taylor. "The Economic Reward for Studying Economics." *Economic Inquiry* 41, no. 3 (2003): 365–377.

Bulow, Jeremy and Paul Klemperer. "The Tobacco Deal." *Brookings Papers on Economic Activity* (1998): 323–394.

Cabral, Luís and Ali Hortaçsu. "The Dynamics of Seller Reputation: Evidence from eBay." *Journal of Industrial Economics* 58, no. 1 (March 2010): 54–78.

Chiappori, Pierre-Andre, Steven Levitt, and Tim Groseclose. "Testing Mixed-Strategy Equilibria When Players Are Heterogeneous: The Case of Penalty Kicks in Soccer." *American Economic Review* 92, no. 4 (September 2002): 1138–1151.

Coase, Ronald. "The Problem of Social Cost." *Journal of Law and Economics* 3 (1960): 1–44.

Cohen, Alma, Rajeev Dehejia, and Dmitri Romanov. "Do Financial Incentives Affect Fertility?" NBER Working Paper, 2007.

Cooper, Russell W. and John C. Haltiwanger. "On the Nature of Capital Adjustment Costs." *Review of Economic Studies* 73, no. 3 (July 2006): 611–633.

Corcoran, Kevin. "The Big Fix." *The Indianapolis Star*, May 6, 2007. A1, A22–A23.

Costa, Dora. "The Wage and the Length of the Work Day: From the 1890s to 1991." *Journal of Labor Economics* 18, no. 1 (2000): 156–181.

Crooker, John R. and Aju J. Fenn. "Estimating Local Welfare Generated by an NFL Team under Credible Threat of Relocation." *Southern Economic Journal* 76, no. 1 (2009): 198–223.

Cutler, David M. and Jonathan Gruber. "Does Public Insurance Crowd Out Private Insurance?" *Quarterly Journal of Economics* 111, no. 2 (1996): 391–430.

de Walque, Damien. "Education, Information, and Smoking Decisions: Evidence from Smoking Histories in the United States, 1940–2000." *Journal of Human Resources* 45, no. 3 (2010): 682–717.

DellaVigna, Stefano and Ulrike Malmendier. "Paying Not to Go to the Gym." *American Economic Review* 96, no. 3 (2006): 694–719.

"Drug Manufacturer Prices Are Higher for Humans than for Animals." U.S. House of Representatives Report, March 16, 2000. http://lobby.la.psu.edu/010_Insuring_the_Uninsured/Congressional_Statements/House/H_Thurman_031600.htm.

Dube, Jean-Pierre. "Product Differentiation and Mergers in the Carbonated Soft Drink Industry." *Journal of Economics and Management Strategy* 14, no. 4 (2005): 879–904.

Dubner, Stephen and Steven Levitt. "What Do Al Gore and Mount Pinatubo Have in Common?" *SuperFreakonomics*. New York: Harper Collins, 2009.

Duranton, Gilles and Matthew A. Turner. "The Fundamental Law of Road Congestion: Evidence from US Cities." *American Economic Review* 101, no. 6 (October 2011): 2616–2652.

Dwyer, Gerald P. Jr. and Cotton M. Lindsay. "Robert Giffen and the Irish Potato." *American Economic Review* 74, no. 1 (1984): 188–192.

Economides, Nicholas, Katja Seim, and V. Brian Viard. "Quantifying the Benefits of Entry into Local Phone Service." *RAND Journal of Economics* 39, no. 3 (2008): 699–730.

Edlin, Aaron and Pinar Karaca-Mandic. "The Accident Externality from Driving." *Journal of Political Economy* 114, no. 5 (2006): 931–955.

Ellison, Glenn and Sara Ellison. "Search, Obfuscation, and Price Elasticities on the Internet." *Econometrica* 77, no. 2 (2009): 427–452.

Finkelstein, Amy and James Poterba. "Selection Effects in the United Kingdom Individual Annuities Market." *Economic Journal* 112, no. 476 (January 2002): 28–50.

Finkelstein, Amy and Robin McKnight. "What Did Medicare Do? The Initial Impact of Medicare on Mortality and Out of Pocket Medical Spending." *Journal of Public Economics* 92, no. 7 (2008): 1644–1668.

"Firefighters Let Home Burn over $75 Fee—Again," April 20, 2012, msnbc.com.

Fleming, Charles. "That Sinking Feeling." *Vanity Fair*, August 1, 1995.

Fleming, Charles. "Fishtar? Why 'Waterworld,' with Costner in Fins, Is Costliest Film Ever." *Wall Street Journal*, January 31, 1996.

Genesove, David and Christopher Mayer. "Loss Aversion and Seller Behavior: Evidence from the Housing Market." *Quarterly Journal of Economics* 116, no. 4 (November 2001): 1233–1260.

Gilley, Otis W. and Marc C. Chopin. "Professional Golf: Labor or Leisure." *Managerial Finance* 26, no. 7 (2000): 33–45.

Goldberg, Pinelopi K. and Frank Verboven. "Cross-Country Price Dispersion in the Euro Era: A Case Study of the European Car Market." *Economic Policy* 19, no. 40 (October 2004): 483–521.

Goldberg, Pinelopi K., Amit K. Khandelwal, Nina Pavcnik, and Petia Topalova. "Multi-Product Firms and Product Turnover in the Developing World: Evidence from India." *Review of Economics and Statistics* 92, no. 4 (2010): 1042–1049.

Goldin, Claudia and Lawrence F. Katz. "The Power of the Pill: Oral Contraceptives and Women's Career and Marriage Decisions." *Journal of Political Economy* 110, no. 4 (2002): 730–770.

Goldin, Claudia, Lawrence F. Katz, and Iliana Kuziemko. "The Homecoming of American College Women: The Reversal of the College Gender Gap." *Journal of Economic Perspectives* 20, no. 4 (2006): 133–156.

Goolsbee, Austan. "Refined Thought: Dependency Paradox." *Fortune*, August 22, 2005. http://money.cnn.com/magazines/fortune/fortune_archive/2005/08/22/8270013/index.htm.

Goolsbee, Austan and Chad Syverson. "How Do Incumbents Respond to the Threat of Entry? Evidence from the Major Airlines." *Quarterly Journal of Economics* 123, no. 4 (2008): 1611–1633.

Government Accountability Office. "National Flood Insurance Program: Actions to Address Repetitive Loss Properties." Statement of William O. Jenkins Jr., March 2004.

Harford, Tim. *The Logic of Life*: *The Rational Economics of an Irrational World*. New York: Random House, 2008. 18–21.

Henrich, Joseph, Robert Boyd, Samuel Bowles, Colin Camerer, Ernst Fehr, Herbert Gintis, and Richard McElreath. "In Search of Homo Economicus: Behavioral Experiments in 15 Small-Scale Societies." *American Economic Review Papers and Proceedings* 91, no. 2 (2001): 73–78.

Hortaçsu, A. and S. Puller. "Understanding Strategic Bidding in Multi-Unit Auctions: A Case Study of the Texas Electricity Spot Market." *RAND Journal of Economics* 39, no. 1 (2008): 86–114.

Hossain, Tanjim and John Morgan. ". . . Plus Shipping and Handling: Revenue (Non) Equivalence in Field Experiments on eBay." *The B.E. Journal of Economic Analysis & Policy* 6, no. 2 (2007): Article 3.

Hsieh, Chang-Tai and Enrico Moretti. "Can Free Entry Be Inefficient? Fixed Commissions and Social Waste in the Real Estate Industry." *Journal of Political Economy* 111, no. 5 (2003): 1076–1122.

Jackson, Joe. *The Thief at the End of the World*: *Rubber, Power and the Seeds of Empire*. New York: Viking, 2008.

Jensen, Robert T. "The Digital Provide: Information (Technology), Market Performance, and Welfare in the South Indian Fisheries Sector." *The Quarterly Journal of Economics* 122, no. 3 (2007): 879–924.

Jensen, Robert T. and Nolan H. Miller. "Giffen Behavior and Subsistence Consumption." *American Economic Review* 98, no. 4 (2008): 1553–1577.

Kreps, David M. and José A. Scheinkman. "Quantity Precommitment and Bertrand Competition Yield

Cournot Outcomes." *The Bell Journal of Economics* 14, no. 2 (Autumn 1983): 326–337.

Leeson, Peter T. "An-*arggh*-chy: The Law and Economics of Pirate Organization." *Journal of Political Economy* 115, no. 6 (2007): 1049–1094.

Levitt, Steven D. and Chad Syverson. "Market Distortions When Agents Are Better Informed: The Value of Information in Real Estate Transactions." *Review of Economics and Statistics* 90, no. 4 (November 2008): 599–611.

Libecap, Gary D. and Steven N. Wiggins. "Contractual Responses to the Common Pool: Prorationing of Crude Oil Production." *American Economic Review* 74, no. 1 (March 1984): 87–98.

List, John. "The Behavioralist Meets the Market: Measuring Social Preferences and Reputation Effects in Actual Transactions." *Journal of Political Economy* 114, no. 1 (February 2006): 1–37.

List, John, Stefano DellaVigna, and Ulrike Malmendier. "Testing for Altruism and Social Pressure in Charitable Giving." *Quarterly Journal of Economics* 121, no.1 (2012): 1-56.

MacDonald, James M. and Michael E. Ollinger. "Scale Economies and Consolidation in Hog Slaughter." *American Journal of Agricultural Economics* 82, no. 2 (2000): 334–346.

Meer, Jonathan and Harvey S. Rosen. "Altruism and the Child Cycle of Alumni Donations." *American Economic Journal: Economic Policy* 1, no. 1 (2009): 258–286.

Mortimer, Julie Holland and Alan Sorensen. "Supply Responses to Digital Distribution: Recorded Music and Live Performances." Preliminary, December 29, 2005. http://www.aeaweb.org/assa/2006/0107_0800_0702.pdf.

Muller, Nicholas Z., Robert Mendelsohn, and William Nordhaus. "Environmental Accounting for Pollution in the United States Economy." *American Economic Review* 101, no. 5 (August 2011): 1649–1675.

Nevo, Aviv. "Measuring Market Power in the Ready-to-Eat Cereal Industry." *Econometrica* 69, no. 2 (2001): 307–342.

"No Pay, No Spray: Firefighters Let Home Burn," October 6, 2010, msnbc.com.

Olson, Mancur. *The Logic of Collective Action: Public Goods and the Theory of Groups.* Cambridge, MA: Harvard University Press, 1965.

Oremus, Will. "Hell Phone: Is There Any Way to Stop the Scourge of Text Message Spam?" *Slate*, April 13, 2012.

Pigou, Arthur C. *The Economics of Welfare.* London: Macmillan, 1920.

Renewable Fuels Association. "Ethanol Industry Overview." Accessed March 28, 2012. http://www.ethanolrfa.org/pages/statistics#EIO.

Rosen, Sherwin. "Potato Paradoxes." *Journal of Political Economy* 107, no. 6 (1999): S294–S313.

Saks, Raven E. "Job Creation and Housing Construction: Constraints on Metropolitan Area Employment Growth." *Journal of Urban Economics* 64, no. 1 (2008): 178–195.

Schelling, Thomas. *The Strategy of Conflict.* Cambridge, MA: Harvard University Press, 1980.

Schmitz, James A. Jr. "What Determines Productivity? Lessons from the Dramatic Recovery of the U.S. and Canadian Iron Ore Industries Following Their Early 1980s Crisis." *Journal of Political Economy* 113, no. 3 (2005): 582–625.

Scott Morton, Fiona M. and Joel M. Podolny. "Love or Money? The Effects of Owner Motivation in the California Wine Industry." *Journal of Industrial Economics* 50, no. 4 (December 2002): 431–456.

Spence, Michael. "Job Market Signaling." *Quarterly Journal of Economics* 87, no. 3 (1973): 355–374.

Symantec. Message Labs Intelligence Report, 2011. http://www.symantec.com/about/news/release/article.jsp?prid=20110426_01.

Teger, Allan I. *Too Much Invested to Quit.* Oxford: Pergamon Press, 1980.

Tversky, Amos and Daniel Kahneman. "Judgment under Uncertainty: Heuristics and Biases." *Science* 185, no. 4157 (1974): 1124–1130.

Tversky, Amos and Daniel Kahneman. "The Framing of Decisions and the Psychology of Choice." *Science* 211, no. 4481 (1981): 453–458.

Waldfogel, Joel. "The Deadweight Loss of Christmas." *American Economic Review* 83, no. 5 (1993): 1328–1336.

Weitzman, Martin. "Prices vs. Quantities." *The Review of Economic Studies* 41, no. 4 (1974): 477–491.

Weitzman, Martin. "On Modeling and Interpreting the Economics of Climate Change." *The Review of Economics and Statistics* 91, no. 1 (2009): 1–19.

Glossary

above par: Description of a bond with a price above its face value, or whose yield is less than its coupon rate. (p. 535)

accounting cost: The direct cost of operating a business, including costs for raw materials. (p. 262)

accounting profit: A firm's total revenue minus its accounting cost. (p. 263)

actuarially fair: Description of an insurance policy with expected net payments equal to zero. (p. 553)

adverse selection: A situation in which market characteristics lead to more low-quality goods and fewer high-quality goods being put on the market. (p. 608)

altruism: Acts motivated primarily by a concern for the welfare of others. (p. 694)

anchoring: A type of framing bias in which a person's decision is influenced by specific pieces of information given. (p. 690)

antitrust law: Laws designed to promote competitive markets by restricting firms from behaviors that limit competition. (p. 377)

arbitrage: The practice of reselling a product at a price higher than its original selling price. (p. 397)

asymmetric information: A situation in which there is an imbalance of information across participants in an economic transaction. (p. 606)

at par: Description of a bond whose price equals its face value, or whose yield equals its coupon rate. (p. 535)

average fixed cost: A firm's fixed cost per unit of output. (p. 274)

average product: The quantity of output produced per unit of input. (p. 223)

average total cost: A firm's total cost per unit of output. (p. 276)

average variable cost: A firm's variable cost per unit of output. (p. 276)

backward induction: The process of solving a multistep game by first solving the last step and then working backward. (p. 498)

bad: A good or service that provides a consumer with negative utility. (p. 132)

barriers to entry: Factors that prevent entry into markets with large producer surpluses. (p. 348)

behavioral economics: Branch of economics that incorporates insights from human psychology into models of economic behavior. (p. 686)

below par: Description of a bond with a price less than its face value, or whose yield is greater than its coupon rate. (p. 535)

Bertrand competition: Oligopoly model in which each firm chooses the price of its product. (p. 450)

block pricing: The practice of reducing the price of a good when the customer buys more of it. (p. 428)

bond: Financial instrument that indicates the issuer is indebted to the purchaser. (p. 534)

budget constraint: A curve that describes the entire set of consumption bundles a consumer can purchase when spending all income. (p. 134)

bundling: A pricing strategy in which the firm sells two or more products together at a single price. (p. 422)

cartel or **collusion:** Oligopoly behavior in which firms coordinate and collectively act as a monopoly to gain monopoly profits. (p. 443)

certainty equivalent: The guaranteed income level at which an individual would receive the same expected utility level as from an uncertain income. (p. 551)

change in demand: A shift of the entire demand curve caused by a change in a determinant of demand other than the good's own price. (p. 20)

change in quantity demanded: A movement *along* the demand curve that occurs as a result of a change in the good's price. (p. 20)

change in quantity supplied: A movement *along* the supply curve that occurs as a result of a change in the good's price. (p. 24)

change in supply: A shift of the entire supply curve caused by a change in a determinant of supply other than the good's own price. (p. 25)

club good: A good that is nonrival and excludable. (p. 672)

Coase theorem: Theorem that states that costless negotiation among market participants will lead to the efficient market outcome regardless of who holds legal property rights. (p. 667)

commodities: Products traded in markets in which consumers view different varieties of the good as essentially interchangeable. (p. 16)

common resource: An economic good that all individuals can access freely and whose value to the individual consumer decreases as others use it. (p. 666)

complement: A good that is purchased and used in combination with another good. (pp. 17, 196)

complete information: Situation in which all participants in an economic transaction know the relevant information. (p. 606)

complete insurance or **full insurance:** An insurance policy that leaves the insured individual equally well off regardless of the outcome. (p. 552)

compounding or **compound interest:** A calculation of interest based on the sum of the original principal and the interest paid over past periods. (p. 529)

constant-cost industry: An industry whose firms' total costs do not change with total industry output. (p. 335)

constant economies of scale: Total cost rises at the same rate as output rises. (p. 287)

constant returns to scale: A production function for which changing all inputs by the same proportion changes the quantity of output by the same proportion. (p. 238)

consumer surplus: The difference between the amount consumers would be willing to pay for a good or service and the amount they actually have to pay. (p. 62)

consumption bundle: A set of goods or services a consumer considers purchasing. (p. 113)

consumption contract curve: Curve that shows all possible Pareto-efficient allocations of goods across consumers. (p. 586)

corner solution: A utility-maximizing bundle located at the "corner" of the budget constraint where the consumer purchases only one of two goods. (p. 147)

cost curve: The mathematical relationship between a firm's production costs and its output. (p. 272)

cost minimization: A firm's goal of producing a specific quantity of output at minimum cost. (p. 225)

coupon payments: Set of scheduled interest payments that recur over a bond's entire life. (p. 534)

coupon rate: The rate of the regular periodic amount paid out to bondholders. (p. 534)

Cournot competition: Oligopoly model in which each firm chooses its production quantity. (p. 453)

credible commitment: A choice or a restriction of choices that guarantees a player will take a particular future action if certain conditions occur. (p. 511)

cross-price elasticity of demand: The percentage change in the quantity demanded of one good associated with a 1% change in the price of another good. (p. 53)

crowding out: A reduction in private economic activity created by greater government presence in a market. (p. 88)

deadweight loss (DWL): The reduction in total surplus that occurs as a result of a market inefficiency. (p. 76)

decreasing-cost industry: An industry whose firms' total costs decrease with increases in industry output. (p. 335)

decreasing returns to scale: A production function for which changing all inputs by the same proportion changes output *less* than proportionately. (p. 238)

demand: The combined amount of a good that all consumers are willing to buy. (p. 15)

demand choke price: The price at which no consumer is willing to buy a good and quantity demanded is zero; the vertical intercept of the inverse demand curve. (pp. 19, 63)

demand curve: The relationship between the quantity of a good that consumers demand and the good's price, holding all other factors constant. (p. 18)

differentiated product market: Market with multiple varieties of a common product. (p. 465)

diminishing marginal product: A feature of the production function; as a firm hires additional units of a given input, the marginal product of that input falls. (p. 221)

direct price discrimination: A pricing strategy in which firms charge different prices to different customers based on observable characteristics of the customers. (p. 399)

diseconomies of scale: Total cost rises at a faster rate than output rises. (p. 287)

diseconomies of scope: The simultaneous production of multiple products at a higher cost than if a firm made each product separately. (p. 290)

diversification: A strategy to reduce risk by combining uncertain outcomes. (p. 552)

dominant strategy: A winning strategy for a player, regardless of her opponents' strategies. (p. 486)

dominated strategy: A losing strategy for a player, regardless of her opponents' strategies. (p. 486)

durable good: A good that has a long service life. (p. 242)

econometrics: Field that develops and uses mathematical and statistical techniques to test economic theory. (p. 696)

economic cost: The sum of a producer's accounting and opportunity costs. (p. 262)

economic profit: A firm's total revenue minus its economic cost. (p. 263)

economic rent: Returns to specialized inputs above what firms paid for them. (p. 336)

economies of scale: Total cost rises at a slower rate than output rises. (p. 287)

economies of scope: The simultaneous production of multiple products at a lower cost than if a firm made each product separately. (p. 290)

Edgeworth box: Graph of an economy with two economic actors and two goods that is used to analyze market efficiency. (p. 581)

efficient level of pollution: The level of emissions necessary to produce the efficient quantity of the good tied to the externality. (p. 652)

egalitarian: Belief that the ideal society is one in which each individual is equally well off. (p. 579)

elastic: A price elasticity with an absolute value greater than 1. (p. 46)

elasticity: The ratio of the percentage change in one value to the percentage change in another. (p. 43)

empirical: Using data analysis and experiments to explore phenomena. (p. 9)

endowment effect: The phenomenon where simply possessing a good makes it more valuable; that is, the possessor must be paid more to give up the good than he would have paid to buy it in the first place. (p. 690)

Engel curve: A curve that shows the relationship between the quantity of a good consumed and a consumer's income. (p. 170)

equilibrium price: The only price at which quantity supplied equals quantity demanded. (p. 26)

exchange efficiency: A Pareto-efficient allocation of a set of goods across consumers. (p. 581)

expansion path: A curve that illustrates how the optimal mix of inputs varies with total output. (p. 246)

expected value: The probability-weighted average payout. (p. 546)

experimental economics: Branch of economics that relies on experiments to illuminate economic behavior. (p. 696)

extensive form or **decision tree:** Representation of a sequential game that shows both the choice and timing of players' actions. (p. 503)

external marginal benefit: The benefit conferred on a third party when an additional unit of a good is produced or consumed. (p. 645)

external marginal cost: The cost imposed on a third party when an additional unit of a good is produced or consumed. (p. 645)

externality: A cost or benefit that affects a third party not directly involved in an economic transaction. (p. 645)

face value or **par value:** The principal that the bond issuer pays interest on. (p. 534)

feasible bundle: A bundle that the consumer has the ability to purchase; lies on or below the consumer's budget constraint. (p. 134)

field experiment: Research method in which randomizations are carried out in real-world settings. (p. 699)

final good: A good that is bought by a consumer. (p. 216)

first-mover advantage: In Stackelberg competition, the advantage gained by the initial firm in setting its production quantity. (p. 462)

First Welfare Theorem: Theorem stating that perfectly competitive markets in general equilibrium distribute resources in a Pareto-efficient way. (p. 596)

fixed cost: An input cost that does not vary with the amount of output. (pp. 239, 265)

free entry: The ability of a firm to enter an industry without encountering legal or technical barriers. (p. 326)

free exit: The ability of a firm to exit an industry without encountering legal or technical barriers. (p. 327)

free-rider problem: A source of inefficiency resulting from individuals consuming a public good or service without paying for it. (p. 674)

game theory: The study of strategic interactions among two or more economic actors. (p. 484)

general equilibrium analysis: The study of market behavior that accounts for cross-market influences and is concerned with conditions present when all markets are simultaneously in equilibrium. (p. 564)

Giffen good: A good for which price and quantity demanded are positively related. (p. 192)

grim trigger strategy (or grim reaper strategy): A strategy in which cooperative play ends when one player cheats. (p. 501)

hyperbolic discounting: Tendency of people to place much greater importance on the immediate present than even the near future when making economic decisions. (p. 688)

imperfect competition: Market structures with characteristics between those of perfect competition and monopoly. (p. 440)

incentive compatibility: The requirement under an indirect price discrimination strategy that the price offered to each consumer group is chosen by that group. (p. 416)

income effect: The change in a consumer's consumption choices that results from a change in the purchasing power of the consumer's income. (pp. 166, 180)

income elasticity: The percentage change in the quantity consumed of a good in response to a 1% change in income. (p. 168)

income elasticity of demand: The percentage change in quantity demanded associated with a 1% change in consumer income. (p. 53)

income expansion path: A curve that connects a consumer's optimal bundles at each income level. (p. 170)

increasing-cost industry: An industry whose firms' total costs increase with increases in industry output. (p. 335)

increasing returns to scale: A production function for which changing all inputs by the same proportion changes output *more* than proportionately. (p. 238)

indifference curve: A mathematical representation of the combination of all the different consumption bundles that provide a consumer with the same utility. (p. 116)

indifferent: The special case in which a consumer derives the same utility level from each of two or more consumption bundles. (p. 116)

indirect price discrimination (second-degree price discrimination): A pricing strategy in which customers pick among a variety of pricing options offered by the firm. (p. 414)

inelastic: A price elasticity with an absolute value less than 1. (p. 46)

infeasible bundle: A bundle that the consumer cannot afford to purchase; lies to the right and above a consumer's budget constraint. (p. 134)

inferior good: A good for which quantity demanded decreases when income rises. (pp. 53, 167)

input efficiency: A Pareto-efficient allocation of inputs across producers. (p. 581)

insurance: A payment from one economic actor to another with the aim of reducing the risk facing the payer. (p. 528)

interest: A periodic payment tied to an amount of assets borrowed or lent. (p. 529)

interest rate: Interest expressed as a fraction of the principal. (p. 529)

interior solution: A utility-maximizing bundle that contains positive quantities of both goods. (p. 147)

intermediate good: A good that is used to produce another good. (p. 216)

inverse demand curve: A demand curve written in the form of price as a function of quantity demanded. (p. 19)

inverse supply curve: A supply curve written in the form of price as a function of quantity supplied. (p. 24)

investment: The purchase of capital in the present with the intent of reaping future benefits. (p. 528)

isocost line: A curve that shows all of the input combinations that yield the same cost. (p. 230)

isoquant: A curve representing all the combinations of inputs that allow a firm to make a particular quantity of output. (p. 226)

lab experiment: Test of an economic theory in a laboratory setting. (p. 697)

learning by doing: The process by which a firm becomes more efficient at production as it produces more output. (p. 239)

lemons problem: An asymmetric information problem that occurs when a seller knows more about the quality of the good he is selling than does the buyer. (p. 606)

Lerner index: A measure of a firm's markup, or its level of market power. (p. 364)

long-run competitive equilibrium: The point at which the market price is equal to the minimum average total cost and firms would gain no profits by entering the industry. (p. 327)

loss aversion: A type of framing bias in which a consumer chooses a reference point around which losses hurt much more than gains feel good. (p. 690)

lump-sum transfer: Transfer to or from an individual for which the size is unaffected by the individual's choices. (p. 598)

luxury good: A good with an income elasticity greater than 1. (pp. 53, 169)

marginal abatement cost (MAC): The cost of reducing emissions by one unit. (p. 653)

marginal cost: The additional cost of producing an additional unit of output. (p. 276)

marginal product: The additional output that a firm can produce by using an additional unit of an input (holding use of the other input constant). (p. 220)

marginal rate of substitution of X for Y (MRS_{XY}): The rate at which a consumer is willing to trade off one good (the good on the horizontal axis X) for another (the good on the vertical axis Y) and still be left equally well off. (p. 121)

marginal rate of technical substitution ($MRTS_{XY}$): The rate at which the firm can trade input X for input Y, holding output constant. (p. 226)

marginal rate of transformation (MRT): The tradeoff between the production of any goods on the market. (p. 592)

marginal revenue: The additional revenue from selling one additional unit of output. (p. 307)

marginal utility: The additional utility a consumer receives from an additional unit of a good or service. (p. 114)

market equilibrium: The point at which the quantity demanded by consumers exactly equals the quantity supplied by producers. (p. 25)

market power: A firm's ability to influence the market price of its product. (p. 348)

market structure: The competitive environment in which firms operate. (p. 304)

markup: The percentage of the firm's price that is greater than its marginal cost. (p. 364)

maturity: The length of a bond's life. (p. 534)

maximin strategy: A strategy in which the player minimizes her exposure to loss. (p. 495)

mental accounting: A type of framing bias in which people divide their current and future assets into separate, nontransferable portions, instead of basing purchasing decisions on their assets as a whole. (p. 691)

microeconomics: The branch of economics that studies the specific choices made by consumers and producers. (p. 2)

mixed bundling: A type of bundling in which the firm simultaneously offers consumers the choice of buying two or more products separately or as a bundle. (p. 424)

mixed strategy: A strategy in which the player randomizes her actions. (p. 493)

monopolist: The sole supplier and price setter of a good on the market. (p. 348)

monopolistic competition: A market structure characterized by many firms selling a differentiated product with no barriers to entry; each firm has some market power but makes zero economic profit in the long run. (pp. 354, 440, 471)

monopoly: A market served by only one firm. (p. 348)

moral hazard: A situation that arises when one party in an economic transaction cannot observe the other party's behavior. (p. 617)

Nash equilibrium: An equilibrium in which each firm is doing the best it can conditional on the actions taken by its competitors. (p. 441)

natural experiment: A randomization or near-randomization that arises by happenstance. (p. 699)

natural monopoly: A market in which it is efficient for a single firm to produce the entire industry output. (p. 348)

necessity good: A normal good for which income elasticity is between zero and 1. (p. 169)

negative externality: A cost imposed on a third party not directly involved in an economic transaction. (p. 645)

net present value (NPV) analysis: The use of the present discounted value to evaluate the expected long-term return on an investment. (p. 537)

network good: A good whose value to each consumer increases with the number of other consumers of the product. (p. 350)

nominal interest rate: Rate of return expressed in raw currency values. (p. 542)

nonbinding price ceiling: A price ceiling set at a level above equilibrium price. (p. 81)

nonbinding price floor: A price floor set at a level below equilibrium price. (p. 83)

noncredible threat: A threat that is not rational for a player to actually carry out. (p. 511)

nonexcludability: A defining property of a common resource, that consumers cannot be prevented from consuming the good. (p. 666)

nonrival: Defining property of a public good that describes how one individual's consumption of the good does not diminish another consumer's enjoyment of the same good. (p. 672)

normal form: The common organization of an economic game into its players, strategies, and the payoffs in a payoff matrix. (p. 487)

normal good: A good for which quantity demanded rises when income rises. (pp. 53, 167)

oligopoly: Market structure in which a few competitors operate. (pp. 354, 440)

operating cost: The cost a firm incurs in producing its output. (p. 267)

operating revenue: The money a firm earns from selling its output. (p. 267)

opportunity cost: The value of what a producer gives up by using an input. (p. 262)

optimal strategy: The action that has the highest expected payoff. (p. 485)

option value of waiting: The value created if an investor can postpone his investment decision until the uncertainty about an investment's returns is wholly or partially resolved. (p. 546)

output efficiency: A Pareto-efficient allocation of inputs and productive outputs in an economy. (p. 581)

overconfidence: A belief that skill and judgment are better than they truly are, or that better outcomes are more likely to happen than their true probability. (p. 687)

own-price elasticities of demand: The percentage change in quantity demanded for a good resulting from a percentage change in the price of that good. (p. 54)

Pareto efficiency: An economic allocation of goods in which the goods cannot be reallocated without making at least one individual worse off. (p. 580)

partial equilibrium analysis: Determination of the equilibrium in a particular market that assumes there are no cross-market spillovers. (p. 564)

payback period: The length of time required for an investment's initial costs to be recouped in future benefits without discounting future flows. (p. 541)

payoff matrix: A table that lists the players, strategies, and payoffs of an economic game. (p. 486)

payoff: The outcome a player receives from playing the game. (p. 485)

perfect competition: A market with many firms producing identical products and no barriers to entry. (p. 304)

perfect complement: A good whose utility level depends on its being used in a fixed proportion with another good. (p. 128)

perfect price discrimination (first-degree price discrimination): A type of direct price discrimination in which a firm charges each customer exactly his willingness to pay. (p. 399)

perfect substitute: A good that a consumer can trade for another good, in fixed units, and receive the same level of utility. (p. 128)

perfectly elastic: A price elasticity that is infinite; any change in price leads to an infinite change in quantity demanded or supplied. (p. 46)

perfectly inelastic: A price elasticity that is equal to zero; there is no change in quantity demanded or supplied for any change in price. (p. 46)

Pigouvian subsidy: A subsidy paid for an activity that creates a positive externality. (p. 656)

Pigouvian tax: A tax imposed on an activity that creates a negative externality. (p. 654)

player: A participant in an economic game, who must decide on actions based on the actions of others. (p. 485)

positive externality: A benefit conferred on a third party not directly involved in an economic transaction. (p. 645)

present discounted value (PDV): The value of a future payment made in terms of equivalent present-period dollars. (p. 529)

price ceiling: A price regulation that sets the highest price that can be paid legally for a good or service. (p. 75)

price discrimination: Pricing strategy in which firms with market power charge different prices to customers for the same product based on their willingness to pay. (pp. 357, 396)

price elasticity of demand: The percentage change in quantity demanded resulting from a 1% change in price. (p. 43)

price floor (or price support): A price regulation that sets the lowest price that can be paid legally for a good or service. (p. 81)

pricing strategy: A firm's method of pricing its product based on market characteristics. (p. 396)

principal: The amount of assets on which interest payments are paid. (p. 529)

principal-agent relationships: Economic transactions that feature information asymmetry between a principal and his hired agent, whose actions the principal cannot fully observe. (p. 623)

prisoner's dilemma: A situation in which the Nash equilibrium outcome is worse for all involved than another (unstable) outcome. (p. 442)

private good: A good that is rival (one person's consumption affects the ability of another to consume it) and excludable (individuals can be prevented from consuming it). (p. 672)

producer surplus: The difference between the price at which producers are willing to sell their good or service and the price they actually receive. (p. 63)

product differentiation: Imperfect substitutability across varieties of a product. (p. 351)

production: The process by which a person, company, government, or non-profit agency creates a good or service that others are willing to pay for. (p. 216)

production contract curve: Curve that shows all Pareto-efficient allocations of inputs across producers. (p. 590)

production function: A mathematical relationship that describes how much output can be made from different combinations of inputs. (p. 216)

production possibilities frontier (PPF): Curve that connects all possible efficient output combinations of two goods. (p. 591)

production technology: The processes used to make, distribute, and sell a good. (p. 22)

profit: The difference between a firm's revenue and its total cost. (p. 306)

public good: A good that is accessible to anyone who wants to consume it, and that remains just as valuable to a consumer even as other people consume it. (p. 671)

pure bundling: A type of bundling in which the firm offers the products only as a bundle. (p. 424)

pure strategy: A strategy in which the player chooses a particular action with certainty. (p. 493)

quantity discount: The practice of charging a lower per-unit price to customers who buy larger quantities. (p. 414)

quota: A regulation mandating that the production or consumption of a certain quantity of a good or externality be limited (negative externality) or required (positive externality). (pp. 83, 658)

Rawlsian social welfare function: Mathematical function that computes society's welfare as the welfare of the worst-off individual. (p. 578)

reaction curve: A function that relates a firm's best response to its competitor's possible actions. In Cournot competition, this is the firm's best production response to its competitor's possible quantity choices. (p. 456)

real interest rate: Rate of return expressed in terms of purchasing power. (p. 542)

rent-seeking: A firm's attempts to gain government-granted monopoly power and, therefore, additional producer surplus. (p. 381)

repeated games: A series of simultaneous games among the same set of economic actors. (p. 484)

residual demand curve: In Cournot competition, the demand remaining for a firm's output given competitor firms' production quantities. (p. 455)

residual marginal revenue curve: A marginal revenue curve corresponding to a residual demand curve. (p. 455)

returns to scale: A change in the amount of output in response to a proportional increase or decrease in all of the inputs. (p. 238)

risk-averse: Suffering an expected utility loss from uncertainty, or equivalently, being willing to pay to have that risk reduced. (p. 551)

risk-free interest rate: Rate of return on an investment that any asset paying a guaranteed return would pay. (p. 555)

risk premium: The amount an individual must be compensated for bearing risk without suffering a loss in expected utility. (p. 551)

Second Welfare Theorem: Theorem stating that any given Pareto-efficient allocation in a perfectly competitive market is a general equilibrium outcome for some initial allocation. (p. 598)

segmenting (third-degree price discrimination): A type of direct price discrimination in which a firm charges different prices to different groups of customers. (p. 403)

sequential games: Games where one player moves first and other players observe this action before making their decisions. (pp. 484, 502)

shortage: The amount by which quantity demanded exceeds quantity supplied when market price is lower than the equilibrium price. (p. 27)

short-run total cost curve: The mathematical representation of a firm's total cost of producing different quantities of output at a fixed level of capital. (p. 281)

side payment: A type of bribe that influences the outcome of a strategic game. (p. 509)

signal: A costly action taken by an economic actor to indicate something that would otherwise be difficult to observe. (p. 631)

signaling: A solution to the problem of asymmetric information in which the knowledgeable party alerts the other party to an unobservable characteristic of the good. (p. 630)

simultaneous game: A game in which participants choose their actions simultaneously without knowing their opponents' strategies. (p. 484)

social benefit: The benefit of an economic transaction to society, equal to the private benefit plus the external benefit. (p. 645)

social cost: The cost of an economic transaction to society, equal to the private cost plus the external cost. (p. 645)

social welfare function: Mathematical function that combines individuals' utility levels into a single measure of society's total utility level. (p. 578)

specific capital: Capital that cannot be used outside of its original application. (p. 266)

Stackelberg competition: Oligopoly model in which firms make production decisions sequentially. (p. 462)

strategic decision: An action made based on the anticipation of others' actions. (p. 484)

strategic move: An action taken early in a game that favorably influences the ultimate outcome of the game. (p. 509)

strategy: The plan of action that a player takes in an economic game. (p. 485)

subsidy: A payment by the government to a buyer or seller of a good or service. (p. 100)

substitute: A good that can be used in place of another good. (pp. 17, 196)

substitution effect: The change in a consumer's consumption choices that results from a change in the relative prices of two goods. (p. 180)

sunk cost: A cost that, once paid, the firm cannot recover. (p. 266)

sunk cost fallacy: The mistake of letting sunk costs affect forward-looking decisions. (pp. 267, 692)

supply: The combined amount of a good that all producers in a market are willing to sell. (p. 15)

supply choke price: The price at which no firm is willing to produce a good and quantity supplied is zero; the vertical intercept of the inverse supply curve. (pp. 24, 64)

supply curve: The relationship between the quantity supplied of a good and the good's price, holding all other factors constant. (p. 23)

surplus: The amount by which quantity supplied exceeds quantity demanded when market price is higher than the equilibrium price. (p. 27)

tax incidence: Who actually pays a tax. (p. 96)

theories and **models:** Explanations of how things work that help us understand and predict how and why economic entities behave as they do. (p. 3)

time-consistent: Consistencies in a consumer's economic preferences in a given economic transaction, whether the economic transaction is far off or imminent. (p. 689)

tit-for-tat: A strategy in which the player mimics her opponent's prior-period action in each round; for example, the player cheats when her opponent cheated in the preceding round, and cooperates when her opponent cooperated in the previous round. (p. 501)

total cost: The sum of a firm's fixed and variable costs. (p. 270)

total cost curve: A curve that shows a firm's cost of producing particular quantities. (p. 246)

total effect: The total change (substitution effect + income effect) in a consumer's optimal consumption bundle as a result of a price change. (p. 181)

total factor productivity growth (or technological change): An improvement in technology that changes the firm's production function such that more output is obtained from the same amount of inputs. (p. 241)

total marginal benefit: The vertical sum of the marginal benefit curves of all of a public good's consumers. (p. 673)

tradable permit: A government-issued permit that allows a firm to emit a certain amount of pollution during production and that can be traded to other firms. (p. 662)

tragedy of the commons: The phenomenon that a common resource is used more intensively than it would be if it were privately owned. (p. 666)

transfer: Surplus that moves from producer to consumer, or vice versa, as a result of a price regulation. (p. 76)

two-part tariff: A pricing strategy in which the payment has two components, a per-unit price and a fixed fee. (p. 429)

unit elastic: A price elasticity with an absolute value equal to 1. (p. 46)

utilitarian social welfare function: Mathematical function that computes society's welfare as the sum of every individual's welfare. (p. 578)

utility: A measure of how satisfied a consumer is. (p. 114)

utility function: A mathematical function that describes the relationship between what consumers actually consume and their level of well-being. (p. 114)

variable cost: The cost of inputs that vary with the quantity of the firm's output. (p. 270)

versioning: A pricing strategy in which the firm offers different product options designed to attract different types of consumers. (p. 419)

welfare economics: The area of economics concerned with the economic well-being of society as a whole. (p. 116)

yield or **yield to maturity:** The interest rate that makes a bond's present discounted value equal to its current market price. (p. 535)

Index

Note: Page numbers followed by f denote a figure; page numbers followed by n denotes a footnote; page numbers followed by t denotes a table.